Topography and Sea-floor Bathymetry

NASA/GSFC, GEBCO

Earth at Night, City Lights

Defense Meteorological Satellite Program (DMSP) NASA/GSFC

D0548794

GEOSYSTEMS

Combination of satellite *Terra* MODIS sensor image and *GOES* satellite image produces a true-color view of North and South America from 35 000 km (22 000 mi) in space. [Courtesy of MODIS Science Team, Goddard Space Flight Center, NASA and NOAA.]

Glacial features dominate this view from the 2993-m summit of Cirque Peak, Banff National Park, Alberta—moraines, tarn lakes, U-shaped valleys, sharp serrated ridges, cirques, and horn peaks—all subjects in Chapter 17. Glaciers advanced and retreated over the continent and through the Canadian Rockies, producing incredible beauty. [Christian Botting.]

GEOSYSTEMS

AN INTRODUCTION TO PHYSICAL GEOGRAPHY THIRD CANADIAN EDITION

ROBERT CHRISTOPHERSON

MARY-LOUISE BYRNE

PHILIP GILES

PEARSON

Toronto

Vice-President, Editorial Director: *Gary Bennett*
Executive Acquisitions Editor: *Cathleen Sullivan*
Senior Marketing Manager: *Kimberly Ukrainec*
Developmental Editor: *Catherine Belshaw, Darryl Kamo*
Assistant Production/Editorial Manager: *Patricia Ciardullo*
Manufacturing Manager: *Susan Johnson*
Full Service Project Management: *Kelly Keeler, Element LLC*
Copy Editor: *Marcia Youngman*
Proofreader: *Sheila Joyce*
Compositor: *MPS Limited*
Permissions Researcher: *Heather Jackson*
Art Studio: *Precision Graphics*
Senior Project Manager, Precision: *JC Morgan*
Art Director: *Julia Hall*
Interior Designer: *Miguel Acevedo*
Cover layout: *Miguel Acevedo*

Cover Photo Credit: Polar bear mom and cub-of-the-year
on ice and snow, near Hudson Bay south of Churchill,
Manitoba. They keep a weary eye for other bears as they
walk through sparse willows in the afternoon light.
[Rinie van Meurs. All rights reserved.]

Dedication Page Quote: Barbara Kingsolver, *Small Wonder*
(New York: Harper Collins, 2002, p. 39.

Credits and acknowledgments for material borrowed from other sources and reproduced, with permission, in this textbook appear on the appropriate page within the text.

If you purchased this book outside the United States or Canada, you should be aware that it has been imported without the approval of the publisher or the author.

Copyright © 2013, 2009, 2006, Pearson Canada Inc. All rights reserved. Manufactured in the United States of America. This publication is protected by copyright and permission should be obtained from the publisher prior to any prohibited reproduction, storage in a retrieval system, or transmission in any form or by any means, electronic, mechanical, photocopying, recording, or likewise. To obtain permission(s) to use material from this work, please submit a written request to Pearson Canada Inc., Permissions Department, 26 Prince Andrew Place, Don Mills, Ontario, M3C 2T8, or fax your request to 416-447-3126, or submit a request to Permissions Requests at **www.pearsoncanada.ca**.

10 9 8 7 6 5 4 3 2 1 CKV

Library and Archives Canada Cataloguing in Publication

Christopherson, Robert W.
    Geosystems: introduction to physical geography/Robert Christopherson, Mary-Louise Byrne,
Philip Giles.—3rd Canadian ed.

Includes bibliographical references and index.

ISBN 978-0-13-210612-2
1. Physical geography—Textbooks. I. Byrne, Mary-Louise, 1961– II. Giles, Philip Thomas, 1967– III. Title.

GB54.5.C47   2012   910'.02   C2011-907455-9

PEARSON

ISBN 978-0-13-210612-2

Environmental Statement

This book is carefully crafted to minimize environmental impact. Pearson Canada is proud to report that the materials used to manufacture this book originated from sources committed to sustainable forestry practices, tree harvesting, and associated land management. The binding, cover, and paper come from facilities that minimize waste, energy usage, and the use of harmful chemicals.

Equally important, Pearson Canada closes the loop by recycling every out-of-date text returned to our warehouse. We pulp the books, and the pulp is used to produce other items such as paper coffee cups or shopping bags.

The future holds great promise for reducing our impact on Earth's environment, and Pearson Canada is proud to be leading the way in this initiative. From production of the book to putting a copy in your hands, we strive to publish the best books with the most up-to-date and accurate content, and to do so in ways that minimize our impact on Earth.

—Dedication—

To all the students and teachers of Earth,
our home planet, and a sustainable future.

To the children and grandchildren,
for it is their future and planet.

The land still provides our genesis,
however we might like to forget
that our food comes from dank,
muddy Earth, that the oxygen in our lungs was
recently inside a leaf, and that every newspaper or
book we may pick up is made from the hearts of
trees that died for the sake of our imagined lives.
What you hold in your hands right now,
beneath these words,
is consecrated air and time and sunlight.

—Barbara Kingsolver

BRIEF CONTENTS

CONTENTS

17 Glacial and Periglacial Processes and Landforms   514

Welcome to *Geosystems: An Introduction to Physical Geography*, Third Canadian Edition! This edition builds on the widespread success of the previous two editions, as well as the companion texts *Geosystems*, Eighth Edition, and *Elemental Geosystems*, Seventh Edition, in the United States. Students and teachers continue to communicate their appreciation of the up-to-date content, systems organization, scientific accuracy, clarity of the summary and review sections, and overall relevancy. *Geosystems* continues to evolve with the geospatial sciences, presenting the latest science and geophysical events, in a student-friendly language that tells a story.

The goal of physical geography is to explain the spatial dimension of Earth's dynamic systems—its energy, air, water, weather, climate, tectonics, landforms, rocks, soils, plants, ecosystems, and biomes. Understanding human-Earth relations is part of the challenge of physical geography—to create a holistic (or complete) view of the planet and its inhabitants. Welcome to physical geography!

The continued popularity of *Geosystems* and its companion text *Elemental Geosystems* made them the leaders in Canadian physical geography. To honour this acceptance and to serve Canadian geographic education, we have produced this updated third Canadian edition of *Geosystems*. As in the previous editions, we include hundreds of Canadian examples, illustrations, photos, maps, and satellite images.

New to the Third Canadian Edition of *Geosystems*

Nearly every page of *Geosystems*, Third Canadian Edition, contains updated material, new features, and new content in both the text and figures—far too many updates to list here.

The following highlights a sampling of the third Canadian edition's features:

- Many figures are new or recast to improve student learning. *Geosystems* continues to use compound figures that integrate art, photos, images, graphs, and schematics to assist the learning task.
- The four Part Openers and 21 Chapter Openers are redesigned with **new photos and images**, the only exception being Chapter 12, with its new integrated map of the ocean floor. Each of these four parts, described on the back cover, features a **new systems schematic**

that portrays the organization of the content. See these for yourself on pages 38, 164, 306, and 552.

- **Key Learning Concepts** appear at the beginning of each chapter, many rewritten for clarity. Each chapter concludes with a **Key Learning Concepts Review,** which is a summary of the chapter organized around these opening concepts.
- New to each chapter is an opening case study feature, **Geosystems Now**. These original, unique essays help focus interest on the chapter content. *Geosystems Now* topics for each chapter include:

Part I:

1. Canada's Southern Border, Not Just a Line on a Map
2. Chasing the Subsolar Point
3. Humans Help Define the Atmosphere
4. How Does Arctic Shipping Impact Albedo and the Surface Energy Balance?
5. Temperature Change Affects St. Kilda's Sheep
6. Ocean Currents Bring Invasive Species

Part II:

7. Earth's Lakes Provide an Important Warming Signal
8. On the Front Lines of Intense Weather
9. Water Resources and Climate Change in the Prairies
10. A Look at Puerto Rico's Climate at a Larger Scale

Part III:

11. Earth's Migrating Magnetic Poles
12. The San Jacinto Fault Connection
13. Human-Caused Mass Scarification at the Athabasca Oil Sands
14. Removing Dams to Restore Natural Stream Conditions
15. Increasing Desertification and Political Action—A Global Environmental Issue
16. Coastal Communities Facing Changes
17. Ice Shelves and Tidewater Glaciers Give Way to Warming

Part IV:

18. High Latitude Soils Emit Greenhouse Gases
19. Species' Distributions Shift with Climate Change
20. Invasive Species Arrive at Tristan da Cunha
21. Seeing Earth and Ourselves from Space

Be sure to read these case study features as you begin each chapter. For instance, "Ocean Currents Bring Invasive Species," in Chapter 6, tracks an oil-drilling platform left adrift in a storm in the South Atlantic Ocean. Months later the platform ran aground in Tristan da Cunha. The *Geosystems Now* in Chapter 20 picks up the story with "Invasive Species Arrive at Tristan da Cunha." The rig was contaminated with nonnative species, introducing them to fragile Tristanian marine ecosystems. The *Geosystems* approach involves such connections and linkages across the chapters and among Earth systems.

- New to each chapter are **Geo Reports,** placed along the bottom of pages. *Geo Reports* offer facts, events related to the chapter discussion, student action items, and new sources of information, among other features. There are 76 *Geo Reports* throughout the book, with topics such as water in the Solar System, why we always see the same side of the Moon, measuring Earth's rotation, polar region warming, Icelandic volcanic ash and aircraft flights, iceberg hazards, tornado and tropical storm records, how water is measured, the Intergovernmental Panel on Climate Change and the Nobel Prize, Earth's weight, how large earthquakes affect the entire Earth system, a saltier Mediterranean Sea, killer waves, high-latitude ice losses, soil losses, ongoing extinction rates, and sources of food and medicine in the rain forest, among many others.
- New to this edition and placed throughout the chapters are 51 carefully crafted **Critical Thinking** items to take you to the next level of learning, offering opportunities to check conceptual understanding and placing you in charge of further inquiry. Topics include finding your location, tracking seasonal change, analyzing your ozone column, assembling your physical geography profile, measuring wind through observation, following clouds, assessing hazard perception, finding your climate, reducing climate forcing, touring the ocean floor, looking at landslide potential, assessing the post-Hurricane Katrina Gulf Coast, relating to rising sea levels, living at an Antarctic polar station, observing ecosystem disturbances, and tracking shifting climates, among others. These bring relevancy to learning physical geography.
- Placed at the end of the text for each chapter is a new **Geosystems Connection** feature. In a brief paragraph, we review what was covered in the chapter and what will unfold in the next chapter, thus "bridging" concepts from one chapter to the next. The final *Geosystems Connection* in Chapter 21 builds a bridge to what comes next, beyond this textbook.
- Climate change science is well established and affects systems in every chapter of *Geosystems*. Part of this revision effort further updates our extensive climate change coverage throughout the chapters. We present a new "Reasons for Concern" to organize the climate discussion. The record year of warmth for land-surface temperatures was 2010 and it tied 2005, with 2007 and 2009 close behind—new monthly temperature records for land and ocean were set. The decade of 2001–2010 was the warmest decade in the entire record. As an integrative spatial science, physical geography is well equipped to analyze related impacts to Earth's systems. *Geosystems* presents all the aspects of climate change and has done so since its first U.S. edition in 1992.
- *Geosystems* continues to embed **Internet URLs** within the text. More than 200 appear in this edition; many are new links, and all are revised and checked. These allow you to pursue topics of interest in greater depth or to obtain the latest information about weather and climate, tectonic events, floods, and the myriad other subjects covered in the book.

Systems Organization Makes *Geosystems* Flow

Each section of this book is organized around the flow of energy, materials, and information. *Geosystems* presents subjects in the same sequence in which they occur in nature. In this way you and your instructor logically progress through topics that unfold according to the flow of individual systems or in accord with time and the flow of events. See Figures 1.9 and 1.10 in the text for an illustration of this systems organization. For flexibility, *Geosystems* is divided into four parts, each containing chapters that link content in logical groupings. A quick check of the table of contents and this illustration shows you the order of chapters within these four parts.

The text culminates with Chapter 21, "Earth and the Human Denominator," a unique capstone chapter that summarizes physical geography as an important discipline in understanding Earth's present status and possible future. Think of the world's population and the totality of our impact as the *human denominator*. Just as the denominator in a fraction tells how many parts a whole is divided into, so the growing human population, the increasing demand for resources, and our rising planetary impact suggest how much the whole Earth system must adjust. This chapter is sure to stimulate further thought and discussion, dealing as it does with the most profound issue of our time, Earth's stewardship.

Geosystems Is a Text That Teaches

Teaching and learning begin with the front cover photograph—A polar bear mom and cub-of-the-year on the snow and ice, with willows, near the shore of Hudson Bay in November. The spatial implications of distant sources of greenhouse gases is interconnected with the fate of the 935 bears remaining in this subregion, as the sea ice disappears owing to increasing temperatures.

To assist you in becoming acquainted with physical geography, this edition of *Geosystems* features hundreds of photographs from around the globe and more than a hundred remote-sensing images from a wide variety of orbital platforms. For spatial analysis and location support, more than 400 maps and illustrations locate and explain concepts. A key to learning is that all these figures are integrated and interlinked with text coverage, giving the student a unified presentation carefully woven to teach as it tells a story.

Three heading levels are used throughout the text and precise topic sentences begin each paragraph to help you outline and review material. **Boldface** words are defined where they first appear in the text. These terms and concepts are collected alphabetically in the Glossary with chapter-number references. *Italics* are used in the text to emphasize other words and phrases of importance. Every figure has a title that summarizes a more detailed caption. Also, in the introduction to each chapter, a feature called "In this chapter" gives you an overview of its contents.

The ***Applied Physical Geography*** and ***Critical Thinking*** features challenge you to take the next step with information from the chapter. These features help you to work your way through exercises and illustrate the processes discussed in the chapter.

The *Geosystems* Learning/Teaching Package

The Third Canadian Edition provides a complete physical geography program for you and your instructor.

For You, the Student:

- **NEW MyGeosciencePlace** (978-0-13-286679-8). Each new copy of *Geosystems: An Introduction to Physical Geography*, Third Canadian Edition, comes with a Student Access Code for MyGeosciencePlace. This new premium website, authored by William Gough of the University of Toronto, is been designed to provide students with useful tools needed for online study and review, augumented by features developed by lead author Robert Christopherson.

  Features include:
  - Self-study quizzes, tests, and exercises, which will expand your understanding of human geography
  - Physical Geography Case Studies
  - Career Links
  - Interactive Animations
  - Satellite Loops and Notebooks
  - MapMaster Interactive Maps
  - Glossary
  - Weblinks
  - eText with links to animations

You can access our premium website by visiting us at www.mygeoscienceplace.ca—a 24/7 personal study portal. Our site provides an excellent platform from which to start using the Internet for the study of physical geography. You will need the access code that has been packaged with your copy of the text to register and log on.

- **Study on the Go** Featured at the end of each chapter, you will find a unique barcode providing access to Study on the Go, an unprecedented mobile integration between text and online content. Students link to Pearson's unique Study on the Go content directly from their smartphones, allowing them to study whenever and wherever they wish! Go to one of the sites below to see how you can download an app to your smartphone for free. Once the app is installed, your phone will scan the code and link to a website containing Pearson's Study on the Go content, including Learning Objectives and Quizzes, which can be accessed anytime.

ScanLife
http://getscanlife.com
NeoReader
http://get.neoreader.com
QuickMark
http://www.quickmark.com.tw

- ***Goode's World Atlas*** (0-321-65200-2): *Goode's World Atlas* has been the world's premiere educational atlas since 1923—and for good reason. It features over 250 pages of maps, from definitive physical and political maps to important thematic maps that illustrate the spatial aspects of many important topics. The 22nd edition includes 160 pages of new, digitally produced reference maps as well as new thematic maps on global climate change, sea-level rise, emissions, polar ice fluctuations, deforestation, extreme weather events, infectious diseases, water resources, and energy production. Your author served on the Editorial Advisory Board for this 22nd edition of *Goode's*.

- ***Dire Predictions*** (978-0-13-604435-2): Reports from the Intergovernmental Panel on Climate Change evaluate the risk of climate change brought on by humans. In just over 200 pages, this practical text presents and expands upon the essential findings in a powerful summary. Scientific findings that provide validity to the implications of climate change are presented in clear-cut graphic elements, striking images, and understandable analogies.

For You, the Instructor:

Geosystems is designed to give you flexibility in presenting your course. The text is comprehensive in that it is true to each scientific discipline from which it draws subject matter. Although this diversity is a strength of physical geography, it makes it difficult to cover the entire book in an academic term. *Geosystems* is organized to help you customize your presentation. You should feel free to use the text based on your specialty or emphasis, rearranging parts and chapters as desired. The four-part structure of chapters, systems organization within each chapter, and *Focus Study* and *Geo Report* features will all assist you in sampling some chapters while covering others in greater depth. The following materials are available to assist you—have a great course!

- **Instructor's Resource DVD (IRDVD)**, (ISBN: 978-0-13-286650-7). Find all your digital resources in one well-organized, easy-to access place. Included on this DVD are:
  - **Figures**—JPEGs of all illustrations and photos from the book.
  - **Animations**—All the animations ready to use in your classroom presentations as PowerPoint slides or Flash files.
  - **PowerPoint Lecture Slides** (978-0-13-286678-1) by Mary-Louise Byrne and Philip Giles—Preauthored slides outline the concepts of each chapter with embedded art for use in the classroom or to customize with other items for your own presentation needs.
  - **TestGen** (978-0-13-286684-2)—by Robert Christopherson, Charlie Thomsen, and Mary-Louise Byrne. This collaboration has produced the most extensive and fully revised test bank available in physical geography. This test bank employs **TestGen** software, a computerized test generator that lets you view and edit test bank questions, transfer questions to tests, and print customized formats.
  - **Instructor's Resource Manual** (978-0-13-286654-5)—by Charlie Thomsen and Mary-Louise Byrne. The Instructor's Resource Manual, intended as a resource for both new and experienced teachers, includes lecture outlines and key terms, additional source materials, teaching tips, and a complete annotation of chapter review questions.
- The Instructor's Resource Manual and TestGen are available for download from the Pearson Canada on-line catalogue at http://catalogue.pearsoned.ca.
- *Aspiring Academics: A Resource Book for Graduate Students and Early Career Faculty* (0-13-604891-9). Drawing on several years of research, this set of essays is designed to help graduate students and early career faculty begin their careers in geography and related social and environmental sciences. This teaching aid stresses the interdependence of teaching, research, and service in faculty work.
- *Teaching College Geography: A Practical Guide for Graduate Students and Early Career Faculty* (0-13-605447-1). This two-part resource provides a starting point for becoming an effective geog-

raphy teacher from the first day of class. Divided in two parts, Part One addresses "nuts-and-bolts" teaching issues. Part Two explores being an effective teacher in the field, supporting critical thinking with GIS and mapping technologies, engaging learners in large geography classes, and promoting awareness of international perspectives and geographic issues.

- ***Practicing Geography: Careers for Enhancing Society and the Environment*** (0-321-81115-1). This National Science Foundation–funded project brings together members of the geography community to discuss workforce needs, expectations, and core competencies in professional geography, profiling the professional applications of and opportunities in geography today.
- **AAG Community Portal for Aspiring Academics and Teaching College Geography**. This web site is intended to support community-based professional development in geography and related disciplines. Here you find activities that can be used in workshops, graduate seminars, brown bags, and mentoring programs offered on campus or within an academic department.

Acknowledgments

Robert, Mary-Louise, and Philip offer their thanks to the many authors and scientists who published research articles and books that enrich this work; to all the colleagues who served as reviewers specifically for this edition, or those who offered helpful suggestions at our national and regional geography meetings; and, although unnamed here, to all the correspondence received from students and instructors from across the globe who shared their comments with the authors—a continuing and much appreciated dialogue. We are grateful to all of them for their generosity of ideas and sacrifice of time.

The authors and publishers thank all of the reviewers who participated in reading material at various stages during the development of all three Canadian editions and previous *Geosystems* editions:

Alec Aitken, *University of Saskatchewan*
Peter Ashmore, *University of Western Ontario*
Chris Ayles, *Camosun College*
Claire Beaney, *University of the Fraser Valley*
Bill Buhay, *University of Winnipeg*
Leif Burge, *Okanagan College*
Ian Campbell, *University of Alberta–Edmonton*
Darryl Carlyle-Moses, *Thompson Rivers University*
Norm Catto, *Memorial University*
Ben Cecil, *University of Regina*
Gail Chmura, *McGill University*
Daryl Dagesse, *Brock University*
Robin Davidson-Arnott, *University of Guelph*
Dirk H. de Boer, *University of Saskatchewan*

Joseph R. Desloges, *University of Toronto*
John Fairfield, *Malaspina University College*
William Gough, *University of Toronto*
Mryka Hall-Beyer, *University of Calgary*
Peter Herren, *University of Calgary*
J. Peter Johnson, Jr., *Carleton University*
David Jordan, *Trinity Western University*
Colin Laroque, *Mount Allison University*
Joyce Lundberg, *Carleton University*
John Maclachlan, *McMaster University*
Robert McClure, *North Island College*
Ben Moffat, *Medicine Hat College*
Catherine Moore, *Concordia University*
Mungandi Nasitwitwi, *Douglas College*
Lawrence C. Nkemdirim, *University of Calgary*
Frédérique Pivot, *Athabasca University*
Sonya Powell, *University of British Columbia*
Sheila Ross, *Capilano University*
Kathy E. Runnalls, *Douglas College*
Anne Marie Ryan, *Dalhousie University*
Dave Sauchyn, *University of Regina*
Cheryl P. Schreader, *Capilano College*
Mark Smith, *Langara College*
Geraldine Sweet, *University of Winnipeg*
Alan Trenhaile, *University of Windsor*
Michael Tripp, *Malaspina University College*
Susan Vajoczki, *McMaster University*
James Voogt, *University of Western Ontario*
Gordon Weary, *Northwest Community College*
Hanna Wilson, *Vancouver Island University*

We extend gratitude to the editorial, production, and sales staff of Pearson Canada and Pearson U.S. Thanks to Gary Bennett, vice president, editorial director, at Pearson Education for his oversight and guidance, and to Cathleen Sullivan, Geosciences editor, for her attention to detail, to Developmental Editors Catherine Belshaw and Darryl Kamo for their tireless work on this edition, and to Robert's Geosciences Editor Christian Botting for his role as we forge this *Geosystems* bridge between two countries. And, as always, thanks and safe travels to the many sales representatives who spend months in the field communicating the *Geosystems* approach—may the wind be at their backs!

From Robert: I give special gratitude to all the students during my 30 years teaching at American River College, for it is in the classroom crucible that the *Geosystems* books are forged. Thanks and admiration go to the many authors and scientists who published research that enriches this work. Thanks for all the dialogue received from students and teachers shared with us through e-mails from across the globe.

I appreciate our Canadian staff at Pearson and the skilled educators that coauthored this edition, led by Mary-Lou Byrne and Philip Giles, who I am honoured to call my colleagues. The Canadian environment is under accelerating climate-change stress that exceeds that

occurring in the lower latitudes. For this reason, *Geosystems*, Third Canadian Edition, takes on an important role to educate and, hopefully, provoke actions toward a slower rate of climate change and a more sustainable future.

At the heart of *Geosystems* and of this life's work is a partner, photographer, and special editorial assistant, my wife Bobbé Christopherson. She has worked tirelessly on all the *Geosystems'* projects. You see her photographs in this third edition, carefully made to illustrate physical geography concepts. And she continues as my best friend, colleague, and expedition companion, by my side on our 12 polar-region expeditions.

Robert W. Christopherson
P. O. Box 128
Lincoln, California 95648
E-mail: bobobbe@aol.com

From Mary-Louise: The incredible journey continues and once again I need to thank so many for their help. I owe my greatest thanks to my immediate family—my husband, Alain Pinard, and our children, Madeleine and Julianne, who continue to be curious about the world around them. To my extended family I am indebted to your honest comments and criticisms.

Robert and Bobbé Christopherson continue to develop an amazing textbook, and I am so pleased to join them on the journey. I am also pleased that Philip Giles has joined us in this endeavour. I thank all my colleagues in the geographic community in Canada who, by comment, communication, or review, helped to shape the contents of this text. I am forever indebted to Brian McCann for teaching me to look at physical processes from many perspectives and to integrate these perspectives in order to form an explanation. He is sadly missed. And Sue Vajoczki, your comments and understanding of geographic education have often informed me while I reviewed the pages of this book. James Hamilton's comments and criticisms are greatly appreciated as we work on team 101, a team that would not be complete without the care and skill of Igor Hoogendoorn.

Finally, to all the students with whom I had contact in 20 years of teaching at Wilfrid Laurier University, your enthusiasm and curiosity keep me focused on the goal of explaining planet Earth. I have had the pleasure of communicating with several current students from across the country who have had positive and constructive criticism about the book. I took your comments seriously and have addressed them where appropriate. It is amazing to hear from you and I encourage you to continue. To future students, our planet is in your hands: Care for it.

Mary-Louise Byrne
Associate Professor
Geography and Environmental Studies
Wilfrid Laurier University
Waterloo, Ontario
N2L 3C5
E-mail: mlbyrne@wlu.ca

From Philip: I am very pleased and grateful to have been given the opportunity to join Robert and Mary-Lou as an author on *Geosystems*, Third Canadian Edition. For many years I have admired Robert's choice of content and writing style, as well as the presentation quality in *Geosystems*, and I used several previous editions as the required textbook in my introductory physical geography course at Saint Mary's University. When selected to join the team, it was an honour to know that I would be contributing to the preparation of this new Canadian edition, which will play an important role for so many students in learning about physical geography. I knew quite early that I wanted to make physical geography my career, so to reach this stage and be playing this new role as an author on a successful and influential textbook is extremely satisfying.

As an undergraduate and graduate student, one is influenced by many people. All of my course instructors and advisors helped me to learn and develop academically, and collectively they deserve recognition. In particular, like Mary-Lou, I also had the pleasure and good fortune to have been taught and advised by Brian McCann during my time at McMaster University. Mary-Lou completed her Ph.D. while I was in the B.Sc. and M.Sc. programs at McMaster; we were both supervised by Brian for our thesis research on coastal sand dunes.

To Yvonne, my parents, and my colleagues in the Department of Geography at Saint Mary's, thank you all for your support over the years.

Whether you are taking this course as a requirement for your major or as an elective, I hope this textbook will help you find pleasure as you develop a better understanding of the physical environment. Robert, Mary-Lou, and I each have a deep passion for this subject and one of the goals of this book is to inspire the same passion in you.

Philip Giles
Associate Professor
Department of Geography
Saint Mary's University
Halifax, Nova Scotia
B3H 3C3
E-mail: philip.giles@smu.ca

And from Robert, Mary-Louise, and Philip: Physical geography teaches us a holistic view of the intricate supporting web that is Earth's environment and our place in it. Dramatic changes that demand our understanding are occurring in many human–Earth relations as we alter physical, chemical, and biological systems. All things considered, this is a critical time for you to be enrolled in a physical geography course! The best to you in your studies—and ***carpe diem!***

CHAPTER 1

Essentials of Geography

Using map, GPS unit, and radar instruments, a course is set through the Antarctic Sound to the Weddell Sea, Antarctica, at 63° 31′ S latitude. A dramatic tabular iceberg from the former Larsen Ice Shelf dominates the horizon. The northern edge of the Larsen Ice Shelf began about 1.5° to the south. [Bobbé Christopherson]

KEY LEARNING CONCEPTS

After reading the chapter, you should be able to:

- **Define** geography and physical geography in particular.
- **Describe** systems analysis, open and closed systems, and feedback information, and **relate** these concepts to Earth systems.
- **Explain** Earth's reference grid: latitude and longitude and latitudinal geographic zones and time.
- **Define** cartography and mapping basics: map scale and map projections.
- **Describe** remote sensing, and **explain** the geographic information system (GIS); both as tools used in geographic analysis.

Canada's Southern Border, Not Just a Line on a Map.

Canada is often called the land "north of the 49th" parallel, which marks the international border between Canada and the United States from Lake of the Woods at the Manitoba–Ontario border, westward to British Columbia (Figure GN 1.1). However, the 49th parallel is not the international boundary in eastern North America, where the border dips southward in Ontario to 41° 41′ N, roughly splitting the Great Lakes, then meanders around the 45th parallel on through the Maritimes to the Bay of Fundy (Figure GN 1.1).

How did this become the southern border? What is its geographic significance and how is it maintained? Because there is no natural feature that clearly marks the boundary between Canada and the United States, the eastern part of the border was negotiated and documented by treaty in the 1700s as land was settled by Europeans. Importantly, in all the editions of *Geosystems* since 1992, the author prepared maps with both countries presented, since the environment does not abruptly change at the unnatural U.S.–Canadian boundary!

With continued westward settlement, following the lead of hunters and trappers trekking into the interior, the need arose for a boundary to separate British territories to the north from the new country to the south. As European settlements moved westward, various treaties were negotiated between Great Britain, on behalf of Canada, and the United States.

The 49th parallel in western North America was first referenced in Hudson Bay Company documents at the beginning of the eighteenth century. Westward U.S. expansion pressed the need for a clearly marked border. The "Convention of 1818" began the resolution of Canada–United States border issues and specified that the 49th parallel from Lake of the Woods to the Strait of Georgia

serve as the border. However, in 1844 the United States made claims to territory west of the Rockies, placing the border of the Oregon Territory at 54° 40′ N. Britain countered with a desire to set the boundary along the Columbia River instead. The 49th parallel became the compromise location in 1846 with the Oregon Treaty.

The International Boundary Commission (IBC) was established in 1908 and made a permanent organization in 1925, although some 20 treaties and agreements preceded this commission. The International Boundary Commission Act passed in Canada in 1960, and recognised by the United States, firmly established not only the boundary, but the government agencies on each side of the border that maintained it. The act was necessary because of deterioration of boundary markers that had been erected in the first half of the nineteenth century. Today, in each country, a commissioner serves as a ministerial chief to oversee staff, equipment, and budgets (see http://www.internationalboundarycommission.org/index-eng.html).

In Canada, this commissioner reports to the Minister for Foreign Affairs, and

in the United States, the commissioner reports to the Secretary of State. The Canadian Boundary Commission is in the Surveyor General Branch of the Department of Natural Resources. Essentially, commissioners of the IBC are charged with:

- Inspecting the border;
- Repairing and rebuilding monuments and placing new monuments;
- Keeping "boundary vistas" open; nearly 2200 km is forested;
- Regulating all construction within 3 m of the boundary;
- Defining the boundary in any legal situation involving the border;
- Implementing an operational GIS in support of IBC operations.

When you walk along most segments of this border you notice that there is no physical barrier. Instead, thousands of markers, or buoys when the boundary is in water, are set to make the boundary a visible reference line. The IBC guides boundary-marker placement on the advice of geospatial surveys. This is part of the longest nonmilitarised border in the world and Canada's only land border

(a)

(b)

FIGURE GN 1.1 Typical border markers.
The Canada–U.S. border: (a) along the 49th parallel; (b) along the St. Croix River that separates New Brunswick and Maine. [David R. Frazier Photolibrary, Inc./GetStock.com.]

FIGURE GN 1.2 Border crossing along the St. Croix River.
Ferry Point International Bridge crosses the St. Croix River between St. Stephen, New Brunswick (left), and Calais, Maine (right). The international border is approximately midchannel. [Bobbé Christopherson.]

the vast distance traversed by this line. (The border with Alaska adds another 2475 km to the total.)

The work of geographers is important when it comes to demarcating the border. There are over 8000 monuments and reference points to inspect and maintain. Each is tied into 1000 survey control points that allow accurate mapping and location of the border. Physically maintaining the border markers and buoys is a continuing challenge. Portions of the international border fall in waterways such as the St. Croix River (Figure GN 1.2); locate this place on the map in GN 1.1b.

In this chapter, we study Geographic Information Systems (GIS) and the Global Positioning System (GPS) as important geospatial tools. These are used by geographers for many tasks, including accurate maps and guidance to IBC activities.

with another country—an incredible line some 6416 km in total length (2878 km on land and 3538 km in water), of which 3013 km lie along the 49th parallel. On a map of North America, find Passamaquoddy Bay and the Strait of Juan de Fuca, respectively, the eastern and western ends of this boundary. Note

---

Welcome to the third Canadian edition of *Geosystems, An Introduction to Physical Geography*! Much has happened since the publication of the previous edition of *Geosystems* in Canada. Imagine the challenge society as a whole, and we in physical geography, face to understand how Earth's systems operate and then to forecast change in these systems to determine what future environments we may expect. In every chapter, *Geosystems* continues to present updated science and information to help you understand our dynamic Earth systems.

Physical geography deals with powerful Earth systems that influence our lives and the many ways humans alter Earth's systems. In this second decade of the twenty-first century, a century that will see many changes to the natural environment, we find ourselves in an exciting time to study physical geography, and learn about the building blocks that form the landscapes, seascapes, atmosphere, and ecosystems upon which we depend. Climate change science will be an overriding topic for the global society this century.

In 1990, the *First Assessment Report* by the Intergovernmental Panel on Climate Change (IPCC, http://www.ipcc.ch/) was published. The IPCC completed its *Fourth Assessment Report* in 2007. The Climate Congress held an International Climate Change Conference in Copenhagen in March 2009 as an update to the IPCC, with 2500 scientists from more than 80 countries in attendance (http://climatecongress.ku.dk/). The Climate Congress concluded:

The *worst-case* IPCC (2007) projections, or even worse, are being realized. . . . Emissions are soaring, projections of sea-level rise are higher than expected,

and climate impacts around the world are appearing with increasing frequency.

The Conference of the Parties held its 15th meeting (COP–15) under the UN Framework Convention on Climate Change (FCCC, http://unfccc.int/2860.php) in Copenhagen in December 2009 and launched the *Copenhagen Accord* in an effort to reduce greenhouse gas emissions that enhance warming. From the First Assessment Report to the present, the level of carbon dioxide, a principal greenhouse gas, rose 16% in Earth's atmosphere, and CO_2 emissions have accelerated 3% per year since 2000. These changes affect systems discussed in every chapter of *Geosystems* and are in evidence across Canada.

During this past decade, the highest temperatures over land and water in the instrumental record were recorded (Figure 1.1). The year 2009 tied 2007 as the second highest year for global temperatures, while 2010 tied 2005 for highest. In the Southern Hemisphere, 2009 had the highest temperatures on record. Temperatures in 2010 for Canada, Russia, Greenland, China, South Asia, and North Africa all set new records. Sea ice was at its smallest recorded aerial extent throughout the Canadian Arctic archipelago. In fact, the Northwest Passage was ice-free long enough for 18 commercial ships to clear customs in Inuvik, Northwest Territories in 2010. A good summary web site is http://climate.nasa.gov/.

Financial data from the world's 15 largest financial institutions indicate that annual weather-related damage losses (drought, floods, hail, tornadoes, damaging winds, tropical systems, monsoon intensity, storm

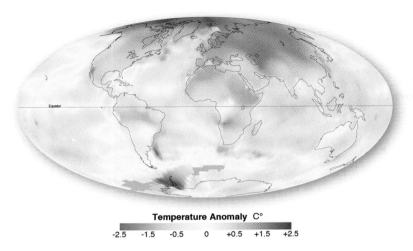

Temperature Anomaly C°

-2.5   -1.5   -0.5   0   +0.5   +1.5   +2.5

FIGURE 1.1 Record temperatures for the decade. Temperature anomalies for the years 2000–2009 compared to the 1951–1980 standard baseline. The decade experienced the highest average air temperatures since record keeping began in 1880, along with the highest temperatures in the global oceans and many lakes. [Map image courtesy of GISS/NASA.]

surges, blizzards and ice storms, and wildfires) could exceed USD $1 trillion by A.D. 2040 (adjusted to current dollars)—up from USD $210 billion in 2005 (Hurricane Katrina alone produced USD $125 billion in losses). Global climate change is driving this increasing total— and at an accelerating pace.

Physical geography explains the operations of Earth systems from a spatial perspective and gives you the tools to understand what is happening all across the globe. In March 2011, a magnitude 9.0 earthquake struck near the coast of Honshu, Japan causing a seismic sea wave that flooded millions of people, killed more than 28 000, and led to 3 core meltdowns in nuclear plants at Fukushima Daiichi. Only a month before, portions of Christchurch, New Zealand were devastated by a 6.3 magnitude quake. Aftershocks in both locations continued for months. A little more than a year earlier—January 2010, a magnitude 7.0 earthquake, with thousands of aftershocks, struck Haiti and literally brought one of the poorest countries on Earth to collapse, killing more than 233 000 people and leaving millions homeless. In Haiti, the problem is one of poor construction, weak infrastructure, and a lack of planning in response to scientific knowledge—although in Haiti poverty blocks hazard perception and preparation. The scene repeated itself with a magnitude 8.8 earthquake that struck the next month in Maule, Chile, southwest of Santiago. These are all examples of how natural processes impact our lives.

Why does the environment vary from equator to midlatitudes, and between deserts and polar regions? How does solar energy influence the distribution of trees, soils, climates, and lifestyles? Why are we experiencing record frequency of wildfires? Why are earthquakes and volcanoes active in certain regions and what is the risk to humans? What produces the patterns of wind, weather, and ocean currents? Why are global sea levels on the rise? Why did the countries of the world join in the International Polar Year (IPY) study of polar regions between 2007 and 2009? How do natural systems affect human populations, and, in turn, what impact are humans having on natural systems? Why are record numbers of plants and animals facing extinction? In this book, we explore these questions, and more, through geography's unique perspective.

In this chapter: Our study of geosystems—Earth systems—begins with a look at the science of physical geography and the geographic tools we use. Physical geography is key to studying entire Earth systems because of its integrative spatial approach.

Physical geographers analyse systems to study the environment. Therefore, we discuss systems and the feedback mechanisms that influence system operations. We then consider location, a key theme of geographic inquiry—the latitude, longitude, and time coordinates that inscribe Earth's surface and the new technologies in use to measure them. The study of longitude and a universal time system provide us with interesting insights into geography. Next, we examine maps as critical tools that geographers use to portray physical and cultural information. This chapter concludes with an overview of the technology that continues to add exciting new dimensions to geography: remote sensing from space and computer-based geographic information systems (GIS).

The Science of Geography

Now is the era of **Earth systems science**. This science contributes to our emerging view of Earth as a complete entity—an interacting set of physical, chemical, and biological systems that produce a whole Earth. Physical geography is at the heart of Earth systems science as we answer the *spatial* questions concerning Earth's physical systems and their interaction with living things.

Geography (from *geo*, "Earth," and *graphein*, "to write") is the science that studies the relationships among natural systems, geographic areas, society, cultural activities, and the interdependence of all of these *over space*. The term **spatial** refers to the nature and character of physical space, its measurement, and the distribution of things within it.

For example, think of how a driver uses knowledge of street patterns, traffic trouble spots, and location of

TABLE 1.1	A Few Geography Organizations
Organization Name	**URL Addresses**
Canadian Association of Geographers	http://www.cag-acg.ca/en/
Geological Association of Canada	http://www.gac.ca/
Canadian Council for Geographic Education	http://www.ccge.org/default.asp
Canadian Federation of Earth Scientists	http://geoscience.ca/
Canadian Geophysical Union	http://www.cgu-ugc.ca
Canadian Geomorphology Research Group	http://cgrg.geog.uvic.ca/index.html
Canadian Society of Soil Science	http://www.csss.ca/index.html
Royal Canadian Geographical Society	http://www.rcgs.org/
American Geographical Society	http://www.amergeog.org/
Association of American Geographers	http://www.aag.org/
National Council for Geographic Education	http://www.ncge.org/
National Geographic Society	http://www.nationalgeographic.com/
Institute of Australian Geographers	http://www.iag.org.au
Australian Geography Teachers Association	http://www.agta.asn.au/
European Geography Association	http://www.egea.eu/
Royal Geographical Society, Institute of British Geographers	http://www.rgs.org/

parking spaces to guide selection of a route to a destination. All of these are spatial considerations that influence human actions.

A list of some geography organizations is presented in Table 1.1. The Canadian Council for Geographic Education (CCGE), established in 1993 to guide geographic education, is mandated to increase emphasis on geography at all levels of education by supporting geography teachers and by facilitating national-level action to strengthen the position of geography in the school curricula, and to foster development of geographic skills. Finally, the CCGE works to promote public awareness of geography and geographic literacy.

We simplify the standards of geographic science using five important spatial themes: **location, region, human–Earth relationships, movement,** and **place,** each of which is illustrated and defined in Figure 1.2. *Geosystems* draws on each theme.

Geographic Analysis

Within these five geographic themes, geography is governed by a *method* rather than a specific body of knowledge. The method is **spatial analysis**. Using this method, geography synthesises (brings together) knowledge from many fields, integrating information to form a whole-Earth concept. Geographers view phenomena as occurring in spaces, areas, and locations. The language of geography reflects this spatial view: *space, territory, zone, pattern, distribution, place, location, region, sphere, province,* and *distance*. Geographers analyse the differences and similarities among places and locations.

Process, a set of actions or mechanisms that operate in some special order, is central to geographic analysis. As examples in *Geosystems*, numerous processes are involved in Earth's vast water–atmosphere–weather system, or in

continental crust movements and earthquake occurrences, or in ecosystem functions. Geographers use spatial analysis to examine how Earth's processes interact over space or area.

Therefore, **physical geography** is the spatial analysis of all the physical elements and process systems that make up the environment: energy, air, water, weather, climate, landforms, soils, animals, plants, and microorganisms. As scientists, geographers employ the **scientific method**, a methodology important to physical geography. Focus Study 1.1 explains this essential process of science.

The Geographic Continuum

Geography is eclectic, integrating a wide range of subject matter from diverse fields; virtually any subject can be examined geographically. Figure 1.3 shows a continuous distribution—a continuum—along which the content of geography is arranged. Physical and life sciences are at one end, and human and cultural sciences are at the other. As the figure shows, specialties within geography draw from these subject areas.

The continuum in Figure 1.3 reflects a basic duality within geography—*physical geography* and *human/cultural geography*. Some societies parallel this duality. Humans at times think of themselves as exempt from physical Earth processes—like actors not paying attention to their stage, props, and lighting. We all depend on Earth's systems to provide oxygen, water, nutrients, energy, and materials to support life. The growing complexity of the human–Earth relationship requires that we shift our study of geographic processes toward the centre of the continuum in Figure 1.3 to attain a more balanced perspective—such is the thrust of *Geosystems*. Many academic departments are offering courses that serve this growing synthesis.

Location
Absolute and relative location on Earth. Location answers the question Where?— the specific planetary address of a location.This road sign, posted along Bruce County Road 9 in Ontario, is located on the 45th parallel of latitude, halfway between the equator and the North Pole.

Place
No two places on Earth are exactly alike. The Bay of Fundy, separating New Brunswick and Nova Scotia, has the highest average tides in the world—up to 17 m in height.

Geographic Science

Region
Areas having uniform characteristics; how they form and change; their relation to other regions. A grain freighter moves through the Welland Canal in the Niagara region of southern Ontario, passing from Lake Ontario (75 m above sea level), rising to Lake Erie (174 m above sea level) in an "upstream" direction. Seven lifting locks bring vessels up 99 m in elevation, connecting the St. Lawrence Seaway and Atlantic Ocean with farms and markets in the Midwest and Prairies.

Movement
Communication, circulation, migration, and diffusion across Earth's surface represent movement in our interdependent world. Snow geese feed and rest along their journey.

Human–Earth Relationships
Human–environment connections include resource exploitation, hazard perception, and environmental pollution and modification. A *Terra* satellite image of the *Deepwater Horizon* oil spill in the Gulf of Mexico, highlighted by a sunglint on the gulf's surface. This human-caused spill is the largest offshore drilling disaster in history.

FIGURE 1.2 Five themes of geographic science.
Drawing from your own experience, can you think of several more examples of each theme? [Location photo by Mary-Louise Byrne; Human–Earth Relationships photo, GSFC/NASA; Region, Movement, and Place photos by Bobbé Christopherson.]

FOCUS STUDY 1.1

The Scientific Method

The term *scientific method* may have an aura of complexity, but it should not. The scientific method is simply the application of common sense in an organised and objective manner. A scientist observes, makes a general statement to summarise the observations, formulates a hypothesis, conducts experiments to test the hypothesis, and develops a theory and governing scientific laws. Sir Isaac Newton (1642–1727) developed this method of discovering the patterns of nature, although the term *scientific method* was applied later.

Complexity dominates nature, making several outcomes possible as a system operates. Science serves an important function in understanding such uncertainty. Yet, the more knowledge we have, the more the uncertainty and the awareness of other possible scenarios (outcomes and events) increase. This in turn demands more precise and progressive science.

Follow the scientific method illustration in Figure 1.1.1,

FIGURE 1.1.1 Scientific method flow chart.
The scientific method process: from perceptions, to observations, reasoning, hypothesis, and predictions, and possibly to general theory and natural laws.

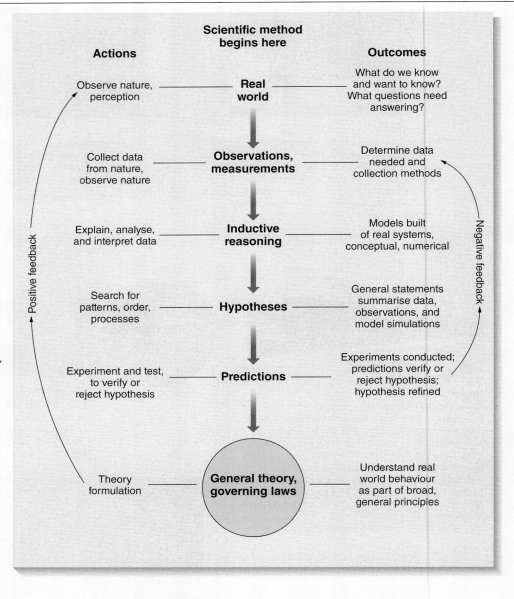

Actions

Observe nature, perception
Collect data from nature, observe nature
Explain, analyse, and interpret data
Search for patterns, order, processes
Experiment and test, to verify or reject hypothesis
Theory formulation

Scientific method begins here

Real world
Observations, measurements
Inductive reasoning
Hypotheses
Predictions
General theory, governing laws

Outcomes

What do we know and want to know? What questions need answering?
Determine data needed and collection methods
Models built of real systems, conceptual, numerical
General statements summarise data, observations, and model simulations
Experiments conducted; predictions verify or reject hypothesis; hypothesis refined
Understand real world behaviour as part of broad, general principles

Positive feedback

Negative feedback

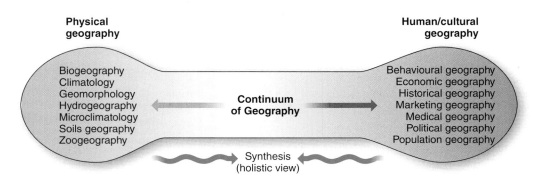

Physical geography
Biogeography
Climatology
Geomorphology
Hydrogeography
Microclimatology
Soils geography
Zoogeography

Continuum of Geography

Human/cultural geography
Behavioural geography
Economic geography
Historical geography
Marketing geography
Medical geography
Political geography
Population geography

Synthesis (holistic view)

FIGURE 1.3 The content of geography.
Geography derives subject matter from many different sciences. The focus of this book is physical geography, but we also integrate some human and cultural components. Movement toward the middle of the continuum suggests a synthesis of Earth topics and human topics.

beginning at the top. The scientific method begins with our perception of the real world and a determination of what we know, what we want to know, and the many unanswered questions that exist.

Scientists who study the physical environment turn to nature for clues that they can observe and measure.

Step 1: *Observe and measure.* Scientists figure out what data are needed and begin to collect those data. These observations are analysed to identify coherent patterns that may exist. This search for patterns requires inductive reasoning, or the process of drawing generalizations from specific facts. This step is important in modern Earth systems science, in which the goal is to understand a whole functioning Earth, rather than isolated, small compartments of information. Such understanding allows the scientist to construct models that simulate general operations of Earth systems.

Step 2: *Form and test a hypothesis.* If patterns are discovered, the researcher may formulate a *hypothesis*—a tentative explanation for the phenomena-observed. Further observations are related to the general principles established by the hypothesis. More data gathering may support or disprove the hypothesis, or predictions made according to it may prove accurate or inaccurate. These findings provide feedback to adjust data collection and model building and to refine the hypothesis statement. Verification of the hypothesis after exhaustive testing may lead to its elevation to the status of a *theory*.

Step 3: *Formulate a theory.* The word theory as used by the media and general public can be confusing. A theory is constructed on the basis of several extensively tested hypotheses. Theories represent truly broad general principles—unifying concepts that tie together the laws that govern nature. Examples include the theory of relativity, theory of evolution, atomic theory, Big Bang theory, stratospheric ozone depletion theory, and plate tectonics theory. A theory is a powerful device with which to understand both order and chaos (disorder) in nature. Using a theory allows predictions to be made about things not yet known, the effects of which can be tested and verified or disproved through tangible evidence. The value of a theory is the continued observation, testing, understanding, and pursuit of knowledge that the theory stimulates. A general theory reinforces our perception of the real world.

Pure science does not make value judgments. Instead, pure science provides people and their institutions with objective information on which to base their own value judgments. Social and political judgments about the applications of science are increasingly critical as Earth's natural systems respond to the impact of modern civilization. Jane Lubchenco, National Oceanic and Atmospheric Administration Administrator, in her 1997 American Association for the Advancement of Science Presidential Address stated:

Science alone does not hold the power to achieve the goal of greater sustainability, but scientific knowledge and wisdom are needed to help inform decisions that will enable society to move toward that end.

The growing awareness that human activity is producing global change places increasing pressure on scientists to participate in decision making. Numerous editorials in scientific journals have called for such applied science involvement.

Earth Systems Concepts

The word *system* pervades our lives daily: "Check the car's cooling system"; "Is a broadband system available for my Internet browser?"; "How does the grading system work?"; "There is a weather system approaching." Systems of many kinds surround us. *Systems analysis* techniques began with studies of energy and temperature (thermodynamics) in the nineteenth century and were further developed in engineering during World War II. Today, geographers use systems methodology as an analytical tool. In this book's four parts and 21 chapters, content is organised along logical flow paths consistent with systems thinking.

Systems Theory

Simply stated, a **system** is any ordered, interrelated set of things and their attributes, linked by flows of energy and matter, as distinct from the surrounding environment outside the system. The elements within a system may be arranged in a series or interwoven with one another. A system may comprise a number of subsystems. Within Earth's systems, both matter and energy are stored and retrieved and energy is transformed from one type to another. (Remember: *Matter* is mass that assumes a physical shape and occupies space; *energy* is a capacity to change the motion of, or to do work on, matter.)

FIGURE 1.4 An open system.
In an open system, inputs of energy and matter undergo conversions and are stored as the system operates. Outputs include energy, matter, and heat energy (waste) that flow from the system. See how the various inputs and outputs are related to the operation of a car—an open system. Expand your viewpoint to the entire system of auto production, from raw materials, to assembly, to sales, to car accidents, to junkyards. Can you identify other open systems that you encounter in your daily life?

Open Systems Systems in nature are generally not self-contained: Inputs of energy and matter flow into the system, and outputs of energy and matter flow from the system. Such a system is an **open system**. Within a system, the parts function in an interrelated manner, acting together in a way that gives each system its operational character (Figure 1.4). Earth is an open system in terms of energy, because solar energy enters freely and heat energy leaves, going back into space. Most natural systems are open in terms of energy.

Most Earth systems are dynamic (energetic, changing) because of the tremendous infusion of radiant energy from thermonuclear reactions deep within the Sun. This energy comes through the outermost edge of Earth's atmosphere to power terrestrial systems, being transformed along the way into various forms of energy, such as *kinetic energy* (of motion), *potential energy* (of position), or as chemical or mechanical energy. Eventually, Earth radiates this energy back to the cold vacuum of space as heat energy.

Closed Systems A system that is shut off from the surrounding environment so that it is self-contained is a **closed system**. Although such closed systems are rarely found in nature, Earth is essentially a closed system in terms of physical matter and resources—air, water, and material resources. The only exceptions are the slow escape of lightweight gases (such as hydrogen) from the atmosphere into space and the input of frequent but tiny meteors and cosmic and meteoric dust. The fact that Earth is a closed material system makes recycling efforts inevitable if we want a sustainable global economy.

System Example Figure 1.5 illustrates a simple openflow system, using plant photosynthesis and respiration as an example. In photosynthesis (Figure 1.5a), plants use sunlight as an energy input and material inputs of water, nutrients, and carbon dioxide. The photosynthetic process converts these inputs to stored chemical energy in the form of plant sugars (carbohydrates). The process also releases an output from the plant system: the oxygen we breathe.

Reversing the process, plants derive energy for their operations from respiration. In respiration, the plant consumes inputs of chemical energy (carbohydrates) and oxygen and releases outputs of carbon dioxide, water, and heat energy into the environment (Figure 1.5b). Thus, a plant acts as an open system, in which both energy and materials freely flow into and out of the plant. (Chapter 19 discusses photosynthesis and respiration processes.)

System Feedback As a system operates, it generates outputs that influence its own operations. These outputs function as "information" that is returned to various points in the system via pathways, or **feedback loops**. Feedback information can guide further system operations. In the plant's photosynthetic system (see Figure 1.5), any changes in daylength (sunlight availability), carbon dioxide, or water produce feedback that changes the growth process; increasing daylength increases the growth process within limits.

If feedback information discourages continued change in the system in response to an initial change, it is **negative feedback**. Negative feedback informs and causes self-regulation in a natural system, stabilizing and maintaining the system. Think of maintaining your healthy body weight—the human body is an open system. When you stand on the scales, the news reported about your weight helps you regulate system activity. If your weight is too high, you will likely decrease your inputs or increase your level of exercise until your weight stabilises.

If feedback information encourages more change in the system, it is **positive feedback**. Positive feedback stimulates further system changes in response to an initial

(a) Plant photosynthesis

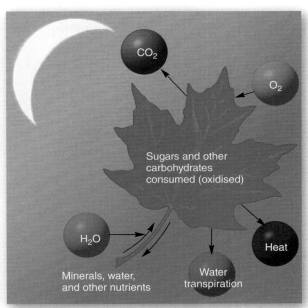
(b) Plant respiration

FIGURE 1.5 A leaf is a natural open system.
A plant leaf provides an example of a natural open system. (a) In the process of photosynthesis, plants consume light, carbon dioxide (CO_2), nutrients, and water (H_2O), and produce outputs of oxygen (O_2) and carbohydrates (sugars) as stored chemical energy. (b) Plant respiration, illustrated here at right, approximately reverses this process.

change. Unchecked positive feedback in a system can create a runaway ("snowballing") condition. In natural systems, such unchecked growth can reach a critical limit, leading to instability, disruption, or even death of organisms.

Global climate change creates an example of positive feedback as meltponds increase on ice sheets, glaciers, and ice shelves worldwide, as illustrated in Chapter 17. Meltponds are darker and reflect less sunlight (there is a lower albedo, or reflectivity, than snow) and therefore absorb more solar energy, which in turn, melts more ice, which forms more meltponds, and so forth. Thus, a positive feedback loop is in operation, further enhancing the effects of higher temperatures and warming trends.

Based on satellite images and aerial surveys, scientists determined a spatial increase in meltpond distribution of 400% across the Arctic region since 2000. Overall ice-mass losses from Greenland more than doubled between 1996 and 2010. The meltponds are symptomatic of climatic warming. Likewise, as sea ice melts, the darker open water absorbs more sunlight, which produces increased air and water temperatures.

Think of the numerous devastating wildfires that occurred in the last decade, including record wildfires in terms of area burned in Australia, the western United States, Canada and elsewhere, as examples of positive feedback. As the fires burned, the heat dried wet shrubs and green wood in areas around the fire, thus providing more fuel for combustion. The greater the fire, the

greater becomes the availability of fuel, and thus more fire is possible—a positive feedback.

System Equilibrium Most systems maintain structure and character over time. An energy and material system that remains balanced over time, in which conditions are constant or recur, is in a *steady-state condition*. When the rates of inputs and outputs in the system are equal and the amounts of energy and matter in storage within the system are constant (or more realistically, as the amounts fluctuate around a stable average, such as a person's body weight), the system is in **steady-state equilibrium**.

However, a steady-state system may demonstrate a changing trend over time, a condition described as **dynamic equilibrium**. These changing trends of either increasing or decreasing system operations may appear gradual. Figure 1.6 illustrates these two equilibrium conditions, steady-state and dynamic.

Note that systems try to maintain their functional operations; they tend to resist abrupt change. However, a system may reach a **threshold**, or *tipping point*, where it can no longer maintain its character, so it lurches to a new operational level. This abrupt change places the system in a *metastable equilibrium*. An example of such a condition is a hillside or coastal bluff that adjusts after a sudden landslide. A new equilibrium is eventually achieved among slope, materials, and energy over time.

This threshold concept raises concern in the scientific community, especially if some natural systems reach

Hillslope system passes a threshold.

(a)

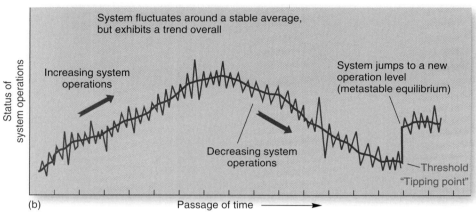

(b)

FIGURE 1.6 System equilibria: steady-state and dynamic.
(a) A steady-state equilibrium over time; system operations fluctuate around a stable average. Other systems are in a condition of dynamic equilibrium, with an increasing or decreasing operational trend as in (b). Rockslide along the Sea to Sky Highway blocked traffic in 2008, a threshold was reached and the cliff failed. [Jonathan Hayward/CP Images.]

their tipping-point limits. The relatively sudden collapse of ice shelves surrounding a portion of Antarctica and the sudden breakup of ice shelves on the north coast of Ellesmere Island serve as examples of systems at a threshold that are changing to a new status—that of disintegration (more on this in Chapter 17).

Thresholds can also be reached in plant and animal communities. The bleaching (death) of living coral reefs worldwide accelerated dramatically after 1997, when warming conditions in oceans combined with pollution to lead coral systems to a threshold. Today, about 50% of the corals on Earth are ailing or nearing collapse (more on this in Chapter 16). Harlequin frogs of tropical Central and South America are another example of species

reaching a tipping point, with increased extinctions since 1986 (Figure 1.7).

Systems Analysis and Species Extinction The key to unraveling what was happening to harlequin frog (*Atelopus varius*) and golden toad (*Bufo periglenes*) species in the Monteverde Cloud Forest Reserve, Costa Rica, and elsewhere in Central and South America was a consideration of climate change and how this alters transmission of diseases and pathogens. One infectious agent, the *chytrid fungus* (*Bactrachochytrium dendrobactidis*), spread as thermal-optimum conditions were reached in its mid-elevation range (1000 m to 2400 m) in the mountain cloud forest.

 GEO REPORT 1.1   *Amphibians at Thresholds*

Amphibian species are a threatened group of animals, with approximately one-third of recognised species now at risk of extinction. According to the Amphibian Specialist Group of the International Union for Conservation of Nature (IUCN, http://www.iucn.org/), two new initiatives are aimed at stopping the amphibian decline: increased habitat protection for species that are found in only a single location and stepped-up efforts at testing antifungal drugs to halt the killer frog disease and ease the current amphibian extinction crisis (more at http://www.amphibians.org).

FIGURE 1.7 **Harlequin frog extinction alarm.**
About two-thirds of harlequin frog species went extinct over the last two decades as a result of climate change. This is "rana dorado" or golden frog, that only survives in captivity. [Dante Fenolio/Photo Researchers, Inc.]

Human-forced climate change is increasing the temperature of the ocean and atmosphere. Higher temperatures cause higher evaporation rates that affect the condensation level (see Chapter 7). As the warm, moist air moves onshore and reaches the mountains, the air mass lifts and cools, and condensation occurs at higher elevations than before (see Chapter 8). Increased clouds affect the daily temperature range: Clouds at night, acting like insulation, raise nighttime minimum temperatures, whereas clouds during the day act as reflectors, lowering daytime maximum temperatures (see Chapter 4).

The chytrid fungus thrives when temperatures are between 17°C and 25°C. The new cloud cover keeps the daytime maximum below 25°C at the forest floor. In these more favourable conditions, the disease pathogen flourishes. Harlequin frogs have moist, porous skin that the fungus penetrates, killing the frog. Between 1986 and 2006, approximately 67% of the 110 known species of harlequin frogs went extinct.

From this example, can you see the power of systems analysis? Global warming affects the hydrologic cycle by raising air and water temperatures and increasing evaporation, all of which change the nature of cloud formations and alter daily temperature patterns.

Mount Pinatubo—Global System Impact A dramatic example of interactions between volcanic eruptions and Earth systems illustrates the strength of spatial analysis. Mount Pinatubo in the Philippines erupted violently in 1991, injecting 15–20 million tons of ash and sulfuric acid mist into the upper atmosphere (Figure 1.8). This was the second greatest eruption during the twentieth century; Mount Katmai in Alaska (1912) was the only one greater. The map in Figure 1.8 notes how the eruption materials from Mount Pinatubo affected Earth systems in several ways.

As you progress through this book, you will see the story of Mount Pinatubo and its implications woven through eight chapters: Chapter 1 (systems theory), Chapter 4 (effects on energy budgets in the atmosphere), Chapter 6 (satellite images of the spread of debris by atmospheric winds), Chapter 10 (temporary effect on global atmospheric temperatures), Chapters 11 and 12 (volcanic processes), Chapter 17 (past climatic effects of

GLOBAL IMPACTS OF MOUNT PINATUBO ERUPTION–JUNE 15, 1991

12 km³ of material was spread by atmospheric winds

Atmospheric albedo (reflectivity) increased 1.5% (4.3 W·m⁻²)

15–20 million tons of ash and sulfuric acid mist blasted into the atmosphere

42% of globe was affected by a thin aerosol cloud (20° S to 30° N)

15° N 120° E

Atmospheric absorption of solar energy increased (2.5 W·m⁻²)

Colourful twilight and dawn skies were seen worldwide

Diffuse sunlight increased; slight enhancement of photosynthesis

Net radiation at Earth's surface temporarily decreased average temperatures in the Northern Hemisphere by 0.5 C°

FIGURE 1.8 **The eruption of Mount Pinatubo.**
The 1991 Mount Pinatubo eruption affected the Earth–atmosphere system on a global scale. Geographers and other scientists use the latest technology to study how such eruptions affect the atmosphere's dynamic equilibrium. A summary of the impacts is in Chapter 12. [Inset photo by Dave Harlow, USGS.]

volcanoes) and Chapter 19 (effects on net photosynthesis). Instead of simply describing the eruption, we show the linkages and global impacts of such a volcanic explosion.

Systems in Geosystems

To further illustrate the systems' organization in this textbook, notice its organization around the flow of energy, materials, and information throughout the chapters and portions of chapters (Figure 1.9). In this way, topics follow a logical progression that unfolds according to the energy and material flows within individual systems or with time and the flow of events.

In Figure 1.9b, you see that Part I begins with Solar energy. The Sun's energy flows across space to the top of

Systems in *Elemental Geosystems*

Inputs
Solar energy to Earth
Earth's modern atmosphere

Actions
Atmosphere and surface energy balances

Human–Earth Relation
Air pollution
Acid deposition
Urban environment
Heat index, Wind chill
Solar energy
Wind power

Outputs
Global temperatures
Wind and ocean currents

PART I
The Energy–Atmosphere System

Inputs
Water
Atmospheric moisture

Actions
Humidity
Atmospheric stability
Air masses

Human–Earth Relation
Weather hazards
Water shortages
Climate change

Outputs
Weather
Water resources
Climatic patterns

PART II
Water, Weather, and Climate Systems

Inputs
Earth
Endogenic systems
Exogenic systems

Actions
Rock and mineral formation
Tectonic processes
Weathering
Erosion, transport, deposition

Human–Earth Relation
Hazard perception
Humans as geomorphic agent
Fluvial impacts; Desertification;
Sealevel rise; Ice-melt

Outputs
Crustal formation
Orogenesis and vulcanism
Landforms: karst, fluvial, eolian, coastal, glacial

PART III
Earth–Atmosphere Interface

Inputs
Insolation
Abiotic and biotic elements
Ecosystem components

Actions
Photosynthesis/respiration
Biogeochemical cycling
Trophic relations, food webs
Evolution, succession

Human–Earth Relation
Biodiversity losses
Soil degradation
Earth and human denominator

Outputs
Soils, plants, animals, life
Biodiversity, communities
Biomes: marine and terrestrial

PART IV
Soils, Ecosystems, and Biomes

FIGURE 1.9 The systems in *Geosystems*.
The sequence of systems flow in the organization of PARTS I, II, III, and IV. [TERRA/NASA.]

the atmosphere and through the atmosphere to the surface and surface energy budgets (Chapters 3 and 4). Then we look at the outputs of temperature (Chapter 5) and winds and ocean currents (Chapter 6). Note the same logical systems flow in the other three parts and in each chapter of this text—Part II and Chapter 16 also are shown as examples.

Models of Systems A **model** is a simplified, idealised representation of the real world. Models are designed with varying degrees of generalization. In your life, you may have built or drawn a model of something that was a simplification of the real thing—such as a model airplane or model house.

The simplicity of a model makes a system easier to understand and to simulate in experiments (for example, the leaf model in Figure 1.5). A good example is a model of the *hydrologic system*, which models Earth's entire water

system, its related energy flows, and the atmosphere, surface, and subsurface environments through which water moves (see Figure 9.1 in Chapter 9). We discuss many system models in this text.

Adjusting the variables in a model produces differing conditions and allows predictions of possible system operations. However, predictions are only as good as the assumptions and accuracy built into the model. A model is best viewed for what it is—a simplification to help us understand complex processes.

Earth's Four "Spheres" Earth's surface is a vast area of 510 million km² where four immense open systems interact. Figure 1.10 shows a simple model of three **abiotic**, or nonliving, systems overlapping to form the realm of the **biotic**, or living, system. The abiotic spheres are the *atmosphere*, *hydrosphere*, and *lithosphere*. The biotic sphere is the *biosphere*.

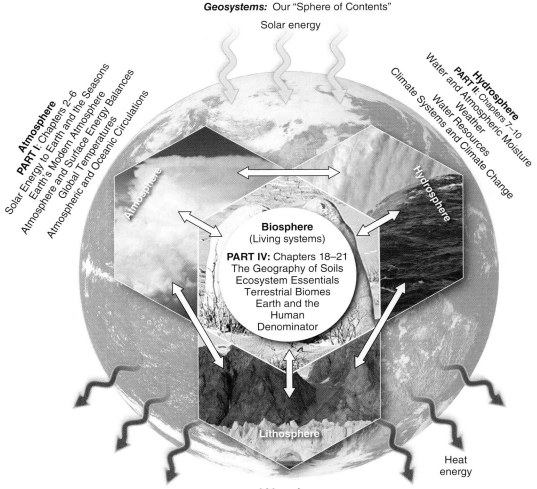

Geosystems: Our "Sphere of Contents"

Solar energy

Atmosphere
PART I: Chapters 2–6
Solar Energy to Earth and the Seasons
Earth's Modern Atmosphere
Atmosphere and Surface Energy Balances
Global Temperatures
Atmospheric and Oceanic Circulations

Hydrosphere
PART II: Chapters 7–10
Water and Atmospheric Moisture
Weather
Water Resources
Climate Systems and Climate Change

Atmosphere

Hydrosphere

Biosphere
(Living systems)

PART IV: Chapters 18–21
The Geography of Soils
Ecosystem Essentials
Terrestrial Biomes
Earth and the
Human
Denominator

Lithosphere

Heat
energy

Lithosphere
PART III: Chapters 11–17
The Dynamic Planet
Tectonics, Earthquakes, and Volcanism
Weathering, Karst Landscapes, and Mass Movement
River Systems and Landforms
Eolian Processes and Arid Landscapes
The Oceans, Coastal Processes, and Landforms
Glacial and Periglacial Processes and Landforms

FIGURE 1.10 Earth's four spheres.
Each sphere is a model of vast Earth systems. This four-part structure is the organizational framework for *Geosystems*. [Bobbé Christopherson.]

As noted in the figure, these four spheres form the Part I–IV structure that guides the grouping of chapters in this book. The various arrows in the figure show that content in each part and among chapters interrelates, as we build our discussion of Earth's abiotic and biotic systems.

- **Atmosphere (Part I, Chapters 2–6)** The **atmosphere** is a thin, gaseous veil surrounding Earth, held in place above the planet by the force of gravity. Formed by gases arising from within Earth's crust and interior and the exhalations of all life over time, the lower atmosphere is unique in the Solar System. It is a combination of nitrogen, oxygen, argon, carbon dioxide, water vapour, and trace gases.

- **Hydrosphere (Part II, Chapters 7–10)** Earth's waters exist in the atmosphere, on the surface, and in the crust near the surface. Collectively, these waters form the **hydrosphere**. That portion of the hydrosphere that is frozen is the **cryosphere**—snow, ice sheets, ice caps and fields, glaciers, ice shelves, sea ice, lake ice, and frozen ground and permafrost. Water of the hydrosphere exists naturally in all three states: liquid (both saline and fresh), solid (ice), and gaseous (water vapour).

- **Lithosphere (Part III, Chapters 11–17)** Earth's crust and a portion of the upper mantle directly below the crust form the **lithosphere**. The crust is quite brittle compared with the layers deep beneath the surface, which move slowly in response to an uneven distribution of heat energy and pressure. The soil layer is the *edaphosphere*, and generally covers Earth's land surfaces. In this text, the chapter on soils represents a bridge between the lithosphere (Part III) and biosphere (Part IV).

- **Biosphere (Part IV, Chapters 18–20)** The intricate, interconnected web that links all organisms with their physical environment is the **biosphere**. The biosphere is the area in which physical and chemical factors form the context of life. The biosphere exists in the overlap among the abiotic, or nonliving, spheres, extending from the seafloor, the upper layers of the crustal rock, to about 8 km into the atmosphere. Life is sustainable within these natural limits. The biosphere evolves, reorganises itself at times, faces extinctions, and still manages to flourish.

A Spherical Planet

We all have heard that some people believed Earth to be flat. Yet understanding of Earth's *sphericity*, or roundness, is not as modern a concept as many think. For instance, more than two millennia ago, the Greek mathematician and philosopher Pythagoras (ca. 580–500 B.C.) determined through observation that Earth is spherical. We do not know what observations led Pythagoras to this conclusion. Can you guess at what led him to deduce Earth's roundness?

He might have noticed ships sailing beyond the horizon and apparently sinking below the water's surface, only to arrive back at port with dry decks. Perhaps he noticed Earth's curved shadow cast on the lunar surface during an eclipse of the Moon. He might have deduced that the Sun and Moon are not just the flat disks they appear to be in the sky, but are spherical, and that Earth must be a sphere as well.

Earth's sphericity was generally accepted by the educated populace as early as the first century A.D. Christopher Columbus, for example, knew he was sailing around a sphere in 1492; that is one reason why he thought he had arrived in the East Indies.

Earth as a Geoid Until 1687, the spherical-perfection model was a basic assumption of **geodesy**, the science that determines Earth's shape and size by surveys and mathematical calculations. But in that year, Sir Isaac Newton postulated that Earth, along with the other planets, could not be perfectly spherical. Newton reasoned that the more-rapid rotational speed at the equator—the equator being farthest from the central axis of the planet and therefore moving faster—would produce an equatorial bulge as centrifugal force pulls Earth's surface outward. He was convinced that Earth is slightly misshapen into an *oblate spheroid*, or more correctly, an *oblate ellipsoid* (*oblate* means "flattened"), with the oblateness occurring at the poles.

Earth's equatorial bulge and its polar oblateness are universally accepted and confirmed with tremendous precision by satellite observations. Figure 1.11 gives Earth's average polar and equatorial circumferences and diameters. The "geoidal epoch" is our modern era of Earth measurement because Earth is a **geoid**, meaning literally that "the shape of Earth is Earth-shaped." Imagine Earth's geoid as a sea-level surface that is extended uniformly worldwide, beneath the continents. Both heights on land and depths in the oceans are measured from this hypothetical surface. Think of the geoid surface as a balance among the gravitational attraction of Earth's mass, the distribution of water and ice along its surface, and the outward centrifugal pull caused by Earth's rotation.

GEO REPORT 1.2 *Water in the Solar System*

Among the planets in the Solar System, only Earth possesses a hydrosphere and surface water in such quantity, some 1.36 billion km³. There are discoveries of subsurface water on the Moon in its polar areas and on Mars, Jupiter's moon Europa, and Saturn's moons Enceladus and Titan. In the Martian polar region, remote spacecraft are studying ground ice and patterned ground phenomena caused by freezing and thawing water, as discussed for Earth in Chapter 17. In the Universe, deep-space telescopes reveal traces of water at nebula and distant planetary objects.

FIGURE 1.11 Earth's dimensions.
Earth's equatorial and polar circumference (a) and diameter (b). The dashed line is a perfect circle for reference to Earth's geoid.

Measuring Earth in 247 B.C.

Eratosthenes (ca. 276–c.a.195 B.C.) served as the librarian of Alexandria in Egypt during the third century B.C. He was a Greek geographer and astronomer in a position of scientific leadership. Alexandria's library was the finest in the ancient world. Among Eratosthenes' achievements was calculating Earth's polar circumference to a high level of accuracy. Here's how he did it. As you read, follow along on Figure 1.12.

Travelers told Eratosthenes that on June 21 they saw the Sun's rays shine directly to the bottom of a well at Syene, the location of present-day Aswan, Egypt. This meant that the Sun was directly overhead on that day. North of Syene in Alexandria, Eratosthenes knew from his own observations that the Sun's rays were never directly overhead, even at noon on June 21, the day when the noon

Sun is at its northernmost position in the sky. He knew objects in Alexandria, unlike objects in Syene, always cast a noontime shadow on June 21. Using his knowledge of geometry, Eratosthenes conducted an experiment to explain the different observations.

In Alexandria at noon on June 21, he measured the angle of a shadow cast by an obelisk (a perpendicular column). Knowing the height of the obelisk and measuring the length of the Sun's shadow from its base, he solved the triangle for the angle of the Sun's noon rays, which he determined to be 7.2° off from directly overhead. However, at Syene on the same day, the angle of the Sun's rays was approximately 0° from a perpendicular, arriving from directly overhead.

Eratosthenes knew from geometry that the distance on the ground between Alexandria and Syene formed an

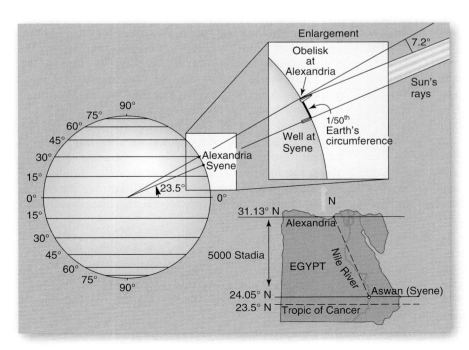

FIGURE 1.12 Eratosthenes' calculation.
Eratosthenes' work teaches the value of observing carefully and integrating all observations. Calculating Earth's circumference required application of his knowledge of Earth–Sun relationships, geometry, and geography.

arc of Earth's circumference equal to the angle of the Sun's rays at Alexandria. Since 7.2° is roughly 1/50 of the 360° in Earth's total circumference (360° ÷ 7.2° = 50), he knew the distance between Alexandria and Syene must represent approximately 1/50 of Earth's total polar circumference.

Next, Eratosthenes determined the surface distance between the two cities as 5000 stadia. A *stadium*, a Greek unit of measure, equals approximately 185 m. He then multiplied 5000 stadia by 50 to determine that Earth's polar circumference is about 250 000 stadia. Eratosthenes' calculations convert to roughly 46 250 km, which is remarkably close to the correct value of 40 008 km for Earth's polar circumference. Not bad for 247 B.C.!

Location and Time on Earth

Geographic science requires an internationally accepted, coordinated grid system to determine location on Earth. From the chapter's opening photograph, you can see the importance of determining the location of the research ship and tracking the locations of tabular icebergs. The terms *latitude* and *longitude* were in use on maps as early as the first century A.D., with the concepts themselves dating back to Eratosthenes and others.

The geographer, astronomer, and mathematician Ptolemy (ca. A.D. 90–168) contributed greatly to the principles used to create modern maps, and many of his terms are still used today. Ptolemy divided the circle into 360 degrees (360°), with each degree having 60 minutes (60') and each minute having 60 seconds (60") in a manner adapted from the ancient Babylonians. He located places using these degrees, minutes, and seconds. However, the precise length of a degree of latitude and a degree of longitude remained unresolved for the next 17 centuries.

Latitude

Latitude is an angular distance north or south of the equator, measured from the centre of Earth (Figure 1.13a). On a map or globe, the lines designating these angles of latitude run east and west, parallel to the equator (Figure 1.13b). Because Earth's equator divides the distance between the North Pole and the South Pole exactly in half, it is assigned the value of 0° latitude. Thus, latitude increases from the equator northward to the North Pole, at 90° north latitude, and southward to the South Pole, at 90° south latitude.

A line connecting all points along the same latitudinal angle is a **parallel**. In Figure 1.13, an angle of 49° N latitude is annotated, and, by connecting all points at this latitude, we have the 49th parallel. Thus, *latitude* is the name of the angle (49° N latitude), *parallel* names the line (49th

(a)

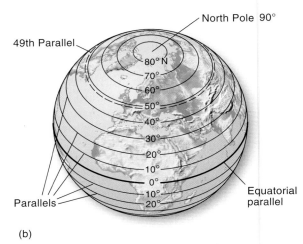

(b)

FIGURE 1.13 Parallels of latitude.
(a) Latitude is measured in degrees north or south of the equator, which is 0°. Earth's poles are at 90°. Note the annotation of 49° latitude. (b) These angles of latitude determine parallels along Earth's surface. Do you know your present latitude?

parallel), and both indicate distance north of the equator. As noted in *Geosystems Now* that opened the chapter, the 49th parallel is significant in the Western Hemisphere, for it forms the boundary between Canada and the United States from Lake of the Woods on the Ontario–Manitoba–Minnesota border to the Strait of Georgia.

Latitude is readily determined by observing *fixed celestial objects* such as the Sun or the stars, a method dating to ancient times. During daylight hours, the angle of the Sun above the horizon indicates the observer's latitude, after adjustment is made for the season and for the time of day. Because Polaris (the North Star) is almost directly overhead

GEO REPORT 1.3   *The Value of a Stadium*

From the Greek *stade*, the value of a Greek stadium varied in time and place. For this calculation related to Eratosthenes' measurement, we used 185 m as a stadium length. This represents an average value in the Greek era. The word for the stadium measure was expanded to be the word to describe the arena in which foot races took place—thus our modern stadiums. Think of Eratosthenes' work when you next see a stadium.

at the North Pole, persons anywhere in the Northern Hemisphere can determine their latitude at night simply by sighting Polaris and measuring its angle above the local horizon. The angle of elevation of Polaris above the horizon equals the latitude of the observation point.

In the Southern Hemisphere, Polaris cannot be seen, because it is below the horizon. Instead, latitude south of the equator is measured by sighting on a constellation that points to a celestial location above the South Pole. This indicator constellation is the Southern Cross (*Crux Australis*).

Latitudinal Geographic Zones Natural environments differ dramatically from the equator to the poles. These differences result from the amount of solar energy received, which varies by latitude and season of the year. "Lower latitudes" are those nearer the equator, whereas "higher latitudes" are those nearer the poles.

Figure 1.14 portrays these zones, their locations, and their names: *equatorial* and *tropical*, *subtropical*, *midlatitude*, *subarctic* or *subantarctic*, and *arctic* or *antarctic*. These generalised latitudinal zones are useful for reference and comparison, but they do not have rigid boundaries; rather, think of them as transitioning from one to another.

█ ▌▌ CRITICAL THINKING 1.1

Latitudinal Zones and Temperature

Refer to the graph in Figure 5.3 that plots annual temperature data for five cities from near the equator to beyond the Arctic Circle. Note the geographic location for each of the five cities on the latitudinal geographic zone map in Figure 1.14. In which zone is each city located? Roughly characterise changing temperature patterns through the seasons as you move away from the equator. Describe what you discover.

The *Tropic of Cancer* (23.5°N parallel) and the *Tropic of Capricorn* (23.5° S parallel) are the most extreme northern and southern parallels that experience perpendicular (directly overhead) rays of the Sun at local noon. When the Sun arrives overhead at these tropics, it marks the first day of summer in each hemisphere. (Further discussion of the tropics is in Chapter 2.) The *Arctic Circle* (66.5° N parallel) and the *Antarctic Circle* (66.5° S parallel) are the parallels farthest from the poles that still experience 24 uninterrupted hours of night, including dawn and twilight, during local winter or 24 uninterrupted hours of day during local summer. In Canada, *north* or *northerly* has meaning beyond a measurement of latitude. In fact, Statistics Canada has developed a measure of northerliness that combines physical, biological, social, economic and cultural measures to define regions that are "north" and have identifiable adaptations (http://www.statcan.gc.ca/pub/16-201-x/2010000/m018-eng.htm).

Longitude

Longitude is an angular distance east or west of a point on Earth's surface, measured from the centre of Earth (Figure 1.15a). On a map or globe, the lines designating these angles of longitude run north and south (Figure 1.15b). A line connecting all points along the same longitude is a **meridian**. In the figure, a longitudinal angle of 60° E is annotated. These meridians run at right angles (90°) to all parallels, including the equator.

Thus, *longitude* is the name of the angle, *meridian* names the line, and both indicate distance east or west of an arbitrary **prime meridian**—a meridian designated as 0° (Figure 1.15b). Earth's prime meridian passes

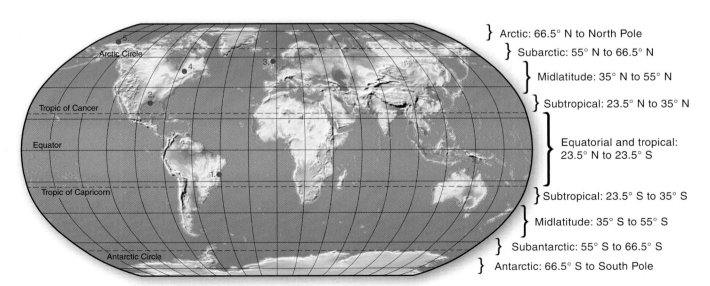

FIGURE 1.14 Latitudinal geographic zones.
Geographic zones are generalizations that characterise various regions by latitude. Think of these as transitional into one another over broad areas. Noted cities: 1. Salvador, Brazil; 2. New Orleans, Louisiana; 3. Edinburgh, Scotland; 4. Montreal, Québec; and 5. Barrow, Alaska.

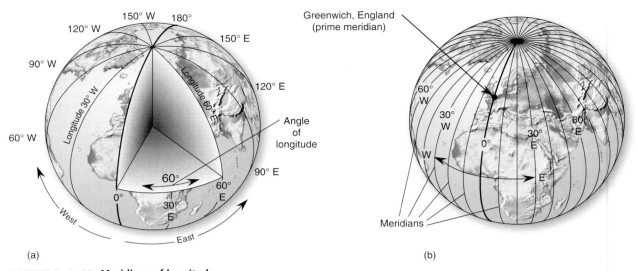

FIGURE 1.15 Meridians of longitude.
(a) Longitude is measured in degrees east or west of a 0° starting line, the prime meridian. Note the annotation of 60° E longitude. (b) Angles of longitude measured from the prime meridian determine other meridians. North America is west of Greenwich; therefore, it is in the Western Hemisphere. Do you know your present longitude?

through the old Royal Observatory at Greenwich, England, as set by treaty in 1884—the *Greenwich prime meridian*.

Determination of Latitude and Longitude
Table 1.2 compares the length of latitude and longitude degrees. Because meridians of longitude converge toward the poles, the actual distance on the ground spanned by a degree of longitude is greatest at the equator (where meridians separate to their widest distance apart) and diminishes to zero at the poles (where meridians converge). In comparison, note the consistent distance represented by a degree of latitude from equator to poles. For your latitude degree and longitude degree, find the nearest linear value for each.

We noted that latitude is determined easily by sighting the Sun or the North Star or by using the Southern Cross as a pointer. In contrast, a method of accurately determining longitude, especially at sea, remained a major difficulty in navigation until after 1760. The key to measuring the longitude of a place lies in accurately knowing time. The relationship between time and longitude and an exciting chapter in human discovery is the topic of Focus Study 1.2.

Great Circles and Small Circles

Great circles and small circles are important concepts that help summarise latitude and longitude (Figure 1.16). A **great circle** is any circle of Earth's circumference whose centre coincides with the centre of Earth. An infinite number of great circles can be drawn on Earth. Every meridian is one-half of a great circle that passes through the poles. On flat maps, airline and shipping routes appear to arch their way across oceans and landmasses. These are *great circle routes*, the shortest distance between two points on Earth (see Figure 1.26).

In contrast to meridians, only one parallel is a great circle—the *equatorial parallel*. All other parallels diminish

TABLE 1.2	Physical Distances Represented by Degrees of Latitude and Longitude	
Latitudinal Location	**Latitude Degree**	**Longitude Degree**
	Length	Length
	km	km
90° (poles)	111.70	0
60°	111.42	55.80
50°	111.23	71.70
40°	111.04	85.40
30°	110.86	96.49
0° (equator)	110.58	111.32

◈ FOCUS STUDY 1.2

The Timely Search for Longitude

Unlike latitude, longitude cannot be determined readily from fixed celestial bodies. Determining longitude is particularly critical at sea where no landmarks are visible. The problem is Earth's rotation, which constantly changes the apparent position of the Sun and stars.

In the early 1600s, Galileo explained that longitude angles could be measured by using two clocks. Any point on Earth takes 24 hours to travel around the full 360° of one rotation (one day). If you divide 360° by 24 hours, you find that any point on Earth travels through 15° of longitude every hour. Thus, if there were a way to measure time accurately at sea, a comparison of two clocks could give a value for the ship's longitudinal position.

One clock would indicate the time back at home port (Figure 1.2.1). The other clock would be reset at local noon each day, as determined by the highest Sun position in the sky (solar zenith). The time difference between the ship and home port would indicate the longitudinal difference traveled: one hour for each 15° of longitude. The principle was sound; all that was needed were accurate clocks. Unfortunately, the pendulum clock invented by Christian Huygens in 1656 and accurate on land was not accurate on the rolling deck of a ship at sea.

In 1707, the British lost four ships and 2000 men in a marine tragedy that was blamed specifically on the longitude problem. In response, Parliament passed an act in 1714—"Publik Reward . . . to Discover the Longitude at Sea"—and authorised a prize worth more than

$2 million in today's dollars to the first successful inventor of an accurate seafaring clock. The Board of Longitude was established to judge any devices submitted.

John Harrison, a self-taught country clockmaker, began work on the problem in 1728 and finally produced his brilliant marine chronometer, known as *Number 4*, in 1760. The clock was tested on a voyage to Jamaica in 1761. When taken ashore and compared to land-based longitude, Harrison's ingenious *Number 4* was only 5 seconds slow, an error that translates to only a distance of 1.25 longitude minutes, or 2.3 km, well within Parliament's standard. After many delays, Harrison finally received most of the prize money in his last years of life.

With his marine clocks, John Harrison tested the waters of space–time. He

succeeded, against all odds, in using the fourth—temporal—dimension to link points on the three-dimensional globe. He wrested the world's whereabouts from the stars, and locked the secret in a pocket watch.*

From the time that Harrison invented his clock, it was possible to determine longitude accurately on land and sea, as long as everyone agreed upon a meridian—which became the Royal Observatory in Greenwich, England—to use as a reference for time comparisons. In this modern era of atomic clocks and GPS satellites in mathematically precise orbits, we have far greater accuracy available for the determination of longitude on Earth.

*From Dava Sobel, *Longitude, The Story of a Lone Genius Who Solved the Greatest Scientific Problem of His Time* (New York: Walker and Co., 1995), p. 175.

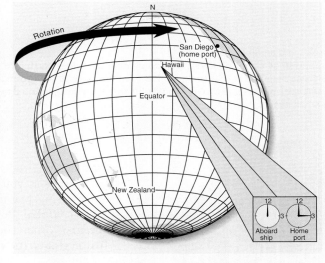

FIGURE 1.2.1 Clock time determines longitude.
If the shipboard clock reads local noon and the clock set for home port reads 3:00 P.M., ship time is 3 hours earlier than home time. Therefore, calculating 3 hours at 15° per hour puts the ship at 45° west longitude from home port.

---

in length toward the poles and, along with any other non-great circles that one might draw, constitute **small circles.** These circles have centres that do not coincide with Earth's centre.

Figure 1.17 combines latitude and parallels with longitude and meridians to illustrate Earth's complete coordinate grid system. Note the dot that marks our measurement of 49° N and 60° E, a location in western Kazakstan. Next time you look at a world globe, follow the parallel and meridian that converge on your location.

▌▌ CRITICAL THINKING 1.2

Where Are You?

Select a location (for example, your campus, home, workplace, or a city) and determine the following: latitude, longitude, and elevation. Describe the resources you used to gather this geographic information, such as an atlas, web site, Google Earth, or Global Positioning System measurement. Finally, using Table 1.2, find the nearest latitude and longitude value for the location you checked, and write down your calculation of the length of a degree of latitude and degree of longitude.

(a) Each pair of meridians forms a great circle

All other parallels form small circles

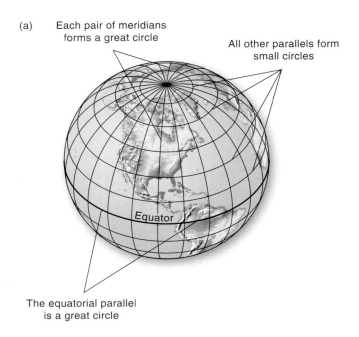

Equator

The equatorial parallel is a great circle

(b)

Great circle

A plane intersecting the globe along a great circle divides the globe into equal halves and passes through its center

(c)

Small circle

A plane that intersects the globe along a small circle splits the globe into unequal sections—this plane does not pass through the center of the globe

FIGURE 1.16 Great circles and small circles.
(a) Examples of great circles and small circles on Earth. (b) Any plane that divides Earth into equal halves will intersect the globe along a great circle; this great circle is a full circumference of the globe and is the shortest distance between any two surface points. (c) Any plane that splits the globe into unequal portions will intersect the globe along a small circle.

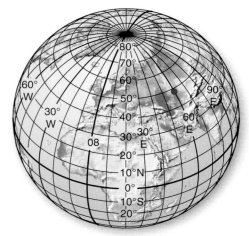

FIGURE 1.17 Earth's coordinate grid system.
Latitude and parallels, longitude and meridians allow all places on Earth to be located precisely. The red dot is at 49° N latitude and 60° E longitude.

Global Navigation Satellite Systems

Today, using a handheld instrument that receives radio signals from satellites, you can accurately calibrate latitude, longitude, and elevation—and even know where your car is as you drive along, often with an electronic voice giving you driving directions. Although the U.S.-owned **Global Positioning System (GPS)** system was the first, other countries have **global navigation satellite systems (GNSS)** in operation or in development: *GLONASS* (Russia), *Galileo* (European Union), and *Compass* (China).

The GPS array comprises 24 orbiting satellites, in six orbital planes, that transmit navigational signals for Earth-bound use (backup GPS satellites have been placed in orbital storage, ready as replacements). Think of the satellites as a constellation of navigational beacons with which you interact to determine your unique location. Every possible square meter of Earth's surface has its own address relative to the latitude–longitude grid.

A GPS receiver, now built into cell phones, digital cameras, and camcorders, senses signals from three or more satellites and triangulates the receiver's location. This is accomplished by calculating the distance between each satellite and receiver using clocks built into each instrument, which time radio signals travelling at the

FIGURE 1.18 **Using satellites to triangulate location through GPS.**
Imagine a ranging sphere around each of three GPS satellites. These spheres intersect at two points, one easily rejected because it is some distance above Earth and the other at the true location of the GPS receiver. In this way, three satellites can determine location; adding a fourth satellite measure elevation.

FIGURE 1.19 **GPS in action.**
Location coordinates on a GPS unit in operation on a research ship as it crosses Earth's equator at 0° latitude. Locate these latitude and longitude coordinates on a globe or map. How far from the nearest land is the ship? What is the name of this ocean? [Bobbé Christopherson.]

speed of light between them (Figure 1.18). The receiver reports latitude, longitude, and elevation (Figure 1.19). Within *Differential GPS (DGPS)*, accuracy increases to between 1 m to 3 m by comparing readings with another base station (reference receiver) for a differential correction. Centimetre-level accuracy can be achieved using a Real-Time Kinematic (RTK) system.

The GPS satellite measurements help refine our knowledge of Earth's exact shape and how this shape is changing. The GPS is useful for diverse applications, such as navigating on the ocean, surveying land, tracking small changes in Earth's crust, managing the movement of fleets of trucks, mining and mapping resources, tracking wildlife migration and behaviour, carrying out police and security work, and conducting environmental planning. Outdoor recreationists and sportspersons commonly carry hand-held GPS devices that allow them to track their own location. Commercial airlines use GPS to improve accuracy of routes flown and thus increase fuel efficiency.

Scientists used GPS technology to determine the height of Mount Everest in the Himalayan Mountains accurately, 8850 m instead of the former measurement of 8848 m (Figure 1.20). GPS measurements of Mount Kilimanjaro also refined the previously determined height of its summit to 5892 m from 5895 m.

In *precision agriculture*, farmers use GPS devices to determine crop yields on specific parts of their farms.

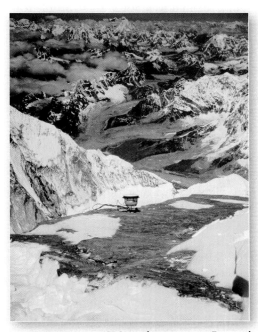

FIGURE 1.20 **GPS used to measure Everest's summit height.**
Installation of a Trimble 4800 GPS unit at Earth's highest benchmark, only 18 m below the 8850 m summit. Previously, the height was measured as 8848 m. Scientists using GPS accurately analysed the rate the mountain range is moving due to tectonic forces. [Photo and GPS installation by adventurer/climber Wally Berg, May 20, 1998.]

 GEO REPORT 1.4 *GPS Origins*

Originally devised in the 1970s by the U.S. Department of Defense for military purposes, the present GPS is commercially available worldwide. In 2000, the Pentagon shut down its Pentagon Selective Availability security control, making commercial resolution the same as military applications. Additional frequencies were added in 2003 and 2006, which increased accuracy significantly to less than 10 m. For a GPS overview, see http://www.colorado.edu/geography/gcraft/notes/gps/gps_f.html.

A detailed plot map is made to guide the farmer on the addition of fertilizer, proper seed distribution, precise irrigation applications, or other work needed. A computer and GPS unit onboard the farm equipment guides the work. This is the science of *variable-rate technology*, made possible by GNSS technology.

GNSS/GPS is important to a locational, spatial geographic science because this precise technology reduces the need to maintain ground control points for location, mapping, and spatial analysis. Instead, geographers working in the field can determine their position accurately as they work. Boundaries and data points in a study area are easily determined and entered into a database, reducing the need for traditional surveys.

Prime Meridian and Standard Time

Coordination of international trade, airline schedules, business and agricultural activities, and daily living depends on a worldwide time system. Today, we take for granted standard time zones and an agreed-upon prime meridian, but such a standard is a relatively recent development.

Setting a standard time was not a great problem in small European countries, most of which are less than 15° wide. But in North America, which spans more than 90° of longitude (the equivalent of six 15° zones), the problem was serious. In 1870, a traveller going from Halifax to Toronto had to change time at Saint John, Québec City, Montréal, Ottawa, and Toronto. When it was noon in Washington, D.C. in the United States, it was 12:54 P.M. in Halifax, 12:14 P.M. in Montreal, and 11:51 A.M. in Toronto!

In 1878, Sanford Fleming, a railway surveyor and engineer who immigrated to Canada from Scotland, suggested a method for standardizing time. Despite early objections, Canada and the United States adopted his system for railway scheduling in 1883. Twenty-seven countries attended the 1884 International Meridian Conference in Washington, D.C. to set a global standard. Before that year, most nations used their own national capital as a prime meridian for their land maps, whereas more than 70% of the world's merchant ships were using Greenwich as a prime meridian on marine charts. After lengthy debate at the conference, most participating nations chose the highly respected Royal Observatory at Greenwich, London, England, as the position for the prime meridian of 0° longitude for all maps. Thus, a world standard was set—**Greenwich Mean Time (GMT)**—

and a consistent Universal Time was established. (See http://wwp.greenwichmeantime.com/.)

The basis of our time system is that Earth revolves 360° every 24 hours, or 15° per hour (360° ÷ 24 = 15°). Thus, 24 time zones of 1 hour are established, each spanning 7.5° on either side of a *central meridian*. Today, with six time zones, only five adjustments to clocks are needed when crossing Canada—from Newfoundland Standard Time to Atlantic, Eastern, Central, Mountain, and Pacific Standard Times—and three changes (with four time zones) across the continental United States.

Assuming it is 9:00 P.M. in Greenwich, then it is 5:30 P.M. in St. John's (UTC +3.5 hr), 5:00 P.M. in Halifax (+4 hr), 4:00 P.M. in Toronto (+5 hr), 3:00 P.M. in Winnipeg (+6 hr), 2:00 P.M. in Edmonton (+7 hr), and 1:00 P.M. in Vancouver (+8 hr). To the east, it is midnight in Ar Riyāḍ, Saudi Arabia (−3hr). The designation A.M. is for *ante meridiem*, "before noon," whereas P.M. is for *post meridiem*, "after noon." A 24-hour clock avoids the use of these designations: 3:00 P.M. is stated 15:00 hours; 3 A.M. is 03:00 hours.

As you can see from the modern international time zones in Figure 1.21, national boundaries and political considerations distort time boundaries. For example, China spans four time zones, but its government decided to keep the entire country operating on the same time. Thus, in some parts of China clocks are several hours different from what we would expect the local time to be based on the height of the Sun. In the United States, parts of Florida and west Texas are in the same time zone.

International Date Line An important corollary of the prime meridian is the 180° meridian on the opposite side of the planet. This meridian is the **International Date Line (IDL)**, which marks the place where each day officially begins (at 12:00 A.M.). From this "line" the new day sweeps westward. This *westward* movement of time is created by Earth's turning *eastward* on its axis and the Sun being in a fixed location. Locating the date line in the sparsely populated Pacific Ocean minimises most local confusion.

At the IDL, the west side of the line is always one day ahead of the east side. No matter what time of day it is when the line is crossed, the calendar changes by one day (Figure 1.22). Note in the illustration the departures of the IDL from the 180° meridian; these deviations are due to local administrative and political preferences.

GEO REPORT 1.5   *Magellan's Crew Loses a Day!*

Early explorers had a problem before the date-line concept. For example, Magellan's crew returned from the first circumnavigation of Earth in 1522, confident from their ship's log that it was Wednesday, September 7. They were shocked when informed by local residents that it was actually Thursday, September 8. Without an International Date Line, they had no idea that they must advance a day somewhere when sailing around the world in a westward direction. Imagine the confusion of the crew arriving home.

FIGURE 1.21 Modern international standard time zones.
Numbers along the bottom of the map indicate how many hours each zone is earlier (minus sign) or later (plus sign) than Coordinated Universal Time (UTC) at the prime meridian. If it is 7:00 P.M. in Greenwich, determine the present time in Moscow, London, Halifax, Chicago, Winnipeg, Edmonton, Vancouver, Fairbanks, Honolulu, Tokyo, and Singapore. [Adapted from Defense Mapping Agency. See http://aa.usno.navy.mil/ faq/docs/world_tzones.html.]

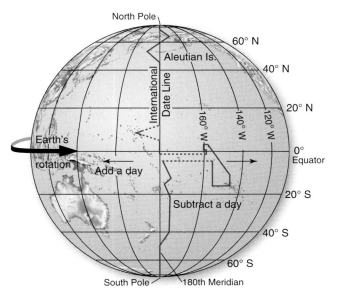

FIGURE 1.22 International Date Line
The International Date Line location is approximately along the 180th meridian (see the IDL location on Figure 1.21). Note the dotted lines on the map—island countries set their own time zones, but their political control extends only 3.5 nautical miles offshore. Officially, you gain one day crossing the IDL from east to west.

Coordinated Universal Time For decades, Greenwich Mean Time (GMT) from the Royal Observatory's astronomical clocks was the world's Universal Time (UT) standard for accuracy. GMT was broadcast using radio time signals as early as 1910. Taking the initiative in 1912, the French government called a gathering of nations to better coordinate radio time signals. At this conference, GMT was made standard, and a new organization was set to be the custodian of "exact" time—the International Bureau of Weights and Measures (BIPM, see http://www.bipm.org/). Progress was made in accurately measuring time with the invention of quartz clocks in 1939 and atomic clocks in the early 1950s.

Accurate time is not a matter of simply keeping track of Earth's rotation, since it is slowing down from the tug of tidal forces and rearrangement of water. Note that 150 million years ago a "day" was 22 hours long and 150 million years in the future a "day" will be approaching 27 hours in length.

The **Coordinated Universal Time (UTC)**[1] time signal system replaced GMT in 1972 and became the

[1]UTC is in use because agreement was not reached on whether to use the English word order, CUT, or the French order, TUC. UTC was the compromise and is recommended for all timekeeping applications; use of the term *GMT* is discouraged.

legal reference for official time in all countries. Although the prime meridian still runs through Greenwich, UTC is based on average time calculations from atomic clocks collected worldwide. You might still see official UTC referred to as GMT or Zulu time.

In Canada, the Institute for Measurement Standards, National Research Council, participates in determining UTC (for the UTC time, call 1-613-745-1578 [English]; or 1-613-745-9426 [French]; for more see http://time5.nrc.ca/JavaClock/timeDisplayWE.shtml). In the United States, Time and Frequency Services of the National Institute for Standards and Technology (NIST, http://nist.time.gov/), U.S. Department of Commerce, operates several of the most advanced clocks.

Daylight Saving Time In 70 countries, mainly in the temperate latitudes, time is set ahead 1 hour in the spring and set back one hour in the fall—a practice known as **daylight saving time**. The idea to extend daylight for early evening activities (at the expense of daylight in the morning), first proposed by Benjamin Franklin, was not adopted until World War I and again during World War II, when Australia, Canada, Germany, Great Britain, and the United States used the practice to save energy (one less hour of artificial lighting needed).

In 1986 for one year, and again permanently in 2007, Canada and the United States lengthened the period of daylight saving time. Time "springs forward" one hour on the second Sunday in March and "falls back" an hour on the first Sunday in November, except in a few places that do not use daylight saving time. In Europe, the last Sundays in March and October are used to begin and end what is called "summer-time period." (See http://webexhibits.org/daylightsaving/.)

Despite standardization efforts, local preferences persist. In Québec, the area east of 63° W does not change to daylight saving time and remains on Atlantic Standard Time year round. In Ontario, Atikokan uses Eastern Time in winter and Central Time in summer; Pickle Lake and New Osnaburgh do not change to daylight saving time, and Big Trout Lake uses Central Time even though it lies in the Eastern Time zone. Most of Saskatchewan does not change to daylight saving time, but uses Central Standard Time throughout the year. Denare Beach and Creighton use daylight saving time even though they are in Saskatchewan. All of Lloydminster uses Mountain Time although it lies in both the Central and Mountain zones. Creston, Fort St. John, and Dawson Creek, British Columbia, ignore daylight saving time by using Mountain Time in winter and Pacific Time in summer.

Maps, Scales, and Projections

The earliest known graphic maps date to 2300 B.C., when the Babylonians used clay tablets to record information about the region of the Tigris and Euphrates rivers (the area of modern-day Iraq). Today, the making of maps and charts is a specialised science as well as an art, blending aspects of geography, engineering, mathematics, graphics, computer science, and artistic specialties. It is similar in ways to architecture, in which aesthetics and utility combine to produce a useful product.

A **map** is a generalised view of an area, usually some portion of Earth's surface, as seen from above and greatly reduced in size. Good maps include a title, border, north arrow, scale, and data source. **Cartography** is that part of geography involving mapmaking. Maps are critical tools with which geographers depict spatial information and analyse spatial relationships.

We all use maps at some time to visualise our location in relation to other places, or maybe plan a trip, or coordinate commercial and economic activities. Have you found yourself looking at a map, planning real and imagined adventures to far-distant places? Maps are wonderful tools! Understanding a few basics about maps is essential to our study of physical geography.

The Scale of Maps

Architects, toy designers, and mapmakers have something in common: They all create scale models. They reduce real things and places to the more convenient scale of a drawing; a model car, train, or plane; a diagram; or a map. An architect renders a blueprint of a structure to guide the building contractors, selecting a scale so that a centimetre on the drawing represents so many metres on the proposed building. Often, the drawing is 1/50 to 1/100 of real size.

The cartographer does the same thing in preparing a map. The ratio of the image on a map to the real world is **scale**; it relates a unit on the map to the same unit on the ground. A 1:1 scale means that a centimetre on the map represents a centimetre on the ground, although this is an impractical map scale, for the map is as large as the area mapped! A more appropriate scale for a local map is 1:10 000, in which 1 unit on the map represents 10 000 of the same units on the ground.

Cartographers express map scale as a representative fraction, a graphic scale, or written scale (Figure 1.23). A *representative fraction* (*RF*, or *fractional scale*) is expressed with either a colon or a slash, as in 1:125 000 or 1/125 000.

FIGURE 1.23 **Map scale.**
Three common expressions of map scale—representative fraction, graphic scale, and written scale.

TABLE 1.3	Sample Representative Fractions and Written Scales for Small-, Medium-, and Large-Scale Maps in Metric		
System		Representative Fraction	Written Scale
Metric	Small	1:1 000 000	1 cm = 10.0 km
	Medium	1:250 000	1 cm = 2.5 km
		1:50 000	1 cm = 500 m
	Large	1:10 000	1 cm = 100 m

No actual units of measurement are mentioned because any unit is applicable as long as both parts of the fraction are in the same unit: 1 cm to 125 000 cm, 1 m to 125 000 m, or even 1 arm length to 125 000 arm lengths, and so on.

A *graphic scale*, or *bar scale*, is a bar graph with units to allow measurement of distances on the map. A *written scale* simply states the ratio in words—for example, "one centimetre to one kilometre." An important advantage of a graphic scale is that if the map is enlarged or reduced, the graphic scale enlarges or reduces along with the map. In contrast, written and fractional scales become incorrect with enlargement or reduction. As an example, you can shrink a map from 1:50 000 to 1:250 000, but a written scale would still say "1 cm to 50 m," instead of the new correct scale of 1 cm to 250 m.

Scales are *small*, *medium*, and *large*, depending on the ratio described. In relative terms, a scale of 1:10 000 is a large scale, whereas a scale of 1:1 000 000 is a small scale. The greater the denominator in a fractional scale (the scale factor, the number on the right in a ratio expression), the smaller the scale and the more abstract the map is in relation to what is being mapped. Examples of selected representative fractions and written scales are listed in Table 1.3 for small-, medium-, and large-scale maps.

❚❚ CRITICAL THINKING 1.3

Find and Calculate Some Scales

Find a globe or map and check the scale at which it was drawn. See if you can find examples of fractional, graphic, and written scales on wall maps, on highway maps, and in atlases. Find some examples of small- and large-scale maps, and note the different subject matter each type portrays.

Consider a world globe that is 61 cm in diameter. We know that Earth has an equatorial diameter of 12 756 km, so the scale of such a globe is the ratio of 61 cm to 12 756 km. To calculate the representative fraction for the globe in centimetres, divide Earth's actual diameter by the globe's diameter (12 756 km/61 cm). (*Hint*: 1 km = 1000 m, 1 m = 100 cm; therefore, Earth's diameter of 12 756 km represents 1 275 600,000 cm; and the globe's diameter is 61 cm.) In general, do you think a world globe is a small- or a large-scale map of Earth's surface?

Map Projections

A globe is not always a helpful map representation of Earth. When you go on a short trip, you need more detailed information than a globe can provide. Consequently, to provide local detail, cartographers prepare large-scale *flat maps*, which are two-dimensional representations (scale models) of our three-dimensional Earth. Unfortunately, such conversion from three dimensions to two causes distortion.

A globe is the only map of Earth that closely represents all of *distance*, *direction*, *area*, *shape*, and *proximity*. A flat map distorts some of these properties. Therefore, in preparing a flat map, the cartographer must decide which characteristics to preserve, for which other characteristics distortion must be accepted, and how much distortion is acceptable. To understand this problem, consider these important properties of a *globe*:

- Parallels always are parallel to each other, always are evenly spaced along meridians, and always decrease in length toward the poles.
- Meridians always converge at both poles and are evenly spaced along any individual parallel.
- The distance between meridians always decreases toward the poles, with the spacing between meridians at the 60th parallel equal to one-half the equatorial spacing.
- Parallels and meridians always cross each other at right angles.

The problem is that all these qualities cannot be reproduced at the same time on a flat surface. Simply taking a globe apart and laying it flat on a table illustrates the challenge faced by cartographers (Figure 1.24). You can see the empty spaces that open up between the sections, or gores, of the globe. This reduction of the spherical Earth to a flat surface is a **map projection**. Thus, no flat map projection of Earth can ever retain all the important properties of a globe. Flat maps always possess some degree of distortion—much less for large-scale maps representing a few square kilometres; much more for small-scale maps covering individual countries, continents, or the entire world.

Properties of Projections   There are many map projections, four of which are shown in Figure 1.25. *The best projection is always determined by its intended use.* The major decisions in selecting a map projection involve the properties of **equal area** (equivalence) and **true shape** (conformality). A decision for one property sacrifices the other, for both properties cannot be shown together on the same flat map.

If a cartographer selects equal area as the desired trait—for example, for a map showing the distribution of world climates—then true shape must be sacrificed by *stretching* and *shearing*, which allows parallels and meridians to cross at other than right angles. On an equal-area map, a coin covers the same amount of Earth surface area no matter where you place it on the map. In contrast, if a cartographer selects the property of true shape, such as for a map used for navigational purposes, then equal area must be sacrificed, and the scale will actually change from one region of the map to another.

FIGURE 1.24 **From globe to flat map.**
Conversion of the globe to a flat map projection requires decisions about which properties to preserve and the amount of distortion that is acceptable. [NASA astronaut photo from *Apollo XVII*, 1972.]

The Nature and Classes of Projections Despite the fact that modern cartographic technology uses mathematical constructions and computer-assisted graphics, the word *projection* is still used. The term comes from times past, when geographers actually projected the shadow of a wire-skeleton globe onto a geometric surface. The wires represented parallels, meridians, and outlines of the continents. A light source then cast a shadow pattern of latitude and longitude lines from the globe onto various geometric surfaces, such as a *cylinder*, *plane*, or *cone*.

Figure 1.25 illustrates the general classes of map projections and the perspectives from which they are generated. The classes shown include the cylindrical, planar (or azimuthal), and conic. Another class of projections, which cannot be derived from this physical-perspective approach, is the nonperspective oval shape. Still other projections derive from purely mathematical calculations.

With projections, the contact line or contact point between the wire globe and the projection surface—called a *standard line* or *standard point*—is *the only place where all globe properties are preserved*. Thus, a *standard parallel* or *standard meridian* is a standard line true to scale along its entire length without any distortion. Areas away from this critical tangent line or point become increasingly distorted. Consequently, this line or point of accurate spatial properties should be centred by the cartographer on the area of interest.

The commonly used **Mercator projection** (from Gerardus Mercator, A.D. 1569) is a cylindrical projection (Figure 1.25a). The Mercator is a true-shape projection, with meridians appearing as equally spaced straight lines and parallels appearing as straight lines that are spaced closer together near the equator. The poles are infinitely stretched, with the 84th N parallel and 84th S parallel fixed at the same length as that of the equator. Note in Figures 1.24 and 1.25a that the Mercator projection is cut around the 80th parallel in each hemisphere because of the severe distortion at higher latitudes.

Unfortunately, Mercator maps present false notions of the size (area) of midlatitude and poleward landmasses. A dramatic example on the Mercator projection is Greenland, which appears to be bigger than all of South America. In reality, Greenland is an island only one-eighth the size of South America and is actually 20% smaller than Argentina alone.

The advantage of the Mercator projection is that a line of constant direction, known as a **rhumb line**, or *loxodrome*, is straight and thus facilitates plotting directions between two points (see Figure 1.26b). Thus, the Mercator projection is useful in navigation and is the standard for nautical charts.

The *gnomonic*, or *planar*, *projection* in Figure 1.25b is generated by projecting a light source at the centre of a globe onto a plane that is tangent to (touching) the globe's surface. The resulting severe distortion prevents showing a full hemisphere on one projection. However, a valuable feature is derived: *All great circle routes, which are the shortest distance between two points on Earth's surface, are projected as straight lines* (Figure 1.26a). The great circle routes plotted on a gnomonic projection then can be transferred to a true-direction projection, such as the Mercator, for determination of precise compass headings (Figure 1.26b).

For more information on maps used in this text and standard map symbols, turn to Appendix A, Maps in This Text and Topographic Maps. Topographic maps are essential tools of landscape analysis. Geographers, other

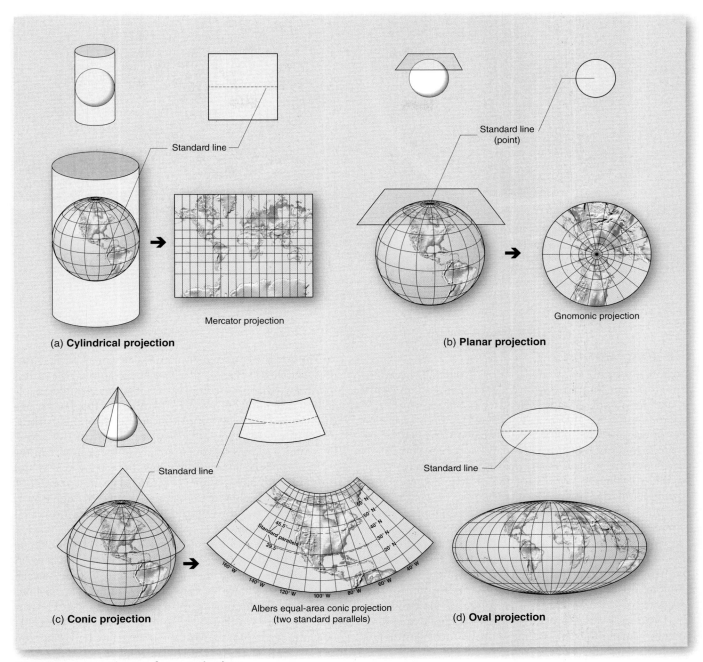

FIGURE 1.25 Classes of map projections.
Four general classes and perspectives of map projections—(a) cylindrical, (b) planar, (c) conic, and (d) oval projections.

scientists, travelers, and anyone visiting the outdoors often use topographic maps. Perhaps you have used a "topo" map in planning a hike.

The National Topographic System (NTS) is the basis for topographic maps in Canada. There is good coverage of the entire country at 1:50 000 and 1:250 000 scales (http://maps.nrcan.gc.ca/index_e.php). Additionally, the *Atlas of Canada* (http://atlas.gc.ca/site/english/index.html) allows you to select and view maps online (in English and French).

Remote Sensing and GIS

Geographers probe, analyse, and map our home planet through remote sensing and geographic information systems (GIS). These technologies enhance our understanding of Earth. Geographers use remote-sensing data to study many subjects in this text and the human activities that produce global change and impact Earth systems.

(a) Gnomonic projection

(b) Mercator projection (conformal, true shape)

FIGURE 1.26 Determining great circle routes.
A gnomonic projection (a) is used to determine the shortest distance—great circle route—between San Francisco and London, because on this projection the arc of a great circle is a straight line. This great circle route is then plotted on a Mercator projection (b), which has true compass direction. Note that straight lines of constant direction (or bearing) on a Mercator projection—rhumb lines—are not the shortest route.

Remote Sensing

In this era of observations from orbit outside the atmosphere, from aircraft within it, and from remote submersibles in the oceans, scientists obtain a wide array of remotely sensed data (Figure 1.27). Remote sensing is nothing new to humans; we do it with our eyes as we scan the environment, sensing the shape, size, and colour of objects from a distance, registering energy from the visible-wavelength portion of the electromagnetic spectrum. Similarly, when a camera views the wavelengths for which its film or sensor is designed, it remotely senses energy that is reflected or emitted from a scene.

Our eyes and cameras are familiar means of obtaining **remote sensing** information about a distant subject without having physical contact. Aerial photographs and satellite images have been used for years to improve the accuracy of surface maps faster and more cheaply than can be done by onsite surveys. Deriving accurate measurements from photographs is the realm of **photogrammetry**, an important application of remote sensing.

Remote sensors on satellites, the International Space Station, and other craft sense a broader range of wavelengths than human eyes. They can be designed to "see" wavelengths shorter than visible light (ultraviolet) and wavelengths longer than visible light (infrared and microwaves).

Following launch, satellites can be set in several types of orbits: geostationary, polar, and Sun-synchronous, illustrated in Figure 1.28. In a geostationary (geosynchronous) orbit, typically about 35 790 km altitude, a satellite paces Earth's rotation speed and therefore remains "parked" above a specific location, usually a point above the equator, which provides a full hemispheric view with the satellite in a "fixed" position—the *GOES* weather satellite is an example.

Figure 1.28b shows a polar-orbiting satellite typically residing at 200 km to 1000 km and passing over every portion of the globe, completing each orbit in 90 minutes. Satellites *Terra* and *Aqua* are examples. Satellites in Sun-synchronous orbits reside at lower altitudes, typically between 600 km and 800 km above Earth's surface (Figure 1.28c). Near-polar Sun-synchronous orbits, where the track is inclined and the satellite close to—but not directly—over the poles, are most common. This orbit is called Sun-synchronous because the satellite shifts its path about 1° per day (365 days in a year, 360° in a circle) which allows it to pass above the equator at the same local Sun time (usually midmorning) on each orbital revolution.

The benefit of a Sun-synchronous orbit is that one variable in illumination conditions is kept constant in series of images of the same part of Earth. The surface below the satellite can be in constat sunlight for visible-wavelength images or in constant darkness for longwave-radiation images. Sun-synchronous orbits are about 90–100 minutes in length, with the exact value depending on orbital altitude.

Satellites do not take conventional-film photographs. Rather, they record *images* that are transmitted to Earth-based receivers in a way similar to television satellite transmissions or a digital camera. A scene is scanned and broken down into pixels (*pic*ture *el*ements), each identified by coordinates named *lines* (horizontal rows) and *samples* (vertical columns). For example, a grid of 6000 lines and 7000 samples forms 42 million pixels, providing great detail. The large amount of data needed to produce a single image requires computer processing and data storage at ground stations.

Digital data are processed in many ways to enhance their utility: simulated natural colour, "false" colour to highlight a particular feature, enhanced contrast, signal filtering, and different levels of sampling and resolution. Active and passive are two types of remote-sensing systems.

Band 1
Band 2
Band 3
Band 4

Numerical values assigned

Composite digital image

A sample of orbital platforms:

CloudSat: Studies cloud extent, distribution, radiative properties, and structure.

ENVISAT: ESA environment-monitoring satellite; 10 sensors, including radar.

GOES: Weather monitoring and forecasting; *GOES-11, -12, -13,* and *-14.*

GRACE: Accurately maps Earth's gravitational field.

JASON-1, -2: Measures sea-level heights.

Landsat: *Landsat-1* in 1972 to *Landsat-7* in 1999, provides millions of images for Earth systems science and global change.

NOAA: First in 1978 through *NOAA-15, -16, -17, -18,* and *-19* now in operation, global data gathering, short- and long-term weather forecasts.

RADARSAT-1, -2: Synthetic Aperture Radar in near-polar orbit, operated by Canadian Space Agency.

SciSat-1: Analyses trace gases, thin clouds, atmospheric aerosols with Arctic focus.

SeaStar: Carries the *SeaWiFS* (Sea-viewing Wide Field-of-View instrument) to observe Earth's oceans and microscopic marine plants.

Terra and Aqua: Environmental change, error-free surface images, cloud properties, through five instrument packages.

TOMS-EP: Total Ozone Mapping Spectrometer, monitoring stratospheric ozone, similar instruments on *NIMBUS-7* and *Meteor-3.*

TOPEX-POSEIDON: Measures sea-level heights.

TRMM: Tropical Rainfall Measuring Mission, includes lightning detection and global energy budget measurements.

For more info see:
http://www.nasa.gov/centers/goddard/missions/index.html

FIGURE 1.27 **Remote-sensing technologies.**
Remote-sensing technology measures and monitors aspects of Earth's systems from orbiting spacecraft, aircraft in the atmosphere, and ground-based sensors. Various wavelengths (bands) are collected from sensors. Computers process the data to produce digital images for analysis. A sample of remote-sensing platforms is listed along the side of the illustration. The Space Shuttle (now retired) is shown in its inverted orbital flight mode.

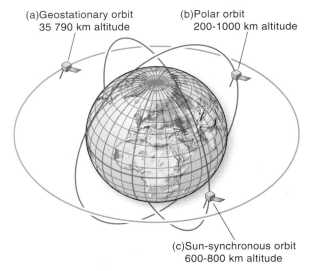

(a)Geostationary orbit
35 790 km altitude

(b)Polar orbit
200-1000 km altitude

(c)Sun-synchronous orbit
600-800 km altitude

FIGURE 1.28 Three satellite orbital paths.
a) Geostationary (geosynchronous) orbit, typically 35 790-km altitude. (b) Polar-orbiting satellites typically are between 200-km and 1000-km altitude. (c) Sun-synchronous orbits shift their nearpolar track from 600-km to 800-km altitude.

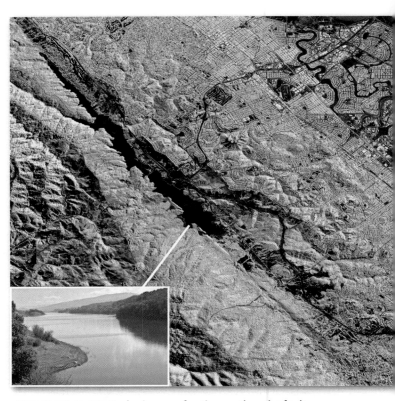

FIGURE 1.29 Radar image of active earthquake fault.
Synthetic aperture radar image made from an aircraft repeatedly over time allows study of stress-accumulating portions of the fault. Discussion of this fault is in Chapter 12. Can you see the fault rift area running from southeast to northwest in this 2009 false-colour image, in the area filled with a reservoir? [UACSAR image by JPL/NASA; photo by Robert Christopherson]

Active Remote Sensing Active systems direct a beam of energy at a surface and analyse the energy reflected back. An example is *radar* (*ra*dio *d*etection *a*nd *r*anging). A radar transmitter emits short bursts of energy that have relatively long wavelengths (0.3 to 10 m) toward the subject terrain, penetrating clouds and darkness. Energy reflected back to a radar receiver for analysis is known as *backscatter*. Several important radar satellites are in orbit at this time, such as *RADARSAT-1* and *-2*, *QuikSCAT*, *ERS-1* and *-2*, and *CloudSat*. Throughout this book you will see examples of remote sensing images from various sensors, including *RADARSAT-1* and *-2*.

A synthetic aperture radar system aboard an aircraft imaged the San Andreas fault near San Mateo, California. NASA and JPL developed systems to repeatedly capture detailed, three-dimensional images along this fault system to track movement and areas that are building up energy that will be released in future earthquakes (Figure 1.29).

Passive Remote Sensing Passive remote-sensing systems record energy reflected or emitted from a surface, particularly visible light, infrared, and microwave. Our own eyes are passive remote sensors, as was the *Apollo XVII* astronaut camera that made the photograph (film) of Earth on the back cover of this book from a distance of 37 000 km.

Since 1972 passive remote sensors on the *Landsat* series of satellites provided a variety of data, as shown in images of the Appalachian Mountains and Mount St. Helens in Chapter 12, river deltas and New Orleans before and after Katrina in Chapter 14, and the Vatnajökull ice cap in Iceland in Chapter 17. Two *Landsats* remain operational in 2011, *Landsat-5* and *-7*; each of *Landsat-1*, *-2*, *-3* and

-4 missions have ended, and *Landsat-6* was launched but failed to reach orbit. See http://landsat.gsfc.nasa.gov/ and http://geo.arc.nasa.gov/sge/landsat/landsat.html for more information and additional links.

A NASA, National Oceanic and Atmospheric Administration (NOAA, see http://www.noaa.gov/), and United Kingdom joint venture, the *Polar Operational Environmental Satellites* (*POES*) complete nearly polar orbits 14 times a day carrying the *advanced very high resolution radiometer* (*AVHRR*). These are in Sun-synchronous orbits aboard *NOAA-15* and *NOAA-17* for morning hours, and *NOAA-16* and *NOAA-18*, and *NOAA-19* for afternoon hours. See http://www.oso.noaa.gov/poesstatus/.

Key to NASA's Earth Observing System (EOS) is satellite *Terra*, which began beaming back data and images in 2000 (see http://terra.nasa.gov/), followed by another satellite in the series called *Aqua*. Five instrument packages observe Earth systems in detail. The image of Earth on the half-title page of this book includes a cloud snapshot from *GOES* added to *Terra* MODIS images.

The *Geostationary Operational Environmental Satellites*, known as *GOES*, became operational in 1994, providing the images you see on weather reports. *GOES-11* is now

FIGURE 1.30 *GOES-14* first image.
GOES-14 made its first image July 27, 2009; the improved technology in this satellite produces 1 km resolution. Can you find the cloud-free southwestern United States? Two tropical waves are visible in the eastern Pacific Ocean. [NASA.]

above 135° W longitude for western North America and eastern Pacific Ocean weather. *GOES-12* sits above 75° W longitude to monitor central and eastern North America and the western Atlantic. Think of these satellites as hovering over these meridians for continuous coverage, using visual wavelengths for daylight hours and infrared for nighttime views. For the future *GOES-13* and *GOES-14* are parked in orbit ready when needed (Figure 1.30). See the Geostationary Satellite Server at http://www.goes.noaa.gov/. The *GOES* Project Science appears at http://rsd.gsfc.nasa.gov/goes/.

SCISAT is a Canadian satellite launched by NASA in 2003 and contains an Ace Fourier Transform Spectrometer and an instrument known as MAESTRO (Measurements of Aerosol Extinction in the Stratosphere and Troposphere Retrieved by Occultation). These instruments measure the concentration and distribution of chemicals in the ozone layer as sunlight passes through Earth's upper atmosphere. *SCISAT* orbits Earth 15 times daily to capture information for 15 sunrises and sunsets. See http://www.space.gc.ca/asc/eng/satellites/default.asp for more on all Canadian satellites. Other satellites that are particularly relevant to Canada and scientists studying snow and ice include *CryoSat* and *ICESat*.

Information about other satellites in Asia, Europe, and Africa is available through the European Space Agency. See the Remote Sensing Virtual Library at http://virtual.vtt.fi/space/rsvlib/ for remote-sensing links; click on "Satellite Data" for specific coverage. For a sampling of global remote sensing coverage from a variety of satellite platforms go to the USGS Global Visualization Viewer (http://glovis.usgs.gov/).

Geographic Information Systems

Techniques such as remote sensing acquire large volumes of spatial data that must be stored, processed, and retrieved in useful ways. A **geographic information system (GIS)** is a computer-based, data-processing tool for gathering, manipulating, and analyzing geographic information. Today's sophisticated computer systems allow the integration of geographic information from direct surveys (on-the-ground mapping) and remote sensing in complex ways never before possible.

Through a GIS, Earth and human phenomena are analysed over time. This can include the study and forecasting of diseases such H1N1 flu and West Nile virus, the population displacement caused by Hurricane Katrina, the destruction from the Haiti and Chilean earthquakes in 2010, or interactive land-cover maps, to name a few examples (Figure 1.31). Whereas printed maps are fixed at time of publication, GIS maps can be modified and evolve instantly.

The beginning component for any GIS is a map, with its associated coordinate system such as latitude–longitude. This establishes reference points against which to position data. The coordinate system is digitised, along with all areas, points, and lines. Increasingly, GNSS units are now used to provide the basic locational data needed for GIS. Remotely sensed imagery and other layers of data can then be added on top of the coordinate system. *Digital elevation models (DEMs)* aid scientific analysis of topography, area-altitude distributions, slopes, and local stream-drainage characteristics, among many applications. The data are then available for computer manipulation, display, and GIS operations.

A GIS is capable of analyzing patterns and relationships within a single data plane, such as the floodplain or soil layer in Figure 1.31a. A GIS also can generate an overlay analysis where two or more data planes interact. When the layers are combined, the resulting synthesis— a *composite overlay*—is a valuable product, ready for use in analyzing complex problems. The utility of a GIS compared with that of a fixed map is the ability to manipulate the variables for analysis and to update the map repeatedly.

The applications of GIS are wide-ranging and cross many disciplines. Geographic information science (GISci) embodies the development, use, and application of GIS. An international conference series on GISci began in 2000 and continues biannually (see http://giscience.org/). These conferences bring together leading scientists from academia, industry, and government to explore emerging research across the disciplines and to seek applications in many fields. An important direction is toward more user-friendly GIS in the future.

Access to GIS is expanding with increased availability of numerous open-source GIS software packages. These

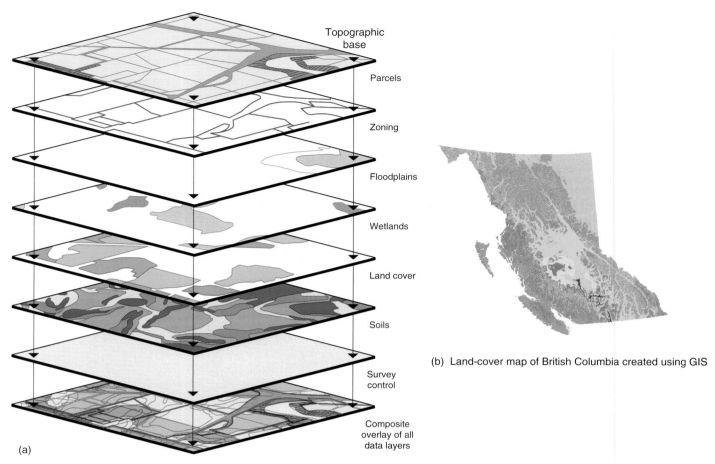

(a)

(b) Land-cover map of British Columbia created using GIS

FIGURE 1.31 A geographic information system (GIS) model.
Layered spatial data in a GIS format. (b) This biogeoclimatic map of British Columbia is a valuable tool for forestry management in the province. [(a) After USGS; (b) © Province of British Columbia. All rights reserved. Reprinted with the permission of the Province of British Columbia, http://www.ipp.gov.bc.ca.]

are usually free, have online support systems, and are updated frequently (see http://opensourcegis.org/).

Programs for visualizing Earth, such as Google Earth, provide three-dimensional viewing of the globe. Google Earth allows the user to "fly" anywhere on Earth and zoom in on landscapes and features of interest, using satellite imagery and aerial photography at varying resolutions. You can find where you live and your campus. Layers can be selected, as in a GIS model, by the user, depending on the task at hand and the composite overlay displayed. To download the free Google Earth software, visit http://earth.google.com.

Career opportunities in GIS, and the field of geoinformatics (encompassing GIS, GNSS, remote sensing, and digital cartography) generally continue to increase. Regardless of your academic major, the ability to analyse data spatially is important. The annual ESRI (Environmental Systems Research Institute) International Users Conference, whose attendance is approaching 15 000 people, continues to be the largest gathering of GIS professionals

to share state-of-the-art applications of GIS technology (http://www.esri.com/).

In Canada, as well as in the United States, GIS degree programs are available at many colleges and universities. GIS curriculum and certificate programs are now available at many community colleges. Many universities have listings of careers and jobs in GIS. Check out the University of Toronto site (http://faculty.geog.utoronto.ca/Boyes/Boyes/Weblinks_General.htm) for a great summary of GIS information. Additionally, the University of British Columbia (http://www.geog.ubc.ca/gislinks/index.php?mode=search&otherk=kgove) has a summary of jobs, careers, web sites, and tools. A consortium of three American universities forms the National Center for Geographic Information and Analysis (NCGIA) for GIS education. See http://www.ncgia.ucsb.edu/.

One of the most extensive and longest operating systems is the Canada Geographic Information system (CGIS). Roger Tomlinson, a Canadian geographer recognised as the father of GIS (see Royal Canadian

Geographic Society award at http://www.rcgs.org/awards/gold_medal/winner_gold2003.asp), was key in the development of the Canadian GIS. To create the system, environmental data about natural features, resources, and land use were taken from maps, aerial photographs, and orbital sources, reduced to map segments, and entered into the CGIS. The development of this system has progressed with the ongoing Canada Land Inventory project; visit the web page at http://geogratis.cgdi.gc.ca/CLI/frames.html. A summary timeline for development of GIS is found at http://www.casa.ucl.ac.uk/gistimeline/welcome.htm.

GEOSYSTEMS CONNECTION

Now that you have background in the essentials of geography and the *Geosystems* approach, we leave on a journey through the chapters in each of Earth's four spheres—Part I Atmosphere; Part II Hydrosphere; Part III Lithosphere; and Part IV Biosphere. Chapter 2 begins with the Sun, including its place in the Universe, operation, and energy flow to Earth. We look at the march of the seasons. We follow solar energy through the atmosphere to the surface and examine the patterns this creates. As outputs in the system we study global temperature patterns and the circulation of air and water in Earth's vast wind and ocean currents.

At the end of each chapter, you will find a *Geosystems Connection* to act as a bridge from one chapter to the next, helping you to cross to the next topic.

KEY LEARNING CONCEPTS REVIEW

To assist you, here is a review in handy summary form of the Key Learning Concepts listed on this chapter's title page. Each concept review concludes with a list of the key terms from the chapter, the corresponding page numbers, and review questions. Such summary and review sections are found at the end of each chapter in the book.

■ **Define** geography and physical geography in particular.

Geography brings together disciplines from the physical and life sciences with those from the cultural and human sciences to attain a holistic view of Earth—physical geography is an essential aspect of the emerging **Earth systems sciences**. **Geography** is a science of method, a special way of analyzing phenomena over space; **spatial** refers to the nature and character of physical space. Geography integrates a wide range of subject matter, and geographic education recognises five major themes: **location**, **region**, **human–Earth relationships**, **movement**, and **place**. Geography's method is **spatial analysis**, used to study the interdependence among geographic areas, natural systems, society, and cultural activities over space or area. **Process**—that is, a set of actions or mechanisms that operate in some special order—is central to geographic synthesis.

Physical geography applies spatial analysis to all the physical elements and process systems that make up the environment: energy, air, water, weather, climate, landforms, soils, animals, plants, and microorganisms. Understanding the complex relations among these elements is important to human survival because Earth's physical systems and human society are intertwined. The development of hypotheses and theories about the Universe, Earth, and life involves the **scientific method**.

    Earth systems science (p. 5)
    geography (p. 5)
    spatial (p. 5)
    location (p. 6)
    region (p. 6)
    human–Earth relationships (p. 6)
    movement (p. 6)
    place (p. 6)
    spatial analysis (p. 6)

    process (p. 6)
    physical geography (p. 6)
    scientific method (p. 6)

1. What is unique about the science of geography? On the basis of information in this chapter, define *physical geography* and review the geographic approach.
2. In general terms, what method might a physical geographer use to analyse water pollution in the Great Lakes?
3. Assess your geographic literacy by examining atlases and maps. What types of maps have you used—political? Physical? Topographic? Do you know what projections were employed? Do you know the names and locations of the four oceans, the seven continents, and most of the individual countries? Can you identify the new countries that have emerged since 1990?
4. Suggest a representative example for each of the five geographic themes and use that theme in a sentence.
5. Have you made decisions today that involve geographic concepts discussed within the five themes presented? Explain briefly.

■ **Describe** systems analysis, open and closed systems, and feedback information, and **relate** these concepts to Earth systems.

A **system** is any ordered, related set of things and their attributes, as distinct from their surrounding environment. Systems analysis is an important organizational and analytical tool used by geographers. Earth is an **open system** in terms of energy, receiving energy from the Sun, but it is essentially a **closed system** in terms of matter and physical resources.

As a system operates, "information" is returned to various points in the system via pathways of **feedback loops**. If the feedback information discourages further change in the system, it is **negative feedback**. Such negative feedback causes self-regulation in a natural system, stabilizing the system. If feedback information stimulates further change in the system, it is **positive feedback**. Unchecked positive feedback in a system can create a runaway ("snowballing") condition. When the rates of inputs and outputs in the system are equal and the amounts of energy and matter in storage within the system are constant (or when there is fluctuation around a stable average), the system is in **steady-state equilibrium**. A system that demonstrates a steady increase or decrease in system operations—a trend over time—is in **dynamic equilibrium**. A **threshold**, or tipping point, is the moment at which a system can no longer maintain its character, so it lurches to a new operational level, one that may not be compatible with previous conditions. To understand natural systems better, geographers often construct a simplified **model** of natural systems to better understand them.

Four immense open systems powerfully interact at Earth's surface: three **abiotic**, or nonliving systems of **atmosphere**, **hydrosphere** (including the **cryosphere**), and **lithosphere**, and a **biotic**, or living system the—**biosphere**.

system (p. 9)
open system (p. 10)
closed system (p. 10)
feedback loops (p. 10)
negative feedback (p. 10)
positive feedback (p. 10)
steady-state equilibrium (p. 11)
dynamic equilibrium (p. 11)
threshold (p. 11)
model (p. 15)
abiotic (p. 15)
biotic (p. 15)
atmosphere (p. 16)
hydrosphere (p. 16)
cryosphere (p. 16)
lithosphere (p. 16)
biosphere (p. 16)

6. Define systems theory as an organizational strategy. What are open systems, closed systems, and negative feedback? When is a system in a steady-state equilibrium condition? What type of system (open or closed) is the human body? A lake? A tree?

7. Describe Earth as a system in terms of both energy and matter; use simple diagrams to illustrate your description.

8. What are the three abiotic (nonliving) spheres that make up Earth's environment? Relate these to the biotic (living) sphere: the biosphere.

■ **Explain** Earth's reference grid: latitude and longitude and latitudinal geographic zones and time.

The science that studies Earth's shape and size is **geodesy**. Earth bulges slightly through the equator and is oblate (flattened) at the poles, producing a misshapen spheroid called a **geoid**. Absolute location on Earth is described with a specific reference grid of **parallels** of **latitude** (measuring distances north and south of the equator) and **meridians** of **longitude** (measuring distances east and west of a prime meridian). A historic breakthrough in navigation and timekeeping occurred with the establishment of an international **prime meridian** (0° through Greenwich, England) and the invention of precise chronometers that enabled accurate measurement of longitude. A **great circle** is any circle of Earth's circumference whose centre coincides with the centre of Earth. Great circle routes are the shortest distance between two points on Earth. **Small circles** are those whose centres do not coincide with Earth's centre. Latitude, longitude, and elevation are accurately calibrated using a handheld **global navigational satellite system (GNSS)** instrument that reads radio signals from satellites.

The prime meridian provided the basis for **Greenwich Mean Time (GMT)**, the world's first universal time system. A corollary of the prime meridian is the 180° meridian, the **International Date Line**. Today, **Coordinated Universal Time (UTC)** is the worldwide standard and the basis for international time zones. **Daylight saving time** is a seasonal change of clocks by 1 hour in summer months.

geodesy (p. 16)
geoid (p. 16)
latitude (p. 18)
parallel (p. 18)
longitude (p. 19)
meridian (p. 19)
prime meridian (p. 19)
great circle (p. 20)
small circle (p. 21)
Global Positioning System (GPS) (p. 22)
global navigational satellite system (GNSS) (p. 22)
Greenwich Mean Time (GMT) (p. 24)
International Date Line (p. 24)
Coordinated Universal Time (UTC) (p. 25)
daylight saving time (p. 26)

9. Draw a simple sketch describing Earth's shape and size.

10. How did Eratosthenes use Sun angles to figure out that the 5000-stadia distance between Alexandria and Syene was 1/50 of Earth's circumference? Once he knew this fraction of Earth's circumference, how did he calculate the entirety of Earth's circumference?

11. What are the latitude and longitude coordinates (in degrees, minutes, and seconds) of your present location? Where can you find this information?

12. Define *latitude* and *parallel* and define *longitude* and *meridian* using a simple sketch with labels.

13. Define a *great circle*, *great circle routes*, and a *small circle*. In terms of these concepts, describe the equator, other parallels, and meridians.

14. Identify the various latitudinal geographic zones that roughly subdivide Earth's surface. In which zone do you live? How do the concepts of north and northerliness describe your location?

15. What does timekeeping have to do with longitude? Explain this relationship. How is Coordinated Universal Time (UTC) determined on Earth?

16. What and where is the prime meridian? How was the location originally selected? Describe the meridian that is opposite the prime meridian on Earth's surface.

17. What is a GNSS and how does it assist you in finding location and elevation on Earth? Give a couple of examples where it was utilised to correct heights for some famous mountains.

■ **Define** cartography and mapping basics: map scale and map projections.

A **map** is a generalised view of an area, usually some portion of Earth's surface, as seen from above, and greatly reduced in size. The science and art of mapmaking is **cartography**. For the spatial portrayal of Earth's physical systems geographers use maps. **Scale** is the ratio of size of the image on a map to the real world size; it relates a unit on the map to an identical unit on the ground. Cartographers create a **map projection** for specific purposes, selecting the best compromise of projection for each application. Compromise is always necessary because Earth's round, three-dimensional surface cannot be exactly duplicated on a flat, two-dimensional map. **Equal area** (equivalence), **true shape** (conformality), true direction, and true distance are all considerations in selecting a projection. The **Mercator projection** is in the cylindrical class; it has true-shape qualities and straight lines that show constant direction. A **rhumb line** denotes constant direction and appears as a straight line on the Mercator.

map (p. 26)
cartography (p. 26)
scale (p. 26)
map projection (p. 27)
equal area (p. 27)
true shape (p. 27)
Mercator projection (p. 28)
rhumb line (p. 28)

18. Define cartography. Explain why it is an integrative discipline.
19. What is map scale? In what three ways may it be expressed on a map?
20. State whether the following ratios are large scale, medium scale, or small scale: 1:2 500 000; 1:25 000; 1:250 000.
21. Describe the differences between the characteristics of a globe and those that result when a flat map is prepared.
22. What type of map projection is used in Figure 1.14? In Figure 1.21? (See Appendix A.)

■ **Describe** remote sensing, and **explain** the geographic information system (GIS); both as tools used in geographic analysis.

Orbital and aerial **remote sensing** are used to analyse the operation of Earth's systems. Satellites do not take photographs, but record images that are transmitted to Earth-based receivers.

Satellite data are recorded in digital form for later processing, enhancement, and image generation. Aerial photographs and satellite images have been used for years to improve the accuracy of surface maps. Deriving accurate measurements from photographs is the realm of **photogrammetry**, an important application of remote sensing.

The mountain of data collected by remote sensing can be put to work in **geographic information system (GIS)** technology. Computers process geographic information from direct surveys and remote sensing in complex ways never before possible. GIS methodology is an important tool for better understanding Earth's systems and is a vital career opportunity for geographers.

The science of physical geography is in a unique position to synthesise the spatial, environmental, and human aspects of our increasingly complex relationship with our home planet—Earth.

remote sensing (p. 30)
photogrammetry (p. 30)
geographic information system (GIS) (p. 33)

23. What is remote sensing? What are you viewing when you observe a weather satellite image on TV or in the newspaper? Explain.
24. Describe the *Terra*, *Landsat*, *GOES*, and *NOAA* satellites and detail them using several examples. Go to the NASA or ESA (European Space Agency) web site and view some satellite images.
25. If you were in charge of planning for development of a large tract of land, how would GIS methodologies assist you? How might planning and zoning be affected if a portion of the tract is a floodplain or prime agricultural land?

MyGeosciencePlace

Visit **www.mygeoscienceplace.ca** for several figure animations, satellite loops, self-study quizzes, flashcards, interactive glossary, career links, RSS feeds, Pearson eText of *Geosystems*, and much more.

INPUTS
Solar energy to Earth
Earth's modern
atmosphere

ACTIONS
Atmosphere and
surface energy
balances

OUTPUTS
Global temperatures
Wind and ocean
currents

**HUMAN-EARTH
RELATION**
Air pollution
Acid deposition
Urban environment
Heat index, Wind chill
Solar energy
Wind power

PART I

The Energy-Atmosphere System

I. Atmosphere

II. Hydrosphere

IV. Biosphere

III. Lithosphere

For more than 4.6 billion years, solar energy has traveled across interplanetary space to Earth, where a small portion of the solar output is intercepted. Our planet and our lives are powered by radiant energy from the star that is closest to Earth—the Sun. Because of Earth's curvature, the energy at the top of the atmosphere is unevenly distributed, creating imbalances from the equator to each pole—the equatorial region experiences energy surpluses; the polar regions experience energy deficits. Also, the annual pulse of seasonal change varies the distribution of energy during the year.

Earth's atmosphere acts as an efficient filter, absorbing most harmful radiation, charged particles, and space debris so that these do not reach Earth's surface. In the lower atmosphere the unevenness of daily energy receipt governs atmospheric and surface energy budgets, giving rise to global patterns of temperature and circulation of wind and ocean currents. Each of us depends on many systems that are set into motion by energy from the Sun. These are the systems of Part I.

Two extratropical cyclones swirl in tandem, November 2006, demonstrating Earth's global circulation. Iceland is in the upper-center area across the page gutter. [NASA].

CHAPTER 2

Solar Energy to Earth and the Seasons

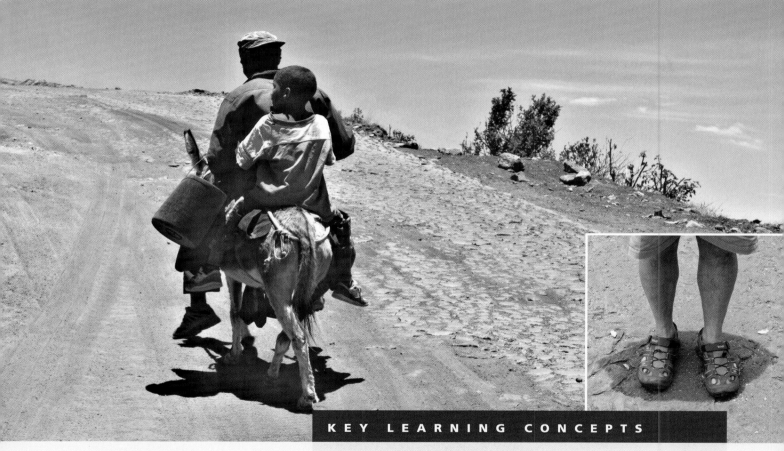

These boys and a donkey haul water on Fogo Island in the tropical West African country of Cape Verde. Note their shadow is cast almost directly beneath them. The inset photo captures the experience of having the Sun directly overhead—the subsolar point. [Bobbé Christopherson.]

KEY LEARNING CONCEPTS

After reading the chapter, you should be able to:

- **Distinguish** among galaxies, stars, and planets, and **locate** Earth.
- **Examine** the origin, formation, and development of Earth, and **construct** Earth's annual orbit about the Sun.
- **Describe** the Sun's internal processes, and **explain** the characteristics of the solar wind and the electromagnetic spectrum of radiant energy.
- **Portray** the intercepted solar energy and its uneven distribution at the top of the atmosphere.
- **Define** solar altitude, solar declination, and daylength, and **describe** the annual variability of each—Earth's seasonality.

Chasing the Subsolar Point

In this chapter we track the march of the seasons. The Sun's subsolar point, where direct overhead rays arrive at the surface, is at the Tropic of Capricorn (about 23.5° S latitude) on December 21–22, migrates northward to the equator on March 20–21, and onward to the Tropic of Cancer (about 23.5° N) on June 20–21. Then turning southward, the Sun's subsolar point returns to the equator on September 22–23, and on to the Tropic of Capricorn in December (see Figure 2.15).

The chapter-opening photo shows an example of the subsolar point, when the Sun's rays were perpendicular to the surface. The moment this photo was taken at this latitude, the Sun was highest in the sky. Outside of the tropics, the Sun is never directly overhead. For example, at 40° N latitude the noon Sun's altitude ranges from 26° above the horizon in December, to 73° in June, never reaching 90°. One of the authors, Robert Christopherson, on an expedition ship, tracked his route and the Sun to find that moment at local noon when his position, either on the ship or on an island in the Atlantic Ocean would encounter the subsolar point. Here is how he calculated this moment.

On most globes, globe designers place an *analemma* in the Eastern Pacific. The analemma is a figure-8-shaped chart where you can check any date, then trace to the *y-axis* to find the Sun's declination, which is the latitude of the subsolar point (Figure GN 2.1). Use the chart to calculate the subsolar point location on your birthday.

The shape of the analemma as the Sun's declination migrates tropic-to-tropic is a result of Earth's axial tilt and elliptical orbit. Earth actually revolves in an elliptical—not a circular—orbit around the Sun, moving faster during December and January, and slower in June and July. This sets the *equation of time*.

An average day of 24 hours (86 400 seconds) sets *mean solar time*. However,

observed solar time occurs each day at noon as the Sun crosses your meridian, and this sets the *apparent solar day*. You see on the chart that in October and November *fast-Sun times* occur and the Sun arrives ahead of local noon (12:00), noted on the *x-axis* along the top of the chart. In February and March the Sun arrives later than local noon (12:00), causing *slow-Sun times*.

The expedition ship chased the subsolar point as it moved from the Equator to the Tropic of Cancer between the March equinox and the June solstice.

According to the analemma, the Sun's declination moves from about 1° N latitude to 15° N between March 23 and May 1, and the ship was in these latitudes from April 25 to May 1.

So when did Robert come the closest to the subsolar point? The Sun was overhead (nearly a 90° angle, perpendicular to a flat surface) on May 1 when he was at 14.8° N, on Fogo Island, Cape Verde. The equation of time was two minutes fast. He measured the Sun's altitude and checked the analemma. He determined his exact location using a GPS receiver.

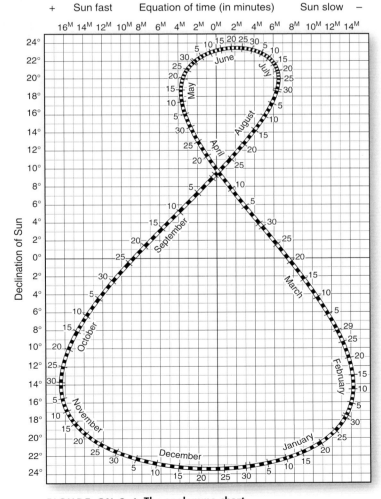

FIGURE GN 2.1 The analemma chart.
Knowing a date, you can determine the Sun's declination and the equation of time. Begin your use of the analemma by looking up your birthday. Where is the subsolar point on that date?

he Universe is populated with at least 125 billion galaxies. One of these is our own Milky Way Galaxy, and it contains about 200 billion stars. Among these stars is an average yellow star we call the Sun, although the dramatic *SOHO* satellite image in Figure 2.2 seems anything but average! Our Sun radiates energy in all directions and upon its family of orbiting planets. Of special interest to us is the solar energy that falls on the third planet, our immediate home.

In this chapter: Incoming solar energy that arrives at the top of Earth's atmosphere establishes the pattern of energy input that drives Earth's physical systems and which influences our lives daily. This solar energy input to the atmosphere, plus Earth's tilt and rotation, produce daily, seasonal, and annual patterns of changing daylength and Sun angle. The Sun is the ultimate energy source for most life processes in our biosphere.

The Solar System, Sun, and Earth

Our Solar System is located on a remote, trailing edge of the **Milky Way Galaxy**, a flattened, disk-shaped mass in the form of a barred-spiral—a spiral with a slightly barred or elongated core of stars (Figure 2.1a, 2.1b). Our Solar System is embedded more than halfway out from the galactic centre, in one of the Milky Way's spiral arms—the Orion Spur of the Sagittarius Arm. A supermassive black hole some 2 million solar masses in size, named *Sagittarius A** (pronounced "*Sagittarius A Star*"), sits in the galactic centre. Our Solar System of eight planets, four dwarf planets, and asteroids is some 30 000 light-years from this black hole at the center of the Galaxy, and about 15 light-years above the plane of the Milky Way.

From our Earth-bound perspective in the Milky Way, the Galaxy appears to stretch across the night sky like a narrow band of hazy light. On a clear night, the unaided eye can see only a few thousand of these billions of stars gathered about us in our "neighbourhood."

Solar System Formation and Structure

According to prevailing theory, our Solar System condensed from a large, slowly rotating and collapsing cloud of dust and gas called a *nebula*. **Gravity**, the mutual attraction exerted by the mass of an object upon all other objects, was the key force in this condensing solar nebula. As the nebular cloud organised and flattened into a disk shape, the early *protosun* grew in mass at the centre,

drawing more matter to it. Small accretion (accumulation) eddies swirled at varying distances from the centre of the solar nebula; these were the *protoplanets*.

The **planetesimal hypothesis**, or *dust-cloud hypothesis*, explains how suns condense from nebular clouds with planetesimals, solid objects that grow from the collision of matter in space, forming in orbits about the central mass. Astronomers study this formation process in other parts of the Galaxy, where planets are observed orbiting distant stars. By spring 2010, astronomers had discovered more than 450 planets orbiting other stars.

By 2011, astronomers had discovered more than 1800 planets orbiting stars. Initial results from the orbiting Kepler Telescope estimate the number of planets in the Milky Way at 50 billion, with some 500 million planets in habitable zones—moderate temperatures and water—a staggering discovery.

Dimensions and Distances The **speed of light** is about 300 000 km · s⁻¹ (kilometres per second)[1]—in other words, about 9.5 trillion kilometres per year. This tremendous distance that light travels in a year is known as a *light-year*, and it is used as a unit of measurement for the vast Universe.

For spatial comparison, our Moon is an average distance of 384 400 km from Earth, or about 1.28 seconds in terms of light speed—for the *Apollo* astronauts this was a 3-day space voyage. Our entire Solar System is approximately 11 light-hours in diameter (Figure 2.1c). In contrast, the Milky Way is about 100 000 light-years across, and the known Universe that is observable from Earth stretches approximately 12 billion light-years in all directions. (See a Solar System simulator at http://space.jpl.nasa.gov/.)

Earth's Orbit Earth's orbit around the Sun is presently *elliptical*—a closed, oval path (Figure 2.1d). Earth's average distance from the Sun is approximately 150 million km, which means that light reaches Earth from the Sun in an average of 8 minutes and 20 seconds. Earth is at **perihelion** (its closest position to the Sun) during the Northern Hemisphere winter on January 3 at 147 255 000 km. It is at **aphelion**, its farthest position from the Sun—152 083 000 km—during the Northern Hemisphere summer on July 4. This seasonal difference in distance from the Sun causes a slight variation in the solar energy incoming to Earth but is not an immediate cause of seasonal change.

[1]To be more precise, light speed is 299 792 km · s⁻¹.

GEO REPORT 2.1   *Sun and Solar System on the Move*

The formation of the Sun and Earth occurred some 4.6 billion years ago. During this vast time span, the Sun, Earth, and the other planets completed 27 orbital trips around the Milky Way Galaxy. When you combine this travel distance with Earth's orbital revolution speed about the Sun of 107 280 km · h⁻¹ and Earth's equatorial rotation on its axis of 1675 km · h⁻¹, you get an idea that "sitting still" is a relative term.

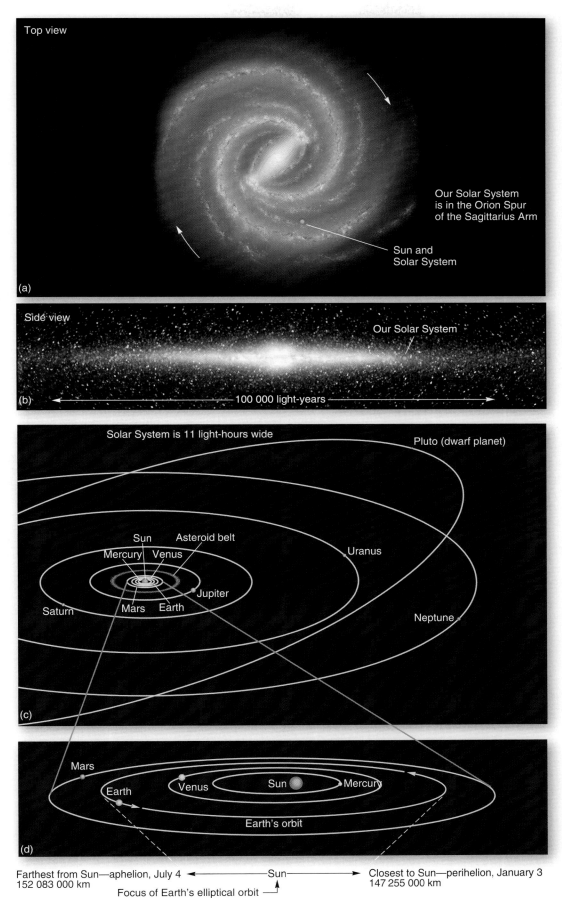

Top view

Our Solar System
is in the Orion Spur
of the Sagittarius Arm

Sun and
Solar System

(a)

Side view

Our Solar System

(b) ◄———————— 100 000 light-years ————————►

Solar System is 11 light-hours wide

Pluto (dwarf planet)

Sun   Asteroid belt

Mercury   Venus

Uranus

Jupiter

Saturn   Mars   Earth

Neptune

(c)

Mars

Earth

Venus   Sun   Mercury

Earth's orbit

(d)

Farthest from Sun—aphelion, July 4   ◄———Sun———►   Closest to Sun—perihelion, January 3
152 083 000 km   147 255 000 km

Focus of Earth's elliptical orbit ┘

FIGURE 2.1
Milky Way Galaxy, Solar System, and Earth's orbit.
(a) The Milky Way Galaxy viewed from above in an artist's conception, and (b) an image in cross-section side view. (c) All of the planets except dwarf Pluto have orbits closely aligned to the plane of the ecliptic. In 2006, Pluto was reclassified as part of the Kuiper Asteroid Belt. (d) The four inner terrestrial planets and the structure of Earth's elliptical orbit, illustrating perihelion (closest) and aphelion (farthest) positions during the year. Have you ever observed the Milky Way Galaxy in the night sky? [Courtesy of NASA/JPL.]

Animation

Nebular Hypothesis

The structure of Earth's orbit is not a constant, but instead exhibits change over long periods. As shown in Chapter 17, Figure 17.31, Earth's distance from the Sun varies more than 17.7 million km during a 100 000-year cycle, placing it closer or farther at different stages of the cycle.

Solar Energy: From Sun to Earth

Our Sun is unique to us but is a commonplace star in the Galaxy. It is only average in temperature, size, and colour when compared with other stars, yet it is the ultimate energy source for most life processes in our biosphere.

The Sun captured about 99.9% of the matter from the original solar nebula. The remaining 0.1% of the matter formed all the planets, their satellites, asteroids, comets, and debris. Consequently, the dominant object in our region of space is the Sun. In the entire Solar System, it is the only object having the enormous mass needed to sustain a natural nuclear reaction and produce radiant energy.

The mass of the Sun produces tremendous pressure and high temperatures deep in its dense interior. Under these conditions, the Sun's abundant hydrogen atoms are forced together, and pairs of hydrogen nuclei are joined in a process called **fusion**. In the fusion reaction, hydrogen nuclei form helium, the second-lightest element in nature, and enormous quantities of energy are liberated—literally, disappearing solar mass becomes energy.

A sunny day can seem so peaceful, certainly unlike the upheaval taking place on the Sun. The Sun's principal outputs consist of the *solar wind* and radiant energy in portions of the *electromagnetic spectrum*. Let us trace each of these emissions across space to Earth.

Solar Activity and Solar Wind

The Sun constantly emits clouds of electrically charged particles (principally hydrogen nuclei and free electrons) that surge outward in all directions from the Sun's surface. This stream of energetic material travels much more slowly than light—at about 50 million km per day—taking approximately 3 days to reach Earth. The term **solar wind** was first applied to this phenomenon in 1958. The *Voyager* and *Pioneer* spacecraft launched in the 1970s are now far beyond our Solar System and have yet to escape the solar wind.

The Sun's most conspicuous features are large **sunspots**, caused by magnetic storms on the Sun. Individual

sunspots may range in diameter from 10 000 to 50 000 km, with some growing as large as 160 000 km, more than 12 times Earth's diameter. These surface disturbances produce flares and prominences (Figure 2.2a). In addition, outbursts of charged material referred to as *coronal mass*

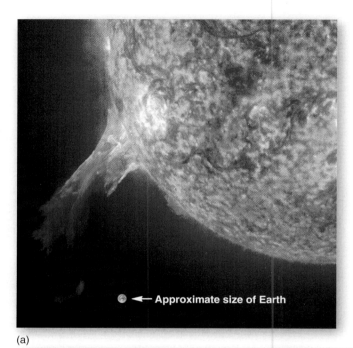

← **Approximate size of Earth**

(a)

(b)

FIGURE 2.2 Image of the Sun and sunspots.
(a) A dramatic image of the Sun captured by instruments aboard the *SOHO* satellite. A prominence rises into the Sun's corona. Earth is shown for scale. (b) The Sun at sunspot activity maximum in July 2000 and minimum in March 2009. Imaged by MDI (Michelson Doppler Imager) aboard satellite *SOHO*. [Images courtesy of *SOHO/EIT* Consortium (NASA and ESA); See http://sohowww.nascom.nasa.gov/.]

GEO REPORT 2.2 *Recent Solar Cycles*

In recent sunspot cycles, a solar minimum occurred in 1976 and a solar maximum in 1979, with more than 100 sunspots visible. Another minimum was reached in 1986, and an extremely active solar maximum followed in 1990–1991, with more than 200 sunspots visible at some time during the year. A sunspot minimum was in 1997, an intense maximum in 2000–2001 of more than 200. The forecast for the maximum in 2013 is that it will be less than the 2000–2001 maximum. The present solar cycle began in 2008 and carries the name *Cycle 24*. The record-tying global temperatures of 2010 took place during a solar minimum. Solar cycles are ruled out by scientists as a cause for increasing temperature trends.

ejections contribute to the solar wind flow of material to space.

A regular cycle exists for sunspot occurrences, averaging 11 years from one period of maximum activity to the next; however, the cycle may vary from 7 to 17 years (Figure 2.2b). A minimum in 2008 and a forecasted maximum in 2013 roughly maintain the average. (For more on the sunspot cycle, see http://solarscience.msfc.nasa.gov/SunspotCycle.shtml; and for the latest space weather, see http://www.spaceweather.com/).

Solar Wind Effects The charged particles of the solar wind first interact with Earth's magnetic field as they approach Earth. The **magnetosphere** is a magnetic field surrounding Earth, generated by dynamo-like motions within our planet. The magnetosphere deflects the solar wind toward both of Earth's poles so that only a small portion of it enters the atmosphere.

Because the solar wind does not reach Earth's surface, research on this phenomenon must be conducted in space. In 1969, the *Apollo XI* astronauts exposed a piece of foil on the lunar surface as a solar wind experiment (Figure 2.3). When examined back on Earth, the exposed foil exhibited particle impacts that confirmed the character of the solar wind.

This interaction of the solar wind and the upper layers of Earth's atmosphere produces the remarkable **auroras** that occur toward both poles. These lighting effects are the *aurora borealis* (northern lights) and *aurora australis* (southern lights) in the upper atmosphere, 80–500 km above Earth's surface. They appear as folded sheets of green, yellow, blue, and red light that undulate across the skies of high latitudes generally poleward of about 50 degrees, as shown in Figure 2.4. During the 2001 solar maximum, auroras were visible as far south as Jamaica.

The solar wind disrupts certain radio broadcasts and some satellite transmissions, and can cause overloads on Earth-based electrical systems. Astronauts working on the International Space Station in November 2003 had to take shelter in the shielded Service Module during a particularly strong outburst. Research continues as to possible links between the sunspot cycle and patterns of drought and periods of wetness—the sunspot–weather connection.

Our understanding of the solar wind is increasing dramatically as data are collected by a variety of satellites: the *THEMIS*, *ACE satellites*, *SOHO* (*Solar and Heliospheric Observatory*), *FAST* (*Fast Auroral Snapshot*), *WIND*, *Ulysses*,

(a)

(b)

FIGURE 2.4 Auroras from an orbital perspective.
(a) Aurora australis and (b) aurora borealis, as seen from orbit.
[(a) *Image* spacecraft, GSFC/NASA. (b) ISS astronaut Don Pettit/NASA.]

FIGURE 2.3 Astronaut and solar wind experiment.
Without a protective atmosphere, the lunar surface receives solar-wind-charged particles and all wavelengths of the Sun's electromagnetic radiation. An *Apollo XI* astronaut in 1969 deploys a sheet of foil in the solar wind experiment. Earth-bound scientists analyzed the foil upon the astronauts' return. Why wouldn't this experiment work if we set it up on Earth's surface? [NASA.]

the *Dynamics Explorer*, and *Genesis* with solar wind collectors, and the new *SDO* (*Solar Dynamics Observatory*), among others. All these satellite data are available on the Internet. (For auroral activity, see http://www.asc-csa.gc.ca/eng/astronomy/auroramax/ or http://www.swpc.noaa.gov/pmap/; and for forecasts, see http://www.gi.alaska.edu/.)

Electromagnetic Spectrum of Radiant Energy

The key essential solar input to life is electromagnetic energy of various wavelengths. Solar radiation occupies a portion of the **electromagnetic spectrum** of radiant energy. This radiant energy travels at the speed of light to Earth. The total spectrum of this radiant energy is made up of different wavelengths. Figure 2.5 shows that a **wavelength** is the distance between corresponding points on any two successive waves. The number of waves passing a fixed point in 1 second is the *frequency*.

The Sun emits radiant energy composed of 8% ultraviolet, X-ray, and gamma-ray wavelengths; 47% visible light wavelengths; and 45% infrared wavelengths. A portion of the electromagnetic spectrum is illustrated in Figure 2.6, with wavelengths increasing from the top of the illustration to the bottom. Note the wavelengths at which various phenomena and human applications of energy occur.

An important physical law, Wein's Displacement Law, states that all objects radiate energy in wavelengths related to their individual surface temperatures: the hotter the object, the shorter the mean wavelengths of maximum intensity emitted. This law holds true for the Sun and Earth. Figure 2.7 shows that the hot Sun radiates shorter wavelength energy, peaking around 0.5 μm (micrometre).

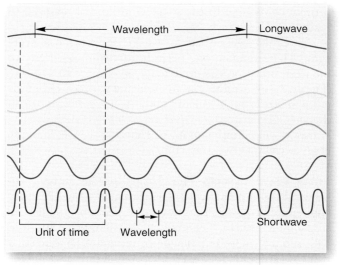

FIGURE 2.5 Wavelength and frequency.
Wavelength and frequency are two ways of describing electromagnetic wave motion. Shorter wavelengths are higher in frequency; longer wavelengths are lower in frequency.

The Sun's surface temperature is about 6000 K (5727 °C), and its emission curve shown in the figure approximates that predicted for an idealised 6000 K surface, or *blackbody radiator* (shown in Figure 2.7). A blackbody absorbs all the radiant energy that it receives and subsequently emits all that it has absorbed. A hotter object like the Sun emits a much greater amount of energy per unit area of its surface than does a similar area of a cooler object like Earth (Stefan-Boltzmann law). Shorter wavelength emissions are dominant at these higher temperatures.

Although cooler than the Sun, Earth radiates nearly all the radiant energy it absorbs. Emission of radiation is at

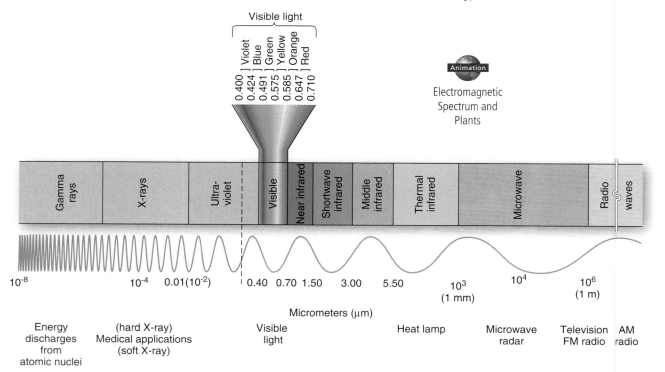

FIGURE 2.6 A portion of the electromagnetic spectrum of radiant energy.
Shorter wavelengths are at top; longer wavelengths toward the bottom.

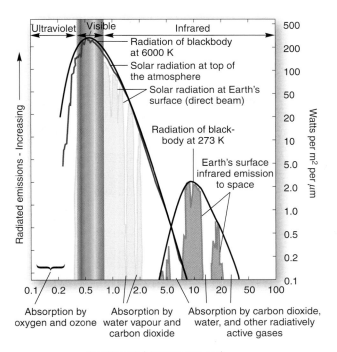

FIGURE 2.7 Solar and terrestrial energy distribution by wavelength.

A hotter Sun radiates shorter wavelengths, whereas a cooler Earth emits longer wavelengths. Dark lines represent ideal blackbody curves for objects with the same temperatures as the Sun and Earth. The dropouts in the plot lines for solar and terrestrial radiation represent absorption bands of water vapour, water, carbon dioxide, oxygen, ozone (O_3), and other gases.
[Adapted from W. D. Sellers, *Physical Climatology* (Chicago: University of Chicago Press), p. 20. Used by permission.]

longer wavelengths, mostly in the infrared portion of the spectrum, centered around 10.0 μm (Figure 2.7). Some of the atmospheric gases vary in their response to radiation received, being transparent to some while absorbing others. Figure 2.8 illustrates the flows of energy into and out of Earth systems. To summarise, the Sun's radiated energy is *shortwave radiation* that peaks in the short visible

wavelengths, whereas Earth's radiated energy is *longwave radiation* restricted to infrared wavelengths. In Chapter 4, we see that Earth, clouds, sky, ground, and objects that are terrestrial radiate longer wavelengths in contrast to the Sun.

Incoming Energy at the Top of the Atmosphere

The region at the top of the atmosphere, approximately 480 km above Earth's surface, is the **thermopause** (see Figure 3.2). It is the outer boundary of Earth's energy system and provides a useful point at which to assess the arriving solar radiation before it is diminished by scattering and absorption in passage through the atmosphere.

Earth's distance from the Sun results in its interception of only one two-billionth of the Sun's total energy output. Nevertheless, this tiny fraction of energy from the Sun is an enormous amount of energy flowing into Earth's systems. Solar radiation that reaches a horizontal plane at Earth is **insolation**, derived from the words *incoming solar radiation*. Insolation specifically applies to radiation arriving at Earth's atmosphere and surface. Insolation at the top of the atmosphere is expressed as the *solar constant*.

Solar Constant Knowing the amount of insolation incoming to Earth is important to climatologists and other scientists. The **solar constant**, with a value of $1372 \text{ W} \cdot \text{m}^{-2}$ (watts per square metre)[2], is the average insolation received at the thermopause when Earth is at its average distance from the Sun. As we follow insolation through the atmosphere to Earth's surface (Chapters 3 and 4), we see that the value of the solar constant is reduced by half

[2] A *watt* is equal to 1 joule (a unit of energy) per second and is the standard unit of power in the International System of Units (SI). (See the conversion tables in Appendix D of this text for more information on measurement conversions.) In nonmetric *calorie* heat units, the solar constant is expressed as approximately 2 calories per square centimetre per minute, or 2 *langleys* per minute (a langley being 1 cal · cm^{-2}). A calorie is the amount of energy required to raise the temperature of 1 gram of water (at 15 °C) by 1 degree Celsius and is equal to 4.184 joules.

FIGURE 2.8 Earth's energy budget simplified.
Inputs of shorter wavelengths arrive at Earth from the Sun. Outputs of longer infrared wavelengths radiate to space from Earth.

FIGURE 2.9 Insolation
receipts and Earth's curved
surface.
Solar insolation angles
determine the concentra-
tion of energy receipts by
latitude.

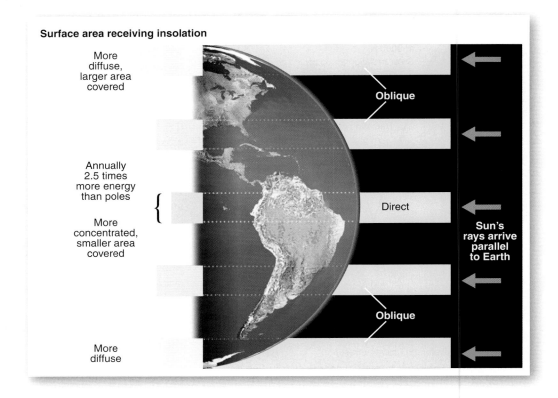

Surface area receiving insolation

More diffuse, larger area covered

Annually 2.5 times more energy than poles

More concentrated, smaller area covered

More diffuse

Oblique

Oblique

Direct

Sun's rays arrive parallel to Earth

or more through reflection, scattering, and absorption of shortwave radiation.

Uneven Distribution of Insolation Earth's curved surface presents a continually varying angle to the incoming parallel rays of insolation (Figure 2.9). Differences in the angle of solar rays at each latitude result in an uneven distribution of insolation and heating. The only point receiving insolation perpendicular to the surface (from directly overhead) is the **subsolar point** (see http://www.timeanddate .com/worldclock/sunearth.html for the location of the subsolar point for any date). During the year this point migrates between the tropics (23.5° N and 23.5° S latitudes), where the energy received is more concentrated. All other places away from the subsolar point receive insolation at an angle less than 90° and thus experience less concentrated energy; this effect is more pronounced at higher latitudes.

The thermopause above the equatorial region receives 2.5 times more insolation annually than the thermopause above the poles. In addition to the lower amount of insolation received per unit area at the thermopause, the lower-angle solar rays must pass through a greater thickness of atmosphere, resulting in greater losses of energy due to scattering, absorption, and reflection.

Figure 2.10 illustrates the daily variations throughout the year of energy at the top of the atmosphere for four locations in watts per square metre ($W \cdot m^{-2}$). The graphs

Energy Receipts at
90°N, 50°N, 0°, and 90°S

North Pole (90° N)

Winnipeg (50° N)

Equator (0°)

South Pole (90° S)

FIGURE 2.10 **Daily insolation received at the top of the atmosphere.**
The total daily insolation received at the top of the atmosphere is charted in watts per square metre per day for four locations (1 $W \cdot m^{-2}$ day^{-1} = 2.064 cal $\cdot$ cm^{-2} $\cdot$ day^{-1}).

show the seasonal changes in insolation northward and southward from the equatorial regions toward the poles. In June, the North Pole receives more than 500 W·m⁻² per day, which is more than is ever received at 40° N latitude or at the equator. Such high values result from long daylengths at the poles in summer—24 hours a day—compared with only 15 hours of daylight at 40° N latitude and 12 hours at the equator. However, at the poles the Sun at noon in summer is low in the sky, so a daylength twice that of the equator yields only about a 100 W·m⁻² difference.

In December, the pattern reverses, as shown on the graphs. Note that the top of the atmosphere at the South Pole receives even more insolation than the North Pole does in June (more than 500 W·m⁻²). This is a function of Earth's closer location to the Sun at perihelion (January 3 on Figure 2.1d). Along the equator, two maximum periods of approximately 430 W·m⁻² occur at the spring and fall equinoxes, when the subsolar point is at the equator.

Global Net Radiation Earth Radiation Budget Experiment (ERBE) instruments aboard several satellites measured shortwave and longwave flows of energy at the top of the atmosphere. ERBE sensors collected the data used to develop the map in Figure 2.11. This map shows *net radiation*, or the balance between incoming shortwave and outgoing longwave radiation—energy inputs minus energy outputs.

Note the latitudinal energy imbalance in net radiation on the map—positive values in lower latitudes and negative values toward the poles. In middle and high latitudes, approximately poleward of 36° north and south latitudes, net radiation is negative. This occurs at these higher latitudes because Earth's climate system loses more energy to space than it gains from the Sun, as measured at the top of the atmosphere. In the lower atmosphere, these polar energy deficits are offset by flows of energy from surpluses in tropical regions (as we will see in Chapters 4 and 6). The largest positive net radiation values, averaging 80 W·m⁻², are above the tropical oceans along a narrow equatorial zone. Net radiation minimums occur over Antarctica.

Of interest is the −20 W·m⁻² area over the Sahara region of North Africa. Here, typically clear skies—which permit great longwave radiation losses from Earth's surface—and light-coloured reflective surfaces act together to reduce net radiation values at the thermopause. In other regions, clouds and atmospheric pollution in the lower atmosphere also affect net radiation patterns at the top of the atmosphere by reflecting more shortwave energy to space.

The atmosphere and ocean form a giant heat engine, driven by differences in energy from place to place and causing major circulations within the lower atmosphere and in the ocean. These circulations include global winds, ocean currents, and weather systems—subjects to follow in Chapters 6 and 8. As you go about your daily activities, let these dynamic natural systems remind you of the constant flow of solar energy through the environment.

Having examined the flow of solar energy to Earth and the top of the atmosphere, let us now look at how

| < -100 | -100 to -80 | -80 to -60 | -60 to -40 | -40 to -20 | -20 to 0 | 0 to 20 | 20 to 40 | 40 to 60 | 60 to 80 | >80 |

FIGURE 2.11 Daily net radiation patterns at the top of the atmosphere.
Averaged daily net radiation flows measured at the top of the atmosphere by the Earth Radiation Budget Experiment (ERBE). Units are W·m⁻². [Data for map courtesy of GSFC/NASA.]

seasonal changes affect the distribution of insolation as Earth orbits the Sun during the year.

The Seasons

Earth's periodic rhythms of warmth and cold, dawn and daylight, twilight and night have fascinated humans for centuries. In fact, many ancient societies demonstrated an intense awareness of seasonal change and formally commemorated these natural energy rhythms with festivals, monuments, ground markings, and calendars (Figure 2.12). Such ancient seasonal monuments and calendar markings are found worldwide, including thousands of sites in North America, demonstrating an ancient awareness of seasons and astronomical relations.

Seasonality

Seasonality refers to both the seasonal variation of the Sun's position above the horizon and changing daylengths during the year. Seasonal variations are a response to changes in the Sun's **altitude**, or the angle between the horizon and the Sun. At sunrise or sunset, the Sun is at the horizon, so its altitude is 0°. If during the day the Sun reaches halfway between the horizon and directly overhead, it is at 45° altitude. If the Sun reaches the point directly overhead, it is at 90° altitude.

The Sun is directly overhead (90° altitude, or *zenith*) only at the *subsolar point*, where insolation is at a maximum, as we demonstrate in the chapter-opening photo described in *Geosystems Now*. At all other surface points, the Sun is at a lower altitude, producing less concentrated insolation.

The Sun's **declination** is the latitude of the subsolar point. Declination annually migrates through 47° of latitude, moving between the Tropic of Cancer (23.5° N) and the Tropic of Capricorn (23.5° S). The subsolar point does not reach Canada; all provinces are too far north.

Seasonality also means changing **daylength**, or duration of exposure to insolation. Daylength varies during the year, depending on latitude. The equator always receives equal hours of day and night: If you live in Ecuador, Kenya, or Singapore, every day and night is 12 hours long, year-round. People living along 40° N latitude (Philadelphia, Madrid, Beijing) or 40° S latitude (Buenos Aires, Capetown, Melbourne) experience about 6 hours difference in daylight between winter (9 hours) and summer (15 hours). At 50° N or S latitude (Winnipeg, Paris, the Falkland [Malvinas] Islands), people experience almost 8 hours of annual daylength variation.

At the North and South Poles, the range of daylength is extreme, with a 6-month period of no insolation—literally the poles experience one long day and one long night each year! Within the Arctic and Antarctic circles, daylength varies with weeks of twilight, then complete darkness, then on to weeks of predawn. Finally, weeks of daylight occur when the Sun does not set, and then the cycle begins again.

▐▐ CRITICAL THINKING 2.1

A Way to Calculate Sunrise and Sunset

For a useful sunrise and sunset calculator for any location, go to http://www.srrb.noaa.gov/highlights/sunrise/sunrise.html. Select a city near you or select "Enter lat/long" and enter your coordinates, enter your time difference offset from UTC (use Figure 1.21) and whether you are on daylight saving time, and enter the date you are checking. Click "Calculate" and you see the equation of time, solar declination, and times for sunrise and sunset. Give this a try.

Reasons for Seasons

Seasons result from variations in the Sun's *altitude* above the horizon, the Sun's *declination* (latitude location of the subsolar point), and *daylength* during the year. These in turn are created by several physical factors that operate in concert: Earth's *revolution* in orbit around the Sun, its daily *rotation* on its axis, its *tilted axis*, the unchanging *orientation of its axis*, and its approximate *sphericity* (Table 2.1). Of course, the essential ingredient is having a single source of radiant energy—the Sun. We now look at each of these

FIGURE 2.12 Stonehenge on the Salisbury Plain, England.
Neolithic peoples beginning about 5000 years ago constructed this complex of standing rock—*sarsen* uprights, topped by *lintel* capstones. Inherent in the layout is an indication of important seasonal dates and precise lunar-cycle predictions. [Bobbé Christopherson.]

TABLE 2.1 Five Reasons for Seasons

Factor	Description
Revolution	Orbit around the Sun; requires 365.24 days to complete at 107 280 km·h^{-1}
Rotation	Earth turning on its axis; takes approximately 24 hours to complete
Tilt	Axis is aligned at about 23.5° angle from a perpendicular to the plane of the ecliptic (the plane of Earth's orbit)
Axial parallelism	Remains in a fixed alignment, with Polaris directly overhead at the North Pole throughout the year
Sphericity	Appears as an oblate spheroid to the Sun's parallel rays; the geoid

FIGURE 2.13 Earth's revolution and rotation. Earth's *revolution* about the Sun and *rotation* on its axis, viewed from above Earth's orbit. Note the Moon's rotation on its axis and revolution are counterclockwise, as well.

factors individually. As we do, please note the distinction between revolution—Earth's travel around the Sun—and rotation—Earth's spinning on its axis (Figure 2.13).

Revolution Earth's orbital **revolution** about the Sun is shown in Figures 2.1d and 2.13. Earth's speed in orbit averages 107 280 km·h^{-1}. This speed, together with Earth's distance from the Sun, determines the time required for one revolution around the Sun and, therefore, the length of the year and duration of the seasons. Earth completes its annual revolution in 365.24 days. This number is based on a *tropical year*, measured from equinox to equinox, or the elapsed time between two crossings of the equator by the Sun.

The Earth-to-Sun distance from aphelion to perihelion might seem a seasonal factor, but it is not significant. It varies about 3% (4.8 million km) during the year, amounting to a 50 W·m^{-2} difference between north and south polar summers. Remember that the Earth–Sun distance averages 150 million km.

Rotation Earth's **rotation**, or turning on its axis, is a complex motion that averages slightly less than 24 hours in duration. Rotation determines daylength, creates the apparent deflection of winds and ocean currents, and produces the twice-daily rise and fall of the ocean tides in relation to the gravitational pull of the Sun and the Moon.

Earth rotates about its **axis**, an imaginary line extending through the planet from the geographic North Pole to the South Pole. When viewed from above the North Pole, Earth rotates counterclockwise around this axis. Viewed from above the equator, Earth rotates west to east, or eastward. This eastward rotation creates the Sun's *apparent* westward daily journey from sunrise in the east to sunset in the west. Of course, the Sun actually remains in a fixed position in the centre of the Solar System.

Although every point on Earth takes the same 24 hours to complete one rotation, the linear velocity of rotation at any point on Earth's surface varies dramatically with latitude. The equator is 40 075 km long; therefore, rotational velocity at the equator must be approximately 1675 km·h^{-1} to cover that distance in one day. At 60° latitude, a parallel is only half the length of the equator, or 20 038 km long, so the rotational velocity there is 838 km·h^{-1}. At the poles, the velocity is 0. This variation in rotational velocity establishes the effect of the Coriolis force, discussed in Chapter 6. Table 2.2 lists the speed of rotation for several selected latitudes.

Earth's rotation produces the diurnal (daily) pattern of day and night. The dividing line between day and night is called the **circle of illumination** (as illustrated in Figure 2.15). Because this day-night dividing circle of illumination intersects the equator, *daylength at the equator is always evenly divided*—12 hours of day and 12 hours

GEO REPORT 2.3 *Why Do We Always See the Same Side of the Moon?*

Note in Figure 2.14 that the Moon both revolves around Earth and rotates on its axis in a counterclockwise direction when viewed from above Earth's North Pole. It completes both of these motions in the same amount of time. The Moon's speed in orbit varies slightly during the month whereas its rotation speed is constant, so we see exactly 50% of the lunar surface at any moment, or about 59% during the month—but always the same side.

TABLE 2.2 Speed of Rotation at Selected Latitudes

Latitude	Speed Km · h⁻¹	Cities at Approximate Latitudes
90°	0	North Pole
60°	838	Seward, Alaska; Oslo, Norway; Saint Petersburg, Russia
50°	1078	Chibougamau, Québec; Winnipeg, Manitoba; Kyyîv (Kiev), Ukraine
40°	1284	Columbus, Ohio; Beijing, China; Valdivia, Chile
30°	1452	New Orleans, Louisiana; Pôrto Alegre, Brazil
0°	1675	Pontianak, Indonesia; Quito, Ecuador

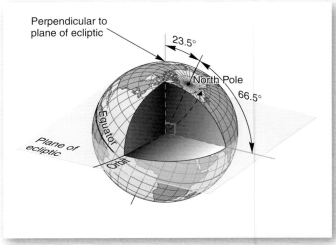

FIGURE 2.14 **The plane of Earth's orbit—the ecliptic—and Earth's axial tilt.**
Note on the illustration that the plane of the equator is inclined to the plane of the ecliptic at 23.5°.

of night. All other latitudes experience uneven daylength through the seasons, except for 2 days a year, on the equinoxes. A true day varies slightly from 24 hours, but by international agreement a day is defined as exactly 24 hours, or 86 400 seconds. This average, called a *mean solar day*, eliminates predictable variations in rotation and revolution that cause the solar day to change slightly in length throughout the year.

Tilt of Earth's Axis To understand Earth's **axial tilt**, imagine a plane (a flat surface) that intersects Earth's elliptical orbit about the Sun, with half of the Sun and Earth above the plane and half below. Such a plane touching all points of Earth's orbit is the **plane of the ecliptic**. Earth's tilted axis remains fixed relative to this plane as Earth revolves around the Sun. The plane of the ecliptic is important to our discussion of Earth's seasons. Now, imagine a perpendicular line (at a 90° angle) passing through the plane. From this perpendicular, Earth's axis is tilted 23.5°. It forms a 66.5° angle from the plane of the ecliptic (Figure 2.14). The axis through Earth's two poles points just slightly away from Polaris, which is named, appropriately, the *North Star*.

This text uses "about" with the tilt angle just described because Earth's axial tilt changes over a complex 41 000-year cycle (see Figure 17.31). The axial tilt ranges roughly between 22° and 24.5° from a perpendicular to the plane of the ecliptic. The present tilt is 23° 27′ (or 66° 33′ from the plane). In decimal numbers, 23° 27′ is approximately 23.45°. For convenience this is rounded off

to a 23.5° tilt (or 66.5° from the plane) in most usage. Scientific evidence shows that the angle of tilt is in a decreasing phase of its 41 000-year cycle.

CRITICAL THINKING 2.2

Astronomical Factors Vary over Long Time Frames

The variability of Earth's axial tilt, orbit about the Sun, and a wobble to the axis is described in Figure 17.31. Please refer to this figure and compare these changing conditions to the information in Table 2.1 and the related figures in this chapter.

What do you think the effect on Earth's seasons would be if the tilt of the axis was decreased? Or if the tilt was increased? You can take a ball or piece of round fruit and mark the poles and move the sphere around a lightbulb, as if revolving it around the Sun. Note the alignment with no tilt and then with a 90° tilt to help complete your analysis. Or what if Earth's orbit was more circular as opposed to its present elliptical shape? Earth's orbit actually does vary like this in a 100 000-year cycle.

Hypothetically, if Earth were tilted on its side, with its axis parallel to the plane of the ecliptic, we would experience maximum variation in seasons worldwide. In contrast, if Earth's axis were perpendicular to the plane of its orbit—that is, with no tilt—we would experience no seasonal changes, with something like a perpetual spring or fall season, and all latitudes would experience 12-hour days and nights. Do you agree with these assertions?

GEO REPORT 2.4 *Measuring Earth's Rotation*

The complexity of Earth's rotation is measured by satellites in precise mathematical orbits: GPS (global positioning system), SLR (satellite-laser ranging), and VLBI (very-long baseline interferometry). All contribute to our knowledge of Earth's rotation. The International Earth Rotation Service at http://www.iers.org/ issues monthly and annual reports. Earth's rotation is gradually slowing, partially owing to the drag of lunar tidal forces. A "day" on Earth today is many hours longer than it was 4 billion years ago.

Axial Parallelism Throughout our annual journey around the Sun, Earth's axis *maintains the same alignment* relative to the plane of the ecliptic and to Polaris and other stars. You can see this consistent alignment in Figure 2.15. If we compared the axis in different months, it would always appear parallel to itself, a condition known as **axial parallelism.**

Sphericity Although Earth is not a perfect sphere, as discussed in Chapter 1, we can refer to Earth's *sphericity* as a part of seasonality, for it produces the uneven receipt of insolation from pole to pole shown in Figures 2.9, 2.10, and 2.11.

The five reasons for seasons are summarised in Table 2.1: revolution, rotation, tilt, axial parallelism, and sphericity. Now, considering all these factors operating together, let us examine the annual march of the seasons.

Annual March of the Seasons

During the march of the seasons on Earth, daylength is the most obvious way of sensing changes in season at latitudes away from the equator. Daylength is the interval between **sunrise**, the moment when the disk of the Sun first appears above the horizon in the east, and **sunset**, that moment when it totally disappears below the horizon in the west.

The extremes of daylength occur in December and June when the subsolar point is farthest from the equator. The times around December 21–22 and June 20–21 are termed *solstices*. Strictly speaking, the solstices are specific points in time at which the Sun's declination is at its highest latitude, either farthest north at the **Tropic of Cancer,** or farthest south at the **Tropic of Capricorn.** Tropic is from *tropicus,* meaning a turn or change, so a tropic latitude is where the Sun's subsolar point appears to

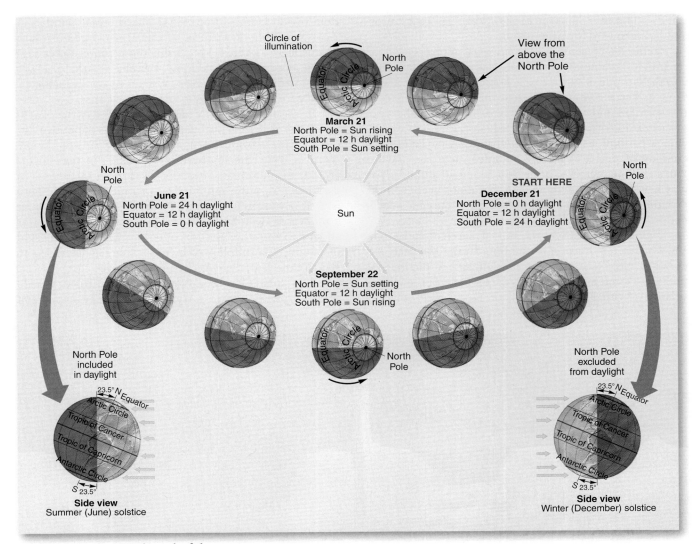

FIGURE 2.15 Annual march of the seasons.
Annual march of the seasons as Earth revolves about the Sun. Shading indicates the changing position of the circle of illumination. Note the hours of daylight for the equator and the poles. As you read, begin on the right side at December 21 and move counterclockwise. Given this illustration, turn to the back cover of this textbook and see whether you can determine the month during which the *Apollo* astronaut made the Earth photo. (The answer is on this book's copyright page.)

Earth–Sun Rotation and Seasons

TABLE 2.3 Annual March of the Seasons

Approximate Date	Northern Hemisphere Name	Latitude of the Subsolar Point
December 21–22	Winter solstice (December solstice)	23.5° S latitude (Tropic of Capricorn)
March 20–21	Vernal equinox (March equinox)	0° (Equator)
June 20–21	Summer solstice (June solstice)	23.5° N latitude (Tropic of Cancer)
September 22–23	Autumnal equinox (September equinox)	0° (Equator)

CRITICAL THINKING 2.3

Measure and Track Seasonal Change

Post a reminder in your notebook to check the position of sunrise and sunset at least twice during the semester from a place where you can see the horizon. If you have a magnetic compass, note the degrees from true north for sunrise and sunset. Be sure and ask your instructor about the *magnetic declination* of your location to adjust your compass readings. *Azimuth* is read from north in a clockwise direction—with 0° and 360° being the same point, north.

If you are new to such observations, the degree of change in the position of where the sun rises and sets over the span of months in a school term might be surprising. Based upon what you have read and your measurements here, make a prediction about sunrise and sunset for the last day of classes.

stand still briefly (Sun stance, or *sol stice*); before it "turns" and heads toward the other tropic.

Table 2.3 presents the key seasonal anniversary dates on which the equinoxes and solstices occur, their names, and the latitude of the subsolar point (declination). Variations in Earth's orbital path determine the exact dates of the solstices and equinoxes each year. During the year, places on Earth outside of the equatorial region experience a continuous but gradual change in daylength, increasing or decreasing a few minutes each day, and the Sun's altitude increases or decreases a small amount. You may have noticed that these daily variations become more pronounced in spring and autumn, when the Sun's declination changes at a faster rate.

Figure 2.15 illustrates the annual march of the seasons and Earth's relationship to the Sun during the year. Let us begin with December, on the right side of the illustration. On December 21 or 22, at the moment of the **winter solstice** ("winter Sun stance"), or **December solstice,**

the circle of illumination excludes the North Pole region (north of 66.5° N) from sunlight but includes the South Pole region (south of 66.5° S). The subsolar point is at 23.5° S latitude, the Tropic of Capricorn. The Northern Hemisphere is tilted away from these more direct rays of sunlight—northern winter—thereby creating a lower angle for the incoming solar rays and thus a less concentrated pattern of insolation.

From about 66.5° N latitude to 90° N (the North Pole), the Sun remains below the horizon the entire day of the winter solstice. This latitude (66.5° N) marks the **Arctic Circle**, the southernmost parallel (in the Northern Hemisphere) that experiences a 24-hour period of darkness. From the autumnal (September) equinox, there is a slow transition from 12 hours of daylight to about a month of twilight followed by the Arctic night. After about two and a half months of darkness, there is a period of extended dawn followed by increasing daylength as the North Pole region emerges from darkness.

The Antarctic sunset photo in Figure 2.16a was made as the expedition ship carrying Robert Christopherson

(a)

(b)

FIGURE 2.16 The Midnight Sun and long days.
(a) Antarctic sunset, 11:30 P.M., approaching the continent of Antarctica at 63° S latitude in December. The low Sun angle produced incredible sunset colours for hours. (b) The Midnight Sun seen from a research ship in the Arctic Ocean at 80° N latitude in June. Can you relate the December and June perspectives to Figure 2.15? [Bobbé Christopherson.]

crossed the Branfield Strait at 63° S, just a week before the December solstice. Sunrise was only a couple of hours later, at 2 A.M. local time—making the sunless period from twilight to dawn only a little over 2 hours!

During the three months following the December solstice, daylength and solar angles gradually increase in the Northern Hemisphere as Earth completes one-fourth of its orbit. The moment of the **vernal equinox** or **March equinox**, occurs on March 20 or 21. At that time, the circle of illumination passes through both poles so that all locations on Earth experience a 12-hour day and a 12-hour night. People living around 45° N latitude (Toronto, Halifax) have gained more than three hours of daylight since the December solstice. At the North Pole, the Sun peeks above the horizon for the first time since the previous September; at the South Pole, the Sun is setting—a dramatic 3-day "moment" for the people working the Scott–Amundson Base—not to be seen again for months.

Spring marches into summer from March to June 20 or 21 and the moment of the **summer solstice**, or **June solstice**. The subsolar point migrates from the equator to 23.5° N latitude, the Tropic of Cancer. Because the circle of illumination now includes the north polar region, everywhere north of the Arctic Circle receives 24 hours of daylight—the *Midnight Sun*.

Figure 2.16b shows the Midnight Sun in June at 80° N latitude on the Arctic Ocean. The camera is pointing due north, seeing the Sun across the North Pole, some 885 km distant. Imagine how strange it would feel to have natural lighting that feels like about 3 P.M., yet have clocks showing midnight. In contrast, the region from the **Antarctic Circle** to the South Pole (66.5°–90° S latitude) is in darkness. Those working in Antarctica call the June solstice *Midwinter's Day*.

September 22 or 23 is the moment in time of the **autumnal equinox,** or **September equinox,** when Earth's orientation is such that the circle of illumination again passes through both poles so that all parts of the planet experience a 12-hour day and a 12-hour night. The subsolar point returns to the equator, with days growing shorter to the north and longer to the south. Researchers stationed at the South Pole see the disk of the Sun just rising, ending their 6 months of darkness. In the Northern Hemisphere, autumn arrives, whereas in the Southern Hemisphere it is spring.

Dawn and Twilight *Dawn* is the period of diffused light that occurs before sunrise. The corresponding evening time after sunset is *twilight*. During both periods, light is scattered by molecules of atmospheric gases and reflected by dust and moisture in the atmosphere. The duration of both is a function of latitude, because the angle of the Sun's path above the horizon determines the thickness of the atmosphere through which the Sun's rays must pass. The illumination may be enhanced by the presence of pollution aerosols and suspended particles from volcanic eruptions or forest and grassland fires.

At the equator, where the Sun's rays are almost directly above the horizon throughout the year, dawn and twilight are limited to 30–45 minutes each. These times increase to 1–2 hours each at 40° latitude, and at 60° latitude they each range upward from 2.5 hours, with little true night in summer. The poles experience about 7 weeks of dawn and 7 weeks of twilight, leaving only 2.5 months of "night" during the 6 months when the Sun is completely below the horizon.

Seasonal Observations In the midlatitudes of the Northern Hemisphere, the position of sunrise on the horizon migrates from day to day, from the southeast in December to the northeast in June. Over the same period, the point of sunset migrates from the southwest to the northwest. The Sun's altitude at local noon at 40° N latitude increases from a 26° angle above the horizon at the winter (December) solstice to a 73° angle above the horizon at the summer (June) solstice—a range of 47° (Figure 2.17).

CRITICAL THINKING 2.4

Measuring the Sun's Changing Altitude

Using the concepts in Figure 2.17, use a protractor and ruler to measure the angle of the Sun's altitude at noon (or 1 P.M., if in daylight saving time). Do not look at the Sun; rather, with your back to the Sun, align the ruler so that it casts the smallest shadow as you measure its angle from the horizontal with the protractor. Record this measurement in your notebook and remember to repeat the measurement near the end of the semester. Compare your records and summarise seasonal change using your different measurements of the Sun's altitude.

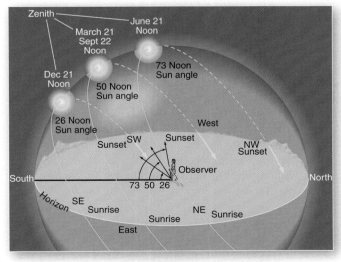

FIGURE 2.17 Seasonal observations—sunrise, noon, and sunset through the year.
Seasonal observations are at 40° N latitude for the December solstice, March equinox, June solstice, and September equinox. The Sun's altitude increases from 26° in December to 73° above the horizon in June—a difference of 47°. Note the changing position of sunrise and sunset along the horizon during the year.

Radiation laws are the set of rules that summarise the way that matter interacts with the electromagnetic spectrum. We can think of radiation, energy, and temperature—the hotter a body, the more energy it radiates, and the shorter the mean wavelength of energy it radiates. Two laws are particularly useful in an examination of energy.

First is the Stefan-Boltzmann Law that gives the total amount of energy being emitted at all wavelengths by a blackbody,

$$E = \sigma T^4$$

where E is the energy measured in $W \cdot m^{-2}$, σ is the Stefan-Boltzmann constant ($5.6705 \times 10^{-8} W \cdot m^{-2} K^{-4}$), and T is the temperature of the surface measured on the Kelvin scale. Kelvin is a scale of temperature that has an absolute zero: Zero Kelvin means there is no temperature. The measurement units are the same distance apart as on the Celsius scale—a relative temperature scale. To change from Kelvin to Celsius, use the following conversion:

$$K = {}^{\circ}C + 273$$

Second is the Wien Displacement Law that gives the wavelength of the peak of the radiation distribution,

$$\lambda_{MAX} = c/T$$

where λ_{MAX} is the wavelength in μm that is the maximum radiation at a given temperature, c is a constant ($2898 \mu m$ K), and T is the surface temperature in K. The numerator is a constant usually measured in angstroms (one 10 billionth of a metre), but can be measured in other units. In this example we use micrometres.

These laws apply only to something known as a blackbody—a perfectly radiating surface. Most surfaces are not perfect radiators, but the differences in radiation are not significant enough to discount the laws.

To see how these laws are applied, consider normal room temperature of 20°C. Convert this temperature to Kelvin by adding 273 to 20. Room temperature in Kelvin is 293 K. Note that we do not use the degree symbol when measuring Kelvins. How much energy is being emitted by a surface at room temperature?

$$\begin{aligned} E &= \sigma T^4 \\ &= (5.6705 \times 10^{-8} \ W \cdot m^{-2} K^{-4}) \\ &\quad \times (293 \ K)^4 \\ &= (5.6705 \times 10^{-8} \ W \cdot m^{-2} K^{-4}) \\ &\quad \times 7.37 \times 10^9 \ K^4 \\ &= 417.9 \ W \cdot m^{-2} \\ &= 418 \ W \cdot m^{-2} \end{aligned}$$

What is the wavelength of the maximum emission?

$$\begin{aligned} \lambda_{MAX} &= c/T \\ &= 2898/293 \ K \\ &= 9.89 \ \mu m \end{aligned}$$

At room temperature, a surface emits $418 \ W \cdot m^{-2}$ of thermal infrared energy at a peak wavelength of $9.89 \ \mu m$.

Seasonal change is quite noticeable across the landscape away from the equator. Think back over the past year. What seasonal changes have you observed in vegetation and weather patterns? All living things respond to changing energy associated with the march of the seasons. Recent scientific observation and measurement indicate that the timing of the seasons is changing as global climates shift in middle and high latitudes. Leafing out is occurring as much as three weeks earlier than expected from previous average conditions. Likewise, the onset of autumn conditions is happening later. Ecosystems are changing in response.

GEOSYSTEMS CONNECTION

We found our place in the Universe, and the relations among Milky Way Galaxy, Sun, planets, and satellites. From the Sun the solar wind and electromagnetic spectrum of radiant energy flow across space to Earth where we look at its distribution along the top of the atmosphere and how this changes in a seasonal rhythm.

Next we construct Earth's atmosphere and examine its composition, temperature, and functions. Electromagnetic energy cascades toward Earth's surface through the layers of the atmosphere where harmful wavelengths are filtered out. Also, we examine human impacts on the atmosphere: the depletion of the ozone layer, acid deposition, and variable atmospheric ingredients, including human air pollution.

KEY LEARNING CONCEPTS REVIEW

■ *Distinguish* among galaxies, stars, and planets, and *locate* Earth.

Our Solar System—the Sun and eight planets—is located on a remote, trailing edge of the **Milky Way Galaxy,** a flattened, disk-shaped mass estimated to contain up to 400 billion stars. **Gravity,** the mutual attracting force exerted by the mass of an object upon all other objects, is an organizing force in the Universe. The process of stars (like our Sun) condensing from nebular clouds with planetesimals (protoplanets) forming in orbits around their central masses is the **planetesimal hypothesis.**

Milky Way Galaxy (p. 42)
gravity (p. 42)
planetesimal hypothesis (p. 42)

1. Describe the Sun's status among stars in the Milky Way Galaxy. Describe the Sun's location, size, and relationship to its planets.
2. If you have seen the Milky Way at night, briefly describe it. Use specifics from the text in your description.
3. Briefly describe Earth's origin as part of the Solar System.
4. Compare the locations of the eight planets of the Solar System.

■ *Examine* the origin, formation, and development of Earth, and *construct* Earth's annual orbit about the Sun.

The Solar System, planets, and Earth began to condense from a nebular cloud of dust, gas, debris, and icy comets approximately 4.6 billion years ago. Distances in space are so vast that the **speed of light** (300 000 km · s^{-1} which is about 9.5 trillion km · yr^{-1}) is used to express distance.

In its orbit, Earth is at **perihelion** (its closest position to the Sun) during our Northern Hemisphere winter (January 3 at 147 255 000 km). It is at **aphelion** (its farthest position from the Sun) during our Northern Hemisphere summer (July 4 at 152 083 000 km). Earth's average distance from the Sun is approximately 8 minutes and 20 seconds in terms of light speed.

speed of light (p. 42)
perihelion (p. 42)
aphelion (p. 42)

5. How far is Earth from the Sun in terms of light speed? In terms of kilometers?
6. Briefly describe the relationship among these features: Universe, Milky Way Galaxy, Solar System, Sun, Earth, and Moon.
7. Diagram a simple sketch of Earth's orbit about the Sun. How much does the distance from the Sun vary during the course of a year?

■ *Describe* the Sun's internal processes, and *explain* the characteristics of the solar wind and the electromagnetic spectrum of radiant energy.

The **fusion process**—hydrogen nuclei forced together under tremendous temperature and pressure in the Sun's interior—generates incredible quantities of energy. Solar energy in the form of charged particles of **solar wind** travels out in all directions from magnetic disturbances on the Sun, such as from large **sunspots.** Solar wind is deflected by Earth's **magnetosphere,** producing various effects in the upper atmosphere, including spectacular **auroras**—the northern and southern lights—which surge across the skies at higher latitudes. Another possible effect of the solar wind in the atmosphere is its possible influence on weather.

Radiant energy across the **electromagnetic spectrum** travels outward in all directions from the Sun. The total spectrum of this radiant energy is made up of different **wavelengths**—the distance between corresponding points on any two successive waves of radiant energy. Eventually, some of this radiant energy reaches Earth.

fusion (p. 44)
solar wind (p. 44)
sunspots (p. 44)
magnetosphere (p. 45)
auroras (p. 45)
electromagnetic spectrum (p. 46)
wavelength (p. 46)

8. How does the Sun produce such tremendous quantities of energy?
9. What is the sunspot cycle? At what stage will the cycle be in the year 2013?
10. Describe Earth's magnetosphere and its effects on the solar wind and the electromagnetic spectrum.
11. Summarise the presently known effects of the solar wind relative to Earth's environment.
12. Describe the various segments of the electromagnetic spectrum, from shortest to longest wavelength. What are the main wavelengths produced by the Sun? Which wavelengths does Earth radiate?

■ *Portray* the intercepted solar energy and its uneven distribution at the top of the atmosphere.

Electromagnetic radiation from the Sun passes through Earth's magnetic field to the top of the atmosphere—the **thermopause,** at approximately 480 km altitude. Incoming solar radiation that reaches a horizontal plane at Earth is **insolation,** a term specifically applied to radiation arriving at Earth's atmosphere and surface. The term **solar constant** describes insolation at the top of the atmosphere: the average insolation received at the thermopause when Earth is at its average distance from the Sun. The solar constant is measured as an average of 1372 W · m^{-2}. The latitude receiving maximum insolation is the **subsolar point,** where solar rays are perpendicular to the surface (radiating from directly overhead). All other locations away from the subsolar point receive slanting rays and less concentrated insolation.

thermopause (p. 47)
insolation (p. 47)
solar constant (p. 47)
subsolar point (p. 48)

13. What is the solar constant? Why is it important to know?

14. Study the graph for Winnipeg at 50° N latitude in Figure 2.10 and record the amount of energy in watts per square metre (W · m⁻²) per day in your notebook for each month throughout the year. Compare this with the amount at the North Pole and at the equator.

15. If Earth were flat and oriented at right angles to incoming solar radiation (insolation), what would be the latitudinal distribution of solar energy at the top of the atmosphere?

■ **Define** solar altitude, solar declination, and daylength, and **describe** the annual variability of each—Earth's seasonality.

The angle between the Sun and the horizon is the Sun's **altitude**. The Sun's **declination** is the latitude of the subsolar point. Declination migrates annually through 47° of latitude, moving between the *Tropic of Cancer* at about 23.5° N (June) and the *Tropic of Capricorn* at 23.5° S (December). Seasonality means an annual change in the Sun's altitude and changing **daylength**, or duration of exposure to insolation.

Earth's distinct seasons are produced in part by interactions of **revolution** (annual orbit about the Sun) and **rotation** (Earth's turning on its **axis**). As Earth rotates, the boundary that divides daylight and darkness is the **circle of illumination**. Additional reasons for seasons include **axial tilt** (at about 23.5° from a perpendicular to the **plane of the ecliptic**) and **axial parallelism** (the parallel alignment of the axis throughout the year), and approximate *sphericity*.

Earth rotates about its axis, an imaginary line extending through the planet from the geographic North Pole to the South Pole. In the Solar System, an imaginary plane touching all points of Earth's orbit is the *plane of the ecliptic*. Daylength is the interval between **sunrise**, the moment when the disk of the Sun first appears above the horizon in the east, and **sunset**, that moment when it totally disappears below the horizon in the west. The **Tropic of Cancer** marks the farthest latitude north the subsolar point migrates during the year, about 23.5° N. The **Tropic of Capricorn** marks the farthest latitude south the subsolar point migrates during the year, about 23.5° S.

On December 21 or 22, at the moment of the **winter solstice** ("winter Sun stance"), or **December solstice**, the circle of illumination excludes the north polar region but includes the south polar region. The Sun remains below the horizon the entire day. This latitude (66.5° N) marks the **Arctic Circle**, the southernmost parallel (in the Northern Hemisphere) that experiences a 24-hour period of darkness, or on June 20–21, a 24-hour period of daylight. The moment of the **vernal equinox**, or **March equinox**, occurs on March 20 or 21. At that time, the circle of illumination passes through both poles so that all locations on Earth experience a 12-hour day and a 12-hour night.

June 20 or 21 is the moment of the **summer solstice**, or **June solstice**. The subsolar point migrates from the equator to 23.5° N latitude, the Tropic of Cancer. Because the circle of illumination now includes the north polar region, everywhere

north of the Arctic Circle receives 24 hours of daylight—the "Midnight Sun." In contrast, the area from the **Antarctic Circle** to the South Pole (66.5°–90° S latitude) is in darkness 24 hours a day, or on December 21, in constant daylight. September 22 or 23 is the time of the **autumnal equinox**, or **September equinox**, when Earth's orientation is such that the circle of illumination again passes through both poles so that all parts of the globe experience a 12-hour day and a 12-hour night.

altitude (p. 50)
declination (p. 50)
daylength (p. 50)
revolution (p. 51)
rotation (p. 51)
axis (p. 51)
circle of illumination (p. 51)
axial tilt (p. 52)
plane of the ecliptic (p. 52)
axial parallelism (p. 53)
sunrise (p. 53)
sunset (p. 53)
Tropic of Cancer (p. 53)
Tropic of Capricorn (p. 53)
winter solstice, December solstice (p. 54)
Arctic Circle (p. 54)
Antarctic Circle (p. 55)
vernal equinox, March equinox (p. 55)
summer solstice, June solstice (p. 55)
autumnal equinox, September equinox (p. 55)

16. Assess the 12-month Gregorian calendar (the calendar currently used in the western world), with its months of different lengths, and leap years, and its relation to the annual seasonal rhythms—the march of the seasons. What do you find?

17. The concept of seasonality refers to what specific phenomena? How do these aspects of seasonality change during a year at 0° latitude? At 45°? At 90°?

18. Differentiate between the Sun's altitude and its declination at Earth's surface.

19. For the latitude at which you live, how does daylength vary during the year? How does the Sun's altitude vary? Does your local newspaper publish a weather calendar containing such information? Can you find this on a weather website?

20. List the five physical factors that operate together to produce seasons.

21. Describe Earth's revolution and rotation and differentiate between them.

22. Define Earth's present tilt relative to its orbit about the Sun.

23. Describe seasonal conditions at each of the four key seasonal anniversary dates during the year. What are the solstices and equinoxes, and what is the Sun's declination at these dates?

MyGeosciencePlace

Visit **www.mygeoscienceplace.ca** for several figure animations, satellite loops, self-study quizzes, flashcards, interactive glossary, career links, RSS feeds, Pearson eText of *Geosystems*, and much more.

CHAPTER 3

Earth's Modern Atmosphere

Sunset at 30 degrees South over the Atlantic Ocean.
[Bobbé Christopherson.]

KEY LEARNING CONCEPTS

After reading the chapter, you should be able to:

- **Construct** a general model of the atmosphere based on three criteria—composition, temperature, and function—and **diagram** this model in a simple sketch.

- **List** the stable components of the modern atmosphere and their relative percentages by volume, and **describe** each.

- **Describe** conditions within the stratosphere; specifically, **review** the function and status of the ozonosphere (ozone layer).

- **Distinguish** between natural and anthropogenic variable gases and materials in the lower atmosphere.

- **Describe** the sources and effects of carbon monoxide, nitrogen dioxide, and sulfur dioxide, and **construct** a simple equation that illustrates photochemical reactions that produce ozone, peroxyacetyl nitrates, nitric acid, and sulfuric acid.

Humans Help Define the Atmosphere

The survival of humans in space depends on our knowledge of the upper atmosphere. Astronaut Mark Lee, on a spacewalk in 1994 (*STS–64*, http://www.nasa.gov/mission_pages/shuttle/shuttlemissions/archives/sts-64.html), was 241 km above the surface, in orbit (Figure GN 3.1). Beyond the protective shield of Earth's atmosphere, he travelled at 28 165 km $\cdot$ h^{-1}, which is almost 9 times faster than a high-speed rifle bullet. Where the Sun hit his spacesuit, temperatures climbed to +120°C, and in the shadows, temperatures dropped to −150°C. The vacuum of space surrounded him. Radiation and solar wind impacted his suit's surface. To survive in the upper atmosphere is an obvious challenge, one that relies on the ability of NASA spacesuits to duplicate Earth's atmosphere.

What features must a spacesuit provide for human survival? The suit must give all the protection provided by the atmosphere, such as blocking radiation and particle impacts. The suit needs to protect the interior from thermal extremes. Earth's oxygen and carbon dioxide processing systems must be replicated in the suit, as must fluid delivery and waste management systems. The suit must maintain an internal air pressure against the space vacuum; for pure oxygen, this is 32.4 kPa; which roughly equals the pressure of oxygen, water vapour, and CO_2 gases together at sea level. All 18 000 parts of the spacesuit work to duplicate what the atmosphere does for us on a daily basis.

In an earlier era before orbital flights, scientists did not know how a human could survive in space or how to design an artificial atmosphere that is supported by the modern spacesuit. In 1960, Air Force Captain Joseph Kittinger, Jr., stood at the opening of a small, unpressurised compartment, dangling from a helium-filled balloon, floating at an altitude of 31.3 km. The air pressure was barely measurable—this altitude is the beginning of space in experimental aircraft testing. He leaped into the stratospheric void and placed himself at tremendous personal risk for an experimental reentry through the atmosphere (Figure GN 3.2). He carried an instrument pack on his seat, his main chute, and pure oxygen supplied to his breathing mask.

Initially frightening to him was that he heard nothing, no rushing sound, for there was not enough air to produce any sound. The fabric of his pressure suit did not flutter, for there was not enough air to create friction against the cloth. His speed was remarkable owing to the lack of air resistance in the stratosphere. Captain Kittinger quickly accelerated to 988 km $\cdot$ h^{-1}, near the speed of sound at sea level.

FIGURE GN 3.2 A remotely triggered camera captures a stratospheric leap into history. [Volkmar Wentzel/NGS Image Collection. Used by permission from the *National Geographic Magazine,* Dec. 1960, p. 855. All rights reserved.]

His free fall took him through the stratosphere and its ozone layer, as the frictional drag of denser layers of atmospheric gases slowed his body. He dropped into the lower atmosphere, finally falling below airplane flying altitudes. His free fall lasted 4 minutes and 25 seconds until the opening of his main chute at 5500 m. He safely drifted to Earth's surface. This remarkable 13-minute, 35-second voyage through 99% of the atmospheric mass remains a record to this day.

The experiences of these two men illustrate the evolution of our understanding of upper atmosphere survival. From Joseph Kittinger's dangerous leap of discovery to the now routine spacewalks of astronauts such as Mark Lee, scientists have gained the ability to duplicate atmospheric conditions artificially. This chapter describes our current knowledge as we explore the Earth's atmosphere.

FIGURE GN 3.1 An untethered STS–64 astronaut Mark Lee as a satellite in Earth orbit on a working spacewalk. [NASA.]

Earth's atmosphere is a unique reservoir of gases, the product of 4.6 billion years of development. It protects us from hostile radiation and particles from the Sun and beyond. The atmosphere serves as an efficient filter. As shown in Geosystems Now, when humans venture away from the lower regions of the atmosphere, they must wear elaborate protective spacesuits that sustain them, providing services the atmosphere normally performs for us all the time.

In this chapter: We examine the modern atmosphere using criteria of composition, temperature, and function. Our look at the atmosphere also includes the spatial aspects of both natural and human-produced air pollution. We all participate in atmospheric processes with each breath we take, the energy we consume, the traveling we do, and the products we buy. Human activities cause stratospheric ozone losses and the blight of acid deposition on ecosystems. These topics are essential to physical geography, for we are influencing the atmospheric composition for the future.

Atmospheric Composition, Temperature, and Function

The modern atmosphere probably is the fourth general atmosphere in Earth's history. It is a gaseous mixture of ancient origin, the sum of all the exhalations and inhalations of life interacting on Earth throughout time. The principal substance of this atmosphere is air, the medium of life as well as a major industrial and chemical raw material. **Air** is a simple mixture of gases that is naturally odourless, colourless, tasteless, and formless, blended so thoroughly that it behaves as if it were a single gas (Figure 3.1).

Viewed from the distance of the Moon, the astonishing thing about Earth, catching the breath, is that it is alive. The photographs show the dry, pounded surface of the Moon in the foreground, dead as an old bone. Aloft, floating free beneath the moist, gleaming membrane of a bright blue sky, is the rising Earth, the only exuberant thing in this part of the cosmos. . . . It has the organized, self-contained look of a live creature, full of information, marvelously skilled in handling the sun. . . . When the Earth came alive it began constructing its own membrane, for the general purpose of editing the sun. . . . Taken all in all, the sky is a miraculous achievement. It works, and for what it is designed to accomplish it is as infallible as anything in nature.

Lewis Thomas

FIGURE 3.1 Earthrise.
Earthrise over the stark and lifeless lunar surface. [JPL/NASA. Quote from "The World's Biggest Membrane" in *The Lives of a Cell* by Lewis Thomas. Copyright © 1973 by the Massachusetts Medical Society.]

As a practical matter, we consider the top of our atmosphere to be around 480 km above Earth's surface, the same altitude we use in Chapter 2 for measuring the solar constant and amounts of insolation received. Beyond that altitude is the **exosphere**, which means "outer sphere," where the rarefied, less dense atmosphere is nearly a vacuum. It contains scarce lightweight hydrogen and helium atoms, to at least 100 000 km from Earth.

Atmospheric Profile

Think of Earth's modern atmosphere as a thin envelope of imperfectly shaped concentric "shells" or "spheres" that grade into one another, all bound to the planet by gravity. We can study the atmosphere by viewing it in layers, each with distinctive properties and purposes. Figure 3.2 charts the atmosphere in a vertical cross-section profile, or side view, and is a useful reference for the following discussion.

(a)

(b)

FIGURE 3.2 **Profile of the modern atmosphere.**
(a) The columns along the left side show the division of the atmosphere by composition, temperature, and function. The plot of temperature by altitude relates to the scale along the bottom axis. The small astronaut and balloon show the heights achieved by Astronaut Mark Lee and by Joseph Kittinger, discussed in Geosystems Now. (b) A sunset from orbit through various atmospheric layers. A silhouetted cumulonimbus thunderhead cloud tops out at the tropopause. [(b) NASA.]

To simplify we use three atmospheric criteria: *composition*, *temperature*, and *function*, noted along the left side of Figure 3.2a.

Earth's atmosphere exerts its weight, pressing downward under the pull of gravity. Air molecules create air pressure through their motion, size, and number. Pressure is exerted on all surfaces in contact with the air. The weight (force per unit area) of the atmosphere, or **air pressure**, pushes against all of us. Fortunately, that same pressure also exists inside us, pushing outward; otherwise, we would be crushed by the mass of air around us.

The atmosphere exerts an average force of approximately 1 kg·cm⁻² at sea level. Gravity compresses air, making it denser near Earth's surface; it thins rapidly with increasing altitude (Figure 3.3a), and with reduced air pressure, less oxygen is carried in each breath a person takes.

Over half the total mass of the atmosphere is compressed below 5500 m, 75% occurs below 10 700 m, and 90% is below 16 000 m. Only 0.1% of the atmosphere exists above an altitude of 50 km, as shown in the pressure profile in Figure 3.3b (percentage column is farthest to the right). At sea level, the atmosphere exerts a pressure of 1013.2 mb (*millibar*, or *mb*; a measure of force per square metre of surface area) as measured by a barometer. In Canada and many other countries, normal air pressure is expressed as 101.32 kPa (*kilopascal*; 1 kPa = 10 mb). More information on air pressure, the instruments that

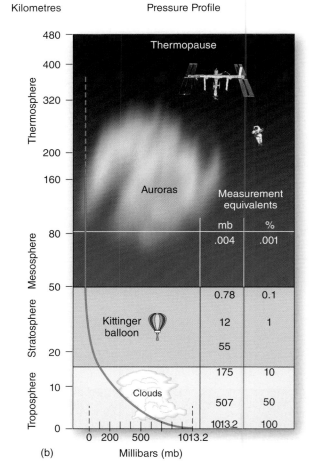

FIGURE 3.3 Density decreases with altitude.
(a) The atmosphere rapidly decreases in density with altitude. Have you experienced pressure changes that you could feel on your eardrums? How high above sea level were you at the time? (b) In this pressure profile, note the rapid decrease in atmospheric pressure with altitude. The troposphere holds about 90% of the atmospheric mass (far right column).

GEO REPORT 3.1 *Outside the Airplane*

Next time you fly somewhere, consider a couple of things. Few people are aware that in routine air travel they are sitting above 80% of the total atmospheric volume and that the air pressure outside is only about 10% of surface air pressure. This means that only 20% of the atmospheric mass is above you. If your plane is at about 11 km, think of Captain Kittinger's jump described in *Geosystems Now*. He started another 20 km higher in altitude than your plane!

measure it, and the role air pressure plays in generating winds is in Chapter 6.

Atmospheric Composition Criterion

Using chemical *composition* as a criterion, the atmosphere divides into two broad regions, the *heterosphere* (80 to 480 km altitude) and the *homosphere* (Earth's surface to 80 km altitude), as shown along the left side of Figure 3.2a. As you read, note that the text follows the same path as incoming solar radiation that travels through the atmosphere to Earth's surface.

Heterosphere The **heterosphere** is the outer atmosphere in terms of composition. It begins at the exosphere and is the transition from interplanetary space, extending to about 80 km altitude (see Figure 3.2). Less than 0.001% of the atmosphere's mass is in this rarefied heterosphere. The International Space Station and most Space Shuttle missions orbit in the middle to upper heterosphere.

As the prefix *hetero-* implies, this region is not uniform—its gases are *not* evenly mixed. Gases in the heterosphere occur in distinct layers sorted by gravity according to their atomic weight, with the lightest elements (hydrogen and helium) at the margins of outer space and the heavier elements (oxygen and nitrogen) dominant in the lower heterosphere. This distribution is quite different from the blended gases we breathe in the homosphere near Earth's surface.

Homosphere Below the heterosphere is the **homosphere**, extending from an altitude of 80 km to Earth's surface. Even though the atmosphere rapidly changes density in the homosphere—pressure increases toward Earth's surface—the blend of gases is nearly uniform throughout. The only exceptions are the concentration of ozone (O_3) in the "ozone layer," from 19 to 50 km, and the variations in water vapour, pollutants, and some trace chemicals in the lowest portion of the atmosphere.

The present blend of gases evolved approximately 500 million years ago. Table 3.1 lists by volume the stable ingredients that constitute dry, clean air in the homosphere. Air sampling occurs at the Mauna Loa Observatory, operational since 1957.

The air of the homosphere is a vast reservoir of relatively inert *nitrogen*, originating principally from volcanic sources. Nitrogen is a key element of life, yet we exhale all the nitrogen we inhale. The explanation for this contradiction is that nitrogen integrates into our bodies not from the air we breathe, but through compounds in food. In the soil, nitrogen is bound to these compounds by nitrogen-fixing bacteria, and it returns to the atmosphere by denitrifying bacteria that remove nitrogen from organic materials. A complete discussion of the nitrogen cycle is in Chapter 19.

Oxygen, a by-product of photosynthesis, also is essential for life processes. Slight spatial variations occur in the percentage of oxygen in the atmosphere because of variations in photosynthetic rates with latitude, seasonal changes, and the lag time as atmospheric circulation slowly mixes the air. Although it comprises about one-fifth of the atmosphere, oxygen forms compounds that compose about half of Earth's crust. Oxygen readily reacts with many elements to form these materials. Both nitrogen and

Mauna Loa Observatory, air sampling tower. [Bobbé Christopherson.]

TABLE 3.1	Stable Components of the Modern Homosphere	
Gas (Symbol)	**Percentage by Volume**	**Parts per Million (ppm)**
Nitrogen (N_2)	78.084	780 840
Oxygen (O_2)	20.946	209 460
Argon (Ar)	0.934	9340
Carbon dioxide (CO_2)*	0.0394	394
Neon (Ne)	0.001818	18
Helium (He)	0.000525	5
Methane (CH_4)	0.00014	1.4
Krypton (Kr)	0.00010	1.0
Ozone (O_3)	Variable	
Nitrous oxide (N_2O)	Trace	
Hydrogen (H)	Trace	
Xenon (Xe)	Trace	

*May 2011 average CO_2 measured at Mauna Loa, Hawai'i (see http://www.esrl.noaa.gov/gmd/ccgg/trends/.)

oxygen reserves in the atmosphere are so extensive that, at present, they far exceed human capabilities to disrupt or deplete them.

The gas *argon*, constituting less than 1% of the homosphere, is completely inert (an unreactive "noble" gas) and unusable in life processes. Argon is a residue from the radioactive decay of an isotope, or chemical form, of potassium called potassium-40 (symbolised ⁴⁰K). All the argon present in the modern atmosphere comes from slow accumulation over millions of years. Because industry has found uses for inert argon (in lightbulbs, welding, and some lasers), it is extracted or "mined" from the atmosphere, along with nitrogen and oxygen, for commercial and industrial uses.

Carbon dioxide *Carbon dioxide* is a natural by-product of life processes. Although its concentration is increasing rapidly, it is included with the homosphere's stable components in Table 3.1. Its present percentage in the atmosphere is small at about 0.0394%, but the amount of CO_2 is important in controlling global temperatures.

Chapters 4, 5, and 10 discuss the role of carbon dioxide as an important greenhouse gas and its role in present global temperature increases. Carbon dioxide concentrations in the atmosphere since 1958 are graphed in Figure 3.4. The annual fluctuation between summer and winter is evidence of seasons and the work of plant photosynthesis. Scientists agree that the increasing trend is human-forced.

Over the past 200 years, the CO_2 percentage increased as a result of human activities, principally the burning of fossil fuels and deforestation. According to ice-core records, CO_2 is higher now than at any time in the past 800 000 years. This increase appears to be accelerating. From 1990 to 1999, CO_2 concentration rose at an average of 1.1% per year; compare this to the average increase since 2000 of 3.1% per year—a 2 to 3 ppm per year increase. Emissions worldwide in 2010 broke all records, increasing 5.9% over the previous year. A distinct climatic threshold is approaching at 450 ppm, forecast for some time in the decade of the 2020s. Beyond this tipping point, there could be irreversible ice-sheet and species losses. Chapter 10 discusses the implications of CO_2 increases for climate change.

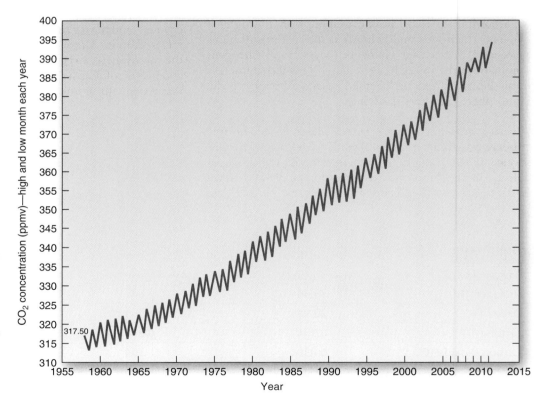

FIGURE 3.4 Carbon dioxide concentrations increase 1958–2011.
Fifty-three years of CO_2 data measured at the Mauna Loa Observatory through May 2010. The highest and lowest average months are plotted for each year on the graph in parts per million by volume (ppmv). [Data posted at ftp://ftp.cmdl.noaa.gov/ccg/co2/trends/co2_mm_mlo.txt.]

 Atmospheric Carbon Dioxide Accelerates

Since 1992, the global concentration of CO_2 in our atmosphere has increased more than 16%, from 354 ppm to 394 ppm in 2011. For comparison, preindustrial levels of CO_2 were about 280 ppm. CO_2 today far exceeds the natural range of 180 to 300 ppm over the last 800 000 years. If this rate of increase continues for the rest of the century, business as usual, then Table 3.1 could read 1400 ppm CO_2 in A.D. 2100, according to several forecasts.

Dr. James Hansen, a NASA scientist at Goddard Institute for Space Sciences, said in 2008:

> If humanity wishes to preserve a planet similar to that on which civilization developed, paleoclimatic evidence and ongoing climate change suggest that CO_2 will need to be reduced to at most 350 ppm [the average in 1987].

Atmospheric Temperature Criterion

Shifting to temperature as a criterion, the atmosphere has four distinct temperature zones—the *thermosphere, mesosphere, stratosphere,* and *troposphere* (labeled in Figure 3.2). Let's look at each of these beginning with the highest in altitude.

Thermosphere The **thermosphere** ("heat sphere") roughly corresponds to the heterosphere (80 km out to 480 km). The upper limit of the thermosphere is the **thermopause** (the suffix -*pause* means "to change"). During periods of a less active Sun when there are fewer sunspots and coronal bursts, the thermopause may lower in altitude from the average 480 km to only 250 km altitude. During periods of a more active Sun, the outer atmosphere swells to an altitude of 550 km, where it can create frictional drag on satellites in low orbit.

The temperature profile in Figure 3.2 (yellow curve) shows that temperatures rise sharply in the thermosphere, to 1200°C and higher. Despite such high temperatures, the thermosphere is not "hot" in the way you might expect. Temperature and heat are different concepts. The intense solar radiation in this portion of the atmosphere excites individual molecules (principally nitrogen and oxygen) to high levels of vibration. This **kinetic energy**, the energy of motion, is the vibrational energy that we measure as *temperature*.

However, the actual heat involved is small. The reason is that the density of molecules is so low. There is little actual **heat** produced, or the flow of kinetic energy from one body to another because of a temperature difference between them. Heating in the atmosphere near Earth's surface is different because the greater number of molecules in the denser atmosphere transmits their kinetic energy as **sensible heat**, meaning that we can measure and feel it. (Density, temperature, and heat capacity determine the sensible heat of a substance.) More on this topic is in Chapters 4 and 5.

Mesosphere The **mesosphere** is the layer from 50 to 80 km above Earth and is within the homosphere. As Figure 3.2 shows, the mesosphere's outer boundary, the *mesopause*, is the coldest portion of the atmosphere, averaging –90°C, although that temperature may vary considerably (25−30 C°). Note in Figure 3.3b the extremely low pressures (low density of molecules) in the mesosphere.

The mesosphere sometimes receives cosmic or meteoric dust, which acts as nuclei around which fine ice crystals form. At high latitudes, an observer may see these bands of ice crystals glow in rare and unusual night **noctilucent clouds**, which are so high in altitude that they still catch sunlight after sunset. For reasons not clearly understood, the occurrence of these unique clouds is on the increase. See, among several sites, http://lasp.colorado.edu/science/atmospheric/.

Stratosphere The **stratosphere** extends from 18 to 50 km from Earth's surface. Temperatures increase with altitude throughout the stratosphere, from –57°C at the tropopause (18 km), warming to 0°C at the stratosphere's outer boundary, the *stratopause* (50 km). Stratospheric changes measured over the past 25 years documented that chlorofluorocarbons are increasing and ozone concentrations are decreasing. With greenhouse gases also on the increase, less infrared radiation reaches the stratosphere. A noted stratospheric cooling is the response. The most recent evidence indicates that ozone loss may have peaked, but there has been no increase in stratospheric ozone rebuilding.

Troposphere The **troposphere** is the final layer encountered by incoming solar radiation surging through the atmosphere to the surface. It is the home of the biosphere, the atmospheric layer that supports life, and the region of principal weather activity.

Approximately 90% of the total mass of the atmosphere and the bulk of all water vapour, clouds, and air pollution occur within the troposphere. An average temperature of −57°C defines the **tropopause**, the troposphere's upper limit, but its exact altitude varies with season, latitude, and surface temperatures and pressures. Near the equator, because of intense heating from the surface, the tropopause occurs at 18 km on average; in the middle latitudes, it occurs at an average of 12 km; and at the North and South poles it averages only 8 km or less above Earth's surface. The marked warming with increasing altitude in the stratosphere above the tropopause causes the tropopause to act like a lid, generally preventing whatever is in the cooler (denser) air below from mixing into the warmer (less dense) stratosphere.

ǁǁ CRITICAL THINKING 3.1

Where Is Your Tropopause?

On your next flight as the plane reaches its highest altitude, ask a flight attendant for the temperature outside the plane. Some planes have video screens that display the outside air temperature. By definition, the tropopause is wherever the temperature –57°C occurs. Depending on the season of the year, altitude and temperature make an interesting comparison. Is the tropopause at higher altitude in summer or winter?

Figure 3.5 illustrates the normal temperature profile within the troposphere during daytime. As the graph shows, temperatures decrease rapidly with increasing altitude at an average of 6.4 C° per kilometre, a rate

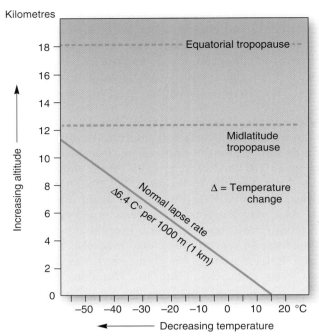

Kilometres

FIGURE 3.5 The temperature profile of the troposphere.
Temperature decreases with increased altitude at a rate known
as the *normal lapse rate*. Scientists use the *standard atmosphere*
as a description of air temperature and pressure changes with
altitude. Note the approximate locations of the equatorial and
midlatitude tropopauses.

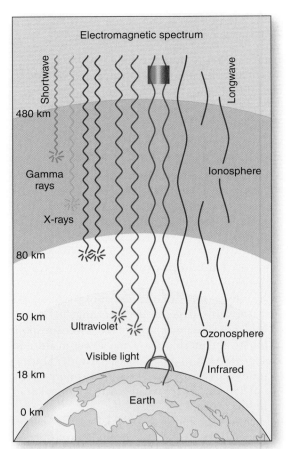

FIGURE 3.6 The atmosphere protects Earth's surface.
As solar energy passes through the atmosphere,
the shortest wavelengths are absorbed. Only a
fraction of the ultraviolet radiation, and most
of the visible light and infrared radiation,
reaches Earth's surface.

Ozone Breakdown
Ozone Hole

known as the **normal lapse rate**. This temperature plot
also appears in the tropospheric portion of Figure 3.2.

The normal lapse rate is an average. The actual
lapse rate may vary considerably because of local weather
conditions: this is the **environmental lapse rate**. This
variation in temperature gradient between normal and
environmental rates in the lower troposphere is central to
our discussion of weather processes in Chapters 7 and 8.

Atmospheric Function Criterion

Looking at our final atmospheric criterion of function, the
atmosphere has two specific zones, the *ionosphere* and the
ozonosphere (*ozone layer*), which remove most of the harmful wavelengths of incoming solar radiation and charged
particles (Focus Study 3.1). Figure 3.6 depicts in a general
way the absorption of radiation by the various functional
layers of the atmosphere.

Ionosphere   The outer functional layer, the **ionosphere**, extends throughout the thermosphere and into
the mesosphere below (see Figure 3.2). The ionosphere
absorbs cosmic rays, gamma rays, X-rays, and shorter
wavelengths of ultraviolet radiation, changing atoms
to positively charged ions and giving the ionosphere its
name. The glowing auroral lights discussed in Chapter 2
occur principally within the ionosphere.

Figure 3.2 shows the average daytime altitudes of four
regions within the ionosphere, known as the D, E, F_1, and F_2
layers. These are important to broadcast communications,

for they reflect certain radio wavelengths, including
AM radio and other shortwave broadcasts, especially at
night. However, during the day the ionosphere actively
absorbs radio signals, preventing distant reception. Normally unaffected are FM or television broadcast wavelengths, which pass through to space, enabling the use of
communication satellites.

Ozonosphere   That portion of the stratosphere that
contains an increased level of ozone is the **ozonosphere**,
or **ozone layer**. Ozone is a highly reactive oxygen molecule made up of three oxygen atoms (O_3) instead of the two
atoms (O_2) that make up oxygen gas. Ozone absorbs certain wavelengths of ultraviolet (principally, all the UVC,
100–290 nm, and about 90% of UVB, 290–320 nm).[1] This
absorbed energy subsequently reradiates at longer wavelengths as infrared radiation and warms the stratosphere.
This process converts most harmful ultraviolet radiation,
effectively "filtering" it and safeguarding life at Earth's

[1]Nanometre (nm) = one-billionth of a metre; 1 nm = 10^{-9} m. For
comparison, a micrometre, or micron, (μm) = one-millionth of a
metre; 1 μm = 10^{-6} m. A millimetre (mm) = one-thousandth of a
metre; 1 mm = 10^{-3}.

surface. UVA, at 320–400 nm, makes up about 98% of all UV radiation that reaches Earth's surface.

The ozone layer is presumed to have been relatively stable over the past several hundred million years. Today, however, it is in a state of continuous change. Focus Study 3.1 presents an analysis of the crisis in this critical portion of our atmosphere.

▌▌ CRITICAL THINKING 3.2

Finding Your Ozone Column

To determine the total ozone column at your present location, go to "What was the total ozone column at your house?" at http://toms.gsfc.nasa.gov/teacher/ozone_overhead.html.

Select a point on the map or enter your latitude and longitude and the date you want to check. The ozone column is measured by the Ozone Monitoring Instrument (OMI) sensor aboard the *Aqua* satellite and is sensitive mainly to stratospheric ozone. (Note also the limitations listed on the extent of data availability.) If you check for several different dates, when did the lowest values occur? The highest values? Briefly explain and interpret the values you found.

UV Index Helps Save Your Skin Newspaper and television weather reports regularly include the *UV Index* (UVI) in daily forecasts, as reported by Environment Canada and, in the United States, the National Weather Service (NWS) and the Environmental Protection Agency (EPA) since 1994. A revision in 2004 aligned the UVI with guidelines adopted by the World Health Organization (WHO) and World Meteorological Organization (WMO). Think of this as a status report on stratospheric functions.

The UVI, as shown in Table 3.2, forecasts the expected risk of exposure to the Sun, using a scale from 1 to 11+. With stratospheric ozone levels at thinner-than-normal conditions, surface exposure to cancer-causing radiation increases. The public, especially babies and children, now is alerted to take extra precautions in the form of sunscreen, hats, protective clothing, and sunglasses. Remember, damage accumulates, and it may be

decades before you experience the ill effects triggered by this summer's sunburn. See http://www.epa.gov/sunwise/uvindex.html for a UVI forecast for your location.

▬ Variable Atmospheric Components

The troposphere contains a variety of other natural and human-caused gases, particles, and other chemicals. Spatial aspects of these variables are important applied topics in physical geography and have important human-health implications.

Air pollution, the contamination of the air with dust, fumes, gas, mist, odour, smoke, or vapour, is not a new problem. Romans complained more than 2000 years ago about the foul air of their cities. Filling Rome's air was the stench of open sewers, smoke from fires, and fumes from ceramic-making kilns and smelters (furnaces) that converted ores into metals. Throughout human civilization, cities have stressed the environment's natural ability to process and recycle waste. Historically, air pollution has occurred around population centres and is closely linked to human production and consumption of energy and resources.

Solutions require regional, national, and international strategies, because the pollution sources often are distant from the observed impact—moving across political boundaries and even crossing oceans. Regulations to curb human-caused air pollution have achieved great success, although much remains to be done. Before we discuss these topics, note that natural pollution sources also exist and will be presented next.

Natural Sources

Natural air contaminant sources produce a greater quantity of pollutants—nitrogen oxides, carbon monoxide, carbon dioxide, and hydrocarbons from plants and trees—than do human-made sources. Table 3.3 lists these along

(text continued on page 72)

TABLE 3.2   UV Index (Environment Canada, EPA, NWS, WHO, WMO)

Exposure Risk Category	UVI Range	Comments
Low	less than 2	Low danger for average person. Wear sunglasses on bright days. Watch out for reflection off snow.
Moderate	3–5	Take covering precautions, such as sunglasses, sunscreen, hats, and protective clothing, and stay in shade during midday hours.
High	6–7	Use sunscreens with SPF of 15 or higher. Reduce time in the Sun between 11 A.M. and 4 P.M. Use protections mentioned above.
Very High	8–10	Minimise Sun exposure 11 A.M. to 4 P.M. Use sunscreens with SPF ratings of higher than 15. Use protections mentioned above.
Extreme	11+	Unprotected skin is at risk of burn in minutes. Apply sunscreen every two hours if out-of-doors. Avoid direct Sun exposure during midday hours. Use protections mentioned above.

⊕ **FOCUS STUDY 3.1**

Stratospheric Ozone Losses: A Continuing Health Hazard

Consider:

- The stratospheric ozone above Antarctica during the Southern Hemisphere spring (September to November) has increased since 1979, with the record lows in 2006 and 2011 at about 30 million km². Subsequent years had similar losses, with 2008 having the fifth largest loss. Recovery is proceeding more slowly than previously thought, despite the slowing rate of accumulation of offending chemicals.

- As stratospheric ozone flows into the depleted region from lower latitudes, ozone thins over southern South America, southern Africa, Australia, and New Zealand. In Ushuaia, Argentina, surface UVB intensity increases more than 225% compared to long-term average levels.

- An international scientific consensus confirmed the anthropogenic, or human-caused, disruption of the ozone layer. See *Scientific Assessment of Ozone Depletion* (http://www.unep.ch/ozone/assessment_Panels/SAP/index.shtml), by NASA, NOAA, UNEP (United Nations Environment Programme), and WMO (World Meteorological Organization).

- At Earth's opposite pole, a similar ozone depletion over the Arctic annually exceeds 30%, to a record 45% loss during spring 1997. The Canadian and U.S. governments report an "ultraviolet index" to help the public protect themselves. See http://www.ec.gc.ca/ozone/ for more information on ozone.

- Increased ultraviolet radiation is affecting atmospheric chemistry, biological systems, oceanic phytoplankton (small photosynthetic organisms that form the basis of the ocean's primary food production), fisheries, crop yields, and human skin, eye tissues, and immune systems.

More ultraviolet radiation than ever before is breaking through Earth's protective ozone layer. What is going on in the stratosphere everywhere and in the polar regions specifically? Why is this happening, and how are people and their governments responding? What effects does this have on you personally?

Monitoring Earth's Fragile Safety Screen

A sample from the ozone layer's densest part (at 29 km altitude) contains only 1 part ozone per 4 million parts of air—compressed to surface pressure, the ozone layer would be only 3 mm thick. Yet, this rarefied layer was in steady-state equilibrium for several hundred million years, absorbing intense ultraviolet radiation and permitting life to proceed safely on Earth.

The ozone layer has been monitored since the 1920s from ground stations. The *Total Ozone Mapping Spectrometer* (TOMS) began operations in 1978 aboard various satellites. Since 2004, the OMI (Ozone Monitoring Instrument) on board NASA's *Aura* satellite has tracked ozone depletion. Figure 3.1.1 shows the 2008 "ozone hole." (See http://ozonewatch.gsfc.nasa.gov/).

Ozone Losses Explained

What is causing the decline in stratospheric ozone? In 1974, two atmospheric chemists, F. Sherwood Rowland and Mario Molina, hypothesised that some synthetic chemicals were releasing chlorine atoms that decompose ozone ("Stratospheric sink for chlorofluoromethanes. . . ," *Nature* 249 [1974]: 810). These **Chlorofluorocarbons**, or **CFCs**, are synthetic molecules of chlorine, fluorine, and carbon.

CFCs are stable, or inert, under conditions at Earth's surface and they possess remarkable heat properties. Both qualities made them valuable as propellants in aerosol sprays and as refrigerants. Also, some 45% of CFCs were solvents in the electronics industry and used as foaming agents. Being inert, CFC molecules do not dissolve in water and do not break down in biological processes. (In contrast, chlorine compounds derived from volcanic eruptions and the ocean are water-soluble and rarely reach the stratosphere.)

Researchers Rowland and Molina hypothesised that stable CFC molecules slowly migrate into the stratosphere, where intense ultraviolet radiation splits them, freeing chlorine (Cl) atoms. This process causes a complex set of reactions that breaks up ozone molecules (O_3) and leaves oxygen gas molecules (O_2) in their place. The effect

Total Ozone (Dobson Units)

110   220   330   440   550

FIGURE 3.1.1 The Antarctic ozone hole.
OMI image for September 12, 2008; the "hole," at nearly 27 million km², ranks fifth in size in the satellite monitoring era; 2011 was the worst depletion year for ozone depletion. Measurements dropped below 100 Dobson units in the region of blue and purple shades. [OMI aboard *Aqua*, GSFC/NASA.]

is severe, for a single chlorine atom decomposes more than 100 000 ozone molecules. The long residence time of chlorine atoms in the ozone layer (40 to 100 years) is likely to produce long-term consequences through this century from the chlorine already in place. Tens of millions of tons of CFCs were sold worldwide and subsequently released into the atmosphere.

Political Realities—an International Response and the Future

As the science became established, sales and production of CFCs declined until a March 1981 U.S. presidential order permitting the export and sales of banned products. Global sales increased and hit a new peak in 1987 at 1.2 million metric tons when an international agreement went into effect halting further sales growth.

Chemical manufacturers once claimed that no hard evidence existed to prove the ozone-depletion model, and they successfully delayed remedial action for 15 years. Today, with extensive scientific evidence and verification of losses, even the CFC manufacturers admit that the problem is serious.

The *Montreal Protocol on Substances That Deplete the Ozone Layer* (1987), as amended five times in 1990, 1992, 1995, 1997, and 1999, aims to reduce and eliminate CFC damage to the ozone layer. With 189 signatory countries, the Protocol is regarded as probably the most successful international environmental protection agreement in history (see http://ozone.unep.org/).

CFC sales continue their decline and all production of harmful CFCs ceased in 2010, although there is concern over some of the substitute compounds and a robust black market for banned CFCs, rivaling drug trafficking at some ports. If the protocol is fully enforced, scientists estimate that the stratosphere will return to more normal conditions in a century. The world without this treaty might prove challenging. Imagine

possible stratospheric ozone losses of two-thirds, producing more cases of malignant melanoma (a skin cancer), and by 2100 a nonexistent ozone layer. We owe much to Doctors Rowland and Molina.

For their work, Rowland, Molina, and another colleague, Paul Crutzen, received the 1995 Nobel Prize for Chemistry. In making the award, the Royal Swedish Academy of Sciences said, "By explaining the chemical mechanism that affects the thickness of the ozone layer, the three researchers have contributed to our salvation from a global environmental problem that could have catastrophic consequences."

Ozone Losses over the Poles

How do Northern Hemisphere CFCs become concentrated over the South Pole? Evidently, chlorine freed in the Northern Hemisphere midlatitudes concentrates over Antarctica through the work of atmospheric winds. Persistent cold temperatures over the South Pole and the presence of thin,

icy clouds in the stratosphere promote development of the ozone hole, which develops in the Antarctic spring and usually peaks in September (Figure 3.1.2). Over the North Pole, conditions are more changeable, so the hole is smaller, although growing each year. Record depletion occurred in 2011 due to a cold and stable stratospheric winter, but this depletion would have been much worse if the Montreal Protocol had not been implemented.

Polar stratospheric clouds (*PSCs*) are thin clouds that are important catalysts in the release of chlorine for ozone-depleting reactions. During the long, cold winter months, a tight circulation pattern forms over the Antarctic continent—the polar vortex. Chlorine that is freed from droplets in PSCs triggers the breakdown of the otherwise inert molecules and frees the chlorine for catalytic reactions.

Make a note to check some of the Internet data sources listed to see how our stratosphere is doing in years to come. What we learn here will be with us for the rest of this century.

FIGURE 3.1.2 The timing and extent of ozone damage.
The area of ozone hole depletion generally peaks in late September, reaching a low 85 Dobson units in 2006 and setting a depletion record in 2011. [Data from GSFC/NASA.]

Southern Hemisphere Ozone 2002–2003

TABLE 3.3	Sources of Natural Variable Gases and Materials in the Atmosphere

Source	Contribution
Volcanoes	Sulfur oxides, particulates
Forest fires	Carbon monoxide and dioxide, nitrogen oxides, particulates
Plants	Hydrocarbons, pollens
Decaying plants	Methane, hydrogen sulfides
Soil	Dust and viruses
Ocean	Salt spray and particulates

with some other natural sources and the substances they contribute to the air. However, any attempt to dismiss the impact of human-made air pollution through a comparison with natural sources is irrelevant, for we evolved with and adapted to the natural ingredients in the air. We did not evolve in relation to the comparatively recent concentrations of *anthropogenic* (human-caused) contaminants in our atmosphere.

A dramatic natural source of pollution was the 1991 eruption of Mount Pinatubo in the Philippines (15° N 120° E), the twentieth century's second largest eruption. This event injected nearly 20 million tons of sulfur dioxide (SO_2) into the stratosphere. The spread of these emissions is shown in a sequence of satellite images in Figure 6.1.

Devastating wildfires on several continents produce natural air pollution as each year's fire season worsens (Figure 3.7). Soot, ash, and gases darken skies and damage health in affected regions. Wind patterns spread the pollution from the fires to nearby cities, closing airports and forcing evacuations to avoid the health-related dangers. Wildfires produce particulate matter (dust, smoke, soot, ash), nitrogen oxides, carbon monoxide, and volatile organic compounds.

Scientists have established a connection between climate change and wildfire occurrence. The linkage between climate-change impacts and wildfires in the western United States also is applicable in Canada:

Higher spring and summer temperatures and earlier snowmelt are extending the wildfire season and increasing the intensity of wildfires . . . large wildfire

(a)

(b)

FIGURE 3.7 Wildfires fill the atmosphere with smoke. (a) Wildfires in northern Alberta and Saskatchewan on May 15, 2011 send smoke into the atmosphere. (b) Sierra Nevada mountain wildfires advance uncontrolled in 2008, consuming millions of acres of drought-damaged forest and chaparral. [(a) Aqua/MODIS Rapid Responde, GSFC/NASA. (b) Bobbé Christopherson.]

activity increased suddenly and markedly in the mid-1980s, with higher large-wildfire frequency . . . longer wildfire durations, and longer wildfire seasons.[2]

[2]A. L. Westerling et al., "Warming and earlier spring increase western U.S. forest wildfire activity," *Science* 313, 5789 (Aug. 18, 2006): 940.

 GEO REPORT 3.3 *New Atmospheric Tools*

Studies of the atmosphere are benefitting from new technology. For example, unmanned aerial vehicles (UAVs) are aircraft guided by remote control or autopilot. These instrumental drones can gather all types of data and carry various remote-sensing devices. In 2010, NASA's unpiloted Global Hawk completed its first scientific flight over the Pacific Ocean, flying for 14 hours on a preprogrammed flight path to altitudes above 18.3 km and carrying instruments to sample ozone depleting substances, aerosols, and other components of air quality in the upper troposphere and lower stratosphere. Aerosol-detecting satellites are in operation, such as *CALIPSO* (Cloud-Aerosol Lidar and IR Pathfinder Satellite); working since 2006, it measures concentrations of atmospheric pollution at altitudes of 1 to 3 km.

These connections occur across the globe, as in drought-plagued Australia, where thousands of wildfires burned millions of hectares in recent years. Each year, worldwide, wildfire acreage breaks the record of the previous year (see http://cwfis.cfs.nrcan.gc.ca/en_CA/index and http://www.usgs.gov/hazards/wildfires/).

Natural Factors That Affect Air Pollution

The problems resulting from both natural and human-made atmospheric contaminants are made worse by several important natural factors. Among these, wind, local and regional landscape characteristics, and temperature inversions in the troposphere dominate.

Winds Winds gather and move pollutants, sometimes reducing the concentration of pollution in one location while increasing it in another. Wind can produce dramatic episodes of dust movement. Dust is defined as particles less than 62 μm (microns). Traveling on prevailing winds, dust from Africa is added to the soils of South America and Europe, and Texas dust ends up across the Atlantic (Figure 3.8). Imagine at any one moment a billion tons of dust aloft in the atmosphere, carried by the winds!

Winds make the atmosphere's condition an international issue. For example, prevailing winds transport air pollution from the United States to Canada, causing much complaint and negotiation between the two governments. Pollution from North America adds to European air problems. In Europe, the cross-boundary drift of pollution is a major issue because of the proximity of countries.

Arctic haze is a term that originated in the 1950s, when pilots noticed decreased visibility, either horizontally or at a slant angle from their aircraft, across the Arctic region. Haze is a concentration of microscopic particles and air pollution that diminishes air clarity. Since there is no heavy industry at these high latitudes and only sparse population, this seasonal haze is a remarkable attribute of industrialization in the Northern Hemisphere.

Also, an increase in wildfires across the Northern Hemisphere and agricultural burning in the midlatitudes contributes to arctic haze. Winds that are part of atmospheric circulation transport pollution to sites far distant from points of origin. There is no comparable haze over the Antarctic continent. Based on this analysis, can you think of why Antarctica lacks such a condition?

Local and Regional Landscapes Local and regional landscapes are another important factor in air pollution. Surrounding mountains and hills can form barriers to air movement or can direct pollutants from one area to another. Some of the worst incidents occur when local landscapes trap and concentrate air pollution.

Places with volcanic landscapes such as Iceland and Hawai'i have their own natural pollution with which to deal. During periods of sustained volcanic activity at Kīlauea, some 2000 metric tons of sulfur dioxide are produced each day. Concentrations are sometimes high enough to merit

(a)

(b)

FIGURE 3.8 Natural variable dust in the atmosphere.
(a) In 2009, dust in eastern Washington state from dryland agricultural fields was moved by winds up to 69 kmph (43 mph), closing some highways at the time. (b) Typical wind-carried dust moves off West Africa, across the Atlantic. The Cape Verde islands are usually in the path of African dust. Beneath such dust near Cape Verde at 15° N latitude, the ocean surface is difficult to distinguish from the sky on the horizon (inset photo). *Terra* MISR is able to gather data obscured by sun glint into the MODIS sensor. [(a) *Terra*, MODIS and (b) *Terra*, MODIS and MISR sensors; both NASA/GSFC; (inset) Bobbé Christopherson.]

broadcast warnings about health concerns. The resulting acid rain and volcanic smog, called *vog* by Hawaiians (for *volcanic smog*), causes losses to agriculture as well as other economic impacts.

Temperature Inversions Vertical temperature and atmospheric density in the troposphere also can worsen pollution conditions. A **temperature inversion** occurs when the typical temperature decrease with altitude reverses trend and begins to increase at some level. This

FIGURE 3.9 Normal and inverted temperature profiles.
(a) A normal temperature profile. (b) A temperature inversion in the lower atmosphere. Note how the warmer air layer prevents mixing of the denser (cooler) air below the inversion, thereby trapping pollution. (c) An inversion layer is visible in the morning hours over a valley. [(c) Bobbé Christopherson.]

can happen at any elevation from ground level to several thousand metres.

Figure 3.9 compares a normal temperature profile with that of a temperature inversion. The normal profile (Figure 3.9a) permits warmer (less dense) air at the surface to rise, ventilating the valley and moderating surface pollution. But the warm-air inversion (Figure 3.9b) prevents the rise of cooler (denser) air beneath, halting the vertical mixing of pollutants with other atmospheric gases. Thus, instead of being carried away, pollutants are trapped under the *inversion layer*.

Inversions most often result from certain weather conditions, such as when the air near the ground is radiatively cooled on clear nights, or from topographic situations that produce cold-air drainage into valleys. In addition, the air above snow-covered surfaces or beneath subsiding air in a high-pressure system may cause a temperature inversion.

Anthropogenic Pollution

Anthropogenic, or human-caused, air pollution remains most prevalent in urbanised regions. Approximately 2% of annual deaths in the United States are attributable to air pollution. Comparable risks are identified in Canada, Europe, Mexico, and Asia, especially China and India.

As urban populations grow, human exposure to pollution increases. By 2012, more than 50% of the world population will live in metropolitan regions, some one-third with unhealthy levels of air pollution. This represents a potentially massive public health issue in this century.

Table 3.4 lists the names, chemical symbols, principal sources, and impacts of variable anthropogenic components in the air. The first seven pollutants in the table result from combustion of fossil fuels in transportation (specifically automobiles, including light trucks). For example, **carbon monoxide (CO)** results from incomplete combustion, or when carbon in fuel does not burn completely. The main anthropogenic source of carbon monoxide is vehicle emissions.

Overall, automobiles contribute more than 60% of United States and 50% of Canadian human-caused air pollution. Reducing air pollution from the transportation sector involves known technologies and strategies, monetary savings for the consumer, and significant health benefits. These facts make the continuing delays in achieving better fuel efficiency all the more confusing.

Stationary sources, such as electric power plants and industrial plants that use fossil fuels, contribute the most sulfur oxides and particulates. For this reason, concentrations are focused in the Northern Hemisphere and the industrial, developed countries. The last three gases shown in Table 3.4 are discussed elsewhere in this text: Water vapour is examined with water and weather

TABLE 3.4   Gases and Materials from Anthropogenic Sources in the Lower Atmosphere

Name	Symbol	Sources	Description and Effects of Criteria Pollutants (Main sources listed for U.S.)
Carbon monoxide	CO	Incomplete combustion of fuels	Odorless, colourless, tasteless gas Toxicity; affinity for hemoglobin Displaces O_2 in bloodstream; 50 to 100 ppm cause headaches and vision and judgment losses *Source:* 78% transportation
Nitrogen oxides	NO_x (NO, NO_2)	High temperature/pressure combustion	Reddish-brown choking gas Inflames respiratory system, destroys lung tissue Damages plants; 3 to 5 ppm is dangerous *Source:* 55% transportation
Volatile organic compounds	VOCs	Incomplete combustion of fossil fuels such as gasoline; cleaning and paint solvents	Prime agents of ozone formation *Sources:* 45% industrial 47% transportation
Ozone	O_3	Photochemical reactions	Highly reactive, unstable gas Oxidises surfaces; dries rubber and elastic Damages plants at 0.01 to 0.09 ppm Agricultural losses at 0.1 ppm; 0.3 to 1.0 ppm irritates eyes, nose, throat
Peroxyacetyl nitrates	PANs	Photochemical reactions	Produced by NO + VOC photochemistry No human health effects Major damage to plants, forests, crops
Sulfur oxides	SO_x (SO_2, SO_3)	Combustion of sulfur-containing fuels	Colourless; irritating smell 0.1 to 1 ppm; impairs breathing, taste threshold Human asthma, bronchitis, emphysema Leads to acid deposition *Source:* 85% fuel combustion
Particulate matter	PM	Dust, dirt, soot, salt, metals, organics; agriculture, construction, roads	Complex mixture of solid and aerosol particles Dust, smoke, and haze affect visibility Various health effects: bronchitis, pulmonary function PM_{10} negative health effects established by researchers *Sources:* 42% industrial 33% fuel combustion 25% transportation
Carbon dioxide	CO_2	Complete combustion, mainly from fossil-fuel consumption	Principal greenhouse gas Atmospheric concentration increasing; 64% of greenhouse warming effect
Methane	CH_4	Organic processes	Secondary greenhouse gas Atmospheric concentration increasing; 19% of greenhouse warming effect
Water vapour	H_2O vapour	Combustion processes, steam	See Chapter 7 for more on the role of water vapour in the atmosphere.

(Chapters 7 and 8); carbon dioxide and methane are discussed with greenhouse gases and climate (Chapters 4, 5, and 10).

Photochemical Smog Pollution Photochemical smog was not generally experienced until the advent of the automobile. Today, it is the major component of anthropogenic air pollution. **Photochemical smog** results from the interaction of sunlight and the combustion products in automobile exhaust (nitrogen oxides and VOCs). The term *smog* was coined by a London physician in A.D. 1900 to describe the combination of fog and smoke containing sulfur gases (sulfur is an impurity in fossil fuels). Although the term *smog* is a misnomer, it is generally used to describe this pollution. Smog is responsible for the hazy sky and reduced sunlight in many of our cities.

The connection between automobile exhaust and smog was not determined until 1953 in Los Angeles, long after society had established its dependence upon cars and trucks. Despite this discovery, widespread mass transit declined, the railroads dwindled, and the polluting, inefficient individual automobile remains North America's preferred transportation.

Figure 3.10 summarises how car exhaust is converted into major air pollutants—PANs, ozone, and nitric acid. The high temperatures in automobile engines produce nitrogen dioxide (NO_2). To a lesser extent nitrogen dioxide is emitted from power plants. Worldwide, the problem with **nitrogen dioxide** production is its concentration in metropolitan regions. North American urban areas may have from 10 to 100 times higher nitrogen dioxide concentrations than nonurban areas. Nitrogen dioxide interacts with water vapour to form nitric acid (HNO_3), a contributor to acid deposition by precipitation, the subject of Focus Study 3.2.

In the photochemical reaction in the illustration, ultraviolet radiation liberates atomic oxygen (O) and a nitric oxide (NO) molecule from the NO_2. The free oxygen atom combines with an oxygen molecule, O_2, to form the oxidant ozone, O_3. In addition, the nitric oxide (NO) molecule reacts with VOCs to produce *peroxyacetyl nitrates* (*PAN*). **Peroxyacetyl nitrates (PAN)** produce no known health effect in humans, but they are particularly damaging to plants, including both agricultural crops and forests.

Ozone is the primary ingredient in photochemical smog. (This is the same gas that is beneficial to us in the stratosphere in absorbing ultraviolet radiation.) The reactivity of ozone is a health threat, for it damages biological tissues. For several reasons, children are at greatest risk from ozone pollution—one in four children in U.S. cities is at risk of developing health problems from ozone pollution. This ratio is significant; it means that more than 12 million children are vulnerable in those metropolitan regions with the worst polluted air (Los Angeles, New York, Atlanta, Houston and Detroit). For more information and city rankings of the worst and the best, see http://www.lungusa.org (enter "city rankings" in the search box on the web site). No similar large scale study has been conducted in Canada, but a Toronto air pollution Burden of Illness study in 2004 found that 1700 premature deaths and 6000 hospital admissions annually in Toronto are related to ground-level ozone. Children accounted for the highest number of those hospital admissions.

The **volatile organic compounds (VOCs)**, including hydrocarbons from gasoline, surface coatings, and combustion at electric utilities, are important factors in ozone formation. States such as California base their standards for control of ozone pollution on VOC emission controls—a scientifically accurate emphasis.

Industrial Smog and Sulfur Oxides Over the past 300 years, except in some developing countries, coal slowly replaced wood as the basic fuel used by society. The Industrial Revolution required high-grade energy to run machines. The changes involved conversion from *animate* energy (energy from animal sources, such as animal-powered farm equipment) to *inanimate* energy (energy from nonliving sources, such as coal, steam, and water). Air pollution associated with coal-burning industries is known as **industrial smog** (Figure 3.11).

Once in the atmosphere, **sulfur dioxide (SO_2)** reacts with oxygen (O) to form sulfur trioxide (SO_3), which is highly reactive and, in the presence of water or water vapour, forms **sulfate aerosols**, tiny particles about 0.1 to 1 μm in diameter. Sulfuric acid (H_2SO_4) can form even in moderately polluted air at normal temperatures. Coal-burning electric utilities and steel manufacturing are the main sources of sulfur dioxide. Sulfur dioxide-laden air

GEO REPORT 3.4 *Smoke Gets in Your Eyes*

As your car idles at a downtown intersection or you walk through a parking garage, you may be exposed to between 50 ppm and 100 ppm of carbon monoxide, a colourless, odourless gas. Smoking a cigarette, CO levels reach 42 000 ppm. Secondhand smoke affects CO levels of anyone breathing nearby. What happens physiologically? CO combines with the oxygen-carrying hemoglobin of the blood; thus, the hemoglobin no longer transports adequate oxygen to vital organs such as the heart and brain.

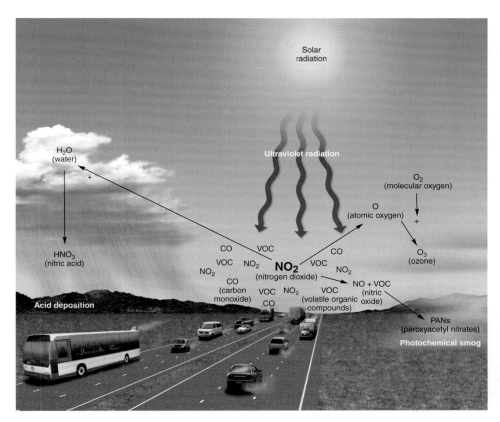

FIGURE 3.10 **Photochemical reactions.**
The interaction of automobile exhaust (NO_2, VOCs, CO) and ultraviolet radiation in sunlight causes photochemical reactions. To the left, note the formation of nitric acid and acid deposition.

is dangerous to health, corrodes metals, and deteriorates stone building materials at accelerated rates. Sulfuric acid deposition, added to nitric acid deposition, has increased in severity since it was first described in the 1970s. Focus Study 3.2 discusses this vital atmospheric issue and recent progress.

Particulates   A diverse mixture of fine particles, both solid and aerosol, that affects human health is **particulate matter (PM)**. Haze, smoke, and dust are visible reminders of particulate material in the air we breathe. Such small particles in the air comprise **aerosols**. Remote sensing now provides a global portrait of such aerosols.

The effects of PM on human health vary with the size of the particle. For comparison, a human hair can range from 50 μm to 70 μm in diameter. $PM_{2.5}$, particulates that are 2.5 μm or less in diameter, pose the greatest health risk. These fine particles, such as combustion particles, organics, and metallic aerosols, can get into the lungs and bloodstream. Coarse particles (PM_{10}) are of less concern, although they can irritate a person's eyes, nose, and throat, and have been linked to increased rates of asthma.

(text continued on page 80)

FIGURE 3.11 **A source of industrial smog.**
Pollution generated by industry and coal-fired electrical generation differs from that produced by transportation. Industrial pollution has high concentrations of sulfur oxides, particulates, and carbon dioxide. This coal-fired power plant at Barentsburg, Svalbard, lacks scrubbers to reduce stack emissions. [Bobbé Christopherson.]

Acid Deposition: Damaging to Ecosystems

Acid deposition is a major environmental problem in some areas of the United States, Canada, Europe, and Asia. Such deposition is most familiar as "acid rain," but it also occurs as "acid snow" and in dry form as dust or aerosols. In addition, winds can carry the acid-producing chemicals many kilometres from their sources before they settle on the landscape, where they enter streams and lakes as runoff and groundwater flows.

Acid deposition is causally linked to serious problems: declining fish populations and fish kills in the northeastern United States, southeastern Canada, Sweden, and Norway; widespread forest damage in these same places and Germany; widespread changes in soil chemistry; and damage to buildings, sculptures, and historic artifacts. In New Hampshire's Hubbard Brook Experimental Forest (http://www.hubbardbrook.org/), a study covering 1960 to the present found half the nutrient calcium and magnesium base cations (see Chapter 18) had been leached from the soil. Excess acids are the cause of the decline.

Despite scientific agreement about the problem, which the U.S. General Accounting Office calls a "combination of meteorological, chemical, and biological phenomena," corrective action was delayed by its complexity and by politics.

The acidity of precipitation is measured on the pH scale, which expresses the relative abundance of free hydrogen ions (H+) in a solution. Free hydrogen ions in a solution are what make an acid corrosive, for they easily combine with other ions. The pH scale is logarithmic: Each whole number represents a tenfold change. A pH of 7.0 is neutral (neither acidic nor basic). Values less than 7.0 are increasingly *acidic,* and values greater than 7.0 are increasingly *basic,* or *alkaline*. A pH scale for soil acidity and alkalinity is portrayed graphically in Chapter 18.

Natural precipitation dissolves carbon dioxide from the atmosphere to form carbonic acid. This process releases hydrogen ions and produces an average pH reading for precipitation of pH 5.65. The normal range for precipitation is 5.3–6.0. Thus, normal precipitation is slightly acidic.

Some anthropogenic gases are converted to acids in the atmosphere and then are removed by wet and dry deposition processes. Specifically, nitrogen and sulfur oxides released in the combustion of fossil fuels can produce nitric acid (HNO_3) and sulfuric acid (H_2SO_4) in the atmosphere.

Acid Precipitation Damage

Precipitation as acidic as pH 2.0 has fallen in the eastern United States, Scandinavia, and Europe. By comparison, vinegar and lemon juice register slightly less than 3.0.

Aquatic plant and animal life perishes when lakes drop below pH 4.8.

More than 50 000 lakes and some 100 000 km of streams in the United States and Canada are at a pH level below normal (that is, below 5.3 pH), with several hundred lakes incapable of supporting any aquatic life. Acid deposition causes the release of aluminum and magnesium from clay minerals in the soil, and both of these are harmful to fish and plant communities.

Also, relatively harmless mercury deposits in lake-bottom sediments in acidified lakes convert into highly toxic *methylmercury,* which is deadly to aquatic life. Local health advisories in two Canadian provinces and 22 U.S. states are regularly issued to warn those who fish of the methylmercury problem. Mercury atoms rapidly bond with carbon and move through biological systems as an *organometallic compound*.

Damage to forests results from the rearrangement of soil nutrients, the death of soil microorganisms, and an aluminum-induced calcium deficiency that is currently under investigation. The most advanced impact is seen in forests in Europe, especially in eastern Europe, principally because of its long history of burning coal and the density of industrial activity. In Germany and Poland, up to 50% of the forests are dead or damaged; in Switzerland, 30% are afflicted (Figure 3.2.1).

FIGURE 3.2.1 Acid deposition blight.
Stressed forests on Mount Mitchell, North Carolina in the Appalachians.
[Will and Deni McIntyre/Photo Researchers, Inc.]

The combined effects of acid deposition and climate change have resulted in a regional-scale decline in forest cover, especially red spruce and sugar maples, in eastern North America. Affected trees are more susceptible to winter cold, insects, and droughts. In red spruce, decline is evidenced by poor crown condition, reduced growth shown in tree ring analyses, and unusually high levels of tree mortality. For sugar maples, an indicator of forest damage is the reduction by almost half of the annual production of U.S. and Canadian maple sugar. Government estimates of damage in the United States, Canada, and Europe exceed $50 billion annually. Because wind and weather patterns are international, efforts at reducing acidic deposition also must be international in scope. Figure 3.2.2 maps the reduction in sulfate deposition between two 5-year periods,

1990–1994 and 1996–2004. However, this progress is only a beginning. Research shows that power plants and other sources must cut sulfur dioxide emissions 80% beyond the Clean Air Act mandate to truly reverse damage trends.

Ten leading acid-deposition researchers reported in an extensive study in *BioScience:*

Model calculations suggest that the greater the reduction in atmospheric sulfur deposition, the greater the magnitude and rate of chemical recovery. Less aggressive proposals for controls of sulfur emissions will result in slower chemical and biological recovery and in delays in regaining the services of a fully functional ecosystem. . . . North America and Europe are in the midst of a large-scale experiment. Sulfuric and nitric

acids have acidified soils, lakes, and streams, thereby stressing or killing terrestrial and aquatic biota.[3]

Acid deposition is an issue of global significance for which science is providing strong incentives for action. Reductions in troublesome emissions are closely tied to energy conservation and therefore directly related to production of greenhouse gases and global climate change concerns—thus, linking these environmental issues.

[3] C. T. Driscoll et al., "Acidic deposition in the northeastern United States: Sources and inputs, ecosystems effects, and management strategies," *BioScience* 51 (March 2001): 195.

1990–1994

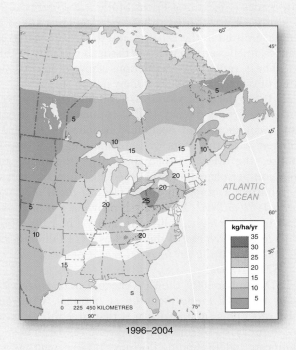

1996–2004

FIGURE 3.2.2 Improvement in sulfate wet deposition rate.
Spatial portrayal of annual sulfate (principally SO_4) wet deposition on the landscape, between two 5-year periods, in kilograms per hectare per year. The Canadian Environmental Protection Act, the Canada–United States Border Air Quality Strategy, and the U.S. Clean Air Act regulations together lowered levels of emissions that add acid to the environment. [Maps from *Cleaner Air through Cooperation, Canada—United States, Progress under the Air Quality Agreement—2003.* © Her Majesty The Queen Right of Canada, Environment Canada, 2003. Reproduced with the permission of the Minister of Public Works and Government Services Canada.]

New studies are implicating even smaller particles, known as *ultrafines*, which are $PM_{0.1}$. These are many times more potent than the larger $PM_{2.5}$ and PM_{10} particles because they can get into smaller channels in lung tissue and cause scarring, abnormal thickening, and damage called *fibrosis*. Asthma prevalence has nearly doubled since 1980 in the United States, a major cause being motor vehicle–related air pollution—specifically, sulfur dioxide, ozone, and fine particulate matter.

We are now contributing significantly to the creation of the **anthropogenic atmosphere**, a tentative label for Earth's next atmosphere. The urban air we breathe today may be just a preview. What is the air quality like where you live, work, and go to university? Where could you search for information about its status?

Benefits of the Clean Air Act

The concentration of many air pollutants declined over the past several decades because of U.S. Clean Air Act (CAA) legislation (1970, 1977, 1990), resulting in the avoidance of trillions of dollars in health, economic, and environmental losses. Despite this reality, air pollution controls are subject to a continuing political debate.

Since 1970 and the CAA, there were significant reductions in atmospheric concentrations of carbon monoxide (−45%), nitrogen oxides (−22%), volatile organic compounds (−48%), PM_{10} particulates (−75%), sulfur oxides (−52%; see Focus Study 3.2, Figure 3.2.2), and lead (−98%). Prior to the CAA, lead was added to gasoline, emitted in the exhaust, and dispersed over great distances, finally settling in living tissues, especially in children. These remarkable reductions show the successful linking of science and public policy.

In 1990, the U.S. Congress requested the Environmental Protection Agency (EPA) to analyse the overall health, ecological, and economic benefits of the CAA compared with the costs of implementing the law. In response, the EPA's Office of Policy, Planning, and Evaluation performed an exhaustive cost–benefit analysis and published a report in 1997: *The Benefits of the Clean Air Act, 1970 to 1990*. The analysis provides a good lesson in cost-benefit analysis, valid to this day. The EPA report estimated the *direct cost* of the Act was $523 billion (1990 U.S. dollars) and the *net financial benefit* of the Clean Air Act is *$21.7 trillion*!

In December 2009, the EPA enacted an *Endangerment Finding* that will guide planning at national, state, and local levels. This finding declares that greenhouse gases "pose a threat to human health and welfare." Scaling such a significant federal finding down to local regulations is a challenge for environmental planners.

Although the U.S. legislation improves air quality irrespective of national borders, there is still no legislation to deal directly with air pollution in Canada. The Canada Clean Air Act was introduced to Parliament in 2006, was greatly debated in Commons Committee, but failed to receive Royal Assent. The Climate Change Accountability Act passed the House of Commons, but was defeated at second reading in the Senate in November of 2010.

As you reflect on this chapter and our modern atmosphere, the treaties to protect stratospheric ozone, and the benefits from the CAA, you should feel encouraged. Scientists did the research and society knew what to do, took action, and reaped enormous economic and health benefits. Decades ago scientists learned to sustain and protect astronauts by providing an "atmosphere" with a spacesuit. Today, we must, in turn, learn to sustain and protect Earth's atmosphere so that it continues to ensure our own survival.

CRITICAL THINKING 3.3
Evaluating Costs and Benefits

In the scientific study *The Benefits of the Clean Air Act, 1970 to 1990*, the EPA determined that the Clean Air Act provided health, welfare, ecological, and economic benefits 42 times greater than its costs (estimated at $21.7 trillion in net benefits compared to $523 billion in costs). Do you think this is significant? Should this be part of the debate about future weakening or strengthening of the Clean Air Act? How should Canada legislate contaminant levels that reduce air quality? In your opinion, why is the public generally unaware of these details? What are the difficulties in informing the public?

Do you think a similar benefit pattern results from laws such as the U.S. Clean Water Act, or hazard zoning and planning, or action on global climate change and the Endangerment Finding by the EPA? Take a moment and brainstorm recommendations for action, education, and public awareness on these issues.

GEOSYSTEMS CONNECTION

We traversed the atmosphere from the thermopause to Earth's surface. You learned the composition, temperature layers, and functions of the ionosphere and ozonosphere and the human impacts on the modern atmosphere. In the next chapter, we follow the flow of energy through the lower portions of the atmosphere as insolation makes its way to the surface. The Earth–atmosphere energy balance is established. Surface energy budgets are powered by this arrival of energy. We explore the possibilities of harvesting some of this solar energy.

Working with Lapse Rates

This chapter introduced the concept of *environmental lapse rates,* the measured change in temperature in the atmosphere for a given change in altitude. The global average of environmental lapse rates is the *normal lapse rate.* We can use lapse rates to calculate temperatures at different altitudes. Being able to do these calculations will benefit your understanding of atmospheric processes described in Chapters 5, 7, and 8.

Expressions of lapse rates are in the form of a change in temperature per unit change in altitude. The normal lapse rate has a value of $\Delta 6.4$ C° 1000 m^{-1}, which in equivalent terms is $\Delta 6.4$ C° km^{-1} (1000 m = 1 km) or $\Delta 0.64$ C° 100 m^{-1}. Δ is the symbol for change. The 100 m, 1000 m, or 1 km in these expressions represents the size of each step in altitude over which the temperature change is measured.

As seen in Figures 3.2 and 3.5, in the troposphere the temperature typically decreases with an increase in altitude. When you see a lapse rate with a positive value, such as $\Delta 4.0$ C° km^{-1}, by convention this represents the usual case of temperature decreasing with increasing altitude. You can interpret $\Delta 4.0$ C° km^{-1} as meaning, "For every 1 km increase in altitude, the temperature decreases by 4 C°." It also means: "For every 1 km *decrease* in altitude, the temperature *increases* by 4 C°."

In Figure 3.5, the temperature at the surface is 15°C. Applying the normal lapse rate, what is the temperature at 10 km altitude?

With $\Delta 6.4$ C° km^{-1} there are 10 1-km steps in altitude between the surface (0 km) and 10 km. Because the new altitude is higher than the starting point, this change is altitude is expressed as a positive value

(10 km − 0 km = +10 km). Set up an equation where the answer ($T_{10\,km}$) is calculated as the initial temperature (15°C at 0 km) minus the lapse rate multiplied by the number of steps in altitude:

$$T_{10\,km} = T_{0\,km} - (6.4 \times 10)$$
$$T_{10\,km} = 15 - (6.4 \times 10)$$
$$T_{10\,km} = 15 - 64 = -49°C$$

Check Figure 3.5 to confirm that the temperature for 10 km was calculated correctly. Note that if the normal lapse rate were expressed as $\Delta 0.64$ C° 100 m^{-1}, there would be 100 steps in altitude instead of 10, but with the corresponding temperature change for each step being 1/10th the magnitude (0.64 C° instead of 6.4 C°), the final answer would be the same as above.

How would we set up the calculation if we started with the temperature of −49°C at 10 km and decreased altitude to 0 km? The altitude difference is 0 km −10 km = −10 km. Compare this setup with the equation above:

$$T_{0\,km} = T_{10\,km} - (6.4 \times -10)$$
$$T_{0\,km} = -49 - (6.4 \times -10)$$
$$T_{0\,km} = -49 - (-64) = -49 + 64$$
$$= 15°C$$

Notice that we set up the right side of the equation as before, initial temperature minus lapse rate multiplied by the number of steps in altitude. The multiplication of the two negative signs results in a positive temperature change for this decrease in altitude.

Lapse rate calculations do not always involve the normal lapse rate or "round" temperatures and differences in altitude. Two examples with these types of variations are now presented.

• First, with an environmental lapse rate of $\Delta 7.6$ C° km^{-1}, what is the change in temperature between a surface at 2 km and a point in the

atmosphere 3 km above it? The altitude of the point for which we want to calculate the temperature is 5 km (3 km above a surface at 2 km), but the change in altitude is only 3 km.

$$T_{5\,km} = T_{2\,km} - (7.6 \times 3)$$
$$T_{5\,km} = T_{2\,km} - (22.8)$$

If the temperature at 2 km is, for example, 28.9°C, then the temperature 3 km above it is 28.9 − 22.8 = 6.1°C.

• Second, if the temperature at Winnipeg (238 m above sea level) is 11.7°C and the environmental lapse rate is $\Delta 5.9$ C° km^{-1}, what is the temperature outside an airplane flying above the city at 12 000 m? The difference in altitude is 12 000 − 238 = 11,762 m or 11.762 km.

$$T_{12\,km} = T_{238\,m} - (5.9 \times 11.762)$$
$$T_{12\,km} = 11.7 - (5.9 \times 11.762)$$
$$T_{12\,km} = 11.7 - 69.4 = -57.7°C$$

Note that sometimes the lapse rate is *inverted*; temperature increases with an increase in altitude. In these cases we need to show the lapse rate as a negative, or state explicitly that the rate is inverted. Moving between the altitudes of 3500 m and 5500 m (a 2 km difference) with an inverted lapse rate of $\Delta 4.5$ C° km^{-1}, what is the temperature change?

$$T_{5.5\,km} = T_{3.5\,km} - (-4.5 \times 2)$$
$$T_{5.5\,km} = T_{3.5\,km} + 9$$

The temperature is 9 C° greater at 5.5 km than at 3.5 km altitude. With an inversion, a decrease in altitude would result in a decrease in temperature. Finally, an *isothermal* condition occurs when there is no change in temperature with a change in altitude. Here the lapse rate would be $\Delta 0$ C° km^{-1}.

KEY LEARNING CONCEPTS REVIEW

■ **Construct** a general model of the atmosphere based on three criteria—composition, temperature, and function—and **diagram** this model in a simple sketch.

Our modern atmosphere is a gaseous mixture so evenly mixed it behaves as if it were a single gas. The principal substance of this atmosphere is air—the medium of life. **Air** is naturally odourless, colourless, tasteless, and formless.

Above about 480 km altitude, the atmosphere is rarefied (nearly a vacuum) and is the **exosphere**, which means "outer sphere." The weight (force per unit area) of the atmosphere, exerted on all surfaces, is **air pressure**. It decreases rapidly with altitude.

By *composition*, we divide the atmosphere into the **heterosphere**, extending from 480 km to 80 km, and the **homosphere**, extending from 80 km to Earth's surface. Within the heterosphere and using *temperature* as a criterion, we identify the **thermosphere**. Its upper limit, called the **thermopause**, is at approximately 480 km altitude. **Kinetic energy**, the energy of motion, is the vibrational energy that we measure and call temperature. The actual amount of heat produced in the thermosphere is very small. The density of the molecules is so low that little actual **heat**, the flow of kinetic energy from one body to another because of a temperature difference between them, is produced. Nearer Earth's surface, the greater number of molecules in the denser atmosphere transmits their kinetic energy as **sensible heat**, meaning that we can feel it.

The homosphere includes the **mesosphere, stratosphere,** and **troposphere**, as defined by temperature criteria. Within the mesosphere, cosmic or meteoric dust acts as nuclei around which fine ice crystals form to produce rare and unusual night clouds called **noctilucent clouds**.

The top of the troposphere is the altitude where a temperature of −57°C is recorded, a transition known as the **tropopause**. The normal temperature profile within the troposphere during the daytime decreases rapidly with increasing altitude at an average of 6.4 C° per km, a value known as the **normal lapse rate**. The actual lapse rate at any particular time and place may deviate considerably because of local weather conditions and is called the **environmental lapse rate**.

We distinguish a region in the heterosphere by its *function*. The **ionosphere** absorbs cosmic rays, gamma rays, X-rays, and shorter wavelengths of ultraviolet radiation and converts them into kinetic energy. A functional region within the stratosphere is the **ozonosphere**, or **ozone layer**, which absorbs life-threatening ultraviolet radiation, subsequently raising the temperature of the stratosphere.

air (p. 62)
exosphere (p. 63)
air pressure (p. 64)
heterosphere (p. 65)
homosphere (p. 65)
thermosphere (p. 67)
thermopause (p. 67)
kinetic energy (p. 67)
heat (p. 67)
sensible heat (p. 67)
mesosphere (p. 67)
noctilucent clouds (p. 67)
stratosphere (p. 67)
troposphere (p. 67)
tropopause (p. 67)
normal lapse rate (p. 68)
environmental lapse rate (p. 68)
ionosphere (p. 68)
ozonosphere, ozone layer (p. 68)

1. What is air? Where did the components in Earth's present atmosphere originate?
2. In view of the spacesuit analogy presented at the beginning of the chapter, characterise the various functions the atmosphere performs that protect the surface environment.
3. What three distinct criteria are employed in dividing the atmosphere for study?
4. Describe the overall temperature profile of the atmosphere, and list the four layers defined by temperature.
5. Describe the two divisions of the atmosphere on the basis of composition.
6. What are the two overall primary functional layers of the atmosphere and what does each do?

■ **List** the stable components of the modern atmosphere and their relative percentages by volume, and **describe** each.

Even though the atmosphere's density decreases with increasing altitude in the homosphere, the blend (proportions) of gases is nearly uniform. This stable mixture of gases has evolved slowly.

The homosphere is a vast reservoir of relatively inert *nitrogen*, originating principally from volcanic sources and from bacterial action in the soil; *oxygen*, a by-product of photosynthesis; *argon*, constituting about 1% of the homosphere and completely inert; and *carbon dioxide*, a natural by-product of life processes and fuel combustion.

7. Name the four most prevalent stable gases in the homosphere measured by volume. Where did each originate? Is the prevalence of any of these changing at this time?

■ **Describe** conditions within the stratosphere; specifically, **review** the function and status of the ozonosphere (ozone layer).

The overall reduction of the stratospheric ozonosphere, or ozone layer, during the past several decades represents a hazard for society and many natural systems and is caused by chemicals introduced into the atmosphere by humans. Since World War II, quantities of human-made **chlorofluorocarbons (CFCs)** and bromine-containing compounds have made their way into the stratosphere. The increased ultraviolet light at those altitudes breaks down these stable chemical compounds, thus freeing chlorine and bromine atoms. These atoms act as catalysts in reactions that destroy ozone molecules.

chlorofluorocarbons (CFCs) (p. 70)

8. Why is stratospheric ozone (O_3) so important? Describe the effects created by increases in ultraviolet light reaching the surface.
9. Summarise the ozone predicament, and describe trends and any treaties that intend to protect the ozone layer.

10. Evaluate Crutzen, Rowland, and Molina's use of the scientific method in investigating stratospheric ozone depletion, and public reaction to their findings.

■ *Distinguish* between natural and anthropogenic variable gases and materials in the lower atmosphere.

Within the troposphere, both natural and human-caused variable gases, particles, and other chemicals are part of the atmosphere. We coevolved with natural "pollution" and thus are adapted to it. But we are not adapted to cope with our own anthropogenic pollution. It constitutes a major health threat, particularly where people are concentrated in cities.

Vertical temperature and atmospheric density distribution in the troposphere can worsen pollution conditions. A **temperature inversion** occurs when the normal temperature decrease with altitude reverses. In other words, temperature begins to increase at some altitude.

temperature inversion (p. 73)

11. Why are anthropogenic gases more significant to human health than those produced from natural sources?
12. In what ways does a temperature inversion worsen an air pollution episode? Why?

■ *Describe* the sources and effects of carbon monoxide, nitrogen dioxide, and sulfur dioxide and *construct* a simple diagram that illustrates photochemical reactions that produce ozone, peroxyacetyl nitrates, nitric acid, and sulfuric acid.

Odourless, colourless, and tasteless, **carbon monoxide (CO)** is produced by incomplete combustion (burning with limited oxygen) of fuels or other carbon-containing substances. Transportation is the major human-caused source for carbon monoxide. The toxicity of carbon monoxide is due to its affinity for blood hemoglobin, which is the oxygen-carrying pigment in red blood cells. In the presence of carbon monoxide, the oxygen is displaced and the blood becomes deoxygenated (Table 3.4).

Photochemical smog results from the interaction of sunlight and the products of automobile exhaust, the single largest contributor of pollution that produces smog. Car exhaust, containing *nitrogen dioxide* and *volatile organic compounds* (*VOCs*), in the presence of ultraviolet light in sunlight converts into the principal photochemical by-products—*ozone, peroxyacetyl nitrates* (*PAN*), and *nitric acid*.

Ozone (O_3) causes negative health effects, oxidizes surfaces, and kills or damages plants. **Peroxyacetyl nitrates (PAN)** produce no known health effects in humans but are particularly damaging to plants, including both agricultural crops and forests. **Nitrogen dioxide (NO_2)** damages and inflames human respiratory systems, destroys lung tissue, and damages plants. Nitric oxides participate in reactions that form nitric acid (HNO_3) in the atmosphere, forming both wet and dry acidic deposition. The **volatile organic compounds (VOCs)**, including hydrocarbons from gasoline, surface coatings, and electric utility combustion, are important factors in ozone formation.

The distribution of human-produced **industrial smog** over North America, Europe, and Asia is related to transportation and electrical production. Such characteristic pollution contains **sulfur dioxide**. Sulfur dioxide in the atmosphere reacts to produce **sulfate aerosols**, which produce sulfuric acid (H_2SO_4) deposition, which can be dangerous to health and affect Earth's energy budget by scattering and reflecting solar energy. **Particulate matter (PM)** consists of dirt, dust, soot, and ash from industrial and natural sources.

Increasing energy conservation and efficiency and reducing emissions are key to reducing air pollution. Earth's next atmosphere most accurately may be described as the **anthropogenic atmosphere** (human-influenced atmosphere).

carbon monoxide (CO) (p. 74)
photochemical smog (p. 76)
nitrogen dioxide (p. 76)
peroxyacetyl nitrates (PAN) (p. 76)
volatile organic compounds (VOCs) (p. 76)
industrial smog (p. 76)
sulfur dioxide (SO_2) (p. 76)
sulfate aerosols (p. 76)
particulate matter (PM) (p. 77)
anthropogenic atmosphere (p. 80)

13. What is the difference between industrial smog and photochemical smog?
14. Describe the relationship between automobiles and the production of ozone and PAN in city air. What are the principal negative impacts of these gases?
15. How are sulfur impurities in fossil fuels related to the formation of acid in the atmosphere and acid deposition on the land?
16. In summary, what were the results from the first 20 years under Clean Air Act regulations?

MyGeosciencePlace

Visit **www.mygeoscienceplace.ca** for several figure animations, satellite loops, self-study quizzes, flashcards, interactive glossary, career links, RSS feeds, Pearson eText of *Geosystems*, and much more.

CHAPTER 4

Atmosphere and Surface Energy Balances

The rapid growth of Metropolitan Toronto between 1986 and 2007 is highlighted in these two Landsat-5 images of southwestern Ontario. Urban growth enhances the urban heat island effect on surface energy budgets. Impervious, artificial surfaces in Toronto cause a 1.5 to 1.8 C° increase in temperature for Metro Toronto. This effect is felt most strongly in winter as the presence of Lake Ontario moderates summer heating. [U.S. Geological Survey.]

KEY LEARNING CONCEPTS

After reading the chapter, you should be able to:

- **Identify** the processes acting on insolation as it passes through the atmosphere to Earth's surface, and **describe** the processes that transfer heat energy in a system.

- **Describe** what happens to insolation when clouds are in the atmosphere, and **analyze** the effect of clouds and air pollution on insolation received at ground level.

- **Review** the energy pathways in the Earth–atmosphere system, the greenhouse effect, and patterns of global net radiation.

- **Plot** the daily radiation curves for Earth's surface, and **label** the key aspects of incoming radiation, air temperature, and the daily temperature lag.

- **Portray** typical urban heat island conditions, and **contrast** the microclimatology of urban areas with that of surrounding rural environments.

How Does Arctic Shipping Impact Albedo and the Surface Energy Balance?

For hundreds of years, explorers searched for the fabled "Northwest Passage"—a sea route connecting the Atlantic and Pacific oceans through the inland waterways of the Canadian Archipelago. The "Northeast Passage," or Northern Sea Route, is another Arctic shipping lane traversing the Russian coast and linking Europe and Asia. These northern routes eliminate the need to go through the Panama and Suez Canals, respectively.

Arctic Ocean sea ice blocked these routes, making them unavailable for shipping—that is, until recently. In 2009, the first commercial navigation of the Northeast Passage by a pair of German container ships was successful owing to reductions in Arctic ice associated with climate change.

The prospect of an ice-free Arctic Ocean is triggering commercial excitement for freighter and oil tanker traffic across these northern passages. With record losses of Arctic sea ice in 2007, the Northwest Passage achieved ice-free status and the Northeast Passage continued its ice-free summer status (Figure GN 4.1). The three years following had comparable ice losses caused by higher ocean and air temperatures across the region.

Given significant losses to multiyear ice, the National Snow and Ice Data Center (NSIDC) forecasted that summer ice-free conditions could happen for the Arctic Ocean before 2015. As the multiyear core ice fails, only the seasonal ice remains. This younger, thinner ice takes less energy

FIGURE GN 4.1 2007 minimum Arctic sea-ice extent.
Trace possible new shipping routes across the Northeast and Northwest Passages on the satellite image. [NASA/GSFC Image.]

to melt. Also, scientists report that strong Arctic winds blow ice southward, where it melts in warmer ocean waters, accounting for nearly a third of sea-ice loss.

The impacts of surface albedo also play a key role in sea ice melting. Day-to-day observations tell us that lighter surfaces tend to reflect sunlight and remain cooler, whereas darker surfaces tend to absorb sunlight and heat up. Snow- and ice-covered surfaces are great natural reflectors; in fact, sea ice reflects about 80%–95% of the insolation it receives. The ocean surface is darker, reflecting only an average of about 10% of insolation. This percentage represents albedo, or the reflective value of a surface. As the ice-covered area in the Arctic retreats, darker water or land receives direct sunlight and absorbs more heat, which adds to further warming—a positive feedback.

Particulates in the atmosphere appear to enhance this albedo impact. Scientists now have evidence that soot and particulate aerosol fallout are significant causes of glacial snow and ice losses across the Himalayas. On the Greenland Ice Sheet, black soot, dust, and particulates accumulate with snow and harden into the ice, darkening the surface. As surface albedo decreases, ice absorbs more insolation, and increased melting causes soot to become even more concentrated and darker. The exhaust from Arctic shipping vessels produce similar impacts.

The 2009 *Arctic Marine Shipping Assessment* (Arctic Council, p. 140) stated that "ship stack emissions in and near the Arctic will increase." Shipping seasons have already expanded by more than three weeks in the Arctic and two months in Hudson Bay since 2000 (Figure GN 4.2). The stack emissions from new freighter and tanker traffic will add soot and particulate material into the Arctic atmosphere. Fallout from these ship emissions could prove to be an albedo disaster, darkening remaining ice shelves and glaciers.

Whether to open the Northwest and Northeast Passages to ship traffic is a question of surface albedo values and the principles we cover in Chapter 4. So far, these surface-energy budget considerations have not entered political or economic discussions.

FIGURE GN 4.2 Ship traffic and shipments in the Arctic Ocean.
[Left—Canadian Coast Guard; right—Peter Andryszak.]

arth's biosphere pulses with flows of solar energy that sustain our lives and empower natural systems. Changing seasons, daily weather conditions, and Earth's variety of climates remind us of this constant flow of energy cascading through the atmosphere. We described Earth's shifting seasonal rhythms in Chapter 2, and a profile of the atmosphere in Chapter 3. Energy and moisture exchanges between Earth's surface and the atmosphere are essential elements of weather and climate, discussed in later chapters.

In this chapter: We follow solar energy through the troposphere to Earth's surface. The *outputs* of reflected light and emitted longwave energy from the atmosphere and surface environment counter the *input* of insolation. Together, these inputs and outputs determine the net energy available to perform work. We examine surface energy budgets and analyze how net radiation is distributed. Focus Study 4.1 discusses solar energy, an applied aspect of surface energy and a renewable energy resource of great potential.

The chapter concludes with a look at the unique energy and moisture environment in our cities. The view across a hot parking lot of cars and pavement in summer is all too familiar—the air shimmers as heat energy radiates skyward. The climate of our urban areas differs measurably from that of surrounding rural areas.

Energy Essentials

When you look at a photograph of Earth taken from space, you clearly see the effects of incoming insolation at the surface (see Earth's photo on the back cover of this book). Land and water surfaces, clouds, and atmospheric gases and dust intercept solar energy. The flows of energy are manifest in swirling weather patterns, powerful oceanic currents, and the varied vegetation of land cover. Specific energy patterns differ for deserts, oceans, mountaintops, plains, rain forests, and ice-covered landscapes. In addition, the presence or absence of clouds may make a 75% difference in the amount of energy that reaches the surface, because clouds reflect incoming energy.

Energy Pathways and Principles

Solar energy that heats Earth's atmosphere and surface is unevenly distributed by latitude, and fluctuates seasonally. Figure 4.1 is a simplified flow diagram of shortwave and longwave radiation in the Earth–atmosphere system, discussed in the pages that follow. You will find it helpful to refer to this figure, and the more detailed energy balance illustration in Figure 4.10, as you read through the following section. We first look at some important pathways and principles for insolation as it passes through the atmosphere to Earth's surface.

Transmission refers to the passage of shortwave and longwave energy through either the atmosphere or water. Our budget of atmospheric energy comprises shortwave radiation *inputs* (ultraviolet light, visible light, and near-infrared wavelengths) and longwave radiation *outputs* (thermal infrared) that pass through the atmosphere by transmission.

Insolation Input

Insolation is the single external energy input driving the Earth–atmosphere system. The world map in Figure 4.2 shows the distribution of average annual solar energy received at Earth's surface. It includes all the radiation that arrives at Earth's surface, both direct and diffuse (scattered by the atmosphere).

Global Warming, Climate Change

Earth-Atmosphere Energy Balance

FIGURE 4.1 Simplified view of the Earth–atmosphere energy system. Energy gained and lost by Earth's surface and atmosphere. Major components include incoming shortwave insolation, reflected shortwave radiation, and outgoing longwave radiation.

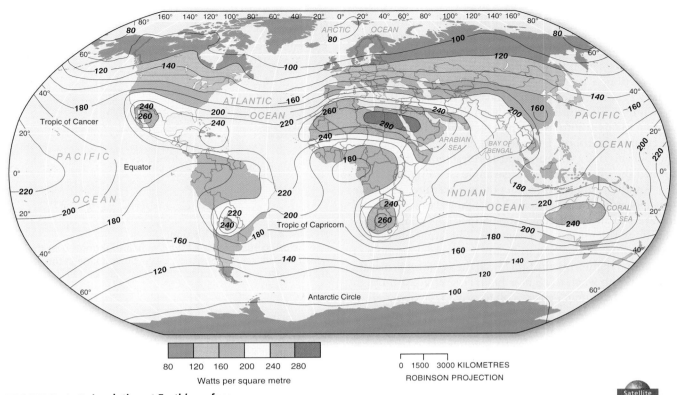

Satellite

Global Shortwave
Radiation

FIGURE 4.2 **Insolation at Earth's surface.**
Average annual solar radiation received on a horizontal surface at ground level in watts per square metre
$(100 \text{ W} \cdot \text{m}^{-2} \cdot \text{year}^{-1} = 75 \text{ kcal} \cdot \text{cm}^{-2} \cdot \text{year}^{-1})$. [After M. I. Budyko, *The Heat Balance of the Earth's Surface*
(Washington, D.C.: U.S. Department of Commerce, 1958), p. 99.]

Several patterns are notable on the map. Insolation decreases poleward from about 25° latitude in the Northern and Southern hemispheres. Consistent daylength and high Sun altitude produce average annual values of 180–220 watts per square metre $(\text{W} \cdot \text{m}^{-2})$ throughout the equatorial and tropical latitudes. In general, greater insolation of 240–280 $\text{W} \cdot \text{m}^{-2}$ occurs in low-latitude deserts worldwide because of frequently cloudless skies. Note this energy pattern in the cloudless subtropical deserts in both hemispheres (for example, the Sonoran, Saharan, Arabian, Gobi, Atacama, Namib, Kalahari, and Australian deserts).

Scattering (Diffuse Radiation) Insolation encounters an increasing density of atmospheric gases as it travels toward the surface. Atmospheric gases, dust, cloud droplets, water vapour, and pollutants physically interact with insolation. The gas molecules redirect radiation, changing the direction of the radiation's movement without altering its wavelength. **Scattering** describes this phenomenon and represents 7% of Earth's reflectivity, or albedo (see Figure 4.10).

Have you wondered why Earth's sky is blue? And why sunsets and sunrises are often red? These simple questions have an interesting explanation, based upon a principle known as Rayleigh scattering (named for English physicist Lord Rayleigh). This principle relates wavelength to the size of molecules or particles that cause the scattering.

The general rule is: *The shorter the wavelength, the greater the scattering; and the longer the wavelength, the lesser the scattering.* Small gas molecules in the air scatter shorter wavelengths of light. Thus, the shorter wavelengths of visible light—the blues and violets—scatter the most and dominate the lower atmosphere. And, because there are more blue than violet wavelengths in sunlight, a blue sky prevails. In addition, a sky filled with smog and haze appears almost white because the larger particles associated with air pollution act to scatter all wavelengths of visible light.

The angle of the Sun's rays determines the thickness of atmosphere the rays must pass through to reach the surface. Therefore, direct rays (from overhead) experience less scattering and absorption than do low- or oblique-angle rays that must travel farther through the atmosphere. Insolation from the low-altitude Sun undergoes more scattering of shorter wavelengths, leaving only the residual oranges and reds to reach the observer at sunset or sunrise.

Some incoming insolation is scattered by clouds and atmosphere and transmits to Earth as **diffuse radiation**, the downward component of scattered light (labelled in Figure 4.10). Such diffuse light is multidirectional and thus casts shadowless light on the ground.

Refraction As insolation enters the atmosphere, it passes from one medium to another, from virtually empty space into atmospheric gases. This occurs when insolation passes from air into water as well. The transition in density subjects the insolation to a change of speed, which also shifts its direction, a bending action called **refraction**. In the same way, a crystal or prism refracts light passing through it, bending different wavelengths to different angles, separating the light into its component colours to display the spectrum. A rainbow is created when visible light passes through myriad raindrops and is refracted and reflected toward the observer at a precise angle (see Figure 4.3).

Another example of refraction is a **mirage**, an image that appears near the horizon where light waves are refracted by layers of air at different temperatures (and consequently of different densities) on a hot day. The atmospheric distortion of the setting Sun in Figure 4.4 is also a product of refraction—light from the Sun low in the sky must penetrate more air than when the Sun is high; it is refracted through air layers of different densities on its way to the observer.

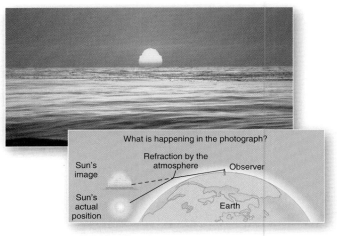

FIGURE 4.4 Sun refraction.
The distorted appearance of the Sun nearing sunset over the ocean is produced by refraction of the Sun's image in the atmosphere. Have you ever noticed this effect? [Robert Christopherson.]

FIGURE 4.3 A rainbow.
Raindrops—and in this photo, moisture droplets from the Niagara River—refract and reflect light to produce a primary rainbow. Note that in the primary (inner) rainbow the colours with the shortest wavelengths are on the inside and those with the longest wavelengths are on the outside. In the secondary bow, note that the colour sequence is reversed because of an extra reflection within each moisture droplet. [Bobbé Christopherson.]

An interesting function of refraction is that it adds approximately 8 minutes of daylight that we would lack if Earth had no atmosphere. We see the Sun's image about 4 minutes before the Sun actually peeks over the horizon. Similarly, as the Sun sets, its refracted image is visible from over the horizon for about 4 minutes afterward. The number of extra minutes varies with atmospheric temperature, moisture, and pollutants.

Reflection and Albedo A portion of arriving energy bounces directly back into space without being absorbed or performing any work—this is the **reflection** process. **Albedo** is the reflective quality, or intrinsic brightness, of a surface. It is an important control over the amount of insolation that is available for absorption by a surface. We state albedo as the percentage of insolation that is reflected (0% is total absorption; 100% is total reflection). Examine the different surfaces and their albedo values in Figure 4.5.

In the visible wavelengths, darker colours have lower albedos, and lighter colours have higher albedos. On water surfaces, the angle of the solar rays also affects albedo values; lower angles produce a greater reflection than do higher angles. In addition, smooth surfaces increase albedo, whereas rougher surfaces reduce it.

GEO REPORT 4.1 *Earthshine*

Some of Earth's reflection of light to space shines on the Moon. We have all seen the effect of *earthshine* as a faint illumination of the dark portion of the Moon, especially in crescent phase, when the dark area of the lunar disk is barely visible. In contrast, the Moon reflects only 6% to 8% of the sunlight that hits its surface, producing the "moonlight" familiar to us all. Scientists from the New Jersey Institute of Technology and California Institute of Technology now measure earthshine at the Big Bear Solar Observatory (see http://www.bbso.njit.edu/). Earthshine studies began in 1925. Think about earthshine the next time you take a moonlit walk.

Global Albedo Values, Global Shortwave Radiation

FIGURE 4.5 Various albedo values.
In general, light-coloured surfaces are more reflective than dark surfaces and thus have higher albedo values.

Specific locations experience highly variable albedo values during the year in response to changes in cloud and ground cover. Earth Radiation Budget (ERB) sensors aboard the *Nimbus*-7 satellite measured average albedos of 19%–38% for all surfaces between the tropics (23.5° N to 23.5° S), whereas albedos for the polar regions measured as high as 80% as a result of ice and snow. Tropical forests are characteristically low in albedo (15%), whereas generally cloudless deserts have higher albedos (35%).

Earth and its atmosphere reflect 31% of all insolation when averaged over a year. By comparison, a full Moon, which is bright enough to read by under clear skies, has only a 6%–8% albedo value. Thus, with *earthshine* being four times brighter than moonlight (four times the albedo), and with Earth four times greater in diameter than the Moon, it is no surprise that astronauts report how startling our planet looks from space.

Clouds, Aerosols, and the Atmosphere's Albedo
Clouds are an unpredictable factor in the tropospheric energy budget and therefore in refining climatic models. They reflect insolation and thus cool Earth's surface. The term **cloud-albedo forcing** refers to an increase in albedo caused by clouds. Yet clouds act as insulation, trapping longwave radiation from Earth and raising minimum temperatures. **Cloud-greenhouse forcing** is an increase in greenhouse warming caused by clouds. Figure 4.6

illustrates the general effects of clouds on shortwave radiation and longwave radiation. Chapter 7 details more on clouds.

The eruption of Mount Pinatubo in the Philippines, which began explosively during June 1991, illustrates how Earth's internal processes affect the atmosphere. Approximately 15–20 megatons of sulfur dioxide were injected into the stratosphere; winds rapidly spread these aerosols worldwide (see the images in Figure 6.1). As a result, atmospheric albedo increased worldwide and produced a temporary average cooling of 0.5 C°.

Other mechanisms affect atmospheric albedo and therefore atmospheric and surface energy budgets. Industrialization is producing a haze of pollution, including sulphate aerosols, soot and fly ash, and black carbon, that is increasing the reflectivity of the atmosphere. Emissions of sulfur dioxide and subsequent chemical reactions in the atmosphere form *sulfate aerosols*. These aerosols act as an insolation-reflecting haze in clear-sky conditions.

Pollution causes both atmospheric warming through absorption by the pollutants and surface cooling through reduction in insolation reaching the surface. An overall term has emerged that describes this decline in insolation reaching Earth's surface—**global dimming**. In determining present temperature increases associated with climate change, the dimming of sunlight is causing an underestimation of the actual amount of warming.

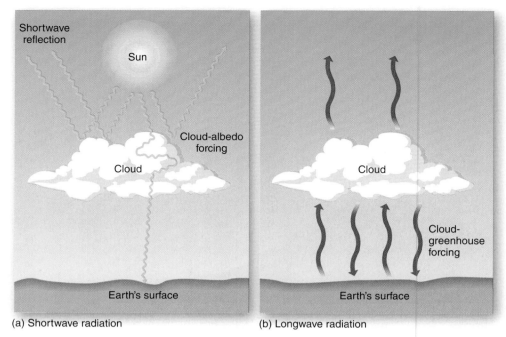

FIGURE 4.6 The effects of clouds on shortwave and longwave radiation.
(a) Clouds reflect and scatter shortwave radiation; a high percentage is returned to space. (b) Clouds absorb and radiate longwave radiation emitted by Earth; some longwave energy returns to space and some toward the surface.

Images from the Clouds and the Earth Radiant Energy System (CERES) in Figure 4.7 show pollution, haze and soot effects on the atmospheric energy budget in the Indian Ocean region. The increased aerosols (1), containing black carbon and particulates, increase reflection off the atmosphere, thus raising atmospheric albedos (2). This causes an increase in atmospheric warming, as aerosols absorb energy (3), and an increase in surface cooling

as less insolation reaches Earth's surface (4). These aerosols reduce surface insolation by 10% and increase energy absorption in the atmosphere by 50%.

Such pollution effects in southern Asia influence the dynamics of the Asian monsoon through alteration of the region's Earth–atmosphere energy budget (see monsoons in Chapter 6). A weakening monsoonal flow will negatively impact regional water resources and agriculture.

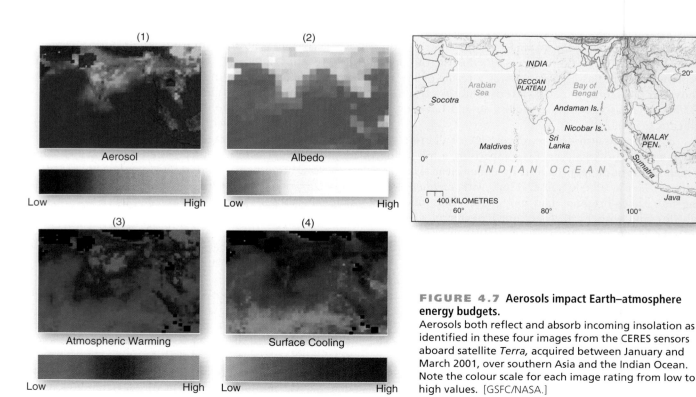

FIGURE 4.7 Aerosols impact Earth–atmosphere energy budgets.
Aerosols both reflect and absorb incoming insolation as identified in these four images from the CERES sensors aboard satellite *Terra,* acquired between January and March 2001, over southern Asia and the Indian Ocean. Note the colour scale for each image rating from low to high values. [GSFC/NASA.]

This research is part of the international, multiagency Indian Ocean Experiment (INDOEX, see http://www-indoex.ucsd.edu/).

Absorption The *assimilation* of radiation by molecules of matter and its conversion from one form of energy to another is **absorption**. Insolation, both direct and diffuse, that is not part of the 31% reflected from Earth's surface and atmosphere is absorbed. Absorbed energy is converted into either longwave radiation or chemical energy by plants in photosynthesis.

The temperature of the absorbing surface is raised in the process, and warmer surfaces radiate more total energy at shorter wavelengths—thus, *the hotter the surface, the shorter the wavelengths that are emitted* (see Chapter 2). Examples are an electric burner beginning to glow as it heats, or molten metal glowing at high temperatures. In addition to absorption by land and water surfaces (about 45% of incoming insolation), absorption also occurs in atmospheric gases, dust, clouds, and stratospheric ozone (about 24% of incoming insolation). Figure 4.10 summarises the pathways of insolation and the flow of heat in the atmosphere and at the surface.

Conduction, Convection, and Advection There are several means of transferring heat energy in a system. **Conduction** is the molecule-to-molecule transfer of heat energy as it diffuses through a substance. As molecules warm, their vibration increases, causing collisions that produce motion in neighbouring molecules, thus transferring heat from warmer to cooler materials.

Different materials (gases, liquids, and solids) conduct sensible heat directionally from areas of higher temperature to those of lower temperature. This heat flow transfers energy through matter at varying rates, depending on the conductivity of the material—Earth's land surface is a better conductor than air; moist air is a slightly better conductor than dry air.

Gases and liquids also transfer energy by movements of **convection** when the physical mixing involves a strong vertical motion. When horizontal motion dominates, the term **advection** applies. In the atmosphere or in bodies of water, warmer (less dense) masses tend to rise and cooler (denser) masses tend to sink, establishing patterns of convection. Sensible heat is transferred physically through the medium in this way.

You commonly experience such energy flows in the kitchen: Energy is conducted through the handle of a pan,

and boiling water bubbles in the saucepan in convective motions (Figure 4.8). Also in the kitchen you may use a convection oven that has a fan to circulate heated air to cook food uniformly.

In physical geography, we find many examples of each physical transfer mechanism:

- *Conduction* includes surface energy budgets, temperature differences between land and water bodies and between darker and lighter surfaces, the heating of surfaces and overlying air, and soil temperatures;
- *Convection* occurs in atmospheric and oceanic circulation, air mass movements and weather systems, internal motions deep within Earth that produce a magnetic field, and movements in the crust and upper mantle; and
- *Advection* involves horizontal movement of winds from land to sea and back, fog that forms and moves to another area, and air-mass movements from source regions.

Now with these pathways and principles in mind, we put it all together to describe the energy budgets of the lower atmosphere.

FIGURE 4.8 A pan of water on the stove illustrates heat transfer processes.
Infrared energy *radiates* from the burner to the saucepan and the air. Energy *conducts* through the molecules of the pan and the handle. The water mixes physically, carrying heat energy by *convection*.

GEO REPORT 4.2 *Monitoring Earth's Radiant Energy Systems*

To understand the role of natural clouds better, NASA began operating sensors aboard satellites in 1997 with the Tropical Rainfall Measuring Mission (TRMM), followed by *Terra* and *Aqua* in 1999 and 2002, respectively. See CERES (Clouds and the Earth Radiant Energy System) at http://ceres.larc.nasa.gov/ to review CERES and the various programs and spacecraft involved in this science.

CRITICAL THINKING 4.1

A Kelp Indicator of Surface Energy Dynamics

Examine the photograph in Figure CT 4.1. In Antarctica, on Petermann Island off the Graham Land Coast, this piece of kelp (a seaweed) was dropped by a passing bird. The kelp was resting about 10 cm deep in the snow, in a hole about the shape of the kelp. In your opinion, what energy factors operated to make this scene?

FIGURE CT 4.1 [Bobbé Christopherson.]

Now expand your conclusion to the issue of mining in Antarctica. There are coal deposits and other minerals in Antarctica. The international Antarctic Treaty blocks mining exploitation, although reconsideration is possible after 2048. Given your energy budget analysis of the kelp in the snow, information on surface energy budgets in this chapter, and the dust and particulate output of mining, construct a case opposed to such mining activities based on these factors. Further, can you think of factors that would favour such mining?

Energy Balance in the Troposphere

The Earth–atmosphere energy system budget naturally balances itself in a steady-state equilibrium. The atmosphere and surface eventually radiate longwave energy back to space, and this energy, together with reflected short-wave energy, equals the initial solar input—think of cash flows into and out of a chequing account and the balance when deposits and cash withdrawals are equal.

Greenhouse gases in the atmosphere effectively delay losses to space and act to warm the lower atmosphere. We examine this greenhouse effect and then develop an overall budget for the troposphere.

The Greenhouse Effect and Atmospheric Warming

Previously, we characterised Earth as a cool-body radiator, emitting more energy in longer (thermal infrared) wavelengths from its surface and atmosphere toward space. However, some of this longwave radiation is absorbed by carbon dioxide, water vapour, methane, nitrous oxide, chlorofluorocarbons (CFCs), and other gases in the lower atmosphere and then emitted back toward Earth.

This absorption and emission of energy is an important factor in warming the troposphere. The rough similarity between this process and the way a greenhouse operates gives the process its name—the **greenhouse effect**.

In a greenhouse, the glass is transparent to shortwave insolation, allowing light to pass through to the soil, plants, and materials inside, where absorption and conduction take place. The absorbed energy is then radiated as long-wave radiation back toward the glass, but the glass physically traps both the longer wavelengths and the warmed air inside the greenhouse. Thus, the glass acts as a one-way filter, allowing shortwave energy in but not allowing long-wave energy out except through conduction. You experience the same process in a car parked in direct sunlight.

Opening the greenhouse roof vent, or the car windows, allows the air inside to mix with the outside environment, thereby removing heat by moving air physically from one place to another by convection. The interior of a car gets surprisingly hot, even on a day with mild temperatures outside. Many people place a sunscreen across the windshield to prevent shortwave energy from entering the car to begin the greenhouse process. Have you taken steps to reduce the insolation input into a car's interior or through windows at home?

Overall, the atmosphere behaves a bit differently. In the atmosphere, the greenhouse analogy does not apply fully because longwave radiation is not *trapped* as in a greenhouse. Rather, its passage to space is *delayed* as the longwave radiation is absorbed by certain gases, clouds, and dust in the atmosphere and is emitted to Earth's surface. According to scientific consensus, today's increasing carbon dioxide concentration is forcing more long-wave radiation absorption in the lower atmosphere, thus producing a warming trend and changes in the Earth–atmosphere energy system.

Clouds and Earth's "Greenhouse"

Clouds affect the heating of the lower atmosphere in several ways, depending on cloud type. Not only is the percentage of cloud cover important but the cloud type, height, and thickness (water content and density) also have an effect. Thin ice-crystal clouds at high altitudes reflect insolation with albedos of about 50%, whereas thick, lower cloud cover reflects about 90% of incoming insolation.

To understand the actual effects on the atmosphere's energy budget, we must consider both transmission of shortwave and longwave radiation and cloud type. Figure 4.9a portrays the *cloud-greenhouse forcing* caused by high clouds (warming effect, because greenhouse effects exceed their albedo effects), and Figure 4.9b portrays the *cloud-albedo forcing* produced by lower, thicker clouds (cooling effect, because albedo effects exceed greenhouse effects).

Jet contrails (*condensation trails*) produce high cirrus clouds (Figure 4.9c and d)—sometimes called *false cirrus clouds*. As shown in Figure 4.9a, these high-altitude ice-crystal clouds are efficient at reducing outgoing longwave radiation and therefore contribute to global

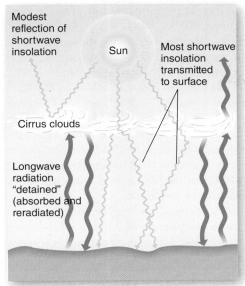

Modest
reflection of
shortwave
insolation

Sun

Most shortwave
insolation
transmitted
to surface

Cirrus clouds

Longwave
radiation
"detained"
(absorbed and
reradiated)

(a) High clouds: net greenhouse forcing and
atmospheric warming

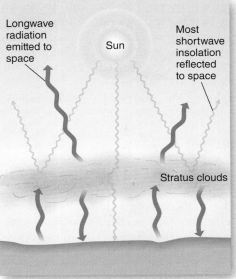

Longwave
radiation
emitted to
space

Sun

Most
shortwave
insolation
reflected
to space

Stratus clouds

(b) Low clouds: net albedo forcing and
atmospheric cooling

FIGURE 4.9 Energy effects of cloud types and contrails. (a) High, ice-crystal clouds (*cirrus*) produce a greater greenhouse forcing and a net warming of Earth. (b) Low, thick clouds (*stratus*) reflect most of the incoming insolation and produce a greater albedo forcing and a net cooling of Earth. (c) Jet aircraft exhaust triggers denser cirrus-cloud development. (d) Compare a more recent, thinner contrail with one spreading to form false cirrus clouds. [(c) NASA/JSC; (d) Bobbé Christopherson.]

(c)

(d)

heating. However, in contrast these contrail-seeded cirrus clouds have a higher density and higher albedo than normal cirrus clouds, thus reducing some surface insolation.

The tragedy that struck the World Trade Center, and humanity, on September 11, 2001, inadvertently provided researchers with a chance to study these effects. Following 9/11 was a three-day grounding of all commercial airline traffic and therefore no contrails across the United States. Weather data from 4000 stations over 30 years were compared with data during the three-day shutdown. *Diurnal temperature range* (DTR)—the difference between daytime maximum and nighttime minimum temperatures—increased during the three days. Specifically, maximum temperatures were more responsive to the missing clouds than were minimum temperatures—slightly higher afternoon and slightly lower nighttime temperature readings.

Later study of synoptic conditions (air pressure, humidity, air mass data—all gathered at a specific time),

analysis of Canadian air space, a check on conditions during adjacent three-day periods, and a look at the few military flights that took place during the halt of air travel served to verify the initial findings and confirmed the energy-budget impacts of contrails.[1]

Earth–Atmosphere Energy Balance

If Earth's surface and its atmosphere are considered separately, neither exhibits a balanced radiation budget. The average annual energy distribution is positive (an energy surplus) for Earth's surface and negative (an energy

[1] See David J. Travis et al., "Contrails reduce daily temperature range," *Nature* 418 (August 8, 2002): 601; and D. J. Travis, A. M. Carleton, and R. G. Lauritsen, "Regional variations in U.S. diurnal temperature range for the 9/11–14/2001 aircraft groundings: Evidence of jet contrail influence on climate," *Journal of Climate* 17 (March 1, 2004): 1123–34.

deficit) for the atmosphere as it radiates energy to space. Considered together, these two equal each other, making it possible for us to construct an overall energy balance.

Figure 4.10 summarises the Earth–atmosphere radiation balance. It brings together all the elements discussed to this point in the chapter by following 100% of arriving insolation through the troposphere. The shortwave portion of the budget is on the left in the illustration; the longwave part of the budget is on the right.

Out of 100% of the solar energy arriving, Earth's average albedo is 31%. Absorption by atmospheric clouds, dust, and gases involves another 21% and accounts for the atmospheric heat input. Stratospheric ozone absorption and radiation account for another 3% of the atmospheric budget. About 45% of the incoming insolation reaches Earth's surface as direct and diffuse shortwave radiation.

The natural energy balance occurs through longwave energy transfers from the surface, which are both *nonradiative* (involving physical motion) and *radiative*. Nonradiative transfers include convection, conduction, and the latent heat of evaporation (energy that is absorbed and dissipated by water as it evaporates and condenses). Radiative transfer is by longwave radiation between the surface, the atmosphere, and space,

as illustrated to the right in the depiction of the greenhouse effect (Figure 4.10).

To summarise, Earth eventually emits the longwave radiation part of the budget into space: 21% (atmosphere heating) + 45% (surface heating) + 3% (ozone emission) = 69%.

Figure 4.11 shows global monthly values in $W \cdot m^{-2}$ flux (meaning energy "flow") of both reflected and emitted radiation in Figure 4.10. In Figure 4.11a, lighter regions indicate where more shortwave radiation is reflected into space than is absorbed—for example, by lighter-coloured land surfaces such as deserts or by cloud cover such as that over tropical lands. Green and blue areas illustrate where less shortwave radiation was reflected.

In Figure 4.11b, orange and red colours indicate regions where more longwave radiation was absorbed and emitted to space; less longwave energy is escaping in the blue and purple regions. Those blue regions of lower longwave emissions over tropical lands are due to tall, thick clouds in the equatorial region (the Amazon, equatorial Africa, and Indonesia); these clouds also cause higher shortwave reflection. Subtropical desert regions exhibit greater longwave radiation emissions owing to the presence of little cloud cover and greater radiative energy losses from surfaces that absorb high amounts of energy.

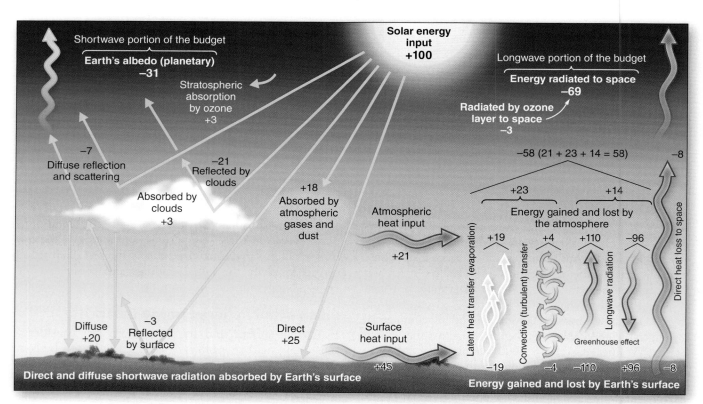

FIGURE 4.10 Detail of the Earth–atmosphere energy balance.
Solar energy cascades through the lower atmosphere (left-hand portion of the illustration), where it is absorbed, reflected, and scattered. Clouds, atmosphere, and the surface reflect 31% of this insolation back to space. Atmospheric gases and dust and Earth's surface absorb energy and radiate longwave radiation (right-hand portion of the illustration). Over time, Earth emits, to space on average, an amount equivalent to 69% of incoming energy. When added to Earth's average albedo (31%, reflected energy), this equals the total energy input from the Sun (100%).

Global Warming, Climate Change

Earth-Atmosphere Energy Balance

(a) Outgoing shortwave – Earth's albedo.

(b) Longwave energy flux to space.

FIGURE 4.11 **Shortwave and longwave images show Earth's radiation budget components.**
The CERES sensors aboard *Terra* made these portraits, capturing (a) outgoing shortwave energy flux reflected from clouds, land, and water—corresponding to Earth's albedo; and (b) longwave energy flux emitted by these surfaces back to space. The scale beneath each image displays values in $W \cdot m^{-2}$. [CERES, Langley Research Center, NASA.]

However, regionally and seasonally Earth absorbs more energy in the tropics and less in the polar regions, establishing the imbalance that drives global circulation patterns. Figure 4.12 summarises the Earth–atmosphere energy balance for all shortwave and longwave energy by latitude:

- At lower latitudes, the angle of incoming insolation is high and daylength is consistent through the year, so more energy is gained than lost annually—*energy surpluses dominate.*
- In the polar regions, the Sun is low in the sky, surfaces are light (ice and snow) and reflective, and for up to 6 months during the year no insolation is received, so more energy is lost than gained—*energy deficits prevail.*
- At around 36° latitude in both hemispheres, a balance exists between energy gains and losses for the Earth–atmosphere system.

The imbalance of net radiation from *tropical surpluses* to the *polar deficits* drives a vast global circulation of both energy and mass. The meridional (north–south) transfer agents are winds, ocean currents, dynamic weather systems, and related phenomena. Dramatic examples of such energy and mass transfers are tropical cyclones—hurricanes and typhoons. Forming in the tropics, these powerful storms mature and migrate to higher latitudes, carrying with them energy, water, and water vapour.

Given this Earth–atmosphere energy balance, we focus next on energy characteristics at Earth's surface and examine energy budgets at ground level, as portrayed in Figure 4.10. The surface environment is the final stage in the Sun–Earth energy system.

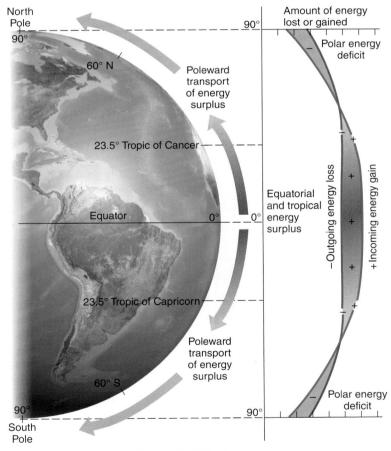

FIGURE 4.12 **Energy budget by latitude.**
Earth's energy surpluses and deficits produce poleward transport of energy and mass in each hemisphere—atmospheric circulation and ocean currents. Outside of the tropics, atmospheric winds dominate the transport of energy toward each pole.

Energy Balance at Earth's Surface

Solar energy is the principal heat source at Earth's surface. Figure 4.10 illustrates the direct and diffuse shortwave radiation and longwave radiation arriving at the ground surface. These radiation patterns at Earth's surface are of great interest to geographers and should be of interest to everyone because these are the surface environments in which we live.

Daily Radiation Patterns

Figure 4.13 shows the daily pattern of incoming shortwave energy absorbed and resultant air temperature. This graph represents idealised conditions above bare soil on a cloudless day in the middle latitudes. Incoming energy arrives during daylight hours, beginning at sunrise, peaking at noon, and ending at sunset.

The shape and height of this insolation curve vary with season and latitude. The peak for such a curve occurs at the time of the summer solstice (around June 21 in the Northern Hemisphere and December 21 in the Southern Hemisphere). The air temperature plot also responds to seasonal cycles and variations in insolation input. Within a 24-hour day, air temperature often peaks in midafternoon and dips to its lowest value at or slightly after sunrise.

The relationship between the insolation curve and the air temperature curve on the graph is interesting—the peaks do not align; there is a time *lag*. The warmest time of day occurs not at the moment of maximum insolation input, but at the moment when the *sum of absorbed insolation* and longwave radiation emitted to the atmosphere from the ground is at a maximum. As long as the total incoming energy to the air above the surface exceeds the outgoing energy, air temperature continues to increase, not peaking until the incoming energy begins to diminish as the afternoon Sun's altitude decreases. In contrast, if you have ever gone camping in the mountains, you no doubt experienced the coldest time of day with a wake-up chill at or just after sunrise!

The annual pattern of insolation and air temperature exhibits a similar lag. For the Northern Hemisphere, January is usually the coldest month, occurring after the December solstice and the shortest days. Similarly, the warmest months of July and August occur after the June solstice and the longest days. Figure 4.14 shows the variation in patterns of bright sunshine across the country.

Simplified Surface Energy Balance

Energy and moisture are continually exchanged at the surface, creating worldwide "boundary-layer climates" of great variety. **Microclimatology** is the science of physical conditions at or near Earth's surface. The following discussion is more meaningful if you visualise an actual surface—perhaps a park, a front yard, or a place on campus.

The surface receives visible light and longwave radiation and it reflects light and radiates longwave according to the following simple scheme:

$+SW\downarrow$	$-SW\uparrow$	$+LW\downarrow$	$-LW\uparrow$	$=$	NET R
(Insolation)	(Reflection)	(Infrared)	(Infrared)		(Net Radiation)

We use SW for shortwave radiation and LW for longwave for simplicity. Other symbols are often used in microclimatology, such as "Q*" for net radiation, "K" for shortwave, and "L" for longwave.

Figure 4.15 shows these components of a surface energy balance. The soil column shown continues to a depth at which energy exchange with surrounding materials or with the surface becomes negligible, usually less than a metre. Sensible heat transfer in the soil is through conduction, predominantly downward during the day or in summer and toward the surface at night or in winter. Energy from the atmosphere that is moving toward the surface is a positive (a gain), and energy that is moving away from the surface, through sensible and latent heat transfers, is a negative (a loss) to the surface account.

Adding and subtracting the energy flow at the surface completes the calculation of **net radiation (NET R)**, or the balance of all radiation at Earth's surface. As the components of this simple equation vary with daylength through the seasons, cloudiness, and latitude, NET R varies continuously. Figure 4.16 illustrates the components of a surface energy balance for a typical summer day at a midlatitude location, showing the daily change in the components of net radiation. The items plotted are direct and diffuse insolation ($+SW\downarrow$), reflected by surface albedo value, ($-SW\uparrow$), and longwave radiation arriving ($+LW\downarrow$) and leaving from the surface ($-LW\downarrow$).

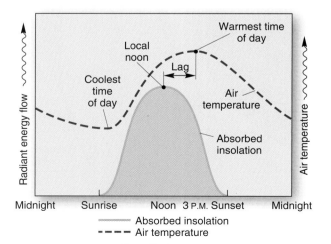

FIGURE 4.13 Daily radiation curves.
Sample radiation plot for a typical day shows the changes in insolation (solid line) and air temperature (dashed line). Comparing the curves demonstrates a lag between local noon (the insolation peak for the day) and the warmest time of day.

Sunniest Places in Canada			
Sunniest month	Eureka, N.W.T.	621 hours	May 1973
Greatest average annual number of sunny hours	Estevan, Sask.	2537 hours	
Major city with greatest annual average number of sunny hours	Saskatoon	2450 hours	
Sunniest small town under 10 000 population	Coronation, Alta.	2490 hours	
Sunniest provincial capital	Regina	2331 hours	
Sunniest year on record	Manyberries, Alta.	2785 hours	1976
Shortest spell of consecutive days without sun	Charlottetown	10 days	
Sunniest summer on average	Yellowknife	1065 hours	June, July, August
Sunniest winter on average	Gimli, Man.	376 hours	December, January, February
Greatest annual number of hours of possible sunshine	Alert, N.W.T.	4580 hours	
Greatest annual average number of sunny days	Calgary	329 days	
Greatest number of sunny days in one year	Medicine Hat	346 days	1976
Greatest number of sunshine recorder sites	Quebec City	84 days	

FIGURE 4.14 Average annual hours of sunshine received across Canada.

The greatest amounts of bright sunshine are received on the prairies even though these areas are farther north than southern Ontario and Quebec. What factors influence this pattern of sunshine? [*The Climates of Canada*, David Phillips, Senior Climatologist. © Environment Canada, 1990. Used by permission.]

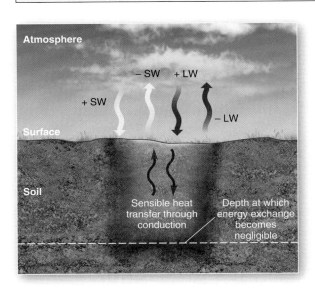

FIGURE 4.15 Surface energy budget.

Idealised input and output energy budget components for surface and a soil column. Sensible heat transfer in the soil is through conduction, predominantly downward during the day or in summer and toward the surface at night or in winter (SW = shortwave, LW = longwave).

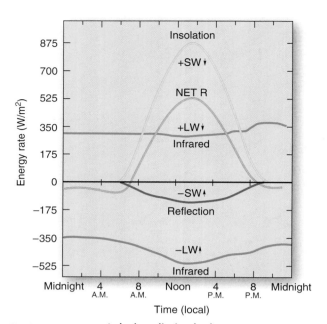

FIGURE 4.16 A day's radiation budget.
Radiation budget on a typical July summer day at a midlatitude location (Matador in southern Saskatchewan, about 51° N). [After T. R. Oke, *Boundary Layer Climates* (New York: Methuen & Co., 1978), p. 21.]

At night, the net radiation value in Figure 4.16 becomes negative because the $+SW\downarrow$ component ceases at sunset and the surface continues to lose longwave radiation to the atmosphere $(-LW\uparrow)$. The surface rarely reaches a zero net radiation value—a perfect balance—at

any one moment. However, over time, Earth's surface naturally balances incoming and outgoing energy.

Net Radiation The net radiation available at Earth's surface is the final outcome of the entire energy-balance process discussed in this chapter. Figure 4.17 displays the global mean annual net radiation at Earth's surface. The abrupt change in radiation balance from ocean to land surfaces is evident. Note that all values shown on this map are positive; negative values probably occur only over ice-covered surfaces poleward of 70° latitude in both hemispheres. The highest net radiation, 185 W·m⁻² per year, occurs north of the equator in the Arabian Sea. Aside from the obvious interruption caused by landmasses, the pattern of values appears generally zonal, or parallel, decreasing away from the equator.

A seasonal look is helpful to see the shifting patterns of NET R. Figure 4.18 shows the solstice months of December and June and the equinox months of March and September. The colour scale gives NET R in W·m⁻², all from the CERES sensors aboard *Terra* and *Aqua*. Positive NET R regions are toward the red colour, with negative NET R regions toward the blue-green colour. Notice tropical surpluses near the equator, balanced values in the midlatitudes, and polar deficits.

Net radiation is expended from a nonvegetated surface through three pathways:

■ *LE*, or *latent heat of evaporation*, is the energy that is stored in water vapour as water evaporates. Water absorbs large quantities of this *latent heat* as it

FIGURE 4.17 Global net radiation.
Distribution of mean annual net radiation (NET R) at surface level in watts per square metre (100 W·m⁻² = 75 kcal·cm⁻²·year⁻¹). Temperature graphs for the five cities noted on the map, and in Figures 4.19 and 4.20, are graphed in Figure 5.4. [After M. I. Budyko, *The Heat Balance of the Earth's Surface* (Washington, D.C.: U.S. Department of Commerce, 1958), p. 106.]

1. Salvador, Brazil
2. New Orleans, Louisiana
3. Edinburgh, Scotland
4. Montreal, Canada
5. Barrow, Alaska

(see Figure 5.4)

Global Net
Radiation

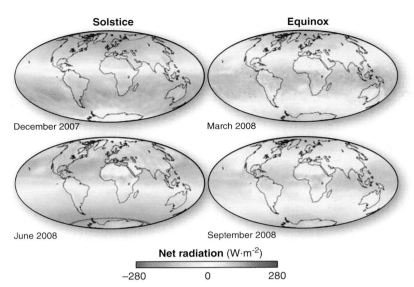

Solstice

December 2007

Equinox

March 2008

June 2008

September 2008

Net radiation (W·m⁻²)

−280   0   280

FIGURE 4.18 Global net radiation through the year.
The seasonal rhythm of NET R from solstice to equinox to solstice to equinox influences the patterns of life on Earth's surface. [CERES, Langley Research Center, NASA.]

changes state to water vapour (discussed in Chapter 7), thereby removing this heat energy from the surface. Conversely, this heat energy is released to the environment when water vapour changes state back to a liquid. Latent heat is the dominant expenditure of Earth's entire NET R, especially over water surfaces.

■ *H*, or *sensible heat*, is the back-and-forth transfer between air and surface in turbulent eddies through convection and conduction within materials. This activity depends on surface and boundary-layer temperatures and on the intensity of convective motion in the atmosphere. About one-fifth of Earth's entire NET R is mechanically radiated as sensible heat from the surface, especially over land.

■ *G*, or *ground heating and cooling*, is the energy that flows into and out of the ground surface (land or water) by conduction. During a year, the overall *G* value is approximately zero because the stored energy from spring and summer is equalled by losses in fall and winter. Another factor in ground heating is energy absorbed at the surface to melt snow or ice. In snow- or ice-covered landscapes, most available energy is in the form of sensible and latent heat used in the melting and warming process.

On land, the highest annual values for latent heat of evaporation (*LE*) occur in the tropics and *LE* decreases toward the poles (Figure 4.19). Over the oceans, the highest *LE* values are over subtropical latitudes, where hot, dry air comes into contact with warm ocean water.

The values for sensible heat (*H*) are distributed differently, being highest in the subtropics (Figure 4.20). Here, vast regions of subtropical deserts feature nearly waterless surfaces, cloudless skies, and almost vegetation-free landscapes. The bulk of NET R is expended as sensible heat in these dry regions. Moist and vegetated surfaces expend less in *H* and more in *LE*, as you can see by comparing the maps in Figures 4.19 and 4.20.

Understanding net radiation is essential to solar energy technologies that concentrate shortwave energy for use. Solar energy offers great potential worldwide and is presently the fastest-growing form of energy conversion by humans. Focus Study 4.1 briefly reviews such direct application of surface energy receipts.

❚❚ CRITICAL THINKING 4.2

Know More about Applied Solar Technologies

You can find several listings of URLs relating to solar energy applications in this chapter of the text. Take some time to explore the Internet for a personal assessment of these technologies (solar-thermal, solar-electric photovoltaic cells, solar-box cookers, and others). As we near the climatic limitations of the fossil-fuel era and the depletion of fossil-fuel resources, renewable energy technologies will be essential to the fabric of our lives. Briefly describe your search results. Given these findings, determine if solar technology is available where you live.

Sample Stations A couple of real locations help complete our discussion. Variation in the expenditure of NET R among sensible heat (*H*, energy we can feel), latent heat (*LE*, energy for evaporation), and ground heating and cooling (*G*) produces the variety of environments we experience in nature. Let us examine the daily energy balance at two locations, El Mirage in California and Pitt Meadows in British Columbia.

El Mirage, at 35° N, is a hot desert location characterised by bare, dry soil with sparse vegetation (Figure 4.21a, b). Our data sample is from a clear summer day, with a light wind in the late afternoon. The NET R value is lower than might be expected, considering the Sun's position close to zenith (June solstice) and the absence of clouds. But the input of energy at this site is countered by surfaces with high albedo and by hot soil surfaces that radiate longwave energy back to the atmosphere throughout the afternoon.

15	25	55	80	135	190	240

Watts per square metre

0 1500 3000 KILOMETRES
ROBINSON PROJECTION

1. Salvador, Brazil
2. New Orleans, Louisiana
3. Edinburgh, Scotland
4. Montreal, Canada
5. Barrow, Alaska

(see Figure 5.4)

FIGURE 4.19 Global latent heat of evaporation.
Annual energy expenditure as the latent heat of evaporation (*LE*) at surface level in watts per square metre ($100 \text{ W} \cdot \text{m}^{-2} \cdot \text{year}^{-1} = 75 \text{ kcal} \cdot \text{cm}^{-2} \cdot \text{year}^{-1}$). Note the high values associated with high sea-surface temperatures in the area of the Gulf Stream and Kuroshio Currents. [Adapted by permission from M. I. Budyko, *The Earth's Climate, Past and Future* (New York: Academic Press, 1982), p. 56.]

Satellite

Global Latent
Heat Flux

-7	0	15	40	65

Watts per square metre

0 1500 3000 KILOMETRES
ROBINSON PROJECTION

1. Salvador, Brazil
2. New Orleans, Louisiana
3. Edinburgh, Scotland
4. Montreal, Canada
5. Barrow, Alaska

(see Figure 5.4)

FIGURE 4.20 Global sensible heat.
Annual energy expenditure as sensible heat (*H*) at surface level in watts per square metre ($100 \text{ W} \cdot \text{m}^2 \cdot \text{year}^{-1} = 75 \text{ kcal} \cdot \text{cm}^{-2} \cdot \text{year}^{-1}$). [Adapted by permission from M. I. Budyko, *The Earth's Climate, Past and Future* (New York: Academic Press, 1982), p. 59.]

Satellite

Global Sensible
Heat

El Mirage has little or no energy expenditure for evaporation (*LE*). With little water and sparse vegetation, most of the available radiant energy dissipates through turbulent transfer of sensible heat (*H*), warming air and soil to high temperatures. Over a 24-hour period, *H* is 90% of NET R; the remaining 10% is for ground heating (*G*). The *G* component is greatest in the morning, when winds are light and turbulent transfers are lowest. In the afternoon, heated air rises off the hot ground and convective heat expenditures are accelerated as winds increase.

Compare graphs for El Mirage (Figure 4.21a) and Pitt Meadows (Figure 4.21c). Pitt Meadows is midlatitude (49° N), vegetated, and moist, and its energy expenditures differ greatly from those at El Mirage. The Pitt Meadows landscape is able to retain much more of its energy because of lower albedo values (less reflection), the presence of more water and plants, and lower surface temperatures than those of El Mirage.

The energy balance for Pitt Meadows is on a cloudless summer day. Higher *LE* values result from the moist environment of rye grass and irrigated mixed-orchard ground cover for the sample area (Figure 4.21d), contributing to the more moderate sensible heat (*H*) levels during the day.

The Urban Environment

An urban landscape produces the temperatures readers of this book feel each day. Urban microclimates differ from those of nearby nonurban areas. In fact, the surface energy

(a) El Mirage, California

(b) Mojave desert landscape

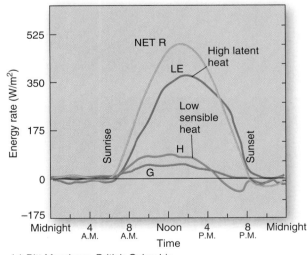

(c) Pitt Meadows, British Columbia

(d) Irrigated blueberry orchards

FIGURE 4.21 Radiation budget comparison for two stations.
(a) Graph of the daily net radiation expenditure for a site at El Mirage, California, east of Los Angeles, at about 35° N; and (b) a typical desert landscape near the hot, dry site. (c) The daily net radiation expenditure for a site at Pitt Meadows in southern British Columbia, at about 49° N; and (d) the irrigated blueberry orchards characteristic of agricultural activity in this moist environment of moderate temperatures. (*H* = turbulent sensible heat transfer; *LE* = latent heat of evaporation; *G* = ground heating and cooling.) [(a) Adapted by permission from W. D. Sellers, *Physical Climatology*, Fig. 33. © 1965 University of Chicago. All rights reserved (b) and (d) Bobbé Christopherson. (c) After T. R. Oke, *Boundary Layer Climates*, © 1978 Methuen & Co.]

Solar Energy Collection and Concentration

Consider the following:

- Earth receives 100 000 terawatts (TW) of solar energy per hour, enough to meet global power needs for a year.[1]
- An average commercial building receives 6 to 10 times more energy from the Sun hitting its exterior than is required to heat the inside.
- Photographs from the early 1900s show solar (flat-plate) water heaters used on rooftops. Today, installed solar water heating is making a comeback, serving 50 million households worldwide.
- Photovoltaic capacity is more than doubling every 2 years. More than 20 000 megawatts of solar-electric power were installed in 2010.

Not only does insolation warm Earth's surface, but also it provides an inexhaustible supply of energy for humanity. Sunlight is direct and widely available, and solar power installations are decentralised, labour-intensive, and renewable. Although collected for centuries using various technologies, sunlight remains underutilised. The utility energy industry appears to prefer indirect, centralised, power-plant-specific, capital-intensive, and nonrenewable sources.

Rural villages in developing countries could benefit greatly from the simplest, most cost-effective solar application—the *solar cooker*. For example, people in Latin America and Africa walk many kilometres collecting fuel wood for cooking fires (Figure 4.1.1a), stripping nearby areas bare. Using solar cookers, villagers are able to cook meals and sanitize their drinking water without scavenging for wood (Figure 4.1.1b). These solar devices in Figure 4.1.1c are simple, yet efficient, reaching temperatures of 107°C–127°C. See http://solarcookers.org/ for more information.

In less-developed countries, the money for electrification (a *centralised* technology) is not available despite the push from more developed countries and energy corporations for large capital-intensive power projects. In reality, the pressing need is for *decentralised* energy sources, appropriate in scale to everyday needs, such as cooking, heating water, and pasteurizing foods. The net per capita (per person) cost for solar cookers is far less than for centralised electrical production, regardless of fuel source.

Collecting and Concentrating Solar Energy

Any surface that receives light from the Sun is a *solar collector*. But the diffuse nature of solar energy received at the surface requires that it be collected, concentrated, transformed, and stored to be useful. Space heating is the simplest application. Windows that are carefully designed and placed allow sunlight to shine into a building, where it is absorbed and converted into sensible heat—an everyday application of the greenhouse effect.

A *passive solar system* captures heat energy and stores it in a "thermal mass," such as water-filled tanks, adobe, tile, or concrete. An *active solar system* involves heating water or air in a collector and then pumping it through a plumbing system to a tank, where it can provide hot water for direct use or for space heating.

Solar energy systems could generate heat energy on an appropriate scale for approximately half the present domestic applications in the United States, which includes space heating and water heating. In marginal climates, solar-assisted water and space heating is feasible as a backup. Several techniques are being used to attain very high temperatures to heat water or other heat-storing fluids. Kramer Junction, California, about 225 km northeast of Los Angeles, in the Mojave Desert near Barstow, has the world's largest operating solar electric–generating system, with a capacity of 150 MW. Long troughs of computer-guided curved

(a)

(b)

(c)

FIGURE 4.1.1 The solar-cooking solution.
(a) Two women and a girl haul firewood many miles in Guatemala. (b) Women in East Africa carry home solar-box cookers that they made at a workshop. Construction is easy, using cardboard components. (c) These simple cookers collect insolation through transparent glass or plastic and trap longwave radiation in an enclosed box or cooking bag. [(a) and (b) Solar Cookers International, Sacramento, California; (c) Bobbé Christopherson.]

[1]Terawatt (10^{12} Watts) = 1 trillion W; gigawatt (10^{9} Watts) = 1 billion W; megawatt (10^{6} Watts) = 1 million W; kilowatt (10^{3} Watts) = 1 thousand W.

mirrors concentrate sunlight to create temperatures of 390°C in vacuum-sealed tubes filled with synthetic oil. The heated oil heats water; the heated water produces steam that rotates turbines to generate cost-effective electricity. The facility converts 23% of the sunlight it receives into electricity during peak hours (Figure 4.1.2a), and operation and maintenance costs continue to decrease.

Electricity Directly from Sunlight

Photovoltaic cells (PVs) were first used to produce electricity in spacecraft in 1958. Familiar to us all are the solar cells in pocket calculators. When light shines upon a semiconductor material in these cells, it stimulates a flow of electrons (an electrical current) in the cell.

The efficiency of these cells, often assembled in large arrays, has improved to the level that they are cost-competitive, especially if government policies and subsidies were to be balanced evenly among all energy sources. The residential installation in Figure 4.1.2b features 36 panels, generating 205 W each, or 7380 W total, at a 21.5% conversion efficiency. People are able to run their electric meters in reverse and supply electricity to the power grid.

The National Renewable Energy Laboratory (NREL, http://www.nrel.gov) and the National Center for Photovoltaics, http://www.nrel.gov/ncpv/, were established in 1974 to coordinate solar energy research, development, and testing in partnership with private industry. At NREL's Outdoor Test Facility in Golden, Colorado, testing is ongoing and includes development of solar cells that broke the 40% conversion efficiency barrier!

Rooftop photovoltaic electrical generation is now cheaper than power line construction to rural sites. PV roof systems provide power to hundreds of thousands of homes in Mexico, Indonesia, Philippines, South Africa, India, and Norway. (See the "Photovoltaic Home Page," at http://www.eere.energy.gov/solar/.) The largest photovoltaic power plant (97 MW) in the world opened officially near Sarnia,

Ontario in October 2010 (Figure 4.1.2c). First Solar, the company that built the PV cells, promises that even larger solar farms will be opening soon.

Obvious drawbacks of both solar-heating and solar-electric systems are periods of cloudiness and night, which inhibit electrical production. Research is under way to enhance energy-storage technologies and to improve battery technology.

The Promise of Solar Energy

Solar energy is a wise choice for the future. Solar is economically preferable to further extraction of our decreasing fossil-fuel reserves, further increases in oil imports and oil tanker spills, and offshore oil-drilling accidents, investment in foreign military incursions, or the addition of more nuclear power, especially in a world with security issues and the threat of natural disasters.

Whether or not we follow the alternative path of solar energy is a matter of political control and not technological innovation. Much of the technology is ready for installation and is cost-effective when all direct and indirect costs are considered for the alternatives.

(a)

(b)

(c)

FIGURE 4.1.2 Solar thermal and photovoltaic energy production.
(a) Kramer Junction solar-electric generating system in southern California. (b) A residence with a 7380-W rooftop solar photovoltaic array generates electricity. Excess electricity is fed to the grid for credits that offset 100% of the home's electric bill. (c) Sarnia Photovoltaic solar farm in southwestern Ontario, the largest photovoltaic plant as of October 2010 producing 97 MW of energy. [(a) and (b) Bobbé Christopherson.] (c) Daniel J. Bellyk.]

characteristics of urban areas are similar to desert locations. Because almost 50% of the world's population lives in cities, urban microclimatology and other specific environmental effects related to cities are important topics for physical geographers.

The physical characteristics of urbanised regions produce an **urban heat island** that has on average both maximum and minimum temperatures higher than nearby rural settings. Table 4.1 lists five urban characteristics and the resulting temperature and moisture effects produced. Figure 4.22 illustrates these traits. Every major city produces its own **dust dome** of airborne pollution, which can be blown from the city in elongated plumes; as noted in the table, such domes affect urban energy budgets.

Table 4.2 compares climatic factors of rural and urban environments. The worldwide trend toward greater urbanization means that more and more people live on urban heat islands. These heat islands increase in size as population and urban sprawl increase. For an average city in North America, the sources of heating are modified surfaces, transportation, buildings, and industrial processes. For example, an average car (using 2.35 l·km^{-1}) produces enough heat to melt a 4.5 kg bag of ice for each km driven.

Many known methods to make cities cooler await application. In addition to lowering urban temperatures, such strategies could reduce energy consumption and fossil-fuel use, thus reducing greenhouse gas emissions. One method being investigated widely in Canada is the

TABLE 4.1   Urban Physical Characteristics and Conditions

Urban Characteristics	Results and Conditions
Urban surfaces typically are metal, glass, asphalt, concrete, or stone, and their energy characteristics respond differently than natural surfaces.	Albedos of urban surfaces are lower, leading to higher net radiation values. Urban surfaces expend more energy as sensible heat than do nonurban areas (70% of the net radiation to *H*). Surfaces conduct up to three times more energy than wet, sandy soil and thus are warmer. During the day and evening, temperatures above urban surfaces are higher than those above natural areas.
Irregular geometric shapes in a city affect radiation patterns and winds.	Incoming insolation is caught in mazelike reflection and radiation "canyons." Delayed energy is conducted into surface materials, thus increasing temperatures. Buildings interrupt wind flows, diminishing heat loss through advective (horizontal) movement. Maximum heat island effects occur on calm, clear days and nights.
Human activity alters the heat characteristics of cities.	In summer, urban electricity production and use of fossil fuels release energy equivalent to 25%–50% of insolation. In winter, urban-generated sensible heat averages 250% greater than arriving insolation, reducing winter heating requirements.
Many urban surfaces are sealed (built on and paved), so water cannot reach the soil.	Central business district surfaces average 50% sealed, producing more water runoff than the suburbs that average 20% sealed surfaces. Urban areas respond as a desert landscape: A storm may cause a flash flood over the hard, sparsely vegetated surfaces, to be followed by dry conditions a few hours later.
Air pollution, including gases and aerosols, is greater in urban areas than in comparable natural settings; this increases possible convection and precipitation.	Pollution increases the atmosphere's reflectivity above a city, reducing insolation and absorbing infrared radiation, reradiating infrared downward. Increased particulates in pollution are condensation nuclei for water vapour, increasing cloud formation and precipitation. Urban-stimulated increases in precipitation may occur downwind from cities.

FIGURE 4.22 The urban environment.
Insolation, wind movements, and a dust dome in a city environment.

green roof system, an engineered roofing system that incorporates vegetation. These systems reduce energy costs for cooling and heating, reduce stormwater runoff from urban structures, reduce the urban heat island effect, provide habitat and increase biodiversity, and can even be used to grow local food. A study in Ottawa found that energy consumption for cooling was reduced by 6%. If all the areas suitable for green roof development in Toronto had these systems installed, a possible improvement in stormwater runoff would result in fewer beach closures. In British Columbia, green roofs were found to reduce heat flow through the roof. The reductions were more effective in summer months than in winter months.

Figure 4.23 illustrates a generalised cross section of a typical urban heat island, showing increasing temperatures toward the central business district. Note that temperatures are lower over areas of trees and parks. Sensible heat is less because of the latent heat of evaporation and plant effects such as transpiration and shade. Urban forests are important factors in cooling cities. Measurements by NASA in an outdoor mall parking lot found temperatures of 48°C, but a small planter with trees in the same lot was significantly cooler at 32°C, 16C° lower in temperature! In New York City's Central Park, daytime temperatures average 5–10 C° cooler than urban areas outside the park.

▌▌ CRITICAL THINKING 4.3

Looking at Your Surface Energy Budget

Given what you now know about reflection, albedo, absorption, and net radiation expenditures, assess your wardrobe (fabrics and colours); house, apartment, or dormitory (colours of exterior walls, especially south and west facing in the Northern Hemisphere); roof (orientation relative to the Sun and roof colour); automobile (colour, use of sun shades); bicycle seat (colour); and other aspects of your environment to determine a personal "Energy Assessment." What grade do you give yourself? Can you roughly assess what this means in general terms of money costs? How could you change your personal energy balance? In Chapter 21 several sources lead you to web sites to assess and reduce your energy use, a direct link to these considerations of orientation, shade, colour, and form of transportation. Be cool!

TABLE 4.2   Average Differences in Climatic Elements between Urban and Rural Environments

Element	Urban Compared with Rural Environs	Element	Urban Compared with Rural Environs
Contaminants		**Precipitation (cont.)**	
Condensation nuclei	10 times more	Snowfall, downwind	10% more
Particulates	10 times more	(to the lee) of city	
Gaseous admixtures	5–25 times more	Thunderstorms	10%–15% more
Radiation		**Temperature**	
Total on horizontal surface	0%–20% less	Annual mean	0.5–3 C° more
Ultraviolet, winter	30% less	Winter minima (average)	1.0–2 C° more
Ultraviolet, summer	5% less	Summer maxima	1.0–3 C° more
Sunshine duration	5%–15% less	Heating degree days	10% less
Cloudiness		**Relative Humidity**	
Clouds	5%–10% more	Annual mean	6% less
Fog, winter	100% more	Winter	2% less
Fog, summer	30% more	Summer	8% less
Precipitation		**Wind Speed**	
Amounts	5%–15% more	Annual mean	20%–30% less
Days with <5 mm	10% more	Extreme gusts	10%–20% less
Snowfall, inner city	5%–10% less	Calm	5%–20% more

Source: H. E. Landsberg, *The Urban Climate*, International Geophysics Series, vol. 28 (1981), p. 258. Reprinted by permission from Academic Press.

FIGURE 4.23 Typical urban heat island profile.
Cross section of a typical urban heat island from rural to downtown. Temperatures steeply rise in urban settings, plateau over the suburban built-up area, and peak where temperature is highest at the urban core. Note the cooling over the park area and river.

When you look across the urban landscape, what strategies do you think would reduce the urban heat island effect? Possibilities include lighter-coloured surfaces for buildings, streets, and parking lots; more reflective roofs; and more trees, parks, and open space. With 60% of the global population predicted to live in cities by 2030 and with rising air and water temperatures from climate change, urban heat island issues will soon emerge as a critical concern. More information is available from the U.S. EPA, including strategies, publications, and hot-topic discussions, at http://www.epa.gov/hiri/.

GEOSYSTEMS CONNECTION

We have tracked the inputs of insolation, followed the cascade of energy through the atmosphere to Earth's surface, and saw the actions of movements and processes. We ended this journey from Sun to Earth analyzing the distribution of energy at the surface and the concepts of energy balance and net radiation available to do work. Now we shift to outputs in the Earth–atmosphere energy system in Chapters 5 and 6—the results and consequences of global temperature patterns, and wind and ocean current circulations driven by these flows of energy.

 APPLIED PHYSICAL GEOGRAPHY *Energy Balance Model*

Energy balance models attempt to account for all incoming and outgoing energy of Earth. In a simple global energy balance, the only variable is the temperature of Earth, signified T_e. The term "balance" suggests that the system is at equilibrium—no energy is accumulated or lost. See the Shodor Education Foundation web site for an energy balance computer model (http://www.shodor.org/).

This energy balance model can be described mathematically as follows:

$$\pi R_E^2 (1 - \alpha) H_0 = 4\pi R_E^2 \sigma T e^4$$

where R_e is the radius of the Earth, H_0 is the solar constant in $W\,m^{-2}$, α is the albedo or reflectivity of the planet, σ is the Stefan-Boltzmann constant ($5.6697 \times 10^{-8}\,W\,m^{-2}K^{-4}$), and T_e is the effective temperature of Earth (the temperature of the Earth as it appears from space).

The above model aims to calculate the effective temperature, T_e. We are interested in the temperature at the surface, or T_s, calculated by:

$$T_s = T_e + dT$$

where dT is the greenhouse increment. At this time, the greenhouse increment is about 33 K, and is a function of the efficiency of the infrared radiation absorption.

This would be fairly simple except that most energy balance models are zonal, not global, models. They focus on the energy balance for a chosen latitude. As such, an equation that accounts for the flow of energy from one latitudinal zone to the next must be used:

$$\frac{\text{Radiation}}{\text{energy in}} = \frac{\text{Radiation}}{\text{energy out}} + \frac{\text{transport into}}{\text{another zone}}$$

Model values of incoming energy from the Sun must account

for the spherical shape and orbital variations of the Earth. Because each zone usually has its own albedo, or reflectivity, each zone also has its own zonal surface temperature (including the greenhouse increment). The zonal model calculates total energy received from the Sun per unit time as given by:

$$\pi Re^2 H_0$$

where R_e is Earth's radius and H_0 is the solar constant.

Given that Earth's total area can be calculated by $4r^2$, the equation can be simplified to :

$$(1 - \alpha) H_0 = \sigma T e^4$$

Therefore, the average extraterrestrial solar flux over the entire surface can be calculated by $H_0/4$.

Because the amount of insolation varies from zone to zone (due to the variation of the incident angle of the Sun to a particular zone), a ratio, γ_i, can be used that corrects the average incoming radiation for a given zone. The incoming solar radiation for a given zone can be calculated as:

Incoming radiation $= \gamma_i H_0 / 4$.

Also, the surface albedo of each zone (α) must be considered. Remember that the albedo depends upon the type of landcover and the varying amounts of land and water on the surface. A critical temperature, T_c, exists below which the land becomes ice covered (typically $-10.0°$ C). If the surface temperature for a zone is below the critical temperature, the albedo for the zone is the albedo of ice, or 0.68. For temperatures above the critical temperature, several equations are used that vary with temperature—a typical equation is:

$$\begin{aligned} \text{albedo of} \\ \text{the zone} \end{aligned} = \begin{aligned} &(1 - \text{fractional cloud} \\ &\quad\text{cover for the zone}) \\ &+ (\text{fractional cloud} \\ &\quad\text{cover} \times \text{albedo of the} \\ &\quad\text{clouds}). \end{aligned}$$

Cloud albedo is typically specified as 0.5. Fractional cloud cover values are a typical input for a standard energy balance model. The transport of energy between zones is given by:

$$F_i = C(T_i - T_s)$$

where C is a constant equal to 3.80 W·m^{-2}·C, T_i is the average temperature of the zone, and T_s is the mean global surface temperature. There are more complicated methodologies, but this equation represents the basic parameters in an energy balance model.

Again, the purpose of the energy balance model is to calculate the temperature of the zone. A final equation for calculating temperatures is as follows:

$$T_i = \frac{[\gamma_i (H_0/4)(1 - \alpha_i) + CT_s - A + 5\varphi_i B]}{B + C}$$

where γ_i is the ratio correction for the zone to incoming radiation, H_0 is the solar constant, α_i is the surface albedo for the zone, C is the constant 3.8 W·m^{-2}·C^{-1}, T_s is the average surface temperature, A is a constant 204 W·m^{-2}, B is a constant 2.17 W·m^{-2}·C^{-1}, φ_i is the fractional cloud cover in each zone.

The equation is repeated for each zone to reach a global energy balance.

KEY LEARNING CONCEPTS REVIEW

■ ***Identify*** the processes acting on insolation as it passes through the atmosphere to Earth's surface, and ***describe*** the processes that transfer heat energy in a system.

Radiant energy from the Sun that cascades through complex circuits to the surface powers Earth's biosphere functions. Our budget of atmospheric energy comprises shortwave radiation *inputs* (ultraviolet light, visible light, and near-infrared wavelengths) and longwave radiation *outputs* (thermal infrared).

Transmission refers to the passage of shortwave and longwave energy through either the atmosphere or water. The gas molecules redirect some radiation, changing the direction of the radiation's movement *without altering its wavelengths.* This phenomenon is known as **scattering** and represents 7% of Earth's reflectivity, or albedo. Dust particles, pollutants, ice, cloud droplets, and water vapour produce further scattering. Some incoming insolation is diffused by clouds and atmosphere and is transmitted to Earth as **diffuse radiation**, the downward component of scattered light. The speed of insolation entering the atmosphere changes as it passes from one medium to another; the change of speed causes a bending action called **refraction**. **Mirage** is a refraction effect when an image appears near the horizon where light waves are refracted by layers of air at different temperatures (and consequently of different densities).

A portion of arriving energy bounces directly back into space without being converted into heat or performing any work. **Albedo** is the reflective quality (intrinsic brightness) of a surface; this returned energy is **reflection**. Albedo is an important control over the amount of insolation that is available for absorption by a surface. We state albedo as the percentage of insolation that is reflected. Earth and its atmosphere reflect 31% of all insolation when averaged over a year.

An increase in albedo and reflection of shortwave radiation caused by clouds is **cloud-albedo forcing**. Also, clouds can act as insulation, thus trapping longwave radiation and raising minimum temperatures. An increase in greenhouse warming caused by clouds is **cloud-greenhouse forcing**. **Global dimming** describes the decline in sunlight reaching Earth's surface owing to pollution, aerosols, and clouds, and may be masking the actual degree of global warming occurring.

Absorption is the assimilation of radiation by molecules of a substance and its conversion from one form to another—for example, visible light to infrared radiation. **Conduction** is the molecule-to-molecule transfer of energy as it diffuses through a substance.

Energy also is transferred in gases and liquids by **convection** (when the physical mixing involves a strong vertical motion) or **advection** (when the dominant motion is horizontal). In the atmosphere or bodies of water, warmer portions tend to rise (they are less dense) and cooler portions tend to sink (they are more dense), establishing patterns of convection.

transmission (p. 86)
scattering (p. 87)
diffuse radiation (p. 87)
refraction (p. 88)
mirage (p. 88)
reflection (p. 88)
albedo (p. 88)

cloud-albedo forcing (p. 89)
cloud-greenhouse forcing (p. 89)
global dimming (p. 89)
absorption (p. 91)
conduction (p. 91)
convection (p. 91)
advection (p. 91)

1. Diagram a simple energy balance for the troposphere. Label each shortwave and longwave component and the directional aspects of related flows.
2. What would you expect the sky colour to be at 50 km altitude? Why? What factors explain the lower atmosphere's blue colour?
3. Define refraction. How is it related to daylength? To a rainbow? To the timing of sunrise and sunset?
4. List several types of surfaces and their albedo values. Explain the differences among these surfaces. What determines the reflectivity of a surface?
5. Using Figure 4.5, explain the differences in albedo values for various surfaces. Based upon albedo alone, which surface is cooler? Which is warmer? Why do you think this is?
6. Define the concepts of transmission, absorption, diffuse radiation, conduction, and convection.

■ **Describe** what happens to insolation when clouds are in the atmosphere, and **analyze** the effect of clouds and air pollution on insolation received at ground level.

Clouds reflect *insolation*, thus cooling Earth's surface—*cloud-albedo forcing*. Yet clouds also act as insulation, thus trapping longwave radiation and raising minimum temperatures—*cloud-greenhouse forcing*. Clouds affect the heating of the lower atmosphere, depending on cloud type, height, and thickness (water content and density). Thin high-altitude, ice-crystal clouds reflect insolation with albedos of about 50% and redirect infrared to the surface, producing a net cloud-greenhouse forcing (warming); thick, lower cloud cover reflects about 90%, producing a net cloud-albedo forcing (cooling). Particulates and water vapour from aircraft exhaust produce **jet contrails,** or *condensation trails*, and can form high cirrus clouds, sometimes called *false cirrus clouds*.

Emissions of sulfur dioxide and the subsequent chemical reactions in the atmosphere form *sulfate aerosols*, which act either as insolation-reflecting haze in clear-sky conditions or as a stimulus to condensation in clouds that increases reflectivity.

jet contrails (p. 92)

7. What counterbalancing roles do clouds play in the Earth–atmosphere radiation balance? Is cloud type important? Compare high, thin cirrus clouds and lower, thick stratus clouds.
8. In what ways do jet contrails affect the Earth–atmosphere balance? Describe some recent scientific findings.
9. In what way does the presence of sulfate aerosols affect solar radiation received at ground level? How does it affect cloud formation?

■ **Review** the energy pathways in the Earth–atmosphere system, the greenhouse effect, and patterns of global net radiation.

The Earth–atmosphere energy system naturally balances itself in a steady-state equilibrium. It does so through energy transfers that are *nonradiative* (convection, conduction, and the latent heat of evaporation) and *radiative* (by longwave radiation between the surface, the atmosphere, and space).

Carbon dioxide, water vapour, methane, CFCs (chlorofluorocarbons), and other gases in the lower atmosphere absorb infrared radiation that is then emitted to Earth, thus delaying energy loss to space. This process is the **greenhouse effect**. In the atmosphere, longwave radiation is not actually trapped, as it would be in a greenhouse, but its passage to space is delayed (heat energy is detained in the atmosphere) through absorption and counterradiation.

In tropical latitudes, high insolation angle and consistent daylength cause more energy to be gained than lost annually, forming energy surpluses. In the polar regions, low insolation angles, highly reflective surfaces, and up to 6 months without insolation cause more energy to be lost annually, forming energy deficits. This imbalance of net radiation—tropical surpluses and polar deficits—drives a vast global circulation of both energy and mass.

Surface energy balances are used to summarise the energy expenditure for any location. Surface energy measurements are used as an analytical tool of **microclimatology**. Adding and subtracting the energy flux at the surface lets us calculate **net radiation (NET R)**, or the balance of all radiation at Earth's surface available to do work—shortwave (SW) and longwave (LW).

greenhouse effect (p. 92)
microclimatology (p. 96)
net radiation (NET R) (p. 96)

10. What are the similarities and differences between an actual greenhouse and the gaseous atmospheric greenhouse? Why is the magnitude of Earth's "greenhouse" changing?
11. In terms of energy expenditures for latent heat of evaporation, describe the annual pattern as mapped in Figure 4.19.
12. Generalise the pattern of global net radiation. How does this pattern drive the atmospheric weather system? (See Figures 4.17 and 4.18.)
13. In terms of surface energy balance, explain the term *net radiation* (NET R).
14. What are the expenditure pathways for surface net radiation? What kind of work is accomplished?
15. What is the role played by latent heat in surface energy budgets?
16. Compare the daily surface energy balances of El Mirage, California, and Pitt Meadows, British Columbia. Explain the differences.

■ **Plot** the daily radiation curves for Earth's surface, and **label** the key aspects of incoming radiation, air temperature, and the daily temperature lag.

The greatest daily insolation input occurs at the time of the summer solstice in the respective hemispheres. Air temperature responds to seasonal cycles and variations in insolation input. Within a 24-hour day, air temperature often peaks in the mid-afternoon and dips to its lowest value at or slightly after sunrise.

Peak air temperature lags behind each day's peak insolation. The warmest time of day occurs not at the moment of maximum insolation, but at that moment when a maximum of shortwave and longwave energy is received.

17. Why is there a temperature lag between the highest Sun altitude and the warmest time of day? Relate your answer to the insolation and temperature patterns during the day.

■ *Portray* typical urban heat island conditions, and *contrast* the microclimatology of urban areas with that of surrounding rural environments.

A growing percentage of Earth's population lives in cities and experiences a unique set of altered microclimatic effects: increased conduction, lower albedos, higher NET R values, increased water runoff, complex radiation and reflection patterns, anthropogenic heating, and the gases, dusts, and aerosols of urban pollution. Urban surfaces of metal, glass, asphalt, concrete, and stone conduct up to three times more energy than wet, sandy soil and thus are warmed, producing an **urban heat island**. Air pollution, including gases and aerosols, is greater in urban areas than in rural ones. Every major city produces its own **dust dome** of airborne pollution.

    urban heat island (p. 104)
    dust dome (p. 104)

18. What is the basis for the urban heat island concept? Describe the climatic effects attributable to urban as compared with nonurban environments.
19. Which of the items in Table 4.2 have you yourself experienced directly? Explain.
20. Assess the potential for solar energy applications in our society. What are some negatives of depending on solar energy? What are some positives?

Arctic Ocean sea-ice extent fell to 4.9 million km² in September 2010. This is 2.14 million km² below the long-term 1979–2000 average. The record minimum occurred during September 2007. Both the Northwest and Northeast Passages were declared open in 2010. Surface energy budgets for these changing landscapes is an important topic for physical geography. [NSIDC image.]

MyGeosciencePlace

Visit **www.mygeoscienceplace.ca** for several figure animations, satellite loops, self-study quizzes, flashcards, interactive glossary, career links, RSS feeds, Pearson eText of *Geosystems,* and much more.

CHAPTER 5

Global Temperatures

Global temperature change is affecting the wild sheep abandoned on this Scottish Isle Hirta of St. Kilda. Stone cleits sheltered the residents of Hirta for thousands of years. Note more rock structures along the hillside in the background. [Bobbé Christopherson.]

KEY LEARNING CONCEPTS

After reading the chapter, you should be able to:

- **Define** the concepts of temperature, kinetic energy, and sensible heat, and **distinguish** among the Kelvin, Celsius, and Fahrenheit temperature scales and how they are measured.

- **List** and **review** the principal controls and influences that produce global temperature patterns.

- **Review** the factors that produce different marine effects and continental effects as they influence temperatures, and **utilise** several pairs of cities to illustrate these differences.

- **Interpret** the pattern of Earth's temperatures from the portrayal of January and July temperature maps and a map of annual temperature ranges.

- **Describe** the human body's response to wind (wind chill) and heat and humidity (Humidex).

Temperature Change Affects St. Kilda's Sheep

On the windswept island of Hirta in Scotland's Outer Hebrides, global temperature change is affecting ecosystems. The wild Soay sheep have shrunk in body size over the past quarter century, a trend that has puzzled scientists. Now, however, the explanation appears clearly linked to milder winters and longer summers associated with recent climate change.

Some 180 km west of the Scottish mainland, the St. Kilda Archipelago comprises three islands—Hirta, Soay, and Dun—centered at 57° 48' N latitude (Figure GN 5.1). Climate conditions are moderate for the latitude because of warm ocean currents from the Gulf Stream (see Figure 5.10). The marine west coast climate is similar to that of Ireland and Britain, but with a cooler summer. January average temperatures are 5.6°C, with July rising to an average of 11.8°C. Snow is a rare occurrence. Monthly precipitation is distributed evenly, an average year receiving 1400 mm. Domestic sheep were introduced to these islands about 2000 years ago and evolved in isolation as a small, primitive breed now known as Soay sheep.

St. Kilda's principal island, Hirta, was continuously occupied over the last 3000 to 4000 years. The people of Hirta lived simply and stored food in sod-roofed stone shelters known as *cleits*. More traditional walled houses of stone did not appear until the nineteenth century. In 1930, the last 30 residents of Hirta were evacuated as their small society failed, and the Soay sheep remained, unmanaged to this day (Figure GN 5.2).

Hirta's sheep provide scientists an ideal opportunity to study an isolated population with no significant competitors or predators. According to evolutionary theory, wild sheep such as the Soay should gradually increase in size over many generations because larger, stronger sheep are more likely to survive winter and reproduce in the spring. This trend follows the principle of natural selection. Remarkably, scientists are seeing the opposite trend as global temperature change affects these sheep.

Present climate change is extending the summer season as spring conditions come a few weeks earlier and fall conditions start a few weeks later across the globe. Also, winters are milder and shorter in length. Scientists began studying the impact of changing climatic conditions on Hirta's wild Soay sheep in 1985 and published their results in 2009. Surprisingly, scientists found that these sheep were not getting larger in size and that evolutionary concepts of adaptive evolution could not explain what was happening.

Since 1985, female Soay sheep of all ages dropped 5% in body mass, with leg length and body weight decreasing.

FIGURE GN 5.2 Wild Soay sheep on Hirta Island.
[Bobbé Christopherson.]

In addition, lambs are not growing as quickly. Scientists found that females are giving birth at younger ages. These sheep can only physically produce offspring that are smaller in size than they were at birth. This "young mum effect" explains why sheep size is not increasing. But why then are sheep shrinking? The explanation ties to warming temperatures. Longer summers increase the availability of grass feed, and milder winters mean that lambs do not need to put on as much weight in their first months, allowing even slower-growing individuals to survive. Smaller lambs that previously would not survive winter are surviving; thus, smaller individuals are becoming more common in the population.

This study indicates that local factors, such as temperature change, can cause rapid *phenotypic change* as a species' genetic makeup interacts with the environment. Such factors can override the pressures of natural selection and evolution. For Chapter 5 and our discussion of global temperatures, we must keep in mind the interconnections among all life and Earth's physical systems as global temperatures increase.

FIGURE GN 5.1 St. Kilda Archipelago, Scotland.

What is the temperature now—both indoors and outdoors—as you read these words? How is it measured, and what does the value mean? How is air temperature influencing your plans for the day? Our bodies subjectively sense temperature, judge comfort, and react to changing temperature. Air temperature plays a remarkable role in our lives, both at the micro level and at the macro and global levels.

Global temperatures have risen an average of 0.17 C° per decade since 1970, and this rate is accelerating. In Figure 5.1, surface temperature anomalies by decade are compared to the standard 1951–1980 base period in the record. Ice-core data and other proxy measures (data that provide an indication of past temperatures when no measurements were recorded) indicate that present temperatures are higher than at any time during the past 125 000 years. This warming trend in air temperature is the subject of much scientific, geographic, and political action.

Temperatures of global land, air, and water set records in 2010. This trend is in response to carbon dioxide concentrations, which have been increasing at 3.0% per year since 2000. As mentioned in Chapter 3, present CO_2 levels in the atmosphere are higher than at any time in the past 800 000 years.

In this chapter: Temperature affects societies, decision making, and resources consumed across the globe. Understanding temperature concepts helps us continue our study of related Earth energy, weather, and climate systems. We look at the principal temperature controls of latitude, altitude and elevation, cloud cover, and land-water heating differences that interact to produce Earth's temperature patterns. We end by examining the effect of temperature on the human body and discussing current temperature trends associated with global warming.

Temperature Concepts and Measurement

Heat and temperature are not the same. *Heat* is a form of energy that flows from one system or object to another because the two are at different temperatures. **Temperature** is a measure of the average kinetic energy (motion) of individual molecules in matter. We feel the effect of temperature as the *sensible heat* transfer from warmer objects to cooler objects. For instance, when you jump into a cool lake, you can sense the heat transfer from your skin to the water as kinetic energy leaves your body and flows to the water.

Temperature and heat are related because changes in temperature are caused by the absorption or emission (gain or loss) of heat energy. The term *heat energy* is frequently used to describe energy that is added to or removed from a system or substance.

Temperature Scales

The temperature at which atomic and molecular motion in matter completely stops is *absolute zero*, "0° absolute temperature." Its value on the different temperature-measuring scales is −273° Celsius (C), −459.4° Fahrenheit (F), and 0 Kelvin (K). Figure 5.2 compares these three scales. On the Kelvin scale, intervals are called kelvins, not degrees, although 1 kelvin is equivalent to 1 C°. Formulas for converting between metric (or SI, Système International), and Imperial units are in Appendix C.

The Fahrenheit scale places the melting point of ice at 32°F, with 180 subdivisions to the boiling point of water at 212°F. The scale is named for its developer Daniel G. Fahrenheit, a German physicist (1686–1736). Note that there is only one melting point for ice, but there are many freezing points for water depending on its purity, volume, and certain conditions in the atmosphere—freezing points for

FIGURE 5.1 Surface temperature anomalies by decade. Increasing temperature patterns are apparent in this decadal look at temperature anomalies for the past four decades, as compared to the 1951–1980 baseline. [GISS/NASA.]

FIGURE 5.3 Instrument shelter.
(a) This standard thermistor shelter is white (for high albedo) and louvered (for ventilation). (b) The Stephenson Screen, a louvered wooden box that houses a minimum and maximum thermometer or a wet bulb thermometer apparatus, provides protection from direct insolation. [(a) Bobbé Christopherson. (b) Dick Hemingway.]

(a)

(b)

is the sum of daily mean temperatures for the month divided by the number of days in the month. An *annual temperature range* expresses the difference between the lowest and highest monthly mean temperatures for a given year. *Climate normals* are 30 year averages used to summarise or describe the average climatic conditions of a particular location. Environment Canada calculates normals at the completion of each decade and uses as many climate characteristics and locations as possible.

Principal Temperature Controls

The interaction of complex physical controls produces Earth's temperature patterns. These principal influences upon temperatures include latitude, altitude and elevation, cloud cover, and land–water heating differences.

Latitude

Insolation is the single most important influence on temperature variations. Figure 2.9 shows how insolation intensity decreases as one moves away from the subsolar point—a point that migrates annually between the Tropic of Cancer

and Tropic of Capricorn (between 23.5° N and 23.5° S). In addition, daylength and Sun angle change throughout the year, increasing seasonal effect with increasing latitude. The five cities graphed in Figure 5.4 demonstrate the effects of latitudinal position on temperature. From equator to poles, Earth ranges from continually warm, to seasonally variable, to continually cold.

Altitude/Elevation

Within the troposphere, temperatures decrease with increasing altitude above Earth's surface. (Recall that the *normal lapse rate* of temperature change with altitude is 6.4 C° per 1000 m; see Figure 3.5.) The density of the atmosphere diminishes with increasing altitude. In fact, the density of the atmosphere at an elevation of 5500 m is about half that at sea level. As the atmosphere thins, there is a loss in its ability to absorb and radiate sensible heat. Thus, worldwide, mountainous areas experience lower temperatures than do regions nearer sea level, even at similar latitudes.

The consequences are that, at high elevations, average air temperatures are lower, nighttime cooling is greater, and the temperature range between day and night is greater than at low elevations. The temperature difference

 GEO REPORT 5.2 *Referring to Heights above Sea Level*

Altitude and elevation are different. Note that *altitude* refers to airborne objects or heights above Earth's surface, whereas elevation usually refers to the height of a point on Earth's surface. Both altitude and elevation are measured in relation to some plane of reference or elevation datum. For example, we ask "The jet flew at what altitude?" and, "The ski resort is at what elevation?"

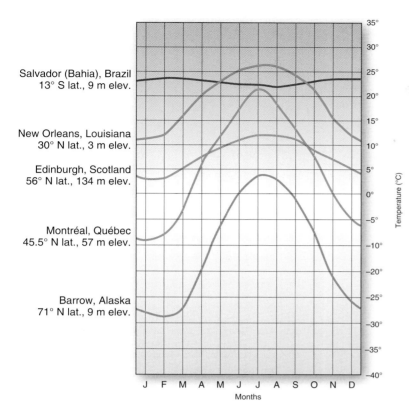

Salvador (Bahia), Brazil
13° S lat., 9 m elev.

New Orleans, Louisiana
30° N lat., 3 m elev.

Edinburgh, Scotland
56° N lat., 134 m elev.

Montréal, Québec
45.5° N lat., 57 m elev.

Barrow, Alaska
71° N lat., 9 m elev.

Located on maps in: Figure 1.14
Figure 4.17 – net radiation
Figure 4.19 – latent heat
Figure 4.20 – sensible heat

FIGURE 5.4 **Latitude affects temperatures.**
A comparison of five cities from near the equator to
north of the Arctic Circle demonstrates changing seasonality and increasing differences between average
minimum and maximum temperatures as one moves
to higher latitudes.

between areas of sunlight and shadow is greater than at sea level. You may have felt temperatures decrease noticeably in the shadows and shortly after sunset in the mountains. Surfaces both gain energy rapidly and lose energy rapidly to the thinner atmosphere.

The snowline seen in mountain areas indicates where snowfall accumulation exceeds the amount of snow lost through melting, evaporation, and sublimation. The snowline's location is a function both of elevation and latitude. Permanent ice fields and glaciers exist on equatorial mountain summits in the Andes and East Africa. In equatorial mountains, the snowline occurs at approximately 5000 m. With increasing latitude, snowlines gradually lower in elevation from 2700 m in the midlatitudes to lower than 900 m in southern Greenland.

Two cities in Bolivia illustrate the combined effects of the two temperature controls, latitude and elevation. Figure 5.5 displays temperature data for the cities of Concepción and La Paz, which are near the same latitude (about 16° S). Note the elevation, average annual temperature, and precipitation for each location noted on the figure.

The hot, humid climate of Concepción at its much lower elevation stands in marked contrast to the cool, dry climate of highland La Paz. People living around La Paz are able to grow wheat, barley, and potatoes—crops characteristic of the cooler midlatitudes—despite the fact that La Paz is 4103 m above sea level (Figure 5.6). (For comparison, the summit of Mount Logan in Yukon Territory is 5959 m, Fairweather Mountain in British Columbia is 4663 m and Pikes Peak in Colorado is 4301 m.)

The combination of elevation and low-latitude location guarantees La Paz nearly constant daylength and moderate temperatures, averaging about 9°C every month. Such moderate temperature and moisture conditions lead to the formation of more fertile soils than those found in the warmer, wetter climate of Concepción, with an annual average temperature of 24°C .

Cloud Cover

Orbiting satellites reveal that approximately 50% of Earth is cloud covered at any given moment. Clouds moderate temperature, and their effect varies with cloud type, height, and density. Cloud moisture reflects, absorbs, and liberates large amounts of energy released upon condensation and cloud formation.

At night, clouds act as insulation and radiate longwave energy, preventing rapid energy loss. During the day, clouds reflect insolation as a result of their high albedo values. In general, clouds lower daily maximum temperatures and raise nighttime minimum temperatures. In the previous chapter, Figures 4.6 and 4.9 portrayed cloud-albedo forcing and cloud-greenhouse forcing as they relate to the presence of clouds and cloud types. Clouds also reduce latitudinal and seasonal temperature differences.

Cloud cover is the most variable factor influencing Earth's radiation budget, making it the subject of much simulation in computer models of atmospheric behaviour. The International Satellite Cloud Climatology Project (http://isccp.giss.nasa.gov/), part of the World Climate Research Programme, is presently in the midst of such

FIGURE 5.5 **Effects of latitude and temperature.**
Comparison of temperature patterns in two Bolivian cities.

Station	Concepción, Bolivia	La Paz, Bolivia
Latitude/longitude	16° 15′ S 62° 03′ W	16° 30′ S 68° 10′ W
Elevation	490 m	4103 m
Avg. ann. temperature	23°C	11°C
Ann. temperature range	6.5 C°	3.5 C°
Ann. precipitation	1212 mm	555 mm
Population	10 000	810 300 (Administrative division 1.6 million)

research. Clouds and the Earth Radiant Energy System (CERES, http://ceres.larc.nasa.gov/) sensors aboard the *TRMM*, *Terra*, and *Aqua* satellites are collecting data to assess cloud effects on longwave, shortwave, and net radiation patterns as never before possible.

FIGURE 5.6 **High-elevation farming.**
People in these high-elevation villages grow potatoes and wheat in view of the permanent ice-covered peaks of the Andes Mountains. The combination of low latitude and high elevation creates consistent, moderate temperatures throughout the year, averaging about +9°C. [Seux Paule/age fotostock.]

Land–Water Heating Differences

Another major control on temperature is the different ways in which land and water respond to insolation. Earth presents these two surfaces in an irregular arrangement of continents and oceans. Each absorbs and stores energy differently than the other and therefore contributes to the global pattern of temperature. Water bodies tend to produce moderate temperature patterns, whereas inland in continental interiors more extreme temperatures occur.

The physical nature of land (rock and soil) and water (oceans, seas, and lakes) is the reason for **land–water heating differences**—land heats and cools faster than water. Figure 5.7 visually summarises the following discussion of the land–water temperature controls: evaporation, transparency, specific heat, movement and ocean currents, and sea-surface temperatures.

Evaporation An estimated 84% of all evaporation on Earth is from the oceans. When water evaporates and thus changes to water vapour, heat energy is absorbed in the process and is stored in the water vapour as latent heat. We saw this process in the map of energy expended for the latent heat of evaporation in Figure 4.19.

You may experience this evaporative heat loss (cooling) by wetting the back of your hand and then blowing on the moist skin. Sensible heat energy is drawn from your

CONTINENTAL
Temperature conditions more extreme—land warms and cools rapidly

Insolation

MARINE
Temperature conditions more moderate—water warms and cools slowly

Insolation

Less evaporation (lower latent heat loss)

Surface is **opaque**

Land has a **lower specific heat**

Land has **no mixing** between layers

Land

Greater evaporaton (higher latent heat loss)

Surface is **transparent**

Water has a **higher specific heat**

Water has **mobility** and mixes in vast ocean currents

Ocean

FIGURE 5.7 Land–water heating differences. The differential heating of land and water produces contrasting marine (more moderate) and continental (more extreme) temperature regimes.

skin to supply some of the energy for evaporation, and you feel the cooling. As surface water evaporates, it absorbs substantial energy from the immediate environment, resulting in a lowering of the temperature. Temperatures over land are not as moderated by evaporative cooling as are marine locations.

Transparency The transmission of light differs between soil and water: Solid ground is opaque, water is transparent. Consequently, a greater proportion of insolation striking a soil surface does not penetrate but is absorbed, heating the ground surface. That energy is accumulated during times of exposure and is rapidly lost at night or in shadows.

Figure 5.8 shows the profile of diurnal (daily) temperatures for a column of soil and the atmosphere above it at a midlatitude location. You can see that maximum and minimum temperatures generally are experienced right at ground level. Below the surface, even at shallow depths, temperatures remain about the same throughout the day. You encounter this at a beach, where surface sand may be painfully hot to your feet, but as you dig in your toes and feel the sand a few centimetres below the surface, it is cooler, offering relief.

In contrast, when light reaches a body of water, it penetrates the surface because of water's **transparency**—water is clear and light transmits through it to an average

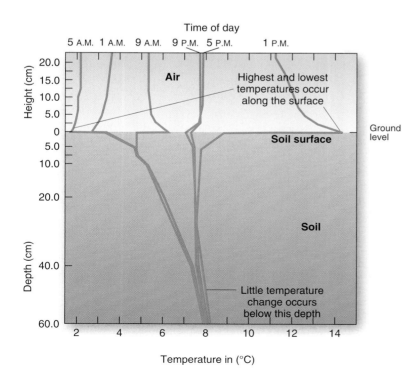

Time of day

5 A.M. 1 A.M. 9 A.M. 9 P.M. 5 P.M. 1 P.M.

Height (cm)

Air

Highest and lowest temperatures occur along the surface

Ground level

Soil surface

Depth (cm)

Soil

Little temperature change occurs below this depth

Temperature in (°C)

FIGURE 5.8 Land is opaque. Profile measurements of air and soil temperatures in Seabrook, New Jersey. Note that little temperature change occurs throughout the year at depth, whereas daily extremes of temperature register along the surface, where insolation is absorbed. [Adapted by permission from John R. Mather, *Climatology: Fundamentals and Applications* (New York: McGraw-Hill, 1974, p. 36).]

FIGURE 5.9 Ocean is transparent.
The transparency of the ocean permits insolation to penetrate to greater depths than on land, increasing the volume of water that absorbs energy. Sunlight empowers myriad forms of life covering the substrate, including a sea urchin. [Bobbé Christopherson]

depth of 60 m in the ocean (Figure 5.9). This illuminated zone is the *photic layer* and has been recorded in some ocean waters to depths of 300 m. This characteristic of water results in the distribution of available heat energy over a much greater depth and volume, forming a larger energy reservoir than that of land surfaces.

Specific Heat When comparing equal volumes of water and land, water requires far more energy to increase its temperature than does land. In other words, *water can hold more heat than can soil or rock*, and therefore water is said to have a higher **specific heat**, the heat capacity of a substance. On average, the specific heat of water is about four times that of soil. A given volume of water represents a more substantial energy reservoir than an equal volume of soil or rock and therefore takes longer to heat and cool. For this reason, day-to-day temperatures near a substantial body of water tend to be moderated.

Movement Land is a rigid, solid material, whereas water is a fluid and is capable of movement. Differing temperatures result in a mixing of cooler and warmer waters, and that mixing spreads the available energy over an even greater volume than if the water were still. Surface water and deeper waters mix, redistributing energy. Both ocean and land surfaces radiate longwave radiation at night, but land loses its energy more rapidly than does the greater mass of the moving oceanic energy reservoir.

Ocean Currents and Sea-Surface Temperatures
The **Gulf Stream** moves northeastward off the east coast of North America, carrying warm water far into the

North Atlantic (Figure 5.10). As a result, the southern third of Iceland experiences much milder temperatures than would be expected for a latitude of 65° N, just south of the Arctic Circle (66.5° N). In Reykjavik, on the southwest coast of Iceland, monthly temperatures average above freezing during all months of the year. Similarly, the Gulf Stream moderates temperatures in coastal Scandinavia and northwestern Europe. In the Pacific Ocean, the Kuroshio, or Japan Current, functions much the same as the Gulf Stream, having a warming effect on Japan, the Aleutian Islands, and the northwestern margin of North America.

Across the globe, ocean water is rarely found warmer than 31°C, although Hurricanes Katrina, Rita, and Wilma intensified as they moved over 33.3°C sea-surface temperatures in the Gulf of Mexico. In contrast, along mid-latitude and subtropical west coasts, cool ocean currents flowing toward the equator influence air temperatures. When conditions in these regions are warm and moist, fog frequently forms in the chilled air over the cooler currents. Chapter 6 discusses ocean currents.

Higher ocean temperatures produce higher evaporation rates and more energy is lost from the ocean as latent heat. As the water vapour content of the overlying air mass increases, the ability of the air to absorb longwave radiation also increases. Therefore, the air mass becomes warmer. The warmer the air and the ocean become, the more evaporation occurs, increasing the amount of water vapour entering the air mass. More water vapour leads to cloud

FIGURE 5.10 **The Gulf Stream.**
Satellite instruments sensitive to thermal infrared wavelengths imaged the Gulf Stream. Temperature differences are noted by computer-enhanced false colours: reds/oranges = 25°–29°C, yellows/greens = 17°–24°C; blues = 10°–16°C; and purples = 2°–9°C. [Imagery by RSMAS, University of Miami.]

formation, which reflects insolation and produces lower temperatures. Lower temperatures of air and ocean reduce evaporation rates and the ability of the air mass to absorb water vapour—an interesting *negative feedback* mechanism.

The Physical Oceanography Distributed Active Archive Center (PODAAC, http://podaac.jpl.nasa.gov/) is responsible for storage and distribution of data relevant to the physical state of the ocean. Sea-level height, currents, and ocean temperatures are measured as part of the effort to understand oceans and climate interactions.

Sea-surface temperature (SST) satellite data correlate well with actual sea-surface measurements. Figure 5.11 displays SST data for January 2010 and July 2009 from satellites in the NOAA/NASA Pathfinder AVHRR program. The Western Pacific Warm Pool is the deep red colour in the southwestern Pacific Ocean, with temperatures above 30°C. This region has the highest average ocean temperatures in the world. Note the seasonal change in ocean temperatures and the cool currents off the west coasts of North and South America, Europe, and Africa.

Mean annual SSTs increased steadily from 1982 through 2010 to record-high levels—with 2010 breaking records for both ocean and land temperatures. Increasing warmth is measured at depths to 1000 m, and even slight increases were found in the temperature of deep bottom water as reported in 2004. Scientists suggest that the ocean's ability to absorb excess heat energy from the atmosphere may be nearing its capacity.

Summary of Marine Effects versus Continental Effects As noted, Figure 5.7 summarises the operation of the land–water temperature controls presented: evaporation, transparency, specific heat, movement, ocean currents, and sea-surface temperatures. The term **marine effect**, or *maritime*, describes locations that exhibit the moderating influences of the ocean, usually along coastlines or on islands. **Continental effect**, a condition of *continentality*, refers to areas less affected by the sea and therefore having a greater range between maximum and minimum temperatures on both a daily and yearly basis.

Vancouver, British Columbia, and Winnipeg, Manitoba, exemplify marine and continental conditions (Figure 5.12). Both cities have similar latitudes, about 49° N and 50° N, respectively. However, Vancouver has

Global Sea-surface Temperatures

(a) January 23, 2010

ICE (°C) 4   10   15   21   27   32

(b) July 23, 2009

FIGURE 5.11 Sea-surface temperatures.
Average annual sea-surface temperatures for (a) January 23, 2010, and (b) July 23, 2009. [Satellite data courtesy of Space Science and Engineering Center, University of Wisconsin, Madison.]

FIGURE 5.12 Cities in maritime and continental locations—Canada.
Comparison of temperatures in coastal Vancouver, British Columbia, and continental Winnipeg, Manitoba. Note that the freezing levels on the two graphs are positioned differently to accommodate the contrasting data. [Vancouver waterfront photo by Robert Christopherson; Winnipeg photo by Eastcott-Momatiuk/The Image Works.]

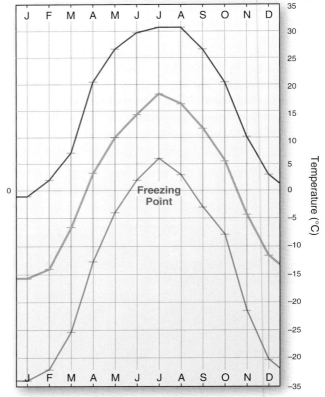

Station: Vancouver, British Columbia
Lat/long: 49°11′ N 123°10′ W
Avg. ann. temp.: 10 °C
Total ann. precip.: 1048 mm
Elevation: sea level
Population: 520 000
Ann. temp. range: 16 C

Station: Winnipeg, Manitoba
Lat/long: 49°54′ N 97°14′ W
Avg. ann. temp.: 2 °C
Total ann. precip.: 517 mm
Elevation: 248 m
Population: 620 000
Ann. temp. range: 38 °C

a more moderate pattern of average maximum and minimum temperatures. Vancouver's annual range of 16.0 C° is far less than Winnipeg's 38.0 C° range. In fact, Winnipeg's continental temperature pattern is more extreme in every aspect than that of maritime Vancouver.

Earth's Temperature Patterns

Let us now look at maps of mean air temperatures worldwide and for the polar regions for January (Figures 5.13 and 5.14) and July (Figures 5.16 and 5.17). To complete the analysis, Figure 5.18 presents the temperature range differences between the January and July maps, or the difference between averages of the coolest and warmest months.

Maps are for January and July instead of the solstice months of December and June because a lag occurs between insolation received and maximum or minimum

temperatures experienced, as explained earlier in Chapter 4. The U.S. National Climate Data Center provided the data for these maps. Some ship reports go back to 1850 and land reports to 1890, although the bulk of the record is representative of conditions since 1950.

The lines on temperature maps are known as *isotherms*. An **isotherm** is an isoline—a line along which there is a constant value—that connects points of equal temperature and portrays the temperature pattern, just as a contour line on a topographic map illustrates points of equal elevation. Isotherms help with the spatial analysis of temperatures.

January Temperature Maps

Figure 5.13 maps January's mean temperatures for the world. In the Southern Hemisphere, the higher Sun altitude causes longer days and summer weather conditions; in the Northern Hemisphere, the lower Sun angle

Global Surface Temperatures, Land and Ocean

FIGURE 5.13 Global mean temperatures for January.
Temperatures in Celsius are taken from separate air-temperature databases for ocean and land. Note the inset map of North America and the equatorward-trending isotherms in the interior. Compare with Figure 5.16. [Adapted by author and redrawn from National Climatic Data Center, *Monthly Climatic Data for the World*, 47 (January 1994), and WMO and NOAA.]

CRITICAL THINKING 5.1

Begin a Record and Physical Geography Profile

With each temperature map (Figures 5.13, 5.16, and 5.18), begin by finding where you live and noting the temperatures indicated by the isotherms for January and July and the annual temperature range. Record the information from these maps in your notebook. Remember that the small scale of these maps permits only generalizations about actual temperatures at specific sites, allowing you to make only a rough approximation for your location.

As you work through the different maps throughout this text, note atmospheric pressure and winds, annual precipitation, climate type, landforms, soil orders, vegetation, and terrestrial biomes. Add this information to your profile in your notebook. By the end of the course, you will have a complete physical geography profile for your regional environment.

causes the short days of winter. Isotherms generally are zonal, trending east–west, parallel to the equator, and are deflected by the presence of landmasses. Isotherms mark the general decrease in insolation and net radiation with distance from the equator.

The **thermal equator** is an isotherm connecting all points of highest mean temperature, roughly 27°C; it trends southward into the interior of South America and Africa, indicating higher temperatures over landmasses. In the Northern Hemisphere, isotherms shift equatorward as cold air chills the continental interiors. The oceans, in contrast, are more moderate, with warmer conditions extending farther north than over land at comparable latitudes.

As an example in Figure 5.13, follow along 50° N latitude and compare isotherms: 3° to 6°C in the North Pacific and 3° to 9°C in the North Atlantic, as contrasted to −18°C in the interior of North America and −24°C to −30°C in central Asia. Also, note the orientation of isotherms over areas with mountain ranges and how they illustrate the cooling effects of elevation. Check the Andes in South America as an example of these elevation effects.

The north and south polar regions (Figure 5.14a and b) are featured on two maps. Remember: the north polar region is an ocean surrounded by land, in contrast to the south polar region, which is the Antarctic continent surrounded by ocean. On the northern map (Figure 5.14a), the island of Greenland has a summit elevation of 3240 m on Earth's second-largest ice sheet, the highest elevation north of the Arctic Circle. Two-thirds of Greenland lies north of the Arctic Circle and its north shore is only 800 km from the North Pole. This combination of high latitude and interior high elevation on the ice sheet produces extremely cold midwinter temperatures.

In Antarctica (Figure 5.14b), it is "summer" in December and January. This is Earth's coldest and highest average elevation landmass. January average temperatures for the three scientific bases noted on the map: McMurdo Station, at the coast on Ross Island, averages −3°C; the Admundsen-Scott Station at the South Pole (elevation 2835 m) averages −28°C; and the Russian Vostok Station at its more continental location (elevation 3420 m) averages −32°C.

January

(a)

(b)

0   1000 Kilometres

0   500 Kilometres

FIGURE 5.14 January mean temperatures for polar regions.
January temperatures in (a) north polar region and (b) south polar region. Note that each map is at a different scale. [Author-prepared maps using same sources as Figure 5.13.]

The coldest continental region other than Antarctica is Russia—and specifically, northeastern Siberia. The intense cold results from winter conditions of consistently clear, dry, calm air; small insolation input; and an inland location far from moderating maritime effects. Verkhoyansk, Russia (located within the −48°C isotherm on the map), actually recorded a minimum temperature of −68°C and experiences a daily average of −50.5°C for January. Verkhoyansk (Figure 5.15) averages 7 months of temperatures below freezing, including at least 4 months below −34°C.

In contrast, Verkhoyansk experienced a maximum temperature of +37°C in July—an incredible 105 C° minimum–maximum range! People do live and work in Verkhoyansk, which has a population of 1400; the town has been occupied continuously since 1638 and today is a secondary mining district.

Trondheim, Norway, is near the latitude of Verkhoyansk and at a similar elevation. But Trondheim's coastal location moderates its annual temperature regime (Figure 5.15). January minimum and maximum temperatures range between −17°C and +8°C, and the minimum–maximum range for July is from 5°C to +27°C. The lowest minimum and highest maximum temperatures ever recorded in Trondheim are −30°C and +35°C—quite a difference from the extremes at Verkhoyansk.

July Temperature Maps

Average July temperatures are presented in Figure 5.16 for the world. The longer days of summer and higher Sun altitude are in the Northern Hemisphere. Winter dominates the Southern Hemisphere, although it is milder than winters north of the equator because continental landmasses are smaller and the dominant oceans and seas store and release more energy. The *thermal equator* shifts northward with the high summer Sun and reaches the Persian Gulf–Pakistan–Iran area. The Persian Gulf is the site of the highest recorded sea-surface temperature of 36°C, difficult to imagine for a large water body.

During July in the Northern Hemisphere, isotherms shift poleward over land, as higher temperatures dominate continental interiors. July temperatures in Verkhoyansk average more than +13°C, which represents a 63 C° seasonal range between winter and summer averages. The Verkhoyansk region of Siberia is Earth's most dramatic example of temperature continentality.

The hottest places on Earth occur in Northern Hemisphere deserts during July. The reasons are simple: clear skies, strong surface heating, virtually no surface water, and few plants. Prime examples are portions of the Sonoran Desert of North America and the Sahara of Africa. The most extreme shade temperature ever recorded, 58°C, occurred on September 13, 1922, at Al 'Azi-zi-yah, Libya.

The highest maximum and annual average temperatures in North America occurred in Death Valley, California, where the Greenland Ranch Station reached 57° C in 1913. The station is at 37° N and is at −54.3 m, below sea level. Chapter 15 discusses such hot, arid lands.

The north and south polar regions (Figure 5.17a and b) are featured on two maps. July is "summer" in the Arctic Ocean (Figure 5.17a) and brings a thinning of multiyear and seasonal pack ice. See the Midnight Sun photo in Figure 2.16b to see what continuous daylight is like. Open cracks and leads stretched all the way to the North Pole over the past several years.

In July, nights in Antarctica are 24 hours long. This lack of insolation contributed to the lowest natural temperature reported on Earth, a frigid −89.2°C recorded on July 21, 1983, at the Russian Vostok Station (noted on Figure 5.17b). Such a temperature is 11°C colder than the freezing point of dry ice (solid carbon dioxide)! If the concentration of carbon dioxide were large enough, such a cold temperature would theoretically freeze tiny carbon dioxide dry-ice particles out of the sky.

The average July temperature around Vostok is −68°C. For average temperature comparisons, the Admundsen–Scott Station at the South Pole experiences −60°C, and McMurdo Station has a −26°C reading. Note that the coldest temperatures in Antarctica are usually in August, not July, just before the equinox sunrise in September at the end of the long polar night.

Annual Temperature Range Map

The temperature range map helps identify areas that experience the greatest annual extremes and, in contrast, the most moderate temperature regimes, as demonstrated in Figure 5.18. As you might expect, the largest temperature ranges occur in subpolar locations within the continental interiors of North America and Asia, where average ranges of 64 C° are recorded. The Southern Hemisphere, in contrast, has little seasonal variation in mean temperatures, owing to the lack of large landmasses and the vast expanses of water to moderate temperature extremes.

Southern Hemisphere temperature patterns are generally maritime and Northern Hemisphere patterns feature continentality; although interior regions in the Southern Hemisphere experience some continentality

GEO REPORT 5.3 *Polar Regions Show Greatest Warming*

Climate change is affecting the higher latitudes at a pace exceeding the middle and lower latitudes. Since 1978, warming has increased in the Arctic region to a rate of 1.2 C° per decade, which means warming over the last 20 years was nearly seven times the rate of the last 100 years. Since 1970, nearly 60% of the Arctic sea ice has disappeared in response to increasing air and ocean temperatures, with record low levels of ice from 2007 through 2010. Similar warming trends are impacting the Antarctic Peninsula and the West Antarctic Ice Sheet, as ice shelves collapse and retreat along the coast (http://nsidc.org/).

Maximum average temperature

Mean monthly temperature

Minimum average temperature

Freezing Point

Temperature (°C)

Temperature (°C)

Station: Trondheim, Norway   **Elevation:** 115 m
Lat/long: 63° 25′ N 10° 27′ E   **Population:** 139 000
Avg. ann. temp.: 5°C   **Ann. temp. range:**
Total ann. precip.: 857 mm   17 C°

Station: Verkhoyansk, Russia   **Elevation:** 107 m
Lat/long: 67° 33′ N 133° 24′ E   **Population:** 1400
Avg. ann. temp.: −15°C   **Ann. temp. range:**
Total ann. precip.: 155 mm   63 C°

FIGURE 5.15 Cities in maritime and continental locations—Eurasia.
Compare temperatures in coastal Trondheim, Norway, and continental Siberian Russia. Note that the freezing levels on the two graphs are positioned differently to accommodate the contrasting data. [Coastal Norway by Bobbé Christopherson; Verkhoyansk photo by Bryan and Cherry Alexander/Arcticphoto.]

Global Surface
Temperatures,
Land and Ocean

FIGURE 5.16 **Global mean temperatures for July.**
Temperatures in Celsius are taken from separate air-temperature data-
bases for ocean and land. Note the inset map of North America and the
poleward-trending isotherms in the interior. Compare with
Figure 5.13. [Adapted by author and redrawn from National Climatic Data
Center, *Monthly Climatic Data for the World*, 47 (July 1994), and
WMO and NOAA.]

effects. For example, in January (Figure 5.13), Australia
is dominated by isotherms of 20°–30°C , whereas in July
(Figure 5.16), Australia is crossed by the 12°C isotherm.
The Northern Hemisphere, with greater land area overall, registers a slightly higher average surface temperature
than does the Southern Hemisphere.

Imagine living in some of these regions and think
of the degree to which you would need to adjust your
personal wardrobe and make other comfort adaptations. See Focus Study 5.1 for more on air temperature and the human body. Summer heat-wave deaths
remain a powerful reminder of the role of temperatures
in our lives.

II CRITICAL THINKING 5.2

What's Your Temperature Comfort Level?

Have you ever experienced discomfort from low-temperature
or high-temperature stress? Where were you at the time of
each experience? Make copies of the *wind-chill* chart and note
Humidex values and consult the *Applied Physical Geography*
feature at the end of this chapter for later reference. On an
appropriate day, check air temperature and wind speed, and
determine the combined effect on skin chilling. In contrast, on
an appropriate warm day, check air temperature and relative
humidity values, and determine the combined effect on your
personal comfort using the Humidex.

FOCUS STUDY 5.1

Air Temperature and the Human Body

We humans are capable of sensing small changes in temperature in the environment around us. Our perception of temperature is described by the term *apparent temperature*, or *sensible temperature*. This perception varies among individuals and cultures. Through complex mechanisms, our bodies maintain an average internal temperature at about 36.8°C, slightly lower in the morning or in cold weather and slightly higher at emotional times or during exercise and work.[1]

Taken together, the water vapour content of air, wind speed, and air temperature affect each individual's sense of comfort. High temperatures, high humidity, and low winds produce the most heat discomfort, whereas low humidity and strong winds enhance cooling rates. Although modern heating and cooling systems, if available and affordable, can reduce the impact of extreme temperatures indoors, the danger to human life from excessive heat or cold persists outdoors. When changes occur in the surrounding air, the human body reacts to maintain its core temperature and to protect the brain at all costs.

Wind Chill

The wind-chill index is important to people who experience winters with freezing temperatures. The wind-chill factor indicates the enhanced rate at which body heat is lost to the air. As wind speeds increase, heat loss from the skin increases. The Meteorological Service of Canada (MSC, http://www.msc.ec.gc.ca/education/windchill/index_e.cfm) and the National Weather Service (NWS, http://www.nws.noaa.gov/om/windchill/) developed the Wind Chill Temperature (WCT) Index in Figure 5.1.1.

Using the chart, if the air temperature is −7°C and the wind is blowing at 32 km · h⁻¹, skin temperatures will be at −16°C. The lower wind-chill values present a serious freezing hazard to exposed flesh. Imagine the wind chill experienced by a downhill ski racer going 130 km · h⁻¹ — frostbite is a definite possibility during a 2-minute run. The wind chill does omit consideration of sunlight intensity, a person's physical activity, and the use of protective clothing, such as a windbreaker, that prevents wind access to a person's skin.

Humidex

Humidex, a Canadian innovation first used in 1965, was devised to describe how hot, humid weather feels to the average person. It represents the heating effect felt as a result of a lack of evaporation from the skin surface, and is only measured in the summer months. Humidex is reported as a temperature—not the recorded temperature, but how hot it "feels" based on humidity. In the United States, the effect of high heat and moisture on the human body is calculated in a similar way in a measure called the heat index (http://www.hpc.ncep.noaa.gov/heat_index.shtml).

Humidex is a calculation based on air temperature and relative humidity and, as mentioned, is reported as an equivalent temperature. Water vapour in the air is expressed as relative humidity, a concept presented in Chapter 7. Although it is used widely in Canada, the areas most commonly affected by high Humidex readings are in southern Ontario and Québec. Here, in summer, the greatest impact of moist tropical air from the Gulf of Mexico is felt. Table 5.1.2 describes the comfort levels associated

FIGURE 5.1.1
Wind Chill Temperature Index for various temperatures and wind speeds.
[© Environment Canada, 2012.]

[1]The traditional value for "normal" body temperature, 37°C , was set in 1868 using old methods of measurement. According to Dr. Philip Mackowiak of the University of Maryland School of Medicine, a more accurate modern assessment places normal at 36.8°C with a range of 2.7 C°, for the human population (*Journal of the American Medical Association*, September 23–30, 1992).

Actual Air Temperature in (°C)

Calm	0°	−5°	−10°	−15°	−20°	−25°	−30°	−35°	−40°	−45°	−50°
8	−2°	−7°	−13°	−19°	−24°	−30°	−36°	−41°	−47°	−53°	−58°
10	−3°	−9°	−15°	−21°	−27°	−33°	−39°	−45°	−51°	−57°	−63°
15	−4°	−11°	−17°	−23°	−29°	−35°	−41°	−48°	−54°	−60°	−66°
20	−5°	−12°	−18°	−24°	−30°	−37°	−43°	−49°	−56°	−62°	−68°
25	−6°	−12°	−19°	−25°	−32°	−38°	−44°	−51°	−57°	−64°	−70°
30	−6°	−13°	−20°	−26°	−33°	−39°	−46°	−52°	−59°	−65°	−72°
35	−7°	−14°	−20°	−27°	−33°	−40°	−47°	−53°	−60°	−66°	−73°
40	−7°	−14°	−21°	−27°	−34°	−41°	−48°	−54°	−61°	−68°	−74°
45	−8°	−15°	−21°	−28°	−35°	−42°	−48°	−55°	−62°	−69°	−75°
50	−8°	−15°	−22°	−29°	−35°	−42°	−49°	−56°	−63°	−69°	−76°
55	−8°	−15°	−22°	−29°	−36°	−43°	−50°	−57°	−63°	−70°	−77°
60	−9°	−16°	−23°	−30°	−36°	−43°	−50°	−57°	−64°	−71°	−78°
65	−9°	−16°	−23°	−30°	−37°	−44°	−51°	−58°	−65°	−72°	−79°
70	−9°	−16°	−23°	−30°	−37°	−44°	−51°	−58°	−65°	−72°	−80°
75	−10°	−17°	−24°	−31°	−38°	−45°	−52°	−59°	−66°	−73°	−80°
80	−10°	−17°	−24°	−31°	−38°	−45°	−52°	−60°	−67°	−74°	−81°

Wind speed, km·h⁻¹

Frostbite times: ☐ Low risk of frostbite   ☐ 30 min.   ☐ 5–10 min.   ☐ 2–5 min.   ☐ 2 min.

with Humidex levels as suggested by the Meteorological Service of Canada.

High Humidex values produce stifling conditions that can be serious, particular-ly to the sick and elderly. In the summer of 2003, Europe was paralyzed by extreme air temperatures that topped 40°C. Official estimates across the continent placed the death count at more than 20 000, triggering controversy as governments were ill-prepared to adequately deal with such a catastrophe.

TABLE 5.1.1   The Human Body's Response to Temperature Stress

At Low Temperatures (Heat-gaining mechanism)	At High Temperatures (Heat-dissipation mechanism)
Temperature-Regulation Methods	
Constriction of surface blood vessels	Dilation of surface blood vessels
Concentration of blood	Dilution of blood
Flexing to reduce surface exposure	Extending to increase exposure
Increased muscle tone	Decreased muscle tone
Decrease in sweating	Sweating
Inclination to increase activity	Inclination to decrease activity
Shivering	
Increased cell metabolism	
Consequent Disturbances	
Increased urine volume	Decreased urine volume
Danger of inadequate blood supply to exposed parts; frostbite	Reduced blood supply to brain; dizziness, nausea, fainting
Discomfort leading to neuroses	Discomfort leading to neuroses
Increased appetite	Decreased appetite
	Mobilization of tissue fluid
	Thirst and dehydration
	Reduced chloride balance; heat cramps
Failure of Regulation	
Falling body temperature	Rising body temperature
Drowsiness	Impaired heat-regulating centre
Cessation of heartbeat and respiration	Failure of nervous regulation; cessation of breathing

Source: Climatology—Arid Zone Research X. © UNESCO. Reproduced by permission of UNESCO.

TABLE 5.1.2   Comfort Levels and Suggested Activities for Ranges of Humidex

Range of Humidex (°C)	Degree of Comfort
Less than 29	No discomfort
30 to 39	Some discomfort; tone down or modify strenuous outdoor activity
40 to 45	Great discomfort; avoid exertion, curtail activity
Above 45	Dangerous
Above 54	Heat stroke is imminent

Source: The Meteorological Service of Canada. Reproduced with the permission of Environment Canada, http://www.qc.ec.gc.ca/meteo/documentation/humidex_e.html.

July

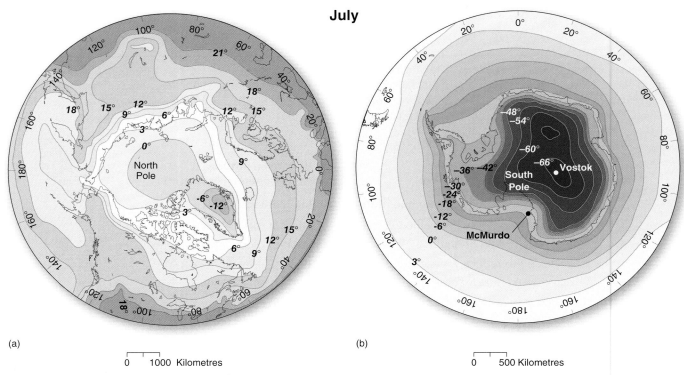

(a)

0   1000 Kilometres

(b)

0   500 Kilometres

FIGURE 5.17 July mean temperatures for polar regions.
July temperatures in (a) north polar region and (b) south polar region. Note that each map is at a different
scale. [Author-prepared maps using same sources as Figure 5.16.]

FIGURE 5.18 Global annual temperature ranges.
The annual range of global temperatures in Celsius degrees, C°. The mapped data show the difference
between average January and July temperature maps.

Record Temperatures and Greenhouse Warming

Humans are experiencing greater temperature-related challenges owing to complex changes now under way in the lower atmosphere. Scientists agree that human activities, principally the burning of fossil fuels, are increasing greenhouse gases that absorb longwave radiation, delaying losses of heat energy to space. We are experiencing human-forced climate change, as Earth's natural greenhouse effect is enhanced.

The Dome C ice core taken from the East Antarctic Plateau shows that the levels of carbon dioxide, methane, and nitrous oxides—all greenhouse gases—are higher in the present decade than any other period in the entire previous 800 000-year record. These are remarkable times in which we live. The last 15 years feature the warmest years in the climate record.

The Intergovernmental Panel on Climate Change (IPCC), through major reports beginning in 1990 with its *Fourth Assessment Report* (*AR4*) in 2007, confirms that global warming is occurring. The IPCC AR4 reached a consensus, in part stating, "Warming of the climate system is unequivocal, as is now evident from observations of increases in global average air and ocean temperatures, widespread melting of snow and ice, and rising global average sea level" (http://www.ipcc.ch/).

The U.S. National Research Council of the National Academy of Sciences (NRC/NAS) released three reports, totalling 825 pages, in May 2010. In the volume *Advancing the Science of Climate Change*, the NRC/NAS stated on page 2:

> Climate change is occurring, is caused largely by human activities, and poses significant risks for—and in many cases is already affecting—a broad range of human and natural systems. . . . Earth is warming. . . . Most of the warming over the last several decades can be attributed to human activities that release carbon dioxide. . . . Global warming is closely associated with a broad spectrum of other climate changes, such as increases in the frequency of intense rainfall, decreases in snow cover and sea ice, more frequent and intense heat waves, rising sea levels, and widespread

ocean acidification. . . . [T]hese changes pose risks for a wide range of human and environmental systems.

Chapter 10 further discusses climate change and Chapter 17 examines the vulnerable polar regions and the ice-core record of climate. Almost every chapter in *Geosystems* is affected in some way by climate change. We address what science has discovered, how global models work, the radiatively active gases that are forcing the warming, the consequences to natural systems, the uncertainties, and what international action is under way to slow the effects of such change by reducing our consumption of fossil fuels—coal, oil, natural gas. Scientific discovery continues.

> By the end of the 21st century, large portions of Earth's surface may experience climates not found at present, and some 20th-century climates may disappear. . . . Novel climates are projected to develop primarily in the tropics and subtropics.[2]

GISS Surface Temperatures Analysis 1891–2006

Global Warming, Climate Change

GEOSYSTEMS CONNECTION

Global temperature patterns are a significant output of the energy–atmosphere system. We examined the complex interactions of several factors that produce these patterns and studied maps of their distributions. In Chapter 6, we shift to another output in this energy–atmosphere system, that of global circulation of winds and ocean currents. We look at the forces that interact to produce these movements of air and water. Such events as the Gulf of Mexico oil disaster that began in April 2010 and the devastating earthquake and tsunami that struck Japan in 2011 make this knowledge important as we see how ocean circulation spreads the toxic debris for thousands of kilometres.

[2]Jack Williams et al., "Projected distributions of novel and disappearing climates by A.D. 2100," *Proceedings of the National Academy of Sciences*, 104, 14 (April 3, 2007): 5738.

 APPLIED PHYSICAL GEOGRAPHY   *Humidex*

Humidex, a calculated parameter that is based on temperature and humidity, can be easily calculated to determine the comfort level of the air at a specific temperature and humidity. It gives a measure of the amount of discomfort felt by the combined effect of the two elements. Humidex is calculated using the following formula:

$$\text{Humidex} = T + 5/9 \times (e - 10)$$

where e = vapour pressure (6.112 $\times$ $10^{(7.5 \times T/(237.7 + T)) \times H/100)}$), T = air

temperature (degrees Celsius), and H = humidity (%).

For example, given a temperature of 25°C with relative humidity of 82%, first determine the vapour pressure, e:

$$e = 6.112 \times 10^{(7.5 \times T/(237.7 + T)) \times H/100}$$

$$= 6.112 \times 10^{(7.5 \times 25(237.7 + 25)) \times 82/100}$$

$$= 6.112 \times 10^{0.5852683}$$

$$= 23.52078.$$

Then use the vapour pressure value in the Humidex equation:

$$\text{Humidex} = T + 5/9 \times (e - 10)$$
$$= 25 + 5/9 \times (23.52078 - 10)$$
$$= 25 + 7.5115444$$
$$= 32.5115444$$
$$= 33°C$$

So on a day with a fairly moderate temperature of 25°C, the high humidity makes it feel much hotter, 33°C.

KEY LEARNING CONCEPTS REVIEW

■ **Define** the concepts of temperature, kinetic energy, and sensible heat, and **distinguish** among the Kelvin, Celsius, and Fahrenheit temperature scales and how they are measured.

Temperature is a measure of the average kinetic energy (motion) of individual molecules in matter. We feel the effect of temperature as the sensible heat transfer from warmer objects to cooler objects when these objects are touching. Temperature scales include:

■ Kelvin scale: 100 units between the melting point of ice (273 K) and the boiling point of water (373 K).
■ Celsius scale: 100 degrees between the melting point of ice (0°C) and the boiling point of water (100°C).
■ Fahrenheit scale: 180 degrees between melting point of ice (32°F) and the boiling point of water (212°F).

The Kelvin scale is used in scientific research because temperature readings start at absolute zero and thus are proportional to the actual kinetic energy in a material.

temperature (p. 112)

1. Distinguish between heat and temperature.
2. What does air temperature indicate about energy in the atmosphere?
3. Compare the three scales that express temperature. Find "normal" human body temperature on each scale and record the three values in your notes.
4. What is your source of daily temperature information? Describe the highest and the lowest temperature you have experienced. From what we have discussed in this chapter, can you identify the factors that may have contributed to these temperatures?

■ **List** and **review** the principal controls and influences that produce global temperature patterns.

Principal controls and influences upon temperature patterns include *latitude* (the distance north or south of the equator), *altitude* and *elevation*, *cloud cover* (reflection, absorption, and reradiation of energy), and *land–water heating differences* (nature of evaporation, transparency, specific heat, movement, and ocean currents and sea-surface temperatures).

5. Describe the effect of altitude/elevation on air temperature. Why is air at higher altitude/elevation lower in temperature? Why does it feel cooler standing in shadows at higher elevation than at lower elevation?
6. What noticeable effect does air density have on the absorption and radiation of energy? What role does elevation play in that process?
7. How is it possible to grow moderate-climate crops such as wheat, barley, and potatoes near La Paz, Bolivia so near the equator?
8. Describe the effect of cloud cover with regard to Earth's temperature patterns. From the previous chapter, review how different cloud types cause cloud-albedo forcing or cloud-greenhouse forcing and relate the concepts with a simple sketch.

■ **Review** the factors that produce different maritime effects and continental effects as they influence temperatures, and **utilise** several pairs of cities to illustrate these differences.

The physical nature of land (rock and soil) and water (oceans, seas, and lakes) is the reason for **land–water heating differences**, the fact that land heats and cools faster than water. Moderate temperature patterns are associated with water bodies, and extreme temperatures occur inland. The controls that cause differences between land and water surfaces are *evaporation, transparency, specific heat, movement,* and *ocean currents and sea-surface temperatures.*

Light penetrates water because of its **transparency**. Water is clearer than land and light transmits to an average depth of 60 m in the ocean. This penetration distributes available heat energy over a much greater volume than occurs on opaque land; thus, a larger energy reservoir is formed. When equal volumes of water and land are compared, water requires far more energy to increase its temperature than does land. In other words, water can hold more energy than can soil or rock, so water has a higher **specific heat**, the heat capacity of a substance, averaging about four times that of soil.

Ocean currents affect temperature. An example of the effect of ocean currents is the **Gulf Stream**, which moves northward off the east coast of North America, carrying warm water far into the North Atlantic. As a result, the southern third of Iceland experiences much milder temperatures than would be expected for a latitude of 65° N, just below the Arctic Circle (66.5°).

Marine effect, or maritime effect, describes locations that exhibit the moderating influences of the ocean, usually along coastlines or on islands. **Continental effect** refers to the condition of areas that are less affected by the ocean and therefore have a greater range between maximum and minimum temperatures diurnally and yearly.

land–water heating differences (p. 116)
transparency (p. 117)
specific heat (p. 118)
Gulf Stream (p. 118)
marine effect (p. 119)
continental effect (p. 119)

9. List the physical aspects of land and water that produce different responses to heating from absorption of insolation. What is the specific effect of transparency in a medium?
10. What is specific heat? Compare the specific heat of water and soil.
11. Describe the pattern of sea-surface temperatures (SSTs) as determined by satellite remote sensing. Where is the warmest ocean region on Earth?
12. What effect does sea-surface temperature have on air temperature? Describe the negative feedback mechanism created by higher sea-surface temperatures and evaporation rates.
13. Differentiate between maritime and continental temperature patterns. Give geographic examples of each from the text: Canada, Norway, and Russia.

■ *Interpret* the pattern of Earth's temperatures from their portrayal on January and July temperature maps and on a map of annual temperature ranges.

Maps for January and July instead of the solstice months of December and June are used for analysis of temperature patterns because of the natural lag that occurs between insolation received and maximum or minimum temperatures experienced. Each line on these temperature maps is an **isotherm**, an isoline that connects points of equal temperature. A set of isotherms portrays temperature patterns.

Isotherms generally are zonal, trending east–west, parallel to the equator. They mark the general decrease in insolation and net radiation with distance from the equator. The **thermal equator** (isoline connecting all points of highest mean temperature) trends southward in January and northward with the high summer Sun in July. In January it extends farther south into the interior of South America and Africa, indicating higher temperatures over landmasses.

In the Northern Hemisphere in January, isotherms shift equatorward as cold air chills the continental interiors. The coldest area on this map is in Russia—specifically northeastern Siberia. The intense cold experienced there results from winter conditions of consistent clear, dry, calm air; small insolation input; and an inland location far from any moderating maritime effects.

isotherm (p. 121)
thermal equator (p. 122)

14. What is the thermal equator? Describe its location in January and in July. Explain why it shifts position annually.
15. Observe trends in the pattern of isolines over North America and compare the January average temperature map with the July map. Why do the patterns shift locations?
16. Describe and explain the extreme temperature range experienced in north-central Siberia between January and July.
17. Where are the hottest places on Earth? Are they near the equator or elsewhere? Explain. Where is the coldest place on Earth?
18. From the maps in Figures 5.13, 5.16 and 5.18, determine the average temperature values and annual range of temperatures for your present location.
19. Compare the maps in Figures 5.13 and 5.16: (a) describe what you find in central Greenland on the January and July maps; (b) look at the south polar region and describe seasonal changes between the two maps. Characterise conditions along the Antarctic Peninsula between January and July (around 60° west longitude).

■ *Describe* the human body's response to wind (wind chill) and heat and humidity (Humidex).

The *wind-chill factor* indicates the enhanced rate at which body heat is lost to the air. As wind speeds increase, heat loss from the skin increases. Humidex indicates the human body's reaction to air temperature and water vapour. The level of humidity in the air affects our natural ability to cool through evaporation from skin.

20. What is the wind-chill temperature on a day with an air temperature of −12°C and a wind speed of 32 km · h⁻¹?
21. Explain what the Canadian *Humidex* measure tells us about sensible temperature and the human body. Give an example based upon your own sense of temperature comfort or discomfort.

MyGeosciencePlace

Visit **www.mygeoscienceplace.ca** for several figure animations, satellite loops, self-study quizzes, flashcards, interactive glossary, career links, RSS feeds, Pearson eText of *Geosystems*, and much more.

CHAPTER 6

Atmospheric and Oceanic Circulations

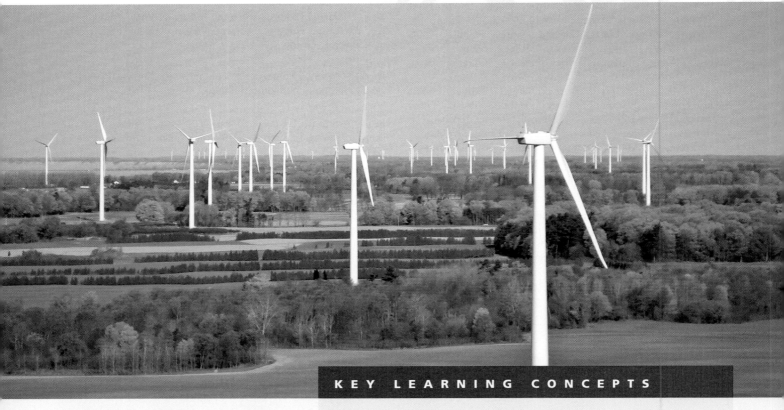

Erie Shores windfarm, Ontario. This 99 MW generating wind farm that stretches from Clear Creek westward to Copenhagen, Ontario, began operations in 2006. During the year ending December 31, 2010, the 66 wind turbines at this location produced about 228 000 megawatt hours of energy. That's enough power to supply 23 000 households. [Courtesy of Erie Shores Wind Farm.]

KEY LEARNING CONCEPTS

After reading the chapter, you should be able to:

- **Define** the concept of air pressure, and **describe** instruments used to measure air pressure.

- **Define** wind, and **explain** how winds are measured, how wind directions are determined, and how winds are named.

- **Explain** the four driving forces within the atmosphere—gravity, pressure gradient force, Coriolis force, and friction force—and **locate** the primary high- and low-pressure areas and principal winds.

- **Describe** upper-air circulation and its support role for surface systems, and **define** the jet streams.

- **Summarise** several multiyear oscillations of air temperature, air pressure, and circulation in the Arctic, Atlantic, and Pacific Oceans.

- **Explain** several types of local winds: land–sea breezes, mountain–valley breezes, katabatic winds, and regional monsoons.

- **Discern** the basic pattern of Earth's major surface ocean currents and deep thermohaline circulation.

Ocean Currents Bring Invasive Species

As human civilization pumps and throws more chemicals and refuse into the oceans, the garbage travels in currents that sweep across the globe. A dramatic episode of such ocean-current transport happened in the South Atlantic in 2006. This story begins here in Chapter 6 and continues with the ecological impacts in *Geosystems Now*, Chapter 20.

High-pressure systems guide the winds and ocean currents in the major oceanic basins. These systems flow clockwise in the Northern Hemisphere and counterclockwise in the Southern Hemisphere. In the South Atlantic, this counterclockwise flow drives the South Equatorial Current westward and the West Wind Drift eastward (Figure GN 6.1). Along the African coast, the cool Benguela Current flows northward, while the warm Brazil Current moves south along the coast of South America. This is the circulation gyre of the South Atlantic.

Along the southeastern portion of this gyre is a remote island group, the Tristan da Cunha Archipelago, comprising four islands, some 2775 km from Africa and 3355 km from South America (see location in Figure GN 6.1). Only 298 people live on Tristan in the village of Edinburgh (Figure GN 6.2).

FIGURE GN 6.2 Village of Edinburgh, Tristan da Cunha.
[Bobbé Christopherson.]

This unique small society practises subsistence farming, collectively grows and exports potatoes, and depends on rich marine life that they carefully manage. The Tristan rock lobster (a crawfish) is harvested, quick frozen at a community factory, and exported around the world. Although Tristan lacks an airport and has no pier or port, several ships a year transport these commodities. In 2006, ocean currents brought to this island a grim reminder of the outside world.

Oil-drilling platforms are like small ships that can be towed to a desired site for drilling undersea wells. Petrobras, Brazil's state-controlled oil company, had such a platform, the *Petrobras XXI*. The oil company towed the 80-m × 67-m × 34-m high platform from Macae, Brazil, on March 5, 2006—destination Singapore. The company chartered a tug, the *Mighty Deliverer,* to do the job. This tug was actually built for inland work as a "pusher" tug, like ones seen in the Great Lakes or on the Mississippi River. Yet it was contracted to haul this drilling rig across the Southern Ocean, easily the most treacherous seas on Earth. The *Deliverer* headed south, encountering rough seas after a couple of weeks. Conditions forced the tug's crew to cut the platform loose on

April 30, and after a few days, it was adrift.

The *Petrobras XXI* was missing in rough seas, caught in the currents of the West Wind Drift and westerlies. Sometime in late May, after almost a month adrift, the oil-drilling platform ran aground on Tristan in Trypot Bay, where it was discovered by Tristanian fishermen on June 7 (Figure GN 6.3).

The owners of the drilling platform followed the usual practice of not cleaning the drilling platform prior to towing, even though clean rigs move through the water with less friction, require less fuel, and result in lower labour costs. Consequently, *Petrobras XXI* carried some 62 nonnative species of marine life, including free-swimming silver porgy and blenny fish that tagged along with the rig as it drifted in the currents.

What marine scientists found when they surveyed the grounded rig was an unprecedented species invasion of Tristan. Exclusive photos by one of the scientist divers, interviewed for this report, follow in Chapter 20. Here in Chapter 6, we learn about wind and ocean circulation, the forces that brought the *Petrobas XXI* to Tristan.

FIGURE GN 6.1 Principal ocean currents of the South Atlantic. Tristan da Cunha is at approximately 37° 4′ S and 12° 19′ W. Note the probable route of the oil-drilling platform shown with the dotted line.

FIGURE GN 6.3 *Petrobras XXI* aground in Trypot Bay, Tristan. [Photo by Sue Scott. All rights reserved.]

After 635 years of dormancy, Mount Pinatubo in the Philippines erupted in 1991 (Figure 6.1a). This event had tremendous atmospheric impact, lofting 15–20 million tons of ash, dust, and sulfur dioxide (SO$_2$) into the atmosphere. As the sulfur dioxide rose into the stratosphere, it quickly formed sulfuric acid (H$_2$SO$_4$) aerosols, which concentrated at 16–25 km altitude. This debris increased atmospheric albedo about 1.5%, giving scientists an estimate of the aerosol volume generated by the eruption (see Figure 6.1).

(a)

Luzon Island, Philippines

6/15 – 6/19/91

(b)

7/4 – 7/10/91

(c)

7/25 – 8/1/91

(d)

Effects cover 42% of globe in just 60 days

8/15 – 8/21/91

(e)

FIGURE 6.1 Volcanic eruption effects spread worldwide by winds. (a) Mount Pinatubo eruption. False-colour images (b–e) of aerosols from Mount Pinatubo, smoke from fires, and dust storms, all swept about the globe by the general atmospheric circulation. The false colour shows aerosol optical thickness (AOT): White is densest, dull yellow indicates medium values, and brown areas have the lowest aerosol concentration. In (b), note the dust moving westward from Africa, smoke from Kuwaiti oil well fires set during the first Persian Gulf War, smoke from forest fires in Siberia, and haze off the East Coast of the United States. [(a) AVHRR satellite image, EROS Data Center; (b–e) AVHRR satellite AOT images, NESDIS/NOAA.]

The AVHRR instrument aboard *NOAA-11* monitored the reflected solar radiation from Mount Pinatubo's aerosols as global winds swept them around Earth. Figure 6.1b–e shows images made at three-week intervals that clearly track the spread of the debris worldwide. Some 60 days after the eruption (the last satellite image in the sequence), the aerosol cloud spanned about 42% of the globe, from 20° S to 30° N. For almost two years, colourful sunrises and sunsets and a small lowering of average temperatures followed. The eruption provided a unique insight into the dynamics of atmospheric circulation.

Today, technology permits a depth of analysis unknown in the past—satellites now track the atmospheric effects from dust storms, forest fires, industrial haze, warfare, and the dispersal of volcanic explosions. For example, millions of tons of dust from African soils cross the Atlantic each year, borne by the winds of atmospheric circulation, visible in Figure 6.1b.

Global winds are certainly an important reason why the United States, the former Soviet Union, and Great Britain signed the 1963 Limited Test Ban Treaty. That treaty banned aboveground testing of nuclear weapons because atmospheric circulation spread radioactive contamination worldwide. Such agreements illustrate how the fluid movement of the atmosphere links humanity more than perhaps any other natural or cultural factor. Our atmosphere makes the world a spatially linked society—one person's or country's exhalation is another's inhalation.

In this chapter: We begin with a discussion of wind essentials, consisting of air pressure and its measurement and a description of wind. The driving forces that produce surface winds are pressure gradient, Coriolis, and friction. We examine the circulation of Earth's atmosphere and the patterns of global winds, including principal pressure systems and winds. We consider Earth's wind-driven oceanic currents and explain multiyear oscillations in atmospheric flows, local winds, and the powerful monsoons. The energy driving all this movement comes from one source: the Sun.

Wind Essentials

The primary circulation of winds across Earth has fascinated travelers, sailors, and scientists for centuries, although only in the modern era is a true picture emerging of global winds. Driven by the imbalance between equatorial energy surpluses and polar energy deficits, Earth's atmospheric circulation transfers both energy and mass on

a grand scale, determining Earth's weather patterns and the flow of ocean currents. Scientists at the U.S. National Center for Atmospheric Research determined that the atmosphere is the dominant medium for redistributing energy from about 35° latitude to the poles in each hemisphere, whereas ocean currents redistribute more heat in a zone straddling the equator between 17° N and S. Atmospheric circulation also spreads air pollutants, whether naturally occurring or human-caused, worldwide, far from their point of origin.

Atmospheric circulation is generally categorised at three levels: primary circulation consisting of general worldwide circulation, secondary circulation of migratory high-pressure and low-pressure systems, and tertiary circulation that includes local winds and temporal weather patterns. Winds that move principally north or south along meridians are known as meridional flows. Winds moving east or west along parallels of latitude are called zonal flows.

Air Pressure and Its Measurement

Air pressure, including its measurement and expression, is key to understanding wind. The motion, size, and number of air molecules—the factors that determine the temperature and density of the air—create **air pressure.** Pressure is exerted on all surfaces in contact with the air.

In 1643, Galileo's pupil Evangelista Torricelli was working on a mine-drainage problem. His work led him to discover a method for measuring air pressure (Figure 6.2a). He knew that pumps in the mine were able to "pull" water upward about 10 m, but no higher, but he did not know why. Careful observation led him to discover that this was caused not by weak pumps but by the atmosphere itself. Torricelli noted that the water level in the vertical pipe fluctuated from day to day. He figured out that air pressure, the weight of the air, varies with weather conditions.

To simulate the problem at the mine, Torricelli devised an instrument at Galileo's suggestion, using a much denser fluid than water—mercury (Hg)—in a glass tube 1 m high. Torricelli sealed the glass tube at one end, filled it with mercury, and inverted it into a dish of mercury (Figure 6.2b). He determined that the average height of the column of mercury in the tube was 760 mm and that it varied day to day as the weather changed. He concluded that the mass of surrounding air was exerting pressure on the mercury in the dish that counterbalanced the column of mercury.

 GEO REPORT 6.1 *Blowing in the Wind*

Dust originating in Africa sometimes increases the iron content of the waters off Florida, promoting the toxic algal blooms (*Karenia brevis*) known as "Red Tides." In the Amazon, soil samples bear the dust print of these former African soils that crossed the Atlantic. Active research on such dust is part of the U.S. Navy's Aerosol Analysis and Prediction System (NAAPS); see links at http://www.nrlmry.navy.mil/aerosol/.

(a)

(c)

(b)

FIGURE 6.2 Developing the barometer.
(a) Torricelli developed the barometer to measure air pressure while trying to solve a mine-drainage problem. Two types of instruments are used to measure atmospheric pressure: (b) a mercury barometer (idealised sketch) and (c) an aneroid barometer. Have you used a barometer? If so, what type was it? Have you tried to reset it using a local weather information source? [(c) Qualimetrics, Inc.]

Using similar instruments, scientists set a standard of *normal sea-level pressure* at 1013.2 mb (*millibar*, or *mb*, which expresses force per square metre of surface area) In Canada and other countries, normal air pressure is expressed as 101.32 kPa (*kilopascal*; 1 kPa = 10 mb).

Any instrument that measures air pressure is a *barometer* (from the Greek *baros*, meaning "weight"). Torricelli developed a **mercury barometer.** A more compact barometer design, which works without a metre-long tube of mercury, is the aneroid barometer, shown in Figure 6.2c. *Aneroid* means "using no liquid." The **aneroid barometer** principle is simple: Imagine a small, flexible chamber, partially emptied of air, which is sealed and connected to a mechanism attached to a needle on a dial. As air pressure increases, it presses on the chamber; as air pressure decreases, it relieves pressure on the chamber—changes in air pressure move the needle. An aircraft altimeter is a type of aneroid barometer that accurately measures altitude because air pressure diminishes with altitude above sea level. For accuracy an altimeter must be adjusted for temperature changes.

Figure 6.3 illustrates comparative scales in millibars and inches used to express air pressure and its relative force. The normal range of Earth's atmospheric pressure from strong high pressure to deep low pressure is about 105.0 to 98 kPa. The figure also indicates the extreme highest and lowest pressures ever recorded in Canada, the United States, and on Earth. Compare Hurricane Wilma (2005), the U.S. record holder, with the lowest central pressures of hurricanes Gilbert (1988), and Rita and Katrina (2005).

Wind: Description and Measurement

Simply stated, **wind** is generally the horizontal motion of air across Earth's surface. Turbulence adds wind updrafts and downdrafts and a vertical component to this definition. Differences in air pressure (density) between one location and another produce wind. Wind's two principal properties are speed and direction, and instruments measure each. An **anemometer** measures wind speed in kilometres per hour ($km \cdot h^{-1}$), miles per hour (mph), metres per second ($m \cdot s^{-1}$), or knots. (A *knot* is a nautical mile per hour, covering 1 minute of Earth's arc in an hour, equivalent to 1.85 $km \cdot h^{-1}$). A **wind vane** determines wind direction; the standard measurement is taken 10 m above the ground to reduce the effects of local topography on wind direction (Figure 6.4).

Wind is named for the direction from which it originates. For example, a wind from the west is a westerly wind (it blows eastward); a wind out of the south is

FIGURE 6.3 Air pressure readings and conversions.
Scales express barometric air pressure in millibars and inches, with average air pressure values and recorded pressure extremes. Canadian values include kilopascal equivalents, 10 mb = 1 kPa. The intensity of the 2005 hurricane season is evident; note the positions of Katrina, Rita, and Wilma on the pressure dial.

Some convenient conversions:
1.0 in. (Hg) = 33.87 mb = 25.40 mm (Hg) = 0.49 lb/in.^{2}
1.0 mb = 0.0295 in. (Hg) = 0.75 mm (Hg) = 0.0145 lb/in.^{2}

1. Hurricane Gilbert 888 mb (26.23 in.) Sept. 1988

2. Hurricane Rita 897 mb (26.46 in.) Sept. 2005

3. Hurricane Katrina 902 mb (26.61 in.) August 2005

a southerly wind (it blows northward). Figure 6.5 illustrates a simple wind compass, naming 16 principal wind directions used by meteorologists.

The traditional Beaufort wind scale is a descriptive scale useful in visually estimating wind speed (Table 6.1). Admiral Beaufort of the British Navy introduced his wind scale in 1806. In 1926, G. C. Simpson expanded Beaufort's scale to include wind speeds on land. The U.S.

FIGURE 6.4 Wind vane and anemometer.
Instruments used to measure wind direction (wind vane, left) and wind speed (anemometer, right) at a weather station installation.
[NOAA Photo Library.]

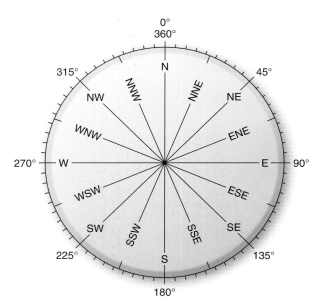

FIGURE 6.5 Sixteen wind directions identified on a wind compass.
Wind is named for the direction from which it originates. For example, a wind from the west is a westerly wind.

National Weather Service (old Weather Bureau) standardised the scale in 1955 (see http://www.hpc.ncep.noaa.gov/html/beaufort.shtml). The scale is still referred to on ocean charts, enabling estimation of wind speed without instruments. Although most ships use sophisticated equipment to perform such measurements, you find the Beaufort scale posted on the bridge of many ships.

CRITICAL THINKING 6.1

Measure the Wind

Use the Beaufort scale in Table 6.1 to estimate wind speed as you walk outside on a day with wind. Estimate wind speed and wind direction at least twice during the day, and record them in your notebook. If possible, check these readings against the reports from a local source of weather information. For wind direction, moisten your finger, hold it in the air, and sense evaporative cooling on one side of your finger to indicate from which direction the wind is blowing. What changes in wind speed and direction do you notice over several days? How did these changes relate to the weather you experienced?

Driving Forces within the Atmosphere

Four forces determine both speed and direction of winds:

- The pressure that Earth's *gravitational force* exerts on the atmosphere is virtually uniform. Gravity equally compresses the atmosphere worldwide, with the density decreasing as altitude increases. The gravitational force counteracts the outward centrifugal force acting on Earth's spinning surface and atmosphere. Without gravity, there would be no atmospheric pressure—or atmosphere, for that matter.
- **Pressure gradient force** drives air from areas of higher barometric pressure (more dense air) to areas of lower barometric pressure (less dense air), thereby causing winds. Without a pressure gradient force, there would be no wind.
- **Coriolis force,** a deflective force, makes wind that actually travels in a straight path appear to be deflected in relation to Earth's rotating surface. Coriolis force deflects wind to the right in the Northern Hemisphere and to the left in the Southern Hemisphere. Without Coriolis force, winds would move along straight paths between high- and low-pressure areas.
- **Friction force** drags on the wind as it moves across surfaces; it decreases with height above the surface. Without friction, winds would simply move in paths parallel to isobars (lines connecting points of equal barometric pressure) and at high rates of speed.

All four of these forces operate on moving air and ocean currents at Earth's surface and influence global wind circulation patterns. The following sections describe the actions of the pressure gradient, Coriolis, and friction forces. (The gravitational force operates uniformly worldwide.)

Pressure Gradient Force

High- and low-pressure areas exist in the atmosphere principally because Earth's surface is unequally heated. For example, cold, dense air at the poles exerts greater pressure than warm, less dense air along the equator. These pressure differences establish a pressure gradient force.

An **isobar** is an *isoline* (a line along which there is a constant value) plotted on a weather map to connect

GEO REPORT 6.2 *A Force Is with Us*

Note that we call Coriolis a *force*. This label is appropriate because, as the physicist Sir Isaac Newton (1643–1727) stated, when something is accelerating over a space, a force is in operation (mass times acceleration). This apparent force (in classical mechanics, an inertial force) acts on moving objects. It is named for Gaspard Gustave Coriolis (1792–1843), a French mathematician and researcher of applied mechanics, who first described the force in 1831. For deeper insight into the physics of this phenomenon, consider an analysis by Anders Persson, "How do we understand the Coriolis force?" in the *Bulletin of the American Meteorological Society* 79, no. 7 (July 1998): 1373–85.

TABLE 6.1 Beaufort Wind Scale

Wind Speed		Beaufort Number	Wind Description	Beaufort Wind Scale	
km · h⁻¹	knots			Observed Effects at Sea	Observed Effects on Land
< 1	< 1	0	Calm	Glassy calm, like a mirror	Calm, no movement of leaves
1–5	1–3	1	Light air	Small ripples; wavelet scales; no foam on crests	Slight leaf movement; smoke drifts; wind vanes still
6–11	4–6	2	Light breeze	Small wavelets; glassy look to crests, which do not break	Leaves rustling; wind felt; wind vanes moving
12–19	7–10	3	Gentle breeze	Large wavelets; dispersed white-caps as crests break	Leaves and twigs in motion; small flags and banners extended
20–29	11–16	4	Moderate breeze	Small, longer waves; numerous whitecaps	Small branches moving; raising dust, paper, litter, and dry leaves
30–38	17–21	5	Fresh breeze	Moderate, pronounced waves; many whitecaps; some spray	Small trees and branches swaying; wavelets forming on inland waterways
39–49	22–27	6	Strong breeze	Large waves, white foam crests everywhere; some spray	Large branches swaying; overhead wires whistling; difficult to control an umbrella
50–61	28–33	7	Moderate (near) gale	Sea mounding up; foam and sea spray blown in streaks in the direction of the wind	Entire trees moving; difficult to walk into wind
62–74	34–40	8	Fresh gale (or gale)	Moderately high waves of greater length; breaking crests forming sea spray; well-marked foam streaks	Small branches breaking; difficult to walk; moving automobiles drifting and veering
75–87	41–47	9	Strong gale	High waves; wave crests tumbling and the sea beginning to roll; visibility reduced by blowing spray	Roof shingles blown away; slight damage to structures; broken branches littering the ground
88–101	48–55	10	Whole gale (or storm)	Very high waves and heavy, rolling seas; white appearance to foam-covered sea; overhanging waves; visibility reduced	Uprooted and broken trees; structural damage; considerable destruction; seldom occurring
102–116	56–63	11	Storm (or violent storm)	White foam covering a breaking sea of exceptionally high waves; small- and medium-sized ships lost from view in wave troughs; wave crests frothy	Widespread damage to structures and trees, a rare occurrence
> 117	> 64	12–17	Hurricane	Driving foam and spray filling the air; white sea; visibility poor to nonexistent	Severe to catastrophic damage; devastation to affected society

points of equal pressure. A pattern of isobars on a weather map provides a portrait of the pressure gradient between an area of higher pressure and one of lower pressure. The spacing between isobars indicates the intensity of the pressure difference, or pressure gradient.

Just as closer contour lines on a topographic map indicate a steeper slope on land, so do closer isobars denote steepness in the pressure gradient. In Figure 6.6a, note the spacing of the isobars (green lines). A steep gradient causes faster air movement from a high-pressure area to one of low pressure. Isobars spaced wider apart from one another mark a more gradual pressure gradient, one that creates a slower airflow. Along a horizontal surface, the pressure gradient force alone acts at right angles to the isobars, so wind blows across isobars at right angles. Note the location of steep ("strong winds") and gradual ("light winds") pressure gradients and their relationship to wind intensity on the map in Figure 6.6b.

(a)

FIGURE 6.6 Pressure gradient determines wind speed.
Pressure gradient (a) portrayed on a weather map (b). See the relationship between pressure gradient and wind strength. Here we see surface winds spiraling clockwise out of a high-pressure system and spiraling counterclockwise into a low-pressure system.

(b)

Figure 6.7 illustrates the forces that direct winds. Figure 6.7a shows the pressure gradient force acting alone. A field of subsiding, or sinking, air develops in a high-pressure area. Air descends in a high-pressure area and diverges outward at the surface in all directions. In contrast, in a low-pressure area, as air rises, it pulls in more air from all directions, causing convergence into the area of lower pressure at the surface.

Coriolis Force

You might expect surface winds to move in a straight line from areas of higher pressure to areas of lower pressure. On a nonrotating Earth, they would. But on our rotating planet, Coriolis force deflects anything that flies or flows across Earth's surface—wind, an airplane, or ocean currents—from a straight path. In simplest terms, this force is an effect of Earth's rotation. Earth's tangential speed varies with latitude, increasing from 0 km·h^{-1} at the poles (surface is at Earth's axis of rotation) to 1675 km·h^{-1} at the equator (surface is farthest from Earth's axis). Table 2.2 lists tangential speeds by latitude.

The deflection occurs regardless of the direction in which the object is moving. Because Earth rotates eastward, objects appear to curve to the right in the Northern Hemisphere and to the left in the Southern Hemisphere (Figure 6.8a). Coriolis force is zero along the equator,

(a) Pressure gradient

Top view and side view of air movement in an idealised high-pressure area and low-pressure area on a nonrotating Earth.

Pressure gradient force alone

(b) Pressure gradient + Coriolis forces (upper level winds)

Earth's rotation adds the Coriolis force and a "twist" to air movements. High-pressure and low-pressure areas develop a rotary motion, and wind flowing between highs and lows flows parallel to isobars.

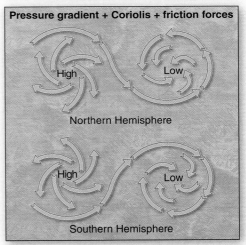

Pressure gradient + Coriolis forces

(c) Pressure gradient + Coriolis + friction forces (surface winds)

Surface friction adds a countering force to Coriolis, producing winds that spiral out of a high-pressure area and into a low-pressure area. Surface winds cross isobars at an angle. Air flows into low-pressure cyclones and turns to the left, because of deflection to the right.

Pressure gradient + Coriolis + friction forces

FIGURE 6.7 Three physical forces that produce winds.
Three physical forces interact to produce wind patterns at the surface and aloft: (a) pressure gradient force; (b) Coriolis force, which counters the pressure gradient force, producing a geostrophic wind flow in the upper atmosphere; and (c) friction force, which, combined with the other two forces, produces characteristic surface winds.

Wind Pattern Development

(a)

(b)

Flight path deflected by Coriolis force

Flight path on a nonrotating Earth

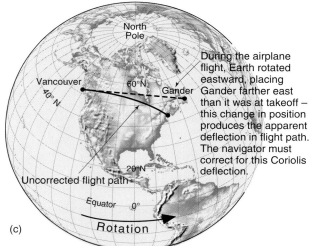

(c)

During the airplane flight, Earth rotated eastward, placing Gander farther east than it was at takeoff – this change in position produces the apparent deflection in flight path. The navigator must correct for this Coriolis deflection.

Coriolis Force

FIGURE 6.8 Coriolis force—an apparent deflection.
Distribution of Coriolis force on Earth: (a) apparent deflection to the right of a straight line in the Northern Hemisphere and apparent deflection to the left in the Southern Hemisphere; (b) Coriolis deflection of a flight path between the North Pole and Quito, Ecuador, which is on the equator; (c) deflection of a flight path between Vancouver and Gander. Deflection from a straight path occurs regardless of the direction of movement.

increases to half the maximum deflection at the 30° N and S latitudes, and reaches maximum deflection at the poles. The effect of Coriolis force increases as the speed of the moving object increases; thus, the faster the wind speed, the greater its apparent deflection. Coriolis force does not normally affect small-scale motions that cover insignificant distance and time.

We work through a simple explanation here focused on the observed phenomena. If you choose you can use physics and identify the variables that interplay to produce these effects. Mathematical formulas explain how the conservation of angular and linear momentum, as our distance to Earth's axis changes with latitudinal location, operates to produce the deflection, as well as the interplay of the opposing gravitational and centrifugal forces.

With this in mind, we observe Coriolis force from different viewpoints. From the viewpoint of an airplane that is passing over Earth's surface, the surface is seen to rotate slowly below. But as we look from the surface at the airplane, the surface seems stationary, and the airplane appears to curve off course. The airplane does not actually deviate from a straight path, but it *appears* to do

GEO REPORT 6.3   *Coriolis: Not a Force on Drains, Sinks, or Toilets*

A common misconception about Coriolis force is that it affects water draining out of a sink, tub, or toilet. Moving water or air must cover some distance across space and time before Coriolis force deflects it noticeably. Long-range artillery shells and guided missiles do exhibit small amounts of deflection that must be corrected for accuracy. But water movements down a drain are too small in spatial extent to be noticeably affected by this force.

so because we are standing on Earth's rotating surface beneath the airplane. Because of this apparent deflection, the airplane must make constant corrections in flight path to maintain its "straight" heading relative to a rotating Earth.

For an example of the effect of this force, see Figure 6.8b. A pilot leaves the North Pole and flies due south toward Quito, Ecuador. If Earth were not rotating, the aircraft would simply travel along a meridian of longitude and arrive at Quito. But Earth is rotating eastward beneath the aircraft's flight path. If the pilot does not allow for this increase in tangential speed, the plane will reach the equator over the ocean along an apparently curved path, far to the west of the intended destination. Likewise flying northward on a return flight, the plane maintains its eastward tangential velocity as it makes its way northward over slower rotational speeds of Earth. Without correction, the plane ends up to the east of the pole, in a right-hand deflection. Pilots must correct for this Coriolis deflection in their navigational calculations.

This effect occurs regardless of the direction of the moving object. A flight from Vancouver to Gander is shown in Figure 6.8c. Coriolis deflection occurs as the airplane flies to Gander because Earth continues to rotate eastward; this increases the centrifugal force acting on the plane (Earth rotation + plane speed), so the plane moves toward the equator in a right-hand deflection (moving farther from Earth's axis at a lower latitude). Unless the pilot corrects for this deflective force, the flight would end up farther to the south. Likewise, flying westward on a return flight opposite Earth's rotation direction, which decreases the centrifugal force (Earth rotation speed − plane speed), the plane moves away from the equator, in a right-hand deflection (moving closer to Earth's axis at a higher latitude).

Coriolis Force and Winds How does Coriolis force affect wind? As air rises from the surface through the lowest levels of the atmosphere, it leaves behind the drag of surface friction and increases speed. This increases Coriolis force, causing winds to spiral to the right in the Northern Hemisphere or to the left in the Southern Hemisphere, generally producing upper-air westerly winds from the subtropics to the poles. In the upper troposphere, Coriolis force just balances the pressure gradient force. Consequently, the winds between higher-pressure and lower-pressure areas in the upper troposphere flow parallel to the isobars.

Figure 6.7b illustrates the combined effect of pressure gradient force and Coriolis force on air currents aloft. Together, these forces produce winds that do not flow directly from high to low, but around the pressure areas, remaining parallel to the isobars. Such winds are called **geostrophic winds** and are characteristic of upper tropospheric circulation. (The suffix -strophic means "to turn.") Note the inset illustration showing the effects of the pressure gradient and Coriolis forces that produce a geostrophic flow of air. Geostrophic winds produce the characteristic pattern shown on the upper-air weather map just ahead in Figure 6.14.

Friction Force

Figure 6.7c adds the effect of friction to Coriolis and pressure gradient forces on wind movements; combining all three forces produces the wind patterns we see along Earth's surface. The effect of surface friction extends to a height of about 500 m and varies with surface texture, wind speed, time of day and year, and atmospheric conditions. In general, rougher surfaces produce more friction.

Near the surface, friction disrupts the equilibrium established in geostrophic wind flows between the pressure gradient and Coriolis forces—note the inset illustration in Figure 6.7c. Because surface friction decreases wind speed, it reduces the effect of Coriolis force and causes winds to move across isobars at an angle. The reason the balance of forces causes the winds to curve to the left into low-pressure cyclones with deflection to the right is shown.

In Figure 6.7c, you can see that the Northern Hemisphere winds spiral out from a high-pressure area *clockwise* to form an **anticyclone** and spiral into a low-pressure area *counterclockwise* to form a **cyclone.** (In the Southern Hemisphere these circulation patterns are reversed, with winds flowing counterclockwise out of anticyclonic high-pressure cells and clockwise into cyclonic low-pressure cells.)

Atmospheric Patterns of Motion

With these forces and motions in mind, we are ready to build a general model of overall atmospheric circulation. The warmer, less-dense air along the equator rises, creating low pressure at the surface, and the colder, denser air at the poles sinks, creating high pressure. If Earth did not rotate, the result would be a simple surface wind flow from the poles to the equator, a meridional flow caused solely by pressure gradient.

However, Earth does rotate, creating a more complex flow system. On a rotating Earth the poles-to-equator flow is predominantly zonal (latitudinal), both at the surface and aloft. Winds are westerly (eastward-moving) in the middle and high latitudes and easterly (westward-moving) in the low latitudes toward the equator in both hemispheres. Earth's global circulation system transfers thermal energy, air, and water masses from equatorial energy surpluses to polar energy deficits, using waves, streams, and eddies on a planetary scale.

Primary High-Pressure and Low-Pressure Areas

The following discussion of Earth's pressure and wind patterns refers often to Figure 6.9, isobaric maps showing average surface barometric pressure in January and July. Indirectly, these maps indicate prevailing surface winds, which are suggested by the isobars.

(a)

(b)

FIGURE 6.9 Global barometric pressures for January and July.
Maps portray average surface barometric pressure (millibars) for (a) January and (b) July. The dashed line marks the general location of the intertropical convergence zone (ITCZ). Compare specific regions for January and July—for instance, the North Pacific, the North Atlantic, and the central Asian land-mass. [Adapted by author and redrawn from National Climatic Data Center, *Monthly Climatic Data for the World*, 46 (January and July 1993), and WMO and NOAA.]

Global Patterns of Pressure   Global Sea-Level Pressure

The primary high- and low-pressure areas of Earth's general circulation appear on these maps as cells or uneven belts of similar pressure that stretch across the face of the planet, interrupted by landmasses. Between these areas flow the primary winds. Secondary highs and lows, from a few hundred to a few thousand kilometres in diameter and hundreds to thousands of metres in height, form within these primary pressure areas. The secondary systems seasonally migrate to produce changing weather patterns in the regions over which they pass.

Four broad pressure areas cover the Northern Hemisphere and a similar set exists in the Southern Hemisphere. In each hemisphere, two of the pressure areas are stimulated by thermal (temperature) factors. These are the **equatorial low-pressure trough** (marked by the ITCZ line on the maps) and the weak **polar high-pressure cells** at the North and South poles (not shown, as the maps are cut off at 80° N and 80° S). The other two pressure areas—the **subtropical high-pressure cells** (H) and **subpolar low-pressure cells** (L)—are formed by dynamic (mechanical) factors. Table 6.2 summarises the characteristics of these pressure areas. We now examine each principal pressure region.

Equatorial Low-Pressure Trough—ITCZ: Warm and Rainy Constant high Sun altitude and consistent daylength (close to 12 hours a day, year-round) make large amounts of energy available in this region throughout the year. The warming creates lighter, less-dense, ascending air, with surface winds converging along the entire extent of the low-pressure trough. This converging air is extremely moist and full of latent heat energy. As it rises, the air expands and cools, producing condensation; consequently, rainfall is heavy throughout this zone.

TABLE 6.2	Pressure Areas in Each Hemisphere		
Name	Cause	Location	Air Temperature/ Moisture
Polar high-pressure cells	Thermal	90° N, 90° S	Cold/dry
Subpolar low-pressure cells	Dynamic	60° N, 60° S	Cool/wet
Subtropical high-pressure cells	Dynamic	20°–35° N, 20°–35° S	Hot/dry
Equatorial low-pressure trough	Thermal	10° N to 10° S	Warm/wet

Vertical cloud columns frequently reach the tropopause, with thunderous strength and intensity.

The combination of heating and convergence forces air aloft and forms the **intertropical convergence zone (ITCZ)**. The ITCZ is identified by bands of clouds associated with the convergence of winds along the equator and is noted on the January and July pressure maps (see Figure 6.9; the maps show the ITCZ as a dashed line). In January, the zone crosses northern Australia and dips southward in eastern Africa and South America. Note this ITCZ location on the satellite image in Figure 6.10 using precipitation patterns. During summer, a marked wet season accompanies the shifting ITCZ over various regions.

Figure 6.10 features satellite images showing the equatorial low-pressure trough of the ITCZ using

(a)

(b)

FIGURE 6.10 Average seasonal rainfall values portray equatorial and subtropical circulation patterns.
(a) January average rainfall 1998–2010 in millimetres per day. Note the uninterrupted band of precipitation along the intertropical convergence zone (ITCZ).
(b) July average rainfall 1998–2010. Compare the pattern between the two images and compare to the pressure maps in Figure 6.9 and the location of the ITCZ. Note to the north and south of the ITCZ in the subtropics several high-pressure systems and clear skies (lacking colouration). [TRMM Microwave Imager on several geosynchronous satellites, courtesy of GSFC/NASA.]

associated precipitation for January and July. A broken band of precipitation accumulation (monthly averages) reveals this low-pressure system and its position slightly north of the equator in July. Note the position of the ITCZ in Figure 6.9 and compare this with the precipitation pattern captured by the TRMM (Tropical Rainfall Measuring Mission) sensors in Figure 6.10. The equatorial low-pressure trough is an elongated, undulating narrow band of low pressure (converging, ascending airflow), cloudiness, and precipitation, which nearly encircles the planet, consistently over the oceans and interrupted over land surfaces.

Figure 6.11 shows two views of Earth's general circulation. The winds converging on the equatorial low-pressure trough are known generally as the **trade winds,** or *trades*. *Northeast trade winds* blow in the Northern Hemisphere,

(a)

(b)

FIGURE 6.11 General atmospheric circulation model.
Two views of the general atmospheric circulation: (a) general circulation schematic; (b) equator-to-pole cross section of the Northern Hemisphere. Both views show Hadley cells, subtropical highs, the polar front, the sub-polar low-pressure cells, and approximate locations of the subtropical and polar jet streams.

and *southeast trade winds* in the Southern Hemisphere. These are labelled in Figure 6.11a. The trade winds were named during the era of sailing ships that carried trade across the seas.

The trade winds pick up large quantities of moisture as they return through the Hadley circulation cell for another cycle of uplift and condensation (shown in cross section in Figure 6.11b). These *Hadley cells* in each hemisphere, named for the eighteenth-century English scientist who described the trade winds, denote the circuit completed by winds rising along the ITCZ. Air moves northward and southward into the subtropics, descending to the surface and returning to the ITCZ as the trade winds. During the year in each hemisphere, this circulation pattern appears most vertically symmetrical near the equinoxes.

Within the ITCZ, winds are calm or mildly variable because of the even pressure gradient and the vertical ascent of air. These equatorial calms are the *doldrums*, a name formed from an older English word meaning "foolish," because of the difficulty sailing ships encountered when attempting to move through this zone. The rising air from the equatorial low-pressure area spirals upward into a geostrophic flow to the north and south. These upper-air winds turn eastward, flowing from west to east, beginning at about 20° N and 20° S, and form descending masses of air and high-pressure systems in the subtropical latitudes.

Subtropical High-Pressure Cells: Hot and Dry

Between 20° and 35° latitude in both hemispheres, a broad high-pressure zone of hot, dry air is evident across the globe (see Figures 6.9 and 6.10). Clear, frequently cloudless skies over the Sahara and the Arabian Desert and portions of the Indian Ocean dominate these regions. Can you identify these desert regions on the TRMM satellite image in Figure 6.10? How about on the photo of Earth on the text's back cover?

The dynamic cause of these subtropical anticyclones is too complex to detail here, but anticyclones generally form as air above the subtropics is mechanically pushed downward and heats by compression on its descent to the surface (shown in Figure 6.11). Warmer air has a greater capacity to absorb water vapour than does cooler air, making this descending warm air relatively dry (large water-vapour capacity, low water-vapour content). The air is also dry because heavy precipitation along the equatorial portion of the circulation removes moisture.

Surface air diverging from the subtropical high-pressure cells generates Earth's principal surface winds: the westerlies and the trade winds. The **westerlies** are the dominant surface winds from the subtropics to high latitudes. They diminish somewhat in summer and are stronger in winter in both hemispheres.

As you examine the global pressure maps in Figure 6.9, you find several high-pressure areas. In the Northern Hemisphere, the Atlantic subtropical high-pressure cell is the **Bermuda high** (in the western Atlantic) or the **Azores high** (when it migrates to the eastern Atlantic in winter). The area in the Atlantic under this subtropical

high features clear, warm waters and large quantities of *Sargassum* (a seaweed) that give the area its name—the Sargasso Sea. The **Pacific high,** or *Hawaiian high*, dominates the Pacific in July, shifting southward in January. In the Southern Hemisphere, three large high-pressure centres dominate the Pacific, Atlantic, and Indian oceans, especially in January, and tend to move along parallels of latitude in shifting zonal positions.

The entire high-pressure system migrates with the summer high Sun, fluctuating about 5°–10° in latitude. The eastern sides of these anticyclonic systems are drier and more stable (exhibit less convective activity) and feature cooler ocean currents than do the western sides. The drier eastern side of these systems and dry-summer conditions influence climate along subtropical and midlatitude west coasts (Figure 6.12). In fact, Earth's major deserts generally occur within the subtropical belt and extend to the west coast of each continent. In Figures 6.12 and 6.20, note that the desert regions of Africa reach the shore in both hemispheres, with the cool, southward-flowing *Canaries Current* offshore in the north, and the cool, northward-flowing *Benguela Current* offshore in the south.

Because the subtropical belts are near 25° N and S latitudes, these areas sometimes are known as the *calms of Cancer* and the *calms of Capricorn*. These zones of windless, hot, dry desert air, so deadly in the era of sailing ships, earned the name *horse latitudes*. Although the term's true origin is uncertain, it is popularly attributed to becalmed and stranded sailing crews of past centuries, who destroyed the horses on board, not wanting to share food or water with the livestock.

Winds ⟶   Warm current ⟶   Cool current ⟶

FIGURE 6.12 **Subtropical high-pressure system in the Atlantic.**
Characteristic circulation in the Northern Hemisphere. Note deserts extend to the shores of Africa, which has offshore cool currents, whereas the southeastern United States is moist and humid, with offshore warm currents.

Subpolar Low-Pressure Cells: Cool and Moist In January, two low-pressure cyclonic cells exist over the oceans around 60° N latitude, near their namesakes: the North Pacific **Aleutian low** and the North Atlantic **Icelandic low** (see Figure 6.9a). Both cells are dominant in winter and weaken or disappear in summer with the strengthening of high-pressure systems in the subtropics. The area of contrast between cold from higher latitudes and warm from lower latitudes air forms the **polar front,** where masses of air with different characteristics battle. This front encircles Earth and is focused in these low-pressure areas.

Figure 6.11 illustrates this confrontation between warm, moist air from the westerlies and cold, dry air from the polar and Arctic regions. Cooling and condensation in the lifted air occurs because of upward displacement of the warm air. Low-pressure cyclonic storms migrate out of the Aleutian and Icelandic frontal areas and may produce precipitation in North America and Europe, respectively. Northwestern sections of North America and Europe generally are cool and moist as a result of the passage of these cyclonic systems onshore—consider the weather in British Columbia, Washington, Oregon, Ireland, and the United Kingdom.

In the Southern Hemisphere, a discontinuous belt of subpolar low-pressure systems surrounds Antarctica. The spiraling cloud patterns produced by these cyclonic systems are visible on the spacecraft image in Figure 6.13.

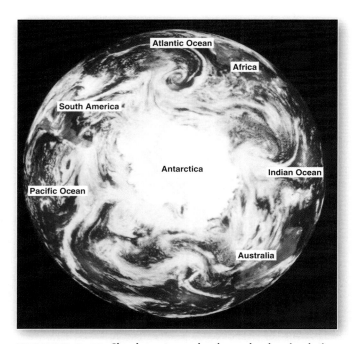

FIGURE 6.13 Clouds portray subpolar and polar circulation patterns.
Centred on Antarctica, this image shows a series of subpolar low-pressure cyclones in the Southern Hemisphere. Antarctica is fully illuminated by a midsummer Sun as the December solstice approaches. The Galileo spacecraft made this image during its December 1990 flyby of Earth. [Image courtesy of the late Dr. W. Reid Thompson, Cornell University.]

Severe cyclonic storms can cross Antarctica, producing strong winds and new snowfall. How many cyclonic systems can you identify around Antarctica on the image?

Polar High-Pressure Cells: Frigid and Dry Polar high-pressure cells are weak. The polar atmospheric mass is small, receiving little energy from the Sun to put it into motion. Variable winds, cold and dry, move away from the polar region in an anticyclonic direction. They descend and diverge clockwise in the Northern Hemisphere (counterclockwise in the Southern Hemisphere) and form weak, variable winds of the **polar easterlies.**

Of the two polar regions, the **Antarctic high** is stronger and more persistent, forming over the Antarctic landmass. Less pronounced is a polar high-pressure cell over the Arctic Ocean. When it does form, it tends to locate over the colder northern continental areas in winter (Canadian and Siberian highs) rather than directly over the relatively warmer Arctic Ocean.

Upper Atmospheric Circulation

Circulation in the middle and upper troposphere is an important component of the atmosphere's general circulation. Just as sea level is a reference datum for evaluating air pressure at the surface, we use a pressure level such as 500 mb as a **constant isobaric surface** for a pressure-reference datum in the upper atmosphere.

On upper-air pressure maps, we plot the height above sea level at which an air pressure of 500 mb occurs. The isobaric chart and illustration for an April day in Figures 6.14a and b illustrate such an undulating isobaric surface, upon which all points have the same pressure. In contrast, on surface weather maps we plot different pressures at the fixed elevation of sea level—a *constant height surface.*

We use this 500-mb level to analyze upper-air winds and the possible support these winds provide for surface weather conditions. Similar to surface maps, closer spacing of the isobars indicates faster winds; wider spacing indicates slower winds. On this constant isobaric pressure surface, altitude variations from the reference datum are ridges for high pressure (with isobars on the map bending poleward) and troughs for low pressure (with isobars on the map bending equatorward). Looking at Figure 6.14a, can you identify such ridges and troughs in the isobaric surface?

The pattern of ridges and troughs in the upper-air wind flow is important in sustaining surface cyclonic (low-pressure) and anticylonic (high-pressure) circulation. Near ridges in the isobaric surface, winds slow and converge (pile up), whereas winds near the area of maximum wind speeds along the troughs in the isobaric surface accelerate and diverge (spread out). Note the wind-speed indicators and labels in Figure 6.14a near the ridge (over Alberta, Saskatchewan, Montana, and Wyoming); now compare these with the wind-speed indicators around the trough (over Kentucky, West Virginia, the New England states, and the Maritimes). Also, note the wind relationships off the Pacific Coast.

FIGURE 6.14 Analysis of a constant isobaric surface for an April day.
(a) Contours show elevation at which 500-mb pressure occurs—a constant isobaric surface. The pattern of contours reveals a 500-mb isobaric surface and geostrophic wind patterns in the troposphere ranging from 5029 to 5822 m in elevation. (b) Note on the map and in the sketch beneath the chart the "ridge" of high pressure over the Intermountain West, at an altitude of 5760 m, and the "trough" of low pressure over the Great Lakes region and off the Pacific Coast, at an altitude of 5460 m. (c) Note areas of convergence aloft (corresponding to surface divergence) and divergence aloft (corresponding to surface convergence).

Cyclones and Anticyclones

Now look at Figure 6.14c. Divergence in the upper-air flow is important to cyclonic circulation at the surface because it creates an outflow of air aloft that stimulates an inflow of air into the low-pressure cyclone (such as what happens when you open a chimney damper to create an upward draft). Convergence aloft, on the other hand, drives descending airflows and divergent winds at the surface, moving out from high-pressure anticyclones.

Rossby Waves Within the westerly flow of geostrophic winds are great waving undulations called **Rossby waves,** named for meteorologist Carl G. Rossby, who first described them mathematically in 1938. The polar front is the line of conflict between colder air to the north and warmer air to the south (Figure 6.15). Rossby waves bring tongues of cold air southward, with warmer tropical air moving northward. The development of Rossby waves in the upper-air circulation is shown in the three-part figure. As these disturbances mature, distinct cyclonic circulation forms, with warmer air and colder air mixing along distinct fronts. These wave-and-eddy formations and upper-air divergences support cyclonic storm systems at the surface. Rossby waves develop along the flow axis of a jet stream.

Jet Streams The most prominent movement in these upper-level westerly wind flows are the **jet streams,** irregular, concentrated bands of wind occurring at several different locations that influences surface weather systems. (Figure 6.11a shows the location of four jet streams.) Rather flattened in vertical cross section, the jet streams normally are 160–480 km wide by 900–2150 m deep, with core speeds that can exceed 300 km·h^{-1}. Jet streams in each

hemisphere tend to weaken during the hemisphere's summer and strengthen during winter as the streams shift closer to the equator. The pattern of ridges and troughs causes variation in jet stream speeds (convergence and divergence).

The *polar jet stream* meanders between 30° and 70° N latitude, at the tropopause along the polar front, at altitudes between 7600 and 10 700 m. The polar jet stream can migrate as far south as Texas, steering colder air masses into North America and influencing surface storm paths travelling eastward. In summer, the polar jet stream exerts less influence on storms by staying at higher latitudes. Figure 6.16 shows a stylised view of a polar jet stream and two jet streams over North America.

In subtropical latitudes, near the boundary between tropical and midlatitude air, the *subtropical jet stream* flows near the tropopause (see Figure 6.11). The subtropical jet stream meanders from 20°–50° N latitude and may occur over North America simultaneously with the polar jet stream—sometimes the two will actually merge for brief episodes.

Multi-year Oscillations in Global Circulation

Several systematic fluctuations that occur in multiyear or shorter periods are important in the global circulation picture, yet an understanding of them is just emerging. The most famous of these is the El Niño–Southern Oscillation (ENSO) phenomenon discussed later in Chapter 10. Multiyear oscillations affect temperatures, air masses, and air pressure patterns, and thus affect global winds and climates. Here we describe three of these hemisphere-scale oscillations in the briefest terms. Please consult the three URLs provided for illustrations and further descriptions.

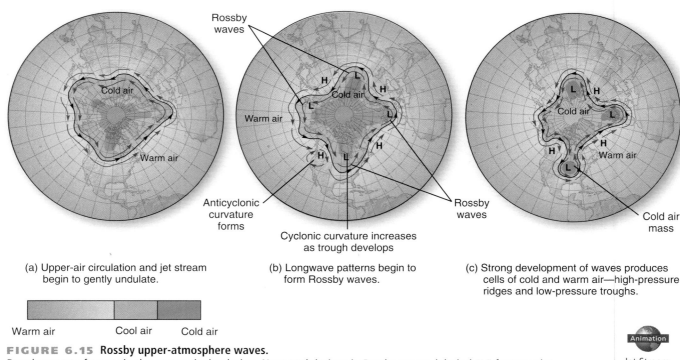

(a) Upper-air circulation and jet stream begin to gently undulate.

(b) Longwave patterns begin to form Rossby waves.

(c) Strong development of waves produces cells of cold and warm air—high-pressure ridges and low-pressure troughs.

FIGURE 6.15 Rossby upper-atmosphere waves.
Development of waves in the upper-air circulation. Note undulations in Rossby waves, labeled "L" for troughs and "H" for ridges.

Jet Stream, Rossby Waves

(a)   (b)

FIGURE 6.16 Jet streams.
(a) Average locations of the two jet streams over North America. (b) Stylised portrait of a polar jet stream.

North Atlantic Oscillation A north–south fluctuation of atmospheric variability marks the *North Atlantic Oscillation* (NAO), as pressure differences between the Icelandic low and the Azores high in the Atlantic alternate in strength. The *NAO Index* is in its *positive phase* when the Icelandic low-pressure system is lower than normal and the Azores (west of Portugal) high-pressure cell is higher than normal. Strong westerly winds and jet stream cross the eastern Atlantic. Northerly winds blow in the Labrador Sea (west of Greenland) and southerly winds move through the Norwegian Sea (east of Greenland). In the eastern United States, winters tend to be less severe in contrast to the strong, warm, wet storms hitting northern Europe; however, the Mediterranean region is dry.

In its *negative phase*, the NAO features a weaker pressure gradient than normal between the Azores and Iceland and reduced westerlies and jet stream. Storm tracks shift southward in Europe, bringing moist conditions to the Mediterranean and cold, dry winters to northern Europe. The eastern United States experiences cold, snowy winters as Arctic air masses plunge to lower latitudes.

With unpredictable flips between positive and negative phases, sometimes changing from week to week, a trend to a phase more positive than negative has emerged since 1960. From 1980 to 2008, the NAO was averaging a more positive phase condition; however, through 2009 and

into early 2010, the NAO was into a more negative phase through the winter (see http://www.ldeo.columbia.edu/res/pi/NAO/).

Arctic Oscillation Variable fluctuations between middle- and high-latitude air mass conditions over the Northern Hemisphere produce the *Arctic Oscillation (AO)*. The AO is associated with the NAO, especially in winter, and the two phases of the *AO Index* correlate with the *NAO Index*. In the *positive phase* of the AO Index (positive NAO), the pressure gradient is affected by lower pressure than normal over the North Pole region and relatively higher pressures at lower latitudes. This sets up stronger westerly winds and a consistently strong jet stream and flow of warmer Atlantic water currents into the Arctic Ocean. Cold air masses do not migrate as far south in winter, whereas winters are colder than normal in Greenland.

In the *negative phase* of the AO Index (negative NAO), the pattern reverses. Higher-than-normal pressure is over the polar region and relatively lower pressure in the central Atlantic. The weaker zonal wind flow allows winter cold air masses into the eastern United States, northern Europe, and Asia, and sea ice in the Arctic Ocean becomes a bit thicker. Greenland is warmer than normal. The Northern Hemisphere winter of 2009–2010 featured unusual flows of cold air into the midlatitudes. In December 2009, the

 GEO REPORT 6.4   *Icelandic Ash Caught in the Jet Stream*

Although smaller than either the Mount St. Helens 1980 eruption or the Mount Pinatubo 1991 eruption, the 2010 eruption of Eyjafjallajökull volcano in Iceland injected about 1/10th of a cubic kilometre of volcanic debris into the jet-stream flow. The ash cloud from Iceland was swept toward the European mainland and the United Kingdom. Aircraft cannot risk ingesting volcanic ash into jet engines; therefore, airports were shut down for days at a time, and thousands of flights were cancelled. People's attention was focused on the guiding jet stream as it affected their flight schedules and lives.

Arctic Index was in its most negative phase since 1970; it was even more negative through 2010 and 2011 (see http://nsidc .org/arcticmet/patterns/arctic_oscillation.html).

Pacific Decadal Oscillation Across the Pacific Ocean, the *Pacific Decadal Oscillation (PDO)*, which lasts 20 to 30 years, is longer-lived than the 2- to 12-year variation in the ENSO. The PDO term came into use only in 1996. Involved are two regions of sea-surface temperatures and related air pressure: the northern and tropical western Pacific (region #1) and the area of the eastern tropical Pacific, along the U.S. west coast (region #2).

Between 1947 and 1977, higher-than-normal temperatures dominated region #1, and lower temperatures were found in region #2; this is the PDO *negative phase* (cool phase). After a switch to a *positive phase* (warm phase) in the PDO from 1977 to the 1990s, lower temperatures were found in region #1 and higher-than-normal

temperatures dominated region #2, coinciding with a time of more intense ENSO events. In 1999, a *negative phase* began for four years, then a mild positive phase for three years, and now the PDO has been in a negative phase since 2008. Unfortunately for the U.S. Southwest, this PDO negative phase can mean a decade or more of drier conditions for the already drought-plagued region.

Causes of the PDO and its cyclic variability over time are unknown. Scientists monitor conditions in the Pacific and look for patterns. A better understanding of the PDO will help scientists predict ENSO events as well as regional drought cycles (see http://jisao.washington .edu/pdo/).

Local Winds

Land and sea breezes occur on most coastlines (Figure 6.17). Different heating characteristics of land and water surfaces create these breezes. Land gains heat

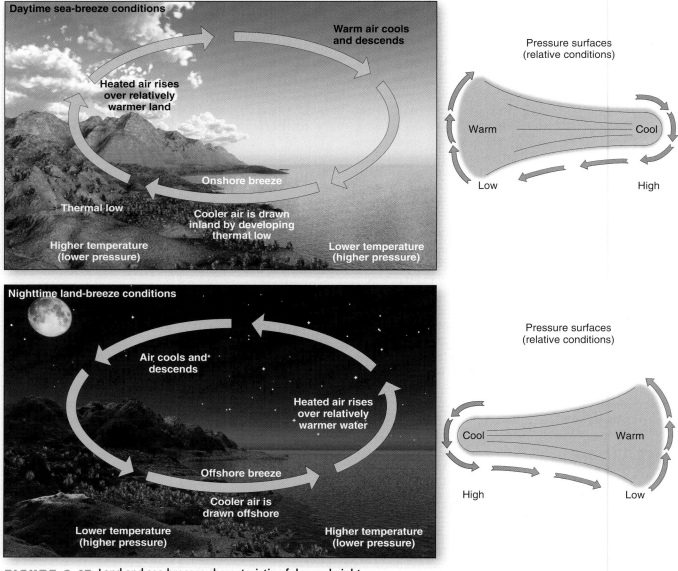

FIGURE 6.17 Land and sea breezes characteristic of day and night.

energy faster and becomes warmer than the water offshore during the day. Because warm air is less dense, it rises and triggers an onshore flow of cooler marine air to replace the rising warm air—the flow is usually strongest in the afternoon. At night, inland areas cool (radiate heat energy) faster than offshore waters. As a result, the cooler air over the land subsides and flows offshore over the warmer water, where the air is lifted. This night pattern reverses the process that developed during the day.

Mountain and valley breezes result when mountain air cools rapidly at night and valley air gains heat energy rapidly during the day (Figure 6.18). Thus, warm air rises upslope during the day, particularly in the afternoon; at night, cooler air subsides downslope into the valleys.

Katabatic winds, or gravity drainage winds, are of larger regional scale and usually stronger than local winds, under certain conditions. An elevated plateau

or highland is essential to their formation, where layers of air at the surface cool, become denser, and flow downslope. Such gravity winds are not specifically related to the pressure gradient. The ferocious winds that can blow off the ice sheets of Antarctica and Greenland are katabatic in nature.

Worldwide, a variety of terrain produces such winds, which bear many local names. The *mistral* of the Rhône Valley in southern France can cause frost damage to vineyards as the cold north winds move over the region to the Golf of Lion and the Mediterranean Sea. The frequently stronger *bora*, driven by the cold air of winter high-pressure systems inland, flows across the Adriatic Coast to the west and south. In Alaska such winds are called the *taku*.

Chinooks are another type of local wind. They occur when a mountain range is exposed to a strong prevailing

Daytime valley-breeze conditions
Warmer air

Nighttime mountain-breeze conditions
Cooler air

FIGURE 6.18 Pattern of valley and mountain breezes day and night.

crosswind. Moist air is forced up the mountains, bringing both clouds and precipitation to the *windward* side. The descending air then warms by compression and becomes drier as it is forced down the *leeward* side of the mountains. The relatively warm, dry, gusty winds that periodically occur on the leeward side of mountain ranges around the world are known by many names. In Canada and the northern United States, the name is *chinooks*, thought to be a native word meaning "snow eater." In parts of Europe these are known as *foehn* or *föhn* winds.

Regionally, wind represents a significant source of renewable energy of increasing importance. Focus Study 6.1 briefly explores wind power as a resource.

▌▌ CRITICAL THINKING 6.2

Construct Your Own Wind-Power Assessment Report

Go to http://www.canwea.ca, http://www.awea.org/ and http://www.ewea.org/, the web sites of the Canadian Wind Energy Association, the American Wind Energy Association and the European Wind Energy Association, respectively. Sample the materials presented as you assess the potential for wind-generated electricity. What are your thoughts concerning this resource—its potential, the reasons for delays, and the competitive economics presented? Propose a brief action plan for the future of this resource.

Monsoonal Winds

Some regional wind systems seasonally change direction. Intense, seasonally shifting wind systems occur in the tropics over Southeast Asia, Indonesia, India, northern Australia, and equatorial Africa. A mild version of such monsoonal-type flow affects the extreme southwestern United States. These winds involve an annual cycle of returning precipitation with the summer Sun. Note the change in rainfall visible on the TRMM images in Figure 6.10; compare January and July.

The Arabic word for season, *mausim*, or **monsoon**, is the source of the name. Specific monsoonal weather, associated climate types, and vegetation regions are discussed in Chapters 8, 10, and 20. The location and size of the Asian landmass and its proximity to the Indian Ocean drive the monsoons of southern and eastern Asia (Figure 6.19). Also important to the generation of monsoonal flows are wind and pressure patterns in the upper-air circulation.

The extreme temperature range from summer to winter over the Asian landmass is due to its continentality (isolation from the modifying effects of the ocean). An intense high-pressure anticyclone dominates this continental landmass in winter (see Figure 6.9a and Figure 6.19a), whereas the equatorial low-pressure trough (ITCZ) dominates the central area of the Indian Ocean. This pressure gradient produces cold, dry winds from the Asian interior over the Himalayas and across India. Average

(a) Winter, dry monsoon

(b) Summer, wet monsoon

(c) Precipitation at Nagpur, India

FIGURE 6.19 The Asian monsoons.
Asian monsoon pressure and wind patterns during (a) winter and (b) summer. Note the shifting location of the ITCZ, the changing pressures over the Indian Ocean, and the different conditions over the Asian landmass. The inset climograph for Nagpur shows the severe contrast in seasonal precipitation. [After Joseph E. Van Riper, *Man's Physical World*, p. 215, McGraw-Hill, 1971.]

Station: Nagpur, India   Elevation: 310 m
Lat/long: 21° 1′ N 79° 1′ E   Total ann. precip.:

temperatures range between 15° and 20°C at lower elevations. These winds desiccate, or dry out, the landscape and then give way to hot weather from March through May.

During the June–September wet period, the subsolar point (rays of sunlight directly overhead) shifts northward to the Tropic of Cancer, near the mouths of the Indus and Ganges rivers. The ITCZ shifts northward over southern Asia, and the Asian continental interior develops a thermal low pressure, associated with high average temperatures (remember the summer warmth in Verkhoyansk, Siberia, from Chapter 5). Meanwhile, subtropical high pressure dominates the Indian Ocean, with a surface temperature of 30°C. As a result of this reversed pressure gradient, hot subtropical air sweeps over the warm ocean, producing extremely high evaporation rates (Figure 6.19b).

By the time this air mass and the convergence zone reach India, the air is laden with moisture in thunderous, dark clouds. When the monsoonal rains arrive from June to September, people welcome the relief from the dust, heat, and parched land of Asia's springtime. Likewise, the annual monsoon is an integral part of Indian music, poetry, and life. In the Himalayas, the monsoon brings snowfall. The photo of the GPS unit in Figure 1.20 was made near the summit of Mount Everest on May 20, 1998, at the end of the spring climbing season in Nepal just before the onset of the summer monsoon.

World-record rainfalls of the wet monsoon drench India. Cherrapunji, India, received both the second-highest average annual rainfall (1143 cm) and the highest single-year rainfall (2647 cm) on Earth.

The fact that the monsoons of southern Asia involve vast global pressure systems leads us to ask whether future climate change might affect present monsoonal patterns. Concern increases following events such as the monsoonal deluge on July 27, 2005, that drowned Mumbai (formerly Bombay)—in only a few hours, 94.2 cm of rain fell, causing widespread flooding. Again in 2007, extensive flooding from an intense monsoon struck across India, and in 2010 Pakistan was devastated by record-breaking monsoon rains.

Scientists forecast higher rainfall if consideration is given to increases in carbon dioxide and its greenhouse warming alone. However, when consideration is given to increases in aerosols—principally sulfur compounds and black carbon—then a drop in precipitation of 7%–14% appears in the model. Air pollution reduces surface heating and therefore decreases the pressure differences at the heart of monsoonal flows. Considering that 70% of the annual precipitation for the entire region comes during the wet monsoon, the actual occurrence of such changes would force difficult societal adjustments to changing water resources. (See the satellite images in Figure 4.7 and review the text discussion.)

Oceanic Currents

The driving force for ocean currents is the frictional drag of the winds, thus linking the atmospheric and oceanic systems. Also important in shaping these currents is the interplay of Coriolis force, density differences caused by temperature and salinity, the configuration of the continents and ocean floor, and astronomical forces (the tides).

Surface Currents

Figure 6.20 portrays the general patterns of major ocean currents. Because ocean currents flow over distance and through time, Coriolis force causes deflection. However, the pattern of deflection is not as tightly circular as in the atmosphere. Compare this ocean-current map with the

FIGURE 6.20 Major ocean currents. [After the U.S. Naval Oceanographic Office.]

Ocean Circulation

FOCUS STUDY 6.1

Wind Power: An Energy Resource for the Present and Future

Understanding of the principles of wind power is ancient, but the technology is modern and the benefits are substantial. Scientists estimate that wind as a resource could potentially produce many times more energy than is currently in demand on a global scale. Yet despite the available technology, wind-power development continues to be slowed mainly by the changing politics of renewable energy.

The Nature of Wind Energy

Power generation from wind depends on site-specific characteristics of the wind resource. Favourable settings for consistent wind are (1) along coastlines influenced by trade winds and westerly winds; (2) where mountain passes constrict airflow and interior valleys develop thermal low-pressure areas, thus drawing air across the landscape; or (3) where localised winds occur, such as an expanse of relatively flat prairies, or in areas with katabatic or monsoonal winds. Many developing countries are located in areas blessed by such steady winds, such as the trade winds across the tropics.

Where winds are sufficient and consistent, electricity is generated by groups of wind turbines, in wind farms, or by individual installations (see the chapter-opening photo and Figure 6.1.1). If winds are reliable less than 25%–30% of the time, only small-scale uses are economically feasible.

The potential of wind power in the United States and Canada is enormous. For example, the winds from the Canadian prairies south through Texas could meet all U.S. and Canadian electrical needs, and investments would benefit rural regions of the country. In the California Coast Ranges, land–sea breezes blow between the Pacific and Central Valley, peaking in intensity from April to October, matching peak electrical demands for air conditioning during the hot summer months. Similar wind-power potential exists along Canadian coastlines.

On the eastern shore of Lake Erie sits a closed Bethlehem Steel mill, contaminated with industrial waste until the site was redeveloped with eight 2.5-MW (megawatts) wind-power turbines in 2007 (Figure 6.1.2). This former *brownfield* site now supplies the equivalent of 75% of the electricity for Lackawanna, New York. Twelve turbines will soon be added, making this a 50-MW electrical generation facility, the largest urban installation in the United States. An additional proposal for 500 MW of wind power from some 167 turbines is planned for an installation offshore in Lake Erie. This former steel town is using wind power to lift itself out of an economic depression with the slogan "Turning the Rust Belt into the Wind Belt."

Wind Power in Canada

The Canadian Wind Energy Association has stated a goal of supplying 20% of Canada's electricity demand by 2025. At the end of 2007, Canada had installed or planned development of more than 4200 MW of wind power capacity. There are wind energy generation installations in 11 provinces and territories. In Yukon Territory, renewable energy programs fund pilot projects. In Alberta and Ontario, private for-profit power developers operate wind farms to supply electricity to competitive wholesale markets. In other regions, partnerships between private companies

(a)

(b)

FIGURE 6.1.1 Wind farms: Kansas and Canada
(a) The Gray County Wind Farm, 40 km (25 mi) west of Dodge City, near Montezuma, Kansas, generates 112 MW of electricity. All the towers and roads combined occupy only 6 acres of land, allowing the balance of 12,000 acres to stay in agricultural production. (b) Wind turbines on Ascension Island (at about 8° S 14° W in the Atlantic Ocean): British installation (left), U.S. installation (right). Four of the U.S. turbines offset the need for the importation of 300,000 barrels of oil per year. [Bobbé Christopherson.]

FIGURE 6.1.2 Wind turbines at a former industrial site.
Known as "The Steel Wind," eight turbines deliver 20 MW of wind power in Lackawanna, New York, on the eastern shore of Lake Erie, south of Buffalo. The former industrial site is set to expand to 50 MW. [Bobbé Christopherson.]

and provincial crown corporations are developing wind-power generation. Table 6.1.1 presents the active wind-power generation capacity by province and territory as of December 2010.

Wind-Power Status and Benefits

Wind-generated energy resources are the fastest-growing energy technology, in terms of new capacity—capacity has risen worldwide in a continuing trend of doubling every three years. Total world capacity exceeded 190 000 MW (190 GW or gigawatts) by the end of 2010 from installations in 81 countries. Globally, the wind-power industry employs more than 550 000 people with investments passing the U.S.$63-billion mark in 2009. Forecasts state that employment will top the million-worker mark in 2012. Average-size wind farms produce more than 100 MW.

In the United States, installed wind capacity exceeded 40 180 MW through 2011, an increase of 300% in 4 years.

This puts U.S-installed wind capacity second-highest on a global level, behind China, with Germany third. The European Wind Energy Association announced installed capacity exceeding 84 000 MW at the end of 2010, a 23% increase in 1 year. Germany has the most, followed by Spain, Italy, France, and the United Kingdom. The European Union has a goal of supplying 20% of all energy from renewable sources by 2020 (see http://www.ewea.org/).

The economic and social benefits from using wind resources are numerous. With all costs considered, wind energy is cost-competitive and actually cheaper than oil, coal, natural gas, and nuclear power. Wind power is renewable and does not cause adverse human health effects or environmental degradation. Relative to concerns about turbines hurting birds, a survey found that wind turbines ranked behind other causes of bird mortality when compared to communication towers, pesticides, high-tension power lines, domestic cats, and collisions with buildings and windows.

To put numbers in meaningful perspective, every 10 000 MW of wind-generation capacity reduces carbon dioxide emissions by 33 million metric tons if it replaces coal, or by 21 million metric tons if it replaces mixed fossil fuels. As an example, if countries rally and create a proposed $600-billion industry by installing 1 250 000 MW of wind capacity by 2020, that would supply 12% of global electrical needs.

Whether or not governments and transnational energy corporations support full-scale implementation of renewable resources such as wind, the energy realities of the near future leave no alternative, and global political realities affirm this urgency. By the middle of this century, wind-generated electricity could be routine, along with other renewable energy sources, conservation, and energy efficiency.

TABLE 6.1.1   Wind Power in Canada

Province/Territory	Installed (MW, end of 2010)	In Development (MW, contracts signed)
British Columbia	325	815
Alberta	519	1618
Saskatchewan	196	226
Manitoba	104	242
Ontario	1410	3816
Québec	1427	2361
Newfoundland	51	0
PEI	72	10
Nova Scotia	72	110
New Brunswick	96	359
Yukon	1	0
Northwest Territory	0	0
Nunavut	0	0
TOTAL	4008	8122

Sources: Canadian Wind Energy Association; Natural Resources Canada.

map showing Earth's pressure systems (see Figure 6.9) and you can see that ocean currents are driven by the circulation around subtropical high-pressure cells in both hemispheres. These circulation systems are known as *gyres* and generally appear to be offset toward the western side of each ocean basin. Remember, in the Northern Hemisphere, winds and ocean currents move *clockwise* about high-pressure cells; in the Southern Hemisphere, circulation is *counterclockwise*, evident on the map. You saw in *Geosystems Now* how these currents guided an oil-drilling platform to Tristan da Cunha, where it ran aground.

In sailing days, the Spanish galleons would leave San Blas and Acapulco, Mexico (16.5° N), and sail southwest, catching the northeast trade winds across the Pacific to Manila (14° N) in the Philippines. Goods would be traded and new commodities obtained. Leaving the Philippines, the ships would move northward to catch the westerlies in the midlatitudes to be blown across the ocean to the shores of present-day Alaska or British Columbia and sail along the coast. The galleons would sail south along North America, fighting the rain, frequent fog, and right-hand Coriolis deflection pushing them away from the coast. The journey would end back in Mexico with cargo from the Orient. Thus the history of the *Manilla Galleons* is a lesson in oceanic currents around the Pacific gyre.

Examples of Gyre Circulation   In 1992, a child at Dana Point, California (33.5° N), a small seaside community south of Los Angeles, placed a letter in a glass juice bottle and tossed it into the waves. Thoughts of distant lands and fabled characters filled the child's imagination as the bottle disappeared. The vast circulation around the Pacific high, clockwise-circulating gyre now took command (Figure 6.21).

Three years passed before ocean currents carried the message in a bottle to the coral reefs and white sands of Mogmog, a small island in Micronesia (7° N). A 7-year-old

child there had found a pen pal from afar. Imagine the journey of that note from California—travelling through storms and calms, clear moonlit nights and typhoons, as it floated on currents as the galleons once had.

In January 1994, a powerful storm ravaged a container ship, loaded with toys and other goods from Hong Kong. One of the containers on board split apart in the wind off the coast of Japan, dumping nearly 30 000 rubber ducks, turtles, and frogs into the North Pacific. Westerly winds and the North Pacific current swept this floating cargo at up to 29 km a day across the ocean to the coast of Alaska, British Columbia, Oregon, and California. Other toys, still adrift, went through the Bering Sea and into the Arctic Ocean (this route is indicated by the dashed line in Figure 6.21).

On August 19, 2006, Tropical Storm Ioke formed about 1285 km south of Hawai'i. The storm's track moved across the Pacific Ocean over Wake Island and Johnston Atoll, becoming the strongest Super Typhoon in recorded history—a category 5, as we discuss in Chapter 8. Turning northward east of Japan and the Kamchatka Peninsula of Russia, the storm moved into higher latitudes. Typhoon Ioke remnants eventually crossed over the Aleutian Islands, reaching 55° N as an extratropical depression. The storm roughly followed the path around the Pacific gyre and along the track of the rubber duckies. Scientists are using incidents such as the message in a bottle and rubber duckies and such remarkable storm tracks to learn more about wind systems and ocean currents.

Equatorial Currents   In Figure 6.20, you can see that trade winds drive the ocean surface waters westward in a concentrated channel along the equator. These currents, called *equatorial currents*, are kept near the equator by Coriolis force, which diminishes to zero at the equator. As these surface currents approach the western margins of the oceans, the water actually piles up against the eastern shores of the continents. The average height of

FIGURE 6.21 Pacific Ocean currents transport human artifacts. The travels of a message in a bottle and toy rubber duckies, and the path of Typhoon Ioke, in currents moving clockwise around the Pacific gyre. During 2011 and 2012 a 51 km² patch of debris, toxics, and chemicals drifted westward across the Pacific Ocean, generated by the March earthquake and tsunami that struck Japan—carried in the path of the westerlies.

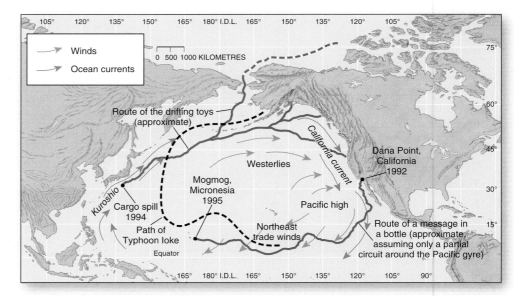

this pileup is 15 cm. This phenomenon is the **western intensification.**

The piled-up ocean water then goes where it can, spilling northward and southward in strong currents, flowing in tight channels along the eastern shorelines. In the Northern Hemisphere, the *Gulf Stream* and the *Kuroshio* (current east of Japan) move forcefully northward as a result of western intensification. Speed and depth increase by the constriction of the area the currents occupy. The warm, deep, clear water of the ribbonlike Gulf Stream (Figure 5.10) usually is 50–80 km wide and 1.5–2.0 km deep, moving at 3–10 km · h⁻¹. In 24 hours, ocean water can move 70–240 km in the Gulf Stream.

Upwelling and Downwelling Flows Where surface water is swept away from a coast, either by surface divergence (induced by Coriolis force) or by offshore winds, an **upwelling current** occurs. This cool water generally is nutrient-rich and rises from great depths to replace the vacating water. Such cold upwelling currents exist off the Pacific coasts of North and South America and the subtropical and midlatitude west coast of Africa. These areas are some of Earth's prime fishing regions.

In other regions where there is an accumulation of water—such as the western end of an equatorial current, or the Labrador Sea, or along the margins of Antarctica—the excess water gravitates downward in a **downwelling current**. These are the deep currents that flow vertically and along the ocean floor and travel the full extent of the ocean basins, carrying heat energy and high salinity water.

Thermohaline Circulation— The Deep Currents

Differences in temperatures and salinity produce density differences important to the flow of deep currents. This is Earth's **thermohaline circulation**, and it is different from wind-driven surface currents. Travelling at slower speeds than surface currents, the thermohaline circulation hauls larger volumes of water. Figure 16.4 illustrates the ocean's physical structure and profiles of temperature, salinity, and dissolved gases; note the temperature and salinity differences with depth on this illustration.

To picture such a deep, salty current, imagine a continuous channel of water beginning with cold-water downwelling in the North Atlantic and along Antarctica, and upwelling in the Indian Ocean and North Pacific (Figure 6.22). Here it warms and then is carried in surface currents back to the North Atlantic. A complete circuit of the current may require 1000 years from downwelling, to deep cold current covering thousands of kilometres, to its reemergence at the surface elsewhere. Even deeper Antarctic bottom water flows northward in the Atlantic Basin beneath the thermohaline currents.

These current systems appear to play a profound role in global climate; in turn, global warming has the potential to disrupt the downwelling in the North Atlantic and the thermohaline circulation. There is a freshening of ocean surface waters in both polar regions, contrasted with large increases in salinity in the surface waters at lower latitudes. Increased rates of glacier, sea-ice, and ice-sheet melting produce these fresh lower-density surface waters that ride on top of the denser saline water. The concern is that such

FIGURE 6.22 Deep-ocean thermohaline circulation.
This global circulation is a vast conveyor belt of water, drawing heat energy from warm shallow currents and transporting it for release in the depths of the ocean basins in cold, deep, salty currents. Four blue areas at high latitudes are where surface water cools, sinks, and feeds the deep circulation.

changes in ocean temperature and salinity could dampen the rate of the North Atlantic Deep Water downwelling in the North Atlantic.

This is a vital research frontier because the oceanic component of Earth's hydrologic cycle is still little understood. Research groups such as Scripps Institution of Oceanography (http://sio.ucsd.edu/), Woods Hole Oceanographic Institution (http://www.whoi.edu/), Institute for the Study of Earth, Oceans, and Space (http://www.eos.sr.unh.edu/), and Bedford Institute of Oceanography (http://www.bio.gc.ca/index-eng.htm), to name only a few of many, are places to periodically check for updated information.

GEOSYSTEMS CONNECTION

With this chapter, you have completed the inputs–actions–outputs through the chapters of PART I, *The Energy–Atmosphere System*. Along the way, we have examined the many ways these Earth systems affect our lives and the many ways human society is affecting these same systems. Given this foundation, we move on to PART II, *The Water, Weather, and Climate Systems*. Water and ice cover 71% of Earth's surface by area, making Earth the water planet. This water is driven by the pattern of energy we have been studying to produce weather, water resources, and climate.

APPLIED PHYSICAL GEOGRAPHY

Describing Wind Regimes

The wind regime for a location can be described by summarizing records of wind speed and direction for a given time period. Mean wind speed ($\bar{u}$) can be calculated as a simple average:

$$\bar{u} = 1/N \sum_{i=1}^{N} u_i$$

where u is wind speed, N is the total number of observations, and $\sum$ is the symbol for summation. It is possible to calculate a value for the mean wind direction—known as a wind resultant—by using vector analysis and some basic trigonometric functions.

$$V_x = -1/N \sum_{i=1}^{N} \sin \theta_i$$

$$V_y = -1/N \sum_{i=1}^{N} \cos \theta_i$$

V_x and V_y are the east–west and north–south components of the resultant and θ is wind direction. The wind resultant direction ($\bar{\theta}$) is calculated by:

$$\bar{\theta} = \arctan \left(V_x/V_y \right) + C$$

The value of C depends on the result of arctan (V_x/V_y). If the result is > 180°, then $C = +180°$ if the result is > 180°, then $C = -180°$. This last step is necessary to produce an answer that describes the mean direction from which the wind blows.

Table APG 6.1 contains a sample data set to show how mean wind speed and direction are calculated for hourly observations over a 12-hour period. For the mean wind speed, $\bar{u} = 118/12 = 9.8$ m·s⁻¹.

TABLE APG 6.1

Observation (i)	Wind Speed, U_i (m · s⁻¹)	Wind Direction, θ_i(°)	sin θ_i	cos θ_i
1	12	270	−1.00	0.00
2	11	280	−0.98	0.17
3	13	280	−0.98	0.17
4	8	260	−0.98	−0.17
5	10	250	−0.94	−0.34
6	10	260	−0.98	−0.17
7	8	250	−0.94	−0.34
8	8	260	−0.98	−0.17
9	6	240	−0.87	−0.50
10	9	230	−0.77	−0.64
11	11	240	−0.87	−0.50
12	12	210	−0.50	−0.87
$\sum$	118		−10.79	−3.36
Mean	9.8		0.90	0.28

For wind direction, $V_x = (-1/12) \times (-10.79) = 0.90$, and $V_y = (-1/12) \times (-3.36) = 0.28$. Consequently, arctan $(V_x/V_y) = 73°$, so the wind resultant is $\bar{\theta} = 73 + 180 = 253°$.

A wind rose is a circular plot that shows the relative distribution of wind direction (from which the wind was blowing), with each petal on the rose portraying data for a range of compass directions. The compass is usually divided into 8, 16, or 36 segments, corresponding to ranges of 45°, 22.5°, or 10°, respectively. As an alternative to summarizing the annual wind regime, it is possible to describe the regime for more specific parts of

the year, such as a particular season or month. When displaying a wind rose, it is important to include the period over which data were collected, and the part of the year that is represented.

Annual wind roses for two locations in Ontario—Windsor and Kapuskasing—for the 30-year period from 1976–2005 are presented in Figure APG 6.1. By plotting both sets of data with the same scales, a visual comparison of the long-term wind regimes can be made. Kapuskasing is located 800 km directly north of Windsor, and comparing the wind roses shows that it has a much different wind regime than Windsor. The data shown represent a summary of almost 263 000 hourly measurements for each location that were collected by the Meteorological Service of Canada[1]. In addition to the directional information, the frequency of wind speeds within each direction category is displayed with coloured segments on the petals.

[1] Wind data source: Canadian Weather Energy and Engineering Datasets (CWEEDS), http://climate.weatheroffice.gc.ca/prods_servs/index_e.html.

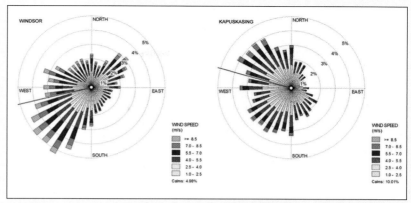

FIGURE APG 6.1 Annual wind roses for Windsor and Kapuskasing, Ontario, 1976–2005.
A wind rose is a visual summary of the distribution of wind directions over a given time period. In this case, the compass is divided into 36 categories, each with a range of 10°; and the distribution of wind speeds within each category is shown with coloured segments on the petals. For Windsor, the mean annual wind speed was 4.4 m · s⁻¹ and the wind resultant was 256°. The corresponding values for Kapuskasing were 3.5 m · s⁻¹ and 286°. Resultant directions are shown with a red line. [Wind rose plotting software program: WRPLOT View (v. 6.5.2) from Lakes Environmental, http://www.weblakes.com/products/wrplot/index.html.]

KEY LEARNING CONCEPTS REVIEW

■ **Define** the concept of air pressure, and **describe** instruments used to measure air pressure.

The weight (created by motion, size, and number of molecules) of the atmosphere is **air pressure**, which exerts an average force of approximately 1 kg · cm⁻². A **mercury barometer** measures air pressure at the surface (mercury in a tube—closed at one end and open at the other, with the open end placed in a vessel of mercury—that changes level in response to pressure changes) as does an **aneroid barometer** (a closed cell, partially evacuated of air, that detects changes in pressure).

air pressure (p. 135)
mercury barometer (p. 136)
aneroid barometer (p. 136)

1. How does air exert pressure? Describe the basic instrument used to measure air pressure. Compare the operation of two different types of instruments discussed.
2. What is normal sea-level pressure in millimetres? Millibars? Kilopascals?

■ **Define** wind, and **explain** how winds are measured, how wind direction is determined, and how winds are named.

Wind is the horizontal movement of air across Earth's surface. Turbulence adds wind updrafts and downdrafts and a vertical component to this definition. Its speed is measured with an **anemometer** (a device with cups that are pushed by the wind) and its direction with a **wind vane** (a flat blade or surface that is directed by the wind). A descriptive scale useful in visually estimating wind speed is the traditional *Beaufort wind scale*.

wind (p. 136)
anemometer (p. 136)
wind vane (p. 136)

3. What is a possible explanation for the beautiful sunrises and sunsets during the summer of 1992 in North America? Relate your answer to global circulation.
4. Explain this statement: "The atmosphere socializes humanity, making all the world a spatially linked society." Illustrate your answer with some examples.
5. Define wind. How is it measured? How is its direction determined?
6. Distinguish among primary, secondary, and tertiary general classifications of global atmospheric circulation.
7. What is the purpose of the Beaufort wind scale? Characterize winds given Beaufort numbers of 4, 8, and 12, and describe specific effects over both water and land.

■ **Explain** the four driving forces within the atmosphere— gravity, pressure gradient force, Coriolis force, and friction force—and **locate** the primary high- and low-pressure areas and principal winds.

The pressure that Earth's gravitational force exerts on the atmosphere operates uniformly worldwide. Winds are driven by the **pressure gradient force** (air moves from areas of high pressure to areas of low pressure). Winds are deflected by the **Coriolis force**, an apparent deflection in the path of winds or ocean currents caused by the rotation of Earth and surface distance from Earth's axis as the gravitational force and centrifugal force work in opposition, deflecting objects to the right in the Northern Hemisphere and to the left in the Southern Hemisphere. Finally, winds are dragged by the **friction force**, in which Earth's varied surfaces exert a drag on wind movements in opposition to the pressure gradient. Maps portray air pressure patterns using the **isobar**—an isoline that connects points of equal pressure. A combination of the pressure gradient and Coriolis forces alone produces **geostrophic winds**, which move parallel to isobars, characteristic of winds above the surface frictional layer.

Winds descend and diverge, spiraling outward to form an **anticyclone** (clockwise in the Northern Hemisphere), and then converge and ascend, spiraling upward to form a cyclone (counterclockwise in the Northern Hemisphere). The pattern of high and low pressures on Earth in generalised belts in each hemisphere produces the distribution of specific wind systems. These primary pressure regions are the **equatorial low-pressure trough**, the weak **polar high-pressure cells** (at both the North and South poles), and the **subtropical high-pressure cells** and **subpolar low-pressure cells**.

All along the equator winds converge into the equatorial low creating the **intertropical convergence zone (ITCZ)**. Air rises along the equator and descends in the subtropics in each hemisphere. The winds returning to the ITCZ from the northeast in the Northern Hemisphere and from the southeast in the Southern Hemisphere produce the **trade winds**.

Winds flowing out of the subtropics to higher latitudes produce the **westerlies** in either hemisphere. The subtropical high-pressure cells on Earth, generally between 20° and 35° in either hemisphere, are variously named the **Bermuda high**, **Azores high**, and **Pacific high**.

Along the polar front and the series of low-pressure cells, the **Aleutian low** and **Icelandic low** dominate the North Pacific and Atlantic, respectively. This region of contrast between colder air toward the poles and warmer air toward the equator is the **polar front**. The weak and variable **polar easterlies** diverge from the polar high-pressure cells, particularly the **Antarctic high**.

pressure gradient force (p. 138)
Coriolis force (p. 138)
friction force (p. 138)
isobar (p. 138)
geostrophic winds (p. 143)
anticyclone (p. 143)
cyclone (p. 143)
equatorial low-pressure trough (p. 145)
polar high-pressure cells (p. 145)
subtropical high-pressure cells (p. 145)
subpolar low-pressure cells (p. 145)
intertropical convergence zone (ITCZ) (p. 145)
trade winds (p. 146)
westerlies (p. 147)
Bermuda high (p. 147)
Azores high (p. 147)
Pacific high (p. 147)
Aleutian low (p. 148)
Icelandic low (p. 148)
polar front (p. 148)
polar easterlies (p. 148)
Antarctic high (p. 148)

8. What does an isobaric map of surface air pressure portray? Contrast pressures over North America for January and July.
9. Describe the effect of Coriolis force. Explain how it apparently deflects atmospheric and oceanic circulations.
10. What are geostrophic winds, and where are these winds encountered in the atmosphere?

11. Describe the horizontal and vertical air motions in a high-pressure anticyclone and in a low-pressure cyclone. How are the patterns different in the Southern Hemisphere compared to the Northern Hemisphere?
12. Construct a simple diagram of Earth's general circulation; begin by labelling the four principal pressure belts or zones, then add arrows between these pressure systems to denote the three principal wind systems.
13. How is the intertropical convergence zone (ITCZ) related to the equatorial low-pressure trough? How does it appear on a satellite image of accumulated precipitation in Figure 6.10?
14. Characterise the belt of subtropical high pressure on Earth: Name the specific cells. Describe the generation of westerlies and trade winds. Discuss sailing conditions.
15. What is the relation among the Aleutian low, the Icelandic low, and migratory low-pressure cyclonic storms in North America? In Europe?

■ **Describe** upper-air circulation and its support role for surface systems, and *define* the jet streams.

A **constant isobaric surface** describes air pressure in the middle and upper troposphere. This is a surface along which the same pressure, such as 500 mb, occurs regardless of altitude. The height of this surface above the ground forms ridges and troughs that support the development of and help sustain surface pressure systems; surface lows are sustained by divergence aloft, and surface highs are sustained by convergence aloft.

Rossby waves are wave motions formed by vast, flowing, longwave undulations in these upper-air westerlies. Prominent streams of high-speed westerly winds in the upper-level troposphere are the **jet streams**. Depending on their latitudinal position in either hemisphere, they are termed the *polar jet stream* or the *subtropical jet stream*.

constant isobaric surface (p. 148)
Rossby waves (p. 150)
jet streams (p. 150)

16. What is the relation between wind speed and the spacing of isobars?
17. How is the constant isobaric surface (ridges and troughs) related to surface pressure systems? To divergence aloft and surface lows? To convergence aloft and surface highs?
18. Relate the jet-stream phenomenon to general upper-air circulation. How is the presence of this circulation related to airline schedules from Halifax to Vancouver and the return trip to Halifax?

■ **Summarise** several multiyear oscillations of air temperature, air pressure, and circulation in the Arctic, Atlantic, and Pacific oceans.

Several system fluctuations that occur in multiyear or shorter periods are important in the global circulation picture. The most famous of these is the *El Niño–Southern Oscillation (ENSO)* phenomenon. A north–south fluctuation of atmospheric variability marks the *North Atlantic Oscillation (NAO)* as pressure differences between the Icelandic low and the Azores high in the Atlantic alternate in strength. The *Arctic Oscillation (AO)* is the variable fluctuation between middle- and high-latitude air mass conditions over the Northern Hemisphere. The AO is associated with the NAO especially in winter, and the two phases of the *AO Index* correlate to the two-phased *NAO Index*. During the winter of 2009–2010, the AO Index was at the lowest negative phase since 1970.

Across the Pacific Ocean the *Pacific Decadal Oscillation* (*PDO*) involves variability between two regions of sea-surface temperatures and related air pressure: the northern and tropical western Pacific (region #1) and the area of the eastern tropical Pacific, along the West Coast (region #2). The PDO switches between positive and negative phases in 20- to 30-year cycles.

19. What phases are identified for the AO and NAO indices? What winter weather conditions generally affect the eastern United States during each phase?
20. What is the apparent relation between the PDO and the strength of El Niño events? Between PDO phases and the intensity of drought in the southwestern United States?

■ **Explain** several types of local winds: land–sea breezes, mountain–valley breezes, katabatic winds, and regional monsoons.

Different heating characteristics of land and water surfaces create **land and sea breezes**. Temperature differences during the day and evening between valleys and mountain summits cause **mountain and valley breezes**. **Katabatic winds**, or gravity drainage winds, are of larger regional scale and are usually stronger than mountain–valley breezes, under certain conditions. An elevated plateau or highland is essential, where layers of air at the surface cool, become denser, and flow downslope.

Intense, seasonally shifting wind systems occur in the tropics over Southeast Asia, Indonesia, India, northern Australia, equatorial Africa, and southern Arizona. These winds involve an annual cycle of returning precipitation with the summer Sun and carry the Arabic word for season, *mausim*, or **monsoon**. The location and size of the Asian landmass and its proximity to the Indian Ocean and the seasonally shifting ITCZ drive the monsoons of southern and eastern Asia.

land and sea breezes (p. 152)
mountain and valley breezes (p. 153)
katabatic winds (p. 153)
monsoon (p. 154)

21. People living along coastlines generally experience variations in winds from day to night. Explain the factors that produce these changing wind patterns.
22. The arrangement of mountains and nearby valleys produces local wind patterns. Explain the day and night winds that might develop.
23. Describe the seasonal pressure patterns that produce the Asian monsoonal wind and precipitation patterns. Contrast January and July conditions.
24. This chapter presents wind power as well developed and cost effective. Given the information presented and your

additional critical thinking work, what conclusions or observations have you made?

■ **Discern** the basic pattern of Earth's major surface ocean currents and deep thermohaline circulation.

Ocean currents are primarily caused by the frictional drag of wind and occur worldwide at varying intensities, temperatures, and speeds, both along the surface and at great depths in the oceanic basins. The circulation around subtropical high-pressure cells in both hemispheres is notable on the ocean circulation map—these *gyres* are usually offset toward the western side of each ocean basin.

The trade winds converge along the ITCZ and push enormous quantities of water that pile up along the eastern shore of continents in a process known as the **western intensification**. Where surface water is swept away from a coast, either by surface divergence (induced by Coriolis force) or by offshore winds, an **upwelling current** occurs. This cool water generally is nutrient-rich and rises from great depths to replace the vacating water. In other portions of the sea where there is an accumulation of water, the excess water gravitates downward in a **downwelling current**. These currents generate important mixing currents that flow along the ocean floor and travel the full extent of the ocean basins, carrying heat energy and high salinity water.

Differences in temperatures and salinity produce density differences important to the flow of deep, sometimes vertical, currents; this is Earth's **thermohaline circulation**. Travelling at slower speeds than wind-driven surface currents, the thermohaline circulation hauls larger volumes of water. There is scientific concern that increased surface temperatures in the ocean and atmosphere, coupled with climate-related changes in salinity, can alter the rate of thermohaline circulation in the oceans.

western intensification (p. 159)
upwelling current (p. 159)
downwelling current (p. 159)
thermohaline circulation (p. 159)

25. Define the western intensification. How is it related to the Gulf Stream and Kuroshio currents?
26. Where on Earth are upwelling currents experienced? What is the nature of these currents? Where are the four areas of downwelling that feed these dense bottom currents?
27. What is meant by deep-ocean thermohaline circulation? At what rates do these currents flow? How might this circulation be related to the Gulf Stream in the western Atlantic Ocean?
28. Relative to Question 27, what relation do these deep currents have to global warming and projected climate changes?

MyGeosciencePlace

Visit **www.mygeoscienceplace.ca** for several figure animations, satellite loops, self-study quizzes, flashcards, interactive glossary, career links, RSS feeds, Pearson eText of *Geosystems*, and much more.

INPUTS
Water
Atmospheric
moisture

ACTIONS
Humidity
Atmospheric stability
Air masses

OUTPUTS
Weather
Water resources
Climatic patterns

HUMAN-EARTH RELATION
Weather hazards
Water shortages
Climate change

I. Atmosphere

II. Hydrosphere

IV. Biosphere

III. Lithosphere

PART II

The Water, Weather, and Climate Systems

Earth is the water planet. Chapter 7 describes the remarkable qualities and properties possessed by water, where it occurs, and how it is distributed. We see the daily dynamics of the atmosphere—the powerful interaction of moisture and energy, the resulting stability and instability, and the variety of cloud forms—all important to understanding weather. Chapter 8 examines weather and its causes. Topics include the interaction of air masses, the daily weather map, and analysis of violent phenomena in thunderstorms, tornadoes, and hurricanes, and the recent trends for each of these.

Chapter 9 explains water circulation on Earth in the hydrologic cycle—an output of the water–weather system. We examine the water-budget concept, which is useful in understanding soil-moisture and water-resource relationships on global, regional, and local scales. Potable (drinking) water is emerging as the critical global political issue in this century. In Chapter 10, we see the spatial implications over time of the energy–atmosphere and water–weather systems and the output of Earth's climatic patterns. In this way, Chapter 10 interconnects all the system elements from Chapters 2 through 9. Part II closes with a discussion of global climate change science, a look at present conditions, and a forecast of future climate trends.

Irrigated lands along the Orange River, forming part of the border between Namibia and South Africa some 100 km from the coast. [*EO-1/* NASA.]

CHAPTER 7

Water and Atmospheric Moisture

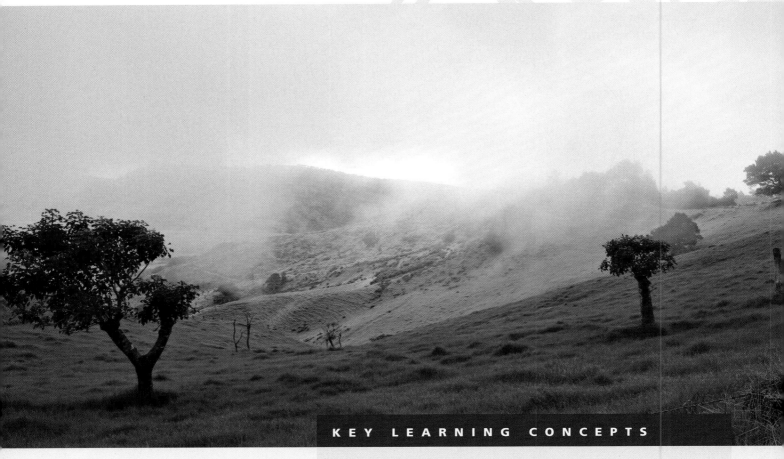

A marine layer fog mist contributes important moisture to this pasture and trees on the island of St. Helena in the middle of the Atlantic Ocean. [Bobbé Christopherson.]

KEY LEARNING CONCEPTS

After reading the chapter, you should be able to:

■ *Describe* the origin of Earth's waters, *define* the quantity of water that exists today, and *list* the locations of Earth's freshwater supply.

■ *Describe* the heat properties of water, and *identify* the traits of its three phases: solid, liquid, and gas.

■ *Define* humidity and the expressions of the relative humidity concept, and *explain* dew-point temperature and saturated conditions in the atmosphere.

■ *Define* atmospheric stability, and *relate* it to a parcel of air that is ascending or descending.

■ *Illustrate* three atmospheric conditions—unstable, conditionally unstable, and stable—with a simple graph that relates the environmental lapse rate (ELR) to the dry adiabatic rate (DAR) and moist adiabatic rate (MAR).

■ *Identify* the requirements for cloud formation, and *explain* the major cloud classes and types, including fog.

Earth's Lakes Provide an Important Warming Signal

All lakes combined contain only 0.33% of freshwater on Earth, yet lakes are significant regionally for water, food, livelihoods, and transport. Most lakes, including the seven major lakes on Earth listed in Table 7.1, are presently being impacted by climate change.

Increasing air temperatures are having a range of effects on lakes throughout the world, from rising lake levels in response to melting of glacial ice, to falling lake levels associated with drought and high evaporation rates. Such warming is damaging to lake ecology and health. Changes in the thermal structure of a lake tend to block the normal mixing between deep and surface waters.

Normally, stratification occurs in the summer in most lakes, with warmer water at the surface and cooler water at depth. This leads to a depletion of nutrients in the shallows and loss of dissolved oxygen at depth by late summer. In the fall, as the surface cools, water sinks, creating a turnover that replenishes surface nutrients and dissolved oxygen levels throughout the lake. In some lakes, wind assists such mixing.

As regional temperatures warm, the summerlike stratification appears earlier in the year and persists later in the fall, and mixing slows or stops. Cold-water species become stressed and invasive warmer-water species flourish.

Lake Tahoe in the Sierra Nevada mountain range along the California–Nevada border is warming at twice the rate of the surrounding region, at about 1.3 C° per decade (Figure GN 7.1). Some 7300 measurements collected over the past 35 years confirm the trend. The rate of warming is highest in the upper 10 m, causing increased thermal stability and resistance to mixing. Invasive large-mouth bass, carp, and Asian clam are on the rise, while cold-water species decline. Such temperature response is seen in the declining snowpack in the surrounding mountains, forecasted to drop some 80% this century.

Lake Tanganyika in East Africa is surrounded by an estimated 10 million people, with most depending on its fish stocks, especially freshwater sardines, for food. Present water temperatures are unprecedented, reaching 26°C, highest in a 1500-year climate record exposed by lake sediment cores. Mixing of surface and deep waters is necessary to replenish nutrients in the upper 200 m of the lake, where the sardines reside. The surface warming and fixed stratification even resist mixing by wind, and scientists fear that fish stocks will continue to decline.

The largest and deepest lake on Earth, Lake Baikal in Russia, is also one of the richest in aquatic biological diversity for lacustrine. Here the effects of warming temperatures are focused around melting ice. Some 60 years of research show that regional temperatures today are higher, especially through winter, with increases in precipitation in response to the warmer air. These changes shorten the amount of time the lake is frozen over and have led to a decrease in the thickness and transparency of the ice.

Microscopic algae are the basis of Lake Baikal's food web and have adapted to the lake's ice cover for growth and reproduction. Present changes in ice thickness and transparency affect the spring algal blooms and decrease growth rates, thus decreasing food for crustaceans that feed on the algae, which decreases food available for fish as the effect moves up the food chain. With earlier spring melting, Lake Baikal's seal population suffers, as this unique freshwater species mates and gives birth on the ice. Climate change is affecting Lake Baikal in other ways, including increased nutrient inputs and industrial pollution from melting permafrost and increased regional precipitation.

These examples illustrate some of the ecosystem impacts of climate change on Earth's lakes. Many of these topics involve "Water and Atmospheric Moisture," covered in this chapter.

FIGURE GN 7.1 Recent warming dominates Lake Tahoe.
[Bobbé Christopherson.]

Water is critical to our daily lives and is an extraordinary compound in nature. In the Solar System, water occurs in significant quantities only on our planet—water covers 71% of Earth by area. Several satellite probes detected ice beneath the poles of the Moon. Elsewhere, three orbiting spacecraft and two robot landers imaged and detected seasonally flowing water on Mars, and one craft landing in Martian high latitudes found itself amongst ice-caused patterned ground. Scientists are finding evidence on Mars of existing subsurface water, polar water and ice, and modern erosional features caused by water. Farther from the Sun, icy expanses can be seen on two of Jupiter's moons, Europa and Calisto and water geysers and ice on Saturn's moon Enceladus—exciting discoveries about water in our Solar System.

Pure water is colourless, odourless, and tasteless; yet because it is a solvent (dissolves solids), pure water rarely occurs in nature. Water weighs $1 g \cdot cm^{-3}$ (gram per cubic centimetre), or $1 kg \cdot l^{-1}$ (kilogram per litre).

Water constitutes nearly 70% of our bodies by weight and is the major ingredient in plants, animals, and our food. A human can survive 50 to 60 days without food but only 3 or 5 days without water. The water we use must be adequate, both in quantity and quality, for its many tasks—everything from personal hygiene to vast national water projects. Water is the medium of life.

In this chapter: We examine water on Earth and the dynamics of atmospheric moisture and stability—the essentials of weather. The key questions answered include these: What is the origin of water? How much water is there? Where is water located? An irony exists with this most common compound because it possesses such uncommon physical characteristics. Water's unique heat properties and existence in all three states in nature are critical in powering Earth's weather systems.

Condensation of water vapour and atmospheric conditions of stability and instability are key to cloud formation. We end the chapter with clouds, our beautiful indicators of atmospheric conditions.

Water on Earth

Earth's hydrosphere contains about 1.36 billion cubic kilometres of water (specifically, $1359208000 km^3$). According to scientific evidence, much of Earth's water originated from icy comets and hydrogen- and oxygen-laden debris that were part of the planetesimals that coalesced to form the planet. In 2007, the orbiting Spitzer Space Telescope observed for the first time the presence of water vapour and ice as planets form in a system 1000 light years from Earth. Such discoveries are evidence that water is abundant throughout the Universe. As a planet forms, water from within migrates to its surface and outgasses.

Outgassing is a continuing process by which water and water vapour emerge from layers deep within and below the crust, 25 km or more below Earth's surface. Figure 7.1 presents two such areas, among many sites worldwide, in New Zealand and Iceland.

In the early atmosphere, massive quantities of outgassed water vapour condensed and then fell to Earth in torrential rains. For water to remain on Earth's surface, land temperatures had to drop below the boiling point of 100°C, something that occurred about 3.8 billion years ago. The lowest places across the face of Earth then began to fill with water—first ponds, then lakes and seas, and eventually ocean-sized bodies of water. Massive flows of water washed over the landscape, carrying both dissolved and solid materials to these early seas and oceans. Outgassing of water has continued ever since and is visible in volcanic eruptions, geysers, and seepage to the surface.

FIGURE 7.1 Water outgassing from the crust.
Outgassing of water from Earth's crust in geothermal areas:
(a) near Wairakei on North Island of New Zealand; and
(b) in southern Iceland west of where the Eyjafjallajökull volcano erupted in 2010. [(a) Bill Bachman/Photo Researchers, Inc.; (b) Bobbé Christopherson.]

(a)

(b)

Worldwide Equilibrium

Today, water is the most common compound on the surface of Earth, having attained the present volume approximately 2 billion years ago. This quantity has remained relatively constant, even though water is continuously being lost from the system. Water is lost when it dissociates into hydrogen and oxygen and the hydrogen escapes Earth's gravity to space, or when it breaks down and forms new compounds with other elements. As pristine water not previously at the surface emerges from within Earth's crust, it replaces lost water in the system. The net result of these water inputs and outputs is that Earth's hydrosphere is in a steady-state equilibrium in terms of quantity.

Despite this overall net balance in water quantity, worldwide changes in sea level do occur. The concept **eustasy** describes the global sea-level condition. Eustatic changes relate to the water volume in the oceans and not changes in the overall quantity of planetary water. Some of these changes result when the amount of water stored in glaciers and ice sheets varies; these are **glacio-eustatic** factors (see Chapter 17). In cooler times, as more water is bound up in glaciers (on mountains worldwide and in high latitudes) and in ice sheets (Greenland and Antarctica), sea level lowers. In warmer times, less water is stored as ice, so sea level rises.

Some 18 000 years ago, during the most recent ice age, sea level was more than 100 m lower than it is today; 40 000 years ago it was 150 m lower. According to the IPCC Fourth Assessment report (2007), mean sea level rose by about 17 cm during the twentieth century and is still rising worldwide at an accelerating pace as higher temperatures melt more ice and cause ocean waters to thermally expand.

Isostasy refers to actual vertical physical movement in landmasses, such as continental uplift or subsidence. Such landscape changes cause apparent changes in sea level relative to coastal environments. Chapter 11 discusses such land elevation changes.

Distribution of Earth's Water Today

From a geographic point of view, ocean and land surfaces are distributed unevenly. If you examine a globe, it is obvious that most of Earth's continental land is in the Northern Hemisphere, whereas water dominates the Southern Hemisphere. In fact, when you look at Earth from certain angles, it appears to have an *oceanic hemisphere* and a *land hemisphere* (Figure 7.2).

The present location of all of Earth's liquid and frozen water—whether fresh or saline, surface or underground—is indicated in Figure 7.3. The oceans contain 97.22% of all water (Figure 7.3a). A table in the figure lists and details the four oceans—Pacific, Atlantic, Indian, and Arctic. The extreme southern portions of the Pacific, Atlantic, and Indian Oceans that surround the Antarctic continent are collectively the "Southern Ocean." Fourth in size among the five oceans, the Southern Ocean lacks precise definition and boundaries, so we meld it into its three parent oceans in the table.

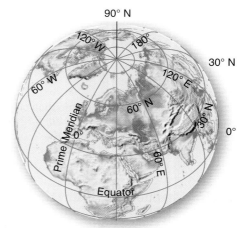

FIGURE 7.2 Land and water hemispheres.
Two perspectives that roughly illustrate Earth's ocean hemisphere and land hemisphere.

Only 2.78% of all of Earth's water is freshwater (non-oceanic). The middle pie chart, along with Table 7.1, details this freshwater portion—surface water and subsurface water (Figure 7.3b). Ice sheets and glaciers are the greatest single repository of surface freshwater; they contain 77.14% of all of Earth's freshwater. Adding subsurface groundwater to frozen surface water accounts for 99.36% of all freshwater.

The remaining freshwater, which resides in lakes, rivers, and streams so familiar to us, actually represents less than 1% of all water (Figure 7.3c). All the world's freshwater lakes total only 125 000 km³, with 80% of this volume in just 40 of the largest lakes and about 50% contained in just 7 lakes (listed with Table 7.1).

The greatest single volume of lake water resides in 25-million-year-old Lake Baikal in Siberian Russia. It contains almost as much water as all five North American Great Lakes combined. Africa's Lake Tanganyika contains the next-largest volume, followed by the five Great Lakes. Overall, 70% of lake water is in North America, Africa, and Asia, with about a fourth of lake water worldwide in small lakes too numerous to count. More than 3 million lakes exist in Alaska alone. Canada has almost 32 000 lakes larger than 3 km² totalling 750 000 km² of surface area. In addition, there are countless smaller lakes.

Earth's Water and the
Hydrologic Cycle

FIGURE 7.3 Ocean and freshwater distribution on Earth.
The location and percentages of (a) all water, (b) freshwater
including subsurface water, and (c) surface water.

Ocean	Earth's Ocean Area (%)	*Area (km²)	*Volume (km³)	Mean Depth of Main Basin (m)
Pacific	48	179 670	724 330	4280
Atlantic	28	106 450	355 280	3930
Indian	20	74 930	292 310	3960
Arctic	4	14 090	17 100	1205

*Values are x 1000: includes all marginal seas.

TABLE 7.1 Distribution of Freshwater on Earth

Location	Amount (km³)	Percentage of Freshwater	Percentage of Total Water
Surface Water			
Ice sheets and glaciers	29 180 000	77.14	2.146
Freshwater lakes	125 000	0.33	0.009
Saline lakes and inland seas	104 000	0.28	0.008
Atmosphere	13 000	0.03	0.001
Rivers and streams	1 250	0.003	0.0001
Total surface water	29 423 250	77.78	2.164
Subsurface Water			
Groundwater—surface to 750 m depth	4 170 000	11.02	0.306
Groundwater—750 to 3950 m depth	4 170 000	11.02	0.306
Soil moisture storage	67 000	0.18	0.005
Total subsurface water	8 407 000	22.22	0.617
Total Freshwater (rounded)	**37 800 000**	**100.00%**	**2.78%**

*Major Freshwater Lakes	Volume (km³)	Surface Area (km²)	Depth (m)
Baikal (Russia)	22 000	31 500	1620
Tanganyika (Africa)	18 750	39 900	1470
Superior (Canada/U.S.)	12 500	83 290	397
Michigan (U.S.)	4920	58 030	281
Huron (Canada/U.S.)	3545	60 620	229
Ontario (Canada/U.S.)	1640	19 570	237
Erie (Canada/U.S.)	485	25 670	64

FIGURE 7.4 Great Salt Lake, a saline lake.
The Great Salt Lake has no outlets other than evaporation and is a remnant of paleoloake Bonneville. At its maximum, some 18 000 years ago, Lake Bonneville extended across eastern Nevada, northern Utah, and southern Idaho—the basin is outlined by ancient shorelines, which scientists actively study. [Bobbé Christopherson.]

Not connected to the ocean are saline lakes and salty inland seas. They usually exist in regions of interior river drainage (no outlet to the ocean), which allows salts to become concentrated. They contain 104 000 km³ of water. Examples of such lakes include Utah's Great Salt Lake (Figure 7.4), California's Mono Lake, Southwest Asia's Caspian and Aral Seas, and the Dead Sea between Israel and Jordan.

Consider all the moisture in the atmosphere and in Earth's thousands of flowing rivers and streams. Combined, they amount to only 14 250 km³, or only 0.033% of freshwater, or 0.0011% of all water! Yet this small amount is dynamic. A water molecule travelling through atmospheric and surface-water paths moves through the entire hydrologic cycle (ocean–atmosphere–precipitation–runoff) in less than two weeks. Contrast this to a water molecule in deep-ocean circulation, groundwater, or a glacier; moving slowly, it takes thousands of years to move through the system.

Unique Properties of Water

Earth's distance from the Sun places it within a most remarkable temperate zone when compared with the locations of the other planets. This temperate location allows all three states of water—ice, liquid, and vapour—to occur naturally on Earth.

Even though water is the most common compound on Earth's surface, it exhibits most uncommon properties. Two atoms of hydrogen and one of oxygen, which readily bond, comprise each water molecule (suggested in Figure 7.5, upper left). Once hydrogen and oxygen atoms join in a covalent, or double, bond, they are difficult to separate, thereby producing a water molecule that remains stable in Earth's environment. This water molecule is a versatile solvent and possesses extraordinary heat characteristics.

The nature of the hydrogen–oxygen bond gives the hydrogen side of a water molecule a positive charge and the oxygen side a negative charge (see Figure 7.5, upper

FIGURE 7.5 Water and water's phase changes.
The three physical states of water: (a) gas, or water vapour; (b) water; and (c) ice. Note the molecular arrangement in each state and the terms that describe the changes from one phase to another. The plus and minus symbols in the phase changes denote whether heat energy is absorbed (+) or liberated (released) (−).

right). As a result of this *polarity*, water molecules attract each other: The positive (hydrogen) side of a water molecule attracts the negative (oxygen) side of another. This bonding between water molecules is *hydrogen bonding*.

The polarity of water molecules also explains why water "acts wet," dissolving many substances. Because of this solvent ability, pure water is rare in nature because something is usually dissolved in it.

The effects of hydrogen bonding in water are observable in everyday life. Hydrogen bonding creates the *surface tension* that allows you to float a steel needle on the surface of water, even though steel is much denser than water. This *surface tension* allows you to slightly overfill a glass with water; webs of millions of hydrogen bonds hold the water slightly above the rim.

Hydrogen bonding is the cause of *capillarity*, which you observe when you "dry" something with a paper towel. The towel draws water through its fibres because hydrogen bonds make each molecule pull on its neighbour. In chemistry laboratory classes, students observe the curved *meniscus*, or surface of the water, which forms in a cylinder or a test tube because hydrogen bonding allows the water to slightly "climb" the glass sides. *Capillary action* is an important component of soil–moisture processes, discussed in Chapters 9 and 18. Without hydrogen bonding to hold molecules together in water and ice, water would be a gas at normal surface temperatures.

Heat Properties

For water to change from one state to another (solid, liquid, or vapour), *heat energy must be absorbed or liberated* (*released*). To cause a change of state, the amount of heat energy must be sufficient to affect the hydrogen bonds between molecules. This relation between water and heat energy is important to atmospheric processes. In fact, the heat exchanged between physical states of water provides more than 30% of the energy that powers the general circulation of the atmosphere.

Figure 7.5 presents the three states of water and the terms describing a change from one state to another, a **phase change**. Along the bottom of the illustration, *melting* and *freezing* describe the familiar phase change between solid and liquid. At the right, the terms *condensation* and *evaporation* (or *vaporization* at boiling temperature) apply to the change between liquid and vapour. At the left, the term **sublimation** refers to the direct change

of ice to water vapour or water vapour to ice, although when water vapour attaches directly to an ice crystal, it is referred to as *deposition*. The deposition of water vapour to ice may form *frost* on surfaces.

Ice, the Solid Phase As water cools, it behaves like most compounds and contracts in volume. However, it reaches its greatest density not as ice, but as water at 4°C. Below that temperature, water behaves differently from other compounds. It begins to expand as more hydrogen bonds form among the slower-moving molecules, creating the hexagonal (six-sided) structures shown in Figures 7.5c and 7.6a. This six-sided preference applies to ice crystals of all shapes: plates, columns, needles, and dendrites (branching or treelike forms). Ice crystals demonstrate a unique interaction of chaos (all ice crystals are different) and the determinism of physical principles (all have a six-sided structure).

This expansion of water and ice that begins at 4°C continues to a temperature of –29°C—up to a 9% increase in volume is possible (Figure 7.6c). This expansion is important in the weathering of rocks, highway and pavement damage, and burst water pipes. For more on ice crystals and snowflakes, see http://www.its.caltech.edu/~atomic/snowcrystals/primer/primer.htm or see http://emu.arsusda.gov/snowsite/default.html. The expansion in volume that accompanies the freezing process results in a decrease in density (the same number of molecules occupy a larger space). Specifically, *pure ice* has 0.91 times the density of water, so it floats. Without this change in density, much of Earth's freshwater would be bound in masses of ice on the ocean floor.

In nature, this density varies slightly given the age of the ice and air content. Therefore, icebergs float with slightly varying displacements that average about one-seventh (14%) of their mass exposed and about six-sevenths (86%) submerged beneath the ocean's surface (Figure 7.6d). With underwater portions melting faster than those above water, icebergs are inherently unstable and will overturn. You see in Figure 7.6b ruffled and fluted ice that was previously underwater.

Chapter 13 discusses the freezing action of ice as an important physical weathering process. Chapter 17 discusses the freeze-and-thaw action of surface and subsurface water affecting approximately 30% of Earth's surface in periglacial landscapes, producing a variety of processes and landforms.

GEO REPORT 7.1 *Breaking Roads and Pipes*

Road crews are busy in the summer repairing winter damage to streets and highways in regions where winters are cold. Rainwater seeps into roadway cracks and then expands as it freezes, thus breaking up the pavement. Perhaps you have noticed that bridges suffer the greatest damage, where cold air can circulate beneath a bridge and produce more freeze–thaw cycles. The expansion of freezing water is powerful enough to crack plumbing or an automobile radiator or engine block. Wrapping water pipes with insulation to avoid damage is a common winter task in many places. Historically, this physical property of water was put to use in quarrying rock for building materials. Holes were drilled and filled with water before winter so that, when cold weather arrived, the water would freeze and expand, cracking the rock into manageable shapes.

FIGURE 7.6 **The uniqueness of ice forms.**
(a) Computer-enhanced photo reveals ice-crystal patterns, dictated by the internal structure between water molecules. (b) Iceberg arch in the Antarctic Sound near 63.5° S. (c) Ice needles form in the freezing process of a meltwater stream. (d) A bergy bit (small iceberg) off the coast of Antarctica illustrates the density–buoyancy state of floating ice. [(a) Photo enhancement © Scott Camazine/Photo Researchers, Inc., after W. A. Bentley; (b), (c), and (d) Bobbé Christopherson.]

▮▮ CRITICAL THINKING 7.1

Iceberg Analysis

Examine the iceberg photographs in Figure 7.6b and Figure 7.6d. These photos show Antarctic waters. Determine what caused the thermal notch above the ocean surface around the iceberg. Why do you think the iceberg appears to be riding higher in the water as it melts? Place an ice cube in a clear glass almost filled with water. Then approximate the amount of ice above the water's surface compared to the amount below water. Pure ice is 0.91 the density of water, whereas ice actually contains air bubbles, so icebergs are about 0.86 the density of water. How do your measurements compare with this range of density?

Water, the Liquid Phase As a liquid, water assumes the shape of its container and is a noncompressible fluid. For ice to change to water, heat energy must increase the motion of the water molecules to break some of the hydrogen bonds (Figure 7.5b). Despite the fact that there is no change in sensible temperature between ice at 0°C and water at 0°C, 80 calories[1] of heat energy must be absorbed for the phase change of 1 g of ice to melt to 1 g of water

(Figure 7.7, upper left). Heat energy involved in the phase change is **latent heat** and is hidden within the structure of water. It becomes liberated whenever the phase reverses and a gram of water freezes. The *latent heat of freezing* or the *latent heat of melting* each involves 80 calories.

To raise the temperature of 1 g of water at 0°C to boiling at 100°C, we must add 100 calories, gaining an increase of 1 C° for each calorie added. No phase change is involved in this temperature gain.

Water Vapour, the Gas Phase Water vapour is an invisible and compressible gas in which each molecule moves independently of the others (Figure 7.4a). The phase change from liquid to vapour at boiling temperature, under normal sea-level pressure, requires the addition of 540 calories for each gram, the **latent heat of vaporization** (Figure 7.6). When water vapour condenses to a liquid, each gram gives up its hidden 540 calories as the **latent heat of condensation**.

---

[1]Remember from Chapter 2 that a calorie (cal) is the amount of energy required to raise the temperature of 1 gram of water (at 15°C) by 1 Celsius degree and is equal to 4.184 joules.

FIGURE 7.7 **Water's heat-energy characteristics.**
The phase changes of water absorb or release a lot of latent heat energy. To transform 1 g of ice at 0°C to 1 g of water vapour at 100°C requires 720 cal: 80 + 100 + 540. The landscape illustrates phase changes between water (lake at 20°C) and water vapour under typical conditions in the environment.

Perhaps you have felt the liberation of the latent heat of condensation on your skin from steam when you have drained steamed vegetables or pasta, or filled a hot teakettle.

In summary, taking 1 g of ice at 0°C and changing its phase to water, then to water vapour at 100°C—from a solid, to a liquid, to a gas—*absorbs* 720 calories (80 cal + 100 cal + 540 cal). Reversing the process, or changing the phase of 1 g of water vapour at 100°C to water then to ice at 0°C, *liberates* 720 calories into the surrounding environment.

Heat Properties of Water in Nature

In a lake or stream or in soil water, at 20°C, every gram of water that breaks away from the surface through evaporation must absorb from the environment approximately 585 cal as the *latent heat of evaporation* (see the natural scene in Figure 7.7). This is slightly more energy than would be required if the water were at a higher temperature such as boiling (540 cal). You can feel this absorption of latent heat as evaporative cooling on your skin when it is wet.

GEO REPORT 7.2 *Iceberg Hazards and the End of a Trip*

A major hazard to ships in higher latitudes is posed by floating ice. Since ice has approximately 0.86 the density of water, an iceberg sits with approximately six-sevenths of its mass below water level. The irregular edges of submarine ice can impact the side of a passing ship. Hitting an iceberg buckled plates and substandard rivets along the side of the RMS *Titanic* on its maiden voyage in 1912, causing it to sink and perhaps triggering a brief lapse in society's faith in technology.

This latent heat exchange is the dominant cooling process in Earth's energy budget.

The process reverses when air cools and water vapour condenses back into the liquid state, forming moisture droplets and thus liberating 585 cal for every gram of water as the *latent heat of condensation*. When you realise that a small, puffy, fair-weather cumulus cloud holds 500–1000 tons of moisture droplets, think of the tremendous latent heat released when water vapour condenses to droplets.

The **latent heat of sublimation** absorbs 680 cal as a gram of ice transforms into vapour. Water vapour freezing directly to ice releases a comparable amount of energy.

Humidity

Humidity refers to water vapour in the air. The capacity of air for water vapour is primarily a function of temperature—the temperatures of both the air and the water vapour, which are usually the same. Humidity can be expressed in several ways, discussed in this section.

We are all aware of humidity in the air, for its relationship to air temperature determines our sense of comfort. North Americans spend billions of dollars a year to adjust humidity, either with air-conditioning (extracting water vapour and cooling) or with air humidifying (adding water vapour). We discussed the relation between humidity and temperature and the Humidex in Chapter 5. To determine the energy available for powering weather, one has to know the water vapour *content* of air and relate this in a ratio to the air's *saturation equilibrium* at a given temperature.

Relative Humidity

After air temperature and barometric pressure, relative humidity is the most common piece of information in local weather broadcasts. **Relative humidity** is a ratio (expressed as a percentage) of the amount of water vapour that is actually in the air compared to the maximum water vapour possible in the air at a given temperature.

Relative humidity varies because of water vapour or temperature changes in the air. The formula to calculate the relative humidity ratio and express it as a percentage places actual water vapour in the air as the numerator and water vapour possible in the air at that temperature as the denominator:

$$\text{Relative humidity} = \frac{\text{Actual water vapour in the air}}{\text{Maximum water vapour possible in the air at that temperature}} \times 100$$

Warmer air increases the evaporation rate from water surfaces, whereas cooler air tends to increase the condensation rate of water vapour to water surfaces. Because there is a maximum amount of water vapour that can exist in a volume of air at a given temperature, the rates of evaporation and condensation can reach equilibrium at some point; the air is then saturated with humidity. Relative humidity tells us how near the air is to saturation and is an expression of an ongoing process of water molecules moving between air and moist surfaces.

In Figure 7.8 at 5 P.M. the evaporation rate exceeds condensation at the higher temperatures of this time of day and relative humidity is at 20%. At 11 A.M. the evaporation rate still exceeds condensation, though not by as much since daytime temperatures are not as high, so the same volume of water vapour now occupies 50% of the maximum possible capacity. At 5 A.M., in the cooler morning air, saturation equilibrium exists and any further cooling or addition of water vapour produces net condensation. When the air is saturated with maximum water vapour for its temperature, the relative humidity percentage is 100%.

Saturation   As stated, air is at **saturation** at 100% relative humidity, when the rate of evaporation and the rate of condensation—the net transfer of water molecules—reach equilibrium. Saturation indicates that any further addition of water vapour or any decrease in temperature that reduces the evaporation rate results in active condensation (clouds, fog, or precipitation).

The temperature at which a given mass of air becomes saturated and net condensation begins to form water droplets is the **dew-point temperature**. *The air is saturated when the dew-point temperature and the air temperature are the same.* When temperatures are below freezing, the term *frost point* is sometimes used.

A cold drink in a glass provides a common example of these conditions (Figure 7.9). The water droplets that form on the outside of the glass condense from the air because the air layer next to the glass is chilled to below its dew-point temperature and thus becomes saturated. Figure 7.9 gives an additional example of saturated air and active condensation above a rock surface in the cooler air layer near the rock. As you walk to classes on some mornings, you perhaps notice damp lawns, an indication of dew-point conditions.

Satellites using infrared sensors now routinely sense water vapour in the lower atmosphere. Water vapour absorbs long wavelengths (infrared), making it possible to distinguish areas of relatively high water vapour from areas of low water vapour. Figure 7.10 includes a global image

GEO REPORT 7.3   *Katrina Had the Power*

Meteorologists estimated that the moisture in Hurricane Katrina (2005) weighed more than 27 trillion metric tons at its maximum power and mass. With 585 cal released for every gram as the latent heat of condensation, a weather event such as a hurricane involves a staggering amount of energy. Do the quick math (585 calories per gram, 1000 g to a kilogram, 1000 kg to a metric ton, times 27 trillion tons).

FIGURE 7.8 Water vapour, temperature, and relative humidity.
The maximum water vapour possible in warm air is greater (net evaporation) than that possible in cold air (net condensation), so relative humidity changes with temperature, even though in this example the actual water vapour present in the air stays the same during the day.

(a)

composite by sensors of the "water-vapour channel." This ability is important to forecasting because it shows the moisture available to weather systems and therefore the available latent heat energy and precipitation potential.

Daily and Seasonal Relative Humidity Patterns
An inverse relation occurs during a typical day between air temperature and relative humidity—as temperature rises, relative humidity falls (Figure 7.11). Relative humidity is highest at dawn, when air temperature is lowest. If you park outdoors, you know about the wetness of the dew that condenses on the car or bicycle overnight. In your own experience, you probably have noticed this pattern—the morning dew on windows, cars, and lawns evaporates by late morning as net evaporation increases with air temperature.

Relative humidity is lowest in the late afternoon, when higher temperatures increase the rate of evaporation.

FIGURE 7.9 Dew-point temperature examples.
(a) The low temperature of the glass chills the surrounding air layer to the dew-point temperature and saturation. Thus, water vapour condenses out of the air and onto the glass as dew.
(b) Cold air above the rain-soaked rocks is at the dew point and is saturated. Water evaporates from the rock into the air and condenses in a changing veil of clouds. [Robert W. Christopherson.]

FIGURE 7.10 Composite mid-infrared image from *GOES* (United States), *Meteosat* (European Space Agency), and *MTSAT* (Japan) of water vapour in the atmosphere.
In this June 21, 2010, image, higher water-vapour content is lighter and lower water-vapour content is darker. [Satellite data courtesy of Space Science and Engineering Center, University of Wisconsin, Madison.]

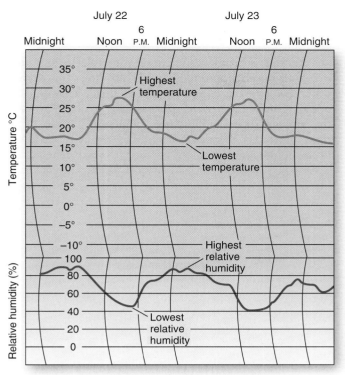

FIGURE 7.11 Daily relative humidity patterns.
Typical daily variations in July demonstrate temperature and
relative humidity relations.

**FIGURE 7.12 Saturation vapour pressure at various
temperatures.**
Saturation vapour pressure is the maximum possible water
vapour, as measured by the pressure it exerts (mb). Inset
compares saturation vapour pressures over water surfaces with
those over surfaces at subfreezing temperatures. Note the
24-mb label for the text discussion.

As shown in Figure 7.8, the actual water vapour present
in the air may remain the same throughout the day. However, relative humidity changes because the temperature,
and therefore the rate of evaporation, varies from morning
to afternoon. Seasonally, January readings are higher than
July readings because air temperatures are lower overall in
winter. Similar relative humidity records at most weather
stations demonstrate the same relation among season,
temperature, and relative humidity.

Expressions of Humidity

There are several ways to express humidity and relative
humidity. Each has its own utility and application. Two
measures involve vapour pressure and specific humidity.

Vapour Pressure As free water molecules evaporate
from surfaces into the atmosphere, they become water
vapour. Now part of the air, water-vapour molecules
exert a portion of the air pressure along with nitrogen
and oxygen molecules. The share of air pressure that is
made up of water-vapour molecules is **vapour pressure**,
expressed in millibars (mb) or the pascal (Pa) in SI units.

As explained earlier, *saturation* is reached when the
movement of water molecules between surface and air is
in equilibrium. Air that contains as much water vapour
as possible at a given temperature is at *saturation vapour
pressure*. Any temperature increase or decrease will change
the saturation vapour pressure.

Figure 7.12 graphs the saturation vapour pressure at
various air temperatures. The graph illustrates that, for

every temperature increase of 10 C°, the saturation vapour
pressure in air nearly doubles. This relation explains why
warm tropical air over the ocean can have so much water
vapour, thus providing much latent heat to power tropical
storms. It also explains why cold air is "dry" and why cold
air toward the poles does not produce a lot of precipitation
(it contains too little water vapour, even though it is near
the dew-point temperature).

As marked on the graph, air at 20°C has a saturation
vapour pressure of 24 mb; that is, the air is saturated if the
water-vapour portion of the air pressure also is at 24 mb.
Thus, if the water vapour actually present is exerting a vapour pressure of only 12 mb in 20°C air, the relative humidity is 50% (12 mb ÷ 24 mb = 0.50 × 100 = 50%). The inset in Figure 7.12 compares saturation vapour pressure over
water and over ice surfaces at subfreezing temperatures.
You can see that saturation vapour pressure is greater above
a water surface than over an ice surface—that is, it takes
more water-vapour molecules to saturate air above water
than it does above ice. This fact is important to condensation processes and rain-droplet formation, both of which
are described later in this chapter.

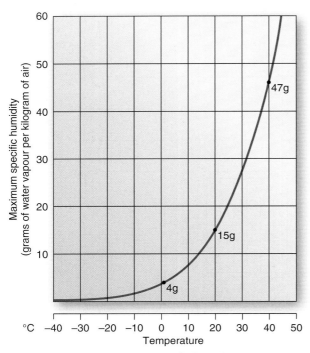

FIGURE 7.13 Maximum specific humidity at various temperatures.
Maximum specific humidity is the maximum possible water vapour in a mass of water vapour per unit mass of air (g/kg). Note the 47-g, 15-g, and 4-g labels for the text discussion.

Specific Humidity A useful humidity measure is one that remains constant as temperature and pressure change. **Specific humidity** is the mass of water vapour (in grams) per mass of air (in kilograms) at any specified temperature. Because it is measured in mass, specific humidity is not affected by changes in temperature or pressure, as when an air parcel rises to higher elevations. Specific humidity stays constant despite volume changes.[2]

The maximum mass of water vapour possible in a kilogram of air at any specified temperature is the *maximum specific humidity*, plotted in Figure 7.13. Noted on the graph is that a kilogram of air could have a maximum specific humidity of 47 g of water vapour at 40°C, 15 g at 20°C, and about 4 g at 0°C . Therefore, if a kilogram of air at 40°C has a specific humidity of 12 g, its relative humidity is 25.5% (12 g ÷ 47 g = 0.255 × 100 = 25.5%). Specific humidity is useful in describing the moisture content of large air masses that are interacting in a weather system and provides information necessary for weather forecasting.

Instruments for Measuring Humidity Various instruments measure relative humidity. The **hair hygrometer** uses the principle that human hair changes as much as 4% in length between 0% and 100% relative humidity. The instrument connects a standardised bundle of human hair

through a mechanism to a gauge. As the hair absorbs or loses water in the air, it changes length, indicating relative humidity (Figure 7.14a).

Another instrument used to measure relative humidity is a **sling psychrometer**. Figure 7.14b shows this device, which has two thermometers mounted side-by-side on a holder. One is the *dry-bulb thermometer*; it simply records the ambient (surrounding) air temperature. The other thermometer is the *wet-bulb thermometer*; it is set lower in the holder and the bulb is covered by a moistened cloth wick. The psychrometer is then spun ("slung") by its handle, or placed where a fan forces air over the wet-bulb wick.

(a)

(b)

FIGURE 7.14 Instruments that measure relative humidity.
(a) The principle of a hair hygrometer. (b) Sling psychrometer with wet and dry bulbs. [Bobbé Christopherson.]

---

[2] Another similar measure used in relative humidity that approximates specific humidity is the *mixing ratio*, that is, the ratio of the mass of water vapour (grams) per mass of dry air (kilograms), as in $g \cdot kg^{-1}$.

The rate at which water evaporates from the wick depends on the relative saturation of the surrounding air. If the air is dry, water evaporates quickly, *absorbing specific heat as the latent heat of evaporation from the wet-bulb thermometer and its wick*, cooling the thermometer and causing its temperature to lower (the *wet-bulb depression*). In conditions of high humidity, little water evaporates from the wick; in low humidity, more water evaporates. After being spun a minute or two, a comparison of temperature on each bulb and a check on a relative humidity (psychrometric) chart gives the relative humidity reading. See Applied Physical Geography at the end of the chapter for more on calculating relative humidity in this manner.

Atmospheric Stability

Meteorologists use the term *parcel* to describe a body of air that has specific temperature and humidity characteristics. Think of an air parcel as a volume of air, perhaps 300 m in diameter, or more. The temperature of the volume of air determines the density of the air parcel. Warm air produces a lower density in a given volume of air; cold air produces a higher density.

Two opposing forces work on a parcel of air: an upward *buoyant force* and a downward *gravitational force*. A parcel of lower density than the surrounding air rises (is more buoyant); a rising parcel expands as external pressure decreases. In contrast, a parcel of higher density descends (is less buoyant); a falling parcel compresses as external pressure increases. Figure 7.15 shows air parcels and illustrates these relationships.

An indication of weather conditions is the relative stability of air parcels in the atmosphere. **Stability** refers to the tendency of an air parcel, with its water-vapour cargo, either to remain in place or to change vertical position by ascending (rising) or descending (falling). An air parcel is *stable* if it resists displacement upward or, when disturbed,

Atmospheric Stability

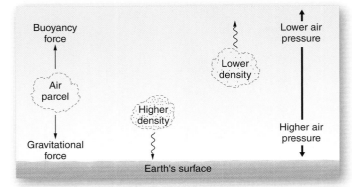

FIGURE 7.15 The forces acting on an air parcel.
Buoyancy and gravitational forces work on an air parcel. Different densities produce rising or falling parcels in response to imbalance in these forces.

FIGURE 7.16 Principles of air stability and balloon launches. Hot-air balloons being launched in southern Utah illustrate the principles of stability. As the temperature inside a balloon increases, the air in the balloon becomes less dense than the surrounding air, and the buoyancy force causes the balloon to rise, acting like a warm-air parcel. [Hemera/Thinkstock.]

tends to return to its starting place. An air parcel is *unstable* if it continues to rise until it reaches an altitude where the surrounding air has a density and temperature similar to its own.

To visualise this, imagine a hot-air balloon launch. The air-filled balloon sits on the ground with the same air temperature inside as in the surrounding environment, like a stable air parcel. As the burner ignites, the balloon fills with hot (less-dense) air and rises buoyantly (Figure 7.16), like an unstable parcel of air. In the photo, why do you think these launches are taking place in the early morning? The concepts of stable and unstable air lead us to the specific temperature characteristics that produce these conditions.

Adiabatic Processes

Determining the degree of stability or instability requires measuring two temperatures: the temperature inside an air parcel and the temperature in the air surrounding the parcel. The contrast of these two temperatures determines stability. Such temperature measurements are made daily with *radiosonde* instrument packages carried aloft by helium-filled balloons at thousands of weather stations.

The *normal lapse rate*, introduced in Chapter 3, is the average decrease in temperature with increasing altitude, a value of $6.4\,C° \cdot 1000\,m^{-1}$. This rate of temperature change is for still, calm air, and it can vary greatly under different weather conditions. Consequently, the *environmental lapse rate* (ELR) is the actual lapse rate at a particular place and time. It can vary by several degrees per thousand metres.

Adiabatic describes the warming and cooling rates for a parcel of expanding or compressing air. *An ascending parcel of air tends to cool by expansion*, responding to the reduced pressure at higher altitudes. In contrast, *descending air tends to heat by compression*. *Diabatic* means occurring with an exchange of heat; *adiabatic* means occurring *without* a loss or gain of heat—that is, without any heat exchange between the surrounding environment and the vertically moving parcel of air. Adiabatic temperatures are measured with one of two specific rates, depending on moisture conditions in the parcel: dry adiabatic rate (DAR) and moist adiabatic rate (MAR).

Dry Adiabatic Rate The **dry adiabatic rate (DAR)** is the rate at which "dry" air cools by expansion (if ascending) or heats by compression (if descending). "Dry" refers to air that is less than saturated (relative humidity is less than 100%). The average DAR is $10\ C° \cdot 1000\ m^{-1}$.

The rising parcel in Figure 7.17a illustrates the principle. To see how a specific example of dry air behaves, consider an unsaturated parcel of air at the surface with a temperature of 27°C. It rises, expands, and cools adiabatically at the DAR as it rises to 2500 m. What happens to the temperature of the parcel? Calculate the temperature change in the parcel, using the dry adiabatic rate:

$$(10\ C° \cdot 1000\ m^{-1}) \times 2500\ m = 25\ C°\ \text{of total cooling}$$

Subtracting the 25 C° of adiabatic cooling from the starting temperature of 27°C gives the temperature in the air parcel at 2500 m as 2°C.

In Figure 7.17b, assume that an unsaturated air parcel with a temperature of –20°C at 3000 m descends to the surface, heating adiabatically. Using the dry adiabatic lapse rate, we determine the temperature of the air parcel when it arrives at the surface:

$$(10\ C° \cdot 1000\ m^{-1}) \times 3000\ m = 30\ C°\ \text{of total warming}$$

Adding the 30 C° of adiabatic warming from the starting temperature of –20°C gives the temperature in the air parcel at the surface as 10°C.

Moist Adiabatic Rate The **moist adiabatic rate (MAR)** is the rate at which an ascending air parcel that is moist, or saturated, cools by expansion. The average MAR is $6\ C° \cdot 1000\ m^{-1}$. This is roughly 4 C° less than the dry adiabatic rate. From this average, the MAR varies with moisture content and temperature and can range from 4 C° (for warm air) to nearly 10 C° (for cool air) per 1000 m. (Note that a descending parcel of saturated air warms at the MAR as well because the evaporation of

(a) Air parcel *cools* adiabatically at the DAR

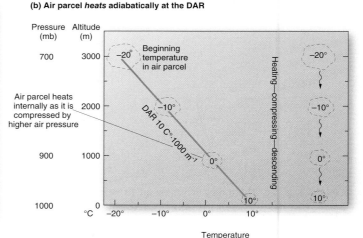

(b) Air parcel *heats* adiabatically at the DAR

Atmospheric Stability

Cooling by expansion

Heating by compression

FIGURE 7.17 Vertically moving air experiences temperature changes—adiabatic cooling and heating.
(a) A rising air parcel that is less than saturated cools adiabatically by expansion at the DAR.
(b) A descending air parcel that is less than saturated heats adiabatically by compression at the DAR.

liquid droplets, absorbing sensible heat, offsets the rate of compressional warming.)

The cause of this variability, and the reason that the MAR is lower than the DAR, is the latent heat of condensation. As water vapour condenses in the saturated air, latent heat is liberated, becoming sensible heat, thus decreasing the adiabatic rate. The release of latent heat may vary with temperature and water vapour content. The MAR is much lower than the DAR in warm air, whereas the two rates are more similar in cold air.

Stable and Unstable Atmospheric Conditions

Now we bring this discussion together to determine atmospheric stability. The relation among the DAR, MAR, and ELR at a given time and place determines the stability of the atmosphere over an area. You see examples of three stability relationships in Figure 7.18.

Temperature relationships in the atmosphere produce the three different conditions: unstable, conditionally unstable, and stable. For the sake of illustration, the three examples in Figure 7.19 begin with an air parcel at the surface at 25°C. In each example, compare the temperatures of the air parcel and the surrounding environment. Assume that a lifting mechanism, such as surface heating, a mountain range, or a weather front, is present to get the parcel started (we examine lifting mechanisms in Chapter 8).

Given unstable conditions in Figure 7.19a, the air parcel continues to rise through the atmosphere because it is warmer (less dense and more buoyant) than the surrounding environment. Note the environmental lapse rate for

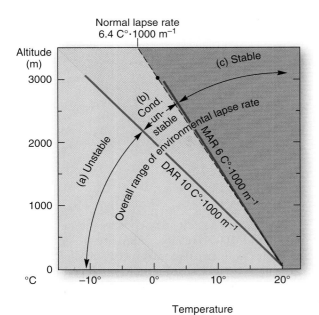

FIGURE 7.18 Temperature relationships and atmospheric stability.
The relationship between dry and moist adiabatic rates and environmental lapse rates produces three atmospheric conditions: (a) unstable (ELR exceeds the DAR), (b) conditionally unstable (ELR is between the DAR and MAR), and (c) stable (ELR is less than the DAR and MAR).

this example is set at 12 C° · 1000 m⁻¹. That is, the air surrounding the air parcel is cooler by 12 C° for every 1000 m increase in altitude. By 1000 m, the rising air parcel has adiabatically cooled by expansion at the DAR from 25°C to 15°C, while the surrounding air has cooled from 25°C at the surface to 13°C. By comparing the temperature in the air parcel and the surrounding environment, you see that the temperature in the parcel is 2 C° warmer than the surrounding air at 1000 m. *Unstable* describes this condition because the less-dense air parcel will continue to lift.

Eventually, as the air parcel continues rising and cooling, it may achieve the dew-point temperature, saturation, and active condensation. This point of saturation forms the *lifting condensation level* that you see in the sky as the flat bottoms of clouds.

The example in Figure 7.19c shows stable conditions resulting when the environmental lapse rate is only 5 C° · 1000 m⁻¹. An ELR of 5 C° · 1000 m⁻¹ is less than both the DAR and the MAR, a condition in which the air parcel has a lower temperature (is more dense and less buoyant) than the surrounding environment. The relatively cooler air parcel tends to settle back to its original position—it is *stable*. The denser air parcel resists lifting, unless forced by updrafts or a barrier, and the sky remains generally cloud-free. If clouds form, they tend to be stratiform (flat clouds) or cirroform (wispy), lacking vertical development. In regions experiencing air pollution, stable conditions in the atmosphere worsen the pollution by slowing exchanges in the surface air.

You may be wondering what stability condition exists if the ELR is somewhere between the DAR and MAR, causing conditions to be neither unstable nor stable. In Figure 7.19b, the environmental lapse rate is measured at 7 C° · 1000 m⁻¹. Under these conditions, the air parcel resists upward movement, unless forced, if it is less than saturated. But if the air parcel becomes saturated and cools at the MAR, it acts unstable and continues to rise.

One example of such conditionally unstable air occurs when stable air is forced to lift as it passes over a mountain range. As the air parcel lifts and cools to the dew point, the air becomes saturated and condensation begins. Now the MAR is in effect and the air parcel behaves in an unstable manner. The sky may be clear and without a cloud, yet huge clouds may develop over a nearby mountain range.

Clouds and Fog

Clouds are more than whimsical, beautiful decorations in the sky; they are fundamental indicators of overall conditions, including stability, moisture content, and weather. They form as air becomes saturated with water. Clouds are the subject of much scientific inquiry, especially regarding their effect on net radiation patterns, as discussed in Chapters 4 and 5. With a little knowledge and practice, you can learn to "read" the atmosphere from its signature clouds.

A **cloud** is an aggregation of tiny moisture droplets and ice crystals that are suspended in air, great enough in volume and concentration to be visible. Fog is simply

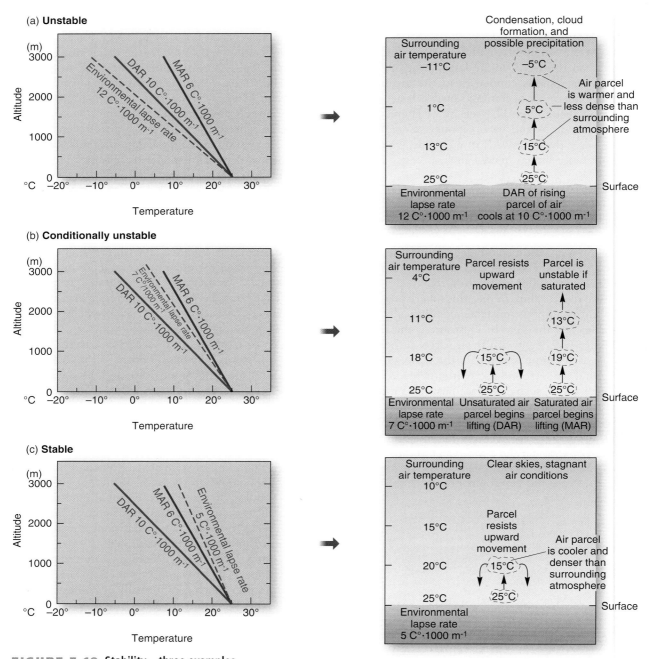

FIGURE 7.19 Stability—three examples.
Specific examples of (a) unstable, (b) conditionally unstable, and (c) stable conditions in the lower atmosphere. Note the response to these three conditions in the air parcel on the right side of each diagram.

a cloud in contact with the ground. Cloud types are too numerous to fully describe here, so we present the most common examples in a simple classification scheme illustrated in Figure 7.21.

Cloud Formation Processes

Clouds may contain raindrops, but not initially. At the outset, clouds are a great mass of moisture droplets, each invisible without magnification. A **moisture droplet** is approximately 20 μm (micrometres) in diameter (0.002 cm). It takes a million or more such droplets to form an average raindrop of 2000 μm in diameter (0.2 cm), as shown in Figure 7.20.

As an air parcel rises it may cool to the dew-point temperature and 100% relative humidity. (Under certain conditions, condensation may occur at slightly less or more than 100% relative humidity.) More lifting of the air parcel cools it further, producing condensation of water vapour into water. Water does not just condense among the air molecules. Condensation requires **cloud-condensation nuclei**, microscopic particles that always are present in the atmosphere.

Continental air masses average 10 billion cloud-condensation nuclei per cubic metre. Ordinary dust, soot, and ash from volcanoes and forest fires and particles from burned fuel, such as sulfate aerosols, typically provide

FIGURE 7.20 Moisture droplets and raindrops. Cloud-condensation nuclei, moisture droplets, and a raindrop enlarged many times—compared at roughly the same scale.

these nuclei. In maritime air masses, nuclei average 1 billion nuclei per cubic metre, including sea salts derived from ocean sprays that supply some of the needed nuclei. The lower atmosphere never lacks cloud-condensation nuclei.

Given the presence of saturated air, the availability of cloud-condensation nuclei, and the presence of cooling (lifting) mechanisms in the atmosphere, condensation occurs. Two principal processes account for the majority of the world's raindrops and snowflakes: the *collision-coalescence process* (for warmer clouds, involving falling coalescing droplets) and the *Bergeron ice-crystal process* (involving supercooled water droplets, which evaporate and are absorbed by ice crystals that grow in mass and fall).

Cloud Types and Identification

As noted, a cloud is a collection of moisture droplets and ice crystals suspended in air in sufficient volume and concentration to be visible. In 1803, English biologist and amateur meteorologist Luke Howard, in his article "On the Modification of Clouds," established a classification system for clouds and coined Latin names for them that we still use. *Altitude* and *shape* are key to cloud classification. Clouds occur in three basic forms—flat, puffy, and wispy—and in four primary altitude classes and 10 basic cloud types. Horizontally developed clouds—flat and layered—are *stratiform* clouds. Vertically developed clouds—puffy and globular—are *cumuliform* clouds. Wispy clouds usually are quite high in altitude and are made of ice crystals; these are *cirroform*.

These three basic forms occur in four altitudinal classes: low, middle, high, and those vertically developed through the troposphere. Table 7.2 presents the basic cloud classes and types and cloud symbols. Figure 7.21

TABLE 7.2 Cloud Classes and Types

Class	Altitude/Composition at Midlatitudes	Type	Symbol	Description
Low clouds (C$_L$)	Up to 2000 m	Stratus (St)		Uniform, featureless, gray, like high fog
	Water	Stratocumulus (Sc)		Soft, gray, globular masses in lines, groups, or waves, heavy rolls, irregular overcast patterns
		Nimbostratus (Ns)		Gray, dark, low, with drizzling rain
Middle clouds (C$_M$)	2000–6000 m	Altostratus (As)		Thin to thick, no halos, Sun's outline just visible, gray day
	Ice and water	Altocumulus (Ac)		Patches of cotton balls, dappled, arranged in lines or groups, rippling waves, the lenticular clouds associated with mountains
High clouds (C$_H$)	6000–13 000 m	Cirrus (Ci)		Mares' tails, wispy, feathery, hairlike, delicate fibres, streaks, or plumes
	Ice	Cirrostratus (Cs)		Veil of fused sheets of ice crystals, milky, with Sun and Moon halos
		Cirrocumulus (Cc)		Dappled "mackerel sky," small white flakes, tufts, in lines or groups, sometimes in ripples
Vertically developed clouds	Near surface to 13 000 m	Cumulus (Cu)		Sharply outlined, puffy, billowy, flat-based, swelling tops, fair weather
	Water below, ice above	Cumulonimbus (Cb)		Dense, heavy, massive, dark thunderstorms, hard showers, explosive top, great vertical development, towering, cirrus-topped plume blown into anvil-shaped head

(a) Altocumulus

(b) Altostratus

High clouds

6000 m—

Cirrocumulus

Halo

Cirrostratus

Altocumulus

Altostratus

Middle clouds

Lenticular

Nimbostratus

Stratus

Stratocumulus

2000 m—
Low clouds

(e) Nimbostratus

(f) Stratus

FIGURE 7.21 Principal cloud types.
Principal cloud types, classified by form (cirroform, stratiform, and cumuliform) and altitude (low, middle, high, and vertically developed across altitude): (a) altocumulus, (b) altostratus, (c) cirrus, (d) cirrostratus, (e) nimbostratus, (f) stratus, (g) cumulus, and (h) cumulonimbus. [(a), (b), (c), (g), and (h) by Bobbé Christopherson; (d), (e), and (f) by Robert Christopherson.]

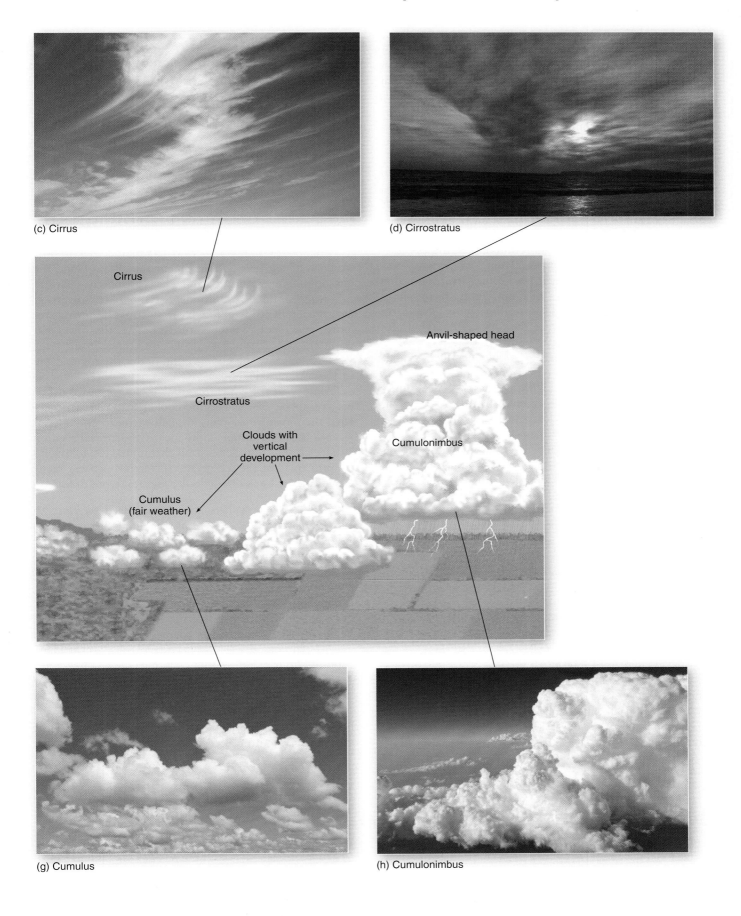

(c) Cirrus

(d) Cirrostratus

Cirrus

Cirrostratus

Anvil-shaped head

Cumulonimbus

Clouds with
vertical
development

Cumulus
(fair weather)

(g) Cumulus

(h) Cumulonimbus

illustrates the general appearance of each type and includes representative photographs.

Low clouds, ranging from the surface up to 2000 m in the middle latitudes, are simply *stratus* or *cumulus* (Latin for "layer" and "heap," respectively). **Stratus** clouds appear dull, grey, and featureless. When they yield precipitation, they become **nimbostratus** (*nimbo-* denotes "stormy" or "rainy"), and their showers typically fall as drizzling rain (Figure 7.21e).

Cumulus clouds appear bright and puffy, like cotton balls. When they do not cover the sky, they float by in infinitely varied shapes. Vertically developed cumulus clouds are in a separate class in Table 7.2 because further vertical development can produce cumulus clouds that extend beyond low altitudes into middle and high altitudes (illustrated at the far right in Figure 7.21 and 7.21h).

Sometimes near the end of the day **stratocumulus** may fill the sky in patches of lumpy, greyish, low-level clouds. Near sunset, these spreading puffy stratiform remnants may catch and filter the Sun's rays, sometimes indicating clearing weather.

The prefix *alto-* (meaning "high") denotes middle-level clouds. They are made of water droplets and, when cold enough, can be mixed with ice crystals. **Altocumulus** clouds, in particular, represent a broad category that occurs in many different styles: patchy rows, wave patterns, a "mackerel sky," or lens-shaped (lenticular) clouds.

Ice crystals in thin concentrations compose clouds occurring above 6000 m. These wispy filaments, usually white except when coloured by sunrise or sunset, are **cirrus** clouds (Latin for "curl of hair"), sometimes dubbed mares' tails. Cirrus clouds look as though an artist took a brush and added delicate feathery strokes high in the sky. Cirrus clouds can indicate an oncoming storm, especially if they thicken and lower in elevation. The prefix *cirro-*, as in *cirrostratus* and *cirrocumulus*, indicates other high clouds that form a thin veil or puffy appearance, respectively.

A cumulus cloud can develop into a towering giant called **cumulonimbus** (again, *-nimbus* in Latin denotes "rain storm" or "thundercloud"; Figure 7.22). Such clouds are *thunderheads* because of their shape and associated lightning and thunder. Note the surface wind gusts, updrafts and downdrafts, heavy rain, and the presence of ice crystals at the top of the rising cloud column. High-altitude winds may then shear the top of the cloud into the characteristic anvil shape of the mature thunderhead.

CRITICAL THINKING 7.2

Be a Cloud and Weather Observer

Using Figure 7.21, begin to observe clouds on a regular basis. See if you can relate the cloud type to particular weather conditions at the time of observation. You may want to keep a log in your notebook during this course. Seeing clouds in this way will help you to understand weather and make studying Chapter 8 easier. See if by the end of this course you can have each type checked off in Table 7.2.

Fog

By international definition, **fog** is a cloud layer on the ground, with visibility restricted to less than 1 km. The presence of fog tells us that the air temperature and the dew-point temperature at ground level are nearly identical, indicating saturated conditions. A temperature-inversion layer generally caps a fog layer (warmer temperatures above and cooler temperatures below the inversion altitude), with as much as 22 C° difference in air temperature between the cool ground under the fog and the warmer, sunny skies above.

Almost all fog is warm—that is, its moisture droplets are above freezing. Supercooled fog, which occurs when the moisture droplets are below freezing, is special because it can be dispersed by means of artificial seeding with ice crystals or other crystals that mimic ice, following the principles of the ice-crystal formation process mentioned earlier. Let's briefly look at several types of fog.

Advection Fog When air in one place *migrates* to another place where conditions are right for saturation, an **advection fog** forms. For example, when warm, moist air overlays cooler ocean currents, lake surfaces, or snow masses, the layer of migrating air directly above the surface becomes chilled to the dew point, and fog develops. Off all subtropical west coasts in the world, summer fog forms in the manner just described (Figure 7.23).

Desert organisms have adapted remarkably to the presence of coastal fog along western coastlines in subtropical latitudes. For example, sand beetles in the Namib Desert in extreme southwestern Africa harvest water from the fog. They hold up their wings so condensation collects and runs down to their mouths. As the day's heat arrives, they burrow into the sand, only to emerge the next night or morning when the advection fog brings in more water

GEO REPORT 7.4 *Luke Howard Knew the Signs for Clouds*

In 1803, when Luke Howard wrote an article and gave a series of lectures on his cloud classification system, he not only designated all the Latin names, but also designed the symbols used for each cloud type. These symbols, shown in Table 7.2, are still in full use to this day.

FIGURE 7.22 Cumulonimbus thunderhead.
(a) Structure and form of a cumulonimbus cloud. Violent updrafts and downdrafts mark the circulation within the cloud. Blustery wind gusts occur along the ground. (b) Space Shuttle astronauts captured a dramatic cumulonimbus thunderhead as it moved over Galveston Bay, Texas. (c) Few acts of nature can match the sheer power released by an intense thunderstorm and related turbulence for air travelers, here rising above the plane's altitude of 10 000 m. [(b) NASA; (c) Bobbé Christopherson.]

for harvesting. Throughout history, people harvested water from fog. For centuries, coastal villages in the deserts of Oman collected water drips deposited on trees by coastal fogs.

In the Atacama Desert of Chile and Peru, residents stretch large nets to intercept advection fog; moisture condenses on the netting and drips into trays, flowing through pipes to a 100 000-l reservoir. Large sheets of plastic mesh along a ridge of the El Tofo Mountains harvest water from advection fog (Figure 7.24). Chungungo, Chile, receives

10 000 l of water from 80 fog-harvesting collectors in a project developed by Canadian (International Development Research Center) and Chilean interests and made operational in 1993. At least 30 countries across the globe experience conditions suitable for this water resource technology. (See http://www.oas.org/dsd/publications/unit/oea59e/ch33.htm.)

Another type of advection fog forms when cold air lies over the warm water of a lake, ocean surface, or even a swimming pool. This wispy **evaporation fog**, or *steam*

FIGURE 7.23 **Advection fog.**
San Francisco's Golden Gate Bridge shrouded by an invading advection fog characteristic of summer conditions along a western coast. [Robert Christopherson.]

fog, may form as water molecules evaporate from the water surface into the cold overlying air, effectively humidifying the air to saturation followed by condensation to form fog (Figure 7.25). When evaporation fog happens at sea, it is a shipping hazard called *sea smoke*.

Advection fog also forms when moist air flows to higher elevations along a hill or mountain. This upslope lifting leads to adiabatic cooling by expansion as the air rises. The resulting **upslope fog** forms a stratus cloud at the condensation level of saturation. Along the Appalachians and the eastern slopes of the Rockies such fog is common in winter and spring. Another advection fog associated with topography is **valley fog**. Because cool air is denser than warm air, it settles in low-lying areas, producing a fog in the chilled, saturated layer near the ground in the valley (Figure 7.26).

FIGURE 7.24 **Fog harvesting.**
In the mountains inland from Chungungo, Chile, polypropylene mesh stretched between two posts captures advection fog for local drinking-water supplies. [Robert S. Schemenauer.]

FIGURE 7.25 **Evaporation fog.**
Evaporation fog, or sea smoke, highlights dawn on a cold morning at Donner Lake, California. Later that morning as air temperatures rose, what do you think happened to the evaporation fog? [Bobbé Christopherson.]

FIGURE 7.26 Valley fog.
Cold air settles in the valleys of the Appalachian Mountains, chilling the air to the dew point and forming a valley fog. [Robert Christopherson.]

FIGURE 7.27 Winter radiation fog.
Radiation fog in the southern Great Valley of California. This fog is locally known as a *tule fog* (pronounced "toolee") because of its association with the tule (bulrush) plants that line the low-elevation islands and marshes of the Sacramento River and San Joaquin River delta regions. [*Terra* MODIS image, GSFC/NASA.]

Radiation Fog When radiative cooling of a surface chills the air layer directly above that surface to the dew-point temperature, creating saturated conditions, a **radiation fog** forms. This fog occurs over moist ground, especially on clear nights; it does not occur over water because water does not cool appreciably overnight. Slight movements of air deliver even more moisture to the cooled area for more fog formation of greater depth (Figure 7.27).

Rime Fog Similar to radiation fog, **rime fog** consists mostly of tiny supercooled droplets that turn into rime frost on contact with freezing objects. It is very common in cold weather, when the air temperature near the surface is below freezing and the air is fairly moist. Rime fog usually happens when the sky is clear on cold mornings. When this type of fog occurs at airports, aircraft have to de-ice before takeoff.

Ice-crystal Fog At low temperatures in a continental Arctic air mass, **ice-crystal fog** may develop (Figure 7.28), for example, when the air becomes full of ice crystals that formed by sublimation. Such an ice-crystal fog seriously limits visibility.

Every year the media carry stories of multicar pileups on stretches of highway where tailgating vehicles continued to speed in foggy conditions. These crash scenes can involve dozens of cars and trucks. Fog is a hazard to drivers, pilots, sailors, pedestrians, and cyclists, and its conditions of formation are quite predictable. The spatial aspects of fog occurrence should be a planning element for any proposed airport, harbour facility, or highway. The prevalence of fog throughout Canada and the United States is shown in Figure 7.29.

FIGURE 7.28 Ice-crystal fog in Whitehorse.
Fog of ice crystals that forms at extremely low temperatures. In this photograph, the air temperature is –42°C. [Murray Lundberg.]

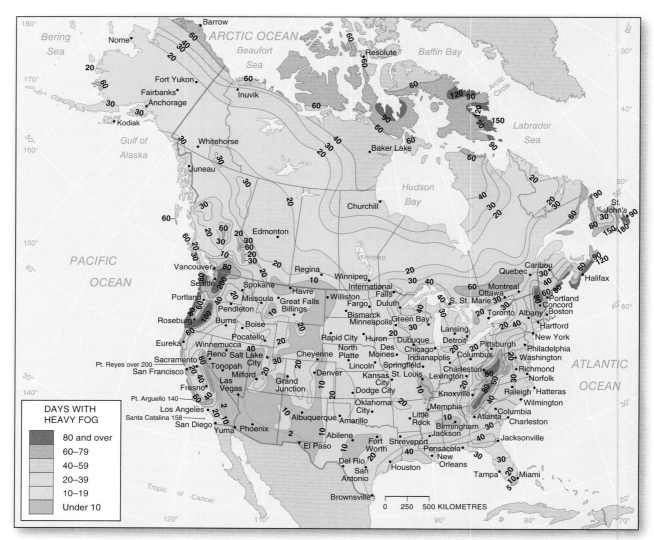

FIGURE 7.29 **Mean annual number of days with heavy fog in the United States and Canada.**
The foggiest spot in the United States is the mouth of the Columbia River where it enters the Pacific Ocean at Cape Disappointment, Washington. One of the foggiest places in the world is Newfoundland's Avalon Peninsula, specifically Argentia and Belle Isle, which regularly exceeds 200 days of fog each year. [Data courtesy of NWS; *Climatic Atlas of Canada*, Atmospheric Environment Service Canada; and *The Climates of Canada*, David Phillips, Senior Climatologist, © Environment Canada, 1990.]

[Geosystems Connection on page 192.]

 APPLIED PHYSICAL GEOGRAPHY   *Measuring Relative Humidity*

How humid is it? Measuring the level of relative humidity is actually a simple matter of reading the temperature simultaneously shown by two ordinary mercury-in-glass thermometers mounted side by side (Figure 7.14b). The first is the dry bulb thermometer, a regular thermometer from which we read the temperature of the air. The other is the same type of thermometer, but with a cloth sleeve that can be wetted, giving the wet bulb temperature. The thermometer with the wet sleeve measures a lower temperature than the dry bulb on any day when the air is less than saturated. This results because moisture evaporates from the cloth sleeve and cools the bulb. The lower the relative humidity, the more rapid the evaporation, the greater the cooling, and the greater the difference in temperatures.

Because the device described above works well only if air is moving rapidly past the wet bulb, a fan can be installed to create a strong air flow. In a sling psychrometer, two thermometers are mounted side by side and are linked to a handle. After the user wets the cloth sleeve, the psychrometer is spun rapidly in a circle to produce the maximum evaporation rate. When the spinning is stopped, the two temperatures, one dry bulb and one wet bulb, are recorded and compared. The difference in temperatures is then used with the relative humidity table (Table 1).

TABLE 1   Relative Humidity Table

(a) Psychrometric chart of relative humidity (in percent)

Depression of the wet bulb (dry-bulb temperature minus wet-bulb temperature, °C)

Dry-bulb temperature (air temperature, °C)

	0.5	1.0	1.5	2.0	2.5	3.0	3.5	4.0	4.5	5.0	7.5	10.0	12.5	15.0	17.5	20.0	22.5	25.0
20	70	41	11															
−17.5	75	51	26	2														
−15	79	58	38	18														
−12.5	82	65	47	30	13													
−10	85	69	54	39	24	10												
−7.5	87	73	60	48	35	22	10											
−5	88	77	66	54	43	32	21	11	1									
−2.5	90	80	70	60	50	42	37	22	12	3								
0	91	82	73	65	56	47	39	31	23	15								
2.5	92	84	76	68	61	53	46	38	31	24								
5	93	86	78	71	65	58	51	45	38	32	1							
7.5	93	87	80	74	68	62	56	50	44	38	11							
10	94	88	82	76	71	65	60	54	49	44	19							
12.5	94	89	84	78	73	68	63	58	53	48	25	4						
15	95	90	85	80	75	70	66	61	57	52	31	12						
17.5	95	90	86	81	77	72	68	64	60	55	36	18	2					
20	95	91	87	82	78	74	70	66	62	58	40	24	8					
22.5	96	92	87	83	80	76	72	68	64	61	44	28	14	1				
25	96	92	88	84	81	77	73	70	66	63	47	32	19	7				
27.5	96	92	89	85	82	78	75	71	68	65	50	36	23	12	1			
30	96	93	89	86	82	79	76	73	70	67	52	39	27	16	6			
32.5	97	93	90	86	83	80	77	74	71	68	54	42	30	20	11	1		
35	97	93	90	87	84	81	78	75	72	69	56	44	33	23	14	6		
37.5	97	94	91	87	85	82	79	76	73	70	58	46	36	26	18	10	3	
40	97	94	91	88	85	82	79	77	74	72	59	48	38	29	21	13	6	
42.5	97	94	91	88	86	83	80	78	75	72	61	50	40	31	23	16	9	2
45	97	94	91	89	86	83	81	78	76	73	62	51	42	33	26	18	12	6
47.5	97	94	92	89	86	84	81	79	76	74	63	53	44	35	28	21	15	9
50	97	95	92	89	87	84	82	79	77	75	64	54	45	37	30	23	17	11

(b) Psychrometric chart of dew-point temperature (in °C)

Depression of the wet bulb (dry-bulb temperature minus wet-bulb temperature, °C)

Dry-bulb temperature (air temperature, °C)

	0.5	1.0	1.5	2.0	2.5	3.0	3.5	4.0	4.5	5.0	7.5	10.0	12.5	15.0	17.5	20.0
−20	−25	−33														
−17.5	−21	−27	−38													
−15	−19	−23	−28													
−12.5	−15	−18	−22	−29												
−10	−12	−14	−18	−21	−27	−36										
−7.5	−9	−11	−14	−17	−20	−26	−34									
−5	−7	−8	−10	−13	−16	−19	−24	−31								
−2.5	−4	−6	−7	−9	−11	−14	−17	−22	−28	−41						
0	−1	−3	−4	−6	−8	−10	−12	−15	−19	−24						
2.5	1	0	−1	−3	−4	−6	−8	−10	−13	−16						
5	4	3	2	0	−1	−3	−4	−6	−8	−10	−48					
7.5	6	6	4	3	2	1	−1	−2	−4	−6	−22					
10	9	8	7	6	5	4	2	1	0	−2	−13					
12.5	12	11	10	9	8	7	6	4	3	2	−7	−28				
15	14	13	12	12	11	10	9	8	7	5	−2	−14				
17.5	17	16	15	14	13	12	12	11	10	8	2	−7	−35			
20	19	18	18	17	16	15	14	14	13	12	6	−1	−15			
22.5	22	21	20	20	19	18	17	16	16	15	10	3	6	−38		
25	24	24	23	22	21	21	20	19	18	18	13	7	0	−14		
27.5	27	26	26	25	24	23	23	22	21	20	16	11	5	−5	−32	
30	29	29	28	27	27	26	25	25	24	23	19	14	9	2	−11	
32.5	32	31	31	30	29	29	28	27	26	26	22	18	13	7	−2	
35	34	34	33	32	32	31	31	30	29	28	25	21	16	11	4	
37.5	37	36	36	35	34	34	33	32	32	31	28	24	20	15	9	0
40	39	39	38	38	37	36	36	35	34	34	30	27	23	18	13	6
42.5	42	41	41	40	40	39	38	38	37	36	33	30	26	22	17	11
45	44	44	43	43	42	42	41	40	40	39	36	33	29	25	21	15
47.5	47	46	46	45	45	44	44	43	42	42	39	35	32	28	24	19
50	49	49	48	48	47	47	46	45	45	44	41	38	35	31	28	23

Applied Physical Geography (*continued*)

Applied Physical Geography (continued)

To use the tables to determine relative humidity (RH, %) and dew point (°C) for a pair of numbers from the sling psychrometer, calculate the difference between the wet bulb and dry bulb temperatures. This difference is called the wet bulb depression. Table 2 gives examples of relative humidity and dew-point temperature based on the differences between wet-bulb and dry-bulb readings. Fill in the spaces in the last two rows using the tables.

TABLE 2

Dry Bulb Temperature (°C)	Wet Bulb Temperature (°C)	Wet Bulb Depression (C°)	Relative Humidity (%)	Dew Point Temperature (°C)
31	14	17	16	−11
35	25	10	44	21
1	−3	4	31	−15
41	28	13	38	23
17.5	—	—	86	—
−10	−12	—	—	—

 GEO REPORT 7.5 *Lenticular clouds signal mountain weather*

Along the mountains of the world, lenticular clouds provide spectacular beauty and photo opportunities. Yet these altostratus clouds may warn of high-speed winds at altitude, sometimes signaling the onset of severe weather. Lenticular, or lens-shaped, clouds form on the lee side of mountain ranges, where winds passing over the terrain develop a wave pattern. These clouds often appear stationary, but they are not. The flow of moist air continuously resupplies the cloud on the windward side as air evaporates from the cloud on the leeward side.

 GEOSYSTEMS CONNECTION

We explored the origins of water, where it is located on earth, and its remarkable physical properties. The role of water in the atmosphere and humidity concepts formed the basis for examining stable or unstable conditions, which lead to clouds and fog formation. With this foundation we move to Chapter 8 and identification of air masses and the conditions that force these to lift, cool, condense, and produce weather phenomena. Also, we look at violent weather events, such as thunderstorms, strong winds, tornadoes, and tropical cyclones.

KEY LEARNING CONCEPTS REVIEW

■ **Describe** the origin of Earth's waters, **define** the quantity of water that exists today, and **list** the locations of Earth's freshwater supply.

The next time it rains where you live, pause and reflect on the journey each of those water molecules made. Water molecules came from within Earth over a period of billions of years, in the **outgassing** process. Thus began endless cycling of water through the hydrologic system of evaporation–condensation–precipitation. Water covers about 71% of Earth. Approximately 97% of it is salty seawater, and the remaining 3% is freshwater—most of it frozen.

The present volume of water on Earth is estimated at 1.36 billion km³, an amount achieved roughly 2 billion years ago. This overall steady-state equilibrium might seem in conflict with the many changes in sea level that have occurred over Earth's history, but is not. **Eustasy** refers to worldwide changes in sea level and relates to the change in volume of water in the oceans. The amount of water stored in glaciers and ice sheets explains these changes as **glacio-eustatic** factors. At present, sea level is rising because of increases in the temperature of the oceans and the record melting of glacial ice.

outgassing (p. 168)
eustasy (p. 169)
glacio-eustatic (p. 169)

1. Approximately where and when did Earth's water originate?
2. If the quantity of water on Earth has been quite constant in volume for at least 2 billion years, how can sea level have fluctuated? Explain.

3. Describe the locations of Earth's water, both oceanic and fresh. What is the largest repository of freshwater at this time? In what ways is this distribution of water significant to modern society?
4. Why would climate change be a concern, given this distribution of water?
5. Why might you describe Earth as the water planet? Explain.

■ **Describe** the heat properties of water, and **identify** the traits of its three phases: solid, liquid, and gas.

Water is the most common compound on the surface of Earth, and it possesses unusual solvent and heat characteristics. Part of Earth's uniqueness is that its water exists naturally in all three states—solid, liquid, and gas—owing to Earth's temperate position relative to the Sun. A change from one state to another is a **phase change**. The change from solid to vapour is **sublimation**; from liquid to solid, freezing; from solid to liquid, melting; from vapour to liquid, condensation; and from liquid to vapour, vaporization, or evaporation.

The heat energy required for water to change phase is **latent heat**, because, once absorbed, it is hidden within the structure of the water, ice, or water vapour. For 1 g of water to become 1 g of water vapour at boiling requires the addition of 540 cal, or the **latent heat of vaporization**. When this 1 g of water vapour condenses, the same amount of heat energy is liberated, as 540 cal of the **latent heat of condensation**. The **latent heat of sublimation** is the energy exchanged in the phase change from ice to vapour and vapour to ice. Weather is powered by the tremendous amount of latent heat energy involved in the phase changes among the three states of water.

phase change (p. 172)
sublimation (p. 172)
latent heat (p. 173)
latent heat of vaporization (p. 173)
latent heat of condensation (p. 173)
latent heat of sublimation (p. 175)

6. Describe the three states of matter as they apply to ice, water, and water vapour.
7. What happens to the physical structure of water as it cools below 4°C? What are some visible indications of these physical changes?
8. What is latent heat? How is it involved in the phase changes of water?
9. Take 1 g of water at 0°C and follow it through to 1 g water vapour at 100°C, describing what happens along the way. What amounts of energy are involved in the changes that take place?
10. Describe the physical structure of water and ice as it applies to Figure 7.6. Explain.

■ **Define** humidity and the expressions of the relative humidity concept, and **explain** dew-point temperature and saturated conditions in the atmosphere.

The amount of water vapour in the atmosphere is **humidity**. The maximum water vapour possible in air is principally a function of the temperature of the air and of the water vapour (usually these temperatures are the same). Warmer air produces higher net evaporation rates and maximum possible water vapour whereas cooler air can produce net condensation rates and lower possible water vapour.

Relative humidity is a ratio of the amount of water vapour actually in the air to the maximum possible at a given temperature. Relative humidity tells us how near the air is to saturation. Relatively dry air has a lower relative humidity value; relatively moist air a higher relative humidity percentage. Air is said to be at **saturation** when the rate of evaporation and the rate of condensation reach equilibrium, and any further addition of water vapour or temperature lowering will result in active condensation (100% relative humidity). The temperature at which air achieves saturation is the **dew-point temperature**.

Among the various ways to express humidity and relative humidity are vapour pressure and specific **humidity**. **Vapour pressure** is that portion of the atmospheric pressure produced by the presence of water vapour. A comparison of vapour pressure with the saturation vapour pressure at any moment yields a relative humidity percentage. **Specific humidity** is the mass of water vapour (in grams) per mass of air (in kilograms) at any specified temperature. Because it is measured as a mass, specific humidity does not change as temperature or pressure changes, making it a valuable measurement in weather forecasting. A comparison of specific humidity with the maximum specific humidity at any moment produces a relative humidity percentage.

Two instruments measure relative humidity, and indirectly the actual humidity content of the air; they are the **hair hygrometer** and the **sling psychrometer**.

humidity (p. 175)
relative humidity (p. 175)
saturation (p. 175)
dew-point temperature (p. 175)
vapour pressure (p. 177)
specific humidity (p. 178)
hair hygrometer (p. 178)
sling psychrometer (p. 178)

11. What is humidity? How is it related to the energy present in the atmosphere? To our personal comfort and how we perceive apparent temperatures?
12. Define relative humidity. What does the concept represent? What is meant by the terms *saturation* and *dew-point temperature?*
13. Using different measures of humidity in the air than those used in the chapter, derive relative humidity values (vapour pressure/saturation vapour pressure; specific humidity/maximum specific humidity) in Figures 7.12 and 7.13.
14. How do the two instruments described in this chapter measure relative humidity?
15. How does the daily distribution of relative humidity compare with the daily trend in air temperature?

■ **Define** atmospheric stability, and **relate** it to a parcel of air that is ascending or descending.

Meteorologists use the term *parcel* to describe a body of air that has specific temperature and humidity characteristics. Think of a parcel of air as a volume of air, perhaps 300 m in diameter. The temperature of the volume of air determines the density of the air parcel. Warm air has a lower density in a given volume of air; cold air has a higher density.

Stability refers to the tendency of an air parcel, with its water-vapour cargo, either to remain in place or to change vertical position by ascending (rising) or descending (falling).

An air parcel is *stable* if it resists displacement upward or, when disturbed, it tends to return to its starting place. An air parcel is *unstable* if it continues to rise until it reaches an altitude where the surrounding air has a density (air temperature) similar to its own.

stability (p. 179)

16. Differentiate between stability and instability relative to a parcel of air rising vertically in the atmosphere.
17. What are the forces acting on a vertically moving parcel of air? How are they affected by the density of the air parcel?

■ *Illustrate* three atmospheric conditions—unstable, conditionally unstable, and stable—with a simple graph that relates the environmental lapse rate (ELR) to the dry adiabatic rate (DAR) and moist adiabatic rate (MAR).

An ascending (rising) parcel of air cools by expansion, responding to the reduced air pressure at higher altitudes. A descending (falling) parcel heats by compression. These temperature changes internal to a moving air parcel are explained by physical laws that govern the behaviour of gases. Temperature changes in both ascending and descending air parcels occur without any significant heat exchange between the surrounding environment and the vertically moving parcel of air. The warming and cooling rates for a parcel of expanding or compressing air are termed **adiabatic**.

The **dry adiabatic rate (DAR)** is the rate at which "dry" air cools by expansion (if ascending) or heats by compression (if descending). The term *dry* is used when air is less than saturated (relative humidity less than 100%). The DAR is 10 C° · 1000 m^{-1}. The **moist adiabatic rate (MAR)** is the average rate at which ascending air that is moist (saturated) cools by expansion, or descending air warms by compression. The average MAR is 6 C° · 1000 m^{-1}. This is roughly 4 C° less than the dry rate. The MAR, however, varies with moisture content and temperature and can range from 4 to 10 C° per 1000 m.

A simple comparison of the dry adiabatic rate (DAR) and moist adiabatic rate (MAR) in a vertically moving parcel of air with that of the environmental lapse rate in the surrounding air determines the atmosphere's stability—whether it is unstable (lifting of air parcel continues), stable (air parcel resists vertical displacement), or conditionally unstable (air parcel behaves as though unstable if the MAR is in operation, and stable otherwise).

adiabatic (p. 179)
dry adiabatic rate (DAR) (p. 180)
moist adiabatic rate (MAR) (p. 180)

18. How do the adiabatic rates of heating or cooling in a vertically displaced air parcel differ from the normal lapse rate and environmental lapse rate?
19. Why is there a difference between the dry adiabatic rate (DAR) and the moist adiabatic rate (MAR)?
20. What atmospheric temperature and moisture conditions would you expect on a day when the weather is unstable? When it is stable? Relate in your answer what you would experience if you were outside watching.
21. Use the "Atmospheric Stability" animation on your *Student Animation CD*. Try different temperature settings on the sliders to produce stable and unstable conditions.

■ *Identify* the requirements for cloud formation, and *explain* the major cloud classes and types, including fog.

A **cloud** is an aggregation of tiny moisture droplets and ice crystals suspended in the air. Clouds are a constant reminder of the powerful heat-exchange system in the environment. **Moisture droplets** in a cloud form when saturated air and the presence of **cloud-condensation nuclei** lead to *condensation*. Raindrops are formed from moisture droplets through either the *collision-coalescence process* or the *Bergeron ice-crystal process*.

Low clouds, ranging from the surface up to 2000 m in the middle latitudes, are **stratus** (flat clouds, in layers) or **cumulus** (puffy clouds, in heaps). When stratus clouds yield precipitation, they are **nimbostratus**. Sometimes near the end of the day, lumpy, greyish, low-level clouds called **stratocumulus** may fill the sky in patches. Middle-level clouds are denoted by the prefix *alto-*. **Altocumulus** clouds, in particular, represent a broad category that occurs in many different styles. Clouds at high altitude, principally composed of ice crystals, are called **cirrus**. A cumulus cloud can develop into a towering giant **cumulonimbus** cloud (*-nimbus* in Latin denotes "rain storm" or "thundercloud"). Such clouds are called *thunderheads* because of their shape and their associated lightning, thunder, surface wind gusts, updrafts and downdrafts, heavy rain, and hail.

Fog is a cloud that occurs at ground level. **Advection fog** forms when air in one place migrates to another place where conditions exist that can cause saturation—for example, when warm, moist air moves over cooler ocean currents. Another type of advection fog forms when cold air flows over the warm water of a lake, ocean surface, or swimming pool. This **evaporation fog**, or steam fog, may form as the water molecules evaporate from the water surface into the cold overlying air. **Upslope fog** is produced when moist air is forced to higher elevations along a hill or mountain. Another fog caused by topography is **valley fog**, formed because cool, denser air settles in low-lying areas, producing fog in the chilled, saturated layer near the ground. Radiative cooling of a surface that chills the air layer directly above the surface to the dew-point temperature creates saturated conditions and a **radiation fog**. **Rime fog**, similar to radiation fog, consists mostly of tiny supercooled droplets that turn into rime frost on contact with freezing objects. It is very common in cold weather, when the air temperature near the surface is below freezing and the air is fairly moist. **Ice-crystal fog** develops at low temperatures, for example in a continental arctic air mass, when the air becomes full of ice crystals that formed by sublimation. Ice-crystal fog seriously limits visibility.

cloud (p. 181)
moisture droplet (p. 182)
cloud-condensation nuclei (p. 182)
stratus (p. 186)
nimbostratus (p. 186)
cumulus (p. 186)
stratocumulus (p. 186)
altocumulus (p. 186)
cirrus (p. 186)
cumulonimbus (p. 186)
fog (p. 186)
advection fog (p. 186)
evaporation fog (p. 187)
upslope fog (p. 188)
valley fog (p. 188)
radiation fog (p. 189)
rime fog (p. 189)
ice-crystal fog (p. 189)

22. Specifically, what is a cloud? Describe the droplets that form a cloud.
23. Explain the condensation process: What are the requirements? What two principal processes are discussed in this chapter?
24. What are the basic forms of clouds? Using Table 7.2, describe how the basic cloud forms vary with altitude.
25. Explain how clouds might be used as indicators of the conditions of the atmosphere and of expected weather.
26. What type of cloud is fog? List and define the principal types of fog.
27. Describe the occurrence of fog in Canada and the United States. Where are the regions of highest incidence?

In this photograph, can you tell which two kinds of fog are pictured from those discussed in this chapter? These questions may help: How does the temperature of the river water compare to that of the overlying air, especially beyond the bend in the river? Could the temperature of the moist farmlands have changed overnight, and if so, how? Might that contribute to fog formation? Can you see any evidence of air movement, such as a light breeze? How might this affect the presence of fog? [Bobbé Christopherson.]

MyGeosciencePlace

Visit **www.mygeoscienceplace.ca** for several figure animations, satellite loops, self-study quizzes, flashcards, interactive glossary, career links, RSS feeds, Pearson eText of *Geosystems*, and much more.

CHAPTER 8

Weather

Elie, Manitoba was devastated by Canada's first F5 Tornado on June 22, 2007. Homes were completely destroyed or damaged beyond use, public buildings were flattened, trees were denuded. Damage costs exceeded a million dollars, but there was no loss of life. [John Woods/CP Images.]

KEY LEARNING CONCEPTS

After reading the chapter, you should be able to:

- **Describe** air masses that affect North America, and **relate** their qualities to source regions.
- **Identify** and **describe** four types of atmospheric lifting mechanisms, and give an example of each.
- **Analyse** the pattern of orographic precipitation, and **describe** the link between this pattern and global topography.
- **Describe** the life cycle of a midlatitude cyclonic storm system, and **relate** this to its portrayal on weather maps.
- **List** the measurable elements that contribute to modern weather forecasting, and **describe** the technology and methods employed.
- **Analyse** various forms of violent weather and their characteristics, and **review** several examples of each.

On the Front Lines of Intense Weather

How do you deal with images of intense weather and the trail of destruction left behind? Imagine what people on the front lines of these events face. Perhaps you have lived through an intense weather event that left an indelible mark on your memory. Improved warning systems have helped to reduce loss of life but the economic costs of intense weather and impacts on human lives remain high.

Each year, some 80–100 tornadoes are *observed* in Canada. Tornadoes occur in all provinces, but the southern Prairies and southwestern Ontario are struck most often. Just days apart in June 2010, tornadoes occurred in the southern Ontario towns of Leamington (rated as F1 on the Enhanced Fujita scale, 138–177 km·h^{-1} winds) and Midland (rated EF2, 178–217 km·h^{-1} winds). Tornadoes usually occur in the late afternoon or early evening, but in Leamington, the tornado struck at 3 A.M. Although warnings were issued by Environment Canada 23 minutes before the tornado struck, most people were asleep. There were a few people with special radios that sound an alarm when an official warning is issued who were alerted to the tornado, but most were not. Ultimately, no major injuries were sustained in Leamington, but nearly 5000 insurance claims were made, totaling $85 million, and over $3.5 million was spent by local governments on the cleanup.

FIGURE GN 8.1 Aftermath of the 2000 Pine Lake, Alberta, tornado.
Twelve people were killed and more than 100 others were critically injured in the Green Acres campground and trailer park when an EF3 tornado struck Pine Lake, 25 km southeast of Red Deer, on July 14, 2000. [Adrian Wyld/CP Images.]

About two weeks later, a tornado tore though Midland in the early evening, causing damage to buildings and power outages. There were some minor injuries, but again the residents were fortunate to avoid serious harm. Considerable damage occurred in Smith's mobile home park near the town where it was reported that 50 families lost their homes. Within a few minutes, an estimated $10–15 million in damage was caused.

The correspondence between significant tornado damage and mobile homes is a recurring story because the trailers are not well anchored to the ground. Fifteen residents of the Evergreen mobile home park in northeast Edmonton died when one of the most destructive and deadly tornadoes in Canadian history occurred on July 31, 1987. The tornado travelled northward on the eastern edge of Edmonton for about a one-hour period, with intensity varying between EF2 and EF4 (winds between 178–322 km·h^{-1}). Another 12 people were killed at a nearby oil refinery complex, and the total cost of damages from the tornado was over $300 million.

Relying on video evidence, officials at Environment Canada rated the Elie, Manitoba tornado of June 22, 2007 to be the first officially documented tornado with EF5 intensity on the Fujita scale in Canada. Maximum wind speeds of 420–510 km·h^{-1} were estimated. After seeing a house on video picked up and moved 300 metres in the air before breaking apart, and a van being tossed around by the tornado, it was upgraded from an initial EF4 rating. This tornado traveled 5.5 km over a 35-minute period, leaving damage in a swath up to 300 metres in width, but it occurred in a less populated area of the country and fortunately, it caused no fatalities or serious injuries.

By the time they reach Atlantic Canada, most hurricanes in the northwest Atlantic have weakened to no greater than tropical storm intensity, but some do retain winds with category

FIGURE GN 8.2 Devastation at the Evergreen mobile home park.
In July 1987, an F4 tornado struck this residential area in northeast Edmonton, killing 15 people. Another 12 people were killed in a nearby industrial area along its path of destruction. [*Edmonton Journal*/Ken Orr/CP Images.]

1 or 2 strength, the lower end of the Saffir-Simpson scale. At its strongest, Hurricane Igor attained category 4 status, but it was a category 1 storm (119–154 km·h^{-1} winds) when it struck Newfoundland on September 21, 2010, and dropped 200 mm of rain in some places. A state of emergency was declared in 30 Newfoundland communities. One man died when the driveway he was standing on collapsed beneath him and he was swept out to sea near Britannia. Igor resulted in $65 million of insurance losses from damage caused by wind, sewer backup, fallen trees, and water entering homes through broken windows, roofs and walls. The figure excludes overland flood damage which is not covered by insurance in Canada.

Tornadoes and hurricanes are not the only intense weather events to affect Canadians. Blizzards, ice storms, and floods caused by high precipitation are other examples. If we are lucky, the damage caused by these events is minor and we are left with just some cleanup to do, but for some people the impact on lives and property can be much greater and longer lasting. Again the question: How do people on the front lines cope with such disaster? Contemplate the human dimension as you work through the weather chapter.

Water has a leading role in the vast drama played out daily on Earth's stage. It affects the stability of air masses and their interactions and produces powerful and beautiful special effects in the lower atmosphere. Air masses come into conflict; they move and shift, dominating now one region, then another, varying in strength and characteristics. Think of the weather as a play, North America (or other parts of the world) as the stage, and the air masses as actors of varying ability.

In this chapter: We follow huge air masses across North America, observe powerful lifting mechanisms in the atmosphere, revisit the concepts of stable and unstable conditions, and examine migrating cyclonic systems with attendant cold and warm fronts. We conclude with a portrait of violent and dramatic weather so often in the news in recent years. 2011 broke records for weather events exceeding USD $1 billion; more than a 500% increase since 1975.

Water, with its ability to absorb and release vast quantities of heat energy, drives this daily drama in the atmosphere. The spatial implications of these weather phenomena and the relationship to human activities strongly link meteorology to physical geography and this chapter.

Weather Essentials

Weather is the short-term, day-to-day condition of the atmosphere, contrasted with *climate*, which is the long-term average (over decades) of weather conditions and extremes in a region. Weather is both a "snapshot" of atmospheric conditions and a technical status report of the Earth–atmosphere heat-energy budget. Important elements that contribute to weather are temperature, air pressure, relative humidity, wind speed and direction, and seasonal factors such as insolation receipt related to day-length and Sun angle.

We can turn for the weather forecast to the Weather Office of the Canadian Meteorological Centre (http://www.weatheroffice.ec.gc.ca), a branch of the Meteorological Service of Canada, Environment Canada, to see current satellite images and to hear weather analysis. In the United States weather is forecast by the National Weather Service (NWS, http://www.nws.noaa.gov). Internationally, the World Meteorological Organization coordinates weather information (see http://www.wmo.int/pages/index_en.html). Many sources of weather information and related topics are found for this chapter on the companion website.

Meteorology is the scientific study of the atmosphere. (*Meteor* means "heavenly" or "of the atmosphere.") Meteorologists study the atmosphere's physical characteristics and motions, related chemical and physical processes, the complex linkages of atmospheric systems, and weather forecasting. Massive computers handle volumes of data from surface, aircraft, and orbital platforms used to accurately forecast near-term weather and to study trends in long-term weather, climatology, and climatic change.

An essential part of understanding weather is Doppler radar (Figure 8.1). Using backscatter from two radar pulses, it detects the direction of moisture droplets toward or away from the radar, indicating wind direction and speed. This information is critical to providing accurate severe storm warnings. As part of the Next Generation Weather Radar (NEXRAD) program, 31 WSR-88D (*W*eather *S*urveillance *R*adar) Doppler radar systems are operational through the Meteorological Service of Canada with another 159 stations in the United States operated through the NWS, Federal Aviation Administration, and Department of Defense.

Air Masses

Each area of Earth's surface imparts its temperature and moisture characteristics to overlying air. The effect of the surface on the air creates regional air masses with a homogenous mix of temperature, humidity, and stability. These masses of air interact to produce weather patterns. Such a distinctive body of air is an **air mass**, and it initially reflects the characteristics of its *source region* and sometimes extends through the lower half of the troposphere. For example, weather forecasters speak of a "cold Arctic air mass" and "moist tropical air mass."

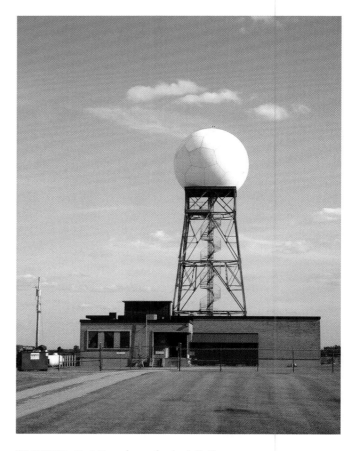

FIGURE 8.1 Doppler radar installation.
Doppler radar installation at Exeter, Ontario, operated by the Meteorological Service of Canada. The radar antenna is sheltered within the dome structure. [Mary-Louise Byrne.]

Air Masses Affecting North America

We classify air masses generally according to the moisture and temperature characteristics of their source regions:

1. *Moisture*—designated **m** for maritime (wet) and **c** for continental (dry).
2. *Temperature* (latitude factor)—designated **A** (Arctic), **P** (polar), **T** (tropical), **E** (equatorial), and **AA** (Antarctic).

The principal air masses that affect North America in winter and summer are mapped in Figure 8.2.

Continental Arctic (cA) air masses originate in Siberia and northern Canada. These cA air masses dominate the extreme north in winter when they cross over the North Pole and spill over to the North American continent. Arctic air, colder than polar air and with a lower dew point, often forms when a high-pressure area becomes nearly stationary over northern Canada, Eastern Alaska, or Siberia. The small amount of winter solar radiation, the abundant surface snow/ice cover, and the continuous emission of radiation from Earth's surface cause the air to become increasingly colder. If the jet stream shifts southward, the cold air spreads into southern Canada and the United States, where it modifies to continental polar air.

Continental polar (cP) air masses form only in the Northern Hemisphere and are most developed in winter and cold weather conditions. These cP air masses are major players in middle- and high-latitude weather. The cold, dense, cP air displaces moist, warm air in its path, producing lifting, cooling, and condensation. An area covered by cP air in winter experiences cold, stable air, clear skies, high pressure, and anticyclonic wind flow—all visible in the weather map in Figure 8.3. The Southern Hemisphere lacks the necessary continental landmasses at high latitudes to create such cP air masses.

Maritime polar (mP) air masses in the Northern Hemisphere exist over the northern oceans. Within them, cool, moist, unstable conditions prevail throughout the year.

FIGURE 8.2 Principal air masses.
Air masses and their source regions influence North America during (a) winter and (b) summer. (*Sea-surface temperature in °C; SH = specific humidity.)

FIGURE 8.3 Winter high-pressure system.
A cP air mass with two high-pressure centres merging north of the Great Lakes Region. These high-pressure systems exceed 1036 mb (103.6 kPa) air pressure. Representative temperatures toward the south are around −9°C, with dew-point temperatures of −18°C. In the northern high-pressure centre temperatures drop to −22°C with dew points as low as −29°C. Associated with these centres are clear, calm, stable conditions that dominate a large area. This is a region of extremely dry air.

The Aleutian and Icelandic subpolar low-pressure cells reside within these mP air masses, especially in their well-developed winter pattern (see the January isobar pressure map in Figure 6.9a).

Two maritime tropical (mT) air masses—the *mT Gulf/ Atlantic* and the *mT Pacific*—influence North America. The humidity experienced in eastern North America and the American Midwest is created by the mT Gulf/Atlantic air mass, which is particularly unstable and active from late spring to early fall. In contrast, the mT Pacific is stable to conditionally unstable and generally lower in moisture content and available energy. As a result, the western United States, influenced by this weaker Pacific air mass, receives lower average precipitation than the rest of the country. Please review Figure 6.12 and the discussion of subtropical high-pressure cells.

Air Mass Modification

As air masses migrate from source regions, the temperature and moisture characteristics slowly take on the characteristics of the land over which the air masses

move. For example, an mT Gulf/Atlantic air mass may carry humidity to Atlanta and on to Toronto but gradually loses its initial characteristics of high humidity and warmth with each day's passage northward.

Similarly, below-freezing temperatures occasionally reach into southern Texas and Florida, brought by an invading winter cP air mass from the north. However, that air mass warms from the –30°C of its winter source region in northern Canada, warming especially after it leaves areas covered by snow.

Modification of cP air as it moves south and east produces snowbelts that lie to the east of each of the Great Lakes. As below-freezing cP air passes over the warmer Great Lakes, it absorbs heat energy and moisture from lake surfaces and becomes *humidified*. This enhancement produces heavy lake-effect snowfall downwind into Ontario, Québec, Michigan, Pennsylvania, and New York—some areas receiving in excess of 250 cm in average snowfall a year (Figure 8.4).

Severity correlates to a low-pressure system positioned north of the Great Lakes, with counterclockwise

FIGURE 8.4 Lake-effect snowbelts of the Great Lakes.
(a) Heavy local snowfall is associated with the lee side of each Great Lake. (b) Processes causing lake-effect snowfall are generally limited to about 50 to 100 km inland. (c) and (d) Satellite images show lake-effect weather in December. [(a) *Climatic Atlas of the United States*, p. 53. (c) *Terra* MODIS image and (d) *OrbView-2* image; both NASA/GSFC.]

winds pushing air across the lakes. With global warming, regional temperatures are increasing, which leads forecasters to predict enhanced lake-effect snowfall over the next several decades, since warmer air can absorb more water vapour. Forecast models show that later in the century, snowfall will decrease as temperatures rise, although rainfall totals will continue to increase over the downwind regions. Temperature and evaporation rates are increasing for all of these lakes.

Atmospheric Lifting Mechanisms

Lifting air masses cool adiabatically (by expansion) to reach the dew-point temperature. Moisture in the saturated air then can condense and form clouds, and perhaps precipitation. Four principal lifting mechanisms operate in the atmosphere:

- Convergent lifting—air flows toward an area of low pressure
- Convectional lifting—stimulated by local surface heating
- Orographic lifting—air is forced over a barrier such as a mountain range
- Frontal lifting—along the leading edges of contrasting air masses

Descriptions of all four mechanisms follow and are shown in Figure 8.5.

Convergent Lifting

Air flowing from different directions into the same low-pressure area is converging, displacing air upward in **convergent lifting** (Figure 8.5a). All along the equatorial region, the southeast and northeast trade winds converge, forming the intertropical convergence zone (ITCZ) and areas of extensive uplift, towering cumulonimbus cloud development, and high average annual precipitation (see Figure 6.10).

Convectional Lifting

When an air mass passes from a maritime source region to a warmer continental region, heating from the warmer land causes lifting and convection in the air mass. Other sources of surface heating might include an urbanized area heat island, or an area of dark soil in a ploughed field—the warmer surfaces produce **convectional lifting**. If conditions are unstable, initial lifting continues and clouds develop. Figure 8.5b illustrates convectional action stimulated by local heating, with unstable conditions present in the atmosphere. The rising air parcel continues its ascent because it is warmer and therefore less dense than the surrounding environment (Figure 8.6).

Florida's precipitation illustrates both convergent and convectional lifting mechanisms. Heating of the land produces convergence of onshore winds from the Atlantic and the Gulf of Mexico. As an example of local heating and convectional lifting, Figure 8.7 depicts a day on which the landmass of Florida was warmer than the surrounding Gulf of Mexico and Atlantic Ocean. Because the Sun's radiation gradually heats the land throughout the day and warms the air above it, convectional showers tend to form in the afternoon and early evening. Thus Florida has the highest frequency of days with thunderstorms in the United States.

Orographic Lifting

The physical presence of a mountain acts as a topographic barrier to migrating air masses. **Orographic lifting** (*oro* means "mountain") occurs when air is forcibly lifted upslope as it is pushed against a mountain. The lifting air cools adiabatically. Stable air forced upward in this manner may produce stratiform clouds, whereas unstable or conditionally unstable air usually forms a line of cumulus and cumulonimbus clouds. An orographic barrier enhances convectional activity and causes additional lifting during the passage of weather fronts and cyclonic systems, thereby extracting more moisture from passing air masses.

Figure 8.8a, page 204 illustrates the operation of orographic lifting under unstable conditions. The wetter intercepting slope facing the oncoming air mass is the *windward slope*, as opposed to the drier far-side slope, known as the *leeward slope*. Moisture condenses from the lifting air mass on the windward side of the mountain; on the leeward side, the descending air mass heats by compression, and any remaining water in the air evaporates (Figure 8.8b). Thus, air beginning its ascent up a mountain can be warm and moist, but finishing its descent on the leeward slope it becomes hot and dry.

 GEO REPORT 8.1 *Killer Snow Squalls*

In December 2010, two remarkable lake effect snow squall events lasted from December 5 to 9 and from December 13 to 14 in Ontario. In the first, cold northwest winds flowed over the ice-free waters of Lake Huron, dumping 75 to 100 cm of snow over an area from Grand Bend to London. In Lucan, accumulations were over 175 cm. The second event targeted Lambton and Middlesex Counties with winds exceeding 70 km·h⁻¹, producing snow, whiteouts, and severe wind chills and leading to the closure of Highway 402. A state of emergency was called as response and recovery workers rescued stranded motorists. Unfortunately, one motorist left his vehicle, became disoriented, and succumbed to the cold.

(a) Convergent lifting

(b) Convectional lifting

(c) Orographic lifting

(d) Frontal lifting, cold front example

FIGURE 8.5 Four atmospheric lifting mechanisms.
(a) Convergent lifting; (b) convectional lifting; (c) orographic lifting; and (d) frontal lifting.

Atmospheric Stability

FIGURE 8.6 Convection activity in unstable conditions.
Work through these unstable atmospheric conditions, with an environmental lapse rate of 12 C° · 1000 m⁻¹. Specific humidity of the air parcel is 8g · kg⁻¹ and the beginning temperature is 25°C. Looking back to Figure 7.13, you find that air with a specific humidity of 8g · kg⁻¹ must be cooled to 11°C to achieve the dew-point temperature. Here the dew point is reached after 14 C° of adiabatic cooling at 1400 m. Note that the DAR (dry adiabatic rate) is used when the air parcel is less than saturated, changing to the MAR (moist adiabatic rate) above the lifting-condensation level at 1400 m.

Convectional Activity over
the Florida Peninsula

FIGURE 8.7 Convectional activity over the Florida peninsula.
Cumulus clouds cover the land, with several cells developing into cumulonimbus thunderheads.
[*Terra* MODIS image, NASA/GSFC.]

The province of British Columbia provides an excellent example of this concept, as shown in Figure 8.9, page 205. The Coast Mountains and the Rocky Mountains orographically lift invading mP air masses from the North Pacific Ocean, squeezing precipitation onto the windward sides of the mountains and allowing dry air to descend the leeward sides. The Egg Island Weather Station demonstrates precipitation on the windward slope of the Coast Mountains, and the Mount Fidelity Station on the edge of Glacier National Park demonstrates the windward slope for the Rockies. The leeward slopes are represented by 100 Mile House in the Caribou (leeward of the Coast Mountains) and Calgary International Airport, both of which show the lesser annual precipitation. Find these stations on the landscape profile and on the precipitation map in Figure 8.9.

In North America, **chinook winds** (called *föhn* or *foehn* winds in Europe) are the warm, downslope airflows characteristic of the leeward side of mountains. Such winds can bring a rapid 20 C° jump in temperature and greatly reduced relative humidity.

The term **rain shadow** is applied to dry regions leeward of mountains. Such rain-shadow patterns dominate east of the Rocky Mountains, including Palliser's Triangle in the southern prairies of Canada described in *Geosystems Now* at the beginning of Chapter 9. In fact, the precipitation pattern of windward and leeward slopes persists worldwide, as confirmed by the precipitation maps for North America (Figure 9.5) and the world (Figure 10.2).

Frontal Lifting (Cold and Warm Fronts)

The leading edge of an advancing air mass is its *front*. Vilhelm Bjerknes (1862–1951) first applied the term while working with a team of meteorologists in Norway during World War I. Weather systems seemed to them to

---

GEO REPORT 8.2 *Mountains Cause Record Rains*

Mount Waialeale, on the island of Kaua'i, Hawai'i, rises 1569 m above sea level. On its windward slope, rainfall averaged 1234 cm a year for the years 1941–1992. In contrast, the rain-shadow side of Kaua'i received only 50 cm of rain annually. If no islands existed at this location, this portion of the Pacific Ocean would receive only an average 63.5 cm of precipitation a year. (These statistics are from established weather stations with a consistent record of weather data; several stations claim higher rainfall values, but do not have dependable measurement records.)

Cherrapunji, India, is 1313 m above sea level at 25° N latitude, in the Assam Hills south of the Himalayas. Summer monsoons pour in from the Indian Ocean and the Bay of Bengal, producing 930 cm of rainfall in one month. Not surprisingly, Cherrapunji is the all-time precipitation record holder for a single year, 2647 cm, and for every other time interval from 15 days to 2 years. The average annual precipitation there is 1143 cm, placing it second only to Mount Waialeale.

Record precipitation occurrences in Canada exist for locations along the Pacific Coast, on the windward side of the mountains. Henderson Lake, on Vancouver Island, is the wettest location in Canada with an average annual precipitation of 666 cm.

(a)

(b)

(c)

FIGURE 8.8 Orographic precipitation, unstable conditions assumed.
(a) Prevailing winds force warm, moist air upward against a mountain range, producing adiabatic cooling, eventual saturation and net condensation, cloud formation, and precipitation. On the leeward slope, as the "dried" air descends, compressional heating warms it and net evaporation dominates, creating the hot, relatively dry rain shadow. (b) Rain shadow produced by descending, warming air contrasts with the clouds of the windward side. Dust is stirred up by leeward downslope winds. (c) The windward slopes of the Coast Mountain Range and leeward rain shadow conditions of the Interior Dry Plateau are clearly visible despite the light dusting of snow in this true-colour MODIS image from the *Terra* satellite. [(b) Robert Christopherson. (c) August 11, 2001, image courtesy of MODIS Rapid Response Team, GSFC/NASA.]

be migrating air-mass "armies," doing battle along fronts. A front is a place of atmospheric discontinuity, a narrow zone forming a line of conflict between two air masses of different temperature, pressure, humidity, wind direction and speed, and cloud development. The leading edge of a cold air mass is a **cold front**, whereas the leading edge of a warm air mass is a **warm front** (Figures 8.10 and 8.11).

Cold Front On weather maps, such as the example in Critical Thinking 8.1 (page 211), a cold front is a line with triangular spikes that point in the direction of frontal movement along an advancing cP or mP air mass. The steep face of the cold air mass suggests its ground-hugging nature, caused by its greater density and uniform physical character compared to the warmer air mass it displaces (Figure 8.10a).

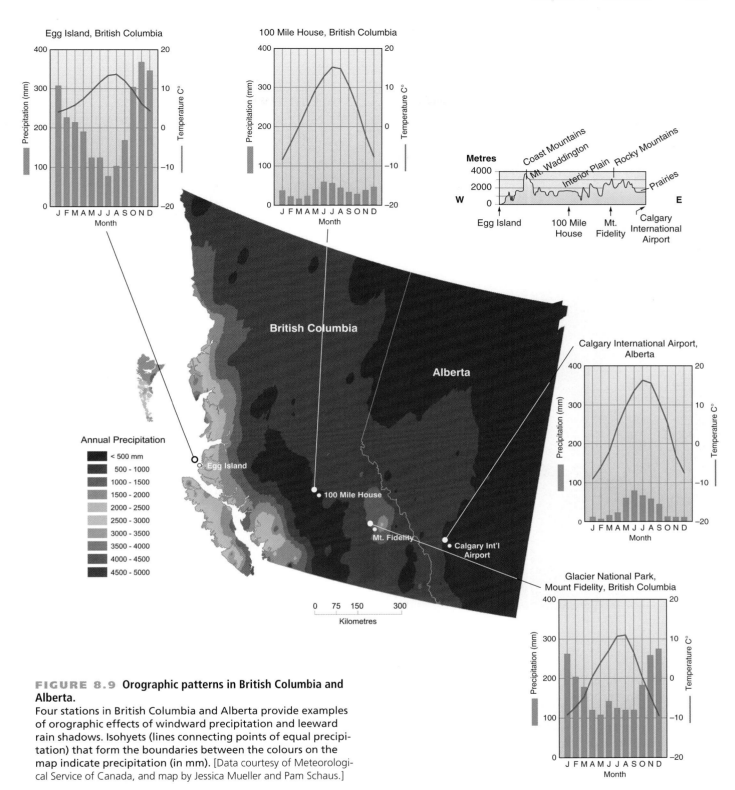

FIGURE 8.9 Orographic patterns in British Columbia and Alberta.
Four stations in British Columbia and Alberta provide examples of orographic effects of windward precipitation and leeward rain shadows. Isohyets (lines connecting points of equal precipitation) that form the boundaries between the colours on the map indicate precipitation (in mm). [Data courtesy of Meteorological Service of Canada, and map by Jessica Mueller and Pam Schaus.]

Warm, moist air in advance of the cold front lifts upward abruptly and experiences the same adiabatic rates of cooling and factors of stability or instability that pertain to all lifting air parcels. A day or two ahead of the cold front's passage, high cirrus clouds appear, telling observers that a lifting mechanism is on the way.

A wind shift, temperature drop, and lowering barometric pressure mark a cold front's advance due to lifting along the front. As the line of most intense lifting passes, usually just ahead of the front itself, air pressure drops to a local low. Clouds may build along the cold front into characteristic cumulonimbus form and may appear as an

(a)

(b)

Cold and Warm Fronts

FIGURE 8.10 A typical cold front.
(a) Denser, advancing cold air forces warm, moist air to lift abruptly. As the air is lifted, it cools by expansion at the DAR, cooling to the dew-point temperature as it rises to a level of condensation and cloud formation. (b) A sharp line of cumulonimbus clouds near the Texas coast and Gulf of Mexico marks a cold front and squall line. The cloud formation rises to 17 000 m. The passage of such a frontal system over land often produces strong winds, cumulonimbus clouds, large raindrops, heavy showers, lightning and thunder, hail, and the possibility of tornadoes. [NASA.]

advancing wall of clouds. Precipitation usually is heavy, containing large droplets, and can be accompanied by hail, lightning, and thunder.

The aftermath of a cold front passage usually brings northerly winds in the Northern Hemisphere and southerly winds in the Southern Hemisphere as anticyclonic high-pressure advances. Temperatures are lower and air pressure rises in response to the cooler, denser air; cloud cover breaks and clears.

The particular shape and size of the North American landmass and its latitudinal position present conditions where cP and mT air masses are best developed and have the most direct access to each other. The resulting contrast can lead to dramatic weather, particularly in late spring, with sizable temperature differences from one side of a cold front to the other.

A fast-advancing cold front can cause violent lifting and create a zone along or slightly ahead of the front, a **squall line**. Along a squall line, such as the one in the Gulf of Mexico shown in Figure 8.10b, wind patterns are turbulent and wildly changing and precipitation is intense. The well-defined frontal clouds in the photograph rise abruptly, with new thunderstorms forming along the front. Tornadoes also may develop along such a squall line.

Warm Front A line with semicircles facing in the direction of frontal movement denotes a warm front on weather maps (see Figure 8.12). The leading edge of an advancing warm air mass is unable to displace cooler, passive air, which is denser along the surface. Instead, the warm air tends to push the cooler, underlying air into a characteristic wedge shape, with the warmer air sliding up

FIGURE 8.11 **A typical warm front.**
Note the sequence of cloud development as the warm front approaches. Warm air slides upward over a wedge of cooler, passive air near the ground. Gentle lifting of the warm, moist air produces nimbostratus and stratus clouds and drizzly rain showers, in contrast to the more dramatic cold-front precipitation.

Cold and Warm Fronts

over the cooler air. Thus, in the cooler-air region a temperature inversion is present, sometimes causing poor air drainage and stagnation.

Figure 8.11 illustrates a typical warm front in which mT air is gently lifted, leading to stratiform cloud development, characteristic nimbostratus clouds, and drizzly precipitation. A warm front presents a progression of cloud development to an observer: high cirrus and cirrostratus clouds announce the advancing frontal system; then clouds lower and thicken to altostratus; and finally the clouds lower and thicken to stratus within several hundred kilometres of the front.

Midlatitude Cyclonic Systems

The conflict between contrasting air masses can develop a **midlatitude cyclone**, or **wave cyclone**. This migrating low-pressure centre with converging, ascending air spirals inward counterclockwise in the Northern Hemisphere and inward clockwise in the Southern Hemisphere. Because of the undulating nature of frontal boundaries and the steering flow of the jet streams, the term *wave* is appropriate. The combination of the *pressure gradient force, Coriolis force*, and *surface friction* generates this cyclonic motion (see discussion in Chapter 6).

Before World War I, weather maps displayed only pressure and wind patterns. Vilhelm Bjerknes added the concept of fronts, and his son Jacob Bjerknes contributed the concept of migrating centres of cyclonic low-pressure systems.

Wave cyclones dominate weather patterns in the middle and higher latitudes of both the Northern and Southern Hemispheres and act as a catalyst for air-mass conflict. Such a midlatitude cyclone can initiate along the polar front, particularly in the region of the Icelandic and Aleutian subpolar low-pressure cells in the Northern Hemisphere. The intense high-speed winds of

the jet streams guide cyclonic systems along their tracks (see Figures 6.15 and 6.16).

Life Cycle of a Midlatitude Cyclone

Figure 8.12 shows the birth, maturity, and death of a typical midlatitude cyclone in several stages, along with an idealized weather map. On the average, a midlatitude cyclonic system takes 3–10 days to progress through these stages from the area where it develops to the area where it finally dissolves. However, chaos rules and every day's weather map departs from the ideal in some manner.

Cyclogenesis The atmospheric process in which low-pressure wave cyclones develop and strengthen is **cyclogenesis**. This process usually begins along the polar front, where cold and warm air masses converge and are drawn into conflict.

The polar front is a discontinuity of temperature, moisture, and winds that establishes potentially unstable conditions. For a wave cyclone to form along the polar front, a compensating area of divergence aloft matches a surface point of air convergence. Even a slight disturbance along the polar front, perhaps a small change in the path of the jet stream, can initiate the converging, ascending flow of air and thus a surface low-pressure system (illustrated in Figure 8.12a).

In addition to the polar front, certain other areas are associated with wave cyclone development and intensification: the eastern slope of the Rockies and other north–south mountain barriers, the Gulf Coast, and along the east coasts of North America and Asia.

Open Stage To the east of the developing low-pressure centre, warm air begins to move northward along an advancing front, while cold air advances southward to the west of the centre. See this organization on Figure 8.12b and around the centre of low pressure, located north of

WEATHER STATION SYMBOLS

FIGURE 8.12 Idealized stages of a midlatitude wave cyclone.
(a) Cyclogenesis is noted where surface convergence and lifting begin. (b) The open stage. (c) The occluded stage. (d) The dissolving stage is reached at the end of the storm track as the cyclone spins down, no longer energized by the latent heat from condensing moisture. Standard weather symbols are in the inset box. After studying the text and the map, can you describe conditions in Vancouver, Calgary, Fort McMurray, Saskatoon, Regina, Winnipeg, Churchill, Toronto, Québec, Halifax, and St. John's depicted on this weather map?

Midlatitude Cyclones

Winnipeg, in the accompanying map. The growing circulation system then vents into upper-level winds. As the midlatitude cyclone matures, the counterclockwise flow draws the cold air mass from the north and west and the warm air mass from the south. In the cross section, you can see the profiles of both a cold front and a warm front and each air mass segment. Compare these with the illustrations in Figures 8.10 and 8.11.

On the map in Figure 8.12, the cold front has passed over Saskatchewan, affecting wind direction, temperature, and humidity. The wind symbol in Regina clearly shows winds are from the southwest. After the passage of the cold front, winds shift to northwest. To the south of the low-pressure centre, southern Manitoba is experiencing temperatures of –3°C with a dew point of –5°C, while to the west of the centre, the temperature is –10°C with a dew point of –15°C.

Occluded Stage Remember the relation between air temperature and the density of an air mass. The colder cP air mass is denser than the warmer mT air mass. This cooler, more unified air mass acts like a bulldozer blade and therefore moves faster than the warm front. Cold fronts can travel at an average 40 km·h⁻¹, whereas warm fronts average roughly half that at 16–24 km·h⁻¹. Thus, a cold front often overtakes the cyclonic warm front, wedging beneath it, producing an **occluded front** (*occlude* means "to close") in Figure 8.12c. The cold front is occluding with the warm front just southwest of the low-pressure system. Precipitation may be moderate to heavy initially and then taper off as the warmer air wedge is lifted higher by the advancing cold air mass. On this idealized map, a cold front and a warm front remain active to the south of the occluded area.

When there is a stalemate between cooler and warmer air masses where airflow on either side is almost parallel to the front, although in opposite directions, a **stationary front** results. Such a front is positioned over the Great Lakes in Figure 8.12. Some gentle lifting might produce light to moderate precipitation. Eventually the stationary front will begin to move, as one of the air masses assumes dominance, evolving into a warm or a cold front.

Dissolving Stage The final, dissolving, stage of the midlatitude cyclone occurs when its lifting mechanism is completely cut off from the warm air mass that was its source of energy and moisture. Remnants of the cyclonic system then dissipate in the atmosphere, perhaps after passage across the country (Figure 8.12d).

Storm Tracks Cyclonic storms—typically 1600 km wide—and their attendant air masses move across the continent along **storm tracks**, which shift in latitude with changes in the Sun's declination and the seasons. Typical storm tracks that cross North America are farther northward in summer and farther southward in winter (Figure 8.13a). Noted on the map are some of the regional names for cyclonic source regions. As the storm tracks

begin to shift northward in the spring, cP and mT air masses are in their clearest conflict. This is the time of strongest frontal activity, featuring thunderstorms and tornadoes. Storm tracks follow the path of upper-air winds, which direct storm systems across the continent.

A map of actual storm tracks for March 1991 in Figure 8.13b demonstrates several areas of cyclogenesis: the northwest over the Pacific Ocean, the Gulf of Mexico (Gulf Lows), the eastern seaboard (Nor'easter, Hatteras Low), and the Arctic. Cyclonic circulation also frequently develops on the lee side of mountain ranges, as along the Rockies from Alberta (Alberta Clipper) south to Colorado (Colorado Low). By crossing the mountains, such systems gain access to the moisture-laden, energy-rich mT air masses from the Gulf of Mexico and are strengthened.

The pattern of storm tracks has important implications for Canadian weather. During winter, when storm tracks are shifted south, much of Canada experiences weather associated with the northern half of low-pressure systems. "Nor'easters" affect the Maritimes, Québec, and many of the American northeast coastal states. These are

(a) Average storm tracks

(b) Actual storm tracks for a typical March

FIGURE 8.13 **Average and actual storm tracks.**
(a) Cyclonic storm tracks over North America vary seasonally. The tracks indicate several locations of cyclogenesis; note the regional names. (b) Actual cyclonic tracks during an average March over North America. [(b) NOAA/NESDIS/NCDC.]

storm conditions generated in the northeastern quadrant of the advancing low-pressure system. Nor'easters pull in moisture from the Atlantic Ocean and can result in large amounts of precipitation.

The Canadian Prairies experience weather associated with expansion and contraction of continental high-pressure systems. The boundary of a strengthening Arctic high-pressure air mass can expand westward, pushing cold air up mountain slopes and resulting in light precipitation from orographic lifting of the dry, cold air. The weather thus approaches from the east or northeast, contrary to the usual west to east movement of frontal weather.

On the West Coast, extreme weather develops when Arctic outflow conditions develop. Normally, mild, moist air comes inland off the Pacific Ocean and flows from west to east. During an Arctic outflow, cold Arctic air moves from the north and gets trapped on the western side of the Rockies. Valleys with a west to east orientation, normally filled with mild moist Pacific air, are filled with cold, dry Arctic air, and drastic temperature changes result.

Analysis of Daily Weather Maps—Forecasting

Synoptic analysis is the evaluation of weather data collected at a specific time. Building a database of wind, pressure, temperature, and moisture conditions is key to *numerical* (computer-based) *weather prediction* and the development of weather-forecasting models. Development of numerical models is a great challenge because the atmosphere operates as a nonlinear system, tending toward chaotic behaviour. Slight variations in input data or slight changes in the basic assumptions of the model's behaviour can produce widely varying forecasts. As our knowledge of the interactions that produce weather increases and as instruments and software improve, so too will the accuracy of our forecasts.

Weather data necessary for the preparation of a synoptic map and forecast include:

- Barometric pressure (sea level and altimeter setting)
- Pressure tendency (steady, rising, or falling)
- Surface-air temperature
- Dew-point temperature
- Wind speed, direction, and character (gusts, squalls)
- Type and movement of clouds
- Current weather observations
- State of the sky (current sky conditions)
- Visibility; vision obstruction (fog, haze)
- Amount of precipitation since last observation

For many related Internet links to weather maps, current forecasts, satellite images, and the latest radar data, please go to the Canadian *Geosystems* companion website, to Chapter 8, and click "Net Search." With the Internet, there is no need to wait for television or the newspaper to bring you the latest satellite images, for the information is at your fingertips.

The Meteorological Service of Canada (MSC; http:// www.ec.gc.ca/meteo-weather/) is responsible for collecting, recording, and reporting accurate and accessible daily weather information. MSC is composed of six directorates, one of which—the Atmospheric Environment Prediction Directorate (AEPD)—provides leadership for all prediction activities of the Atmospheric Environment Program.

The Canadian Meteorological Centre (CMC) carries out synoptic analysis. Its four branches—Informatics, Operations, Development, and Atmospheric and Climate Science—provide forecast guidance to regional prediction centres. The Informatics Branch provides centralized computing and telecommunications services, and operates and maintains the supercomputer facility in Dorval, Québec, and various telecommunications networks. The Operations Branch is responsible for the meteorological operations of numerous production systems for weather, climate, air quality, and environmental programs at the CMC. The Development Branch has the responsibility for developing new systems and for technology transfer from research to operations of the Canadian environmental prediction effort. The Atmospheric and Climate Science Branch is responsible for conducting research on mechanisms controlling atmospheric evolution to forecast atmospheric change and assist adaptation and mitigation of climate change impacts.

(a)

(b)

FIGURE 8.14 AWOS weather instruments and workstation display.
(a) Automated Weather Observation System (AWOS) weather station—Thunder Bay, Ontario. (b) Workstation on which data are analyzed. MetManager is a software package used to display and overlay many different data types. [Courtesy of Environment Canada.]

Typical instrumentation and displays are illustrated in Figure 8.14. Automated stations use the Automatic Weather Observation System (AWOS) developed in partnership between the Atmospheric Environment Service and a private corporation. Canada currently has 31 upper air stations that send two radiosondes up each day at 1200 UTC and 0000 UTC. Additionally, there are six emergency stations and five Department of National Defence stations that occasionally produce upper air soundings. Nationally, there are 31 Doppler weather radar installations, 84 stations in the Canadian Lightning Detection Network, and over 800 hourly weather observation sites across the country. This includes 243 NAV Canada aviation observation sites, Department of National Defence sites, and differing types of automated observation sites that have various types of observation equipment. There are 302 Reference Climate Stations (RCS sites) that record maximum and minimum temperatures and precipitation amounts twice a day. Finally, there are 1425 climate stations operated by volunteers. The numbers of hourly observation stations, reference climate stations, and volunteer climate stations change frequently.

AWOS sensor instrument arrays are a primary surface weather-observing network (Figure 8.14a). An AWOS installation includes the following: rain gauge (tipping bucket), temperature/dew-point sensor, barometer, present weather identifier, wind speed indicator, direction sensor, cloud height indicator, freezing rain sensor, thunderstorm sensor, and visibility sensor, among other items.

CRITICAL THINKING 8.1
Analyzing a Weather Map

After studying the text, test your knowledge by determining the conditions in Fort McMurray, Calgary, Saskatoon, Regina, Winnipeg, and Toronto as depicted on the weather map in Figure 8.12.

Next, look at the weather map showing a classic open stage midlatitude cyclone in Figure CT 8.1.1 for February 19, 2004, along with a *GOES-12* infrared satellite image at that time. Using the legend in Figure 8.12 for weather map symbols, briefly analyze this map: Find the centre of low pressure, note the counterclockwise winds, compare temperatures on either side of the cold front, note air temperatures and dew-point temperatures, explain the location of the fronts on the map, and locate the centre of high pressure.

Think about the air and dew-point temperatures in the Great Lakes Basin as compared to those along the Atlantic coast. At 8:00 A.M., the air temperature in Halifax was −4°C and dew-point temperature was −4°C, while in Toronto at the same time the temperature was −4°C and dew-point temperature was −6°C. To become saturated, the air in Toronto needed to cool to −6°C, whereas the air in Halifax was already at saturation. In the far north, find Kuujjuarapik on the eastern shore of Hudson Bay. The air and dew-point temperatures were −23°C and −27°C, respectively, and the state of the sky was clear. If you were there, what would you have experienced at this time? Why would you have been reaching for the lip balm?

Describe the pattern of air masses on this weather map. How are these air masses interacting, and what kind of frontal activity do you see? What does the pattern of isobars tell you about high- and low-pressure areas?

(a)

(b)

FIGURE CT 8.1.1 Weather map and *GOES-12* infrared image over eastern North America, February 19, 2004. [(a) Satellite *GOES-12* image courtesy of NOAA. (b) Map data from Environment Canada.]

Preparing a weather report and forecast requires analysis of daily weather maps and the use of standard weather symbols, such as those in Figure 8.12. Although the actual pattern of cyclonic passage over North America is widely varied in shape and duration, you can apply this general model, along with your understanding of warm and cold fronts, to reading the daily weather map. A weather map is a useful tool, especially when weather turns dramatic in violent episodes.

Violent Weather

Weather provides a continuous reminder of the flow of energy across the latitudes that at times can set into motion destructive, violent weather conditions. Environment Canada issues severe weather warnings, watches, and advisories to the public via the media, weather outlets, and Weatheradio Canada (see http://www.ec.gc.ca/meteo-weather/default.asp?lang=En&n=D9553AB5-1 for a summary of different types of warnings, watches, and advisories).

Weather is often in the news. Weather-related destruction has risen more than 500% over the past two decades as population has increased in areas prone to violent weather and as climate change intensifies weather anomalies. Global weather-related losses exceeded $10 billion per year through the 1990s, eclipsing the previous annual average of less than $2 billion. Each year of the twenty-first century has far surpassed the past decade. Hurricane Katrina and the 2005 season caused $130 billion in damages and Hurricanes Gustav and Ike (in 2008) caused $100 billion in damages! 2011 experienced losses greater than any year over the past 10 years—12 events in North America exceeded USD $1 billion in 2011. MSC includes a branch for severe weather. In the United States, government research and monitoring of violent weather is centred at NOAA's National Severe Storms Laboratory and Storm Prediction Center in several cities (see http://www.nssl.noaa.gov). Consult these sites for each of the topics that follow.

Ice Storms

Ice storms (freezing rain, ice glaze, and ice pellets), snow blizzards, and low temperatures are forms of violent weather. Freezing precipitation occurs when *supercooled* moisture freezes on contact with a surface. The most common types of freezing precipitation are *freezing rain* and *freezing drizzle*, both of which can accumulate on surfaces and cause great damage (Figure 8.15a). Ice storms are a hazard in all parts of Canada except the far north. They are especially common in the southern and eastern parts of the country, in a swath from southern Ontario to Newfoundland (Figure 8.15b). The thickness of ice accumulation associated with a storm, the storm's duration, and the extent of area affected determine the severity of the event. Typically, an ice storm lasts for 45 to 65 hours and deposits, at most, 30 to 40 mm of ice.

The ice storm of January 1998 was an exceptional event that knocked out power for several weeks over a wide area—affecting eastern Ontario, southern Québec, the Fundy coast of New Brunswick and Nova Scotia, and the American Northeast. During the 1998 storm there were over 80 hours of freezing rain and drizzle, and in some areas near Montréal, over 100 mm of ice accumulated. This particular storm was extraordinary because it hit some of the largest populated and urbanized areas of North America—and affected more people than any previous weather event in Canadian history. Three weeks after the storm, more than 700 000 people were still without electricity!

Eastern Canada suffered widespread effects from the 1998 ice storm. Tragically, hypothermia claimed 25 human lives. Additionally, thousands of dairy cattle died from mastitis and related illnesses after mechanized milking equipment failed due to power outages. The storm sparked the largest peacetime deployment of Canadian troops—nearly 16 000 Canadian Forces personnel assisted with rebuilding the power grid. More than one-third of the cropland in Québec and almost one-quarter of that in Ontario were in the storm zone and many farmers suffered substantial losses. Additionally, more than 5 million sugar maple taps located in the affected areas had a subsequent decrease in sap output. Recovery could take 30 to 40 years before syrup production returns to normal. In all, economic losses for Montréal, and Ottawa and surrounding areas were estimated at $585 million and $114 million, respectively. As of 2011, this storm is still ranked by the Insurance Bureau of Canada as the most expensive insured disaster in Canadian history.

Thunderstorms

Tremendous energy is liberated by the condensation of large quantities of water vapour. This process locally heats the air, causing violent updrafts and downdrafts as rising air parcels pull surrounding air into the column and as the frictional drag of raindrops pulls air toward the ground. Giant cumulonimbus clouds can create dramatic weather moments—squall lines of heavy precipitation, lightning, thunder, hail, blustery winds, and tornadoes. Thunderstorms may develop within an air mass, in a line along a front (particularly a cold front), or where mountain slopes cause orographic lifting.

Thousands of thunderstorms occur on Earth at any given moment. Equatorial regions and the ITCZ experience many of them, exemplified by the city of Kampala in Uganda, East Africa (north of Lake Victoria), which sits virtually on the equator and averages a record 242 days a year of thunderstorms. Figure 8.16 shows the annual distribution of days with thunderstorms across Canada and the United States. In North America, most thunderstorms occur in areas dominated by mT air masses.

Atmospheric Turbulence Most airplane flights experience at least some turbulence—the encountering of air of different densities or air layers moving at different speeds and directions. This is a natural state of the atmosphere

(a)

FIGURE 8.15 **Freezing precipitation and ice storms.**
(a) A series of Hydro-Québec high voltage towers near St-Bruno, Québec, south of Montréal, collapsed after a severe ice storm hit southwest Québec in January 1998. The storm left over one million households without electricity for several weeks as crews worked to replace transmission lines. (b) Average annual hours of freezing precipitation in Canada. [(a) Jacques Boissinot/CP Images; (b) Courtesy of Environment Canada. Used by permission of the Minister of Public Works and Government Services Canada.]

(b)

and passengers are asked to keep seat belts fastened when in their seats to avoid injury, even when the seat-belt light is turned off.

Thunderstorms can produce severe turbulence in the form of downbursts, which are exceptionally strong downdrafts. Downbursts are classified by size: a *macroburst* is at least 4 km wide and in excess of 210 km · h⁻¹; a *microburst* is smaller in size and speed. A microburst causes rapid changes in wind speed and direction and it causes the dreaded *wind shear* that can bring down aircraft. Such turbulence events are short-lived and hard to detect,

although the Forecast Systems Laboratory, among others, is making progress in developing forecasting methods.

Lightning and Thunder An estimated 8 million lightning strikes occur each day on Earth. **Lightning** refers to flashes of light caused by enormous electrical discharges—tens of millions to hundreds of millions of volts—that briefly superheat the air to temperatures of 15 000–30 000°C. A buildup of electrical energy polarity between areas within a cumulonimbus cloud or between the cloud and the ground creates lightning. The violent expansion

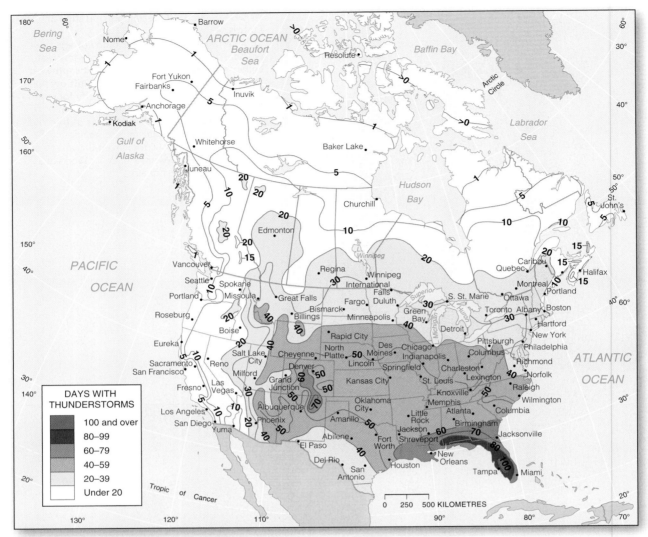

FIGURE 8.16 Thunderstorm occurrence.
Average annual number of days experiencing thunderstorms. [Data courtesy of NWS; Map Series 3; *Climatic Atlas of Canada*, Atmospheric Environment Service, Canada.]

of this abruptly heated air sends shock waves through the atmosphere as the sonic bang of **thunder**.

Lightning poses a hazard to aircraft, people, animals, trees, and structures. The CN Tower in Toronto, the tallest freestanding structure in the Western Hemisphere, is particularly susceptible to lightning. It is struck so often that observations and measurements of lightning activity have been conducted at the tower since 1978. The tower was struck 460 times between 1978 and 1994, an average of 75 times per year.

NASA's Lightning Imaging Sensor (LIS) aboard the *Tropical Rainfall Measuring Mission* (*TRMM*) satellite monitors lightning and other phenomena. The LIS can image lightning strikes day or night, within clouds or between cloud and ground. The sensor's data show that about 90% of all strikes occur over land in response to increased convection over relatively warmer continental surfaces. Strikes shift with expected seasonal shifts of the Sun's declination, as shown in Figure 8.17a and b (see http://thunder.msfc.nasa.gov/lis/).

GEO REPORT 8.3   *You Can Feel the Warning*

If the hair on your head or neck begins to stand on end, get indoors, or if you are in the open, get low to the ground, crouched on both feet and not lying down, in a low spot, if possible. Your hair is telling you that a lightning charge is building in that area. The place *not* to seek shelter is beneath a tree, for trees are good conductors of electricity and often are hit by lightning.

(a)

Winter (Dec. 1999, Jan. and Feb. 2000)

| 1 | 2 | 3 | 4 | 5 | >5 | >10 | >15 | >25 | >50 | >100 | >150 |

Flash scale

(b)

Summer (June, July, August 2000)

FIGURE 8.17 Seasonal images show global lightning.
A composite of 3 months' worth of data derived from NASA's Lightning Imaging Sensor (LIS) records of all lightning strikes between 35° N and 35° S latitudes during (a) winter (December 1999–February 2000) and (b) summer (June, July, August 2000). The LIS is aboard the *Tropical Rainfall Measuring Mission* satellite launched in 1997. (c) Multiple lightning strikes in southern Arizona captured in a time-lapse photo. [(a) and (b) *TRMM* images courtesy of NASA's Global Hydrology and Climate Center, MSC. (c) Keith Kent/Photo Researchers, Inc.]

(c)

Hail Ice pellets called **hail** form most frequently within a cumulonimbus cloud. Raindrops circulate repeatedly above and below the freezing level in the cloud, adding layers of ice until the circulation in the cloud can no longer support their weight (Figure 8.18). Hail may also grow from the addition of moisture on a snow pellet.

Pea-sized and marble-sized hail is common, although hail the size of golf balls and baseballs happens at least once or twice a year somewhere in North America. For larger hail to form, the frozen pellets must stay aloft for longer periods. The largest authenticated hailstone in the world

FIGURE 8.18 Hailstones and ruler for measurement.
[Weatherstock/Photolibrary/Getty Images.]

landed in Aurora, Nebraska, on June 22, 2003; it measured 17.8 cm in diameter and was 47.6 cm in circumference!

Hail is common in Canada and the United States, although somewhat infrequent at any given place, occurring perhaps every 1 or 2 years in the highest-frequency areas. Hail typically occurs in Canada in heavy but localized showers associated with mature thunderstorms. Most hailstorms develop in the continental interior, namely central Alberta's "hailstorm alley," in the lee of the Rockies and the southernmost part of Saskatchewan, east of Cypress Hills. These areas experience four to six major hail events each year. The period of most frequent hail occurrence is May to July, with nearly three-quarters of all hailstorms occurring between noon and 6:00 P.M.

In Canada, hailstorms cause the greatest economic losses of any natural hazard in terms of property and crop damage. This is why, collectively, farmers pay millions of dollars each year for crop insurance. The pattern of hail occurrence across Canada and the United States is similar to that of thunderstorms shown in Figure 8.16.

Damaging Winds

Although tornadoes and hurricanes grab headlines, linear winds associated with thunderstorms and bands of showers cause significant damage and crop losses. These strong winds in excess of 26 m · s^{-1} are known as **straight-line winds**, **downbursts**, **microbursts**, or **plough winds**. The first two terms are used commonly in eastern Canada while the last is more frequently used in the west. A microburst is used to describe damage to an area less than 4 km². Wind outbursts from convective storms can produce groups of downburst clusters from a thunderstorm system and tend to blast in linear paths fanning out along curved-wind fronts over a wide swath of land. These winds pose distinct hazards to summer outdoor activities by overturning boats, hurling flying objects, and causing broken trees and limbs. Their highest frequency (about 70%) is from May to August.

Derechos, a term for straight-line winds used in the U.S. and elsewhere, describes this type of damaging wind event specifically linked to large, organized, fast-moving areas of thunderstorms. Derechos are capable of producing widespread and long-lived—over a number of hours—wind damage on the order of hundreds of kilometres.

Tornadoes

The updrafts associated with a cold-front squall line and cumulonimbus development appear on satellite images as pulsing bubbles of clouds. According to one hypothesis, a spinning, cyclonic, rising column of midtroposphere-level air forms a mesocyclone. Ranging up to 10 km in diameter, a **mesocyclone** rotates vertically within a *supercell cloud* (the parent cloud) to a height of thousands of metres (Figure 8.19a). A well-developed mesocyclone will produce heavy rain, large hail, blustery winds, and

lightning. Some mature mesocyclones will generate tornado activity.

As more moisture-laden air draws up into the circulation of a mesocyclone, more energy is liberated and the rotation of air increases speed. The narrower the mesocyclone, the faster the spin of converging air parcels being sucked into the rotation. The swirl of the mesocyclone itself is visible, as are smaller, dark grey **funnel clouds** that pulse from the bottom side of the parent cloud. The potential of this stage of development is the lowering of such a funnel to Earth—a **tornado** (Figure 8.19b).

A tornado can range from a few metres to a few hundred metres in diameter and can last from a few seconds to tens of minutes. Tornadoes have been increasing in average speed and duration over the last two decades. Greensburg, Kansas, was essentially erased from the map by an EF-5 tornado in May 2007. The statistics are unprecedented: Winds exceeded 330 km · h^{-1} in the 2.7-km-wide funnel that was on the ground along a 35-km track. A photograph taken one year later (Figure 8.19c) shows block after block of empty lots in what was a residential district. Greensburg is attempting to rebuild, following Leadership in Energy and Environmental Design (LEED) "green" standards for energy conservation and efficiency.

A tornado's scoured path is visible on the ground in a series of semicircular "suction" prints and, of course, in the trail of damage, such as in the image of a tornado's path through Maryland (Figure 8.19d). When tornado circulation occurs over water, a **waterspout** forms, and surface water is drawn some 3–5 m up into the funnel. The rest of the waterspout funnel is made visible by the rapid condensation of water vapour.

The chapter-opening photo shows the aftermath of an EF-5 tornado at Elie, Manitoba, and *Geosystems Now* discusses the impacts of tornadoes in some detail. The power of these tornadoes may seem abstract until you see the resultant damage in person. Multiply the destruction times the near doubling of average occurrences and an increase in EF–3, –4, and –5 events in North America, and it does take one's breath away.

Tornado Measurement and Totals Air pressures inside a tornado usually are about 10% less than those in the surrounding air. The inrushing convergence created by such a horizontal pressure gradient causes high wind speeds. The late Theodore Fujita, a noted meteorologist from the University of Chicago, designed the Fujita Scale (1971), which classifies tornadoes according to wind speed as indicated by related property damage. A refinement in the scale, adopted in February 2007, is the *Enhanced Fujita Scale*, or *EF Scale* (Table 8.1; http://www.tornadoproject.com/fscale/fscale.htm). The revision filled the need to better assess damage, correlate wind speed to damage caused, and account for structural construction quality. To assist with wind estimates, the EF Scale contains Damage Indicators relating to types of structures and vegetation

(a)

(b)

(c)

(d)

FIGURE 8.19 Mesocyclone and tornado formation.
(a) Strong wind aloft establishes spinning; as updraft from thunderstorm development tilts the rotating air, a mesocyclone forms as a rotating updraft within the thunderstorm. If one forms, a tornado will descend from the lower portion of the mesocyclone. (b) A supercell tornado descends from the cloud base near Spearman, Texas. Strong hail is falling to the left of the tornado. (c) 2007 EF-5 tornado leveled whole neighbourhoods in Greensburg, Kansas; photograph taken in 2008. (d) A tornado leaves its mark, as this *Landsat-7* image captures. The damage path tracks for 39 km where an EF-4 tornado tore through La Plata, Maryland. More than 900 homes and 200 businesses were destroyed. [(b) © Howard B. Bluestein; (c) Bobbé Christopherson. (d) *Landsat-7* image, USGS/EROS.]

TABLE 8.1   The Enhanced Fujita Scale

EF-number	3-Second Gust Wind Speed; Damage Specs
EF-0 Gale	105–137 km·h⁻¹; *light damage*: branches broken, chimneys damaged.
EF-1 Weak	138–177 km·h⁻¹; *moderate damage*: beginning of hurricane wind-speed designation, roof coverings peeled off, mobile homes pushed off foundations.
EF-2 Strong	178–217 km·h⁻¹; *considerable damage*: roofs torn off frame houses, large trees uprooted or snapped, box cars pushed over, small missiles generated.
EF-3 Severe	218–266 km·h⁻¹; *severe damage*: roofs torn off well-constructed houses, trains overturned, trees uprooted, cars thrown.
EF-4 Devastating	267–322 km·h⁻¹; *devastating damage*: well-built houses leveled, cars thrown, large missiles generated.
EF-5 Incredible	More than 322 km·h⁻¹; *incredible damage*: house lifted and carried a distance to disintegration, car-sized missiles fly farther than 100 m, bark removed from trees.

Note: See http://www.wind.ttu.edu/EFScale.pdf for details.

affected, along with Degrees of Damage ratings, both of which you can view at the URL listed in the table note. As of July 2011, Environment Canada researchers still use the original Fujita Scale, but the enhanced scale will likely be adopted in 2012.

North America experiences more tornadoes than anywhere on Earth because its latitudinal position and topography permit contrasting air masses to confront one another. Tornadoes have struck all 50 states and all the Canadian provinces and territories, although Fujita-scale ratings are usually lower in Canada than in the United States. May and June are the peak months, as you see in Figure 8.20, based on 51 years of records.

Canada's Worst Tornadoes Canada places second to the United States in the world for tornado occurrences. In Canada, on average, there are 80 tornadoes causing two deaths, 20 injuries, and tens of millions of dollars in property damage each year. The actual number of tornadoes may be higher as tornadoes that strike unpopulated areas remain undetected. Canada's "tornado alleys" are southern Ontario, Alberta, southeastern Québec, and a band stretching from southern Saskatchewan and Manitoba through to Thunder Bay, Ontario. Other tornado zones occur in the interior of British Columbia and in New Brunswick. In Canada, annual tornado numbers have been increasing since 1990.

In the United States, 54 030 tornadoes were recorded in the years from 1950 through 2010, including 29 tornadoes in December 2010. In these 60 years, tornadoes caused over 5000 deaths, or about 85 deaths per year. Of note is the fact that these tornadoes resulted in more than 80 000 injuries and property damage of over $28 billion for this period of record. The yearly average of $500 million in damage is rising each year. Record-setting tornado outbreaks occurred in 2011.

The long-term annual average number of tornadoes before 1990 was 787. Interestingly, since 1990 the average per year has risen to over 1000. In 1998, the annual average reached 1270 tornadoes; the peak year was 2004, with 1820 tornadoes;1156 tornadoes were reported in 2009, and 1180 tornadoes in 2010, and 1725 in 2011.

Importantly, the number of EF-4 and EF-5 tornadoes is on the increase, reaching more than a dozen each season. Note on the graph in Figure 8.20 that the number of tornadoes nearly doubled in March and more than doubled in September for the 2003-2009 period as compared to the longer record, meaning that access to maritime tropical air masses is occurring earlier in spring and later in fall, suggesting that climate change is forcing this trend.

Reasons for the annual increase in tornado frequency in North America range from climate change and more intense thunderstorm activity to better reporting through Doppler Radar and a larger population with videotape recorders. Researchers are pursuing many questions with an enthusiasm for the science and an awe of the subject,

GEO REPORT 8.4   *Tornado Records Fall*

During April 2011, 875 tornadoes struck in some 20 U.S. states. This is far above the average for April—and more tornadoes for any single month since 2003. The previous record for April was in 1974 with 267 tornadoes.The results caused more than 361 deaths and hundreds of millions of dollars in property damage. In contrast, in Canada, there were fewer tornadoes reported than average for the same time period.

The previous record month was May 2003. Eighty-four tornadoes hit on Sunday, May 4, in a path across eight states. Tornado damage ratings indicated four EF-4s and eight EF-3s struck in the Midwest. Five tornadoes struck in or near Kansas City. One of the Kansas City EF-4 tornadoes achieved a funnel-base width of 450 m. Some damage appeared to be from downbursts and straight-line wind effects. (For an animation of satellite images, see http://www.osei.noaa.gov/Events/Severe/US_Midwest/2003/SVRusMW125_G12.avi.)

(a)

(b)

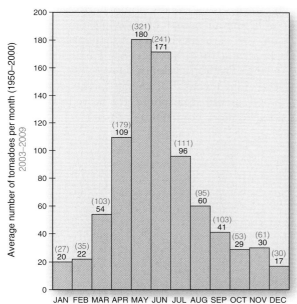

(c)

FIGURE 8.20 Tornado occurrence and frequency.
Since tornado sightings are often concentrated around population centres, many tornadoes in rural areas may go unreported. (a) Average number of tornadoes per 10 000 km² for 1950 to 2003 in Canada. (b) Average number of tornadoes per 26 000 km² for 1950 to 2003 in the United States. Differences in the classification of data and different scales used explain the mapping variation along the border. (c) Average number of tornadoes per month 1950–2000 in the United States. Remarkably, the 7-year period from 2003 to 2009 has seen a significant increase in the average number of tornadoes per month (marked in red). [Data courtesy of (a) David A. Etkin, York University; (b) and (c) the Storm Prediction Center, National Weather Service, and NOAA sources.]

as summarized by Howard Bluestein, foremost tornado researcher and meteorologist:

> Our quest for discovery has not taken away from the respect we have for the awesome power the tornado harbors, nor the thrill for viewing the violent motions in the tornado or the beauty of the storm. We eagerly await the next act in the atmospheric play starring the tornado.[1]

[1]H. Bluestein, *Tornado Alley, Monster Storms of the Great Plains* (New York: Oxford University Press, 1999), p. 162.

Tropical Cyclones

A powerful manifestation of the Earth–atmosphere energy budget is the **tropical cyclone**, which originates entirely within tropical air masses. Approximately 80 tropical cyclones occur annually worldwide. Some 45 per year are powerful enough to be classified as hurricanes, typhoons, and cyclones (different regional names for the same type of tropical storm). Table 8.2 presents the criteria for classification of tropical cyclones based on wind speed.

| TABLE 8.2 | Tropical Cyclone Classification |

Designation	Winds	Features
Tropical disturbance	Variable, low	Definite area of surface low pressure; patches of clouds
Tropical depression	Up to 34 knots or 63 km·h⁻¹	Gale force, organizing circulation; light to moderate rain
Tropical storm	35–63 knots or 64–118 km·h⁻¹	Closed isobars; definite circular organization; heavy rain; assigned a name
Hurricane (Atlantic and East Pacific) Typhoon (West Pacific) Cyclone (Indian Ocean, Australia)	Greater than 64 knots or 119 km·h⁻¹	Circular, closed isobars; heavy rain, storm surges; tornadoes in right-front quadrant

Cyclonic systems forming in the tropics are quite different from midlatitude cyclones because the air of the tropics is essentially homogeneous, with no fronts or conflicting air masses of differing temperatures. In addition, the warm air and warm seas ensure abundant water vapour and thus the necessary latent heat to fuel these storms. Tropical cyclones convert heat energy from the ocean into mechanical energy in the wind—the warmer the ocean and atmosphere, the more intense the conversion and more powerful the storm.

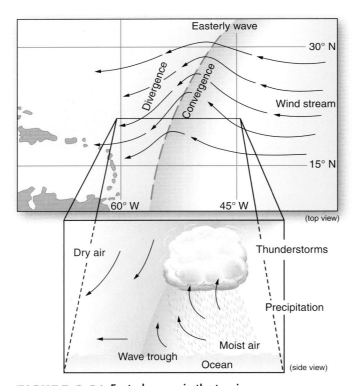

FIGURE 8.21 Easterly wave in the tropics.
A low-pressure centre develops along an easterly (westward-moving) wave. Moist air rises in an area of convergence at the surface to the east of the wave trough. Wind flows bend and converge before the trough and diverge downwind from the trough.

What mechanism triggers the development of a tropical cyclone? Meteorologists now think that cyclonic motion begins with slow-moving easterly waves of low pressure in the trade-wind belt of the tropics (Figure 8.21). For these processes, sea-surface temperatures must exceed approximately 26°C. Tropical cyclones form along the eastern (leeward) side of these migrating troughs of low pressure, a place of convergence and rainfall. Surface airflow then converges into the low-pressure area, ascends, and flows outward aloft. This important divergence aloft acts as a chimney, pulling more moisture-laden air into the developing system. To maintain and strengthen this vertical convective circulation, there must be little or no wind shear to interrupt or block the airflow.

Hurricanes, Typhoons, and Cyclones Tropical cyclones are potentially the most destructive storms experienced by humans, claiming thousands of lives each year worldwide. This is especially true when wind speeds and low-pressure areas attain readings that upgrade tropical cyclone status to a full-fledged **hurricane**, **typhoon**, or *cyclone* (>64 knots, >119 km·h⁻¹). Across the globe, such storms bear these three different names, among others: *hurricane* around North America, *typhoon* in the western Pacific (Japan, Philippines), and *cyclone* in Indonesia, Bangladesh, and India. Worldwide, about 10% of all tropical disturbances have the necessary ingredients to become hurricanes, typhoons, or cyclones. For coverage and reporting, see the National Hurricane Center at http://www.nhc.noaa.gov/ or the Joint Typhoon Warning Center at http://www.usno.navy.mil/JTWC. Information from the Canadian Hurricane Centre can be found at http://www.ec.gc.ca/ouragans-hurricanes/default.asp?lang=En.

The map in Figure 8.22a shows areas in which tropical cyclones form and some of the characteristic storm tracks travelled. The map indicates the range of months during which tropical cyclones are most likely to appear. For example, storms that strike the southeastern United States do so mostly between August and October. Officially, tropical cyclone season for the Atlantic region

Satellite
Hurricane Isabel
9/6–9/19/04

Satellite
Florida Hurricanes
Satellite Coverage

Super Typhoon Ioke
Central Pacific
August 2006

June–November

Tropic of Cancer

PACIFIC
OCEAN

June–December

June–October

Equator

August–October

H

ATLANTIC
OCEAN

June–November

ARCTIC
OCEAN

Arctic Circle

(b)

INDIAN
OCEAN

Coral
Sea

January–March

January–March

Tropic of Capricorn

INDIAN
OCEAN

C

Super Cyclone
Gonu
June 2007

0   1500   3000 KILOMETRES
ROBINSON PROJECTION

Antarctic Circle

H – Hurricane   ——— – Tropical cyclones
T – Typhoon   ——— – Wave cyclones
C – Cyclone

(a)

BRAZIL   Sao Paulo   Rio de Janeiro
                                          25°S
        Laguna
Porto Alegre
                                          30°S
                        Atlantic
                        Ocean
        50°W   45°W   40°W

TD   TS   1   2   3   4   5
Saffir-Simpson Intensity Scale

(d)   (c)

FIGURE 8.22 Worldwide pattern of the most intense tropical cyclones.
(a) Typical tropical storm tracks with principal months of occurrence and regional names. Super Typhoon
Ioke (2006) and Super Cyclone Gonu (2007) are noted. (b) The remnants of Tropical Storm Vince hit Spain in
October 2005, the first storm to take such a track from the tropics. (c) Hurricane Catarina approaches Brazil's
southeastern coast, March 27, 2004—a unique occurrence in recorded history. (d) Global tropical cyclone
tracks from 1856 to 2006. Can you find Hurricane Catarina on the map? [(b) October 11, 2005, *Meteosat–7*
image, University of Ulm. (c) *Terra* MODIS image, NASA/GSFC. (d) R. Rohde/NASA/GSFC.]

GEO REPORT 8.5 *Tropical Cyclone Peak*

For the North Atlantic region from 1871 to 2009, 1229 tropical cyclones (storms and hurricanes) developed. The peak day in
this region (assuming a 9-day moving average calculation) is September 10, with 73 cyclones for the 139-year period.

is from June 1 to November 30 each year. (For comparison, the average midlatitude cyclonic storm tracks are in blue on the map.)

Relative to North and Central America, tropical depressions (low-pressure areas) intensify into tropical storms during the journey across the Atlantic. A rule of thumb has emerged: If tropical storms mature early along the track, the tendency is for storms to curve northward toward the North Atlantic, missing the United States and Atlantic Canada. The critical position is approximately 40° W longitude. If a tropical storm matures after it reaches the longitude of the Dominican Republic (70° W), then it has a higher probability of hitting the United States.

In contradiction to these average conditions, in October 2005, the remnants of Tropical Storm Vince became the first Atlantic tropical cyclone to strike Spain (Figure 8.22b). In the Southern Hemisphere, no hurricane was ever observed turning from the equator into the south Atlantic (note on the map). However, in March 2004 Hurricane Catarina made landfall in Brazil south of the resorts at Laguna, state of Santa Catarina. NASA's *Terra* satellite in Figure 8.22c clearly shows an organized hurricane, with characteristic central eye and rain bands. Compare the circulation patterns between Hurricane Gilbert (see

Figure 8.23a) to this satellite image of Catarina. What do you see? Note the effect of Coriolis force counterclockwise in the Northern Hemisphere and clockwise in the Southern Hemisphere.

Then in 2006, the first tropical storm to become a category 5 super typhoon developed in the Central Pacific, some 1285 km south of Hawaiʻi. Super Typhoon Ioke continued for almost 3 weeks, with final remnants causing large-scale erosion along Alaskan shores. And in 2007, Super Cyclone Gonu became the strongest tropical cyclone on record occurring in the Arabian Sea, eventually hitting Oman and the Arabian Peninsula. Another tropical cyclone, Phet, took an unusual path into the Arabian Peninsula during June 2010. These storms apparently are signalling changes under way in tropical meteorology relative to the increased occurrence and intensity of cyclonic systems, as related to higher oceanic and atmospheric temperatures.

When you hear meteorologists speak of a "category 4" hurricane, they are using the *Saffir–Simpson Hurricane Damage Potential Scale* to estimate possible damage from hurricane-force winds. Table 8.3 presents this scale, which ranks hurricanes and typhoons in five categories using wind speeds and central pressure criteria, from category 1 for smaller

(a)

(b)

(c)

FIGURE 8.23 Profile of a hurricane.
For the Western Hemisphere, Hurricane Gilbert attained the record size (1600 km in diameter) and second lowest barometric pressure (888 mb). Gilbert's sustained winds reached 298 km · h⁻¹, with peaks exceeding 320 km · h⁻¹. Hurricane Gilbert, September 13, 1988: (a) *GOES-7* satellite image. (b) A stylized portrait of a mature hurricane, drawn from an oblique perspective (cutaway view shows the eye, rain bands, and wind-flow patterns). (c) *SLAR* (side-looking airborne radar) image from an aircraft flying through the center of the storm. Rain bands of greater cloud density are false-coloured in yellows and reds. The clear sky in the central eye is portrayed dramatically. [(a) and (c) NOAA and the NHC.]

Hurricane Wind Patterns   Hurricane Georges

TABLE 8.3 Saffir–Simpson Hurricane Damage Potential Scale

Category	Wind Speed Central Pressure (mb)	Notable Atlantic Examples (landfall rating)
1	64–82 knots 119–154 km·h⁻¹ [> 980 mb]	
2	83–95 knots 155–178 km·h⁻¹ [965–979 mb]	1954, Hazel; 1999, Floyd; 2003, Isabel (was a cat. 5), Juan; 2004, Francis; 2008, Dolly; 2010, Alex
3	96–113 knots 179–210 km·h⁻¹ [945–964 mb]	1985, Elena; 1991, Bob; 1995, Roxanne, Marilyn; 1998, Bonnie; 2003, Kate; 2004, Ivan (was a cat. 5), Jeanne; 2005, Dennis; Rita, and Wilma (were cat. 5); 2007, Henrietta; 2008, Gustav, Ike (were cat. 4)
4	114–135 knots 211–250 km·h⁻¹ [920–944 mb]	1979, Frederic; 1985, Gloria; 1995, Felix, Luis, Opal; 1998, Georges; 2004, Charley; 2005, Emily, Katrina (were cat. 5)
5	> 135 knots > 250 km·h⁻¹ [< 920 mb]	1935, No. 2; 1938, No. 4; 1960, Donna; 1961, Carla; 1969, Camille; 1971, Edith; 1977, Anita; 1979, David; 1980, Allen; 1988, Gilbert, Mitch; 1989, Hugo; 1992, Andrew; 2004, Ivan; 2007, Dean, Felix

storms to category 5 for extremely dangerous storms. Damage depends on the degree of property development at a storm's landfall site, how prepared citizens are for the blow, the height of storm surge, the presence of embedded tornadoes, and the overall intensity of the storm. Related central pressure levels are included for comparison.

Physical Structure Fully organized tropical cyclones have an intriguing physical appearance (Figure 8.23). They range in diameter from a compact 160 km, to 1000 km, to some western Pacific super typhoons that attain diameters of 1300–1600 km. Vertically, these storms dominate the full height of the troposphere.

The inward-spiraling clouds form dense rain bands, with a central area designated the *eye*. Around the eye swirls a thunderstorm cloud called the *eyewall*, which is the area of most intense precipitation. The eye remains an enigma, for in the midst of devastating winds and torrential rains the eye is quiet and warm with even a glimpse of blue sky or stars possible. The structure of the rain bands, central eye, and eyewall is clearly visible for Hurricane Gilbert in Figure 8.23a (top view), 8.23b (oblique view from an artist's perspective), and Figure 8.23c (side-radar view).

The strongest winds of a Northern Hemisphere tropical cyclone are usually recorded in its right-front quadrant (relative to the storm's directional path), where dozens of fully developed tornadoes may be embedded. For example, Hurricane Camille in 1969 had up to 100 tornadoes embedded in that quadrant.

A tropical cyclone moves along at 16–40 km·h⁻¹. When it makes **landfall**, or moves ashore, the storm pushes seawater inland, causing dangerous **storm surges** often several metres in depth. Storm surges frequently catch people by surprise and cause the majority of hurricane drownings. In 1998, Hurricanes Bonnie, Georges, and Mitch moved slowly onshore, producing damaging storm surges along North Carolina, Mississippi, and Central America, respectively. The slow progress of these storms produced extensive flooding from sustained rains.

The storm surge from Hurricane Katrina in 2007 (see Focus Study 8.1, Figure 8.1.1, page 227) caused failure in numerous poorly conceived and constructed levees and canals; therefore we discuss this in Chapter 14 under floodplain management. The flood disaster that befell New Orleans after Katrina resulted more from human engineering and construction errors than from the storm itself, which was actually downgraded to a category 3 hurricane when it made landfall.

Hurricane Juan—2003 One of the most powerful and damaging hurricanes ever to affect Canada made landfall in Nova Scotia on September 29, 2003. Hurricane Juan, a category 2 storm, packed sustained winds of 158 km·h⁻¹ with gusts to 185 km·h⁻¹. Juan began as Tropical Depression Number 15 about 470 km southeast of Bermuda on September 25. Within 6 hours it had developed into tropical storm Juan, and 18 hours later, Juan attained hurricane status 255 km east of Bermuda. The storm made landfall and ripped northward through Nova Scotia, arriving at Prince Edward Island as a marginal hurricane. A satellite image clearly displays the hurricane as it moved on its track over Nova Scotia (Figure 8.24).

Rainfall amounts caused by Hurricane Juan ranged from 25 to 44 mm, with storm surges of 1.0 to 1.5 m. Halifax Harbour, over which the eastern eyewall passed, recorded a storm surge of 290 cm, resulting in widespread flooding in the Historic Properties and surrounding areas along the waterfront. The largest significant waves resulted from the storm outside Halifax Harbour, where significant wave heights (average of the highest one-third of waves) reached 9 m and maximum waves reached 19.9 m.

In comparison with some of the hurricanes that have made landfall in the United States, Hurricane Juan was

(a)

(b)

FIGURE 8.24 Hurricane Juan.
(a) *GOES-12* colourised visible image of Hurricane Juan, September 28, 2003, as it approached Nova Scotia (b) A 4-hour plot of Hurricane Juan's track on September 29, as it made landfall and crossed Nova Scotia. Top wind speed in knots and km·h⁻¹ are noted. [(a) *GOES-12* image courtesy of NOAA; (b) map courtesy of the Canadian Hurricane Centre.]

not a particularly large or fierce storm. However, this hurricane claimed the lives of eight people and resulted in millions of dollars in property damage. Hundreds of thousands of Nova Scotians and Prince Edward Islanders were affected by the storm's passage, and it took two weeks to restore power to all. There was also widespread damage to wharfs and marinas along the eastern shore. Perhaps the greatest damage, other than loss of life, was the loss of trees throughout both provinces. Streets and sidewalks were impassable for days. Especially hard hit were Halifax's Point Pleasant Park and Public Gardens, where the reestablishment of trees will take decades. The World Meteorological Organization recognized the impact of Juan on Maritime Canada in April 2004 by retiring the name from its list of hurricane names. Reaching Canada in 2010, Hurricanes Earl and Igor and in 2011 Irene, Maria, and Ophelia, produced varying impacts of wind damage, power outages, trees down, and heavy rainfall from their remnants.

Sample Devastating Tropical Cyclones The tropical cyclone that struck Bangladesh in 1970 killed an estimated 300 000 people, and the one in 1991 claimed over 200 000 lives. In the United States, death tolls are much lower, but still significant. The Galveston, Texas, hurricane of 1900 killed 6000; Hurricane Katrina and related engineering failures killed more than 1000 in Louisiana, Mississippi, and Alabama in 2005. Other storms resulting in significant fatalities include Hurricane Audry (1957), 400; Hurricane Gilbert (1988), 318; Hurricane Camille (1969), 256; and Hurricane Agnes (1972), 117. Canada's most famous hurricane was Hurricane Hazel in 1954 which struck southern Ontario and resulted in 81 deaths and estimated damage of $100 million (1954 dollars). In 1998, Hurricanes Bonnie and Georges damaged property and took lives. Hurricane Mitch (October 26–November 4, 1998) was the deadliest Atlantic hurricane in two centuries, killing more than 12 000 people in Central America. In 2007, for the first time in history in a single Atlantic season, two category 5 hurricanes simultaneously made landfall, Hurricane Dean (Yucatán) and Hurricane Felix (Honduras).

In September 2003, Hurricane Isabel struck the Outer Banks and Cape Hatteras of North Carolina, causing extensive flooding and wind damage to these fragile barrier islands as well as 36 deaths and about $2 billion in damages. Hurricane Charley brought category 4 winds to Florida's Gulf Coast in 2004, causing approximately $12 billion in damage and taking about two dozen lives (Figure 8.25a).

The 2008 season was notable for seven landfalls featuring four major storms, including Hurricanes Gustav hitting Louisiana and Ike hitting Galveston, the southeastern Texas coast, and southern Louisiana. Hurricane Ike reached category 4 status in the Caribbean, crossed Cuba, and maintained category 2 as it grew in overall size. On September 13, it made landfall on Galveston Island with the worst storm surge and damage striking to the east on the Bolivar Peninsula, where 80% to 95% of homes were destroyed (Figure 8.25b); see the photograph and discussion in *Geosystems Now* for this chapter and more coverage of barrier islands in Chapter 16.

The tragedy of Hurricane Andrew, which struck Florida in 1992, is that the storm destroyed or seriously damaged 70 000 homes and left 200 000 people homeless between Miami and the Florida Keys. The Everglades, the coral reefs north of Key Largo, some 4000 hectares of mangrove wetlands, and coastal southern pine forests all had significant damage from Andrew. Scientific assessments judge the Everglades to be quite resilient because the region's ecosystems evolved naturally with periodic hurricanes over the millennia. In fact, urbanization, agriculture, pollution, and water diversion pose a greater ongoing threat to the Everglades than do hurricanes.

Thus, tropical cyclones usually damage human structures more than they damage natural systems. This recurrent, yet avoidable, cycle—construction, devastation,

[text continued on page 228]

(a)

(b)

FIGURE 8.25 Damage from Hurricanes Charley and Ike.
(a) Category 4 Hurricane Charley in 2004 devastated Punta Gorda, near Port Charlotte, Florida; U.S. damage totaled at $15 billion. (b) Category 2 Hurricane Ike devastated Bolivar Peninsula and the Texas coast, with damage of $40 billion. [Bobbé Christopherson.]

Atlantic Hurricanes and the Future

Forecasters at the National Hurricane Center (NHC) in Miami were busy throughout the 1995–2010 hurricane seasons. This was the most active 16-year period in the history of the NHC, with 226 named tropical storms, including 123 hurricanes (53 of which were intense, meaning category 3 or higher). This was a record level of activity and individual storm intensity despite the reduced number of tropical cyclones during the 1997 El Niño season. The Atlantic hurricane season officially begins June 1 and lasts until November 30.

Statistically, the damage caused by tropical cyclones is increasing substantially as more and more development occurs along susceptible coastlines, whereas loss of life is decreasing in most parts of the world owing to better forecasting of these storms. The journal *Science* offered this "Perspective":

> The risk of human losses is likely to remain low . . . because of a well-established warning and rescue system and ongoing improvements in hurricane prediction. A main concern is the risks of high damage costs (up to $100 billion in a single event) because of ongoing population increases in coastal areas and increasing investment in buildings and extensive infrastructure in general.[2]

As an example, the 2005 Atlantic hurricane season broke several records, including the most named tropical storms in a single year, totalling 27 (the average is 10); the most hurricanes, totalling 15 (the average is 5); and the highest number of intense hurricanes, category 3 or higher, totalling 7 (the average is 2). The 2005 season was the first time that three category 5 storms (Katrina, Rita, and Wilma) occurred in the Gulf of Mexico and the first time that three category 3 or above hurricanes made U.S. landfall in subsequent years (2004 and 2005). The 2005 season also recorded the greatest damage total in one year, at more than $130 billion. Hurricane Wilma is now the most intense storm (lowest central pressure) in recorded history for the Atlantic.

The Gulf Coast and Atlantic seaboard sustained hits and near misses in 2005 from Hurricanes Cindy, Dennis, Katrina, Ophelia, Rita, Wilma, and Gamma; and when added to Charley, Francis, Ivan, and Jeanne in 2004 and to Dolly, Fay, Gustav, and Ike in 2008, the United States sustained more than $250 billion in damages and a loss of more than 2500 lives.

In the aftermath of Hurricane Ike in 2008, government delays held up water, ice, and food supplies for the 2 million evacuees until 4 or 5 days after landfall, thus repeating mistakes made after Katrina (Figure 8.25b). As we learn through hearings and investigations of the post-storm failure to respond and assist these regions and as we see continuing mistakes in planning and engineering, the case for an integrated scientific approach is clearly made. We discuss related issues for this region, including engineering, floodplain management, and levee considerations, in Chapter 14.

Prediction and the Future

The Tropical Prediction Center, at the NHC in Miami, Florida, posts tropical cyclone forecasts on its Web site (http://www.nhc.noaa.gov/). Their analysis of weather records for the period 1900–2006 disclosed a significant causal relationship between Atlantic tropical storms, including hurricanes that make landfall along the U.S. Gulf and East Coasts, and several meteorological variables, such as sea-surface temperatures, the presence of upper tropospheric crosswinds that cause shearing of vertical tropical storm circulation, and conditions in the Pacific Ocean, among other factors.

Subsequent research published in 2005 correlates longer storm lifetimes and greater storm intensity with rising sea-surface temperatures,[3] a link that was further reinforced in 2008:

> Atlantic tropical cyclones are getting stronger on average, with a 30-year trend that has been related to an increase in ocean temperatures. . . . The results presented here are conclusive in showing significant increasing trends in the satellite-derived lifetime-maximum wind speeds of the strongest tropical cyclones globally, and are quantitatively consistent with the heat-engine theory of cyclone intensity. Thus, as seas warm, the ocean has more energy that can be converted to tropical cyclone wind.[4]

Hurricanes Katrina, Rita, and Wilma in 2005 and Dean and Felix in 2007 all recorded remarkable central pressure drops as they passed over record sea-surface temperatures (see the satellite image of Katrina in Figure 8.1.1a). Wilma experienced a 100-mb central pressure drop in a little over 24 hours on October 19, 2005. The record sea-surface temperatures that are being recorded across the globe produce warmer water to depth, and the natural mixing that such storms trigger only brings up more heat to fuel the circulation. Many scientists now suggest that future warming with climate change, when considered alongside increased coastal population settlement, will produce substantial hurricane-related damage losses (Figure 8.1.1b and c).

Ironically, the relatively mild hurricane seasons from 1971 to 1994 encouraged weak zoning and rapid development of vulnerable coastal lowlands. New buildings, apartments, and government offices open quickly adjacent to piles of rubble and bare foundation pads. Unfortunately, public or private

---

[2]L. Bengtsson, "Hurricane threats," *Science* 293 (July 20, 2001): 441.

[3]K. Emanuel, "Increasing destructiveness of tropical cyclones over the past 30 years," *Nature* 436 (August 4, 2005): 686–688.

[4]J. B. Elsner, J. P. Kossin, and T. H. Jagger, "The increasing intensity of the strongest tropical cyclones," *Nature* 455 (September 4, 2008): 92–95.

decision makers practice thoughtful hazard planning infrequently, whether along coastal lowlands, river floodplains, or earthquake fault zones. The consequence is that our entire society bears the financial cost of planning failure, not to mention those victims who directly shoulder the physical, emotional, and economic hardships of the event.

No matter how accurate storm forecasts become, coastal and lowland property damage will continue to increase until better hazard zoning and development restrictions are in place. The property insurance industry appears to be

taking action to promote these improvements. It is requiring tougher building standards to obtain coverage—or, in some cases, it is refusing to insure property along vulnerable coastal lowlands. Given the increased intensity and "power dissipation" of these storms and a rise in sea level, the public, politicians, and business interests must respond to somehow mitigate this hazardous predicament. Given what we have experienced and what we know of Earth systems, has society learned anything? The Atlantic hurricane season begins each June 1.

(a)

2005: 27 Storms, Arlene to Zeta

FIGURE 8.1.1 Katrina surge clears neighbourhoods and destroys highway bridge.
(a) Hurricane Katrina, August 28, 2005, 11 A.M. CDT, category 5 strength. (b) NOAA aerial photo shows the power of wind and storm surge as entire Mississippi Gulf Coast neighbourhoods are obliterated, such as here in Long Beach, with the debris carried by storm surge a kilometre from shore. (c) Remnants of the U.S. 90 bridge and causeway out of Bay St. Louis, Mississippi. [(a) *Terra* image, NASA/GSFC. (b) NOAA. (c) Randall Christopherson.]

(b)

(c)

reconstruction, devastation—was reinforced ironically in *Fortune* magazine more than 40 years ago after the destruction caused by Hurricane Camille:

> Before long the beachfront is expected to bristle with new motels, apartments, houses, condominiums, and office buildings. Gulf Coast businessmen, incurably optimistic, doubt there will ever be another hurricane like Camille, and even if there is, they vow, the Gulf Coast will rebuild bigger and better after that.[5]

Sadly, Hurricane Katrina obliterated the same Gulf Coast towns in 2005—Waveland, Bay Saint Louis, Pass Christian, Long Beach, Gulfport, among others—that Camille washed away in 1969. The below-sea-level sections of New Orleans may never recover their former status; however, we are told that "the Gulf Coast will rebuild bigger and better."

[5] *Fortune*, October 1969, p. 62.

▌▌ CRITICAL THINKING 8.2

Hazard Perception and Planning: What Seems to be Missing?

Relative to coastal devastation from tropical weather, the following statement appears in the text: "This recurrent, yet avoidable, cycle—construction, devastation, reconstruction, devastation. . . ." This describes the ever-increasing dollar losses to property from tropical storms and hurricanes at a time when improved forecasts have resulted in a significant reduction in loss of life. Given rising sea levels along coastlines and the doubling of total power dissipation in these tropical storms since 1970, in your opinion, what is the solution to halting this cycle of destruction and increasing losses? How would you implement your ideas?

⊞ GEOSYSTEMS CONNECTION

Weather is the expression of energy, water, water vapour, and the atmosphere at any given moment. The patterns of precipitation produced across the globe form the input to water resource analysis. In the next chapter, we use the water balance model and examine inputs and outputs of the water budget. A budget can be established for any time frame or area, from a house plant to a front lawn, to a region, or country. Issues of water quality and quantity and the availability of potable water loom as major issues for global society.

 APPLIED PHYSICAL GEOGRAPHY *Adiabatic Warming and the Rain Shadow*

When Europeans first came to the "New World," they encountered a place of abrupt climate zonation. Nowhere else on the globe are great marginal mountain chains such as the Andes, Cascades, Sierra Nevada, and Coast Mountains found in the zone of the prevailing westerly winds, adjacent to low interior plains or basins to the east. Intense rain-shadow deserts in middle latitudes—for example, the Palliser Triangle in southern Alberta—are unique to the Americas. For many emigrants seeking the paradise of west coasts by the overland route, these rain-shadow deserts were deadly. The cause of these rain shadows lies in the adiabatic process, working first on air rising up a slope and then on air sinking down a slope. It is nature's process of wringing out the available moisture by forced ascent of air over a mountain barrier.

Imagine a mountain barrier, 4000 m in elevation, rising from sea level and located in the prevailing westerly winds that blow onshore from the ocean. The initial air temperature is 28°C as the air mass strikes the mountain along the windward side (westward-facing slope). The air mass then rises to the top of the mountain, where it crosses the crest and descends the leeward side (eastward-facing slope) of the mountain barrier. What happens to the air temperature as it rises up the slope? How much change occurs? What lapse rate applies? If the initial air had a dew-point temperature of 12°C, using the dew-point lapse rate, at what altitude will condensation begin?

Refer to Figure 8.8a on page 204. The air temperature decreases as it rises up the slope. If there is no condensation, temperature decreases by 10 C° per 1000 m, so at 1000 m the temperature is 18°C, at 2000 m the temperature is 8°C, and so forth.

However, we are given the initial dew-point temperature at sea level (12°C) and the dew-point lapse rate (2 C° · 1000 m⁻¹). So at sea level, the dew-point temperature is 16 C° lower than the air temperature. At 1000 m, it is 10°C, and at 2000 m, 8°C. The temperature of the air and the dew-point temperature are the same at 2000 m. Cloud formation begins at this altitude, the lifting condensation level—an altitude at which air temperature is at the dew point. Continued lifting will no longer be at the dry adiabatic rate. Instead, because condensation releases latent heat that warms the atmosphere, the lower, moist adiabatic rate must be used. From 2000 m upward, the air will cool at an average rate of 6 C° per 1000 m. So at 3000 m the air will be at 2°C and at 4000 m, −4°C.

Now, imagine the leeward-slope descent. Starting with an air temperature of −4°C at an elevation of 4000 m, what will happen to the cold, dry air on the leeward side of the mountain?

Cold, dry air at the mountaintop will subside and warm adiabatically—its temperature will increase at the dry adiabatic rate and no condensation will occur. At 3000 m, the temperature will be 6°C; at 2000 m, 16°C; at 1000 m, 26°C; and at 500 m, 31°C. At 500 m, the air is warmer and, because no moisture has been added in its descent, drier than it was at the same elevation on the windward side of the mountain barrier—thus, a rain shadow.

KEY LEARNING CONCEPTS REVIEW

Weather is the short-term condition of the atmosphere; **meteorology** is the scientific study of the atmosphere. The spatial implications of atmospheric phenomena and the relationship to human activities strongly link meteorology to physical geography.

weather (p. 198)
meteorology (p. 198)

■ *Describe* air masses that affect North America, and *relate* their qualities to source regions.

Specific conditions of humidity, stability, and cloud coverage occur in a regional, homogenous **air mass**. The longer an air mass remains stationary over a region, the more definite its physical attributes become. The homogeneity of temperature and humidity in an air mass sometimes extends through the lower half of the troposphere. Air masses are categorized by moisture content—**m** for maritime (wetter) and **c** for continental (drier)—and temperature, a function of latitude—designated **A** (Arctic), **P** (polar), **T** (tropical), **E** (equatorial), and **AA** (Antarctic).

air mass (p. 198)

1. How does a source region influence the type of air mass that forms over it? Give specific examples of each basic category.
2. Of all the air masses, which are of greatest significance to Canada and the United States? What happens to air masses that migrate to locations different from the source regions? Give an example of air-mass modification.

■ *Identify* and *describe* four types of atmospheric lifting mechanisms, and give an example of each.

Air masses can rise through **convergent lifting** (airflows conflict, forcing some of the air to lift); **convectional lifting** (air passing over warm surfaces gains buoyancy); **orographic lifting** (passage over a topographic barrier); and *frontal lifting*. In North America, **chinook winds** (called *föhn* or *foehn* winds in Europe) are the warm, downslope airflows characteristic of the leeward side of mountains. Orographic lifting creates wetter windward slopes and drier leeward slopes situated in the **rain shadow** of the mountain. Conflicting air masses at a front produce a **cold front** (and sometimes a zone of strong wind and rain) or a **warm front**. A zone at or slightly ahead of the front, called a **squall line**, is characterized by turbulent and wildly changing wind patterns and intense precipitation.

convergent lifting (p. 201)
convectional lifting (p. 201)
orographic lifting (p. 201)
chinook winds (p. 203)
rain shadow (p. 203)
cold front (p. 204)
warm front (p. 204)
squall line (p. 206)

3. Explain why it is normally necessary for an air mass to be lifted if there is to be saturation, condensation, and precipitation.
4. What are the four principal lifting mechanisms that cause air masses to ascend, cool, condense, form clouds, and perhaps produce precipitation? Briefly describe each.
5. Differentiate between the structure of a cold front and a warm front.

■ *Analyse* the pattern of orographic precipitation, and *describe* the link between this pattern and global topography.

The physical presence of a mountain acts as a topographic barrier to migrating air masses. *Orographic lifting* (oro- means "mountain") occurs when air is lifted forcibly upslope as it is pushed against a mountain. It cools adiabatically. An orographic barrier enhances convectional activity. The precipitation pattern of windward and leeward slopes persists worldwide. The provinces of British Columbia and Alberta are presented in the chapter as exhibiting excellent examples of this concept.

6. When an air mass passes across a mountain range, many things happen to it. Describe each aspect of a moist air mass crossing a mountain. What is the pattern of precipitation that results?
7. Explain how the distribution of precipitation in British Columbia is influenced by the principles of orographic lifting.

■ *Describe* the life cycle of a midlatitude cyclonic storm system, and *relate* this to its portrayal on weather maps.

A **midlatitude cyclone**, or **wave cyclone**, is a vast low-pressure system that migrates across the continent, pulling air masses into conflict along fronts. **Cyclogenesis**, the birth of the low-pressure circulation, can occur off the west coast of North America, along the polar front, along the lee slopes of the Rockies, in the Gulf of Mexico, or along the East Coast. A midlatitude cyclone can be thought of as having a life cycle of birth, maturity, old age, and dissolution. An **occluded front** is produced when a cold front overtakes a warm front in the maturing cyclone. Sometimes a **stationary front** develops between conflicting air masses, where air flow is parallel to the front on both sides. These systems are guided by the jet streams of the upper troposphere along seasonally shifting **storm tracks**.

midlatitude cyclone (p. 207)
wave cyclone (p. 207)
cyclogenesis (p. 207)
occluded front (p. 209)
stationary front (p. 209)
storm tracks (p. 209)

8. Differentiate between a cold front and a warm front as types of frontal lifting, and describe what you would experience with each one.

9. How does a midlatitude cyclone act as a catalyst for conflict between air masses?

10. What is meant by cyclogenesis? In what areas does it occur and why? What is the role of upper-tropospheric circulation in the formation of a surface low?

11. Diagram a plan view of a midlatitude cyclonic storm during its open stage. Label each of the components in your illustration, and add arrows to indicate wind patterns in the system.

■ *List* the measurable elements that contribute to modern weather forecasting, and *describe* the technology and methods employed.

Synoptic analysis involves the collection of weather data at a specific time, as shown on the synoptic weather maps inserted in Figures 8.3, 8.12, and CT 8.1.1. The standard weather station symbols used on these maps are identified in the legend to Figure 8.12. Building a database is key to computer-based weather prediction and the development of weather-forecasting models, including the following:

■ Barometric pressure (sea level and altimeter setting)
■ Pressure tendency (steady, rising, or falling)
■ Surface air temperature
■ Dew-point temperature
■ Wind speed, direction, and character (gusts, squalls)
■ Type and movement of clouds
■ Current weather observations
■ State of the sky (current sky conditions)
■ Visibility; vision obstruction (fog, haze)
■ Amount of precipitation since last observation

Technology employed includes Doppler radar, wind profilers, workstations, AWOS instrument arrays, various satellite platforms, and GNSS.

12. What is your principal source of weather data, information, and forecasts? Where does your source obtain its data? Have you used the Internet and World Wide Web to obtain weather information? What benefits do you see?

■ *Analyse* various forms and characteristics of violent weather, and *review* several examples of each.

The violent power of some weather phenomena poses a hazard to society. Severe ice storms involve freezing precipitation, ice glaze, and ice pellets, snow blizzards, and crippling ice coatings on roads, power lines, and crops. Thunderstorms produce **lightning** (electrical discharges in the atmosphere), **thunder** (sonic bangs produced by the rapid expansion of air after intense heating by lightning), and **hail** (ice pellets formed within cumulonimbus clouds).

Strong linear winds in excess of $26 \text{ m} \cdot \text{s}^{-1}$ known as **straight-line winds**, **downbursts**, **microbursts**, **plough winds**, and **derechos**, are associated with thunderstorms and bands of showers crossing a region. Straight-line winds can cause significant damage and crop losses. A spinning, cyclonic column rising to mid-troposphere level—a **mesocyclone**—is sometimes visible as the swirling mass of a cumulonimbus cloud, especially in a *supercell* system. Dark grey **funnel clouds** pulse from the bottom side of the parent cloud. A **tornado** is formed when the funnel connects with Earth's surface. A **waterspout** forms when a tornado circulation occurs over water.

Within tropical air masses, large low-pressure centres can form along easterly wave troughs. Under the right conditions, a tropical cyclone is produced. Depending on the central pressure, a **tropical cyclone** can become a **hurricane**, **typhoon**, or cyclone; this occurs when winds exceed 64 knots (119 km·h⁻¹). As forecasting of weather-related hazards improves, loss of life decreases, although property damage continues to increase. Great damage occurs to occupied coastal lands when hurricanes make **landfall** and when winds drive ocean water inland in **storm surges**.

ice storm (p. 212)
lightning (p. 213)
thunder (p. 214)
hail (p. 215)
straight-line wind (p. 216)
downburst (p. 216)
microburst (p. 216)
plough wind (p. 216)
derechos (p. 216)
mesocyclone (p. 216)
funnel cloud (p. 216)
tornado (p. 216)
waterspout (p. 216)
tropical cyclone (p. 219)
hurricane (p. 220)
typhoon (p. 220)
landfall (p. 223)
storm surge (p. 223)

13. What constitutes a thunderstorm? What type of cloud is involved? What type of air mass would you expect in an area of thunderstorms in North America?

14. Lightning and thunder are powerful phenomena in nature. Briefly describe how they develop.

15. Describe the formation process of a mesocyclone. How is this development associated with that of a tornado?

16. Evaluate the pattern of tornado activity in Canada and the United States. Where is Tornado Alley? What generalizations can you make about the distribution and timing of tornadoes? Do you perceive a trend in tornado occurrences in North America? Explain.

17. What are the different categories for tropical cyclones? List the various names used worldwide for hurricane strength tropical cyclones. Have any hurricanes ever occurred in the south Atlantic?

18. What factors contributed to the incredible damage cost of Hurricane Katrina in 2005 and subsequent years? Why have such damage figures increased even though loss of life has decreased over the past 30 years?

19. What have scientists said to explain the intensity of tropical cyclones since 1970? Put in your own words the quotations in this chapter from scientific journals related to changes in storm intensity.

20. Relative to improving weather forecasting, what are some of the technological innovations discussed in this chapter?

Hurricane Irene, August 25, 2011, is on track for landfall in North Carolina, the Northeast, and Canadian Maritimes, as its rainbands cover the Atlantic off Florida. The turquoise areas along Irene's southern flank are the coral reefs of the Bahamian platform, and elsewhere. The hurricane's eye is just touching Abaco Island, with category 3 sustained winds of 185 kmph. Irene moved along the East Coast as a category 1 hurricane with rainbands stretching out some 725 km. Damage estimates exceeded USD $10 billion with 45 lives lost. Irene crossed into New Brunswick and on into Québec as an extratropical storm with 88 mm of rain and winds topping 93 kmph along the coast. [*Terra* MODIS image, NASA/GSFC.]

MyGeosciencePlace

Visit **www.mygeoscienceplace.ca** for several figure animations, satellite loops, self-study quizzes, flashcards, interactive glossary, career links, RSS feeds, Pearson eText of *Geosystems*, and much more.

Water Resources

1983
July

2009
March

The western United States, particularly the Southwest, is experiencing a prolonged drought. Hoover Dam on the Arizona–Nevada border backs up Lake Mead on the Colorado River. The maximum reservoir elevation of 374.6 m is shown in the July 1983 photo of Lake Mead. Twenty-six years later, in March 2009, Lake Mead was at 331 m elevation, or about 43.6 m lower than 1983. The lake level dropped to 300 m in 2010, some 74.6 m lower than 1983. The roadway over the dam was closed in late 2010 as a new bypass bridge opened. More on this in Focus Study 15.1, Chapter 15. [(1983) Robert Christopherson. (2009) Bobbé Christopherson.]

KEY LEARNING CONCEPTS

After reading the chapter, you should be able to:

- ***Illustrate*** the hydrologic cycle with a simple sketch, and ***label*** it with definitions for each water pathway.

- ***Relate*** the importance of the water balance concept to your understanding of the hydrologic cycle, water resources, and soil moisture for a specific location.

- ***Construct*** the water balance equation as a way of accounting for the expenditures of water supply, and ***define*** each of the components in the equation and their specific operation.

- ***Describe*** the nature of groundwater, and ***define*** the elements of the groundwater environment.

- ***Identify*** critical aspects of freshwater supplies for the future, and ***cite*** specific water resource issues and potential remedies for any shortfalls.

Water Resources and Climate Change in the Prairies

In 1863, Captain John Palliser described a semiarid region extending from the foothills of the Rocky Mountains to southwestern Manitoba (Figure GN 9.1) a region of grasslands and sandy soil indicative of a dry climate. The area, now known as Palliser's Triangle, was promoted to prospective settlers as mostly treeless, requiring little clearing of forests for agricultural activities. The dryness should have served as a warning that the climate provided limited water resources and that drought could be a frequent occurrence.

In spite of the semiarid climate conditions, settlement took place in the nineteenth and twentieth centuries in the southern prairies. Today Alberta, Saskatchewan, and Manitoba have a combined population of 6 million people, with numbers increasing. The majority of people in these provinces live in or near Palliser's Triangle.

There are concerns of an impending water crisis in this region. Future water supplies will not be adequate to meet the growing demand at current per capita usage. Changes in water policies are required to accommodate population growth, fluctuations in climatic cycles, and the impacts of global climate change.

Many people are fooled by the "myth of abundance"; a belief in the idea that with so much freshwater, Canada could not possibly have concerns about water supplies. While Canada does indeed have large volumes of freshwater, much of it exists in areas of low population density, such as the North. In the southern prairies, where precipitation is low and evapotranspiration is high, particularly in the summer, water availability is dependent on rivers transferring supplies from areas with water surpluses to areas with water deficits.

"Natural water tower" is a description that applies to mountainous and highland regions on Earth, from which excess water is available to supply rivers. The Rocky Mountains are an example of a natural water tower feeding the

North Saskatchewan and South Saskatchewan Rivers that flow eastward through the southern prairies (Figure GN 9.1). Present intensive water extraction from these rivers and their tributaries is mainly for domestic water supplies and for large-scale irrigation.

The South Saskatchewan River, is, "Canada's most threatened river" as cited by the World Wildlife Fund Canada. The factors that led to this designation include: disruption of natural habitats and flow patterns by hundreds of dams in the basin; the annual extraction of 70% of water flow for agricultural and urban use; and predicted effects of ongoing climate change. A report on water supply and demand in the South Saskatchewan River basin is in the October 2010 issue of *Canadian Geographic* (see: http://www.canadiangeographic.ca/magazine/oct10/south_saskatchewan_river.asp).

Studies of climate in the southern prairies over the past two centuries—the time of nonnative settlement—confirm a view that the climate was actually more moist than in previous centuries. Climatic records interpreted from evidence such as tree rings and sediments in closed lake basins, suggest that droughts were more common and more severe in the past, and that climate for this settlement period was a departure from a drier past.

Climate change is bringing back a drier trend and adding stress to water resources[1]. An important component to the water-tower supply is glacial-ice melt, yet glaciers in the Rocky Mountains are diminishing as temperatures rise. Increased melt rates have raised spring and summer discharge in mountain streams, but as glacier masses decrease the contribution of melt water to river flows will decline. Furthermore, climate change is expected to cause temperatures to increase and precipitation to decrease in the southern

FIGURE GN 9.1 The southern prairies, the Palliser Triangle, and the North Saskatchewan and South Saskatchewan River basins.
Mean annual precipitation is 410 mm at Calgary, 390 mm at Regina, and 515 mm at Winnipeg. In the southern prairies, the annual water budget deficit averages 35%–50% of water need—water resource concepts discussed in Chapter 9. Rivers originating in the Rocky Mountains, fed by snow and ice melt, are critical to supplying water to this region.

prairie region. This will lead to greater aridity, reduced soil moisture, and greater pressure on limited groundwater supplies, particularly in summer.

It is clear that with climate change, diminishing water resources, and increasing population, human activity and water use policies in the southern prairie provinces must adapt.

Greater emphasis on water conservation and more efficient use of water is needed. However, even with such measures, activities in areas with marginal water supplies may have to shift location, or cease. For example, land currently on the edges of the viable farming region may transition into less-intensive ranch land. Clearly, water resource issues in this region need our attention.

[1]A key scientific report is: Henderson, N. and Sauchyn, D., 2008, *Climate Change Impacts on Canada's Prairie Provinces: A Summary of Our State of Knowledge*, Prairie Adaptation Research Collaborative Report No. 08-01, available at http://www.parc.ca/pdf/research_publications/summary_docs/SD2008-01.pdf.

The physical reality of life is defined by water. Our lives are bathed and infused with water. Our own bodies are about 70% water, as are plants and animals. We use water to cook, bathe, wash clothing, and dilute our wastes. We water small gardens and vast agricultural tracts. Most industrial processes would be impossible without water. It is the essence of our existence and is therefore the most critical resource supplied by Earth systems—the essential resource for life.

Water is not always naturally available where and when we want it. Consequently, we rearrange surface-water resources to suit our needs. We drill wells, build cisterns and reservoirs, and dam and divert streams to redirect water either spatially (geographically, from one area to another) or temporally (over time, from one part of the calendar to another). All of this activity constitutes water-resource management.

Fortunately, water is a renewable resource, constantly cycling through the environment. Even so, some 1.1 billion people lack safe drinking water. People in 80 countries face impending water shortages, either in quantity or quality, or both. Approximately 2.4 billion people lack adequate sanitary facilities, 80% of people in Africa, 13% in Asia. This leads to approximately 2 million deaths a year due to lack of water and 5 million deaths a year from waterborne infections and disease. An investment in safe drinking water, sanitation, and hygiene could decrease these numbers.

During the first half of this century, global water availability per person will drop by 74% as population increases and adequte water decreases, especially in the tropical, arid and semi-arid regions where population growth is greatest. Author Peter Gleick summarized:

> The overall economic and social benefits of meeting basic water requirements far outweigh any reasonable assessment of the costs of providing those needs. . . . Water-related diseases cost society on the order of $125 billion per year. . . . Yet the cost of providing new infrastructure needs for all major urban water sectors has been estimated at around $25 to $50 billion per year.[2]

[2]P. Gleick, *The World's Water*, a biennial report (Washington, DC: Island Press, 2008), http://www.worldwater.org/.

Thus the role for geographic science with its integrative, spatial approach is key in analyzing a systematic, comprehensive global portrait, a world-water economy approach, to more effectively allocate investment to mitigate better the coming crisis (see World Water Assessment Program, UNESCO, http://www.unesco.org/water/wwap/).

In this chapter: We begin with the hydrologic cycle, which gives us a model for understanding the global water balance. We look at resources using a water balance approach—similar in many ways to a money budget—in which we examine water "receipts" and "expenses" at specific locations. This budget approach can be applied at any scale, from a small garden, to a farm, to a regional landscape such as Palliser's Triangle described in *Geosystems Now*.

In Canada about 6 million people draw freshwater from the groundwater resource, yet groundwater is tied to surface-water supplies for recharge. This chapter concludes by considering the quantity and quality of the water we withdraw and consume for irrigation, industrial, and municipal uses—our specific water supply. Water supplies of adequate quantity and quality loom as the most important resource issue for many parts of the world this century.

The Hydrologic Cycle

Vast currents of water, water vapour, ice, and energy are flowing about us continuously in an elaborate, open, global plumbing system. Together these form the **hydrologic cycle**, which has operated for billions of years, from the lower atmosphere to several kilometres beneath Earth's surface. The cycle involves the circulation and transformation of water throughout Earth's atmosphere, hydrosphere, lithosphere, and biosphere.

A Hydrologic Cycle Model

Figure 9.1 is a simplified model of this complex system. Let's use the ocean as a starting point for our discussion, although we could jump into the model at any point. More than 97% of Earth's water is in the ocean, and here most evaporation and precipitation occur. We can trace 86% of all evaporation to the ocean. The other 14% is from the land, including water moving from the soil into plant

GEO REPORT 9.1   *The Water We Use*

On an individual level, Canadians use an average of 326 litres of water per person per day, but this figure varies widely by location. The daily domestic use in litres per person per day varies from 156 litres in Charlottetown, to 470 litres in Hamilton, Ontario, to 659 litres in St. John's. Take a moment and speculate why there is a difference (compare rural vs. urban populations). However, overall individual water use is actually much higher than these figures because of indirect use, such as consuming food and beverages made using water-intensive practices. See http://www.worldwater.org/data.html, *World's Water 2008–2009*, Table 19, for more on these indirect uses of water. Canadian examples are documented by the Sustainable Water Project at http://poliswaterproject.org/publication/27.

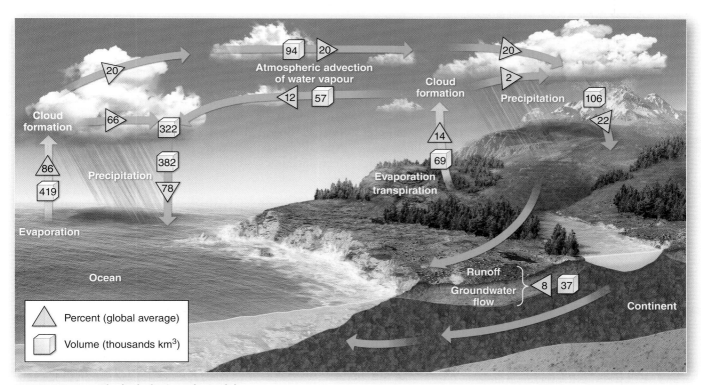

FIGURE 9.1 The hydrologic cycle model.
Water travels endlessly through the hydrosphere, atmosphere, lithosphere, and biosphere. The triangles show global average values as percentages. Note that all evaporation (86 + 14 = 100) equals all precipitation (78 + 22 = 100), and advection in the atmosphere is balanced by surface and subsurface water runoff when all of Earth is considered.

roots and passing through their leaves (the process of *transpiration*, described later in this chapter). Estimates of the volume of water involved in these pathways are given in thousands of km³.

In the figure, you can see that of the 86% of evaporation rising from the ocean, 66% combines with 12% advected (moving horizontally) from the land to produce the 78% of all precipitation that falls back into the ocean. The remaining 20% of moisture evaporated from the ocean, plus 2% of land-derived moisture, produces the 22% of all precipitation that falls over land. Clearly, the bulk of continental precipitation comes from the oceanic portion of the cycle. Regionally, various parts of the cycle will vary, creating imbalances and, depending on climate, surpluses in one region and shortages in another.

Surface Water

Precipitation that reaches Earth's surface follows two basic pathways: It either flows overland or soaks into the soil. Along the way **interception** occurs when precipitation strikes vegetation or other ground cover. Intercepted water that drains across plant leaves and down their stems to the ground is *stem flow* and can be an important route to the ground for moisture. Precipitation that falls directly to the ground, coupled with drips from vegetation (excluding stem flow), constitutes *throughfall*. Water soaks into the subsurface through **infiltration**, or penetration of the

soil surface. It further permeates soil or rock through the downward movement of **percolation**. These concepts are shown in Figure 9.2.

The atmospheric advection of water vapour from sea to land and land to sea at the top of Figure 9.1 appears to be unbalanced: 20% (94 000 km³) moving inland but only 12% (57 000 km³) moving out to sea. However, this exchange is balanced by the 8% (37 000 km³) that is land runoff, which flows to the sea. Most of this runoff—about 95%—comes from surface waters that wash across land as overland flow and streamflow. Only 5% of runoff is slow-moving subsurface groundwater. These percentages indicate that the small amount of water in rivers and streams is dynamic. In contrast, the large quantity of subsurface water is sluggish and represents only a small portion of total runoff.

The residence time for a water molecule in any part of the hydrologic cycle determines its relative importance in affecting Earth's climates. The short time spent by water in transit through the atmosphere (an average of 10 days) plays a role in temporary fluctuations in regional weather patterns. Long residence times, such as the 3000–10 000 years in deep-ocean circulation, groundwater aquifers, and glacial ice, act to moderate temperature and climatic changes. These slower parts of the cycle work as a "system memory"; the long periods over which heat energy is stored and released can buffer the effects of system changes.

To observe and describe the hydrologic cycle and its related energy budgets, scientists established in 1988 the Global Energy and Water Cycle Experiment (GEWEX). This is part of the World Climate Research Program and represents an important focus in climate-change studies. Canada's contribution to the program was the Mackenzie GEWEX Study (MAGS, http://www.usask.ca/geography/MAGS/). The goal was to improve understanding of water and energy cycles of the Mackenzie River Basin in particular and cold regions in general. A major objective of the study was to develop coupled models of atmospheric and hydrologic processes that could be used to evaluate the impact of both human-induced climate change and natural climate variability on Canada's water resources. Now that you are acquainted with the hydrologic cycle, let's examine the concept of the soil-water budget as a method of assessing water resources.

Soil-Water Balance Concept

An effective method for assessing water resources is to establish a **soil-water budget** for any area of Earth's surface—a continent, country, region, field, or front yard. Key is measuring the precipitation "supply" input and its distribution to satisfy the "demand" outputs of plants, evaporation, and soil moisture storage in the area considered. Such a budget can examine any time frame, from minutes to years.

Think of a soil-water budget as a money budget: Precipitation income must be balanced against expenditures of evaporation, transpiration, and runoff. Soil-moisture storage acts as a savings account, accepting deposits and withdrawals of water. Sometimes all expenditure demands are met, and any extra water results in a surplus. At other times, precipitation and soil moisture income are inadequate to meet demands, and a deficit, or water shortage, results.

Geographer Charles W. Thornthwaite (1899–1963) pioneered applied water-resource analysis and worked with others to develop a water balance methodology. They applied water balance concepts to solving problems, especially related to irrigation, which requires accurate quantity and timing of water application to maximize crop yields. Thornthwaite also developed methods for estimating evaporation and transpiration. He recognized the important relation between water supply and local water demand as an essential climatic element. In fact, his initial use of these techniques was to develop a climatic classification system.

The Soil-Water Balance Equation

To understand Thornthwaite's water balance methodology and "accounting" or "bookkeeping" procedures, we must first understand some terms and concepts. Figure 9.2 illustrates the essential aspects of a soil-water budget. Precipitation (mostly rain and snow) provides the moisture input. The object, as with a money budget, is to account for the ways in which this supply is distributed: actual water taken by evaporation and plant transpiration, extra water that exits in streams and subsurface groundwater, and recharge or utilization of soil-moisture storage.

Figure 9.3 organizes the water balance components into an equation. As in all equations, the two sides must balance; that is, the precipitation receipt (left side) must be fully accounted for by expenditures or by changes in soil moisture (right side). Follow this water balance equation as you read the following paragraphs. To help you learn these concepts, we use letter abbreviations (such as P) for the components.

Precipitation Input The moisture supply to Earth's surface is **precipitation (P)**. It arrives in several different forms depending upon temperature and moisture supply. Table 9.1 summarizes the different types of precipitation. As you read through this table, recall which types of precipitation you have experienced—rain, sleet, snow, and hail being most common.

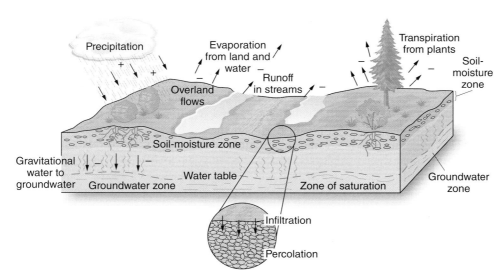

FIGURE 9.2 The soil-moisture environment.
The principal pathways for precipitation include interception by plants; throughfall to the ground; collection on the surface, forming overland flow to streams; transpiration and evaporation from plants; evaporation from land and water; and gravitational water moving to subsurface groundwater.

Water balance equation:

Explanation:

FIGURE 9.3 The water balance equation explained.
The outputs (components to the right of the equal sign) are an accounting of expenditures from the precipitation moisture-supply input (to the left).

Satellite

Global Water Balance Components

TABLE 9.1   Types of Precipitation

Type	Characteristic	Typical Amounts
Dew	Condensation on surfaces, especially vegetation; hoar frost when frozen, formed by direct deposition	0.1 to 1.0 mm per night; small input to supply; may be locally significant
Fog-drip	Deposited on vegetation and other surfaces from fog; rime when frozen	Can be 0.1 mm per night; a small input to supply; may be significant in foggy climates
Drizzle (mist)	Numerous, uniform water drops	Light 0.3 mm/hr; moderate 0.3–0.5 mm/hr; heavy > 0.5 mm $\cdot$ hr^{-1}; if over 1.0 mm $\cdot$ hr^{-1} it's rain
Hail	Roughly spherical, irregular lumps of ice > 5 mm in diameter, with a layered structure of opaque and clear ice in cross section; produced in convective clouds, almost always cumulonimbus	Highly variable, can cover the ground; hailstones can go to more than 15 cm diameter
Rain	Water drops > 0.5 mm in diameter, or widely scattered drops might be smaller	Light < 0.25 cm $\cdot$ hr^{-1} Moderate 0.26–0.76 cm $\cdot$ hr^{-1} Heavy > 0.76 cm $\cdot$ hr^{-1}
Snowflakes	Cluster of ice crystals, or a single crystal, that fall from a cloud; an aggregate can exceed 6 cm diameter	Highly variable
Snow grains (granular snow)	Quite small, flat, opaque grains of ice; solid equivalent of drizzle	Highly variable
Snow pellets (graupel or soft hail)	Opaque, approximately round pellets of ice, 2 to 5 mm in diameter, falling in showers; often before or with snow	Highly variable
Ice pellets	Clear ice encasing a snowflake or snow; transparent pellets of ice < 5 mm diameter	Highly variable

Precipitation is measured with the **rain gauge**. A rain gauge is essentially a large measuring cup that collects rainfall and snowfall so the water can be measured by depth, weight, or volume (Figure 9.4). Wind can cause an undercatch because the drops or snowflakes are not falling vertically. For example, a wind of 37 km·h⁻¹ produces an undercatch as great as 40%, meaning that an actual 2.5 cm rainfall might gauge at only 1 cm. The *wind shield* you see above the gauge's opening reduces this error by catching raindrops that arrive at an angle. According to the World Meteorological Organization (http://www.wmo.ch/), more than 100 000 weather-monitoring stations (including automatic weather stations), with more than 40 000 places measuring precipitation.

Figure 9.5 maps precipitation patterns for Canada and the United States. Note the patterns of wetness and dryness, as you remember our discussion of air masses and lifting mechanisms in Chapter 8. (Chapter 10 presents a world precipitation map in Figure 10.2.) P is the principal input to the water balance equation (Figure 9.3). All the components discussed next are outputs or expenditures of this water.

Actual Evapotranspiration As discussed in Chapters 5 and 7, **evaporation** is the net movement of free water molecules away from a wet surface into air that is less than saturated. **Transpiration** is a cooling mechanism in plants. When a plant transpires, it moves water through

FIGURE 9.4 A rain gauge.
A funnel guides water into a bucket that is sitting on an electronic weighing device. The gauge minimises evaporation, which would cause underestimated readings. The wind shield around the top of the gauge minimises the undercatch produced by wind. [Bobbé Christopherson.]

small openings called stomata in the underside of its leaves. The water evaporates, cooling the plant, much as perspiration cools humans. Transpiration is partially regulated by the plants themselves. Control cells around the stomata conserve or release water. Transpired quantities can be significant: On a hot day, a single tree can transpire hundreds of litres of water; a forest, millions of litres. Evaporation and transpiration are combined into one term—**evapotranspiration**—14% of global evapotranspiration occurs from land surfaces and plants. Now, let's examine ways to estimate evapotranspiration rates.

Potential Evapotranspiration Evapotranspiration is an actual expenditure of water. In contrast, **potential evapotranspiration (PE)** is the amount of water that would evaporate and transpire under optimum moisture conditions when adequate precipitation and adequate soil-moisture supply are present.

Filling a bowl with water and letting the water evaporate illustrates this concept: When the bowl becomes dry, is there still an evaporation demand? Yes, the demand remains, of course, regardless of whether the bowl is dry. If you always kept water in the bowl, the actual amount of water that would evaporate or transpire is equal to the PE, or the optimum demand given a constant supply of water. If you let the bowl dry out, the amount of PE demand that went unmet is the shortage, or deficit (D). Note that in the water balance equation, when we subtract the deficit from the potential evapotranspiration, we derive the amount that actually evapotranspirated—AE.

Figure 9.6 presents PE values derived using Thornthwaite's approach for Canada and the United States. Note that higher values occur in the south, with highest readings in the southwest, where higher average air temperature and lower relative humidity exist. Lower PE values are found at higher latitudes and elevations, which have lower average temperatures.

Compare this PE (demand) map with the P (supply) map in Figure 9.5. The relation between the two determines the remaining components of the water balance equation in Figure 9.3. From the two maps, can you identify regions where P is greater than PE annually (for example, the lower Great Lakes Basin)? Or where PE is greater than P (for example, the southwestern United States)? Where you live, is the water demand usually met by the precipitation supply? Or does your area experience a natural shortage? How might you find out?

Determining PE Although exact measurement is difficult, one method of measuring PE employs an **evaporation pan**, or *evaporimeter*. As evaporation occurs, water in measured amounts is automatically replaced in the pan, equalling the amount that evaporated. Mesh screens over the pan protect against overmeasurement due to wind, which accelerates evaporation.

A more elaborate measurement device is a **lysimeter**. A tank, approximately a cubic metre in size or larger, is buried in a field with its upper surface left open. The lysimeter

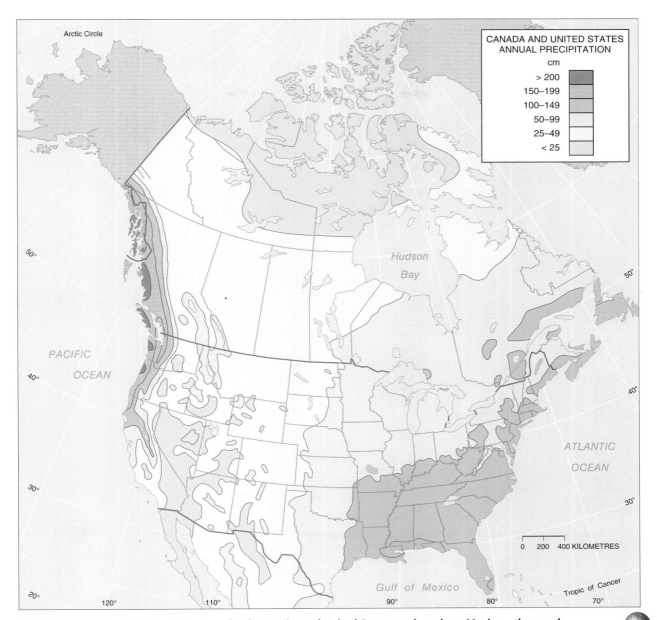

FIGURE 9.5 Precipitation (P) in Canada, the continental United States, and northern Mexico—the supply. Annual precipitation (water supply, P) in Canada and the United States. [Adapted from NWS, US Department of Agriculture and Environment Canada.]

Global Water Balance Components

isolates a representative volume of soil, subsoil, and plant cover, thus allowing measurement of the moisture moving through the sampled area. A weighing lysimeter has this embedded tank resting on a weighing scale (Figure 9.7). A rain gauge next to the lysimeter measures the precipitation input.

The number of lysimeters and evaporation pans is somewhat limited across North America, but these instruments still provide a database from which to develop ways of estimating PE. Several methods of estimating PE on the basis of meteorological data are widely used and easily implemented for regional applications. Thornthwaite developed one of these methods.

He discovered that if you know monthly mean air temperature and daylength, you could approximate PE.

These data are readily available, so calculating PE is easy and fairly accurate for most midlatitude locations. (Recall that daylength is a function of a station's latitude.) His method can work with data from hourly, daily, or annual time frames or with historical data to re-create water conditions in past environments.

Thornthwaite's method works better in some climates than in others. It ignores warm or cool air movements across a surface, sublimation and surface-water retention at subfreezing temperatures, poor drainage, and frozen soil (*permafrost*, Chapter 17), although there is allowance for snow accumulations. Nevertheless, we use his water balance method here because of its great utility as a teaching tool and its overall ease of application and acceptable results for geographic studies.

FIGURE 9.6 Potential evapotranspiration (PE) for Canada and the continental United States—the demand.
[From C.W. Thornthwaite, "An approach toward a rational classification of climate," *Geographical Review* 38 (1948): 64. Adapted by permission from the American Geographical Society. Canadian data from M. Sanderson, "The climates of Canada according to the new Thornthwaite classification," *Scientific Agriculture* 28 (1948): 501–17.]

Global Water Balance Components

FIGURE 9.7 A weighing lysimeter for measuring evaporation and transpiration. The various pathways of water are tracked: Some water remains as soil moisture, some is incorporated into plant tissues, some drains from the bottom of the lysimeter, and the remainder is credited to evapotranspiration. Modelling natural conditions, the lysimeter measures actual evapotranspiration. [Adapted from illustration courtesy of Lloyd Owens, Agricultural Research Service, USDA, Coshocton, Ohio.]

Deficit The PE demand can be satisfied in three ways: by P, by moisture stored in the soil, or through artificial irrigation. If these three sources are inadequate to meet moisture demands, the location experiences a moisture shortage. This unsatisfied PE is **deficit (D)**.

By subtracting D from PE, we determine the **actual evapotranspiration (AE)** that takes place (see Figure 9.3). Under ideal conditions for plants, potential and actual amounts of evapotranspiration are about the same, so plants do not experience a water shortage; droughts result from deficit conditions.

Surplus If PE is satisfied and the soil is full of moisture, then additional water input becomes **surplus (S)**. This excess water might sit on the surface in puddles, ponds, and lakes, or it might flow across the surface toward stream channels or percolate through the soil underground. The **overland flow** combines with precipitation and groundwater flows into river channels to make up the **total runoff**. Because surplus water generates most streamflow, or runoff, the water balance approach is useful for indirectly estimating streamflow.

Soil-Moisture Storage A "savings account" of water that receives recharge "deposits" and provides for utilization "withdrawals" is **soil-moisture storage (Δ ST)**. This is the volume of water stored in the soil some of which is accessible to plant roots. The delta symbol, Δ, means that this component includes both *recharge* and *utilization* of soil moisture; the Δ in math means "change." Soil moisture comprises three categories of water—hygroscopic, gravitational, and capillary—but only capillary water is accessible to plants (Figure 9.8a).

Hygroscopic water is inaccessible to plants because it is a molecule-thin layer that is tightly bound to each soil particle by the hydrogen bonding of water molecules (Figure 9.8a, left). Hygroscopic water exists even in the desert, but it is unavailable to meet PE demands. Relative to plants, soil is at the **wilting point** when all that remains is this inaccessible water; plants wilt and eventually die after a prolonged period of such moisture stress.

Capillary water is generally accessible to plant roots because it is held against the pull of gravity in the soil by hydrogen bonds between water molecules, which causes surface tension, and by hydrogen bonding between water molecules

(a)

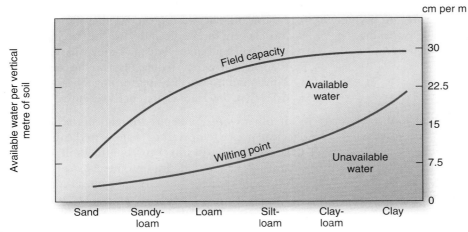

(b)

FIGURE 9.8 Types of soil moisture and its availability.
(a) Hygroscopic and gravitational water is normally unavailable to plants; only capillary water that is not bound hygroscopically to soil is available. (b) The relation between soil-moisture availability and soil texture determines the distance between the two curves that show field capacity and wilting point. A loam soil (one-third each of sand, silt, and clay) has roughly the most available water per vertical depth of soil exposed to plant roots.
[(a) After D. Steila, *The Geography of Soils,* © 1976, p. 45, © Pearson Prentice Hall, Inc. (b) After U.S. Department of Agriculture, *1955 Yearbook of Agriculture—Water,* p. 120.]

and the soil. Most capillary water that remains in the soil is **available water** in soil-moisture storage. After some water drains from the larger pore spaces, the amount of available water remaining for plants is termed **field capacity**, or storage capacity. It is removable to meet PE demands through the action of plant roots and surface evaporation (Figure 9.8, centre). Field capacity is specific to each soil type, and the amount can be determined by soil surveys.

When soil becomes saturated after a precipitation event, any water surplus in the soil body becomes **gravitational water**. It percolates from the shallower capillary zone to the deeper groundwater zone (Figure 9.8a, right).

Figure 9.8b shows the relation of soil texture to soil-moisture content. Different plant species send roots to different depths and therefore reach different amounts of soil moisture. A soil blend that maximizes available water is best for plants. On the basis of Figure 9.8b, can you determine the soil texture with the greatest quantity of available water?

As **soil-moisture utilization** removes soil water, the plants must exert greater effort to extract the amount of moisture they need. As a result, even though a small amount of water may remain in the soil, plants may be unable to exert enough pressure to use it. The resulting *unsatisfied demand* is a *deficit*. Avoiding a deficit and reducing plant growth inefficiencies are the goals of irrigation, for the harder plants must work to get water, the less their yield and growth will be.

Whether from natural precipitation or artificial irrigation, water infiltrates the soil and replenishes available water, the process of **soil-moisture recharge**. The texture and the structure of the soil dictate available pore spaces, or **porosity**. The property of the soil that determines the rate of soil-moisture recharge is its **permeability**. Permeability depends on particle sizes and the shape and packing of soil grains.

Water infiltration is rapid in the first minutes of precipitation and slows as the upper soil layers become saturated, even though the deeper soil is still dry. Agricultural practices, such as ploughing and adding sand or manure to loosen soil structure, can improve both soil permeability and the depth to which moisture can efficiently penetrate to recharge soil-moisture storage. You may have found yourself working to improve soil permeability with a houseplant or garden—that is, working the soil to increase the rate of soil-moisture recharge.

Drought

Drought might seem a simple thing to define: Less precipitation and higher temperatures make for drier conditions over an extended period of time. However, scientists and resource managers use four technical definitions for **drought**. The key is to consider not only precipitation, temperature, and soil-moisture content, but also the water-resource demand as it relates to the lack of water.

- *Meteorological drought* is defined by the degree of dryness, as compared to a regional average, and the duration of dry conditions. This definition is region-specific since it relates to atmospheric conditions that change from area to area.
- *Hydrological drought* relates to the effects of precipitation shortages (both rain and snow) on water supply, such as when streamflow decreases, reservoir levels drop, mountain snowpack declines, and groundwater mining increases.
- *Agricultural drought* occurs when shortages of precipitation and soil moisture affect crop yields. Losses can be significant and are running in the tens of billions of dollars each year in North America, although agricultural drought evolves slowly and gets little media coverage.
- *Socioeconomic drought* results when reduced water supply causes the demand for goods to exceed the supply, such as when hydroelectric power production declines with reservoir depletion. This is a more comprehensive measure that considers loss of life, water rationing, wildfire events, and other widespread impacts of water shortfalls.

The National Drought Mitigation Center, University of Nebraska–Lincoln (NDMC, http://www.drought.unl.edu/), publishes a weekly "Drought Monitor" map, released each Thursday, and a newsletter *DroughtScape*. In Canada, Agriculture and Agri-Food Canada provide a drought watch map and assessment; see http://www.agr.gc.ca/pfra/drought/.

Droughts of various intensities are occurring on every continent through 2011. Australia is in a decade-long drought, its worst drought in 110 years. 2010 was the driest in Western Australia history. Regarding the U.S. Southwest drought, under way since late 2000, scientists reported that this remarkable situation links directly to global climate change:

> The projected future climate of intensified aridity in the Southwest is caused by . . . a poleward expansion of the subtropical dry zones. The drying of subtropical land areas . . . imminent or already underway is unlike any climate state we have seen in the instrumental record. It is also distinct from the multi-decadal mega-droughts that afflicted the American Southwest during Medieval times. . . . The most severe future droughts will still occur during persistent La Niña events, but they will be worse than any since the Medieval period, because the La Niña conditions will be perturbing a base state that is drier than any state experienced recently.[3]

In other words, previous droughts in the region related to sea-surface temperature changes in the distant tropical Pacific Ocean will still occur, but they will be worsened by climate change and the unwanted expansion farther into the region of the hot, dry subtropical high-pressure

[3]Richard Seager et al., "Model projections of an imminent transition to a more arid climate in southwestern North America," *Science* 316, no. 5828 (May 25, 2007): 1184.

system and summertime continental tropical (cT) air masses. The spatial implications of such semipermanent drought in a region of explosive population growth and urbanisation are serious and tie in directly to the need for water resource planning.

Sample Water Budgets

Using all of these concepts, we graph the water balance components for several representative cities. Let's begin by looking at Hamilton, Ontario Airport, Ontario, on the western end of Lake Ontario at 43.25° N, 79.85° W, elevation 237 m (data are from Hamilton airport).

Figure 9.9 graphs the water balance components for long-term supply and demand, using monthly averages. The monthly values for P and PE smooth the actual daily and hourly variability. On the graph, a comparison of P and PE by month determines whether there is a *net supply* or a *net demand* for water. The cooler time from October to May shows a net surplus, but the warm days from June to September create a net water demand. If we assume a soil-moisture storage capacity of 300 mm, typical of shallow-rooted plants, the net water-demand months are satisfied through soil-moisture utilization (green area), with a small summer soil-moisture deficit.

Obviously, not all stations experience the surplus moisture patterns of this humid continental region. Different climatic regimes experience different relations among water balance components. Figure 9.10 presents water balance graphs for several other cities in North America and the Caribbean Sea region. Among these examples, compare the summer precipitation of Vancouver, British Columbia, with that of Seabrook, New Jersey; the drier prairies of Saskatchewan with the more humid conditions in Ottawa; and the precipitation receipts of San Juan, Puerto Rico, with the arid desert of Phoenix, Arizona.

CRITICAL THINKING 9.1
Your Local Water Budget

Select your campus, yard, or perhaps a house plant and apply the water balance concepts. Where does the water supply originate—its source? Estimate the ultimate water supply and demand for the area you selected. For a general idea of P and PE, find your locale on Figures 9.5 and 9.6. Consider the seasonal timing of this supply and demand, and estimate water needs and how these needs vary as components of the water balance change.

Water Budget and Water Resources

Water distribution is uneven over space and time. Because humans require a steady supply, we build large-scale management projects intended to redistribute the water resource either geographically, by moving water from one place to another, or over time, by storing water from time of receipt until it is needed. In this way, deficits are reduced, surpluses are held for later release, and water availability is improved to satisfy evapotranspiration and society's demands. The water balance permits analysis of the contribution streams make to water resources.

Streams may be *perennial* (constantly flowing; *perennial* is Latin for "through the year") or *intermittent*. In either case, the total runoff that moves through them comes from surplus surface-water runoff, subsurface throughflow, and groundwater. Figure 9.11 maps annual global river runoff for the world. Highest runoff amounts are along the equator within the tropics, reflecting the frequent rainfall along the intertropical convergence zone (ITCZ). Southeast Asia also experiences high runoff, as do northwest coastal mountains in the Northern Hemisphere. In countries having great seasonal fluctuations in runoff, groundwater becomes an important reserve water supply. Regions of lower runoff coincide with Earth's subtropical deserts, rain-shadow areas, and continental interiors, particularly in Asia.

The new Three Gorges Dam controls the treacherous Yangtze River in China (Figure 9.12). At a length of 2.3 km and a height of 185 m, it is the largest dam and related construction in the world in overall size. Forced relocation of entire cities and more than one million people made room for the 600-km long reservoir. Controversies surrounded the immense scale of environmental, historical, and cultural losses. Gained is flood control, water resources for redistribution, and power production. Electrical production capacity is 22 000 MW.

FIGURE 9.9 Sample water budget for Hamilton, Ontario. Compare the average monthly values of precipitation inputs and potential evapotranspiration outputs to determine the condition of the soil-moisture environment. A typical pattern of spring surplus, summer soil-moisture utilization, a small summer deficit, autumn soil-moisture recharge, and early winter surplus highlights the year. Snow accumulation occurs in January and February when average temperatures are below freezing. During this time, snow is stored on top of the ground and does not recharge soil moisture. In March, when temperatures warm, snow melts, the ground thaws, and soil-moisture storage returns to 300 mm.

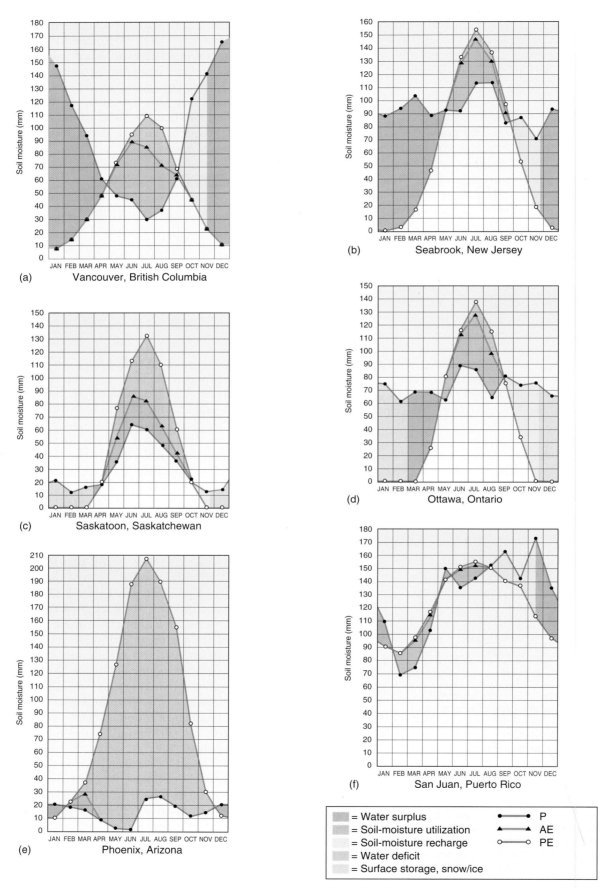

(a) Vancouver, British Columbia

(b) Seabrook, New Jersey

(c) Saskatoon, Saskatchewan

(d) Ottawa, Ontario

(e) Phoenix, Arizona

(f) San Juan, Puerto Rico

= Water surplus   ● ● P
= Soil-moisture utilization   ▲ ▲ AE
= Soil-moisture recharge   ○ ○ PE
= Water deficit
= Surface storage, snow/ice

FIGURE 9.10 Sample water budgets for selected stations.

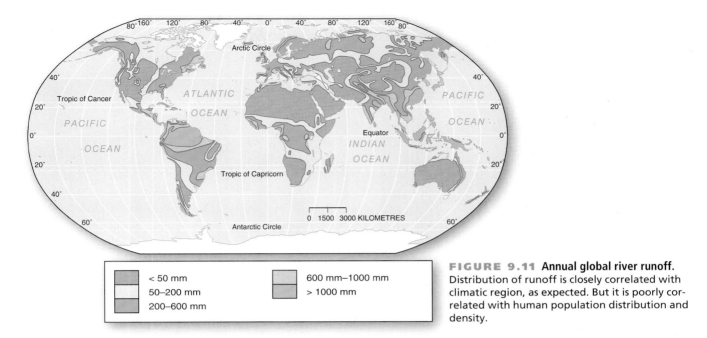

< 50 mm	600 mm–1000 mm
50–200 mm	> 1000 mm
200–600 mm	

FIGURE 9.11 Annual global river runoff.
Distribution of runoff is closely correlated with climatic region, as expected. But it is poorly correlated with human population distribution and density.

In Canada, the Nelson River project in Manitoba, the Churchill Falls project in Newfoundland and Labrador, and the proposed $12 billion Gull Island Dam and related hydroelectric projects in Québec are significant. The Gull Island project, as originally proposed, would be second only to the Three Gorges Dam with regard to the size of proposed construction.

In the United States, several large water-management projects already operate: the Bonneville Power Authority (BPA, Figure 9.13a) in Washington State, the Tennessee Valley Authority in the Southeast, the California Water Project, and the Central Arizona Project. BPA comprises 31 hydroelectric dams and a transmission grid and began operation in 1937.

Literally, the California Water Project rearranges the water budget in the state, holding back winter runoff for release in summer and pumping water from the north to the south. Completed in 1971, this 1207-km-long "river"

flows from the Sacramento River delta to the Los Angeles region, servicing irrigated agriculture in the San Joaquin Valley along the way (Figure 9.13b).

Canada and the United States share a long history of water supply issues. Rivers define several areas of their common border, and the Great Lakes are a significant boundary water resource; thus friction can develop when water supply diminishes. Bulk water export is an often-discussed political issue. The International Joint Commission (IJC), established by the Boundary Waters Treaty of 1909, is an independent binational organization whose purpose is to help prevent and resolve disputes relating to the use and quality of boundary waters and to advise Canada and the United States on related questions. The IJC has more than 20 boards that assist in dispute resolution. Visit the IJC website for a complete overview of its mission and a description of the boards (http://www.ijc.org/en/home/main_accueil.htm).

FIGURE 9.12 Major dam in China.
Satellite views in 2000 (construction) and 2006 (completion) of the $25 billion Three Gorges Dam on the Yangtze River, flowing from upper left to right. For scale, the main portion of the dam is 2.3 km in length. This is the world's largest individual construction project. The channel to the north of the dam contains a system of locks for shipping. [Terra ASTER images, NASA/GSFC/MITI/ERSDAC/JAROS.]

Global Water Balance
Components

(a) Grand Coulee Dam, BPA, Washington

(b) California Aqueduct

FIGURE 9.13 **Two major water projects in the United States.**
(a) Grand Coulee Dam holds back the Columbia River, as part of the federal Bonneville Power Administration, in Washington State. (b) The California Aqueduct transports water as part of the California Water Project. The Palmdate Reservoir beyond the aqueduct is in a depression of the San Andreas fault zone. [(a) Robert Christopherson. (b) Bobbé Christopherson.]

The best sites for multipurpose hydroelectric projects are already taken, so battles among conflicting interests and analysis of negative environmental impacts invariably accompany new project proposals. Chapter 14 discusses river management through such construction in further detail.

Groundwater Resources

Groundwater is an important part of the hydrologic cycle, although it lies beneath the surface, beyond the soil-moisture root zone. It is tied to surface supplies through pores in soil and rock. Groundwater is the largest potential freshwater source in the hydrologic cycle—larger than all surface lakes and streams combined. Between Earth's land surface and a depth of 4 km worldwide, some 8 340 000 km³ of water resides, a volume comparable to 70 times all the freshwater lakes in the world. Groundwater is generally free of sediment, colour, and disease-bearing organisms, although polluted groundwater conditions are considered irreversible. Pollution threatens groundwater quality, and overconsumption depletes groundwater volume in quantities beyond natural replenishment rates.

Remember: *Groundwater is not an independent source of water, for it is tied to surface supplies for recharge.* An important consideration in many regions is that groundwater accumulation occurred over millions of years, so care must be taken not to exceed this long-term buildup with excessive short-term demands.

About 6 million people in Canada (two-thirds of them in rural areas) rely on groundwater for domestic needs—1.5 billion m³ per year. About 50% of the U.S. population derives a portion of its freshwater from groundwater sources. In some states, such as Nebraska, groundwater supplies 85% of water needs and may reach 100% in rural areas. Between 1950 and 2000, annual groundwater withdrawal in the United States and Canada increased more than 150%. Figure 9.14 shows potential groundwater resources in both countries.

Groundwater Profile and Movement

Figure 9.15 brings together many groundwater elements in a single illustration, and it is the basis for the following discussion. Groundwater begins as surplus water, which percolates downward as gravitational water from the zone of capillary water. This excess surface water moves through the **zone of aeration**, where soil and rock are less than saturated (some pore spaces contain air).

The *porosity* of any rock layer depends on the arrangement, size, and shape of its individual particles, the nature of any cementing elements between them, and their degree of compaction. Subsurface rocks are either *permeable* or *impermeable*. Their permeability depends on whether they conduct water readily (higher permeability) or tend to obstruct its flow (lower permeability).

Eventually, the water reaches an area where subsurface water accumulates, the **zone of saturation**. Here the pores are completely filled with water. Like a hard sponge made of sand, gravel, and rock, the saturation zone stores water in its countless pores and voids. An **aquifer** is a rock layer that is permeable to groundwater flow adequate for wells and springs. An **aquiclude** (also called an *aquitard*) is a body of rock that does not conduct water in usable amounts. The saturated zone may include the saturated portion of the aquifer and a part of the underlying *aquiclude*, even though the latter has such low permeability that its water is inaccessible.

The upper limit of the water that collects in the zone of saturation is the **water table**. It is the surface where the zone of saturation, a narrow capillary fringe layer, meets the zone of aeration above (all across Figure 9.15). The slope of the water table, which generally follows the contours of the land surface, controls groundwater movement.

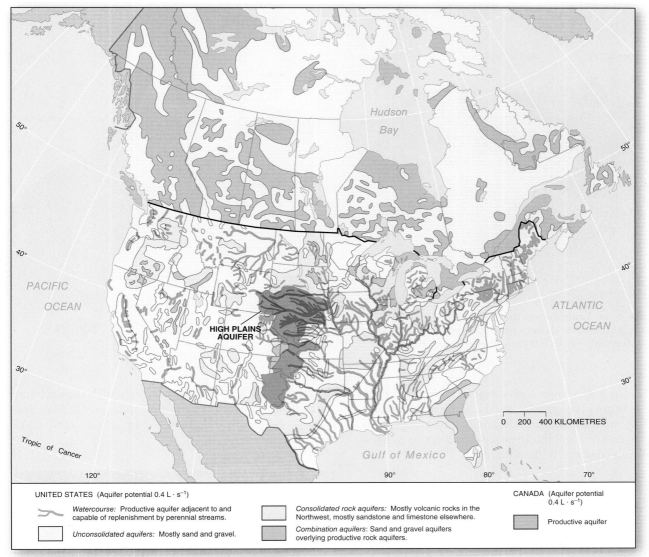

FIGURE 9.14 **Groundwater resource potential for Canada and the continental United States.**
Highlighted areas of the United States are underlain by productive aquifers capable of yielding freshwater to
wells at 3.3 L·s⁻¹ or more (for Canada, 0.4 L·s⁻¹). [Courtesy of Water Resources Council for the United States. *Currents
of Change: Final Report - Inquiry on Federal Water Policy*, p. 26, Environment Canada, 1985. Reproduced with the permission of the Minister of Public Works and Government Services Canada, 2011.]

Aquifers, Wells, and Springs

For many people, adequate water supply depends on a good aquifer beneath them that is accessible with a well or exposed on a hillside where water emerges as a spring. Is any of the water you consume from a well or spring?

Confined and Unconfined Aquifers Whether an aquifer is confined or unconfined affects its behaviour. A **confined aquifer** is bounded above and below by impermeable layers of rock or sediment. An **unconfined aquifer** has a permeable layer on top and an impermeable one beneath (see Figure 9.15).

Confined and unconfined aquifers differ in the size of their recharge area, which is the ground surface where water enters an aquifer to recharge it. For an unconfined aquifer, the **aquifer recharge area** generally extends above the entire aquifer; the water simply percolates down to the water table. But in a confined aquifer, the recharge area is far more restricted, as you can see in Figure 9.15. Pollution of this limited recharge area causes groundwater contamination; note in the illustration the improperly located disposal pond on the aquifer recharge area, contaminating wells to the right.

Confined and unconfined aquifers also differ in their water pressure. A well drilled into an unconfined aquifer (see Figure 9.15) must be pumped to make the water level rise above the water table. In contrast, the water in a confined aquifer is under the pressure of its own weight, creating a pressure level to which the water can rise on its own, the **potentiometric surface**.

The potentiometric surface actually can be above ground level (right side in Figure 9.15). Under this condition, **artesian water**, or groundwater confined under pressure, may rise in a well and even flow at the surface without pumping if

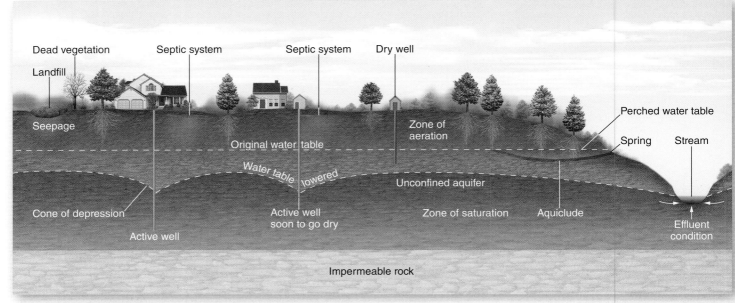

FIGURE 9.15 Groundwater characteristics.
Subsurface groundwater characteristics, processes, water flows, and human interactions. Follow the concepts across the illustration from left to right as you read along in the text.

Why Is There a
Water Table?

the top of the well is lower than the potentiometric surface. (These wells are called *artesian*, for the Artois area in France where they are common.) In other wells, however, pressure may be inadequate, and the artesian water must be pumped the remaining distance to the surface.

Wells, Springs, and Streamflows Water wells can work only if they penetrate the water table. Too shallow a well will be a "dry well"; too deep a well will punch through the aquifer and into the impermeable layer below, also yielding little water. This is why water wells should be drilled in consultation with a *hydrogeologist*.

Where the water table intersects the surface, it creates springs (Figure 9.16). Such an intersection also occurs in lakes and riverbeds. Ultimately, groundwater may enter stream channels to flow as surface water (stream near centre in Figure 9.15). In fact, during dry periods, the water table may sustain river flows.

Figure 9.17 illustrates the relation between the water table and surface streams in two different climatic settings. In humid climates, where the water table generally supplies a continuous base flow to a stream and is higher than the stream channel, the stream is *effluent* because it receives the water flowing out (effluent) from the surrounding ground. The Mississippi River and countless other streams are examples. In drier climates, with lower water tables, water from *influent* streams flows into the adjacent ground, sustaining vegetation along the stream. The Colorado River and the Rio Grande of the American West are examples of influent streams.

The Arkansas River no longer flows across western and central Kansas. As you see in Focus Study 9.2, "High Plains Aquifer Overdraft," groundwater mining is prevalent throughout this region. When the bottom of

the stream bed is no longer in contact with the declining water table, streamflow seeps into the aquifer. These influent conditions produce dry river, stream, and creek beds across the region.

FIGURE 9.16 An active spring.
Springs provide evidence of groundwater emerging at the surface. [Robert Christopherson.]

Forming a Cone
of Depression

Overuse of Groundwater

As water is pumped from a well, the surrounding water table within an unconfined aquifer may experience **drawdown**, or become lowered. Drawdown occurs if the pumping rate exceeds the replenishment flow of water into the aquifer or the horizontal flow around the well. The resultant lowering of the water table around the well is a **cone of depression** (see Figure 9.15, left).

Overpumping Aquifers frequently are pumped beyond their flow and recharge capacities, a condition known as **groundwater mining**. A major area of overuse of groundwater in Canada is the Regional Municipality of Waterloo in Ontario—the largest urban groundwater municipality in Canada. Here, nearly a half a million people rely on groundwater for municipal supplies. The depletion of

groundwater aquifers has led to extensive conservation efforts and exploration of other water sources.

In the United States today, large tracts experience chronic groundwater overdrafts in the Midwest, West, lower Mississippi Valley, Florida, and the intensely farmed Palouse region of eastern Washington State. In many places, the water table or artesian water level has declined more than 12 m. In the United States, groundwater mining is of special concern in the great High Plains aquifer (see Figure 9.14 for its location), which has declined over 30 m in some areas.

About half of India's irrigated water and half of industrial and urban water needs are met by the groundwater reserve. In rural areas, groundwater supplies 80% of domestic water from some 3 million hand-pumped bore holes. And in approximately 20% of India's agricultural districts, groundwater

[text continued on page 252.]

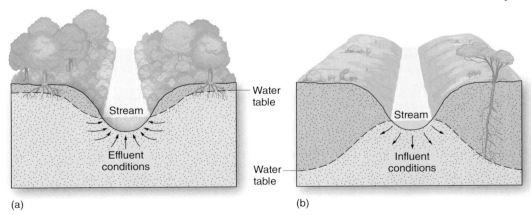

(a)   (b)

FIGURE 9.17 Groundwater interaction with streamflow.
(a) Effluent stream base flow is partially supplied by a high water table, characteristic of humid regions.
(b) Influent stream supplies a lower water table, characteristic of drier regions. The water table may drop below the stream channel, effectively drying it out.

FOCUS STUDY 9.1

High Plains Aquifer Overdraft

North America's largest known aquifer is the High Plains aquifer. It lies beneath the American High Plains, an eight-state, 450 600-km² area from southern South Dakota to Texas (Figure 9.1.1). Annual precipitation over the region varies from 30 cm in the southwest to 60 cm in the northeast.

For several hundred thousand years, the aquifer's sand and gravel were charged with meltwaters from retreating glaciers. However, heavy mining of High

FIGURE 9.1.1 High Plains aquifer.
(a) Average saturated thickness. (b) Water level changes, using 1950 to represent "predevelopment." The colour scale in the legend indicates widespread declines and a few areas of water-level rise. [Maps: (a) After D. E. Kromm and S. E. White, "Interstate groundwater management preference differences: The High Plains region," *Journal of Geography* 86, no. 1 (January–February 1987): 5. (b) Adapted from "Water-Level Changes in the High Plains Aquifer, Predevelopment to 2002, 1980 to 2002, and 2001 to 2002," by V. L. McGuire, USGS Fact Sheet 2004–3026, Fig. 1.]

Plains groundwater began 100 years ago, intensifying after World War II with the introduction of centre-pivot irrigation (Figure 9.1.2). These large, circular devices provide vital water to wheat, sorghums, cotton, corn, and about 40% of the grain fed to cattle in the United States. The USGS began monitoring this groundwater mining from more than 7000 wells in 1988.

A 2004 USGS map of the water-level changes from predevelopment (about 1950) to 2002 appears in Figure 9.1.1.b. Wells were measured in the winter or early spring when water levels were recovered from the previous irrigation season. Declining water levels are most severe in northern Texas, where the saturated thickness of the aquifer is least, through the Oklahoma panhandle and into western Kansas. Rising water levels are noted in portions of south-central Nebraska and a portion of Texas due to recharge from surface irrigation, a period of above-normal precipitation years, and downward percolation from canals and reservoirs. (See http://co.water.usgs.gov/nawqa/hpgw/HPGW_home.html.)

The High Plains aquifer irrigates about one-fifth of all U.S. cropland: 120,000 wells provide water for 5.7 million hectares. This is down from the peak of 170,000 wells in 1978. In 1980, water was pumped from the aquifer at the rate of 26 billion m^3 a year, an increase of more than 300% since 1950. By the turn of this century, withdrawals had decreased 10% due to declining well yields and increasing pumping costs.

During the past five decades, the water table in the aquifer dropped more than 30 m, and throughout the 1980s, it averaged a 2-m drop each year. The USGS estimates that recovery of the High Plains aquifer (those portions that have not collapsed) would take at least 1000 years if groundwater mining stopped today!

Obviously, billions of dollars of agricultural activity cannot be abruptly halted, but neither can profligate water mining continue. This issue raises tough questions: How do we best manage cropland? Can extensive irrigation continue? Can the region continue to meet the demand to produce commodities for export? Should we continue high-volume farming of certain crops that are in chronic oversupply? Should we rethink federal policy on crop subsidies and price supports? What changes will biofuels production force? What would be the impact on farmers and rural communities of any changes to the existing system?

Present irrigation practices, if continued, will deplete about half of the High Plains aquifer resource (and two-thirds of the Texas portion) by 2020. Add to this the approximate 10% loss of soil moisture due to increased evapotranspiration demand caused by climatic warming for this region by 2050, as forecast by computer models, and we have a portrait of a major regional water problem and a challenge for society.

FIGURE 9.1.2 Center-pivot irrigation.
Myriad centre-pivot irrigation systems water crops in the western Great Plains. A growing season for corn requires from 10 to 20 revolutions of the sprinkler arm, depending on the weather. The arm delivers about 3 cm of water per revolution (rainfall equivalent). [Bobbé Christopherson]

mining through more than 17 million wells (motorized dug wells and tube wells) is beyond recharge rates.

In the Middle East, conditions are even more severe. The groundwater resource beneath Saudi Arabia accumulated over tens of thousands of years, forming "fossil aquifers," but the increasing withdrawals are not being naturally recharged due to the desert climate—in essence, groundwater has become a *nonrenewable* resource. Some researchers suggest that groundwater in the region will be depleted in a decade, although worsening water-quality problems will no doubt arise before this. Imagine having the hottest economic issue in the Middle East become water, not oil!

> Like any renewable resource, groundwater can be tapped indefinitely as long as the rate of extraction does not exceed the rate of replenishment. But just like a bank account, a groundwater reserve will dwindle if withdrawals exceed deposits. Few governments have established and enforced rules and regulations to insure that groundwater sources are exploited at a sustainable rate…. No government has yet adequately tackled the issue of groundwater depletion, but it is at least getting more attention.[4]

Collapsing Aquifers A possible effect of water removal from an aquifer is that the aquifer, which is a layer of rock or sediment, will lose its internal support. Water in the pore spaces between rock grains is not compressible, so it adds structural strength to the rock. If the water is removed through overpumping, air infiltrates the pores. Air is readily compressible, and the tremendous weight of overlying rock may crush the aquifer. On the surface, the visible result may be land subsidence, cracked house foundations, and changes in drainage.

Houston, Texas, provides an example. The removal of groundwater and crude oil caused land within an 80-km radius of Houston to subside more than 3 m over the years. Yet another example is the Fresno area of California's San Joaquin Valley. After years of intensive pumping of groundwater for irrigation, land levels have dropped almost 10 m because of a combination of water removal and soil compaction from agricultural activity.

Surface mining ("strip mining") for coal in eastern Texas, northeastern Louisiana, Wyoming, Arizona, and other

[4] L. Brown et al. and the Worldwatch Institute, *Vital Signs: The Environmental Trends That Are Shaping Our Future* (New York: W. W. Norton & Co., 2000), pp. 122, 123.

locales also destroys aquifers. Aquifer collapse is an increasing problem in West Virginia, Kentucky, and Virginia, where low-sulfur coal is mined to meet current air-pollution requirements for coal-burning electric power plants.

Unfortunately, collapsed aquifers may not be rechargeable, even if surplus gravitational water becomes available, because pore spaces may be permanently collapsed. The water-well fields that serve the Tampa Bay–St. Petersburg, Florida, area are a case in point. Pond and lake levels, swamps, and wetlands in the area are declining and land surfaces subsiding as the groundwater drawdown for export to the cities increases.

An additional problem arises when aquifers are overpumped near the ocean or coastal areas. Along a coastline, fresh groundwater and salty seawater establish a natural interface, or *contact surface*, with the less-dense freshwater flowing on top. But excessive withdrawal of freshwater can cause this interface to migrate inland. As a result, wells near the shore may become contaminated with saltwater, and the aquifer may become useless as a freshwater source. Figure 9.15 illustrates this seawater intrusion (far-right side). Pumping freshwater back into the aquifer may halt contamination by seawater, but once contaminated, the aquifer is difficult to reclaim.

Pollution of Groundwater

When surface water is polluted, groundwater inevitably becomes contaminated because it is recharged from surface-water supplies. Surface water flows rapidly and flushes pollution downstream, but slow-moving groundwater, once contaminated, remains polluted virtually forever.

Pollution can enter groundwater from many sources: industrial injection wells (wastes pumped into the ground), septic tank outflows, seepage from hazardous-waste disposal sites, industrial toxic waste, agricultural residues (pesticides, herbicides, fertilizers), and urban solid-waste landfills. Groundwater pollution from agricultural practices is the topic of Focus Study 9.2.

For management purposes, about 35% of pollution is *point source*, such as a gasoline tank or septic tank; 65% is *nonpoint source*, coming from a broad area, such as an agricultural field or urban runoff. Nitrates contaminate nearly all the groundwater that underlies agricultural land in Canada. The levels are below the guidelines for Canadian drinking water quality but, while historical data suggest that nitrate levels have not changed in the last 50 years, the incidence of bacteria in well water has almost doubled in

GEO REPORT 9.2   *Water Pipelines in the Middle East*

One water pipeline proposal brings water overland from Turkey to the Middle East through two branches. The Gulf water line would run southeast through Jordan and Saudi Arabia, with extensions into Kuwait, Abu Dhabi, and Oman. The other branch would run south through Syria, Jordan, and Saudi Arabia to the cities of Makkah (Mecca) and Jeddah. This pipeline would cover some 1500 km, the distance from Montreal to Moncton, New Brunswick. (See the links listed in Middle East Water Information Network at http://www.columbia.edu/cu/lweb/indiv/mideast/cuvlm/water.html.)

Walkerton, Ontario: Groundwater Contamination, Water System Mismanagement, and Tragedy

In May 2000, the town of Walkerton, Ontario (Figure 9.2.1), was the site of water resources mismanagement that ultimately led to the illnesses of 2300 residents and the deaths of seven people. A period of heavy precipitation in early May resulted in local flooding, which had a tragic impact on the drinking water supply.

The town of Walkerton is among many in a part of Ontario that relies heavily on groundwater. The town has six wells that supply its municipal water needs. During the May 2000 precipitation event, Well 5, an extremely shallow well, directly connected to surface water, became contaminated. Contamination may have entered the well via overland flow but is more likely to have been transported through boreholes (fence posts) and fractures in the bedrock. The groundwater contamination probably occurred after water percolated rapidly through the thin soil that was spread with animal waste from feedlots. Rapid

percolation is enhanced by the drawdown around the well when water is pumped.

A secondary source of contamination was from Well 7. This artesian well had an overflow device, allowing excess water to run out when the well was not operating. During periods of heavy precipitation, as in May 2000, the excess water flows out of the wellhead and floods surrounding depression areas. When Well 7 was turned on, the small plastic flap valve was not able to prevent water from flowing down the pipe into the well. In Figure 9.15 you can see how the surface water, seepage from pollution sources, and groundwater wells are interrelated.

On May 19, 2000, several people contacted the regional Medical Health Office (MHO) to relate symptoms including bloody diarrhea, vomiting, cramps, and fever. The MHO began to investigate a possible source of bacterial contamination—beginning with the

water system. The Public Utilities Commission (PUC) that managed the water system assured the MHO that the water was safe and that wells were routinely sampled.

As the MHO continued the investigation, more people became ill. Again, the PUC reassured officials that the water was safe. Regardless, the MHO issued a boil water advisory, took its own water sample, and found that the local drinking water was contaminated with *Escherichia coli*, more commonly known as E. coli. The bacteria had been washed into wells and seeped into the groundwater in the area. A judicial inquiry was called to investigate the event.

The results of the inquiry summarized that seven people died and more than 2300 became ill. Many of those who became ill, especially children, will have lasting effects as a result of the E. coli contamination. The bacteria entered Municipal Well 5 on or about May 12, 2000, when heavy precipitation and local flooding resulted in runoff from fields spread with uncomposted manure. During the precipitation event, the well was not continuously monitored and chlorine levels were not measured. The results of the inquiry determined that the PUC had mismanaged the water system for years. Government budget cutbacks for water monitoring and minimising water management standards compounded the problem.

Judicial inquiry recommendations included planning and standards for drinking water quality, the management of runoff and other contaminant pathways, increases in monitoring and licencing of water managers, and establishment of electronic access to drinking water information. As of 2011, much remains to be done to insure safety in public water supply infrastructure. See the drinking water portal website for updates on drinking water safety in Ontario (http://www.ontario.ca/ONT/portal61/drinkingwater/General?docId=STEL01_047769&breadcrumbLevel=1&lang=en).

FIGURE 9.2.1 Walkerton, Ontario.
Walkerton is typical of the small towns in southern Ontario that rely on groundwater for freshwater supply. [Map created by Pam Schaus.]

the same time period. The 1996 State of Canada's Environment Report noted that, in some areas, nitrate levels were more than four times greater than the Canadian drinking water guidelines. The Canadian Environmental Sustainability Indicators website reports that there has been no change at monitoring sites in nitrate levels for 60% of the sites between 1990 and 2006 (http://www.ec.gc.ca/indicateurs-indicators/default.asp?lang=En&n=2102636F-1).

Regardless of the spatial nature of the source, pollution can spread over a great distance, as illustrated in Figure 9.15. Since the nature of aquifers makes them inaccessible, the extent of groundwater pollution is underestimated.

In the face of government inaction, and even attempts to reverse some protection laws, serious groundwater contamination continues throughout North America, adding validity to a quote from more than 25 years ago:

> One characteristic is the practical irreversibility of groundwater pollution, causing the cost of clean-up to be prohibitively high.... It is a questionable ethical practice to impose the potential risks associated with groundwater contamination on future generations when steps can be taken today to prevent further contamination.[5]

Our Water Supply

Human thirst for adequate water supplies, both in quantity and quality, will be a major issue in this century. Internationally, increases in per capita water use are double the rate of population growth. Since we are so dependent on water, it seems that humans should cluster where good water is plentiful. But accessible water supplies are not well correlated with population distribution or the regions where population growth is greatest.

Table 9.2 provides statistics that, taken together, indicate the unevenness of Earth's water supply. These data include population, land area, annual streamflow, and projected population change for six world regions. Also note 2006 data on carbon dioxide emissions per person for each region. Earth's water supply is tied, first, to climatic variability and, second, to water demand, which is,

[5] J. Tripp, "Groundwater protection strategies," in *Groundwater Pollution: Environmental and Legal Problems* (Washington, DC: American Association for the Advancement of Science, 1984), p. 137. Reprinted by permission.

in turn, tied to level of development, affluence, and per capita consumption.

For example, North America's mean annual discharge is 5960 km³ and Asia's is 13 200 km³. However, North America has only 6.7% of the world's population, whereas Asia has 60%, with a population-doubling time less than half of North America's. In northern China, 550 million people living in approximately 500 cities lack adequate water supplies. For comparison, note that the 1990 floods cost China $10 billion, whereas water shortages cost the Chinese economy more than $35 billion a year in costs to the Chinese economy. An analyst for the World Bank stated that China's water shortages pose a more serious threat than floods during this century, yet in news coverage, we hear only about floods.

CRITICAL THINKING 9.2
Water on Your Campus
How much do you know about the water on your campus? If the campus has its own wells, how is the quality tested? Who on campus is in charge of supervising these wells? Lastly, what is your subjective assessment of the water you use: taste, smell, hardness, clarity? Write a brief critique following a taste test. Compare these perceptions with others in your class.

In Africa, 56 countries draw from a varied water-resource base; these countries share more than 50 river and lake watersheds. Increasing population growth and a rising percentage of urban dwellers cause water demands to rise and lead to an overexploitation of the resource. Twelve African countries experience water stress (less than 1700 m³ per person per year) and 14 have water scarcity (less than 1000 m³ per person per year).

Water resources differ from other resources in that there is no alternative substance to water. Water-resource stress related to quantity and/or quality shortfalls will dominate future political agendas. Water shortages increase the probability for international conflict, endanger public health, reduce agricultural productivity, and damage life-supporting ecological systems. For the twenty-first century a transition to a new approach is required, away from large, centralized structures toward decentralized, community-based strategies, focused on demand management and efficient technologies.

Water Supply in Canada

The Canadian water supply derives from surface and groundwater sources. The supply of freshwater and some of

GEO REPORT 9.3 *The Water It Takes for Food and Necessities*

Simply providing the variety of food we enjoy requires voluminous water. For example, 77 g of broccoli requires 42 L of water to grow and process; producing 250 ml of milk requires 182 L of water; producing 28 g of cheese requires 212 L; producing 1 egg requires 238 L; and producing a 113 g beef patty requires 2314 L. And then there are the toilets, the majority of which still flush approximately 16 L of water. Imagine the spatial complexity of servicing the desert city of Las Vegas, with toilets flushing in 150 000 hotel rooms each day; of providing all support services for 38 million visitors per year, plus 38 golf courses. One hotel confirms that it washes 14 000 pillowcases a day.

TABLE 9.2 Regional Comparison of Factors Influencing Global Water Supply

Region	2010 Population (in millions)	Share of Global Population	Land Area in Thousands of km²	Share of Global Land Area	Mean Annual Streamflow km³/yr	Share of Annual Streamflow	2050 population as a multiple of 2010	Metric Tons of CO_2 Emissions per Person (2006)
Africa	1030	15%	30 600	23%	4220	11%	2.0	0.9
Asia	4157	60%	44 600	33%	13 200	34%	1.3	3.0
Australia–Oceania	37	0.5%	8 420	6%	1960	5%	1.6	19.0 (Australia) 8.9 (New Zealand)
Europe	739	10.8%	9 770	7%	3150	8%	1.0	8.4
North America[a]	455	6.7%	22 100	16%	5960	15%	1.4	18.4 (U.S. and Canada) 4.0 (Mexico)
Central and South America	474	7%	17 800	13%	10 400	27%	1.3	3.1
Global (excluding Antarctica)	6892		134 000		38 900		1.4	More developed: 11.5 Less developed: 2.4

[a]Includes Canada, Mexico, and the United States.
Note: Population data from *2010 World Population Data Sheet* (Washington, DC: Population Reference Bureau, 2010). Population change forecast is at present growth rates. Numbers are rounded. Metric tons × 1.1 for short (U.S.) tons.

the threats to it are outlined on the National Water Research Institute's website (http://www.ec.gc.ca/inre-nwri/default.asp?lang=En&n=0CD66675-1&offset=10&toc=show). Canada has about 9% of Earth's renewable water distributed over 7% of Earth's landmass. Water is accessed through rivers, lakes, ponds and reservoirs, groundwater aquifers, the snowpack, glaciers, ice fields, and the liquid and solid precipitation that replenishes all other sources. Measurements of precipitation recorded across the country are difficult to aggregate because the hydrology of the landmass varies so greatly.

Figure 9.18 is a map of the streamflow in Canada found on the National Atlas Web site (http://atlas.gc.ca/site/english/maps/archives/5thedition/environment/water/mcr4178). Insets portray the distribution of low flows, peak flows, and runoff. Peak flows occur earlier in the year to the south and are later to the north. Often, this results in spring flooding caused by ice jams as the northern mouths of rivers are still frozen when the southern headwaters have melted. The map depicts volumes of flow in major streams and the width of the

red colouration represents the volume of flow in cubic metres per second ($m \cdot s^{-1}$). This surface runoff (runoff plus streamflow), which varies between 75 000 $m \cdot s^{-1}$ in low flow times to over 134 500 $m \cdot s^{-1}$ in high flow times, is available for use.

The seeming abundance of water is misleading when you consider that about 60% of Canada's freshwater drains to the north, while about 85% of the population lives within 300 km of our southern border. In other words, much of our water is not available in the heavily populated areas where it is most needed.

The difference between supply and demand is growing with increasing urbanisation. All sources of freshwater are now under pressure from the growing, and often conflicting, demands for domestic water supplies for municipalities, for agriculture and industry, and for maintaining adequate streamflow in rivers that support aquatic ecosystems. There is also the added stress from the uncertain, but predicted, effects of climate change. Despite these growing stresses, many Canadians assume that governments will protect and sustain the freshwater supply.

GEO REPORT 9.4 *Metering Personal Water Use in Canada*

Canadians are second only to the United States as the highest per capita users of water in the world. Water use for municipal supply stresses surface reservoirs and groundwater aquifers. Treating and distributing water uses energy and has a heavy economic cost. After use, the released water is usually poorer in quality, diminishing the condition of the downstream supply.

The direct costs of supplying water are often unnoticed by the average user. In a 1999 national water survey, unmetered households used 433 litres of water per person per day. In metered households where water was paid for by the volume used, the daily residential water use was 288 litres per person per day. Water meters are clearly an effective conservation mechanism, saving the consumer money on water bills and future outlays for more water-supply infrastructure.

FIGURE 9.18 Streamflows n Canada.
The greatest volume of streamflow in Canada exits northward through the Mackenzie River. This streamflow represents the surface runoff from that drainage basin. Next in volume is the flow to the Atlantic from the Great Lakes through the St. Lawrence River. The hydrographs show the effects of seasonality on the timing of the melt. [Map and data used with permission of Natural Resources Canada.]

Instream, Nonconsumptive, and Consumptive Uses

Surface runoff available for use can be classified according to the type of use:

- *Instream* uses are those that use stream water in the channel, without removing it: Examples include navigation, wildlife and ecosystem preservation, waste dilution and removal, hydroelectric power production, fishing resources, and recreation.
- *Nonconsumptive uses*, sometimes called **withdrawal** or *offstream use*, remove water from the supply, use it, and then return it to the same supply. Nonconsumptive water is used by industry, agriculture, municipalities, and in steam–driven electric power generation. A portion of water withdrawn is consumed.
- **Consumptive uses** remove water from a stream but do not return it, so it is not available for a second or third use. Some consumptive examples include water that evaporates or is vaporized in steam-electric plants.

When water returns to the system, water quality usually is altered—water is contaminated chemically with pollutants, or waste, or thermally with heat energy. This portion of the budget is returned to runoff and eventually the ocean. This wastewater represents an opportunity to extend the resource through reuse.

Contaminated or not, returned water becomes a part of all water systems downstream. Canada uses only 9% of its withdrawn water for agriculture and 80% for industry. Figure 9.19 compares regions by their use of withdrawn water during 1998, graphically illustrating the differences between more-developed and less-developed parts of the world.

CRITICAL THINKING 9.3

That Next Glass of Water

You may have had no doubt had several glasses of water between when you awoke this morning and the time you are reading these words. Where did this water originate? Obtain the name of the water company or agency, determine whether it is using surface or groundwater to meet demands, and check how the water use is metered and billed. If your province requires water-quality reporting, obtain a copy from the water supplier of this analysis of your tap water.

Desalination

Desalination of seawater to augment diminishing groundwater supplies is becoming increasingly important as a freshwater source. More than 12,000 desalination plants are now in operation worldwide, and plant construction is expected to increase 140% between 2009 and 2017, amounting to some $60 billion in investments. Approximately 50% of all desalination plants are in the Middle East. Desalination is an alternative to further groundwater mining and saltwater intrusion under Saudi Arabia; in fact, 30 desalination plants currently supply 70% of the country's drinking water needs (Figure 9.20a). In the United States, along the coast of southern California and in Florida, desalination is slowly increasing in use.

The Tampa–St. Petersburg area in Florida took a giant step forward with the opening of its own Tampa Bay desalination plant, which produces 95 million litres per day, about 10% of the region's drinking water supply, making it the largest in the United States. This output is about 12% of the production at the Jabal plant in Saudi Arabia. The seawater intake is from the Big Bend Power Station's cooling

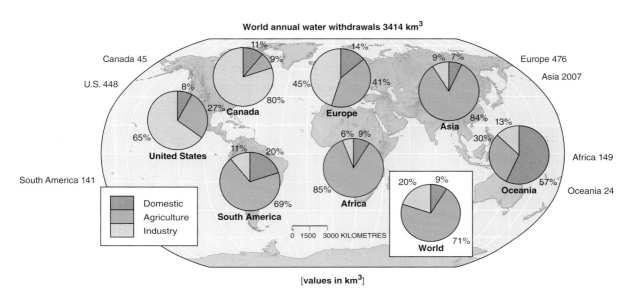

FIGURE 9.19 Water withdrawal by sector.
World annual water withdrawal estimated total is 3414 km³. Compare industrial water use among the geographic areas, as well as agricultural and municipal uses. [After World Resources Institute. *World Resources 2000-2001*, Data Table FW.1, pp. 276-77.]

The international aspect of the water-resource problem is illustrated by the 200 major river drainage basins in the world. One hundred and forty-five countries possess territory within an international river drainage basin—truly a global commons.

Working Group II, *Climate Change Impacts, Adaptation, and Vulnerability*—part of the Intergovernmental Panel on Climate Change's *Fourth Assessment Report* (2007), concluded that global climate change and greenhouse warming will cause added water problems:

> By mid-century, annual average river runoff and water availability are projected to increase 10–40% at high latitudes and in some wet tropical areas, and decrease by 10–30% over some dry regions at mid-latitudes and in the dry tropics, some of which are presently water-stressed areas.... Drought-affected areas will likely increase in extent.... In the course of the century, water supplies stored in glaciers and snow cover are projected to decline, reducing water availability in regions supplied by meltwater from major mountain ranges, where more than one-sixth of the world population currently lives.

Clearly, cooperation is needed, yet we continue toward a water crisis without a concept of a *world water economy* as a frame of reference. The geopolitical question is: When will more international coordination begin, and which country or group of countries will lead the way to sustain future water resources? The water balance approach detailed in this chapter is a place to start.

(a) Saudi Arabia

(b) Tampa Bay Florida

FIGURE 9.20 Water desalination.
(a) Freshwater is supplied to Saudi Arabia from the Jabal water desalination plant along the Red Sea. (b) The Tampa Bay desalination plant provides 95 million litres per day to the region's water resources through filtration and reverse osmosis processes.
[(a) Liaison Agency. (b) Tampa Bay Water.]

GEOSYSTEMS CONNECTION

In this chapter, we looked at water resources through a water balance approach. Such a systems view, considering both water supply and water demand, is the best method to understand the water resource. The ongoing drought in the western United States brings the need for such a water balance strategy to the forefront. With water resources as the ultimate output of the water–weather system, we now shift our attention to climate. The examination of world climates in Chapter 10 completes our journey from Chapter 2, which began with solar energy flowing through the atmosphere to Earth's surface, then moved to the outputs of temperature and wind and ocean circulation, and finally shifted to water and weather. The synthesis in the next chapter will bring us to the end of Part II.

water discharge. The Tampa Bay plant produces drinking water through a series of filters to remove algae and particles and a reverse-osmosis process where the water is forced through semipermeable membranes (Figure 9.20b).

In Sydney, Australia, a reverse-osmosis desalination plant opened in 2010. The $17 billion Kurnell plant supplies about 15% of the region's water needs. Some 67 wind turbines are required to supply the energy demands for the operation.

Future Considerations

When precipitation is budgeted, the limits of the water resource become apparent. How can we satisfy the growing demand for water? Water availability per person declines as population increases, and individual demand increases with economic development, affluence, and technology. Thus, world population growth since 1970 reduced per capita water supplies by one-third. Also, pollution limits the water-resource base, so that even before *quantity* constraints are felt, *quality* problems may limit the health and growth of a region.

APPLIED PHYSICAL GEOGRAPHY   *A Thornthwaite Water Balance Problem*

Table 1 presents, in random order, data (in mm) in rows for potential evapotranspiration (PE), precipitation (P), soil moisture storage (ST), actual evapotranspiration (AE), water deficit (D), and water surplus (S) for a Northern Hemisphere station. Determine which of these variables each row represents and explain your reasoning.

A moisture deficit commonly occurs in conjunction with a decrease in precipitation, and there are only two rows that show a decrease in values. Row #1 has nonzero values in all months and shows a decrease that begins the month before the deficit appears. This decrease continues across the summer months and then increases into the fall

the demand that the atmosphere makes on the available water supply. Remember also that if P > PE, then AE = PE, and that D occurs when P < PE. Therefore, we can say that D = PE−AE. An examination shows that the two remaining rows have equal values from January to April and from October to December. But

TABLE 1   Weather Station Data

	J	F	M	A	M	J	J	A	S	O	N	D	TOTAL
Row #1	147	117	94	61	48	45	30	37	61	122	141	165	1068
Row #2	8	15	30	48	72	89	85	71	64	45	23	11	561
Row #3	139	102	64	13	0	0	0	0	0	0	35	154	507
Row #4	300	300	300	300	276	232	177	143	140	217	300	300	—
Row #5	0	0	0	0	2	6	24	29	5	0	0	0	66
Row #6	8	15	30	48	74	95	109	100	69	45	23	11	627

To solve this problem, we apply the Thornthwaite water balance described earlier in this chapter. To identify the rows, follow a logical sequence of reasoning. To begin, although soil-moisture storage and field capacity can vary depending on soil type and the crop planted, we set it at 300 mm for this example. Therefore, Row #4 is ST because the number 300 does not change from January to April. It decreases from May to September and then increases through October to become fully recharged in November.

Now consider Row #5, immediately below the row identified as storage. When storage falls below 300 mm, water is being utilized. Water is removed from storage only when precipitation alone is unable to meet demand. Because of the decrease in storage from soil-moisture utilization and the increase in values in Row #5, this row is D—the unmet demand. Note soil-moisture recharge begins in October and continues into November when field capacity is restored.

when the deficit ends. Row #3 also shows a similar pattern, but it has values of zero for some of the year. We can therefore conclude that Row #1 is P and Row #3 is S.

This leaves two rows, #2 and #6, to be labelled. These two rows contain values that are remarkably similar. They represent AE and PE. But which one is which? Remember, potential evapotranspiration is the amount of evapotranspiration (evaporation + transpiration) that would occur if an unlimited water supply were available. It represents

when the deficit occurs in the summer months, Row #2 is less than Row #6. So Row #6 is PE and Row #2 is AE.

A graph of P, PE, and AE can be used to determine the type of climate depicted (Figure 1). Here we see that the precipitation is greatest during winter months. Both PE and AE increase in summer and both decrease in winter. We describe climate types in the next chapter. You will see that this graph is typical of a Marine West Coast climate, with all months averaging above freezing, a cool summer, and abundant precipitation.

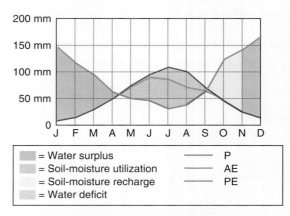

FIGURE 1 Sample water balance graph.

KEY LEARNING CONCEPTS REVIEW

■ *Illustrate* the hydrologic cycle with a simple sketch, and *label* it with definitions for each water pathway.

The **hydrologic cycle** is a model of Earth's water system, which has operated for billions of years from the lower atmosphere to several kilometres beneath Earth's surface. **Interception** occurs when precipitation strikes vegetation or other ground cover. Water soaks into the subsurface through **infiltration**, or penetration of the soil surface. It further permeates soil or rock through vertical movement called **percolation**.

> hydrologic cycle (p. 234)
> interception (p. 235)
> infiltration (p. 235)
> percolation (p. 235)

1. Sketch and explain a simplified model of the complex flows of water on Earth—the hydrologic cycle.
2. What are the possible routes that a raindrop may take on its way to through the soil surface?
3. Compare precipitation and evaporation volumes from the ocean with those over land. Describe advection flows of moisture and countering surface and subsurface runoff.

■ *Relate* the importance of the water balance concept to your understanding of the hydrologic cycle, water resources, and soil moisture for a specific location.

A **soil-water budget** can be established for any area of Earth's surface by measuring the precipitation input and the output of various water demands in the area considered. Understanding both the supply of the water resource and the natural demands on the resource is essential to sustainable human interaction with the hydrologic cycle. Water resources represent the ultimate output of Earth's water system. Rivers and streams represent only a tiny fraction of all water (1250 km³), the smallest volume of any of the freshwater categories. Yet rivers and streams supply four-fifths of all the water we use. Groundwater is the largest potential freshwater source in the hydrologic cycle and is tied to surface supplies.

> soil-water budget (p. 236)

4. How might an understanding of the hydrologic cycle in a particular locale, or a soil-moisture budget, of a site assist you in assessing water resources? Give some specific examples.

■ *Construct* the water balance equation as a way of accounting for the expenditures of water supply, and *define* each of the components in the equation and its specific operation.

The moisture supply to Earth's surface is **precipitation (P)**, arriving most often as rain, freezing precipitation, snow, and hail. Precipitation is measured with a **rain gauge**. **Evaporation** is the net movement of free water molecules away from a wet surface into air. **Transpiration** is the movement of water through plants and back into the atmosphere; it is a cooling mechanism for plants. Evaporation and transpiration are combined into one term—**evapotranspiration**. The ultimate demand for moisture is **potential evapotranspiration (PE)**, the amount of water that *would* evaporate and transpire under optimum moisture conditions (adequate precipitation and adequate soil moisture). Evapotranspiration is measured with an **evaporation pan** (*evaporimeter*) or the more elaborate **lysimeter**.

Unsatisfied PE is **deficit (D)**. By subtracting D from PE, we determine **actual evapotranspiration**, or AE. Ideally, PE and AE are about the same, so that plants have sufficient water. If PE is satisfied and the soil is full of moisture, then additional water input becomes **surplus** (S), which may puddle on the surface, flow across the surface toward stream channels, or percolate underground through the soil. The **overland flow** to streams includes precipitation and groundwater flows into river channels to make up the **total runoff** from the area.

A "savings account" of water that receives deposits and provides withdrawals as water balance conditions change is the **soil-moisture storage (ST)**. This is the volume of water stored in the soil that is normally accessible to plant roots. In soil, **hygroscopic water** is inaccessible because it is a molecule-thin layer that is tightly bound to each soil particle by hydrogen bonding. As available water is utilized, soil reaches the **wilting point** (all that remains is unextractable water). **Capillary water** is generally accessible to plant roots because it is held in the soil by surface tension and hydrogen bonding between water and soil. Almost all capillary water that remains in the soil is **available water** in soil-moisture storage. After water drains from the larger pore spaces, the available water remaining for plants is termed **field capacity**, or storage capacity. When soil is saturated after a precipitation event, surplus water in the soil becomes **gravitational water** and percolates to groundwater. As **soil-moisture utilization** removes soil water, the plants work harder to extract the same amount of moisture, whereas **soil-moisture recharge** is the rate at which needed moisture enters the soil.

The texture and the structure of the soil dictate available pore spaces, or **porosity**. The soil's **permeability** is the degree to which water can flow through it. Permeability depends on particle sizes and the shape and packing of soil grains.

Drought does not have a simple water balance definition; rather, it can occur in at least four forms: *meteorological drought, hydrologic drought, agricultural drought,* and/or a *socioeconomic drought.*

> precipitation (P) (p. 236)
> rain gauge (p. 238)
> evaporation (p. 238)
> transpiration (p. 238)
> evapotranspiration (p. 238)
> potential evapotranspiration (PE) (p. 238)
> evaporation pan (p. 238)
> lysimeter (p. 238)
> deficit (D) (p. 241)
> actual evapotranspiration (AE) (p. 241)
> surplus (S) (p. 241)
> overland flow (p. 241)
> total runoff (p. 241)
> soil-moisture storage (ST) (p. 241)
> hygroscopic water (p. 241)
> wilting point (p. 241)
> capillary water (p. 241)
> available water (p. 242)
> field capacity (p. 242)
> gravitational water (p. 242)
> soil-moisture utilization (p. 242)
> soil-moisture recharge (p. 242)
> porosity (p. 242)
> permeability (p. 242)
> drought (p. 242)

5. Explain the meaning of this statement: "The soil-water budget is an assessment of the hydrologic cycle at a specific site."

6. What are the components of the water balance equation? Construct the equation and place each term's definition below its abbreviation in the equation.

7. Explain how to derive actual evapotranspiration (AE) in the water balance equation.

8. What is potential evapotranspiration (PE)? How do we go about estimating this potential rate? What factors did Thornthwaite use to determine this value?

9. Using the annual water balance graph (Figure 9.9, p. 243) for Hamilton, Ontario, work the concepts through the water balance equation as you interpret the relationship of AE to P.

10. Explain the operation of soil-moisture storage, soil-moisture utilization, and soil-moisture recharge. Include discussion of field capacity, capillary water, and wilting point concepts.

11. In the case of silt-loam soil from Figure 9.8, roughly what is the available water capacity? How is this value derived?

12. Describe the four types of drought. Why do you think media coverage of drought seems lacking? If wars in the twenty-first century are accurately predicted to be about water availability in quantity and quality, what action could we take to understand the issues and avoid the conflicts?

■ **Describe** the nature of groundwater, and **define** the elements of the groundwater environment.

Groundwater is a part of the hydrologic cycle, but it lies beneath the surface beyond the soil-moisture root zone. Groundwater does not exist independently because its replenishment is tied to surface surpluses. Excess surface water moves through the **zone of aeration**, where soil and rock are less than saturated. Eventually, the water reaches the **zone of saturation**, where the pores are completely filled with water.

The *permeability* of subsurface rock depends on whether it conducts water readily (higher permeability) or tends to obstruct its flow (lower permeability). Rocks can even be impermeable. An **aquifer** is a rock layer that is permeable to groundwater flow in usable amounts. An **aquiclude** (aquitard) is a body of rock that does not conduct water in usable amounts.

The upper limit of the water that collects in the zone of saturation is the **water table**; it is the contact surface between the zones of saturation and aeration. A **confined aquifer** is bounded above and below by impermeable layers of rock or sediment. An **unconfined aquifer** has a permeable layer on top and an impermeable one beneath. The **aquifer recharge area** extends over an entire unconfined aquifer. Water in a confined aquifer is under the pressure of its own weight, creating a pressure level to which the water can rise on its own, the **potentiometric surface**, which can be above ground level. Groundwater confined under pressure is **artesian water**; it may rise up in wells and even flow out at the surface without pumping, if the head of the well is below the potentiometric surface.

As water is pumped from a well, the surrounding water table within an unconfined aquifer will experience **drawdown**, or become lower, if the rate of pumping exceeds the horizontal flow of water in the aquifer around the well. This excessive pumping causes a **cone of depression**. Aquifers frequently are pumped beyond their flow and recharge capacities, a condition known as **groundwater mining**.

groundwater (p. 246)
zone of aeration (p. 246)
zone of saturation (p. 246)
aquifer (p. 246)
aquiclude (p. 246)
water table (p. 246)
confined aquifer (p. 247)
unconfined aquifer (p. 247)
aquifer recharge area (p. 247)
potentiometric surface (p. 247)
artesian water (p. 247)
drawdown (p. 249)
cone of depression (p. 249)
groundwater mining (p. 249)

13. Are groundwater resources independent of surface supplies, or are the two interrelated? Explain your answer.

14. Make a simple sketch of the subsurface environment, labelling zones of aeration and saturation and the water table in an unconfined aquifer. Then add a confined aquifer to the sketch.

15. At what point does groundwater utilization become groundwater mining? Use the High Plains aquifer example to explain your answer.

16. What is the nature of groundwater pollution? Can contaminated groundwater be cleaned up easily? Explain.

■ **Identify** critical aspects of freshwater supplies for the future, and **cite** specific water-resource issues and potential remedies for any shortfalls.

Nonconsumptive uses, or water **withdrawal** or *offstream use*, remove water from the supply, use it, and then return it to the stream. **Consumptive uses** remove water from a stream but do not return it, so the water is not available for a second or third use. Regional and global water-resource planning, using water balance principles, is essential if Earth's societies are to have enough water of adequate quality. **Desalination** as a water resource involves the removal of organics, debris, and salinity from seawater through distillation or reverse osmosis. This processing yields potable water for domestic uses.

withdrawal (p. 257)
consumptive uses (p. 257)
desalination (p. 257)

17. What is the difference between withdrawal and consumptive use of water resources? Compare these with instream uses.

18. Characterize each of the sectors withdrawing water: irrigation, industry, and municipalities. What are the present usage trends in more-developed and less-developed nations?

19. Briefly assess the status of world water resources. What challenges exist in meeting the future needs of an expanding population and growing economies?

MyGeosciencePlace

Visit **www.mygeoscienceplace.ca** for several figure animations, satellite loops, self-study quizzes, flashcards, interactive glossary, career links, RSS feeds, Pearson eText of *Geosystems*, and much more.

CHAPTER 10

Climate Systems and Climate Change

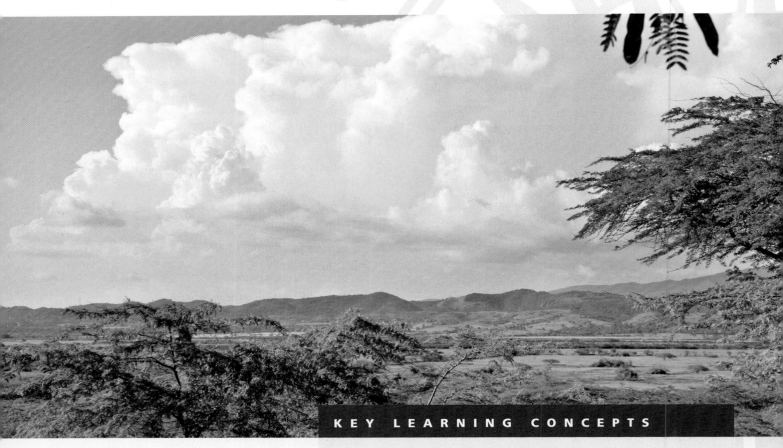

Across southern Puerto Rico in the rain shadow of the Cordillera Central, drier conditions produce tropical savanna climate conditions. The acacia trees in the foreground are suggestive of similar savanna landscapes in Africa and coastal Southeast Asia. The area in the photo receives about 69 cm of rainfall annually, with five months receiving less than 6 cm. [Bobbé Christopherson.]

KEY LEARNING CONCEPTS

After reading the chapter, you should be able to:

- **Define** climate and climatology, and **explain** the difference between climate and weather.
- **Review** how temperature, precipitation, air pressure, and air mass patterns are used to delineate climatic regions.
- **Review** the development of climate classification systems, and **compare** genetic and empirical systems as ways of classifying climates.
- **Describe** the principal climate classification categories other than deserts, and **locate** the corresponding regions on a world map.
- **Explain** the precipitation and moisture efficiency criteria used to determine the desert (arid and semiarid) climates, and **locate** these regions on a world map.
- **Explain** the causes and potential consequences of climate change, and **outline** future climate patterns from forecasts presented.

A Look at Puerto Rico's Climate at a Larger Scale

Examining the small-scale maps in this text, such as the map of world climates in Figure 10.6, you see generalisations of spatial patterns. On a larger-scale map of an island such as Puerto Rico we can see more climatic detail and responses to local elevation and orientation to trade winds. Similarly, on the map of terrestrial biomes in Figure 20.4, all of Puerto Rico is designated as rain forest. A larger-scale map in Figure GN 10.1 shows three biomes— rain forest, seasonal

outstanding natural harbour. The 18th parallel runs along Puerto Rico's south coast, positioning it to receive trade winds from the northeast. The island is nearly rectangular, comprising 9104 km² and stretching 65 km from north to

Forest, administered by the National Park Service. The moisture-intercepting northern and eastern slopes are in contrast to the rain shadow southern slopes and flatlands. Across Puerto Rico, all months average above 18°C, qualifying it as a tropical climate.

On the map, you see the extent of tropical rain forest climates, where precipitation exceeds 6 cm every month. The mountains of the Cordillera Central

San Juan, 150.9 cm

El Yunque National Forest, 508 cm

FIGURE GN 10.1
Climates, representative photos, and rainfall data.
What do you see in the photos that indicates differences in annual rainfall? [All photos by Bobbé Christopherson.]

Pico del Este, 434.5 cm

add an orographic component to the climate, increasing annual precipitation. In the leeward south, we find a tropical monsoon climate where precipitation is less than 6 cm for 3 to

Near Ponce, 69.7 cm

North of Adjuntas, 198.3 cm

forest and scrub, and savanna, as you can see in the photos.

Puerto Rico is centred between the Greater and Lesser Antilles island chains, separating the Atlantic Ocean and the Caribbean Sea, a key location in the history of the entire region. Puerto Rico is within important shipping lanes to the Panama Canal, a situation of historical importance. The capital, San Juan, has an

south and 180 km from east to west. Puerto Rico is an official territory of the United States, sharing the same currency and president but with nonvoting representation in Congress.

The mountains of the Cordillera Central, rising to 1338 m, divide Puerto Rico lengthwise, and the Sierra de Luquillo in the east, rising to 650 m, is home to the tropical rain forest of El Yunque National

5 months during the year. Ponce and the south coast have a tropical savanna climate, where rainfall for 6 months is less than 6 cm, and feature an acacia–savanna landscape, as shown in the chapter-opening photo and in Figure GN 10.1. With this closer look at spatial variations in climate in mind, we shift our perspective to examine climate categories across the globe.

arth experiences an almost infinite variety of *weather*—conditions of the atmosphere at any given time and place. But if we consider the weather over many years, including its variability and extremes, a pattern emerges that constitutes **climate**. Think of climatic patterns as dynamic rather than static, owing to the fact that we are witnessing climate change. Climate is more than a consideration of simple averages of temperature and precipitation.

Today, climatologists know that intriguing global-scale linkages exist in the Earth–atmosphere–ocean system. For instance, strong monsoonal rains in West Africa are correlated with the development of intense Atlantic hurricanes. One year an El Niño event in the Pacific was linked to rains in the American West, floods in Louisiana and Northern Europe, and a weak Atlantic hurricane season. Yet the persistent La Niña events in 2007 and 2010 strengthened drought conditions in the West. The spring wildflower bloom in Death Valley provides visible evidence of the resultant heavy rains during El Niño conditions (Figure 10.1a), as compared to normal desert conditions. The departure from climate norms, such as the El Niño/La Niña phenomenon, is the subject of Focus Study 10.1.

Climatologists, among other scientists, are analysing global climate change—record-breaking global average temperatures, glacial ice melt, drying soil-moisture conditions, changing crop yields, spreading of infectious disease, changing distributions of plants and animals, declining coral reef health and fisheries, and the thawing of high-latitude lands and ice cover. Climatologists are concerned about observed changes occurring in the global climate, as these are at a pace not evidenced in the records of the past millennia. Climate and natural vegetation shifts during the next 50 years could exceed the total of all changes since the peak of the last ice-age episode, some 18 000 years ago.

Geographer Jack Williams and two colleagues summarised the issue:

> By the end of the 21st century, large portions of the Earth's surface may experience climates not found at present, and some 20th-century climates may disappear. . . . Novel climates are projected to develop primarily in the tropics and subtropics. . . . Disappearing climates increase the likelihood of species extinctions and community disruption for species endemic to particular climatic regimes, with the largest impacts projected for poleward and tropical montane regions.[1]

We need to realize that the boundaries delineating climate regions we study in this chapter are not fixed but are on the move as temperature and precipitation relationships alter. The impacts of changing climates on plants and animals is discussed in more detail in *Geosystems Now*, Chapter 19.

In this chapter: Climates are so diverse that no two places on Earth's surface experience exactly the same climatic conditions; in fact, Earth is a vast collection of microclimates. However, broad similarities among local climates permit their grouping into climatic regions.

Many of the physical elements of the environment that we studied in the first nine chapters of this text, link together to explain climate characteristics. Here we survey the patterns of climate using a series of sample cities and towns. *Geosystems* uses a simplified classification system based on physical factors that help uncover the "why" question—why climates are found in certain locations. Though imperfect, this method is easily understood and is based on a widely used classification system

[1] J. W. Williams, S. T. Jackson, and J. E. Kutzbach, "Projected distributions of novel and disappearing climates by 2100 AD," *Proceedings of the National Academy of Sciences* 104 (April 3, 2007): 5739.

(a) 1998, during El Niño

(b) 2002, during La Niña

FIGURE 10.1 El Niño's impact on the desert.
Death Valley, in southeastern California, during spring in (a) full bloom following record rains triggered by El Niño and (b) the same scene in its stark desert grandeur during a La Niña a few years later. This dramatic effect is caused by changes in the distant tropics of the Pacific Ocean described in Focus Study 10.1.
[Bobbé Christopherson.]

devised by climatologist Wladimir Köppen (pronounced KUR-pen). For reference, Appendix C details the Köppen climate classification system and all its criteria.

Climatologists use powerful computer models to simulate changing complex interactions in the atmosphere, hydrosphere, lithosphere, and biosphere. This chapter concludes with a discussion of climate change and its vital implications for society. Climate patterns are changing at an unprecedented rate. Especially significant are changes occurring in the polar regions of the Arctic and Antarctic, and high latitude countries such as Canada.

Earth's Climate System and Its Classification

Climatology, the study of climate and its variability, analyses long-term weather patterns over time and space, and the controls that produce Earth's diverse climatic conditions. One type of climatic analysis locates areas of similar weather statistics and groups them into **climatic regions**. Observed patterns grouped into regions are at the core of climate classification.

The climate in a particular place may be humid with distinct seasons, or dry with consistent warmth, or moist and cool—almost any combination is possible. There are places where it rains more than 20 cm each month, with monthly average temperatures remaining above 27°C year-round. Other places may be without rain for a decade at a time. A climate may have temperatures that average above freezing every month yet still threaten severe frost problems for agriculture. Students reading *Geosystems* in Singapore experience precipitation every month, ranging from 13.1 to 30.6 cm, or 228 cm during an average year, whereas students at university in Karachi, Pakistan, measure only 20.4 cm of rain over an entire year.

Climates greatly influence *ecosystems*, the natural, self-regulating communities formed by plants and animals in their nonliving environment. On land, the basic climatic regions determine to a large extent the location of the world's major ecosystems. These regions, called *biomes*, include forest, grassland, savanna, tundra, and desert. Plant, soil, and animal communities are associated with these biomes. Because climate cycles through periodic change, it is never really stable; therefore, ecosystems should be thought of as being in a constant state of adaptation and response.

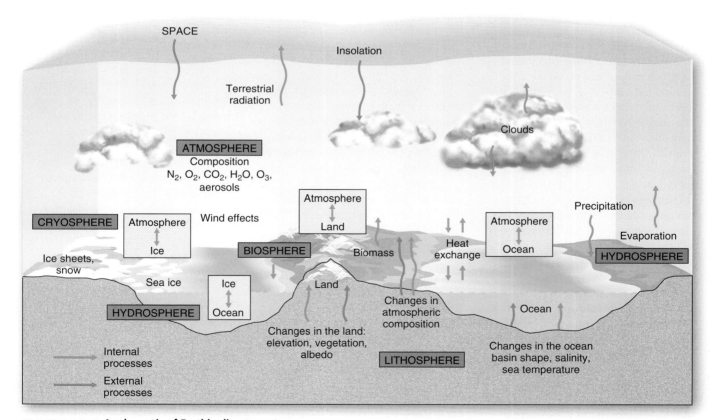

FIGURE 10.2 A schematic of Earth's climate system.
Imagine you are hired to write a computer program that simulates Earth's climates. *Internal processes* that influence climate involve the atmosphere, hydrosphere (streams and oceans), cryosphere (polar ice masses and glaciers, and all frozen water), biosphere, and lithosphere (land)—all energised by insolation. Human activity and other processes external to the climate system affect this climatic balance and force climate change.
[After J. Houghton, *The Global Climate* (Cambridge, England: Cambridge University Press, 1984); and the Global Atmospheric Research Program (coordinated by WMO).]

The El Niño Phenomenon—Global Linkages

Climate is the average behaviour of weather over time, but average weather conditions also include extremes that depart from normal. The El Niño–Southern Oscillation (ENSO) in the Pacific Ocean forces the greatest interannual variability of temperature and precipitation on a global scale. The two strongest ENSO events in 120 years occurred in 1982–1983 and 1997–1998. Peruvians coined the name El Niño ("the boy child") because these episodes seem to occur around the traditional December celebration time of Christ's birth. Actually, El Niños can occur as early as spring and summer and persist through the year.

Revisit Figure 6.20 and see that the northward-flowing Peru Current dominates the region off South America's west coast. These cold waters move toward the equator and join the westward movement of the South Equatorial Current.

The Peru Current is part of the normal counterclockwise circulation of winds and surface ocean currents around the subtropical high-pressure cell dominating the eastern Pacific in the Southern Hemisphere. As a result, a location such as Guayaquil, Ecuador, normally receives 91 cm of precipitation each year under dominant high pressure, whereas islands in the Indonesian archipelago receive more than 254 cm under dominant low pressure. This normal alignment of pressure is shown in Figure 10.1.1a.

What Is ENSO?

Occasionally, for unexplained reasons, pressure patterns and surface ocean temperatures shift from their usual locations. Higher pressure than normal develops over the western Pacific and lower pressure develops over the eastern Pacific. Trade winds, normally moving from east to west, weaken and can be reduced or even replaced by an eastward (west-to-east) flow. The shifting of atmospheric pressure and wind patterns across the Pacific is the

Southern Oscillation. Chapter 6 discussed the Pacific Decadal Oscillation (PDO) and its interrelation with ENSO.

Sea-surface temperatures increase, sometimes more than 8°C above normal in the central and eastern Pacific during an ENSO, replacing the normally cold, upwelling, nutrient-rich water along Peru's coastline. Such ocean-surface warming, the "warm pool," may extend westward as far as the International Date Line. This surface pool of warm water is known as El Niño. Thus, the designation ENSO—El Niño–Southern Oscillation— is derived. This condition is shown in Figure 10.1.1b in illustration and satellite image.

The expected interval for recurrence is 3 to 5 years, but the interval may range from 2 to 12 years. The frequency and intensity of ENSO events increased through the twentieth century, a topic of extensive scientific research looking for a link to global climate change. Recent studies suggest ENSO might be more responsive to global change than previously thought.

The thermocline (boundary of colder, deep-ocean water) lowers in depth in the eastern Pacific Ocean. The change in wind direction and warmer surface water slow the normal upwelling currents that control nutrient availability. This loss of nutrients affects the phytoplankton and food chain, depriving many fish, marine mammals, and predator birds of nourishment.

Scientists at the National Oceanographic and Atmospheric Administration (NOAA) speculate that ENSO events have occurred more than a dozen times since the fourteenth century. The latest El Niño subsided in May 2010, followed by a brief neutral period and then intensification of La Niña conditions in December 2010 and 2011. See the satellite images in Figure 10.1.1 b–j.

La Niña—El Niño's Cousin

When surface waters in the central and eastern Pacific cool to below normal by 0.4°C or more, the condition is dubbed

La Niña, Spanish for "the girl." This is a weaker condition and less consistent than El Niño. There is no correlation in the strength or weakness of each. For instance, following the record 1997–1998 ENSO event, the subsequent La Niña was not as strong as predicted and shared the Pacific with lingering warm water (Figure 10.1.1c, d, h, and j). The satellites that produced the images in Figure 10.1.1 use radar altimeters to accurately measure sea-surface heights, and therefore sea-surface temperatures.

Global Effects Related to ENSO and La Niña

Effects related to ENSO and La Niña occur worldwide: droughts in South Africa, southern India, Australia, and the Philippines; strong hurricanes in the Pacific, including Tahiti and French Polynesia; and flooding in the United States in the southwestern and mountain states, Bolivia, Cuba, Ecuador, and Peru. In India, every drought for more than 400 years seems linked to ENSO events. The Atlantic hurricane season weakens during El Niño years and strengthens during La Niñas.

Precipitation in the southwestern United States is greater in El Niño than in La Niña years. The Pacific Northwest is wetter with La Niña than with El Niño. Discovery of these truly Earthwide relations and spatial impacts is at the heart of physical geography. The climate of one location is related to climates elsewhere. "It is fascinating that what happens in one area can affect the whole world. . . . Scientists are trying to make order out of chaos," says NOAA scientist Alan Strong. (For ENSO monitoring and forecasts, see the National Climate Prediction Center at http://www.cpc.ncep. noaa.gov/, the Jet Propulsion Laboratory at http://sealevel.jpl.nasa.gov/science/ el-nino.html, or NOAA's El Niño Theme Page at http://www.pmel.noaa.gov/toga- tao/el-nino/nino-home.html.)

FIGURE 10.1.1 Normal, El Niño, and La Niña conditions in the Pacific.
(a) Normal patterns in the Pacific. (b) El Niño wind and weather patterns across the Pacific Ocean and *TOPEX/Poseidon* satellite image for November 1997 (white and red colours indicate warmer surface water—a warm pool). (c) *TOPEX/Poseidon* image of La Niña conditions in transition in the Pacific in October 12, 1998 (purple and blue colours for cooler surface water—a cool pool). (d) A persistent La Niña in a March 2000 satellite image. (e) Image from June 7, 2001, of neutral conditions. (f) Neutral to a mild La Niña off South America, July 12, 2004, image. (g) More neutral conditions February 22, 2005. (h) La Niña growing in size, August 26, 2007. (i) El Niño conditions on January 3, 2010. (j) as La Niña conditions intensify December 26, 2010.
[(a) and (b) adapted and author corrected from C. S. Ramage, "El Niño." © 1986 by *Scientific American*, Inc.
(b)–(e) *TOPEX/Poseidon* and (f)–(i) *Jason–1* and OSTM–*Jason-2* images courtesy of Jet Propulsion Laboratory, NASA.]

The present global climatic warming trend is producing changes in plant and animal distributions. Figure 10.2 presents a schematic view of Earth's climate system, showing both internal and external processes and linkages that influence climate and thus regulate such changes.

Climate Components: Insolation, Temperature, Pressure, Air Masses, and Precipitation

The principal elements of climate are insolation, temperature, pressure, air masses, and precipitation. The first nine chapters discussed each of these elements. We review them briefly here. Insolation is the energy input for the climate system, but it varies widely over Earth's surface by latitude (see Chapter 2 and Figures 2.9, 2.10, and 2.11). Daylength varies seasonally and temperature patterns vary diurnally (daily) and seasonally. The principal controls of temperature are latitude, altitude, elevation, land–water heating differences, and cloud cover. The pattern of world temperatures and annual temperature ranges are covered in Chapter 5 (see Figures 5.13, 5.16, 5.17, and 5.18).

Temperature variations result from a coupling of dynamic forces in the atmosphere to Earth's pattern of atmospheric pressure and resulting global wind and ocean systems (see Figures 6.9 and Figures 6.11). Important, too, are the location and physical characteristics of air masses, those vast bodies of homogeneous air that form over oceanic and continental source regions.

Moisture, the remaining input to climate, is represented by precipitation in all its forms. The hydrologic cycle transfers moisture, with its tremendous latent heat energy, through Earth's climate system (see Figure 9.1). Figure 10.3 shows the worldwide distribution of precipitation, our moisture supply. Average temperatures and daylength help us approximate PE (potential evapotranspiration), a measure of natural moisture demand.

Most of Earth's desert regions, areas of permanent water deficit, are in lands dominated by subtropical high-pressure cells, with bordering lands grading to grasslands and to forests as precipitation increases. The most consistently wet climates on Earth straddle the equator in the Amazon region of South America, the Congo region of Africa, and Indonesia and Southeast Asia, all of which are influenced by equatorial low pressure and the intertropical convergence zone (ITCZ; see Figure 6.10).

Simply relating the two principal climatic components—temperature and precipitation—reveals general climate types (Figure 10.4). Temperature and precipitation patterns, plus other weather factors, provide the key to climate classification.

Classification of Climatic Regions

Classification is the process of grouping data or phenomena into related classes. Such generalizations are important organizational tools in science and are especially useful for the spatial analysis of climatic regions. A climate classification based on *causative* factors—for example, the interaction of air masses—is a **genetic classification**. This approach explores the "why" question as to the

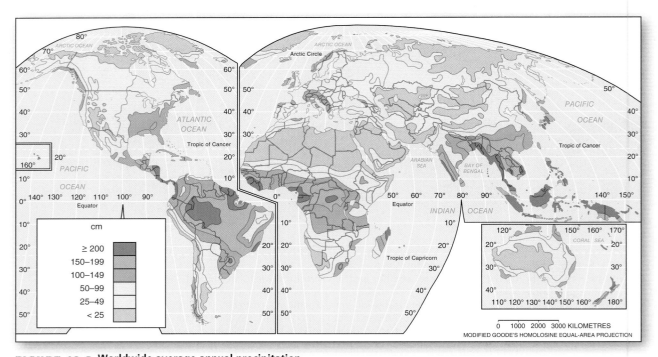

FIGURE 10.3 Worldwide average annual precipitation.
The causes that produce these patterns should be recognizable to you: temperature and pressure patterns; air mass types; convergent, convectional, orographic, and frontal lifting mechanisms; and the general energy availability that decreases toward the poles.

FIGURE 10.4 Climatic relationships.
A temperature and precipitation schematic reveals climatic relationships. Based on general knowledge of your location, can you identify its approximate location on the schematic diagram? Now locate the region of your birthplace.

mix of climatic ingredients in certain locations. A climate classification determined by *statistical data* of observed effects is an **empirical classification**.

Climate classifications based on temperature and precipitation data are examples of empirical classifications. One empirical classification system published by C. W. Thornthwaite identified moisture regions using aspects of the water-balance approach (discussed in Chapter 9) and vegetation types. Another empirical classification system is the Köppen classification system, designed by Wladimir Köppen (1846–1940), a Russian/German climatologist and botanist. His classification work began with an article on heat zones in 1884 and continued throughout his career. The first wall map showing world climates, coauthored with his student Rudolph Geiger, was introduced in 1928 and soon was widely adopted. Köppen continued to refine it until his death. In Appendix C you will find a description of his system and the detailed criteria he used to distinguish climatic regions and their bondaries.

Classification Categories The basis of any classification system is the choice of criteria or causative factors used to draw lines between regions. As we devise categories and spatial boundaries, we must remember that boundaries really are transition zones of gradual change. The trends and overall patterns of boundary lines are more important than their precise placement, especially with the small scales generally used for world maps.

For the *Geosystems* classification, we focus on temperature and precipitation measurements, and for the desert areas, moisture efficiency. Keep in mind these are measurable results produced by the climatic elements listed above. Figure 10.5 portrays six basic climate categories and the regional types that provide us with a structure for our discussion in this chapter.

- Tropical (tropical latitudes)
    rain forest (rainy all year)
    monsoon (6 to 12 months rainy)
    savanna (less than 6 months rainy)
- Mesothermal (midlatitudes, mild winter)
    humid subtropical (hot to warm summers)
    marine west coast (warm to cool summers)
    Mediterranean (dry summers)
- Microthermal (mid and high latitudes, cold winter)
    humid continental (hot to warm summers)
    subarctic (cool summers to very cold winters)
- Polar (high latitudes and polar regions)
    tundra (high latitude or high elevation)
    ice caps and ice sheets (perpetually frozen)
    polar marine

 GEO REPORT 10.1   *Ancient Thinking on Climate Classifications*

The ancient Greeks simplified their view of world climates into three zones: The "torrid zone" referred to warmer areas south of the Mediterranean; the "frigid zone" was to the north; and the area where they lived was labelled the "temperate zone," which they considered the optimum climate. They believed that travelling too close to the equator or too far north would surely end in death. But the world is a diverse place, and Earth's myriad climatic variations are more complex than these simple views.

FIGURE 10.5 Climate regions generalised.
Six general climate categories, keyed to the legend and colouration in the Figure 10.6 map. Relative to the question asked about your campus and birthplace in the caption to Figure 10.4, locate these two places on this climate map.

■ Highland (high elevations at all latitudes; highlands have lower temperatures)

Only one climate category is based on moisture efficiency as well as temperature:

■ Desert (permanent moisture deficits)

   arid deserts (tropical, subtropical hot, and midlatitude cold)

   semiarid steppes (tropical, subtropical hot, and midlatitude cold)

Global Climate Patterns Adding detail to Figure 10.5, we develop the world climate map presented in Figure 10.6. The following sections describe specific climates, organized around each of the main climate categories listed previously. An opening box at the beginning of each climate section gives (1) a simple description of the climate category and causal elements that are in operation and (2) a world map showing distribution and the featured representative cities. The names of the climates appear in italics in the chapter.

GEO REPORT 10.2 *Boundary Considerations and Changes Under Way*

The boundary between mesothermal and microthermal climates is sometimes placed along the isotherm where the coldest month is −3°C or lower. That might be an accurate criterion for Europe, but for conditions in North America, the 0°C isotherm is considered more appropriate. The difference between the 0°C and −3°C isotherms covers an area about 350 km wide. In Figure 10.6, you see the 0°C boundary used.

Climate change means these statistical boundaries are shifting. The Intergovernmental Panel on Climate Change (IPCC; discussed later in this chapter) predicts a 150- to 550-km range of possible poleward shift of climatic patterns in the midlatitudes during this century. Such change in climate would place Saskatchewan and Manitoba within climate regimes now experienced in Wyoming and South Dakota. As you examine North America in Figure 10.6, use the graphic scale to get an idea of the magnitude of these potential shifts.

Selected cities represent each climate category, with their information on a **climograph**, a graph that shows monthly temperature and precipitation for a station. Also included are the location coordinates, average annual temperature, total annual precipitation, elevation, local population, annual temperature range, annual hours of sunshine (if available, as an indication of cloudiness), and a location map for each city. Along the top of each climograph are the dominant weather features that are influential in that climate. Discussions of soils, vegetation, and major terrestrial biomes that fully integrate these global climate patterns are in Part IV of this text.

CRITICAL THINKING 10.1
Finding your climate

The caption text for Figures 10.4 and 10.5 asked that you locate the climate conditions for your campus and your birthplace. Now, mark these locations with a dot on Figures 10.4 through 10.6. For these places, obtain monthly precipitation and temperature data. Briefly describe the information sources you used. Now, refer to Appendix C to refine your assessment of climate for the two locations. Briefly show how you worked through the Köppen climate criteria given in the appendix that established the climate classification for your two locations.

Tropical Climates (tropical latitudes)

Tropical climates, the most extensive, occupy about 36% of Earth's surface, including both ocean and land areas. The tropical climates straddle the equator from about 20° N to 20° S, roughly between the Tropics of Cancer and Capricorn, thus the name. Tropical climates stretch northward to the tip of Florida and south-central Mexico, central India, and Southeast Asia, and southward to northern Australia, Madagascar, central Africa, and southern Brazil. These climates do not have a cold season. Important causal elements include:

- Consistent daylength and insolation input, which produce consistently warm temperatures;
- Effects of the ITCZ, which brings rain as it shifts seasonally with the high Sun; and
- Warm ocean temperatures and unstable maritime air masses.

Tropical climates have three distinct regimes: *tropical rain forest* (ITCZ present all year), *tropical monsoon* (ITCZ present for 6 to 12 months), and *tropical savanna* (ITCZ present for less than 6 months).

Tropical Rain Forest Climates

The *tropical rain forest* climate is constantly moist and warm. Convectional thunderstorms, triggered by local heating and trade-wind convergence, peak each day from midafternoon to late evening inland and earlier in the day where marine influence is strong along coastlines. Precipitation follows the migrating ITCZ (Chapter 6). The ITCZ shifts northward and southward with the summer Sun throughout the year, but it influences *tropical rain forest* regions all year long. Not surprisingly, water surpluses are enormous, creating the world's greatest stream discharges in the Amazon and Congo rivers.

High rainfall sustains lush evergreen broadleaf tree growth, producing Earth's equatorial and tropical rain forests. The leaf canopy is so dense that little light diffuses to

the forest floor, leaving the ground surface dim and sparse in plant cover. Dense surface vegetation occurs along riverbanks, where light is abundant.

High temperature promotes energetic bacterial action in the soil, so that organic material is quickly consumed. Heavy precipitation washes away certain minerals and nutrients. The resulting soils are somewhat sterile and can support intensive agriculture only if supplemented by fertilizer.

Uaupés, Brazil (Figure 10.7), is characteristic of a *tropical rain forest* location. On the climograph you can see that the lowest-precipitation month receives nearly 15 cm, and the annual temperature range is barely 2 C°. In all such climates, the diurnal (day-to-night) temperature range exceeds the annual average maximum–minimum (coolest to warmest) range: Day–night temperatures can

[text continued on page 274]

OCEAN CURRENTS (Fig. 6.20)

→ Warm current

→ Cool current

INTERTROPICAL CONVERGENCE
ZONE

     Figs. 6.9, 6.11

     — ITCZ July

     — — ITCZ January

AIR PRESSURE SYSTEMS (Fig. 6.9)

SH Subtropical high

L Low

H High

AIR MASSES (Fig. 8.2)

mP Maritime polar (cool, humid)

cP Continental polar (cool, cold, dry)

mT Maritime tropical (warm, humid)

cA Continental Arctic (very cold, dry)

cT Continental tropical (hot, dry summer only)

mE Maritime equatorial (warm, wet)

TROPICAL CLIMATES

Tropical rain forest
    Rainy all year
Tropical monsoon
    6 to 12 months rainy

Tropical savanna
    Less than 6 months rainy

DRY CLIMATES

Arid deserts
    Tropical, subtropical hot
    Midlatitude cold

Semiarid steppes
    Tropical, subtropical hot
    Midlatitude cold

FIGURE 10.6 World climate classification.
Annotated on this map are selected air masses, near-shore ocean currents, pressure systems, and the January and July
locations of the ITCZ. Use the colours in the legend to locate various climate types; some labels of the climate names
appear in italics on the map to guide you.

Polar front (variable)

ARCTIC OCEAN
Arctic Circle
Ice cap
mP
60°
cA Tundra
Tundra
Subarctic
Subarctic
Tundra
cP
mP
40°
Polar front (variable)
Marine west coast
Highland
Humid continental
Steppe
Desert
Steppe
Desert
Humid continental
PACIFIC
Mediterranean
Steppe
Steppe
Highland
30°
SH
Desert
Desert
Humid subtropical
OCEAN
mT
0°
Tropical monsoon
Tropic of Cancer
ITCZ July
cT
Desert
ARABIAN SEA
Tropical monsoon
Tropical savanna
mT
Tropical Monsoon
20°
opical nsoon
Steppe
Highland
mT
BAY OF BENGAL
140°
10°
mE
mE
Tropical rain forest
Equator
mE
Tropical rain forest
mE
0°
10°
INDIAN
OCEAN
0°
ATLANTIC
Tropical savanna
10°
OCEAN
ITCZ January
SH
Desert
Steppe
SH
20°
SH
mT
Mediterranean
Desert
Steppe
Humid subtropical
mT
Tropic of Capricorn
30°
40°
mP
50°
mP
Polar front (variable)
mP
50°

120° Tropical Savanna 140° 150° 160° 170°
ITCZ January
Steppe
CORAL SEA
20°
Desert
SH
Desert
20°
cT
30°
Mediterranean
Steppe
30°
Marine west coast
40°
40°
110° 120° 130° 140° 150° 160° 180°

0 1000 2000 3000 KILOMETRES
MODIFIED GOODE'S HOMOLOSINE EQUAL-AREA PROJECTION

MESOTHERMAL CLIMATES

- Humid subtropical
  Moist all year, hot summer
- Humid subtropical
  Winter-dry, hot to warm summers
- Marine west coast
  Moist all year, warm to cool summers
- Mediterranean
  Summer dry, hot to warm summers

MICROTHERMAL CLIMATES

- Humid continental
  Hot summers: moist all year
  Asian winter-dry
- Humid continental
  Mild summers: moist all year
  Asian winter-dry
- Subarctic regions
  Cool summers
- Subarctic regions
  Very cold winters

POLAR CLIMATES HIGHLANDS

- Tundra
- Ice cap and ice sheets
  Highland temperature effects

Station: Uaupés, Brazil   **Elevation:** 86 m
Lat/long: 0° 08′ S 67° 05′ W   **Population:** 10 000
Avg. Ann. Temp.: 25°C   **Ann. Temp. Range:** 2 C°
Total Ann. Precip.: 291.7 cm   **Ann. Hr of Sunshine:** 2018

FIGURE 10.7 Tropical rain forest climate.
(a) Climograph for Uaupés, Brazil. (b) The rain forest along the Rio Negro River, Amazonas state, Brazil. [(b) Gerard & Margi Moss/ Peter Arnold/Getty Images.]

range more than 11 C°, more than 5 times the annual monthly average range.

The only interruption of *tropical rain forest* climates across the equatorial region is in the highlands of the South American Andes and in East Africa (see Figure 10.6). There, higher elevations produce lower temperatures; Mount Kilimanjaro is less than 4° south of the equator, but at 5895 m it has permanent glacial ice on its summit (although this ice is shrinking due to higher air temperatures). Such mountainous sites fall within the highland climate category.

Tropical Monsoon Climates

Tropical monsoon climates feature a dry season that lasts one or more months. Rainfall brought by the ITCZ falls in these areas from 6 to 12 months of the year. (Remember, the ITCZ affects the *tropical rain forest* climate region throughout the year.) The dry season occurs when the convergence zone is not overhead. Yangon, Myanmar (formerly Rangoon, Burma), is an example of this climate type, as illustrated by the climograph and photograph in Figure 10.8. Mountains prevent cold air masses from central Asia reaching Yangon, resulting in its high average annual temperatures.

About 480 km north is another coastal city, Sittwe (Akyab), Myanmar, on the Bay of Bengal, where annual precipitation rises to 515 cm compared to Yangon's 269 cm. Therefore, Yangon is in a drier *tropical monsoon* area than farther north along the coast, but still receives more than the 250-cm criteria in use for this classification.

Tropical monsoon climates lie principally along coastal areas within the tropical rain forest climatic realm and experience seasonal variation of wind and precipitation. Evergreen trees grade into thorn forests on the drier margins near the adjoining savanna climates.

Tropical Savanna Climates

Tropical savanna climates exist poleward of the *tropical rain forest* climates. The chapter-opening photo from Puerto Rico is from such a region. The ITCZ reaches these

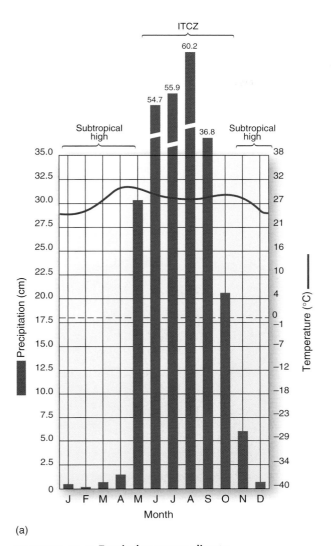

ITCZ

60.2

55.9

54.7

36.8

Subtropical high   Subtropical high

Station: Yangon, Myanmar*
Lat/long: 16° 47′ N 96° 10′ E
Avg. Ann. Temp.: 27.3°C
Total Ann. Precip.: 268.8 cm

Elevation: 23 m
Population: 6 000 000
Ann. Temp. Range: 5.5 C°

*(Formerly Rangoon, Burma)

(a)

(b)

FIGURE 10.8 Tropical monsoon climate.
(a) Climograph for Yangon, Myanmar (formerly Rangoon, Burma) (*tropical monsoon*); city of Sittwe also noted on map.
(b) Mixed monsoonal forest and scrub characteristic of the region. [shaileshnanal/Shutterstock.]

climate regions for about 6 months or less of the year as it migrates with the summer Sun. Summers are wetter than winters because convectional rains accompany the shifting ITCZ when it is overhead. This produces a notable dry condition when the ITCZ is farthest away and high pressure dominates. Thus, PE (natural moisture demand) exceeds P (natural moisture supply) in winter, causing water-budget deficits.

Temperatures vary more in *tropical savanna* climates than in *tropical rain forest* regions. The *tropical savanna* regime can have two temperature maximums during the year because the Sun's direct rays are overhead twice—before and after the summer solstice in each hemisphere as the Sun moves between the equator and the tropics.

Dominant grasslands with scattered trees, drought-resistant to cope with the highly variable precipitation, characterise the *tropical savanna* regions (Figure 10.9).

Arusha, Tanzania, is a characteristic *tropical savanna* city (Figure 10.9). This metropolitan area of more than 14 million people is east of the famous Serengeti Plains savanna and Olduvai Gorge, site of human origins, and north of Tarangire National Park. Temperatures are consistent with tropical climates, despite the elevation (1387 m) of the station. Note the marked dryness from June to October, which defines changing dominant pressure systems rather than annual changes in temperature. This region is near the transition to the dryer *desert hot-steppe* climates to the northeast.

Station: Arusha, Tanzania
Lat/long: 3° 24′ S 36° 42′ E
Avg. Ann. Temp.: 26.5°C
Total Ann. Precip.: 119 cm

Elevation: 1387 m
Population: 1 368 000
Ann. Temp. Range: 4.1 C°
Ann. Hr of Sunshine: 2600

(a)

FIGURE 10.9 Tropical savanna climate.
(a) Climograph for Arusha, Tanzania; note the intense dry period. (b) Characteristic landscape in the Ngorongoro Conservation Area, Tanzania, near Arusha, with plants adapted to seasonally dry water budgets. [Blaine Harrington III/Latitude/Corbis.]

(b)

Mesothermal Climates (midlatitudes, mild winters)

Mesothermal, meaning "middle temperature," describes these warm and temperate climates where true seasonality begins and seasonal contrasts in vegetation, soil, and human lifestyle adaptations are evident. More than half of the world's population resides in these mesothermal climates. These climates occupy about 27% of Earth's land and sea surfaces, the second largest percentage behind the tropical climates. Together the tropical and mesothermal climates dominate over half of Earth's oceans and about one-third of its land area.

The mesothermal climates, and nearby portions of the microthermal (cold winter) climates, are regions of great weather variability, for these are the latitudes of greatest air mass interaction. Causal elements include:

- Shifting of maritime and continental air masses, as they are guided by upper-air westerly winds and undulating Rossby waves and jet streams.
- Migration of cyclonic (low-pressure) and anticyclonic (high-pressure) systems, bringing changeable weather conditions and air mass conflicts.
- Effects of sea-surface temperatures on air mass strength: Cooler temperatures along west coasts weaken air masses, and warmer temperatures along east coasts strengthen air masses; and

- Latitudinal effects on insolation and temperature, as summers transition from hot to warm to cool, moving poleward from the tropics.

Mesothermal climates are humid, except where subtropical high pressure produces dry-summer conditions. The four distinct regimes based on precipitation variability are *humid subtropical hot-summer* (moist all year), *humid subtropical winter-dry* (hot to warm summers, in Asia), *marine west coast* (warm to cool summers, moist all year), and *Mediterranean* (warm to hot summers).

Humid Subtropical Climates

Humid subtropical hot-summer climates are either moist all year or have a pronounced winter-dry period, as occurs in eastern and southern Asia. Maritime tropical air masses generated over warm waters off eastern coasts influence *humid subtropical hot-summer* climates during summer. This warm, moist, unstable air produces convectional showers over land. In fall, winter, and spring, maritime tropical and continental polar air masses interact, generating frontal activity and frequent midlatitude cyclonic storms. These two mechanisms produce year-round precipitation. Overall, precipitation averages 100–200 cm a year.

Nagasaki, Japan (Figure 10.10) is characteristic of an Asian *humid subtropical hot-summer* station, whereas Columbia, South Carolina, is characteristic of the North American *humid subtropical hot-summer* climate found across the southeastern United States (Figure 10.11). Unlike the winter precipitation of the *humid subtropical hot-summer* cities in the United States (Atlanta, New Orleans, and Columbia), Nagasaki's winter precipitation is less because of the effects of the Asian monsoon. However, the lower precipitation of winter is not quite dry enough to change its category to a *humid subtropical winter-dry* climate. In comparison to higher rainfall amounts in Nagasaki (196 cm), Columbia's precipitation totals 127 cm (Figure 10.11b); compare this to Atlanta's 122 cm annually.

Humid subtropical winter-dry climates are related to the winter-dry, seasonal pulse of the monsoons. They extend poleward from tropical savanna climates and have a summer month that receives 10 times more precipitation than their driest winter month. A representative station is Chengdu, China. Figure 10.12 demonstrates the strong correlation between precipitation and the high-summer Sun.

The habitability of the humid *subtropical hot-summer* and *humid subtropical winter-dry* climates and their ability to sustain populations are borne out by the concentration of people in north-central India, the bulk of China's 1.3 billion people, and the many who live in climatically similar portions of the United States.

The intense summer rains of the Asian monsoon can cause problems, as they did during many years of the last decade, producing floods in India and Bangladesh. The monsoonal winter-dry climates hold several precipitation records, as discussed in Chapter 8. Sometimes dramatic thunderstorms and tornadoes are notable in the southeastern United States.

Marine West Coast Climates

Marine west coast climates, featuring mild winters and cool summers, dominate Europe and other middle-to-high-latitude west coasts (see Figure 10.6). In the United States, these climates with their cooler summers are in

Station: Nagasaki, Japan
Lat/long: 32° 44′ N 129° 52′ E
Avg. Ann. Temp.: 16°C
Total Ann. Precip.: 195.7 cm
Elevation: 27 m
Population: 1 585 000
Ann. Temp. Range: 21 C°
Ann. Hr of Sunshine: 2131

(a)

(b)

FIGURE 10.10 Humid subtropical hot-summer climate, Asian region.
(a) Climograph for Nagasaki, Japan.
(b) Landscape on Kitakyujukuri Island, near Nagasaki and Sasebo, Japan, in spring season.
[(b) JTB Photo/Photolibrary/Getty Images.]

Station: Columbia, South Carolina
Lat/long: 34° 0′ N 81° 2′ W
Avg. Ann. Temp.: 17.3°C
Total Ann. Precip.: 126.5 cm

Elevation: 96 m
Population: 116 000
Ann. Temp. Range: 20.7 C°
Ann. Hr of Sunshine: 2800

(a)

(b)

(c)

FIGURE 10.11 Humid subtropical hot-summer climate, American region.
(a) Climograph for Columbia, South Carolina. Note the more consistent precipitation pattern compared to Nagasaki, as Columbia receives seasonal cyclonic storm activity and summer convection showers within maritime tropical air. (b) The mixed evergreen forest of cypress and pine, with water lilies in southern Georgia. (c) This is the humid subtropical portion of Argentina along the Paraná River with a makeshift dock, northwest of Buenos Aires. [(b) and (c) Bobbé Christopherson.]

contrast to the *humid subtropical hot-summer* climate of the Southeast.

Maritime polar air masses—cool, moist, unstable—dominate *marine west coast* climates. Weather systems forming along the polar front and maritime polar air masses move into these regions throughout the year, making weather quite unpredictable. Coastal fog, annually totaling 30 to 60 days, is a part of the moderating marine influence. Frosts are possible and tend to shorten the growing season.

Marine west coast climates are unusually mild for their latitude. They extend along the coastal margins of the Aleutian Islands in the North Pacific, cover the southern third of Iceland in the North Atlantic and coastal Scandinavia, and dominate the British Isles. It is hard to imagine that such high-latitude locations can have

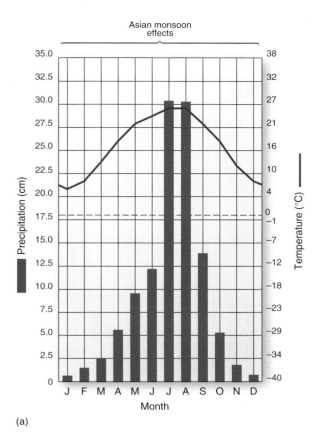

Asian monsoon
effects

(a)

Station: Chengdu, China
Lat/long: 30° 40′ N 104° 04′ E
Avg. Ann. Temp.: 17°C
Total Ann. Precip.: 114.6 cm

Elevation: 498 m
Population: 2 500 000
Ann. Temp. Range: 20 C°
Ann. Hr of Sunshine: 1058

(b)

FIGURE 10.12 Humid subtropical winter-dry climate.
(a) Climograph for Chengdu, China. Note the summer-wet
monsoonal precipitation. (b) People flee high-rise buildings
following a major earthquake in Chengdu. [(b) Oded Balilty/
AP Photo/CP Images.]

average monthly temperatures above freezing throughout the year.

Unlike the extensive influence of marine west
coast regions in Europe, mountains restrict this climate to coastal environs in Canada, Alaska, Chile,
and Australia. The temperate rain forest of Vancouver
Island is representative of these moist and cool conditions (Figure 10.13).

The climograph for Dunedin, New Zealand, demonstrates the moderate temperature patterns and the
annual temperature range for a *marine west coast* city in the
Southern Hemisphere (Figure 10.14).

An interesting anomaly occurs in the eastern United
States. In portions of the Appalachian highlands, increased
elevation lowers summer temperatures in the surrounding
humid subtropical hot-summer climate, producing a *marine
west coast* cooler summer. The climograph for Bluefield, West Virginia (Figure 10.15), reveals marine west
coast temperature and precipitation patterns, despite its
location in the east. Vegetation similarities between the
Appalachians and the Pacific Northwest have enticed
many emigrants from the East to settle in these climatically familiar environments in the Northwest.

Mediterranean Dry-Summer Climates

The Mediterranean dry-summer climate designation speci-
fies that at least 70% of annual precipitation occurs during
the winter months. This is in contrast to the majority of the

FIGURE 10.13 A marine west coast climate.
Temperate rain forest along the Little Qualicum River, central
Vancouver Island, adjacent to the Macmillan Provincial Park,
British Columbia. [Bobbé Christopherson.]

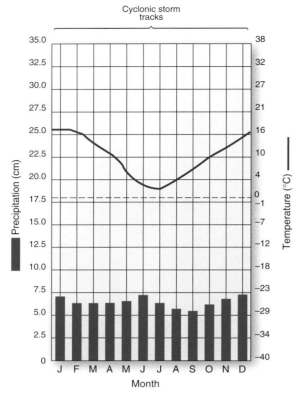

Cyclonic storm tracks

Station: Dunedin, New Zealand
Lat/long: 45° 54′ S 170° 31′ E
Avg. Ann. Temp.: 10.2°C
Total Ann. Precip.: 78.7 cm

Elevation: 1.5 m
Population: 120 000
Ann. Temp. Range: 14.2 C°

(a)

(b)

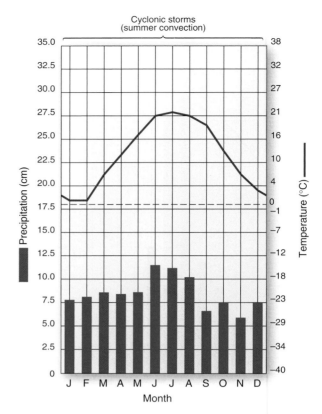

Cyclonic storms (summer convection)

Station: Bluefield, West Virginia
Lat/long: 37° 16′ N 81° 13′ W
Avg. Ann. Temp.: 12°C
Total Ann. Precip.: 101.9 cm

Elevation: 780 m
Population: 11 000
Ann. Temp. Range: 21 C°

(a)

(b)

FIGURE 10.14 A Southern Hemisphere marine west coast climate.
(a) Climograph for Dunedin, New Zealand. (b) Meadow, forest, and mountains on South Island, New Zealand. [Brian Enting/Photo Researchers, Inc.]

FIGURE 10.15 Marine west coast climate in the Appalachians of the eastern United States.
(a) Climograph for Bluefield, West Virginia. (b) Characteristic mixed forest in Appalachia in winter. [Robert Christopherson.]

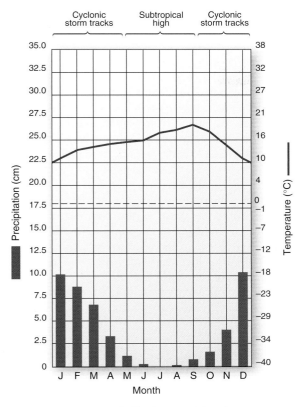

Cyclonic storm tracks | Subtropical high | Cyclonic storm tracks

Station: San Francisco, California
Lat/long: 37° 37′ N 122° 23′ W
Avg. Ann. Temp.: 14.6°C
Total Ann. Precip.: 56.6 cm
Elevation: 5 m
Population: 777 000
Ann. Temp. Range: 11.4 C°
Ann. Hr of Sunshine: 2975

(a)

Station: Sevilla, Spain
Lat/long: 37° 22′ N 6° W
Avg. Ann. Temp.: 18°C
Total Ann. Precip.: 55.9 cm
Elevation: 13 m
Population: 1 764 000
Ann. Temp. Range: 16 C°
Ann. Hr of Sunshine: 2862

(b)

(c)

(d)

FIGURE 10.16 Mediterranean climates, California and Spain.
Climographs for (a) San Francisco, California, with its cooler dry summer, and (b) Sevilla, Spain, with its hotter dry summer.
(c) Central California Mediterranean landscape of oak savanna.
(d) Near Sevilla, Spain, the El Penon mountains in the distance.
[(c) Bobbé Christopherson. (d) Michael Thornton/Design Pics/Corbis.]

world that experiences summer-maximum precipitation, or evenly-distributed precipitation. Across the planet during summer months, shifting cells of subtropical high pressure block moisture-bearing winds from adjacent regions. This shifting of stable, warm to hot, dry air over an area in summer and away from these regions in the winter creates a pronounced dry-summer and wet-winter pattern. For example, in summer the continental tropical air mass over the Sahara in Africa shifts northward over the Mediterranean region and blocks maritime air masses and cyclonic storm tracks.

Worldwide, cool offshore ocean currents (California, Canary, Peru, Benguela, and West Australian currents) produce stability in overlying air masses along west coasts, poleward of subtropical high pressure. The world climate map (see Figure 10.6) shows Mediterranean dry-summer climates along the western margins of North America, central Chile, and the southwestern tip of Africa, as well as across southern Australia and the Mediterranean Basin—the climate's namesake region. Examine the offshore currents along each of these regions on the world climate map.

Figure 10.16 on page 281 compares the climographs of the *Mediterranean dry-summer* cities of San Francisco, California, and Sevilla (Seville), Spain. Coastal maritime effects moderate San Francisco's climate, producing a cooler summer. The transition to a hot summer occurs no more than 24–32 km inland from San Francisco.

The *Mediterranean dry-summer* climate brings summer water-balance deficits. Winter precipitation recharges soil moisture, but water use usually exhausts soil moisture by late spring. Large-scale agriculture requires irrigation, although some subtropical fruits, nuts, and vegetables are uniquely suited to these conditions. Natural vegetation features a hard-leafed, drought-resistant variety known locally as *chaparral* in the western United States. (Chapter 20 discusses local names for this type of vegetation in other parts of the world.)

Microthermal Climates (mid and high latitudes, cold winters)

Humid microthermal climates have a winter season with some summer warmth. Here the term *microthermal* means cool temperate to cold. Approximately 21% of Earth's land surface is influenced by these climates, equaling about 7% of Earth's total surface.

These climates occur poleward of the mesothermal climates and experience great temperature ranges related to continentality and air mass conflicts. Temperatures decrease with increasing latitude and toward the interior of continental landmasses, and result in intensely cold winters. In contrast to moist-all-year regions (the northern tier across Canada and the United States, eastern Europe through the Ural Mountains) is the winter-dry association with the Asian dry monsoon and cold air masses across the region.

In Figure 10.6, note the absence of microthermal climates on land in the Southern Hemisphere. Because the Southern Hemisphere lacks substantial landmasses, in the latitudinal range suitable for microthermal climates, these climates develop there only in highlands. Important causal elements include:

- Increasing seasonality (daylength and Sun altitude) and greater temperature ranges (daily and annually).
- Upper-air westerly winds and undulating Rossby waves, which bring warmer air northward and colder air southward for cyclonic activity, and convectional thunderstorms from mT air masses in summer.
- An Asian winter-dry pattern associated with continental high pressure and related air masses, increasing east of the Ural Mountains to the Pacific Ocean and eastern Asia.

Hot, humid continental	Subarctic, cool summers
Warm, humid continental	Subarctic, very cold winters

- Hot summers cooling northward, with insolation and net radiation declines from the mesothermal climates, and short spring and fall seasons surrounding winters that are cold to very cold.
- Continental interiors serving as source regions for intense continental polar air masses that dominate winter, blocking cyclonic storms.

Microthermal climates have four distinct regimes based on increasing cold with latitude and precipitation variability: *humid continental hot-summer* (Chicago, New York); *humid continental mild-summer* (Toronto, Duluth, Moscow); *subarctic cool summer* (Churchill, Manitoba); and the formidable extremes of frigid, *subarctic with very cold winters* (Verkhoyansk and northern Siberia).

Humid Continental Hot-Summer Climates

Humid continental hot-summer climates are differentiated by their annual precipitation distribution. In summer, maritime tropical air masses influence both *humid continental moist-all-year* and *humid continental winter-dry* climates. In North America, frequent weather activity is possible between conflicting air masses—maritime tropical and continental polar—especially in winter. The

Cyclonic storm tracks
(summer convection)

Station: New York, New York
Lat/long: 40° 46′ N 74° 01′ W
Avg. Ann. Temp.: 13°C
Total Ann. Precip.: 112.3 cm
Elevation: 16 m
Population: 8 092 000
Ann. Temp. Range: 24 C°
Ann. Hr of Sunshine: 2564

(a)

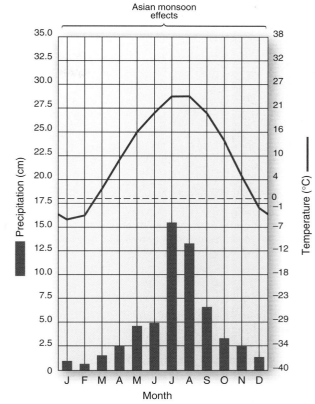

Asian monsoon
effects

Station: Dalian, China
Lat/long: 38° 54′ N 121° 54′ E
Avg. Ann. Temp.: 10°C
Total Ann. Precip.: 57.8 cm
Elevation: 96 m
Population: 5 550 000
Ann. Temp. Range: 29 C°
Ann. Hr of Sunshine: 2762

(b)

(c)

(d)

FIGURE 10.17 Humid continental hot-summer climates, New York and China.
Climographs for (a) New York City (humid continental hot-summer climate that is moist all year) and (b) Dalian, China (humid continental hot-summer climate that is dry in winter). (c) Belvedere Castle, 1872, in New York's Central Park; location of weather station from 1919 to 1960. (d) Dalian, China, cityscape and park in summer. [(c) Bobbé Christopherson. (d) Top Photo/Asia Photo Connection/Henry Westheim Photography/Alamy/GetStock.com.]

FIGURE 10.18 **Cornfields in the humid continental prairie.**
East of Minneapolis near the boundary between humid continental
hot- and mild-summer climate regions. [Bobbé Christopherson.]

climographs and photos for New York City and Dalian,
China (10.17, page 283), illustrate these two hot-summer
microthermal climates. The Dalian, China, climograph
demonstrates a dry-winter tendency caused by the intruding cold continental air that forces dry monsoon
conditions.

Before European settlement, forests covered the
humid continental hot-summer climatic region of the United
States as far west as the Indiana–Illinois border. Beyond
that approximate line, tall-grass prairies extended westward to about the 98th meridian (98° W in central Kansas)
and the approximate location of the 51-cm isohyet (line of

equal precipitation). Further west the short-grass prairies
reflected lower precipitation receipts.

Deep sod made farming difficult for the first settlers
of the American prairies, as did the climate. However,
native grasses soon were replaced with domesticated
wheat and barley. In the United States today, the *humid
continental hot-summer* region is the location of corn,
soybean, hog, feed crop, dairy, and cattle production
(Figure 10.18).

The region milder summers poleward of these hot
summer climates is in a climatic transition related to
ongoing global climate change. Milder summers will
become hotter as the boundary between these climatic subtypes shifts to higher latitudes. The forests of the
Great Lakes Lowlands and the northeastern portions of
North America in the latter half of this century will shift
from the present maple–beech–birch forests, with some
elm and ash, to a dominant oak–hickory–hemlock mix.
Such shifting of climatic boundaries and their related
ecosystems are occurring worldwide.

Humid Continental Mild-Summer Climates

Soils are thinner and less fertile in the cooler microthermal climates, yet agricultural activity is important.
Frost-free periods range from fewer than 90 days in
the north to as many as 225 days in the south. Overall,
precipitation is less than in the hot-summer regions to
the south; however, notably heavier snowfall is important to soil moisture recharge when it melts. Various
snow-capturing strategies are in use, including fences
and tall stubble left standing after harvest in fields to

Station: Moscow, Russia
Lat/long: 55° 45′ N 37° 34′ E
Avg. Ann. Temp.: 4°C
Total Ann. Precip.: 57.5 cm

Elevation: 156 m
Population: 11 460 000
Ann. Temp. Range: 29 C°
Ann. Hr of Sunshine: 1597

FIGURE 10.19 **Humid continental mild-summer climate.**
(a) Climograph for Moscow, Russia. (b) Landscape between Moscow and St. Petersburg along the Volga River. (c) Winter scene of pathway through mixed forest near Brunswick, Maine. [(b) Dave G. Houser/Corbis; (c) Bobbé Christopherson.]

create snowdrifts and thus more moisture retention on the soil.

Characteristic cities are Duluth, Minnesota, and Saint Petersburg, Russia. Figure 10.19 presents a climograph for Moscow, which is at 55° N, or about the same latitude as the southern shore of Hudson Bay in Canada.

The dry winter aspect of the mild-summer climate occurs only in Asia, in a far-eastern area poleward of the winter-dry mesothermal climates. A representative *humid continental mild-summer* climate along Russia's east coast is

Vladivostok, usually one of only two year-round ice-free ports in that country.

Subarctic Climates

Farther poleward, seasonal change becomes greater. The short growing season is more intense during long summer days. The *subarctic* climates include vast stretches of Canada, Alaska, and northern Scandinavia with their cool summers, and Siberian Russia with its very cold winters. Discoveries of minerals and petroleum reserves and the

Station: Churchill, Manitoba
Lat/long: 58° 45′ N 94° 04′ W
Avg. Ann. Temp.: −7°C
Total Ann. Precip.: 44.3 cm

Elevation: 35 m
Population: 921
Ann. Temp. Range: 40 C°
Ann. Hr of Sunshine: 1732

FIGURE 10.20 Subarctic cool-summer climate.
(a) Climograph for Churchill, Manitoba. (b) Winter scene in Churchill showing the port facilities on Hudson Bay.
(c) Polar bear mom and older cub taking protective shelter near Hudson Bay, waiting for the ice. [Bobbé Christopherson.]

Arctic Ocean sea-ice losses have led to new interest in portions of these regions, such as the port expansion in Churchill (see Figure 10.20b).

Areas that receive 25 cm or more of precipitation a year on the northern continental margins and are covered by the so-called snow forests of fir, spruce, larch, and birch are the *boreal forests* of Canada and the *taiga* of Russia. These forests are in transition to the more open northern woodlands and to the tundra region of the far north. Forests thin out to the north when the warmest month drops below an average temperature of 10°C. During the decades ahead, the boreal forests are shifting northward into the tundra in response to climate change with higher temperatures.

Soils are thin in these lands once scoured by glaciers. Precipitation and potential evapotranspiration both are low, so soils are generally moist and either partially or totally frozen beneath the surface, a phenomenon known as *permafrost* (discussed in Chapter 17).

The Churchill, Manitoba, climograph (Figure 10.20) shows average monthly temperatures below freezing for 7 months of the year, during which time light snow

cover and frozen ground persist. High pressure dominates Churchill during its cold winter—this is the source region for the continental polar air mass. Churchill is representative of the *subarctic cool summer* climate, with an annual temperature range of 40 C° and low precipitation of 44 cm.

The *subarctic* climates that feature a dry and very cold winter occur only within Russia. The intense cold of Siberia and north-central and eastern Asia is difficult to comprehend, for these areas experience an average temperature lower than freezing for 7 months; minimum temperatures of below −68°C were recorded there, as described in Chapter 5. Yet summer maximum temperatures in these same areas can exceed +37°C.

An example of this extreme *subarctic climate with very cold winters* is Verkhoyansk, Siberia (Figure 10.21). For 4 months of the year, average temperatures fall below −34°C. Verkhoyansk has probably the world's greatest annual temperature range from winter to summer: a remarkable 63 C°. Winters feature brittle metals and plastics, and temperatures that render straight antifreeze a solid and require triple-glazed windowpanes.

Station: Verkhoyansk, Russia **Elevation:** 137 m
Lat/long: 67° 35′ N 133° 27′ E **Population:** 1500
Avg. Ann. Temp.: −15°C **Ann. Temp. Range:** 63 C°
Total Ann. Precip.: 15.5 cm

(a)
(b)

FIGURE 10.21 Extreme subarctic cold winter climate.
(a) Climograph for Verkhoyansk, Russia. (b) A summer scene in this unique continental location; the top layers of permafrost thaw, creating many ponds. [Dean Conger/Corbis.]

Polar and Highland Climates

The polar regions have no true summer like that in lower latitudes. Dominating the South Pole is the Antarctic continent, surrounded by the Southern Ocean, whereas the North Pole region is the Arctic Ocean, surrounded by the continents of North America and Eurasia. Poleward of the Arctic and Antarctic circles, daylength increases in summer until daylight becomes continuous, yet average monthly temperatures never rise above 10°C. These temperature conditions do not allow tree growth. See the polar temperature maps for January and July in Figure 5.14 and Figure 5.17. Principal causal elements in these frozen and barren regions are the following:

- Low Sun altitude even during the long summer days is the principal climatic factor.
- Extremes of daylength between winter and summer.
- Extremely low humidity produces low precipitation amounts—these regions are Earth's frozen deserts.
- Light-coloured surfaces of ice and snow reflect substantial energy away from the ground surface, thus reducing net radiation.

Polar climates have three regimes: *tundra* (high latitude, or elevation); *ice caps* and *ice sheet* (perpetually frozen);

Tundra
Ice cap and ice sheet
Highland

Antarctica

and *polar marine* (oceanic association, slight moderation of extreme cold).

Also in this climate category we include highland climates. Even at low latitudes the effects of elevation can produce tundra and polar conditions. Glaciers on tropical mountain summits attest to the cooling effects of altitude. Highland climates on the map follow the pattern of Earth's mountain ranges.

Tundra Climate

In a *tundra* climate, land is under continuous snow cover for 8–10 months, with the warmest month above 0°C yet never warming above 10°C. When spring arrives and the snow melts, numerous plants appear—stunted sedges, mosses, flowering plants, and lichens—and persist through the short summer (Figure 10.22a). Some of the dwarf willows (7.5 cm tall) can exceed 300 years in age. Much of the area experiences permafrost and ground ice conditions; these are Earth's periglacial regions (see Chapter 17).

Global warming is bringing dramatic changes to the tundra. In parts of Canada and Alaska, registered temperatures as much as 5 C° above seasonal average are a regular occurrence, setting many records. As organic peat deposits in the tundra thaw, vast stores of carbon are released to the atmosphere, further adding to the greenhouse gas problem. Temperatures in the Arctic are warming at a rate twice that of the global average increase.

Tundra climates are strictly in the Northern Hemisphere, except for elevated mountain locations in the Southern Hemisphere and a portion of the Antarctic Peninsula.

Ice-Cap and Ice-Sheet Climate

Earth's two ice sheets cover the Antarctic continent and most of the island of Greenland. Thus, most of Antarctica and central Greenland fall within the *ice sheet* climate regime, as does the North Pole, with all months averaging below freezing. These regions are dominated by dry, frigid air masses, with vast expanses that never warm above freezing. In fact, winter minimum temperatures in central Antarctica (July) frequently drop below the temperature of solid carbon dioxide or "dry ice" (−78°C).

The area of the North Pole is actually a sea covered by ice, whereas Antarctica is a substantial continental landmass. Antarctica is constantly snow-covered, but receives less than 8 cm of precipitation each year. However, Antarctic ice has accumulated to several kilometres deep and is the largest repository of freshwater on Earth.

Ice caps are smaller in extent than ice sheets, roughly less than 50 000 km², yet completely bury the landscape like an ice sheet. The Vatnajökull Ice Cap in southeastern Iceland is an example.

Figure 10.23 shows two scenes of the repositories of multiyear ice on the Antarctic and Greenland Ice Sheets. This ice contains a vast historical record of Earth's atmosphere. Within it, evidence of thousands of past volcanic eruptions from all over the world and ancient combinations of atmospheric gases lies trapped in frozen bubbles. Chapter 17 presents analysis of ice cores taken from Greenland and the latest one taken from Antarctica, which pushed the climate record to 800 000 years before the present.

FIGURE 10.22 Greenland tundra and a research settlement.
(a) Late September in East Greenland with fall colours and muskoxen. (b) In summer, utilidors (raised shelters that carry water and sewage) and housing in the scientific settlement of Ny-Ålesund, Spitsbergen (Svalbard). [Bobbé Christopherson.]

FIGURE 10.23 Earth's ice sheets—Antarctica and Greenland.
These are Earth's frozen freshwater reservoirs. (a) In the Antarctic Sound, between Bransfield Strait and the Weddell Sea, mountains rise from the mist behind a flank of tabular icebergs. (b) Glaciers move toward the ocean into Davis Strait from West Greenland and the ice sheet on the horizon. [Bobbé Christopherson.]

Polar Marine Climate

Polar marine stations are more moderate than other polar climates in winter, with no month below −7°C, yet they are not as warm as *tundra* climates in summer. Because of marine influences, annual temperature ranges are low. This climate exists along the Bering Sea, the southern tip of Greenland, northern Iceland, Norway, and in the Southern Hemisphere, generally over oceans between 50° S and 60° S. Macquarie Island at 54° S in the Southern Ocean, south of New Zealand, is *polar marine*.

South Georgia Island is *polar marine*, made famous as the place where Ernest Shackleton sought rescue help for himself and his men in 1916 after their failed Antarctic expedition (Figure 10.24). Although the island is in the Southern Ocean and part of Antarctica, the annual temperature range is only 8.5 C° (average January is 7°C and July is −1.5°C), with 7 months averaging slightly above freezing. Although cold at between 0°C and 4°C, the ocean temperatures moderate the climate despite its location at 54° S latitude. Average precipitation is 150 cm, and it can snow during any month.

FIGURE 10.24 **South Georgia Island, a polar marine climate.** Here is the abandoned whaling station at Grytviken, South Georgia, that processed more than 50 000 whales between 1904 and 1964, about a third of all whale processed on South Georgia among seven factories. The whales of the Southern Ocean were driven almost to extinction. [Bobbé Christopherson.]

Dry Climates (permanent moisture deficits)

For understanding the dry climates, we consider moisture efficiency along with temperature. These dry regions occupy more than 35% of Earth's land area and are by far the most extensive climate over land. Sparse vegetation leaves the landscape bare; water demand exceeds precipitation water supply throughout, creating permanent water deficits. The extent of this dryness distinguishes two types of dry climatic regions: *arid deserts*, where precipitation supply is roughly less than one-half of the natural moisture demand; and *semiarid steppes*, where the precipitation supply is roughly more than one-half of natural moisture demand. (See specific annual and daily desert temperature regimes, including the highest recorded temperatures and surface energy budgets, in Chapters 4 and 5; desert landscapes in Chapter 15; and desert environments in Chapter 20.)

Important causal elements in these drylands include:

- The dominant presence of dry, subsiding air in subtropical high-pressure systems;
- Locations in the rain shadow (or leeward side) of mountains, where dry air subsides after moisture has been intercepted on the windward slopes;
- Location in continental interiors, particularly central Asia, are far from moisture-bearing air masses; and

Arid deserts Semiarid steppes

- Shifting subtropical high-pressure systems produce semiarid steppes around the periphery of arid deserts.

Dry climates are distributed by latitude and the amount of moisture deficits in four distinct regimes: arid climates include *tropical, subtropical hot desert and midlatitude cold desert*, semiarid climates include *tropical, subtropical hot steppe* and *midlatitude cold steppe*.

Characteristics of Dry Climates

The world climate map in Figure 10.6 reveals the pattern of Earth's dry climates, which cover broad regions between 15° and 30° N and S latitudes. In these areas, subtropical high-pressure cells predominate, with subsiding, stable air and low relative humidity (Figure 10.25). Under generally cloudless skies, these subtropical deserts extend to western continental margins, where cool, stabilizing ocean currents operate offshore and summer advection fog forms. The Atacama Desert of Chile, the Namib Desert of Namibia, the Western Sahara of Morocco, and Australia's Great Sandy Desert each lie adjacent to such a coastline.

Orographic lifting intercepts moisture-bearing weather systems to create rain shadows along mountain ranges that extend these dry regions into higher latitudes. Note these rain shadows in North and South America on the climate map. The isolated interior of Asia, far distant from any moisture-bearing air masses, also falls within the *dry arid and semiarid* climates.

(a)

(b)

FIGURE 10.25 Desert landscapes.
(a) Desert vegetation such as these plants in the Anza-Borrego Desert in California is typically *xerophytic*: drought-resistant, with waxy, hard leaves, or no leaves, to reduce water loss by transpiration. (b) Sand dunes get their colouration from the parent material in the rocky cliffs in southern Utah. [Bobbé Christopherson.]

Dry climates are subdivided into deserts and steppes, which are distinguished by the amount of moisture deficit; deserts have greater moisture deficits than do steppes, but both have permanent water shortages. Important is whether precipitation falls principally in the winter with a dry summer, falls principally in the summer with a dry winter, or is evenly distributed. Winter rains are most effective because they fall at a time of lower moisture demand. Relative to temperature, the lower-latitude deserts and steppes tend to be hotter with less seasonal change than the midlatitude deserts and steppes, where mean annual temperatures are below 18°C and freezing winter temperatures are possible.

A **steppe** is a regional term referring to the vast semiarid grassland biome of Eastern Europe and Asia (the equivalent biome in North America is called shortgrass prairie; in Africa, the savanna; see Chapter 20). In this chapter, we use steppe in a climatic context; a steppe climate is considered too dry to support forest, but too moist to be a desert.

Tropical, Subtropical Hot Desert Climates

Tropical, subtropical hot desert climates are Earth's true tropical and subtropical deserts and feature annual average temperatures above 18°C. They generally are found on the western sides of continents, although Egypt, Somalia, and Saudi Arabia also fall within this classification. Rainfall is from local summer convectional showers. Some regions receive almost no rainfall, whereas others may receive up to 35 cm of precipitation a year. A representative *subtropical hot desert* city is Ar Riyāḍ (Riyadh), Saudi Arabia (Figure 10.26).

Along the Sahara's southern margin is a drought-tortured region. Human populations suffered great hardship as desert conditions gradually expanded over their homelands. The arid environment sets the stage for a rugged lifestyle and subsistence economies, such as on volcanic Fogo Island in Cape Verde, a West African country (Figure 10.26c). Chapter 15 presents the process of desertification (expanding desert conditions).

Death Valley, California (Figure 10.1), features a *subtropical hot desert* climate with an average annual temperature of 24°C. July and August average temperatures are 46°C and 45°C, respectively. Temperatures over 50°C are not uncommon.

In recent years, the media have focused on the Iraq war and related political events. What seemed overlooked in many reports was the fact the air temperatures in Baghdad (located on the map in Figure 10.26) were actually higher than those in Death Valley during some days in July and August. Soldiers and civilians experienced temperatures of 50°C and higher in the city. Such readings broke records for Baghdad in 2007. In January, averages for Death Valley (11°C) and Baghdad (9.4°C) are comparable. Death Valley is drier, with 6 cm of precipitation annually, compared to 14 cm in Baghdad, both low amounts. Baghdad's May to September period is remarkable, with zero precipitation, as it is dominated by an intense subtropical high-pressure system. Keep these hot desert climates in mind as you follow events in the news.

Midlatitude Cold Desert Climates

Midlatitude cold desert climates cover only a small area: the countries along the southern border of Russia, the Gobi Desert, and Mongolia in Asia; the central third of Nevada and areas of the American Southwest, particularly at high elevations; and Patagonia in Argentina. Because of lower temperatures and lower moisture-demand values, rainfall must be low for a station to qualify as a *midlatitude cold desert* climate; consequently, total annual average rainfall is only about 15 cm.

A representative station is Albuquerque, New Mexico, with 21 cm of annual precipitation and an annual average temperature of 14°C (Figure 10.27). Note the precipitation increase from summer convectional showers on the climograph. A characteristic expanse of *midlatitude cold desert* stretches across central Nevada, over the region of

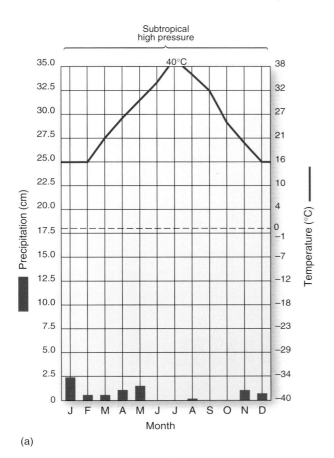

Subtropical
high pressure

(a)

Station: Ar Riyāḍ (Riyadh),
Saudi Arabia
Lat/long: 24° 42′ N 46° 43′ E
Avg. Ann. Temp.: 26°C
Total Ann. Precip.: 8.2 cm

Elevation: 609 m
Population: 5 024 000
Ann. Temp. Range: 24 C°

(c)

(b)

FIGURE 10.26 Tropical, subtropical hot desert climate.
(a) Climograph for Ar Riyāḍ (Riyadh), Saudi Arabia. (b) The Arabian desert landscape of Red Sands near Ar Riyāḍ. (c) The desert landscape on Fogo Island, Cape Verde, viewed from a higher elevation with enough moisture to support scattered trees.
[(b) Andreas Wolf/age fotostock; (c) Bobbé Christopherson.]

the Utah-Arizona border and into northern New Mexico (Figure 10.27b).

Tropical, Subtropical Hot Steppe Climates

Tropical, subtropical hot steppe climates generally exist around the periphery of hot deserts, where shifting subtropical high-pressure cells create a distinct summer-dry and winter-wet pattern. Average annual precipitation in *subtropical hot steppe* areas is usually below 60 cm. Walgett, in interior New South Wales, Australia, provides a Southern Hemisphere example of this climate (Figure 10.28). This climate is seen around the Sahara's periphery and in the Iran, Afghanistan, Turkmenistan, and Kazakhstan region.

Midlatitude Cold Steppe Climates

The *midlatitude cold steppe* climates occur poleward of about 30° latitude and the *midlatitude cold desert* climates. Such midlatitude steppes are not generally found in the Southern Hemisphere. As with other dry climate regions, rainfall in the steppes is widely variable and undependable, ranging from 20 to 40 cm. Not all rainfall is convectional, for cyclonic storm tracks penetrate the continents; however, most storms produce little precipitation.

Figure 10.29 presents a comparison between Asian and North American *midlatitude cold steppes*. Consider Semey (Semipalatinsk) in Kazakhstan with its greater temperature

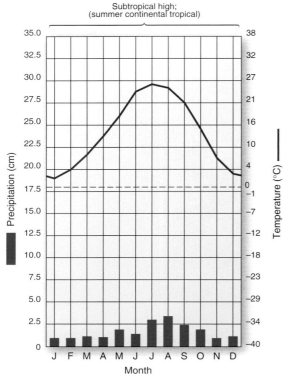

Subtropical high;
(summer continental tropical)

(a)

Station: Albuquerque,
New Mexico
Lat/long: 35° 03′ N 106° 37′ W
Avg. Ann. Temp.: 14°C
Total Ann. Precip.: 20.7 cm

Elevation: 1620 m
Population: 522 000
Ann. Temp. Range: 24 C°
Ann. Hr of Sunshine: 3420

(b)

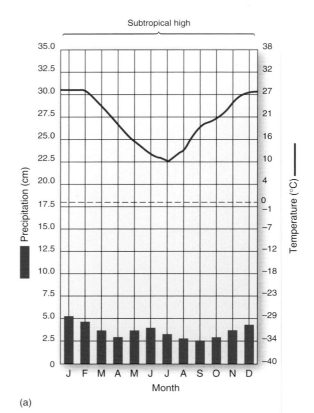

Subtropical high

(a)

Station: Walgett, New South
Wales, Australia
Lat/long: 30° S 148° 07′ E
Avg. Ann. Temp.: 20°C
Total Ann. Precip.: 45.0 cm

Elevation: 133 m
Population: 8200
Ann. Temp. Range: 17 C°

(b)

FIGURE 10.27 Midlatitude cold desert climate.
(a) Climograph for Albuquerque, New Mexico. (b) A winter scene near the New Mexico–Arizona border. [Bobbé Christopherson.]

FIGURE 10.28 Tropical, subtropical hot steppe climate.
(a) Climograph for Walgett, New South Wales, Australia.
(b) Vast plains characteristic of north-central New South Wales. [iStockphoto/Thinkstock.]

(a)

(b)

Station: Semey (Semipalatinsk), Kazakhstan
Lat/long: 50° 21′ N 80° 15′ E
Avg. Ann. Temp.: 3°C
Total Ann. Precip.: 26.4 cm

Elevation: 206 m
Population: 270,500
Ann. Temp. Range: 39 °C

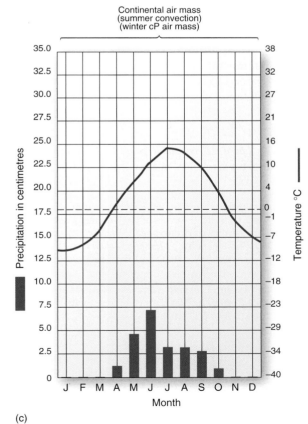

(c)

Station: Lethbridge, Alberta
Lat/long: 49° 42′ N 110° 50′ W
Avg. Ann. Temp.: 2.9°C
Total Ann. Precip.: 25.8 cm

Elevation: 910 m
Population: 73 000
Ann. Temp. Range: 24.3 C°

(d)

FIGURE 10.29 Midlatitude cold steppe climates, Kazakhstan and Canada.
(a) Climograph for Semey (Semipalatinsk) in Kazakhstan. (b) Aerial view of Semey and the Ertis River.
(c) Climograph for Lethbridge in Alberta. (d) Grain elevators highlight an Alberta, Canada, landscape.
[(b) Dinara Sagatova; (d) Design Pics/Bilderbuch/Getty Images.]

range and more evenly distributed precipitation, and Leth-bridge, Alberta, with its lesser temperature range and summer maximum convectional precipitation.

Global Climate Change

Let us begin this important section of *Geosystems* with a bottom line. The gas that is the primary cause of climate change, as we learned in Chapter 3 and Figure 3.4, is carbon dioxide, and its atmospheric volume has been increasing at about 3.1% per year since 2000. The measurements of CO_2 in the lower atmosphere, beginning in 1958, are made at the Mauna Loa station in Hawai'i, and are worth reviewing:

- May 2005 = 382 ppm
- May 2006 = 385 ppm
- May 2007 = 387 ppm
- May 2008 = 389 ppm
- May 2009 = 390 ppm
- May 2010 = 393 ppm
- May 2011 = 394 ppm

Over the past 800 000 years, CO_2 levels in the atmosphere ranged between 100 ppm and 300 ppm—never over 300. You can check the data yourself and see what the level of CO_2 is during the month when you are working on this chapter (http://www.esrl.noaa.gov/gmd/ccgg/trends/index.html). May and October are the highest and lowest months, respectively, for CO_2 readings during the year.

Scientists think that we are already in the danger zone and that to avoid irreversible ice sheet and species loss, we must avoid crossing the 450 ppm threshold for maximum CO_2. You can do the math using the rate of accelerated growth in emissions for the past 10 years to find out when we might reach this threshold. Further, to obtain climate stability, scientists tell us that we should implement policies to return the level of CO_2 to 350 ppm.[2] This is the bottom line based on actual levels of carbon dioxide.

Significant climatic change has occurred on Earth in the past and most certainly will occur in the future. Society can do little about long-term climatic influences that cycle Earth

through swings from ice ages to warmer periods. However, our global society must address short-term changes that are influencing global temperatures within the life span of present generations. This is especially true since these changes are due to human activities—an anthropogenic forcing of climate. Article 2 of the United Nations Framework Convention on Climate Change (UNFCCC), signed in 1992, commits countries to stabilize greenhouse gases at levels that will "prevent dangerous anthropogenic interference with the climate system."

Record-high global temperatures have dominated the past two decades—for both land and ocean and for both day and night. Two years tie for the record year for warmth—2005 and 2010—and all the years since 1995 were near this record. Air temperatures are the highest since recordings began in earnest more than 140 years ago and higher than at any time in the last 120 000 years, according to the ice-core record. This warming trend is *very likely*[3] due to a buildup of greenhouse gases from the burning of fossil fuels (coal, oil, natural gas); about 94% of CO_2 emissions come from the combustion of fossil fuels and the rest from cement manufacturing and other industries.

Remember the 2007 Intergovernmental Panel on Climate Change (IPCC) *Fourth Assessment Report* (*AR4*) concluded:

> Warming of the climate system is unequivocal, as is now evident from observations of increases in global average air and ocean temperatures, widespread melting of snow and ice, and rising global average sea level. . . . Most of the observed increase in globally averaged temperatures since the mid-20th century is *very likely* due to the observed increase in anthropogenic greenhouse gas concentrations.[4]

"Reasons for Concern"

In the IPCC's *Third Assessment Report* (*TAR*), published in 2001, "Reasons for Concern" were detailed in Chapter 19

---

[2]Among many sources, see J. Hansen et al., "Target atmospheric CO_2: Where should humanity aim?" *Open Atmospheric Science Journal* 2 (March 2008): 217–231; and K. Zickfeld, M. Eby, H. D. Matthews, and A. J. Weaver, "Setting cumulative emissions targets to reduce the risk of dangerous climate change," *Proceedings of the National Academy of Sciences* 106, 38 (September 22, 2009): 16129–16134.

[3]As a standard scientific reference on climate change, the IPCC uses the following to indicate levels of confidence: *Virtually certain* > 99% probability of occurrence; *Extremely likely* > 95%; *Very likely* > 90%; *Likely* > 66%; *More likely than not* > 50%; *Unlikely* < 33%; *Very unlikely* < 10%; and *Extremely unlikely* < 5%.

[4]IPCC, Working Group I, *Fourth Assessment Report: Climate Change 2007: The Physical Science Basis* (Geneva, Switzerland: IPCC Secretariat, 2007), pp. 5, 10.

 GEO REPORT 10.3   *The UNFCCC Process and Annual Meetings*

The UNFCCC was a product of the 1992 Earth Summit in Rio de Janeiro. The leading body of the Convention is the Conference of the Parties (COP), maintained by the 192 countries that ratified the FCCC Treaty. Meetings were then held in Berlin (*COP-1*, 1995) and Geneva (*COP-2*, 1996). These meetings set the stage for *COP-3* in Kyoto, Japan, in December 1997, where 10 000 participants adopted the *Kyoto Protocol* by consensus. Nineteen national academies of science endorsed the Kyoto Protocol, and 84 countries are signatories. For updates on the status of the Kyoto Protocol, see http://unfccc.int/2860.php. The 2011 gathering, COP–17, was in Durban, South Africa, with a 2012 meeting in Qatar, on the Persian Gulf.

of the volume, entitled *Vulnerability to Climate Change and Reasons for Concern: A Synthesis* (pp. 911–967), prepared by Working Group II. Scientists grouped together categories of concern with specific observations and impact analyses, proposals for future research, and indications that specific impacts were underway.

In the *Fourth Assessment Report (AR4)*, IPCC scientists continued with *Assessing Key Vulnerabilities and the Risk from Climate Change* (pp. 779–810), from Working Group II, and found that "the 'reasons for concern' identified in the TAR remain a viable framework for assessing vulnerabilities." Further, that evidence suggests that smaller increases in global mean temperature are needed to produce significant impacts described within the five reasons for concern.

In the years since the *TAR* and *AR4* were published, more confirming evidence and a deeper understanding have emerged. The lead scientist authors of the 2001 and 2007 chapters, Joel Smith and the late Stephen Schneider, respectively, gathered a group to update the "Reasons for Concern" in their paper "Assessing Dangerous Climate Change Through an Update of the IPCC 'Reasons for Concern'" [*Proceedings of the National Academy of Sciences* 106, 11 (March 17, 2009): 4133–4137]. The following summary is drawn from all three publications.

Figure 10.30 summarizes the five "Reasons for Concern" as they each inform climate change science. As you explore climate change, perhaps this framework can assist you in organizing your approach. The five IPCC reasons for concern are

A. **Risks to Unique and Threatened Systems**—Risks include irreversible losses to physical systems (e.g., glaciers, coral reefs, lakes, barrier islands, small islands) and biological systems (e.g., biodiversity hotspots, mangroves, ecosystem migrations, species extinctions), among others.

B. **Risks of Extreme Weather Events**—Risks include extreme event magnitude and frequency increase; intense precipitation and floods, tropical cyclone and tornado intensity increases, heat waves, droughts, and wildfires, among others.

C. **Uneven Distribution of Climate Change Impacts**—Impacts are greatest in low-latitude and less-developed countries and for circumpolar Arctic indigenous peoples; disparity occurs among economic classes of people; range and seasonality

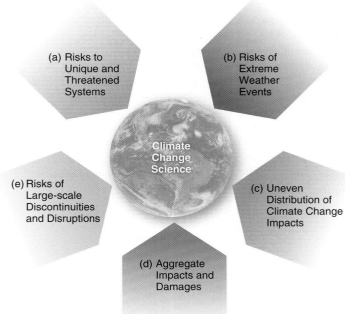

FIGURE 10.30 Summary of IPCC's five "Reasons for Concern." [Based on sources presented in the text.]

of disease vectors and health impacts tend to impact lower-latitude countries.

D. **Aggregate Impacts and Damages**—Effects are combined to assess total monetary damage and lives changed or lost; few developing countries or poor people have the financial, technical, or institutional base to support adaptation.

E. **Risks of Large-Scale Discontinuities and Disruptions**—Abrupt and dramatic system responses occur at thresholds where systems fluctuate above and below an average, yet show a trend over time—a dynamic equilibrium. As conditions change, the system can no longer maintain that operational level and spasms to a new equilibrium; that moment is a "tipping point." Resulting disruptions include the melting of mountain glaciers, Greenland and West Antarctic Ice Sheet losses, ocean acidification, permafrost melt and CO_2 liberation, and rapid sea-level rise, among others.

The fact that climate change is occurring is an accepted consensus among mainstream scientists. Determining the accelerating rate of this change is essential. In geologic time, changes in the environment occurred over millions of years, whereas elements of climate change today are happening over the span of decades.

 GEO REPORT 10.4   *The IPCC and the Nobel Peace Prize*

The IPCC, formed in 1988, is an organization operating under the United Nations Environment Programme (UNEP) and the World Meteorological Organization (WMO), and is the scientific organization coordinating global climate-change research, climate forecasts, and policy formulation. In 2007, the IPCC shared the Nobel Peace Prize with former U.S. Vice-President Albert Gore for its two decades of work raising understanding and awareness about global climate-change science.

The 800 000-year climate record from the Antarctic Dome-C ice core, discussed in Chapter 17, revealed that atmospheric CO_2 has never changed 30 ppm upward or downward during a period of less than 1000 years. Yet today, we see that atmospheric CO_2 rose 30 ppm in only the last 12 years. The rate of change affects the amount of time available for physical and biological systems to adapt. The accelerating rate of change is a key factor in all five "Reasons for Concern."

The International Scientific Conference on Climate Change met in March 2009 in Copenhagen to update the *AR4*. The conclusions from these meetings reinforce the "Reasons for Concern" in part:

- "The worst-case IPCC projections, or even worse, are being realized,"
- "Emissions are soaring, projections of sea-level rise are higher than expected,"
- "The acceleration of Greenland's and Antarctica's ice losses of mass are very clearly in evidence in satellite images,"
- "Inaction is inexcusable, weaker emissions targets for 2020 increases the risk of crossing numerous tipping points."[5]

Table 10.1 presents a sampling of major scientific organisations and websites dealing with climate change topics and reports.

[5]Summarized in E. Kintisch, "Global warming: projections of climate change go from bad to worse, scientists report," *Science* 323, 5921 (March 20, 2009): 1546–1547.

TABLE 10.1   Sources of Information for Global Climate Change Research

United Nations Environment Programme	http://www.unep.ch/
World Meteorological Organization	http://www.wmo.ch/
World Climate Research Programme	http://wcrp.wmo.int/
Global Climate Observing System	http://gosic.org/ios/GCOS-main-page.htm
Intergovernmental Panel on Climate Change	http://www.ipcc.ch/
Arctic Council	http://www.arctic-council.org/
Arctic Climate Impact Assessment	http://www.acia.uaf.edu/
Arctic Monitoring and Assessment Program	http://www.amap.no/
Conservation of Flora and Fauna	http://www.caff.is/
International Arctic Science Committee	http://www.arctic-council.org/
Environment Canada	http://climate.weatheroffice.gc.ca/
Canada's Action on Climate Change	http://www.climatechange.gc.ca/
U.S. Global Change Research Program	http://www.globalchange.gov.
U.S. Environmental Protection Agency	http://www.epa.gov/climatechange/
Goddard Institute for Space Studies	http://www.giss.nasa.gov/
Global Hydrology and Climate Center	http://www.ghcc.msfc.nasa.gov
National Climate Data Center	http://www.ncdc.noaa.gov/
National Environmental Satellite, Data, and Information Service	http://www.nesdis.noaa.gov/
NASA Global Climate Change	http://climate.nasa.gov/
NWS Climate Prediction Center	http://www.cpc.ncep.noaa.gov/
Climate Institute	http://www.climate.org/
Pew Center on Global Climate Change	http://www.pewclimate.org/
National Ice Center	http://www.natice.noaa.gov/
National Snow and Ice Data Center	http://nsidc.org/
National Center for Atmospheric Research	http://www.ncar.ucar.edu/
British Antarctic Survey	http://www.antarctica.ac.uk/
International Union for the Conservation of Nature and Natural Resources	http://www.iucn.org/
World.Org 100 Top Climate Change Sites	http://www.world.org/weo/climate

FIGURE 10.31 **A thousand years of record and the covariance of carbon dioxide and temperature.**
Carbon emissions, CO_2 concentrations, and temperature change correlate over the past 1000 years. This graph was prepared before the record-setting temperatures of 2005 and 2010. By May 2011, CO_2 levels were at 394 ppm. Earth systems are in record territory. [Illustration from ACIA, *Impacts of a Warming Arctic* (London: Cambridge University Press, 2004), p. 2. Used by permission of ACIA.]

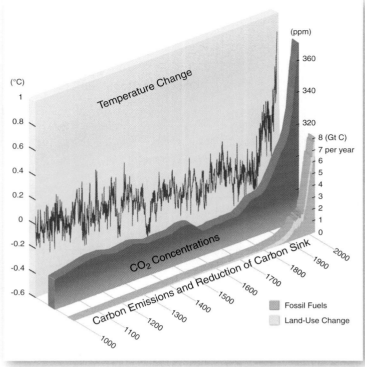

Climate Change Measurements

In the field of **paleoclimatology**, the science that studies past climates (discussed in Chapter 17), scientists use a number of proxy, or substitute, indicators for climate reconstruction. Data from ice cores, lake and ocean sediments, coral reefs, ancient pollen, and tree-ring density, among others, point to the present time as the warmest in the last 120 000 years. These proxy indicators also suggest that the increase in temperature during the twentieth century is *very likely* the largest in any century over the past 1000 years (Figure 10.31). Earth is less than 1 C° from equaling the highest average temperature of the past 125 000 years.

Figure 10.32a plots observed annual land-surface air temperatures and 5-year mean temperatures from 1880 through 2009. The record year for warmth for land-surface temperatures was tied between 2005 and 2010, with 2007, 2009, and 1998 the second, third, and fourth warmest. For the Southern Hemisphere, 2009 was the warmest in the modern record. The decade of 2001–2010 was the warmest decade in the entire record.

The map in Figure 10.32b uses the same base period as the graph (1951–1980) to give you an idea of temperature anomalies across the globe for 2010. Refer back to the temperature anomaly maps for several decades in Figure 1.1. Note the Arctic region through Hudson Bay, Canada, where new records for land and water temperatures and sea-ice melt were set. Anomalies exceeding 4.0 C° were measured in the Canadian Arctic and the Antarctic Peninsula.

Scientists are determining the difference between *forced fluctuations* (human-caused) and *unforced fluctuations* (natural) as a key to predicting future climate trends. Figure 10.33 shows a comparison of climate models, which include

natural forcing (shaded blue area) and anthropogenic forcing (shaded pink area) for Earth. The black line on the graph plots observations from 1906 to 2005. Clearly, only those coupled climate models that include human factors accurately simulate increasing temperatures. Solar variability and volcanic output alone do not explain the increase.

Because the enhanced greenhouse gases are anthropogenic in origin, various management strategies are possible to reduce human-forced climatic changes. Let's begin by examining the problem at its roots.

Greenhouse Gases Carbon dioxide and water vapour are the principal radiatively active gases causing Earth's natural greenhouse effect. *Radiatively active* gases include atmospheric gases, such as carbon dioxide (CO_2), methane (CH_4), nitrous oxide (N_2O), chlorofluorocarbons (CFCs), and water vapour, which absorb and radiate longwave energy. Figure 10.34 plots changes in three of these greenhouse gases over the past 10 000 years.

 GEO REPORT 10.5   *Professional Consensus on Climate Change*

The American Association for the Advancement of Science (AAAS) reported in "The Scientific Consensus on Climate Change," by Naomi Oreskes, [*Science* 306, 5702 (December 3, 2004): 1686], on the results of a survey of all 928 climate-change papers published between 1993 and 2003 and concluded: "Remarkably, none of the papers disagreed with the consensus position."

The Association of American Geographers (AAG; 11 000 members) passed the AAG Resolution Requesting Action on Climate Change in 2006. This resolution places the AAG in line with other professional organizations and many national academies of sciences, now on record for action to slow rates of climate change. The American Meteorological Society (AMS; 13 000 members) published its AMS Statement on Climate Change in 2007. The American Physical Society (APS; 46 000 members) adopted its APS National Policy on Climate Change in 2007, declaring that "human causes of climate change are well understood and beyond dispute." The Geological Society of America (GSA, 22 000) adopted its strong "Climate Change Statement" that global climate has warmed and that human activities (greenhouse gases) account for it.

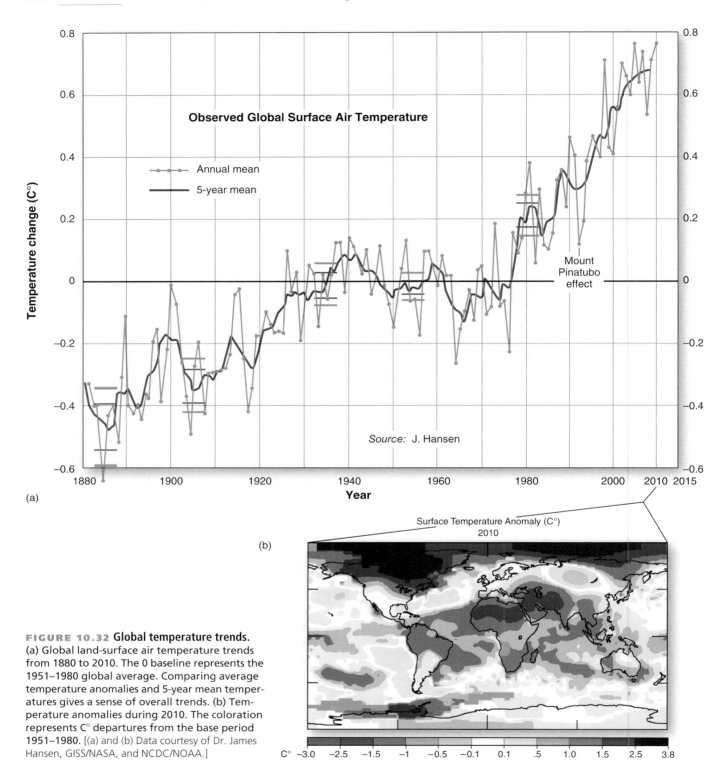

FIGURE 10.32 Global temperature trends.
(a) Global land-surface air temperature trends from 1880 to 2010. The 0 baseline represents the 1951–1980 global average. Comparing average temperature anomalies and 5-year mean temperatures gives a sense of overall trends. (b) Temperature anomalies during 2010. The coloration represents C° departures from the base period 1951–1980. [(a) and (b) Data courtesy of Dr. James Hansen, GISS/NASA, and NCDC/NOAA.]

Over the past several years, China produced the most carbon dioxide emissions, with the United States a close second. China, with 19.5% of global population, produces 4.9 metric tons per person, whereas the United States, with 4.5% of world population, is at 19.2 metric tons of CO_2 emissions per person. Clearly, per capita CO_2 emissions in the United States are far above what an average person in China produces. In comparison, Canada ranks seventh in world total emissions of CO_2 with only 00.5% of the world population, placing it third

(behind the U.S. and Australia) in per capita ranking at 17.3 metric tons per person.

Another radiatively active gas contributing to the overall greenhouse effect is methane (CH_4), which is increasing at a rate even faster than carbon dioxide. In ice cores, methane levels never topped 750 ppb in the past 800 000 years, yet in Figure 10.34 we see present levels at 1780 ppb. We are at an atmospheric concentration of methane that is higher than at any time in the past 800 millennia.

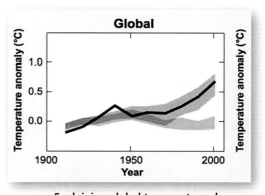

FIGURE 10.33 Explaining global temperature changes.
Computer models accurately track observed temperature change (black line) when they factor in human-forced influences on climate (pink shading). Solar activity and volcanoes do not explain the increases (blue shading). [IPCC, Working Group I, *Fourth Assessment Report: Climate Change 2007: The Physical Science Basis* (Geneva, Switzerland: IPCC Secretariat, February 2007), Fig. SPM-4, p. 11.]

▌▌ CRITICAL THINKING 10.2

The Forcing Element of Fuel Economy

Transportation is the major sector producing carbon dioxide emissions. In effect since 1975 in the United States, corporate average fuel economy (CAFE) requirements for automobiles are presently set at 8.55 L · 100 km^{-1}. For light trucks (including SUVs), these requirements were set at 10.6 L · 100 km^{-1} in 2007 and changed to 10 in 2010. In Figure 10.2.1, examine the higher standards in all the other countries sampled, including Canada.

A 24 litre per 100 km increase in efficiency could save more than a million barrels of oil per day, or more than half what the United States imports from the Persian Gulf states, making a 7 litre per 100 kilometres goal for 2020 quite appealing. Increased numbers of drivers and driving will negate some of these savings, making the solution more complex than just having more-fuel-efficient cars and trucks. Study the graph, and ponder the relative inefficiency of North American vehicles. Why are North American fuel standards about half those of the European Union and so far below the standard enforced in China? Why is having higher CAFE standards such a hard sell, given the price of fuel and all the problems involved with importing oil (conflicts, oil spills, balance of trade deficits), and drilling for oil? How do we communicate the upfront savings in money for drivers and the improved air quality that higher standards would bring?

FIGURE 10.2.1 Fuel economy standards for selected countries.
[Adapted from IPCC, *Climate Change 2007: Mitigation and Climate Change* (Geneva, Switzerland: IPCC Secretariat, February 2007), Fig. 5.18, p. 373.]

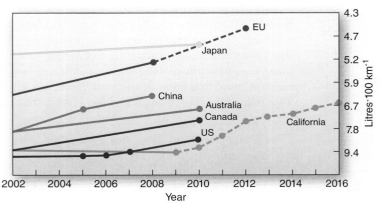

Changes in Greenhouse Gases from Ice-Core and Modern Data

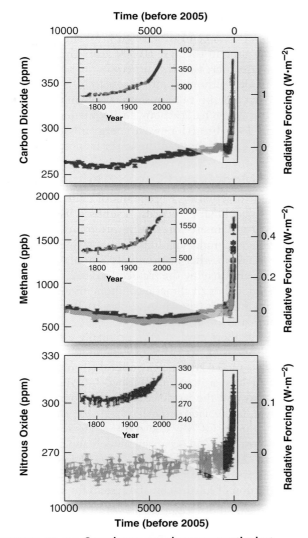

FIGURE 10.34 Greenhouse gas changes over the last 10 000 years.
Ice-core and modern data show the trends in carbon dioxide, methane, and nitrous oxide over the last 10 000 years. We are living in unique territory on these graphs. To update, during May 2010, CO_2 passed the 393 ppm level, CH_4 was at 1780 ppb, and N_2O approached 330 ppb. [IPCC, Working Group I, *Fourth Assessment Report: Climate Change 2007: The Physical Science Basis* (Geneva, Switzerland: IPCC Secretariat, February 2007), Fig. SPM-1, p. 3.]

Methane is generated by such organic processes as digestion and rotting in the absence of oxygen (anaerobic processes). About 50% of the excess methane comes from bacterial action in the intestinal tracts of livestock and from organic activity in flooded rice fields. Burning of vegetation causes another 20% of the excess, and bacterial action inside the digestive systems of termite populations also is a significant source. Methane is thought responsible for at least 19% of the total atmospheric warming. Melting permafrost is thought to be an important source of methane that will rise in prominence with continued global warming.

Nitrous oxide (N_2O) is the third most important greenhouse gas that is forced by human activity—up 17% in atmospheric concentration since 1750 and now higher than at any time in the past 10 000 years (Figure 10.34). Fertilizer use increases the processes in soil that emit nitrous oxide, although more research is needed to fully understand the relationships. Chlorofluorocarbons (CFCs) and other halocarbons also contribute to global warming. CFCs absorb longwave energy missed by carbon dioxide and water vapour in the lower troposphere.

Climate Models and Future Temperatures

In addition to actual measurements of climatic elements and the paleoclimatic records, scientists use computer models to run climate-forecasting programs. The scientific challenge in understanding climate change is to sense climatic trends in what is essentially a nonlinear, chaotic natural system. Imagine the tremendous task of building a computer model of all climatic components and programming these linkages (shown in Figure 10.2) over different time frames and at various scales.

Using mathematical models originally established for forecasting weather, scientists developed a complex computer climate model known as a **general circulation model (GCM)**. At least a dozen established GCMs are now in operation around the world. Submodel programs for the atmosphere, ocean, land surface, cryosphere, and biosphere operate within a GCM. The most sophisticated models couple atmosphere and ocean submodels and are known as *Atmosphere-Ocean General Circulation Models (AOGCMs)*.

The first step in describing a climate is to define a manageable portion of Earth's climatic system for study. Climatologists create dimensional "grid boxes" that extend from beneath the ocean to the tropopause, in multiple layers (Figure 10.35). Resolution of these boxes in the atmosphere is about 250 km in the horizontal and 1 km in the vertical; in the ocean the boxes use the same horizontal resolution and a vertical resolution of about 200 to 400 m. Analysts deal not only with the climatic components within each grid layer but also with the interaction among the layers on all sides.

A comparative benchmark among the operational GCMs is *climatic sensitivity* to doubling of carbon dioxide levels in the atmosphere. GCMs do not predict specific temperatures, but do offer various scenarios of global warming. GCM-generated maps correlate well with the observed global warming patterns experienced since 1990.

The 2007 IPCC *Fourth Assessment Report*, using a variety of GCM forecast scenarios, predicted a range of average surface warming for this century. Figure 10.36 illustrates six of these scenarios, each with its own assumptions of economics, population, degree of global cooperation, and greenhouse gas emission levels. The orange line is the simulation experiment where greenhouse gas emissions are held at 2000 values with no increases. The grey bars give you the best estimate and likely ranges of outcomes; for example, from a "low forecast" in B1 to a

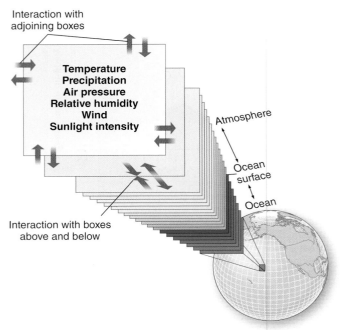

FIGURE 10.35 A general circulation model scheme. Temperature, precipitation, air pressure, relative humidity, wind, and sunlight intensity are sampled in myriad grid boxes. In the ocean, sampling is limited, but temperature, salinity, and ocean current data are considered. The interactions within a grid layer, and between layers on all six sides, are modeled in a general circulation model program.

"high forecast" in A1Fl. Even the "B" scenario represents a significant increase in global land and ocean temperatures and will produce consequences.

Changes in Sea Level Sea-level rise is occurring, and the rate is accelerating. The rate in the late twentieth century was about three times that of the late nineteenth century. Since the 1990s, the rate is about six times greater, at $3 \text{ mm} \cdot \text{yr}^{-1}$. During the last century, sea level rose 10–20 cm, a rate 10 times higher than the average during the last 3000 years. Sea level is rising because of melting ice sheets and glaciers that add water and because of thermal expansion that occurs as the ocean absorbs heat energy and warms. There is more on this subject in Chapters 16 and 17.

The 2007 IPCC forecast scenarios for global mean sea-level rise this century are already being exceeded. Unfortunately, new measurements of Greenland's ice-loss acceleration and Antarctica's ice losses were not within the time frame for the *AR4* report. Scientists are considering at least a 1.4-m "high case" for estimates of sea-level rise sometime this century as more realistic, given Greenland's present losses coupled with mountain glacial ice losses worldwide. Keep in mind that a 0.3-m rise in sea level would produce a shoreline retreat of 30 m on average. Here is the concern:

> The data now available raise concerns that the climate system, in particular sea level, may be responding more quickly than climate models indicate. . . . The rate of sea-level rise for the past 20 years is 25% faster than the rate of rise in any

Multi-model Averages and Assessed Ranges for Surface Warming

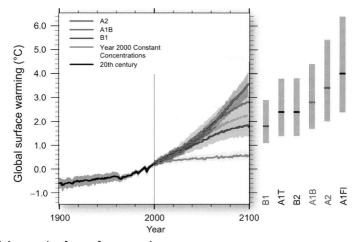

FIGURE 10.36 Model scenarios for surface warming.
Ranging from business as usual, lack of international cooperation, and continuation of the use of fossil fuels
(A2FI) to a low-emission scenario (B1), each scenario spells climatic catastrophe to some degree. Holding
emissions at the 2000 concentration (orange line plot) is predicted to result in the least temperature impacts.
[Graph from IPCC, Working Group I, *Fourth Assessment Report: Climate Change 2007: The Physical Science Basis*
(Geneva, Switzerland: IPCC Secretariat, February 2007), Fig. SPM-5, p. 14.]

20-year period in the preceding 115 years. . . . Since 1990 the observed sea-level has been rising faster than the rise projected by models.[6]

These increases would continue beyond 2100 even if greenhouse gas concentrations were stabilized.

A quick survey of world coastlines shows that even a moderate rise could bring change of unparalleled proportions. At stake are the river deltas, lowland coastal farming valleys, and low-lying mainland areas, all contending with high water, high tides, and higher storm surges. Particularly tragic social and economic consequences will affect small island states, which are unable to adjust within their present country boundaries—disruption of biological systems, loss of biodiversity, reduction in water resources, and evacuation of residents are among the impacts that will be felt as water rises.

The future may bring both internal and international migration of affected human populations, spread over decades, as people move away from coastal flooding caused by the sea-level rise—a 1-m rise would displace 130 million people. Presently there is no body of world law that covers "environmental refugees." In Chapter 16, maps present what coastlines will experience in the event of such a 1-m rise in sea level.

"No Regrets"

Reading through all this climate change science must seem pretty "heavy." Instead, think of this information as empowering and motivating people to take action—personally, locally, regionally, nationally, and globally.

The IPCC declared that "no regrets" opportunities to reduce carbon dioxide emissions are available in most countries and are defined as follows:

[6]S. Rahmstorf et al., "Recent climate observations compared to projections," *Science* 316, 5825 (May 4, 2007): 709.

No regrets options are by definition greenhouse gas emissions reduction options that have negative net costs, because they generate direct and indirect benefits that are large enough to offset the costs of implementing the options.

Benefits that equal or exceed their cost to society include reduced energy cost, improved air quality and health, reduction in tanker spills and oil imports, and deployment of renewable and sustainable energy sources, with the growth of new related business opportunities, among others. This holds true without even considering the benefits of slowing the rate of climate change.

For Europe, scientists determined that carbon emissions could be reduced to less than half the 1990 level by 2030, at a negative cost. A study by the U.S. Department of Energy's national laboratories found that the United States can meet the Kyoto carbon emission reduction targets with negative overall costs (cash benefit savings) ranging from −$7 to −$34 billion. Of course, one key to "no regrets" is untapped energy-efficiency and conservation potentials.

The most comprehensive economic analysis is *The Economics of Climate Change: The Stern Review*, prepared by Nicholas Stern for the British government (Cambridge, England: Cambridge University Press, 2007; 692 pages). This report concluded as follows:

- There is still time to avoid the worst impacts of climate change, if we take strong action now.
- Climate change could have very serious impacts on growth and development.
- The costs of stabilizing the climate are significant but manageable; delay would be dangerous and much more costly.
- Action on climate change is required across all countries, and it need not cap the aspirations of growth in rich and poor countries.

- A range of options exists to cut emissions; strong, deliberate policy action is required to motivate their uptake.
- Climate change demands an international response, based on shared understanding of long-term goals and agreement on frameworks for action.

Twenty-three years ago climatologists Richard Houghton and George Woodwell described the present climatic condition:

CRITICAL THINKING 10.3

Thinking Through an Action Plan to Reduce Human Climate Forcing

Many external factors force climate, as you can see in Figure 10.3.1. Let us work with the chart to see how the variables influence climate change decisions.

The estimates of radiative forcing (RF) in watts-per-square-metre ($W \cdot m^{-2}$) units are given on the x-axis (horizontal axis). In the far-right column, LOSU refers to "level of scientific understanding." Those bars that extend to the right of the "0" value (in red, orange, and yellow) indicate warming, or *positive forcing*, such as "long-lived greenhouse gases." Bars that go to the left of the "0" value (in blue) indicate cooling, or *negative forcing*, such as cloud-albedo effect. Each bar also includes an estimate of the uncertainty range.

Assume you are a policy maker with a goal of reducing the rate of climate change—that is, reducing positive radiative forcing of the climate system. What strategies do you suggest to alter the extent of the columns and adjust the mix of elements that cause temperature increases? Assign priorities to each suggested strategy to denote the most- to least-effective strategies in moderating climate change. Brainstorm and discuss your strategies with others.

The world is warming. Climatic zones are shifting. Glaciers are melting. Sea level is rising. These are not hypothetical events from a science fiction movie; these changes and others are already taking place, and we expect them to accelerate over the next years as the amounts of carbon dioxide, methane, and other trace gases accumulating in the atmosphere through human activities increase.[7]

[7]R. Houghton and G. Woodwell, "Global climate change," *Scientific American* (April 1989): 36.

GEOSYSTEMS CONNECTION

Chapter 10 is a synthesis of systems in Chapters 2 through 9 of *Geosystems* and marks the end of Part II. Climate classification categories give us a portrait of energy and moisture and of solar insolation and surface energy budgets and provide a baseline that we can use to track changing climatic boundaries, given climate change. Next, we move to Part III, where Earth and the atmosphere interface—where the systems of each meet. We begin with the endogenic system in Chapters 11 and 12, where energy wells up from within Earth—with such power that crustal plates are dragged and pushed around, sometimes in dramatic episodes. We study rock-forming processes and the nature of deformation by folding, faulting, and displacement, and we spend time with earthquakes and volcanic eruptions.

Analysis of Radiative Forcing of Temperature

FIGURE 10.3.1 **Analysis of radiative forcing of temperatures.** [IPCC, Working Group I, *Fourth Assessment Report: Climate Change 2007: The Physical Science Basis* (Geneva, Switzerland: IPCC Secretariat, February 2007), Figure SPM-2, p. 4, and Figure 2.20, p. 203.]

APPLIED PHYSICAL GEOGRAPHY *Calculating a Climate-Change Index*

Is it possible to reduce the relative magnitude of complex climate changes into just one number, analogous to a stock market index? A group of scientists representing the International Geosphere Biosphere Program has done just that by creating the IGBP Climate-Change Index (http://www.igbp.net/4.1b8ae20512db692f2a680001647.html). The index combines data for four key climate change indicators: global average temperature, atmospheric CO_2 concentration, global mean sea level, and Arctic sea ice cover.

The index is calculated annually and can be summed over a number of consecutive years to show accumulated change over time. For the period 1980–2007, 25 of the 28 years had positive index values, with only 1982, 1992, and 1996 being the exceptions. Cumulatively, the unequivocal increasing trend in the index indicates a persistent shift away from relatively stable climate.

To calculate the index for a sample data set (2001–2007), annual values of the four indicator variables are required (Table 1). Year-to-year changes are calculated and the maximum recorded annual change in the series is noted for each variable. Then the ratio of each value of annual change is normalized to a scale of −100 to +100, with +100 representing the maximum recorded annual change and 0 corresponding to no annual change. (Note that decreases in Arctic sea ice cover are multiplied by −1 to produce positive scaled values.)

The calculation of normalized values results in the measurement units cancelling out, so the values ranging from −100 to +100 are dimensionless ratios. Converting annual changes into normalized values means that changes in variables with different units can be compared and combined into a single overall index.

For example, scaled values of annual temperature change (ΔTj) are calculated as:

$$\Delta Tj = (Tj - Ti)/\Delta T_{max} \times 100$$

where i and j are two consecutive years and ΔT_{max} is the maximum recorded change in annual temperature in the series. For 2001, the scaled change in temperature is:

$$\Delta T_{2001} = (T_{2001} - T_{2000})/\Delta T_{max} \times 100$$
$$= (14.55 - 14.41)/0.19 \times 100$$
$$= 0.14/0.19 \times 100$$
$$= 73.7$$

The annual climate-change index is calculated as the average of the scaled values of the four indicator variables (Table 2). To show the trend over time, the annual values are then cumulated. Note that the index value for a given year may vary, depending on the values of maximum recorded annual changes within the time period analyzed that are used in the calculations. IGBP scientists are considering how the index might be modified, such as whether the indicator variables should have different weights or whether the list of variables should be expanded.

TABLE 1 2000–2007 Dataset for Calculating IGBP Climate-Change Index

Year	Global Average Temperature (°C) Original Data*	Atmospheric CO_2 Concentration (ppmv)	Global Mean Sea Level (mm)	Minimum Arctic Sea Ice Cover (million km²)
2000	14.41	369.48	114.15	6.32
2001	14.55	371.02	115.24	6.75
2002	14.68	373.10	115.28	5.96
2003	14.66	375.64	121.73	6.15
2004	14.58	377.38	123.41	6.05
2005	14.77	379.67	128.05	5.57
2006	14.66	381.84	141.67	5.92
2007	14.75	383.55	137.64	4.30
Year–to–Year Differences (maximum difference underlined)				
2001	0.14	1.54	1.09	0.43
2002	0.13	2.08	0.04	−0.79
2003	−0.02	<u>2.54</u>	6.45	0.19
2004	−0.08	1.74	1.68	−0.10
2005	<u>0.19</u>	2.29	4.64	−0.48
2006	−0.11	2.17	<u>13.62</u>	0.35
2007	0.09	1.71	−4.03	<u>−1.62</u>

*Data sources: temperature—NASA (http://data.giss.nasa.gov/gistemp/tabledata/GLB.Ts.txt); CO_2— Carbon Dioxide Information Analysis Center, Mauna Loa (http://cdiac.ornl.gov/ftp/trends/co2/maunaloa.co2); sea level—CSIRO (http://www.psmsl.org/products/reconstructions/church.php); and sea ice—NOAA (ftp://sidads.colorado.edu/DATASETS/NOAA/G02135/Sep/N_09_area.txt).

TABLE 2	IGBP Climate-Change Index for 2001–2007					
Year	Scaled Difference Values (dimensionless)				Annual Index	Cumulative Index
	Temperature	CO_2	Sea Level	Sea Ice		
2001	73.7	60.6	8.0	−26.5	+29	+29
2002	68.4	81.9	0.3	48.8	+50	+79
2003	−10.5	100.0	47.4	−11.7	+31	+110
2004	−42.1	68.5	12.3	6.2	+11	+121
2005	100.0	90.2	34.1	29.6	+63	+185
2006	−57.9	85.4	100.0	−21.6	+26	+211
2007	47.4	67.3	−29.6	100.0	+46	+258

KEY LEARNING CONCEPTS REVIEW

■ **Define** climate and climatology, and *explain* the difference between climate and weather.

Climate is dynamic, not static. **Climate** is a synthesis of weather phenomena at many scales, from planetary to local, in contrast to weather, which is the condition of the atmosphere at any given time and place. Earth experiences a wide variety of climatic conditions that can be grouped by general similarities into climatic regions. **Climatology** is the study of climate and attempts to discern similar weather statistics and identify **climatic regions**.

climate (p. 264)
climatology (p. 265)
climatic regions (p. 265)

1. Define climate and compare it with weather. What is climatology?
2. Explain how a climatic region synthesizes climate statistics.
3. How does the El Niño phenomenon produce the largest interannual variability in climate? What are some of the changes and effects that occur worldwide?

■ **Review** how temperature, precipitation, air pressure, and air mass patterns are used to delineate climatic regions.

Climatic inputs include insolation (pattern of solar energy in the Earth–atmosphere environment), temperature (sensible heat energy content of the air), precipitation (rain, sleet, snow, and hail—the supply of moisture), air pressure (varying patterns of atmospheric density), and air masses (regional-sized homogeneous units of air). Climate is the basic element in ecosystems, the natural, self-regulating communities of plants and animals that thrive in specific environments.

4. How do radiation receipts, temperature, air pressure inputs, and precipitation patterns interact to produce climate types? Give an example from a humid environment and one from an arid environment.
5. **Describe** the relationships among a climatic region, ecosystem, and biome.

■ **Review** the development of climate classification systems, and **compare** genetic and empirical systems as ways of classifying climates.

Classification is the process of ordering or grouping data in related categories. A **genetic classification** is based on causative factors, such as the interaction of air masses. An **empirical** classification is one based on statistical data, such as temperature or precipitation. This text analyzes climate using aspects of both approaches, with a map based on climatological elements.

classification (p. 268)
genetic classification (p. 268)
empirical classification (p. 269)

6. What are the differences between genetic and empirical classification systems?
7. What are some of the climatological elements used in classifying climates? Why each of these? Use the approach on the climate classification map in Figure 10.6 in preparing your answer.

■ **Describe** the principal climate classification categories other than deserts, and **locate** these regions on a world map.

Keep in mind the classification of climate is produced by analysis of the interacting elements of weather and climate. These data are plotted on a **climograph** to display the characteristics of the climate.

There are six basic climate categories. Temperature and precipitation considerations form the basis of five climate categories and their regional types:

■ Tropical (tropical latitudes)
rain forest (rainy all year)
monsoon (6 to 12 months rainy)
savanna (less than 6 months rainy)

■ Mesothermal (midlatitudes, mild winters)
humid subtropical (hot to warm summers)
marine west coast (warm to cool summers)
Mediterranean (dry summers)

■ Microthermal (mid and high latitudes, cold winters)
humid continental (hot to warm, mild summers)
subarctic (cool summers to very cold winters)

■ Polar (high latitudes and polar regions)
tundra (high latitude or high elevation)
ice caps and ice sheets (perpetually frozen)
polar marine

■ Highland (high elevations at all latitudes; highlands have lower temperatures)

Only one climate category is based on moisture efficiency as well as temperature:

- Desert (permanent moisture deficits)

arid deserts (tropical, subtropical hot, and midlatitude cold)

semiarid steppes (tropical, subtropical hot, and midlatitude cold)

    climograph (p. 271)

8. List and discuss each of the principal climate categories. In which one of these general types do you live? Which category is the only type associated with the annual amount and distribution of precipitation?
9. What is a climograph, and how is it used to display climatic information?
10. Which of the major climate types occupies the most land and ocean area on Earth?
11. Characterise the tropical climates in terms of temperature, moisture, and location.
12. Using Africa's tropical climates as an example, characterize the climates produced by the seasonal shifting of the ITCZ with the high Sun.
13. Mesothermal climates (midlatitudes, mild winter) occupy the second-largest portion of Earth's entire surface. Describe the temperature, moisture, and precipitation characteristics of these climates.
14. Explain the distribution of the *humid subtropical hot-summer* and *Mediterranean dry-summer* climates at *similar latitudes* and the difference in precipitation patterns between the two types. Describe the difference in vegetation associated with these two climate types.
15. Which climates are characteristic of the Asian monsoon region?
16. Explain how a *marine west coast* climate type can occur in the Appalachian region of the eastern United States.
17. What role do offshore ocean currents play in the distribution of the *marine west coast* climates? What type of fog is formed in these regions?
18. Discuss the climatic conditions for the coldest places on Earth outside the poles.

- **Explain** the precipitation and moisture efficiency criteria used to determine the desert (arid and semiarid) climates, and **locate** these regions on a world map.

The dry and semi-arid climates are described by precipitation rather than temperature.

Major subdivisions are *arid deserts* in tropical and midlatitude areas (precipitation—natural water supply—less than one-half of natural water demand) and *semiarid steppes* in tropical and midlatitude areas (precipitation more than one-half of

natural water demand). A **steppe** is a regional term referring to the vast semiarid grassland biome of Eastern Europe and Asia (the equivalent biome in North America is called shortgrass prairie; in Africa, the savanna).

    steppe (p. 290)

19. In general terms, what are the differences among the four desert classifications? How are moisture and temperature distributions used to differentiate these subtypes?
20. Relative to the distribution of arid and semiarid climates, describe at least three locations where these climates occur across the globe and the reasons for being present in these locations.

- **Explain** the causes and potential consequences of climate change, and **outline** future climate patterns from forecasts.

Various activities of present-day society are producing climatic changes, particularly a global warming trend. The highest average annual temperatures experienced since the advent of instrumental measurements have dominated the last 25 years. There is a scientific consensus that global warming is related to the anthropogenic impacts on the natural greenhouse effect.

The 2007 *Fourth Assessment Report* affirms this consensus. The IPCC predicted surface-temperature response to a doubling of carbon dioxide. Natural climatic variability over the span of Earth's history is the subject of **paleoclimatology**. A **general circulation model (GCM)** forecasts climate patterns and is providing greater capability and accuracy than in the past. People and their political institutions can use GCM forecasts to form policies aimed at reducing unwanted climate change.

    paleoclimatology (p. 297)

    general circulation model (GCM) (p. 300)

21. Explain climate forecasts. How do general circulation models (GCMs) produce such forecasts?
22. Describe the potential climatic effects of global warming on polar and high-latitude regions. What are the implications of these climatic changes for persons living at lower latitudes?
23. How is climatic change affecting agricultural and food production? Natural environments? Forests? The possible spread of disease?
24. What are the actions being taken at present to delay the effects of global climate change? What is the Kyoto Protocol? What is the current status of Canadian and U.S. government action on the Protocol?

MyGeosciencePlace

> Visit **www.mygeoscienceplace.ca** for several figure animations, satellite loops, self-study quizzes, flashcards, interactive glossary, career links, RSS feeds, Pearson eText of *Geosystems*, and much more.

INPUTS
Earth
Endogenic systems
Exogenic systems

ACTIONS
Rock and mineral
formation
Tectonic processes
Weathering
Erosion, transport,
deposition

OUTPUTS
Crustal deformation
Orogenesis and
volcanism
Landforms: karst,
fluvial, eolian,
coastal, glacial

**HUMAN-EARTH
RELATION**
Hazard perception,
Humans as
geomorphic agent,
Fluvial impacts. Sea-
level rise, Ice-melt

USA: Louisiana
Weiss and Overpeck
The University of Arizona

PART III

I. Atmosphere

II. Hydrosphere

IV. Biosphere

III. Lithosphere

The Earth-Atmosphere Interface

Earth is a dynamic planet whose surface is shaped by active physical agents of change. Two broad systems—endogenic and exogenic—organize these agents in Part III. The **endogenic system** (Chapters 11 and 12) encompasses internal processes that produce flows of heat and material from deep below Earth's crust. Radioactive decay principally powers these processes. The materials involved constitute the solid realm of Earth. Earth's surface responds by moving, warping, and breaking, sometimes in dramatic episodes of earthquakes and volcanic eruptions, constructing the crust.

At the same time, the **exogenic system** (Chapters 13 through 17) involves external processes that set into motion air, water, and ice, all powered by solar energy—this is the fluid realm of Earth's environment. These media carve, shape, and reduce the landscape. One such process, weathering, breaks up and dissolves the crust. Erosion picks up these materials; transports them in rivers, winds, coastal waves, and flowing glaciers; and deposits them along the way. Thus, Earth's surface is the interface between two vast open systems: one that builds the landscape and topographic relief and one that tears it down into sedimentary plains.

The Gulf of Oman enters the Straits of Hormuz into the Persian Gulf, as dust storms move south across Iran and the Zagros Crush Zone. [*Terra* NASA/GSFC.]

CHAPTER 11

The Dynamic Planet

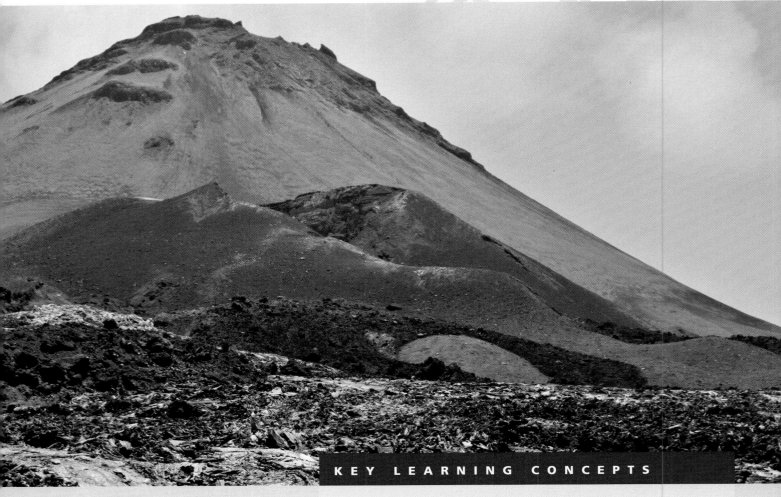

Pico de Fogo volcano, in the Cape Verde Islands in the Atlantic Ocean, rises to 2830 m. An eruption from the small vent cone on the slopes of Pico (stained with sulfur compounds) happened in 1995. This forced the evacuation of the village Chã das Caldeiras, located in the crater of the larger volcano Chã, with a previous history of almost continuous eruptions between 1500 and 1760. Farming, including some vineyards and coffee, is done in the volcanic soils; homes are built with blocks of basaltic rock. [Bobbé Christopherson.]

KEY LEARNING CONCEPTS

After reading the chapter, you should be able to:

- **Distinguish** between the endogenic and exogenic systems, **determine** the driving force for each, and **explain** the pace at which these systems operate.

- **Diagram** Earth's interior in cross section, and **describe** each distinct layer.

- **Illustrate** the geologic cycle, and **relate** the rock cycle and rock types to endogenic and exogenic processes.

- **Describe** Pangaea and its breakup, and **relate** several physical proofs that crustal drifting is continuing today.

- **Portray** the pattern of Earth's major plates, and **relate** this pattern to the occurrence of earthquakes, volcanic activity, and hot spots.

Earth's Migrating Magnetic Poles

In this chapter, we journey to the center of Earth and study Earth's core, divided between a solid inner core and a dense, but fluid, outer core. Earth's magnetic field is principally generated by motions in this outer core. In Chapter 1, we discussed the north geographic pole—the axial pole centred where the meridians of longitude converge. This is *true north* and is a fixed point. However, Earth's magnetic field is focused at a different set of poles, which move at a measurable rate.

When we use a compass to find directions, the needle points to the *North Magnetic Pole* (NMP). At this pole, the magnetic field is directed vertically downward, the magnetic dip, relative to Earth's surface. This is the observed magnetic pole, located and mapped by magnetic surveys.

Consider North at the top of a circle and *azimuth* as the degrees of arc clockwise around the circle from North. This makes due East 90°, due South 180°, due West 270°, and returning to North at 360° or 0°. The compass points to the NMP. Based on the location where you are measuring with the compass, there could be an angular distance in degrees between the NMP and true north: this is the magnetic declination. Use the declination calculator provided by the Geological Survey of Canada (GSC) at http://geomag.nrcan.gc.ca/apps/mdcal-eng.php to determine magnetic declination where you live.

As the magnetic field of Earth changes, the NMP slowly drifts across the Canadian Arctic. Scientists have traced a long history of change in the location of the NMP.

As a surface expression of Earth's magnetic field, the NMP moved 1100 km just this past century. The GSC tracks the motion of the NMP (see http://gsc.nrcan.gc.ca/geomag/nmp/northpole_e.php).

Surveys are a collaborative effort between the GSC and the Bureau de Recherches Géologiques et Minières in France. Presently the NMP is moving northwestward toward Siberia at approximately 50 km per year. The observed positions for 1831–2012 are mapped in Figure GN 11.1. Approximate NMP coordinates are presented in Table GN 11.1 for the years 2001 to a prediction for 2015. Each day the actual magnetic pole migrates in a small oval pattern around the average locations given on the map.

The NMP is near 85° N 147° W in 2012 in the Canadian Arctic. Its antipode, or opposite pole, is the *South Magnetic Pole* (SMP), which lies off the coast of Wilkes Land, Antarctica. The SMP moves separately from the NMP and is presently headed northwest at just 5 km per year. This chapter discusses the changing intensity of Earth's magnetic field and how the field periodically reverses polarity.

0   125   250
KILOMETRES

FIGURE GN 11.1

TABLE GN 11.1	Approximate North Magnetic Pole Coordinates 2001 to 2015	
Year	**Latitude (°N)**	**Longitude (°W)**
2001	81.3	110.8
2002	81.6	111.6
2003	82	112.4
2004	82.3	113.4
2005	82.7	114.4
2006	83.9	119.9
2007	84.4	121.7
2008	84.2	124.9
2009	84.9	131.0
2010	85.0	132.6
2011	85.1	134
2012	85.9	147
2015 prediction	86.1	153

Discoveries have revolutionized our understanding of Earth system science and how continents and oceans came to be arranged as we see today. A new era of understanding is emerging, combining various sciences within the study of physical geography. One task of physical geography is to explain the *spatial implications* of all this new information.

In this chapter: Earth's interior is organized as a core surrounded by roughly concentric shells of material. It is heated unevenly by the radioactive decay of unstable elements. A rock cycle produces three classes of rocks through igneous, sedimentary, and metamorphic processes. Internal processes coupled with the rock cycle, hydrologic cycle, and tectonic cycle result in a varied crustal surface featuring irregular fractures, extensive mountain ranges both on land and the ocean floor, drifting continental masses and ocean floors, and frequent earthquakes and volcanic events. All of this movement of materials results from endogenic forces within Earth—the subject of this chapter.

The Pace of Change

The **geologic time scale**, shown in Figure 11.1, is a summary timeline since Earth was formed. It reflects currently accepted names of time intervals for each segment of Earth's history, from vast *eons* through briefer *eras*, *periods*, and *epochs*. Present knowledge places Earth's age at 4.6 billion years, with the Moon about 30 million years younger, formed when a Mars-sized object struck early Earth.

The time scale depicts two important kinds of time: *relative* (what happened in what order) and *absolute* (actual number of years before the present). Also on the geologic time scale, note the labels denoting the six major extinctions of life forms in Earth history. Rather than being complete extinctions, think of some of these spasms in planetary life as significant *depletions*. These range from 440 million years ago (m.y.a.) to the ongoing present-day episode caused by modern civilization.

Relative time corresponds to the *sequence* of events, based on the relative positions of rock strata above or below each other. Relative time is based on the important general principle of *superposition*, which states that *rock and sediment always are arranged with the youngest beds "superposed" toward the top of a rock formation and the oldest at the*

base, assuming that the beds have not been disturbed and tilted. The study of these sequences is called *stratigraphy*. Thus, relative time places the Precambrian Eon at the bottom (beginning) of the time scale and the Holocene Epoch (today) at the top. Important time clues—namely, *fossils*, the remains of ancient plants and animals—lie embedded within these strata. Since approximately 4.0 billion years ago, life has left its evolving imprint in the rocks.

Scientific methods such as radiometric dating determine *absolute time*, the actual "millions of years ago" shown on the time scale. These absolute ages permit scientists to update geologic time actively, refining the time-scale sequence and lending greater accuracy to relative dating sequences. For more on the geologic time scale, see http://www.ucmp.berkeley.edu/exhibit/geology.html.

Holocene is the name given to the youngest epoch in the geologic time scale, characteristic of the last 11 500 years since the retreat of the continental glaciers. Because of the impact of human society on planetary systems, discussion is underway about designating a new name for the human epoch. A proposal is to call this time the *Anthropocene*.

However, when would such a time begin? Some think the beginning of the Industrial Revolution in the eighteenth century is the best starting point, whereas others think an appropriate time is some 5000 years ago when Asians began flooding rice fields that released methane gas into the atmosphere. Or perhaps 8000 years ago is a better chronology with the spread of domesticated crops, widespread clearing of forests, and the human use of fire to modify environments. Human impacts on the atmosphere began at the roots of civilization.

> **▮▮ CRITICAL THINKING 11.1**
>
> ### Thoughts about an "Anthropocene" Epoch
>
> Take a moment to explore this concept of naming our human epoch in the geologic time scale. Determine some arguments for such a change, considering landscape alteration, deforestation, and climate change. If we were to designate the late Holocene as the Anthropocene, what do you think the criteria for the beginning date should be?

A guiding principle of Earth science is **uniformitarianism**, which assumes that *the same physical processes active in the environment today have been operating throughout geologic*

GEO REPORT 11.1 *RADIOACTIVE DATING AND EARTH TIME*

Radiometric dating of Earth materials involves the steady decay of certain atoms. An atom contains protons and neutrons in its nucleus. Certain forms of atoms called *isotopes* have unstable nuclei; that is, the protons and neutrons do not remain together indefinitely. As particles break away and the nucleus disintegrates, radiation is emitted, and the atom decays into a different element—this process is *radioactivity*. This provides the steady time clock needed to measure the age of ancient rocks, since the decay rates for different isotopes are determined precisely. Scientists compare the amount of original isotope in the sample with the amount of decayed end product in the sample to determine the date the rock formed. See Applied Physical Geography at the end of the chapter for more information on radioactive dating and decay.

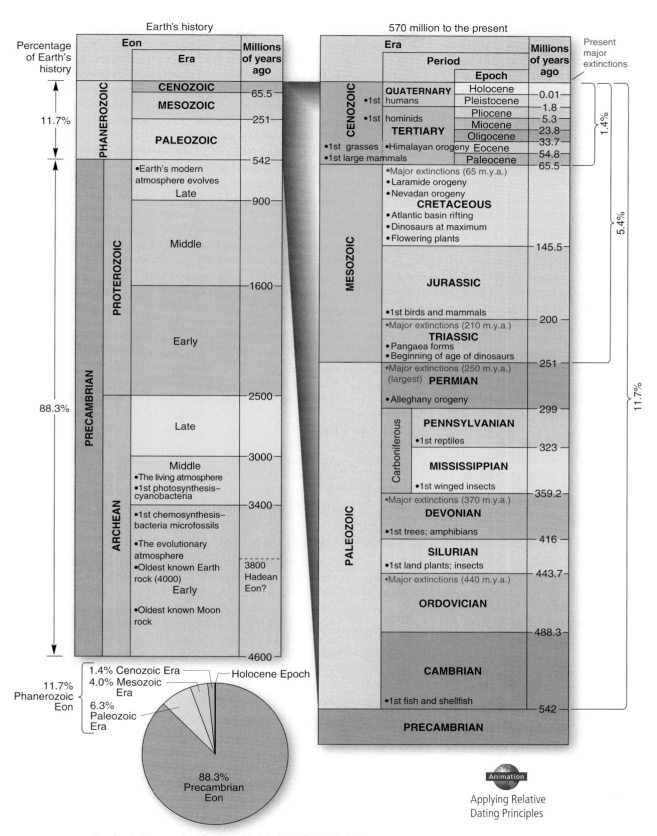

Applying Relative Dating Principles

FIGURE 11.1 Geologic time scale, showing highlights of Earth's history.
The six major extinctions or depletions of life forms are shown in red. The sixth extinction episode is under way at the present time. In the column to the left, note that 88.3% of geologic time occurred during the Precambrian Eon. Dates appear in m.y.a. (million years ago) [Data and update from Geological Society of America and *Nature* 429 (May 13, 2004): 124–125.]

time. For example, if streams carve valleys now, streams must have done so 500 m.y.a. The phrase "the present is the key to the past" describes this principle. Evidence from exploration and from the landscape record of volcanic eruptions, earthquakes, and exogenic processes support uniformitarianism. The concept was first proposed by James Hutton in *Theory of the Earth* (1795) and was later amplified by Charles Lyell in *Principles of Geology* (1830).

Within the principle of uniformitarianism, catastrophic events such as massive landslides, earthquakes, volcanic eruptions, extraterrestrial asteroid impacts, and sometimes recurring episodes of mountain building punctuate geologic time. Vast superfloods occurred as huge quantities of water were released from ice-dammed lakes such as glacial Lake Missoula, in the later days of the last ice age which left evidence across a broad region. These localized catastrophic events occur as small interruptions in the generally uniform processes that shape the slowly evolving landscape. Here the *punctuated equilibrium* concept (interruptions occur in the flow of events: systems jump to new operation levels) studied in the life sciences and palaeontology might apply to aspects of Earth's long developmental history.

We start our journey deep within the planet. Knowledge of Earth's internal structure and energy is key to understanding the surface.

Earth's Structure and Internal Energy

Along with the other planets and the Sun, Earth is thought to have condensed and congealed from a nebula of dust, gas, and icy comets about 4.6 billion years ago (Chapter 2). Until recently, the oldest known surface rocks on Earth were in northwestern Canada. The Acasta Gneiss is a 3.96 billion-year-old formation; other Slave Province rocks date to 4.03 billion year old. Some rocks from Greenland date back to 3.8 billion years old.

Detrital zircons (particles of preexisting zirconium silica oxides that formed rock) in Western Australia date to between 4.2 and 4.4 billion years old and are possibly the oldest materials in Earth's crust. Research in 2008 found mineral grains in the Nuvvuagittuq greenstone belt of northern Quebec, Canada, that date to 4.3 billion years old. These discoveries tell us something significant: Earth was forming continental crust at least 4 billion years ago, during the Archean Eon. Although not an official designation, in Figure 11.1 note the Hadean Eon, the proposed name for the period before the Archean.

As Earth solidified, gravity sorted materials by density. Heavier substances such as iron gravitated slowly to its centre, and lighter elements such as silica slowly welled upward to the surface and became concentrated in the crust. Consequently, Earth's interior is sorted into roughly concentric layers (see Figure 11.2), each one distinct in either chemical composition or temperature. Heat energy migrates outward from the centre by conduction and by physical convection in the more fluid or plastic layers in the mantle and nearer the surface.

Our knowledge of Earth's *internal differentiation* into these layers is acquired entirely through indirect evidence, because we are unable to drill more than a few kilometres into Earth's crust. For example, when an earthquake or underground nuclear test sends shock waves through the planet, the cooler areas, which generally are more rigid, transmit these **seismic waves** at a higher velocity than do the hotter areas, where seismic waves are slowed to lower velocity. Plastic zones simply do not transmit some seismic waves; they absorb them. Some seismic waves are reflected where densities of materials change, whereas others are refracted, or bent, as they travel through Earth.

Thus, the distinctive ways in which seismic waves pass through Earth and the time they take to travel between two surface points help seismologists deduce the structure of Earth. This is the science of *seismic tomography*, as if Earth is subjected to a kind of CT scan with every earthquake.

Figure 11.3 illustrates the dimensions of Earth's interior compared with surface distances in North America to give you a sense of size and scale. An airplane flying from Anchorage, Alaska, across Canada to Miami, Florida, would travel the same distance as that from Earth's centre to its surface. Note that in this figure, Earth's thin crust extends only about 30 km inland from the coast.

Earth's Core and Magnetism

A third of Earth's entire mass, but only a sixth of its volume, lies in its dense core. The **core** is differentiated into two regions—*inner core* and *outer core*—divided by a transition zone several hundred kilometres wide (see Figure 11.2b). The inner core is thought to be solid iron that is well above the melting temperature of iron at the surface but remains solid because of tremendous pressure. Scientists believe that the inner core formed before the outer core, shortly after Earth condensed. The iron is not pure, but probably combined with silicon and possibly oxygen and sulphur. The outer core is molten, metallic iron with a lighter density than the inner core.

The fluid outer core generates at least 90% of Earth's magnetic field and the magnetosphere that surrounds and protects Earth from the solar wind and cosmic radiation. One hypothesis explains that circulation in the outer core converts thermal and gravitational energy into magnetic

GEO REPORT 11.2 *Earth on the Scales*

How much does our planet weigh? A revised estimate of Earth's mass, or weight, calculated in 2000 set its weight at 5.972 sextillion metric tons (5972 followed by 18 zeros).

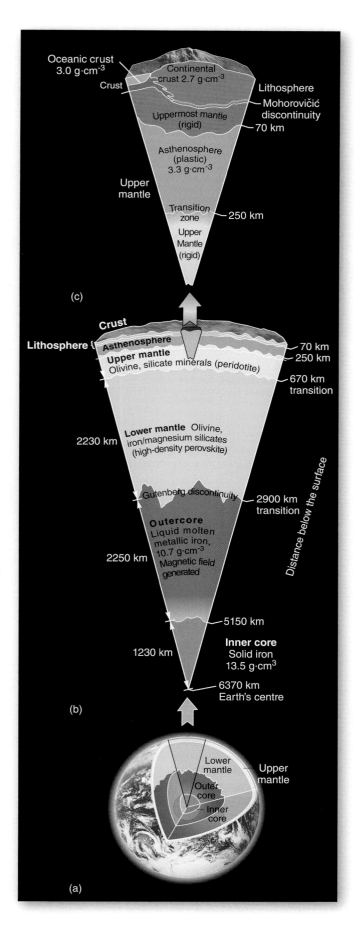

Oceanic crust
3.0 g·cm⁻³

Continental
crust 2.7 g·cm⁻³

Crust

Lithosphere

Mohorovičić
discontinuity
70 km

Uppermost mantle
(rigid)

Asthenosphere
(plastic)
3.3 g·cm⁻³

Upper
mantle

Transition
zone   250 km

Upper
Mantle
(rigid)

(c)

Crust

Lithosphere { Asthenosphere   70 km
Upper mantle   250 km
Olivine, silicate minerals (peridotite)

670 km
transition

Lower mantle Olivine,
2230 km   iron/magnesium silicates
(high-density perovskite)

Gutenberg discontinuity   2900 km
transition

Outer core
Liquid molten
metallic iron,
10.7 g·cm⁻³
2250 km   Magnetic field
generated

Distance below the surface

5150 km

Inner core
Solid iron
1230 km   13.5 g·cm³

6370 km
Earth's centre

(b)

Lower
mantle   Upper
mantle
Outer
core

Inner
core

(a)

FIGURE 11.2 Earth in cross section.
(a) Cutaway showing Earth's interior. (b) Earth's interior in cross
section, from the inner core to the crust. (c) Detail of the
structure of the lithosphere and its relation to the asthenosphere.
(For comparison to the densities noted, the density of water is
1.0 g cm⁻³, and mercury, a liquid metal, is 13.0 g cm⁻³.) [Photo
from NASA.]

energy, producing Earth's magnetic field. The locations
of the north and south magnetic poles are surface expressions of Earth's magnetic field and migrate as plotted on
the map in the *Geosystems Now* opening for this chapter.

An intriguing feature of Earth's magnetic field is
that its polarity sometimes fades to zero and then returns
to full strength, with north and south magnetic poles
reversed. In the process, the field does not blink on and
off but instead diminishes slowly to low intensity, perhaps
25% strength, and then rapidly regains full power. This
geomagnetic reversal has taken place nine times during
the past 4 million years and hundreds of times over Earth's
history. During the transition interval of low strength,
Earth's surface receives higher levels of cosmic radiation
and solar particles, but note that past reversals do not correlate with species extinctions. The evolution of life has
weathered many of these transitions.

The average length of time between magnetic reversals is about 500 000 years; several hundred documented
occurrences varied from as short as 20 000 to 30 000 years
to 50 million years. Transition periods of low intensity
last from 1000 to 10 000 years. The last reversal was
790 000 years ago, preceded by a transition ranging
2000 years in length along the equator to 10 000 years in
the midlatitudes. Given present rates of magnetic field
decay over the last 150 years, we are perhaps 1000 years
away from entering the next phase of field changes,
although there is no expected pattern to forecast the timing. An apparent trend in recent geologic time is toward
more frequent reversals. The obvious question for us is,
Why does this happen?

The reasons for these magnetic reversals are unknown. However, the spatial patterns that are created at
Earth's surface are a key tool in understanding the evolution of landmasses and the movements of the continents.
When new iron-bearing rocks solidify from molten material (lava) at Earth's surface, the small magnetic particles
in the rocks align according to the orientation of the magnetic poles at that time. As the rocks cool and solidify, this
alignment is locked in place. When Earth is without polarity in its magnetic field, a random pattern of magnetism
in crustal rock results.

All across Earth, rocks of the same age bear an
identical record of magnetic reversals in the form of
measurable magnetic "stripes" in any magnetic material they contained within, such as iron particles. These
stripes illustrate global patterns of changing magnetism.
Matching segments allow scientists to reassemble past
continental arrangements. Later in this chapter we see the
importance of observing these magnetic reversals.

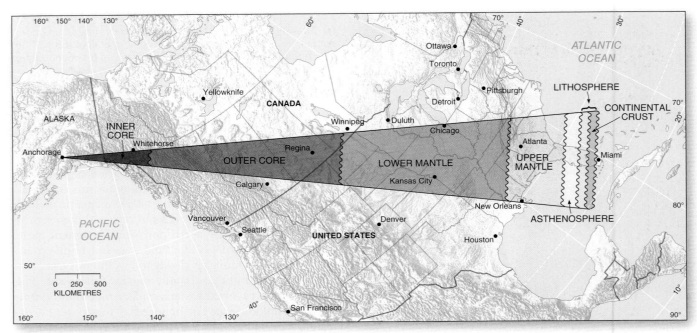

FIGURE 11.3 Distances from core to crust.
The distance from Anchorage, Alaska, to Miami, Florida, is the same distance as that from Earth's center to its outer crust. The continental crust thickness extends only an equivalent distance to the outskirts of Fort Lauderdale and its suburbs, some 30 km along this profile.

Earth's Mantle

Figure 11.2b shows a transition zone several hundred kilometres wide, at an average depth of about 2900 km, dividing Earth's outer core from its mantle. This zone is a discontinuity, or a place where physical differences occur between adjoining regions in Earth's interior. Scientists at the California Institute of Technology analyzed more than 25 000 earthquakes and determined that this transition area, called the *Gutenberg discontinuity*, is uneven, with ragged peak-and-valley-like formations. Experts think that this zone of rough texture and low velocity creates some of the motion in Earth's mantle.

The lower and upper **mantle** represent about 80% of Earth's total volume. The mantle is rich in oxides of iron and magnesium and silicates (FeO, MgO, and SiO_2), which are dense and tightly packed at depth, grading to lesser densities toward the surface. A broad transition zone of several hundred kilometres, centred between 410 and 660 km below the surface, separates the upper mantle from the lower mantle. The entire mantle experiences a gradual temperature increase with depth and a stiffening due to increased pressures. The denser lower mantle is thought to contain a mixture of iron, magnesium, and silicates, with some calcium and aluminum. One hypothesis states that a tremendous amount of water is bound up with minerals in the mantle.

The upper mantle divides into three fairly distinct layers: upper mantle, asthenosphere, and *uppermost mantle*, shown in Figure 11.2c. The **asthenosphere**, or plastic layer (from the Greek *asthenos*, meaning "weak"), extends from about 70 km below the surface down to 250 km. It contains pockets of increased heat from radioactive decay and is susceptible to slow convective currents in these hotter, and therefore less dense, materials. The uppermost mantle is a high-velocity zone just below the crust, where seismic waves transmit through a rigid, cooler layer. This uppermost mantle, along with the crust, makes up the *lithosphere*, approximately 45–70 km thick.

Because of its dynamic condition, the asthenosphere is the least rigid region of the mantle, with densities averaging $3.3 \text{ g} \cdot \text{cm}^{-3}$ (or $3300 \text{ kg} \cdot \text{m}^{-3}$). About 10% of the asthenosphere is molten in uneven patterns and hot spots. The resulting slow movement in this zone disturbs the overlying crust and creates tectonic activity—the folding, faulting, and general deformation of surface rocks. The depth affected by convection currents is the subject of much scientific research. One body of evidence states that mixing occurs throughout the entire mantle, upwelling from great depths at the core–mantle boundary, sometimes in small blobs of material and other times "megablobs" of mantle that convect toward and away from the crust. Another view states that mixing in the mantle is layered, segregated above and below the 660-km boundary. Presently, evidence indicates some truth in both positions.

As an example, there are hot spots on Earth, such as those under Hawai'i, Easter Island, and Tahiti, that appear to be at the top of tall plumes of rising mantle rock that are anchored deep in the lower mantle, where the upward flow of warmer, less-dense material begins. The plume beneath Iceland appears to begin at the 660-km transition. Yet there are other surface hot spots that sit atop smaller plumes going down only some 200 km.

Earth's Lithosphere and Crust

The lithosphere includes the **crust** and uppermost mantle to about 70 km in depth (Figure 11.2c). An important internal boundary between the crust and the high-velocity portion of the uppermost mantle is another discontinuity, called the **Mohorovičić discontinuity**, or **Moho** for short. It is named for the Yugoslavian seismologist who determined that seismic waves change at this depth owing to sharp contrasts of materials and densities.

Figure 11.2c illustrates the relation of the crust to the rest of the lithosphere and the asthenosphere below. Crustal areas beneath mountain masses extend deep, perhaps to 50–60 km, whereas the crust beneath continental interiors averages about 30 km in thickness. Oceanic crust averages only 5 km. The crust is only a small fraction of Earth's overall mass. Drilling through the crust into the uppermost mantle remains an elusive scientific goal.

The longest-lasting deep-drilling attempt is on the northern Kola Peninsula near Zapolyarny, Russia, 250 km north of the Arctic Circle—the *Kola Superdeep Borehole (KSDB)*. Twenty years of high-technology drilling (1970–1989) produced a hole 12.26 km deep, purely for exploration and science. Crystalline rock 1.4 billion years old at 180°C was reached. The site has other active boreholes. (See an analysis log at http://www.icdp-online.de/.) A record holder for depth for a gas well is in Oklahoma; it was stopped at 9750 m when the drill bit ran into molten sulfur.

Oceanic crust is thinner than continental crust and is the object of several drilling attempts. The Integrated Ocean Drilling Program (IODP), a cooperative effort among the governments of Japan, the United States, and the European Union, replaced the former Ocean Drilling Program (ODP) effort directed by Texas A&M University. Over the past 40 years, about 1700 boreholes were completed, yielding 160 km of sediment and rock cores and more than 35 000 samples for researchers. Much of this science windfall helped put together the puzzle of geologic time and plate tectonics. See http://www.oceandrilling.org/ for the IODP home page information.

Japan's *Chikyu*, the largest deep-ocean drilling ship, began work in 2007. The ship is the first capable of drilling in the Arctic (Figure 11.4). The *Chikyu* is "riserless" in that it uses seawater as the primary drilling fluid. It can drill to 7 km, more than three times the capability of the drilling ship *JOIDES Resolution*, operated by the United States as its Scientific Ocean Drilling Vessel. The *JOIDES*, workhorse of the former ODP, has now been converted to riserless status as well (see http://joidesresolution.org/).

The composition and texture of continental and oceanic crusts are quite different, and this difference is a key to the concept of drifting continents. The oceanic crust is denser than continental crust. In collisions, the denser oceanic material plunges beneath the lighter, more buoyant continental crust.

- *Continental crust* is essentially **granite**; it is crystalline and high in silica, aluminum, potassium, calcium, and

FIGURE 11.4 Ocean drilling ship.
The new *Chikyu* research ship began drilling core samples from the ocean floor in 2007. [IODP.]

sodium. (Sometimes continental crust is called *sial*, shorthand for *si*lica and *al*uminum.) Continental crust is relatively low in density, averaging 2.7 g·cm⁻³ (or 2700 kg·m⁻³).

- *Oceanic crust* is **basalt**; it is granular and high in silica, magnesium, and iron. (Sometimes oceanic crust is called *sima*, shorthand for *si*lica and *ma*gnesium.) It is denser than continental crust, averaging 3.0 g·cm⁻³ (or 3000 kg·m⁻³).

Buoyancy is the principle that something less dense, such as wood, floats in something denser, such as water. The principles of buoyancy and balance were combined in the 1800s into the important principle of **isostasy**, which explains certain vertical movements of Earth's crust.

Think of Earth's crust as floating on the denser layers beneath, much as a boat floats on water. Where the load is greater, owing to glaciers, sediment, or mountains, the crust tends to sink, or ride lower in the asthenosphere. Without that load (for example, when a glacier melts), the crust rides higher, in a recovery uplift known as *isostatic rebound*. Thus, the entire crust is in a constant state of compensating adjustment, or isostasy, slowly rising and sinking in response to its own burdens, as it is pushed, and dragged, and pulled over the asthenosphere (Figure 11.5). An interesting development in Alaska relates this concept of isostatic rebound and climate change.

The retreat of glacial ice following the last ice-age cycle unloaded much weight off the crust in Alaska, among those regions affected. Researchers from the Geophysical Institute at the University of Alaska–Fairbanks, using an array of global positioning system (GPS) receivers, measured isostatic rebound of the crust following glacial ice losses. They expected to find a slowed rate of crustal rebound in southeastern Alaska as compared to the more rapid response in the distant past when the ice first retreated.

Instead, they detected some of the most rapid vertical motion on Earth, averaging about 36 mm per year. Scientists attribute this isostatic rebound to the loss of

FIGURE 11.5 Isostatic adjustment of the crust.
Earth's entire crust is in a constant state of compensating adjustment, as suggested by these three sequential stages: (a) The mountain mass slowly sinks, displacing mantle material. (b) Because of the loss of mass through erosion and transportation, the crust isostatically adjusts upward, and sediments accumulate in the ocean. (c) As the continent thins and rises, the heavy sediment load offshore begins to deform the lithosphere beneath the ocean. (d) The melting of ice from the last ice age and losses of overlying sediments are thought to produce an ongoing isostatic uplift of portions of the Sierra Nevada batholith. [Bobbé Christopherson.]

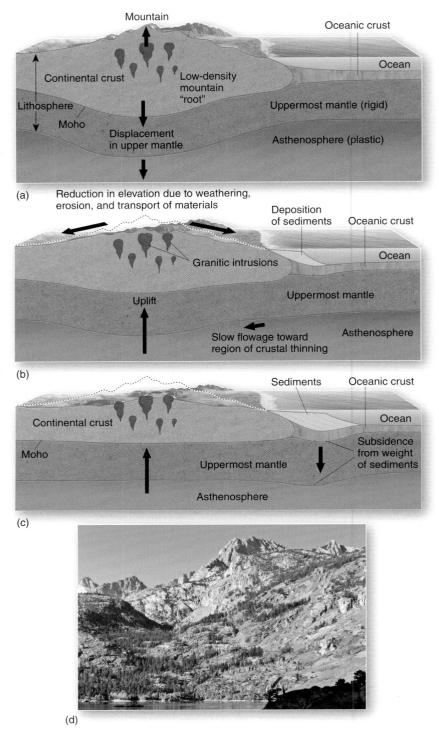

glaciers in the region, especially the areas from Yakutat Bay and the Saint Elias Mountains in the north, through Glacier Bay, Juneau, and on south through the inland passage. This rapid rebound is attributable to glacial melt and retreat over the past 150 years and correlates with record warmth across Alaska.

Earth's crust, an irregular, brittle layer, is the outermost shell, residing restlessly on a dynamic and diverse interior. Let us examine the processes at work on this crust and the variety of rock types that compose the landscape.

The Geologic Cycle

Earth's crust is in an ongoing state of change, being formed, deformed, moved, and broken down by physical, chemical, and biological processes. While the endogenic (internal) system is at work building landforms, the exogenic (external) system is busily wearing them down. This vast give-and-take at the Earth–atmosphere–ocean interface is the **geologic cycle**. It is fueled from two sources—Earth's internal heat and solar energy from space—influenced by the ever-present leveling force of Earth's gravity.

Figure 11.6 illustrates the geologic cycle, combining many of the elements presented in this text. As you can see in the figure, the geologic cycle is composed of three principal subcycles—hydrologic, rock, and tectonic. Through erosion, transportation, and deposition, the *hydrologic cycle*, along the top of Figure 11.6, processes Earth materials with the chemical and physical action of water, ice, and wind. The *rock cycle* produces the three basic rock types found in the crust—igneous, metamorphic, and sedimentary. The *tectonic cycle* brings heat energy and new material to the surface and recycles material, creating movement and deformation of the crust.

(a)

(b)

FIGURE 11.6 The geologic cycle.
(a) The geologic cycle is a model showing the interactive relation among the hydrologic cycle, rock cycle, and tectonic cycle. (b) Earth's surface is where two dynamic systems—the endogenic (internal) and exogenic (external)—interact.

Convection in a Lava Lamp

The Rock Cycle

Only eight natural elements compose 98.5% of Earth's crust, and only two of these—oxygen and silicon—account for 74.3% (Table 11.1). Oxygen is the most reactive gas in the lower atmosphere, readily combining with other elements. For this reason, the percentage of oxygen is higher in the crust than the 21% concentration in the atmosphere. The internal differentiation process, in which less dense elements migrate toward the surface, explains the relatively large percentages of lightweight elements such as silicon and aluminum in the crust.

Minerals and Rocks Earth's elements combine to form minerals. A **mineral** is an inorganic, or nonliving, natural compound having a specific chemical formula and possessing a crystalline structure. The combination of elements and the crystal structure give each mineral its characteristic hardness, colour, density, and other properties. For example, the common mineral *quartz* is silicon dioxide, SiO_2, with a distinctive six-sided crystal. Note that mercury, a liquid metal, is an exception to this definition, for it has no crystalline structure; also note that water is not a mineral for the same reason, but ice does fit the definition of a mineral.

Of the more than 4200 minerals, about 30 comprise the *rock-forming minerals* most commonly encountered. *Mineralogy* is the study of the composition, properties, and classification of minerals. For more on minerals see http://webmineral.com/.

One of the most widespread mineral families on Earth is the *silicates*, because silicon and oxygen are so common and because these elements readily combine with each other and with other elements. Roughly 95% of Earth's crust is made up of silicates. This mineral family includes quartz, feldspar, clay minerals, and numerous gemstones. *Oxides* are another group of minerals in which oxygen combines with metallic elements, such as iron, to form hematite, Fe_2O_3. Also, there are the *sulphides* and *sulphates* groups in which sulphur compounds combine with metallic elements to form pyrite (FeS_2) and anhydrite ($CaSO_4$), respectively.

Another important mineral family is the *carbonate* group, which features carbon in combination with oxygen and other elements such as calcium, magnesium, and potassium. An example is the mineral calcite ($CaCO_3$), a form of calcium carbonate.

A **rock** is an assemblage of minerals bound together (such as granite, a rock containing quartz, feldspar and other minerals), or a mass of a single mineral (such as rock salt), or undifferentiated material (such as the noncrystalline glassy obsidian), or even solid organic material (such as coal). Thousands of different rocks have been identified. All can be sorted into one of three kinds, depending on the processes of formation: *igneous* (melted), *sedimentary* (from settling out), and *metamorphic* (altered). Figure 11.7 illustrates these three processes and the interrelations among them that constitute the **rock cycle**. Figure 11.8 maps the distribution of these rock types across Canada. Let us examine each rock-forming process.

Igneous Processes

An **igneous rock** is one that solidifies and crystallizes from a molten state. Familiar examples are granite, basalt, and rhyolite. Igneous rocks form from **magma**, which is molten rock beneath the surface (hence the name *igneous*, which means "fire-formed" in Latin). Magma is fluid, highly gaseous, and under tremendous pressure. Either it *intrudes* into crustal rocks, cools, and hardens, or it *extrudes* onto the surface as **lava**.

The cooling history of an igneous rock—how fast it cooled and how steadily its temperature dropped—determines its crystalline physical characteristics, or crystallization. Igneous rocks range from coarse-grained

TABLE 11.1	Common Elements in Earth's Crust
Element	**Percentage of Earth's Crust by Weight**
Oxygen (O)	46.6
Silicon (Si)	27.7
Aluminum (Al)	8.1
Iron (Fe)	5.0
Calcium (Ca)	3.6
Sodium (Na)	2.8
Potassium (K)	2.6
Magnesium (Mg)	2.1
All others	1.5
Total	100.0

Note: A quartz crystal (SiO_2) consists of Earth's two most abundant elements, silicon (Si) and oxygen (O). Inset photo iStockphoto/Thinkstock.

A quartz crystal (SiO_2)

FIGURE 11.7 **The rock cycle.**
A rock-cycle schematic demonstrates the relation among igneous, sedimentary, and metamorphic processes. The arrows indicate that each rock type can enter the cycle at various points and be transformed into other rock types. [Photos by Bobbé Christopherson.]

The Rock Cycle

(slower cooling, with more time for larger crystals to form) to fine-grained or glassy (faster cooling).

Igneous rocks comprise approximately 90% of Earth's crust, although sedimentary rocks (sandstone, shale, limestone), soil, or oceans frequently cover them. Figure 11.9 illustrates the variety of occurrences of igneous rocks, both on and beneath Earth's surface.

Intrusive and Extrusive Igneous Rocks Intrusive igneous rock that cools slowly in the crust forms a

pluton, a general term for any intrusive igneous rock body, regardless of size or shape, that invaded layers of crustal rocks. The Roman god of the underworld, Pluto, is the namesake. The largest pluton form is a **batholith**, defined as an irregular-shaped mass with a surface area greater than 100 km² (Figure 11.10a). Batholiths form the mass of many large mountain ranges—for example, the Sierra Nevada batholith in California, the Idaho batholith, and the Coast Range batholith of British Columbia and Washington State.

FIGURE 11.8 **Bedrock geology and physiography of Canada.**
Distribution of igneous, sedimentary, and metamorphic rocks within the various physiographic regions of Canada. Intrusive igneous rocks, volcanic rocks, and metamorphic rocks dominate the geology of the Canadian Shield. The geology of the Appalachian Orogen and Cordilleran Orogen represents a mixture of intrusive igneous rocks, volcanic rocks, metamorphic rocks, and deformed sedimentary rocks. Deformed sedimentary rocks with minor intrusive igneous and volcanic rocks dominate the geology of the Innuitian Orogen. Clastic and chemical sedimentary rocks dominate the geology of the various sedimentary platforms (Great Lakes–St. Lawrence, Hudson Bay, Arctic, Interior). The geology of the Arctic Coastal Plain consists largely of unlithified clastic sediments. [Map by Keith Bigelow, University of Saskatchewan. Data used by permission of the Minister of Public Works and Government Services Canada; Natural Resources Canada, Geological Survey of Canada.]

Smaller plutons include the magma conduits of ancient volcanoes that have cooled and hardened. Those that form parallel to layers of sedimentary rock are *sills*; those that cross layers of rock are *dikes*. You see these two forms in Figure 11.9 at Petermann Island, Antarctica. Magma also can bulge between rock strata and produce a lens-shaped body called a *laccolith*, a type of sill. In addition, magma conduits themselves may solidify in roughly cylindrical forms that stand starkly above the landscape when finally exposed by weathering and erosion. Shiprock *volcanic neck* in New Mexico is such a feature, rising above the surrounding plain, as suggested by the art in Figure 11.9 and shown in the inset photos; note the radiating dikes in the aerial photo. Striking examples of smaller plutons can be seen in the Monteregian Hills east of Montreal (Figure 11.10c). Weathering action of air, water, and ice can expose all of these intrusive forms.

Volcanic eruptions and flows produce extrusive igneous rock, such as lava that cools and forms basalt (Figure 11.10b). Chapter 12 presents volcanism and treats this phenomenon in detail.

Classifying Igneous Rocks Mineral composition and texture usually classify igneous rocks (Table 11.2). The two broad categories are:

1. *Felsic* igneous rocks—derived both in composition and name from *fel*dspar and *sili*ca. Felsic minerals are generally high in silica, aluminum, potassium, and sodium and have low melting points. Rocks formed from felsic minerals generally are lighter in colour and are less dense than mafic mineral rocks.
2. *Mafic* igneous rocks—derived both in composition and name from *ma*gnesium and *fer*ric (Latin for

Aerial view, Shiprock

Landscape view,
Shiprock, NM

Radiating dike   Volcanic neck

Laccolith exposed
by erosion

Sill

Country
rock (surrounding
igneous rock)

Lava
flows
(basalt)

Volcano

Dike

Volcanic
conduit

Rock strata

Dike

Laccolith
(granite)

Batholith
(granite)

Magma

Granite

Dike and sill—
Petermann Island, Antarctica

Basalt

FIGURE 11.9 Igneous rock types and landforms.
The variety of igneous rocks, both intrusive (below the surface) and extrusive (on the surface), and associated
landforms. Inset photographs show samples of granite (intrusive), basalt (extrusive), and other igneous
forms. [Photos of rock samples and aerial by Bobbé Christopherson; surface photo of Shiprock volcanic neck by Robert
Christopherson.]

iron). Mafic minerals are low in silica, high in magnesium and iron, and have high melting points. Rocks formed from mafic minerals are darker in colour and of greater density than felsic mineral rocks.

The same magma that produces coarse-grained granite (when it cools slowly beneath the surface) can form fine-grained *rhyolite* (when it cools above the surface—see inset photo in Table 11.2). If it cools quickly, magma

having silica content comparable to granite and rhyolite can form the dark, smoky, glassy-textured rock called *obsidian*, or volcanic glass (see inset photo in Table 11.2). Another glassy rock, *pumice*, forms when escaping gases bubble a frothy texture into the lava. Pumice is full of small holes, is light in weight, and is low enough in density to float in water (see inset photo in Table 11.2).

On the mafic side, basalt is the most common fine-grained extrusive igneous rock. It makes up the bulk of

(a)

(b)

(c)

FIGURE 11.10 **Intrusive and extrusive rocks.**
(a) Exposed intrusive granite, part of a batholith. (b) Basaltic lava flows on Hawai'i. The glowing opening is a skylight into an active lava tube where molten lava flows; the shiny surface is where lava recently flowed out of the skylight. (c) Astronaut photograph of the Monteregian Hills to the east of Montreal: circular features are Mont St. Hilaire, Rougemont, and Mont Yamaska. The rectangular pattern results from agriculture in the rich lowland soils between the hills. [(a) and (b) Bobbé Christopherson. (c) NASA.]

the ocean floor, accounting for 71% of Earth's surface. It appears in lava flows such as those on the big island of Hawai'i (Figure 11.10b). An intrusive counterpart to basalt, formed by slow cooling of the parent magma, is *gabbro*.

Sedimentary Processes

Solar energy and gravity drive the process of *sedimentation*, with water as the principal transporting medium. Existing rock is disintegrated and dissolved by weathering, picked up and moved by erosion and transportation, and deposited along river, beach, and ocean sites, where burial initiates the rock-forming process. The formation of **sedimentary rock** involves **lithification** processes of cementation, compaction, and a hardening of sediments.

Most sedimentary rocks derive from fragments of existing rock or organic materials. Bits and pieces of former rocks—principally quartz, feldspar, and clay minerals—erode and then are mechanically transported by water, ice (glacial action), wind, and gravity. Materials are transported from "higher-energy" sites, where the carrying medium has the energy to pick up and move particles, to "lower-energy" sites, where the material is deposited.

The common sedimentary rocks are *sandstone* (cemented sand), *shale* (compacted mud), *limestone* (lithified bones and shells or calcium carbonate that precipitated in ocean and lake waters), and *coal* (ancient plant remains that became compacted into rock).

Various cements, depending on availability, fuse rock particles together. Lime, or calcium carbonate ($CaCO_3$),

TABLE 11.2   Igneous Rock Minerals

		Felsic Minerals (feldspars and silica)			Mafic Minerals (magnesium and iron)		Ultramafic Minerals (low silica)	
General characteristics		Higher ⟵———————— Silica content ————————⟶ Lower						
		Higher ⟵———————— Resistance to weathering ——————⟶ Lower						
		⟵— Increased potassium and sodium. Increased calcium, iron, and magnesium —⟶						
		Lower ⟵———————— Melting temperatures ————————⟶ Higher						
		Lower ⟵———————— Coloration ————————⟶ Darker						
Mineral families	Quartz	Feldspars			Mica	Amphibole	Pyroxene	Olivine
		Potassium feldspars SiO₂, K, Al, Si (Orthoclase)	Sodium feldspars Na, Al, Si (Plagioclase) (aluminosilicates)	Calcium feldspars Ca, Al, Si	K, Fe, Mg, Al, Si (biotite: black; muscovite: white)	Fe, Mg, Al, Si, Ca, Na (complex) (hornblende: black)	Fe, Mg, Si (dark)	Mg, Fe, SiO₄ (dark green) (no quartz, no feldspars)
Coarse-grained texture (intrusive, slower cooling rate)		Granite	Diorite				Gabbro	Peridotite
Fine-grained texture (extrusive, faster cooling rate)		Rhyolite	Andesite Dacite (sodic feldspar) (Mount St. Helens)				Basalt	
Other textures		Obsidian (glassy)	Pumice (vesicular)				Scoria (Vesicular)	

Source: [inset left (rhyolite) Tyler Boyes/Shutterstock; inset middle (osbidian) Hemera/Thinkstock; inset right (pumice) iStockphoto/Thinkstock.]

is the most common, followed by iron oxide (Fe₂O₃) and silica (SiO₂). Drying (dehydration), heating, or chemical reactions can also unite particles.

Some minerals, such as calcium carbonate, dissolve into solution and form sedimentary deposits by precipitating from those solutions to form rock. This is an important process in both the oceanic and karst (weathered limestone; see Chapter 13) environments.

The layered strata of sedimentary rocks form an important record of past ages. **Stratigraphy** is the study of the sequence (superposition), thickness, and spatial distribution of strata. These sequences yield clues to the age and origin of the rocks. Figure 11.11a shows a sandstone sedimentary rock in a desert landscape. Note the multiple layers in the formation and how the layers resist weath-

ering processes differently. The climatic history of this rock's formation environment is disclosed in the stratigraphy. Figure 11.11c shows sedimentary rock strata on Mars that imply water deposition of sediments sometime in the distant Martian past.

The two primary sources of sedimentary rocks are *clastic sediments*, formed from the mechanically transported fragments of older rock, and *chemical sediments* from the dissolved minerals in solution, some having organic origins.

Clastic Sedimentary Rocks Weathered and fragmented rocks that are further worn in transport provide *clastic sediments*. Table 11.3 lists the range of *clast* sizes—everything from boulders to microscopic clay particles—and the form they take as *lithified rock*. Common

(a)

(b)

Sandstone

Limestone   Limestone landscape

(c)   Martian sedimentary formations

FIGURE 11.11 **Sedimentary rock types.**
(a) Hoodoos developed in weakly cemented Cretaceous sandstone, near Drumheller, Alberta. Physical weathering by frost action, associated with the repeated freezing (expansion) and thawing (contraction) of water, acts to break up the rocks to create these landforms. (b) Ball's Falls, Jordan Harbour, Ontario, along the length of the Niagara Escarpment in southern Ontario. The exposed cliff face is attacked by the action of running water that erodes the softer shale at the base of the cliff, progressively undermining the Paleozoic limestone until it collapses. Inset photos show whole shells and some clasts (parts) cemented together and a typical limestone landscape. (c) Ancient sediment deposition through repeated cycles of erosion and deposition is evident in the Martian western Arabia Terra (8° N and 7° W). [(a) Barna Tanko/Shutterstock; inset photos by Bobbé Christopherson; (b) Barrett & MacKay/All Canada Photos; (c) image from Mars Global Surveyor courtesy of NASA/JPL/Malin Space Science Systems.]

sedimentary rocks from clastic sediments include siltstone or mudstone (silt-sized particles), shale (clay to silt-sized particles), and sandstone (sand-sized particles ranging from 0.06 to 2 mm in diameter).

Chemical Sedimentary Rocks *Chemical sedimentary* rocks are formed not from physical pieces of broken rock but instead from dissolved minerals, transported in solution and chemically precipitated from solution (these

TABLE 11.3   Clast Sizes and Related Sedimentary Rock Form

Unconsolidated Sediment	Grain Size	Rock Form
Boulders, cobbles	>80 mm	Conglomerate (breccia, if pieces are angular)
Pebbles, gravel	>2 mm	Conglomerate
Coarse sand	0.5–2.0 mm	Sandstone
Medium-to-fine sand	0.062–0.5 mm	Sandstone
Silt	0.0039–0.063 mm	Siltstone (mudstone)
Clay	<0.0039 mm	Shale

are essentially nonclastic). The most common chemical sedimentary rock is **limestone**, which is lithified calcium carbonate, derived from inorganic and organic sources. A similar form is *dolomite*, which is lithified calcium–magnesium carbonate, $CaMg(CO_3)_2$. Limestone from marine organic origins is most common; it is biochemical—derived from shell and bone produced by biological activity (see inset photo in Figure 11.11b). Once formed, these rocks are vulnerable to chemical weathering, which produces unique landforms, as discussed in the weathering section of Chapter 13.

Chemical sediments from inorganic sources are deposited when water evaporates and leaves behind a residue of salts. These *evaporites* may exist as common salts, such as gypsum or sodium chloride (table salt) and often appear as flat, layered deposits across a dry landscape. The pair of photographs in Figure 11.12 dramatically demonstrates this process; one was made in Death Valley National Park one day after a record 2.57-cm rainfall, and the other photo was made one month later at the exact same spot.

Chemical deposition also occurs in the water of natural hot springs from chemical reactions between minerals and oxygen. This is a sedimentary process related to *hydrothermal activity*. An example is the massive deposit of travertine, a form of calcium carbonate, at Mammoth Hot Springs in Yellowstone National Park (Figure 11.13a).

Hydrothermal activity also occurs on the ocean floor along the rift valleys formed by sea-floor spreading. These "black smokers" belch dark clouds of hydrogen sulphides, minerals, and metals that hot water (in excess of 380°C) leached from the basalt. In contact with seawater, metals and minerals precipitate into deposits (Figure 11.13b). Along the Mid-Atlantic Ridge, one region of hydrothermal activity has 30- to 60-m towering chimney vents of calcium carbonate that are at least 30 000 years old, and still active.

Metamorphic Processes

Any rock, either igneous or sedimentary, may be transformed into a **metamorphic rock** by going through profound physical or chemical changes under pressure and increased temperature. (The name *metamorphic* comes from a Greek word meaning "to change form.") Metamorphic rocks generally are more compact than the original rock and therefore are harder and more resistant to weathering and erosion (Figure 11.14).

Several conditions can cause metamorphism. Most common is when subsurface rock is subjected to high temperatures and high compressional stresses occurring over millions of years. Igneous rocks become compressed during collisions between slabs of Earth's crust (see the discussion of plate tectonics later in this chapter). Sometimes rocks simply are crushed under great weight when a crustal area is thrust beneath another piece of the crust. In another setting, igneous rocks may be sheared and stressed along earthquake fault zones, causing metamorphism.

Metamorphic rocks comprise the ancient roots of mountains. Exposed at the bottom of the inner gorge of the Grand Canyon in Arizona, a Precambrian (Archean) metamorphic rock, the Vishnu Schist, is a remnant of such an ancient mountain root (Figure 11.14b). Despite the fact that the schist is harder than steel, the Colorado River has cut down into the uplifted Colorado Plateau, exposing and eroding these ancient rocks.

Another metamorphic condition occurs when sediments collect in broad depressions in Earth's crust and, because of their own weight, create enough pressure in the bottommost layers to transform the sediments into metamorphic rock, a process called *regional metamorphism*. Also, molten magma rising within the crust may "cook" adjacent rock, a process called *contact metamorphism*.

Metamorphic rocks may be changed both physically and chemically from the original rocks. Table 11.4

(a)

(b)

FIGURE 11.12 Death Valley, wet and dry.
(a) One day after a record rainfall when the valley was covered by several square kilometres of water only a few centimetres deep. (b) One month later the water evaporated, and the playa was coated with evaporites (borated salts), shown in close-up inset photo. [Robert W. Christopherson.]

(a)

(b)

FIGURE 11.13 Hydrothermal deposits.
(a) Mammoth Hot Springs, Yellowstone National Park, is an example of a hydrothermal deposit principally composed of travertine (CaCO$_3$), deposited as a chemical precipitate from heated spring water as it evaporated. (b) Hydrothermal vents with black smokers rise along the Mid-Atlantic Ridge. [(a) Robert Christopherson. (b) Scripps Institution of Oceanography.]

(a)

(b)

FIGURE 11.14 Metamorphic rocks.
(a) A metamorphic rock outcrop in Greenland, the Amitsoq Gneiss, at 3.8 billion years old, one of the oldest rock formations on Earth. (b) Precambrian Vishnu Schist makes up these rock cliffs in the inner gorge of the Grand Canyon in northern Arizona. These metamorphic rocks lie beneath many layers of sedimentary rocks deep in the continent. [(a) Kevin Schafer/Peter Arnold/Getty Images; (b) Robert Christopherson.]

Foliation (Metamorphic Rock)

lists some metamorphic rock types, the parent rocks, and resultant textures. If the mineral structure demonstrates a particular alignment after metamorphism, the rock is *foliated*, and some minerals may appear as wavy striations (streaks or lines) in the new rock. The four inset photographs in Table 11.4 demonstrate foliated and non-foliated textures. Which form do you see—foliated or non-foliated—in Figure 11.14a or in the far-right inset photo of metamorphic rock from Livingston Island in Figure 11.7?

On the Isle of Lewis (Outer Hebrides), northwest of the Scottish coast, people constructed the Standing Stones of Calanais (Callanish) beginning approximately 5000 years ago (Table 11.4, far-right inset). These Neolithic people used the 3.1-billion-year-old metamorphic Lewisian gneiss and arranged the monument with the foliations aligned vertically. The standing stone in the photo is about 3.5 m tall.

Now you see how the rock-forming processes yield the igneous, sedimentary, and metamorphic materials of Earth's crust. Next, we look at how vast *tectonic processes* press, push, and drag portions of the crust in large-scale movements, causing the continents to *drift*.

TABLE 11.4 Metamorphic Rocks

Parent Rock	Metamorphic Equivalent	Texture
Shale (clay minerals)	Slate	Foliated
Granite, slate, shale	Gneiss	Foliated
Basalt, shale, peridotite	Schist	Foliated
Limestone, dolomite	Marble	Nonfoliated
Sandstone	Quartzite	Nonfoliated

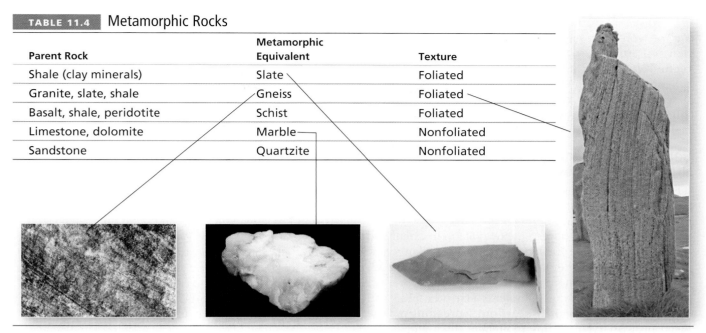

Note: Slate and standing stone photos by Bobbé Christopherson; gneiss photo by Les Palenik/Shutterstock; marble photo by Hemera/Thinkstock.

Plate Tectonics

Have you ever looked at a world map and noticed that a few of the continental landmasses appear to have matching shapes, like pieces of a jigsaw puzzle—particularly South America and Africa? The incredible reality is that the continental pieces indeed once were fitted together! Continental landmasses not only migrated to their present locations but continue to move at speeds up to 6 cm per year. We say that the continents are *adrift* because convection currents in the asthenosphere and upper mantle are dragging continents around. The key point is that the arrangement of continents and oceans we see today is not permanent, but is in a continuing state of change.

A continent, such as North America, is actually a collage of crustal pieces that migrated from elsewhere to form the landscape we know. Through a historical chronology, let us trace the discoveries that led to the plate tectonics theory—a major revolution in Earth systems science.

A Brief History

As early mapping gained accuracy, some observers noticed the symmetry among continents, particularly the fit between South America and Africa. Abraham Ortelius (1527–1598), a geographer, noted the apparent fit of some continental coastlines in his *Thesaurus Geographicus* (1596). In 1620, English philosopher Sir Francis Bacon noted gross similarities between the edges of Africa and South America (although he did not suggest that the landmasses had drifted apart). Benjamin Franklin wrote in 1780 that the crust must be a shell that can break and shift by movements of fluid below. Others wrote—unscientifically—about such apparent relationships, but it was not until much later that a valid explanation came forward.

In 1912, German geophysicist and meteorologist Alfred Wegener publicly presented in a lecture his idea that Earth's landmasses migrate. His book, *Origin of the Continents and Oceans*, appeared in 1915. Today, Wegener is regarded as the father of this concept, which he first called **continental drift**. Scientists at the time were unreceptive to Wegener's revolutionary proposal. Thus, a great debate began, lasting almost 50 years until a scientific consensus developed that Wegener was correct after all.

Wegener thought that all landmasses formed one supercontinent approximately 225 m.y.a., during the Triassic Period. **Pangaea** is the name he gave this one landmass, meaning "all Earth" (see Figure 11.18b). Although his initial model kept the landmasses together too long and his proposal included an incorrect driving mechanism for the moving continents, Wegener's arrangement of Pangaea and its breakup was correct, Pangaea being only the latest of earlier supercontinent arrangements over the span of Earth history.

To come up with his Pangaea fit, he studied the geologic record represented in the rock strata, the fossil record, and the climatic record for the continents. He concluded that South America and Africa correlated in many complex ways. Wegener decided that the large mid-latitude coal deposits, which date to the Permian and Carboniferous Periods (251–354 m.y.a.), exist because these regions once were nearer the equator and therefore covered by lush vegetation that eventually became coal.

As modern scientific capabilities built the case for continental drift, the 1950s and 1960s saw a revival of interest in Wegener's concepts and, finally, confirmation. Aided by an avalanche of discoveries, the plate tectonics theory today is universally accepted as an accurate model of the way Earth's surface evolves.

Tectonic, from the Greek *tektonikùs*, meaning "building" or "construction," refers to changes in the configuration of Earth's crust as a result of internal forces. **Plate tectonic** processes include upwelling of magma; lithospheric plate movements; sea-floor spreading and lithospheric subduction; earthquakes; volcanic activity; and lithospheric deformation such as warping, folding, and faulting.

Sea-Floor Spreading and Production of New Crust

The key to establishing the theory of continental drift was a better understanding of the seafloor. The seafloor has a remarkable feature: an interconnected worldwide mountain chain, forming a ridge some 64 000 km in extent and averaging more than 1000 km in width. A striking view of this great undersea mountain chain opens Chapter 12. How did this global mountain chain get there?

In the early 1960s, geophysicists Harry H. Hess and Robert S. Dietz proposed **sea-floor spreading** as the mechanism that builds this mountain chain and drives continental movement. Hess said that these submarine mountain ranges were **mid-ocean ridges** and the direct result of upwelling flows of magma from hot areas in the upper mantle and asthenosphere and perhaps from the deeper lower mantle. These are sites of intense hydrothermal activity, as mentioned earlier.

When mantle convection brings magma up to the crust, the crust fractures, and the magma extrudes onto the seafloor and cools to form new seafloor. This process builds the mid-ocean ridges as the seafloor spreads laterally, rifting as the two sides move apart. The concept is illustrated in Figure 11.15, which shows how the ocean floor is rifted (moves apart) and scarred along mid-ocean ridges and includes a remote-sensing image of the mid-ocean ridge and map of the system in the Atlantic.

Figure 11.15d shows a portion of the mid-ocean ridge system that surfaces at Thingvellir, Iceland, forming these rifts—the North American plate along one side and the European plate on the other. Iceland's first Althing (parliament) met here in A.D. 930; leaders used the acoustics of the rift walls to be heard by the gathering. Only in Iceland does a portion of Earth's 64 000-km mid-ocean ridge system protrude above sea level.

As new crust generates and the seafloor spreads, magnetic particles in the lava orient with the magnetic field in force at the time the lava cools and hardens. The particles become locked in this alignment as new seafloor forms, creating a magnetic recording in the seafloor. The continually forming oceanic crust records each magnetic reversal and reorientation of Earth's polarity.

Figure 11.16 illustrates just such a recording from the Mid-Atlantic Ridge south of Iceland. The colours denote the alternating magnetic polarization preserved in the minerals of the oceanic crust. Note the mirror images that develop on either side of the rift as a result of the nearly symmetrical spreading of the seafloor; the relative ages of the rocks increase with distance from the ridge. These periodic reversals of Earth's magnetic field are a valuable clue to understanding sea-floor spreading, helping scientists fit together pieces of Earth's crust.

These sea-floor recordings of Earth's magnetic-field reversals and other measurements allowed the age of the seafloor to be determined. The complex harmony of the two concepts of plate tectonics and seafloor spreading thus became clearer. The youngest crust anywhere on Earth is at the spreading centres of the mid-ocean ridges, and, with increasing distance from these centres, the crust gets steadily older (Figure 11.17). The oldest seafloor is in the western Pacific near Japan, dating to the Jurassic Period. Note on the map in the figure the distance between this basin and its spreading centre in the South Pacific west of South America.

Overall, the seafloor is relatively young—nowhere does it exceed 208 million years—remarkable when you remember that Earth's age is 4.6 billion years. The reason is that oceanic crust is short-lived—the oldest sections, farthest from the mid-ocean ridges, are slowly plunging beneath continental crust along Earth's deep oceanic trenches. The discovery that the seafloor is young demolished earlier thinking that the oldest rocks would be found there.

Subduction of the Lithosphere

In contrast to the upwelling zones along the mid-ocean ridges are the areas of descending lithosphere elsewhere. On the left side of Figure 11.15a, note how one plate of the crust is diving, or being dragged beneath another, into the mantle. Recall that the basaltic ocean crust has a density of 3.0 g cm^{-3}, whereas continental crust averages 2.7 g cm^{-3}. As a result, when continental crust and oceanic crust slowly collide, the denser ocean floor will grind beneath the less dense continental crust, thus forming a **subduction zone**, as shown in the figure.

The subducting slab of crust exerts a gravitational pull on the rest of the plate—an important driving force in plate motion. This plate motion can trigger through shear traction along the base of the lithosphere as a flow in the mantle material beneath. Thus, subduction and plate motion are complex processes.

The world's deep ocean trenches coincide with these subduction zones and are the lowest features on Earth's surface. Deepest is the Mariana Trench near Guam, which descends below sea level to −11 030 m; next deepest is the Tonga Trench, also in the Pacific, which drops to −10 882 m. For comparison, in the Atlantic Ocean, the Puerto Rico Trench drops to −8605, and, in the Indian Ocean, the Java Trench drops to −7125.

The subducted portion of lithosphere travels down into the asthenosphere, where it melts and eventually is recycled as magma, rising again toward the surface through deep fissures and cracks in crustal rock. Volcanic mountains such as the Andes in South America and the Cascade Range from Southern British Columbia to northern California form inland of these subduction zones as a result of rising plumes of magma, as suggested in Figure 11.15a. Sometimes the diving plate remains

(b)

|← 4 km →|

(c)

(d)

Mid-Atlantic Ridge

Atlantic Ocean floor

Andes Mountains

South America

Oceanic crust

Sea-floor spreading

Africa

Ocean trench

Lithosphere

Asthenosphere

Lithosphere

Asthenosphere

Indian Ocean floor

Continental crust

Rising magma

Upwelling of basaltic magma along mid-ocean ridge

Mantle

Subduction zone

Pacific Ocean floor

Diving plate

(a)

FIGURE 11.15 Crustal movements.
(a) Sea-floor spreading, upwelling currents, subduction, and plate movements, shown in cross section. Arrows indicate the direction of the spreading. (b) A 4-km-wide image of the Mid-Atlantic Ridge showing linear faults, a volcanic crater, a rift valley, and ridges. The image was taken by the TOBI (towed ocean-bottom instrument) at approximately 29° N latitude. (c) Detail from ocean-floor map. (d) The mid-Atlantic rift surfaces through Iceland, where the North American and European plates of Earth's crust diverge. [(b) Image courtesy of Deborah K. Smith, Woods Hole Oceanographic Institution. (c) Heezen and Tharp, courtesy of Office of Naval Research. (d) Bobbé Christopherson.]

Sea-Floor Spreading, Subduction

FIGURE 11.16 Magnetic reversals recorded in the seafloor.
Magnetic reversals recorded in the seafloor south of Iceland along the Mid-Atlantic Ridge.
[Adapted from J. R. Heirtzler, S. Le Pichon, and J. G. Baron, *Deep-Sea Research* 13, © 1966, Pergamon Press, p. 247.]

FIGURE 11.17 Relative age of the oceanic crust.
Compare the dark-brown color near the East Pacific rise in the eastern Pacific Ocean with the same dark-brown color along the Mid-Atlantic Ridge. What does the difference in width of similarly-shaded zones tell you about the rates of plate motion in the two locations? [Adapted from Deep-Sea Research 13, J.R. Heirtzler, X. Le Pichon and J.G. Baron, Magnetic anomalies over the Reykjanes Ridge, © 1966, Elsevier, p. 247.]

m.y. = millions of years

0–2 m.y.	58–66 m.y.
2–5 m.y.	66–84 m.y.
5–24 m.y.	84–117 m.y.
24–37 m.y.	117–144 m.y.
37–58 m.y.	144–208 m.y.

intact for hundreds of kilometres, whereas at other times it can break into large pieces; this is thought to be the case under the Cascade Range based on its distribution of volcanoes.

Spreading ridges and subduction zones are areas of earthquake and volcanic activity that provide important proof of plate tectonics. Now, using current scientific findings, let us go back and reconstruct the past, and Pangaea.

The Formation and Breakup of Pangaea

The supercontinent of Pangaea and its subsequent break-up into today's continents represent only the last 225 million years of Earth's 4.6 billion years, or only the most recent 1/21 of Earth's existence. During the other 20/21 of geologic time, other things were happening and the landmasses as we know them were unrecognizable.

Figure 11.18a begins with the pre-Pangaea arrangement of 465 m.y.a. (during the middle Ordovician Period). Researchers are discovering other, older arrangements of continents. One proposal is for an ancient supercontinent, tentatively called *Rodinia*, which formed approximately a billion years ago, with breakup at about 700 m.y.a., the late Proterozoic.

Figure 11.18b illustrates an updated version of Wegener's Pangaea, 225–200 m.y.a. (Triassic–Jurassic periods). Plate movements that occurred by 135 m.y.a. (the beginning of the Cretaceous Period) are in Figure 11.18c. Figure 11.18d presents the arrangement 65 m.y.a. (shortly after the beginning of the Tertiary Period). Finally, the present arrangement in modern geologic time (the late Cenozoic Era) is in Figure 11.18e.

Earth's present crust is divided into at least 14 plates, of which about half are major and half are minor, in terms of area (Figure 11.19). Literally hundreds of smaller pieces and perhaps dozens of microplates that migrate together comprise these broad plates. The arrows in the figure indicate the direction in which each plate is presently moving, and the length of the arrows suggests the rate of movement during the past 20 million years.

Compare Figure 11.19 with the image of the ocean floor in Figure 11.20. In the image, satellite radar-altimeter measurements determined the sea-surface height to a remarkable accuracy of 3 cm. The sea-surface elevation is far from uniform; it is higher or lower in direct response to the mountains, plains, and trenches of the ocean floor beneath it. This sea-floor topography causes slight differences in Earth's gravity.

For example, a massive mountain on the ocean floor exerts a high gravitational field and attracts water to it, producing higher sea level above the mountain; over a trench there is less gravitational attraction, resulting in a drop in sea level. A mountain 2000 m high that is 20 km across its base creates a 2-m rise in the sea surface. Scripps Institution of Oceanography and the National Oceanic and Atmospheric Administration developed this use of satellite technology to provide a comprehensive map of the ocean *floor*, derived from remote sensing of the ocean *surface*!

The illustration of the seafloor that begins Chapter 12 also is helpful in identifying the plate boundaries in the following discussion. Try correlating the features illustrated in Figures 11.19 and 11.20 with the sea-floor map.

❚❚ CRITICAL THINKING 11.2

Tracking Your Location since Pangaea

Using the maps in this chapter, determine your present location in relation to the pattern of Earth's crustal plates. Now, using Figure 11.18b, approximately identify where your present location was 225 m.y.a.; express it in a rough estimate using the equator and the longitudes noted on the map.

Plate Boundaries

The boundaries where plates meet clearly are dynamic places, although slow-moving within human time frames. The block diagram inserts in Figure 11.18e show the three general types of motion and interaction that occur along the boundary areas:

- *Divergent boundaries* (lower left in figure) are characteristic of sea-floor spreading centres, where upwelling material from the mantle forms new seafloor and lithospheric plates spread apart—a constructional process. The spreading makes these zones of tension. An example noted in the figure is the divergent boundary along the East Pacific rise, which gives birth to the Nazca plate (moving eastward) and the Pacific plate (moving northwestward). Whereas most divergent boundaries occur at mid-ocean ridges, there are a few within continents themselves. An example is the Great Rift Valley of East Africa, where crust is rifting apart.
- *Convergent boundaries* (upper left) are characteristic of collision zones, where areas of continental and oceanic lithosphere collide. These are zones of compression and crustal loss—a destructional process. Examples include the subduction zone off the west coast of South and Central America and the area along the Japan and Aleutian Trenches. Along the western edge of South America, the Nazca plate collides with and is subducted beneath the South American plate. This convergence creates the Andes Mountains chain and related volcanoes. The collision of India and Asia is another example of a convergent boundary, shown in Figure 11.19.
- *Transform boundaries* (lower right) occur where plates slide laterally past one another at right angles to a sea-floor spreading centre, neither diverging nor converging, and usually with no volcanic eruptions. These are the right-angle fractures stretching across the mid-ocean ridge system worldwide.

Related to plate boundaries, another piece of the tectonic puzzle fell into place in 1965 when University

FIGURE 11.18 Continents adrift, from 465 m.y.a. to the present. Observe the formation and breakup of Pangaea and the types of motions occurring at plate boundaries.
[(a) From R. K. Bambach, "Before Pangaea: The geography of the Paleozoic world," *American Scientist* 68 (1980): 26–38, reprinted by permission. (b–e) From R. S. Dietz and J. C. Holden, Reconstruction of Pangaea: Breakup and Dispersion of Continents, Permian to Present, *Journal of Geophysical Research* 75, no. 26 (September 10, 1970): 4939–4956, © The American Geophysical Union. (f) Remote-sensing image courtesy of Robert Detrick.]

Correlating Processes and Plate Boundaries

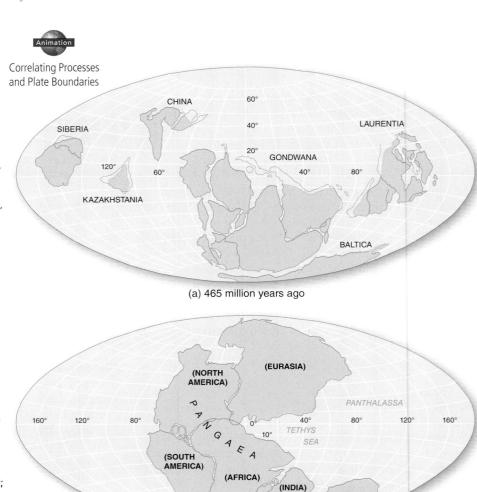

(a) 465 million years ago

Pangaea—all Earth. Panthalassa ("all seas") became the Pacific Ocean, and the Tethys Sea (partly enclosed by the African and the Eurasian plates) became the Mediterranean Sea; trapped portions of former ocean became the present-day Caspian Sea. The Atlantic Ocean did not exist.

Africa shared a common connection with both North and South America. Today, the Appalachian Mountains in the eastern United States and the Lesser-Atlas Mountains of northwestern Africa reflect this common ancestry; these are, in fact, portions of the same mountain range, torn thousands of kilometres apart.

(b) 225 million years ago

New seafloor that formed since the last map is highlighted (gray tint). An active spreading centre rifted North America away from landmasses to the east, shaping the coast of Labrador. India was farther along in its journey to collide with Eurasia, with a spreading centre to the south and a subduction zone to the north; the leading edge of the India plate was diving beneath Eurasia.

The outlines of South America, Africa, India, Australia, and southern Europe appear within the continent called *Gondwana* in the Southern Hemisphere. North America, Europe, and Asia make up *Laurasia*, the northern portion.

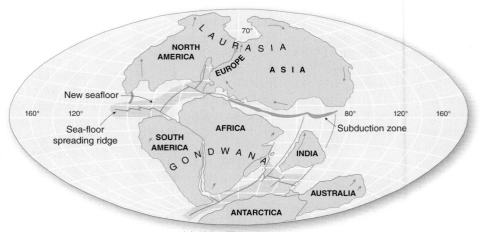

(c) 135 million years ago

Forming a Divergent Boundary

(d) 65 million years ago

Along the Mid-Atlantic Ridge, the seafloor spread some 3000 km in 70 million years. Africa moved northward about 10° in latitude, leaving Madagascar split from the mainland and opening up the Gulf of Aden. The rifting along what would be the Red Sea began. The India plate moved three-fourths of the way to Asia, as Asia continued to rotate clockwise. Of all the major plates, India travelled the farthest—almost 10 000 km.

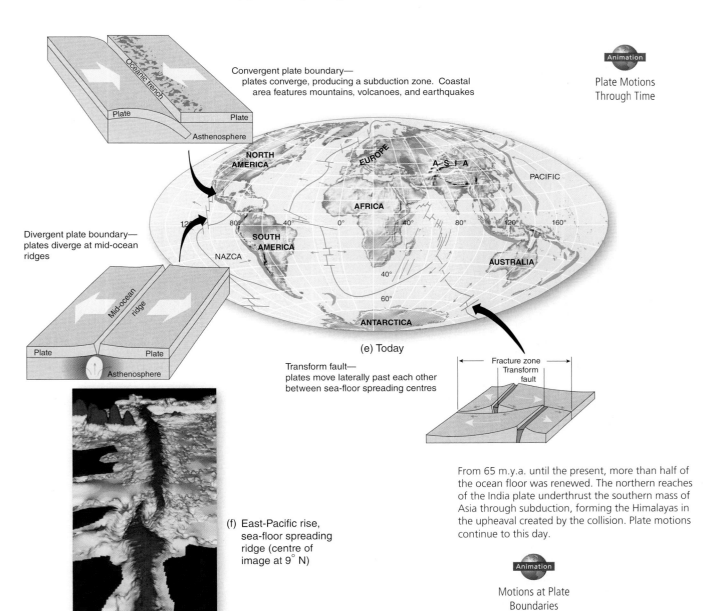

Convergent plate boundary—plates converge, producing a subduction zone. Coastal area features mountains, volcanoes, and earthquakes

Divergent plate boundary—plates diverge at mid-ocean ridges

(e) Today

Transform fault—plates move laterally past each other between sea-floor spreading centres

Plate Motions Through Time

(f) East-Pacific rise, sea-floor spreading ridge (centre of image at 9° N)

From 65 m.y.a. until the present, more than half of the ocean floor was renewed. The northern reaches of the India plate underthrust the southern mass of Asia through subduction, forming the Himalayas in the upheaval created by the collision. Plate motions continue to this day.

Motions at Plate Boundaries

Plate Boundaries

Animation

India Collision
with Asia

Notebook

Plate Boundaries

FIGURE 11.19 **Earth's major lithospheric plates and their movements.**
Each arrow represents 20 million years of movement. The longer arrows indicate that the Pacific and Nazca plates are moving more rapidly than are the Atlantic plates. Compare the length of these arrows with those light-gray areas on Figure 11.17. [Adapted from U.S. Geodynamics Committee, National Academy of Sciences and National Academy of Engineering.]

FIGURE 11.20 **The ocean floor revealed.**
A global gravity anomaly map derived from *Geosat* and *ERS-1* altimeter data. The radar altimeters measured sea-surface heights. Variation in sea-surface elevation is a direct indication of the topography of the ocean floor. [Image courtesy of D. T. Sandwell, Scripps Institution of Oceanography. All rights reserved, 1995.]

of Toronto geophysicist J. Tuzo Wilson first described the nature of transform boundaries and their relation to earthquake activity. All spreading centres on Earth's crust feature these perpendicular scars. Some are a few hundred kilometres long; others, such as those along the East Pacific rise, stretch out 1000 km or more. Across the entire ocean floor, spreading-centre mid-ocean ridges are the location of **transform faults**. The faults generally are parallel to the direction in which the plate is moving. How do these occur?

Mid-ocean ridges are not simple straight lines (Figure 11.19). When a mid-ocean rift begins, it opens at points of weakness in the crust. The fractures visible in the figure began as a series of offset breaks in the crust in

each portion of the spreading centre. As new material rises to the surface, building the mid-ocean ridges and spreading the plates, these offset areas slide past each other, in horizontal faulting motions. The resulting fracture zone, which follows these breaks in Earth's crust, is active only along the fault section between ridges of spreading centres, as shown in Figure 11.21.

Along transform faults (the fault section between C and D in Figure 11.21) the motion is one of horizontal displacement—no new crust is formed or old crust subducted. In contrast, beyond the spreading centres, the two sides of the fracture zones join and are inactive. In fact, the plate pieces on either side of the fracture zone are moving in the same direction, away from the spreading centre

FIGURE 11.21 Transform faults.
Appearing along fracture zones, a transform fault is only that section between spreading centres where adjacent plates move in opposite directions—between C and D. [Adapted from B. Isacks, J. Oliver, and L. R. Sykes, *Journal of Geophysical Research* 73 (1968): 5855–5899, © The American Geophysical Union.]

(the fracture zones between A and B and between E and F in the figure).

The name *transform* was assigned because of this apparent transformation in the direction of the fault movement. The famous San Andreas fault system in California, where continental crust has overridden a transform system, relates to this type of motion. The fault that triggered the 1995 Kobe earthquake in Japan also has this type of horizontal motion, as does the North Anatolian fault in Turkey and its 1999 and later quakes.

Earthquake and Volcanic Activity

Plate boundaries are the primary location of earthquake and volcanic activity, and the correlation of these phenomena is an important aspect of plate tectonics. In 2010, the massive earthquakes that hit Haiti and Chile and the volcanic eruption in Iceland focused world attention on these principles. The March 11, 2011, earthquake in Japan demonstrated the power of one of the largest magnitude earthquakes ever recorded. The next chapter discusses earthquakes and volcanic activity in more detail.

Figure 11.22 maps earthquake zones, volcanic sites, hot spots, and plate motion. The "ring of fire" surrounding the Pacific Basin, named for the frequent incidence of volcanoes, is evident. The subducting edge of the Pacific plate thrusts deep into the crust and mantle, producing

molten material that makes its way back toward the surface. The upwelling magma forms active volcanoes along the Pacific Rim. Such processes occur similarly at plate boundaries throughout the world, including the Pacific Coast of Canada (Focus Study 11.1).

Hot Spots

A dramatic aspect of Earth's internal dynamics is the estimated 50 to 100 **hot spots** across Earth's surface (shown in Figure 11.22). These are individual sites of upwelling material arriving at the surface in tall plumes from the mantle or rising from near the surface that produce thermal effects in groundwater and crust. Some of these sites can be developed for geothermal power (Focus Study 11.2). Hot spots occur beneath both oceanic and continental crust. Some hot spots are anchored deep in the stiff lower mantle, tending to remain fixed relative to migrating plates; others appear to be above plumes that move themselves, or shift with plate motion. Thus, the area of a plate that is above a hot spot is locally heated for the brief geologic time it is there (a few hundred thousand or million years).

The Pacific plate moved across a hot, upward-erupting plume for the last 80 million years, creating a string of volcanic islands stretching northwestward away from the hot spot. This hot spot produced, and continues to form, the Hawaiian–Emperor Islands chain (Figure 11.23). Thus,

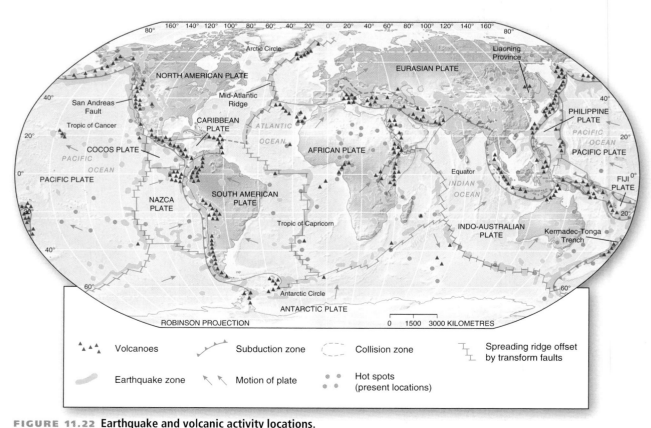

FIGURE 11.22 Earthquake and volcanic activity locations.
Earthquake and volcanic activity in relation to major tectonic plate boundaries and principal hot spots.
[Earthquake, volcano, and hot spot data adapted from USGS.]

(a)

Hot Spot Volcano
Tracks

FIGURE 11.23 Hot spot tracks across the North Pacific.
Hawai'i and the linear volcanic chain of islands known as
the Emperor Seamounts. (a) The islands and seamounts in
the chain are progressively younger toward the southeast.
Ages, in m.y.a., are shown in parentheses. Note that Midway Island is 27.7 million years old, meaning that the site
was over the plume 27.7 m.y.a. (b) Lö'ihi is forming 975 m
beneath the Pacific Ocean off South Point; presently an
undersea volcano (seamount), it is growing into the next
Hawaiian island. [(a) After D. A. Clague, "Petrology and K–Ar
(Potassium–Argon) ages of dredged volcanic rocks from the
western Hawaiian ridge and the southern Emperor seamount
chain," *Geological Society of America Bulletin* 86 (1975): 991;
inset from global gravity anomaly map image, Scripps Institution
of Oceanography. (b) Bobbé Christopherson.]

(b)

Tectonic Setting of the Pacific Coast of Canada

The Pacific Coast is the most seismically active region of Canada. This region is one of the few areas in the world where divergent, convergent, and transform plate boundaries occur in proximity to one another (Figure 11.1.1), resulting in significant earthquake activity. More than 100 earthquakes of magnitude 5 or greater (capable of causing damage) were recorded offshore in the past 70 years.

The oceanic Juan de Fuca plate, which extends from the northern tip of Vancouver Island to northern California

(Figure 11.1.1), is moving toward North America. The Juan de Fuca plate is sliding beneath the North American plate within the Cascadia subduction zone at a convergence rate of about 40 mm per year. Earthquake activity in this region is unusual in that instruments record few small (low magnitude) earthquakes and infrequent large magnitude events (Figure 11.1.2). A magnitude 7.3 earthquake that occurred in June 1946 on central Vancouver Island (Figure 11.1.3a) caused considerable structural damage in communities on Vancouver Island and resulted in two deaths.

Farther north, in a region extending from northern Vancouver Island to Haida Gwaii (Queen Charlotte Islands), the oceanic Pacific plate is sliding northwestward relative to North America at a rate of 60 mm per year (Figure 11.1.1). The transform boundary separating the Pacific and North American plates is known as the Queen Charlotte fault, the Canadian equivalent of the San Andreas fault. A magnitude 8.1 earthquake, Canada's largest earthquake, in recorded history occurred on this fault in August 1949

(Figure 11.1.3b). Limited structural damage in mainland communities such as Prince Rupert resulted.

The Canadian and American governments have established a network of Global Positioning System (GPS) receivers to monitor the motion of the Earth's surface in response to compression and shearing occurring along convergent plate boundaries (Cascadia subduction zone) and transform plate boundaries (San Andreas fault–Queen Charlotte fault, that separates the Pacific and North American plates), respectively. The Western Canada Deformation Array (WCDA), a network of eight GPS stations in southwestern British Columbia, is linked to the Pacific Northwest Geodetic Array (PANGA), which operates in the northwestern United States. Data from these networks indicate that the Cascadia subduction zone is currently locked (http://gsc.nrcan.gc.ca/geodyn/cascadia_e.php) and that Vancouver Island is being compressed at a rate of 10 mm per year. Earth scientists believe that the energy currently being stored along the Cascadia subduction zone will be released in a future megathrust earthquake.

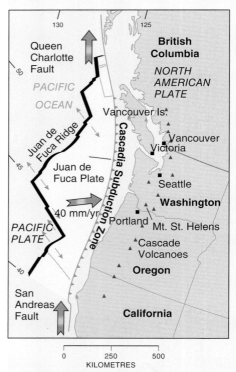

FIGURE 11.1.1 Plate tectonic setting of western North America. The Juan de Fuca plate is currently being subducted beneath the North American continent; the convergent plate boundary is indicated by the Cascadia subduction zone along the eastern margin of the Juan de Fuca plate. The blue arrow indicates the movement of this plate. A divergent plate boundary (indicated by green arrows) marks the western margin of the Juan de Fuca plate. This region is characterized by active volcanism and seismic activity. The San Andreas Fault–Queen Charlotte fault lies adjacent to the coastline of western North America. Blue arrows indicate movement along this fault. Seismic activity along this fault produces infrequent, large-magnitude (megathrust) earthquakes. [Reproduced with the permission of Natural Resources Canada, 2011. Courtesy of the Geological Survey of Canada.].

the ages of the islands or seamounts in the chain increase northwestward from the island of Hawai'i, as you can see from the ages marked in the figure. The oldest island in the Hawaiian part of the chain is Kaua'i, approximately 5 million years old; it is weathered, eroded, and deeply etched with canyons and valleys.

To the northwest of this active hot spot in Hawai'i, the island of Midway rises as a part of the same system. From there, the Emperor seamounts follow northwestward to an age of about 40 m.y.a. At that point, this linear island chain shifts direction northward. This bend in the chain

is now thought to be from both movement in the plume and a possible change in the plate motion itself. The former thinking that the plumes remained fixed relative to the migrating plate has been revised. At the northernmost extreme, the seamounts that formed about 80 m.y.a. are now approaching the Aleutian Trench and eventually will be subducted beneath the Eurasian plate. Perhaps some 80 million years hence, the Hawaiian Islands too will slowly disappear into the trench. Aloha!

The big island of Hawai'i, the newest, actually took less than 1 million years to build to its present stature.

FIGURE 11.1.2 Seismic activity in western North America.
The nature of seismic activity along the Cascadia subduction zone and the Queen Charlotte fault. Note that seismic activity along the Queen Charlotte fault is characterized by a wide range of intensities—low-magnitude events (M = 3) occur frequently while large-magnitude events (M > 8) rarely occur. In contrast, the Cascadia subduction zone exhibits a distinctly different level of seismic activity characterized by infrequent large-magnitude (M > 8) events. The box (red colour) in the bottom-right corner of the graph indicates that earthquakes in the Cascadia subduction zone exhibit magnitudes in the 8 to 9 range. [Reproduced with the permission of Natural Resources Canada, 2011. Courtesy of the Geological Survey of Canada.]

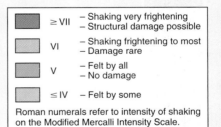

FIGURE 11.1.3 Earthquake intensity and damage in British Columbia.
The magnitude of seismic activity generated by the two greatest earthquakes recorded in British Columbia in the twentieth century: (a) 1946 and (b) 1949. Both earthquakes resulted in structural damage to buildings with little loss of human lives. [Used by permission of the Minister of Public Works and Government Services Canada; Natural Resources Canada, Geological Survey of Canada.]

≥ VII	– Shaking very frightening – Structural damage possible
VI	– Shaking frightening to most – Damage rare
V	– Felt by all – No damage
≤ IV	– Felt by some

Roman numerals refer to intensity of shaking on the Modified Mercalli Intensity Scale.

█ █ CRITICAL THINKING 11.3

How Fast Is the Pacific Plate Moving?

Relative to the motion of the Pacific plate shown in Figure 11.23 (note the map's graphic scale in the lower-left corner), the island of Midway formed 27.7 m.y.a. over the hot spot that is active under the southeast coast of the big island of Hawai'i today. Given the scale of the map, roughly determine the average annual speed of the Pacific plate in centimetres per year for Midway to have travelled this distance.

The island is a huge mound of lava, melded from several sea-floor fissures through five volcanoes, rising from the seafloor 5800 m to the ocean surface. From sea level, its highest peak—Mauna Kea—rises to 4205 m elevation. This total height of almost 10 000 m represents the highest mountain on Earth, if measured from the seafloor.

The youngest island in the Hawaiian chain is still a seamount, a submarine mountain that does not reach the surface. It rises 3350 m from its base but is still 975 m beneath the ocean surface. Even though this new

Heat from Earth—Geothermal Energy and Power

A tremendous amount of endogenic energy flows from Earth's interior toward the surface. Temperatures at the base of Earth's crust range from 200°C–1000°C. Convection and conduction transport this geothermal energy in enormous quantities from the mantle to the crust, yet geothermal power development is limited in extent to certain locations (Figure 11.2.1).

What Is Geothermal Energy?

Geothermal energy is produced when pockets of magma and hot portions of the crust heat groundwater. This energy is transmitted to the surface by heated water or steam accessed through the drilling of wells. For an effective *underground thermal reservoir* to form, an aquifer must have high porosity and high permeability

that allows heated water to move freely through connecting pore spaces. Ideally, this aquifer should heat groundwater from 180°C to 350°C and be accessible to drilling within 3 km of the surface, although 6–7 km depths are feasible.

Geothermal energy literally refers to heat from Earth's interior, whereas *geothermal power* relates to specific

(a)   (b)

FIGURE 11.2.1 Surface geothermal activity in Iceland.
(a) This is the original Geysir, in Haukadalur, Iceland, from which we derive the name for all other geysers on Earth; historical accounts of Geysir's activity date back to A.D. 1294. (b) The popular Blue Lagoon Spa is filled with hot geothermal waters. The Svartsengi power plant is in the distance in this geothermal field near Reykjavik, Iceland. [Bobbé Christopherson.]

 GEO REPORT 11.3 *A Lot of Basalt in Hawai'i*

A mass of basalt forms the Big Island of Hawai'i. From seafloor to summits, it contains about 40 000 km³ of basalt, which is enough to cover all of Nova Scotia (55 490 km²) to a depth of about 0.7 km.

island will not experience the tropical Sun for about 10 000 years, it is already named Lō'ihi (noted on the map).

Iceland is a result of an active hot spot sitting astride a mid-ocean ridge—visible on the different maps and images of the seafloor (see Figure 11.15d). It is an excellent example of a segment of mid-ocean ridge rising above sea level. This hot spot has generated enough material to form Iceland, and eruptions continue from deep in the mantle as happened in 2010 and again in 2011. As a result, Iceland is still growing in area and volume. This is further evidence that, indeed, Earth is a dynamic planet.

GEOSYSTEMS CONNECTION

Beginning with the internal structure of Earth, we tracked the flow of energy toward the surface. Owing to these internal dynamics, the crust is subject to forces and it moves in sections, and gravity pulls on heavier elements. Plate tectonics is the science studying these continent-sized migrating pieces of crust that can move on a collision course with other plates. Earth's present surface map is the result of the vast forces and motions. In Chapter 12, we look at the surface expressions of all this energy and matter in motion: the stress and strain of folding, faulting, and deformation; the building of mountains; and the sometimes dramatic activity of earthquakes and volcanoes.

applied strategies of geothermal electric or geothermal direct applications. *Geothermal electric* uses steam, or hot water that flashes to steam, to drive a turbine-generator. In *geothermal direct*, hot water is used to heat buildings and to cool buildings using a heat-exchange system; to heat greenhouses, to heat soil, to heat swimming pools, and for manufacturing processes and aquaculture, among many other uses.

Geothermal Power Production

The first geothermal electrical generating station was built in Larderello, Italy, in 1904—it has operated continuously since 1913 with an installed capacity of 360 MWe (megawatts electric). Today, geothermal applications are in use in 30 countries, through some 200 plants, producing an output of 8000 MWe and direct heat of 12 000 MWt (megawatts thermal). In Reykjavík, Iceland, the majority of space heating (87%) and some of the electrical production (18%) is geothermal. The Svartsengi power plant (40 MWe) on the Reykjavík Peninsula is an example of such a modern facility

(Figure 11.2.2). In the same area, a large array of wells collects heat from hot water and pumps it to the city for geothermal direct applications.

In the Paris Basin, France, some 25,000 residences are heated using geothermal direct 70°C water. In the Philippines, almost 30% of total electrical production is generated with geothermal energy. The top seven countries for installed geothermal electrical generation are the United States, Philippines, Italy, Mexico, Indonesia, New Zealand, and Iceland. Worldwide operational capacity is 8933 MWe of a potential estimated to be in excess of 80 000 MWe and hundreds of thousands of MWt. The United States, China, and Iceland lead in thermal installations.

In Canada, a proposed project at Mount Meager, B.C., will produce elec-

FIGURE 11.2.2 Svartsengi geothermal power plant. On the Reykjavík Peninsula, southwest of Iceland's capital, the Svartsengi power plant produces electricity and provides hot water for homes and businesses. The plant's name means "Black Meadow," referring to the extensive lava beds throughout this region of Iceland. [Bobbé Christopherson.]

tricity; geothermal direct heats buildings at Carleton University, Ottawa; and some direct operations are in development in Nova Scotia. For more information, see http://www1.eere.energy.gov/geothermal/ or http://geothermal.marin.org/, or http://www.geothermal.org/, or http://www.smu.edu/geothermal/.

 APPLIED PHYSICAL GEOGRAPHY   *Radioactivity: Earth's Time Clock*

The age of Earth and the age of the earliest known crustal rock are outstanding, for we think in terms of Earth's trips around the Sun and the pace of our own lives. We need something greater than human time to measure the vastness of geologic time. Nature has provided a way: *radiometric dating*. It is based on the steady, exponential decay of certain atoms.

An atom contains protons and neutrons in its nucleus. Certain forms of atoms called *isotopes* have unstable nuclei; that is, the protons and neutrons do not remain together indefinitely. As particles break away and the nucleus disintegrates,

radiation is emitted and the atom decays into a different element—this process is *radioactivity*.

Radioactivity provides the steady time clock needed to measure the age of ancient rocks. It works because the decay rates for different elements are determined precisely, and they do not vary beyond established uncertainties. The decay rate of an element is commonly expressed as its *half-life*, the time required for one-half of the unstable "parent" atoms in a sample to decay into stable "daughter" atoms.

Some examples of unstable elements that become stable elements

(with their half-lives in parentheses) are thorium-232 to lead-280 (14.1 billion years); uranium-238 to lead-206 (4.5 billion years); potassium-40 to argon-40 (1.3 billion years); and, in organic materials, carbon-14 to nitrogen-14 (5730 years).

The presence of a decaying element and its stable end product in a sample of sediment or rock allows scientists to apply the known decay rate and read the radiometric "clock." The formula for the age of a sample is:

$$t = \frac{1}{\lambda} \ln\left(1 + \frac{D}{P}\right)$$

where:

t is the age of the sample,

λ is the decay constant for the parent element,

ln is the natural logarithm (that is, the logarithm to base e),

D is the number of atoms in the daughter isotope product today, and

P is the number of atoms in the parent isotope today.

D and P in a sample are measured with a mass spectrometer. λ is related to the half-life ($t_{1/2}$) of the parent element with:

$$\lambda = \frac{\ln 2}{t_{1/2}} = \frac{0.693}{t_{1/2}}$$

For example, the 5730 year half-life of carbon-14 equates to a decay constant of 1.21×10^{-4} yr^{-1}.

Errors can occur if the sample was disturbed or subjected to natural weathering processes that might alter its radioactivity. To increase accuracy, investigators may check the age of a sample using more than one radiometric measurement, or by cross-checking a result against other dating methods such as tree-ring or fossil analysis.

KEY LEARNING CONCEPTS REVIEW

■ **Distinguish** between the endogenic and exogenic systems, **determine** the driving force for each, and **describe** the pace at which these systems operate.

The Earth–atmosphere interface is where the **endogenic system** (internal), powered by heat energy from within the planet, interacts with the **exogenic system** (external), powered by insolation and influenced by gravity. These systems work together to produce Earth's diverse landscape. The **geologic time scale** is an effective device for organizing the vast span of geologic time. It depicts the sequence of Earth's events (relative time) and the approximate actual dates (absolute time).

The most fundamental principle of Earth science is **uniformitarianism**. Uniformitarianism assumes that the *same physical processes active in the environment today have been operating throughout geologic time*, although dramatic episodes, such as massive landslides, asteroid impacts, or volcanic eruptions, can interrupt the smooth flow of events, leading to a state of *punctuated equilibrium*.

endogenic system (p. 307)
exogenic system (p. 307)
geologic time scale (p. 310)
uniformitarianism (p. 310)

1. To what extent is Earth's crust active at this time in its history?
2. Define the endogenic and the exogenic systems. Describe the driving forces that energize these systems.
3. How is the geologic time scale organized? What is the basis for the time scale in relative and absolute terms? What era, period, and epoch are we living in today?
4. Contrast uniformitarianist science and catastrophist beliefs as models for Earth's development.

■ **Diagram** Earth's interior in cross section, and **describe** each distinct layer.

We have learned about Earth's interior from indirect evidence—the way its various layers transmit **seismic waves**. The **core** is differentiated into an inner core and an outer core, divided by a transition zone. Earth's magnetic field is generated almost entirely within the outer core. Polarity reversals in Earth's magnetism are recorded in cooling magma that contains iron minerals. The patterns of **geomagnetic reversal** frozen in rock help scientists piece together the story of Earth's mobile crust.

Above Earth's core lies the **mantle**, differentiated into lower mantle and upper mantle. It experiences a gradual temperature increase with depth and a stiffening due to increased pressures. The upper mantle is divided into three fairly distinct layers. The uppermost mantle, along with the crust, makes up the *lithosphere*.

Below the lithosphere is the **asthenosphere**, or *plastic layer*. It contains pockets of increased heat from radioactive decay and is susceptible to slow convective currents in these hotter materials. An important internal boundary between the **crust** and the high-velocity portion of the uppermost mantle is the **Mohorovičić discontinuity**, or **Moho**. *Continental crust* is basically **granite**; it is crystalline and high in silica, aluminum, potassium, calcium, and sodium. *Oceanic crust* is **basalt**; it is granular and high in silica, magnesium, and iron. The principles of buoyancy and balance were combined in the 1800s into the important principle of **isostasy**. Isostasy explains certain vertical movements of Earth's crust, such as isostatic rebound when the weight of ice is removed.

seismic waves (p. 312)
core (p. 312)
geomagnetic reversal (p. 313)
mantle (p. 314)
asthenosphere (p. 315)
crust (p. 315)
Mohorovičić discontinuity (Moho) (p. 315)
granite (p. 315)
basalt (p. 315)
isostasy (p. 315)

5. Make a simple sketch of Earth's interior, label each layer, and list the physical characteristics, temperature, composition, and range of size of each on your drawing.
6. How does Earth generate its magnetic field? Is the magnetic field constant, or does it change? Explain the implications of your answer.
7. Describe the asthenosphere. Why is it also known as the plastic layer? What are the consequences of its convection currents?
8. What is a discontinuity? Describe the principal discontinuities within Earth.
9. Define isostasy and isostatic rebound, and explain the crustal equilibrium concept.
10. Diagram the uppermost mantle and crust. Label the density of the layers in grams per cubic centimetre. What two types of crust were described in the text in terms of rock composition?

■ **Illustrate** the geologic cycle, and **relate** the rock cycle and rock types to endogenic and exogenic processes.

The **geologic cycle** is a model of the internal and external interactions that shape the crust. A **mineral** is an inorganic natural compound having a specific chemical formula and possessing a crystalline structure. A **rock** is an assemblage of minerals bound together (such as granite, a rock containing quartz, feldspar, and other minerals), or it may be a mass of a single mineral (such as rock salt).

The geologic cycle comprises three sub-cycles: the *hydrologic cycle*, the *tectonic cycle*, and the **rock cycle**. The rock cycle describes the three principal rock-forming processes and the rocks they produced. **Igneous rocks** form from **magma**, which is molten rock beneath the surface. Magma is fluid, highly gaseous, and under tremendous pressure. Either it *intrudes* into crustal rocks, cools, and hardens, or it *extrudes* onto the surface as **lava**. Intrusive igneous rock that cools slowly in the crust forms a **pluton**. The largest pluton form is a **batholith**.

Lithification is the cementation, compaction, and hardening of sediments into **sedimentary rocks**. These layered strata form important records of past ages. **Stratigraphy** is the study of the sequence (superposition), thickness, and spatial distribution of strata that yield clues to the age and origin of the rocks.

Clastic sedimentary rocks are derived from the fragments of weathered rocks. Chemical sedimentary rocks are dissolved minerals, transported in solution, and chemically precipitated out of solution (these are essentially nonclastic). The most common chemical sedimentary rock is **limestone**, which is lithified calcium carbonate, $CaCO_3$.

Any rock, either igneous or sedimentary, may be transformed into a **metamorphic rock** by going through profound physical or chemical changes under pressure and increased temperature.

geologic cycle (p. 316)
mineral (p. 318)
rock (p. 318)
rock cycle (p. 318)
igneous rock (p. 318)
magma (p. 318)
lava (p. 318)
pluton (p. 319)
batholith (p. 319)
sedimentary rock (p. 322)
lithification (p. 322)
stratigraphy (p. 323)
limestone (p. 325)
metamorphic rock (p. 325)

11. Illustrate the geologic cycle, and define each component: rock cycle, tectonic cycle, and hydrologic cycle.
12. What is a mineral? A mineral family? Name the most common minerals on Earth. What is a rock?
13. Describe igneous processes. What is the difference between intrusive and extrusive types of igneous rocks?
14. Characterize felsic and mafic minerals. Give examples of both coarse- and fine-grained textures.
15. Briefly describe sedimentary processes and lithification. Describe the sources and particle sizes of sedimentary rocks.
16. What is metamorphism, and how are metamorphic rocks produced? Name some original parent rocks and their metamorphic equivalents.

■ *Describe* Pangaea and its breakup, and *relate* several physical proofs that crustal drifting is continuing today.

The present configuration of the ocean basins and continents is the result of *tectonic processes* involving Earth's interior dynamics and crust. Alfred Wegener coined the phrase **continental drift** to describe his idea that the crust is moved by vast forces within the planet. **Pangaea** was the name he gave to a single assemblage of continental crust some 225 m.y.a. that subsequently broke apart. Earth's lithosphere is fractured into huge slabs or plates, each moving in response to their own motion of gravitational pull and to flowing currents in the mantle that create frictional drag on the plate. The all-encompassing theory of **plate tectonics** includes **sea-floor spreading** along **mid-ocean ridges** and denser oceanic crust diving beneath lighter continental crust along **subduction zones**.

continental drift (p. 327)
Pangaea (p. 327)
plate tectonics (p. 327)
sea-floor spreading (p. 328)
mid-ocean ridge (p. 328)
subduction zone (p. 328)

17. Briefly review the history of the theory of continental drift, sea-floor spreading, and the all-inclusive plate tectonics theory. What was Alfred Wegener's role?
18. Define upwelling, and describe related features on the ocean floor. Define subduction, and explain the process.
19. What was Pangaea? What happened to it during the past 225 million years?
20. Characterize the three types of plate boundaries and the actions associated with each type.

■ *Portray* the pattern of Earth's major plates, and *relate* this pattern to the occurrence of earthquakes, volcanic activity, and hot spots.

Occurrences of often-damaging earthquakes and volcanoes are correlated with plate boundaries. Three types of plate boundaries form: divergent, convergent, and transform. Along the offset portions of mid-ocean ridges, horizontal motions produce **transform faults**.

As many as 50 to 100 **hot spots** exist across Earth's surface, where plumes of magma—some anchored in the lower mantle, others originating from shallow sources in the upper mantle—generate a flow upward. **Geothermal energy** literally refers to heat from Earth's interior, whereas *geothermal power* relates to specific applied strategies of geothermal electric or geothermal direct applications.

transform faults (p. 335)
hot spots (p. 336)
geothermal energy (p. 340)

21. What is the relation between plate boundaries and volcanic and earthquake activity? How is this activity manifested along the Pacific Coast of Canada?
22. What is the nature of motion along a transform fault? Name a famous example of such a fault.

MyGeosciencePlace

Visit **www.mygeoscienceplace.ca** for several figure animations, satellite loops, self-study quizzes, flashcards, interactive glossary, career links, RSS feeds, Pearson eText of *Geosystems*, and much more.

Tectonics, Earthquakes, and Volcanism

WORLD OCEAN F
BY BRUCE C. HEEZEN AND MARI

UNITED STATES NAVY OFFICE OF N

The scarred ocean floor is clearly visible: sea-floor spreading centres marked by oceanic ridges that stretch over 64 000 km, subduction zones indicated by deep oceanic trenches, and transform faults slicing across oceanic ridges. [*World Ocean Floor* by Bruce C. Heezen and Marie Tharp, 1977, Office of Naval Research.]

KEY LEARNING CONCEPTS

After reading the chapter, you should be able to:

- **Describe** first, second, and third orders of relief, and **relate** examples of each from Earth's major topographic regions.

- **Describe** the different origins of continental crust, and **define** displaced terranes.

- **Explain** the compressional processes of folding and faulting, and **describe** four principal types of faults and their characteristic landforms.

- **Relate** the three types of plate collisions associated with orogenesis, and **identify** specific examples of each.

- **Explain** the nature of earthquakes, including characteristics, measurement, fault mechanics, and forecasting methods.

- **Distinguish** between effusive and explosive volcanic eruptions, and **describe** related landforms, using specific examples.

The San Jacinto Fault Connection

The San Jacinto fault is an active fault in southern California. It is part of the San Andreas fault system, which is made up of hundreds of horizontally moving faults. These faults are produced by the relative motion of the northwestward-moving Pacific plate against the southwestward-moving North American plate; some 5 cm per year of motion builds stress and accumulated strain. The San Jacinto fault runs from north of the Mexican border to the "Inland Empire" of San Bernardino, somewhat parallel to the Elsinore fault, which continues on into Orange County, and the Whittier fault, which runs into Los Angeles. Numerous other related faults run through the region with this same alignment (Figure GN 12.1).

From the small inland communities in the Mojave Desert to the sprawling coastal population centres of metropolitan Los Angeles, the people of southern California live with earthquakes. One overriding question for everyone is, When will the "Big One" occur? The U.S. Geological Survey (USGS) regards the San Jacinto fault as capable of an M 7.5 quake ("M" is the abbreviation for *moment magnitude* and refers to an earthquake rating scale discussed in this chapter). The San Jacinto fault's relation to the Elsinore, Whittier, and other fault lines in the San Andreas system indicates the potential for major earthquakes across the metropolitan southern California landscape. An M 7.5 would release almost 30 times more energy than that produced by the 1994 Northridge earthquake—thus, a major quake compared to a strong quake. The Northridge quake remains the most costly in terms of property damage in U.S. history.

Scientific evidence regarding the nature of faulting and crustal movement suggests that a major earthquake may be preceded by a number of small earthquakes in an area. Recent evidence points to a "wavelike pattern" of small quakes as rupturing spreads along the fault plane. The latest earthquake activity along the San Jacinto and Elsinore faults may be following this pattern.

Records show that at least six quakes have occurred along the San Jacinto fault in the last 50 years: an M 5.8 and M 6.5 in 1968, an M 5.3 in 1980, and an M 5.0 in 2005. Then an M 4.1 hit on February 13, 2010, about 40 km south of Palm Springs. The largest of the sequence was an M 7.2 Sierra El Mayor-Cucapah quake April 4, 2010, some 65 km south-southeast of El Centro, in Baja California. An aftershock of M 5.7 occurred on June 15.

The April 2010 quake transferred strain to the San Jacinto fault, with large clusters of aftershocks toward the north in the fault structure. Continuing the pattern, an M 5.4 quake occurred along the San Jacinto fault on July 7, 2010, the Borrego quake, with aftershocks again spread to the northwest. If strain is moving northward along the system, then there should be much concern. A network of 100 global positioning system (GPS) stations monitors crustal change across the region that might indicate an upcoming earthquake. More on earthquake forecasting is ahead in this chapter.

As said so many times in this text, such a situation adds to the importance of Earth systems science toward education of the public to ensure proper planning, zoning, and preparation. Zoning could block new construction in particularly vulnerable areas and require the retrofitting of poorly built infrastructure. A great quake along the San Jacinto and related faults should not be a surprise, but should be anticipated with adaptation and mitigation actions in place.

FIGURE GN 12.1 Southern California seismic map.

arth's endogenic systems produce flows of heat and material toward the surface to form crust. Ongoing processes produce continental landscapes and oceanic sea-floor crust, sometimes in dramatic episodes. Earth's physical systems move to the front pages whenever a strong earthquake strikes or after one of the nearly 50 volcanic eruptions a year that threaten a built-up area.

In Haiti and Chile in 2010 and in New Zealand and Japan in 2011, the world was again riveted to images of the effects of massive earthquakes as unstable plate boundaries snapped into new positions. The 2011 quake along northeastern Honshu Island produced a devastating tsunami, 30 000 deaths, and an estimated USD $325 billion in damage (Figure 12.1). More on these recent events is contained in Focus Study 12.2 in this chapter.

Volcanic eruptions pose threats to life and property to those who live in proximity to the hazard. Earth systems science is providing analysis and warnings to affected populations as never before. For instance, in April 2010 the Eyjafjallajökull volcano in southern Iceland erupted (see Figure 12.23). Previously, this mountain had erupted in 1821 and 1823. The ash cloud rose to 10 660 m and quickly dispersed toward Europe and its commercial airline corridors. European airspace was closed for five days, cancelling more than 100 000 flights. When flights resumed, routes were changed to avoid lingering ash. Because ash from this eruption was essentially restricted to a horizontal layer in the lower atmosphere, there was not a significant climate signature in Earth's atmosphere, as occurred from Mount Pinatubo in 1991.

In this chapter: We examine processes that construct Earth's surface and create world structural regions. Tectonic processes deform, recycle, and reshape Earth's crust. These processes occur sometimes in dramatic episodes but most often in slow, deliberate motions that build the landscape. Continental crust has been forming throughout most of Earth's 4.6-billion-year existence.

The arrangement of continents and oceans, the origin of mountain ranges, the topography of the land and the sea-floor, and the locations of earthquake and volcanic activity are all evidence of our dynamic Earth. Principal seismic and volcanic zones occur along plate boundaries and hot-spot locations, thus linking plate tectonics to the potential devastation of earthquakes and local threats of major volcanic eruptions and their attendant global climatic impact.

We begin our look at tectonics and volcanism on the ocean floor, hidden from direct view. The illustration that opens this chapter is a striking representation of the concepts learned in the previous chapter, laying the foundation for this and subsequent chapters. Be sure to take the quick tour presented in Critical Thinking 12.1 for a closer look. Try to correlate this sea-floor illustration with the maps of crustal plates and plate boundaries shown in Figures 11.18 and the gravity anomaly image in Figure 11.19.

CRITICAL THINKING 12.1
Ocean Floor Tectonics Tour

Using the chapter-opening map, follow the ocean ridge and spreading centre known as the East Pacific Rise northward as it trends beneath the west coast of the North American plate, disappearing under earthquake-prone California. Locate the continents, the offshore-submerged continental shelves, and the expanses of the sediment-covered abyssal plains on the map.

On the floor of the Indian Ocean, you see the wide track along which the India plate travelled northward to its collision with the Eurasian plate. Vast deposits of sediment cover the Indian Ocean floor, south of the Ganges River and to the east of India. Sediments derived from the Himalayan Range blanket the floor of the Bay of Bengal (south of Bangladesh) to a depth of 20 km. These sediments result from centuries of erosion in the land of the monsoons.

In the area of the Hawaiian Islands, a chain of islands and seamounts marks a hot-spot track from the Pacific plate from Hawai'i to the Aleutian Islands. Visible as dark trenches are subduction zones south and east of Alaska and Japan and along the western coast of South and Central America. Follow the Mid-Atlantic Ridge spreading centre the full length of the Atlantic to where it passes through Iceland, sitting astride the ridge. Take time with this map and, when you have finished reading this chapter, note the many concepts discussed in Chapters 11 and 12.

FIGURE 12.1 Earthquake and tsunami damage in Japan.
Damage scene four days after the March 11, 2011, quake and tsunami in Ofunato, Japan, north of Sendai.
[U.S. Navy photo by Mass Communication Specialist 1st Class Matthew M. Bradley.]

Earth's Surface Relief Features

Relief refers to vertical elevation differences in the landscape. Examples include the low relief of the prairie provinces, medium relief in foothill regions, and high relief in the Rocky and Himalaya Mountain ranges. The undulating configuration, including relief, that give Earth's surface its texture is called **topography**, portrayed so effectively on topographic maps—the lay of the land.

The relief and topography of Earth's landforms has played a vital role in human history: High mountain passes both protected and isolated societies, ridges and valleys dictated transportation routes, and vast plains necessitated developing faster methods of communication and travel. Earth's topography has stimulated human invention and spurred adaptation.

Crustal Orders of Relief and Hypsometry

Modern computer capabilities and tools for determining location and elevation, such as the GPS, assist in studying Earth's relief and topography. Scientists put elevation data in digital form for computer manipulation and display in *digital elevation models* (*DEMs*).

For convenience of description, geographers group the landscape's topography into three *orders of relief.* These orders classify landscapes by scale, from vast ocean basins and continents down to local hills and valleys. The first order of relief is the coarsest level of landforms, consisting of the continents and oceans. **Continental landmasses** are those portions of crust that reside above or near sea level, including the undersea continental shelves along the coastlines. **Ocean basins**, featured in the chapter-opening illustration, are entirely below sea level. Approximately 71% of Earth is covered by water.

The second order of relief is the intermediate level of landforms, for both continental and ocean-basin features. Continental features in the second order of relief include mountain masses, plains, and lowlands. A few examples are the Alps, Canadian and American Rockies, west Siberian lowland, and Tibetan Plateau. The great rock "shields" that form the heart of each continental mass are of this second order. In the ocean basins, second order of relief includes continental rises, slopes, abyssal plains, mid-ocean ridges, submarine canyons, and oceanic trenches (subduction zones)—all visible in the sea-floor illustration that opens this chapter.

The third and most-detailed order of relief includes individual mountains, cliffs, valleys, hills, and other landforms of smaller scale. Groups of these features are identifiable as local landscapes.

Figure 12.2 is a *hypsographic curve* (from the Greek *hypsos* meaning "height") that shows the distribution of Earth's surface by area and elevation in relation to sea level. Relative to Earth's diameter of 12,756 km, the surface is of low relief, only about 20 km from highest peak to lowest oceanic trench. For perspective, the summit of Mount Everest is 8.8 km above sea level and the bottom of the Mariana Trench is 11 km below sea level.

The average elevation of Earth's solid surface is actually below mean sea level at −2070 m. The average elevation for exposed land is only +875 m. For the ocean depths, average elevation is −3800 m. From this description you can see that, on average, the oceans are much deeper than continental regions are high. Overall, the underwater ocean basins, ocean floor, and submarine mountain ranges form Earth's largest "landscape."

Earth's Topographic Regions

The three orders of relief can be further generalized into six topographic regions: plains, high tablelands, hills and low tablelands, mountains, widely spaced mountains, and depressions (Figure 12.3). An arbitrary elevation or descriptive limit that is in common use defines each type of topography (see the map legend).

Four of the continents possess extensive *plains*, areas with local relief of less than 100 m and average slope angles of 5° or less. Some plains have high elevations of more than 600 m; in the United States, the high plains attain elevations above 1220 m. The Colorado Plateau, Greenland, and Antarctica are notable *high tablelands* (the latter two formed of ice), with elevations exceeding 1520 m. *Hills* and *low tablelands* dominate Africa.

Mountain ranges, characterized by local relief exceeding 600 m, occur on each continent. Earth's relief and topography are undergoing constant change as a result of processes that form crust.

▮▮ CRITICAL THINKING 12.2

Scaling Topographic Regions to Your Area

Using the topographic regions map in Figure 12.3, assess the region within 100 km and 1000 km of your location. Describe the topographic character and the variety of relief within these two regional scales. You may want to consult local maps and atlases in your analysis. Do you perceive that this type of topographic region influences lifestyles? Economic activities? Transportation? Was it influential in the history of the region?

 GEO REPORT 12.1   *Mount Everest at New Heights*

The announcement came on November 11, 1999, in Washington, DC: Mount Everest had a new revised elevation, determined by direct GPS placement on the mountain's icy summit. This was a continuation of a measurement effort begun in 1995 by the late Bradford Washburn, renowned mountain photographer and explorer.

Everest's new elevation of 8850 m is close to the previous official measure of 8848 m set in 1954 by the Survey of India. Also measured was the fact that the Himalayas are moving northeastward, as the mountain range is being driven farther into Asia by plate tectonics—the continuing collision of Indian and Asian landmasses.

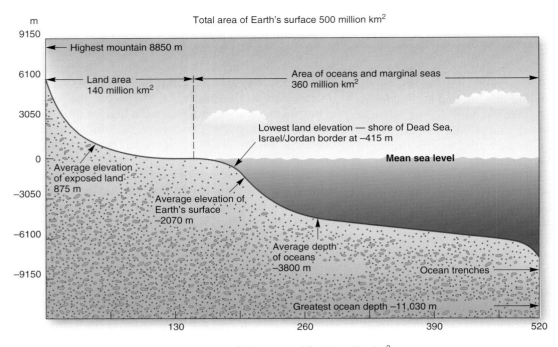

FIGURE 12.2 Earth's hypsometry.
Hypsographic curve of Earth's surface area and elevation as related to mean sea level. From the highest
point above sea level (Mount Everest) to the deepest oceanic trench (Mariana Trench), Earth's overall relief is
almost 20 km.

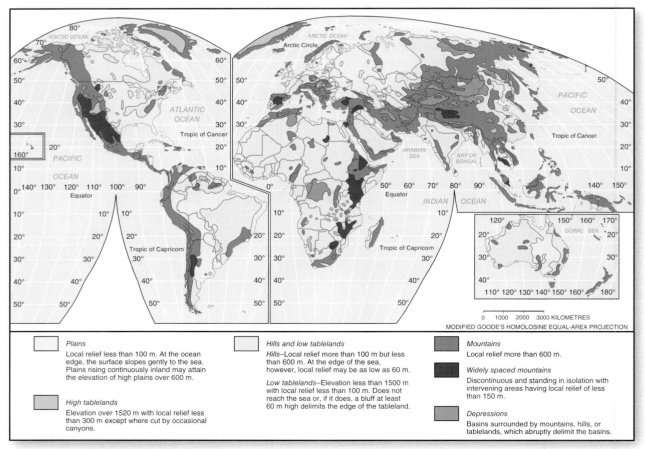

FIGURE 12.3 Earth's topographic regions.
Compare the map and legend to the world physical map inside the back cover of this book. [After R. E. Murphy,
"Landforms of the world," *Annals of the Association of American Geographers* 58, 1 (March 1968).]

Crustal Formation Processes

How did Earth's continental crust form? What gave rise to the three orders of relief just discussed? Earth's surface is a battleground of opposing processes: On the one hand, tectonic activity, driven by our planet's internal energy, builds crust; on the other hand, the exogenic (external) processes of weathering and erosion tear down crust, powered by the Sun through the actions of air, water, waves, and ice.

Tectonic activity generally is slow, requiring millions of years. Endogenic (internal) processes result in gradual uplift and new landforms, with major mountain building occurring along plate boundaries. These uplifted crustal regions are quite varied, but we think of them in three general categories, all discussed in this chapter:

■ Residual mountains and stable continental cratons, formed from inactive remnants of ancient tectonic activity;

■ Tectonic mountains and landforms, produced by active folding, faulting, and crustal movements; and

■ Volcanic features, formed by the surface accumulation of molten rock from eruptions of subsurface materials.

Thus, several distinct processes operate in concert to produce the continental crust we see around us.

Continental Shields

All continents have a nucleus of ancient crystalline rock around which the continent "grows" with the addition of crustal fragments and sediments. This nucleus is the *craton*, or heartland region, of the continental crust. Cratons generally have been eroded to a low elevation and relief. Most date to the Precambrian Era and can exceed two billion years of age. The lack of basaltic components in these cratons offers a clue to their stability. The lithosphere is thicker in cratonic regions, which consist of crust and the lithospheric uppermost mantle, than beneath younger portions of continents and oceanic crust.

A **continental shield** is a region where a craton is exposed at the surface. Figure 12.4 shows the principal

FIGURE 12.4 Continental shields.
(a) Portions of major continental shields exposed by erosion. Adjacent portions of these shields remain covered by younger sedimentary layers. (b) Canadian shield landscape in northern Québec, stable for hundreds of millions of years, stripped by past glaciations and marked by intrusive igneous dikes (magmatic intrusions). Can you see evidence in the photo of directional flow of the continental glaciers? [(a) After R. E. Murphy, "Landforms of the world," *Annals of the Association of American Geographers* 58, 1 (March 1968). (b) Bobbé Christopherson.]

areas of exposed shields and a photo of the Canadian shield in Québec. Layers of younger sedimentary rock surround these shields and appear quite stable over time. Examples of such stable *platforms* are the region that stretches from east of the Rockies to the Appalachians and northward into central and eastern Canada, a large portion of China, eastern Europe to the Ural Mountains, and portions of Siberia.

Building Continental Crust and Terranes

The formation of continental crust is complex and takes hundreds of millions of years. It involves the entire sequence of sea-floor spreading and formation of oceanic crust, its later subduction and remelting, and its subsequent rise as new magma, all summarized in Figure 12.5.

To understand this process, study Figure 12.5 and the inset photos, and revisit Figure 11.15. Begin with the magma that originates in the asthenosphere and wells up along the mid-ocean ridges. Basaltic magma is formed from minerals in the upper mantle that are rich in iron and magnesium. Such magma has less than 50% silica and

has a low-viscosity (thin) texture—it tends to flow. This mafic material rises to erupt at spreading centres and cools to form new basaltic seafloor, which spreads outward to collide with continental crust along its far edges. The denser oceanic crust plunges beneath the lighter continental crust, into the mantle, where it remelts. New magma then rises and cools, forming more continental crust, in the form of intrusive granitic igneous rock.

As the subducting oceanic plate works its way under a continental plate, it takes with it trapped seawater and sediment from eroded continental crust. The remelting incorporates the seawater, sediments, and surrounding crust into the mixture. As a result, the magma, generally called a *melt*, that migrates upward from a subducted plate contains 50%–75% silica and aluminum (called andesitic or silicic, depending on silica content). The melt has a high-viscosity (thick) texture—it tends to block and plug conduits to the surface.

Bodies of such silica-rich magma may reach the surface in explosive volcanic eruptions, or they may stop short and become subsurface intrusive bodies in the crust, cooling

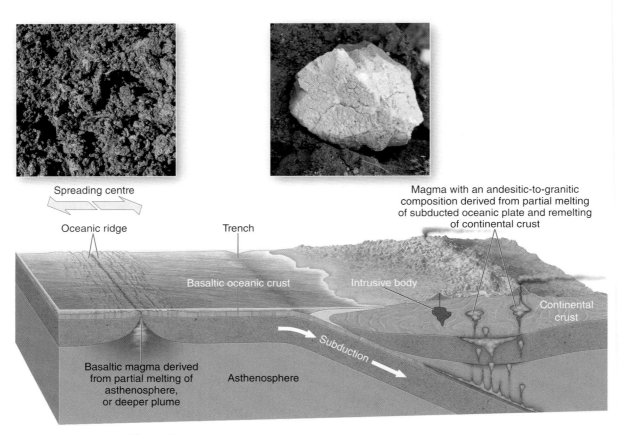

FIGURE 12.5 Crustal formation.
Material from the asthenosphere upwells along sea-floor spreading centres. Basaltic ocean floor is subducted beneath lighter continental crust, where it melts, along with its cargo of sediments, water, and minerals. This melting generates magma, which makes its way up through the crust to form igneous intrusions and extrusive eruptions. The dacite volcanic bomb (lighter rock on right, higher in silica) is from Mount St. Helens, and the basalt lava rock (darker rock on left, lower in silica) is from Hawai'i. What does this colouration tell you about the rocks' history and composition? Find these rock types in Table 11.2. [Bobbé Christopherson.]

slowly to form granitic crystalline plutons such as batho-liths (see Figures 11.9 and 11.10a). Note that this compo-sition is quite different from the magma that rises directly from the asthenosphere at sea-floor spreading centres. In these processes of crustal formation, you can literally fol-low the cycling of materials through the tectonic cycle.

Each of Earth's major lithospheric plates actually is a collage of many crustal pieces acquired from a variety of sources. Crustal fragments of ocean floor, curving chains (or arcs) of volcanic islands, and other pieces of continental crust all have been forced against the edges of continen-tal shields and platforms. These slowly migrating crustal pieces, which have become attached or accreted to the plates, are called **terranes** (not to be confused with "ter-rain," which refers to the topography of a tract of land). These displaced terranes, sometimes called *microplate* or *exotic terranes*, have histories different from those of the continents that capture them. Terranes are usually framed by fault-zone fractures and differ in rock composition and structure from their new continental homes.

In the region surrounding the Pacific, accreted ter-ranes are particularly prevalent. At least 25% of the growth of western North America can be attributed to the accre-tion of at least 50 terranes since the early Jurassic Period (190 million years ago). A good example is the Wrangell Mountains, which lie just east of Prince William Sound and the city of Valdez, Alaska. The *Wrangellia terranes*—a former volcanic island arc and associated marine sedi-ments from near the equator—migrated approximately 10,000 km to form the Wrangell Mountains and three other distinct formations along the western margin of the continent (Figure 12.6). Focus Study 12.1 gives greater detail of the principal geomorphic belts that contain exotic terranes in western Canada.

The Appalachian Mountains, extending from the southern United States to the Maritime Provinces, possess bits of land once attached to ancient Europe, Africa, South America, Antarctica, and various oceanic islands. The dis-covery of terranes, made only in the 1980s, demonstrates one of the ways continents are assembled.

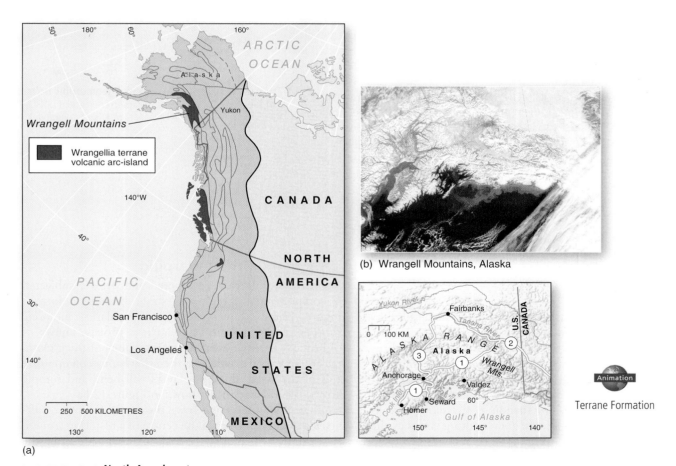

(b) Wrangell Mountains, Alaska

Terrane Formation

(a)

FIGURE 12.6 North American terranes.
(a) Wrangellia terranes occur in four segments, highlighted in red among the outlines of other terranes along the western margin of North America. (b) Snow-covered Wrangell Mountains north of the Chugach Moun-tains in this November 7, 2001, image in east-central Alaska and across the Canadian border. Note Denali (Mount McKinley) at 6194 m, the highest elevation in North America, in the upper-left part of the image, north of Cook Inlet. [(a) Based on data from USGS. (b) *Terra* MODIS image, NASA/GSFC.]

FOCUS STUDY 12.1

Geomorphic Belts Contain Exotic Terranes in Western Canada

The Western Cordillera is subdivided into five belts aligned parallel to the northwest–southeast trend of this mountain system (see Figure 12.18). Distinctive combinations of bedrock geology and landforms characterize each belt (see Natural Resources Canada website http://gsc.nrcan.gc.ca/). Moving from east to west, the belts are: Foreland, Omineca, Intermontane, Coast, and Insular (Figure 12.1.1). Contained within each belt are various exotic terranes that have been captured by continental North America.

The Rocky Mountains represent the Foreland Belt. The belt is underlain by an immense thickness of Precambrian and Phanerozoic sedimentary rocks, deposited offshore of the old North American craton that, during mountain building between 100 and 55 million years ago, were folded and thrust eastward for at least 150 km onto the edge of the old continent.

The Omineca Belt derives its name from the Omineca Mountains of central British Columbia. This belt also includes the Purcell, Selkirk, Columbia, Monashee, and Cariboo mountain ranges of southern British Columbia. Metamorphic rocks

with lesser amounts of granitic rocks dominate the bedrock geology of the Omineca Belt. The metamorphic rocks are complexly folded and faulted, and represent the roots of an ancient mountain chain that formed between 180 and 60 million years ago.

High plateaux and deep river valleys characterize the landscapes of the Intermontane Belt. This belt is underlain by a variety of Paleozoic and Mesozoic volcanic, granitic, and sedimentary rocks. The presence of volcanic and granitic rocks in the Intermontane Belt, the intense metamorphism of these same rocks represented in the Omineca Belt, and the folding and thrust faulting of sedimentary rocks in the Foreland Belt, together record the initial phase of mountain building (180 to 100 m.y.a.) associated with the accretion of exotic terranes along the western margin of the North American craton.

The Coast Belt includes the Coast and Cascade mountains and the Fraser Lowland near

FIGURE 12.1.1 Five principal geomorphic belts of western Canada. [Map adapted courtesy of LITHO-PROBE Secretariat, The University of British Columbia.]

Crustal Deformation Processes

Rocks, whether igneous, sedimentary, or metamorphic, are subjected to powerful stress by tectonic forces, gravity, and the weight of overlying rocks. Figure 12.7 shows three types of stress: *tension* (stretching), *compression* (shortening), and *shear* (twisting or tearing).

Strain is how rocks respond to stress. Strain is expressed in rocks by *folding* (bending) or *faulting* (breaking). Think of stress as a force and resulting strain as the deformation in the rock. Whether a rock bends or breaks depends on several factors, including composition and how much pressure is on the rock. An important quality is whether the rock is *brittle* or *ductile*. The patterns created by these processes are clearly visible in the landforms we see today, especially in mountain areas. Figure 12.7 illustrates each type of stress and its resulting strain and the surface expressions that develop.

Folding and Broad Warping

When rock strata that are layered and flat are subjected to compressional forces, the strata become deformed (Figure 12.8). Convergent plate boundaries intensely compress rocks, deforming them in a process known as **folding**. As an analogy, if we take sections of thick cloth, stack them flat on a table, and then slowly push on opposite ends of the stack, the cloth layers will bend and rumple into folds similar to those shown in Figure 12.8a.

If we then draw a line down the centre axis of a resulting ridge, and a line down the centre of a resulting trough, we see how the names of the folds are assigned. Along the *ridge* of a fold, layers *slope downward away from the axis*, which is called an **anticline**. In the *trough* of a fold, layers *slope downward toward the axis*, called a **syncline**.

If the axis of either type of fold is not "level" (horizontal, or parallel to Earth's surface), the fold axis then *plunges*, inclined (dipped down) at an angle. Knowledge of how folds are angled with respect to Earth's surface, the city of Vancouver. Long, deep fjords that were created by glacial erosion during Pleistocene glaciations dissect the mountain ranges. The bedrock consists largely of granite in the form of plutons and batholiths that intrude into folded, faulted, and metamorphosed volcanic and sedimentary rocks. The granitic rocks represent the roots of deeply eroded volcanoes that formed at various times throughout the Mesozoic and early Cenozoic eras (170 to 45 m.y.a.).

The Insular Belt includes the mountain ranges on Vancouver Island and Haida Gwaii (Queen Charlotte Islands), as well as the rocks that underlie the continental shelf (Figure 12.1.2). This belt is composed of Paleozoic and Mesozoic volcanic and sedimentary rocks that have been intruded by Mesozoic and Cenozoic granitic rocks.

The presence of youthful mountain ranges in both the Insular and Coast belts underlain by metamorphosed Paleozoic rocks and Mesozoic and Cenozoic granitic intrusions records a second phase of mountain building (84 to 40 m.y.a.). This phase is associated with the accretion of exotic terranes along the western margin of North America.

The Pacific Ocean floor started to move strongly northward along the margin of the advancing North American plate about 85 million years ago. Portions of the North American plate became coupled with the underlying oceanic plate and started to move northward with it. This movement caused widespread faulting within the Western Cordillera and the displacement of accreted terranes several hundreds of kilometres northward.

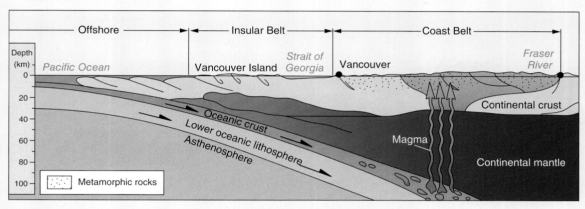

FIGURE 12.1.2 Plate tectonic setting of the Cascadia subduction zone. [Cross-section adapted courtesy of LITHOPROBE Secretariat, The University of British Columbia, http://www.lithoprobe.ca.]

and where they are located, is important for the petroleum industry. For example, petroleum geologists know that oil and natural gas collect in the upper portions of anticlinal folds in permeable rock layers such as sandstone.

Figure 12.8a further illustrates the landforms that result from the effects of weathering and other exogenic processes in folded landscapes:

- A residual "synclinal ridge" may form within a syncline because different rock strata offer greater resistance to weathering processes. A synclinal ridge is exposed in Figure 12.8 to the right.
- Compressional forces often push folds far enough that they actually overturn upon their own strata (producing an "overturned anticline").
- Further stress eventually fractures the rock strata along distinct lines, and some overturned folds are thrust upward, causing a considerable shortening of the original strata ("thrust fault"). Areas of intense stress and compressional folding

are visible in a road cut in the Canadian Rockies (Figure 12.8b).

The Canadian Rocky Mountains, the Appalachian Mountains, and areas of the Middle East illustrate the complexity of folded landscapes. Satellites allow us to view many of these structures from an orbital perspective, as in Figure 12.9, north of the Persian Gulf and the Zagros Mountains of Iran. This area was a dispersed terrane that separated from the Eurasian plate. However, the collision produced by the northward push of the Arabian block is now shoving this terrane back into Eurasia and forming an active margin known as the Zagros crush zone, a zone of continuing collision more than 400 km wide. In the satellite image, anticlines form the parallel ridges; active weathering and erosion processes are exposing the underlying strata.

In addition to the rumpling of rock strata just discussed, broad warping actions also affect Earth's continental crust. These actions produce similar up-and-down

FIGURE 12.7 Three kinds of stress and strain and the resulting surface expressions.
The bulldozers represent the stress, or force, on the rock strata. (a) Tension stress produces a stretching
and thinning of the crust and a *normal fault.* (b) Compression produces shortening and folding and *reverse
faulting* of the crust. In a back-and-forth horizontal motion, (c) shear stress produces a bending of the crust
and, on breaking, a *strike-slip fault.*

bending of strata, but the bends are far greater in extent than those produced by folding. Warping forces include mantle convection, isostatic adjustment such as that caused by the weight of previous ice loads across northern Canada, or crustal swelling above an underlying hot spot. Warping features can be small, individual, foldlike structures called *basins* and *domes* (Figure 12.10a, b) or regional features the size of the Richat Dome in Mauritania or the Isachsen dome on Ellef Rignes Island in Nunavut (Figure 12.10c, d).

In the Queen Elizabeth Islands of Arctic Canada (Figure 12.10e), upwarped domes composed of the evaporite minerals gypsum ($CaSO_4 \cdot 2H_2O$) and anhydrite ($CaSO_4$)—known as *piercement domes*—represent distinctive landforms. The thick evaporite deposits (approximately 400 m) accumulated within a large sedimentary basin during the Carboniferous and Permian Periods (approximately 290 m.y.a.). In the middle of the Cenozoic Era, a mountain-building event (Eurekan orogeny) resulted in folding and thrust faulting of the sedimentary rocks. The evaporite rocks were driven

upward through the overlying Mesozoic sedimentary rocks (mostly sandstone and shale) to produce the piercement domes. The piercement domes attain heights of several hundreds of metres and diameters up to 10 km.

Faulting

A freshly poured concrete sidewalk is smooth and strong. But stress the sidewalk by driving heavy equipment over it, and the resulting strain might cause a fracture. Pieces on either side of the fracture may move up, down, or horizontally, depending on the direction of stress. Similarly, when rock strata are stressed beyond their ability to remain a solid unit, the strata express the strain as a fracture. Rocks on either side of the fracture displace relative to the other side in a process known as **faulting**. Thus, *fault zones* are areas where fractures in the rock demonstrate crustal movement. At the moment of fracture, a sharp release of energy occurs, called an **earthquake** or *quake.*

The fracture surface along which the two sides of a fault move is the *fault plane.* The names of the three basic

Axis of Syncline

Axis of anticline

Overturned anticline

Thrust fault

Synclinal ridge

Anticlinal valley

Plunge angle

Horizontal plane

Anticline

Syncline

(a)

Fault plane

(c) Folded strata along San Andreas fault

(b) Folded landscape, Canadian Rocky Mountains

FIGURE 12.8 Folded landscapes.
(a) Folded landscape and the basic types of fold structures. (b) Interbedded limestone and shale strata in the Canadian Rocky Mountains that have been intensely folded in response to compression of the crust. (c) Folding, squeezing, and uplift from strong compressional and shearing forces show well in a road cut along the San Andreas fault zone, beside the Antelope Valley freeway. [(b) Gunter Marx Photography/ Encyclopedia/Corbis; (c) Bobbé Christopherson.]

Folds, Anticlines, and Synclines

FIGURE 12.9 Folding in the Zagros crush zone, Iran.
The Zagros Mountains are a product of the Zagros crush zone between the Arabian and Eurasian plates, where the northward push of the Arabian block is causing the folded mountains shown. [NASA.]

FIGURE 12.10 Domes and basins.
(a) An upwarped dome. (b) A structural basin. Denudation of weak (soft) rock strata has produced valleys and depressions in these landscapes. In contrast, strong (hard) rock strata stand in positive topographic relief forming ridges. (c) The Richat dome structure of Mauritania. (d) Isachsen dome, Ellef Ringnes Island, Nunavut, Canada. This piercement dome consists of Carboniferous evaporite rocks (represented by bright tones in the photograph) flanked by steeply dipping beds of Cretaceous shale (represented by dark tones in the photograph). (e) The distribution of piercement domes within the Queen Elizabeth Islands, Arctic Canada. [(c) Image courtesy SRTM Team NASA/JPL/NIMA; (d) ASTER image from NASA and the Earth Remote Sensing Data Analysis Center; (e) Adapted with the permission of Natural Resources Canada, 2012, from *Geology and economic minerals of Canada*, R. J. W. Douglas, ed. Geological Survey of Canada, *Economic Geology Report No. 1*, (ed. 5), 1970, Fig. X-8, p. 570.]

types of faults, illustrated in Figure 12.11, are based on the tilt and orientation of the fault plane. A normal fault forms when rocks are pulled apart by tensional stress. A thrust or reverse fault results when rocks are forced together by compressional stress. A strike-slip fault forms when rocks are torn by lateral-shearing stress.

When forces pull rocks apart, the tension causes a **normal fault**, or *tension fault*. When the break occurs, rock on one side moves vertically along an inclined fault plane (Figure 12.11a). The downward-shifting side is the *hanging wall*; it drops relative to the *footwall block*. The exposed fault plane sometimes is visible along the base of faulted mountains, where individual ridges are truncated by the movements of the fault and appear as triangular facets at the ends of the ridges. A cliff formed by faulting is commonly called a *fault scarp*, or *escarpment*.

Compressional forces associated with converging plates force rocks to move *upward* along the fault plane. This is a **reverse fault**, or *compression fault* (Figure 12.11b).

On the surface, it appears similar to a normal fault, although more collapses and landslides may occur from the hanging wall component. In England, when miners worked along a reverse fault, they would stand on the lower side (*foot*wall) and hang their lanterns on the upper side (*hanging* wall), giving rise to these terms.

If the fault plane forms a low angle relative to the horizontal, the fault is termed a **thrust fault**, or *overthrust fault*, indicating that the overlying block has shifted far over the underlying block (see Figure 12.8, "thrust fault"). Place your hands palms-down on your desk, with fingertips together, and slide one hand up over the other—this is the motion of a low-angle thrust fault, with one side pushing over the other.

In the Alps, several such overthrusts result from compressional forces of the ongoing collision between the African and Eurasian plates. Beneath the Los Angeles Basin, overthrust faults produce a high risk of earthquakes and caused many quakes in the twentieth century,

(a) Normal fault (tension)

(b) Thrust or reverse fault (compression)

(c) Strike-slip fault (lateral shearing)

* Viewed from either dot on each road,
movement to opposite side is *to the right*.
** Viewed from either dot on each road,
movement to opposite side is *to the left*.

FIGURE 12.11 Types of faults.
(a) A normal fault produced by tension in the crust, visible along the edge of mountain ranges in California and along the Wasatch Front in Utah. (b) A thrust, or reverse fault, produced by compression in the crust, visible in these offset strata in coal seams and volcanic ash in British Columbia. (c) A strike-slip fault produced by lateral shearing, clearly seen looking southeast along the San Andreas fault rift zone, with the Carrizo Plain—Pacific plate to the right and the North American plate to the left. (d) Can you find the San Andreas fault on the satellite image? Look for a linear rift stretching from southeast to northwest, at the edge of the coastal mountains and the San Joaquin Valley. Use the arrows as guides. [(a) Bobbé Christopherson. (b) Fletcher and Baylis/Photo Researchers, Inc. (c) USGS; (d) *Terra* MISR image, NASA/GSFC/JPL.]

Animation

Fault Types, Transform
Faults, Plate Margins

including the $30 billion 1994 Northridge earthquake. These blind thrust faults (unknown until they rupture) beneath the Los Angeles region remain a major earthquake threat.

If movement along a fault plane is horizontal, such as produced along a transform fault, it forms a **strike-slip fault** (Figure 12.11c; refer to Figure 12.20 for review). The movement is *right-lateral* or *left-lateral*, depending on the motion perceived when you observe movement on one side of the fault relative to the other side.

Although strike-slip faults do not produce cliffs (scarps), as do the other types of faults, the movements can create linear rift valleys. This is the case with the San Andreas fault system of California. The rift valley is clearly visible in Figure 12.11c, where the edges of the North American and Pacific plates are grinding past one another as a result of transform-fault movement.

The evolution of the San Andreas fault system is shown in Figure 12.12. Note in the figure how the East Pacific rise developed as a spreading centre with associated transform faults (1), while the North American plate was progressing westward after the breakup of Pangaea. Forces then shifted the transform faults toward a northwest–southeast alignment along a weaving axis (2). Finally, the western margin of North America overrode those shifting transform faults (3). Note the convergence rate is a rapid 4 cm per year.

In *relative* terms, the motion along this series of transform faults is right-lateral, whereas in *absolute* terms the North American plate is still moving southwestward. Consequently, the San Andreas system is a series of faults that are *transform* (associated with a former spreading centre), *strike-slip* (horizontal in motion), and *right-lateral* (one side is moving to the right relative to the other side).

Faults in Concert Combinations of faults can produce distinctive landscapes. In the U.S. interior west, the *Basin and Range Province* (featuring a roughly parallel series of faulted mountains and valleys) experienced tensional forces caused by uplifting and thinning of the crust (illustrated later in Chapter 15, Figure 15.22). This movement cracked the surface to form aligned pairs of normal faults and a distinctive landscape (Figure 12.13a).

The term **horst** applies to upward-faulted blocks; **graben** refers to downward-faulted blocks. One example of a horst-and-graben landscape is the Great Rift Valley of East Africa (associated with crustal spreading); it extends northward to the Red Sea, which fills the rift formed by parallel normal faults (Figure 12.13b). Another example is the Rhine graben, through which the Rhine River flows in Europe.

Orogenesis (Mountain Building)

Orogenesis literally means the birth of mountains (*oros* comes from the Greek for "mountain"). An *orogeny* is a mountain-building episode, occurring over millions of years. It can occur through large-scale deformation and

uplift of the crust. An orogeny may include the capture of migrating exotic terranes, adding by accretion to the continental margins, or the intrusion of granitic magmas to form plutons. The net result of this accumulating material is a thickening of the crust. The granitic plutons often become exposed by erosion following uplift. Uplift is the final act of an orogenic cycle of mountain building. Earth's major chains of folded and faulted mountains, called *orogens*, are remarkably well correlated with the plate tectonics model.

No orogeny is a simple event; many involve previous developmental stages dating back far into Earth's past, and the processes are ongoing today. Major mountain ranges, and the orogenies that caused them, include:

- Rocky Mountains of North America—*Laramide orogeny*, 40–80 million years ago (m.y.a.); beginning 170 m.y.a., including Sevier Orogeny;
- Sierra Nevada and Klamath Mountains of California—*Nevadan orogeny*, with faulting 29–35 m.y.a. and older batholithic intrusion emplacements dating back 80 to 180 million years;
- Appalachian Mountains and the Ridge and Valley Province (nearly parallel ridges and valleys) of the eastern United States and Canadian Maritime Provinces—*Alleghany orogeny*, 250–300 m.y.a., associated with the collision of Africa and North America, preceded by at least two earlier orogenies; in Europe this is contemporary with the *Hercynian orogeny*;
- Alps of Europe—*Alpine orogeny*, 2 to 66 m.y.a., principally in the Teriary Period and continuing to the present across southern Europe and the Mediterranean, with many earlier episodes (Figure 12.14);
- Himalayas of Asia—*Himalayan orogeny*, 45–54 m.y.a., beginning with the collision of the India plate and Eurasia plate and continuing to the present.

Types of Orogenies

Figure 12.15 illustrates three types of convergent plate collisions that cause orogenesis:

(a) **Oceanic plate–continental plate collision orogenesis.** This type of convergence is now occurring along the Pacific coast of the Americas and has formed the Andes, the Sierra of Central America, the Rockies, and other western mountains. We see folded sedimentary formations, with intrusions of magma forming granitic plutons at the heart of these mountains. The buildup has been augmented by capturing displaced terranes, accreted during collision with the continental mass. Also, note the associated volcanic activity inland from the subduction zone, the eruption of plateau (flood) basalts (see Figures 12.27 and 12.31), and the development of composite volcanoes (see Figure 12.33).

(b) **Oceanic plate–oceanic plate collision orogenesis.** Such collisions can produce either simple volcanic island arcs or more complex arcs, such as Indonesia

(a) Evolution of West Coast plate boundary

(c) Plate boundary

(b) Fault and earthquake map

FIGURE 12.12 San Andreas fault formation.
(a) Formation of the San Andreas fault system as a series of transform faults in three successive stages.
(b) Enlargement shows the portion of southern California where the 1992 Landers, 1994 Northridge (Reseda), 1999 Hector Mine, and 2010 Redlands, Borrego, and El Mayor earthquakes occurred. Note the January 2001 M 6.8 Nisqually quake in Washington State, related to the subduction zone offshore on map (a). (c) Trail sign near the epicentre of the 1906 San Francisco earthquake roughly marks the Pacific–North American plate boundary, Marin County, Point Reyes National Seashore, California. [(c) Robert Christopherson.]

(a)

(b)

FIGURE 12.13 **Faulted landscapes.**
(a) Pairs of faults produce a horst-and-graben landscape. (b) The Red Sea occupies a down-dropped block that
is part of the rift system through East Africa, a graben. [(b) NASA *Gemini.*]

and Japan, which include deformation and meta-morphism of rocks, and granitic intrusions. These processes formed the chains of island arcs and volcanoes that continue from the southwestern Pacific to the western Pacific, the Philippines, the Kuril Islands, and on through portions of the Aleutian Islands.

Both (a) oceanic–continental and (b) oceanic–oceanic collision types are active around the Pacific Rim. Both are thermal in nature, because the diving plate melts and migrates back toward the surface as molten rock. The region of active volcanoes and earthquakes around the Pacific is known as the **circum-Pacific belt** or, more popularly, the **Ring of Fire**.

FIGURE 12.14 **European Alps.**
Western (France), central (Italy), and eastern (Austria) segments make up the crescent shape of the Alps.
Complex overturned faults and crustal shortening due to compressional forces occur along convergent plates.
The Alps are some 1200 km in length, occupying 207 000 km². Note the snow coverage in this December
image. [*Terra* MODIS image, NASA/GSFC.]

FIGURE 12.15 **Three types of plate convergence.**
(a) Oceanic plate–continental plate (example: Nazca plate–South American plate collision and subduction).
(b) Oceanic plate–oceanic plate (example: New Hebrides Trench near Vanuatu, 16° S 168° E). (c) Continental plate–continental plate (example: India plate and Eurasian landmass collision and resulting Himalayan Mountains. Can you identify more of these plate convergence areas on the chapter-opening map?

Plate Boundaries

(c) **Continental plate–continental plate collision orogenesis.** Here the orogenesis is mechanical; large masses of continental crust are subjected to intense folding, overthrusting, faulting, and uplifting. The converging plates crush and deform both marine sediments and basaltic oceanic crust. The formation of the European Alps is a result of such compression forces and includes considerable crustal shortening, forming great overturned folds, called *nappes*.

As mentioned earlier, the collision of the Indian subcontinent with the Eurasian landmass produced the Himalayan Mountains. That collision is estimated to have shortened the overall continental crust by as much as 1000 km and to have produced telescoping sequences of thrust faults at depths of 40 km. The Himalayas feature the tallest mountains above sea level on Earth, including Mount Everest at 8850 m elevation, and all 10 of Earth's highest peaks (measured from sea level).

The disruption created by this plate collision has reached far under China, and frequent earthquakes there signal the continuation of this rapid-paced collision, as India moves northward at about 2 m a year. As evidence of this ongoing strain, the January 2001 quake in Gujarat, India, was along a shallow, east–west-tending thrust fault that gave way under the pressure of the northward-pushing India plate. More than one million buildings were destroyed or damaged during this event, along the 2500-km fault zone that marks this plunging Indian subcontinent. Another 40-km segment snapped in October 2005, when an M 7.6 quake hit the Kashmir region of Pakistan, resulting in the deaths of more than 83 000 people.

The Appalachian Mountains

The old, eroded, fold-and-thrust belt of southeastern Canada and the eastern United States has origins dating to the formation of Pangaea and the collision of Africa and North America (250–300 million years old). The Appalachians contrast with the higher mountains of western North America (35–80 million years old). As noted, the complexity of the *Alleghany orogeny* derives from at least two earlier orogenic cycles of uplift and the accretion of several captured terranes.

Each orogenic event was separated by long periods of time during which rock weathering and erosion gradually stripped material from the mountain summits. The end result of these processes was the production of upland plateaux with elevations equal to or greater than 700 m above sea level throughout much of Atlantic Canada, excluding Prince Edward Island.[1] Fluvial and glacial erosion has created steep-sided valleys that dissect the edge of the upland plateaux (Figure 12.16).

Structure and composition link the mountain ranges separated by the Atlantic Ocean and the Pangaea collision and separation. In fact, the Lesser (or Anti-) Atlas Mountains of Mauritania and northwestern Africa were connected to the Appalachians at some time in the past, but the mountains embedded in the African plate rafted apart from the Appalachians.

The Western Cordillera

The rugged topography that characterizes much of this region developed in response to volcanism and tectonism accompanying the accretion of exotic terranes through-

[1]A. S. Trenhaile, *Geomorphology: A Canadian Perspective* (Oxford University Press, 2003).

out the Mesozoic and early Tertiary Periods (180 to 45 m.y.a.). Mountain peaks commonly exceed elevations of 3000 m above sea level (Figure 12.17). Mount Logan, its peak the highest point in Canada at an elevation of 5959 m above sea level, occurs within the St. Elias mountain range (Figure 12.17c). The terrain in this region is composed of a variety of intrusive and extrusive igneous rocks, metamorphic rocks, and sedimentary rocks that have experienced folding and faulting.

Pleistocene alpine glaciation widened and deepened river valleys, creating mountain passes and deep fjords. These important breaks in the mountain ridges greatly influenced European exploration of the region in the eighteenth and nineteenth centuries. The routes selected for several transcontinental railways in the latter part of the nineteenth century were guided by this topography.

The Innuitian Mountains

This region occupies the northeastern margin of the Queen Elizabeth Islands in Arctic Canada. Folding and thrust faulting of sedimentary rocks during the *Ellesmerian orogeny* in the late Paleozoic Period (Devonian-Pennsylvanian) initiated mountain building. This orogeny also involved the eruption of basaltic lava and the intrusion of granite plutons. Volcanism and folding and thrust faulting of sedimentary rocks during the mid-Cenozoic period *Eurekan orogeny* characterized a later phase of mountain building. Mountains in this region may attain elevations up to 2400 m above sea level (Figure 12.18d).

World Structural Regions

Examine the first two maps in this chapter (the map opening the chapter and Figure 12.3) and you note two vast alpine systems on the continents. In the Western Hemisphere, the *Cordilleran system* stretches from Tierra del Fuego at

(a)

(b)

FIGURE 12.16 Landscapes at the northern end of the Appalachian Mountains.
(a) The upland plateau of Cape Breton Island. (b) The Long Range Mountains in Newfoundland. The upland plateau surfaces represent ancient erosion created by intense weathering and fluvial erosion, most likely under the warmer and moister climates of the late Cretaceous and early Tertiary Periods. River valleys dissect the margins of the plateaux. The valleys were initiated as the plateaux were uplifted in preglacial times and progressively deepened by fluvial and glacial erosion. [(a) Irwin Barrett/firstlight.ca; (b) Len Wagg/CP Images.]

(a)

(b)

(c)

(d)

FIGURE 12.17 Canadian Rockies, the Bow River Valley, and Mount Logan.
(a) Rugged topography and scenic vistas characterize the Canadian Rockies in the Banff region along the Alberta–British Columbia border. Orogenesis during the late Paleozoic and Mesozoic Eras occurred earlier than the American Rockies. (b) Sculpting by rivers and the work of Pleistocene glaciers give us such natural beauty in this eastern portion of the Canadian Cordillera. (c) Mount Logan, the highest point in Canada and second highest in North America, is located in the St. Elias Range, Yukon Territory. A team of six climbers made the first ascent in 1925. (d) Mountains of the Princess Margaret Range, Axel Heiberg Island, Nunavut, Canada. [(a) and (b) by Robert Christopherson; (c) M. Beedell, Parks Canada, no. 11.110.07.08 (21); (d) Jerry Kobalenko/firstlight.ca.]

the southern tip of South America to the peaks of Alaska, including the relatively young Rocky and Andes Mountains along the western margins of the North and South American plates. In the Eastern Hemisphere, the *Eurasian–Himalayan system* stretches from the European Alps across Asia to the Pacific Ocean and contains younger and older components.

These mountain systems also are shown on the structural region map as the *Alpine system* (Figure 12.18). The map defines seven fundamental structural regions that possess distinctive types of landscapes, grouped because of shared physical characteristics. Looking at the distribution of these regions helps summarize the three rock-forming processes (igneous, sedimentary, and metamorphic), plate tectonics, landform origins and construction, and overall orogenesis.

As you examine the map, identify the continental shields at the heart of each landmass. Continental platforms composed of younger sedimentary deposits surround these areas. Various mountain chains, rifted

Alpine System
The world-girdling system of mountain chains and ranges formed since the Jurassic Period.*

Laurasian Shields
North of the great east–west portion of the Alpine system; areas of stable, massive blocks of Earth's crust where rocks formed an encircling enclosure with no gap of more than 320 km (200 mi) between outcrops.

Rifted Shield Areas
Block-faulted areas of shields forming grabens together with associated horsts and volcanic features.

Gondwana Shields
South of the great east–west portion of the Alpine system.

Sedimentary Covers
Areas of sedimentary layers that have not been subject to orogenesis. These areas of sedimentary rock form continuous covers over underlying structures.

Caledonian and Hercynian (or Appalachian Remnants)
Remains of mountain chains and ranges formed during the Paleozoic and Mesozoic Eras prior to the Cretaceous Period and experiencing no orogenesis since then.*

Isolated Volcanic Areas
Areas of volcanoes, active or extinct, with associated volcanic features, lying outside the Alpine mountain system and the rifted shield areas.

*Please refer to Figure 11.1, the geologic time scale.

FIGURE 12.18 World structural regions and major mountain systems.
Some of the regions appear larger than the structures themselves because each region includes related landforms adjacent to the central feature. (Correlate aspects of this map with Figures 12.3 and 12.4.) Structural regions in the Western Hemisphere are visible on the composite false-colour *Landsat* image inset (vegetation is portrayed in red). [After R. E. Murphy, "Landforms of the world," *Annals of the Association of American Geographers* 58, 1 (March 1968). Inset image EROS Data Center/USGS.]

regions, and isolated volcanic areas are noted on the map. On the continent of Australia, there are older mountain sequences to the east, sedimentary layers covering basement rocks west of these ranges, and portions of the original Gondwana, an ancient landscape in the central and western region. Remember that Gondwana was a landmass that included Antarctica, Australia, South America, Africa, and the southern portion of India; it broke away from Pangaea some 200 million years ago.

Earthquakes

Crustal plates do not glide smoothly past one another. Instead, tremendous friction exists along plate boundaries. The stress (a force) of plate motion builds strain (a deformation) in the rocks until friction is overcome and the sides along plate boundaries or fault lines suddenly break loose. The two sides of the fault plane then lurch into new positions, moving from centimetres to several metres, and release enormous amounts of seismic energy into the surrounding crust. This energy radiates throughout the planet, diminishing with distance, but sufficient enough to register on instruments worldwide.

In 2007, southern Sumatra, Indonesia, was hit with M 8.4 and M 7.9 quakes, near the same plate boundary where there were four other quakes greater than M 7.9 since 1998. At this boundary, the Australian Plate moves northeast, subducting beneath the Sunda Plate on which Sumatra rides, at a relative speed of 6.6 cm per year. This is where the M 9.1 earthquake struck December 26, 2004, triggering the devastating Indian Ocean tsunami (more on this in Chapter 16); the quake and tsunami took 228 000 lives. For complete listings of these and other earthquakes, go to http://earthquake.usgs.gov/earthquakes/.

What are the mechanisms that produce such dramatic tectonic events? Why do most quakes strike in total surprise, such as in Haiti and Chile in 2010 and New Zealand and Japan in 2011? See Focus Study 12.2.

Focus, Epicentre, Foreshock, and Aftershock

The subsurface area along a fault plane, where the motion of seismic waves is initiated, is the *focus*, or hypocentre, of an earthquake (see labels in Figure 12.19). The area at the surface directly above the focus is the *epicentre*. Shock waves produced by an earthquake radiate outward through the crust from the focus and epicentre. Some of the seismic waves are conducted throughout the planet to distant instruments. Scientists explore Earth's interior using these seismic wave patterns and the nature of their transmission through the layers of the planet.

An *aftershock* may occur after the main shock, sharing the same general area of the epicentre; some aftershocks rival the main tremor in magnitude. A *foreshock*, which precedes the main shock, also is possible. The pattern of foreshocks is now regarded as an important consideration in the forecasting effort. Before the 1992 Landers earthquake in southern California, at least two dozen foreshocks occurred along the soon-to-erupt portion of the fault.

Earthquake Intensity and Magnitude

Tectonic earthquakes are those quakes associated with faulting. A worldwide network of more than 4000 **seismograph** instruments record vibrations transmitted as waves of energy throughout Earth's interior and in the crust. Using this device and actual observations, scientists rate earthquakes on two kinds of scales: a *qualitative* damage intensity scale and a *quantitative* magnitude-of-energy-released scale.

A damage *intensity scale* is useful in classifying and describing damage to terrain and structures after an earthquake. Earthquake damage intensity is rated on the arbitrary *Mercalli scale*, a Roman numeral scale from I to XII representing "barely felt" to "catastrophic total destruction." It was designed in 1902 and modified in 1931. Table 12.1 shows this scale and the number of quakes in each category that are expected each year. The strongest recorded earthquake thought to have struck was the M 9.6 in Chile in 1960, producing Mercalli XII damage. The fault-line break in the crust extended over 1000 km after that quake.

In 1935, Charles Richter designed a system to estimate earthquake magnitude. In this method, a seismograph located at least 100 km from the epicentre of the quake records the amplitude of seismic waves. The measurement is then charted on the **Richter scale**. The relation of magnitude to energy released is still a useful feature of his scale. See Applied Physical Geography at the end of this chapter.

The Richter scale is logarithmic: Each whole number on it represents a 10-fold increase in the measured wave amplitude. Translated into energy, each whole number signifies a 31.6-fold increase in energy released. Thus, a magnitude of 3.0 on the Richter scale represents 31.6 times

---

GEO REPORT 12.2 *Large Earthquakes Affect the Entire Earth System*

Scientific evidence is mounting that Earth's largest earthquake events have a global influence. The 2004 Sumatra–Andaman earthquake appears to have affected fault strengths and global seismicity as changes in measured stress and strain increased. Related to this was an unusual increase in M 8.0 and higher quakes after 2004.

An M 7.9 quake near Denali National Park, Alaska, was the largest on Earth in 2002. This quake triggered far-reaching effects: more than 200 small earthquakes in Yellowstone, seismic crustal waves that were felt in Texas, and altered water tables and well water in Pennsylvania. Earth indeed behaves as a vast, integrated tectonic system.

FOCUS STUDY 12.2

Earthquakes in Haiti, Chile, and Japan: A Comparative Analysis

Let us take a summary look at three quakes that struck in 2010 and 2011. As we compare, use this information to further your understanding of the relation between plate tectonics and quake occurrences. Table 12.2.1 summarizes these three events, whereas Table 12.2 details significant earthquakes in history.

The first setting was the impoverished country of Haiti, January 12, 2010, just before 5 P.M., when an M 7.0 earthquake struck. The epicentre was 15 km southwest of the capital, Port-Au-Prince. Seven minutes later an aftershock of M 6.0 con-

tinued the tragedy. More than 222 000 people died, with another 300 000 injured. Almost 300 000 houses were destroyed or damaged. Total damage exceeded the country's $14 billion annual gross domestic product (GDP).

The fault plane solution—that is, the orientation of the fault plane and the direction of slip motion—determined that the Caribbean plate moved eastward relative to the North American plate's southwestward shift, in a horizontal strike-slip motion along a 50-km section of the Enriquillo–Plaintain Garden fault.

Having this fault segment snap added more stress to the eastern segment of the fault, which is some 600 km in length. The entire fault system is accumulating elastic energy at the same rate as the section that broke in the quake.

Six weeks later the Nazca plate, moving eastward beneath the westward-moving South American plate, suddenly shifted, generating an M 8.8 quake southwest of Santiago, near Maule, Chile. This is near Concepción and the epicentre of the greatest earthquake of the twentieth century, the M 9.6 that

TABLE 12.2.1 Summary of Three Major Earthquakes in 2010 and 2011

Location, date, and time	Map	Moment magnitude*	Focus depth	Epicentre distance to nearest city	Type of fault motion	Tectonic plate location	Human dimension	Damage cost (USD)
Port-Au-Prince, Haiti Jan. 12, 2010 4:53 P.M.	Haiti	M 7.0	13 km Ocean	15 km southwest from Port-Au-Prince	Strike-slip fault	Transform boundary: Caribbean plate moving eastward with respect to the North America plate	222 570 killed 300 000 injured 1.3 million displaced	$25 billion
Maule, Chile Feb. 27, 2010 3:34 A.M.	Chile	M 8.8	35 km Ocean	95 km from Santiago	Thrust fault at subduction zone	Convergent boundary: Nazca plate subducting beneath South American plate	521 killed, 12 000 injured, 800 000 displaced	$30 billion
Tohoku, Honshu, Japan Mar. 11, 2011 2:46 P.M.	Honshu, Japan	M 9.0	32 km Ocean	129 km from Sendai	Thrust fault at subduction zone	Convergent boundary: Pacific plate subducting beneath North American plate	~30 000 deaths	~$325 billion

*Reported by USGS.

struck in 1960. Some of the fault-slip zone from that record quake matched areas for the February 27, 2010, event. Damage in 2010 exceeded $30 billion, compared to Chile's Gross Domestic Product of USD $204 billion. The deaths of 521 people and injuries to 12,000 marked the human dimension. At least two tsunami were generated, arriving in Hilo, Hawai'i, about 15 hours later, each only a metre in height.

The fault plane solution here was a subduction zone earthquake. This area of convergence and subduction is moving at a relative speed of 7 m per century. Damage limitation across Chile was aided by strict building codes that went into effect in 1985.

Japan rocked on the afternoon of March 11, 2011 when an M 9.0 quake struck at 5:46 UTC (12:46 a.m. EST). Off the northeast coast of Honshu Island, the focus was at a depth of 32 km along the subduction boundary between the converging North American and Pacific plates—this was the Tohoku earthquake along the Japan Trench. The epicentre surface expression was at 38.3° N 142.4° E—about 370 km northeast of Tokyo. Imagine an area some 340 km (N–S) by 150 km thrust faulting, abruptly lifting 30–40 m and displacing the ocean above it. The nearest coastal city is Sendai (Figure 12.2.1).

The westward-moving Pacific plate is pulled and dives beneath the Eurasian plate east of the Japan Trench at a rate averaging 83 mm per year. In the ocean-floor map that begins this chapter, you can see several microplates that form this complex plate boundary.

Foreshocks began about 48 hours before the main quake, whereas several

FIGURE 12.2.1 Search efforts complicated by tsunami and radiation threat. Fire trucks line up along what was a city street in Sukuiso, Japan, 6 days after the quake and tsunami. Radiation dangers from the Fukushima nuclear power station disaster delay the search for casualties. [U.S. Navy photo by Mass Communication Specialist 3rd Class Dylan McCord.]

hundred aftershocks continued for weeks, registering between M 5.0 and M 7.0, with a maximum of M 7.1. The number of people killed will probably never be known exactly, but an estimate of 30 000 is suggested by the known dead and missing as of summer 2011. Damage estimates from the quake and tsunami are USD $325 billion.

The tremendous energy released by the fault movement also radiated across

the Pacific Ocean in a massive tsunami. The deep coastal embayments along the coast of Honshu magnify tsunami energy and make this region particularly vulnerable. This reality means that the coastal siting of six nuclear reactors at the Fukushima Daiichi plant, south of Sendai, was a poor planning decision. The quake and tsunami damaged cooling systems, and subsequent hydrogen explosions destroyed three secondary containment structures, leading to massive radiation releases to the land, atmosphere, and ocean.

The tsunami averaged 10 m at Miyagi. Where the wave entered the narrow Ofunate harbour, wave heights reached nearly 30 m as it funnelled up the valley three km. Even Japan's strict hazard preparedness standards were of no avail as the deep, swift wave travelled inland. The Pacific Tsunami Warning System alerted the countries around the Pacific basin. Damage occurred on Maui and Hawai'i and in the harbours of Crescent City and Santa Cruz on the California coast.

FIGURE 12.2.2 Tsunami moves ashore overwhelming Iwanuma, Japan. Houses, cars, and city debris are carried kilometres inland over farmlands. Iwanuma is 20 km south of Sendai and 30 km north of the Fukushima Daiichi nuclear plants. [Kyodo News/AP Images.]

FIGURE 12.19 Anatomy of an earthquake.
(a) The fault-plane solution for the 1989 Loma Prieta, California, earthquake shows the lateral and vertical (thrust) movements occurring at depth. There was no surface expression of this fault plane. (b) In only 15 seconds, more than 2 km of the Route 880 Cypress Freeway collapsed. (c) Section failure in the San Francisco–Oakland Bay Bridge. [(a) After USGS. (b) and (c) Courtesy of California Department of Transportation.]

Animation

P- and S-waves, Seismology

more energy than a 2.0, and 992 times more energy than a 1.0. A revised, more quantitative scale, the moment magnitude scale, was introduced. Revision was needed because the scale did not properly measure or differentiate between quakes of high intensity. Seismologists wanted to know more about what they call the *seismic moment* to understand a broader range of possible motions during an earthquake.

The **moment magnitude scale**, in use since 1993, is more accurate for large earthquakes than is Richter's *amplitude magnitude* scale. Moment magnitude considers the amount of fault slippage produced by the earthquake, the size of the surface (or subsurface) area that ruptured, and the nature of the materials that faulted, including how resistant the materials were to failure. The moment magnitude scale considers extreme ground acceleration

TABLE 12.1 Magnitude, Intensity, and Frequency of Earthquakes

Description	Effects on Populated Areas	Moment Magnitude Scale	Modified Mercalli Scale	Average Number per Year[1]
Great	Damage nearly total	8.0 and higher	XII	1
Major	Great damage	7.0–7.9	X–XI	17
Strong	Considerable-to-serious damage to buildings; railroad tracks bent	6.0–6.9	VIII–IX	134
Moderate	Felt by all, with slight building damage	5.0–5.9	V–VII	1319
Light	Felt by some to felt by many	4.0–4.9	III–IV	13 000 (estimated)
Minor	Slight, some feel it	3.0–3.9	I–II	130 000 (estimated)
Very minor	Not felt, but recorded	2.0–2.9	None to I	1 300 000 (estimated)

[1]Based on observations since 1990.
Source: USGS, Earthquake Information Center.

 Seismograph, How it Works

(movement upward), a characteristic that the Richter amplitude magnitude method underestimated.

A reassessment of past quakes has increased the magnitude rating of some and decreased that of others. As an example, the 1964 earthquake at Prince William Sound in Alaska had an amplitude magnitude of 8.6, but on the moment magnitude scale it increases to a magnitude M 9.2. Note that Table 12.2 includes more earthquakes for the period following 1960 than for the years before 1960. This is not because earthquake frequency has increased; rather, it reflects an effort to include recent events that affected high population densities in vulnerable areas.

Seismologists record an average of 1500 earthquakes in Canada each year. Figure 12.20 illustrates the intensity of seismic activity within Canada and the location of 15 significant twentieth-century Canadian earthquakes. The magnitude of these 15 seismic events is presented in Table 12.3. The regions that experienced large magnitude earthquakes (M > 5) include the Ottawa River and St. Lawrence River valleys in eastern Canada, the Western Cordillera, the Mackenzie River valley, and the continental shelf of northwestern Baffin Bay.

The U.S. National Earthquake Information Center in Golden, Colorado, reports earthquake epicentres. For references, see http://earthquake.usgs.gov/regional/neic/ and the National Geophysical Data Center at http://www.ngdc.noaa.gov/hazard/. In Canada, a listing of significant Canadian earthquakes is at http://earthquakescanada.nrcan.gc.ca/index-eng.php.

The Nature of Faulting

We earlier described types of faults and faulting motions. The specific mechanics of how a fault breaks remain under study, but **elastic-rebound theory** describes the basic process. Generally, two sides along a fault appear to be locked by friction, resisting any movement despite the powerful forces acting on the adjoining pieces of crust. Stress continues to build strain along the *fault plane* surfaces, storing elastic energy like a wound-up spring. When the strain buildup finally exceeds the frictional lock, both sides of the fault abruptly move to a condition of less strain, releasing a burst of mechanical energy.

Think of the fault plane as a surface with irregularities that act as sticking points, preventing movement, similar to two pieces of wood held together by drops of glue of different sizes rather than an even coating of glue. Research scientists at the USGS and the University of California identify these small areas of high strain as *asperities*. They are the points that break and release the sides of the fault.

If the fracture along the fault line is isolated to a small asperity break, the quake will be small in magnitude. As some asperities break (perhaps recorded as small foreshocks), the strain increases on surrounding asperities that remain intact. Thus, small earthquakes in an area may be precursors to a major quake. However, if the break involves the release of strain along several asperities, the quake will be greater in extent and will involve the shifting of massive amounts of crust. The latest evidence points to a wavelike pattern, as rupturing spreads along the fault plane, rather than the entire fault surface giving way at once.

The buildup and release of stress and strain accumulates as the two sides of the fault attempt to move laterally past one another, yet remain locked (Figure 12.21). Stress forces continue to build strain until it overwhelms the frictional sticking points and the two sides snap violently and at great speed into new positions. An earthquake strikes.

TABLE 12.2 A Sampling of Significant Earthquakes**

Year	Date	Location	Number of Deaths	Mercalli Intensity	Moment Magnitude (Richter)
1556	Jan. 23	Shaanxi Province, China	830 000	*	*
1737	Oct. 11	Calcutta, India	300 000	*	*
1812	Feb. 7	New Madrid, Missouri	Several	XI–XII	*
1857	Jan. 9	Fort Tejon, California	*	X–XI	*
1870	Oct. 21	Montreal to Québec, Canada	*	IX	*
1886	Aug. 31	Charleston, South Carolina	*	IX	6.7
1906	Apr. 18	San Francisco, California	3000	XI	7.7 (8.25)
1923	Sept. 1	Kwanto, Japan	143 000	XII	7.9 (8.2)
1939	Dec. 27	Erzincan, Turkey	40 000	XII	7.6 (8.0)
1960	May 22	Southern Chile	5700	XII	9.6 (8.6)
1964	Mar. 28	Southern Alaska	131	X–XII	9.2 (8.6)
1970	May 31	Northern Peru	66 000	*	7.9 (7.8)
1971	Feb. 9	San Fernando, California	65	VII–IX	6.7 (6.5)
1972	Dec. 23	Managua, Nicaragua	5000	X–XII	6.2 (6.2)
1976	July 28	Tangshan, China	250 000	XI–XII	7.4 (7.6)
1978	Sept. 16	Iran	25 000	X–XII	7.8 (7.7)
1985	Sept. 19	Mexico City, Mexico	7000	IX–XII	8.1 (8.1)
1988	Dec. 7	Armenia–Turkey border	30 000	XII	6.8 (6.9)
1989	Oct. 17	Loma Prieta (near Santa Cruz, California)	66	VII–IX	7.0 (7.1)
1991	Oct. 20	Uttar Pradesh, India	1700	IX–XI	6.2 (6.1)
1994	Jan. 17	Northridge (Reseda), California	66	VII–IX	6.8
1995	Jan. 17	Kobe, Japan	5500	XII	6.9
1996	Feb. 17	Indonesia	110	X	8.1
1997	Feb. 28	Armenia–Azerbaijan	1100	XII	6.1
1997	May 10	Northern Iran	1600	XII	7.3
1998	May 30	Afghanistan–Tajikistan	4000	XII	6.9
1998	July 17	Papua New Guinea	2200	X	7.1
1999	Jan. 26	Armenia, Colombia	1000	VIII–IX	6.0
1999	Aug. 17	Izmit, Turkey	17 100	VIII–XI	7.4
1999	Sept. 7	Athens, Greece	150	VI–VIII	5.9
1999	Sept. 20	Chi-Chi, Taiwan	2500	VI–X	7.6
1999	Sept. 30	Oaxaca, Mexico	33	VI	7.5
1999	Oct. 16	Hector Mine, California	0	*	7.1
1999	Nov. 12	Düzce, Turkey	700	VI–X	7.2
2001	Jan. 26	Gujarat state, India	19 998	X–XII	7.7
2002	Nov. 3	Near Denali National Park, Alaska	1	X	7.9
2003	Dec. 26	Bam, Iran	30 000	X–XII	6.9
2004	Dec. 26	Northern Sumatra (west coast)	228 000+***	X–XII	9.3
2005	Oct. 8	Kashmir region, Pakistan	83 000+	X–XII	7.6
2008	May 12	Chengdu, China	87 000+	X–XII	7.9
2010	Jan. 12	Port-Au-Prince, Haiti	223 000	X–XII	7.0
2010	Feb. 27	Maule, Chile	521	IX–XI	8.8
2011	Feb. 21	Christchurch, New Zealand	166	VI–VIII	6.3
2011	Mar. 11	Tohoku/Sendai, Japan****	30 000	X–XII	9.0

*Data not available.

**Note that earthquakes are not on the increase; rather, the list reflects a greater sample for recent years.

***Estimated deaths in 11 countries from the quake and resulting tsunami that travelled across the Indian Ocean.

****Combined deaths from earthquake and tsunami.

 Seismograph, How it Works

Natural Resources Canada   Ressources naturelles Canada

Magnitude
· 3
· 4
· 5
● 6
● 7
● 8
● 9

Earthquakes in or near Canada, 1627 - 2010

EarthquakesCanada.nrcan.gc.ca

FIGURE 12.20 Seismic activity in or near Canada, 1627 to 2010 Canada.
Damaging earthquakes (M > 5) are strongly associated with the Western Cordillera and the valleys of the Ottawa and St. Lawrence Rivers. [Used by permission of the Minister of Public Works and Government Services Canada; Natural Resources Canada, Geological Survey of Canada.]

TABLE 12.3 Significant Canadian Earthquakes of the Twentieth Century

Year	Date	Location	Moment Magnitude
1918	Dec. 6	Vancouver Island, British Columbia	7.0
1925	Mar. 1	Charlevoix–Kamouraska Region, Québec	6.2
1929	May 26	South of Haida Gwaii (formerly Queen Charlotte Islands), British Columbia	7.0
1929	Nov. 18	Atlantic Ocean south of Newfoundland	7.2
1933	Nov. 20	Baffin Bay northeast of Baffin Island, Nunavut	7.3
1935	Nov. 1	Temiscamingue Region, Ontario–Québec border	6.1
1944	Sept. 5	Cornwall region, Ontario–New York border	5.8
1946	June 23	Vancouver Island, British Columbia	7.3
1949	Aug. 22	South of Haida Gwaii (formerly Queen Charlotte Islands), British Columbia	8.1
1958	July 10	Near the British Columbia–Alaska border	7.9
1970	June 24	South of Haida Gwaii (formerly Queen Charlotte Islands), British Columbia	7.4
1979	Feb. 28	Yukon–Alaska border	7.2
1982	Jan. 9	Miramichi region, New Brunswick	5.7
1982	Jan. 11	Miramichi, New Brunswick	5.4
1985	Dec. 23	Nahanni region, Northwest Territories	6.9
1988	Nov. 25	Saguenay region, Québec	5.9
1989	Dec. 25	Ungava region, Québec	6.3

Source: Important Canadian Earthquakes, www.earthquakescanada.nrcan.gc.ca/historic-historique/map-carte-eng.php. Data from 1918 to 1989. Natural Resources Canada. Reproduced with the permission of the Minister of Public Works and Government Services Canada, 2012.

Elastic Rebound

(a)   (b)

FIGURE 12.21 Buildup and release of stress and strain along a fault system.
The elastic-rebound mechanism applies to strike-slip faults such as the San Andreas system of faults in California, North Anatolian fault in Turkey, Enriquillo fault in Haiti, and Nojima fault zone near Kobe, Japan. Note the fence that crosses the fault line. This stress continues to build to the break point, the two sides snap into new positions, strain is released, and the fence no longer forms a continuous property line. The segments of the fault that remain locked now have added strain. A coulomb is a unit of shear-stress failure overcoming friction and resistance to movement; the colour scale ranges from blue (decreased stress) to red (increased stress). [Illustrations courtesy of Serkan Bozkurt, USGS.]

Earthquake Forecasting and Planning

The maps in Figure 12.22 plot earthquake hazards in Canada and the United States. These occurrences give some indication of relative risk by region. The challenge is to discover how to predict the *specific time and place* for a quake in the short term in these regions of past earthquake experience.

Actual implementation of an action plan to reduce death, injury, and property damage from earthquakes is difficult. The political environment adds complexity since studies show that an accurate earthquake prediction may threaten a region's economy. Research examining the potential socioeconomic impact of earthquake

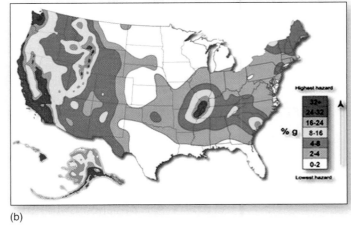

(a)   (b)

FIGURE 12.22 Earthquake hazard maps.
(a) Relative seismic hazard across Canada for one- to two-storey, single-family dwellings. In the regions of highest hazard (Vancouver and regions off the west coast, isolated portions of Yukon and the high Arctic, and a small area in the St. Lawrence estuary), the probability of strong shaking that can significantly damage buildings is 30 times greater for a 50-year period than in the regions of lowest hazard. There is a 5% to 15% chance that significant damage will occur in a 50-year period in regions of moderate hazard. (b) Earthquake ground accelerations having a 10% probability of being topped in the next 50 years. Acceleration is expressed as a percentage of 1 g (gravity), with red being the highest shaking. Active seismic regions include the West Coast, the Wasatch Front of Utah northward into Canada, the central Mississippi Valley, the southern Appalachians, and portions of South Carolina, upstate New York, and Ontario. [(a) Reproduced with the permission of Natural Resources Canada, 2011. Courtesy of the Geological Survey of Canada; (b) USGS; see http://eqhazmaps.usgs.gov/.]

prediction on an urban community shows surprising negative economic impacts in the period before the quake hits. Imagine a chamber of commerce, bank, real estate agent, tax assessor, or politician who would welcome an earthquake prediction and such negative publicity for their city. These factors work against effective planning and preparation.

How do you forecast an earthquake? One approach is to examine the history of each plate boundary and determine the frequency of past earthquakes, a study called *paleoseismology*. Paleoseismologists construct maps that provide an estimate of expected earthquake activity based on past performance. An area that is seismically quiet and overdue for an earthquake is a *seismic gap*; such an area forms a gap in the earthquake occurrence record and is therefore a place that possesses accumulated strain. The area along the Aleutian Trench subduction zone had three such gaps until the great 1964 Alaskan earthquake filled one of them.

The areas around San Francisco and northeast of Los Angeles represent other such gaps where the San Andreas fault system appears to be locked by friction and stress is producing accumulating strain. The USGS in 1988 predicted a 30% chance of an M 6.5 earthquake occurring within 30 years in the Loma Prieta portion of the fault system. The actual 1989 quake dramatically filled a portion of the seismic gap in that region. The 1995 Nojima fault in the area of Kobe occurred in another gap.

A second approach to forecasting is to observe and measure phenomena that might precede an earthquake. *Dilitancy* refers to the slight increase in volume of rock produced by small cracks that form under stress and accumulated strain. The affected region may tilt and swell in response to strain. Tiltmeters measure these changes in suspect areas. Another indicator of dilitancy is an increase in radon (a naturally occurring, slightly radioactive gas) dissolved in groundwater. At present, some earthquake hazard zones have thousands of radon monitors taking samples in test wells; increases in gas levels, however, have come before quakes and yet also happened when there was no subsequent quake.

In the absence of effective forecasting weeks, months, or years ahead, earthquake warning systems can be useful. Following the 1989 Loma Prieta earthquake near San Francisco, highway-repair workers were linked to a broadcast system that gave them 20-second alerts of aftershocks from distant epicentres. In southern California, the USGS is coordinating a Southern California Seismographic Network (SCSN at http://www.scsn.org/) to correlate 350 instruments for immediate earthquake location analysis and disaster coordination. A seismic network in operation in Mexico City is providing 70-second warnings of arriving seismic-wave energy from distant epicentres.

The science behind earthquake forecasting is informed by a range of data that is integrated to predict future events. The most intensely studied seismic area in the world is along the San Andreas fault outside Parkfield, California. The area features tiltmeter instruments, gas-monitoring wells, *lidar* laser-ranging measurements, and a newly completed drill hole where instruments are placed in the fault at a depth between 2 km and 3 km—the San Andreas Fault Observatory at Depth (SAFOD). A similar drilling project has been completed in the Nojima fault, which caused the Kobe, Japan, earthquake in 1995. The goal is to sample material at the seismogenic depth that is in the subsurface area of fault slippage.

A synthetic-aperture radar image of a portion of the San Andreas fault zone in San Mateo, California, is shown in Figure 1.29. Even the slightest movements in the build-up to a quake are sensed, which is critical to forecasting an earthquake. In addition, all the movement during the quake and the settling down of aftershocks following a quake are tracked and measured.

In the San Francisco Bay Area, the present forecast predicts a 62% chance of an M 6.7, or higher, striking between 2000 and 2030 along the San Andreas system of faults. Added to this is a 14% chance of a significant earthquake occurring along some yet unknown fault. Adding to the risk is the extent of landfill in the Bay Area, where about half the original bay is now filled and the reclaimed land is occupied by buildings. In an earthquake, such fill fails in a process of liquefaction, where shaking brings water to the surface and liquefies the soil.

Someday accurate earthquake forecasting may be a reality, but several questions remain: How will humans respond to a forecast? Can a major metropolitan region be evacuated for short periods of time? Can a city relocate after a disaster to an area of lower risk?

Long-range planning is a complex subject. After the Loma Prieta earthquake in 1989, the U.S. National Research Council concluded as follows in a report:

> One of the most jarring lessons from these quakes may be that earthquake professionals have long known many of the things that could have been done to reduce devastation. . . . The cost-effectiveness of mitigation and the importance of closing the knowledge gap among researchers, building professionals, government officials, and the public are only two of the many lessons from the Loma Prieta that need immediate action.

A valid and applicable generalization is that *humans and their institutions seem unable or unwilling to perceive hazards in a familiar environment.* In other words, we tend to feel secure in our homes and communities, even if they are sitting on a quiet fault zone. Such an axiom of human behaviour certainly helps explain why large populations continue to live and work in earthquake-prone settings. Similar questions also can be raised about populations in areas vulnerable to floods, droughts, hurricanes, and coastal storm surges and in settlements on barrier islands. See the Natural Hazards Center at the University of Colorado at http://www.colorado.edu/hazards/index.html, home of the publication *Natural Hazards Observer*.

FIGURE 12.23 **The Eyjafjallajökull eruption in April 2010.**
[Rakal Osk Sigurdardottir/Nordic Photo.]

Volcanism

Volcanic eruptions across the globe remind us of Earth's internal energy. Ongoing eruption activity matches plate tectonic activity, as shown on the map in Figure 11.21. A few recent eruptions include Eyjafjallajökull and Grímsvötn (Iceland), Kīlauea (Hawai'i), Soufriere Hills on Montserrat (Lesser Antilles), Mount Etna (Sicily, Italy), several on the Kamchatka Peninsula (Russia), Rabaul (Papua, New Guinea), Axial Summit and the Jackson Segment (sea-floor spreading centre off the coast of Oregon), and Shishaldin (Unimak Island, Alaska; see Figure 12.33).

The Eyjafjallajökull eruption on April 13, 2010, was notable because its ash forced a 5-day closure of European airspace, grounding some 100 000 flights (Figure 12.23). Iceland's Meteorological Office monitored the effusive eruption with its 56-station seismic network, implemented with risk assessment and evacuation plans in 1999. Such subglacial eruptions do produce floodwaters and sometimes explosive reactions between meltwater and lava. No large cities were threatened. The region near the volcano is mainly rural farm and pasture land (see Figure 7.1a).

Over 1300 identifiable volcanic cones and mountains exist on Earth, although fewer than 600 are active (have had at least one eruption in recorded history). In an average year, about 50 volcanoes worldwide erupt, varying from modest activity to major explosions. (An index to the world's volcanoes is at http://vulcan.wr.usgs.gov/Volcanoes/framework.html, and the National Museum of Natural History Global Volcanism Program lists information for more than 8500 eruptions at http://www.nmnh.si.edu/gvp/. For more volcanic eruption listings, check http://www.geo.mtu.edu/volcanoes/links/observatories.html for links to volcano observatories across the globe.)

Eruptions in remote locations and at depths on the seafloor go largely unnoticed, but the occasional eruption of great magnitude near a population centre makes headlines. North America has about 70 volcanoes (mostly inactive) along the western margin of the continent. Mount St. Helens in Washington State is a famous recently active example, and over one million visitors a year travel to Mount St. Helens Volcanic National Monument to see the effects of volcanism for themselves.

Volcanic Features

A **volcano** forms at the end of a central vent or pipe that rises from the asthenosphere and upper mantle through the crust into a volcanic mountain. A **crater**, or circular surface depression, usually forms at or near the summit. Magma rises and collects in a magma chamber deep below the volcano until conditions are right for an eruption. This subsurface magma emits tremendous heat; in some areas it boils groundwater, producing *geothermal energy*, as seen in the thermal springs and geysers of Yellowstone National Park and elsewhere in the world.

Lava (molten rock), gases, and **pyroclastics**, or *tephra* (pulverized rock and clastic materials of various sizes ejected violently during an eruption), pass through the vent to the surface and build the volcanic landform. Flowing basaltic lava takes two principal forms, both named in Hawaiian terms (Figure 12.24). One form, called **aa**, is rough and jagged with sharp edges. This texture happens

(a) Aa

(b) Pahoehoe

Tectonic Settings and
Volcanic Activity

FIGURE 12.24 **Two types of basaltic lava—Hawaiian examples, close up.**
(a) A rough, sharp-edged lava, aa is said to get its name from the sounds people make if they attempt to walk on it. The gold-coloured strands are clumps of natural spun glass formed by the lava as it blew out into the air—called *Pele's hair*. (b) Pahoehoe forms ropy chords in twisted folds. [Bobbé Christopherson.]

FIGURE 12.25 Many cinder cones on Ascension Island. Ascension Island is a massive composite volcano that rises over 3000 m from the ocean floor, with 858 m above sea level. It is classified as inactive. [Bobbé Christopherson.]

because the lava loses trapped gases, flows slowly, and develops a thick skin that cracks into the jagged surface. Another principal lava texture that is more fluid than aa is **pahoehoe**. As this lava flows it forms a thin crust that develops folds and appears "ropy," like coiled, twisted rope. Both forms can come from the same eruption, and sometimes pahoehoe will become aa as the flow progresses. Other types of basaltic magma are described later in this section.

A **cinder cone** is a small, cone-shaped hill usually less than 450 m high, with a truncated top formed from cinders that accumulate during moderately explosive eruptions. Cinder cones are made of pyroclastic material and *scoria* (cindery rock, full of air bubbles). For example, about 100 cinder cones and craters are found on the Ascension Islands, located about 8° S latitude in the Atlantic Ocean (Figure 12.25).

A **caldera** (Spanish for "kettle") is a large, basin-shaped depression. It forms when summit material on a volcanic mountain collapses inward after an eruption or other loss of magma. A caldera may fill with rainwater, as it did in beautiful Crater Lake in southern Oregon.

The Long Valley caldera (Figure 12.26), near the California–Nevada border, was formed by a powerful volcanic eruption 760 000 years ago. The oval-shaped caldera is about 15 by 30 km long in a north–south direction at an elevation of 2000 m. About 1100 metric tons of carbon

dioxide are coming up through the soil in the old caldera each day, killing about 69 hectares of forest in six different areas over the past 20 years. The source is active and moving magma at a depth of some 3 km. These gas emissions signal volcanic activity and are useful indicators of potential eruptions. For updates, see http://lvo.wr.usgs.gov/.

On Fogo Island in the Cape Verde Islands (15° N 24.5° W), the Cha caldera opens onto the sea on the eastern side (see the chapter-opening photo). The best farmland is in the caldera, so the people choose to live and work there. Eruptions began in 1995, destroying farmland and forcing the evacuation of 5000 people. Previously, eruptions occurred between A.D. 1500 and 1750, followed by six more in the nineteenth century, each destroying houses and crops. The population returned to work the volcanic soils and to develop the beginnings of an ecotourism business when the eruption sequence subsided.

Location and Types of Volcanic Activity

The location of volcanic mountains on Earth is a function of plate tectonics and hot-spot activity. Volcanic activity occurs in three settings (with representative examples):

1. Along subduction boundaries at continental plate–oceanic plate convergence (such as Mount St. Helens and Kliuchevskoi, Siberia) or oceanic plate–oceanic plate convergence (Philippines and Japan).
2. Along sea-floor spreading centres on the ocean floor (Iceland on the Mid-Atlantic Ridge, or off the coast of British Columbia, Oregon, and Washington) or areas of rifting on continental plates (the rift zone in east Africa).
3. At hot spots, where individual plumes of magma rise to the crust (such as Hawai'i and Yellowstone National Park).

Figure 12.27 illustrates these three settings for volcanic activity, which you can compare with the active volcano sites and plate boundaries shown in Figure 11.21.

Effusive Eruptions

Effusive eruptions are relatively gentle and produce enormous volumes of lava annually on the seafloor. These direct eruptions from the asthenosphere and upper mantle

Formation of Crater Lake

FIGURE 12.26 Forest death from CO_2 emission, Long Valley caldera, California. A warning sign signals the danger from CO_2 gassing up through soils from subsurface magma and related volcanic activity. The hazard has killed one person to date. [Bobbé Christopherson.]

FIGURE 12.27 Tectonic settings of volcanic activity.
Magma rises and lava erupts from rifts, through crust above subduction zones, and where thermal plumes at hot spots break through the crust. [Adapted from U.S. Geological Survey, *The Dynamic Planet* (Washington, DC: Government Printing Office, 1989).]

Forming Types of
Volcanoes

produce a low-viscosity magma that is fluid and cools to form a dark, basaltic rock low in silica (less than 50% silica and rich in iron and magnesium). Gases readily escape from this magma because of its low viscosity, adding to a gentle effusive eruption that pours out on the surface, with relatively small explosions and few pyroclastics. However, dramatic fountains of basaltic lava sometimes shoot upward, powered by jets of rapidly expanding gases.

An effusive eruption may come from a single vent or from the flank of a volcano, through a side vent. Vents that form a linear opening are *fissures;* these sometimes

erupt in a dramatic *curtain of fire* (sheets of molten rock spraying into the air). Rift zones capable of erupting tend to converge on the central crater, or vent, as they do in Hawai'i. The interior of such a crater, often a sunken caldera, may fill with low-viscosity magma during an eruption, forming a molten lake, which then may overflow lava downslope in dramatic rivers and falls of molten rock.

On the island of Hawai'i, the continuing Kīlauea eruption is the longest in recorded history, active since January 3, 1983 (Figure 12.28). Although this eruption is

(a)

(b)

FIGURE 12.28 Kīlauea landscape.
(a) Aerial photo of the newest land on the planet produced by the massive flows of basaltic lavas from the Kīlauea volcano, Hawai'i Volcano National Park. In the distance, ocean water quenches the intense 1200°C lava on contact, producing steam and hydrochloric acid mist. This entire area is slowly slipping toward the sea. (b) Dramatic Hawaiian active lava flows form the Kamoamoa bench as it builds into the sea. The glowing lava is clearly visible through the steam. Even at the safe distance of this aerial photo, the radiated heat from the lava flow is incredible to feel. [Bobbé Christopherson.]

located on the slopes of the massive Mauna Loa volcano, scientists have determined that Kīlauea has its own magma plumbing system extending some 60 km into Earth, allowing it to produce more lava than any other vent in recorded history. To date, the eruption has produced 3.1 km³ of lava, covering 117 km². During 1989–1990, lava flows from Kīlauea actually consumed several visitor buildings in the Hawai'i Volcanoes National Park. Beginning on Mother's Day 2002 (May 12), an aggressive eruption sequence intensified, flowing over the Chain of Craters Road and continuing for several years to send streams of lava to the ocean (Figure 12.28b). Fourteen kilometres of Chain of Craters Road are now covered by lava flows,

making National Park Service rangers keep their end-of-road checkpoint for tourists movable.

Pu'u O'o is the active crater on Kīlauea and is presently continuing to erupt. In 2007, a portion of Pu'u O'o crater's west side collapsed, filled with lava, and collapsed again (Figure 12.29)—see http://hvo.wr.usgs.gov/.

In 2008, a vent blasted open a pit crater in the floor of the Halema'uma'u Crater within Kīlauea. This is within full view of the USGS Hawaiian Volcano Observatory and a dedicated web cam with hourly updated views (http://volcanoes.usgs.gov/hvo/cams/KIcam/). The vent in the crater floor is directly below the former tourist overlook and parking area on the rim of Halema'uma'u

(a)

(b)

(c)

FIGURE 12.29 Dynamic and active Pu'u O'o, at Kīlauea, Hawai'i.
(a) The cracked and faulted crater of Pu'u O'o in 1999. Note the changes that happened (b) by 2007 and (c) by 2011. Portions of the crater wall collapsed in summer 2007, refilled with lava, and collapsed again. Active lava continues to fill the crater from the spatter cones. [(a) Bobbé Christopherson. (b), (c) USGS Hawaiian Volcano Observatory.]

(a) (b)

FIGURE 12.30 Halema'uma'u crater eruptions from 2008 to the present.
Halema'uma'u crater is 100 m deep, roughly circular, and about 800 m in diameter. A pit crater formed and began eruptions in 2008. The writer Mark Twain witnessed and described eruptions in his travels in 1866.
[USGS 2009 photos.]

FIGURE 12.31 Shield and composite volcanoes compared.
Comparison of Mauna Loa in Hawai'i, a shield volcano, and Mount Rainier in Washington State, a composite volcano. Their strikingly different profiles signify their different tectonic origins. Note the gently sloped shield shape in the inset photo.
[After U.S. Geological Survey, *Eruption of Hawaiian Volcanoes* (Washington, DC: Government Printing Office, 1986). Inset photo by Bobbé Christopherson.]

(Figure 12.30). Since 2008, the vent has cycled through lava filling and draining events and through debris collapses blocking the vent and then clearing. This activity is producing enormous quantities of sulfur dioxide, which contributes to Hawai'i's volcanic smog problem, *vog*.

A typical mountain landform built from effusive eruptions is gently sloped, gradually rising from the surrounding landscape to a summit crater. The shape is similar in outline to a shield of armour lying face up on the ground and therefore is called a **shield volcano**. The shield shape and size of Mauna Loa in Hawai'i is distinctive when compared with Mount Rainier in Washington, which is a different type of volcano (explained shortly) (Figure 12.31).

The height of the Mauna Loa shield is the result of successive eruptions, flowing one on top of another. Mauna Loa is one of five shield volcanoes that make up

GEO REPORT 12.3 *Slow Slip Events across Kīlauea's South Flank*

The entire south flank of the Kīlauea volcano is in a long-term motion toward the ocean, along a low-angle fault at a rate of about 7 cm per year—see the area in Figure 12.28a. GPS units, tiltmeters, and small earthquakes mark the slow movement. In February 2010, in one 36-hour period, a slow slip event of 3 cm occurred, accompanied by a flurry of small earthquakes. A bench collapse or failure of this new basaltic landscape into the sea is possible, but the eventual outcome of these slow slip events is unknown.

FIGURE 12.32 Earth's extensive igneous provinces.
(a) Plateau basalts form large igneous provinces across the globe. Many are ancient and inactive. The largest known is the Ontong Java Plateau, which covers nearly 2 million km² on the Pacific Ocean floor. Black dots are areas of ancient volcanism along continental margins. (b) In the foreground are plateau (flood) basalts characteristic of the Columbia Plateau in Oregon. Mount Hood, in the background to the west of the plateau, is a composite volcano. [(a) After M. F. Coffin and O. Eldholm, "Large igneous provinces," *Scientific American* (October 1993): 42–43. © Scientific American, Inc. (b) Robert Christopherson.]

the island of Hawai'i. At least one million years were needed to accumulate the volcano's mass. Mauna Kea is 35 m taller, but Mauna Loa is the most massive single mountain on Earth.

In another volcanic setting, effusive eruptions send material out through hot spots or elongated fissures, such as a continental rift valley, forming extensive sheets of basaltic lava on the surface (see Figure 12.27). The Columbian Plateau of the northwestern United States, some 2–3 km thick, is the result of the eruption of **plateau basalts**, or *flood basalts* (inset photo Figure 12.32b).

More than double the size of the Columbian Plateau is the Deccan Traps, which dominates west-central India. *Trap* is Dutch for "staircase," referring to the typical steplike eroded lavas. The Siberian Traps is more than twice the area of that in India and is exceeded only by the Ontong Java Plateau, which covers an area of the seafloor in the Pacific (Figure 12.32). These regions are sometimes referred to as *plateau basalt provinces.* Of these extensive igneous provinces, no presently active sites come close in size to the largest of the extinct igneous provinces, some of which formed more than 200 million years ago.

Explosive Eruptions

Volcanic activity inland from subduction zones produces the infamous explosive volcanoes. Magma produced by the melting of subducted oceanic plate and other materials is thicker (more viscous) than magma from effusive volcanoes. It is 50%–75% silica and high in aluminum; consequently, it tends to block the magma conduit inside the volcano. The blockage traps and compresses gases, causing pressure to build for a possible **explosive eruption**.

From this magma, a lighter dacitic rock forms at the surface, as illustrated in the comparison in Figure 12.5 (see *dacite* in Table 11.2). Unlike the volcanoes in Hawai'i Volcanoes National Park, where tourists gather at observation platforms or hike out across the cooling lava flows to watch the relatively calm effusive eruptions, these explosive eruptions can explode with little warning and do not invite close inspection.

The term **composite volcano** describes these explosively formed mountains. (Composite volcanoes are sometimes called *stratovolcanoes* because alternating layers of ash, rock, and lava build up, but shield volcanoes also can exhibit a stratified structure, so *composite* is the preferred term.) Composite volcanoes tend to have steep sides, and are also known as *composite cones*. If a single summit vent erupts repeatedly, a remarkable symmetry may develop as the mountain grows in size, as demonstrated by Mount Orizaba in Mexico, Mount Shishaldin in Alaska (Figure 12.33), Mount Fuji in Japan, and the pre-1980-eruption shape of Mount St. Helens in Washington.

Owing to its chemical makeup and high viscosity, rising magma in a composite volcano forms a plug near the surface. The blockage causes tremendous pressure to build, keeping the trapped gases compressed and liquefied. When the blockage can no longer hold back this pressurized inferno, explosions equivalent to megatons of TNT blast the tops and sides off the mountain. This type of eruption produces much less lava than effusive eruptions but larger amounts of *pyroclastics*, which include volcanic *ash* (<2 mm in diameter), dust, cinders, lapilli (up to 32 mm in diameter), scoria (volcanic slag), pumice, and aerial bombs (explosively ejected blobs of incandescent lava).

Probably the most studied and photographed composite volcano on Earth is Mount St. Helens, located in southern Washington State. Mount St. Helens is the youngest and most active of the Cascade Range of volcanoes, which form a line from Mount Lassen in California to Mount Meager in British Columbia. The Cascade Range is the product of the Juan de Fuca sea-floor spreading centre off the coast of northern California, Oregon, Washington, and British Columbia and the plate subduction that occurs offshore, as identified in the upper right of Figure 12.12a. Focus Study 12.3 details the highly publicized 1980 eruption of

Mount St. Helens that so drastically altered the landscape (Figure 12.34).

Mount Pinatubo Eruption In June 1991, after 600 years of dormancy, Mount Pinatubo in the Philippines erupted. The summit of the 1460-m volcano exploded, devastating many surrounding villages and permanently closing Clark Air Force Base, operated by the United States. Fortunately, scientists from the USGS and local scientists accurately predicted the eruption. A timely evacuation of the surrounding countryside saved thousands of lives, but nevertheless 800 people were killed.

Although volcanic eruptions are local events, the spatial implications can be regional to worldwide. The single volcanic eruption of Mount Pinatubo was significant to the global environment, as discussed in Chapters 1, 3, 4, 5, and 10 (see Figure 1.8). Here is a summary of effects:

- 4–18 million metric tons (15–20 million tons) of ash and sulphuric acid mist were blasted into the atmosphere, concentrating at 16–25 km altitude
- 12 km³ of material was ejected and extruded by the eruption (12 times the volume from Mount St. Helens)
- 60 days after the eruption, about 42% of the globe was affected (from 20° S to 30° N) by the thin, spreading aerosol cloud in the atmosphere
- Colourful twilight and dawn skies were observed worldwide
- An increase in atmospheric albedo of 1.5% (4.3 W · m⁻²) occurred

(a)

(b)

FIGURE 12.33 A composite volcano.
(a) A typical composite volcano with its cone-shaped form in an explosive eruption. (b) Mount Shishaldin, Unimak Island, in the eastern Aleutian Islands, Alaska, is a 2857-m composite volcano. Here shown during a 1995 eruption; it was active through 2001. [(b) © AeroMetric, Inc.]

FIGURE 12.34 **Mount St. Helens before and after the eruption—days and years later.**
(a) Mount St. Helens prior to the 1980 eruption. (b) The devastated and scorched land shortly after the
eruption in 1980. The scorched earth and tree blowdown area covered some 38 950 hectares. (c) A landscape
in recovery as life moves back in and takes hold to establish new ecosystems in 1999 along the Toutle River
and debris flow. [(a) Tom & Pat Lesson/Photo Researchers, Inc. (b) Images & Volcans/Photo Researchers, Inc. (c) Bobbé
Christopherson.]

- An increase in the atmospheric absorption of insolation followed (2.5 W · m^{-2})
- A decrease in net radiation at the surface and a lowering of Northern Hemisphere average temperatures of 0.5 C° were measured

Atmospheric scientists and volcanologists were able to study the eruption aftermath using satellite-borne orbiting sensors and general circulation model computer simulations.

Canadian Volcanoes

The Pacific Coast of Canada is one of the few areas in the world where divergent, convergent, and transform plate boundaries occur in proximity to one another, giving rise to various types of volcanic activity (Figure 12.35). Mount Baker, Mount Garibaldi, Mount Meager, and Mount Edziza are among the most prominent volcanic landforms in western Canada. Mount Baker is a large, active, composite volcano situated in the Cascade Mountain Range of Washington State, approximately 100 km southeast of the city of Vancouver. Mount Garibaldi and Mount Meager are large composite volcanoes situated 80 km north and 150 km north of the city of Vancouver, respectively. Mount Edziza is situated in northwestern British Columbia and consists of four large composite volcanoes built on top of plateau

basalts: It represents one of the most extensive volcanic regions in Canada, covering an area of 1300 km^2.

Ash clouds, lava flows, and pyroclastic flows have dominated the post-glacial volcanic activity of all of these volcanoes and represent a threat to large population centres

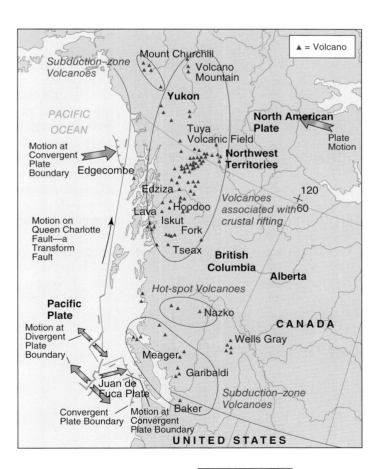

FIGURE 12.35 **Volcanoes and the tectonic environment in western Canada.**
Volcanic activity occurs in three tectonic settings: (1) along convergent plate boundaries experiencing subduction (for example, Mount Garibaldi, Mount Meager); (2) in regions of rifting on continental plates (for example, Mount Edziza, Mount Iskut); and (3) at hot spots where plumes of magma break through the crust (for example, Mount Nazko). The green lines indicate transform faults, while the circled areas indicate the boundaries of different types of volcanism. [Adapted with the permission of Natural Resources Canada, 2011. Courtesy of the Geological Survey of Canada (Bulletin 548).]

The 1980 Eruption of Mount St. Helens

Quiet since 1857, Mount St. Helens awoke in March 1980, with a sharp earthquake registering an M 4.1. The first eruptive outburst occurred one week later, beginning with an M 4.5 quake and continuing with a thick black plume of ash and the development of a small summit crater. Ten days later, after scientists hurriedly placed instruments around the volcano, the first volcanic earthquake, called a *harmonic tremor,* registered. Harmonic tremors are slow, steady vibrations, unlike the sharp releases of energy associated with tectonic earthquakes and faulting. These vibrations indicated that magma was on the move within the mountain.

Also developing was a massive bulge on Mount St. Helens' north side, indicating the direction of the magma flow within the volcano. A bulge represents the greatest risk from a composite volcano, for it could signal a potential lateral burst through the bulge and across the landscape.

Early on Sunday, May 18, the area north of the mountain was rocked by an M 5.0 quake, the strongest to date. The mountain, with its distended 245-m bulge, was shaken, but nothing happened. Then a second quake (M 5.1) hit a few minutes later, loosening the bulge and launching the eruption. David Johnston, a volcanologist with the U.S. Geological Survey, was only 8 km from the mountain, servicing instruments, when he saw the eruption begin. He radioed headquarters in Vancouver, Washington, saying, "Vancouver, Vancouver, this is it!" He perished in the eruption. For a continuously updated live picture of Mount St. Helens from Johnston's approximate observation point and other specifics, go to http://www. fs.fed.us/gpnf/mshnvm/volcanocam. The camera is mounted below the roofline

at the Johnston Ridge Observatory. The observatory is open to the public.

As the contents of the mountain exploded, a surge of hot gas (about 300°C), steam-filled ash, pyroclastics, and a *nuée ardente* (rapidly moving, very hot, explosive ash and incandescent gases) moved northward, hugging the ground and travelling at speeds up to 400 km $\cdot$ h^{-1} for a distance of 28 km.

The slumping north face of the mountain produced the greatest landslide witnessed in recorded history; about 2.75km^3 of rock, ice, and trapped air, all fluidized with steam, surged at speeds approaching 250 km $\cdot$ h^{-1}. Landslide materials travelled for 21 km into the valley, blanketing the forest, covering a lake, and filling the rivers below. A series of photographs, taken at 10-second intervals from the east looking west, records this sequence (Figure 12.3.1). The eruption continued with intensity for 9 hours, first clearing out old rock from the throat of the volcano and then blasting new material.

As destructive as such eruptions are, they also are constructive, for this is the way in which a volcano eventually builds its height. Before the eruption, Mount St. Helens was 2950 m tall; the eruption blew away 418 m. Today, Mount St. Helens is building a lava dome within its crater. The thick lava rapidly and repeatedly plugs and breaks in a series of lesser dome eruptions that may continue for several decades. The several domes are more than 300 m high, so a new mountain is being born from the eruption of the old.

The lava dome is covered with a dozen survey benchmarks and several tiltmeters to monitor the status of the volcano. Swarms of minor earthquakes along the north flank of the mountain began in November 2001, marking

this mountain as still unstable. Dome eruptions of varying intensities occurred through 2007. Intensive scientific research and monitoring has paid off, as every eruption since 1980 was successfully forecasted from days to as long as 3 weeks in advance, with the exception of one small eruption in 1984.

An ever-resilient ecosystem is recovering, as shown in the dramatic comparison photos from 1983 and 1999 in Figure 19.28. More than three decades have passed, yet strong interest in the area continues; scientists and more than one million tourists visit the Mount St. Helens Volcanic National Monument each year. For more information, see the Cascades Volcano Observatory at http:// vulcan.wr.usgs.gov/. The attention drawn to Mount St. Helens over these three decades is deserved, especially when you think of the status of volcanic science 30 years ago, before cell phones, laptops, and GPS. A recent paper summarizes this well:

> The eruption remains a seminal historical event—studying it and its aftermath revolutionized the way scientists approach the field of volcanology. Not only was the eruption spectacular, but also it occurred in daytime, at an accessible volcano, in a country with the resources to transform the disaster into scientific opportunity, amid a transformation in digital technology. Lives lost and the impact of the eruption on people and infrastructure downstream and downwind made it imperative for scientists to investigate events and work with communities to lessen losses from future eruptions.*

* J. W. Vallance et al., "Mount St. Helens: A 30-year legacy of volcanism," *EOS, Transactions* (American Geophysical Union), May 11, 2010, p. 169.

FIGURE 12.3.1 The Mount St. Helens eruption sequence and corresponding schematics. [© 1980 Keith Ronnholm.]

Debris Avalanche and eruption
of Mount St. Helens

in British Columbia and Washington. Airborne ash can result in severe damage to aircraft and represents the most important short-term hazard risk for the Canadian public. Debris flows (*lahars*) and floods (*jökulhlaups*) produced by the rapid melting of ice and snow on mountain summits can flow rapidly downslope and be extremely destructive.

Volcano Forecasting and Planning

The USGS and the Office of Foreign Disaster Assistance operate the Volcano Disaster Assistance Program (VDAP) in the United States. For a listing of more than two dozen projects, see http://vulcan.wr.usgs.gov/Vdap/framework. html. The need for such a program is evident in that over the past 30 years, volcanic activity has killed 29 000 people, forced more than 800 000 to evacuate their homes, and caused more than $3 billion in damage. The program was established after 23 000 people died in the eruption of Nevado del Ruiz, Colombia, in 1985. The U.S. VDAP is in place to help local scientists with eruption forecasts by setting up mobile volcano-monitoring systems at the most-threatened sites.

An effort such as this led to the life-saving evacuation of 60 000 people hours before Mount Pinatubo exploded. In addition, satellite remote sensing is helping VDAP to monitor eruption cloud dynamics, atmospheric emissions and climatic effects, and lava and thermal measurements; to make topographic measurements; to estimate volcanic

hazard potential; and to enhance geologic mapping—all in an effort to better understand our dynamic planet. Integrated seismographic networks and monitoring are making possible early warning systems.

In this era of the Internet you can access "volcano cams" positioned around the world to give you 24-hour surveillance of many volcanoes. For an exciting visual adventure, go to the following URL and add it to your bookmarks (and note whether it is day or night for the location you are checking): http://vulcan.wr.usgs.gov/Photo/volcano_cams.html.

GEOSYSTEMS CONNECTION

This completes the examination of crust-building processes of Earth's endogenic systems covered in Chapters 11 and 12. Earth's surface topography results from formation and deformation processes powered by radioactive-decay heat radiating from Earth's interior. Mountain building, earthquakes, and volcanism are the resulting outputs of these systems. We now move on to the exogenic system, where solar energy empowers weathering, erosion, and deposition through the agents of water, wind, waves, and ice. These processes reduce relief and the height of the landscape.

 APPLIED PHYSICAL GEOGRAPHY   *Comparing the Sizes of Earthquakes*

Two scales for measuring the size of earthquakes were described in this chapter: the *amplitude magnitude* scale (commonly known as the Richter Scale) and the *moment magnitude* scale. Although each scale measures a different phenomenon and there is not perfect agreement, the USGS explains that both magnitude scales should yield approximately the same value for an earthquake[1], although the moment magnitude scale is more accurate for measuring the size of the largest earthquakes.

Both the amplitude and moment scales are logarithmic. Each increase of one unit on a logarithmic scale represents an increase of 10 on the corresponding numerical scale, an increase of two logarithmic units represents an increase of $10 \times 10 = 10^2 = 100$ on the numerical scale,

and so on. We can compare the numerical difference between two earthquakes if we are given magnitude values.

For earthquakes with measured wave amplitudes of 7.0 and 4.0, the difference is $10^{7.0} - 10^{4.0}$. This is $10^{(7.0 - 4.0)}$ or $10^{3.0}$, and $10^{3.0}$ is $10 \times 10 \times 10 = 1000$. So the amplitude of the 7.0 earthquake was three logarithmic units larger than the 4.0 earthquake—but this means it was 1000 times larger numerically.

How much larger is magnitude 5.7 than magnitude 3.4? Calculate: $10^{(5.7 - 3.4)} = 10^{2.3} =$ about 200 times larger.

The calculations above compare the size of two earthquakes on the amplitude magnitude scale. But that scale does not directly measure the amount of energy released during an earthquake. The actual amount of energy

released is approximately $10^{1.5}$ times the amplitude, or approximately 31.6 as much. Let's now compare the released energy in the same examples as above.

We substitute $10^{1.5}$ before raising to the power of the amplitude magnitude, so the energy released by a 7.0 earthquake is $10^{(1.5) \times (7.0 - 4.0)} = 10^{(1.5 \times 3.0)} = \sim31,600$ times compared to magnitude 4.0. For the second example, $10^{(1.5) \times (5.7 - 3.4)} = 10^{(1.5 \times 2.3)} = \sim2820$ times as much energy released. With these examples, it is easy to see why the infrequent great earthquakes with magnitudes of 8 and 9 are so destructive: there are incredible amounts of energy released at one time compared to smaller earthquakes that occur with greater frequency.

[1]USGS Earthquake Hazards Program, http://earthquake.usgs.gov/learn/glossary/?termID=118.

KEY LEARNING CONCEPTS REVIEW

■ **Describe** first, second, and third orders of relief, and **relate** examples of each from Earth's major topographic regions.

Tectonic forces generated within the planet dramatically shape Earth's surface. **Relief** is the vertical elevation difference in a local landscape. The undulating physical surface of Earth, including relief, is **topography**. Convenient descriptive categories are termed *orders of relief.* The coarsest level of landforms includes the **continental landmasses** and **ocean basins**; the finest comprises local hills and valleys.

> relief (p. 347)
> topography (p. 347)
> continental landmasses (p. 347)
> ocean basins (p. 347)

1. How does the map of the ocean floor in the chapter-opening illustration exhibit the principles of plate tectonics? Briefly analyze.
2. What is meant by an "order of relief"? Give an example from each of the three orders.
3. Explain the difference between relief and topography.

■ **Describe** the different origins of continental crust, and **define** displaced terranes.

A continent has a nucleus of ancient crystalline rock called a *craton.* A region where a craton is exposed is a **continental shield**. As continental crust forms, it is enlarged through accretion of dispersed **terranes**. An example is the Insular Belt of the Western Cordillera that includes Vancouver Island and Haida Gwaii (formerly Queen Charlotte Islands).

> continental shield (p. 349)
> terranes (p. 351)

4. What is a craton? Relate this structure to continental shields and platforms, and describe these regions in North America.
5. What is a migrating terrane, and how does it add to the formation of continental masses?
6. Briefly describe the journey and destination of the Wrangellia terrane.

■ **Explain** the compressional processes of folding and faulting, and **describe** four principal types of faults and their characteristic landforms.

Folding and broad warping, and faulting deform the crust and produce characteristic landforms. Compression causes rocks to deform in a process known as **folding**, during which rock strata bend and may overturn. Along the *ridge* of a fold, layers *slope downward away from the axis*, which is an **anticline**. In the *trough* of a fold, however, layers *slope downward toward the axis*; this is a **syncline**.

When rock strata are stressed beyond their ability to remain a solid unit, they express the strain as a fracture. Rocks on either side of the fracture are displaced relative to the other side in a process known as **faulting**. Thus, *fault zones* are areas where fractures in the rock demonstrate crustal movement. At the moment of fracture, a sharp release of energy, an **earthquake** or *quake*, occurs. When forces pull rocks apart, the tension causes a **normal fault**, sometimes visible on the landscape as an escarpment, or scarp. Compressional forces associated with converging plates force rocks to move upward, producing a **reverse fault**. A low-angle fault plane is referred to as a **thrust fault**. Horizontal movement along a fault plane that produces a linear rift valley is a **strike-slip fault**. In the U.S. interior west, the Basin and Range Province is an example of aligned pairs of normal faults and a distinctive horst-and-graben landscape. The term **horst** is applied to upward-faulted blocks; **graben** refers to downward-faulted blocks.

> folding (p. 352)
> anticline (p. 352)
> syncline (p. 352)
> faulting (p. 354)
> earthquake (p. 354)
> normal fault (p. 356)
> reverse fault (p. 356)
> thrust fault (p. 356)
> strike-slip fault (p. 358)
> horst (p. 358)
> graben (p. 358)

7. Diagram a simple folded landscape in cross section, and identify the features created by the folded strata.
8. Define the four basic types of faults. How are faults related to earthquakes and seismic activity?

■ **Relate** the three types of plate collisions associated with orogenesis, and **identify** specific examples of each.

Orogenesis is the birth of mountains. An orogeny is a mountain-building episode, occurring over millions of years, that thickens continental crust. It can occur through large-scale deformation and uplift of the crust. It also may include the capture of migrating terranes and cementation of them to the continental margins, and the intrusion of granitic magmas to form plutons.

Oceanic plate–continental plate collision orogenesis is now occurring along the Pacific coast of the Americas and has formed the Andes, the Sierra of Central America, the Rockies, and other western mountains. *Oceanic plate–oceanic plate* collision orogenesis produces either simple volcanic island arcs or more complex arcs such as Japan, the Philippines, the Kuril Islands, and portions of the Aleutian Islands. The region around the Pacific contains expressions of each type of collision in the **circum-Pacific belt**, or the **Ring of Fire**.

Continental plate–continental plate collision orogenesis occurs when large masses of continental crust, such as the Himalayan Range, are subjected to intense folding, overthrusting, faulting, and uplifting.

> orogenesis (p. 358)
> circum-Pacific belt (p. 360)
> Ring of Fire (p. 360)

9. Define *orogenesis*. What is meant by the birth of mountain chains?
10. Name some significant orogenies.
11. Identify on a map Earth's two large mountain ranges. What processes contributed to the development of these ranges?
12. How are plate boundaries related to episodes of mountain building? Explain how different types of plate boundaries produce differing orogenic episodes and different landscapes.
13. Relate tectonic processes to the formation of the Western Cordillera.

■ **Explain** the nature of earthquakes, including characteristics, measurement, fault mechanics, and forecasting methods.

Earthquakes generally occur along plate boundaries; major ones can be disastrous. Earthquakes result from faults, which are under continuing study to learn the nature of faulting, stress and the buildup of strain, irregularities along fault-plane surfaces, the way faults rupture, and the relationship among active faults. Earthquake prediction and improved planning are active concerns of *seismology*, the study of earthquake waves and Earth's interior. Seismic motions are measured with a **seismograph**.

Charles Richter developed the **Richter scale**, a measure of earthquake magnitude. A more precise and quantitative scale that assesses the *seismic moment* is now used, especially for larger quakes; this is the **moment magnitude scale**. The specific mechanics of how a fault breaks are under study, but the **elastic-rebound theory** describes the basic process. In general, two sides along a fault appear to be locked by friction, resisting any movement. This stress continues to build strain along the fault surfaces, storing elastic energy like a wound-up spring. When energy is released abruptly as the rock breaks, both sides of the fault return to a condition of less strain.

seismograph (p. 365)
Richter scale (p. 365)
moment magnitude scale (p. 368)
elastic-rebound theory (p. 369)

14. What is the relationship between an epicentre and the focus of an earthquake? Give an example from the Honshu, Japan earthquake.
15. Differentiate among the Mercalli, moment magnitude, and amplitude (Richter) scales. How are these used to describe an earthquake? Why has the Richter scale been replaced?
16. How do the elastic-rebound theory and asperities help explain the nature of faulting?
17. Describe the San Andreas fault and its relationship to ancient sea-floor spreading movements along transform faults.
18. How are paleoseismology and the seismic gap concept related to expected earthquake occurrences?
19. What do you see as the biggest barrier to effective earthquake prediction?

■ **Distinguish** between effusive and explosive volcanic eruptions, and **describe** related landforms, using specific examples.

Volcanoes offer direct evidence of the makeup of the asthenosphere and uppermost mantle. A **volcano** forms at the end of a central vent or pipe that rises from the asthenosphere through the crust into a volcanic mountain. A **crater**, or circular surface depression, usually forms at the summit. Areas where magma is near the surface may heat groundwater, allowing for the extraction of *geothermal energy*.

Eruptions produce **lava** (molten rock), gases, and **pyroclastics** (pulverized rock and clastic materials ejected violently during an eruption) that pass through the vent to openings and fissures at the surface and build volcanic landforms. Basaltic lava flows occur in two principal textures: **aa**, rough and sharp-edged lava, and **pahoehoe**, smooth, ropy folds of lava. Volcanic activity produces landforms such as a **cinder cone**, a small hill, or a large basin-shaped depression sometimes caused by collapse of a volcano's summit, forming a **caldera**.

Volcanoes are of two general types, based on the chemistry and the viscosity of the magma involved. An **effusive eruption** produces a **shield volcano** (such as Kīlauea in Hawai'i) and extensive deposits of **plateau basalts**, or flood basalts. Magma of higher viscosity leads to an **explosive eruption** (such as Mount Pinatubo in the Philippines), producing a **composite volcano**. Volcanic activity has produced some destructive moments in history but constantly creates new seafloor, land, and soils.

volcano (p. 374)
crater (p. 374)
lava (p. 374)
pyroclastics (p. 374)
aa (p. 374)
pahoehoe (p. 375)
cinder cone (p. 375)
caldera (p. 375)
effusive eruption (p. 375)
shield volcano (p. 378)
plateau basalts (p. 379)
explosive eruption (p. 379)
composite volcano (p. 379)

20. What is a volcano? In general terms, describe some related features.
21. Where do you expect to find volcanic activity in the world? Why?
22. Compare effusive and explosive eruptions. Why are these different? What distinct landforms are produced by each type? Give examples of each.
23. Describe several recent volcanic eruptions, such as in Hawai'i and Iceland. What is the present status in each place?

Ageless Mount Etna on the Isle of Sicily.
Mount Etna erupts in view of the International Space Station (ISS). Visible is the ash and steam from a vigorous eruption. Gas emissions are along the north slope (lower left) through a series of vents. Smoke on the lower slope is from wildfires set by lava flows. View is to the southeast across the island of Sicily. Ashfall from this episode reached North Africa. [October 30, 2002, ISS photo courtesy of Earth Science and Image Analysis Laboratory, JSC, NASA.]

MyGeosciencePlace

Visit **www.mygeoscienceplace.ca** for several figure animations, satellite loops, self-study quizzes, flashcards, interactive glossary, career links, RSS feeds, Pearson eText of *Geosystems*, and much more.

CHAPTER 13

Weathering, Karst Landscapes, and Mass Movement

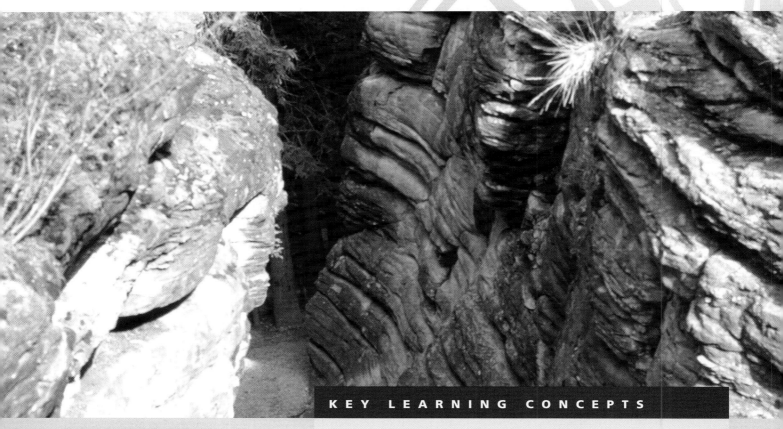

Weathering processes and stream actions formed the gaps between the layers of rock in the walls of Athabasca Canyon near Athabasca Falls in Alberta. Weakened rock then fell to the canyon floor where stream erosion and transport continued the overall process of denudation. [Mary-Louise Byrne.]

KEY LEARNING CONCEPTS

After reading the chapter, you should be able to:

- **Define** the science of geomorphology.
- **Illustrate** the forces at work on materials residing on a slope.
- **Define** weathering, and **explain** the importance of the parent rock, and of joints and fractures in rock.
- **Describe** frost action, salt-crystal growth, and pressure-release jointing as physical weathering processes.
- **Describe** the susceptibility of different minerals to the chemical weathering processes called hydration, hydrolysis, oxidation, carbonation, and solution.
- **Review** the processes and features associated with karst topography.
- **Portray** the various types of mass movements, and **identify** examples of each in relation to moisture content and speed of movement.

Human-Caused Scarification at the Athabasca Oil Sands

Natural processes powered by gravity move billions of metric tons of Earth material every year and are important agents controlling the appearance and development of landscapes. Added to natural processes of mass movement, humans move vast quantities of Earth material while undertaking activities such as mining natural resources, mountaintop removal, building houses, and constructing roads. In fact human activity is now a greater geomorphic agent than all natural processes combined.

Scarification results from such human-caused mass movements. Instead of gravity that drives natural processes, most mass movement related to human activity done by machines and the burning of fossil fuels.

A stark example of human impact on Earth's surface is in the Athabasca oil sands of northeastern Alberta (Figure GN 13.1 and 13.3). Estimates of the reserves of oil in the Athabasca oil sands are about 174 billion barrels, or 13% of global proven oil reserves. However, supporters and opponents of oil sands development debate over its benefits and its negative impacts. Scarification is just one of the environmental impacts of oil-sands extraction and should be part of this discussion.

Two principal methods of extraction are in use depending on the depth of oil-bearing deposits. The Athabasca oil

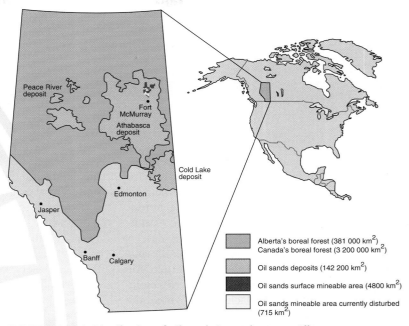

FIGURE GN 13.1 Distribution of oil sands in northeastern Alberta.
Most of the oil sands lie at depths requiring in situ mining, whereas other deposits are accessible through surface mining. Clearly, this is a major example of human-caused mass movement, or scarification. [Adapted with permission from the Government of Alberta.]

sands include about 4800 km^2 of shallow deposits, less than 75 m below the surface. Shallow deposits are exploited by *surface mining* as shown in Figure GN 13.2. To begin, overburden material is stripped from the site, exposing a sticky mixture of sand and bitumen, a form of heavy oil. Next, massive shovels and huge trucks haul loads of oil sands to plants where the sand and bitumen are separated and the production of crude oil results. As of 2009, about 600 km^2 near Fort McMurray were torn up in surface mining.

Once oil is removed, *tailings* remain. About 1.25 m^3 of tailings are created for each barrel of oil (159 litres) produced. The tailings are mixed with water, and various chemical by-products, and collected in settling ponds. Solid materials in the tailings settle as the water evaporates. Over decades, the ponds fill up and the oil producers are charged with reclaiming and re-vegetating the land. Successful reclamation projects are

experimental and only a few reclaimed hectares have received official certification from the Alberta government.

Tailing ponds are basins surrounded by dikes, covering tens of square kilometres. Also, there are former mine pits that result from oil-sand extraction.

In addition to concerns about slow seepage of liquids through dikes,

FIGURE GN 13.3 Oil sand mining along the Athabasca River.
Mining activity follows along the dark-brown waters of the Athabasca River. This true-colour satellite image shows open-pit mines, tailing ponds, and the removal of boreal forest. [*EO-1* image, NASA.]

FIGURE GN 13.2 Surface mining at the Shell Albian Sands mine near Fort McMurray, AB.
Tens of metres of overburden are removed to expose shallow oil sand deposits.
[Jay McIntosh/CP Images.]

questions have been raised about the stability of older dikes, and the possibility of a catastrophic failure and release of toxic material into the adjacent Athabasca River.

The second mining oil-sands method is *in situ* extraction, used for deeper deposits that require less human-mass

movement than surface mining. In this process steam is injected underground into the oil sands, heats the oil, and separates it from sand. The oil is then pumped to the surface. Significant quantities of water are used and polluted in this process. In northern Alberta, *in situ* methods are used for the majority of oil

sands that are distributed over more than 142 000 km².

Significant environmental impacts occur from both *surface mining* and *in situ* mining, as both are human scarification processes—a topic discussed later in this chapter.

Here we begin a five-chapter examination of exogenic processes at work on the landscape. This chapter examines weathering and mass movement of Earth's crust. The next four chapters look at the actions and effects of specific exogenic agents and their handiwork—river systems, wind-influenced landscapes, deserts in water-deficit regions, coastal processes and landforms, and regions worked by ice and glaciers. Whether you enjoy time along a river, love the desert or the waves along a coastline, or live in a place where glaciers once carved the land, you will find something of interest in these chapters.

In this chapter: We look at physical (mechanical) and chemical weathering processes that break up, dissolve, and generally reduce the landscape. Such weathering releases essential minerals from bedrock for soil formation or enrichment. In limestone regions, chemical weathering produces sinkholes, caves, and caverns. In these karst environments, water has created enormous underground worlds of mystery and darkness, yet many caves remain undiscovered.

In addition, we examine mass-movement processes that continually operate in and upon the landscape. News broadcasts may describe an avalanche in Austria; a mudflow in Mexico, China, or Pakistan; a tragic landslide in China, Turkey, or Indonesia; a massive rockfall in the Rockies; or the prediction of an imminent mudflow down the slopes in a southern California suburb. In 2008, Haiti was deluged by three hurricanes that caused massive landslides and mudflows from deforested mountain slopes. This chapter discusses the processes that caused these events.

Landmass Denudation

Geomorphology is the science of landforms—the study of origin, evolution, form, and spatial distribution of landforms. This science is an important aspect of physical geography. **Denudation** is any process that wears away landforms or rearranges landform materials. The principal denudation processes affecting surface materials include *weathering, mass movement, erosion, transportation,* and *deposition,* as produced by the agents of moving water, air, waves, and ice—all influenced by the pull of gravity.

Interactions between the structural elements of the land and denudation processes are complex. They represent a continuing struggle between Earth's internal and external processes, between the resistance of materials and weathering and erosional processes. The iconic 15-story-tall Delicate Arch in Utah is dramatic evidence of this struggle (Figure 13.1). Differing resistances of the rock layers, coupled with variations in the processes at work on the rock, are carving this delicate sculpture—an example of **differential weathering**, where a more resistant cap rock protects supporting strata below.

Ideally, endogenic processes build *initial landscapes,* whereas exogenic processes develop *sequential landscapes* of low relief, gradual change, and relative stability. These countering processes must be viewed as going on simultaneously. Several hypotheses have been proposed to model denudation processes and to account for the appearance of the landscape.

Dynamic Equilibrium Approach to Landforms

A landscape is an open system, with highly variable inputs of energy and materials: Uplift creates the *potential energy of position* above sea level and therefore disequilibrium, an imbalance, between relief and energy. The Sun provides radiant energy that converts into *heat energy.* The hydrologic cycle imparts *kinetic energy* through mechanical motion. *Chemical energy* is made available from the atmosphere and various reactions within the crust.

As physical factors fluctuate in an area, the surface constantly responds in search of equilibrium. Every change produces compensating actions and reactions. The balancing act between tectonic uplift and reduction by weathering and erosion, between the resistance of rocks and the ceaseless attack of weathering and erosion, is the **dynamic equilibrium model.** According to current thinking, landscapes in a dynamic equilibrium show ongoing adaptations to the ever-changing conditions of rock structure, climate, local relief, and elevation.

Endogenic events, such as faulting or lava flow, or exogenic events, such as heavy rainfall or forest fire, may provide new sets of relationships for the landscape. Following such destabilizing events, a landform system

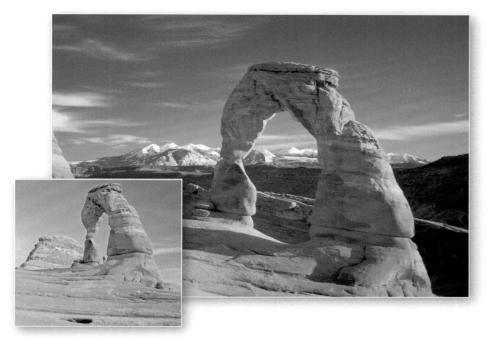

FIGURE 13.1 Delicate Arch, Arches
National Park, Utah.
Resistant rock strata at the top of the
structure helped preserve the arch
beneath as surrounding rock eroded
away. Note the person standing at the
base in the inset photo for a sense of
scale. In the distance are the snow-
covered Manti LaSal Mountains, extinct
volcanoes. [Robert Christopherson.]

arrives at a **geomorphic threshold**—the point at which
energy overcomes resistance against movement. At this
threshold, the system breaks through to a new set of equilibrium relationships as the landform and its slopes enter a period of adjustment and realignment. The pattern
over time follows a sequence: (1) equilibrium stability,
in which the system fluctuates around some average,
(2) a destabilizing event, (3) a period of adjustment, and
(4) development of a new and different condition of
equilibrium stability. Slow, continuous-change events,
such as soil development and erosion, tend to maintain
an approximate equilibrium condition. Dramatic events
such as a major landslide require longer recovery times
before equilibrium is re-established. The disturbed
hillslope in Figure 13.2 is in the midst of compensating adjustment. The failure of saturated slopes caused
a landslide into the river and created a condition of disequilibrium. As a consequence, the new dam of material
threw the stream into disequilibrium between its flow
and sediment load. Refer to Figure 1.6, which graphically
illustrates the distinction between steady-state equilibrium and dynamic equilibrium, as well as the occurrence
of a geomorphic threshold.

Slopes

Material loosened by weathering is susceptible to erosion and transportation. However, if gravity is to move
loosened material downslope, the agents of erosion must
overcome the forces of friction, inertia (the resistance to
movement), and the cohesion of particles to each other
(Figure 13.3a). If the slope angle is steep enough for
gravity to overcome frictional forces, or if the impact of
raindrops or moving animals or even wind dislodges material, then erosion of particles and transport downslope
can occur.

Slopes or *hillslopes* are inclined surfaces, often with
straight or curved segments, that connect flatter parts of a
landscape. Figure 13.3b illustrates basic slope components
that vary among slopes with conditions of rock structure
and climate. Slopes generally feature an upper *waxing slope*
near the top (*waxing* means "increasing"). This convex
surface curves downward and grades into the *free face*
below. The presence of a free face indicates an outcrop of
resistant rock that forms a steep scarp or cliff.

Downslope from the free face is a *debris slope*, which
receives rock fragments and materials from above. The
condition of a debris slope reflects the local climate. In
humid climates, continually moving water carries material away, lowering the debris slope. But in arid climates,

FIGURE 13.2 A slope in disequilibrium.
Unstable, saturated soils gave way, leaving a debris dam partially
blocking the river. The hillslope, river, and forest ecosystem is
in disequilibrium as adjustments to new conditions proceed.
[Robert Christopherson.]

debris slopes accumulate material. A debris slope grades into a *waning slope*, a concave surface along the base of the slope that forms a *pediment*, or broad, gently sloping erosional surface.

Slopes are open systems and seek an *angle of equilibrium* among the forces described here. Conflicting forces work simultaneously on slopes to establish an optimum compromise incline that balances these forces. You can identify these slope components and conditions on the actual hillslope shown in Figure 13.3c. When any condition in the balance is altered, all forces on the slope compensate by adjusting to a new dynamic equilibrium.

The relation between rates of weathering and breakup of slope materials, coupled with the rates of mass movement and material erosion, forms the shape of the slope. A slope is *stable* if its strength exceeds these denudation

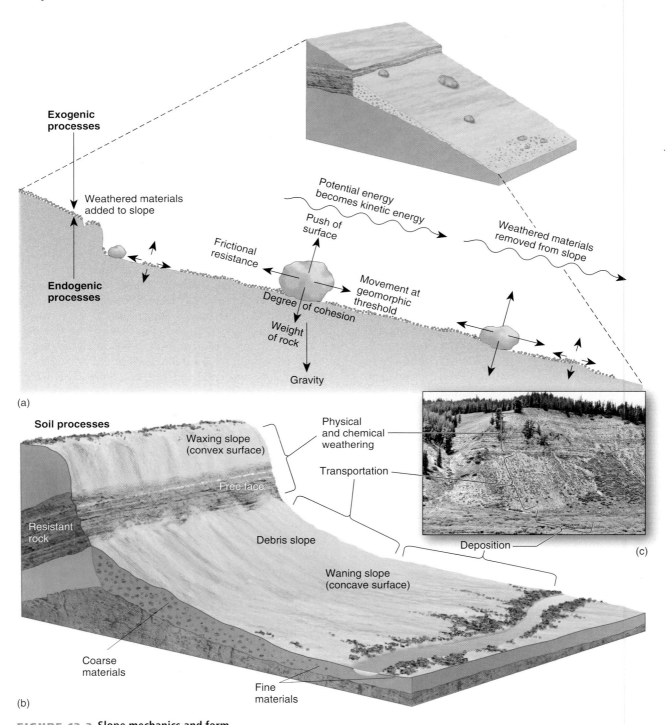

FIGURE 13.3 Slope mechanics and form.
(a) Directional forces (noted by arrows) act on materials along an inclined slope. (b) The principal elements of a slope. (c) A hillslope example; note the role of the rock outcrop as a slope interruption and the rock fragments loosened from the outcrop by frost action. [Robert Christopherson.]

processes and *unstable* if materials are weaker than these processes. Why are hillslopes shaped in certain ways? How do slope elements evolve? How do hillslopes behave during rapid, moderate, or slow uplift? These are topics of active scientific study and research. Now, let us examine specific processes that operate to wear away landforms.

■ **■ CRITICAL THINKING 13.1**

Find a Slope; Apply the Concepts

Locate a slope, possibly near campus or your home. Using Figure 13.3a, b, and c, can you identify the forces and forms of a hillslope at your site? How would you go about assessing the stability of the slope? Do you see evidence of slope instability near your campus or the region in which you are located—perhaps at a construction site or road cut?

▬ Weathering Processes

Weathering processes break down rocks at Earth's surface and to some depth below the surface, either disintegrating rock into mineral particles or dissolving it with water. Weathering processes may be physical (mechanical) or chemical. The interplay of the two is complex, often forming a synergy, a combined action, as the suite of processes work the rock.

Weathering does not transport the materials; it simply generates them for erosion and transport by the agents of water, wind, waves, and ice—all influenced by gravity. In most areas, the upper surface of bedrock undergoes continual weathering, creating broken-up rock called **regolith**. As regolith continues to weather, or is transported and deposited, loose surface material is formed (Figure 13.4a). In

(a)

(b)

(c)

(d)

FIGURE 13.4 Regolith, soil, and parent materials.
(a) A cross section of a typical hillside. (b) A cliff exposes hillside components. (c) The red sand beaches of Prince Edward Island derive colour from the red sandstone parent material of the cliff. (d) This image, from a larger panoramic scene, was made by the Mars Exploration Rover *Spirit* on March 12, 2004. Looking toward the Columbia Hills, you can see weathered rocks and windblown sand in approximate true colours. [(b) Robert Christopherson; (c) Mary-Louise Byrne; (d) Mars image courtesy of NASA/JPL and Cornell University.]

some areas, regolith may be missing or undeveloped, thus exposing an outcrop of unweathered bedrock.

Bedrock is the *parent rock* from which weathered regolith and soils develop. Wherever a soil is relatively youthful, its parent rock is traceable through similarities in composition. For example, the sand in Figure 13.4c derives its colour and character from the parent rock in the cliff, just as the sediment on Mars derives its characteristics from the weathered parent material present (Figure 13.5d). Such small, unconsolidated fragmental material, known as **sediment**, combines with weathered rock to form the **parent material** from which soil evolves.

Factors Influencing Weathering Processes

A number of factors influence weathering processes. Important controls on weathering rates include

- *Rock composition and structure (jointing)*—Weathering is greatly influenced by the character of the bedrock: hard or soft, soluble or insoluble, broken or unbroken. *Jointing* in rock is important for weathering processes. **Joints** are fractures or separations in rock that occur without displacement of the sides (as would be the case in faulting). The presence of these usually flat spaces increases the surface area of rock exposed to both physical and chemical weathering.
- *Climate*—Precipitation, temperature, and freeze-thaw cycles are the most important factors affecting weathering.
- *Subsurface water*—Influences in weathering processes include both the position of the water table and water movement within soil and rock structures.
- *Slope orientation*—The *geographic orientation* of a slope—whether it faces north, south, east, or west—controls the slope's exposure to sunlight, wind, and precipitation. Slopes facing away from the Sun's rays tend to be cooler, moister, and more vegetated than are slopes in

direct sunlight. This effect of orientation is especially noticeable in the middle and higher latitudes.

- *Vegetation*—Although vegetative cover can protect rock by shielding it from raindrop impact and providing roots to stabilize soil, it also produces organic acids from the partial decay of organic matter; these acids contribute to chemical weathering. Plant roots can enter crevices and break up a rock, exerting enough pressure to force rock segments apart, thereby exposing greater surface area to other weathering processes (Figure 13.5a). You may have observed how tree roots can heave the sections of a sidewalk or driveway sufficiently to raise and crack concrete.

The scale at which we analyze weathering processes is important. Research at *microscale* levels reveals a more complex relationship between climate and weathering than previously thought. At the small scale of actual reaction sites on the rock surface, both physical and chemical weathering processes can occur across varied climate types. Soil moisture (hygroscopic water and capillary water) activates chemical weathering processes, even in the driest landscape. (Review sections in Chapter 9, Figure 9.8, for types of soil moisture.)

Imagine all the factors that influence weathering rates as operating in concert, although we separate these processes here for convenience of study. In the complexity of nature, physical and chemical weathering processes usually operate together. Of course, in all of this, *time* is the crucial factor, for these processes require long periods of time to operate.

Physical Weathering Processes

When rock is broken and disintegrated without any chemical alteration, the process is **physical weathering** or *mechanical weathering*. By breaking up rock, physical weathering produces more surface area on which chemical

(a)

(b)

Physical Weathering

FIGURE 13.5 Physical weathering examples.
(a) Tree roots exert a force on the sides of joints in rock. (b) Frost action shattered this marble, a metamorphic rock; ice expansion forced the rock segments apart. [Bobbé Christopherson.]

weathering may operate. A single rock that becomes broken into eight pieces has doubled its surface area susceptible to weathering processes. We look briefly at three physical weathering processes: frost action, crystallization, and pressure-release jointing.

Frost Action When water freezes, its volume expands by as much as 9% (see Chapter 7). Such expansion creates a powerful mechanical force, **frost action**, or *freeze–thaw action*, which can exceed the tensional strength of rock (Figure 13.5b). Repeated freezing (expanding) and thawing (contracting) of water breaks rocks apart. Freezing actions are important in the humid microthermal climates (*humid continental* and *subarctic*) and polar climates, and occur at higher elevations in mountains worldwide in the highland climates. In arctic and subarctic climates, frost action dominates soil conditions (discussed in further detail in Chapter 17).

The work of ice begins in small openings, gradually expanding until rocks are cleaved, or split. Figure 13.6a shows a block field in northwestern Manitoba. This rock surface was shattered and heaved by frost action. *Felsenmeer*, a result of a cold-climate process, usually forms in coarser grained rocks that contain few fine particles and results in a surface composed of coarse, angular blocks with soil absent from the upper layers. Frost action also causes *joint block separation* along existing joints and fractures (Figure 13.6b and c). This weathering action, called *frost-wedging*, creates varied shapes in the rocks depending on the rock structure. In Figure 13.6b, the softer supporting rock underneath the slabs is weathering at a faster pace in *differential weathering*.

Frost action can have a dramatic effect on rock in areas of permafrost. In these areas where the ground temperature has remained below freezing for many years, exposed bedrock surfaces can be covered with mounds of heaved rock called *rock blisters* that are 1–3 m high and 3–5 m in diameter. In the centre of Figure 13.7 is a rock blister in granite. The rock is broken along joint planes into equally sized blocks. In the background, the undisturbed bedrock is covered with glacially transported boulders. Rock blisters can occur on any type of rock. *Frost-heaving* in jointed, horizontally bedded, competent bedrock—such as dolomite in western Nunavut—produces significant rock domes that date from early postglacial times when permafrost was establishing in the region.

(a)

(b)

(c)

FIGURE 13.6 Physical weathering examples—joint block separation.
(a) Close-up view of felsenmeer (block fields) in the boreal forest, Kasmere Lake, northwestern Manitoba. This rock was shattered by frost action. (b) Joint-block separation in slate at Alkehornet, Isfjord, on Spitsbergen Island in the Arctic Ocean where freezing is intense. (c) Physical weathering along joints in rock produces discrete blocks in the backcountry of Canyonlands National Park, Utah. [Photos by (a) Courtesy of the Geological Survey of Canada. Photo 2001-131 by Lynda Dredge. Reproduced with the permission of Natural Resources Canada. © 2012; (b) Bobbé Christopherson; (c) Robert Christopherson.]

Frost action was important to various cultures as a force to quarry rock. Pioneers in the early American West drilled holes in rock, poured water in the holes, and then plugged the holes. During the cold winter months, expanding ice broke off large blocks along lines determined by the drill-hole patterns. In spring, they hauled the blocks to town for construction material. Frost action also produces unwanted fractures that damage road pavement and cause water pipes to burst. Perhaps you have noticed rough and broken highways in areas that experience freezing temperatures. The pavement breaks into chunks each winter and develops potholes.

Spring can be a risky time to venture into mountainous terrain. As rising temperatures melt the winter's ice, newly fractured rock pieces fall without warning and may even initiate rock slides. The falling rock pieces may physically shatter on impact—another form of physical weathering (Figure 13.8).

Salt-Crystal Growth (Salt Weathering) Especially in arid climates, dry weather draws moisture to the surface of rocks. As the water evaporates, dissolved minerals in the water grow crystals—crystallization. Over time, the crystals grow and exert a force great enough to spread apart individual mineral grains, and begin breaking up the rock. Such *salt-crystal growth*, or *crystallization*, is a form of physical weathering.

In the Colorado Plateau region of the American Southwest, salty water slowly flows from rock strata. As this salty water evaporates, crystallization loosens the sand grains. Subsequent erosion and transportation by water and wind complete the sculpturing process. Deep indentations develop in sandstone cliffs, especially where the sandstone lies above an impervious layer such as shale. More than 1000 years ago, Native Americans built entire villages in these weathered niches at several locations, including Mesa Verde in Colorado and Arizona's Canyon de Chelly (pronounced "canyon duh shay"; Figure 13.9).

Pressure-Release Jointing Recall from Chapter 11 how rising magma that is deeply buried and subjected to high pressure forms intrusive igneous rocks called plutons. These plutons cool slowly and produce coarse-grained, crystalline, granitic rocks. As the landscape is subjected to uplift, the regolith overburden is weathered, eroded, and transported away, eventually exposing the pluton as a mountainous batholith (a plutonic batholiths is illustrated in Figure 11.8).

As the tremendous weight of overburden is removed from the granite, the pressure of deep burial is relieved. Over millions of years, the granite slowly responds with an enormous physical heave. In a process known as *pressure-release jointing*, layer after layer of rock peels off in curved slabs or plates, thinner at the top of the rock structure

FIGURE 13.7 Rock blisters.
Rock blister on granite, Eokuk Lake, Nunavut. [Courtesy of the Geological Survey of Canada. Photo 2001-237 by Lynda Dredge. Reproduced with the permission of Natural Resources Canada. © 2012.]

(a)

(b)

FIGURE 13.8 Rockfall.
(a) Shattered rock debris from a large rockfall in Yosemite National Park. Freshly exposed, light-coloured rock shows where the rockfall originated. (b) A large slab failure produces a rockfall in Zion National Park. The small opening in the cliff base is a window blasted through to the highway tunnel that was excavated inside the cliff (see red arrow). [Robert Christopherson.]

(a)

(b)

FIGURE 13.9 Physical weathering in sandstone.
(a) Cliff dwelling site in Canyon de Chelly, Arizona, occupied by the ancient Pueblo people until about 900 years ago. The niche in the rock formed partially by crystallization, which forced apart mineral grains and broke up the rock. The dark streaks on the rock are thin coatings of desert varnish, composed of iron and manganese and wind-blown clay. (b) Water and an impervious rock layer helped concentrate weathering processes in a niche in the overlying sandstone. [Robert Christopherson.]

and thicker at the sides. These slabs subsequently slip off in the process of **sheeting**. This *exfoliation process* creates arch-shaped and dome-shaped features on the exposed landscape, sometimes forming an **exfoliation dome** (Figure 13.10). Such domes are probably the largest weathering features on Earth (in areal extent). Smaller exfoliation features also develop.

Chemical Weathering Processes

Chemical weathering refers to the chemical breakdown of the constituent minerals in rock, always in the presence of water. The rate of chemical decomposition and decay increases as both temperature and precipitation increase. Although individual minerals vary in susceptibility, all rock-forming minerals are responsive to some degree of chemical weathering.

A familiar example of chemical weathering is the eating away of cathedral façades and the etching of tombstones by acid precipitation. In Europe, where increasingly acidic rains resulted from the burning of coal, chemical weathering processes are visible on many buildings. As an example, Saint Magnus Cathedral, in Kirkwell, Orkney Islands, north of Scotland, was built of red and yellow sandstone. Almost nine centuries of chemical weathering dissolved cementing materials in the sandstone, breaking down the rock and making many of the sculptured design elements unrecognizable, as if they "melted" or became "out-of-focus" (Figure 13.11).

 GEO REPORT 13.1 *Weathering on Bridges in Central Park, NYC*

In New York City's Central Park, 36 bridges are built out of a variety of rock from sources across the U.S. Northeast and Canada. For more than 135 years, physical and chemical processes have weathered these bridges. As air pollution from the burning of fossil fuels has increased, acidity in rain and snow has hastened weathering rates, a problem that has been compounded by the use of salt on the roads in winter. Design elements on the bridges are now disappearing as weathering wears at the surface rock. Some heavily weathered sandstone blocks have had to be replaced by cast concrete.

(a)

(b)

(c)

(d)

FIGURE 13.10 Exfoliation in granite.
Exfoliation processes loosen slabs of granite, freeing pieces for further weathering and downslope movement. (a) Great arches form in the White Mountains of New Hampshire. (b) Exfoliated layers of rock are visible in characteristic dome formations in granites. The loosened slabs of rock are susceptible to further weathering and downslope movement. This view is from the east side of Half Dome in Yosemite National Park, California. (c) Half Dome perspective from the west; relief is approximately 1500 m from the top of the dome to the bottom of the glaciated valley below. (d) Rock sheeting exposed along Beverly Sund, Nordaust-landet Island, in the Arctic Ocean. [Photos by (a) and (d) Bobbé Christopherson; (b) and (c) Robert Christopherson.]

FIGURE 13.11 Chemical weathering attacks sandstone cathedral.
The west-front entrance of Saint Magnus Cathedral, in Kirkwell, Orkney Islands, Scotland, shows the signs of chemical weathering as processes attack the cementing materials in the rock. Construction of this edifice began in A.D. 1137. [Bobbé Christopherson.]

As an example of the way chemical weathering attacks rock, consider **spheroidal weathering**. The sharp edges and corners of rocks are rounded as the alteration of minerals progresses through the rock. Joints in the rock offer more surfaces available for weathering. Water penetrates joints and fractures and dissolves the rock's weaker minerals or cementing materials. A boulder can be attacked from all sides, shedding spherical shells of decayed rock, like the layers of an onion. The resulting rounded edges are the basis for the name *spheroidal*. Spheroidal weathering of rock resembles exfoliation, but it does not result from pressure-release jointing. This type of weathering is visible in Figure 13.12; note the spheroidal rock form.

Hydration and Hydrolysis Although these two processes are different, we group them together because both decompose rock using water—one by a simple combination of water with a mineral and the other by a chemical reaction of water with a mineral.

Hydration, meaning "combination with water," involves little chemical change. Water becomes part of the chemical composition of the mineral (such a hydrate is gypsum, which is hydrous calcium sulphate: $CaSO_4 \cdot 2H_2O$). The expansion caused by hydration creates a strong mechanical effect or wedging pressure that stresses the rock, forcing grains apart as in physical weathering.

A cycle of hydration and dehydration can lead to granular disintegration and further susceptibility of the rock to chemical weathering. Hydration works together with carbonation and oxidation to convert feldspar, a common mineral in many rocks, to clay minerals and silica. The hydration process is also at work on the sandstone niches shown in the cliff-dwelling photo (Figure 13.9); the water and minerals are consumed in the process, becoming a new compound.

When minerals chemically react with water, the process is **hydrolysis**. Hydrolysis is a decomposition process that breaks down silicate minerals in rocks. Compared with hydration, in which water simply combines with minerals in the rock, the hydrolysis process involves water and elements in chemical reactions to produce different compounds.

For example, the weathering of feldspar minerals in granite can be caused by a reaction to the normal mild acids dissolved in precipitation:

feldspar (K, Al, Si,O) + carbonic acid and water →
residual clays + dissolved minerals + silica

The by-products of chemical weathering of feldspar in granite include clay (such as kaolinite) and silica. As clay forms from some minerals in the granite, quartz (SiO_2) particles are left behind. The resistant quartz may wash downstream, eventually becoming sand on some distant beach. Clay minerals become a major component in soil and in shale, a common sedimentary rock.

When weaker minerals in rock are changed by hydrolysis, the interlocking crystal network breaks down, so the rock fails and *granular disintegration* takes place. Such disintegration in granite may make the rock appear etched, corroded, and softened, or even crumbly (Figure 13.12b).

In Table 11.2, the second line shows resistance to chemical weathering in igneous rocks. On the ultramafic side of the table (right side), the low-silica minerals olivine and peridotite are most susceptible to chemical weathering. Stability gradually increases toward the high-silica minerals such as feldspar. On the far left side of the table, quartz is resistant to chemical weathering.

Oxidation Another example of chemical weathering occurs when certain metallic elements combine with oxygen to form oxides. This is a chemical weathering process known as **oxidation**. Perhaps the most familiar oxidation

(a)

(b)

FIGURE 13.12 Chemical weathering and spheroidal weathering.
(a) Chemical weathering processes act on the joints in granite to dissolve weaker minerals, leading to a rounding of the edges of the cracks in the Alabama Hills. Mount Whitney is visible on the crest of the Sierra Nevada in the background. (b) Rounded granite outcrop demonstrates spheroidal weathering and the subsequent disintegration of rock. The surface is actually crumbly. [Bobbé Christopherson.]

(a)

(b)

FIGURE 13.13 Oxidation processes in rock and soil.
(a) Oxidation of iron minerals produces these brilliant red colours in the sandstone formations of the cliffs on the north shore of Prince Edward Island. (b) Soil is coloured by the red humo-ferric Podzolic soil is coloured by the red sandstone parent material common to most of the province. [Mary-Louise Byrne.]

form is the "rusting" of iron in rocks or soil that produces a reddish-brown stain of iron oxide (Fe_2O_3). Tools or nails left outside may be found weeks later, coated with iron oxide. The rusty colour is visible on the surfaces of rock and in heavily oxidized soils such as those in Prince Edward Island, New Brunswick, the southeastern United States, southwestern deserts, or the tropics (Figure 13.13). Here is a simple oxidation reaction in iron:

iron (Fe) + oxygen (O_2) → iron oxide (hematite; Fe_2O_3)

As iron is removed from the minerals in a rock, the disruption of the crystal structures in the rock's minerals makes the rock more susceptible to further chemical weathering and disintegration.

Dissolution of Carbonates Chemical weathering also occurs when a mineral dissolves into *solution*—for example, when sodium chloride (common table salt) dissolves in water. Water is the "universal solvent" because it is capable of dissolving at least 57 of the natural elements and many of their compounds.

Water vapour readily dissolves carbon dioxide, thereby yielding precipitation containing carbonic acid (H_2CO_3). This acid is strong enough to dissolve many minerals, especially limestone. This process is **carbonation**, a reaction whereby carbon combines with and dissolves minerals.

Such chemical weathering transforms minerals that contain calcium, magnesium, potassium, and sodium. When rainwater attacks formations of limestone (which is calcium carbonate, $CaCO_3$), the constituent minerals dissolve and wash away with the mildly acidic rainwater:

calcium carbonate + carbonic acid and water → calcium bicarbonate ($Ca_2^{2+} \cdot CO_2 \cdot H_2O$)

Walk through an old cemetery and you can observe the dissolution of marble, a metamorphic form of limestone (Figure 13.14). Weathered limestone and marble, in tombstones or in rock formations, appear pitted and worn wherever adequate water is available for dissolution. In this

FIGURE 13.14 Dissolution of limestone.
A marble tombstone is chemically weathered beyond recognition in a Scottish churchyard. Marble is a metamorphic form of limestone. Based upon readable dates on surrounding tombstones, this one is about 230 years old. [Bobbé Christopherson.]

era of human-induced increases of acid precipitation, carbonation processes are greatly enhanced (see Focus Study 3.2, "Acid Deposition: Damaging to Ecosystems").

Chemical weathering involving dissolution of carbonates dominates entire landscapes composed of limestone. These are the regions of karst topography, which we examine next.

Karst Topography and Landscapes

Soluble carbonate rocks like limestone are abundant on Earth and composes many landscapes (Figure 13.15). These areas are quite susceptible to chemical weathering, which creates a specific landscape of pitted, bumpy surface topography, poor surface drainage, and well-developed solution channels (dissolved openings and conduits) underground. Weathering and erosion caused by groundwater may also result in remarkable mazes of underworld caverns.

These are the hallmarks of **karst topography**, named for the Krš Plateau in Slovenia (formerly Yugoslavia), where karst processes were first studied. Approximately 15% of Earth's land area has some karst features, with outstanding examples found in southern China, Japan, Puerto Rico, Cuba, the Yucatán of Mexico, the United States and Canada. As an example, approximately 38% of the state of Kentucky has sinkholes and related karst features noted on topographic maps.

Formation of Karst

For a limestone landscape to develop into karst topography, several conditions are necessary:

- The limestone formation must contain 80% or more calcium carbonate for dissolution processes to proceed effectively.
- Complex patterns of joints in the otherwise impermeable limestone are needed for water to form routes to subsurface drainage channels.
- An aerated (containing air) zone must exist between the ground surface and the water table.
- For more rapid dissolution, vegetation cover is required to supply varying amounts of organic acids that enhance the solution process.

The role climate plays in providing optimum conditions for karst processes remains under debate, although the amount and distribution of rainfall appear important. Karst occurs in arid regions, but it is primarily due to former climatic conditions of greater humidity. Karst is rare in the Arctic and Antarctic regions because the water, although present, is generally frozen.

As with all weathering processes, time is a factor. Early in the twentieth century, karst landscapes were thought to progress through evolutionary stages of development, as if aging. Evidence has not supported this theory, and today these landscapes are thought to be locally unique,

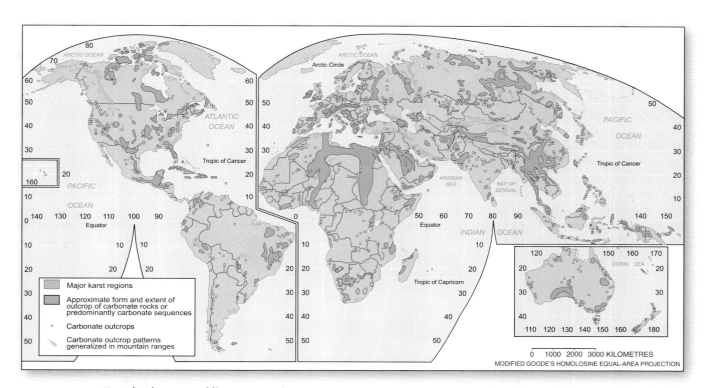

FIGURE 13.15 Karst landscapes and limestone regions.
Major karst regions exist on every continent. The outcrops of carbonate rocks or predominantly carbonate sequences are limestone and dolomite (calcium magnesium carbonate), but may contain other carbonate rocks. [Map adapted by Pam Schaus, after USGS sources; and D. C. Ford and P. Williams, *Karst Geomorphology and Hydrology*, p. 601. © 1989 by Kluwer Academic Publishers. Adapted by permission.]

FIGURE 13.16 Sinkhole in Guatemala City.
This huge sinkhole collapsed in northern Guatemala City in June 2010. Rains from Tropical Storm Agatha are thought to be what triggered the collapse of the sinkhole, which was probably forming for decades. A similar sinkhole collapsed nearby in 2007. [Moises Castillo/AP Photo/CP Images.]

a result of specific conditions. Nonetheless, mature karst landscapes do display certain characteristic forms.

Sinkhole Landscapes

The weathering of limestone landscapes creates many solution **sinkholes**, which form in circular depressions. (Traditional studies may call a sinkhole a *doline*.) A *collapse sinkhole* forms if a solution sinkhole collapses through the roof of an underground cavern, sometimes dramatically, such as in Guatemala City in June 2010 (Figure 13.16). A 91-m deep, 18-m wide sinkhole suddenly collapsed, taking a three-story

building and parts of two streets with it. Probably years in the making, the collapse was likely caused by heavy rains from a tropical storm, which finally brought the system to a geomorphic threshold. Investigators are trying to determine the cause of this sinkhole and whether limestone or subsurface drainage issues were involved.

A gently rolling limestone plain might be pockmarked by slow subsidence of surface materials in *solution sinkholes* with depths of 2–100 m and diameters of 10–1000 m, as shown in Figure 13.17a. Through continuing solution and collapse, sinkholes may coalesce to form a *karst valley*—an elongated depression up to several kilometres long.

The area southwest of Orleans, Indiana, has an average of 1022 sinkholes per 2.6 km². In this area, the Lost River, a "disappearing stream," flows more than 13 km through underground solution channels before it resurfaces at the Lost River rise near the Orangeville rise shown in Figure 13.17e. The Lost River flow diverts from the surface through sinkholes and solution channels. Its dry bed can be seen on the lower left of the topographic map in Figure 13.17b.

In Florida, several sinkholes have made news because water tables lowered by pumping from municipal wells caused collapses into underground solution caves, taking with them homes, businesses, and even new cars from an auto dealership. One such sinkhole collapsed in a suburban area in 1981, and others in 1993 and 1998 (Figure 13.18). These examples remind us of the effects of disruptions to groundwater, especially in complex karst landscapes.

In the wet tropics, karst topography forms in deeply jointed, thick limestone beds. Weathering leaves isolated resistant limestone blocks standing, such as these limestone knobs in Puerto Rico (Figure 13.19, page 404). These resistant cones and knobs are most remarkable in several areas of China, where *tower karst* up to 200 m high interrupts an otherwise level plain.

A complex landscape in which sinkholes intersect is a *cockpit karst*. The sinkholes can be symmetrically shaped in certain circumstances; one at Arecibo, Puerto Rico, is shaped perfectly for a radio telescope installation (Figure 13.20).

Also, gypsum is affected by solutional processes. Parts of the island of Newfoundland and Cape Breton Island are affected by the solution of gypsum layers. The

---

GEO REPORT 13.2 *Human-caused Sinkholes*

Along Bushkill Creek, downstream from the Hercules mining quarry enterprise, several dozen sinkholes have collapsed since 2000, taking down one of the bridges from State Route 33 and threatening neighborhoods in Stockertown, Northampton County, Pennsylvania. Sinkhole development correlated with groundwater pumping at the nearby quarry, which lowered water tables. A new bridge was completed in 2006 for the main highway. A group of citizens pressed the case for mitigating action, blaming quarry operators; the outcome is pending.

(c) Rolling karst landscape

(d) Pond in sinkhole depression

(a)

Sinkholes   Karst valley   Disappearing streams

Deeply entrenched permanent stream   Karst valley   Limestone   Shale

(b)

(e) Orangeville rise

FIGURE 13.17 Features of karst topography in Indiana.
(a) Idealized features of karst topography in southern Indiana. (b) Karst topography southwest of the town of Orleans, Indiana, on a topographic map; note the contour lines and the depressions, which are indicated with small hachures (tick marks) on the downslope side of the contour lines. (c) Gently rolling karst landscape and cornfields near Orleans, Indiana. (d) This pond is in a sinkhole depression near Palmyra, Indiana. (e) The Orangeville rise, near Orangeville, Indiana, is just north of the Lost River rise. During periods of high rainfall, this rise is almost filled with water. [(b) Mitchell, Indiana quadrangle, USGS. (c), (d), and (e) Bobbé Christopherson.]

(a)

(b)

FIGURE 13.18 **The Winter Park sinkholes.**
(a) Florida sinkhole in Winter Park, a suburb of Orlando. (b) Karst area 25 km north of Winter Park depicted on a topographic map.
Note that the depressions are marked by small hachures (tick marks). [(a) AP Photo/CP Images; (b) Orange City quadrangle, USGS.]

topography of the surface reflects a hummocky terrain with depressions and disorganized valleys that are typical of this type of gypsum karst landscapes (Figure 13.21).

Caves and Caverns

Caves form in limestone because it is so easily dissolved by carbonation. The largest limestone caverns in the United States are Mammoth Cave in Kentucky (also the longest surveyed cave in the world at 560 km), Carlsbad Caverns in New Mexico, and Lehman Cave in Nevada.

FIGURE 13.19 **Karst landscape near Manati, Puerto Rico.**
Note the numerous limestone hills and knobs. [iStockphoto/Thinkstock.]

Carlsbad Caverns are in 200-million-year-old limestone formations deposited when shallow seas covered the region. Regional uplifts associated with the building of the Rockies (the Laramide orogeny, 40–80 million years ago) elevated the region above sea level, subsequently leading to active cave formation.

Caves generally form just beneath the water table, where later lowering of the water level exposes them to further development. *Dripstones* form as water containing dissolved minerals slowly drips from the cave ceiling. Calcium carbonate precipitates out of the evaporating solution, literally one molecular layer at a time, and accumulates at a point below on the cave floor. Forming depositional features, *stalactites* grow from the ceiling and *stalagmites* build from the floor; sometimes the two grow until they connect and form a continuous *column* (Figure 13.22b). A dramatic subterranean world is thus created.

Cave science is an aspect of geomorphology where amateur cavers make important discoveries about these unique habitats and new life forms—*biospeleology*. More than 90% of known caves have not been biologically surveyed, and it is estimated that some 90% of possible caves worldwide still lie undiscovered, making this a major research frontier. For more on caves and related formations, see the Canadian Cave and Karst Information Server http://www.cancaver .ca/ or http://www.goodearthgraphics.com/ virtcave/virtcave.html.

Cave habitats are unique, nearly closed, self-contained ecosystems with simple food chains

FIGURE 13.20 Deep-space research facility constructed in cockpit karst topography.
Cockpit karst topography near Arecibo, Puerto Rico, is the setting for Earth's largest radio telescope. The discolouration of the dish does not affect telescope reception. The suspended movable receivers, where the signals focus, are 168 m above the dish. [Bobbé Christopherson; inset Cornell University Photography.]

and great stability. In total darkness, bacteria synthesize inorganic elements and produce organic compounds that sustain many types of cave life, including algae, small invertebrates, amphibians, and fish—a chemosynthesis-based food web.

In a cave discovered in 1986, near Movile in southeastern Romania, cave-adapted invertebrates were discovered after millions of years of sunless isolation. Thirty-one of these organisms were previously unknown. Without sunlight, the ecosystem in Movile is sustained on sulfur-metabolizing bacteria that synthesize organic matter using energy from oxidation processes. These chemosynthetic bacteria feed other bacteria and fungi that, in turn, support cave animals. The sulfur bacteria produce sulfuric acid compounds that may prove to be important in the chemical weathering of some caves.

FIGURE 13.21 Cape Breton gypsum karst.
The lowland areas contain gypsum beds that were dissolved, producing an irregular hummocky terrain. Isolated flats are the remnants of the original, bevelled slope on the intervening sandstone and shale. Underlying the steeper, interior hills beyond is resistant volcanic rock. [Raymond Gehman/Documentary Value/Corbis.]

Mass-Movement Processes

Nevado del Ruiz, northernmost of two dozen dormant (not extinct, sometimes active) volcanic peaks in the Cordilleran Central of Colombia, had erupted six times during the past 3000 years, killing 1000 people during its last eruption in 1845. On November 13, 1985, at 11 P.M., after a year of earthquakes and harmonic tremors, a growing bulge on its northeast flank, and months of small summit eruptions, Nevado del Ruiz violently erupted in a lateral explosion. The mountain was back in action.

On this night, the familiar pyroclastics, lava, and blast were not the worst problem. The hot eruption quickly melted ice on the mountain's snowy peak, liquefying mud and volcanic ash, sending a hot mudflow downslope. Such a flow is a *lahar*, an Indonesian word referring to mudflows of volcanic origin. This lahar moved rapidly down the Lagunilla River toward the villages below. The wall of mud was at least 40 m high as it approached Armero, a regional centre with a population of 25 000. The city slept as the

 GEO REPORT 13.3 *Amateurs Make Cave Discoveries*

In the early 1940s, George Colglazier, a farmer southwest of Bedford, Indiana, awoke to find his farm pond at the bottom of a deep, collapsed sinkhole. This sinkhole is now the entrance to an extensive cave system that includes a subterranean navigable stream. The exploration and scientific study of caves is *speleology*. Although professional physical and biological scientists carry on investigations, amateur cavers, or "spelunkers," have made many important discoveries.

The mystery, intrigue, and excitement of cave exploration lie in the variety of dark passageways, enormous chambers that narrow to tiny crawl spaces, strange formations, and underwater worlds that can be accessed only by cave diving. Private-property owners and amateur adventurers discovered many of the major caves, a fact that keeps this popular science/sport very much alive. For nearly a thousand worldwide links and more information, see the http://www.cbel.com/speleology web site.

(b) Near column

(c) Sinkhole

Near column
Surface stream
Sinkhole
Collapsed sinkhole
Lost River
Soluble rock (limestone)
Waterfall
Stalactite
Drip curtain
Collapse blocks
Column
Drip stones
Chamber
Collapse blocks
Stalagmite
(a)
Cave pool
Underground stream

(d) Dripstone drapery

(e) Flowstone and pool

(f) Soda straws

FIGURE 13.22 Cavern features.
(a) An underground cavern and related forms in limestone. (b) A column forms where stalactites from the ceiling and stalagmites from the floor connect; here nearly attached. (c) A sinkhole in a Florida pasture dropping through to a void in limestone. (d), (e), and (f) Cave depositional features forming one molecular layer at a time. All cave photos from Marengo Caves, Marengo, Indiana.
[(c) Thomas M. Scott, Florida Geological Survey. (b), (d), (e), and (f) Bobbé Christopherson.]

lahar buried its homes: 23 000 people were killed; thousands were injured; 60 000 were left homeless across the region. The volcanic debris flow is now a permanent grave for its victims. Not all mass movements are this destructive, but such processes play an important role in the denudation of the landscape.

For more on mass-movement hazards, including landslides, see the web site of the Natural Hazards Center at the University of Colorado, Boulder, at http://www. Colorado.edu/hazards/ or the USGS Geologic Hazards page at http://landslides.usgs.gov/.

Mass-Movement Mechanics

Physical and chemical weathering processes create an overall weakening of surface rock, which makes it more susceptible to the pull of gravity. The term **mass movement** applies to any unit movement of a body of material, propelled and controlled by gravity, such as the lahar just described. Mass movements can be surface processes or they can be submarine landslides beneath the ocean. Mass-movement content can range from dry to wet, slow to fast, or small to large, and from free-falling to gradual or intermittent (see Figure 13.24).

The term *mass movement* is sometimes used interchangeably with **mass wasting**, which is the general process involved in mass movements and erosion of the landscape. To combine the concepts, we can say that the mass movement of material works to waste slopes and provide raw material for erosion, transportation, and deposition.

The Role of Slopes All mass movements occur on slopes under the influence of gravitational stress. If we pile dry sand on a beach, the grains will flow downslope until equilibrium is achieved. The steepness of the resulting slope depends on the size and texture of the grains; this steepness is the **angle of repose**. This angle represents a balance of the driving force (gravity) and resisting force (shearing strength). The angle of repose for various materials commonly ranges between 33° and 37°(from horizontal (and between 30° and 50° for snow avalanche slopes).

The *driving force* in mass movement is gravity. It works in conjunction with the weight, size, and shape of the surface material; the degree to which the slope is over-steepened (how far it exceeds the angle of repose); and the amount and form of moisture available (frozen or fluid). The greater the slope angle, the more susceptible the surface material is to mass wasting processes.

The *resisting force* is the shearing strength of slope material—that is, the combination of cohesiveness and internal friction, which work against gravity and mass wasting. To reduce shearing strength is to increase shearing stress, which eventually reaches the point when gravity overcomes friction and shearing strength, initiating slope failure.

Clays, shales, and mudstones are highly susceptible to hydration (physical swelling in response to the presence of water). If such materials underlie rock strata in a slope, the strata will require less driving-force energy to move. Wet clay surfaces deform slowly in the direction of movement, and when saturated a viscous fluid forms with little shearing strength (resistance to movement) to hold back the slope. However, if the rock strata are such that material is held back from slipping, then more driving-force energy may be required, such as that generated by an earthquake.

Madison River Canyon Landslide In the Madison River Canyon near West Yellowstone, Montana, a blockade of dolomite (a magnesium-rich carbonate rock) held back a deeply weathered and *over-steepened slope* (40° to 60° slope angle) for untold centuries (white area in Figure 13.23). Then, shortly after midnight on August 17, 1959, an M 7.5 earthquake broke the dolomite structure along the foot of the slope. The break released 32 million m³ of mountainside, which moved downslope at 95 km · h⁻¹, causing gale-force winds through the canyon. Momentum carried the material more than 120 m up the opposite canyon slope, trapping several hundred campers under about 80 m of rock, killing 28 people.

The mass of material also effectively dammed the Madison River and created a new lake, dubbed Quake Lake. The landslide debris dam established a new temporary equilibrium for the river and canyon. A channel was quickly excavated by the U.S. Army Corps of Engineers to prevent a disaster below the dam, for if Quake Lake overflowed the landslide dam, the water would quickly erode a channel and thereby release the entire contents of the new lake onto farmland downstream. This channel-dredging relief procedure in a landslide "dam" was exactly what engineers had to do on the Chaping River, Hubei Province, China, in 2008. The M 7.9 Wenchuan quake produced more than 100 of these landslide dams; engineers prioritized the highest-risk dams to receive channel dredging first.

Classes of Mass Movements

In any mass movement, gravity pulls on a mass until the critical shear-failure point is reached—*a geomorphic threshold.* The material then can *fall, slide, flow,* or *creep*—the four classes of mass movement. Figure 13.24 summarizes these classes. Note the speed and moisture gradients in the margins of the illustration, which show the relation between water content and movement rate. The Madison River Canyon event was a type of slide, whereas the Nevado del Ruiz lahar mentioned earlier was a flow. We now look at specific mass-movement classes.

Falls and Avalanches This class of mass movement includes rockfalls and debris avalanches. A **rockfall** is simply a volume of rock that falls through the air and hits a surface. During a rockfall, individual pieces fall independently and characteristically form a cone-shaped pile of irregular broken rocks in a **talus slope** at the base of a steep incline, where several *talus cones* coalesce (Figure 13.25).

A **debris avalanche** is a mass of falling and tumbling rock, debris, and soil. It is differentiated from a slower debris slide or landslide by the velocity of onrushing material. This speed often results from ice and water that fluidize the debris. The extreme danger of a debris avalanche results from its tremendous speed and lack of warning.

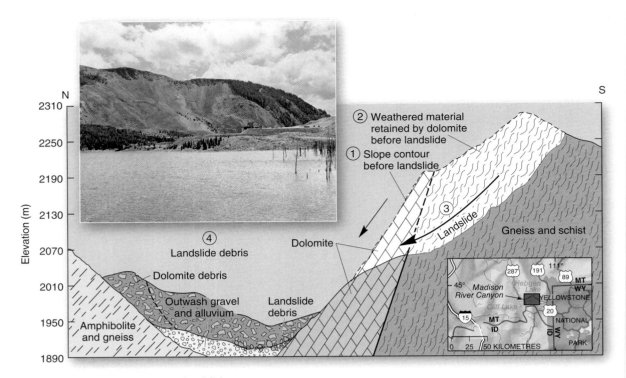

FIGURE 13.23 Madison River landslide.
Cross section showing geologic structure of the Madison River Canyon in Montana, where an earthquake triggered a landslide in 1959: (1) prequake slope contour; (2) weathered rock that failed; (3) direction of landslide; and (4) landslide debris blocking the canyon and damming the Madison River, visible in the inset photo. [USGS Professional Paper 435-K, August 1959, p. 115. Inset photo by Bobbé Christopherson.]

In 1962 and again in 1970, debris avalanches roared down the west face of Nevado Huascarán, the highest peak in the Peruvian Andes. The 1962 debris avalanche contained an estimated 13 million m³ of material, burying the city of Ranrahirca and eight other towns, killing 4000 people. An earthquake initiated the 1970 event (Figure 13.26). This time, upward of 100 million m³ of debris buried the city of Yungay, where 18 000 people perished. This avalanche attained velocities of 300 km · h⁻¹.

A dramatic example of a debris flow that did not kill occurred in Banff National Park, Alberta, in August 1999. The failure was unexpected and resulted from an intense rainfall that was unrecorded because local weather stations were outside the area of focused precipitation. Debris blocked the highway for 24 hours, and delayed thousands of travellers in Banff for a few days while cleanup occurred (Figure 13.27).

Landslides A sudden rapid movement of a cohesive mass of regolith or bedrock that is not saturated with moisture is a **landslide**—a large amount of material failing simultaneously. Surprise creates the danger, for the downward pull of gravity wins the struggle for equilibrium in an instant. Focus Study 13.1 describes one such surprise event that struck near Frank, Alberta, in 1903.

To eliminate the surprise element, scientists are using the Global Positioning System (GPS) to monitor landslide movement. With GPS, scientists measure slight land shifts in suspect areas for clues to possible mass wasting. GPS was applied in two cases in Japan and effectively identified pre-landslide movements of 2–5 cm per year, providing information to expand the area of hazard concern and warning.

Slides occur in one of two basic forms: translational or rotational (see Figure 13.24 for an idealized view of each). *Translational slides* involve movement along a planar (flat)

GEO REPORT 13.4 *Rockfalls in Yosemite*

Records indicate that at least 600 rockfalls have occurred in Yosemite Valley, located in the Sierra Nevada of California, in the past 150 years. In July 1996, a 162 000-ton granite slab shocked Yosemite Valley, a crashing drop of 670 m at 260 km · h⁻¹, pulverizing into a light dust that covered 20 hectares and felled more than 500 trees. In 1999, another rockfall occurred that took a life. Large rockfalls from Half Dome (Figure 13.10b and c) in 2006, Glacier Point in 2008, and Ahwiyah Point in 2009 are of recent notice. A National Park Service (NPS) map of rockfalls from 1857 to 2009 is at http://www.nps.gov/yose/naturescience/rockfall.htm. Note from the NPS map that winter and spring events dominate the record, although large rockfalls can occur during the warmer months as well.

FIGURE 13.24 Mass movement classes.
Principal types of mass movement and mass wasting events. Variations in water content and rates of movement produce a variety of forms. (a) A 1995 slide in La Conchita, California, also the site of a 2005 mudslide event. (b) Saturated hillsides fail, Santa Cruz County, California. (c) Mudflows 2 m deep, also in Santa Cruz County. [(a) Robert L. Schuster/USGS. (b) Alexander Lowry/Photo Researchers, Inc. (c) James A. Sugar/National Geographic Society]

Mass Movement

surface roughly parallel to the angle of the slope, with no rotation. The Madison Canyon landslide described earlier was a translational slide. Flow and creep patterns also are considered translational in nature.

FIGURE 13.25 Talus slope.
Rockfall and talus deposits at the base of a steep slope along Duve Fjord, Nordaustlandet Island. Can you see the lighter rock strata above that are the source for the three talus cones? [Bobbé Christopherson.]

Rotational slides occur when surface material moves along a concave surface. Frequently, underlying clay presents an impervious surface to percolating water. As a result, water flows along the clay surface, undermining the overlying block and lubricating the contact, thereby reducing the friction force. The simplest form of rotational slide is a rotational slump, in which a small block of land shifts downward. The upper surface of the slide appears to rotate backward and often remains intact. The surface may rotate as a single unit, or it may present a stepped appearance.

Flows Flows include *earthflows* and more fluid **mudflows**. When the moisture content of moving material is high, the suffix *-flow* is used (see Figure 13.24). Heavy rains can saturate barren mountain slopes and initiate movement. Figure 13.28 shows an earthflow in the Machiche River valley, in Trois-Rivières, Québec, known as the St. Boniface landslide. It occurred in late April 1996, causing approximately seven million cubic metres of sediment to slide into the Machiche River valley, damming the river. This type of retrogressive earthflow can occur within

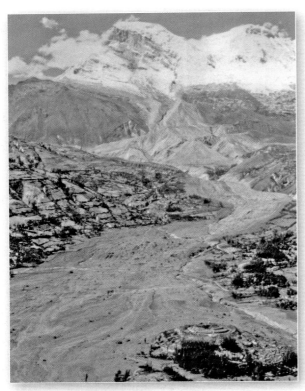

FIGURE 13.26 Debris avalanche, Peru.
A 1970 debris avalanche falls more than 4100 m down the west face of Nevado Huascarán, burying the city of Yungay, Peru. The same area was devastated by a similar avalanche in 1962 and by others in pre-Columbian times. A great danger remains for the towns in the valley from possible future mass movements.
[George Plafker, USGS.]

FIGURE 13.27 Five Mile Creek, Alberta, 1999.
In August 1999, an intense localized rainfall triggered this debris flow approximately 5 km west of Banff, in Banff National Park.
[Courtesy of the Geological Survey of Canada. Photo 2002-584 by Réjean Couture. Reproduced with the permission of Natural Resources Canada. © 2012.]

sensitive glaciomarine sediments common to the St. Lawrence Lowlands and Ottawa Valley regions. In these flows, the headwall erodes back into the valley side, and the landslide debris flows toward the river, away from the scarp. In January 2005, more than 300 mm of rain in less than a week saturated the mountainside in North Vancouver, resulting in mudslides that caused millions of dollars of damage and claimed one life.

Creep A persistent, gradual mass movement of surface soil is **soil creep**. In creep, individual soil particles are lifted and disturbed by the expansion of soil moisture as it freezes; by cycles of moistness and dryness; by diurnal temperature variations; or by grazing livestock or digging animals.

In the freeze–thaw cycle, particles are lifted at right angles to the slope by freezing soil moisture, as shown in Figure 13.29a and b. When the ice melts, however, the particles fall straight downward in response to gravity. As the process repeats, the surface soil gradually creeps its way downslope.

Figure 13.29c illustrates a **solifluction** rampart in Nunavut. Abundant soil water is available during spring snowmelt and causes the soil to liquefy and flow downslope. As water drains from the front of the flowing mass, movement ceases, leaving a "rampart" of soil. Because the process illustrated here is happening over permafrost, the specific type of solifluction occurring here is **gelifluction**.

The overall wasting of a slope may cover a wide area and may cause fence posts, utility poles, and even trees to lean downslope. Various strategies are used to arrest the mass movement of slope material—grading the terrain, building terraces and retaining walls, planting ground cover—but the persistence of creep nearly always wins.

Human-Induced Mass Movements (Scarification)

Every human disturbance of a slope—highway roadcut, surface mining, or building of a shopping mall, housing development, or home—can hasten mass wasting. The

GEO REPORT 13.5 *Landscaping Choices, Watering, and Landslides*

In October 2007, mass-movement realities struck upscale La Jolla, California, damaging more than 100 homes along Soledad Mountain Road. The rotational slump along a hillside pulled material from beneath the highway, causing a sinkhole-like collapse. The area is inherently unstable, having experienced three other collapse events since 1961, with early warning signs of this occurrence beginning in July. Homeowners were allowed to irrigate lawns and gardens with no restrictions, feeding drainage runoff water into subsurface strata and, as a result, increasing instability and lubricating slides. In an area such as this, it is difficult to understand how standard cut-and-fill housing pads were allowed on unstable slopes in the zoning and planning stages prior to construction.

FIGURE 13.28 St. Boniface landslide, Québec, April 1996
The St. Boniface landslide, a retrogressive earthflow, occurred in late April 1996. Here, the landslide debris forms a series of concentric ridges, visible in the centre of the photograph, effectively damming the river when it occurred [Courtesy of the Geological Survey of Canada. Photo 2002-703 by Greg Brooks. Reproduced with the permission of Natural Resources Canada. © 2012.]

newly destabilized and oversteepened surfaces are thrust into a search for a new equilibrium.

Large open-pit surface mines—such as the iron ore mine near Labrador City, the Bingham Copper Mine west of Salt Lake City, the Berkeley Pit in Butte, Montana, and numerous large coal surface mines in the U.S. East and West, such as Black Mesa (Figure 13.30a)—are examples of human-induced mass movements, generally called **scarification** (Figure 13.30).

At the Bingham Copper Mine, a mountain literally was removed since mining began in 1906, forming a pit 4 km wide and 1 km deep (Figure 13.30b). This is the largest human-made excavation on Earth, with ores containing copper, gold, silver, and molybdenum. The disposal of tailings (mined ore of little value) and waste material is a significant problem at any mine. Such large excavations produce tailing piles that are unstable and susceptible to further weathering, mass wasting, or wind dispersal. The leaching of toxic materials from tailings and waste piles

(a)

(b)   (c)

FIGURE 13.29 Soil creep and its effects.
(a) Typical soil-creep features. (b) Note the subsurface effects on rock strata caused by surface creep.
(c) Solifluction, rapid soil creep, in Nunavut. The rampart seen in the foreground is about 1 m high. [(b) Bobbé Christopherson; (c) Courtesy of the Geological Survey of Canada. Photo 2002-452 by Lynda Dredge. Reproduced with the permission of Natural Resources Canada. © 2012.]

FOCUS STUDY 13.1

Frank Slide: Coal Mining and an Early Morning Disaster

On April 29, 1903, at 4:10 A.M., an estimated 82 million metric tons of rock and sediment slid down the east side of Turtle Mountain in southwestern Alberta at speeds nearing 140 km·h⁻¹. The slide buried the wetland at the base of the mountain, roared through the southern edge of the town of Frank, continued across the valley, and came to a stop upslope on the opposite side of the valley. It took just 90 seconds for the mass of material to travel 1.5 km and to cover an area up to 3 km² at an average depth of 14 m. One estimate counted 70 lives lost in Canada's deadliest landslide.

More than a century has passed since the Frank Slide, and scientists still do not agree about what caused the slide. The mountain is made of interbedded Paleozoic limestone and shale topping Mesozoic sandstone, with shale and coal at its base. A coal-mining shaft was sunk at the base of the mountain below the Turtle Mountain thrust fault (Figure 13.1.1). Mining at the base of the mountain was likely one of the final triggers that sent the rock downslope. The rockslide took place along the easterly dipping beds of the main geological structure—the Turtle Mountain anticline.

The actual mechanism of failure is complex and includes limestone creep over shales, siltstones, sandstones, and coal; adverse jointing and faulting of the rock mass; underground coal mining at the base of the mountain; ice wedging in cracks and discontinuities of the rock mass; excessive rainfall in the four years preceding the slide; and seismic loading. All these factors contributed to the

FIGURE 13.1.1 Cross section through the central part of the Frank Slide. Rock structure creates a natural instability in the rock of Turtle Mountain. Splay refers to a minor fault that branches off a major fault. [Illustration reprinted by permission of John Krahn, P. Eng.]

failure, but the greatest influence came from the geological instability.

The mechanism of movement of the material in the slide has also been the subject of considerable academic debate. One theory states that the debris in the slide remained in contact with the surface through most of its travel down the mountainside, across the valley bottom, and up the facing slope. A second theory proposes that the material had to be lubricated at the base by either compressed air or steam and that this compressed layer allowed the slide material to move freely downslope, across the valley, and up the other side.

The slide affected an entire face of the mountain (Figure 13.1.2), buried part of the town, the Canadian Pacific Railway, and the highway that passed through town, and dammed the Crowsnest River,

forming a temporary lake. The continued threat from the geological instability of the mountain led to the relocation of much of the town—out of the potential path of future landslides. The road was rebuilt and the rail line reconstructed. The mine reopened, but closed again soon after.

In Canada, thousands of slides change the terrain every year in all parts of the country. From 1850 to the present, landslides have caused about 600 fatalities in Canada. From an economic perspective, slides have cost between $100 million and $200 million in property damage, blocked rail lines and roads, and caused pipeline explosions. Environmental damages, the costs of which are difficult to estimate, include damage to spawning grounds and localized deforestation and habitat destruction. Natural factors cause most slides, owing to

poses an ever-increasing problem to streams, aquifers, and public health across the country (Figure 13.30c).

In eastern Pennsylvania, commercial slate deposits formed over millions of years. The Dally slate quarry in Pen Argyl is now working a second pit that is 55 m deep (Figure 13.30d). The grain of the metamorphic rock guides the slate removal so as to produce the flattest pieces. Slate is mined for shingles and countertops. The local county turned the first quarry into a landfill—a practical use for the abandoned pit.

The Carol Project, Labrador City, mines about 38 million metric tons of crude iron ore per year and

produces 21 million metric tons of tailings. Mine dewatering and flow from tailings and flotation plant effluent all discharge into Wabush Lake, producing significant pollution (Figure 13.30e).

Where underground mining is common, particularly for coal in the Appalachians, land subsidence and collapse produce further mass movements. Homes, highways, streams, wells, and property values are severely affected. Another controversial form of mining called *mountaintop removal* is done by removing ridges and summits and dumping the debris into stream valleys, thereby exposing the coal seams for mining and burying stream channels. A change in

(a)

(b)

FIGURE 13.1.2 **The Frank Slide in 1903 and 2003.**
(a) From a distance, you can see how the entire side of the mountain moved downslope. (b) The town was in the path of destruction: to the left are the buried remains of the miner's houses, to the right are the buildings that remained intact. (c) The slide scar in 2003 still clearly shows the path of movement of the slide. [(a) Glenbow Archives, NA 3011-7; (b) Glenbow Archives, NA 411-9; (c) courtesy of Frank Slide Visitors' Centre.]

(c)

geology, water, ice, wind, and temperature changes. However, human activities such as urbanization, deforestation, and mining may also play a role as triggers to mass movement. The results remain a part of the landscape, such as Turtle Mountain—a reminder of times when mountains moved. For current information on landslides in Canada, see the Natural Resources Canada Landslides web page at http://gsc.nrcan.gc.ca/landslides/index_e.php.

the U.S. Clean Water Act in 2002 to protect flows removed a 20-year-old restriction that barred dumping within 30 metres of a stream. Figure 13.30f is an aerial view of mountaintop removal on Kayford Mountain, West Virginia. The 20-story-tall dragline machine is visible centre-right. In the background, forest cover and litter are removed using fire to prepare the site for minimal reclamation, although this is difficult since the landscape has essentially been changed beyond recognition. Some 2000 km of streams are now filled with tailings and mountaintop scenery is gone.

Scientists can informally quantify the scale of human-induced scarification for comparison with natural denudation processes. Geologist R. L. Hooke, then at the University of Minnesota, used estimates of U.S. excavations for new housing, mineral production (including the three largest—stone, sand and gravel, and coal), and highway construction. He then prorated these quantities of moved material for all countries, using their gross domestic product (GDP), energy consumption, and agriculture's effect on river sediment loads. From these he calculated a global estimate for human material movement.

Hooke estimated that humans, as a geomorphic agent, annually move 40–45 billion metric tons (40−45 $Gt \cdot y^{-1}$)

(a)

(b)

(c)

(d)

(e)

(f)

FIGURE 13.30 **Scarification.**
(a) Black Mesa, Arizona, strip-mining for coal. (b) Bingham Canyon, Utah, west of Salt Lake City, strip-mining for copper and other minerals. (c) Spoil banks of tailings in a West Virginia coal-mining area. (d) The 55-m-deep Dally slate quarry in Pen Argyl, Pennsylvania. (e) The Carol Project, Labrador City, Newfoundland and Labrador. (f) Mountaintop removal coal strip-mining on Kayford Mountain, West Virginia. [(a) and (c) Robert Christopherson; (b) and (d) Bobbé Christopherson; (e) Courtesy of Iron Ore Company of Canada; (f) Dr. Chris Mayda, Eastern Michigan University, all rights reserved.]

of the planet's surface material. Compare this quantity with natural river sediment transfer ($14 \ \mathrm{Gt \cdot y^{-1}}$), movement through stream meandering ($39 \ \mathrm{Gt \cdot y^{-1}}$), haulage by glaciers ($4.3 \ \mathrm{Gt \cdot y^{-1}}$), movement due to wave action and erosion ($1.25 \ \mathrm{Gt \cdot y^{-1}}$), wind transport ($1 \ \mathrm{Gt \cdot y^{-1}}$), sediment movement by continental and oceanic mountain building ($34 \ \mathrm{Gt \cdot y^{-1}}$), or deep-ocean sedimentation ($7 \ \mathrm{Gt \cdot y^{-1}}$). As Hooke concluded about us,

> *Homo sapiens* has become an impressive geomorphic agent. Coupling our earth-moving prowess with our

APPLIED PHYSICAL GEOGRAPHY   *The Role of Gravity in Landform Development*

Endogenic processes produce land-forms through uplift and tectonism, while exogenic processes wear the forms away. Gravity has an important role to play in moving mineral matter and water downslope.

Gravity is the mutual force exerted by the masses of objects that are attracted to one another, and is produced in an amount proportional to each object's mass. It results in potential energy differences between the continents that have been uplifted and the ocean basins.

Mass movement is the downslope movement of material under the influence of gravity. The rate and method of the movement depends upon the slope, the cohesion of the material, and the moisture content (Figure 1).

When W sin θ exceeds F, movement occurs. F is proportional to W cos θ as:

$$F = f\,W \cos \theta$$

Where: *F* is the frictional force, f is the coefficient of friction, θ is the slope angle, and W is weight,

Decreasing f, or increasing θ leads to movement.

Water has a dual effect in that it can help stabilize sediments, but it can also contribute to failure. Water adds weight and increases the cohesiveness of soils (although too much water can cause failure). This increases F and stabilizes the slope. Water also lubricates the potential

m = mass
g = acceleration due to gravity
W = weight
F = frictional force
f = coefficient of friction

F

$W\cos\theta$ $W\sin\theta$
θ
$W = mg$
θ

FIGURE 1 Mass movement.

slip faces, decreasing f and, in consequence F, leading to slope failure.

Soil saturated with water experiences increased water pressure that acts to decrease the contact pressure between soil grains, forcing the granular framework apart and decreasing stability.

In Focus Study 13.1, we learned that an estimated 82 million metric tons of rock and sediment failed, sliding down the side of Turtle Mountain at speeds nearing 140 km · h^{-1}. The material moved across the valley bottom and up the opposite side. In 90 seconds, the mass of material travelled 1.5 km and covered an area up to 3 km^2, with an average depth of 14 m.

The slide started as potential energy on the mountainside. When gravity overcame cohesion, the potential energy was converted to kinetic energy as the mass moved downslope. Kinetic energy dissipated as heat due to friction as the movement came to an end.

What force was applied by this moving mass?

$$F = m \times g$$

where F is the force, m is the mass of the object, and g is acceleration due to gravity (9.8 m · s^{-2}). Filling in the numbers from the Turtle Mountain slide,

$$\begin{aligned}F &= m \times g \\ &= 8.2 \times 10^{10} \text{ kg} \times 9.8 \text{ m} \cdot \text{s}^{-2} \\ &= 8.036 \times 10^{11} \text{ N}\end{aligned}$$

The SI units of force are newtons (N). (Work is measured in joules, J, and power in Watts, W.) From this force, we can determine the *work* done.

$$W = F \times d$$

where W is work, F is force, and d is distance.

$$\begin{aligned}W &= F \times d \\ &= 8.036 \times 10^{11} \text{ N} \times 1500 \text{ m} \\ &= 1.21 \times 10^{15} \text{ J}\end{aligned}$$

We can now calculate power from this measure of work (T is time in seconds).

$$\begin{aligned}P &= W/T \\ &= 1.21 \times 10^{15} \text{ J}/90 \text{ s} \\ &= 1.34 \times 10^{13} \text{ W}\end{aligned}$$

This is greater by far than the average rate of consumption of electric power in North America annually. The overwhelming power released by gravity in a slope failure is an illustration of the ability of nature to sculpt the landscape.

---

inadvertent adding of sediment load to rivers and the visual impact of our activities on the landscape, one is compelled to acknowledge that, for better or for worse, this biogeomorphic agent may be the premier geomorphic agent of our time.[1]

In 2000, Dr. Hooke asked an important question in another paper on this subject: "One may well ask how long such rates of increases [in human geomorphic impacts] can be sustained, and whether it will be rational behavior or catastrophe that brings them to an end."[2]

GEOSYSTEMS CONNECTION

The basics of landmass denudation and morphology of slopes are at the core of exogenic processes. The physical and chemical weathering of rock, dissolution of limestone landscapes, and mass-movement processes deliver materials for erosional transport. In the next chapter, we examine river systems and landforms that result from these fluvial processes. The erosional and depositional agents of running water, wind, waves and coastal actions, and ice flow through the next four chapters.

---

[1]R. L. Hooke, "On the efficacy of humans as geomorphic agents," *GSA Today* (The Geological Society of America), 4, 9 (September 1994): 217–226.

[2]R. L. Hooke, "On the history of humans as geomorphic agents," *Geology*, 28, 9 (September 2000): 843–846.

■ *Define* the science of geomorphology.

Geomorphology is the science that analyzes and describes the origin, evolution, form, and spatial distribution of landforms. The exogenic system, powered by solar energy and gravity, wears down the landscape through processes of landmass **denudation** involving weathering, mass movement, erosion, transportation, and deposition. Different rocks offer differing resistance to weathering processes and produce a pattern on the landscape of **differential weathering**.

Agents of change include moving air, water, waves, and ice. Since the 1960s, research and understanding of the processes of denudation have moved toward the **dynamic equilibrium model**, which considers slope and landform stability to be consequences of the resistance of rock materials to the attack of denudation processes.

geomorphology (p. 390)
denudation (p. 390)
differential weathering (p. 390)
dynamic equilibrium model (p. 390)

1. Define geomorphology, and describe its relationship to physical geography.
2. Define *landmass denudation*. What processes are included in the concept?
3. What is the interplay between the resistance of rock structures and differential weathering?
4. Describe the process at work to produce the landform in Figure 13.1.
5. What are the principal considerations in the dynamic equilibrium model?

■ *Illustrate* the forces at work on materials residing on a slope.

Slopes are shaped by the relation between rate of weathering and breakup of slope materials and the rate of mass movement and erosion of those materials. In this struggle against gravity, a slope may reach a **geomorphic threshold**—the point at which potential energy overcomes resistance against movement. **Slopes** that form the boundaries of landforms have several general components: *waxing slope, free face, debris slope,* and *waning slope*. Slopes seek an angle of equilibrium among the operating forces.

geomorphic threshold (p. 391)
slope (p. 391)

6. Describe conditions on a hillslope that is precisely at the geomorphic threshold. What factors might push the slope beyond this point?
7. Given all the interacting variables, do you think a landscape may ever reach a stable, old-age condition? Explain.
8. What are the general components of an ideal slope?
9. Relative to slopes, what is meant by an *angle of equilibrium*? Can you apply this concept to the photograph in Figure 13.2?

■ *Define* weathering, and *explain* the importance of parent rock, and of joints and fractures in rock.

Weathering processes disintegrate both surface and subsurface rocks into mineral particles or dissolve them in water. The upper layers of surface material undergo continual weathering and create broken-up rock called **regolith**. Weathered **bedrock** is the *parent rock* from which regolith forms. The small unconsolidated,

fragmented material that develops after weathering is **sediment**, which along with weathered rock forms the **parent material** from which soil evolves.

Important in weathering processes are **joints**, the fractures and separations in the rock. Jointing opens up rock surfaces on which weathering processes operate. Factors that influence weathering include character of the bedrock (hard or soft, soluble or insoluble, jointed or unjointed), climatic elements (temperature, precipitation, freeze–thaw cycles), position of the water table, slope orientation, surface vegetation and its subsurface roots, and time.

weathering (p. 393)
regolith (p. 393)
bedrock (p. 394)
sediment (p. 394)
parent material (p. 394)
joints (p. 394)

10. Describe weathering processes operating on an open expanse of bedrock. How does regolith develop? How is sediment derived?
11. Describe the relationship between mesoscale climatic conditions and rates of weathering activities. At microscale levels, describe weathering processes.
12. What is the relation among parent rock, parent material, regolith, and soil?
13. What role do joints play in the weathering process? Give an example from one of the illustrations in this chapter.

■ *Describe* frost action, salt-crystal growth, and pressure-release jointing as physical weathering processes.

Physical weathering refers to the breakup of rock into smaller pieces with no alteration of mineral identity. The physical action of water when it freezes (expands) and thaws (contracts) is a powerful agent in shaping the landscape. This **frost action** may break apart any rock. Working in joints, expanded ice can produce *joint-block separation* through the process of *frost-wedging*. Another process of physical weathering is *salt-crystal growth* (*salt weathering*); as crystals in rock grow over time and force apart mineral grains to break up rock.

As overburden is removed from a granitic batholith, the pressure of deep burial is relieved. The granite slowly responds with *pressure-release jointing*, with layer after layer of rock peeling off in curved slabs or plates. Slabs slip off in the process of **sheeting**. This *exfoliation process* creates an arch-shaped or dome-shaped feature on the exposed landscape, forming an **exfoliation dome**.

physical weathering (p. 394)
frost action (p. 395)
sheeting (p. 397)
exfoliation dome (p. 397)

14. What is physical weathering? Give an example.
15. Why is freezing water such an effective physical weathering agent?
16. What weathering processes produce a granite dome? Describe the sequence of events.

■ *Describe* the susceptibility of different minerals to the chemical weathering processes, including hydration, hydrolysis, oxidation, carbonation, and solution.

Chemical weathering is the chemical decomposition of minerals in rock. It can cause **spheroidal weathering**, in which chemical weathering occurs in cracks in the rock. As cementing and binding materials are removed, the rock begins to disintegrate, and sharp edges and corners become rounded.

Hydration occurs when a mineral absorbs water and expands, thus creating a strong mechanical force that stresses rocks, similar to physical weathering processes. **Hydrolysis** breaks down silicate minerals in rock, as in the chemical weathering of feldspar into clays and silica. Water actively participates in many chemical weathering reactions. **Oxidation** is the reaction of oxygen with certain metallic elements, the most familiar example being the rusting of iron, producing iron oxide. The dissolution of materials into *solution* is considered chemical weathering. For instance, a mild acid such as carbonic acid in rainwater will cause **carbonation**, wherein carbon combines with certain minerals, such as calcium, magnesium, potassium, and sodium.

chemical weathering (p. 397)
spheroidal weathering (p. 399)
hydration (p. 399)
hydrolysis (p. 399)
oxidation (p. 399)
carbonation (p. 400)

17. What is chemical weathering? Contrast this set of processes to physical weathering.
18. What is meant by the term *spheroidal weathering*? How does spheroidal weathering occur?
19. What is hydration? What is hydrolysis? Differentiate between these processes. How do the processes affect rocks?
20. Iron minerals in rock are susceptible to which form of chemical weathering? What characteristic colour is associated with this type of weathering?
21. With what kind of minerals do carbon compounds react, and under what circumstances does the dissolution of carbonate minerals occur? What is this weathering process called?

■ **Review** the processes and features associated with karst topography.

Karst topography refers to distinctively pitted and weathered landscapes. Surface circular **sinkholes** form and may extend to form a *karst valley*. A sinkhole may collapse through the roof of an underground cavern, forming a *collapse sinkhole*. The formation of caverns is part of karst processes and groundwater erosion. Limestone caves feature many unique erosional and depositional features.

karst topography (p. 401)
sinkholes (p. 402)

22. Describe the development of limestone topography. What is the name applied to such landscapes? From what area was this name derived?
23. Differentiate among sinkholes, karst valleys, and cockpit karst. Within which form is the radio telescope at Arecibo, Puerto Rico?
24. In general, how would you characterize the region southwest of Orleans, Indiana?

25. What are some of the unique erosional and depositional features you find in a limestone cavern?

■ **Portray** the various types of mass movements, and **identify** examples of each in relation to moisture content and speed of movement.

Any movement of a body of material, propelled and controlled by gravity, is **mass movement**, also called **mass wasting**. The **angle of repose** of loose sediment grains represents a balance of driving and resisting forces on a slope. Mass movement of Earth's surface produces some dramatic incidents, including: **rockfalls** (a volume of rock that falls), which can form a **talus slope** of loose rock along the base of the cliff; **debris avalanches** (a mass of tumbling, falling rock, debris, and soil moving at high speed); **landslides** (a large amount of material failing simultaneously); **mudflows** (material in motion with a high moisture content); and **soil creep** (a persistent movement of individual soil particles that are lifted by the expansion of soil moisture as it freezes, by cycles of wetness and dryness, by temperature variations, or by the impact of animals). **Solifluction** (a form of mass movement characterized by a slow movement of soil material downslope under the influence of gravity) creates lobe-shaped features in environments that experience cycles of freeze-thaw. **Gelifluction** (a class of solifluction that occurs in areas of permafrost), which is characterized by the movement of soil downslope under the influence of gravity over a permafrost layer, also produces lobe-shaped features. In addition, human mining and construction activities have caused massive **scarification** of landscapes.

mass movement (p. 407)
mass wasting (p. 407)
angle of repose (p. 407)
rockfall (p. 407)
talus slope (p. 407)
debris avalanche (p. 407)
landslide (p. 408)
mudflows (p. 409)
soil creep (p. 410)
solifluction (p. 410)
gelifluction (p. 410)
scarification (p. 411)

26. Define the role of slopes in mass movements, using the terms *angle of repose*, *driving force*, *resisting force*, and *geomorphic threshold*.
27. What events occurred in the Madison River Canyon in 1959?
28. What are the classes of mass movement? Describe each briefly and differentiate among these classes.
29. Name and describe the type of mudflow associated with a volcanic eruption.
30. Describe the difference between a landslide and what happened on the slopes of Nevado Huascarán.
31. What is scarification, and why is it considered a type of mass movement? Give several examples of scarification. Why are humans a significant geomorphic agent?

MyGeosciencePlace

Visit **www.mygeoscienceplace.ca** for several figure animations, satellite loops, self-study quizzes, flashcards, interactive glossary, career links, RSS feeds, Pearson eText of *Geosystems*, and much more.

River Systems and Landforms

The Mackenzie River flows from Great Slave Lake through the Northwest Territories to the Beaufort Sea and Arctic Ocean (see map in Figure 14.7). More than 25 000 small lakes dot the river's marshy delta. Distributaries lace through the delta carrying a heavy sediment load, the visible plume interacting with currents and open pack ice. The delta is approximately 200 km in length and 60 wide. [*Terra* image, August 2001, courtesy of MODIS Rapid Response Team NASA/GSFC.]

KEY LEARNING CONCEPTS

After reading the chapter, you should be able to:

■ **Define** the term *fluvial*, and **explain** processes of fluvial erosion, transportation, and deposition.

■ **Construct** a basic drainage basin model, and **identify** different types of drainage patterns, with examples.

■ **Describe** the relations among velocity, depth, width, and discharge.

■ **Develop** a model of a meandering stream, including point bar, undercut bank, and cutoff, and **explain** the role of stream gradient in this model.

■ **Define** a floodplain, and **analyze** the behaviour of a stream channel during a flood.

■ **Differentiate** the types of river deltas, and **detail** each.

■ **Explain** flood probability estimates, and **review** strategies for mitigating flood hazards.

Removing Dams to Restore Natural Ecosystems

In September 2011, demolition began on the 32-m high Elwha dam in Washington, the largest dam removal in the United States to date. The deconstruction of the Elwha and Glines Canyon dams is part of the $325 million Elwha River restoration project. This dam removal was followed a few weeks later by the demolition of Condit Dam on the White Salmon River, also in Washington, to restore historic salmon runs.

Dams on rivers have a number of benefits, such as water storage, hydroelectric power generation, and flood control. However, the downstream effects of dams on river ecosystems are profound: changes in river discharge, sediment supply, and water temperature impact the entire system. Channel form, riparian vegetation, fisheries, and recreation are all negative effects on native species. Dams create an obvious barrier to fish migration; reservoirs inundate habitat and create "lentic" (related to still water) rather than "lotic" (related to moving water) conditions for aquatic species.

As occurred with other such removals, a free-flowing Elwha River should enable the return of five species of Pacific salmon to the watershed, with numbers expected to increase from 3000 to 390 000 over the next 30 years. Construction of the Elwha Dam in 1913 and the Glines Canyon Dam in 1927, built to generate hydropower, blocked salmon and other fish from accessing all but the lowest 8 km of the river. Such species are *anadromous* (from the Greek *anadromos*, "running up"), meaning they migrate from the sea into freshwater rivers to spawn. Many dam removals in the United States are for restoration of these important species.

In 1999, Edwards Dam was deconstructed from the Kennebec River in Augusta, Maine, marking the first U.S. dam removal for ecological reasons. Migratory fish such as shad, sturgeon, Atlantic salmon, and striped bass rebounded quickly in the Kennebec as the natural connection between the river and the sea was restored. In 2000, the removal of Finlayson Dam on the Big East River in the Muskoka district of Ontario marked the first Canadian dam removal that followed an intricately planned process. The goal was habitat restoration to enhance the brook trout fishery; post-project monitoring shows that brook trout have successfully moved into the former reservoir area and that habitat restoration is ongoing.

Although removal of large dams is not yet common in Canada, deconstruction of small dams for habitat restoration is becoming a new priority. In November 2010, local conservation groups spearheaded removal of a dam on Marden Creek near Guelph, Ontario, to restore brook trout habitat (Figure GN 14.1). In northern New Brunswick, the gates of the Eel River Dam were opened in summer 2010, beginning the process of removing the 47-year old dam. A newly

FIGURE GN 14.1 Excavator removing the concrete dam on Marden Creek near Guelph, Ontario, in 2010.
Although only a small structure, the dam modified streamflow conditions and aquatic habitats. Its removal has reestablished a free flowing stream and allowed brook trout to access the lower reaches. [Courtesy of Emily Giles/WWF Canada.]

free-flowing river will reestablish fish passage, restore salt marsh wetlands, and restore habitat for soft-shelled clams and other shellfish.

In some cases, dam "decommissioning" (making a dam inactive) involves dam breaching rather than full removal. In 2003, the 40-year old Coursier Dam near Revelstoke in British Columbia was breached for safety reasons. Rather than removing this aging, earthfill dam, engineers cut a notch in the berm, effectively draining much of the reservoir and establishing a new channel feature, a "riffle," at the lake outlet. Habitat near the outlet and in the upper reaches of Cranberry Creek is recovering.

As more dams become outdated and unsafe, these types of projects will remain on the increase, especially with an increasing societal emphasis on environmental restoration. Are there obsolete dams in your area? For more information on dams, reservoirs, and flow regulation in Canada, see http://www.ec.gc.ca/inre-nwri/default.asp?lang=En&n=0CD66675-1&offset=7&toc=show.

Earth's rivers and waterways form vast arterial networks that drain the continents. Rivers are Earth's lifeblood, inasmuch as rivers redistribute mineral nutrients important for soil formation and plant growth and serve society in many ways. Rivers also shape the landscape by removing the products of weathering, mass movement, and erosion and transporting them downstream.

Rivers not only provide essential water supplies, but also receive, dilute, and transport wastes, provide critical cooling water for industry, and form one of the world's most important transportation networks. Rivers have been significant throughout human history. Each devastating flood event, such as the August 2010 catastrophe that drowned large areas of Pakistan along the Indus River, demonstrates the interrelationship between rivers and society.

Stream-related processes are **fluvial** (from the Latin *fluvius*, meaning "river"). Fluvial systems, like all natural systems, have characteristic processes and produce recognizable landforms. Yet a river system can behave with randomness and seeming disorder. The term *river* is applied to a trunk, or main stream; a network of tributaries forms a *river system*. *Stream* is a more general term not necessarily related to size. There is much overlap in usage between the terms *river* and *stream*.

Hydrology is the science of water and its global circulation, distribution, and properties—specifically water at and below Earth's surface. For hydrology links on the web, see The Water Survey of Canada at http://www.ec.gc.ca/rhc-wsc/, The Hydrology Web at http://hydrologyweb.pnl.gov/index.asp, http://hydrology.pnnl.gov/, or the Global Hydrology and Climate Center at http://weather.msfc.nasa.gov/surface_hydrology/.

In this chapter: We begin with a look at the largest rivers on Earth. Essential fluvial concepts of base level, drainage basin, and drainage density and patterns follow. With this foundation, we define stream discharge, "Q," the essential element in fluvial processes. We discuss factors that affect flow characteristics and the work performed by flowing water, including erosion and transport. Depositional features such as deltaic forms are illustrated with a detailed look at the Mississippi River Delta. We look at the effects of urbanization on hydrology. Human response to floods and floodplain management are important aspects of river management, with details of the New Orleans levee and floodwall disaster and tragedy concluding the chapter.

Basic Fluvial Concepts

At any moment, approximately 1250 km³ of water is flowing through Earth's waterways. Even though this volume is only 0.003% of all freshwater, the work performed by this energetic flow makes it a dominant agent of landmass denudation. Of the world's rivers, those with the greatest *discharge* (streamflow volume past a point in a given unit of time) are the Amazon of South America (Figure 14.1), the Congo of Africa, the Chàng Jiang (Yangtze) of Asia, and the Orinoco of South America (Table 14.1). The Amazon's leading discharge delivers millions of tons of sediment from its drainage basin, which is as large as the Australian continent. In North America, the greatest discharges are from the Missouri–Ohio–Mississippi, Saint Lawrence, and Mackenzie river systems.

Insolation and gravity power the hydrologic cycle and are the driving forces of fluvial systems. Individual streams vary greatly from one another, depending on the climate, the composition of the surface, topography, the nature of vegetation and plant cover, and the length of time the stream has been operating in a specific setting.

Water dislodges, dissolves, or removes surface material in the **erosion** process. Flowing water causes fluvial erosion, in which weathered sediment is picked up for transport to new locations. Thus, a stream is a mixture of water and solids; the solids are carried by mechanical **transport** or move in dissolved solution. Materials are laid down by another process, **deposition**. The general term

(a)

(b)

FIGURE 14.1 Amazon River drainage basin and mouth. (a) Shuttle Radar Topography Mission (SRTM) images showing elevation are combined with digitally mapped stream channels in this view of the Amazon basin. Elevations range from sea level in green to above 4,500 m in white. In 2007, Brazilian researchers reported finding a new source for the Amazon (white box), near Mount Mismi in southern Peru, and a new length measurement of 6800 km, making it longer than the Nile. (b) The mouth of the Amazon is 160 km wide and discharges a fifth of all the freshwater that enters the world's oceans. Large islands of sediment are deposited where the flow enters the Atlantic Ocean. [(a) NASA SRTM image by Jesse Allen, University of Maryland, Global Land Cover Facility; stream data World Wildlife Fund, HydroSHEDS project (see http://hydrosheds. cr.usgs.gov/). (b) *Terra* image, NASA/ GSFC/JPL.]

TABLE 14.1   Largest Rivers on Earth Ranked by Discharge

Rank by Discharge	Average Discharge at Mouth (× 1000 m³ s⁻¹)	River (with Major Tributaries)	Outflow/Location	Length (km)	Rank by Length
1	180	Amazon (Ucayali, Tambo, Ene, Apurimac)	Atlantic Ocean/ Amapá-Pará, Brazil	6570	1*
2	41.0	Congo (Lualaba)	Atlantic Ocean/ Angola, Congo	4630	10
3	34.0	Yangtze or Chàng Jiang	East China Sea/ Kiangsu, China	6300	3
4	30.0	Orinoco	Atlantic Ocean/Venezuela	2737	27
5	21.8	La Plata estuary (Paraná)	Atlantic Ocean/Argentina	3945	16
6	19.6	Ganges (Brahmaputra)	Bay of Bengal/India	2510	23
7	19.4	Yenisey (Angara, Selenga or Selenge, Ider)	Gulf of Kara Sea/Siberia	5870	5
8	18.2	Mississippi (Missouri, Ohio, Tennessee, Jefferson, Beaver-head, Red Rock)	Gulf of Mexico/Louisiana	6020	4
9	16.0	Lena	Laptev Sea/Siberia	4400	11
17	9.7	St. Lawrence	Gulf of St. Lawrence/ Canada and United States	3060	21
36	2.8	Nile (Kagera, Ruvuvu, Luvironza)	Mediterranean Sea/ Egypt	6690	2*

* Measurements in 2007 places the Amazon first in length; see Figure 14.1.

for the clay, silt, sand, gravel, and mineral fragments deposited by running water is **alluvium**, which may be sorted or semisorted sediment on a floodplain, delta, or streambed.

Base Level

Base level is a level below which a stream cannot erode its valley. In general, the *ultimate base level* is sea level. Imagine base level as a surface extending inland from sea level, inclined gently upward under the continents. Ideally, this is the lowest practical level for all denudation processes (Figure 14.2a).

American geologist and ethnologist John Wesley Powell (1834–1902) put forward the idea of base level in 1875. He was a director of the U.S. Geological Survey, first director of the U.S. Bureau of Ethnology, an explorer of the Colorado River, and a pioneer in understanding the western landscape.

Powell recognized that not every landscape has degraded all the way to sea level; clearly, other intermediate base levels are in operation. *A local base level*, or temporary one, may control the lower limit of local streams for a region. The local base level may be a river, a lake, a layer of resistant rock, or a human-made dam (Figure 14.2b). In arid landscapes, with their intermittent precipitation, valleys, plains, or other low points provide local base level control.

Over time, the work of streams modifies the landscape dramatically. Landforms are produced by two basic processes: (1) erosive action of flowing water and (2) deposition of stream-transported materials. Before we introduce streamflow characteristics, let us begin by examining a basic fluvial unit—the drainage basin.

Drainage Basins

Figure 14.3 illustrates drainage basin concepts. Every stream has a **drainage basin** (also called a *watershed*), ranging in size from small to vast. Ridges form *drainage divides* that define the catchment (water-receiving) area of every drainage basin. That is, the ridges are the dividing lines that control into which basin runoff water from precipitation drains. In any drainage basin, water initially moves downslope in a thin film of **sheetflow**, or *overland flow*. High ground that separates one valley from another and directs sheetflow is termed an *interfluve*. Surface runoff concentrates in *rills*, or small-scale downhill grooves that may develop into deeper *gullies* and then on to a stream course in the valley.

The drainage basin acts as a collection system of water comprised of many subsystems from erosion in the headwaters, transportation throughout, to deposition in the lower portions. Figure 14.4 illustrates the drainage basin system operation from the smallest rills and gullies, to the main tributaries and stream trunk, to the dispersing lower extremities and mouth where the river meets the ocean or another water body.

Drainage Divides and Basins Several high drainage divides, called **continental divides**, are situated in Canada and the United States. These are extensive mountain and highland regions separating drainage basins, sending flows to the Pacific, the Gulf of Mexico, the Atlantic, Hudson Bay, or the Arctic Ocean. The principal drainage divides and drainage basins in Canada and the United States are mapped in Figure 14.5. These divides form water-resource regions and provide a spatial framework for water-management planning.

A major drainage basin system is made up of many smaller drainage basins. Each drainage basin gathers and delivers its precipitation and sediment to a larger basin, concentrating the volume into the main stream. A good example from Figure 14.5 is the Peace–Athabasca–Liard–Mackenzie river system.

Precipitation falling in any area collects in streams and may travel vast distances. Consider the precipitation that falls in southcentral Alberta. This water collects in hundreds of small streams that join the Athabasca River.

FIGURE 14.2 Ultimate and local base levels.
(a) The concepts of ultimate base level (sea level) and local base level (natural, such as a lake, or artificial, such as a dam). Note how base level curves gently upward from the sea as it is traced inland; this is the theoretical limit for stream erosion. (b) Glen Canyon Dam became a local base level on the Colorado River when it closed off the canyon, in effect starving the Grand Canyon of needed sediment. [Bobbé Christopherson.]

(a)

(b)

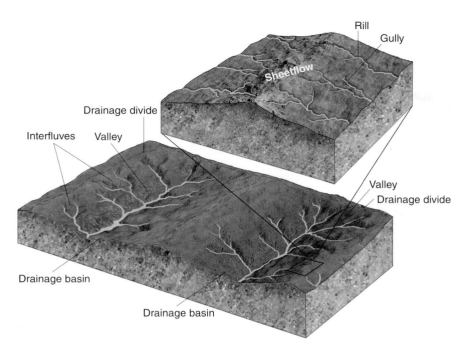

FIGURE 14.3 A drainage basin.
A drainage divide separates the drainage basin and its watershed from other basins.

FIGURE 14.4 A drainage basin system.
Beginning with intricate drainage patterns, water and sediment are collected and delivered to the stream tributaries. This fluidized mass transports to the main trunk and the dispersing system at the end of the stream, where it enters another water body. [After W. K. Hamblin and E. H. Christiansen, *Earth's Dynamic System*, 10th ed., Pearson Prentice Hall, 2004; Figure 12.3, p. 300.]

At the same time, precipitation in northern Alberta feeds hundreds of streams that flow into the Peace River. The Peace and Athabasca rivers flow into Lake Athabasca, and then into the Slave River, which, in turn, empties into Great Slave Lake. Water from Great Slave Lake flows into the Mackenzie River. The Liard River collects the outflow of all the streams that gathered precipitation in northeastern British Columbia and then joins the Mackenzie at Fort Simpson, and continues northward past Inuvik into the Beaufort Sea and the Arctic Ocean. Each contributing tributary, large or small, adds its flow and sediment load to the larger river. When water collects in lakes, sediment accumulates. Sediment weathered and eroded in south-central Alberta and northeastern British Columbia is carried by rivers and deposited in the Peace, Athabasca, Slave River, and Mackenzie river deltas.

Imagine the complexity of an international drainage basin, such as the Danube River in Europe, that flows 2850 km from western Germany's Black Forest to the Black Sea. The river crosses or forms the borders between nine countries (Figure 14.6). A total area of 817 000 km² falls within the drainage basin, including some 300 tributaries.

The Danube serves many economic functions: commercial transport, municipal water source, agricultural irrigation, fishing, and hydroelectric-power production. An international struggle is underway to save the river from its burden of industrial and mining wastes, sewage, chemical discharge, agricultural runoff, and drainage from ships. The many shipping canals actually spread pollution and worsen biological conditions in the river. All of this pollution passes through Romania and the deltaic ecosystems in the Black Sea. The river is widely regarded as one of the most polluted on Earth.

Political changes in Europe in 1989 allowed the first scientific analysis of the entire river system. The United Nations Environment Programme (UNEP) and the European Union, along with other organizations, are dedicated to clearing the Danube, saving deltaic ecosystems, and restoring the environment of this valuable resource; see http://www.icpdr.org/.

Drainage Basins as Open Systems Drainage basins such as the Danube are open systems. Inputs include precipitation and the minerals and rocks of the regional geology. Energy and materials are redistributed as the stream

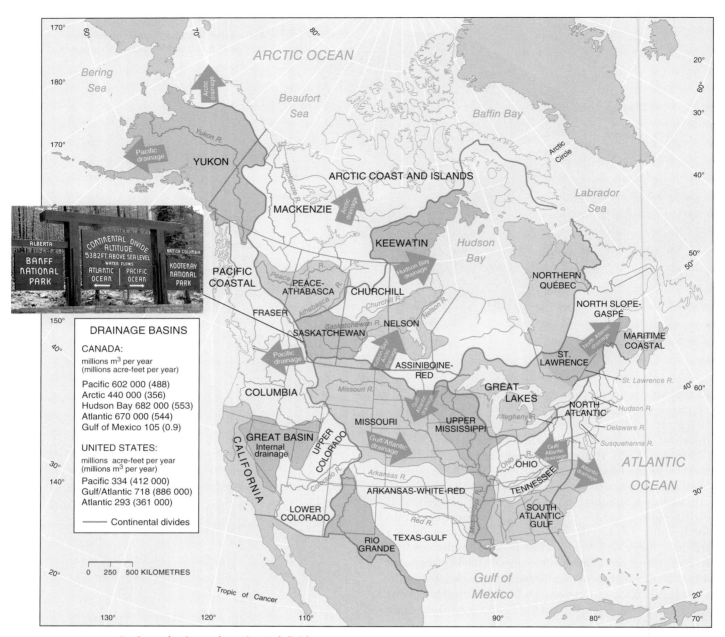

FIGURE 14.5 Drainage basins and continental divides.
Continental divides (blue lines) separate the major drainage basins that empty into the Pacific, Atlantic, and Gulf of Mexico and, to the north, through Canada into Hudson Bay and the Arctic Ocean. Subdividing these large-scale basins are major river basins. The sign in the inset photo should actually indicate the divide between "Arctic" and "Pacific" drainage. [After US Geological Survey; The National Atlas of Canada, 1985, Energy, Mines, and Resources Canada; and Environment Canada, *Currents of Change: Final Report - Inquiry on Federal Water Policy*, p. 26, 1985. Adapted with the permission of the Minister of Public Works and Government Services, 2011. Photo by Robert Christopherson.]

CRITICAL THINKING 14.1

Locate Your Drainage Basin

Determine the name of the drainage basin within which your institution is located. Is there a major river? Where are its headwaters? Where is the river's mouth? In Canada use Figure 14.5 to locate the larger drainage basins and divides for your region. Does any regulatory organization oversee planning and coordination for the drainage basin you identified? Does the library or your geography department have topographic maps on file that cover this region?

constantly adjusts to its landscape. System outputs of water and sediment disperse through the mouth of the river into a lake, another river, or the ocean, as shown in Figure 14.4.

Change that occurs in any portion of a drainage basin can affect the entire system. The stream adjusts to carry the appropriate load of sediment relative to its discharge. If a river system is brought to a threshold where it can no longer maintain its present form, the river system may become destabilized, initiating a transition period to a more stable condition. A river system constantly struggles toward

Danube River delta

FIGURE 14.6 An international drainage basin—the Danube River.
The Danube crosses or forms the border of ten countries as it flows across Europe to the Black Sea. The river carries polluted discharge into the Black Sea through its arcuate-form delta. [*Terra* image, June 15, 2002, NASA/GSFC.]

equilibrium among the interacting variables of discharge, sediment load, channel shape, and channel steepness.

An Example: Mackenzie River Basin Let us take a closer look at the Mackenzie River basin within the Arctic Ocean drainage region (Figure 14.7). The main headwaters of the Mackenzie River are in the Peace River and the Athabasca River. The basin encompasses 1.8 million km² and is the longest river in Canada. The Mackenzie River's discharge at its mouth is 9700 m³·s⁻¹ and is second, in Canada, only to that of the St. Lawrence. Although peak discharge occurs in June, the flow is generally uniform due to the flatness of the land surrounding the river and because the land east of the river contains many large lakes that help sustain its flow throughout the year. From the head of the Finlay River, a tributary of the Peace, the Mackenzie River system is 4241 km long, second longest in North America after the Mississippi–Missouri river system.

The Mackenzie Basin includes six subbasins, three major deltas, three great lakes, and more than 30 000 lakes of various sizes. From its headwaters to the Beaufort Sea, it crosses three climatic regions—the boreal, the subarctic, and the arctic regions—and four physiographic regions: the Western Cordillera, the Canadian Shield, the Interior Plains, and the Mackenzie Delta. Almost 75% of the basin is affected by permafrost; the average monthly temperature is about −2.5°C, and the mean annual precipitation is 410 mm with mean annual evapotranspiration of 237 mm.

More than 90% of the 360 000 residents of the Mackenzie Basin live in the southern part of the basin. The river system is a source of water, power, and transportation. The management of this resource will be critically important as climate change proceeds.

Internal Drainage Most streams find their way to progressively larger rivers and eventually into the ocean. In some regions, however, stream drainage does not reach the

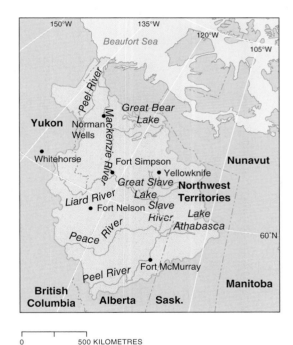

FIGURE 14.7 The Mackenzie River drainage basin.
The basin is under study by a group of Earth scientists to assess the potential impact of global warming on a northern river system. [Map courtesy of the Mackenzie River Board and Aurora Research Institute.]

ocean. Instead, such streams terminate in areas of **internal drainage** and the water leaves the drainage basin only by means of evaporation or subsurface gravitational flow.

Portions of Asia, Africa, Australia, Mexico, and the western United States have regions with internal drainage patterns. Internal drainage defines the region of the Great Basin of the western United States, as shown on maps in Figures 14.5 and 15.22a. For example, the Humboldt River flows west across Nevada, where evaporation and seepage losses to groundwater make it disappear into the

Humboldt "sink." Many streams and creeks flow into the Great Salt Lake, but its only outlet is evaporation, so it exemplifies a region of internal drainage. The Dead Sea region in the Middle East and the areas around the Aral Sea and Caspian Sea in Asia have no outlet to the ocean.

Drainage Density and Patterns A primary feature of any drainage basin is its **drainage density**, determined by dividing the total length of all stream channels in the basin by the area of the basin. The number and length of channels in a given area reflects the climate and the landscape's regional geology and topography. The **drainage pattern** is the arrangement of stream channels in an area.

The *Terra* satellite image and topographic map in Figure 14.8 are of a portion of the province of Québec north of the Ottawa River. The drainage pattern here is *deranged*—the geometry of the drainage is not clear and there is no organized pattern of stream channels. The drainage pattern developed in this manner because glaciation removed much of the sediment covering the bedrock

in the area. The Canadian Shield is close to the surface. Rivers do not have the ability to easily erode downward into the rock and will therefore follow preexisting, glacially scoured, low areas in the rock surface. Over a much longer period of time (the glaciers melted only about 10 000 years ago), the rivers will be able to erode downward into the rock and create a more organized drainage pattern.

Common Drainage Patterns The seven most common drainage patterns are shown in Figure 14.9. A most familiar pattern is *dendritic drainage* (Figure 14.9a). This treelike pattern (Greek *dendron*, or "tree") is similar to that of many natural systems, such as capillaries in the human circulatory system, the vein patterns in leaves, and tree roots. Energy expended by this drainage system is efficient because the overall length of the branches is minimized.

The *trellis drainage* pattern (Figure 14.9b) is characteristic of dipping or folded topography. Such drainage exists in the nearly parallel mountain folds of the Ridge and

(a)

(b)

FIGURE 14.8 Deranged drainage in Québec.
(a) Deranged drainage on the Canadian Shield in Québec, north of the Ottawa River. The box indicates the area shown in the topographic map. (b) Topographic map covering a portion of the area in the satellite image. [Image (a) courtesy of NASA/GSFC; (b) map from the Canada Centre for Remote Sensing, Natural Resources Canada. Used by permission of the Minister of Public Works and Government Services.]

0   125   250 KILOMETRES

Valley Province in the eastern United States. The inset sketch to Figure 14.9b suggests that a headward-eroding part of one stream (to the lower right of the inset) could break through a drainage divide and *capture* the headwaters of another stream in the next valley, and indeed this does happen. The dotted line is the abandoned former channel. The sharp bends in two of the streams in the illustration are called *elbows of capture* and are evidence that one stream has breached a drainage divide. This type of capture, or *stream piracy*, can also occur in other drainage patterns.

The remaining drainage patterns in Figure 14.9c–g are responses to other specific structural conditions:

- A *radial* drainage pattern (c) results when a stream flows off a central peak or dome, such as occurs on a volcanic mountain.
- *Parallel* drainage (d) is associated with steep slopes.
- A *rectangular* pattern (e) is formed in a faulted and jointed landscape, which directs stream courses in patterns of right-angle turns.
- *Annular* patterns (f) are produced by structural domes, with concentric patterns of rock strata guiding stream courses. Figure 12.10c provides an example of annular drainage on a dome structure.
- In areas having disrupted surface patterns, such as the glaciated shield regions of Canada, northern Europe, and some parts of Michigan and other states, a deranged pattern (g) is in evidence, with no clear geometry in the drainage and no organized stream valley pattern (see Figure 17.14a).

CRITICAL THINKING 14.2

Identifying Drainage Patterns

Examine the photograph in Figure CT 14.2.1, where you see two distinct drainage patterns. Of the seven types illustrated in Figure 14.9, which two patterns are most like those in the aerial photo, made in central Montana? Looking back in this discussion to the example in Figure 14.4, which drainage pattern do you assign to it? Explain. The next time you fly in an airplane, remember to get a window seat so that you can observe drainage patterns.

FIGURE CT 14.2.1 Two drainage patterns dominate this scene from central Montana, in response to local relief and rock structure. [Bobbé Christopherson.]

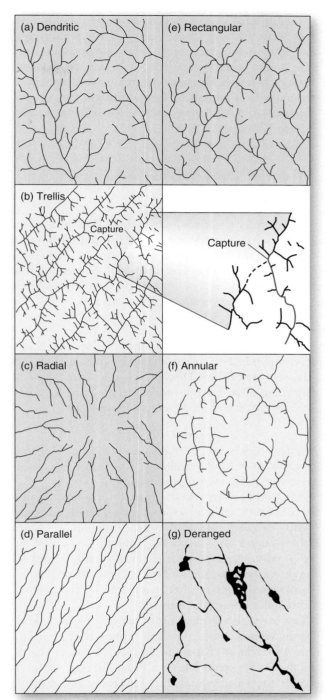

FIGURE 14.9 The seven most common drainage patterns. Each pattern is a visual summary of all the geologic and climatic conditions of its region. [(a) through (g) after A. D. Howard, "Drainage analysis in geological interpretation: A summation," *Bulletin of American Association of Petroleum Geologists* 51 (1967): 2248, adapted by permission.]

Occasionally, drainage patterns occur that are discordant with the surrounding landscape. For example, a drainage system may flow in apparent conflict with older, buried structures that have been uncovered by erosion, so that the streams appear to be *superimposed*. Where an existing stream flows as rocks are uplifted, the stream keeps its original course, cutting into the rock in a pattern contrary to its structure. Such a stream is a *superposed stream* (the stream cuts across weak and resistant rocks alike). A few examples include Wills Creek, cutting a water gap through Haystack Mountain at Cumberland, Maryland; the Columbia River through the Cascade Mountains of Washington; and the River Arun that cuts across the Himalayas.

Fluvial Processes and Landforms

A mass of water positioned above base level in a stream has potential energy. As the water flows downslope, or downstream, under the influence of gravity, this energy becomes kinetic energy. The rate of this conversion from potential to kinetic energy depends on the steepness of the stream channel and volume of water involved.

Stream Discharge

Discharge, or the stream's volume of flow per unit of time, is dependent on stream channel width and depth and on the velocity of flow. Discharge is calculated by multiplying these three variables for a specific cross section of the channel, as stated in the simple expression:

$$Q = wdv$$

where Q = discharge, w = channel width, d = channel depth, and v = stream velocity. Discharge is typically expressed in cubic metres per second ($m^3 \cdot s^{-1}$).

As Q increases in a downstream direction with inflow from tributaries, channel width, channel depth, or stream velocity—or more commonly some combination of these variables—must also increase. Note that velocity may increase with greater discharge downstream, despite the common misperception that flow becomes more sluggish. The increased velocity often is masked by the apparent smooth, quiet flow of the water.

Discharge also changes over time at any specific channel cross section, especially during periods of high flow. Figure 14.10 shows changes in the San Juan River channel in Utah that occurred during a flood. Greater discharge increases the velocity and therefore the capacity of the river to transport sediment as the flood progresses. As a result, the river's ability to scour materials from its bed is enhanced. Such scouring represents a powerful clearing action, especially in the excavation of alluvium.

You can see in Figure 14.10 that the San Juan River's channel was deepest on October 14, when floodwaters were highest (blue line). Then, as the discharge returned to normal, the kinetic energy of the river was reduced, and the bed again filled as sediments were redeposited. You can see this process in the progression of the red, green, and purple lines. The flood and scouring process graphed in Figure 14.10 moved a depth of about 3 m of sediment from this channel cross section. This type of channel adjustment occurs as the system continuously works

September 15, 1941

(b)

(a)

FIGURE 14.10 A flood affects a stream channel.
(a) Channel cross sections showing the effects of a 1941 flood on the San Juan River near Bluff, Utah. (b) Detail of channel profile on September 15, 1941. [USGS Professional Paper 252, p. 32.]

toward equilibrium, in an effort to balance discharge and sediment load with channel form.

Dam-Controlled Discharge and Sediment Redistribution

Glen Canyon Dam on the Colorado River near the Utah–Arizona border controls discharge and blocks sediment from flowing into the Grand Canyon downstream (see the map in Focus Study 15.1, Figure 15.1.1). Consequently, over the years, the river's sediment supply was cut off, starving the river's beaches for sand, disrupting fisheries, and depleting backwater channels of nutrients.

In 1996, 2004, and 2008, an unprecedented series of scouring–redistribution–deposition experiments took place as the Grand Canyon was artificially flooded with dam-controlled releases. The first test lasted for 7 days. The later tests were of shorter duration and were timed to coincide with floods in tributaries that supplied fresh sediment to the system.

The results were mixed and the benefits turned out to be limited, as ecosystems were disrupted and some sediment deposits were immediately eroded away. Present thinking is that the problem is sediment supply—that is, not enough sediment is present in the system to build beaches and improve habitat. Sediment redistribution is still being monitored. See http://www.gcmrc.gov/ for progress reports and analysis.

Exotic Streams

In most river basins in humid regions, discharge increases in a downstream direction. The Mississippi River is typical. It starts as many small streams and grows to a mighty river pouring into the Gulf of Mexico. However, if a stream originates in a humid region and subsequently flows through an arid region, this relationship may change. High potential evapotranspiration rates in the arid regions may cause discharge to decrease with distance downstream. Such a stream is an **exotic stream** (*exotic* means "of foreign origin").

The Nile River exemplifies exotic streams. This great river, Earth's longest, drains much of northeastern Africa. But as it courses through the deserts of Sudan and Egypt, it loses water instead of gaining it, because of evaporation and withdrawal for agriculture. By the time it empties into the Mediterranean Sea, the Nile's flow has dwindled so much that it ranks only 36th in discharge.

In the United States, the Colorado River is notable as an exotic stream. Discharge decreases with distance from its source; in fact, the river no longer produces enough discharge to reach its mouth in the Gulf of California—only some agricultural runoff remains at its delta. The exotic Colorado River is depleted not only by passage across dry,

desert lands but also by upstream removal of water for agriculture and municipal uses; see Focus Study 15.1.

Stream Erosion and Transportation

A stream's erosional turbulence and abrasion carve and shape the landscape through which it flows. **Hydraulic action** is the work of flowing water alone. Running water causes hydraulic squeeze-and-release action that loosens and lifts rocks. As this debris moves along, it mechanically erodes the streambed further, through the process of **abrasion**, with rock particles grinding and carving the streambed like liquid sandpaper.

The upstream tributaries in a drainage basin usually have small and irregular discharges, and most of the stream's energy is expended in turbulent eddies. As a result, hydraulic action in these upstream sections is at a maximum, whereas the coarse-textured load of such a stream is small. The downstream portions of a river move much larger volumes of water past a given point and carry larger suspended loads of sediment (Figure 14.11).

You may have watched a river or stream after a rainfall, the water coloured brown by the high sediment load being transported. The amount of material available to a stream depends on topographic relief, the nature of rock and soil through which the stream flows, climate, vegetation, and human activity in a drainage basin. *Competence*, which is a stream's ability to move particles of a specific size, is a function of stream velocity and the available energy to suspend materials. *Capacity* is the total possible sediment load that a stream can transport at a particular discharge. Four processes transport eroded materials:

(a)

(b)

FIGURE 14.11 Stream velocity and discharge increase together.
(a) A low-volume, low-velocity (but turbulent) mountain stream, the Athabasca River in Jasper National Park. (b) High-discharge, high-velocity (but laminar, smooth water flow) portion of the Bow River in Banff National Park. [Robert Christopherson.]

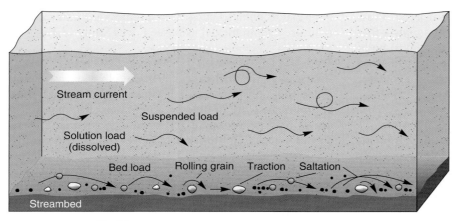

FIGURE 14.12 Fluvial transport.
Fluvial transportation of eroded materials through
suspension, solution, saltation, and traction.

solution, suspension, saltation, and traction; each is shown in action in Figure 14.12.

Solution refers to the **dissolved load** of a stream, especially the chemical solution derived from minerals such as limestone or dolomite or from soluble salts. The main contributor of material in solution is chemical weathering. Sometimes the undesirable salt content that hinders human use of some rivers comes from dissolved rock formations and from springs in the stream channel; as an example, the San Juan and Little Colorado rivers that flow into the Colorado River near the Utah–Arizona border add dissolved salts to the system.

The **suspended load** consists of fine-grained, clastic particles (bits and pieces of rock). These particles are held aloft in the stream, with the finest grains not deposited until the stream velocity slows nearly to zero. Turbulence in the water, with random upward motion, is an important mechanical factor in holding a load of sediment in suspension.

Bed load refers to coarser materials that are dragged, rolled, or pushed along the streambed by **traction** or that are moved by **saltation**, where particles bounce along in short hops and jumps (from the Latin *saltim*, which means "by leaps or jumps"). Particles transported by saltation are too large to remain in suspension but are not limited to the sliding and rolling motion of traction. These processes relate directly to a stream's velocity and its ability to retain particles in suspension. With increased kinetic energy, parts of the bed load are rafted upward and become suspended load.

If the load (bed and suspended) exceeds a stream's capacity, sediments accumulate as **aggradation** (the opposite of degradation) and the stream channel builds up through deposition. With excess sediment, a stream becomes a maze of interconnected channels that form a **braided stream** pattern (Figure 14.13). Braiding often occurs when reduced discharge lowers a stream's transporting ability, such as after flooding, or when a landslide occurs upstream, or from increased load where weak banks of sand or gravel exist. Braided rivers commonly occur in glacial environments, which have abundant supplies of sediment and steep channel slopes, as in the case of the Sunwapta River in Alberta. Glacial materials also exceed stream capacity in the 15-km stretch of the Brahmaputra River about 35 km south of Lhasa, Tibet (Figure 14.13b).

Flow and Channel Characteristics

Flow characteristics of a stream are best seen in a cross-sectional view. The greatest velocities in a stream are near the surface at the centre of the channel (Figure 14.14), corresponding to the deepest part of the stream channel. Velocities decrease closer to the sides and bottom of the channel because of the frictional drag on the water flow. The portion of the stream flowing at maximum velocity moves diagonally across the stream from bend to bend in a meandering stream, and corresponds to the deepest part of the channel termed the *thalweg*.

Flow becomes *turbulent* in shallow streams, or where the channel is rough, as in a section of rapids. Small eddies are caused by friction between streamflows and the channel sides and bed. Complex turbulent flows propel sand, pebbles, and even boulders, increasing the suspension, traction, and saltation.

Where slope is gradual, stream channels develop a sinuous (snakelike) form, weaving across the landscape. This action produces a **meandering stream**. The tendency to meander is evidence of a river system's struggle to operate with least effort, between self-organizing order (equilibrium) and chaotic disorder in nature.

The outer portion of each meandering curve is subject to the fastest water velocity and therefore the greatest scouring erosive action; it can be the site of a steep bank, the **undercut bank**, or *cutbank* (Figure 14.14 and 14.15).

GEO REPORT 14.1   *River Rumbles*

The early explorers who visited the Grand Canyon reported in their journals that they were kept awake at night by the thundering sound of the river and rapids and bed load. Imagine the tremendous quantity of material being moved along by the natural Colorado River before any dams were built. Dams and reservoirs now trap much of the sediment that formerly contributed to the river's bed load.

(a)   (b)

FIGURE 14.13 **A braided stream.**
(a) Sunwapta River, along the Icefields Parkway, southern Jasper National Park, Alberta. (b) A 15-km stretch along the braided Brahmaputra River channel some 35 km south of Lhasa, Tibet, in a narrow valley south of the Tibetan Plateau. These streams reflect excessive sediment load associated with glacial meltwaters filled with fine sediments, or "glacial flour." [Photos (a) Courtesy of the Geological Survey of Canada. Photo 2002-597 by Réjean Couture and Gianluca Bianchi Fasani. Reproduced with the permission of Natural Resources Canada. © 2012. (b) October 13, 2001, International Space Station astronaut, courtesy of Earth Science and Image Analysis Lab, JSC/NASA.]

In contrast, the inner portion of a meander experiences the slowest water velocity and thus receives sediment fill, forming a **point bar** deposit. As meanders develop, these scour-and-fill features gradually work at stream banks. As a result, the landscape near a meandering river bears meander scars of residual deposits from previous river channels (see Figure 14.22). The photograph of the Itkillik River in Alaska, Figure 14.15a, shows both meanders and meander scars.

FIGURE 14.14 **Meandering stream profile.**
Oblique view and cross sections of a meandering stream, showing the location of maximum flow velocity, point bar deposits, and areas of undercut bank erosion.

GEO REPORT 14.2   *The First Meanders*

The term *meander* comes from the ancient Greek Maiandros River in Asia Minor (the present-day Menderes River in Turkey). The Maiandros appears in Greek mythology and written accounts as early as the second century B.C. Its meandering channel came to describe this pattern in other river channels.

FIGURE 14.15 Meandering stream development.
(a) Itkillik River in Alaska. (b) Development of a river meander and an oxbow lake simplified in four stages. [(a) USGS.]

Stream Processes, Floodplains, Oxbow Lake Formation

Meandering streams create a remarkable looping pattern on the landscape, as shown in the four-part sequence in Figure 14.15b. In this model (1), the stream erodes its outside bank as the curve migrates downstream, forming a neck. In (2), the narrowing neck of land created by the looping meander eventually erodes through and forms a *cutoff* in (3). A cutoff marks an abrupt change in the stream's lateral movements—the stream becomes straighter.

When the former meander becomes isolated from the rest of the river, the resulting **oxbow lake** (4) may gradually fill with organic debris and silt or may again become part of the river when it floods. Changing patterns of flow affect the river over time. How many of these stream features—meanders, oxbow lakes, cutoffs—can you spot in the aerial photo in Figure 14.16, looking east across northern Argentina?

Streams often form natural political boundaries, and it is easy to see how disagreements might arise when boundaries are based on river channels that change course. There are several locations between Canada and the United States where rivers are used as the divide for the international boundary. The International Boundary Commission (IBC) is responsible for maintaining the boundary between the two countries in a clearly marked fashion and for defining the location of the boundary for any legal situation involving the border.

FIGURE 14.16 Meandering stream.
Meandering streams catch the morning light over northern Argentina. Identify where former meanders were cut off, oxbow lakes, and former stream channels. Several inversion layers are visible in the far distance, as the burning of tropical rain forest to the north fills the air with smoke. [Bobbé Christopherson.]

FIGURE 14.17 The St. Croix River.
The boundary between New Brunswick and Maine is determined by the thalweg of the St. Croix River.

An interesting case of river boundaries involves the determination of the St. Croix River as the boundary between Maine in the United States and New Brunswick in Canada (Figure 14.17). In 1783 with the Treaty of Paris, the boundaries between the United States and what is now Canada were drawn up. It was agreed that the St. Croix River would be the boundary. Disputes arose over whether the channel margins, channel midline, or some other location was the actual boundary. The St. Croix River was the first to have an identification attached that was based on the function of the river. The boundary was determined to be the *thalweg* (zone of maximum depth) of the river. Recognizing that the thalweg changed over time with erosion and deposition along the riverbank, the commissioners relied on river soundings taken by the United States Coast Guard and the Geodetic Survey to determine the location of the thalweg. The thalweg was then mathematically calculated and plotted on a map. So, although the river was used as the boundary, potential disputes were resolved through reference to the stream's hydrology. Ideally boundaries should not be fixed to river locations because border disputes result when river channels change course.

Stream Gradient

Every stream has a degree of inclination or **gradient**, which is the rate of elevation decline from its headwaters to its mouth. A stream's gradient generally forms a concave-shaped slope (Figure 14.18). Characteristically, the *longitudinal profile* of a stream (a side view) has a steeper slope upstream and a more gradual slope downstream. This curve assumes its shape for complex reasons related to the stream's ability to do enough work to accomplish the transport of the load it receives.

Streams tend to adjust their gradient and other channel characteristics so that discharge can move the sediment supply. A **graded stream** condition occurs when channels adjust their slope, size, and shape so that a stream has just enough energy to transport its sediment load. This condition is a state of *dynamic equilibrium* among discharge, sediment load, and channel form. The stream, channel, and landscape work together to maintain this balance within a drainage basin. Both high-gradient and low-gradient streams can achieve a graded condition. A stream's profile tells geographers about characteristics of slope, discharge, and load.

> A graded stream is one in which, over a period of years, slope is delicately adjusted to provide, with available *discharge* and with prevailing *channel characteristics*, just the velocity required for transportation of the load supplied from the drainage basin.[1]

[1] J. H. Mackin, "Concept of the graded river," *Geological Society of America Bulletin* 59 (1948): 463.

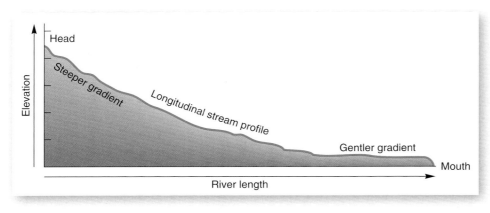

FIGURE 14.18 An ideal longitudinal profile.
The sloping profile of a stream is its gradient. Upstream segments have a steeper gradient; downstream, the gradient is gentler. The middle and lower portions in the illustration appear graded, or in dynamic equilibrium.

Attainment of a graded condition does not mean that the stream is at its lowest gradient, but rather that it has reached a balance among erosion, transportation, and deposition over time along a specific portion of the stream. One problem with applying the graded stream concept is that an individual stream can have both graded and ungraded portions. It may have graded sections without having an overall graded slope. In fact, variations and interruptions are the rule rather than the exception.

Stream gradient may be affected by tectonic uplift of the landscape, which changes the base level. If tectonic forces slowly lift the landscape, the stream gradient will increase, stimulating renewed erosional activity. A meandering stream flowing through the uplifted landscape becomes *rejuvenated*; that is, the river actively returns to downcutting and can eventually form entrenched *meanders* in the landscape. Figure 14.19 depicts actual rejuvenated landscapes.

Nickpoints When the longitudinal profile of a stream shows an abrupt change in gradient, such as at a waterfall or an area of rapids, the point of interruption is a **nickpoint** (also spelled *knickpoint*). At a nickpoint, the conversion of potential energy in the water at the lip of the falls to concentrated kinetic energy at the base works

to eliminate the nickpoint interruption and smooth out the gradient. Figure 14.20a shows a stream with two such interruptions.

Nickpoints can result when a stream flows across a zone of hard, resistant rock or from various tectonic uplift episodes, such as might occur along a fault line. Temporary blockage in a channel, caused by a landslide or a logjam, also could be considered a nickpoint; when the logjam breaks, the stream quickly readjusts its channel to its former grade.

Waterfalls are interesting and beautiful gradient breaks. At the edge of a fall, a stream is free-falling, moving at high velocity under the acceleration of gravity, causing increased abrasion and hydraulic action in the channel below. The increased action generally undercuts the waterfall. Eventually the excavation will cause the rock ledge at the lip of the fall to collapse, and the waterfall will shift a bit farther upstream. The height of the waterfall is gradually reduced as debris accumulates at its base (see Figure 14.21b). Thus, a nickpoint migrates upstream, sometimes for kilometres, until it becomes a series of rapids and is eventually eliminated.

At Niagara Falls on the Ontario–New York border, glaciers advanced over the region and then receded some 13 000 years ago. In doing so, the glaciers exposed resistant

(a)

(b)

FIGURE 14.19 Aerial views of entrenched meanders.
(a) The San Juan River near Mexican Hat, Utah, cuts down into the uplifted Colorado Plateau landscape, producing the entrenched meanders of the Goosenecks of the San Juan. (b) Entrenched meanders near Hall's Creek along Waterpocket Fold in Capitol Reef National Park, Utah. [Bobbé Christopherson.]

(a)

FIGURE 14.20 Nickpoints interrupt a stream profile.
(a) Longitudinal stream profile showing nickpoints produced by resistant rock strata. Potential energy is converted into kinetic energy and concentrated at the nickpoint, accelerating erosion, which will eventually eliminate the feature. (b) Falls and rapids break the flow of the Big Sioux River in Sioux Falls, South Dakota. [Bobbé Christopherson.]

(b)

(a)

(b)

(c)

(d)

FIGURE 14.21 Retreat of Niagara Falls.
(a) Headward retreat of Niagara Falls from the Niagara escarpment. It has taken the falls about 12 000 years to reach this position at a pace of about 1.3 m per year. (b) The escarpment seen from below American Falls. (c) Niagara Falls, with the American Falls portion almost completely shut off by upstream controls for engineering inspection. Horseshoe Falls in the background is still flowing over its 57-m plunge. (d) In contrast to (c), American Falls in full discharge. [(a) After W. K. Hamblin, *Earth's Dynamic Systems*, 6th ed., Pearson Prentice Hall, Inc. © 1992, Figure 12.15, p. 246. (c) Courtesy of the New York Power Authority. (b) and (d) Bobbé Christopherson.]

Niagara Falls

rock strata that are underlain by less-resistant shales. This tilted formation is a *cuesta*, which is a ridge with a steep slope on one side and beds gently sloping away on the other side (Figure 14.21a). This Niagara escarpment actually stretches across more than 700 km from east of the falls, northward through Ontario, the Upper Peninsula of Michigan, curving south through Wisconsin along the western shore of Lake Michigan and the Door Peninsula. As this less-resistant material continues to weather away, the overlying rock strata collapse, allowing Niagara Falls to erode farther upstream toward Lake Erie.

Niagara Falls is a place where natural processes labour to eliminate a nickpoint and reduce this portion of the river to a series of mere rapids. In fact, the falls have retreated more than 11 km from the steep face of the Niagara escarpment. A nickpoint is a relatively temporary and mobile feature on the landscape. In the past, engineers have used control facilities upstream to reduce flows over the American Falls at Niagara for inspection of cliff erosion; compare this reduced flow (Figure 14.21c) to normal discharge (Figure 14.21d).

Stream Deposition and Landforms

After weathering, mass movement, erosion, and transportation, deposition is the next logical event in the sequence.

In *deposition*, alluvium, or unconsolidated sediments, settles out from the streamflow, thereby creating depositional landforms, such as floodplains, terraces, or deltas.

As discussed earlier, stream meanders tend to migrate downstream through the landscape. Over time, the landscape near a meandering river comes to bear meander scars of residual deposits from former, abandoned channels. Former point-bar deposits leave low-lying ridges, creating a *bar-and-swale relief* (a swale is a gentle low area), forming a *scroll topography*. The *Landsat* image in Figure 14.22 exhibits characteristic meandering scars: meander bends, oxbow lakes, natural levees, point bars, and undercut banks.

Floodplains The flat, low-lying area flanking many stream channels that is subjected to recurrent flooding is a **floodplain**. It is formed when the river overflows its channel during times of high flow. Thus, when floods occur, the floodplain is inundated. When the water recedes, it leaves behind alluvial deposits that generally mask the underlying rock with accumulating thickness. The present river channel is embedded in these alluvial deposits. Figure 14.23 illustrates a characteristic floodplain, related features in photos, and a representative topographic map of an area near Philipp, Mississippi.

FIGURE 14.22 The Mississippi River's shifting meanders through history.
The former river channels for 1765, 1820, 1880, and 1944 are noted for the portion of the river north of the Old River Cutoff. [Army Corps of Engineers, *Geological Investigation of the Alluvial Valley of the Lower Mississippi*, 1944; *Landsat*, NASA and UMD Global Land Cover Facility, http://glcf.umiacs.umd.edu/index.shtml.]

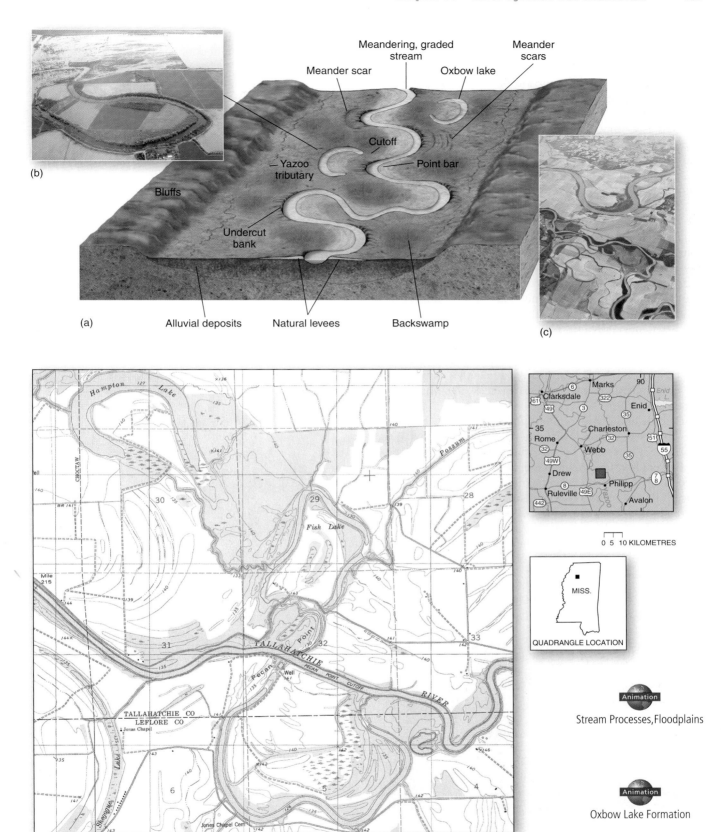

FIGURE 14.23 A floodplain.
(a) Typical floodplain landscape and related landscape features. (b) An oxbow lake. (c) Levees, oxbow lakes, yazoo tributary, and farmland on a typical floodplain in the upper Midwest. (d) A portion of the Philipp, Mississippi, topographic map quadrangle. [(b) and (c) Bobbé Christopherson. (d) USGS topographic map.]

On either bank of some streams, **natural levees** develop as by-products of flooding. When floodwaters rise, the river overflows its banks, loses stream velocity as it spreads out, and drops a portion of its sediment load to form the levees. Larger, sand-sized particles drop out first, forming the principal component of the levees, with finer silts and clays deposited farther from the river. Successive floods increase the height of the levees (*levée* is French for "raising"). The levees may grow in height until the river channel becomes elevated, or *perched*, above the surrounding floodplain.

On the topographic map (Figure 14.23d), you can see the natural levees represented by several contour lines that run immediately adjacent to the Tallahatchie River. These contour lines (5-ft interval) denote a height of 10–15 ft (3–4.5 m) above the river and the adjoining floodplain. Next time you have an opportunity to see a river and its floodplain, look for levees, which may be low and subtle.

Notice in Figure 14.23a the backswamp area and the yazoo tributary stream. The natural levees and elevated channel of the river prevent this **yazoo tributary** from joining the main channel, so it flows parallel to the river and through the **backswamp** area. The name comes from the Yazoo River in the southern part of the Mississippi floodplain.

People build cities on floodplains despite the threat of flooding because floodplains are nearly level and are next to water. There may be historic momentum for settlement. People often are encouraged by government assurances of artificial protection from floods and disaster assistance if floods occur. Government assistance may provide for the building of artificial levees on top of natural levees. Artificial levees do increase the capacity in the channel, but can also lead to even greater floods when overtopped by floodwaters or when levee failure occurs, as happened in New Orleans (Figure 14.24).

Perhaps the best use of some floodplains is for crop agriculture because inundation generally delivers nutrients to the land with each new alluvial deposit. A significant example is the Nile River in Egypt, where annual flooding enriches the soil. However, floodplains that are covered with coarse sediment—sand and gravel—are less suitable for agriculture. If floodplains are present where you live, what is your impression of present land-use patterns, local planning and zoning, and people's hazard perception overall?

Stream Terraces An uplifting of the landscape, a lowering of base level, or a change in climatic condition may rejuvenate stream energy so that a stream again scours downward with renewed vigour and increased erosion. The resulting entrenchment of the river deeper into its own floodplain produces **alluvial terraces** on either side of the valley, which look like topographic steps above the river. Alluvial terraces generally appear paired at similar elevations on each side of the valley (Figure 14.25). If more than one set of paired terraces is present, the valley probably has undergone more than one episode of rejuvenation.

Alluvial terraces (paired)

(a)

(b)

FIGURE 14.25 Alluvial stream terraces.
(a) Alluvial terraces are formed as a stream cuts into a valley. (b) Alluvial terraces along the Rakaia River in New Zealand. [(a) After W. M. Davis, *Geographical Essays* (New York: Dover, 1964 [1909]), p. 515. (b) Bill Bachman/Photo Researchers, Inc.]

Animation

Stream Terrace
Formation

FIGURE 14.24 Levee break and devastation in New Orleans.
August 30, 2005, view across the Inner Harbor Navigation Canal, as broken levees allow floodwaters to drown the city. A dramatic failure of engineering, levee design and construction, and proper planning. [Vincent Laforet/Pool/Reuters/Corbis.]

If the terraces on either side of the valley do not match in elevation, then entrenchment actions must have been continuous as the river meandered from side to side, with each meander cutting a terrace slightly lower in elevation. Thus, alluvial terraces represent an original depositional feature, a floodplain, subsequently eroded by a stream that has experienced a change in gradient and is downcutting.

River Deltas   The mouth of a river is where it reaches a base level at the edge of a larger, standing body of water such as the sea or a lake. The river's forward velocity rapidly decelerates as it enters the body of water. The reduced stream competence and capacity cause deposition of the sediment load. Coarse sediment such as sand and gravel drops out first and is deposited closest to the river's mouth. Finer clays are carried farther and form the extreme end of the deposit, which may be *subaqueous*, or underwater, even at low tide. The level or nearly level depositional plain that forms at the mouth of a river is a **delta** for its characteristic triangular shape, after the Greek letter delta (Δ).

Each flood stage deposits a new layer of alluvium over the surface of the delta so that it grows outward. Channels divide into smaller courses known as *distributaries*, which appear as a reverse of the dendritic drainage pattern of tributary streams discussed earlier. Here are a few examples:

- The Ganges River delta features an extensive lower delta plain formed in relation to high tidal ranges in an *arcuate* (arc-shaped) pattern. It is covered by an intricate maze of distributaries. Bountiful alluvium carried from slopes upstream, especially those that are deforested, provides excess sediment that is deposited to form many deltaic islands (Figure 14.26). The combined delta complex of the Ganges and Brahmaputra rivers is the largest in the world at some 60 000 km².
- The Nile River delta is an *arcuate* delta (Figure 14.27). Also arcuate are the Danube River delta in Romania, where it enters the Black Sea, and the Indus River delta.
- The Tiber River in Italy has an *estuarine delta*, one that is in the process of filling an **estuary**, which is the seaward mouth of a river where freshwater flow encounters seawater.

Mississippi River Delta   Over the past 120 million years, the Mississippi has transported alluvium throughout its vast basin into the Gulf of Mexico. During the past 5000 years, the river has formed a succession of seven distinct deltaic complexes along the Louisiana coast.

Each generalized lobe in Figure 14.28a reflects a distinct course change in the Mississippi River, probably where the river broke through its natural levees during

FIGURE 14.26 The Ganges River enters the Bay of Bengal.
The complex distributary pattern in the "many mouths" of the Ganges River delta in Bangladesh and extreme eastern India from the Terra satellite. Imagine the devastation to this barely-above-sea-level delta when Tropical Storm Sidr, a category 4, plowed through in November 2007, killing thousands of people on the low-lying islands. [*Terra* MODIS, NASA.]

FIGURE 14.27 **The arcuate Nile River delta.**
Intensive agricultural activity and small settlements are visible on the delta and along the Nile River flood-plain in this true-colour image. Cairo is at the apex of the delta. You can see the two main distributaries: Damietta to the east and Rosetta to the west. [January 30, 2001, *Terra* image, NASA/GSFC/JPL.]

episodes of severe flooding, thus changing the configuration of the delta. The seventh and current delta has been building for at least 500 years and is a classic example of a bird's-foot delta—a long channel with many distributaries and sediments carried beyond the tip of the delta into the Gulf of Mexico.

The Mississippi River delta clearly is dynamic over time as new alluvial material accumulates and the distributaries shift (Figure 14.28b). The main channel persists because of much effort and expense directed at maintaining the artificial levee system. The 3.25 million-km² Mississippi drainage basin produces about 550 million metric tons of sediment annually—enough to extend the Louisiana coast 90 m a year; however, several factors are

actually causing losses to the delta each year. In fact, most of coastal Louisiana, which represents about 40% of the coastal marshes in the United States, is profoundly altered and disrupted by dam and levee construction, flow alterations, oil and gas exploration and pumping, pipelines, and dredging for navigation, logging, and industrial needs. Approximately 65 km² of these Louisiana coastal lowlands are flooded by the Gulf of Mexico in an average year.

Compaction and the tremendous weight of the sediments in the Mississippi River create isostatic adjustments in Earth's crust. These adjustments are causing the entire region of the delta to subside, thereby placing ever-increasing stress on natural and artificial levees and other structures along the lower Mississippi. The many

GEO REPORT 14.3 *The Nile River Delta Is Disappearing*

The Aswân High Dam, built in 1964, caused a decrease in the supply of sediment to the Nile River delta. Also, over the centuries, more than 9000 km of canals were built in the delta to augment the natural distributary system. As the river discharge enters the network of canals, flow velocity is reduced, stream competence and capacity are decreased, and sediment load is deposited far short of the delta margin at the Mediterranean Sea. River flows no longer effectively reach the sea. As a result, the delta coastline continues to actively recede at an alarming rate of 50 to 100 m per year. Seawater is intruding farther inland in both surface water and groundwater. Human action and reaction to this evolving situation will no doubt determine the delta's future.

canals and waterways excavated through the delta by the oil and gas industry and shipping interests have worked to deprive the delta of new alluvial building materials. Also, the pumping of tremendous quantities of oil and gas from thousands of onshore and offshore wells is thought to be a cause of regional land subsidence.

An additional problem for the lower Mississippi Valley is the possibility, in a worst-case flood, that the river could break from its existing channel and seek a new route to the Gulf of Mexico. If you examine the map in Figure 14.28c and the sediment plume to the west of the main delta in the satellite image, an obvious alternative to the Mississippi's present channel is the Atchafalaya River. The Atchafalaya would provide a much shorter route to the Gulf of Mexico,

less than half the present distance, and it has a steeper gradient than the Mississippi. Presently, this alternative-route distributary carries about 30% of the Mississippi's total discharge. For the Mississippi to bypass New Orleans entirely would be a blessing, for it would remove the flood threat. However, this shift would be a financial disaster, as a major U.S. port would silt up and seawater would intrude into freshwater resources.

At present, artificial barriers block the Atchafalaya from reaching the Mississippi at the point shown; without the floodgates the two rivers do connect. The Old River Control Project (1963) maintains three structures and a lock about 320 km from the Mississippi's mouth to keep these rivers in their channels (Figure 14.28d). Many floods have hit the

(a) Seven deltas in 5000 years

[Shaded areas denote areas of previous deltas.]

(b) Mississippi River delta

(c)

(d) Old River Control Auxilliary Structure

FIGURE 14.28 The Mississippi River delta.
(a) Evolution of the present delta, from 5000 years ago (1) to the present (7). (b) The bird's-foot delta of the Mississippi River receives a continuous sediment supply, focused by controlling levees, although subsidence of the delta and rising sea level have diminished the overall surface area. (c) Location map of the Old Control Structures and potential capture point (arrow) where the Atchafalaya River may one day divert the present channel. (d) Old River Control Auxiliary Structure, one of the dams to keep the Mississippi in its channel.
[(a) Adapted from C. R. Kolb and J. R. Van Lopik, "Depositional environments of the Mississippi River deltaic plain," in *Deltas in Their Geologic Framework* (Houston, TX: Houston Geological Society, 1966). (b) *Terra* image courtesy of Liam Gumley, Space Science and Engineering Center, University of Wisconsin, and NASA. (d) Bobbé Christopherson.]

lower Mississippi in the past, such as that in 2003, and Hurricanes Cindy, Katrina, and Rita in 2005 and Gustav in 2008 resulted in major storm surges and flooding. Another major flood—one that might cause the river channel to switch to the Atchafalaya course—is only a matter of time.

Fraser River Delta The Fraser River delta was formed as sediment accumulated where the Fraser River now flows into the Strait of Georgia (Figure 14.29). Deglaciation of the region and the rapid development of the Fraser River floodplain westward down a glacially scoured, partially submerged trough preceded initial delta growth. As the floodplain extended westward, fluvial, deltaic, marine, and lacustrine sediments covered the floor of the trough.

About 10 000 years ago, the Fraser River began to empty directly into the Strait of Georgia through a gap in the Pleistocene uplands at New Westminster. Deposition has advanced the delta front seaward 25 km over the past 10 000 years, creating a landform that covers about 1000 km². Floods deposited silt and clay on the Fraser delta plain until the 1900s, when dikes were constructed for protection of human development. The dikes stabilized the river channel, stifling natural processes. Dredging maintains shipping channels downstream from New Westminster and dredged sand does not make its way to the delta front. The impact of human activity was to decrease the rate of sediment delivery to the edge of the delta. Erosion dominates in some areas, increasing the delta slope and the risk of delta-slope failure. Prehistoric and historic failures are in evidence across the submarine slope of the Fraser delta.

The delta is an important agricultural area with deep, fertile sediment and a favourable climate. Infringing on

FIGURE 14.29 The Fraser Delta.
The delta is located where the river empties into the Strait of Georgia between the lower mainland of British Columbia and Vancouver Island. [*Terra* image NASA/GSFC.]

 GEO REPORT 14.4   *What Is a Bayou?*

Bayou is a general term for several water features in the lower Mississippi River system, including creeks and secondary waterways. These sometimes stagnant, winding watercourses pass through coastal marshlands and swamps and allow tidal waters access to deltaic lowlands.

this land use are urban development and industrial growth in Richmond, Ladner, and Delta, a coal port at Point Roberts, and a ferry terminal at Tsawwassen. The area is also valuable as habitat for migratory waterfowl and salmon fry. These competing uses of the delta are threatened by earthquake hazard. Liquefaction, the fluidization of water-saturated sediment when shaken, will cause subsidence of the delta plain and may cause buildings that are not properly anchored to tilt or collapse. Small earthquakes are common in the area, but a large-scale quake has not happened in the last hundred years. It is only a matter of time until the "big one" hits.

Rivers without Deltas Earth's highest-discharge river is the Amazon; it discharges more than 175 000 m³ · s⁻¹ and carries sediment far into the deep Atlantic deep offshore. Yet the Amazon lacks a true delta. Its mouth, 160 km wide, has formed a subaqueous deposit on a sloping continental shelf. As a result, the Amazon's mouth is braided into a broad maze of islands and channels (see Figure 14.1). The Paraná and Uruguay Rivers form the Rio de la Plata, which also lacks a delta.

A river may lack a deltaic formation if it does not deposit significant amounts of sediment or if it discharges into strong erosive currents. The Columbia River of the U.S. Northwest lacks a delta because offshore currents remove sediment before it can accumulate into a delta.

Floods and River Management

Throughout history, civilizations have settled floodplains and deltas, especially since the agricultural revolution of 10 000 years ago, when the fertility of floodplain soils was discovered. Early villages generally were built away from the area of flooding, or on stream terraces, because the floodplain was dedicated exclusively to farming. However, as commerce grew, competition for sites near rivers grew, because these locations were important for transportation. Port and dock facilities were built, as were river bridges. Because water is a basic industrial raw material used for cooling and for diluting and removing wastes, waterside industrial sites became desirable. These competing human activities on vulnerable flood-prone lands place lives and property at risk during floods.

Catastrophic floods continue to be a threat, especially in less-developed regions of the world. Bangladesh is perhaps the most persistent example: it is one of the most densely populated countries on Earth, and more than *three-fourths* of its land area is a floodplain. The country's vast alluvial plain sprawls over an area the size of the Maritime Provinces (130 000 km²).

The flooding severity in Bangladesh is a consequence of human economic activities, along with heavy precipitation episodes. Excessive forest harvesting in the upstream portions of the Ganges–Brahmaputra River drainage basins increased runoff. Over time, the increased sediment

load carried by the river was deposited in the Bay of Bengal, creating new islands (see Figure 14.26). These islands, barely above sea level, became sites for new farming villages. Subsequently, about 150 000 people perished in the 1988 and 1991 floods and storm surges.

The Indus River, which flows through Pakistan into the Arabian Sea, is another recent example of flooding in a developing part of the world. Heavy monsoon rains in August 2010 swelled the Indus and its many tributaries beyond any previous level in recorded history. Destruction was greater than that from the 2004 Indian Ocean tsunami. More than 20 million Pakistanis were left homeless (Figure 14.30). For information on floods worldwide, see the Dartmouth Flood Observatory at http://www.dartmouth.edu/~floods/Archives/index.html or a daily flood summary at http://www.nws.noaa.gov/oh/hic/current/.

Engineering Failures in New Orleans, 2005

Normally, the city of New Orleans is almost entirely below the level of the Mississippi River, with about half of the city below sea level in elevation. Severe flooding is a certainty for existing and planned settlements unless further intervention or urban relocation occurs. The building of artificial earthen levees, concrete floodwalls, and multiple flood-control structures by the U.S. Army Corps of Engineers apparently have only delayed the peril, as demonstrated by recent flooding. The events of 2005, following the passage of Hurricane Katrina, will remain for many years as one of the greatest engineering failures by the government. Four major levee breaks and at least four dozen levee breaches, in which water flows over the embankment, permitted the inundation of a major city. The polluted water remained for days.

Figure 14.31 from *Landsat*–7 presents matching images of New Orleans along the shore of Lake Pontchartrain on April 24 and August 30, 2005. The map helps you locate the areas that are below sea level, the levees and floodwalls, and the four major breaches. The darker areas on image (b) indicate flooding; some neighbourhoods were submerged up to 6.1 m. At the time of image (b), New Orleans was approximately 80% underwater.

Six investigations by civil engineers, scientists, and political bodies agreed that in concept, design, construction, and maintenance, the "protection" system was flawed. Many of the structures failed before they reached design-failure limits. After all, Hurricane Katrina was diminished in power as it moved onshore. Several of the levee floodwalls and pilings were not anchored to the design depth, such as along the 17th Street Canal (Figure 14.32). This inadequate achoring depth made parts of the system inherently weak. In 2007, inspections by civil engineers found that the composition of levee fill materials throughout the city is too low in clays and too high in sand—a recipe for future problems.

Repair and recovery work in New Orleans is ongoing, and elements of the completed sections appear inadequate

FIGURE 14.30 Indus River flooding, 2010. The image combines visible light and infrared to enhance contrast between the flooded river and land; water appears blue and clouds blue-green. Similar heavy monsoon rains fell across Asia. [*Terra* image NASA/GSFC.]

and positioned for repeat disasters, which nearly occurred in 2008 as Hurricane Gustav followed a track just west of New Orleans. Most levees held, some were overtopped, and extensive flooding occurred in the parishes west and south of the city that had no levees. Hurricane Gustav is regarded as a near-miss from being another Katrina-level disaster for New Orleans.

CRITICAL THINKING 14.3

Review and Assessment of the Post-Katrina Gulf Coast

Using your Internet search engine or browser, type in "New Orleans flooding, 2005" or "Gulf Coast damage, Katrina" or "New Orleans levee failures." Allow some time to sample through at least 10 of the links. Describe what you find. Did you find photo galleries, engineering reports, or news coverage? What did you learn about this region of the lower Mississippi River, including New Orleans and other Gulf Coast cities? What future direction should they take: rebuild things as they were; rethink the hazards and adopt a new strategy of replacing urban with low-density recreation zones; establish possible setback hazard zoning; walk away except for necessary port functions; or abandon the region? Are there other options you think are important?

Rating Floodplain Risk

A **flood** is a high water flow that overflows the natural bank along any portion of a stream. Floods are rated statistically for the expected time intervals between them, based upon historical data. Thus, you hear about "10-year floods," "50-year floods," and so on. A *10-year flood* is likely to occur with an average interval of 10 years. This also means that a flood of this size has only a 10% likelihood of occurring in any one year and is likely to occur about 10 times each century. For any given floodplain, such a frequency indicates a moderate threat.

A 50-year or 100-year flood is of greater and perhaps catastrophic consequence, but it is also less likely to occur in a given year (2% or 1% chance of occurrence in any year, respectively). These probability ratings of flood levels are mapped for an area, and each defined floodplain that results is then labelled a "50-year floodplain" or a "100-year floodplain."

These statistical estimates are probabilities that events will occur randomly during any single year of the specified period. Of course, two decades might pass without

(a) April 24, 2005

(b) August 30, 2005

FIGURE 14.31 **New Orleans before and after the Katrina disaster.** *Landsat–7* images made (a) April 24, 2005, and (b) August 30, 2005, clearly show canal locations and flooded portions of the city; compare features to the locator map. Numerous levee breaks and breaches put 80% of the city underwater for more than a week. [USGS *Landsat* Image Gallery.]

17th St. Canal

FIGURE 14.32 **Levee breach and break.**
The Lakeview neighborhood is under water (to the right) from the 17th Street Canal levee failure, whereas the Metairie neighborhood is essentially dry (to the left). You see debris caught up north of the bridge where steel beams were placed in an attempt to curb flows. Flotsam, or floating debris, is visible in the photo. [NOAA.]

a 50-year flood, or a 50-year level of flooding could occur two years in a row. The record-breaking Mississippi River Valley floods in 1993 easily exceeded a 1000-year flood probability, as did the 2005 Katrina catastrophe. See Focus Study 14.1 for more about floodplain hazards and management strategies.

Stream Discharge Measurement

Flood patterns in a drainage basin are as complex as the weather, for floods and weather are equally variable and both include a level of unpredictability. Measuring and analyzing the behaviour of each large watershed and stream enables engineers and concerned parties to develop the best possible flood-management strategy. Unfortunately, reliable data often are not available for small basins or for the changing landscapes of urban areas.

The key to flood avoidance or management is to possess extensive measurements of a stream's discharge and information on how it performs during a precipitation event (Figure 14.33a). Three measurements are needed at a stream cross section in order to calculate discharge: width, depth, and velocity. Field measurements of these variables may be difficult to obtain, depending on a stream's size and flow. Velocity for different subsections of the stream cross section is most commonly measured using a movable current meter. Width and depth for each subsection are then combined with velocity to compute subsection discharge, and then the subsection discharges across the stream are totalled (see Figure 14.33). Since channel beds are often composed of alluvial deposits that may change over short time

Floodplain Measurement and Strategies

Detailed records of streamflows and flood records have been kept for only about the last 100 years in Canada. The coverage of stream gauging stations is concentrated in the southern part of the country, with stations on lakes, rivers, and streams of many sizes. Data from these recording stations are limited both spatially and temporally. However, hydrological engineers can use these data to model the flows of most rivers in the country. From these models, flooding hazards can be determined. Recurrence intervals of floods are calculated and the most commonly recognized standard is the 100-year flood. This standard is used for floodplain mapping to determine zones where development is limited. Floodplain delineation, assessment of flood risk, and flood forecasting are nonstructural means of flood damage reduction.

In some cases, these do not limit development, and where development occurred prior to modern risk assessment, floods can cause catastrophic damage. A common scenario might go like this: (1) Minimal zoning precautions are not carefully supervised; (2) a flooding disaster occurs; (3) the public is outraged at being caught off guard; (4) businesses and homeowners are surprisingly resistant to stricter laws and enforcement; (5) eventually another flood refreshes the memory and promotes a knee-jerk

reaction. As strange as it seems, there is little indication that our risk perception improves as the risk increases.

Bypass Channels as a Planning Strategy

A planning strategy used in some large river systems is to develop artificial floodplains; this is done by constructing *bypass channels* to accept seasonal or occasional floods. When not flooded, the bypass channel can serve as farmland, often benefitting from the occasional soil-replenishing inundation. When the river reaches flood stage, large gates called *weirs* are opened, allowing the water to enter the bypass channel. This alternate route relieves the main channel of the burden of carrying the entire discharge. The bypass channel around Winnipeg saved the city from damage during the 1997 record flood.

Along the lower Mississippi River north of New Orleans, the Bonnet Carré spillway is such a weir (Figure 14.1.1a). During high-water events, water is directed through a floodway into a bypass between a pair of guide levees. The bypass diverts the flood 9.7 km into Lake Pontchartrain, as it has done seven times since 1937, to protect New Orleans. For more details, see http://www.mvn.usace.army.mil/pao/bcarre/bcarre.htm.

In the Sacramento Valley, California, such weirs lead to bypass channels that

take floodwaters around metropolitan areas. See Figure 14.1.1b and c for the Sacramento weir and bypass farmland.

Floodplain-Management Considerations

The benefit of any levee, bypass, or other project intended to prevent flood destruction is measured in avoided damage and is used to justify the cost of the protection facility. Thus, ever-increasing damage leads to the justification of ever-increasing flood-control structures. All such strategies are subjected to cost–benefit analysis, but bias is a serious drawback because such an analysis usually is prepared by an agency or bureau with a vested interest in building more flood-control projects.

As suggested in an article titled "Settlement Control Beats Flood Control,"[1] published over 50 years ago, there are other ways to protect populations than with enormous, expensive, sometimes environmentally disruptive projects. Strictly zoning the floodplain is one approach. However, the flat, easily developed, and often picturesque floodplains are desirable for housing and thus weaken political resolve. A reasoned zoning strategy would set aside the floodplain for farming; passive recreation, such as a riverine park, golf course, or plant and wildlife sanctuary; or other uses that are not hurt by natural

periods, stream depth is measured as the height of the stream surface above a constant reference elevation (a datum) and is called the stage. Scientists may use a *staff gauge* (a pole marked with water levels) or a *stilling well* on the stream bank with a gauge mounted in it to measure stage (Figure 14.33c).

Environment Canada's Water Survey of Canada maintains more than 3000 gauging stations (see

http://www.ec.gc.ca/rhc-wsc/). In the political climate surrounding hazards and planning, such hydrologic monitoring by the stream gauging network is under continual threats of budget cuts. In the United States, there are over 11,000 stream gauging stations, many automated and sending data by telemetry to regional centres. Scientists hope that adequate funding to maintain such hydrologic monitoring by stream gauging networks will

(a)

FIGURE 14.1.1 Weir and bypass channels to divert floodwaters.
(a) The Bonnet Carré spillway (a weir), on the lower Mississippi, New Orleans District, is opened in flood events to let water flow to Lake Pontchartrain and bypass New Orleans to the south. (b) The Sacramento weir awaits floodwaters from the Sacramento River, which it will direct through a channel into the Yolo Bypass visible in the distance in (c). The bypass is used for farmland crops when flood waters recede. [Bobbé Christopherson.]

Stream processes, Floodplains

(b)

(c)

floods. This study concludes that "urban and industrial losses would be largely obviated [avoided] by set-back levees and zoning and thus cancel the biggest share of the assessed benefits which justify big dams."

[1] Walter Kollmorgen, "Settlement control beats flood control," *Economic Geography* 29, 3 (July 1953): 215.

continue, for the data are essential to hazard assessment and proper planning.

Hydrographs A graph of stream discharge over time for a specific place is a **hydrograph**. The hydrograph in Figure 14.34a shows the relation between precipitation input (the bar graph) and stream discharge (the curves). During dry periods, at low-water stages, the flow is described as *base flow* and is largely maintained by input from local groundwater (dark blue line).

When rainfall occurs in some portion of the watershed, the runoff collects and is concentrated in streams and tributaries. The amount, location, and duration of the rainfall episode determine the *peak flow*. Also important is the nature of the surface in a watershed, whether permeable or impermeable. A hydrograph for a specific portion

FIGURE 14.33 **Stream discharge measurement.**
(a) A typical flow measurement installation may use a variety of devices. (b) An automated hydrographic station and (c) a stilling well sends telemetry to a satellite for collection by the USGS. (d) Lee's Ferry cable towers and cable from which current meters are lowered. [(b) California Department of Water Resources. (c) and (d) by Bobbé Christopherson.]

of a stream changes after a forest fire or following urbanization of the watershed.

Human activities have enormous impact on water flow in a basin. The effects of urbanization are quite dramatic, both increasing and hastening peak flow, as you can see by comparing pre-urban streamflow (purple curve) and urbanized streamflow (light blue) in Figure 14.34a. In fact, urban areas produce runoff patterns quite similar to those of deserts. The sealed surfaces of the city drastically reduce infiltration and soil-moisture recharge; the effect is similar to that of the usually hard surfaces in the desert. A significant part of urban flooding occurs because of the increased area covered by impervious surfaces, which produces shortened concentration times; peak flows may strike with little warning.

These issues will intensify as urbanization of vulnerable areas continues. The flooded region in Figure 14.34b was flooded in 1986 and again in 1997.

GEOSYSTEMS CONNECTION

We followed the flow of moving water through streams, examining fluvial processes and landforms, and the river system outputs of discharge, deposition, and floods. The human society's relationship to river dynamics and related flood hazards and floodplain landscapes is an integral aspect of our ability to perceive hazards in a familiar environment. In the next chapter, we study the agent of wind as it operates to erode, transport, and deposit sediment. Also, in the chapter we look at arid lands and some unique aspects of Earth's desert landscapes.

(b)

(a)

FIGURE 14.34 Effect of urbanization on a typical stream hydrograph.
(a) Normal base flow is indicated with a dark blue line. The purple line indicates discharge after a storm, before urbanization. Following urbanization, stream discharge dramatically increases, as shown by the light blue line. (b) Severe flooding of an urban area in Linda, California, after levee breaks along the Sacramento River in 1986. Linda flooded again in 1997. [(b) California Department of Water Resources.]

 APPLIED PHYSICAL GEOGRAPHY   *Flood Frequency Analysis*

The degree to which any phenomenon is a hazard depends on its magnitude and its frequency of occurrence. The frequency with which a flood of a certain magnitude can be expected to occur is called its recurrence interval. Recurrence intervals can be determined wherever long-term river-gauging records are available, and are given by the formula:

$$T_r = (n + 1)/m$$

where T_r is the recurrence interval, n is the number of years of record,

and m is the number of floods of the given magnitude or larger during the years of record.

Table 1 shows peak discharges for a river-gauging station for a period of record from 1980 to 2009.

If we want to calculate the recurrence of a flood of magnitude 425 $m^3 \cdot s^{-1}$, for example, we note in Table 1 that 425 $m^3 \cdot s^{-1}$ was exceeded four times in the 30 year period.

$$T_r(425) = 31/4$$
$$= 7.75$$
$$= 7.8$$

Statistically, we then expect a flood of magnitude 425 $m^3 \cdot s^{-1}$ to occur on average once every 7 to 8 years.

This relationship can also be expressed as the chance or probability of a flood of given magnitude occurring in any given year. This is the reciprocal of the recurrence interval in percent:

$$P(425) = m/(n+1) \times 100$$
$$= 4/31 \times 100$$
$$= 12.9$$

There is a 12.9% chance of a flood of this magnitude occurring in any given year.

TABLE 1   Peak Discharges 1980–2009

Year	Peak Discharge $m^3 \cdot s^{-1}$	Year	Peak Discharge $m^3 \cdot s^{-1}$	Year	Peak Discharge $m^3 \cdot s^{-1}$
1980	113	1990	227	2000	113
1981	71	1991	2407	2001	241
1982	170	1992	411	2002	113
1983	212	1993	198	2003	311
1984	85	1994	255	2004	184
1985	42	1995	311	2005	198
1986	297	1996	113	2006	991
1987	57	1997	595	2007	71
1988	1770	1998	212	2008	28
1989	57	1999	227	2009	283

■ **Define** the term fluvial, and **explain** processes of fluvial erosion, transportation, and deposition.

Fluvial processes are stream-related. **Hydrology** is the science of water and its global circulation, distribution, and properties—specifically, water at and below Earth's surface. Water dislodges, dissolves, or removes surface material in the **erosion** process, in which weathered sediment is picked up for **transport**, and moved to new locations. Sediments are laid down by another process, **deposition**. **Alluvium** is the general term for the clay, silt, sand, gravel, or other unconsolidated rock and mineral fragments deposited by running water as sorted or semisorted sediment on a floodplain, delta, or streambed.

Base level is the lowest elevation limit of stream erosion in a region. A local base level occurs when something interrupts the stream's ability to achieve base level, such as is created by a dam or a landslide that blocks a stream channel.

fluvial (p. 420)
hydrology (p. 420)
erosion (p. 420)
transport (p. 422)
deposition (p. 422)
alluvium (p. 422)
base level (p. 422)

1. Define the term *fluvial*. What is a fluvial process?
2. What role is played by rivers in the hydrologic cycle?
3. What are the five largest rivers on Earth in terms of discharge? Relate these to the weather patterns in each area and to regional potential evapotranspiration (POTET) and precipitation (PRECIP)—concepts studied in Chapter 9.
4. What is the sequence of events that takes place as a stream dislodges material?
5. Explain the base-level concept. What happens to a local base level when a reservoir is constructed?

■ **Construct** a basic drainage basin model, and **identify** different types of drainage patterns, with examples.

The basic fluvial system is a **drainage basin** (or watershed), which is an open system. *Drainage divides* define the drainage-basin catchment (water-receiving) area of the drainage basin. In any drainage basin, water initially moves downslope in a thin film called **sheetflow**, or overland flow. This surface runoff concentrates in *rills*, or small-scale downhill grooves, which may develop into deeper *gullies* and a stream course in a valley. High ground that separates one valley from another and directs sheetflow is an *interfluve*. Extensive mountain and highland regions act as **continental divides** that separate major drainage basins. Some regions have **internal drainage** that does not reach the ocean, the only outlets being evaporation and subsurface gravitational flow.

Drainage density is determined by the number and length of channels in a given area and is an expression of a landscape's topographic surface appearance. **Drainage pattern** refers to the arrangement of channels in an area as determined by the steepness, variable rock resistance, variable climate, hydrology, relief of the land, and structural controls imposed by the landscape. Seven basic drainage patterns are generally found in nature: dendritic, trellis, radial, parallel, rectangular, annular, and deranged.

drainage basin (p. 422)
sheetflow (p. 422)
continental divides (p. 422)

internal drainage (p. 425)
drainage density (p. 426)
drainage pattern (p. 426)

6. What is the spatial geomorphic unit of an individual river system? How is it determined on the landscape? Define the several relevant key terms used.
7. In Figure 14.5, follow the Missouri–Ohio–Mississippi river system to the Gulf of Mexico. Analyze the pattern of tributaries, and describe the channel. What role do continental divides play in this drainage?
8. Describe drainage patterns. Define the various patterns that commonly appear in nature. What drainage patterns exist in your region?

■ **Describe** the relations among stream velocity, depth, width, and discharge.

Stream channels vary in *width* and *depth*. The water that flows in stream channels varies in velocity and in the *sediment* load it carries. All of these factors may increase with increasing discharge. **Discharge**, a stream's volume of flow per unit of time, is calculated by multiplying the velocity of the stream by its width and depth for a specific cross section of the channel. Most streams increase discharge downstream. But some **exotic streams** originate in a humid region and flow through an arid region, such that discharge decreases with distance.

Hydraulic action is the work of *turbulence* in the water. Running water causes hydraulic squeeze-and-release action to loosen and lift rocks and sediment. As this debris moves along, it mechanically erodes the streambed further, through a process of **abrasion**.

Solution refers to the **dissolved load** of a stream, especially the chemical solution derived from minerals such as limestone or dolomite or from soluble salts. The **suspended load** consists of fine-grained, clastic particles held aloft in the stream, with the finest particles not deposited until the stream velocity slows nearly to zero. **Bed load** refers to coarser materials that are dragged, pushed and rolled along the streambed by **traction** or that bounce and hop along by **saltation**. If the load in a stream exceeds its capacity, sediments accumulate through deposition on the bed and the stream channel builds through **aggradation**. With excess sediment, a stream becomes a maze of interconnected channels that form a **braided stream** pattern.

discharge (p. 428)
exotic stream (p. 429)
hydraulic action (p. 429)
abrasion (p. 429)
dissolved load (p. 430)
suspended load (p. 430)
bed load (p. 430)
traction (p. 430)
saltation (p. 430)
aggradation (p. 430)
braided stream (p. 430)

9. What was the impact of flood discharge on the channel of the San Juan River near Bluff, Utah? Why did these changes take place?
10. How does stream discharge do its erosive work? What are the processes at work in the channel?
11. Differentiate between stream competence and stream capacity.
12. How does a stream transport its sediment load? What processes are at work?

■ *Develop* a model of a meandering stream, including point bar, undercut bank, and cutoff, and *explain* the role of stream gradient in this model.

Where the slope is gradual, stream channels develop a sinuous form called a **meandering stream**. The outer portion of each meandering curve is subject to the fastest water velocity and can be the site of a steep **undercut bank**. On the other hand, the inner portion of a meander experiences the slowest water velocity and forms a **point-bar** deposit. When a meander neck is cut off as two undercut banks merge, the meander becomes isolated and forms an **oxbow lake**.

Every stream develops its own **gradient** and establishes a longitudinal profile. A **graded stream** condition occurs when a channel has just enough energy to transport its sediment load; this represents a balance among slope, discharge, channel characteristics, and the load supplied from the drainage basin. An interruption in a stream's longitudinal profile is called a **nickpoint**. This abrupt change in gradient can occur as the stream flows across hard, resistant rock or after tectonic uplift episodes.

    meandering stream (p. 430)
    undercut bank (p. 430)
    point bar (p. 431)
    oxbow lake (p. 432)
    gradient (p. 433)
    graded stream (p. 433)
    nickpoint (p. 434)

13. Describe the flow characteristics of a meandering stream. What is the pattern of flow in the channel? What are the erosional and depositional features and the typical landforms created?

14. Explain these statements: (a) All streams have a gradient, but not all streams are graded. (b) Graded streams may have ungraded segments.

15. Why is Niagara Falls an example of a nickpoint? Without human intervention, what do you think will eventually take place at Niagara Falls?

■ *Define* a floodplain, and *analyze* a stream channel during a flood.

Floodplains have been an important site of human activity throughout history. Rich soils, bathed in fresh nutrients by floodwaters, attract agricultural activity and urbanization. Despite our historical knowledge of devastation by floods, floodplains are settled, raising issues of human perception of hazard. The flat low-lying area along a stream channel that is subjected to recurrent flooding is a **floodplain**. It is formed when the river overflows its channel during times of high flow. On either bank of some streams, **natural levees** develop as by-products of flooding. On the floodplain, backswamps and yazoo tributaries may develop. The natural levees and elevated channel of the river prevent a **yazoo tributary** from joining the main channel, so it flows parallel to the river and through the **backswamp** area. Entrenchment of a river into its own floodplain forms **alluvial terraces**.

    floodplain (p. 436)
    natural levees (p. 438)
    yazoo tributary (p. 438)

    backswamp (p. 438)
    alluvial terraces (p. 438)

16. Describe the formation of a floodplain. How are natural levees, oxbow lakes, backswamps, and yazoo tributaries produced?

17. Identify any of the features listed in Question 16 on the Philipp, Mississippi, topographic quadrangle in Figure 14.23d.

18. Describe any floodplains near where you live. Have you seen any of the floodplain features discussed in this chapter? If so, which ones?

■ *Differentiate* the several types of river deltas, and *detail* each.

A depositional plain formed in a body of water at the mouth of a river is called a **delta**. When the mouth of a river enters the sea and is inundated by seawater in a mix with freshwater, it is called an **estuary**.

    delta (p. 439)
    estuary (p. 439)

19. What is a river delta? What are the various deltaic forms? Give some examples.

20. Based on materials in this chapter and in Chapter 8, assess what occurred in New Orleans in 2005. How might New Orleans change later in this century? Explain. In your opinion, did Hurricane Katrina cause the disaster, or was it a result of engineering failures and hazard-planning shortfalls?

21. Describe the Ganges River delta. What factors upstream explain its form and pattern? Assess the consequences of settlement on this delta.

22. What is meant by the statement "the Nile River delta is disappearing"?

■ *Explain* flood probability estimates, and *review* strategies for mitigating flood hazards.

A **flood** occurs when high water overflows the natural riverbank along any portion of a stream. Both floods and the adjacent floodplains are rated statistically for the expected time interval between floods. A 10-year flood is the greatest level of flooding that is likely to occur, on average, once every 10 years. A graph of stream discharge over time for a specific place is called a **hydrograph**.

Collective efforts by government agencies undertake to reduce flood probability. Such management attempts include the construction of artificial levees, bypasses, straightened channels, diversions, dams, and reservoirs. Society is still learning how to live in a sustainable way with Earth's dynamic river systems.

    flood (p. 444)
    hydrograph (p. 447)

23. Specifically, what is a flood? How are such flows measured and tracked?

24. Differentiate between a hydrograph from a natural terrain and one from an urbanized area.

25. What do you see as the major consideration regarding floodplain management? How would you describe the general attitude of society toward natural hazards and disasters?

26. What do you think the author of the article "Settlement Control Beats Flood Control" meant by the title? Explain your answer, using information presented in the chapter.

MyGeosciencePlace

Visit **www.mygeoscienceplace.ca** for several figure animations, satellite loops, self-study quizzes, flashcards, interactive glossary, career links, RSS feeds, Pearson eText of *Geosystems*, and much more.

Eolian Processes and Arid Landscapes

Active sand dunes in the Great Sand Hills of Southwestern Saskatchewan are evidence of cyclic dune activity. Sand transport and dune growth cycle between active and stable states. Activity increases with climatic disturbances such as drought, and even small disturbances can result in longer time periods of dune activity. [Courtesy of the Geological Survey of Canada. Photo 2002-649 by S. A. Wolfe. Reproduced with the permission of Natural Resources Canada. © 2012.]

KEY LEARNING CONCEPTS

After reading the chapter, you should be able to:

- **Characterize** the unique work accomplished by wind and eolian processes.
- **Describe** eolian erosion, including deflation, abrasion, and the resultant landforms.
- **Describe** eolian transportation, and **explain** saltation and surface creep.
- **Identify** the major classes of sand dunes, and **present** examples within each class.
- **Define** loess deposits and their origins, locations, and landforms.
- **Portray** desert landscapes, and **locate** these regions on a world map.

Increasing Desertification and Political Action—A Global Environmental Issue

We are witnessing an unwanted expansion of Earth's deserts in a process known as **desertification**. This is a worldwide phenomenon along the margins of semi-arid and arid lands—Earth's dry lands, one of the subjects in this chapter.

Desertification is due in part to poor agricultural practices such as overgrazing and activities that abuse soil structure and fertility, improper soil-moisture management, erosion, salinization, and deforestation. A worsening causative force is global climate change, which is shifting temperature and precipitation patterns and causing poleward movement of Earth's subtropical high-pressure systems, discussed elsewhere in *Geosystems*.

Figure GN 15.1 portrays regions of desertification risk, as defined by the loss of agricultural activity. The severity of this problem is magnified by poverty in many of the affected areas, since most people lack the capital to change agricultural practices and implement conservation strategies. Many of the highest-risk lands are in India and central Asia. In fact, a 2009 mapping project showed that 25% of India is undergoing desertification. Throughout central Asia, overexploitation of water resources has combined with drought to cause the expansion of desert conditions. The Aral Sea, formerly one of the four largest lakes in the world, has

steadily shrunk in size since the 1960s as inflowing rivers have increasingly been diverted. As the lake level has fallen, fine sediment and alkali dust have become available for wind deflation, leading to massive dust storms.

In Africa, the Sahel is the transition region between the Sahara Desert in the subtropics and the wetter equatorial regions. The southward expansion of desert conditions through portions of the Sahel region has left many African peoples on land that no longer experiences the same amount of rainfall it received just three decades ago. Yet climate change is only part of the story: Other factors contributing to desertification in the Sahel are population increases, poverty, land degradation (deforestation, overgrazing), and the lack of a coherent environmental policy.

The United Nations estimates that degraded lands cover some 800 million hectares; many millions of additional hectares are added each year. An immediate need is to improve the database of degraded land across the globe for a more accurate accounting of the problem and a better understanding of desertification processes.

One of the successes coming from the 1992 Earth Summit in Rio de Janeiro was the Convention to Combat Desertification, an initiative that began operations in 1994

and is still active. Efforts continue to get these issues to the forefront for action.

In August 2010, the *International Conference: Climate, Sustainability, and Development in the Semi-Arid Regions* met for a second time (http://www.unccd.int/). Related issues from more than 100 countries were on the agenda. Launched at this meeting was a global effort for the next decade—the United Nations Decade for Deserts and the Fight against Desertification (UNDDD).

All this was geared to increase public and government attention to the issue of desertification in preparation for the important *Rio + 21 Earth Summit* in Rio de Janeiro in 2012. The conference call was for action on many issues: sustainable development and climate change, political involvement on behalf of dryland peoples, integration of and focus on global environmental initiatives, development of financing, education, and recognition of the urgency of the problem, among other items.

About a billion people are being affected by desertification, with their livelihoods threatened. Further delays in addressing the problem will result in far higher costs when compared to taking action within the next few years. For more on global arid lands, see http://www.undp.org/drylands/.

FIGURE GN 15.1 Area at risk of desertification. [Map prepared by U.S. Department of Agriculture–Natural Resources Conservation Service, Soil Survey Division, and includes consideration of population densities in affected regions provided by the National Center for Geographic Information Analysis at University of California, Santa Barbara.]

RISK

- Low
- Moderate
- High
- Very High
- Not considered

ind is an agent of geomorphic change. Like moving water, moving air causes erosion, transportation, and deposition of materials; moving air is a fluid and it behaves similarly, although it has a lower viscosity (it is less dense) than water. Although lacking the lifting ability of water, wind processes can modify and move large quantities of materials in deserts, along coastlines, and elsewhere.

Wind can contribute to soil formation in places far from a sediment source area. Fine particles may be transported long distances from regions where glaciers once were active. Fallow fields (those not planted) give up their soil resource to destructive wind erosion. Scientists are only now getting an accurate picture of the amount of windblown dust that fills the atmosphere and crosses the oceans between continents. Chemical fingerprints and satellites trace windblown dust from African soils to North and South America and from Asian landscapes to Europe. Winds even spread living organisms. One study found related mosses, liverworts, and lichens distributed thousands of kilometres between islands in the Southern Ocean.

Earth's dry lands stand out in stark contrast on the water planet. In desert environments, an overall lack of moisture and stabilizing vegetation allows wind to create extensive sand seas and dunes of infinite variety. The polar regions are deserts as well, so there should be no surprise that weather-monitoring stations in Yuma, Arizona, and in Antarctica report the same amount of annual precipitation. These polar and high-latitude deserts possess unique features related to their cold, dry environment—aspects covered in Chapter 17.

Consistent local wind can prune and shape vegetation and sculpt ice and snow surfaces (Figure 15.1). Arid landscapes display distinctive landforms and life forms: "Instead of finding chaos and disorder the observer never fails to be amazed at a simplicity of form, an exactitude of repetition and a geometric order."[1]

In this chapter: We examine the work of wind, associated erosion, transport, depositional processes, and resulting landforms. Windblown fine particles form vast loess deposits, the basis for rich agricultural soils. We include the discussion of arid lands in this chapter. Most deserts are rocky and covered with desert pavement, whereas other dry landscapes are covered in sand dunes. In desert environments, landscapes lacking moisture and stabilizing vegetation are set off in sharp, sun-baked relief. Surprising to many, water is the major erosional agent in the desert, yet water is the limiting resource for human development. We examine the causes and distribution of Earth's desert landscapes. The troubled Colorado River and the western drought are the subject of an important focus study.

The Work of Wind

The work of the wind—erosion, transportation, and deposition—is **eolian** (also spelled *aeolian*). The word comes from Aeolus, ruler of the winds in Greek mythology. British Army major Ralph Bagnold, an engineering

[1]R. A. Bagnold, *The Physics of Blown Sand and Desert Dunes* (London, England: Methuen, 1941).

(a)

(b)

FIGURE 15.1 **The work of wind.**
(a) Wind-sculpted tree near South Point, Hawai'i. Nearly constant tradewinds keep this tree naturally pruned.
(b) Blowing wind shapes ice and snow in formations of *sastrugi*. Can you tell the direction of the prevailing winds from looking at the ice and snow? [Bobbé Christopherson.]

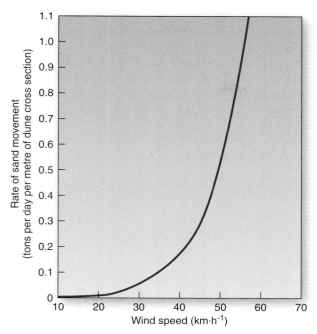

FIGURE 15.2 Sand movement and wind velocity.
Sand movement relative to wind velocity, as measured over a metre cross section of ground surface. [After R. A. Bagnold, 1941.]

officer, while stationed in Egypt in the 1920s and 1930s, accomplished much eolian research. In the deserts west of the Nile, Bagnold measured, sketched, and developed hypotheses about the wind and desert forms. Imagine the scene in the 1920s: A Model-T Ford chugs across the desert west of Cairo taking Bagnold to his research area. He laid rolls of chicken wire over treacherous stretches of sand to prevent getting stuck. Bagnold's often-cited work, *The Physics of Blown Sand and Desert Dunes*, was published in 1941.

The ability of wind to move materials is actually small compared with that of other transporting agents such as water and ice, because air is so much less dense than those other media. Yet, over time, wind accomplishes enormous amounts of work. Bagnold studied the ability of wind to transport sand over the surface of a dune. Figure 15.2 shows that a steady wind of 50 km·h^{-1} can move approximately one-half ton of sand per day over a metre cross

section of dune. The graph also demonstrates how rapidly the amount of transported sand increases with wind speed.

Grain size is important in wind erosion. Intermediate-sized grains move most easily—these can bounce along. It is the largest and the smallest sand particles that require the strongest winds to move. The large particles are heavier and thus require stronger winds. Small particles are difficult to move because they exhibit a mutual cohesiveness and because they usually present a smooth surface (more aerodynamic) to the wind. Yet the finest dust, once aloft, can be carried from continent to continent.

Eolian Erosion

Two principal wind-erosion processes are **deflation**, the removal and lifting of individual loose particles, and **abrasion**, the grinding of rock surfaces with a "sandblasting" action by particles captured in the air. Deflation and abrasion produce a variety of distinctive landforms and landscapes.

Deflation   Deflation literally blows away loose or noncohesive sediment and works with rainwater to form a surface resembling a cobblestone street: a **desert pavement** that protects underlying sediment from further deflation and water erosion. Traditionally, deflation was regarded as a key formative process, eroding fine dust, clay, and sand away, leaving behind a concentration of pebbles and gravel as desert pavement (Figure 15.3a).

Another hypothesis that explains some desert pavement surfaces states that deposition of windblown sediments, not removal, is the formative agent. Windblown particles settle between and below coarse rocks and pebbles that are gradually displaced upwards. Rainwater is involved as wetting and drying episodes swell and shrink clay-sized particles. The gravel fragments are gradually lifted to surface positions to form the pavement (Figure 15.3b). Desert pavements are so common that many provincial names are used for them—for example, *gobi* in China; and in Africa, *lag gravels* or *serir*, or *reg* desert if some fine particles remain.

Heavy recreational activity damages fragile desert landscapes, especially in the United States, where more than 15 million off-road vehicles (ORVs) are now in use. Such vehicles crush plants and animals; disrupt desert

GEO REPORT 15.1   *Bagnold Was Ahead of His Time*

Ralph Bagnold's work in the desert described sand dunes as complex self-organizing systems—with order and regularity arising from chaos and disorder. Today, this is the science of complex system behaviour, where system components interact in a self-enhancing manner. For example, consider the ripple patterns in sand: The ripple captures increasing amounts of sand as it grows in size, which reduces the amount of sand grains in the air, forcing the distance between ripples to increase. In Chapter 17, we study self-organizing behaviour in periglacial regions and how freeze–thaw cycles organize rock sorting and resulting patterns.

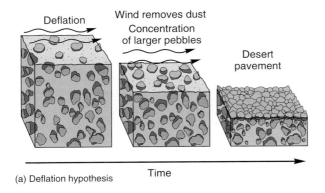

Deflation | Wind removes dust Concentration of larger pebbles | Desert pavement

(a) Deflation hypothesis — Time

Deflation | Rain washes dust downward | Gravel displacement upward | Desert pavement

(b) Sediment-accumulation hypothesis

(c)

FIGURE 15.3 Desert pavement.
(a) Desert pavement may be formed when larger rocks and fragments are left behind after deflation and sheetwash remove finer dust, silt, and clays. (b) Other desert pavements seem to be formed by wind delivering fine particles that settle and wash downward; through cycles of swelling and shrinking, the gravels gradually migrate upward to form pavement. (c) A typical desert pavement. [Bobbé Christopherson.]

pavement, leading to greater deflation; and create ruts that easily concentrate sheetwash to form gullies.

Wherever wind encounters loose sediment, deflation may remove enough material to form basins called **blow-out depressions**. These depressions range from small indentations less than a metre wide up to areas hundreds

of metres wide and many metres deep. Chemical weathering, although slow in the desert owing to the lack of water, is important in the formation of a blowout, for it removes the cementing materials that give particles their cohesiveness. Large depressions in the Sahara Desert are at least partially formed by deflation. The enormous Munkhafad el Qaṭṭâra (Qaṭṭâra Depression), which covers 18 000 km^2 just inland from the Mediterranean Sea in the Western Desert of Egypt, is now about 130 m below sea level at its lowest point.

Abrasion You may have seen work crews sandblasting surfaces on buildings, bridges, or streets to clean them or to remove unwanted markings. Sandblasting uses a stream of compressed air filled with sand grains to quickly abrade a surface. Abrasion by windblown particles is nature's slower version of sandblasting, and it is especially effective at polishing exposed rocks when the abrading particles are hard and angular. Variables that affect the rate of abrasion include the hardness of surface rocks, wind velocity, and wind constancy. Abrasive action is restricted to the area immediately above the ground, usually no more than a metre or two in height, because sand grains are lifted only a short distance.

Rocks exposed to eolian abrasion appear pitted, fluted (grooved), or polished. Abraded rocks are often aerodynamically shaped in a specific direction, according to the consistent flow of airborne particles carried by prevailing winds. Rocks that have such evidence of eolian erosion are **ventifacts** (literally, "artifacts of the wind"). On a larger scale, deflation and abrasion are capable of streamlining rock structures that are aligned parallel to the most effective wind direction, leaving behind distinctive, elongated ridges or formations called **yardangs**. These wind-sculpted features can range from metres to kilometres in length and up to many metres in height.

On Earth, some yardangs are large enough to be detected on satellite imagery. The Ica Valley of southern Peru contains yardangs reaching 100 m in height and several kilometres in length, and yardangs in the Lut Desert of Iran attain 150 m in height. Abrasion is concentrated on the windward end of each yardang, with deflation operating on the leeward portions. Wind-sculpted formations are shown in Figure 15.4.

Eolian Transportation

Atmospheric circulation can transport fine material—such as volcanic debris, fire soot and smoke, and dust—worldwide within days. Wind exerts a drag, or frictional pull, on surface particles until they become airborne, just as water in a stream picks up sediment (again, remember that air is a fluid). The distance that wind is capable of transporting particles in suspension varies greatly with particle size. Only the finest dust particles travel significant distances, so the finer material suspended in a dust storm is lifted much higher than the coarser particles of a sandstorm.

(a)   (b)

FIGURE 15.4 **A yardang.**
(a) A small wind-sculpted rock formation located in Snow Canyon outside St. George, Utah. (b) Consistent winds shape this exposed rock on Bear Island in the North Atlantic. The rock sits on a surface of patterned ground and periglacial features (see Chapter 17). [Bobbé Christopherson.]

(a)

(b)

People living in areas of frequent dust storms are faced with infiltration of very fine particles into their homes and businesses through even the smallest cracks. Figure 3.8 illustrates such dust storms. People living in desert regions and along sandy beaches, where frequent sandstorms occur, contend with the sandblasting of painted surfaces and etched window glass.

Both human and natural sand erosion and transport from a beach are slowed by conservation measures such as the introduction of stabilizing native plants, the use of fences, and the restriction of pedestrian traffic to walkways (Figure 15.5). As human settlement encroaches on coastal dunes, sand transport becomes problematic.

The term *saltation* was used in Chapter 14 to describe one type of movement of particles by water. The term also describes the wind transport of grains, usually larger than 0.2 mm, along the ground. About 80% of wind transport of particles is accomplished by this skipping and bouncing action (Figure 15.6). Compared with fluvial transport, in which saltation is accomplished by hydraulic lift, eolian saltation is executed by aerodynamic lift, elastic bounce, and impact (compare Figure 15.6a with Figure 14.12).

FIGURE 15.5 **Preventing sand transport.**
(a) Pinery Provincial Park, Ontario. Further erosion and transport of coastal dunes can be controlled by stabilizing strategies, planting native plants, and confining pedestrian traffic to walkways. (b) Tufts of grass are planted to stabilize sand with a fence installed to prevent human foot traffic. [(a) Mary-Louise Byrne. (b) Bobbé Christopherson.]

(a)

(b)

(c)

(d)

FIGURE 15.6 How the wind moves sand.
(a) Eolian suspension, saltation, and surface creep are mechanisms of sediment transportation. Compare with the saltation and traction that occur in another fluid, water, in Figure 14.12. (b) Sand grains saltating along the surface in the Stovepipe Wells dune field, Death Valley. (c) Sand deposited by eolian processes oversteepens the slope, and failure results in sand flow. (d) Sand deposition buried this abandoned, two-storey life-saving station on Sable Island, Nova Scotia. [(b) Robert Christopherson. (c) and (d) Mary-Louise Byrne.]

How Wind Moves Sand

On impact, grains hit other grains and knock them into the air. Saltating particles crash into other particles, knocking them both loose and forward. This type of movement is **surface creep**, which slides and rolls particles too large for saltation and affects about 20% of the material being transported. Once in motion, particles continue to be transported by lower wind velocities. In a desert or along a beach, sometimes you can hear a slight hissing sound, almost like steam escaping, produced by the myriad saltating grains of sand bouncing along and colliding with surface particles.

GEO REPORT 15.2 *Conflicts Feed the Sand Seas*

Military activities can threaten desert landscapes. A serious environmental impact of the ongoing wars in Iraq and Afghanistan is the disruption of desert pavement by explosives and the movement of heavy vehicles. As thousands of square kilometres of stable desert pavement break apart, nearby cities and farms experience increased dust and sand invasions.

The Registan Desert of southern Afghanistan, south of the city of Kandahar, is an example of such a sand sea over a flat terrain. A result of drought conditions and war-disrupted desert pavement surfaces, the migrating sand is overtaking areas of sparse agricultural activity and has covered more than 100 villages.

(a)

FIGURE 15.7 **Sand ripples.**
(a) Sand ripple patterns later may become lithified into fixed patterns in rock. The area in the photo is about 1 m wide.
(b) Planed-off ripples reveal the structures created by the migration of ripples on Cavendish Spit, Prince Edward Island.
[(a) Robert Christopherson. (b) Mary-Louise Byrne.]

(b)

Eolian Depositional Landforms

The smallest features shaped by individual saltating grains are ripples (Figure 15.7). Eolian ripples are similar to fluvial ripples, although impact of saltating grains is slight in water. Ripples form in crests and troughs, positioned transversely (at a right angle) to the direction of the wind. The interception of sand grains from the wind stream deprives the downwind area of grains and determines the distance between ripples—this is self-enhancing behavior in a complex system.

Many people know arid landscapes only from the movies, which leave the impression that most deserts are covered by sand. Instead, desert pavements predominate across most subtropical arid landscapes; only about 10% of desert areas are fully covered with sand. Sand grains generally are deposited as transient ridges or hills called dunes.

A **dune** is a wind-sculpted accumulation of sand. An extensive area of dunes, such as that found in North Africa, is characteristic of an **erg desert**, or **sand sea**. The Grand Erg Oriental in the central Sahara exceeds 1200 m in depth and covers 192 000 km², about 2.5 times the size of New Brunswick. This sand sea has been active for more than 1.3 million years. Similar sand seas, such as the Grand Ar Rub'al Khālī Erg, are active in Saudi Arabia.

In eastern Algeria, the Issaouane Erg covers 38 000 km². Winds from varying directions produce star dunes with multiple slipfaces (Figure 15.8a). *Star dunes* are the mountainous giants of the sandy desert. They are pinwheel-shaped, with several radiating arms rising and joining to form a common central peak that approach 200 m in height. Some in the Sonoran Desert also approach this size. In Figure 15.8a, you can also see some barchan dunes, which suggest the region has experienced changing wind patterns over time, as barchans form with a single principal wind flow. Dunes are present on Mars as well as in semi-arid areas such as the Great Plains of the United States (Figure 15.8b) and in the Great Sand Hills of southwestern Saskatchewan (chapter-opening photo).

Dune Movement and Form Dune fields, whether in arid regions or along coastlines, tend to migrate in the direction of effective, sand-transporting winds. In this regard, stronger seasonal winds or winds from a passing storm may sometimes prove more effective than average prevailing winds. When saltating sand grains encounter small patches of sand, the kinetic energy (motion) is dissipated and sand grains accumulate. As height increases above about 30 cm, a **slipface** and characteristic dune features form.

By studying the dune model in Figure 15.9 you can see that winds characteristically create a gently sloping *windward side* (stoss side), with a more steeply sloped slipface on the *leeward side*. A dune usually is asymmetrical in one or more directions. The angle of a slipface is the steepest angle at which loose material is stable—its *angle of repose*. Thus, the constant flow of new material makes a slipface a type of *avalanche slope*. Sand builds up as it moves over the crest of the dune to the brink; then it avalanches, falling and cascading as the slipface continually adjusts, seeking

(a) Issaouane Erg, Algeria

(b) Melas Chasma, Mars

FIGURE 15.8 Seas of sand.
(a) The Issaouane Erg of eastern Algeria is a blend of principally star dunes, some barchan dunes, and linear dunes in the far upper-left—all disclose the prevailing wind history of the region. (b) Sand dunes are found on the Martian surface in the southern area of Melas Chasma in Valles Marineris. Note the dust devil in the lower left. The area covered is about 2 km wide. [(a) *ISS* astronaut photo, NASA/GSFC; (b) Mars Global Surveyor, Mars Orbiter Camera image courtesy of NASA/JPL/Malin Space Science Systems.]

its angle of repose (usually 30° to 34°, see Figure 15.6c). Together with sand transported over the brink, this avalanching process causes a dune to migrate downwind, as suggested by the successive dune profiles in Figure 15.9.

Dunes have many wind-shaped styles that make classification difficult. We simplify dune forms into three classes—*crescentic* (crescent, curved shape), *linear* (straight form), and massive *star dunes*. Each is summarized in Figure 15.10. The ever-changing form of these eolian deposits

is part of their beauty, eloquently described by one author: "I see hills and hollows of sand like rising and falling waves. Now at midmorning, they appear paper white. At dawn they were fog gray. This evening they will be eggshell brown."[2]

[2]J. E. Bowers, *Seasons of the Wind* (Flagstaff, AZ: Northland Press, 1985), p. 1.

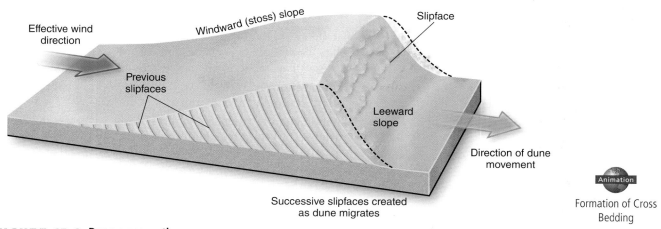

FIGURE 15.9 Dune cross section.
Successive slipfaces exhibit a distinctive pattern as the dune migrates in the direction of the effective wind.

The map in Figure 15.11 shows the correlation of active sand regions with deserts (tropical, continental interior, and coastal). Note the extent of desert area covered by active sand dunes—only about 10% of all continental land between 30° N and 30° S. Also noted on the map are dune fields in humid climates outside of this range, such as along coastal Oregon, the shore of Lake Huron (Figure 15.11b), along the Gulf and Atlantic coastlines, in Europe, and elsewhere.

These same dune-forming principles and terms (for example, *dune* and *slipface*) apply to snow-covered landscapes. *Snow dunes* are formed as wind deposits snow in drifts. In semiarid farming areas, capturing drifting snow with fences and tall stubble left in fields contributes significantly to soil moisture when the snow melts.

Loess Deposits

Approximately 15 000 years ago, in several episodes, Pleistocene glaciers retreated in many parts of the world, leaving behind large glacial outwash deposits of fine-grained clays and silts. Some of these materials were blown great distances by the wind and redeposited in unstratified, homogeneous (evenly mixed) deposits. Peasants working along the Rhine River Valley in Germany gave these deposits the name **loess** (pronounced "luss"). No specific landforms were created; instead, loess covered existing landforms with a thick blanket of material that assumed the general topography of the existing landscape.

Because of its own binding strength and its internal coherence, loess weathers and erodes into steep bluffs, or vertical faces. When a bank is cut into a loess deposit,

 The Dust Bowl

Wind transport of soils including loess produced a catastrophe in the North American Great Plains in the 1930s—the Dust Bowl. More than a century of overgrazing and intensive agriculture left soil susceptible to drought and deflation processes. Reduced precipitation amounts and above-normal temperatures triggered the multiyear period of severe dust storms and loss of farmlands.

The deflation of many centimetres of soil occurred in the southern prairies in Canada, in southern Nebraska, Kansas, Oklahoma, Texas, and eastern Colorado in the United States, and even in northern Mexico. The transported dust darkened the skies of cities, which left the streetlights on throughout the day, and drifted over farmland to depths that covered failing crops. The largest migration in North American history occurred as 2 million people had moved out of the prairie provinces and plains states by 1940.

The Prairie Farm Rehabilitation Administration (PFRA), a branch of Agriculture Canada, was established to combat the outmigration of prairie farmers as the drought caused them to abandon their land. Through soil and water conservation and the development of innovative farming practices, the PFRA assisted farmers through the Dust Bowl of the Dirty Thirties and allowed agriculture to continue in Canada's breadbasket. The PFRA today continues its role in soil and water conservation.

Tree-ring analyses show that droughts of similar intensity happened about twice a century over the past 400 years. One such intense drought in what is now Nebraska in the thirteenth century appears to have lasted nearly 40 years. The Dust Bowl weather conditions seem to correlate with sea-surface temperatures that are cool in the Pacific Ocean and warm in the Atlantic Ocean. Chapter 6 discussed the Pacific Decadal Oscillation and its relation to drought occurrences in the United States. For more on the Dust Bowl, see http://www.pbs.org/wgbh/americanexperience/films/dustbowl/.

Class	Type	Description
Crescentic	Barchan	Crescent-shaped dune with horns pointed downwind. Winds are constant with little directional variability. Limited sand available. Only one slipface. Can be scattered over bare rock or desert pavement or commonly in dune fields.
	Transverse	Asymmetrical ridge, transverse to wind direction (right angle). Only one slipface. Results from relatively ineffective wind and abundant sand supply.
	Parabolic	Role of anchoring vegetation important. Open end faces upwind with U-shaped "blowout" and arms anchored by vegetation. Multiple slipfaces, partially stabilized.
	Barchanoid ridge	A wavy, asymmetrical dune ridge aligned transverse to effective winds. Formed from coalesced barchans; looks like connected crescents in rows with open areas between them.

Barchan

Transverse

Parabolic

Barchanoid ridge

FIGURE 15.10 Major dune forms.
See table for dune descriptions. Arrows show wind direction.
[Adapted from E. D. McKee, *A Study of Global Sand Seas*, USGS Professional Paper 1052 (Washington, DC: U.S. Government Printing Office, 1979).]

it generally will stand vertically, although it can fail if saturated (Figure 15.12). There are historical accounts of American Civil War soldiers in the Vicksburg, Mississippi, area excavating places to live in loess banks; in areas of China, dwellings are carved from the loess.

Figure 15.13 shows the worldwide distribution of loess deposits. Large and deep loess deposits do not occur in Canada; however, significant accumulations throughout the Mississippi and Missouri river valleys in the United States form continuous deposits of loess 15–30 m thick. Loess deposits also occur in eastern Washington State and Idaho. The hills and gullies in the Loess Hills of Iowa in Figure 15.12b reach heights of about 60 m above the nearby prairie farmlands and Missouri River and run north and south more than 320 km. Only China has deposits that exceed these dimensions. This

Class	Type	Description
Linear	Longitudinal	Long, slightly sinuous, ridge-shaped dune, aligned parallel with the wind direction; two slipfaces. Average 100 m high and 100 km long, and the "draa" at the extreme in size can reach to 400 m high. Results from strong, effective winds varying in one direction.
	Seif	After Arabic word for "sword"; a more sinuous crest and shorter than longitudinal dunes. Rounded toward upwind direction and pointed downwind. (Not illustrated.)
Star dune		The giant of dunes. Pyramidal or star-shaped with three or more sinuous, radiating arms extending outward from a central peak. Slipfaces in multiple directions. Results from effective winds shifting in all directions. Tend to form isolated mounds in high, effective winds and connected sinuous arms in low, effective winds.
Other	Dome	Circular or elliptical mound with no slipface. Can be modified into barchanoid forms; vegetation can play role in coastal locales.
	Reversing	Asymmetrical ridge form that is intermediate between star dune and transverse dune. Wind variability can alter shape between forms.

Longitudinal

Star

Dome

Reversing

silt explains the fertility of the soils in these regions, for loess deposits are well drained and deep, and have excellent moisture retention. Loess deposits also cover much of Ukraine, central Europe, China, the Pampas–Patagonia regions of Argentina, and lowland New Zealand. The soils derived from loess help form some of Earth's "breadbasket" farming regions. Transport of loess soils occurred in the catastrophic 1930s Dust Bowl in the United States.

In Europe and North America, loess is thought to be derived mainly from glacial and periglacial sources. The vast deposits of loess in China, covering more than 300 000 km^2, are derived from windblown desert sediment rather than glacial sources. Accumulations in the Loess Plateau of China exceed 300 m in thickness, forming complex weathered badlands and some good agricultural land. These windblown deposits are interwoven with much of Chinese history and society.

(a)

(b)

(c)

FIGURE 15.11 Sandy regions of the world.
(a) Worldwide distribution of active and stable sand regions. (b) Sand dunes along the shore of Lake Huron in Pinery Provincial Park, Ontario. (c) Coastal dunes can be large features as exemplified by "The Grand Canyon" at the east lighthouse on Sable Island, Nova Scotia. [(a) After R. E. Snead, *Atlas of World Physical Features*, p. 134, © 1972 by John Wiley & Sons; (b) and (c) Mary-Louise Byrne.]

(a)

(b)

FIGURE 15.12 Example of loess deposit.
(a) A loess bluff in western Iowa; note the vertical structural strength. (b) The Loess Hills of western Iowa give evidence of the last ice age, as the finely ground sediments left by the glaciers were windblown to this setting. [Bobbé Christopherson.]

FIGURE 15.13 Loess deposits worldwide.
Areas of major accumulations of loess. Dots represent small, scattered loess formations. [Adapted from NRCS, FAO, and USGS data.]

CRITICAL THINKING 15.1

The Nearest Eolian Features

What eolian features are nearest to your present location? Are they coastal, lakeshore, or desert dunes, or are they loess deposits? Which causative factors discussed in this chapter explain the location or form of these features? Are you able to visit the site?

Overview of Earth's Deserts

Arid climates occupy about 26% of Earth's land surface. If all semiarid climates are considered, perhaps as much as 35% of all land area tends toward dryness, constituting the largest single climatic region on Earth (see Figures 10.4 and 10.5 for the location of these *arid deserts* and *semiarid steppe* climate regions and Figure 20.5 for the distribution of these desert environments).

Deserts occur worldwide as topographic plains, such as the Great Sandy and Simpson Deserts of Australia, the Arabian and Kalahari Deserts of Africa, and portions of the extensive Taklimakan Desert, which covers some 270,000 km² in the central Tarim Basin of China. Deserts also are found in mountainous regions: interior Asia, from Iran to Pakistan, and in China and Mongolia. In South America, the rugged Atacama Desert lies between the ocean and the Andes. Desert conditions can also be found on small islands, such as the Cape Verde Islands off the West African coast at around 15° N latitude (see Figure 15.14d). Earth's deserts are expanding, as discussed in *Geosystems*

Now. Now, let us look at the link between climate and Earth's deserts.

Desert Climates

The spatial distribution of dry lands is related to three climatological settings:

- Areas dominated by subtropical high-pressure cells between 15° and 35°, for both N and S latitudes (see Figures 6.9 and 6.11);
- Rain shadow areas on the lee side of mountain ranges (see Figure 8.8); and
- Areas at great distance from moisture-bearing air masses, such as central Asia.

Figure 15.14 portrays this distribution according to the climate classification used in this text and presents photographs of four major desert regions.

The daily surface energy balance for El Mirage, California, presented in Figure 4.20a and b, highlights the high sensible heat conditions and intense ground heating in the desert. Such areas receive a high input of insolation through generally clear skies and experience high radiative heat losses at night. A typical desert water balance includes high potential evapotranspiration demand, low precipitation supply, and prolonged summer water deficits.

Desert Fluvial Processes

In desert landscapes, running water is the most significant agent of erosion. Rivers and streams in deserts can be described by the type of flow, which may be perennial,

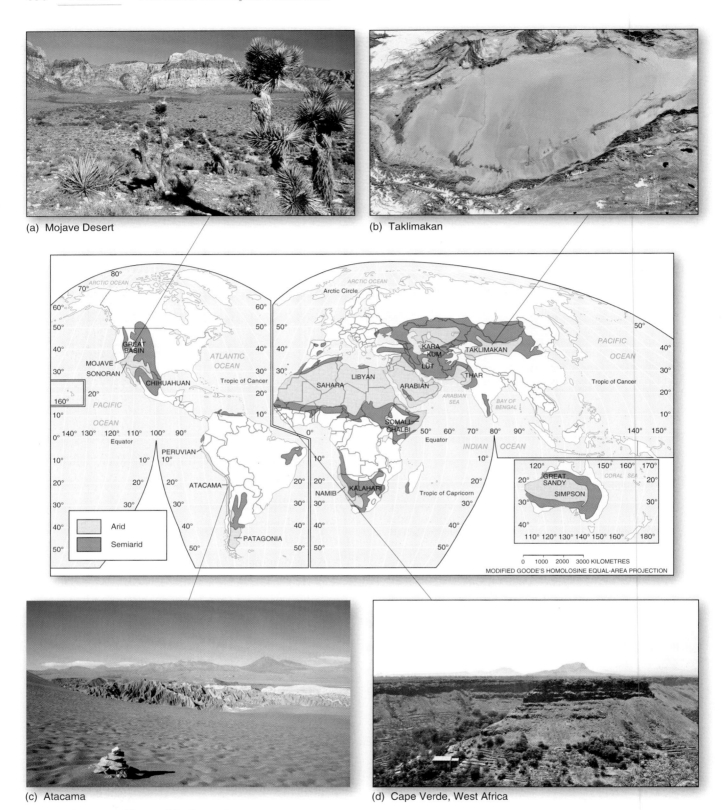

(a) Mojave Desert

(b) Taklimakan

(c) Atacama

(d) Cape Verde, West Africa

FIGURE 15.14 The world's dry regions.
Worldwide distribution of arid lands (*arid desert* climates) and semiarid lands (*semiarid steppe* climates).
(a) Mojave Desert in the American Southwest. (b) Taklimakan Desert in central Asia from orbit. (c) Atacama
Desert in subtropical Chile near Baquedano. (d) São Tiago Island desert in Cape Verde; note the light-coloured
sky filled with dust from Africa. [(a) Robert W. Christopherson; (b) *Terra* image, NASA/GSFC; (c) Hemera/Thinkstock;
(d) Bobbé Christopherson.]

FIGURE 15.15 Water through a dry land.
The Virgin River is a tributary of the Colorado River. This perennial stream is prone to flash floods during precipitation events. The riparian vegetation includes willow, cottonwood, and the water-drawing tamarisk, or salt cedar. [Bobbé Christopherson.]

ephemeral, or intermittent. *Perennial streams* flow all year, fed by snowmelt, rainfall, or groundwater, often in some combination (Figure 15.15). *Ephemeral streams* flow only after precipitation events and are not connected to groundwater systems. Years may pass between flow events in these usually dry stream channels. *Intermittent streams* flow for several weeks or months each year and may have some groundwater inputs. Fluvial processes in deserts are most often characterized by such intermittent running water, with hard, poorly vegetated surfaces of thin, immature soils yielding high runoff during rainstorms.

Precipitation events in a desert may be rare indeed, even years apart, but when a rainstorm occurs, a dry streambed can fill with a torrent, a **flash flood**. These channels may fill in a few minutes and surge briefly during and after a storm. Depending on the region, such a

dry streambed is known as a **wash**, an *arroyo* (Spanish), or a *wadi* (Arabic). Signs are usually posted where a desert highway crosses a wash to warn drivers not to proceed if rain is in the vicinity, for a flash flood can suddenly arise and sweep away anything in its path. If a long, steady precipitation event occurs, material on slopes may become saturated and flow into canyons. *Debris flows* occur as moving masses of mud, soil, and rock fragments mixed with enough water to keep the material flowing. Debris flows can travel at high speed down steep canyons, often leaving unsorted alluvium as the velocity slows and material is deposited.

When washes fill with surging flash flood waters, a unique set of ecological relationships quickly develops. Crashing rocks and boulders break open seeds that respond to the timely moisture and germinate. Other plants and animals also spring into brief life cycles as the water irrigates their limited habitats.

At times of intense rainfall, remarkable scenes fill the desert. Figure 15.16 shows two photographs taken just one month apart in a sand dune field in Death Valley, California. A rainfall event produced 2.6 cm of precipitation in one day, in a place that receives an average of 4.6 cm per year. The stream in the photograph continued to run for hours and then collected in low spots on hard, underlying clay surfaces. The water was quickly consumed by the high evaporation demand so that, in just a month, these short-lived watercourses were dry and covered with accumulations of alluvium. Such evaporation pans coated with salt are visible on a large scale in Figure 15.8a in Algeria (bluish-white areas).

The 1985 precipitation event just described was exceeded by one August 15, 2004, when several thunderstorm cells stalled over the mountains along the east side of Death Valley. Rainfall totals reached 6.4 cm in little more than an hour. Cars were swept away from the Furnace Creek Inn parking lot, about five kilometres off Highways

[text continued on page 470]

(a)

(b)

FIGURE 15.16 An improbable river in Death Valley.
The Stovepipe Wells dune field of Death Valley, California, shown (a) the day after a 2.6-cm rainfall and (b) one month later (identical location). This 1985 rainfall event was exceeded by one in 2004. [Robert Christopherson.]

FOCUS STUDY 15.1

The Colorado River: A System Out of Balance

The headwaters of an exotic stream rise in a region of water surpluses, but the stream flows mostly through arid lands for the rest of its journey to the sea. Exotic streams have few incoming tributaries. Consequently, an exotic stream has a discharge pattern that is different than a typical humid-region stream: Instead of discharge increasing downstream, it decreases (see Chapter 14). The Nile and Colorado rivers are prominent examples.

Orographic precipitation totalling 102 cm per year falls mostly as snow in the American Rockies, feeding the Colorado River headwaters in Rocky Mountain National Park (Figure 15.1.1a). But at Yuma, Arizona, near the river's mouth, annual precipitation is a scant 8.9 cm, an extremely small amount when compared with the high annual potential evapotranspiration demand in the Yuma region of 140 cm.

From its source region, the Colorado River quickly leaves the humid Rockies and spills out into the arid desert of western Colorado and eastern Utah. At Grand Junction, Colorado, near the Utah border, annual precipitation is only 20 cm (upstream from Figure 15.1.1b, on the map). After carving its way through the Utah canyonlands, the river enters Lake Powell, behind Glen Canyon Dam (Figure 15.1.1c), and then flows on through the Grand Canyon. The river then turns southward, marking its final 640 km at the Arizona–California border. Along this stretch sits the Hoover Dam, just east of Las Vegas (Figure 15.1.1d); Davis Dam, built to control the releases from Hoover (Figure 15.1.1e); Parker Dam, for the water needs of Los Angeles; three more dams for irrigation water (Palo Verde, Imperial, and Laguna, Figure 15.1.1f); and finally, Morelos Dam at the Mexican border. Mexico owns the

end of the river and whatever water is left. Hydrologically exhausted, the river no longer reaches its mouth in the Gulf of California (Figure 15.1.1g).

Figure 15.1.1h shows the annual water discharge and suspended sediment load for the Colorado River at Yuma, Arizona, from 1905 to 1964. The completion of Hoover Dam in the 1930s dramatically reduced suspended sediment. Subsequent dams upstream from Yuma reduced both discharge and sediment to nearly zero by the mid-1960s.

Overall, the drainage basin encompasses 641 025 km² of mountain, plateau, canyon, basin-and-range, and hot desert landscapes in parts of seven states and two countries. A discussion of the Colorado River is included in this chapter because of its crucial part in the history of the Southwest and its role in the future of this drought-plagued region.

Dividing Up the Colorado's Dammed Water

John Wesley Powell (1834–1902) was the first European-American of record to successfully navigate the Colorado River through the Grand Canyon. Powell perceived that the challenge of the West was too great for individual efforts and believed that solutions to problems such as water availability could be met only through private cooperative efforts. His 1878 study, *Report of the Lands of the Arid Region of the United States* (reprinted 1962), is a conservation landmark.

Today, Powell probably would be skeptical of the intervention by government agencies in building large-scale water projects. An anecdote in Wallace Stegner's book *Beyond the Hundredth Meridian* tells of an 1893 international irrigation conference held in Los Angeles,

where development-minded delegates bragged that the entire West could be conquered and reclaimed from nature and that "rain will certainly follow the plow." Powell spoke against that sentiment: "I tell you, gentlemen, you are piling up a heritage of conflict and litigation over water rights, for there is not sufficient water to supply the land."[1] He was booed from the hall, but history has shown Powell to be correct.

The Colorado River Compact was signed by six of the seven basin states in 1923. (The seventh state, Arizona, signed in 1944, the same year as the Mexican Water Treaty.) With this compact, the Colorado River basin was divided into an upper basin and a lower basin, arbitrarily separated for administrative purposes at Lees Ferry near the Utah–Arizona border (noted on the map in Figure 15.1.1). The U.S. Congress adopted the Boulder Canyon Act in 1928, authorizing Hoover Dam as the first major water project on the river. Also authorized was the All-American Canal into the Imperial Valley, which required an additional dam. Los Angeles then began its project to bring Colorado River water 390 km from still another dam and reservoir on the river to the city.

Shortly after Hoover Dam was finished and downstream enterprises were thus offered flood protection, the other projects were quickly completed. There are now eight major dams on the river and many irrigation works. The most recent effort to redistribute Colorado River water is the Central Arizona Project, which carries water to the Phoenix and Tucson areas.

[1]W. Stegner, *Beyond the Hundredth Meridian* (Boston, MA: Houghton Mifflin, 1954), p. 343.

FIGURE 15.1.1 The Colorado River drainage basin.
The Colorado River basin, showing division of the upper and lower basins near Lees Ferry in northern Arizona. (a) River headwaters near Mount Richthofen in the Colorado Rockies. (b) The river near Moab, Utah. (c) Glen Canyon Dam, a regulatory, administrative facility near Page, Arizona. (d) Hoover Dam and Lake Mead with declining water levels. (e) Davis Dam in full release during flood. (f) Irrigated fresh-cut flowers in the Imperial Valley, refrigerated trucks in the field, and a cargo jet at a local airport await shipments to distant markets. (g) The Colorado River (far upper left) stops short of its former delta. (h) Dam construction affects river discharge and sediment yields. [(a), (c), (d), and (f) Bobbé Christopherson; (b) and (e) Robert Christopherson; (g) *Terra* image, NASA/ GSFC; (h) Data from U.S. Geological Survey, *National Water Summary 1984*, Water Supply Paper 2275 (Washington, DC: Government Printing Office, 1985), p. 55.]

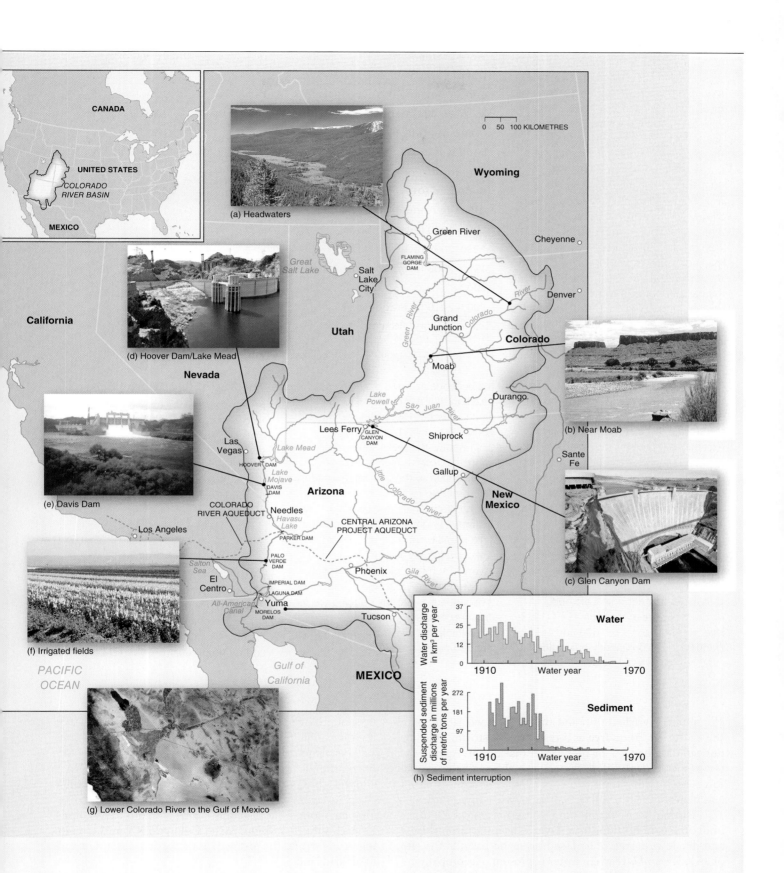

CANADA

UNITED STATES

COLORADO
RIVER BASIN

MEXICO

(a) Headwaters

0   50   100 KILOMETRES

Wyoming

Green River

Cheyenne

FLAMING
GORGE
DAM

Denver

Great
Salt Lake

Salt
Lake
City

California

(d) Hoover Dam/Lake Mead

Nevada

Utah

Grand
Junction

Colorado

Moab

(b) Near Moab

Lake
Powell

Durango

San Juan River

Las
Vegas

Lake Mead

Lees Ferry

GLEN
CANYON
DAM

Shiprock

Sante
Fe

(e) Davis Dam

Lake
Mojave

DAVIS
DAM

HOOVER DAM

Arizona

Gallup

New
Mexico

COLORADO
RIVER AQUEDUCT

Needles

Havasu
Lake

PARKER DAM

CENTRAL ARIZONA
PROJECT AQUEDUCT

Little Colorado River

(c) Glen Canyon Dam

Los Angeles

PALO
VERDE
DAM

Phoenix

Gila River

Salton
Sea

El
Centro

IMPERIAL DAM

LAGUNA DAM

Yuma

All-American
Canal

MORELOS
DAM

Tucson

(f) Irrigated fields

PACIFIC
OCEAN

Gulf of
California

MEXICO

Water discharge
in km³ per year

37

25

12

0

1910   Water year   1970

Water

Suspended sediment
discharge in millions
of metric tons per year

272

181

97

0

1910   Water year   1970

Sediment

(h) Sediment interruption

(g) Lower Colorado River to the Gulf of Mexico

Highly Variable River Flows

The flaw in all this planning and water distribution is that exotic streams have highly variable flows, and the Colorado is no exception. In 1917, the discharge measured at Lees Ferry totalled 29.6 km³, whereas in 1934 it was only 6.2 km³, about 80% lower than 1917. In 1977, the discharge dropped again to 6.2 km³, but in 1984 it rose to an all-time high of 30.4 km³. Yet, in contrast, from 2000 to 2006 river discharge fell to exceptionally low levels, with 2002 dropping to a record low of 3.8 km³, and 2003 to 7.9 km³. The 2002 to 2006 water years marked the lowest 5-year average flow in the total record. Revisit the chapter-opening pair of photos for Chapter 9, showing the comparison of Lake Mead water levels at Hoover Dam in July 1983 and March 2009 as evidence of this variability. By 2009, lake levels had dropped 43.6 m below the 375-m capacity reached in 1983.

As a planning basis for the Colorado River Compact, the government used average river discharges from 1914 up to the compact signing in 1923, an exceptionally high average of 23.2 km³. That amount was perceived as more than enough for the upper and lower basins, each to receive 9.3 km³, and, later, for Mexico to receive 1.9 km³ in the 1944 Mexican Water Treaty.

Should long-range planning be based on such a short time period on a river with highly variable flows? Tree-ring analyses of past climates have disclosed that the only other time Colorado discharges were at the high 1914–1923 level was between A.D. 1606 and 1625. Planners have consistently overestimated

the dependable flows of the river, a situation that has created shortfalls as demand exceeds supply in the water budget (Table 15.1.1).

Presently, the seven states *ideally* want rights that total as high as 30.8 km³. When added to the guarantee for Mexico, this comes up to 32.7 km³ of demands. And six states share one common opinion: California's right to the water must be limited to a court-ordered 5.4 km³, which it exceeded every year until California's access to surplus Colorado River water was stopped in 2002. At present, there is no surplus during the ongoing western drought. And U.S. water planners continue to think that Canadian water resources could somehow be brought south.

TABLE 15.1.1 Estimated Colorado River Budget through 2009

Water Demand	Quantity (km³)
Upper basin, 9.25; lower basin, 9.25[a]	18.5
Central Arizona Project (rising to 3.5 km³)	1.2
Mexican allotment (1944 Treaty)	1.9
Evaporation from reservoirs (when full)	1.9
Bank storage at Lake Powell (when full)	0.6
Phreatophytic losses (water-demanding plants)	0.6
Budgeted total demand	**24.7 km³**
Average Annual Flows at Lees Ferry	
1906–1930 (average flow)	21.8
1930–2003 (average flow)	17.4
1990–2006 (average flow)	14.0
2002	3.8
2003–2010 (average flow)	9.1

Source: Bureau of Reclamation and states of Arizona, California, and Nevada. A water year runs from October 1 to September 30.

[a]In-basin consumptive uses are 75% agricultural.

Colorado River Water Losses

Several natural processes associated with reservoirs and river flow regulation cause water losses and increase overall water demand, as observed in Table 15.1.1. Glen Canyon Dam, located 27 km north of Lees Ferry, the division point between the upper and lower basins, serves as an example.

Glen Canyon Dam was completed in 1963 and began impounding water in Lake Powell. Glen Canyon Dam's primary purpose, according to the Bureau of Reclamation, was to regulate flows between the upper and lower basins. Additional benefits are the production of hydroelectric power and a new recreation and tourism industry around Lake Powell,

190 and 178 washed out, and there were two fatalities in the Zabriskie Point area as a result of the storm. One annex building had a 3-m-high water mark on it. Again, water is sparse in the deserts, yet it is the major erosional force—sometimes dramatically so. For recent information and maps of Death Valley, see http://www.nps.gov/deva/.

As runoff water evaporates, salt crusts may be left behind on the desert floor in a **playa**. This intermittently wet and dry lowest area of a closed drainage basin is the site of an *ephemeral lake* when water is present. Accompanying our earlier discussion of evaporites, in Chapter 11, Figure 11.11 shows such a playa, covered with salt-crust

precipitate over fine clays just one month after the 1985 record rainfall event.

Permanent lakes and continuously flowing rivers are uncommon features in the desert, although the Nile River and the Colorado River are notable exceptions. Both these rivers are *exotic streams*, having headwaters in a wetter region and courses, for the most part, through arid regions. Focus Study 15.1 discusses the Colorado River, the ongoing drought, and the problem of increasing water demands in an arid land.

In arid and semiarid climates, a prominent landform is an **alluvial fan**, which occurs at the mouth of a canyon as previously inaccessible desert scenery now can be reached by boat.

Lake Powell inundated 300 km of former river channel, which cuts through porous Navajo sandstone for much of its length. This sandstone absorbs an estimated 0.6 km^3 of the river's overall annual discharge as bank storage when the reservoir is full—the higher the lake level, the greater the loss into the sandstone. The reservoir also experiences evaporative losses as hot, dry winds flow across an open water body in an arid region. Evaporation accounts for another 0.6 km^3 of discharge lost annually from the reservoir, equaling about a third of all Colorado River reservoir evaporation losses—again, higher lake levels mean more losses.

In the upper reaches of large reservoirs where water levels fluctuate, as well as along reaches of regulated river flow below dams throughout the basin, sand bars and banks have become near-permanent features. Riparian vegetation has colonized those surfaces, including dense thickets of water-demanding plants called phreatophytes. These species extract and transpire an additional 0.6 km^3 per year of the river flow. The three water losses discussed here—bank storage, evaporation, and water use by vegetation—are an increasingly large percentage of the overall river discharge as drought conditions persist.

Ongoing Drought in the Colorado River Basin

A ongoing period of drought began in the Colorado River basin in 2000. Continuing population growth throughout the region compounds the problem of increasing water demand coupled with decreased river flows. The drought itself appears directly linked to the shifting of subtropical high-pressure systems with climate change. This expansion of subtropical dry zones has given scientists a new approach to understanding drought. In regions such as the American Southwest, application of the term *drought* is changing to consideration of a change in *permanent average climate*. When future droughts occur—for example, during a Pacific Ocean La Niña condition—these will be in addition to this new base state of a drier climate. This is unprecedented in the climate record for this region.

In contrast, basin streamflow increased in 2011 as the La Niña weather pattern shifted, causing high snowpack and producing a late spring melt across the Colorado River headwaters and Rockies. By July 2011, Lake Powell was up to 72% of capacity, its highest level since October 2001. Lake Mead was 46% of capacity, up from a low of 41% in 2010. However, scientists agree that the overall trend of declining snowfall and ongoing drought appears set and will continue to cause declining reservoir levels. Climate change is in fact increasing such natural system variability.

Engineers estimate that it could take 13 normal winters of snowpack in the Rockies and basin-wide precipitation to "reset" the system. Such a recovery is much slower than previous drought recoveries because of increasing evaporation associated with increasing temperatures across the Southwest as well as increasing human water use. Present probabilities for the period after 2016 put the chances of surplus streamflow occurring in the Colorado River system in any given year at only 20%.

Government stopgap measures to address water shortages came to a head in December 2007 when the Department of the Interior signed a historic Record of Decision, an agreement representing a consensus among the stakeholders. This agreement sets the rules for dealing with water shortages during the drought and determining where water deliveries will be cut; guides the operation rules for Lake Mead and Lake Powell (see http://www.usbr.gov/lc/region/programs/strategies/RecordofDecision.pdf).

Conservation (using less water) and efficiency (using water more effectively) are not yet being stressed as ways to reduce the tremendous demand for water across the Southwest. For instance, southern Nevada has launched a campaign to replace lawns with drought-tolerant xeriscaping—desert landscaping—but with 150 000 hotel rooms, we might question planning efforts. Las Vegas receives 90% of its water from the Colorado River and could save 30% of its usage by simply requiring water-efficient fixtures and appliances in hotels and residences.

Limiting or halting further metropolitan construction and population growth in the Colorado River Basin is not part of present strategies to lower demand. The focus remains on water supply. We might wonder what John Wesley Powell would think if he were alive today to witness such errant attempts to control the mighty and variable Colorado River. He foretold such a "heritage of conflict and litigation."

where an ephemeral stream channel exits into a valley (Figure 15.17). The fan is produced whenever flowing water abruptly loses velocity as it leaves the constricted channel of the canyon, or wherever the stream gradient suddenly decreases, and therefore drops layer upon layer of sediment along the base of the mountain block. Water then flows over the surface of the fan and produces a braided drainage pattern, sometimes shifting from channel to channel. A continuous apron, or **bajada** (Spanish for "slope"), may form if adjacent alluvial fans coalesce into one sloping surface (see Figure 15.22c and d). Fan formation of any sort is reduced in humid climates because perennial streams constantly carry away sediment, preventing its deposition.

An aspect of an alluvial fan is the natural sorting of materials by size. Near the mouth of the canyon at the apex of the fan, coarser materials are deposited, grading slowly to pebbles and finer gravels with distance out from the mouth. Then sands and silts are deposited, with the finest clays and dissolved salts carried in suspension and solution all the way to the valley floor. Dissolved minerals accumulate as evaporite deposits on the valley floor left after evaporation of the water from the playa, and from salt-laden, upward moving groundwater. Figure 15.18 shows the edge

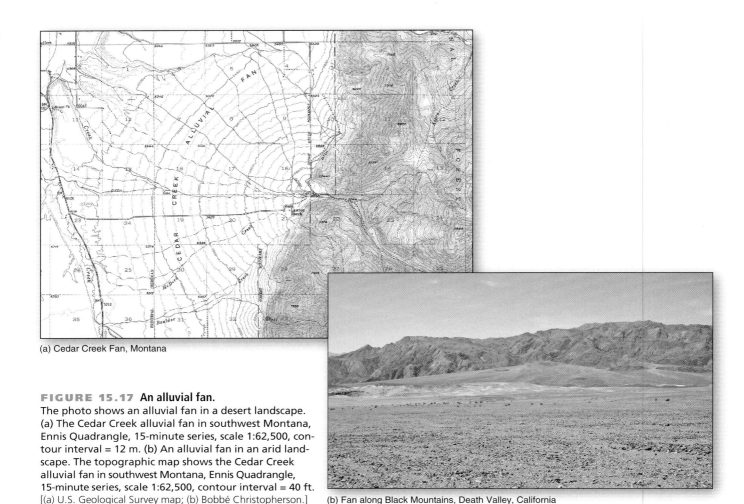

(a) Cedar Creek Fan, Montana

FIGURE 15.17 An alluvial fan.
The photo shows an alluvial fan in a desert landscape.
(a) The Cedar Creek alluvial fan in southwest Montana,
Ennis Quadrangle, 15-minute series, scale 1:62,500, contour interval = 12 m. (b) An alluvial fan in an arid landscape. The topographic map shows the Cedar Creek
alluvial fan in southwest Montana, Ennis Quadrangle,
15-minute series, scale 1:62,500, contour interval = 40 ft.
[(a) U.S. Geological Survey map; (b) Bobbé Christopherson.]

(b) Fan along Black Mountains, Death Valley, California

**FIGURE 15.18 Sand and playa—natural sorting of
materials.**
Playa of dissolved and finer materials (top of photo), sand dunes
(middle), and coarser particles on slopes along the mountains
(lower area) demonstrate the natural sorting that occurs in desert landscapes. [Bobbé Christopherson.]

of a playa and active dune field, so there is a natural sorting
of materials by grain size, with sands dropped in the dunes,
silts and clays moving farther toward the playa, and the finest and dissolved materials in the playa.

Well-developed alluvial fans also can be a major source
of groundwater. Some cities—San Bernardino, California,
for example—are built on alluvial fans and extract their
municipal water supplies from them. In other parts of the
world, such water-bearing alluvial fans are known as *qanat*
(Iran), *karex* (Pakistan), or *foggara* (western Sahara).

CRITICAL THINKING 15.2

Water in the Desert

Water is the major erosion and transport medium in the desert,
although less frequently available than in humid regions.
Respond to this concept. How is it possible for this to be true
when deserts are so dry? What have you learned from this
chapter that proves this statement true? Review some of the
examples presented.

Desert Landscapes

Deserts are not wastelands, for specially adapted plants and animals abound. Moreover, the limited vegetation and distant vistas produce starkly beautiful landscapes. The desert's visual enchantment is keyed to light and naked rock formations. The shimmering heat waves and related mirage effects are products of light refraction through layers of air that have developed a temperature gradient near the hot ground. And all deserts are not the same: For example, North American deserts have more vegetation cover than do the generally more barren Asian desert expanses, as we saw in Figure 15.14.

Deserts possess unique landscapes created by the interaction of intermittent precipitation events, weathering processes, and wind with the underlying geology. The buttes, pinnacles, and mesas of the U.S. Southwest are resistant horizontal rock strata that have eroded differentially. Removal of the less-resistant sandstone strata produces unusual desert sculptures—arches, windows, pedestals, and delicately balanced rocks. The upper layers of sandstone along the top of an arch or butte or tower are more resistant to weathering and protect the sandstone rock beneath (Figure 15.19).

The removal of surrounding rock through differential weathering leaves enormous buttes as residuals on the landscape. If you imagine a line intersecting the tops of the Mitten Buttes shown in Figure 15.20, you can gain some idea of the quantity of material that has been removed. These buttes exceed 300 m in height, similar to First Canadian Place in Toronto or the Chrysler Building in New York City.

Desert landscapes are places where stark erosional remnants can stand above the surrounding terrain as knobs or hills. Such a bare, exposed rock is an *inselberg* (island mountain), as exemplified by Uluru (Ayers) Rock in Australia. The formation is 348 m high and 2.5 km long by 1.6 km wide. Uluru Rock is sacred to Aboriginal peoples and is protected as part of Uluru National Park, established in 1950.

In semiarid regions, weak surface material may weather to a complex, rugged topography, usually of relatively low and varied relief. Such a landscape is a **badland**, probably so named because in the American West it offered little economic value and was difficult to traverse in 19th-century wagons. The Badlands region of Alberta, the Dakotas and northcentral Arizona (the Painted Desert) are so named.

Patterns of cross bedding, or *cross-stratification*, are sometimes present in desert sandstone, formed by lithification of sand dunes that existed in ancient deserts. When such a dune was accumulating, sand cascaded down its slipface and distinct bedding planes (layers) were established that remained after the dune lithified (Figure 15.21). Ripple marks, animal tracks, and fossils also are found preserved in these sandstones.

Basin and Range Province

A physiographic province is a large region that is identified by several geologic or physiographic traits. We find alternating basins (valleys) and mountain ranges that lie in the rain shadow of mountains to the west characterizing the **Basin and Range Province** of the western United

(a) Balanced Rock in Utah

(b) Spider Rock in Arizona

FIGURE 15.19 A balanced rock—Differential weathering.
(a) Balanced Rock in Arches National Park, Utah. The overall feature is 39 m tall and composed of Entrada sandstone. The balance-rock portion is 17 m tall and weighs 3255 metric tons. (b) Spider Rock towers 244 m above the canyon floor of Canyon de Chelly, Arizona, in winter—a dramatic monolith; note the lighter colour in the capstone rock.
[(a) Robert Christopherson; (b) Bobbé Christopherson.]

FIGURE 15.20 Monument Valley landscape.
(a) Mitten Buttes, Merrick Butte, and rainbow in Monument Valley, Navajo Tribal Park, which have appeared
as a backdrop in many movies, along the Utah–Arizona border. (b) A schematic of the tremendous removal
of material by weathering, erosion, and transport. (c) Aerial view of Monument Valley. (d) View just east of
(c), showing the residual spires of the Yie Bi Chei rock formation that ends with Totem Pole, 137 m tall and only
10 m wide. [(a) and (d) inset by Robert Christopherson; (c) and (d) Bobbé Christopherson.]

States (Figure 15.22). This region lies in the rain shadow
of the Sierra Nevada mountains, giving it a *midlatitude cold
desert* climate. The climate and geology combine to give
the province few permanent streams and *internal drainage*
that lacks any outlet to the ocean (in Figure 14.5, see the
Great Basin and its internal drainage).

The vast Basin and Range Province—almost
800 000 km^2—was a major barrier to early settlers in their
migration westward. The combination of desert climate
and north–south trending mountain ranges presented
harsh challenges. Today, U.S. Highway 50 across Nevada
crosses five passes of more than 1950 m and traverses

(a) Valley of Fire

(b) Red Rocks

FIGURE 15.21 **Cross bedding in sedimentary rocks.**
The bedding pattern of cross stratification in these sandstone rocks tells us about dune environments before lithification (hardening into rock). [Bobbé Christopherson.]

numerous basins. It is difficult to imagine crossing this topography with wagons and oxen (Figure 15.22e).

John McPhee captured the feel of this desert province in his book *Basin and Range*:

> Supreme over all is silence. Discounting the cry of the occasional bird, the wailing of a pack of coyotes, silence—a great spatial silence—is pure in the Basin and Range. It is a soundless immensity with mountains in it. You stand . . . and look up at a high mountain front, and turn your head and look fifty miles down the valley, and there is utter silence.[3]

The Basin and Range formed as a result of tectonic processes. As the North American plate lumbered westward, it overrode former oceanic crust and hot spots at such a rapid pace that slabs of subducted material literally were run over. The crust was uplifted and stretched, creating a tensional landscape fractured by many faults. The present landscape consists of nearly parallel sequences; some are tilted-fault blocks, others have pairs of faults on either side of *horsts* of upward-faulted blocks, which are the "ranges," and *grabens* of downward fault-bounded blocks, which are the "basins." Figure 15.22c shows this pattern of normal faults and tensional stretching.

Basin-and-range relief is abrupt, and rock structures are angular and rugged. As the ranges erode, transported materials accumulate to great depths in the basins, gradually producing extensive desert plains. The basin's elevation averages roughly 1200–1500 m above sea level,

with mountain crests rising higher by another 900–1500 m. Death Valley, California, is the lowest of these basins, with an elevation of –86 m. However, to the west of the valley, the Panamint Range rises to 3368 m at Telescope Peak—almost 3.5 vertical kilometres of desert mountain relief.

In Figure 15.22c and d, note the **bolson**, a slope-and-basin area between the crests of two adjacent ridges in a dry region of internal drainage. Figure 15.22c also identifies a *playa* (central pan), a *bajada* (coalesced alluvial fans), and a mountain front in retreat from weathering and erosional attack. A *pediment* is an area of bedrock that is layered with a thin veneer, or coating, of alluvium. It is an erosional surface, as opposed to the depositional surface of the bajada.

Vast arid and semiarid lands remain an enigma on the water planet. These areas challenge our technology to access water, our courage, and personal need for water. Yet these lands hold a fascination, perhaps because they are so lacking in the moisture that infuses our lives.

█ ▌▌   CRITICAL THINKING 15.3

Relating to the Colorado River Crisis

Relative to the Colorado River system, define, compare, and contrast what you think is meant by a *supply strategy* or a *demand strategy*. How does each strategy relate to the present Colorado River water budget (Table 15.1.1, Focus Study 15.1)? What political and economic forces do you think are at play in planning for the river and its dependent region? Who are the stakeholders? With your analysis, briefly speculate as to what you think needs to happen.

[3]J. McPhee, *Basin and Range* (New York, NY: Farrar, Straus, Giroux, 1981), p. 46.

(a)

(b)

(c)

(d) Death Valley bolson

(e) Playas in Nevada

FIGURE 15.22 Basin and Range Province in the western United States.
(a) Map and (b) *Landsat* image of the area. Scientific discoveries extend this province south through northern and central Mexico. (c) Parallel faults produce a series of ranges and basins, including a bolson. (d) Death Valley features a central playa, parallel mountain ranges, alluvial fans, and bajadas along the bases of the ranges. (e) Playas can be seen in several basins. [(b) NASA; (d) Robert Christopherson; (e) Bobbé Christopherson.]

FIGURE 15.23 Sensitivity to wind erosion with climate change.
Risk for erosion of unprotected soils in areas sensitive to climate change is greatest in the southern and central Prairies and in southernmost Ontario. [Map adapted from *The Atlas of Canada*, with the permission of Natural Resources Canada.]

Climate Change and Increased Aridity in Canada

Greenhouse gas emissions are increasing annually and a doubling of carbon dioxide emissions may take place within the next 50 years. Since 2000, atmospheric carbon dioxide increased at a rate of 3.1% per year, which can lead to a doubling in as little as 20 years. Some climate models predict that changes in precipitation and temperature caused by this doubling will force grasslands to shift northward and to grow in regions now covered by boreal plant forest communities. As grasslands shift northward and to higher elevations, the present day grasslands are predicted to become semidesert. And in turn, the boreal forest is shifting northward, encroaching on the tundra regions.

When plant communities shift in response to temperature and precipitation changes, the nature of geological processes that act in an area are likely to change as well, so increased aridity may influence the distribution and intensity of eolian processes. Climate change can cause dramatic reduction of vegetation, exposing soil surfaces. Thus, changes in the timing and amount of precipitation and variations in temperature regime may cause changes in eolian erosion.

The Geological Survey of Canada (GSC) modelled the sensitivity of eolian processes to climate change on the basis of predicted shifts of vegetation communities. Climate model results indicate that reactivation and increased movement of sand dunes and the increased erosion of unprotected, bare soils are likely to occur as climate changes. If predicted changes in vegetation cover and moisture conditions increase soil moisture deficits, sensitivity to eolian erosion increases.

A survey of the sensitivity of dune areas in Canada that will be affected by climate change is illustrated in Figure 15.23. The least sensitive regions to potential increased wind erosion include the arctic, subarctic, boreal, cool temperate forest, and transitional grassland have a low sensitivity to changes in eolian processes.

Moderately sensitive areas include the existing boreal regions that may change to grassland and cool temperate regions that may change to moderate temperate regions. In these moderate regions—central Saskatchewan, some regions of Manitoba, Ontario, Québec, and the Maritimes—some reactivation of sand dunes and some soil erosion are likely. Areas that are currently grassland and moderate temperate regions are likely to become more arid. These regions of increased aridity are predicted to be highly sensitive to climate change, and may experience significant increases in eolian and dune activity. These regions are predicted to change to semi-desert. The Palliser Triangle, including the Great Sand

Hills of Saskatchewan and Alberta, has severe sensitivity to eolian activity. Figure 15.23 reflects wind erosion risk as well throughout these low, moderate, and high sensitivity regions.

We now have the first circumarctic scientific analysis of the impact of global warming on the Arctic Region. The Arctic Council empowered the Arctic Monitoring and Assessment Programme (AMAP), Conservation of Arctic Flora and Fauna (CAFF), and the International Arctic Science Committee (IASC) to conduct this study and prepare a comprehensive report. The Arctic Climate Impact Assessment (ACIA—http://www.acia.uaf.edu), released in November 2004 following 4 years of study by 300 scientists and indigenous peoples, stated in one section of the ACIA report regarding the impact of warming and potential desertification in the high latitudes:

> Because the rate of evaporation increases as temperatures climb, if precipitation does not rise enough to keep up with that increase, land areas would dry out. . . followed by desertification in some areas as warming continues.

 APPLIED PHYSICAL GEOGRAPHY   *Wind Erosion*

The ability of wind to move objects is small when compared with other transporting agents (e.g., water, ice, gravity), but over time, the amount of material moved can be large. The exponential increase in the rate of sand movement with an increase in wind velocity is illustrated in Figure 15.2. Erosion of surface material, especially soil, has been a concern to Prairie farmers for a long time. The dry climate, the intensity of farming, and the open spaces of the Canadian Prairies make them especially susceptible to wind erosion.

Wind erosion of the soil occurs in three stages. First, individual soil particles must be detached. This is usually accomplished by frost action, mineral expansion and contraction, alternate wetting and drying, mechanical shear, or abrasion. Once detached, soil particles are available to be transported. Wind speed is lowest at the ground surface and increases exponentially

TABLE 1	Soil Loss from 1992 Windstorm and Breakdown of Soil Movement for Two Sites in Manitoba[a]		
		Site 1	**Site 2**
Total soil loss (metric tons per hectare)		16.25	18.45
% Soil loss from:			
Surface creep		1	1
Saltation		81	69
Suspension		18	30

[a]The field length was 400 m. Soil loss was calculated in kg on an area of 0.04 hectare (1 m wide and 400 m long). Wind speed for this event was 50–75 km·h[-1].

Source: Manitoba Agriculture, Food and Rural Initiatives, http://www.gov.mb.ca/agriculture/soilwater/soil/fbd01s01.html.

upward until surface friction is overcome.

The most important factors to consider when calculating wind erosion are air velocity and turbulence; soil structure, density, and moisture content; and surface roughness, cover, obstructions, and topographic features. Mathematical models calculate soil losses by combining these factors. Table 1 shows the calcula-

tions of soil loss for a 1992 windstorm in Manitoba.

The loss of soil in metric tons per hectare is a volume measurement. What does this mean for depth of soil lost? If we assume a bulk density of 1mg·m[-3], then 10 metric tons per hectare of soil loss is equal to 1 mm of soil depth. So at Site 1, 1.6 mm of soil and, at Site 2, 1.8 mm of soil were lost during a single storm.

GEOSYSTEMS CONNECTION

Wind is an agent of geomorphic change, causing erosion, transportation, and deposition of sediments, sometimes redistributing materials among continents. Sand accumulations form dunes of several types, including crescentic, linear, and star dunes. Wind also transports fine-grained clays and silts to form loess deposits. Wind and scarce water operate in Earth's desert regions, where both sandy and rocky surfaces are found. In the next chapter, we examine coastal processes involved with the agents of waves, tides, and currents that sculpt Earth's erosional and depositional coastlines. A significant portion of the human population lives in coastal areas, making hazard perception and planning in times of predicted rising sea level important applied aspects of Chapter 16.

KEY LEARNING CONCEPTS REVIEW

■ *Desertification* is the ongoing process that leads to an unwanted expansion of the Earth's desert lands; presently, some 1 billion people are affected, and a new international effort is framed under the United Nations Decade for Deserts and the Fight against Desertification.

> desertification (p. 453)

1. What is meant by desertification? Using the maps in Figures GN 15.1, 15.14 and 15.22 and the text description, locate several of the regions affected by desert expansion.

■ *Characterize* the unique geomorphic work accomplished by wind and eolian processes.

The movement of the atmosphere in response to pressure differences produces wind. Wind is a geomorphic agent of erosion, transportation, and deposition. **Eolian** processes modify and move sand accumulations along coastal beaches and deserts. Wind's ability to move materials is small compared with that of water and ice.

> eolian (p. 454)

2. Explain the term *eolian* and its application in this chapter. How would you characterize the ability of wind to move material as shown in Figure 15.2?
3. Who was Ralph Bagnold? What was his contribution to eolian studies?

■ *Describe* eolian erosion, including deflation, abrasion, and the resultant landforms.

Two principal wind-erosion processes are **deflation**, the removal and lifting of individual loose particles, and **abrasion**, the "sandblasting" of rock surfaces with particles captured in the air. Deflation literally blows away loose or noncohesive sediment and works with rainwater to form a surface resembling a cobblestone street: a **desert pavement** that protects underlying sediment from further deflation and water erosion. Wherever wind encounters loose sediment, deflation may remove enough material to form basins. Called **blowout depressions**, they range from small indentations less than a metre wide up to areas hundreds of metres wide and many metres deep. Rocks that bear evidence of eolian erosion are called **ventifacts**. On a larger scale, deflation and abrasion are capable of streamlining rock structures, leaving

behind distinctive rock formations or elongated ridges called **yardangs**.

> deflation (p. 455)
> abrasion (p. 455)
> desert pavement (p. 455)
> blowout depressions (p. 456)
> ventifacts (p. 456)
> yardangs (p. 456)

4. Describe the erosional processes associated with moving air.
5. Explain deflation and give an overview of each hypothesis on the processes that produce desert pavement.
6. How are ventifacts and yardangs formed by the wind?

■ *Describe* eolian transportation, and *explain* saltation and surface creep.

Wind may exert a drag or frictional pull on surface particles to cause the particles to become airborne. The finer material suspended in a dust storm is lifted much higher than the coarser particles of a sandstorm; only the finest dust particles travel significant distances. Saltating particles bounce along and crash into other particles, knocking them both loose and forward. The motion of **surface creep** slides and rolls particles too large for saltation.

> surface creep (p. 458)

7. Differentiate between a dust storm and a sandstorm.
8. What is the difference between eolian saltation and fluvial saltation?
9. Explain the concept of surface creep.

■ *Identify* the major classes of sand dunes, and *present* examples within each class.

In arid and semiarid climates and along some coastlines where sand is available, dunes accumulate. A **dune** is a wind-sculpted accumulation of sand. An extensive area of dunes, such as that found in North Africa, is characteristic of an **erg desert**, or **sand sea**. When saltating sand grains encounter small patches of sand, the kinetic energy (motion) is dissipated and grains start to accumulate into a dune. As height increases above 30 cm, a steeply sloping **slipface** on the lee side and characteristic dune features are formed. Dune forms are broadly classified as *crescentic, linear,* and *star*.

> dune (p. 459)
> erg desert (p. 459)
> sand sea (p. 459)
> slipface (p. 459)

10. What is the difference between an erg and a reg desert? Which type is a sand sea? Are all deserts covered by sand? Explain.
11. What are the three classes of dune forms? Describe the basic types of dunes within each class. What do you think is the major shaping force determining the shape of sand dunes?
12. Which form of dune is the mountain giant of the desert? What are the characteristic wind patterns that produce such dunes?

■ *Define* loess deposits and their origins, locations, and landforms.

Eolian-transported materials may contribute to soil formation in places far from source areas. Windblown **loess** deposits occur worldwide and can develop into good agricultural soils. These fine-grained clays and silts are moved by the wind many kilometres, and are redeposited as an unstratified, homogeneous blanket of material.

> loess (p. 461)

13. How are loess materials generated? What form does loess assume when deposited?
14. Name a few examples of significant loess deposits on Earth.

■ *Portray* desert landscapes, and *locate* these regions on a world map.

Dry and semiarid climates occupy about 35% of Earth's land surface. The spatial distribution of these dry lands is related to subtropical high-pressure cells between 15° and 35° N and S, to rain shadows on the lee side of mountain ranges, or to areas at great distance from moisture-bearing air masses, such as central Asia.

Precipitation events are rare, yet running water is still the major erosional agent in deserts. When precipitation events do occur, a dry streambed fills with a torrent called a **flash flood**. Such a dry streambed is known as a **wash**. As runoff water evaporates, salt crusts may be left behind on the desert floor. This intermittently wet and dry low area in a region of closed drainage is called a **playa**, site of an *ephemeral lake* when water is present.

In arid climates, a prominent landform is an **alluvial fan** at the mouth of a canyon where it exits into a valley. The fan is produced by flowing water that abruptly loses velocity as it leaves the constricted channel of the canyon and deposits a layer of sediment along the mountain block. A continuous apron, or **bajada**, may form if adjacent alluvial fans coalesce. In a desert area, weak surface material may weather to a complex, rugged topography, usually of relatively low and varied relief. Such a landscape is a **badland**. A *province* is a large region that is characterized by several geologic or physiographic traits. The **Basin and Range Province** of the western United States consists of alternating basins and mountain ranges. A slope-and-basin area between the crests of two adjacent ridges in a dry region of internal drainage is a **bolson**.

> flash flood (p. 467)
> wash (p. 467)
> playa (p. 470)
> alluvial fan (p. 470)
> bajada (p. 471)
> badland (p. 473)
> Basin and Range Province (p. 473)
> bolson (p. 475)

15. Characterize desert energy and water-balance regimes. What are the significant patterns of occurrence for arid landscapes in the world?
16. How would you describe the water budget of the Colorado River? What was the basis for agreements regarding distribution of the river's water? Why has thinking about the river's discharge been so optimistic? Provide an overview of current conditions of the Colorado River system in light of the ongoing drought and increasing water demands.
17. Describe a desert bolson from crest to crest. Draw a simple sketch with the components of the landscape labelled.
18. Where is the Basin and Range Province? Briefly describe its appearance and character.
19. With climate change, what changes are predicted for eolian processes in Canada? Which areas are most likely to experience change? Where will sand dunes most likely be active?

MyGeosciencePlace

Visit **www.mygeoscienceplace.ca** for several figure animations, satellite loops, self-study quizzes, flashcards, interactive glossary, career links, RSS feeds, Pearson eText of *Geosystems*, and much more.

CHAPTER 16

The Oceans, Coastal Processes, and Landforms

Turtle Beach, Ascension Island, where female green sea turtles (*Chelonia mydas*) leave the sea and climb the beach to lay their eggs in nests dug in the sand. Upon hatching, the young make their way back to the ocean. The turtles migrate great distances from their feeding areas of seagrass to these nesting/hatching beaches. On this volcanic island, the light sand originates from formations of calcarious algae that fish consume to make the sand. Ascension Island is 8° S 14.5° W; the beach is near Georgetown. [Bobbé Christopherson.]

KEY LEARNING CONCEPTS

After reading the chapter, you should be able to:

- **Describe** the chemical composition of seawater and the physical structure of the ocean.
- **Identify** the components of the coastal environment, and **list** the physical inputs to the coastal system, including tides and mean sea level.
- **Describe** wave motion at sea and near shore, and **explain** coastal straightening as a product of wave refraction.
- **Describe** barrier islands and associated hazards that relate to human settlement.
- **Assess** living coastal environments: corals, wetlands, salt marshes, and mangroves.
- **Construct** an environmentally sensitive model for settlement and land use along the coast.

Coastal Communities Facing Changes

Coastlines are dynamic environments at the interface between land and bodies of water, constantly changing as energy associated with the movements of water is absorbed and redistributed. This chapter shows how the absorption of energy contained in wave, tide, and current motions explains coastal processes and the creation of coastal landforms. We created many present-day problems by building communities at coastlines without fully recognizing the effect this could have on the dynamic coastal environment. In many places we are now forced to deal with resulting coastal hazards and implement adaptive strategies to accommodate coastal changes.

While sea level rise is not always the cause of coastal erosion or flooding, rising sea level linked to global climate change is increasing the severity and frequency of these processes. The town of Tuktoyaktuk, Northwest Territories, on the Beaufort Sea coast is experiencing the effects of sea level rise (3–4 mm per year) but those effects are being further compounded by two related impacts of warming climate: melting permafrost which destabilizes the ground, and reduced sea ice in the Arctic Ocean which eliminates an important buffer against wave energy.

Tuktoyaktuk is located on a low-lying peninsula at the northern edge of the Mackenzie River delta. Shoreline erosion is threatening the continued existence of this community. A recent study of Arctic shorelines showed average erosion rates of 0.5 m per year with the highest rates along the Beaufort Sea coast; about double the average value. Localized rates of erosion can be up to 8 m per year.

In 1994 an engineering study commissioned by the municipality showed that shoreline erosion was a problem at Tuktoyaktuk and recommended complete relocation of the town. To date this has not occurred, and some buildings have been lost or relocated. Instead, the problem was addressed by trying to slow erosion rates with the placement of concrete, rocks, and sandbags (Figure GN 16.1). Wave energy is absorbed better by the heavier materials, thus protecting smaller sediment particles from being eroded. These measures are unlikely to succeed in the long-term as the ground becomes destabilized with melting permafrost and as sea level continues to rise. Also, sea ice dampens the effects of storms, but with less sea ice there will be more frequent high-energy waves generated in the open water able to cause erosion along an unprotected coastline.

Halifax, Nova Scotia, is an example of a larger community that is seeing the effects of sea level rise. Land use for much of the waterfront around Halifax Harbour consists of a mixture of commercial, industrial, and residential infrastructure (Figure GN 16.2). Recent storms, including Hurricane Juan in 2003, Earl and Igor

FIGURE GN 16.1 Shoreline protection measures at Tuktoyaktuk, NWT
Sandbags were placed on a beach to protect it from storm waves in an attempt to slow the rate of coastal erosion. [© Gunter Marx Stock Photos.]

FIGURE GN 16.2 Downtown Halifax waterfront.
Recent storms have caused damage to areas along the waterfront, and the occurrence of flooding is expected to increase as sea level rises. [Dan Doucette/Infotography.]

in 2010, and Irene, Maria, and Ophelia in 2011, caused erosion and flooding around the harbour. Similar impacts are being observed throughout the Maritimes, where much of the coastline has been rated as highly sensitive to sea level rise by Geological Survey of Canada–Atlantic scientists. (See the CoastWeb site, http://www.nrcan.gc.ca/earth-sciences/geography-boundary/coastal-research/7191, for more information on coastal change issues and research conducted by the GSC.)

While British Columbia's coast will not be immune to sea level rise, it is considered to have low to moderate sensitivity because it generally is composed of hard rock and slopes steeply away from the shoreline. However, there are some places where rapid change is occurring, such as on the northeast coast of Graham Island in the Haida Gwaii archipelago.

The Fraser River delta—including much of the metropolitan Vancouver region—is a low-lying area that is particularly vulnerable to sea level rise. Parts of the delta, particularly the cities of Richmond and Delta, are sinking at rates of 1–2 mm per year, with some areas having subsidence rates of 5–10 mm per year. This is caused by the compaction of sediments from the weight of human infrastructure combined with the fact that the river no longer replenishes the surface with sediment during flood periods. Instead, humans have constructed protective levees that prevent flooding and force sediment to be carried out into the Strait of Georgia.

As well as having coastlines on three oceans, Canada has many large lakes where other coastal processes operate. As you progress through this chapter, look for examples of how human activities can disrupt natural coastal processes—and how natural coastal processes can affect humans. To understand coastlines in inhabited areas and how best to accommodate and adapt to changes, we need to study and understand basic coastal controls and processes.

Walk along a shoreline and you witness the dramatic interaction of Earth's vast oceanic, atmospheric, and lithospheric systems. At times, the ocean attacks the coast in a stormy rage of erosive power; at other times, the moist sea breeze, salty mist, and repetitive motion of the water are gentle and calming. Coastlines are areas of dynamic change and beauty. Few have captured this confrontation between land and sea as well as biologist Rachel Carson:

> The edge of the sea is a strange and beautiful place. All through the long history of Earth it has been an area of unrest where waves have broken heavily against the land, where the tides have pressed forward over the continents, receded, and then returned. For no two successive days is the shoreline precisely the same. Not only do the tides advance and retreat in their eternal rhythms, but the level of the sea itself is never at rest. It rises or falls as the glaciers melt or grow, as the floors of the deep ocean basins shift under its increasing load of sediments, or as the Earth's crust along the continental margins warps up or down in adjustment to strain and tension. Today a little more land may belong to the sea, tomorrow a little less. Always the edge of the sea remains an elusive and indefinable boundary.[1]

Commerce and access to sea routes, fishing, and tourism prompt many people to settle near the ocean. A scientific assessment estimates that about 40% of Earth's population lives within 100 km of coastlines. More than 42% of Canada's population lives in areas designated as *coastal* (this includes the Great Lakes coasts).

Therefore, an understanding of coastal processes and landforms is important to a high proportion of the world's population. And because these processes along coastlines often produce dramatic change, it is essential to consider these in planning and development. A World Resources Institute study found as much as 50% of the world's coastlines at some risk of loss through things like erosion and rising sea level or disruption from pollution.

The ocean is a vast ecosystem, intricately linked to life on the planet and to life-sustaining systems in the atmosphere, the hydrosphere, and the lithosphere. Oceans act as a vast buffering system, absorbing excess atmospheric carbon dioxide and thermal energy, yet the system is overwhelmed with the rate of change over the past several decades. In 2009, the second meeting of the Conference on the Ocean Observing System for Climate took place in Venice, Italy; the first meeting was 10 years earlier. The 2009 program noted the profound changes that had transpired in the ocean system and set a goal for a new physical and carbon ocean observing system by 2015—see http://www.oceanobs09.net/.

In this chapter: We begin the chapter with a brief look at our global oceans and seas. We discuss the physical and chemical properties of seawater. Our coverage includes discussions about tides, waves, coastal erosional and depositional landforms, beaches, and barrier islands. Important organic processes produce corals, wetlands, salt marshes, and mangroves. A systems framework of specific inputs (components and driving forces), actions (movements and processes), and outputs (results and consequences) organizes our discussion of coastal processes. We conclude with a look at the considerable human interaction and impact on coastal environments.

---

[1]"The Marginal World," in *The Edge of the Sea* by Rachel Carson. © 1955 by Rachel Carson, renewed 1983 by R. Christie (Boston: Houghton Mifflin), 11.

▬ Global Oceans and Seas

The ocean is one of Earth's last great scientific frontiers and is of great interest to geographers. Remote sensing from orbit, aircraft, surface vessels, and submersibles is providing a wealth of data and a new capability to understand the oceanic system. The pattern of sea-surface temperatures is presented in Figure 5.11 and ocean currents both surface and deep in Figures 6.20 and 6.22. The world's oceans, and oceanic area, volume, and depth, are listed in a table in Figure 7.3. The locations of oceans and major seas are shown and listed alphabetically in Figure 16.1.

Chemical Composition of Seawater

Water is the "universal solvent," dissolving at least 57 of the 92 elements found in nature. In fact, most natural elements and the compounds they form are found in the seas as dissolved solids, or *solutes*. Thus, seawater is a solution, and the concentration of dissolved solids is **salinity**.

Seawater is a remarkably homogeneous mixture. The ratio of individual salts does not change, despite there being minor fluctuations in overall salinity. In 1874, the British HMS *Challenger* sailed around the world, taking surface and depth measurements and collecting samples of seawater. Analyses of those samples first demonstrated the nearly uniform composition of seawater.

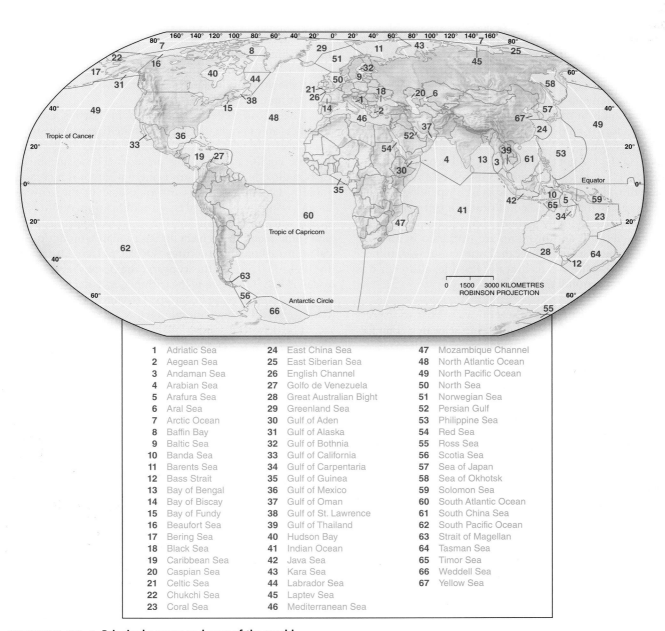

1	Adriatic Sea	24	East China Sea	47	Mozambique Channel
2	Aegean Sea	25	East Siberian Sea	48	North Atlantic Ocean
3	Andaman Sea	26	English Channel	49	North Pacific Ocean
4	Arabian Sea	27	Golfo de Venezuela	50	North Sea
5	Arafura Sea	28	Great Australian Bight	51	Norwegian Sea
6	Aral Sea	29	Greenland Sea	52	Persian Gulf
7	Arctic Ocean	30	Gulf of Aden	53	Philippine Sea
8	Baffin Bay	31	Gulf of Alaska	54	Red Sea
9	Baltic Sea	32	Gulf of Bothnia	55	Ross Sea
10	Banda Sea	33	Gulf of California	56	Scotia Sea
11	Barents Sea	34	Gulf of Carpentaria	57	Sea of Japan
12	Bass Strait	35	Gulf of Guinea	58	Sea of Okhotsk
13	Bay of Bengal	36	Gulf of Mexico	59	Solomon Sea
14	Bay of Biscay	37	Gulf of Oman	60	South Atlantic Ocean
15	Bay of Fundy	38	Gulf of St. Lawrence	61	South China Sea
16	Beaufort Sea	39	Gulf of Thailand	62	South Pacific Ocean
17	Bering Sea	40	Hudson Bay	63	Strait of Magellan
18	Black Sea	41	Indian Ocean	64	Tasman Sea
19	Caribbean Sea	42	Java Sea	65	Timor Sea
20	Caspian Sea	43	Kara Sea	66	Weddell Sea
21	Celtic Sea	44	Labrador Sea	67	Yellow Sea
22	Chukchi Sea	45	Laptev Sea		
23	Coral Sea	46	Mediterranean Sea		

FIGURE 16.1 Principal oceans and seas of the world.
A sea is generally smaller than an ocean; sometimes the term refers to a large, inland, salty body of water. Match the alphabetized name and number with its location on the map.

Although ocean chemistry was thought to be fairly constant during the Phanerozoic Eon (the past 542 million years), recent evidence suggests that seawater chemistry has varied over time within a narrow range. The variations are consistent with changes in sea-floor spreading rates, volcanism, and sea level. Evidence is gathered from fluid inclusions in marine formations such as in limestone and evaporite deposits, which contain ancient seawater.

Ocean Chemistry   Ocean chemistry is a result of complex exchanges among seawater, the atmosphere, minerals, bottom sediments, and living organisms. In addition, significant flows of mineral-rich water enter the ocean through hydrothermal (hot water) vents in the ocean floor. These vents are the "black smokers" noted for the dense, black, mineral-laden water that spews from them (Figure 11.12b.) The uniformity of seawater results from complementary chemical reactions and continuous mixing—after all, the ocean basins interconnect, and water circulates among them.

Seven elements account for more than 99% of the dissolved solids in seawater. These are (with corresponding ionic form) chlorine (as chloride, Cl^-), sodium (as Na^+), magnesium (as Mg^{2+}), sulphur (as sulphate, SO_4^{2-}), calcium (as Ca^{2+}), potassium (as K^+), and bromine (as bromide, Br^-). Seawater also contains dissolved gases (such as carbon dioxide, nitrogen, and oxygen), suspended and dissolved organic matter, and a multitude of trace elements.

Commercially, only sodium chloride (common table salt), magnesium, and bromine are extracted in any significant amount from the ocean. Future mining of minerals from the seafloor is technically feasible, although it is presently uneconomical.

Average Salinity: 35‰   Several ways exist to express salinity (dissolved solids by volume) in seawater. The following methods use the worldwide average value:

- 3.5% (parts per hundred)
- 35 000 ppm (parts per million)
- 35 000 mg·l^{-1}
- 35 g·kg^{-1}
- 35‰ (‰ = parts per thousand)—the most common notation

Salinity worldwide normally varies between 34‰ and 37‰ in the open oceans; variations are attributable to atmospheric conditions above the water and to the volume of freshwater inflows. In equatorial water, precipitation is high throughout the year, diluting salinity values to slightly lower than average (34.5‰). In subtropical oceans—where evaporation rates are greatest because of the influence of hot, dry, subtropical high-pressure cells—salinity is more concentrated, increasing to 36‰. In these regions, salinity is rising as increased evaporation rates rise with temperature.

The term **brine** is applied to water that exceeds the average of 35‰ salinity. **Brackish** applies to water that is less than 35‰ salts. In general, oceans are lower in salinity near landmasses because of freshwater runoff and river discharges. Extreme examples include the Baltic Sea (north of Poland and Germany) and the Gulf of Bothnia (between Sweden and Finland), which average 10‰ or less salinity because of heavy freshwater runoff and low evaporation rates.

In contrast, the Sargasso Sea, within the North Atlantic subtropical gyre, averages 38‰. The Persian Gulf has a salinity of 40‰ as a result of high evaporation rates in a nearly enclosed basin. Deep pockets, or "brine lakes," along the floor of the Red Sea and the Mediterranean Sea register up to a salty 225‰.

The ocean reflects conditions in Earth's environment. As an example, the high-latitude oceans have freshened over the past decade. Another change underway is oceanic acidification, taking place as the ocean absorbs carbon dioxide from the atmosphere where it is increasing rapidly. Hydrolysis forms carbonic acid in the seawater and a lowering of ocean pH—an acidification. A more acid ocean will cause certain marine organisms such as corals and some plankton to have difficulty maintaining external calcium carbonate structures. Ocean pH could decrease by −0.4 to −0.5 units this century; the oceans' average pH today is 8.2. The scale is logarithmic, so a decrease of 0.1 equals a 30% increase in acidity. Oceanic biodiversity and food webs will change in unknown ways.

The dissolved solids remain in the ocean, but the water recycles endlessly through the hydrologic cycle, driven by energy from the Sun. The water you drink today may have water molecules in it that not long ago were in the Pacific Ocean, in the Yangtze River, in groundwater in Sweden, or airborne in the clouds over Peru.

Physical Structure of the Ocean

The basic physical structure of the ocean is layered, as shown in Figure 16.2. The figure also graphs four key aspects of the ocean, each of which varies with increasing depth: average temperature, salinity, dissolved carbon dioxide, and dissolved oxygen.

GEO REPORT 16.1   *The Mediterranean Sea Is Getting Saltier*

The Mediterranean Sea is warming at a faster rate than the oceans. Increased salinity and temperatures are occurring in the deep layers, below 600 m to the sea bed. Saltier conditions change the water density and cause outflows past the Strait of Gibraltar, thus blocking natural mixing with the Atlantic Ocean. These changes are expected as climate changes. This warming is disrupting the natural mixing in such water bodies, as reported in the *Geosystems Now* in Chapter 7.

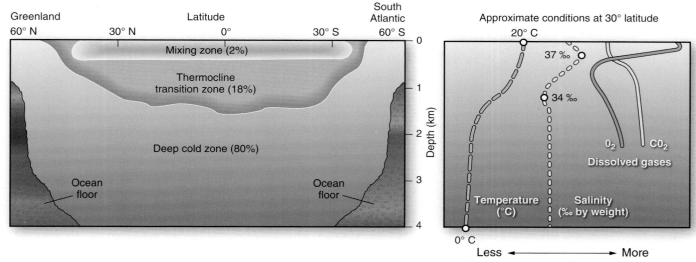

FIGURE 16.2 **The ocean's physical structure.**
Schematic of average physical structure observed throughout the ocean's vertical profile as sampled along a line from Greenland to the South Atlantic. Temperature, salinity, and dissolved gases are shown plotted by depth.

Midlatitude Productivity

The ocean's surface layer is warmed by solar insolation and is wind driven. Variations in water temperature and solutes are blended rapidly in a *mixing zone* that represents only 2% of the oceanic mass. Below the mixing zone is the *thermocline transition zone*, a more than 1-km-deep region of decreasing temperature gradient that lacks the motion of the surface. Friction at these depths dampens the effect of surface currents. In addition, colder water temperatures at the lower margin tend to inhibit any convective movements.

From a depth of 1–1.5 km to the ocean floor, temperature and salinity values are quite uniform. Temperatures in this *deep cold zone* are near 0°C. Water in the deep cold zone does not freeze because of its salinity and the intense pressures at those depths; while seawater freezes at about –2°C at the surface. Generally, the coldest water is along the bottom. Now let us shift to the edge of the sea and examine Earth's coastlines.

Coastal System Components

Earth's surface features, such as mountains and crustal plates, were formed over millions of years. However, most of Earth's coastlines are relatively young, the present state of the coastline being a temporary state within a longer-term trend of continuous change. The land, ocean, atmosphere, Sun, and Moon interact to produce tides, currents, waves, erosional features, and depositional features along the continental margins.

Inputs to the coastal environment include many elements we have already discussed:

- *Solar energy* input drives motions in the atmosphere and the hydrosphere. The conversion of insolation to kinetic energy produces prevailing winds, weather systems, and climate.

- *Atmospheric winds*, in turn, generate ocean currents and waves, key inputs to the coastal environment.
- *Climatic regimes*, which result from insolation and moisture, strongly influence coastal geomorphic processes.
- The *nature of coastal rock* and coastal processes are important in determining rates of erosion and sediment production.
- *Human activities* are an increasingly significant input to coastal change.

All of these inputs occur within the ever-present influence of gravity's pull—not only from Earth, but also from the Moon and Sun. Gravity provides the potential energy for materials in motion and produces the tides. A dynamic equilibrium among all these components produces coastline features of infinite variety and beauty.

The Coastal Environment and Sea Level

The coastal environment is the **littoral zone**, from the Latin word for "shore." Figure 16.3 illustrates the littoral zone and includes specific components discussed later in the chapter. The littoral zone spans some land as well as water. Landward, it extends to the highest waterline that occurs on shore during a storm. Seaward, it extends to where water is too deep for storm waves to move sediment on the seafloor—usually around 60 m in depth. The specific contact line between the sea and the land is the *shoreline*, although this line shifts with tides, storms, and sea-level adjustments. The *coast* continues inland from the high tide line to the first major landform change and may include areas considered to be part of the coast in local usage.

Because the level of the ocean varies, the littoral zone naturally shifts position from time to time. A rise in sea

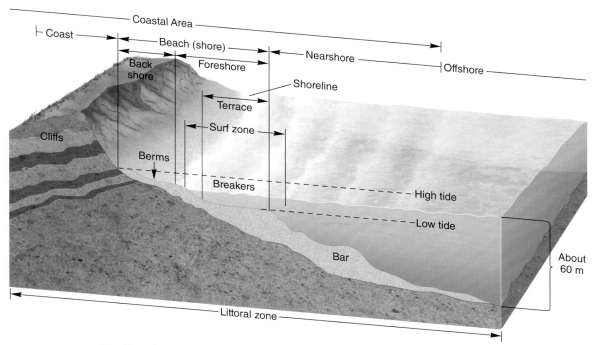

FIGURE 16.3 The littoral zone.
The littoral zone includes the coast, beach, and nearshore environments.

level causes submergence of land, whereas a fall in sea level exposes new areas to coastal action. In addition, uplift and subsidence of the land itself initiate changes in the littoral zone.

Sea level is an important concept. Every elevation you see in an atlas or on a map is referenced to mean sea level. Yet this average sea level changes daily with the tides and over the long term with changes in climate, tectonic plate movements, and glaciation. Thus, *sea level* is a relative term. At present, no international system exists to determine exact sea level over time. The Global Sea Level Observing System (GLOSS) is an international group actively working on sea-level issues and is part of the larger Permanent Service for Mean Sea Level, which you can find at http://www.pol.ac.uk/psmsl/programmes/.

Mean sea level (MSL) is a value based on average tidal levels recorded hourly at a given site over many years. MSL varies spatially because of ocean currents and waves, tidal variations, air temperature, pressure differences and wind patterns, ocean temperature variations, slight variations in Earth's gravity, and changes in oceanic volume.

Changes in Sea Level

Over the long term, sea-level fluctuations expose a range of coastal landforms to tidal and wave processes. As average global temperatures cycle through cold or warm climatic spells, the quantity of ice locked up in the ice sheets of Antarctica and Greenland and in hundreds of mountain glaciers can increase or decrease and result in sea-level changes accordingly. At the peak of the most recent Pleistocene glaciation about 18 000 B.P. (years before the present), sea level was about 130 m lower than it is today. On the other hand, if Antarctica and Greenland ever became ice free (if the ice sheets fully melted), mean sea level would rise at least 65 m worldwide.

Just 100 years ago sea level was 38 cm lower along the coast of southern Florida. Venice, Italy, has experienced a rise of 25 cm since 1890. During the last century, sea level rose 10–20 cm, a rate 10 times higher than the average rate during the last 3000 years. Since 1930, sea-level rise has continued at an increasing rate, with any variability explained by global construction and artificial reservoir impoundments of water. The present sea-level rise

GEO REPORT 16.2   *Sea Level Varies along the Coastline*

Sea level varies along the full extent of North American shorelines. The mean sea level (MSL) of the U.S. Gulf Coast is about 25 cm higher than that of Florida's east coast, which is the lowest in North America. MSL rises northward along the eastern coast, to 38 cm higher in Maine than in Florida. Along the U.S. western coast, MSL is higher than Florida's by about 58 cm in San Diego and by about 86 cm in Oregon. Overall, North America's Pacific Coast MSL averages about 66 cm higher than the Atlantic Coast MSL.

FIGURE 16.4 Ocean topography as revealed by satellite radar altimetry.
Sea-level data noted by the colour scale are given in centimetres above or below Earth's geoid. The overall relief portrayed in the image is about 2 m. The maximum sea level is in the western Pacific Ocean (white). The minimum is around Antarctica (blue and purple). [*TOPEX/Poseidon* image JPL and NASA/GSFC.]

is spatially uneven; for instance, the rate along the coast of Argentina is nearly 10 times the rate along the coast of France. About 50% of the present sea-level rise is from thermal expansion produced by warmer water temperatures. The remainder is from worldwide losses in glacial mass and ice caps, and from the ice sheets in Greenland and Antarctica.

Given these trends and the predicted climatic change, sea level will continue to rise and potentially be devastating for many coastal locations. A rise of only 0.3 m would cause shorelines worldwide to move inland (transgress) an average of 30 m. This elevated sea level would inundate some valuable real estate along coastlines all over the world. Some 20 000 km² of land along North American shores alone would be drowned, at a staggering loss of more than a trillion dollars. A 95-cm sea-level rise could inundate 15% of Egypt's arable land, 17% of Bangladesh, and many island nations and communities. However, uncertainty exists in these forecasts, and the pace of the rise should be slow enough for humans to react and adapt.

The 2007 Intergovernmental Panel on Climate Change (IPCC) forecast for global mean sea-level rise this century, given regional variations, is a range from 0.18 to 0.59 m. However, the new 2006–2007 measurements of Greenland's ice loss were not included in the forecasts, and data appear to suggest an acceleration of ice melt and rising sea level. Scientists are carefully monitoring the growing instability of the West Antarctic Ice Shelf. A fair working estimate for sea-level rise this century now stands

at 1.0 to 1.4 m; the state of California is using a rise of 1.4 m in its planning models.

Remote-sensing technology augments these measurements, including the *TOPEX/Poseidon* satellite launched in 1992 (see http://topex-www.jpl.nasa.gov/, click on the "Sea Level Viewer"). This satellite has two radar altimeters that measured changes in mean sea level at any one location every 10 days between 66° N and 66° S latitudes. These measurements are made to a precision of 4.2 cm (Figure 16.4). *TOPEX/Poseidon* portraits of El Niño and La Niña in the Pacific are included in Focus Study 10.1. Another ocean surface topography satellite launched in December 2001, named *Jason-1*, is extending the science of determining mean sea level, ocean topography, atmosphere–ocean interactions, and ocean circulation. *Jason-2* was launched in 2008, and SARAL is scheduled to launch in 2012.

The University of Arizona's Environmental Studies Laboratory prepared a dramatic map series related to rising sea level. Using digital elevation model (DEM) data, the scientists plotted 1-m to 6-m increases in sea level and the amount of coastal inundation (Figure 16.5). As you examine the three maps, consider what adjustments to human settlement will be required.

A recent study completed by a team from Natural Resources Canada, Environment Canada, Dalhousie University, the Centre of Geographic Sciences of the Nova Scotia Community College, the City of Charlottetown, and other partners, assessed the physical and socioeconomic

FIGURE 16.5 Coastal inundation of a 1-m rise in sea level.
Along three portions of U.S. coastline, scientists at the University of Arizona using U.S. Geological Survey digital elevation data produced these maps to show a 1-m sea-level rise and its impact. [Maps prepared by Weiss and Overpeck, Environmental Studies Laboratory, Department of Geosciences, University of Arizona. Used by permission.]

impacts of climate change and the potential accelerated sea-level rise on the coast of Prince Edward Island. The study findings estimate the cost associated with flooding of property in Charlottetown at between $190 million and $202 million and the value of property lost to erosion on Prince Edward Island's north shore to be $22 000 per year for cottages to $1100 per year for noncottage property. These losses result from increased frequency and extent of storm surge flooding in Charlottetown and increased erosion from a decrease in sea ice, and an increase in wind energy with the resulting increase in wave energy on the north shore of the province.

The study suggests three levels of adaptation to these changes in the coastal zone depending on the type of coastal land use. The first adaptation is shore protection, but because protection is costly and has limited long-term effectiveness, it should only be used to armour structures that are in immediate risk of flooding or erosion. The second adaptation is accommodation through redesign of structures and efforts to increase natural resilience in the coastal ecosystem. The most effective adaptation is retreat from the coastal zone through restrictive zoning laws, although progress is slow.

CRITICAL THINKING 16.1
Thinking through a Rising Sea Level

Based upon coastal inundation shown in Figure 16.5, what is your assessment of southern Louisiana if sea level rises 1 m? What is the region's future? Go to the website where these maps were created, http://www.geo.arizona.edu/dgesl/; click on "maps of areas potentially impacted by sea level rise"; and proceed to select a coastal area of interest to you. Initially, enter a 1-m rise and examine the map generated. Try other values. Briefly analyze what you find. Certainly, any calculations of the costs of slowing fossil-fuel burning to lower emissions of greenhouse gases should be balanced against damage estimates from such coastal inundation. What do you think?

Coastal System Actions

The coastal system is the scene of complex tidal fluctuation, winds, waves, ocean currents, and the occasional impact of storms. These forces shape landforms, ranging from gentle beaches to steep cliffs, and sustain delicate ecosystems.

Tides

Tides are complex daily oscillations in sea level, ranging worldwide from barely noticeable to several metres. Tides are experienced to varying degrees along every ocean shore around the world. Tidal action is a relentless energy agent for geomorphic change. As tides flood (rise) and ebb (fall), the daily migration of the shoreline landward and seaward causes significant changes that affect sediment erosion and transportation.

Tides are important in human activities, including navigation, fishing, and recreation. Tides are especially important to ships because the entrance to many ports is limited by shallow water, and thus high tide is required for passage. Tall-masted ships may need a low tide to clear overhead bridges. Tides also exist in large lakes, but because the tidal range is small, tides are difficult to distinguish from changes in water level caused by wind. Lake Superior, for instance, has a tidal variation of only about 5 cm.

Causes of Tides Tides are produced by the gravitational pull of both the Sun and the Moon. Chapter 2 discusses Earth's relation to the Sun and the Moon, and the reasons for the seasons. Despite its greater size, the Sun's influence is only about half that of the Moon's because of the Sun's greater distance from Earth, although it is still a significant force. Figure 16.6 illustrates the relation among the Moon, the Sun, and Earth and the generation of variable tidal bulges on opposite sides of the planet.

The gravitational pull of the Moon tugs on Earth's atmosphere, oceans, and lithosphere. The same is true for

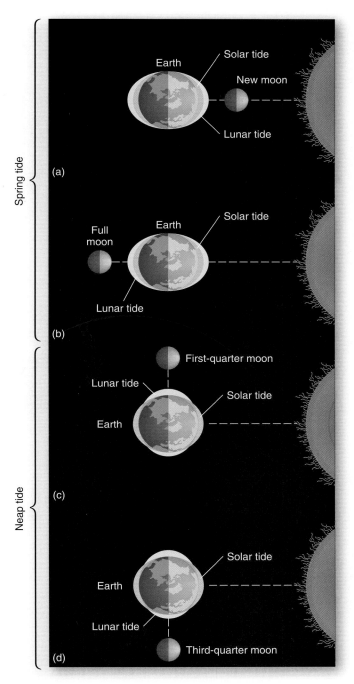

Spring tide

Neap tide

FIGURE 16.6 The cause of tides.
Gravitational relations of Sun, Moon, and
Earth combine to produce spring tides (a, b)
and neap tides (c, d). (Tide heights are
greatly exaggerated for illustration.)

Monthly Tidal Cycles

two bodies. *Inertia* is the tendency of objects to stay still if
motionless or to keep moving in the same direction if in
motion. The gravitational effect on the side of Earth facing
the Moon or Sun is greater than that experienced by the far
side, where inertial forces are slightly greater. This difference exists because gravitational influences decrease with
distance. In effect, from this inertial point of view, as the
nearside water and Earth are drawn toward the Moon and
Sun, the farside water is left behind because of the slightly
weaker gravitational pull. This arrangement produces the
two opposing tidal bulges on opposite sides of Earth.

Tides appear to move in and out along the shoreline, but do not actually do so in the open ocean. Instead,
Earth's surface rotates into and out of the relatively "fixed"
tidal bulges as Earth changes its position in relation to the
Moon and Sun. Every 24 hours and 50 minutes, any given
point on Earth rotates through two bulges as a direct result of this rotational positioning. Thus, every day, most
coastal locations experience two high (rising) tides, known
as **flood tides**, and two low (falling) tides, known as **ebb
tides**. The height difference between consecutive high
and low tides is considered the *tidal range*.

Spring and Neap Tides The combined gravitational
effect of the Sun and Moon is strongest in the conjunction alignment and results in the greatest tidal range between high and low tides, known as **spring tides**. (*Spring*
means to "spring forth"; it has no relation to the season
of the year.) Figure 16.6b shows the other alignment that
gives rise to spring tides, when the Moon and Sun are at
opposition. In this arrangement, the Moon and Sun cause
separate tidal bulges, affecting the water nearest to each of
them. In addition, the left-behind water resulting from the
pull of the body on the opposite side augments each bulge.

When the Moon and the Sun are neither in conjunction nor in opposition but are more or less in the positions
shown in Figure 16.6c and d, the gravitational influences
are offset and counteract each other, producing a lesser
tidal range known as **neap tide**. (*Neap* means "without the
power of advancing.")

Tides also are influenced by other factors, including
ocean basin characteristics (size, depth, and topography),
latitude, and shoreline shape. These factors cause a great
variety of tidal ranges. For example, some locations may
experience almost no difference between high and low
tides. The highest tides occur when open water is forced
into partially enclosed gulfs or bays. The Bay of Fundy
in Nova Scotia records the greatest tidal range on Earth,
a difference of 16 m (Figure 16.7a and b). The comparison in Figure 16.7c shows a smaller tidal range along
England's east coast. For more on tides and tide prediction and a complete listing of links, see http://ocean
.peterbrueggeman.com/tidepredict.html.

Tidal Power The fact that sea level changes daily with
the tides suggests an opportunity: Could these predictable
flows be harnessed to generate electricity? The answer is
yes, given the right conditions. Bays and estuaries tend to

the Sun, to a lesser extent. Earth's solid and fluid surfaces
all experience some stretching as a result of this gravitational pull. The stretching raises large *tidal bulges* in the
atmosphere (which we can't see), smaller tidal bulges in
the ocean, and very slight bulges in Earth's rigid crust.
Our concern here is the tidal bulges in the ocean.

Gravity and inertia are essential elements in understanding tides. *Gravity* is the force of attraction between

(a)

(b)

(c)

(d)

FIGURE 16.7 Tidal range and tidal power.
Tidal range is great in some bays and estuaries, such as Halls Harbour near the Bay of Fundy at flood tide
(a) and ebb tide (b). (c) Tidal variation of about 3 m in the harbour at Bamburgh, Northumbrian, England,
over several hours. (d) The flow of water between high and low tide is ideal for turning turbines and generating electricity, as is done at the Annapolis Tidal Generating Station, near the Bay of Fundy in Nova Scotia,
in operation since 1984. [(a) Jeff Newbery, (b) through (d) Bobbé Christopherson.]

focus tidal energy, concentrating it in a smaller area than in the open ocean. This circumstance provides an opportunity to construct a dam with water gates, locks to let ships through, and turbines to generate power.

Only 30 locations in the world are suited for tidal power generation. At present, only three are producing electricity. Two are outside North America—a 4-megawatt–capacity station in Russia in operation since 1968 (at Kislaya-Guba Bay on the White Sea) and a facility in France operating since 1967 (on the Rance River estuary on the Brittany coast). The tides in the Rance estuary fluctuate up to 13 m, and power production has been almost continuous there, providing an electrical-generating capacity of a moderate 240 megawatts (about 20% of the capacity of Hoover Dam).

The third area is the Bay of Fundy in Nova Scotia. At one of several favourable sites on the bay, the Annapolis Tidal Generating Station was built in 1984. Nova Scotia

Power Incorporated operates this 20-megawatt plant (Figure 16.7d). According to the Canadian government, tidal power generation at ideal sites is economically competitive with fossil fuel plants.

Another kind of tidal power taking form in Norway involves sea-floor devices that harness the motion of coastal currents. Windmill-like turbines are set in motion by the tides and currents, as are paddle-driven turbines. Electrical production using this method began in 2003. Research into the feasibility of similar devices is presently being conducted in the upper Bay of Fundy for possible future power generation.

Waves

Friction between moving air (wind) and the ocean surface generates undulations of water called **waves**. Waves travel in groups of *wave trains*. Wave phenomena vary widely in scale: On a small scale, a moving boat creates a wake of small waves; at a larger scale, storms generate large groups of wave trains. At the extreme is the wind wake produced by the presence of the Hawaiian Islands, traceable westward across the Pacific Ocean surface for 3000 km. The islands disrupt the steady trade winds and produce related surface temperature and wind changes.

A stormy area at sea is called a *generating region* for large wave trains, which radiate outward in all directions. The ocean is crisscrossed with intricate patterns of these multidirectional waves. The waves seen along a coast may be the product of a storm centre thousands of kilometres away.

Regular patterns of smooth, rounded waves, the mature undulations of the open ocean, are **swells**. As waves leave the generating region, these swells—which can range from small ripples to very large flat-crested waves—continue to transfer wave energy across the ocean. A wave leaving a deep-water generating region tends to extend its wavelength horizontally for many metres. Tremendous energy occasionally accumulates to form unusually large waves. One moonlit night in 1933, the crew on the U.S. Navy tanker *Ramapo* reported a wave in the Pacific higher than its mainmast, at about 34 m!

As you watch waves in open water, it appears that water is migrating in the direction of wave travel, but only a slight amount of water is actually advancing. It is the *wave energy* that is moving through the flexible medium of water. Water within a wave in the open ocean is simply transferring energy from molecule to molecule in simple cyclic undulations; these are *waves of transition* (Figure 16.8). Individual water particles follow a vertically circular pattern and move forward only slightly.

The diameter of the paths formed by the orbiting water particles decreases with depth. As a deep-ocean wave approaches the shoreline and enters shallower water (10–20 m), the orbiting water particles are vertically restricted. This restriction causes more-elliptical, flattened orbits to form near the bottom. This change from circular to elliptical orbits slows the entire wave, although more waves continue arriving. This results in closer-spaced waves, growing in height and steepness, with sharper wave crests. As the crest of each wave rises, a point is reached when its height exceeds its vertical stability and the wave falls into a characteristic **breaker**, crashing onto the beach (Figure 16.8b).

In a breaker, the orbital motion of transition gives way to elliptical *waves of translation* in which both energy and water move toward shore. The slope of the shore determines wave style. Plunging breakers indicate a steep bottom profile, whereas spilling breakers indicate a gentle,

shallow bottom profile. In some areas, unexpected high waves can arise suddenly. It is a good idea to learn to recognize severe wave conditions before you venture along the shore in these areas.

When the backwash of water flows to the ocean from the beach in a concentrated column, usually at a right angle to the line of breakers, it is a *rip current*. A person caught in one of these can be swept offshore, but usually only a short distance. These brief, short torrents of water can be dangerous (Figure 16.8c).

Various wave trains moving along in the open sea interact by *interference*. These interfering waves sometimes align so that the wave crests and troughs from one wave train are in phase with those of another. When this in-phase condition occurs, the height of the waves is amplified, sometimes dramatically. The resulting "killer waves" or "sleeper waves" can sweep in unannounced and overtake unsuspecting victims. Signs along portions of the coastlines in British Columbia, Washington, Oregon, and California warn beachcombers to watch for "killer waves." In August 2009, despite warnings from park rangers, a person was killed as several giant waves hit Acadia National Park on the coast of Maine. Hurricane Bill in the Atlantic was the source of the wave energy. The same energy caused rogue waves at Peggy's Cove in Nova Scotia that swept hikers off the rocks. In contrast, out-of-phase wave trains will dampen wave energy at the shore. When you observe the breakers along a beach, the changing beat of the surf actually is produced by the patterns of *wave interference* that occurred in far-distant areas of the ocean.

Wave Refraction In general, wave action tends to straighten a coastline. Waves approaching an irregular coast bend around headlands, protruding landforms generally composed of resistant rocks (Figure 16.9). The submarine topography refracts, or bends, approaching waves. The refracted energy is focused around headlands and dissipates in coves, bays, and the submerged coastal valleys between headlands. Thus, headlands receive the brunt of wave attack along a coastline. This **wave refraction** redistributes wave energy so that different sections of the coastline vary in erosion potential, with the long-term effect of straightening the coast.

Figure 16.10 (page 496) shows waves approaching the coast at an angle, as the crests usually arrive at some angle other than parallel. The waves enter shallow water and are refracted as the shoreline end of the wave slows first. The end of the wave in deeper water moves faster in comparison, thus producing a current parallel to the coast, zigzagging in the prevalent direction of the incoming

GEO REPORT 16.3 *Sea-wave Amplification Kills*

On March 3, 2010, a large cruise ship in the western Mediterranean Sea, off the coast of Marseilles, France, was struck by three surprise waves about 8 m in height. Two passengers were killed and many injured. Rescue personnel took the injured to hospitals in Barcelona, Spain.

(a)

(b)

(c)

(d)

FIGURE 16.8 Wave formation and breakers.
(a) The orbital tracks of water particles change from circular motions and swells in deep water (waves of transition) to more elliptical orbits near the bottom in shallow water (waves of translation). (b) Cascades of waves attack the shore along Baja California, Mexico. (c) A dangerous rip current interrupts approaching breakers. Note the churned-up water where the rip current enters the surf. (d) Wave trains on the Gulf of St. Lawrence-side of Blooming Point Spit in Prince Edward Island, expending energy before reaching the shoreline. [(b) and inset and (c) Bobbé Christopherson; (d) Mary-Louise Byrne.]

Wave Motion/Wave
Refraction

(b) Headland

(c) Cove

(d) Lighthouse on headland bluff

FIGURE 16.9 Coastal straightening.
(a) The process of coastal straightening is brought about by wave refraction. Wave energy is concentrated as it converges on headlands (b) and is diffused as it diverges in coves and bays (c). (d) Headlands are frequent sites for lighthouses such as the Farne light on Farne Island, England. At least six species of birds nest on the island, including Atlantic Puffins, Kittiwakes, and Arctic Terns. [Bobbé Christopherson.]

waves. This **longshore current**, or *littoral current*, depends on wind direction and resultant wave direction. A longshore current is generated only in the surf zone and works in combination with wave action to transport large amounts of sand, gravel, sediment, and debris along the shore as *longshore drift*, or **littoral drift**, the more comprehensive term.

Particles on the beach also are moved along as **beach drift**, shifting back and forth between water and land with each *swash* and *backwash* cycle of the surf. Individual sediment grains trace arched paths along the beach. You have perhaps stood on a beach and heard the sound of myriad sand grains and seawater in the backwash of surf. These dislodged materials, which can be significant volumes, are available for transport and eventual deposition in coves and inlets.

Tsunami, or Seismic Sea Wave An occasional wave that momentarily, but powerfully influences coastlines is the tsunami. Japanese for "harbour wave," a **tsunami** is named for its devastating effect when its energy is focused in harbours. Often tsunami are reported incorrectly as "tidal waves," but there is no relation to the tides. Sudden, sharp motions in the seafloor, caused by earthquakes, submarine landslides, or eruptions of undersea volcanoes, produce tsunami. Thus, tsunami properly are *seismic sea waves*.

A large undersea disturbance usually generates a solitary wave of great wavelength. Tsunami generally exceed

100 km in wavelength (crest to crest) but are only a metre or so in height. The waves travel at great speeds in deep-ocean water—velocities of 600–800 km·h^{-1} are not uncommon—but often pass unnoticed on the open sea because their great wavelength makes the rise and fall of water hard to observe.

As a tsunami approaches a coast, the shallow water forces the wavelength to shorten. As a result, the wave height may increase up to 15 m or more. Such a wave has the potential to devastate a coastal area, causing property damage and death. For example, in 1992 the citizens of Casares, Nicaragua, were surprised by a 12-m tsunami that took 270 lives. In Papua New Guinea in 1998 a massive undersea landslide of about 4 km^3 launched a tsunami that killed 2000. During the twentieth century, there were 141 damaging tsunami and perhaps 900 smaller ones, with a total death toll of about 70 000. Nearly 30 000 people were killed by the March 11, 2011 tsunami that was initiated by a Magnitude 9.0 earthquake near Sendai, Japan.

Hawai'i is vulnerable to tsunami because of its position in the open central Pacific, surrounded by the Ring of Fire that outlines the Pacific Basin. The U.S. Army Corps of Engineers has reported 41 damaging tsunami in Hawai'i during the past 142 years—statistically, one every 3.5 years on average. Forecasters watch the unstable Kīlauea region of the southeast coast of Hawai'i, where the

(a)

(b)

(c)

Animation

Beach Drift, Coastal Erosion

FIGURE 16.10 Longshore current and beach drift.
(a) Longshore currents are produced as waves approach the surf zone and shallower water. Longshore and beach drift results as substantial volumes of material are moved along the shore. (b) Processes at work along Point Reyes Beach, Point Reyes National Seashore, California. (c) Shoals in the nearshore area in Prince Edward Island develop through an interaction of the tides and the longshore currents. Over time, with a great enough sediment supply, these may become subaerially exposed. [(b) Robert Christopherson; (c) Mary-Louise Byrne.]

possible collapse of a 40-km by 20-km by 2000-m thick portion of relatively new and unstable crustal basalt could affect the Pacific Basin. In the Atlantic Basin, continuing threat exists from volcanic island collapses, such as the closely watched Cumbre Vieja volcano in the Canary Islands.

Because tsunami travel such great distances so quickly and are virtually undetectable in the open ocean, accurate forecasts are difficult and occurrences are often unexpected. A warning system now is in operation for nations surrounding the Pacific, where the majority of tsunami occur. A warning is issued whenever seismic stations detect a significant quake or landslide under water, where it might generate a tsunami. A new tsunami hazard-mitigation network began operating in 2004 with the deployment of six pressure sensors on the ocean floor with accompanying surface buoys—this is the Deep-ocean Assessment and Reporting of Tsunamis (DART). Three instruments are along the Aleutian Islands, south of Alaska, two along the U.S. West Coast, and one near the equator off South America. The challenge to the

world community is to apply this technology so that early warnings are possible in all vulnerable oceans, such as the Indian Ocean.

On December 26, 2004, a M 9.3 earthquake (fourth largest in a century) struck off the west coast of northern Sumatra, triggering a massive tsunami across the Indian Ocean—the Sumatra–Andaman earthquake and tsunami. No warning system was in place when this occurred. The earthquake trigger was the continuing underthrust of the Indo-Australian plate beneath the Burma plate along the Sunda Trench subduction zone. Imagine the island of Sumatra springing up about 13.7 m in elevation! You can find this oceanic trench on the Chapter 12 opening map of the ocean floor, stretching along the coast of Indonesia in the eastern Indian Ocean basin.

Radar images from four Earth-orbiting satellites at the time clearly show the tsunami wave energy travelling across the Indian Ocean. In Figure 16.11 we see two of these images, one at 2:05 hours and the other at 7:10 hours after the event. Energy from this tsunami wave actually

FIGURE 16.11 Satellites track tsunami waves across the Indian Ocean, 2004.
(a) A *Jason-1* image 2 hours after the M 9.3 earthquake showing wave heights of 60 cm radiating outward from the epicenter off Sumatra. (b) The *Geosat Follow On* (*GFO*) satellite radar captured the wave patterns 7 hours and 10 minutes after the earthquake. [NOAA, Laboratory for Satellite Altimetry.]

travelled several times around the global ocean basins before settling down. With Earth's mid-ocean mountain chain acting as a guide, related large waves arrived at the shores of Eastern Canada, Antarctica, and Peru.

Geophysicists even picked up slight changes in Earth's rotation (which was slowed, resulting in 3 microseconds less daylength) and a shift in the North Pole location by 2.5 cm in response to this event. Total deaths from the quake and tsunami exceeded 150 000, and a final count may never be known. Recovery will take years. In response to this tsunami the Indian Ocean Tsunami Warning and Mitigation System was created as part of a United Nations tsunami warning system project.

Warnings always should be heeded, despite the many false alarms, for the causes lie hidden beneath the ocean and are difficult to monitor in any consistent manner, although the temporal resolution of remote-sensing devices is increasing. For the tsunami research program, see http://nctr.pmel.noaa.gov/. The tsunami home page is at http://www.ess.washington.edu/tsunami/index.html. Strangely, despite hazard warnings following a recent February 2010 Chilean earthquake for tsunami activity in New Zealand and Hawai'i, it seemed to attract onlookers and even some surfers. Fortunately, the tsunami waves were only about a metre in height. Hotels on Oahu did evacuate staff and guests to the third-floor level around the time of tsunami arrival. Visit the Atlas of Canada online to learn about tsunami history and geography in Canada (http://atlas.nrcan.gc.ca/site/english/maps/environment/naturalhazards/tsunami/tsunami).

Coastal System Outputs

As you can see, coastlines are active places, with energy and sediment being delivered continuously to a narrow environment. The action of tides, currents, wind, waves,

and changing sea level produces a variety of erosional and depositional landforms. We look first at erosional coastlines, then at depositional coastlines. In this era of rising sea level, coastlines are becoming more dynamic.

Erosional Coastal Processes and Landforms

The active margin of the Pacific Ocean along North and South America is a typical erosional coastline. *Erosional coastlines* tend to be rugged, of high relief, and tectonically active, as expected from association with the leading edge of drifting lithospheric plates (review the plate tectonics discussion in Chapter 11). Figure 16.12 presents features commonly observed along an erosional coast. Within this erosional setting, depositional processes can also occur, producing some depositional landforms.

Sea cliffs are formed by the undercutting action of the sea. As indentations slowly grow at water level, a sea cliff becomes notched and eventually will collapse and retreat. Other erosional forms evolve along cliff-dominated coastlines, including *sea caves*, *sea arches*, and *sea stacks*. As erosion continues, arches may collapse, leaving isolated stacks in the water (Figure 16.12b). Parts of the east coast of Canada, parts of the Great Lakes coastlines, and the coasts of southern England and Oregon are prime examples of such erosional landscapes.

The combined effect of wave action, weathering, and several other processes can cut a horizontal bench in the intertidal zone, extending from a sea cliff out into the sea. Such a structure is a **wave-cut platform**, or *shore platform* (Figure 16.12f). If the relation between the land and sea level has changed over time, multiple platforms or terraces may rise like stair steps back from the coast. These marine terraces are remarkable indicators of a changing relation between the land and sea, with some terraces more than 370 m above sea level.

(b) Notched cliff

(c) Arch

(d) Stacks, erosional coast

Former
sea cliffs

Terrace

Sea cave

Wave-cut platform (terrace)

Sea arch

(a)

Sea cliff

Landslides

Notched cliff

Sea stack

(e) Collapsing cliffs

(f) Wave-cut platform

FIGURE 16.12 Erosional coastal features.
(a) Characteristic coastal erosional landforms: (b) notched cliff, Bjørnøya (Bear Island), Barents Sea;
(c) headlands and an arch, Ascension Island, Atlantic Ocean; (d) stacks and headlands, Gough Island, Southern
Ocean; (e) notched cliffs at Joggins, Nova Scotia; (f) wave-cut platform, or shore platform, cut into soft
sandstone of Les Iles de la Madeleine, Québec. [(b) through (d) Bobbé Christopherson; (e) and (f) Mary-Louise Byrne.]

Depositional Coastal Processes and Landforms

Depositional coasts generally are along land of gentle relief, where sediments from many sources are available. Such is the case with the Atlantic and Gulf coastal plains of the United States, which lay along the relatively passive, trailing edge of the North American lithospheric plate. Erosional processes and inundation influence depositional coasts, particularly during storm activity.

Sediment budgets are important considerations for depositional coastlines. A sediment budget is a calculation of the flow of sediment within the coastal system. It accounts for sediment sources, sinks, and transport pathways. In locations where the sediment budget is positive, there is more sediment coming into an area than leaving.

In areas where sediment budget is negative, more sediment leaves an area than comes in. Depositional coastlines have a positive sediment budget. Sediment budget is calculated for an area based on the *littoral cell*—a self-contained shoreline system that has no movement of sediment across its boundaries. The longshore limits of the cell are defined by natural formations or artificial barriers where net sediment movement changes direction or becomes zero. Littoral cells usually contain littoral drift that moves in a more or less continuous direction, with some variation due to local or temporal shifts in wind and current directions. The direction of sediment movement in a littoral cell determines the growth of depositional features.

Figure 16.13 illustrates characteristic landforms deposited by waves and currents. One notable deposition

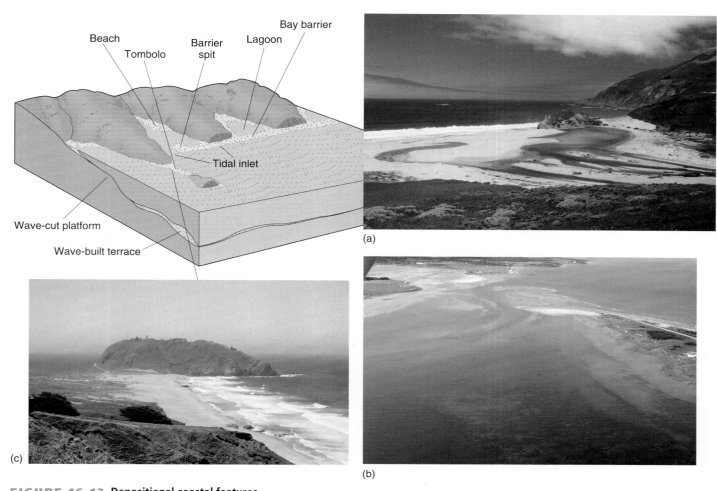

FIGURE 16.13 **Depositional coastal features.**
Characteristic coastal depositional landforms: beaches, spits, barriers, lagoons, and tombolos. (a) The Little
Sur River enters the Pacific Ocean; a barrier spit nearly blocks its way. (b) Barrier spit forming across the
North Rustico Harbour, north shore Prince Edward Island. (c) A tombolo at Point Sur along the central
California coast, where sediment deposits connect the shore with an island. [(a) and (c) Bobbé Christopherson;
(b) Mary-Louise Byrne.]

landform is the **barrier spit**, which consists of material deposited in a long ridge extending out from a coast. It partially crosses and blocks the mouth of a bay. Classic examples of
a barrier spit include Cavendish Spit, Prince Edward Island,
and Cape Cod, Massachusetts. The Little Sur River in
California (Figure 16.13a) and North Rustico Harbour Inlet
in Prince Edward Island (Figure 16.13b) have barrier spits
extending partway across the mouths of a river and a bay.

If a spit grows to completely cut off the bay from the
ocean and form an inland lagoon, it becomes a **bay barrier**, or *baymouth bar*. Spits and barriers are made up of
materials that have been eroded and transported by *littoral drift* (considered beach and longshore drift combined).
For much sediment to accumulate, offshore currents must
be weak; since strong currents carry material away before it can be deposited. Tidal flats and salt marshes are
characteristic low-relief features wherever tidal influence
is greater than wave action. As noted earlier, if these deposits completely cut off the bay from the ocean, an inland **lagoon** is formed. A **tombolo** occurs when sediment

deposits connect the shoreline with an offshore island or
sea stack by accumulating on an underwater wave-built
terrace (Figure 16.13c).

Beaches Of all the features associated with a depositional
coastline, beaches probably are the most familiar. Beaches
vary in type and permanence, especially along coastlines
dominated by wave action. Technically, a **beach** is that
place along a coast where an accumulation of sediment is
in motion, subject to the actions of waves and currents.
Material from the land temporarily resides on the beach
while it is in active transit along the shore.

On average, the beach zone spans from about 5 m
above high tide to 10 m below low tide (see Figure 16.3).
However, the specific limits vary greatly along individual
shorelines. Worldwide, quartz (SiO_2) dominates beach
sands because it resists weathering and therefore remains
after other minerals are removed. In volcanic areas, beaches
are derived from wave-processed lava. Hawai'i and Iceland,
for example, feature some black-sand beaches.

Many beaches, such as those in southern France and western Italy, lack sand and are composed of pebbles and cobbles—a type of *shingle beach*. Some shores have no beaches at all; scrambling across bedrock may be the only way to move along the coast. The coasts of Maine and portions of Canada's Atlantic provinces are classic examples. These coasts, composed of resistant granite rock, are scenically rugged and have few beaches.

A beach acts to stabilize a shoreline by absorbing wave energy, as is evident by the amount of material that is in almost constant motion (see "sand movement" in Figure 16.10). Some beaches are stable. Others cycle seasonally: Sediment accumulates during one summer, is moved offshore by winter storm waves, forming a submerged bar, and is re-deposited onshore the next summer. Protected areas along a coastline tend to accumulate sediment, which can lead to the formation of large coastal sand dunes landward

of the beach. Prevailing winds often drag such coastal dunes inland, sometimes burying trees and highways.

Maintaining Beaches Changes in coastal sediment transport can disrupt human activities—beaches are lost, harbours are closed, and coastal highways and beach houses can be inundated with sediment. Thus, people use various strategies to interrupt littoral drift and beach drift. The goal is either to halt sand accumulation or to force accumulation in a desired way through construction of engineered structures, called "hard" shoreline protection.

Figure 16.14 illustrates common approaches: a *jetty* to block material from harbour entrances, a *groyne* to slow drift action along the coast, and a *breakwater* to create a zone of still water near the coastline. However, interrupting the littoral drift that is the natural replenishment for beaches may lead to unwanted changes in sediment distribution downcurrent.

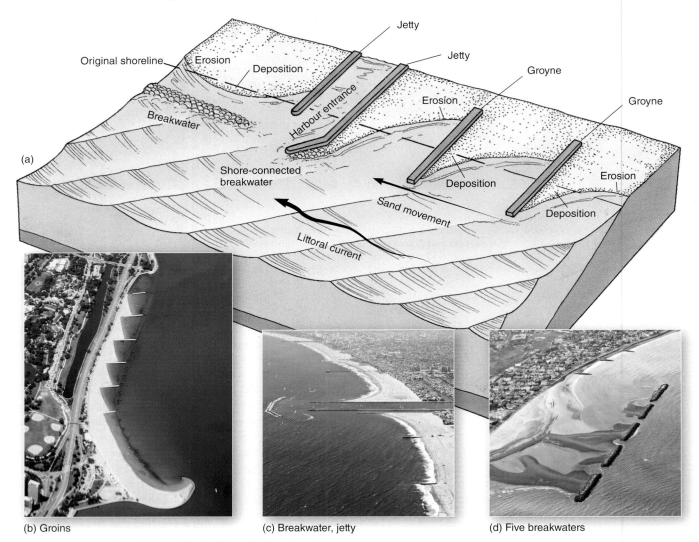

(b) Groins   (c) Breakwater, jetty   (d) Five breakwaters

FIGURE 16.14 Interfering with the littoral drift of sand.
(a) Various constructions attempt to control littoral drift and beach drift along a coast: breakwater, jetty, and groyne. Aerial photographs of coastal constructions: (b) Note the disruption of sediment movement by each groyne along the coast of Lake Michigan, north of Chicago; (c) a breakwater and jetties protect the entrance to Marina del Rey, California; (d) the Five Sisters breakwaters in Winthrop, Massachusetts (near Boston)—note coarse gravels and sand accumulating in bars behind the breakwaters since their construction in the 1930s. [Bobbé Christopherson.]

Coastal Stabilization Structures

Careful planning and impact assessment should be part of any strategy for preserving or altering a beach.

In contrast to the term *hard structures*, the hauling of sand to replenish a beach is considered "soft" shoreline protection. *Beach nourishment* refers to the artificial replacement of sand along a beach. Through such efforts, a beach that normally experiences a net loss of sediment will be "nourished" with imported sand. Years of human effort and expense to build beaches can be erased by a single storm, as occurred when Hurricane Camille completely eliminated offshore islands along the Gulf Coast in 1969, or in 2004 when hurricanes Charley, Frances, Ivan, and Jeanne devastated coastal Florida beaches and barrier islands. Unforeseen environmental impact may accompany the addition of sand to a beach, especially if the sand is from an unmatched source, in terms of its ecological traits. If the new sand does not physically and chemically match the existing varieties, disruption of coastal marine life is possible.

Barrier Beach Formation Barrier chains are long, narrow, depositional features, generally composed of sand, that form offshore roughly parallel to the coast. Common forms are **barrier beaches** or the broader, more extensive landform, **barrier islands**. Tidal variation in the area usually is moderate to low, with adequate sediment supplies coming from nearby coastal plains. Figure 16.15 illustrates the many features of barrier chains, using North

Carolina's famed Outer Banks as an example, including Cape Hatteras, across Pamlico Sound from the mainland. The area presently is designated as one of 10 national seashore reserves supervised by the U. S. National Park Service.

On the landward side of a barrier formation are tidal flats, marshes, swamps, lagoons, coastal dunes, and beaches, visible in Figure 16.15. Barrier beaches appear to adjust to sea level and may naturally shift position from time to time in response to wave action and longshore currents. A break in a barrier forms an inlet that connects a bay with the ocean. The name *barrier* is appropriate, for these formations take the brunt of storm energy and actually shield the mainland. Various hypotheses have been proposed to explain the formation of barrier islands. These features may begin as offshore bars or low ridges of submerged sediment near shore and then gradually migrate toward shore as sea level rises.

Barrier beaches and islands are quite common worldwide, lying offshore of nearly 10% of Earth's coastlines. Examples are found offshore of Africa, India's eastern coast, Sri Lanka, Australia, Alaska's northern slope, and the shores of the Baltic and Mediterranean seas. Earth's most extensive chain of barrier islands is along the U.S. Atlantic and Gulf coasts, extending some 5000 km from Long Island to Texas and Mexico.

Barrier Island Vulnerabilities and Hazards Because many barrier islands seem to be migrating landward,

(a)

(b)   (c)

FIGURE 16.15 Barrier island chain.
(a) *Landsat* image of barrier island chain along the North Carolina coast. You can see key depositional forms: spit, island, beach, lagoon, and inlet. A sound is a large inlet of the ocean; Pamlico Sound is an example. (b) The path, partially a parking lot, along which the Cape Hatteras lighthouse was moved inland in 1999 to safer ground. (c) Cape Hatteras lighthouse in its new location 488 m farther inland. [(a) *Terra* MODIS image, NASA/GSFC; (b) and (c) Bobbé Christopherson.]

these landforms are an unwise choice for home sites or commercial building. Nonetheless, barrier islands are a common choice, despite the brunt of storm energy that must be absorbed frequently. The hazard represented by the settlement of barrier islands was made graphically clear when Hurricane Hugo assaulted South Carolina in 1989. In the Charleston area, Hugo swept away beachfront houses, barrier-island developments, and millions of tonnes of sand; the hurricane destroyed up to 95% of the single-family homes in one community. The southern portion of one island was torn away. With increased development and continuing real estate appreciation, each future storm can be expected to cause ever-increasing capital losses.

Vulnerable settlements fill the Outer Banks and Cape Hatteras and are repeatedly slammed by tropical storms—Hurricanes Emily, 1993; Dennis, Floyd, and Irene, 1999; Isabel, 2003; Alex and Bonnie, 2004; Ophelia, 2005; Hanna, 2008; and Earl, 2010—causing damage and beach erosion. Because of the continuing loss of sand, the famous Cape Hatteras lighthouse was moved inland in 1999 to safer ground (Figure 16.15b). Its new position is about 500 m from the ocean, or approximately the distance it was from the water in 1870 when it was built—that much sand was lost back to the sea. See http://www.ncsu.edu/coast/chl/ for details of the extraordinary effort to save this landmark.

The barrier islands off the Louisiana shore are disappearing. The islands are affected by subsidence through compaction of Mississippi delta sediments, a changing sea level that is rising at 1 cm per year in the region, and an increase in tropical storm intensity. In 1998, Hurricane Georges destroyed large tracts of the Chandeleur Islands, located 30 to 40 km from the Louisiana and Mississippi Gulf Coast, leaving the mainland with reduced protection (Figure 16.16). Louisiana's increasingly exposed wetlands are disappearing at rates of 65 km^2 per year. Hurricane Katrina (2005) alone removed this area of wetlands and swept away most of the remaining Chandeleur Islands (Figure 16.16c, d). The regional office of the U.S. Geological Survey predicts that in a few decades the barrier islands may disappear.

Figure 16.17a is an aerial photo of development along the Bolivar Peninsula, a barrier spit near Galveston on the Texas Gulf Coast. Portions of the barrier island chain are experiencing beach erosion rates averaging 2 m per year as sea level continues to rise. Hurricane Ike (September 13, 2008) struck Galveston Island, Bolivar Peninsula, and the Texas–Louisiana Coast—landfall was in the area pictured in Figure 16.17a. The barrier island urbanization was devastated as $30 billion in structures were swept away along with more than 200 lives—the third costliest hurricane on record for the United States. Surveys found 80% to 95% of homes were destroyed. The devastation is visible in Figure 16.17c a year after the event.

Biological Processes: Coral Formations

Not all coastlines form by purely physical processes. Some form as the result of biological processes, such as coral growth. A **coral** is a simple marine animal with a small, cylindrical, saclike body called a *polyp*; it is related to other marine invertebrates, such as anemones and jellyfish. Corals secrete calcium carbonate ($CaCO_3$) from the lower half of their bodies, forming a hard, calcified external skeleton.

Corals live in a *symbiotic* relationship with algae: They live together in a mutually helpful arrangement, each dependent on the other for survival. Corals cannot photosynthesize, but they do obtain some of their own nourishment. Algae perform photosynthesis and convert solar energy to chemical energy in the system, providing the coral with about 60% of its nutrition and assisting the coral with the calcification process. In return, corals provide the algae with nutrients.

Coral reefs are the most diverse marine ecosystems. Preliminary estimates of coral species place the number at a million worldwide, yet, as in most ecosystems in water or on land, biodiversity is declining in these communities.

Figure 16.18 shows the distribution of living coral formations. Corals mostly thrive in warm tropical oceans, so the difference in ocean temperature between the western coasts and eastern coasts of continents is critical to their distribution. Western coastal waters tend to be cooler, thereby discouraging coral activity, whereas eastern coastal currents at the same latitude are warmer and thus enhance coral growth.

Living colonial corals range in distribution from about 30° N to 30° S. Corals occupy a very specific ecological zone: 10–55 m depth, 27‰–40‰ salinity, and 18° to 29°C water temperature—30°C is the upper threshold; above that temperature the corals begin to bleach and die. Corals have low genetic diversity worldwide and long generation times, which together mean that corals are slow to adapt and vulnerable to changing conditions.

However, an interesting exception to these environmental parameters for corals are the unique species of cool corals that exist in cold, dark water and deep ocean, at temperatures as low as 4°C and in depths to 2000 m, well beyond the expected range of tropical corals. Scientists study these remarkable oddities, for they do not rely on algae but harvest nutrients from plankton and particulate matter. Corals require clear, sediment-free water and consequently do not locate near the mouths of sediment-charged freshwater streams. For example, note the lack of these structures along the U.S. Gulf Coast.

Coral Reefs Corals exist as both solitary and colonial formations. It is the colonial corals that produce enormous structures. Their skeletons accumulate, forming coral rock. Through many generations, live corals near the ocean's surface build on the foundation of older coral skeletons, which in turn may rest upon a volcanic seamount or some other submarine feature built up from the ocean floor. *Coral reefs* form by this process. Thus, a coral reef is a biologically derived sedimentary rock. It can assume one of several distinctive shapes.

In 1842, Charles Darwin hypothesized an evolution of reef formation. He suggested that, as reefs developed

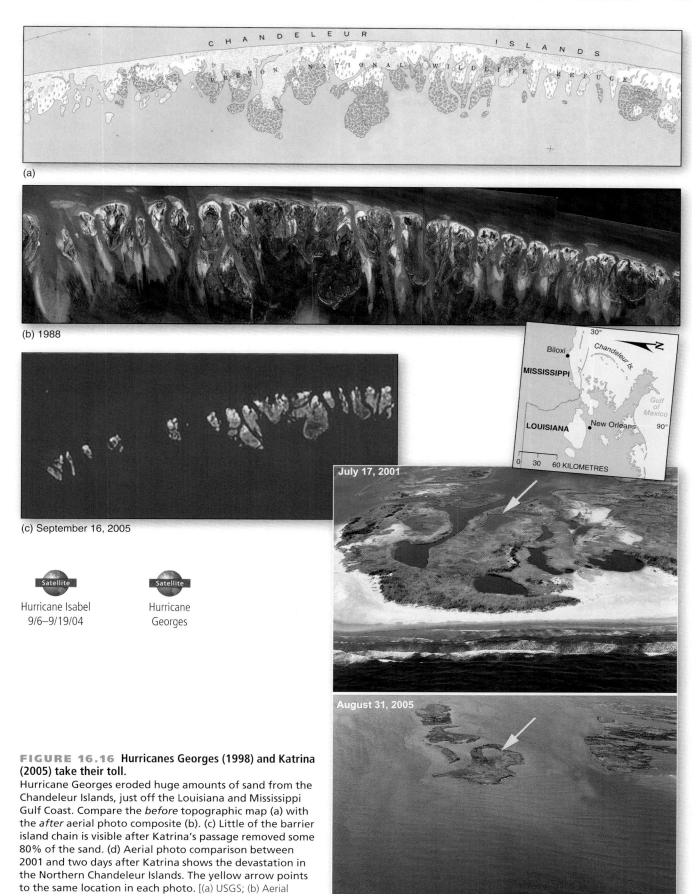

(a)

(b) 1988

(c) September 16, 2005

Satellite
Hurricane Isabel
9/6–9/19/04

Satellite
Hurricane
Georges

July 17, 2001

August 31, 2005

FIGURE 16.16 **Hurricanes Georges (1998) and Katrina (2005) take their toll.**
Hurricane Georges eroded huge amounts of sand from the Chandeleur Islands, just off the Louisiana and Mississippi Gulf Coast. Compare the *before* topographic map (a) with the *after* aerial photo composite (b). (c) Little of the barrier island chain is visible after Katrina's passage removed some 80% of the sand. (d) Aerial photo comparison between 2001 and two days after Katrina shows the devastation in the Northern Chandeleur Islands. The yellow arrow points to the same location in each photo. [(a) USGS; (b) Aerial Data Service, Earth Imaging; (c) and (d) USGS Hurricane Impact Studies.]

(d)

(a) Bolivar peninsula

(b) Hurricane Ike approaching landfall

(c) Empty foundation pads, houses gone

FIGURE 16.17 **Coastal barrier formations devastated along the Texas Gulf Coast.**
(a) Bolivar Peninsula, a barrier spit, stands between Texas and the Gulf of Mexico. Note the Intercoastal Waterway for shipping along Bolivar Peninsula. The scene is between Crystal Beach and Gilcrist, in the distance, where the spit narrows. (b) Hurricane Ike moves toward this coast September 12, 2008. The red dot notes the location of photo (a). (c) Devastation of Crystal Beach, Texas, on the Bolivar Peninsula. Debris from former homes and businesses is still being collected and burned. [(a) and (c) Bobbé Christopherson; (b) *Terra* image, SSEC/NASA.]

Hurricane Ike (2008) Bolivar Peninsula Damage

FIGURE 16.18 **Worldwide distribution of tropical living coral formations.**
Yellow areas include prolific reef growth and atoll formation. The red dotted line marks the geographical limits of coral activity. Colonial corals range in distribution from about 30° N to 30° S. [NOS/NOAA, 2008.]

around a volcanic island and the island itself gradually subsided, equilibrium is maintained between the subsidence of the island and the upward growth of the corals. This idea, generally accepted today, is portrayed in Figure 16.19. Note the specific examples of each reef stage: *fringing reefs* (platforms of surrounding coral rock),

barrier reefs (forming enclosed lagoons), and *atolls* (circular, ring-shaped).

Earth's most extensive fringing reef is the Bahamian platform in the western Atlantic (Figure 16.19c), covering some 96 000 km². The largest barrier reef, the Great Barrier Reef along the shore of the state of Queensland,

(a)

(b) Tikehau Atoll

(c) Bahamian coral platform

FIGURE 16.19 Coral forms.
(a) Common coral formations in a sequence of reef growth formed around a subsiding volcanic island: fringing reefs, barrier reefs, and an atoll. (b) Satellite image of the Tikehau Atoll, French Polynesia; note the airport runway and village in the far south (15° S 148° 10′ W). (c) The Bahamas: The lighter areas feature ocean depths to 10 m; the darker blues indicate depths dropping off to 4000 m. [(a) After D. R. Stoddart, *The Geographical Magazine* 63 (1971): 610; (b) *EO-1* image, NASA; (c) *Terra* image, NASA/GSFC.]

Australia, exceeds 2000 km in length, is 16–145 km wide, and includes at least 700 coral-formed islands and keys (coral islets or barrier reefs).

Coral Bleaching   Coral reefs may experience a phenomenon known as *bleaching*, which occurs as normally colourful corals turn stark white by expelling their own nutrient-supplying algae. Exactly why the corals eject their symbiotic partner is unknown, for without algae the corals die. Scientists are currently tracking this worldwide phenomenon, which is occurring in the Caribbean Sea and the Indian Ocean, as well as off the shores of Australia, Indonesia, Japan, Kenya, Florida, Texas, and Hawai‘i.

Possible causes include local pollution, disease, sedimentation, changes in salinity, and increasing oceanic acidity. One acknowledged cause is the 1 to 2 C° warming

 GEO REPORT 16.4   *Ocean Acidification Impact on Corals*

An early study of increasing ocean acidification and its impact on corals occurred from 1991 to 1993 in *Biosphere 2*—the closed habitat experiment located north of Tucson, Arizona. The habitat suffered from high carbon dioxide levels, and the model ocean in *Biosphere 2* quickly absorbed massive amounts of the excessive carbon dioxide. The model ocean became more acidic, which in turn chemically attacked the corals in the ocean. This same process is now occurring in the global oceans as CO_2 levels rise—here in ‘Biosphere 1’—with much research focused on the effects of acidification on oceanic flora and fauna.

of sea-surface temperatures linked to greenhouse warming of the atmosphere. In the *Status of Coral Reefs of the World: 2000*, a report from the Global Coral Reef Monitoring Network, warmer water was found to be a greater threat to corals than local pollution or other environmental problems (see http://www.coris.noaa.gov/).

Although a natural process, coral bleaching is now occurring at an unprecedented rate as average ocean temperatures climb higher, thus linking the issue of climate change to the health of all living coral formations. By the end of 2000, approximately 30% of reefs were lost, especially following the record El Niño event of 1998. In 2010, scientists reported one of the most rapid and severe coral bleaching and mortality events on record near Aceh, Indonesia, on the northern tip of the island of Sumatra. Some species declined 80% in just a few months, in response to sea-surface temperature anomalies across the region. Many of these corals previously were resilient to other ecosystem disruptions, such as the Sumatra–Andaman tsunami in 2004.

As sea-surface temperatures continue to rise, forecasts state that coral losses will continue. In the 2007 IPCC *Fourth Assessment Report*, Working Group II (SPM, p. 12) states, "Increases in sea surface temperatures of about 1 to 3 C° are projected to result in more frequent coral bleaching events and widespread mortality." For more information, see http://www.usgs.gov/coralreef.html and the Coral Reef Monitoring Network at http://www.gcrmn.org/.

CRITICAL THINKING 16.2

Exploring Corals

Google "Coral reef facts" and "coral reef in danger" and sample some of the links on these pages. Do you find any information about the damage to and bleaching of coral reefs reported in 1998 or at present? In which places in the world is bleaching being reported? Are the suspect causes presented in *Geosystems* mentioned in "Bleaching Hot Spots" or any of the "Coral Reef Alliance" references?

Wetlands, Salt Marshes, and Mangrove Swamps

Some coastal areas have great *biological productivity* (plant growth; spawning grounds for fish, shellfish, and other organisms) stemming from trapped organic matter and sediments. A rich coastal marsh environment can greatly outproduce a wheat field in raw vegetation per hectare. Thus, coastal marshes can support rich wildlife habitats. Unfortunately, these wetland ecosystems are quite fragile and are threatened by human development. Shoreline planning is the subject of Focus Study 16.1.

Wetlands are saturated with water enough of the time to support *hydrophytic vegetation* (plants that grow in water or wet soil). Wetlands usually occur on poorly drained soils. Geographically, wetlands occur not only along coastlines but also as northern bogs (peatlands with high water tables), as potholes in prairie lands, as cypress swamps (with standing or gently flowing water), as river bottomlands and floodplains, and as arctic and subarctic environments that experience permafrost during the year.

Coastal Wetlands

Coastal wetlands are of two general types—salt marshes and mangrove swamps. In the Northern Hemisphere, **salt marshes** tend to form north of the 30th parallel, whereas **mangrove swamps** form equatorward from that latitude in the Eastern and Western hemispheres. This distribution is dictated by the occurrence of freezing conditions which control the survival of mangrove seedlings. Roughly the same latitudinal limits apply in the Southern Hemisphere.

Salt marshes usually form in estuaries and behind barrier beaches and spits. An accumulation of mud produces a site for the growth of *halophytic* (salt-tolerant) plants. This vegetation then traps additional alluvial sediments and adds to the salt marsh area. Because salt marshes are in the intertidal zone (between the farthest reaches of high and low tides), sinuous, branching channels are produced as tidal waters flood into and ebb from the marsh (Figure 16.20).

FIGURE 16.20 Coastal salt marsh.
Salt marshes are productive ecosystems commonly occurring poleward of 30° latitude in both hemispheres. This is Gearheart Marsh, part of the Arcata Marsh system on the Pacific Coast in northern California. [Bobbé Christopherson.]

(a) Mangrove island

FIGURE 16.21 Mangroves.
(a) Mangroves take root and collect sediments to extend this island south of Puerto Rico. (b) Mangroves at sunset in J.N. "Ding" Darling National Wildlife Refuge, Sanibel Island, Florida; you can see the roots above the water line. (c) Underwater mangrove roots form a habitat for numerous plants and animals in a specific ecosystem. [Bobbé Christopherson.]

(b) Mangroves

(c) Mangrove ecosystem underwater

Sediment accumulation on tropical coastlines provides the site for mangrove trees, shrubs, and other small trees. The prop roots of the mangrove are constantly finding new anchorages. The roots are visible above the waterline but reach below the water surface, providing a habitat for a multitude of specialized life forms. Mangrove swamps often secure and fix enough material to form islands (Figure 16.21).

The World Resources Institute and the U.N. Environment Programme estimate that from pre-agricultural times to today, mangrove losses are running between 40% (examples, Cameroon and Indonesia) and nearly 80% (examples, Bangladesh and Philippines). Deliberate removal was a common practice by many governments in the early days of settlement because of a falsely conceived fear of disease or pestilence in these swamplands.

Human Impact on Coastal Environments

Development of modern societies is closely linked to estuaries, wetlands, barrier beaches, and coastlines. Estuaries provide natural harbours, a food source, and convenient sewage and waste disposal and are therefore important sites of human settlement. Society depends on daily tidal flushing of

estuaries to dilute the pollution created by waste disposal. Thus, the estuarine and coastal environment is vulnerable to abuse and destruction if development is not carefully planned. We are also approaching a time when most barrier islands will be developed and occupied (Figure 16.22).

FIGURE 16.22 Barrier island subdivisions.
The town of Barnegat Light abruptly stops where Long Beach Island is protected in Barnegat Lighthouse State Park, New Jersey. The protected area is almost entirely composed of replenished sand. [Bobbé Christopherson.]

An Environmental Approach to Shoreline Planning

Coastlines are places of wonderful opportunity, such as ecosystem preservation, recreation, and development. These areas also are zones of specific constraints, and are vulnerable to shoreline processes. Poor understanding of this resource and a lack of environmental analysis often go hand in hand, surrounded by intense developmental pressures for economic gain.

For example, Cape Cod, Massachusetts, is a narrow coastal sandy peninsula composed of glacial outwash and moraInal deposits. With much of its land protected as part of the Cape Cod National Seashore Reserve in 1961, Cape Cod is still subject to extensive human impacts and aggressive coastal processes. Urbanization along the cape has developed in a patchwork in and around protected areas, making a complex mix of private and public jurisdiction, land use, and plans (Figure 16.1.1).

Settlements outside the reserve are vulnerable to sea-level rise, storm surges, and saltwater intrusion into groundwater systems. Houses and businesses are barely above sea level and use septic systems with leach fields for waste disposal. These systems and most structures will be increasingly vulnerable to future sea-level rise. See http://pubs .usgs.gov/of/2002/of02-233/ for a report on the concept of coastal vulnerability along Cape Cod. Scientists are working to understand this dynamic environment better. Proper planning and thinking

about the future are difficult as various stakeholders defend their positions.

Beaches and Dunes—Where to Build?

In his book *Design with Nature*, the late ecologist and landscape architect Ian McHarg discusses the New Jersey coast. He shows how proper understanding of a coastal environment could have avoided problems from major storms and coastal development. Figure 16.1.2 illustrates the New Jersey shore from ocean to back bay. Let us walk across this landscape and discover how it might be treated under ideal conditions. Remember that much of this applies to coastal areas elsewhere.

We begin our walk at the water's edge and proceed across the beach. Sand beaches are the primary natural defence against the ocean, acting as bulwarks against the pounding of a stormy sea. The shoreline tolerates recreation, but not construction, because of its shifting, changing nature during storms, daily tidal fluctuations, and the potential effects of rising sea level. Beaches are susceptible to pollution and require environmental protection to control nearshore dumping of dangerous materials.

Walking inland, we encounter the primary dune. Even more sensitive than the beach, it is fragile, easily disturbed, and vulnerable to erosion, and it cannot tolerate the passage of people trekking to the beach. Some vegetation is present, but it

has only a small effect on sand stabilization. Carefully controlled access points to the beach should be designated, and restricted access should be enforced. (See two examples of beach stabilization in Figure 15.5.)

The trough behind the primary dune is relatively tolerant of limited recreation and building. The plants send roots down to fresh groundwater reserves and anchor the sand in the process. Thus, if construction should inhibit the surface recharge of that water supply, the natural protective ground cover could die and destabilize the environment. Or subsequent saltwater intrusion might contaminate well water. Clearly, groundwater resources and the location of recharge aquifers must be considered in planning. The continuing use of septic sewage systems in the trough is not sustainable.

Behind the trough is the secondary dune, a second line of defence against the sea. It, too, is tolerant of some use, yet is vulnerable to destruction. Next is the backdune, more suitable for development than any zone between it and the sea. Further inland are the bayshore and the bay, where no dredging or filling and only limited dumping of treated wastes and toxics should be permitted. This zone is tolerant of intensive recreation. In reality, of course, the opposite of such careful assessment and planning often prevails.

FIGURE 16.1.1 Vulnerable coastal settlements along Beach Point on Cape Cod, Massachusetts.
[Bobbé Christopherson.]

Science and Political Reality

Before an intensive government study of the New Jersey shore was completed in 1962, no analysis of coastal hazards had been done outside of academic circles. What is common knowledge in science classrooms and laboratories still has not filtered through to financial, developmental, and real estate interests. As a result, on the New Jersey shore and along much of the Atlantic and Gulf coasts, improper development of the fragile coastal zone (primary dunes, trough, and secondary dunes) led to extensive destruction during storms in 1962, 1992, 2004, and 2005, and a near miss in 2010, among other times.

Scientists estimate that the U.S. Atlantic and Gulf coastlines will continue to erode—in some cases, tens of metres in a few decades. Society should reconcile ecology and economics if these coastal environments are to be sustained, especially in a time of increased storm intensity and sea-level rise. Similar rates of sea level rise in Atlantic Canada mean that similar inundation and erosion is to be expected.

FIGURE 16.1.2 Coastal environment and planning along the New Jersey shore.
(a) A planning perspective from ocean to bay. Note letters on the illustration to identify photo location. (b) Light trucks and SUV tracks in the protected Island Beach State Park. These vehicles are banned from developed stretches of beach. (c) Houses once distant from the surf are hit by waves. Sand is brought in to strengthen defenses. (d) Development along the primary dunes—an amusement park— challenges the natural setting. (e) The primary dune in a somewhat natural state. (f) An undeveloped trough behind the primary dune. (g) The former trough, paved and developed, barely above high-tide levels. (h) Development and commerce in the bayshore and bay. [(a) After *Design with Nature* by Ian McHarg. Copyright © 1969 by Ian L. McHarg; (b) through (h) Bobbé Christopherson.]

Barrier islands and coastal beaches migrate over time. Houses that were more than 1600 m from the sea in the Hamptons along the southeastern shore of Long Island, New York, are now within only 30 m of it. The time remaining for these homes can be quickly shortened by a single hurricane or by a sequence of storms. Hurricane Earl in 2010 passed close by to these coastal environments, causing sand inventory losses.

Despite our understanding of beach and barrier-island migration, the effect of storms, and warnings from scientists and government agencies, coastal development proceeds. Society behaves as though beaches and barrier islands are stable and fixed, or as though these features can be engineered to be permanent. Experience has shown that severe erosion generally cannot be prevented, as we have seen with the cliffs of southern California, the shores of the Great Lakes, the New Jersey shore, the devastation of Hurricane Hugo, and the devastation along the Gulf Coast and the disappearances of islands caused by Hurricane Georges.

A reasonable conclusion seems to be that the key to protective environmental planning and zoning is to *allocate responsibility and cost in the event of a disaster*. A system might place a hazard tax on land, based on assessed risk, and restrict the government's responsibility to fund reconstruction or an individual's right to reconstruct on frequently damaged sites. Comprehensive mapping of erosion-hazard areas would help avoid the ever-increasing costs from recurring disasters.

GEOSYSTEMS CONNECTION

In these last four chapters, we examined aspects of weathering, erosion and transportation, and deposition, through the agents of streams, wind, and waves. In this chapter, the systems approach moved you through coastal system inputs, actions, and outputs and analyzed human perceptions of and impacts on coastal environments. Next, we look at the agents of change in the cryosphere and the ice environments on Earth: systems that are undergoing the highest rate of change as climates shift.

 APPLIED PHYSICAL GEOGRAPHY   *Coastal Geomorphology—Sediment Budgets*

Figures 1 and 2 portray two different types of coasts. Tables 1 and 2 summarize the gains and losses for each type of coast (see *Nearshore Total* line in the tables) and the volume of offshore sediment gained or lost.

In Figure 1, the amount of longshore sediment transport increases by 100 × 10³ m³·y⁻¹ because there are more gains of sediment to the longshore zone than losses. The greatest

contributions to the sediment budget come from the input of sediment delivered by the rivers and the material added to the coastal system as a result of cliff erosion. If the cliffs were protected from erosion, the coastal sediment budget would be reduced by 45 × 10³ m³·y⁻¹.

The question mark and dashed line at A in the offshore region represent the loss of sediment to the

submarine canyon (called *offshore out*). Material transported here is effectively lost from the coastal system. If 80% of the sediment could be captured from this location before it moved into the canyon, losses would be limited to 7 × 10³ m³·y⁻¹, leaving an extra 28 × 10³ m³·y⁻¹ for the *longshore out* component and dune accretion.

FIGURE 1 High hinterland coast. Volumes of sediment moved through the sediment budget are portrayed in this example. Waves from offshore break on the accreting beach. See Table 1. [Figure by Mary-Louise Byrne and Brian McCann.]

Often dams are constructed in the hinterland. If dams were constructed at B and C, the sand input from rivers would be trapped by the dams, reducing the input by 90%. In calculating the balance, a reduction of 11×10^3 m³·y⁻¹ at B and a reduction of 99×10^3 m³·y⁻¹ at C would occur. Balance in the system would be maintained through decreased values of longshore out, offshore out, and dune accretion.

Figure 2 shows a spit and barrier system. The barriers are maintaining position through dune accretion and beach erosion. The lagoon is infilling due to large inputs of sediment through the inlets.

Overall, the coastal reach portrayed in Figure 1 is experiencing greater erosion than accretion in the nearshore—there is a net loss of sediment to this system through longshore and offshore movement of sediment. In Figure 2, the coastal system is in balance with some losses of sediment to the longshore offset by gains of sediment to the lagoon through the inlet. Sediment is being added to the nearshore from offshore sources.

FIGURE 2 Low hinterland coast. Barrier islands and spits are separated from the mainland by a lagoon so waves from offshore expend their energy before reaching the mainland. The focus of the sediment budget is on these nearshore features. See Table 2. [Figure by Mary-Louise Byrne and Brian McCann.]

TABLE 1   Sediment Gains and Losses—High Hinterland Coast

Potential Gains	(10³ m³·y⁻¹)	Potential Losses	(10³ m³·y⁻¹)
Longshore in	140	Longshore out	240
Beach erosion	0	Beach accretion	5
Rivers	230	Dune accretion and overwash	135
Cliff erosion	45	Inlets	0
Nearshore Total	415	Nearshore Total	380
Offshore in	0	Offshore out	35

There are greater potential gains than losses of sediment in this environment. Although there are large amounts of sediment moved out of this cell by longshore processes, cliff erosion and rivers carry more sediment in than is lost.

TABLE 2   Sediment Gains and Losses—Low Hinterland Coast

Potential Gains	(10³ m³·y⁻¹)	Potential Losses	(10³ m³·y⁻¹)
Longshore in	10	Longshore out	90
Beach erosion	195	Beach accretion	0
Rivers	0	Dune accretion and overwash	165
Cliff erosion	0	Inlets	215
Nearshore Total	315	Nearshore Total	470
Offshore in	155	Offshore out	0

There are more potential losses than gains in this environment through coastal processes. Large amounts of sediment are brought into the system through the inlets. This volume of sediment is deposited in the lagoon and represents a loss. Over time, the barriers will maintain their shape, but be driven landward by wave action. [Tables by Mary-Louise Byrne and Brian McCann.]

KEY LEARNING CONCEPTS REVIEW

■ **Describe** the chemical composition of seawater and the physical structure of the ocean.

Water is the "universal solvent," dissolving at least 57 of the 92 elements found in nature. Seawater is a solution, and the concentration of dissolved solids is **salinity**. **Brine** exceeds the average 35‰ (parts per thousand) salinity; **brackish** applies to water that is less than 35‰. The ocean is divided by depth into a narrow mixing zone at the surface, a thermocline transition zone, and the deep cold zone.

> salinity (p. 485)
> brine (p. 486)
> brackish (p. 486)

1. Describe the salinity of seawater: its composition, amount, and distribution.
2. Analyze the latitudinal distribution of salinity as shown in Figure 16.2. Why is salinity less along the equator and greater in the subtropics?
3. What are the three general zones relative to physical structure within the ocean? Characterize each by temperature, salinity, dissolved oxygen, and dissolved carbon dioxide.

■ **Identify** the components of the coastal environment, and **list** the physical inputs to the coastal system, including tides and mean sea level.

The coastal environment is the **littoral zone** and exists where the tide-driven, wave-driven sea confronts the land. Inputs to the coastal environment include solar energy, wind and weather, climatic variation, the nature of coastal geomorphology, and human activities.

Mean sea level (MSL) is based on average tidal levels recorded hourly at a given site over many years. MSL varies spatially because of ocean currents and waves, tidal variations, air temperature and pressure differences, ocean temperature variations, slight variations in Earth's gravity, and changes in oceanic volume. MSL worldwide is rising in response to global warming of the atmosphere and oceans.

Tides are complex daily oscillations in sea level, ranging worldwide from barely noticeable to many metres. Tides are produced by the gravitational pull of both the Moon and the Sun. Most coastal locations experience two high (rising) **flood tides** and two low (falling) **ebb tides** every day. The difference between consecutive high and low tides is the tidal range. **Spring tides** exhibit the greatest tidal range, when the Moon and Sun are either in conjunction or opposition. **Neap tides** produce a lesser tidal range.

> littoral zone (p. 487)
> mean sea level (MSL) (p. 488)
> tides (p. 490)
> flood tide (p. 491)
> ebb tide (p. 491)
> spring tide (p. 491)
> neap tide (p. 491)

4. What are the key terms used to describe the coastal environment?
5. Define mean sea level. How is this value determined? Is it constant or variable around the world? Explain.

6. What interacting forces generate the pattern of tides?
7. What characteristic tides are expected during a new Moon or a full Moon? During the first-quarter and third-quarter phases of the Moon?
8. What is meant by a flood tide? An ebb tide?
9. Explain briefly how tidal power is being used to generate electricity. Are there any sites doing this in North America? If so, name the location and briefly describe the operation.

■ **Describe** wave motion at sea and near shore, and **explain** coastal straightening as a product of wave refraction.

Friction between moving air (wind) and the ocean surface generates undulations of water that we call **waves**. Wave energy in the open sea travels through water, but the water itself remains virtually in place after the wave has passed. Regular patterns of smooth, rounded waves, the mature undulations of the open ocean, are **swells**. Near shore, the restricted depth of water slows the wave, forming *waves of translation*, in which both energy and water actually move forward toward shore. As the crest of each wave rises, the wave falls into a characteristic **breaker**.

Wave refraction redistributes wave energy so that different sections of the coastline vary in erosion potential. Headlands are eroded, whereas coves and bays receive materials, with the long-term effect of straightening the coast. As waves approach a shore at an angle, refraction produces a **longshore current** of water moving parallel to the shore. This current produces the *longshore drift* of sand, sediment, and gravel and assorted. **Littoral drift** is transport of materials along the shore. Particles move along the beach as **beach drift**, shifting back and forth between water and land. A **tsunami** is a seismic sea wave triggered by an undersea landslide or earthquake. It travels at great speeds in the open sea and gains height as it comes ashore, posing a major coastal hazard.

An *erosional coast* features wave action that cuts a horizontal bench in the tidal zone, extending from a sea cliff out into the sea. Such a structure is a **wave-cut platform**, or *wave-cut terrace*. In contrast, *depositional coasts* generally are located along land of gentle relief, where depositional sediments are available from many sources. Characteristic landforms deposited by waves and currents are a **barrier spit** (material deposited in a long ridge extending out from a coast); a **bay barrier**, or *baymouth bar* (a spit that cuts off the bay from the ocean and forms an inland **lagoon**); a **tombolo** (where sediment deposits connect the shoreline with an offshore island or sea stack); and a **beach** (land along the shore where sediment, deposited by waves and currents, is in motion). A beach helps to stabilize the shoreline, although it may be unstable seasonally.

> wave (p. 492)
> swell (p. 493)
> breaker (p. 493)
> wave refraction (p. 493)
> longshore current (p. 495)
> littoral drift (p. 495)
> beach drift (p. 495)
> tsunami (p. 495)
> wave-cut platform (p. 497)
> barrier spit (p. 499)

bay barrier (p. 499)
lagoon (p. 499)
tombolo (p. 499)
beach (p. 499)

10. What is a wave? How are waves generated? Does the water travel with the wave as it moves across the ocean?
11. Describe the refraction process that occurs when waves reach an irregular coastline. Why is the coastline straightened?
12. Define the components of beach drift and the longshore current and longshore drift.
13. Explain how a seismic sea wave attains such tremendous velocities. Why is it given a Japanese name—tsunami?
14. What is meant by an erosional coast? What are the expected features of such a coast?
15. What is meant by a depositional coast? What are the expected features of such a coast?
16. How do people attempt to modify littoral drift? What strategies are used? What are the positive and negative impacts of these actions?
17. Describe a situation in which a tombolo forms.

■ *Describe* barrier islands and associated hazards that relate to human settlement.

Barrier chains are long, narrow, depositional features, generally of sand, that form offshore parallel to the coast. Common forms are **barrier beaches** and the broader, more extensive **barrier islands**. Barrier formations are transient coastal features, constantly on the move, and they are a poor, but common, choice for development.

barrier beach (p. 501)
barrier island (p. 501)

18. On the basis of the information in the text and any other sources at your disposal, do you think barrier islands and beaches should be used for development?

■ *Assess* living coastal environments: corals, wetlands, salt marshes, and mangroves.

A **coral** is a simple marine invertebrate that forms a hard, calcified, external skeleton. Over generations, corals accumulate in large reef structures. Corals live in a *symbiotic* (mutually helpful) relationship with algae; each is dependent on the other for survival.

Wetlands are lands saturated with water that support specific plants adapted to wet conditions. Wetlands occur along coastlands and inland in bogs, swamps, and river bottomlands. Coastal wetlands form as **salt marshes** poleward of the 30th parallel in each hemisphere and as **mangrove swamps** equatorward of these latitudes.

coral (p. 502)
wetlands (p. 506)
salt marshes (p. 506)
mangrove swamps (p. 506)

19. How are corals able to construct reefs and islands?
20. Describe a trend in corals that is troubling scientists, and discuss some possible causes.
21. Why are the coastal wetlands poleward of 30° N and S latitude different from those that are equatorward? Describe the differences.

■ *Construct* an environmentally sensitive model for settlement and land use along the coast.

Coastlines are zones of specific constraints. Poor understanding of this resource and a lack of environmental analysis often go hand in hand, producing frequent disasters to coastal ecosystems and real property losses. Society must reconcile ecology and economics if these coastal environments are to be sustained.

22. What type of environmental analysis is needed for rational development and growth in a region like the New Jersey shore? Evaluate the approach to coastal hazards and protection in the focus study and in Figure 16.1.2.

MyGeosciencePlace

Visit **www.mygeoscienceplace.ca** for several figure animations, satellite loops, self-study quizzes, flashcards, interactive glossary, career links, RSS feeds, Pearson eText of *Geosystems*, and much more.

CHAPTER 17

Glacial and Periglacial Processes and Landforms

Chauveau Glacier calves into Ayerfjorden (Ayer Fjord), as seen from morainal deposits. The scene is at 79° 40′ N latitude. Less than 10 years ago, this glacier filled the entire fjord. This fjord is an inlet of the larger Raudfjorden on Spitsbergen's north coast. [Bobbé Christopherson.]

KEY LEARNING CONCEPTS

After reading the chapter, you should be able to:

- **Differentiate** between alpine and continental glaciers, and **describe** the principal features of each type.
- **Explain** the process of glacial ice formation, and **portray** the mechanics of glacial movement.
- **Describe** characteristic erosional and depositional landforms created by alpine glaciation and by continental glaciation.
- **Analyze** the spatial distribution of periglacial processes and related permafrost and frozen ground, and **explain** the present thaw under way.
- **Explain** the Pleistocene ice-age epoch and related glacials and interglacials, and **describe** some of the methods used to study paleoclimatology.
- **Define** each polar region, and **list** climatic changes taking place and associated impacts.

Ice Shelves and Tidewater Glaciers Giving Way to Warming

Along the coasts of Canada, Greenland, and Antarctica are numerous *ice shelves*, extending over the sea while still attached to continental ice. These shelves are often found in sheltering inlets and bays, cover thousands of square kilometres, and reach thicknesses of 1000 m. Also in these regions are *tidewater glaciers*, which end in the sea. Warming temperatures appear to be hastening the flow, calving (breaking off), and thinning of ice shelves and tidewater glaciers. While the loss of these ice shelves does not significantly raise sea level, since the ice already displaces seawater, the concern is the possible surge of grounded continental ice and outlet glaciers that many of the ice shelves hold back from the sea.

In 2005, there were six ice shelves remaining along the northern coast of Ellesmere Island in Canada. Two of these have collapsed completely—Ayles in 2005 and Markham in 2008—and are now floating ice islands in the Arctic Ocean (Figure GN 17.1). The other four ice shelves are disintegrating as large sections calve off periodically (Serson ice shelf lost 122 km², 60% of its area, in 2008), and the warming climate means these shelves will not reform. Ward Hunt Ice Shelf, largest in the Arctic, began to break up in 2003 after remaining stable for at least 4500 years. Backed up behind the Ward Hunt Ice Shelf was an *epishelf lake*, an extensive freshwater accumulation some 43 m deep. As the ice-shelf dam failed, this epishelf lake—largest in the Northern Hemisphere—drained. A unique biological community of fresh- and brackish-water plankton was lost and delicate ecosystems disrupted.

Along the northwest coast of Greenland, the tidewater portion of Petermann Glacier is breaking up. On August 5, 2010, a section 251 km² in area broke loose (Figure GN 17.2). The new iceberg is the largest to form in the Arctic in 50 years and is more than 25% of this glacier's entire floating ice shelf. As warmer air melts ice from above, and higher sea temperatures melt ice from below, the rate of glacial loss increases. On the satellite image, note the numerous meltponds on the glacier, some filling surface cracks (pale blue in color), and new cracks opening upstream, demonstrating the forward-moving stress. The symptomatic meltponds represent a positive feedback mechanism caused by increasing temperatures.

In the south polar region, similar melt events are under way. Along the Antarctic Peninsula, the Wilkins Ice Shelf has an area of about 10 300 km². Intact for the past 10 000 years, this ice shelf breakup began in 2008 and scientists predict it will soon collapse completely (Figure GN 17.3). The ongoing ice loss is likely a result of the 2.5 C° temperature increase in the peninsula region during the last 50 years. As in the Arctic, warmth is melting the shelf along both the ocean and the atmosphere surfaces.

To the west of the peninsula, the Pine Island Glacier flows as an outlet glacier from the West Antarctic Ice Sheet (WAIS) to the Amundsen Sea (noted on Figure 17.32c). The flow is accelerating, increasing some 400% in rate between 1995 and 2006. The 40-km wide ice shelf is also calving and thinning at higher rates than previously recorded: Over the past 10 000 years, thinning was a few centimetres per year, yet over the past 20 years, the thinning reached over 1 m per year.

These tidewater outlet glaciers and ice shelves hold back flows of grounded ice upstream in the Arctic and Antarctic—and in the WAIS in particular. These grounded masses of ice are not yet displacing ocean water, but they are moving toward the sea. As the ice shelf portions disappear, their buttressing effect is lost. If the warming trends continue as predicted, these ice masses may reach the ocean and add to increasing sea level across the globe.

FIGURE GN 17.2 Greenland tidewater glacier breaks up.
Note the meltponds, crevasses, and cracks on the ice surfaces of the Petermann Glacier. Notice that there are at least five tributary glaciers. [*EO-1,* NASA/USGS.]

FIGURE GN 17.1 Collapse of Ayles Ice Shelf, north coast of Ellesmere Island, Canada, in 2005.
After breaking up, the ice shelf (circled) became a 66 km² ice island drifting in the Arctic Ocean. [*Terra* MODIS image, NASA/GSFC.]

FIGURE GN 17.3 Wilkins Ice Shelf breakup, Antarctica.
This image is from 2008; active disintegration continued through 2010. [*Terra* MODIS image, NASA/GSFC.]

About 77% of Earth's freshwater is frozen, with the bulk of that ice occurring in just two places—Greenland and Antarctica. The remaining ice covers various mountains and fills some alpine valleys. A volume of more than 32.7 million km³ of water is tied up as ice in Greenland (2.38 million km³), Antarctica (30.1 million km³), and ice caps and mountain glaciers worldwide (180 000 km³).

These accumulations provide an extensive frozen record of Earth's climatic history over the past several million years and perhaps some clues to its climatic future. This is Earth's *cryosphere*, the portion of the hydrosphere and groundwater that is perennially frozen, generally at high latitudes and high elevations. The cryosphere is in a state of dramatic change, as worldwide glacial and polar ice inventories melt. In 2007, Arctic Ocean sea ice decreased to its smallest extent in the past century, as regional temperatures set records of more than 5 C° above normal. The ice loss in 2008 was second to this record, with 2009 and 2010 tying for third.

In this chapter: We focus on Earth's extensive ice deposits—their formation, movement, and the ways in which they produce various erosional and depositional landforms. Glaciers, transient landforms themselves, leave behind a variety of landscape features. The fate of glaciers is intricately tied to changes in global temperature and rising or falling sea level, which ultimately concerns us all. We discuss the methods used to decipher past climates—the science of *paleoclimatology*—and the clues for understanding future climate patterns. Exciting discoveries are arising from ice cores taken from Earth's two ice sheets; one core dates back 800 000 years from the present.

We examine the cold world of permafrost and periglacial geomorphic processes. Approximately 25% of Earth's land area is subject to freezing conditions and frost action characteristic of periglacial regions, including areas that have specific related features of relict, or past, permafrost. The chapter ends with a look at the polar regions.

Rivers of Ice

A **glacier** is a large mass of ice resting on land or floating as an ice shelf in the sea adjacent to land. Glaciers are not frozen lakes or groundwater ice. Instead, glaciers form by the continual accumulation of snow that recrystallizes under its own weight into an ice mass. Glaciers are not stationary; the ice moves slowly under the pressure of its own great weight and the pull of gravity. In fact, glaciers move slowly in streamlike patterns, merging as tributaries into large rivers of ice, as you can see in the satellite image and aerial photos in Figure 17.1. In Greenland and Antarctica, vast sheets of ice dominate, slowly flowing outward toward the ocean.

Today, these slowly flowing rivers and sheets of ice dominate about 11% of Earth's land area. As much as 30% of continental land was covered by glacial ice during colder episodes in the past. Through these "ice ages," below-freezing temperatures prevailed at lower latitudes more than is the case today, allowing snow to accumulate year after year.

(a)

(b)

(c)

FIGURE 17.1 Rivers and sheets of ice.
(a) Alpine glaciers merge from adjoining glacial valleys in the northeast region of Ellesmere Island in the Canadian Arctic. (b) Numerous glaciers flow toward the coast of Greenland; note the morainal deposit marking the flow. (c) These peaks, known as *nunataks*, rise above the Greenland Ice Sheet, an accumulation perhaps 100 000 years in the making; note the ice stream flowing. [(a) *Terra* ASTER image, NASA/GSFC/ERSDAC/JAROS; (b) and (c) Bobbé Christopherson.]

Glaciers form in areas of permanent snow, both at high latitudes and at high elevations at any latitude. A **snowline** is the lowest elevation where snow can persist

(a)

(b)

(c)

FIGURE 17.4 Glacial ice calving into the sea and icebergs.
(a) When glaciers reach the sea, large pieces break off, forming icebergs, such as these massive bergs in southern Greenland. (b) A tabular iceberg off Antarctica, in the Bransfield Strait near the Antarctic Sound. (c) This iceberg tower in East Greenland is about 60 m tall; imagine its keel extending some 360 m below the surface. [Bobbé Christopherson.]

Continental Glaciers

On a much larger scale than individual alpine glaciers, a continuous mass of ice is a **continental glacier**. In its most extensive form, it is an **ice sheet**. Most of Earth's glacial ice exists in the ice sheets that blanket 81% of Greenland and 90% of Antarctica. Antarctica alone has 92% of all the glacial ice on the planet. A composite of satellite imagery reveals the Antarctic continent in Figure 17.5.

The Antarctic and Greenland ice sheets have such enormous mass that large portions of each landmass beneath the ice are isostatically depressed (pressed down by weight) below sea level. Each ice sheet has a maximum thickness of more than 3000 m, with average thickness around 2000 m, burying all but the highest peaks, known as *nunataks*.

Two additional types of continuous ice cover associated with mountain locations are *ice caps* and *ice fields*. An **ice cap** is roughly circular and, by definition, covers an area of less than 50 000 km². Ice caps are found in polar regions and, like ice sheets, are not constrained by the existing relief, but completely bury the underlying relief. The ice exerts a modifying effect on the climate, cooling the local area. In Canada, there are well-developed ice caps in the high Arctic (Agassiz Ice Cap, Northern Ellesmere Island; Melville Island South Ice Cap; Devon Ice Cap; Meighen Ice Cap, White Glacier on Axel Heiberg Island; Penny and Barnes ice caps on Baffin Island). The Barnes

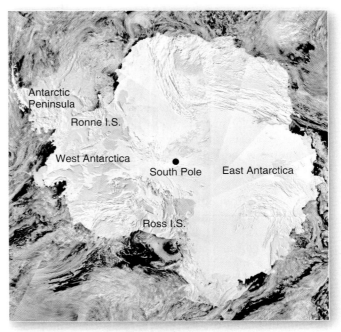

FIGURE 17.5 Antarctic Ice Sheet.
A composite of *Aqua* MODIS images from January 2009 portrays the Antarctic continent—containing 92% of Earth's glacial ice. Reference the map of Antarctica in Figure 17.32c. [*Aqua* MODIS image, NASA/GSFC.]

(a)

(b)

FIGURE 17.6 Ice cap and ice field.
(a) The Vatnajökull Ice Cap in southeastern Iceland outlined by the red line (*jökull* means "ice cap" in Danish). This image was made after the Eyjafjallajökull Volcano began erupting in April 2010; see the ash cloud flowing southeastward toward European airspace. (b) The southern Patagonian ice field of Argentina. [(a) NASA/GSFC; (b) NASA Headquarters.]

Ice Cap on Baffin Island is the last remnant of the Laurentide Ice Sheet that covered almost all of Canada and a portion of the northern United States at the peak of the Wisconsinan glaciation. The ice in the Barnes Ice Cap is over 100 000 years old, making it Canada's oldest.

The volcanic island of Iceland features several ice caps, such as the Vatnajökull Ice Cap in the *Landsat* image in Figure 17.6a. Volcanoes lie beneath these icy surfaces. Iceland's Grímsvötn Volcano erupted in 1996, and again in 2004, producing large quantities of melted glacial water and floods, a flow Icelanders call a *jökulhlaup*.

An **ice field** is not extensive enough to form the characteristic dome of an ice cap; instead, it extends in a characteristic elongated pattern in a mountainous region. A fine example is the Patagonian ice field of Argentina and Chile, one of Earth's largest. It attains only 90 km width, but stretches 360 km, from 46° to 51° S latitude (equivalent in latitude from South Dakota to central Manitoba in the Northern Hemisphere).

In Canada, the Columbia Icefield (see Figure 17.3) straddles the continental divide between Banff and Jasper, Alberta. The highest elevation on the ice field, Snow Dome, reaches 3520 m and represents the triple point in the drainage divide system of North America: Arctic, Atlantic, and Pacific. Eight glaciers flow out from the ice field, including the Athabasca, Saskatchewan, Dome, Stutfield, Castleguard, and Columbia. Covering an area of about 325 km², the Columbia Icefield is one of the largest in the Rocky Mountains.

Continuous ice sheets or ice caps are drained by rapidly moving, solid *ice streams* on the periphery, moving to the sea or to lowlands. Such frozen ice streams flow from the edges of Greenland and Antarctica, through stationary and slower-moving ice. An *outlet glacier* flows out from an ice sheet or ice cap but is constrained by a mountain valley or pass. Can you see the ice stream flowing past the nunataks in Figure 17.1c?

Glacial Processes

A glacier is a dynamic body, moving relentlessly downslope at rates that vary within its mass, excavating the landscape through which it flows. The mass is dense ice that is formed from snow and water through a process of compaction, recrystallization, and growth. A glacier's *mass budget* consists of net gains or losses of this glacial ice, which determine whether the glacier expands or retreats. Let us now look at glacial ice formation, mass balance, movement, and erosion before we discuss the fascinating landforms produced by these processes.

Formation of Glacial Ice

Consider for a moment the nature of ice. You may be surprised to learn that ice is both a mineral (an inorganic natural compound of specific chemical makeup and crystalline structure) and a rock (a mass of one or more minerals). Ice is a frozen fluid, a trait that it shares with igneous rocks. The accumulation of snow in layered deposits is similar to sedimentary rock formations. Glaciers develop when snow and ice are transformed under pressure, recrystallizing into a type of metamorphic rock. Glacial ice is a remarkable material!

The essential input to a glacier is snow that accumulates in a snowfield, a glacier's accumulation zone (Figure 17.7a and c). Snowfields typically are at the highest elevation of an ice sheet, ice cap, or head of a valley glacier, usually in a cirque. Avalanches from surrounding mountain slopes can add to the snowfield.

As the snow accumulation deepens in sedimentary-like layers, the increasing thickness results in increased

FIGURE 17.7 **A retreating alpine glacier and mass balance.**
(a) Cross section of a typical retreating alpine glacier. (b) Annual mass balance of a glacial system, showing how the relation between accumulation and ablation controls the location of the equilibrium line. (c) The accumulation zone for a glacier in Antarctica. (d) At least four tributary glaciers flow into a compound valley glacier in Greenland. (e) A terminal moraine marks the farthest advance of this glacier on Nordaustlandet Island, Arctic Ocean. (f) Morainal rock in lateral moraines merges to form a medial moraine, leading to a terminal moraine left by the retreating glacier. These merging glaciers along Beverlysundet, Nordaustlandet Island, haul erratic boulders that have cracked off the cliffs through frost action and fallen onto the glacier surfaces. [Bobbé Christopherson.]

Budget of a Glacier, Mass Balance, Flow of Ice Within a Glacier.

(a)

Neoglacial maximum
(around 1840)

(b)

FIGURE 17.8 Photo comparison of Peyto Glacier.
(a) Peyto Glacier in 1966, at the beginning of the mass balance record. (b) In 2001, dashed line represents the extent
of glacial ice in 1966 and illustrates the quantity of ice that has retreated since the mass balance was recorded.
[(a) Peyto Glacier-One Century of Science, p. x, National Water Research Institute. © 2006 Environment Canada. Photo by
W. E. S. Henoch. Reproduced with the permission of the Minister of Public Works and Government Services Canada, 2012;
(b) Peyto Glacier-One Century of Science, p. x, National Water Research Institute. © 2006 Environment Canada. Photo by
M. N. Demuth. Reproduced with the permission of the Minister of Public Works and Government Services Canada, 2012.]

weight and pressure on underlying ice. Rain and summer snowmelt then contribute water, which stimulates further melting, and that meltwater seeps down into the snowfield and refreezes. Snow surviving the summer and into the following winter begins a slow transformation into glacial ice. Air spaces among ice crystals are pressed as snow packs to a greater density. The ice recrystallizes and consolidates under pressure. In a transition step to glacial ice, snow becomes **firn**, which has a compact, granular texture.

As this process continues, many years pass before dense glacial ice is produced. Formation of **glacial ice** is analogous to metamorphic processes: Sediments (snow and firn) are pressured and recrystallized into a dense metamorphic rock (glacial ice). In Antarctica, glacial ice formation may take 1000 years because of the dryness of the climate (minimal snow input), whereas in wet climates, the time is reduced to just a few years because of rapid, constant snow input to the system.

Glacial Mass Balance

A glacier is an open system, with *inputs* of snow and *outputs* of ice, meltwater, and water vapour. Snowfall and other moisture in the *accumulation zone* feed the glacier's upper reaches (Figure 17.7a). This area ends at the **firn line**, indicating where the winter snow and ice accumulation survived the summer melting season. Toward a glacier's lower end, it is wasted (reduced) through several processes: melting on the surface, internally, and at its

base; ice removal by deflation (wind); the calving of ice blocks; and sublimation (recall from Chapter 7 that this is the direct evaporation of ice). Collectively, these losses are **ablation**.

The zone where accumulation gain balances ablation loss is the *equilibrium line* (Figure 17.7a and b). This area of a glacier generally coincides with the firn line. A glacier achieves *positive net balance* of mass—grows larger—during cold periods with adequate precipitation. In warmer times, the equilibrium line migrates up-glacier, and the glacier margin retreats—grows smaller—because of its *negative net balance*. Internally, gravity continues to move a glacier forward even though its lower terminus might be in retreat owing to ablation.

As part of a global trend, the net mass balance of the Peyto Glacier in Alberta demonstrated significant losses between 1965 and 2009. As a result of this negative mass balance, sometimes the terminus retreated tens of metres in a year. The glacier has retreated nearly every year in the record—only 6 years saw advance. Figure 17.8 is a photo comparison of the Peyto Glacier between 1966 and 2001.

A comparison of the trend of this glacier's mass balance with that of others in the world shows that temperature changes apparently are causing widespread reductions in middle- and lower-elevation glacial ice. The present wastage (ice loss) from alpine glaciers worldwide is thought to contribute to over 25% of the rise in sea level.

 GEO REPORT 17.2 *Alaskan Ice Losses Related to Isostatic Rebound*

Researchers from the Geophysical Institute at the University of Alaska–Fairbanks, using an array of Global Positioning System (GPS) receivers in southeast Alaska, measured isostatic rebound of the crust following modern glacial ice losses. They detected some of the most rapid vertical motion on Earth, averaging about 36 mm per year. Scientists attribute this isostatic rebound to the huge weight reduction caused by the loss of glacial ice in the region, especially from around Yakutat Bay and the St. Elias Mountains in the north, through the Glacier Bay and Juneau areas, and on south through the Inland Passage.

Glacial Movement

We generally think of ice as those small, brittle cubes from the freezer, but glacial ice is quite different. In fact, glacial ice behaves in a plastic (pliable) manner, for it distorts and flows in its lower portions in response to weight and pressure from above and the degree of slope below. In contrast, the glacier's upper portions are quite brittle. Rates of flow range from almost nothing to a kilometre or two per year on a steep slope. The rate of accumulation of snow in the formation area is critical to the speed.

Glaciers are not rigid blocks that only slide downhill. The greatest movement within a valley glacier occurs *internally*, below the rigid surface layer, which fractures as the underlying zone moves forward (Figure 17.9a). At the same time, the base creeps and slides along, varying its speed with temperature and the presence of any lubricating water or saturated sediment beneath the ice. This *basal slip* usually is much slower than the internal plastic flow of the glacier, so the upper portion of the glacier flows ahead of the lower portion.

Unevenness in the landscape beneath the ice may cause the pressure to vary, melting some of the basal ice by compression at one moment, but allowing it to refreeze later. This process is *ice regelation*, meaning to refreeze, or re-gel. Such melting/freezing action incorporates rock debris into the base of the glacier. Consequently, the basal ice layer, which can extend tens of metres above the base of the glacier, has a much greater debris content than the ice above.

A flowing alpine glacier or ice stream in a continental glacier can develop vertical cracks known as **crevasses** (Figure 17.9b and c). Crevasses result from friction with valley walls, or tension from stretching as the glacier passes over convex slopes, or compression as the glacier passes over concave slopes. Traversing a glacier, whether an alpine glacier or an ice sheet, is dangerous because a thin veneer of snow sometimes masks the presence of a crevasse.

Glacier Surges   Although glaciers flow plastically and predictably most of the time, some will lurch forward with little or no warning in a **glacier surge**. A surge is not quite as abrupt as it sounds; in glacial terms, a surge can be tens of metres per day. The Jakobshavn Glacier on the western Greenland coast, for example, is one of the fastest moving at between 7 and 12 km a year.

There was a doubling of ice-mass loss from Greenland between 1996 and 2005 with some glaciers surging forward. In southern Greenland in 2007 outlet glaciers were averaging movement of 22.8 m per year, a significant increase from the 1999 average flow rate of 1.8 m per year. Scientists determined that Greenland experienced more

(a)

(b)

(c)

FIGURE 17.9 Glacial movement.
(a) Cross section of a glacier, showing its forward motion, brittle cracking at the surface, and flow along its basal layer.
(b) Surface crevasses and cracks are evidence of a glacier's forward motion on Elephant Island, Antarctica. (c) Crevasses mark the jumbled surface of this glacier in Spitsbergen; for scale, note the two Zodiac rafts in the water. [Bobbé Christopherson.]

FIGURE 17.10 Glacial sandpapering polishes rock.
Glacial polish and striations are examples of glacial abrasion
and erosion. The polished, marked surface is seen beneath a
glacial erratic—a rock left behind by a retreating glacier. [Bobbé
Christopherson.]

days of melting snow at higher elevations than average in
2006–2007, thereby contributing to faster glacial movement. The meltwater works its way to the basal layer,
lubricating underlying *soft beds* of clay. In addition, the
warmer surface waters draining beneath the glacier deliver
heat that increases basal melt rates.

The exact cause of such a glacier surge is being studied.
Some surge events result from a buildup of water pressure
under the glacier—sometimes enough to actually float the
glacier slightly, detaching it from its bed during the surge.
As a surge begins, ice quakes are detectable and ice faults
are visible. Surges can occur in dry conditions as well, as
the glacier plucks (picks up) rock from its bed and moves
forward. Another cause of glacier surges is the presence of
a water-saturated layer of sediment—a so-called *soft bed*—
beneath the glacier as discussed for Greenland. This is a
deformable layer that cannot resist the tremendous sheer
stress produced by the moving ice of the glacier. Scientists
examining cores taken from several ice streams now accelerating through the West Antarctic Ice Sheet think they
have identified this as a cause of glacial surges—although
water pressure is still important.

Glacial Erosion The way in which a glacier erodes the
land is similar to a large excavation project, with the glacier
hauling debris from one site to another for deposition. The
passing glacier mechanically plucks rock material and carries
it away. Debris is carried on its surface and is also transported
internally, or *englacially*, embedded within the glacier itself.
Evidence indicates that rock pieces actually freeze to the

basal layers of the glacier in a *glacial plucking*, or a picking-up
process, and once embedded, enable the glacier to scour and
sandpaper the landscape as it moves—a process of **abrasion**.
This abrasion and gouging produces a smooth surface on exposed rock, which shines with *glacial polish* when the glacier
retreats. Larger rocks in the glacier act much like chisels,
gouging the underlying surface and producing glacial *striations* parallel to the flow direction (Figure 17.10).

Glacial Landforms

Glacial erosion and deposition produce distinctive landforms that differ greatly from the way the land looked
before the ice came and went. You might expect all glaciers
to create the same landforms, but alpine and continental
glaciers each generate characteristic landscapes. We look
first at erosional landforms created by alpine glaciers,
then at alpine depositional landforms. Finally, we examine
landscapes that result from continental glaciation.

Erosional Landforms Created by Alpine Glaciation

Alpine glaciers create spectacular, dramatic landforms
that bring to mind the Canadian Rockies, the Swiss Alps,
or vaulted Himalayan peaks. Geomorphologist William
Morris Davis depicted the stages of a valley glacier in draw-
ings published in 1906 and redrawn here in Figures 17.11
and 17.12. Study of these figures reveals the handiwork of
ice as sculptor:

- In Figure 17.11a, you see a typical stream-cut valley
  as it existed before glaciation. Note the prominent
  V-shaped valley.
- In 17.11b, you see the same landscape during subsequent glaciation. Glacial erosion and transport
  actively remove much of the regolith (weathered
  bedrock) and the soils that covered the stream-valley
  landscape. As the *cirque* walls erode away, sharp
  ridges form, dividing adjacent cirque basins. These
  arêtes ("knife-edge" in French) become the *sawtooth*,
  serrated ridges in glaciated mountains. Two eroding
  cirques may reduce an arête to a saddlelike depression or pass, called a **col**. A **horn** (pyramidal peak)
  results when several cirque glaciers gouge an individual mountain summit from all sides. Most famous
  is the Matterhorn in the Swiss Alps, but many others
  occur worldwide. A **bergschrund** forms when a
  crevasse or wide crack opens along the headwall of a
  glacier, most visible in summer when covering snow
  is gone.

GEO REPORT 17.3 *Greenland Ice Sheet Losses Increasing*

The Greenland Ice Sheet is experiencing a greater amount of ice loss and a greater area of surface melting than at any time
since systematic satellite monitoring started. Changes in glacial outlet velocity to the ocean are contributing to these losses, with
rates of flow more than double previous estimates. In 1996, Greenland lost an estimated 91 km³ of ice mass, which by 2007
had risen to 251 km³ per year—this is 230 billion metric tonnes of ice per year and rising, compared to the West Antarctic Ice
Sheet losses estimated at 132 billion metric tonnes a year, and also increasing.

FIGURE 17.11 Alpine glaciers occupy valleys.
(a) A preglacial landscape with **V**-shaped stream-cut valley. (b) The same landscape filled with valley glaciers. Note inset photos of a *horn, cirque basin, sawtooth ridge,* and *bergschrund* from Antarctica, Greenland, and Spitsbergen.
[Bobbé Christopherson.]

■ In Figure 17.12, you see the same landscape at a time of warmer climate when the ice has retreated. The glaciated valleys now are **U**-shaped, greatly changed from the previous stream-cut **V** form. You can see the steep sides and the straightened course of the valleys. Physical weathering from the freeze-thaw cycle has loosened rock along the steep cliffs, where it has fallen to form *talus slopes* along the valley sides. Retreating ice leaves behind transported rocks as *erratics*.

Note in Figure 17.12 that in the cirques where the valley glaciers originated, small mountain lakes called **tarns** have formed. One cirque contains small, circular, stair-stepped lakes called **paternoster** ("our father") **lakes** for their resemblance to rosary (religious) beads. Paternoster lakes may have formed from the differing resistance of rock to glacial processes or from damming by glacial deposits.

The valleys carved by tributary glaciers are left stranded high above the valley floor, because the trunk valley glacier eroded the valley floor so deeply. These *hanging valleys* are the sites of spectacular waterfalls. See how many of the erosional forms from Figures 17.11 and 17.12 (arête, col, horn, cirque, cirque glacier, sawtooth ridge, **U**-shaped valley, erratic, tarn, and truncated spur, among others) you can identify in Figure 17.13.

Where a glacial trough intersects the ocean, the glacier can continue to erode the landscape, even below sea level. As the glacier retreats, the trough floods and forms a deep **fjord** in which the sea extends inland, filling the lower reaches of the steep-sided valley (Figure 17.14). The fjord may be flooded further by rising sea level or by changes in the elevation of the coastal region. All along the glaciated coast of Alaska, glaciers now are in retreat, thus opening many new fjords that previously were blocked by ice. Coastlines with notable fjords include those of Norway, Greenland, Chile, the South Island of New Zealand, Alaska, and British Columbia.

▌▌ CRITICAL THINKING 17.1

Looking for Glacial Features on Closer Inspection

The text asks you to look at Figure 17.13 to identify glacial features. Now examine the photos in the chapter opener and Figures 17.1, 17.3, and 17.4, and re-examine Figure 17.13. List all the glacial formations that you can identify in these photos. Are there any erosional landforms that you find on all the photos other than the glaciers themselves?

FIGURE 17.12 **The geomorphic handiwork of alpine glaciers.** As the glaciers retreat, the new landscape is unveiled. Note inset photos of *glacial erratics,* a *hanging valley* and waterfall, a *tarn,* and characteristic **U**-shaped glacial valleys as **U**-shaped troughs in surface and aerial views from Norway. [Bobbé Christopherson; waterfall by Robert Christopherson.]

Glacial erratics

Horn

Arete

Col

Paternoster lakes

Hanging valley

Cirques

U-shaped glacial trough

Hanging waterfall

Postglacial

U-shaped valley

U-shaped valley, aerial

Tarn

Hanging waterfall

Tarn

U-shaped valley

Depositional Landforms Created by Alpine Glaciation

You have just seen how glaciers excavate tremendous amounts of material and create fascinating erosional landforms in the process. Glaciers produce a different set of distinctive landforms when they melt and deposit their debris cargo at the glacier's *terminus*. Figures 17.7a, e, and f show that after the glacier melts, debris accumulates in moraines to mark the former margins of the glacier, both its end and sides.

Glacial Drift The general term for all glacial deposits, both unsorted and sorted, is **glacial drift**. **Till** describes direct ice deposits left as unstratified and unsorted debris. Sediments deposited by glacial meltwater are sorted by size and are **stratified drift**.

As a glacier flows to a lower elevation, a wide assortment of rock fragments becomes *entrained* (carried along) on its surface or embedded within its mass or in its base. As

the glacier melts, this unsorted cargo is deposited on the ground surface. Such till is poorly sorted and the presence of larger stones makes it difficult to cultivate for farming, but the clays and finer particles can provide a basis for soil development.

Retreating glaciers leave behind large rocks (sometimes house-sized), boulders, and cobbles that are "foreign" in composition and origin from the ground on which the rocks were deposited. These *glacial erratics*, lying in strange locations with no obvious means of transport, were an early clue that blankets of ice once had covered the land (pictured in Figure 17.12).

Moraines The deposition of glacial sediments produces a specific landform, a **moraine**. Several types of moraines are associated with alpine glaciations. A **lateral moraine** forms along each side of a glacier (Figure 17.15a). If two glaciers with lateral moraines join, a **medial moraine** may form (see Figures 17.1 and 17.7e and f). Other moraines

FIGURE 17.13 **Erosional features of alpine glaciation.** Many of the erosional glacial features appear in this scene from southern Greenland. How many of the erosional features illustrated in Figures 17.11 and 17.12 can you find in the photo? See Critical Thinking 17.1. [Bobbé Christopherson.]

are associated with both alpine and continental glaciation. Eroded debris that is dropped at the glacier's farthest extent is a **terminal moraine**. *Recessional moraines* may also be present, formed at other points where a glacier paused after reaching a new equilibrium between accumulation and ablation. *End moraines* exist at the end of the ice and represent the active depositional area for material in transit by the glacier. In landscapes of continental glaciation, moraines are much larger in scale. A deposition of till that is generally spread across a surface is a *ground moraine*, or *till plain*, and may cover the former landscape. Such plains

are found in portions of the Canadian Prairies and southern Ontario, as well as the upper U.S. Midwest.

Lakes may form behind terminal and end moraines after a glacier's retreat, with the moraine acting as a dam. The large terminal moraine deposit in Figure 17.15b forms an island, when just 9 years earlier it was a peninsula at the edge of a small ice cap visible in the distance. The ice cap rapidly retreated more than a kilometre in this time frame.

Tributary valley glaciers merge to form a *compound valley glacier*. The flowing movement of a compound

(a)

(b)

FIGURE 17.14 **Norwegian fjords.**
(a) A beautiful fjord where an inlet of the sea fills a **U**-shaped, glacially carved valley. (b) Sediment carried in runoff is visible in this fjord. [Bobbé Christopherson.]

(a)

(b)

FIGURE 17.15 Depositional features of alpine glaciation.
(a) Retreating ice leaves behind a substantial lateral moraine; the retreating Gaffelbreen (Gaffel Glacier) is seen in the background. (b) A terminal moraine forms this island, separated from its ice-cap glacier by more than a kilometre of ocean, at Isispynten Island, Arctic Ocean. [Bobbé Christopherson.]

Erosional and Depositional Features of Continental Glaciation

The extent of the most recent continental glaciation in North America and Europe, which ended about 18 000 years ago, is portrayed several pages ahead in Figure 17.28. Because continental glaciers form under different circumstances—not in mountains, but across broad, open landscapes—the intricately carved alpine features, lateral moraines, and medial moraines all are lacking in continental glaciation.

Figure 17.17 illustrates some of the most common depositional features associated with the retreat of a continental glacier. A **till plain** forms behind an end moraine; it features *unstratified* coarse till, has low and rolling relief, and has a deranged drainage pattern (see Figure 17.17b and Figure 14.9). Beyond the morainal deposits lies the **outwash plain** of *stratified drift* featuring stream channels that are meltwater fed, braided, and overloaded with sorted materials.

A sinuously curving, narrow ridge of coarse sand and gravel is an **esker**. It forms along the channel of a meltwater stream that flows beneath a glacier, in an ice tunnel, or between ice walls. As a glacier retreats, the steep-sided esker is left behind in a pattern roughly parallel to the path of the glacier. The ridge may not be continuous and in places may even appear to be branched, following

valley glacier is different from that of a river with tributaries. Tributary glaciers flow into a compound glacier and merge alongside one another by extending and thinning rather than by blending, as do rivers. Each tributary maintains its own patterns of transported debris (dark streaks, visible in the photo in Figure 17.7d, e, and f).

All of these till types are poorly sorted and unstratified. In contrast, streams of glacial meltwater can carry and deposit sorted and stratified glacial drift beyond a terminal moraine. Meltwater-deposited material down-valley from a glacier is a *valley train deposit*. Peyto Glacier in Alberta, Canada, produces such a valley train that continues into Peyto Lake (Figure 17.16). Distributary stream channels appear braided across its surface. The picture also shows the milky meltwater associated with glaciers, laden with finely ground "rock flour." Meltwater comes from glaciers at all times, not just during phases of retreat.

FIGURE 17.16 A valley train deposit.
Peyto Glacier in Alberta, Canada, is in extensive retreat. Note the valley train, braided stream, and milky-colored glacial meltwater. [Robert Christopherson.]

FIGURE 17.17 Continental glacier depositional features.
(a) Common depositional landforms produced by glaciers; note the esker, drumlin field, recessional moraine, kames, kettle lake, till, and outwash plain of stratified drift. (b) Deranged drainage tells us continental glaciers advanced and retreated across the prairies of central Saskatchewan, Canada. [Bobbé Christopherson.]

the path set by the subglacial watercourse. Commercially valuable deposits of sand and gravel are quarried from some eskers.

Sometimes an isolated block of ice, perhaps more than a kilometre across, remains buried in a ground moraine, an outwash plain, or valley floor after a glacier has retreated. As much as 20 to 30 years is required for it to melt. In the interim, material continues to accumulate around the melting ice block. When the block finally melts, it leaves behind a steep-sided hole. Such a feature then frequently fills with water. This feature is a **kettle**. Thoreau's famous Walden Pond in Massachusetts is such a glacial kettle.

Another feature of outwash plains is a **kame**, a small hill, knob, or mound of poorly sorted sand and gravel that is deposited directly by water, by ice in crevasses, or in ice-caused indentations in the surface. Kames also can be found in deltaic forms and in terraces along valley walls.

Glacial action also forms two types of streamlined hills. One is erosional, called a *roche moutonnée*, and the other is depositional, called a *drumlin*. A **roche moutonnée** ("sheep rock" in French) is an asymmetrical hill of exposed bedrock. Its gently sloping upstream side (stoss side) has been polished smooth by glacial action, whereas its downstream side (lee side) is abrupt and steep where the glacier plucked rock pieces (Figure 17.18).

(a)

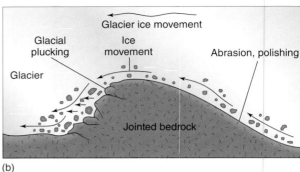

(b)

FIGURE 17.18 Glacially eroded streamlined rock.
Roche moutonnée, as exemplified by (a) this formation on
the Melville Peninsula, Nunavut, and (c) Lembert Dome in the
Tuolumne Meadows area of Yosemite National Park, California.
[(a) Courtesy of the Geological Survey of Canada. Photo 2002-499 by
Lynda Dredge. Reproduced with the permission of Natural Resources
Canada. © 2012; (b) With glacial ice movement right to left, the
landform develops; (c) Robert W. Christopherson.]

(c)

A **drumlin** is deposited till that has been streamlined
in the direction of continental ice movement, blunt end
upstream and tapered end downstream. Drumlins occur
in fields across the landscape in all parts of Canada, with
particularly good examples in Nova Scotia and Ontario.
Sometimes the shape is that of an elongated teaspoon bowl,
lying face down. Drumlins attain lengths of 100–5000 m
and heights up to 200 m. Figure 17.19a shows an area
near Peterborough, Ontario, that experienced continental glaciation during the Wisconsinan glacial (discussed
shortly). The remotely sensed image in Figure 17.19b
allows you to see the drumlins on the surface. From the
orientation of the drumlins on the map and in the photo,
can you determine the direction of continental ice movement? (Look for gentle, tapered slopes in the downstream
direction of each drumlin.)

Periglacial Landscapes

In 1909, Polish geologist W. Lozinski coined the term
periglacial to describe frost weathering and freeze-
thaw rock shattering in the Carpathian Mountains.
These periglacial regions occupy over 20% of Earth's
land surface (Figure 17.20). Periglacial landscapes are
found in cold regions that are seasonally snow free.

Under these conditions, a unique set of periglacial processes operates.

Climatologically, these regions are in *subarctic* and
polar climates, especially *tundra* climate. Such climates occur
either at high latitude (tundra and boreal forest environments) or at high elevation in lower-latitude mountains
(alpine environments). Processes that are related to physical weathering, mass movement (Chapter 13), climate
(Chapter 10), and soil (Chapter 18) dominate periglacial
regions.

Geography of Permafrost

When soil or rock temperatures remain below 0°C for
at least two consecutive years, **permafrost** ("permanent
frost") develops. An area of permafrost that is not covered
by glaciers is considered periglacial. Note that this criterion is based solely on *temperature* and has nothing to do
with how much or how little frozen water is present. Two
other factors also contribute to permafrost: the presence of
fossil permafrost from previous ice-age conditions and the
insulating effect of snow cover or vegetation that inhibits
heat loss. As much as 50% of Canada and 80% of Alaska
have permafrost conditions. In central Eurasia, the effects
of continentality and elevation produce discontinuous permafrost that extends equatorward to the 50th parallel.

(a)

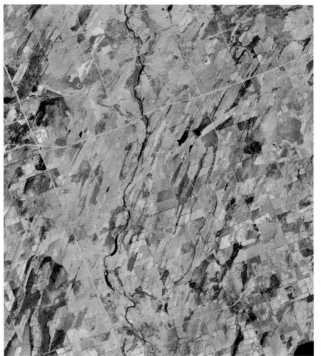

FIGURE 17.19 Glacially deposited streamlined features.
(a) Topographic map of Peterborough, Ontario, featuring
numerous drumlins indicated by the elongated oval patterns of
brown contour lines. (b) Aerial photo of Peterborough Drumlin
Field. [From Ontario Ortho Photos, Natural Resources Canada. Used
by permission of the Minister of Public Works and Government
Services.]

(b)

Continuous and Discontinuous Zones Permafrost
regions are divided into two general categories: continuous and discontinuous, which merge along a general
transition zone. *Continuous permafrost* is the region of
severest cold and is perennial, roughly poleward of the
–7°C mean annual temperature isotherm (purple area in
Figure 17.20). Continuous permafrost affects all surfaces
except those beneath deep lakes or rivers. The depth of
continuous permafrost may exceed 1000 m, averaging approximately 400 m.

Unconnected patches of *discontinuous permafrost*
gradually coalesce poleward toward the continuous zone.
Equatorward permafrost becomes scattered or sporadic
until it gradually disappears, bounded by the –1°C mean
annual temperature isotherm (dark blue area on map).
In the discontinuous zone, permafrost is absent on sun-
exposed south-facing slopes, areas of warm soil, or areas
insulated by snow. In the Southern Hemisphere, north-
facing slopes experience increased warmth.

These discontinuous zones are most susceptible to thawing with climate change. Affected peat-rich soils (Gelisols,
Organic, Cryosols—Chapter 18), contain twice the amount
of carbon in the atmosphere, making a powerful positive
feedback as soils thaw and oxidation releases more carbon
dioxide to the atmosphere. Additionally, the losses of carbon
in thawing exceed any increases in carbon uptake that the
warmer conditions and higher carbon dioxide levels create,
making permafrost thaw an important source of greenhouse
gases—a real-time positive feedback mechanism.

In the Mackenzie Mountains (62–65° N), continuous
permafrost exists in areas as low as 1200 m in elevation, and
discontinuous permafrost occurs throughout the range. The
Colorado Rockies (38–40° N) experience continuous permafrost above 3400 m and discontinuous permafrost above
1700 m.

Behavior of Permafrost We looked at the spatial distribution of permafrost; now let us examine how

FIGURE 17.20 **Permafrost distribution.**
Distribution of permafrost in the Northern Hemisphere. Alpine permafrost is noted except for small occurrences in Hawai'i, Mexico, Europe, and Japan. Subsea permafrost occurs in the seabed beneath the Arctic Ocean along the margins of the continents, as shown. Note the towns of Resolute and Coppermine (Kugluktuk) in Nunavut (formerly part of NWT) and Hotchkiss in Alberta. A cross section of the permafrost beneath these towns is shown in Figure 17.21. [Adapted from T. L. Péwé, "Alpine permafrost in the contiguous United States: A review," *Arctic and Alpine Research* 15, no. 2 (May 1983): 146. © University of Colorado. Used by permission.]

permafrost behaves. Figure 17.21 is a stylized cross section from approximately 75° N to 55° N, using the three sites located on the map in Figure 17.20. The **active layer** is the zone of seasonally frozen ground that exists between the subsurface permafrost layer and the ground surface.

The active layer is subjected to consistent daily and seasonal freeze-thaw cycles. This cyclic melting of the active layer extends to as little as 10 cm depth in the north (Ellesmere Island, 78° N), up to 2 m in the southern margins (55° N) of the periglacial region, and 15 m in the alpine permafrost of the Colorado Rockies (40° N).

Higher temperatures degrade (reduce) permafrost and increase the thickness of the active layer; lower temperatures gradually aggrade (increase) permafrost depth and reduce active-layer thickness. Although somewhat sluggish in response, the active layer is a dynamic open system driven by energy gains and losses in the subsurface

environment. As you might expect, most permafrost exists in disequilibrium with environmental conditions and therefore actively adjusts to inconstant climatic conditions.

With the significantly warmer temperatures recorded in the Canadian and Siberian Arctic since 1990, more disruption of surfaces is occurring—leading to highway, railway, and building damage. In Siberia, many lakes have disappeared in the discontinuous permafrost region as subsurface drainage opens; yet new lakes have formed in the continuous region as thawed soils become waterlogged. In Canada, hundreds of lakes have disappeared simply from excessive evaporation into the warming air. These trends are measurable from satellite imagery.

A *talik* is unfrozen ground that may occur above, below, or within a body of discontinuous permafrost or beneath a water body in the continuous region. Taliks occur beneath deep lakes and may extend to bedrock and noncryotic soil

GEO REPORT 17.4 *Feedback Loops from Fossil-fuel Exploration to Permafrost Thawing*

The thaw in the active layer in the Alaskan tundra has shortened the number of days that oil exploration equipment can operate. Previously, the frozen ground lasted more than 200 days, permitting the heavy rigs and trucks to operate on the solid surface. With the thawing and unstable soft surfaces, exploration is now restricted to only 100 days a year. Think in a systems view: The exploration is for fossil fuels, which, when burned, increase the carbon dioxide levels in the atmosphere, which enhances greenhouse warming, which increases temperatures and permafrost thawing, which decreases the number of days to explore for fossil fuels—a negative feedback into the system.

Closed talik (under
pressure from aggraded
permafrost)

Thinner active
layer (<0.5 m)

Small deep
lake

Large deep
lake

Former lake
basin (bog)

Thicker active
layer (>3.0 m)

**Continuous
permafrost**

Open talik

Through
talik

45 m

Permafrost

10 m

**Discontinuous
permafrost**

400 m

North

Unfrozen
(noncryotic) soil
and rock

Resolute, Nunavut
(74° N)

Coppermine, (Kugluktuk), Nunavut
(68° N)

South

Hotchkiss, Alberta
(57° N)

(a)

FIGURE 17.21 **Periglacial environments.**
(a) Cross section of a periglacial region in northern Canada, showing typical forms of permafrost, the active
layer, talik, and ground ice. The three sites noted are shown on the map in Figure 17.19. (b) Poor drainage,
with some standing water and hummocks, and (c) irregular ice-forced bumps of tundra turf indicate permafrost.
[Bobbé Christopherson.]

beneath large, deep lakes (see Figure 17.21). Taliks form connections between the active layer and groundwater, whereas in continuous permafrost groundwater is essentially cut off from surface water. In this way, permafrost disrupts aquifers and taliks, leading to water-supply problems.

Ground-Ice and Frozen-Ground Phenomena

In regions of permafrost, frozen subsurface water is termed *ground ice*. The moisture content of areas with ground ice varies from nearly none in drier regions to almost 100% in saturated soils. From the area of maximum energy loss, freezing progresses through the ground along a *freezing front*, or boundary between frozen and unfrozen soil. The presence of frozen water in the soil initiates geomorphic processes associated with *frost action* and the expansion of water as it freezes.

The 9% expansion of water as it freezes produces strong mechanical forces. Such frost action shatters rock, producing angular pieces that form a *block field*, or *felsenmeer*.

The felsenmeer accumulates as part of the arctic and alpine periglacial landscape, particularly on mountain summits and slopes.

If sufficient water freezes, the saturated soil and rocks are subjected to *frost-heaving* (vertical movement) and *frost-thrusting* (horizontal movement). Boulders and rock slabs may be thrust to the surface. Soil horizons (layers) may be disrupted by frost action and appear to be stirred or churned, a process termed *cryoturbation*. Frost action also can produce contractions in soil and rock, opening up cracks for ice wedges to form. Also, there is a tremendous increase in pressure in the soil as ice expands, particularly if there are multiple freezing fronts trapping unfrozen soil and water between them.

An *ice wedge* develops when water enters a crack in the permafrost and freezes (Figure 17.22). Thermal contraction in ice-rich soil forms a tapered crack—wider at the top, narrowing toward the bottom. Repeated seasonal freezing and melting progressively enlarge the wedge, which may widen from a few millimetres to 5–6 m and up to 30 m in

(a)

(c)

(b)

Frozen active layer

Thawed active layer

Open crack (thermal contraction)

Ice

Permafrost

Permafrost

Winter

Fall

Mounded sediments in response to subsurface volume of ice

Frozen active layer

Thawed active layer

Open crack

Developed ice wedge

Permafrost

Permafrost

500th Winter

500th Fall

FIGURE 17.22 **Evolution of an ice wedge.**
Sequential illustration of ice-wedge formation: (a) A crack forms in the tundra. (b) The crack evolves into an ice wedge over a time span of hundreds of years. (c) An example of an ice wedge and ground ice in northern Canada with a person for scale. [(a) Bobbé Christopherson; (b) Illustration adapted from A. H. Lachenbruch, "Mechanics of thermal contraction and ice-wedge polygons in permafrost," *Geological Society of America Bulletin Special Paper 70* (1962); (c) H. M. French.]

depth. Widening may be small each year, but after many years the wedge can become significant, like the sample shown in Figure 17.22b. In summer, when the active layer thaws, the wedge itself may not be visible. However, the presence of a wedge beneath the surface is noticeable where the ice-expanded sediments form raised, upturned ridges.

Frost-Action Landforms Large areas of frozen ground (soil-covered ice) can develop a heaved-up, circular, ice-cored mound called a *pingo*. It rises above the flat landscape, occasionally exceeding 60 m in height. Pingos rise when freezing water expands, sometimes as a result of pressure developed by artesian water injected into permafrost (Figure 17.23).

A *palsa* (from the Swedish word for "elliptical") is a rounded or elliptical mound of peat that contains thin perennial ice lenses rather than an ice core, as in a pingo. Palsas can be 2–30 m wide by 1–10 m high and usually are covered by soil or vegetation over a cracked surface.

Fascinating research identified unique synergies at work to form **patterned ground**. The expansion and contraction of frost action result in the movement of soil particles, stones, and small boulders. Self organization begins during this freeze–thaw process. Imagine a process where stones move toward stone domains (stone-rich areas) and soil particles move toward soil domains (soil-rich areas). What emerges is patterned ground that may take centuries to form. Added to this is the role of slope angle—greater slopes produce striped patterns (Figure 17.24e), whereas lesser slopes result in sorted polygons (Figure 17.24a, b, and c).

The stone-centred polygons in Figure 17.24b indicate higher stone concentrations, and the soil-centred polygons in Figure 17.24c indicate higher soil particle concentrations with lesser availability of stones. The amount of stone confinement by frozen soil domains helps determine the form: More circular forms occur when sorting is dominant; more polygons occur when confinement of stone domains is dominant. This means that such landscapes are self-making, self-maintaining, and self-organizing—all traits of living systems, making this an interesting path for future research in Earth systems. (See M. A. Kessler and B. T. Warner, "Self-organization of patterned ground," *Science* 299, 5606 [Jan. 17, 2003]: 380–383.)

Such polygon nets in patterned ground provide vivid evidence of frozen subsurface water on Mars (Figure 17.24f).

FIGURE 17.23 **A pingo.**
An ice-cored pingo resulting from hydraulic pressures that pushed the mound upward above the landscape. Coastal erosion exposed the ice core. This pingo is near Tuktoyaktuk, Mackenzie Delta, NWT, Canada. [H. M. French.]

FIGURE 17.24 Patterned-ground phenomena.
(a) Patterned ground in Beacon Valley of the McMurdo Dry Valleys of East Antarctica.
(b) Polygons and circles (about a metre across) in a stone-dominant area near Duvefjord, Nordaustlandet Island, Arctic Ocean. (c) Polygons and circles in a soil-dominant area, Spitsbergen Island. (d) Intermediate organization in progress on Bear Island (74° 30′ N).
(e) Patterned ground in stripes near Sundbukta, Barents Island. (f) Polygons in the Martian northern plains; each cell averages a little more than 100 m across. [(a) © Joan Myers; (b), (c), (d), and (e) Bobbé Christopherson; (f) *Mars Global Surveyor*, NASA/JPL/Malin Space Science Systems.]

(a) (b) (c) (d) (e) (f)

In this 1999 image, the *Mars Global Surveyor* captured a region of these features on the Martian northern plains. To date, some 600 different sites on Mars demonstrate such patterned ground, and in 2008, the *Phoenix* lander set down in the middle of a Martian arctic plain covered with polygonal forms. The craft dug into the Martian surface and verified the presence of ground (water) ice.

Hillslope Processes: Gelifluction and Solifluction
Soil drainage is poor in areas of permafrost and ground ice. The active layer of soil and regolith is saturated with soil moisture during the thaw cycle (summer), and the whole layer commences to flow from higher to lower elevation if the landscape is even slightly inclined. This flow of soil is generally called *solifluction* and may occur in all climate conditions. In the presence of ground ice or permafrost, the more specific term *gelifluction* is applied. In this ice-bound type of soil flow, movement up to 5 cm per year can occur on slopes as gentle as a degree or two.

The cumulative effect of this landflow can be an overall flattening of a rolling landscape, with identifiable

sagging surfaces and scalloped and lobed patterns in the downslope soil movements. Other types of periglacial mass movement include failure in the active layer, producing translational and rotational slides and rapid flows associated with melting ground ice. Periglacial mass movement processes are related to slope dynamics and processes discussed in Chapter 13.

Thermokarst Landscapes As ground ice melts, irregular features develop across the landscape, creating *thermokarst* topography. These forms result from thermal subsidence and erosion caused by ice-wedge melting and poor drainage. (Note that thermokarst refers only to the topographic style and has nothing to do with the solution processes and chemical weathering that cause limestone karst.)

Thermokarst topography is hummocky, marked by cave-ins, bogs, small depressions, pits, standing water, and small lakes. More thermokarst landforms are found in Siberia and Scandinavia than in North America. In Canada and Alaska, rounded thaw lakes, or cave-in lakes, are thermokarst features.

FIGURE 17.25 Permafrost melting and structure collapse.
Building failure due to improper construction and the melting of permafrost, south of Fairbanks, Alaska. [Steve McCutcheon, McCutcheon Collection; Anchorage Museum, B1990.14.4.permafrost.11570.]

Humans and Periglacial Landscapes

In areas of permafrost and frozen-ground phenomena, people face several related problems. Because thawed ground above the permafrost zone frequently shifts, highways and rail lines become warped, twisted, and fail and utility lines are disrupted. In addition, any building placed directly on frozen ground will settle into the defrosting soil, creating subsidence in structures (Figure 17.25).

In periglacial regions, structures are often constructed above the ground to allow air circulation beneath. This airflow allows the ground to cycle through its normal annual temperature pattern. Utilities such as water and sewer lines must be built above ground in "utilidors" (utility corridors) to protect them from freezing and thawing ground (Figure 17.26). Likewise, the trans-Alaska oil pipeline was constructed aboveground on racks for 675 of its 1285-km length to avoid melting the frozen ground, causing shifting that could rupture the line. The pipeline that is underground uses a cooling system to keep the permafrost around the pipeline stable.

The Pleistocene Ice-Age Epoch

Imagine almost a third of Earth's land surface buried beneath ice sheets and glaciers—most of Canada, the northern U.S. Midwest, the British Isles, and northern Europe, and many mountain ranges in other regions, beneath thousands of metres of ice. This occurred at the height of the Pleistocene Epoch of the late Cenozoic Era.

In addition, periglacial regions along the margins of the ice during the last ice age covered about twice the present areal extent.

The Pleistocene is thought to have begun about 1.65 million years ago and is one of the more prolonged cold periods in Earth's history. It featured not just one glacial advance and retreat, but at least 18 expansions of ice over Europe and North America, each obscuring and confusing the evidence from the one before. Apparently, ice-age scale glaciation can last about 100 000 years, whereas deglaciation is rapid, requiring less than about 10 000 years to melt away the accumulation.

The term **ice age**, or *glacial age*, is applied to any extended period of cold (not a single brief cold spell), which may last several million years. An ice age is a time of generally cold climate that includes one or more *glacials*, interrupted by brief warm spells known as *interglacials*. Each glacial and interglacial is given a name that is usually based on the location where evidence of the episode is prominent—for example, "Wisconsinan glacial."

One method for determining Pleistocene temperatures is by evidence from deep-sea cores—specifically, from the oxygen isotope fluctuations in fossil plankton, which are tiny marine organisms with a calcareous shell. Glaciologists currently recognize the Illinoian glacial and Wisconsinan glacial intervals, with the Sangamon interglacial between the two. These events span the 300 000-year interval prior to our present Holocene Epoch. The chart in Figure 17.27 shows that the Illinoian glacial actually consisted of two glacials occurring during marine (oxygen) isotope stages (MISs) 6 and 8, as did the

Average height 1.5 to 3.0 m

Pipeline 1.2 m diameter

(b)

(a)

FIGURE 17.26 Special structures for permafrost.
(a) Proper construction in periglacial environments requires the raising of buildings above ground and the running of water and sewage lines in elevated "utilidors," here in Barentsburg, a Russian settlement on Spitsbergen Island. (b) Supporting the trans-Alaska oil pipeline on racks protects the permafrost from additional heat. [(a) Bobbé Christopherson; (b) ZUMA Press/Newscom.]

Wisconsinan (MISs 2 and 4), which are dated at 10 000 to 35 000 years ago. To overcome local bias in deep-sea-core records, investigators correlate oxygen isotope data with other global climate indicators, such as ice cores. Note the label on the chart in Figure 17.27 at MIS 20.2 for the Dome-C ice-core extent of 800 000 years; an ice core extracted from the East Antarctic Plateau. For web links on the Pleistocene Epoch and glaciers generally, see http://userpages.umbc.edu/~miller/geog111/glacierlinks.htm.

Sea-surface temperatures 18 000 years ago averaged between 1.4°C and 1.7°C lower than today. During the coldest portion of the Pleistocene ice age, air temperatures were as much as 12°C colder than today's average, although milder periods ranged to within 5°C of present air temperatures.

Changes in the Landscape

The continental ice sheets covered portions of Canada, the United States, Europe, and Asia about 18 000 years ago, as illustrated on the polar map projection in Figure 17.28. Ice sheets ranged in thickness to more than 2 km. In North America, the Ohio and Missouri river systems mark the southern terminus of continuous ice at its greatest extent during the Pleistocene. The ice sheet had disappeared by 7000 years ago.

Retreating alpine and continental glaciers exposed a drastically altered landscape: the rocky soils of New England, the polished and scarred surfaces of Canada's Atlantic Provinces, the sharp crests of the Sawtooth Range and Tetons of Idaho and Wyoming, the scenery of the Canadian Rockies and the Sierra Nevada, the Great Lakes of Canada and the United States, the Matterhorn of Switzerland, and much more. In the Southern Hemisphere, there is evidence of this ice age in the form of fjords and sculpted mountains in New Zealand and Chile.

The continental glaciers advanced and retreated several times over the region we know as the Great Lakes (Figure 17.29). The ice enlarged and deepened stream valleys to form the basins of the future lakes. This complex history produced five lakes that today cover 244 000 km² and hold some 18% of all the lake water on Earth. Figure 17.29 shows the final formation of the Great Lakes, which involved two advancing and two retreating stages—between 13 200 and 10 000 years before the present. During the final retreat, tremendous quantities of glacial meltwater flowed into the isostatically depressed basins—that is, basins that are lowered by the weight of the ice. Drainage at first was to the Mississippi River via the Illinois River, to the St. Lawrence River via the Ottawa River, and to the Hudson River in the east. In recent times, drainage has shifted through the present St. Lawrence system.

 GEO REPORT 17.5 *Glacial Ice Might Protect Underlying Mountains*

Researchers are studying the effect of glacial ice on the underlying topography during the last glacial maximum. The temperature at the base of the ice is important. In the southernmost Patagonian Andes, conditions were so cold that the glacial ice froze to the bedrock. It appears that this protected the bedrock from erosion and typical glacial excavation, resulting in higher mountain peaks and a wider mountain belt in the southern Andes than in the northern part of the range, where mountain surfaces were ground down and narrowed by glacial action.

scientists have mapped outlets to the south, east, north, and northwest. About 11 000 years ago, an outlet opened into the basin of present-day Lake Superior and the level of Lake Agassiz fell. As the lake level fell, the rivers that flowed into the lake—the Assiniboine and Saskatchewan rivers—cut downward into their delta sediments. By 7800 years ago, Lake Agassiz, this largest of all North American glacial lakes, disappeared as the ice sheet disintegrated and water drained into Hudson Bay. All that remains of the former greatest lake are lakes Manitoba, Winnipeg, Dauphin, and Winnipegosis and Lake of the Woods.

Sea levels 18 000 years ago were approximately 100 m lower than today because so much of Earth's water was frozen and tied up in the glaciers instead of being in the ocean. Imagine the coastline of Nova Scotia being 100 km farther east, Alaska and Russia connected by land across the Bering Strait, and England and France joined by a land bridge. Sea ice extended southward into the North Atlantic and Pacific and northward from Antarctica about 50% farther than it does today.

Paleolakes

The American West was dotted with large lakes 12 000–30 000 years ago. Except for the Great Salt Lake in Utah (remnants of ancient Lake Bonneville) and a few smaller lakes, only dry basins, ancient shorelines, and lake sediments remain today. These ancient lakes are called **paleolakes**.

The term *pluvial* (Latin: "rain") describes any period of wet conditions, such as occurred during the Pleistocene Epoch. During pluvial periods, lake levels increased in arid regions. The drier periods between pluvial, called *interpluvials*, are marked with *lacustrine deposits*, the name for lake sediments that form terraces along former shorelines.

Are paleolakes of glacial origin like the Great Lakes? Earlier researchers attempted to correlate pluvial and glacial ages, given their coincidence during the Pleistocene. However, few sites actually demonstrate such a simple correlation. For example, in the western United States, the estimated volume of melted ice from glaciers is only a small portion of the actual water volume that was in the paleolakes. Also, these lakes tend to predate glacial times and are correlated instead with periods of wetter climate, or periods thought to have had lower evaporation rates. The term *paleolake* is used in the scientific literature to describe these lakes and to separate such occurrences from specific glacial stages.

Paleolakes existed in North and South America, Africa, Asia, and Australia. Today, the Caspian Sea in Kazakhstan and southern Russia has a level of 30 m below mean world sea level, but ancient shorelines are visible about 80 m above the present lake level. In North America, the two largest late Pleistocene paleolakes were in the Basin and Range Province of the West—Lake Bonneville and Lake Lahontan.

New evidence reveals that the occurrence of these lakes in North America was related to specific changes in the polar jet stream that steered storm tracks across the region,

FIGURE 17.27 Temperature record of the past two million years.
Twenty-three MISs cover 900 000 years, with names assigned for the past 300 000 years. [After N. J. Shackelton and N. D. Opdyke, *Oxygen-Isotope and Paleomagnetic Stratigraphy of Pacific Core V28-239, Late Pliocene to Latest Pleistocene*, Geological Society of America Memoir 145. ©1976 by the GSA. Adapted by permission.]

Glacial Lake Agassiz began to form about 11 700 years ago when water was trapped between the Manitoba Escarpment and the retreating Laurentide ice sheet (Figure 17.29b, c, d, and detailed in e). The ice margin determined the locations of outlet channels. Earth

18 000 years ago

FIGURE 17.28 **Extent of Pleistocene glaciation.**

Earlier episodes produced continental glaciation of slightly greater extent. Note the depth of the continental ice sheets in North America (in metres). [From A. McIntyre, *CLIMAP* (Climate: Long-Range Investigation, Mapping, and Prediction) Project, Lamont-Doherty Earth Observatory. © 1981 by the GSA. Adapted by permission.]

9500 years ago

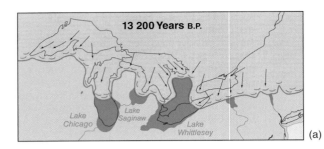

13 200 Years B.P.

(a)

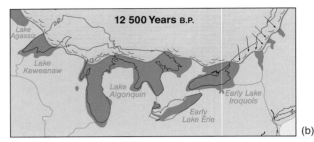

12 500 Years B.P.

(b)

11 800 Years B.P.

(c)

10 000 Years B.P.

(d)

11 000 Years B.P.

0 125 250 KILOMETRES

- - - - Extent of Glacial
Lake Agassiz

(e)

FIGURE 17.29 Late stages of Great Lakes formation and glacial Lake Agassiz.
(a)–(d) Four "snapshots" of the Great Lakes' evolving development during the waning of the Wisconsinan glaciation. Note the change in stream drainage between (b) and (d). (e) Note the massive Lake Agassiz at approximately 11 000 B.P. (before the present), when an outlet opened into the Lake Superior basin. The largest of the glacial Great Lakes was trapped between higher ground to the south and the retreating ice sheet. The dashed line delineates the maximum extent of the ancient lake. The lake was never fully this size; it represents the total area that the lake covered throughout its history, some 4000 years. All that remains of the former greatest lake are lakes Manitoba, Winnipeg, Dauphin, and Winnipegosis in Manitoba and Lake of the Woods in Ontario. [(a) through (d) After *The Great Lakes—An Environmental Atlas and Resource Book*, Environment Canada, U.S. EPA, Brock University, and Northwestern University (Toronto: Environment Canada, 1987), p. 7; (e) adapted from A. S. Trenhaile, *Geomorphology: A Canadian Perspective,* from Teller, in Karrow and Calkin, 1985.]

creating pluvial conditions. The continental ice sheet evidently influenced changes in average jet-stream position.

Deciphering Past Climates: Paleoclimatology

Glacials and interglacials occur because Earth's climate has fluctuated in and out of warm and cold ages. Evidence for this fluctuation now is traced in ice cores from Greenland and Antarctica, in layered ocean deposits of silts and clays, in the extensive pollen record from ancient plants, and in the relation of past coral productivity to sea level. This evidence is analyzed with radioactive dating methods and other techniques. One especially interesting fact is emerging from these studies: We humans (*Homo erectus* and *H. sapiens* of the last 1.9 million years) have never experienced Earth's normal (more moderate, less extreme) climate, most characteristic of our planet's entire 4.6 billion-year span.

Apparently, Earth's climates fluctuated slowly until the past 1.2 billion years, when temperature patterns with cycles of 200–300 million years became more pronounced. The Pleistocene Epoch began in earnest 1.65 million years ago and it may still be in progress. The Holocene Epoch began approximately 10 000 years ago, when average temperatures abruptly increased 6 C°. The period we live in may represent an end to the Pleistocene, or it may be merely a mild interglacial time. Figure 17.30 details the climatic record of the past 160 000 years.

Medieval Warm Period and Little Ice Age

In A.D. 1001, Leif Eriksson inadvertently ventured to the North American continent, perhaps the first European to do so. He and his fellow Vikings were favoured by a medieval warming episode as they sailed the less-frozen North Atlantic to settle Iceland and Greenland.

The mild climatic episode that lasted from about A.D. 800 to 1200 is known as the *Medieval Warm Period*.

FIGURE 17.30 **Recent climates determined from an ice core.**
Temperature and snow accumulation patterns for the last 20 000 years, based on data from the GISP-2 ice core, Greenland. An abrupt temperature increase began about 12 000 years ago, at the end of the Younger Dryas cold period of the Pleistocene. Note the Medieval Warm Period and Little Ice Age during the Holocene. [From R. B. Alley, "The Younger Dryas cold interval as viewed from central Greenland," *Quaternary Science Reviews* 19 (January 2000): 213–226; NCDC/NOAA.]

During the warmth, grape vineyards were planted far into England some 500 km north of present-day commercial plantings. Oats and barley were planted in Iceland, and wheat was planted as far north as Trondheim, Norway. The shift to warmer, wetter weather influenced migration patterns and settlement pushed northward in North America, Europe, and Asia.

However, from approximately 1400–1900, a *Little Ice Age* took place. Parts of the North Atlantic froze, and expanding glaciers blocked many key mountain passes in Europe. Snowlines in Europe lowered about 200 m in the coldest years. The Greenland colonies were deserted. Cropping patterns changed, and northern forests declined, along with human population in those regions. In the winter of 1779–1780, New York's Hudson and East rivers and the entire Upper Bay froze over. People walked and hauled heavy loads across the ice between Staten and Manhattan Islands!

But the Little Ice Age was not consistently cold throughout its 500-year reign. Reading the record of the Greenland ice cores, scientists have found many mild years among the harsh. More accurately, this was a time of rapid, short-term climate fluctuations that lasted only decades.

Ice cores drilled in Greenland have revealed a record of annual snow and ice accumulation that, when correlated with other aspects of the core sample, is indicative of air temperature. Figure 17.30c presents this record since A.D. 500. The warmth of the Medieval Warm Period is evident, whereas the Little Ice Age appears mixed with warmer conditions around 1400 and 1700.

Mechanisms of Climate Fluctuation

What mechanisms cause short-term fluctuations? And why is Earth pulsing through long-term climatic changes that span several hundred million years? The ice-age concept is being researched and debated with an unprecedented intensity for three principal reasons: (1) Continuous ice cores from Greenland and Antarctica are providing a new, detailed record of weather and climate patterns, volcanic eruptions, and trends in the biosphere (discussed in Focus Study 17.1); (2) to understand present and future climate change and to refine general circulation models, we must understand the natural variability of the atmosphere and climate; (3) anthropogenic global warming, and its relation to ice ages, is a major concern.

Because past occurrences of low temperature appear to have followed a pattern, researchers have looked for causes that also are cyclic in nature. They have identified a complicated mix of interacting variables that appear to influence long-term climatic trends. Let us take a look at several of them.

Climate and Celestial Relations As our Solar System revolves around the distant centre of the Milky Way, it crosses the plane of the galaxy approximately every 32 million years. At that time, Earth's plane of the ecliptic aligns parallel to the galaxy's plane, and we pass through regions in space of increased interstellar dust and gas, which may have some climatic effect.

Milutin Milankovitch (1879–1954), a Yugoslavian astronomer who studied Earth–Sun orbital relations,

FOCUS STUDY 17.1

Ice Cores Reveal Earth's Climate History

The Greenland Ice Core Project (GRIP) was launched in 1989. A site was selected near the summit of the Greenland Ice Sheet at 3200 m so that the maximum thickness of ice history would be accessed (Figure 17.1.1). After 3 years, the drills hit bedrock 3030 m below the site—or, in terms of time, 250 000 years into the past. The core is 10 cm in diameter.

A year later, about 32 km west of the summit, the Greenland Ice Sheet Project (GISP-2) produced a core slightly larger in diameter, at 13.2 cm, which collects about twice the data. The existence of a second core helped scientists compensate for some folds or disturbed sections they

encountered below 2700 m, or about 115 000 years in the past, in the first core.

What was discovered from these ice cores? Locked into the cores is a record of past precipitation and air bubbles of past atmospheres, which indicate ancient gas concentrations. Of special interest are the greenhouse gases, carbon dioxide and methane. Chemical and physical properties of the atmosphere and the snow that accumulated each year are frozen in place.

Pollutants are locked into the ice-core record. For example, during cold periods, high concentrations of dust were present, brought by winds from distant dry lands. An invaluable record of past volcanic eruptions is included in the layers, as if on a calendar. Even the beginning of the Bronze Age—about 3000 B.C.—is recorded in the ice core. When the Greeks and later the Romans began smelting copper, they produced ash and smoke that the winds carried to this distant place. The presence of ammonia indicates ancient forest fires at lower latitudes. And, as an important analog of past temperatures on the ice-sheet surface when each snowfall occurred, the ratio between stable forms of oxygen is measured.

Dome-C Ice Core

On the East Antarctic Plateau, approximately 900 km from the coast and 1750 km from the South Pole, sits Dome C. This is the point on the Antarctic continent where the ice sheet is the thickest (see Figure 17.32 for the location and Figure 17.1.2). Here the ice is 3310 m

FIGURE 17.1.2 Dome-C station. An overview of the Dome-C scientific station, at 75.1° S, 123.3° E, with its gathering of tents and semipermanent structures. [Chris Gilbert/British Antarctic Survey, www.photo.antarctica.ac.uk.]

deep. The mean annual surface temperature is −54.5°C; however, the science crews experience temperatures that range from −50°C when they arrive to −25°C by midsummer. Dome C is 560 km from the Vostok Station, where the previous coring record of 400 000 years was set. The Dome-C project is part of a 10-country European Project for Ice Coring in Antarctica (EPICA).

The mechanical drill bit used for coring was 10 cm wide and provided a high-resolution record of ancient atmospheric gases, ash from volcanic eruptions, and materials from other atmospheric events. By December 2004, coring to a depth of 3270.20 m brought up 800 000 years of Earth's past climate history (Figure 17.1.3). In Figure 17.27, this is MIS 20.2. This remarkable record contains eight glacial and interglacial

FIGURE 17.1.1 Greenland ice-core locations.
GRIP is at 72.5° N, 37.5° W. GISP-2 is at 72.6° N, 38.5° W. [Map courtesy of GISP-2 Science Management Office.]

proposed other possible astronomical factors. Milankovitch wondered whether the development of an ice age relates to seasonal astronomical factors—Earth's revolution around the Sun, rotation, and tilt—extended over a longer time span (Figure 17.31). In summary:

- Earth's elliptical orbit about the Sun is not constant. The shape of the ellipse varies by more than 17.7 million kilometres during a 100 000-year cycle, from nearly circular to an extreme ellipse (Figure 17.31a).
- Earth's axis "wobbles" through a 26 000-year cycle, in a movement much like that of a spinning top winding down. Earth's wobble is called *precession*. As you can

see in Figure 17.31b, precession changes the orientation of hemispheres and landmasses to the Sun.
- Earth's present axial tilt of 23.5° varies from 22° to 24.5° during a 41 000-year period (Figure 17.31c).

Milankovitch calculated, without the aid of today's computers, that the interaction of these Earth–Sun relations creates a 96 000-year climatic cycle. His glaciation model assumes that changes in astronomical relations affect the amounts of insolation received.

Milankovitch died in 1954, his ideas still not accepted by a skeptical scientific community. Now, in the era of computers, remote-sensing satellites, and worldwide efforts to

(a) Dome-C core removed

(b) Ice-core section

(c) Glacial ice bubbles

FIGURE 17.1.3 Dome-C ice-core analysis.
(a) Two members of the British Antarctic Survey carefully inspect one of the ice-core segments. A quarter-section of each ice core is kept at Dome-C in case there is an accident in transport back to labs in Europe. (b) Light shining through a thin section from the ice core; Earth's ancient atmosphere is trapped in the ice awaiting analysis. (c) You can see the trapped air bubbles in this chunk of glacial ice. [(a) and (b) Chris Gilbert/British Antarctic Survey, www.photo.antarctica.ac.uk; (c) Bobbé Christopherson.]

Confirmed are the findings that the present concentrations of carbon dioxide, methane, and nitrous oxide in the atmosphere are the highest in the past 800 000 years and that these changing levels have marched in step with higher and lower temperatures throughout this time span.

Go to Figure 17.27, and find MIS 11, which indicates an additional item of importance at Dome C. This warm spell at MIS 11, from 425 000 to 395 000 years ago, is perfectly recorded in the Dome-C core and is of interest because CO_2 in the atmosphere during MIS 11 was similar to our preindustrial level of 280 ppm. Earth's orbital alignment was similar to that of today as well. The MIS 11 analogy means that a return to the next glacial period is perhaps 16,000 years in the future.

Ice-core drilling projects planned, under way, or completed bring the total cores to nearly 30 in Antarctica and 16 in Greenland. The Ice Core Gateway site of NOAA Paleoclimatology lists and links to coring projects (http://www.ncdc .noaa.gov/paleo/icgate.html). The Byrd Polar Research Center at Ohio State University presents information on the worldwide efforts of its Ice Core Paleoclimatology Research Group at http://bprc .osu.edu/Icecore/.

Understanding the past helps decode future trends. The challenge for physical geographers is to analyze these data spatially and find the linkages to other Earth systems and to human economies and societies in an effort to understand what is happening in Earth's cryosphere.

cycles. Scientists found the Dome-C record affirms the Vostok findings and correlates perfectly with the deep-sea core of oxygen isotope fluctuations in foraminifera shells (microfossils) from the Atlantic Ocean.

decipher past climates, Milankovitch's valuable work has stimulated much research to explain climatic cycles and has experienced some confirmation. A roughly 100 000-year climatic cycle is confirmed in such diverse places as ice cores in Greenland and the accumulation of sediment in Lake Baykal, Siberia. Milankovitch cycles appear to be the primary cause of glacial-interglacial cycles, although there are other factors that cause second-order effects such as changes in the North Atlantic Ocean, gains or losses of Arctic sea ice, and variable carbon dioxide levels.

Climate and Solar Variability If the Sun significantly varies its output over the years, as some other stars do, that variation would seem a convenient and plausible cause of ice-age timing. However, lack of evidence that the Sun's radiation output varies significantly over long cycles argues against this hypothesis. Nonetheless, inquiry about the Sun's variability actively continues and research using deep-space satellites is under way. As we saw in Chapter 10, with data from the Intergovernmental Panel on Climate Change *Fourth Assessment Report* in Figure 10.33, solar variability is not correlated to temperature increases occurring in the atmosphere and oceans.

Climate and Tectonics Major glaciations also can be associated with plate tectonics because some landmasses

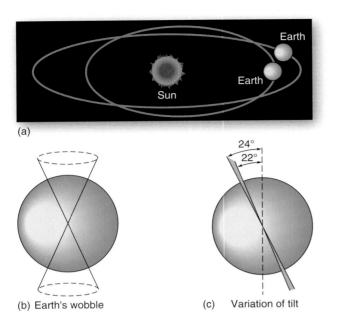

(a)

(b) Earth's wobble (c) Variation of tilt

FIGURE 17.31 Astronomical factors that may affect broad climatic cycles.
(a) Earth's elliptical orbit varies widely during a 100 000-year cycle, stretching out to an extreme ellipse. (b) Earth's 26 000-year axial wobble. (c) Variation in Earth's axial tilt has a 41 000-year cycle.

have migrated to higher, cooler latitudes. Chapters 11 and 12 explain that the shape and orientation of landmasses and ocean basins have changed greatly during Earth's history. Continental plates have drifted from equatorial locations to polar regions, and vice versa, thus exposing the land to a gradual change in climate. Gondwana (the southern half of Pangaea) experienced extensive glaciation that left its mark on the rocks of parts of present-day Africa, South America, India, Antarctica, and Australia. Landforms in the Sahara, for example, bear the markings of even earlier glacial activity. These markings are partly explained by the fact that portions of Africa were centred near the South Pole during the Ordovician Period, 465 million years ago (see Figure 11.18a).

Episodes of mountain building over the past billion years have forced mountain summits above the snowline, where snow remains after the summer melt. Mountain chains influence downwind weather patterns and jet-stream circulation, which in turn guides weather systems. More dust was present during glacial periods, suggesting drier weather and more extensive deserts beyond the frozen regions.

Climate and Atmospheric Factors Some events alter the atmosphere and produce climate change. A volcanic eruption might produce lower temperatures for a year or two. The lower temperatures could initiate a buildup of long-term snow cover at high latitudes. These high-albedo snow surfaces then would reflect more insolation away from Earth to further enhance cooling in a positive feedback system.

The fluctuation of atmospheric greenhouse gases could trigger higher or lower temperatures. Ice cores taken from Greenland and Antarctica contain trapped air samples that show carbon dioxide levels varying from 180 ppm to 290 ppm. Higher levels of carbon dioxide generally correlate with

each interglacial, or warmer, period. In the first decade of this century, atmospheric carbon dioxide increased dramatically, principally a result of anthropogenic (human-caused) forcing. Refer to the carbon dioxide records in Figures 10.31 (1000-year record) and 10.34 (10 000-year record).

Climate and Oceanic Circulation Finally, changes in oceanic circulation patterns may affect climate. For example, the Isthmus of Panama formed about 3 million years ago and effectively separated the circulation of the Atlantic and Pacific oceans. Changes in ocean basin configuration, surface temperatures, and salinity and in upwelling and downwelling rates affect air mass formation and air temperature.

Our understanding of Earth's climate—past, present, and future—is unfolding. We are learning that climate is a multicyclic system controlled by an interacting set of cooling and warming processes, all founded on celestial relations, tectonic factors, changes in oceanic circulation, and human impacts.

Arctic and Antarctic Regions

Climatologists use environmental criteria to define the Arctic and the Antarctic regions. The 10°C isotherm for July defines the **Arctic region** (green line on the map in Figure 17.32a). This line coincides with the visible tree line—the boundary between the northern forests and tundra. The Arctic Ocean is covered by two kinds of ice: *floating sea ice* (frozen seawater) and *glacier ice* (frozen freshwater). This pack ice thins in the summer months and sometimes breaks up (Figure 17.32b).

As mentioned elsewhere, the volume of the Arctic ice pack has reduced by almost half since 1970 due to regional-scale warming. The year 2007 broke the record for lowest sea-ice extent, falling below the previous record low in 2005 by 24%. The fabled Northwest Passage across the Arctic from the Atlantic to the Pacific was ice-free in September 2007, as the Arctic ice continues to melt. The Northeast passage, north of Russia, has been ice-free in the summer for the past several years.

The Antarctic convergence defines the **Antarctic region** in a narrow zone that extends around the continent as a boundary between colder Antarctic water and warmer water at lower latitudes. This boundary follows roughly the 10°C isotherm for February, the Southern Hemisphere summer, and is located near 60° S latitude (green line in Figure 17.32c). The Antarctic region that is covered just with sea ice represents an area greater than North America, Greenland, and Western Europe combined. For more information on polar-region ice, see the Canadian Ice Service at http://ice-glaces.ec.gc.ca/app/WsvPageDsp .cfm/ and the U.S. National Ice Center at http://www .natice.noaa.gov.

The Antarctic landmass is surrounded by ocean and is much colder overall than the Arctic, which is an ocean surrounded by land. In simplest terms, Antarctica can be thought of as a continent covered by a single enormous glacier, although it contains distinct regions such as the East Antarctic and West Antarctic ice sheets, which respond differently to

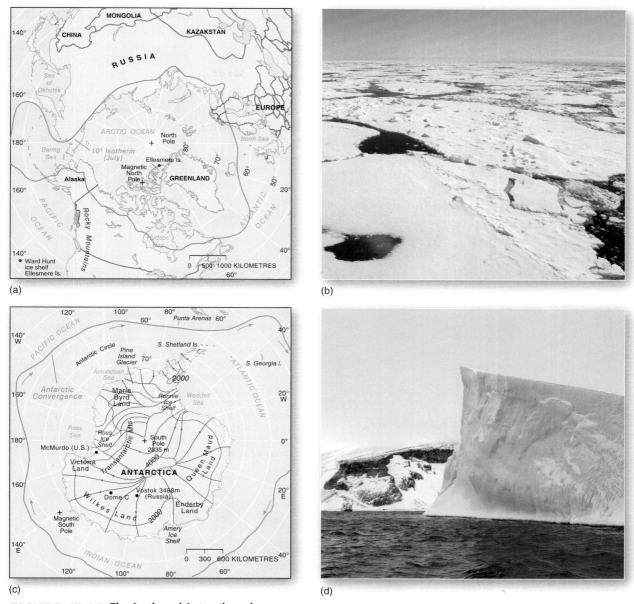

(a)

(b)

(c)

(d)

FIGURE 17.32 The Arctic and Antarctic regions.
In (a), note the 10°C isotherm in midsummer, which designates the Arctic region, dominated by pack ice.
(b) Arctic sea ice about 965 km from the North Pole. In (c), the Antarctic convergence designates the Antarctic region. Arrows on the ice sheet show the general direction of ice movement on Antarctica. Note the location of the Dome-C and Vostok Stations. (d) View across the Antarctic Sound from Brown Bluff; for scale, note the ship compared to the huge tabular iceberg. [Bobbé Christopherson.]

slight climatic variations. These ice sheets are in constant motion, as indicated by the arrows in Figure 17.32c.

The fact that Antarctica is so remote from civilization makes it an excellent laboratory for sampling past and present evidence of human and natural variables that are transported by atmospheric and oceanic circulation to this pristine environment. High altitude, winter cold and darkness, and distance from pollution sources make the polar region an ideal location for certain astronomical and atmospheric observations. Fifty scientists and support people work through the winter (February to October), and 130 personnel, or more, research and work there during the brief summer.

█ ▌▌ CRITICAL THINKING 17.2

A Sample of Life at the Polar Station

After reading a summary of the *New South Polar Times*, 1993–1998, on the *Geosystems* web site under this chapter, imagine what duty would be like at the South Pole. Of the 50 people who winter over at the station, some serve as scientists, technicians, and support staff. The station commander and reporter for the 1998 season was Katy McNitt-Jensen, in her third tour at the pole. Although dated, her personal observations are interesting. Remember, the last airplane leaves mid-February, and the first airplane lands mid-October—such is the isolation. What do you see as the positives and negatives of such service? How would you combat the elements, the isolation, and the dark conditions?

Changes Under Way in the Polar Regions

Review the "Global Climate Change" section in Chapter 10, where a portrait of high-latitude temperatures and ongoing physical changes to pack ice, ice shelves, and glaciers is presented.

An important indicator of changing surface conditions is an increase in meltponds across the polar regions, as these meltponds represent positive feedback—meltponds are darker, absorb more insolation, and become warmer, which melts more ice, making more meltponds, and so forth. The *Landsat*-7 satellite, in tandem with aircraft equipped with video cameras, spotted this increase in meltpond occurrence on glaciers, icebergs, ice shelves, and the Greenland Ice Sheet.

Figure 17.33a is a scene from western Greenland in June 2003 made by the *Terra* satellite. Examine the bare rock along the eastern margin, indicating that the snowline has retreated to higher elevations. The image shows rapidly increasing numbers of meltponds and areas of water-saturated ice in the *melt zone*, which advanced 400% from 2001 to 2003. The meltponds look like small blue dots across the ice. In Figure 17.33b, you can see the meltponds and melt streams in southwest Greenland as of June 2008.

The streams sometimes melt through the ice sheet, forming a *moulin*, or drainage channel, that works its way to the base of the glacier (Figure 17.33c). The glacial water can flow through the basal layers of fine clays, thus

meltponds,
water-saturated ice

(a)

(b)

(c)

(d)

FIGURE 17.33 Meltponds, melt streams, and moulins on the increase in Greenland.

Meltponds are on the increase in the Arctic on icebergs, ice shelves, and the Greenland Ice Sheet. (a) Image of western Greenland demonstrates these conditions. Between the rocky landscape with outlet glaciers and fjords to the west (left) and the ice sheet to the east (right), examine the extent of the melt zone—water-saturated surface ice and meltponds (blue specks). (b) Meltponds and melt streams flow across southwest Greenland to a moulin. (c) Meltwater flows into a moulin. (d) Sometimes moulin drainage outlets emerge from the face of a glacier. (e) and (f) Meltponds are positive-feedback climate indicators. [(a) *Terra* MODIS image, NASA/GSFC; (b) and (c) JPL/NASA; (d), (e), and (f) Bobbé Christopherson.]

(e)

(f)

January 31, 2002   March 7, 2002

FIGURE 17.34 **Disintegrating ice shelves along the Antarctic coast.**
Disintegration and retreat of the Larsen-B ice shelf between January 31 and March 7, 2002. Note the meltponds in the January image. [*Terra* images, NASA.]

lubricating and causing acceleration of glacial flow rates; even hydrostatically lifting the ice is possible. Sometimes these moulin channels exit from the glacier's face and flow into the sea (Figure 17.33d).

Numerous ice shelves surround the margins of Antarctica, and constitute about 11% of its ice-covered surface area. Although ice shelves constantly break up to produce icebergs, more large sections are breaking free than expected. You read about a recent breakup of the Wilkins Ice Shelf in Geosystems Now for this chapter. In 1998, an iceberg the size of Delaware broke off the Ronne Ice Shelf, southeast of the Antarctic Peninsula. In March 2000, an iceberg tagged B-15, measuring 300 km by 40 km, broke off the Ross Ice Shelf (some 3027 km, west of the Antarctic Peninsula).

Since 1993, seven ice shelves have disintegrated in Antarctica. More than 8000 km² of ice shelf are gone, changing maps, freeing up islands to circumnavigation, and creating thousands of icebergs. The Larsen Ice Shelf, along the east coast of the Antarctic Peninsula, was retreating slowly for years. Larsen-A suddenly disintegrated in 1995. In only 35 days in early 2002, Larsen-B collapsed into icebergs (Figure 17.34). Larsen-B was at least 11 000 years old, meaning this collapse was farther south than any previously during the Holocene Epoch. Larsen-C, the next segment to the south, is losing mass on its underside, since the water temperature is warmer by 0.65 C° than the melting point for ice at a depth of 300 m—warmth is melting the shelf from both the oceanic and the atmospheric sides. This ice loss is likely a result of this warmer water and the 2.5 C° air temperature increase in the peninsula region during the last 50 years. In response to the increasing warmth, the Antarctic Peninsula is experiencing previously unseen vegetation growth, reduced sea ice, and disruption of penguin feeding, nesting, and fledging activities; ticks are a new problem for these animals.

CRITICAL THINKING 17.3

The IPY Accomplishment Continues

The International Polar Year (IPY) ran from March 2007 to March 2009, covering two polar summer seasons—it was the fourth IPY conducted since 1882. This global interdisciplinary research, exploration, and discovery effort involved 50 000 scientists in hundreds of collaborative projects. A systems approach was key, finding the linkages and connections among ecosystems and human activity. About 65% of the research was in the Arctic region and 35% in the Antarctic region. Results are still being published, and the IPY is stimulating conferences and educational activity. Traditional knowledge of indigenous peoples that are experiencing climate change firsthand was part of the research effort—the actual experiences of the First Nations people.

Use your critical-thinking skills in a brief exploration of this IPY. Begin at the web site http://www.ipy.org. From the "What is IPY" frame: (1) Click "Polar Weeks," and follow the chronology of links; (2) click "About IPY" for background and urgent issues; and (3) click "IPY Project Database," then click "Browse all EOIs" ("Expressions of Intent") and sample some projects. The list is too long for a complete examination; just do a brief survey of the research.

Glacier Mass Balance

Mass balance calculation is a method used to monitor the behaviour of glaciers and can give an indication, if a long enough time series exists, of the regional warming or cooling of climate. Net mass balance is total accumulation (gains of mass) minus total ablation (losses of mass) over a given time which is normally one year. A positive net balance implies that the glacier accumulation is greater than the ablation in a given time period; a negative net balance implies that there is greater ablation than accumulation. Across the surface of the glacier, there is an elevation where accumulation and ablation annually are equal—this is marked by the equilbrium line.

Table 1 shows a sample mass balance data set for a 15-year period. Values in the table are expressed with units metres of water equivalent (m w.e.). Total mass gained or lost by

the glacier has been converted into the equivalent depth of liquid water (density of 1 $g \cdot cm^{-3}$) averaged over the entire glacier surface area. Mass balance values are provided for the "winter season" (when accumulation exceeds ablation; thus mass balance is positive) and the "summer season" (when ablation exceeds accumulation; mass balance is negative). Annual net balance can be calculated as the sum of winter and summer values.

To discern whether there is a trend in a glacier's mass balance, cumulative net mass balance is calculated. To cumulate values in a series, each value is added to the sum of the previous values. For year 1, there is no previous value, so the cumulative net balance is the net balance of year 1 (−0.05 m w.e.). For year 2, the annual net balance of year 2 (+0.12 m w.e.) is added to the value for year 1, giving a cumulative value of +0.07 m w.e.

For year 3, the annual net balance of year 3 (−0.04 m w.e.) is added to the previous sum (+0.06 m w.e.), giving +0.03 m w.e. This procedure is continued down to the end of the series.

Inspection of the mass balance graph in Figure APG 17.1 reveals that the amount of accumulation in a given year is not a direct indication of the amount of ablation. Note that for the first eight years in this sample data set, accumulation, ablation, and net glacer mass values fluctuate annually but there is little cumulative change (+0.19 m w.e.). For the last seven years, however, all of the net mass balance values are negative, the cumulative mass balance is −2.94 m w.e., and there is a clear trend—the glacier is losing mass and shrinking. Such a trend is indicative of climate change (higher air and ocean temperatures)—an accelerating anthropogenic warming.

TABLE 1	Sample Glacier Mass Balance Data[a]

(Values in Metres of Water Equivalent)

Year in Series	Winter Season	Summer Season	Net Mass Balance	Cumulative Balance
1	0.95	−1.00	−0.05	−0.05
2	1.12	−1.00	0.12	0.07
3	1.57	−1.61	−0.04	0.03
4	0.69	−1.60	−0.91	−0.88
5	0.71	−0.25	0.46	−0.42
6	1.29	−0.95	0.34	−0.08
7	1.08	−1.39	−0.31	−0.39
8	1.44	−0.86	0.58	0.19
9	0.55	−1.64	−1.09	−0.90
10	1.12	−1.35	−0.23	−1.13
11	0.96	−1.88	−0.92	−2.05
12	1.39	−1.60	−0.21	−2.26
13	0.98	−1.17	−0.19	−2.45
14	1.35	−1.77	−0.42	−2.87
15	1.13	−1.20	−0.07	−2.94

[a]Winter and summer mass balance data for Gulkana Glacier, Alaska, acquired from USGS Alaska Science Center, Water Resources Office (http://alaska.usgs.gov/science/water/index.php).

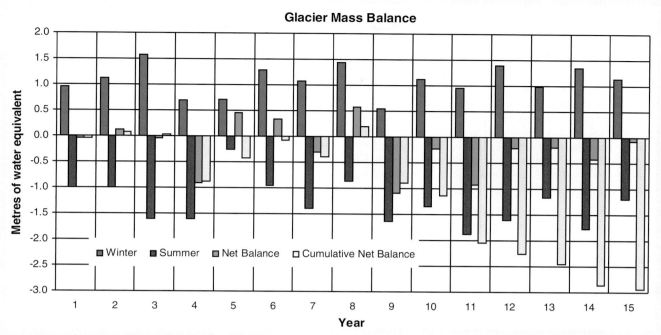

FIGURE APG 17.1 Glacier mass balance graph.
Positive values indicate net accumulation; negative values indicate net ablation. [Philip Giles using data from Gulkana Glacier, Alaska, acquired from USGS Alaska Science Center, Water Resources Office (http://alaska.usgs.gov /science/water/index.php.]

GEOSYSTEMS CONNECTION

Our look at the cryosphere and glacial processes and landforms ends Part III, The Earth–Atmosphere Interface. We examined past and present alpine and continental glaciations. Earth's landscapes bear the mark of past glacial phases. One method by which scientists study paleoclimatology is by analyzing ice cores, with the record going back to 800 000 years before the present. The polar regions are undergoing rapid change at a pace faster than the lower latitudes. We shift now to Part IV, Soils, Ecosystems, and Biomes, a synthesis of the other three parts in this text, focused on the biosphere and the subdiscipline of biogeography.

KEY LEARNING CONCEPTS REVIEW

■ **Differentiate** between alpine and continental glaciers, and **describe** the principal features of each type.

More than 77% of Earth's freshwater is frozen. Ice covers about 11% of Earth's surface, and periglacial features occupy another 20% of ice-free but cold-dominated landscapes. A **glacier** is a mass of ice sitting on land or floating as an ice shelf in the ocean next to land. Glaciers form in areas of permanent snow. A **snowline** is the lowest elevation where snow occurs year-round and its altitude varies by latitude—higher near the equator, lower poleward.

A glacier in a mountain range is an **alpine glacier**. If confined within a valley, it is termed a *valley glacier*. The area of origin

is a snowfield, usually in a bowl-shaped erosional landform called a **cirque**. Where alpine glaciers flow down to the sea, calving forms **icebergs**. A **continental glacier** is a continuous mass of ice on land. Its most extensive form is an **ice sheet;** a smaller, roughly circular form is an **ice cap;** and the least extensive form, usually in mountains, is an **ice field**.

glacier (p. 516)
snowline (p. 516)
alpine glacier (p. 517)
cirque (p. 517)
iceberg (p. 518)

continental glacier (p. 519)
ice sheet (p. 519)
ice cap (p. 519)
ice field (p. 520)

1. Describe the location of most freshwater on Earth today.
2. What is a glacier? What is implied about existing climate patterns in a glacial region?
3. Differentiate between an alpine glacier and the three types of continental glaciers. Which occurs in mountains? Which covers Antarctica and Greeenland?
4. How are icebergs generated? Describe iceberg buoyancy characteristics from this discussion and the section on ice in Chapter 7. Why do you think an iceberg overturns from time to time as it melts?

■ **Explain** the process of glacial ice formation, and **portray** the mechanics of glacial movement.

Snow becomes glacial ice through accumulation, increasing thickness, pressure on underlying layers, and recrystallization. Snow progresses through transitional steps from **firn** (compact, granular) to a denser **glacial ice** after many years.

A glacier is an open system. A **firn line** is the lower extent of a fresh snow-covered area. A glacier is fed by snowfall and is wasted by **ablation** (losses from its upper and lower surfaces and along its margins). Accumulation and ablation achieve a mass balance in each glacier.

As a glacier moves downhill, vertical **crevasses** may develop. Sometimes a glacier will move rapidly in a **glacier surge**. The presence of water along the basal layer appears to be important in glacial movements. As a glacier moves, it plucks rock pieces and debris, incorporating them into the ice, and this debris scours and sandpapers underlying rock through **abrasion.**

firn (p. 522)
glacial ice (p. 522)
firn line (p. 522)
ablation (p. 522)
crevasse (p. 523)
glacier surge (p. 523)
abrasion (p. 524)

5. Trace the evolution of glacial ice from fresh fallen snow.
6. What is meant by glacial mass balance? What are the basic inputs and outputs underlying that balance?
7. What is meant by a glacier surge? What do scientists think produces surging episodes?

■ **Describe** characteristic erosional and depositional landforms created by alpine glaciation and by continental glaciation.

Extensive valley glaciers have profoundly reshaped mountains worldwide, carving **V**-shaped stream valleys into **U**-shaped glaciated valleys, producing many distinctive erosional and depositional landforms. As cirque walls erode away, sharp **arêtes** (sawtooth, serrated ridges) form, dividing adjacent cirque basins. Two eroding cirques may reduce an arête to a saddlelike **col**. A **horn** results when several cirque glaciers gouge an individual mountain summit from all sides, forming a pyramidal peak. A **bergschrund** forms when a crevasse or wide crack opens along the headwall of a glacier, most visible in summer when covering snow is gone. An ice-carved rock basin left as a glacier retreats may fill with water to form a **tarn**; tarns in a string separated by moraines are called **paternoster lakes.** Where a glacial valley trough joins the ocean, and the glacier retreats, the sea extends inland to form a **fjord.**

All glacial deposits, whether ice-borne or meltwater-borne, constitute **glacial drift**. Glacial meltwater deposits are sorted and are called **stratified drift**. Direct deposits from ice, called **till**, are unstratified and unsorted. Specific landforms produced by the deposition of drift are **moraines**. A **lateral moraine** forms along each side of a glacier; merging glaciers with lateral moraines form a **medial moraine**; and eroded debris dropped at the glacier's terminus is a **terminal moraine**.

Continental glaciation leaves different features than does alpine glaciation. A **till plain** forms behind end moraines, featuring unstratified coarse till, low and rolling relief, and deranged drainage. Beyond the morainal deposits, **outwash plains** of stratified drift feature stream channels that are meltwater fed, braided, and overloaded with debris that is sorted and deposited across the landscape. An **esker** is a sinuously curving, narrow ridge of coarse sand and gravel that forms along the channel of a meltwater stream beneath a glacier. An isolated block of ice left by a retreating glacier becomes surrounded with debris; when the block finally melts, it leaves a steep-sided **kettle**. A **kame** is a small hill, knob, or mound of poorly sorted sand and gravel that is deposited directly by water or by ice in crevasses.

Glacial action forms two types of streamlined hills: the erosional **roche moutonnée** is an asymmetrical hill of exposed bedrock, gently sloping upstream and abruptly sloping downstream; the depositional **drumlin** is deposited till, streamlined in the direction of continental ice movement (blunt end upstream and tapered end downstream).

arête (p. 524)
col (p. 524)
horn (p. 524)
bergschrund (p. 524)
tarn (p. 525)
paternoster lakes (p. 525)
fjord (p. 525)
glacial drift (p. 526)
stratified drift (p. 526)
till (p. 526)
moraine (p. 526)
lateral moraine (p. 526)
medial moraine (p. 526)
terminal moraine (p. 527)
till plain (p. 528)
outwash plain (p. 528)
esker (p. 528)
kettle (p. 529)
kame (p. 529)
roche moutonnée (p. 529)
drumlin (p. 530)

8. How does a glacier accomplish erosion?
9. Describe the evolution of a **V**-shaped stream valley to a **U**-shaped glaciated valley. What features are visible after the glacier retreats?
10. How is an arête formed? A col? A horn? Briefly differentiate between these landforms.
11. Differentiate between two forms of glacial drift—till and outwash.
12. What is a morainal deposit? What specific moraines are created by alpine glaciers and by continental glaciers?
13. What are some common depositional features encountered in a till plain?
14. Contrast a roche moutonnée and a drumlin regarding appearance, orientation, and the way each forms.

■ *Analyze* the spatial distribution of periglacial processes and related permafrost and frozen ground, and *explain* the present thaw under way.

The term **periglacial** describes cold-climate processes, landforms, and topographic features that exist along the margins of glaciers, past and present. When soil or rock temperatures remain below 0°C for at least two consecutive years, **permafrost** ("permanent frost") develops. Note that this criterion is based solely on temperature and has nothing to do with how much or how little water is present. The **active layer** is the zone of seasonally frozen ground that exists between the subsurface permafrost layer and the ground surface. **Patterned ground** forms in the periglacial environment, where freezing and thawing of the ground create polygonal forms of circles, polygons, stripes, nets, and steps.

periglacial (p. 530)
permafrost (p. 530)
active layer (p. 532)
patterned ground (p. 534)

15. In terms of climatic types, describe the areas on Earth where periglacial landscapes occur. Include both higher latitude and higher altitude climate types.
16. Define two categories that describe how permafrost is distributed, and differentiate the occurrence of these categories on Earth. What are the characteristics of each?
17. Describe the active zone in permafrost regions, and relate the degree of development to specific latitudes.
18. What is a talik? Where might you expect to find taliks, and to what depth do these occur?
19. What is the difference between permafrost and ground ice?
20. Describe the role of frost action in the formation of various landform types in the periglacial region, such as a pingo and patterned ground.
21. Relate some of the specific problems humans encounter with developing infrastructure in periglacial landscapes.

■ *Explain* the Pleistocene ice-age epoch and related glacials and interglacials, and *describe* some of the methods used to study paleoclimatology.

An **ice age** is any extended period of cold. The late Cenozoic Era featured pronounced ice-age conditions in an epoch called the Pleistocene. During this time, alpine and continental glaciers covered about 30% of Earth's land area in at least 18 glacials, punctuated by interglacials of milder weather. Beyond the ice, **paleolakes** formed because of wetter conditions. Evidence of ice-age conditions is gathered from ice cores drilled in Greenland and Antarctica, from ocean sediments, from coral growth in relation to past sea levels, and from rock. The study of past climates is *paleoclimatology*.

The apparent pattern followed by these low-temperature episodes indicates cyclic causes. A complicated mix of interacting variables appears to influence long-term climatic trends: celestial relations, solar variability, tectonic factors, atmospheric variables, and oceanic circulation. The present anthropogenic forcing of temperatures is thought to be overwhelming the natural cycle.

ice age (p. 536)
paleolake (p. 538)

22. What is paleoclimatology? Describe Earth's past climatic patterns. Are we experiencing a normal climate pattern in this era, or have scientists noticed any significant trends indicating climate change?
23. Define an ice age. When was the most recent? Explain "glacial" and "interglacial" in your answer.
24. Summarize what science has learned about the causes of ice ages by listing and explaining at least four possible factors in climate change.
25. Describe the role of ice cores in deciphering past climates. What records are preserved? Where were these cores drilled?

■ *Define* each polar region, and *list* climatic changes taking place and associated impacts.

The 10°C isotherm for July defines the **Arctic region**. This line coincides with the visible tree line—the boundary between the northern forests and tundra. The Antarctic convergence defines the **Antarctic region** in a narrow zone that extends around the continent as a boundary between colder Antarctic water and warmer water at lower latitudes. This boundary follows roughly the 10°C isotherm for February, the Southern Hemisphere summer, and is located near 60° S latitude.

Arctic region (p. 544)
Antarctic region (p. 544)

26. Explain the relationship between the criteria defining the Arctic and Antarctic regions. Is there any coincidence between the Arctic criteria and the distribution of Northern Hemisphere forests?
27. Based on information in this chapter and elsewhere in *Geosystems*, summarize a few of the changing conditions under way in each polar region. Are there any conditions that seem of greatest concern to you after studying them?

MyGeosciencePlace

Visit **www.mygeoscienceplace.ca** for several figure animations, satellite loops, self-study quizzes, flashcards, interactive glossary, career links, RSS feeds, Pearson eText of *Geosystems*, and much more.

INPUTS
Insolation
Abiotic and biotic
elements
Ecosystem
components

ACTIONS
Photosynthesis/
respiration
Biogeochemical
cycling
Trophic relations,
food webs
Evolution, succession

OUTPUTS
Soils, plants,
animals, life
Ecosystems
Biodiversity
Biomes: marine and
terrestrial

**HUMAN-EARTH
RELATION**
Biodiversity losses
Soil degradation
Desertification
Earth and human
denominator

ABIOTIC COMPONENTS   BIOTIC COMPONENTS

CANADA
0   400 MI
0   400 KM

NITROGEN
DELIVERED TO GULF
(KILOGRAMS PER
HECTARE PER YEAR)
☐ Low (< 3)
☐ Medium (3–8)
☐ High (> 8)
☐ Dead zone

UNITED STATES   40°

30°

MEXICO   Gu
Pollution plume after Katrina   2010 BP oil spill

I. Atmosphere

II. Hydrosphere

IV. Biosphere

III. Lithosphere

Soils, Ecosystems, and Biomes

Earth is the home of the only known biosphere in the Solar System—a unique, complex, and interactive system of abiotic (nonliving) and biotic (living) components working together to sustain a tremendous diversity of life. Energy enters the biosphere through conversion of solar energy by photosynthesis in the leaves of plants. Soil is the essential link among the lithosphere, plants, and the rest of Earth's physical systems. Thus, soil helps sustain life and is a bridge between Part III and Part IV of this text.

Life is organized into a feeding hierarchy from producers to consumers, ending with decomposers. Taken together, the soils, plants, animals, and all abiotic components produce aquatic and terrestrial ecosystems, generally grouped together in various biomes. Today, we face crucial issues—principally, the preservation of the diversity of life in the biosphere. Patterns of land and ocean temperatures, precipitation, weather phenomena, and stratospheric ozone, among many elements, are changing as global climate systems shift. The resilience of the biosphere as we know it is being tested in a real-time, one-time experiment. These important issues of biogeography are considered in Part IV.

Massive phytoplankton bloom in the Atlantic Ocean off the coast of Argentina, December 21, 2010. Imaged using seven spectral bands in the MODIS sensor aboard *Aqua*. [NASA/GSFC.]

CHAPTER 18

The Geography of Soils

Fertile soils overlie glacial till in the Region of Durham, east of Toronto. In summertime, green fields are evidence of the richness of the soils in this area. [Helen Filatova/Shutterstock.]

KEY LEARNING CONCEPTS

After reading the chapter, you should be able to:

- **Define** soil and soil science, and **describe** a pedon, a polypedon, and a typical soil profile.
- **Describe** soil properties, including colour, texture, structure, consistence, porosity, and soil moisture.
- **Explain** basic soil chemistry, including cation-exchange capacity, and **relate** these concepts to soil fertility.
- **Evaluate** the principal soil formation factors, including the human element.
- **Describe** the principal pedogenic processes that lead to the formation of soils under different environmental conditions.
- **Describe** the 10 soil orders of the Canadian System of Soil Classification, and **explain** the general occurrence of these orders.

High-Latitude Soils Emit Greenhouse Gases

Throughout this book, we have discussed effects of recently warming temperatures in the polar regions. As sea ice, ice shelves, and tidewater glaciers melt, the possible effects are wide ranging—from altered surface albedo, to accelerated sea-level rise, to losses of high-latitude species as habitats change. Science is focused on these warming polar regions as one of the main indicators of climate change.

However, another process in the northern polar regions has the potential to increase the rate of global warming by releasing substantial amounts of greenhouse gases into the atmosphere. This process is related not to ice, but rather to soil—specifically, the effects of thawing permafrost.

Cryosolic soils, in the Canadian Soil Classification System, are the permafrost-affected soils of the northern latitudes. These soils contain about half of the pool of global carbon, much of which is normally locked up in organic matter in the permafrost (Figure GN 18.1). (These are the Gelisols in the U.S. Soil Taxonomy and the Cryozems in the Russian system.) The latest estimate of the carbon contained in these periglacial soils is 1.5 trillion metric tonnes, which is double the amount mentioned in the Intergovernmental Panel on Climate Change (IPCC) *Fourth Assessment Report* (2007). This fact, mostly unknown to the general public, is sometimes left out of climate change discussions.

The higher latitudes are warming at more than double the rate of the middle and lower latitudes. Cryosolic soils can quickly become wet and soggy with only a slight shift in their thermal balance. As this thaw happens, the poorly decomposed organic content begins to decay, with decomposition releasing enormous quantities of carbon dioxide into the atmosphere through increased respiration. Another greenhouse gas, methane, is released as well. Researchers stated the linkage in these systems in 2009:

We show that approximately 1 C° warming accelerated total ecosystem respiration rates on average by 60% in spring and 52% in summer. ... We find that at least 69% of the increase in respiration rate originated from carbon in peat towards the bottom of the active layer above the permafrost. ... Our findings suggest a large, long-lasting, positive feedback of carbon stored in northern peatlands to the global climate system.[1]

A 2010 publication—*Soil Atlas of the Northern Circumpolar Region* (Figure GN 18.2)—completed as part of the International Polar Year and published by the Joint Research Center of the European Commission (Luxembourg: European Union, 2010), brings all this together. Seven international agencies were part of this effort, and the final atlas is an excellent reference for periglacial environments and permafrost-affected soils. The atlas is available for download at http://eusoils.jrc.ec.europa.eu/library/maps/Circumpolar/.

In this atlas, regional soil distributions, mapped at high resolution, are portrayed on maps derived using Geographic Information System (GIS) technology. The atlas draws special attention to the relationship between climate change and properties of soils and to the general impact of climate on soil characteristics, both of which are expanded on in our Chapter 18, "The Geography of Soils."

As the science community moves forward in the preparation of the IPCC *Fifth Assessment Report*, this northern soil and environment atlas will be an important resource. As summarized in the atlas (pages 7 and 12):

Anthropogenic pressures on northern ecosystems and soil resources are rapidly increasing. ... The atlas illustrates vividly the great diversity of circumpolar soils and northern landscapes while encouraging the general public and governments to develop policies for the protection of these fragile regions. ... The poles are recognized as sensitive barometers of environmental change. Polar science is crucial to understanding our planet and our impact on it.

[1]E. Dorrepaal et al., "Carbon respiration from subsurface peat accelerated by climate warming in the subarctic," *Nature* 460 (July 30, 2009): 616.

FIGURE GN 18.1 Gelisols—permafrost-affected soils.
(a) Cryosolic soils and tundra green in the brief summer season on Spitsbergen Island, as the active layer thaws. (b) Turning over a clod exposes the fibrous organic content and slow decomposition on this Arctic island location. [Bobbé Christopherson.]

FIGURE GN 18.2 Soil Atlas of the Northern Circumpolar Region.

Earth's landscape generally is covered with soil. **Soil** is a dynamic natural material composed of fine particles in which plants grow, and it contains both mineral fragments and organic matter. The soil system includes human interactions and supports all human, other animal, and plant life. If you have ever planted a garden, tended a houseplant, or been concerned about famine and soil loss, this chapter will interest you. Knowledge of soil is at the heart of agriculture and food production.

You kneel down and scoop a handful of prairie soil, compressing it and breaking it apart with your fingers. You are holding a historical object, one that bears the legacy of the last 15 000 years or more. This lump of soil contains information about the last ice age and intervening warm intervals, about distinct and distant source materials, about several physical processes. Soils develop slowly, and we are using and abusing this legacy at rates much faster than it is being formed.

Soil science is the interdisciplinary study of soils, involving physics, chemistry, biology, mineralogy, hydrology, taxonomy, climatology, and cartography. Physical geographers are interested in the spatial patterns formed by soil types and the environmental factors that interact to produce them. As an integrative science, physical geography is well suited to the study of soils. *Pedology* concerns the origin, classification, distribution, and description of soil (*ped* from the Greek *pedon*, meaning "soil" or "earth"). *Edaphology* (from the Greek *edaphos*, meaning "soil" or "ground") focuses on soil as a medium for sustaining higher plants.

Soil science deals with a complex substance whose characteristics vary continuously across Earth's surface. In many locales, an *agricultural extension service* can provide specific information and perform a detailed analysis of local soils. Soil surveys and local soil maps are available for most Canadian provinces and counties in the United States. Agriculture Canada's soil information system is available on the web (http://sis.agr.gc .ca/cansis/intro.html), and the soil landscape of Canada can be viewed online (http://sis.agr.gc.ca/cansis/nsdb /slc/intro.html). For the United States, the National Soil Survey Center's site is at http://soils.usda.gov/ and for links related to world soils, see http://soils.usda.gov /use/worldsoils/.

In this chapter: The geography of soils concerns the inputs and actions that produce a substance with such varied characteristics. We begin with soil characteristics and basic soil sampling and soil mapping units. The soil profile is a dynamic structure, mixing and exchanging materials and moisture across its horizons. Properties of soils include texture, structure, porosity, moisture, and chemistry—all integrating to form soil types. The chapter discusses both natural and human factors that affect soil formation. A global concern exists over the loss of soils to erosion, mistreatment, and conversion to other uses. The chapter concludes with a brief examination of the Canadian System

of Soil Classification (CSSC) and a comparison with other systems that are widely used.

Soil Characteristics

Classifying soils is similar to classifying climates (Chapter 10) because both involve interacting variables. Before we look at soil classification, let us examine the physical properties that distinguish soils developing through time in response to climate, relief, and topography.

Soil Profiles

As a book cannot be judged by its cover, so soils cannot be evaluated at the surface alone. Instead, a soil profile should be studied from the surface to the deepest extent of plant roots, or to where unweathered bedrock is encountered. Such a profile is a **pedon**, a hexagonal column measuring 1 to 10 m^2 in top surface area (Figure 18.1). At the sides of the pedon, the various layers of the soil profile are visible in cross section and are labelled with letters. *A pedon is the basic sampling unit used in soil surveys*.

Many pedons together in one area make up a **polypedon**, which has distinctive characteristics differentiating it from surrounding polypedons. A polypedon is an essential soil individual, comprising an identifiable soil series in an area. It can have a minimum dimension of about 1 m^2 and no specified maximum size. *The polypedon is the basic mapping unit used in preparing local soil maps*.

Soil Horizons

Each distinct layer exposed in a pedon is a **soil horizon**. A horizon is roughly parallel to the pedon's surface and has characteristics distinctly different from horizons directly above or below. The boundary between horizons usually is distinguishable when viewed in profile, such as along a road cut, using the properties of colour, texture, structure, consistence (meaning soil consistency or cohesiveness), porosity, presence or absence of certain minerals, moisture, and chemical processes (Figure 18.2). Soil horizons are the building blocks of soil classification.

At the top of a typical soil profile is the *O (organic) horizon*, named for its organic composition, derived from plant and animal litter that was deposited on the surface and transformed into humus. **Humus** is not just a single material; it is a mixture of decomposed and synthesized organic materials, usually dark in colour. Microorganisms work busily on this organic debris, performing a portion of the *humification* (humus-making) process. The O horizon is 20%–30% or more organic matter, which is important because of its ability to retain water and nutrients and for the way it acts in a complementary manner to clay minerals.

At the bottom of the soil profile is the *R (rock) horizon*, consisting of either unconsolidated (loose) material or consolidated bedrock. When bedrock physically and chemically weathers into regolith, it may or may not contribute to overlying soil horizons. The A, Ae, B, and C horizons mark differing mineral strata between O and R.

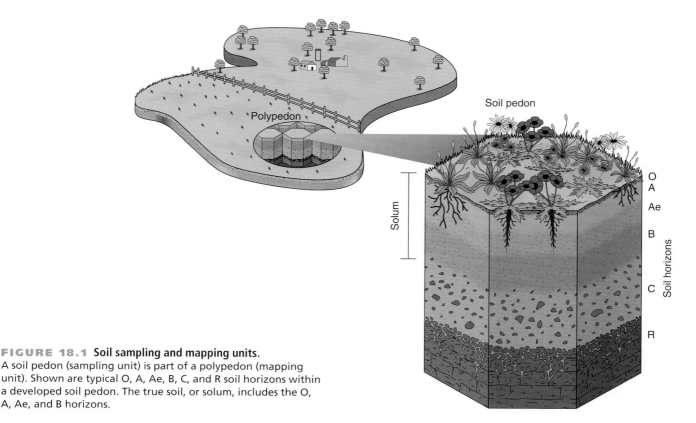

FIGURE 18.1 Soil sampling and mapping units.
A soil pedon (sampling unit) is part of a polypedon (mapping unit). Shown are typical O, A, Ae, B, C, and R soil horizons within a developed soil pedon. The true soil, or solum, includes the O, A, Ae, and B horizons.

These middle layers are composed of sand, silt, clay, and other weathered by-products. (Table 11.3 in Chapter 11 presents a description of grain sizes for these weathered soil particles.)

The *A horizon* is a primarily mineral layer that forms at or near the surface. It exists in the zone of maximum accumulation of organic matter, or in the zone of leaching of materials either in solution or suspension, or both. The accumulation of organic material usually results in a darkening of the surface soil. The A horizon can be enriched in organic matter (Ah) or depleted in mineral matter (Ae). The Ae horizon is lighter in colour, coarser in texture, and is the transition from the A horizon to the B horizon.

The removal of fine particles and minerals by water, leaving behind sand and silt, is termed **eluviation**—thus the "e" notation in Ae. Silicate clays and oxides of aluminum and iron are removed by water, or leached, and carried to lower horizons with the water as it percolates through the soil. More soluble material can be fully removed from the soil quickly, while iron and aluminum oxides are residual and may move more slowly.

FIGURE 18.2 A typical soil profile.
This is a Gleysol from southern Ontario. The parent material is till and glaciolacustrine sediment, and the soil is poorly drained. The dark O and A horizons are above the #7 and transition into the Ae horizon to the #13. Below the #13 is the mottled B horizon.
[Courtesy of Agriculture and Agri-Food Canada, http://sis2.agr.gc.ca/cansis/images/index.html. Reproduced with the permission of the Minister of Public Works and Government Services Canada, 2012.]

The accumulation or enrichment of organic matter, oxides, or clay dominates the B horizon. The deposition of these materials is known as **illuviation**. Accumulated organic material (Bh) results in a layer darker in colour relative to the *C horizon*. Finer soil texture or coatings of clay on the peds and in the pores results from clay accumulation (Bt). Soil structure may also develop in the B horizon with prismatic or columnar units and coating or stainings, significant amounts of exchangeable sodium, or other changes of structure from the parent material.

Some materials occurring in the B horizon may have formed in place from weathering processes rather than arriving there by *translocation*, or migration. In the humid tropics, these layers often develop to a considerable depth. Likewise, clay losses in an A horizon may be caused by destructive processes and not eluviation. Research to better understand erosion and deposition of clays between soil horizons is one of the challenges in modern soil science.

The combination of the A and Ae horizons and the B horizon is designated the **solum**, considered the true definable soil of the pedon. The A, Ae, and B horizons experience active soil processes (labelled in Figure 18.1).

Below the solum is the *C horizon* of weathered bedrock or weathered parent material. This zone is identified as *regolith* (although the term sometimes is used to include the solum as well). The C horizon is not much affected by soil processes in the solum and lies outside the biological influences experienced in the shallower horizons. Plant roots and soil microorganisms are rare in the C horizon. It lacks clay concentrations and generally is made up of carbonates, gypsum, or soluble salts, or of iron and silica, which form cemented soil structures. In dry climates, calcium carbonate commonly forms the cementing material of these hardened layers. In many glaciated parts of North America, the C horizon consists of glacial deposits, commonly till.

Soil Properties

Soils are complex and varied, as this section reveals. Observing a real soil profile will help you identify colour, texture, structure, and other soil properties. A good opportunity to observe soil profiles is at a construction site or excavation, or at a road cut along a highway. Manuals for describing, mapping, surveying, and analyzing soils can be found at the Agriculture and Agri-Food website (http://sis.agr.gc.ca/cansis/publications/index.html).

Soil Colour

Colour is important, for it sometimes suggests composition and chemical makeup. If you look at exposed soil, colour may be the most obvious trait. Among the many possible hues are the reds and yellows found in soils of New Brunswick and Prince Edward Island and in soils of the southeastern United States (high in iron

FIGURE 18.3 A Munsell Soil Color Chart page. A soil sample is viewed through the hole to match it with a colour on the chart. Hue, value, and chroma are the characteristics of colour assessed by this system. [Gretag Macbeth, Munsell Color.]

oxides); the blacks of the prairie soils in parts of southern Alberta and Saskatchewan and portions of the U.S. grain-growing regions and Ukraine (richly organic); and white-to-pale hues found in soils containing silicates and aluminum oxides. However, colour can be deceptive: Soils of high humus content are often dark, yet clays of warm–temperate and tropical regions with less than 3% organic content are some of the world's blackest soils.

To standardize colour descriptions, soil scientists describe a soil's colour by comparing it with a *Munsell Color Chart* (developed by artist and teacher Albert Munsell in 1913). These charts display 175 colours arranged by *hue* (the dominant spectral colour, such as red), *value* (degree of darkness or lightness), and *chroma* (purity and saturation of the colour, which increase with decreasing greyness). A Munsell notation identifies each colour by a name, so soil scientists can make worldwide comparisons of soil colour. Soil colour is checked against the chart at various depths within a pedon (Figure 18.3).

Soil Texture

Soil texture, perhaps a soil's most permanent attribute, refers to the mixture of sizes of its particles and the proportion of different sizes. Individual mineral particles are *soil separates*. All particles smaller in diameter than 2 mm, such as very coarse sand, are considered part of the soil. Larger particles, such as pebbles, gravel, or cobbles, may exist within the soil column but are not considered part of the soil. (Sands are graded from coarse to medium to fine, down to 0.05 mm; silt to 0.002 mm; and clay at less than 0.002 mm.)

Figure 18.4 is a *soil texture triangle* showing the relation of sand, silt, and clay concentrations in soil. Each corner of the triangle represents a soil consisting solely of the particle size noted (although rarely are true soils composed of a single separate). Every soil on Earth is defined somewhere in this triangle.

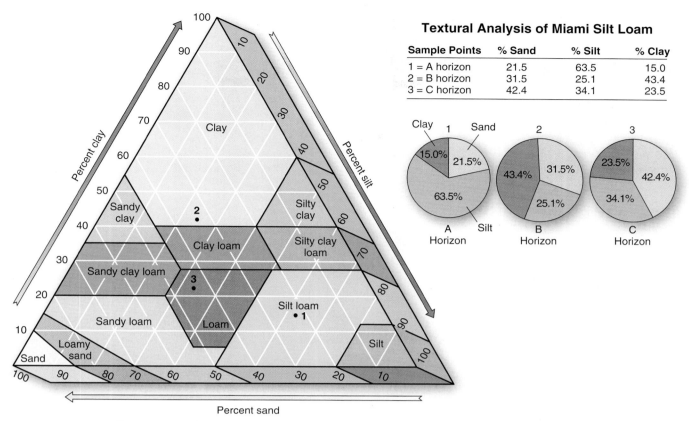

Textural Analysis of Miami Silt Loam

Sample Points	% Sand	% Silt	% Clay
1 = A horizon	21.5	63.5	15.0
2 = B horizon	31.5	25.1	43.4
3 = C horizon	42.4	34.1	23.5

FIGURE 18.4 Soil texture triangle.
Measures of the ratio of clay, silt, and sand determine soil texture. As an example, points 1 (horizon A),
2 (horizon B), and 3 (horizon C) designate samples taken at three different horizons in the Miami silt loam in
Indiana. Note the ratio of sand to silt to clay shown in the three pie graphs and table. [After USDA–NRCS, *Soil
Survey Manual*, Agricultural Handbook No. 18, p. 138 (1993).]

Figure 18.4 includes the common designation **loam**, which is a balanced mixture of sand, silt, and clay that is beneficial to plant growth. Farmers consider ideal a sandy loam with clay content below 30% (lower left) because of its water-holding characteristics and ease of cultivation. Soil texture is important in determining water-retention and water-transmission traits.

To see how the soil texture triangle works, consider a *Miami silt loam* soil type from Indiana. Samples from this soil type are plotted on the soil texture triangle as points 1, 2, and 3. A sample taken near the surface in the A horizon is recorded at point 1, in the B horizon at point 2, and in the C horizon at point 3. Textural analyses of these samples are summarized in the three pie graphs to the right of the triangle. Note that silt dominates the near-surface, clay the B horizon, and sand the C horizon. Soil survey manuals present guidelines for estimating soil texture by feel, a relatively accurate method when used by an experienced person. However, laboratory methods using graduated sieves and separation by mechanical analysis in water allow more precise measurements.

Soil Structure

Soil *texture* describes the size of soil particles, but soil *structure* refers to the *arrangement* of particles. Structure can partially modify the effects of soil texture. The smallest natural lump or cluster of particles is a *ped*. The shape of soil peds determines which of the structural types the soil exhibits: crumb or granular, platy, blocky, prismatic, or columnar (Figure 18.5).

Peds separate from each other along zones of weakness, creating voids, or pores, that are important for moisture storage and drainage. Rounded peds have more pore space between them and greater permeability than other shapes and are therefore better for plant growth than are blocky, prismatic, or platy peds, despite comparable fertility. Terms used to describe soil structure include fine, medium, or coarse. Adhesion among peds ranges from weak to strong.

Soil Consistence

In soil science, the term *consistence* is used to describe the consistency of a soil or cohesion of its particles.

FIGURE 18.5 Types of soil structure.
Structure is important because it controls drainage, rooting of plants, and how well the soil delivers nutrients to plants. The shape of individual peds, shown here, controls a soil's structure. [National Soil Survey Center, NRCS, USDA, Soil Survey Staff.]

Consistence is a product of texture (particle size) and structure (ped shape). Consistence reflects a soil's resistance to breaking and manipulation under varying moisture conditions:

- A *wet soil* is sticky between the thumb and forefinger, ranging from a little adherence to either finger to sticking to both fingers to stretching when the fingers are moved apart. *Plasticity*, the quality of being moldable, is roughly measured by rolling a piece of soil between your fingers and thumb to see whether it rolls into a thin strand.
- A *moist soil* is filled to about half of field capacity (the usable water capacity of soil), and its consistence grades from loose (noncoherent) to *friable* (easily pulverized) to firm (not crushable between thumb and forefinger).
- A *dry soil* is typically brittle and rigid, with consistence ranging from loose to soft to hard to extremely hard.

Soil particles are sometimes cemented together to some degree. Soils are described as weakly cemented, strongly cemented, or *indurated* (hardened). Calcium carbonate, silica, and oxides or salts of iron and aluminum all can serve as cementing agents. The cementation of soil

particles that occurs in various horizons is a function of consistence and may be continuous or discontinuous.

Soil Porosity

Soil porosity, permeability, and moisture storage were discussed in Chapter 9. Pores in the soil horizon control the movement of water—its intake, flow, and drainage—and air ventilation. Important porosity factors are pore *size*, pore *continuity* (whether pores are interconnected), pore *shape* (whether pores are spherical, irregular, or tubular), pore *orientation* (whether pore spaces are vertical, horizontal, or random), and pore *location* (whether pores are within or between soil peds).

Porosity is improved by the biotic actions of plant roots, animal activity such as the tunnelling of gophers or worms, and human intervention through soil manipulation (ploughing, adding humus or sand, or planting soil-building crops). Much of a farmer's soil preparation work before planting, and for the home gardener as well, is done to improve soil porosity.

Soil Moisture

Examining Figures 9.8 and 9.9 in Chapter 9 (soil moisture types and availability) will help you understand this section. Plants operate most efficiently when the soil is at *field capacity*, which is the maximum water availability for plant use after large pore spaces have drained of gravitational water. Soil type determines field capacity. The depth to which a plant sends its roots determines the amount of soil moisture to which the plant has access. If soil moisture is removed below field capacity, plants must exert increased energy to obtain available water. This moisture removal inefficiency worsens until the plant reaches its wilting point. Beyond this point, plants are unable to extract the water needed, and the result is death. Soil moisture regimes and their associated climate types shape the biotic and abiotic properties of the soil more than any other factor.

Soil Chemistry

Recall that soil pores may be filled with air, water, or a mixture of the two. Consequently, soil chemistry involves both air and water. The air within soil pores consists mostly of nitrogen, oxygen, and carbon dioxide. Nitrogen concentrations are about the same as in the atmosphere, but oxygen is less and carbon dioxide is greater because of ongoing respiration processes.

Water present in soil pores is the *soil solution*. It is the medium for chemical reactions in soil. This solution is critical to plants as the source of nutrients, and it is the foundation of *soil fertility*. Carbon dioxide combines with the water to produce carbonic acid, and various organic materials combine with the water to produce organic acids. These acids are then active participants in soil processes, as are dissolved alkali and salts.

To understand how the soil solution behaves, let us go through a quick chemistry review. An *ion* is an atom, or group of atoms, that carries an electrical charge (examples: Na^+, Cl^-, HCO_3^-). An ion has either a positive charge or a negative charge. For example, when NaCl (sodium chloride) dissolves in solution, it separates into two ions: Na^+, a *cation* (positively charged ion), and Cl^-, an *anion* (negatively charged ion). Some ions in soil carry single charges, whereas others carry double or even triple charges (e.g., sulphate, SO_4^{2-}; and aluminum, Al^{3+}).

Ions in soil are retained by **soil colloids**. These tiny particles of clay and organic material (humus) carry a negative electrical charge and consequently attract any positively charged ions in the soil (Figure 18.6). The positive ions, many metallic, are critical to plant growth. If it were not for the negatively charged soil colloids, the positive ions would be leached away in the soil solution and thus would be unavailable to plant roots.

Individual clay colloids are thin and platelike, with parallel surfaces that are negatively charged. Clay colloids are more chemically active than silt and sand particles but less active than organic colloids. Metallic cations attach to the surfaces of the colloids by *adsorption* (not *absorption*, which means "to enter"). Colloids can exchange cations with the soil solution, an ability called **cation-exchange capacity (CEC)**, which is the measure

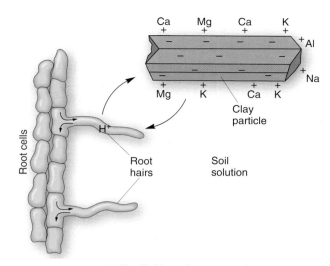

FIGURE 18.6 Soil colloids and cation-exchange capacity (CEC).
This typical soil colloid retains mineral ions by adsorption to its surface (opposite charges attract). This process holds the ions until they are absorbed by root hairs.

of soil fertility. A high CEC means that the soil colloids can store or exchange more cations from the soil solution, an indication of good soil fertility (unless there is a complicating factor, such as a soil that is too acid).

Therefore, **soil fertility** is the ability of soil to sustain plants. Soil is fertile when it contains organic substances and clay minerals that absorb water and adsorb certain elements needed by plants. Billions of dollars are expended to create fertile soil conditions, yet the future of Earth's most fertile soils is threatened because soil erosion is on the increase worldwide.

Soil Acidity and Alkalinity

A soil solution may contain significant hydrogen ions (H^+), the cations that stimulate acid formation. The result is a soil rich in hydrogen ions, or an *acid soil*. On the other hand, a soil high in base cations (calcium, magnesium, potassium, sodium) is a *basic* or *alkaline soil*. Such acidity or alkalinity is expressed on the pH scale (Figure 18.7).

Pure water is nearly neutral, with a pH of 7.0. Readings below 7.0 represent increasing acidity; readings above 7.0 indicate increasing alkalinity. Acidity usually is regarded as strong at 5.0 or lower on the pH scale, whereas 10.0 or above is considered strongly alkaline.

The major contributor to soil acidity in this modern era is acid precipitation (rain, snow, fog, or dry deposition). Acid rain actually has been measured below pH 2.0—an incredibly low value for natural precipitation, as acid as lemon juice. Increased acidity in the soil solution accelerates the chemical weathering of mineral nutrients and increases their depletion rates. Because most crops are sensitive to specific pH levels, acid soils below pH 6.0 require treatment to raise the pH. This soil treatment is

FIGURE 18.7 pH scale.
The pH scale measures acidity (lower pH)
and alkalinity (higher pH). (The complete pH scale ranges between 0 and 14.)

accomplished by the addition of bases in the form of minerals that are rich in base cations, usually lime (calcium
carbonate, $CaCO_3$).

Soil Formation Factors and Management

Soil is an open system involving physical inputs and
outputs. Soil-forming factors are both *passive* (parent
material, topography and relief, and time) and *dynamic*
(climate, biology, and human activities). These factors
work together as a system to form soil. The roles of these
factors are considered here and in the soil-order discussions that follow.

Natural Factors

Physical and chemical weathering of rocks in the upper
lithosphere provides the raw mineral ingredients for soil
formation. These rocks supply the parent materials, and
their composition, texture, and chemical nature help determine the type of soil that forms. Clay minerals are the
principal weathered by-products in soil.

Climate types correlate closely with soil types
worldwide. The moisture, evaporation, and temperature regimes of climates determine the chemical reactions, organic activity, and eluviation rates of soils. Not
only is the present climate important but many soils
exhibit the imprint of past climates, sometimes over
thousands of years. Most notable is the effect of glaciations. Among other contributions, glaciation produced
the loess soil materials that have been windblown thousands of kilometres to present locations (discussed in
Chapter 15).

Vegetation, animal, and bacterial activity determine
the organic content of soil, along with all that is living
in soil—algae, fungi, worms, and insects. The chemical
makeup of the vegetation contributes to the acidity or alkalinity of the soil solution. For example, broadleaf trees
tend to increase alkalinity, whereas needleleaf trees tend
to produce higher acidity. Thus, when civilization moves
into new areas and alters the natural vegetation by logging
or ploughing, the affected soils are likewise altered, often
permanently.

Topography also affects soil formation. Slopes that are
too steep cannot have full soil development because gravity and erosional processes remove materials. Lands that
are nearly level inhibit soil drainage and can become waterlogged. The compass orientation of slopes is important
because it controls exposure to sunlight. In the Northern
Hemisphere, a south-facing slope is warmer overall
through the year because it receives direct insolation.
Water-balance relations are affected because north-facing
slopes are colder, causing slower snowmelt and a lower
evaporation rate, providing more moisture for plants than
is available on south-facing slopes, which tend to dry faster.

All of the identified natural factors in soil development
(parent material, climate, biological activity, landforms,
and topography) require *time* to operate. Over geologic
time, plate tectonics has redistributed landscapes and thus
subjected soil-forming processes to diverse conditions.

The Human Factor

Human intervention has a major impact on soils. Millennia
ago, farmers in most cultures learned to plant slopes "on
the contour"—to make rows or mounds around a slope at
the same elevation, not vertically up and down the slope.
Planting on the contour creates a terraced pattern that
prevents water from flowing straight down the slope and
thus reduces soil erosion. Farmers often planted and harvested floodplains, while living on higher ground nearby.
Floods were celebrated as blessings that brought water,
nutrients, and more soil to the land. Society is drifting
away from these commonsense strategies.

A few centimetres' thickness of prime farmland soil
may require *500 years* to mature. Yet this same thickness
is being lost annually through soil erosion when the soil-
holding vegetation is removed and the land is ploughed,
regardless of topography. Flood control structures block
sediments and nutrients from replenishing floodplain soils,
leading to additional soil losses. Over the same period,
exposed soils may be completely leached of needed cations, thereby losing fertility.

Unlike living species, soils do not reproduce, nor can
they be re-created. Some 35% of farmlands are losing soil
faster than it can form—a loss exceeding 23 billion metric
tonnes (25 billion tons) per year. Soil depletion and loss
are at record levels from Iowa to China, Peru to Ethiopia,

and the Middle East to the Americas. The impact on society is potentially disastrous as population and food demands increase.

Soil erosion can be compensated for in the short run by using more fertilizer, increasing irrigation, and planting higher-yielding strains. But the potential yield from prime agricultural land will drop by as much as 20% over the next 20 years if only moderate erosion continues. One study tabulated the market value of lost nutrients and other variables in the most comprehensive soil-erosion study to date. The sum of direct damage (to agricultural land) and indirect damage (to streams, society's infrastructure, and human health) was estimated at more than $25 billion a year in the United States and hundreds of billions of dollars worldwide. Of course, this is a controversial assessment in the agricultural industry. The cost to bring erosion under control in the United States is estimated at approximately $8.5 billion, or about 30 cents compared to every dollar of damage and loss. In Canada as well, erosion prevention is cheaper than the cost of losses from soil erosion. Figure 18.8 maps regions of soil loss. An article by scientist David Montgomery well summarizes our predicament:

> Recent compilations of data from around the world show that soil erosion under conventional agriculture exceeds both rates of soil production and geological erosion rates by several orders of magnitude. Consequently, modern agriculture—and therefore global society—faces a fundamental question over the upcoming centuries. Can an agricultural system capable of feeding a growing population safeguard both soil fertility and the soil itself?[2]

‖ CRITICAL THINKING 18.1

Soil Losses—What to Do?

Given the information you just read in "The Human Factor," break down the issue of soil loss into the forcing causes, impacts produced, and possible actions to slow soil degradation and loss. Based on this analysis, suggest possible scales of response, moving from individual to local to regional to provincial and finally to national in scope. Given the problem and the scale at which you determine solutions are best implemented, what actions do you suggest to reverse the situation of soil degradation here and abroad?

Soil Classification

Classification of soils is complicated by the continuing interaction of physical properties and processes just discussed. This interaction creates thousands of distinct soils, with well over 15 000 soil series identified in Canada and the United States alone. Not surprisingly, different classification systems are in use worldwide. Canada, the United States, the United Kingdom, Germany, Australia, Russia, and the United Nations Food and Agricultural Organization each have their own soil classification system. Each system reflects the environment of its country. For example, the National Soil Survey Committee of Canada developed a system suited to its great expanses of boreal forest, tundra, and cool climatic regimes. The remainder of this chapter will outline the Canadian System of Soil Classification (CSSC). Appendix B contains information about the U.S. Soil Taxonomy system for classifying soils. For information on tropical soils not in the CSSC, refer to the Soil Taxonomy in Appendix B.

Pedogenic Regimes Soil-forming processes are linked to climatic regions, a connection that serves as the basis for **pedogenic regimes**. Before the present soil classification systems in Canada and the United States, these pedogenic regimes were used to describe soils. Although each pedogenic process may be active in several soil orders and in different climates, not all are present in Canada, such as the lateritic processes in the tropics. Such climate-based regimes are convenient for relating climate and soil processes. However, both the Canadian and U.S. soil classification systems *recognize the great uncertainty and inconsistency in basing soil classification on such climatic variables.* Aspects of several pedogenic processes are discussed with appropriate soil orders:

- **Laterization:** a leaching process active in humid and warm climates (in the tropics and subtropics, but not in Canada);
- **Salinization:** a process that concentrates salts in soils in climates with excessive potential evapotranspiration (PE) rates, discussed with the Solonetzic order

[2]D. R. Montgomery, "Is agriculture eroding civilization's foundation?" *GSA Today,* October 2007, p. 4.

 GEO REPORT 18.1 *Slipping through Our Fingers*

About half of all cropland in Canada and the United States is experiencing excessive rates of soil erosion—these countries are two of the few that monitor loss of topsoil. The U.S. General Accounting Office estimates that from 1.2 to 2.0 million hectares of prime farmland are lost each year in the United States through mismanagement or conversion to nonagricultural uses. Worldwide, about one-third of potentially farmable land has been lost to erosion, much of that in the past 40 years. The Canadian Environmental Advisory Council estimated that the organic content of cultivated prairie soils has declined by as much as 40% compared with noncultivated native soils. In Ontario and Québec, losses of organic content increased to as much as 50%, and losses are even higher in the Atlantic Provinces, which were naturally low in organic content before cultivation. The causes for degraded soils, in order of severity, include: overgrazing, vegetation removal, agricultural activities, overexploitation, and industrial and bioindustrial use.

(a)

(b)

FIGURE 18.8 Soil degradation.
(a) Approximately 1.2 billion hectares of Earth's soils suffer degradation through erosion caused by human misuse and abuse. (b) An example of soil loss through sheet and gully erosion on a northwest Iowa farm. One millimetre of soil lost from a hectare weighs about 11 metric tons. [(a) *A Global Assessment of Soil Degradation*, adapted from UNEP, International Soil Reference and Information Centre, "Map of Status of Human-Induced Soil Degradation," Nairobi, Kenya; (b) USDA/NRCS.]

- **Calcification:** a process that produces an illuviated accumulation of calcium carbonates in continental climates, discussed with the Chernozemic order (Figure 18.11);
- **Podzolization:** a process of soil acidification associated with forest soils in cool climates, discussed with the Podzolic order (Figure 18.19);
- **Gleysation:** a process that includes an accumulation of humus and a thick, water-saturated grey layer of clay beneath, and is usually found in cold, wet climates and poor drainage conditions. It is discussed with the Gleysolic order.

The Canadian System of Soil Classification (CSSC)

Canadian efforts at soil classification began in 1914 with the partial mapping of Ontario's soils by A.J. Galbraith. Efforts to develop a taxonomic system spread countrywide,

anchored by universities in each province. Regional differences in soil classification emerged, further confused by a lack of specific soil details. By 1936, only 1.7% of Canadian soil (15 million hectares) had been surveyed.

Canadian scientists needed a taxonomic system based on observable and measurable properties in soils specific to Canada. This meant a departure from Marbut's 1938 U.S. classification. Canada's first taxonomic system, the **Canadian System of Soil Classification (CSSC)**, was introduced in 1955, splitting away from the soil classification effort in the United States. Classification work progressed through the Canada Soil Survey Committee after 1970 and was replaced by the Expert Committee on Soil Survey in 1978, all under the purview of Agriculture Canada. This committee worked on interpretation, mapping systems, soil degradation, and soil classification and produced the second edition of the *Canadian System of Soil Classification* in 1987. Work continued with the classification of Vertisols and further development of the CSSC. The third edition of the *Canadian System of Soil Classification* was published in 1998.

The Canadian System of Soil Classification provides taxa for all soils presently recognized in Canada and is adapted to Canada's expanses of forest, tundra, prairie, frozen ground, and colder climates. As in the U.S. Soil Taxonomy system, the CSSC classifications are based on observable and measurable properties found in real soils that may result from the interactions of genetic processes rather than idealized soils. The system is flexible in that its framework can accept new findings and information in step with progressive developments in the soil sciences.

Categories of Classification in the CSSC

Categorical levels are at the heart of a taxonomic system. These categories are based on soil profile properties organized at five levels, nested in a hierarchical pattern to permit generalization at several levels of detail. Each level is referred to as a category of classification. The levels in the CSSC are briefly described here, as adapted from the third edition of *The Canadian Soil Classification System*.

- *Order:* Each of 10 soil orders has pedon properties that reflect the soil environment and effects of active soil-forming processes.
- *Great group:* Subdivisions of each order reflect differences in the dominant processes or other major contributing processes. As an example, in Luvic Gleysols (great group name followed by order) the dominant process is gleying—reduction of iron and other minerals—resulting from poor drainage under either grass or forest cover with Aeg and Btg horizons (see Table 18.2).
- *Subgroup:* Subgroups are differentiated by the content and arrangement of horizons that indicate the relation of the soil to a great group or order or the subtle transition toward soils of another order.
- *Family:* This is a subdivision of a subgroup. Parent material characteristics such as texture and mineralogy, soil climatic factors, and soil reactions are important.
- *Series:* Detailed features of the pedon differentiate subdivisions of the family—the essential soil-sampling unit. Pedon horizons fall within a narrow range of colour, texture, structure, consistence, porosity, moisture, chemical reaction, thickness, and composition.

Soil Horizons in the CSSC

Soil horizons are named and standardized as diagnostic in the classification process. Several mineral and organic horizons and layers are used in the CSSC. Three mineral horizons are recognized by capital letter designation,

followed by lowercase suffixes for further description. Principal soil-mineral horizons and suffixes are presented in Table 18.1.

Four organic horizons are identified in the Canadian classification system. O is further defined through subhorizon designations. Note that for organic soils, such layers are identified as *tiers*. These organic horizons are detailed in Table 18.2.

The 10 Soil Orders of the CSSC

At the heart of the Canadian System of Soil Classification are 10 general orders. These orders were developed specifically for soils in Canada and are presented here with their associated great groups and subgroups. The 10 orders of the CSSC, and related great groups, are summarized below with a general description of properties, related great groups, an estimated percentage of land area for the soil order, a fertility assessment, and any applicable soil taxonomy equivalent. Figure 18.9 is a generalized map of the soil landscapes of Canada. This map illustrates the great variation of soils across the country.

The *Soil Landscapes of Canada* (SLC) site at http://sis.agr.gc.ca/cansis/ provides a useful assortment of landscape and soil profile photographs, arranged geographically across Canada from east to west. The site also has an interactive GIS online mapping application. Version 2.2 SLC Component Mapping (December 1996) is operational and involves the CSSC and the Canadian Land Resource Network (CLRN). The component mapping involves a GIS model consisting of layers that include the major characteristics of soil and land for all of Canada. You can select a spatial area and a variety of attributes to display on the map (drainage class, soil type, rooting depth, local surface form, slope, and vegetation cover, among others).

Brunisolic Order The **Brunisolic** order is the first order alphabetically. These soils are sufficiently developed to exclude them from the Regosolic order, but the degree of development of soil horizons is so low that these horizons are differentiated from other orders (Figure 18.10). These soils form under mixed forest and have brownish Bm horizons, although various colours are possible. Brunisolic soils can also develop under shrubs and grassland. The B horizon is the most diagnostic feature with Bm, Bfj, thin Bf, or Btj horizons. Brunisols develop under well- to imperfectly drained conditions and lack the Podzolic B horizon of the Podzols, although Brunisols are surrounded by Podzolic soils in the St. Lawrence Lowlands. The soils of this order are rated as medium and variable in fertility and account for 14% of the surface area of Canada. The great groups of the Brunisolic order include Melanic Brunisol, Eutric Brunisol, Sombric Brunisol, and Dystric Brunisol. There are 18 subgroups within this order.

Some Brunisolic and Chernozemic soils and other soil orders are highly calcareous. *Calcification*

TABLE 18.1   Three Mineral Horizons and Mineral Horizon Suffixes Used in the CSSC

Symbol	Mineral Horizon Description
A	Forms at or near the surface; experiences *eluviation*, or leaching, of finer particles or minerals. Several subdivisions are identified, with the surface usually darker and richer in organic content than lower horizons (*Ah*); or a paler, lighter zone below that reflects removal of organic matter with clays and oxides of aluminum and iron leached (removed) to lower horizons (*Ae*).
B	Experiences *illuviation*, a depositional process, as demonstrated by accumulations of clays (*Bt*), sesqui-oxides of aluminum or iron, and possibly an enrichment of organic debris (*Bh*), and the development of soil structure. Colouration is important in denoting whether hydrolysis, reduction, or oxidation processes are operational for the assignment of a descriptive suffix.
C	Exhibits little effect from pedogenic processes operating in the *A* and *B* horizons, except the process of gleysation associated with poor drainage and the reduction of iron, denoted (*Cg*), and the accumulation of calcium and magnesium carbonates (*Cca*) and more soluble salts (*Cs*) and (*Csa*).

Symbol	Horizon Suffix Description
b	A buried soil horizon.
c	Irreversible cementation of a pedogenic horizon; e.g., cemented by $CaCO_3$.
ca	Lime accumulation of at least 10 cm thickness that exceeds in concentration that of the unenriched parent material by at least 5%.
cc	Irreversible cemented concretions, typically in pellet form.
e	Used with *A* mineral horizons (*Ae*) to denote eluviation of clay, Fe, Al, or organic matter.
f	Enriched principally with illuvial iron and aluminum combined with organic matter, reddish in upper portions and yellowish at depth, determined through specific criteria. Used with *B* horizons alone.
g	Grey to blue colours, prominent mottling, or both, produced by intense chemical reduction. Various applications to *A*, *B*, and *C* horizons.
h	Enriched with organic matter: accumulation in place or biological mixing (*Ah*) or subsurface enrichment through illuviation (*Bh*).
j	A modifier suffix for *e, f, g, n*, and *t* to denote limited change or failure to meet specified criteria denoted by that letter.
k	Presence of carbonates as indicated by visible effervescence with dilute hydrochloric acid (HCl).
m	Used with *B* horizons slightly altered by hydrolysis, oxidation, or solution, or all three to denote a change in colour or structure.
n	Accumulation of exchangeable calcium (Ca) in ratio to exchangeable sodium (Na) that is 10 or less, with the following characteristics: prismatic or columnar structure, dark coatings on ped surfaces, and hard consistence when dry. Used with *B* horizons alone.
p	*A* or *O* horizons disturbed by cultivation, logging, and habitation. May be used when ploughing intrudes on previous *B* horizons.
s	Presence of salts, including gypsum, visible as crystals or veins or surface crusts of salt crystals, and by lowered crop yields. Usually with *C* but may appear with any horizon and lowercase suffixes.
sa	A secondary enrichment of salts more soluble than Ca or Mg carbonates, exceeding unenriched parent material, in a horizon at least 10 cm thick.
t	Illuvial enrichment of the *B* horizon with silicate clay that must exceed overlying *Ae* horizon by 3% to 20%, depending on the clay content of the *Ae* horizon.
u	Markedly disrupted by physical or faunal processes other than cryoturbation.
x	Fragipan formation—a loamy subsurface horizon of high bulk density and very low organic content. When dry, it has a hard consistence and seems to be cemented.
y	Affected by cryoturbation (frost action) with disrupted and broken horizons and incorporation of materials from other horizons. Application to *A*, *B*, and *C* horizons and in combination with other suffixes.
z	A frozen layer.

(Figure 18.11, page 569) is the accumulation of calcium carbonate or magnesium carbonate in the B and C horizons. Calcification by calcium carbonate ($CaCO_3$), among others, forms a diagnostic subsurface horizon along the boundary between dry and humid climates.

These deposits harden or cement to become *caliche*, which can form in the southern prairies.

Chernozemic Order The **Chernozemic** order includes well- to imperfectly drained soils of the steppe–grassland–

TABLE 18.2 Four Organic Horizons Used in the CSSC

Symbol	Description
O	Organic materials, mainly mosses, rushes, and woody materials
L	Mainly discernible leaves, twigs, and woody materials
F	Partially decomposed, somewhat recognizable **L** materials
H	Indiscernible organic materials

O is further defined through subhorizon designations:

Of	Readily identifiable fibric materials
Om	Mesic materials of intermediate decomposition
Oh	Humic material at an advanced stage of decomposition—low fibre, high bulk density

FIGURE 18.9 Generalized soils of Canada.
Distribution of the 10 soil orders of Canada. [Thematic Soil Maps of Canada: Soil Order, http://sis.agr.gc.ca/cansis/nsdb/slc/intro.html, Agriculture and Agri-Food Canada ©, 2010. Reproduced with the permission of the Minister of Public Works and Government Services, 2012.]

forest transition in southern Alberta; Saskatchewan; Manitoba; Okanagan Valley, British Columbia, and Palouse Prairie, British Columbia, and accounts for 4% of the solid surface area of Canada. The surface horizons are darkened by organic matter accumulation that results from decomposition of grasses and forbs in the vegetation cover (Figure 18.12, page 570). Most soils are frozen in winter and dry in summer with a mean annual soil temperature greater than or equal to 0°C, but usually less than 5.5°C.

Chernozemic soils have high fertility, especially for growing wheat, but can be subject to salinization.

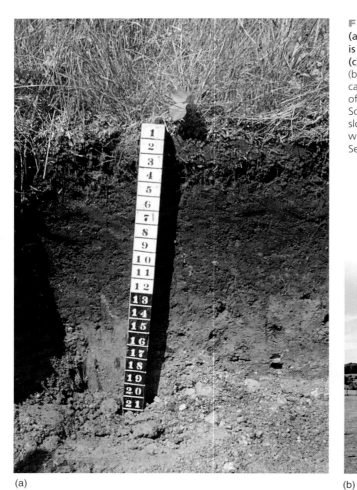

(a)

FIGURE 18.10 Brunisolic order.

(a) Soil profile from southern Ontario. (b) Hay and pastureland that is typical of the Melanic Brunisolic landscape in southern Ontario. (c) Distribution of Brunisolic order in Canada. [Photos by (a) and (b) Courtesy of Agriculture and Agri-Food Canada, http://sis2.agr.gc.ca/cansis/images/index.html. Reproduced with the permission of the Minister of Public Works and Government Services Canada, 2012; (c) Thematic Soil Maps of Canada: Brunisolic order, http://sis.agr.gc.ca/cansis/nsdb/slc/intro.html, Agriculture and Agri-Food Canada ©, 2010. Reproduced with the permission of the Minister of Public Works and Government Services, 2012.]

(b)

Brunisolic Order Map of Canada

Sombric Brunisol

Eutric Brunisol

Dystric Brunisol

Melanic Brunisol

0   500
Kilometres

(c)

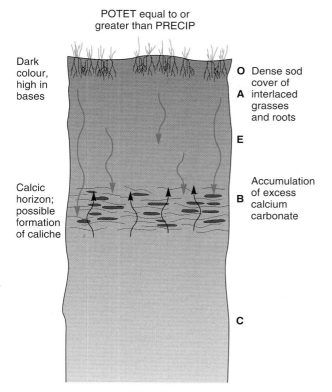

Dark colour, high in bases

POTET equal to or greater than PRECIP

O Dense sod
A cover of interlaced grasses and roots

E

Calcic horizon; possible formation of caliche

B Accumulation of excess calcium carbonate

C

FIGURE 18.11 Calcification in soil.
The calcification process in drier Brunisolic soils (in the U.S. the Aridisol/Mollisol soils) occurs in climatic regimes that have potential evapotranspiration equal to or greater than precipitation.

Salinization, discussed below in the Solonetzic order, creates deposits that appear as subsurface salty horizons, which will damage or kill plants when the horizons occur near the root zone. This process is especially of concern where soils are irrigated. Focus Study 18.1 (pages 572–73) outlines the problems associated with salinization and the buildup of toxic materials in the soil. The great groups of the Chernozemic order are Brown Chernozem, Dark Brown Chernozem, Black Chernozem, and Dark Grey Chernozem. There are 38 subgroups within this order. Figure 18.13 (page 571) shows the transition between great groups within the Chernozem order, principally in response to climate differences.

Cryosolic Order The **Cryosolic** order dominates the northern third of Canada, with permafrost closer to the surface and composed of mineral and organic soil deposits. Generally, Cryosolic soils are found north of the treeline, in fine-textured soils in the subarctic forest, or in some organic soils in Boreal forests (Figure 18.14, page 574). The Ah horizon is lacking or thin. Cryoturbation (frost action) is common and is often denoted by patterned ground circles, polygons, and stripes. Cryosols have a mean annual temperature less than or equal to 0°C. The subgroups of this order are based on the degree of

cryoturbation and the nature of the mineral or organic soil material. Fertility ratings are not applicable to these soils that cover 28% of Canada's land area. The great groups are Turbic Cryosol, Static Cryosol, and Organic Cryosol, and there are 15 subgroups in this order.

Gleysolic Order *Gleysation* is a soil-forming process in poorly drained conditions where organic matter accumulates in the upper soil layers and mottling occurs in the lower layers resulting from reduction of iron and other elements. The **Gleysolic** order of soils is defined on the basis of colour and mottling that results from chronic reducing conditions inherent in poorly drained mineral soils under wet conditions. A high water table and long periods of water saturation are common to these soils. Gleysolic soils are spotty in areal distribution, appearing within other soil orders, occasionally being the dominant soil of an area (Figure 18.15, page 575), and account for 3% of the land surface. A diagnostic Bg horizon is present in these soils that are rated as high to medium in fertility. The great groups of this order are Luvic Gleysol, Humic Gleysol, and Gleysol. There are 13 subgroups.

Luvisolic Order *Eluviation-illuviation* processes produce a light-coloured Ae horizon and a diagnostic Bt horizon. Soils of this order develop beneath the mixed deciduous–coniferous forests. There are major occurrences of **Luvisolic** soils in the St. Lawrence Lowlands. Luvisolic soils occur from the zone of permafrost to the southern extremity of Ontario and from Newfoundland to British Columbia. The greatest areal extent is in the northern Interior Plains under deciduous, mixed, and coniferous forest (Figure 18.16, page 576). The fertility rating is high for these soils that cover 7% of the land surface. The great groups of the Luvisolic order are Gray Brown Luvisol and Gray Luvisol and include 18 subgroups.

Organic Order Soils of the **Organic** order are composed largely of organic materials. These include peat, bog, and muck soils and are commonly saturated with water for prolonged periods of time (Figure 18.17, page 577). Organic soils are widespread and are associated with poorly to very poorly drained depressions, but can be found under upland forest environments (Folisols) and account for 9% of the land surface. To qualify as organic, these soils must contain greater than 17% organic carbon and exceed 30% organic matter by weight overall. Organic soils are rated as high to medium in fertility depending upon drainage and the available nutrients. The great groups contained in this order are Fibrisol, Mesisol, Humisol, and Folisol and include 31 subgroups.

Podzolic Order **Podzolic** soils develop beneath coniferous forests and sometimes heath vegetation and result from leaching of the overlying horizons in moist, cool to cold climates (Figure 18.18, page 578). These soils result from

(a)

(b)

FIGURE 18.12 Chernozemic order.

(a) Soil profile from southern Prairies. Chernozemic landscape images associated with dry grasslands can be seen in Figure 18.13. (b) Distribution of the Chernozemic order in Canada. [(a) Courtesy of Agriculture and Agri-Food Canada, http://sis2.agr.gc.ca/cansis/images/index.html. Reproduced with the permission of the Minister of Public Works and Government Services Canada, 2012; (b) Thematic Soil Maps of Canada: Chernozemic Order, http://sis.agr.gc.ca/cansis/nsdb/slc/intro.html, Agriculture and Agri-Food Canada ©, 2010. Reproduced with the permission of the Minister of Public Works and Government Services, 2012.]

podzolization, a soil-forming process in which a highly leached soil with strong surface acidity develops in cool, moist climates (Figure 18.19, page 579). The Boreal forest that encircles the globe in northern latitudes is largely underlain by Podzolic soils. Iron, aluminum, and organic matter form the L, F, and H horizons and are redeposited in the Podzolic B horizon. A diagnostic Bh, Bhf, or Bf horizon is present depending upon the great group. Podzolic soils dominate in western British Columbia, Ontario, Québec, and Atlantic Canada and account for

FIGURE 18.13 **Soils of the southern Prairies.**
(a) Brown Chernozemic soils in the west, Dark Brown Chernozemic in the central portions, and Black Cherno-zemic in the east—a soil continuum in the southern Canadian Prairies. (b) Brown Chernozemic soil landscape—soils developed in the short grass prairie of the southwestern Prairies in Alberta and Saskatchewan. Photo from south-central Saskatchewan shows typical crops. (c) Black Chernozem landscape—soils are typical of the mixed to tall grass prairie found in eastern Saskatchewan and southern Manitoba. [(a) Illustration based on N. C. Brady, *The Nature and Properties of Soils*, 10th ed., © 1990 by Macmillan Publishing Company; photos (b) and (c) Courtesy of Agriculture and Agri-Food Canada, http://sis2.agr.gc.ca/cansis/images/index.html. Reproduced with the permission of the Minister of Public Works and Government Services Canada, 2012.]

most of the agricultural surface cover in Canada, 14% of the total land area. The fertility rating for Podzolic soils is low to medium depending on acidity. The great groups in the Podzolic order are Humic, Ferro-humic Podzol, and Humo-ferric Podzol and include 25 subgroups.

Regosolic Order Soils of the **Regosolic** order are weakly developed as a result of a number of contributing factors that include young materials, fresh alluvial deposits, material instability, mass-wasted slopes, and dry, cold cli-matic conditions. Regosolic soils lack Solonetzic, illuvial,

Selenium Concentration in Soils: The Death of Kesterson

About 95% of the irrigated acreage in Canada and the United States lies west of the 98th meridian, a region that is increasingly troubled with salinization and waterlogging problems. Drainage of agricultural wastewater poses a particular problem in semiarid and arid lands, where river discharge is inadequate to dilute and remove field runoff. Fields are often purposely overwatered to keep salts away from the effective rooting depth of the crops. One solution is to place field drains beneath the soil to collect gravitational water (Figure 18.1.1). But agricultural drain water must go somewhere, and for the San Joaquin Valley of central California, this problem triggered a 25-year controversy surrounding toxic levels of selenium in the wetland ecosystem of Kesterson Reservoir.

California's western San Joaquin Valley is one of at least nine sites in the western United States experiencing contamination from increasing selenium concentrations. Selenium is a trace element that occurs naturally in bedrock, particularly Cretaceous shales found throughout the western United States. Toxic effects

FIGURE 18.1.1 Fields drain into canals. Soil drainage canal collects contaminated water from field drains and directs it into the Salton Sea. Such soil-moisture tile drains and collection channels are used in the San Joaquin Valley. [Robert Christopherson.]

of selenium were reported during the 1980s in some domestic animals grazing on grasses grown in selenium-rich soils in the Great Plains. In California, the coastal mountain ranges are a significant source region for selenium. As parent materials weather, selenium-rich alluvium washes into valleys, forming Solonetzic soils (aridisols in the US Taxonomy) that become productive with the addition of irrigation water. Selenium then becomes concentrated by evaporation in farmlands

and may become mobilized by irrigation drainage into wetlands where it bioaccumulates to toxic levels.

Central California's potential drain outlets for agricultural wastewater are limited. Yet by the late 1970s a drain about 130 kilometres long was built in the western San Joaquin Valley, without an outlet or the completion of a formal plan. Large-scale irrigation of corporate-owned farms continued, supplying the field drains with salty, selenium-laden runoff that made its way to the Kesterson National Wildlife Refuge in the northern portion of the San Joaquin Valley east of San Francisco. The unfinished drain abruptly stopped at the boundary to the refuge (Figure 18.1.2).

The selenium-tainted drainage took only three years to contaminate the wildlife refuge, which was officially declared a toxic waste site. Selenium was first taken in by aquatic life forms (e.g., marsh plants, plankton, and insects) and then made its way up the food chain and into the diets of higher life forms in the refuge. According to U.S. Fish and Wildlife Service scientists, the toxicity causes genetic abnormalities and death in wildlife, including all varieties of birds that nested

---

or Podzolic B horizons (Figure 18.20, page 580), and do not exist where permafrost is within 1 m of the surface or within 2 m of cryoturbated soil. Regosolic soils may have L, F, H, or O horizons or a thin Ah horizon (less than 10 cm thick). Regosolic soils, which account for 2% of the land surface, dominate in the Northwest Territories and northern Yukon, and are rated as low (variable) in fertility. There are two great groups in the Regosolic order—Regosol and Humic Regosol. These contain eight subgroups.

Solonetzic Order   **Solonetzic** soils are associated with saline or alkaline. These well- to imperfectly-drained soils develop under grasses in semiarid to subhumid climates and have B horizons that are very hard when dry and swell to a sticky mass of very low permeability when wet. Solonetzic soils, existing in limited areas of central and north-central Alberta (Figure 18.21, page 581), account for only 1% of Canada's surface area and are rated as having variable fertility. Solonetzic soils differ from saline

soils in that the bedrock under Solonetzic soils is saline or alkaline and is quite close to the surface. Because of imperfect drainage, salts are distributed throughout Solonetzic soils and can occur over wide areas. These soils were originally called blowout soils and have a hardened layer close to the surface called a hardpan that prevents the free flow of water in the soil and restricts root growth. The three great groups of the Solonetzic order—Solonetz, Solodized Solonetz, and Solod—contain 27 subgroups.

Salinization results from excessive potential evapotranspiration rates in deserts and semiarid regions. Salts dissolved in soil water migrate to surface horizons, which will damage or kill plants when the horizons occur near the root zone. The salt accumulation in Figure 18.21b is an example of this process. Under such semiarid conditions, commercial evaporite mineral deposits can develop (Figure 18.22, page 581).

Salinization complicates farming in these drier lands. The introduction of irrigation water may either waterlog at Kesterson; approximately 90% of the exposed birds perished or were injured. Because this refuge was a major migration flyway and stopover point for birds from throughout the Western Hemisphere, its contamination also violated several multinational wildlife protection treaties.

The field drains were sealed and removed in 1986, following a court order that forced the federal government to uphold existing laws. Irrigation water then immediately began backing up in the corporate farmlands, producing both water logging and selenium contamination. The Kesterson Unit became part of the San Luis National Wildlife Refuge—and selenium control and restoration became a priority.

Frustrated, large-scale corporate agricultural interests pressured the federal government to finish the drain, either to San Francisco Bay or to the ocean. In 1996, the Grasslands Bypass Project was implemented by the U.S. Bureau of Reclamation to prevent the discharge of agricultural drainage water into wetlands and wildlife refuges of central California. Thus, agricultural drain water now moves through the old San Luis Drain to Mud Slough, a natural waterway through the

FIGURE 18.1.2 Kesterson locator map.
The source of selenium is in the Coast Ranges; surface runoff delivers this element over thousands of years to the soils of the region. The agricultural drains complete the delivery systems to the refuge. [USGS.]

San Luis National Wildlife Refuge, and then on to the San Joaquin River, the San Joaquin–Sacramento delta, and eventually San Francisco Bay. Initially, selenium levels increased in those channels, although fluctuations downward in concentrations were noted as well. Biological monitoring continues.

There are nine such threatened sites in the western United States; Kesterson was simply the first of these to fail from contamination. Such damage to a wildlife refuge presents a real warning to human populations—remember where we are, at the top of the food chain.

poorly drained soils or lead to salinization. Nonetheless, vegetation does grow where soils are well drained and low in salt content. Focus Study 18.1 discusses the battle between salinization and waterlogging in irrigated lands in California.

Vertisolic Order Vertisolic soils occur in heavy-textured material that is high in clay content (≥ 60% clay), especially smectite, a shrinking and swelling clay. These soils have little development of horizons, and are marked by slickensides (a smooth, polished rock surface) and severe disruption. The shrinking and swelling of the clays resulting from wetting and drying cycles are strong enough to groove and polish surfaces along internal shear planes in the soil and prevent horizons from fully developing. However, Vertisolic soils may have an A horizon similar to Chernozemic soils, or may have features similar to Gleysolic soils. Vertisolic soils occur primarily in the cool, subarid to subhumid grassland portion of the Interior

Plains of western Canada (Figure 18.23, page 582) and account for just over 0.28% of the land area. This order may also occur to a more minor extent in valleys of the Cordilleran Region, in parts of the South Boreal Region, and in the cool temperate regions of central Canada. The two great groups of the Vertisolic order are Vertisol and Humic Vertisol, and these contain six subgroups.

CSSC and Worldwide Soil Taxonomy

Numerous systems of soil taxonomy exist in many countries throughout the world. The Canadian System of Soil Classification was designed to classify the soils that exist in Canada, whether or not the soils are likely to be cultivated. The CSSC system was not designed to be a comprehensive system to classify the world's soils. Other systems are more useful in the countries where the systems were developed. The FAO–UNESCO Soil Map of the World is helpful for correlating the different

(a)

(b)

Cryosolic Order Map of Canada

Static Cryosol

Turbic Cryosol

Organic Cryosol

0   500
Kilometres

(c)

(d)

FIGURE 18.14 Cryosolic order.
(a) Soil profile of Turbic Cryosolic soil from Northwest Territories. (b) Turbic Cryosolic landscape in Northwest Territories in which patches of soil support vegetation growth. (c) Distribution of Cryosolic order in Canada. (d) Turning over the upper organic layer exposes the fibrous organic content and slow decomposition; permafrost is just below this layer that briefly thaws in summer in the Arctic. [Photos (a) and (b) Courtesy of Agriculture and Agri-Food Canada, http://sis2.agr.gc.ca/cansis/images/index.html. Reproduced with the permission of the Minister of Public Works and Government Services Canada, 2012; (c) Thematic Soil Maps of Canada: Cryosolic Order, http://sis.agr.gc.ca/cansis/nsdb/slc/intro.html, Agriculture and Agri-Food Canada ©, 2010. Reproduced with the permission of the Minister of Public Works and Government Services, 2012; (d) Bobbé Christopherson.]

soil classifications in use. (See http://www.itc.nl/~rossiter/research/rsrch_ss_class.html#FAO.)

Perhaps the closest to a comprehensive system is the Soil Taxonomy of the Natural Resources Conservation Service (NRCS) in the United States, a system under development since 1951. The Soil Taxonomy is of major influence on the design and development of the Canadian system and is presented and mapped in Appendix B. Table 18.3 on page 579 presents the approximate equivalents of the soil orders and great groups in the Canadian system with the FAO-UNESCO system and the U.S. system (also, see Figure B.2). This table is

(a)

(b)

Gleysolic Order Map of Canada

■ Gleysolic Order

0   500
Kilometres

(c)

FIGURE 18.15 Gleysolic order.
(a) Soil profile of Gleysol from Atlantic Canada. (b) Poorly drained soils of the Gleysolic landscape in Atlantic
Canada are often used for forage crops. These soils are highly fertile when drainage is improved. (c) Distribution
of Gleysolic order in Canada. [Photos (a) and (b) Courtesy of Agriculture and Agri-Food Canada, http://sis2.agr.gc.ca/cansis/
images/index.html. Reproduced with the permission of the Minister of Public Works and Government Services Canada, 2012;
(c) Thematic Soil Maps of Canada: Gleysolic Order, http://sis.agr.gc.ca/cansis/nsdb/slc/intro.html, Agriculture and Agri-Food
Canada ©, 2010. Reproduced with the permission of the Minister of Public Works and Government Services, 2012.]

adapted from the *Canadian System of Soil Classification*.
Both the Soil Taxonomy and CSSC are hierarchical
and each defines taxa on the basis of measurable soil
properties. However, the Canadian system is designed
only to classify soils within Canada, whereas the U.S.
system classifies soils of the world. The U.S. system
has "suborders," a category that does not exist in the
Canadian system. The greatest difference between
the two systems is that the Canadian system uses all
horizons that are present to diagnose the soil, whereas
the Soil Taxonomy system emphasizes the depth of soil
reached through ploughing.

(a)

(b)

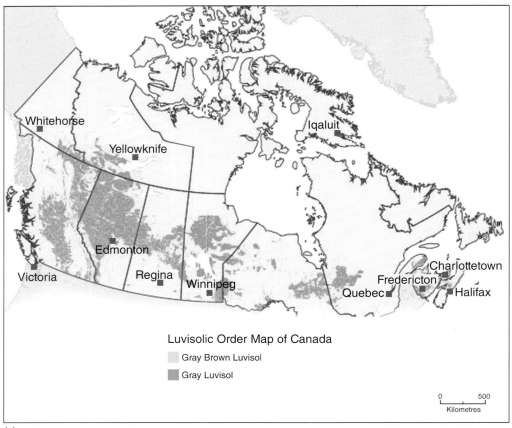

Luvisolic Order Map of Canada

☐ Gray Brown Luvisol

☐ Gray Luvisol

0   500
Kilometres

(c)

FIGURE 18.16 Luvisolic order.
(a) Soil profile of Gray Luvisol from Atlantic Canada.
(b) Coniferous forests are typical of the Gray Luvisol landscape in Atlantic Canada.
(c) Distribution of Luvisolic order in Canada. [Photos (a) and (b) Courtesy of Agriculture and Agri-Food Canada, http://sis2.agr.gc.ca/cansis/images/index.html. Reproduced with the permission of the Minister of Public Works and Government Services Canada, 2012; (c) Thematic Soil Maps of Canada: Luvisolic order, http://sis.agr.gc.ca/cansis/nsdb/slc/intro.html, Agriculture and Agri-Food Canada ©, 2010. Reproduced with the permission of the Minister of Public Works and Government Services, 2012.]

(b)

(a)

(c)

FIGURE 18.17 Organic order.
(a) Organic soil profile from Southern Ontario. (b) Vegetable and market crops are often grown on drained organic soils in southern Ontario. (c) Distribution of Organic order in Canada. [Photos (a) and (b) Courtesy of Agriculture and Agri-Food Canada, http://sis2.agr.gc.ca/cansis/images/index.html. Reproduced with the permission of the Minister of Public Works and Government Services Canada, 2012; (c) Thematic Soil Maps of Canada: Organic Order, http://sis.agr.gc.ca/cansis/nsdb/slc/intro.html, Agriculture and Agri-Food Canada ©, 2010. Reproduced with the permission of the Minister of Public Works and Government Services, 2012.]

(b)

(a)

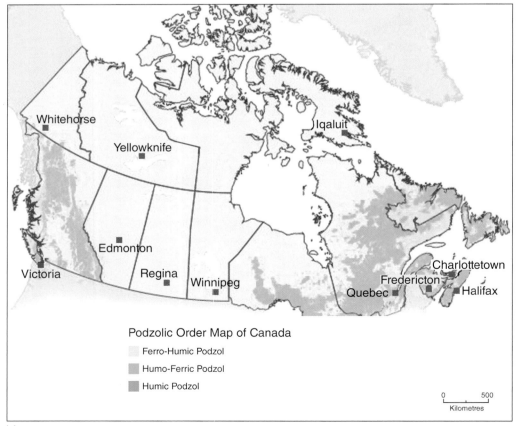

Podzolic Order Map of Canada

Ferro-Humic Podzol

Humo-Ferric Podzol

Humic Podzol

0   500
Kilometres

(c)

FIGURE 18.18 **Podzolic order.**
(a) Humo-ferric Podzol from coastal forest, British Columbia. (b) Characteristic temperate forest and Podzolic soils in the cool, moist climate of central Vancouver Island. (c) Distribution of Podzolic order in Canada. [Photos (a) Courtesy of Agriculture and Agri-Food Canada, http://sis2.agr .gc.ca/cansis/images/index.html. Reproduced with the permission of the Minister of Public Works and Government Services Canada, 2012; (b) by Bobbé Christopherson; (c) Thematic Soil Maps of Canada: Podzolic Order, http://sis.agr.gc.ca/cansis/ nsdb/slc/intro.html, Agriculture and Agri-Food Canada ©, 2010. Reproduced with the permission of the Minister of Public Works and Government Services, 2012.]

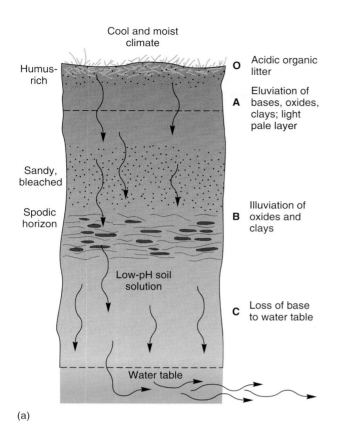

(a)

Cool and moist climate

Humus-rich

O — Acidic organic litter

A — Eluviation of bases, oxides, clays; light pale layer

Sandy, bleached

Spodic horizon

B — Illuviation of oxides and clays

Low-pH soil solution

C — Loss of base to water table

Water table

(b)

FIGURE 18.19 **Podzolization.**
(a) The podzolization process is typical in cool and moist climatic regimes. (b) Freshly ploughed Podosols near Lakeville, Nova Scotia, being prepared for planting vegetables. Formed beneath coniferous forests, the land is cleared for crops and apple orchards (visible in the distance). [(b) Bobbé Christopherson.]

TABLE 18.3   Canadian Soil Orders Correlated to World Reference Base for Soil Orders (Food and Agriculture Organization UNESCO) and the U.S. Soil Taxonomy[a]

Canadian System of Soil Classification	World Reference Base (FAO-UNESCO)	U.S. Soil Taxonomy
Chernozemic	Kastanozem, Chernozem, Greyzem, Phaeozem	Mollisols (Borolls)
Solonetzic	Solonetz	Mollisols, Alfisols (Natric great groups); some Aridisols
Luvisolic	Luvisol	Alfisols (Boralfs and Udalfs)
Podzolic	Podzol	Spodosols, some Inceptisols
Brunisolic	Cambisol	Inceptisols, Aridisols (Psamments)
Regosolic	Fluvisol, Regosol	Entisols
Gleysolic	Gleysol, Planosol	Several orders: "Aqu-" suborders
Organic	Histosol	Histosols
Cryosolic	Cryosol	Gelisols
Vertisolic	Vertisol	Vertisols (six suborders)

[a]Only generalizations are possible; these are nearest equivalents or orders (or suborders), if applicable.

Source: Canadian System of Soil Classification, 3rd ed., Table 18.4, Canadian Soil Orders, Agriculture and Agri-Food Canada. © 1998. Reproduced with the permission of the Minister of Public Works and Government Services, 2012.

(a)

(b)

(c)

FIGURE 18.20 Regosolic order.
(a) Marine Regosol in Atlantic Canada—
note the absence of a B horizon. (b) Fertile
farm fields on marine Regosol landscape.
(c) Alluvial Regosol. (d) Alluvial Regosolic
landscape where streams and creeks deposit
the sediments that create this fertile soil.
(e) Distribution of the Regosolic order in
Canada. [Photos (a) to (d) Courtesy of Agriculture and Agri-Food Canada, http://sis2.agr.gc.ca/
cansis/images/index.html. Reproduced with the
permission of the Minister of Public Works and Government Services Canada, 2012; (e) Thematic Soil Maps of Canada:
Regosolic Order, http://sis.agr.gc.ca/cansis/nsdb/slc/intro.html, Agriculture and Agri-Food Canada ©, 2010. Reproduced
with the permission of the Minister of Public Works and Government Services, 2012.]

(d)

Regosolic Order Map of Canada

■ Regosolic Order

Whitehorse
Iqaluit
Yellowknife
Edmonton
Victoria
Regina
Winnipeg
Charlottetown
Fredericton
Quebec
Halifax

0   500
Kilometres

(e)

(a)

(b)

Whitehorse

Yellowknife

Iqaluit

Victoria

Edmonton

Regina

Winnipeg

Charlottetown

Fredericton

Quebec

Halifax

Solonetzic Order Map of Canada

■ Solonetzic Order

0   500
Kilometres

(c)

FIGURE 18.21 **Solonetzic order.**
(a) Solodized Solonetzic profile in Alberta. (b) Saline landscape in Alberta. The salt pan in the foreground is an example of extreme salinization of the soil. (c) Distribution of Solonetzic order in Canada. [Photos (a) and (b) Courtesy of Agriculture and Agri-Food Canada, http://sis2.agr .gc.ca/cansis/images/index.html. Reproduced with the permission of the Minister of Public Works and Government Services Canada, 2012; (c) Thematic Soil Maps of Canada: Solonetzic Order, http://sis.agr.gc.ca/cansis/nsdb/ slc/intro.html, Agriculture and Agri-Food Canada ©, 2010. Reproduced with the permission of the Minister of Public Works and Government Services, 2012.]

FIGURE 18.22 **Commercial lake-bed evaporite mineral deposits.**
Although a mineral and not a soil, these deposits of sodium sulphate (Na_2SO_4) are mined from a lakebed near Chaplin, in southcentral Saskatchewan. Such deposits form in an environment where evaporation exceeds precipitation, thus the evaporites accumulate. This type of water-balance regime can lead to salinization in soils. This semiarid region features some mixed prairie, seen in the foreground. [Photo by Robert Christopherson.]

(a)

Vertisolic Order Map of Canada

■ Humic Vertisol

■ Vertisol

0   500
Kilometres

(b)

FIGURE 18.23 Vertisolic order.
(a) Distribution of Vertisolic order in Canada. (b) Vertisolic soil profile in Saskatchewan. [(a) Thematic Soil Maps of Canada: Vertisolic order, http://sis.agr.gc.ca/cansis/nsdb/slc/intro.html, Agriculture and Agri-Food Canada ©, 2010. Reproduced with the permission of the Minister of Public Works and Government Services, 2012; (b) Photo by Darwin Anderson, University of Saskatchewan.]

GEOSYSTEMS CONNECTION

Soil science forms the bridge between Parts I, II, and III, the abiotic systems, and Part IV, the biotic systems. Soil formation is affected by temperature, moisture, parent material, topography, and living organisms, including humans. Thus, in this chapter, we combine the energy–atmosphere and water, weather, and climate systems, and the weathering processes that are the source for soil particles and minerals, into a study of this basic covering over Earth's surface. Given this soil foundation, we move to the essentials of Earth's ecosystems and the biotic operations that fuel living systems and the communities that organize life.

APPLIED PHYSICAL GEOGRAPHY   *Soil Density and Porosity*

Soil density is a mass per unit volume and can be measured either as bulk density or particle density, both of which are described below.

Calculation of *bulk density* is based on the naturally existing volume of soil (volume of the soil as it would be in the field) after it has been dried. This measure includes the pore spaces that may be filled with either air or water, and organic material. Typically bulk density for mineral soils ranges from 1.0 g·cm^{-3} to 1.8 g·cm^{-3}, but can exist outside that range. Bulk density of terrestrial soils is used as an indicator of soil compaction.

Particle density is the density of the solid soil particle and excludes pore spaces (that may be filled by air or water). Typically particle density for mineral soil is approximately equal to 2.65 g·cm^{-3}.

Soil Sample	Volume (cm³)	Wet Weight (g)	Dry Weight (g)
Sample A	83.6	115.7	88.8
Sample B	63.6	121.2	101.4

Pores in the soil control the movement of water. Porosity, with units of percent, is the measure of the volume of soil that is air or water, and can be calculated using the bulk density of the soil.

Porosity = 100 − (BD / 2.65 × 100)

where *BD* is bulk density.

Given the two soil samples above, calculate the porosity of each.

To calculate the porosity of each sample, first, calculate bulk density using the dry weight divided by volume. Bulk density is a mass per unit volume.

A 88.8g / 83.6 cm³ = 1.06 g·cm³
B 101.4g / 63.6 cm³ = 1.59 g·cm³

Then calculate the porosity using:
Porosity = 100 − (BD / 2.65 × 100)

A Porosity = 100 − (1.06 g·cm³ /
           2.65 g·cm³ × 100)
         = 100 − (40)
         = 60
Sample A has a porosity of 60%

B Porosity = 100 − (1.59 g·cm³ /
           2.65 g·cm³ × 100)
         = 100 − (60)
         = 40
Sample B has a porosity of 40%

Each sample has adequate pore space for the movement of moisture through the soil, but the second sample is more compacted than the first.

KEY LEARNING CONCEPTS REVIEW

■ **Define** soil and soil science, and **describe** a pedon, a polypedon, and a typical soil profile.

Soil is a dynamic natural body composed of fine materials and contains both mineral and organic matter. **Soil science** is the interdisciplinary study of soils involving physics, chemistry, biology, mineralogy, hydrology, taxonomy, climatology, and cartography. *Pedology* deals with the origin, classification, distribution, and description of soil. *Edaphology* specifically focuses on the study of soil as a medium for sustaining the growth of plants.

The basic sampling unit used in soil surveys is the **pedon**. The **polypedon** is the soil unit used to prepare local soil maps and may contain multiple pedons. Each discernible layer in an exposed pedon is a **soil horizon**. The horizons are designated O (contains **humus**, a complex mixture of decomposed and synthesized organic materials), A (rich in humus and clay, darker), Ae (zone of **eluviation**, the removal of fine particles and minerals by water), B (zone of **illuviation**, the deposition of clays and minerals translocated from elsewhere), C (*regolith*, weathered bedrock), and R (bedrock). Soil horizons A, Ae, and B experience the most active soil processes and together are designated the **solum.**

soil (p. 556)
soil science (p. 556)
pedon (p. 556)

polypedon (p. 556)
soil horizon (p. 556)
humus (p. 556)
eluviation (p. 557)
illuviation (p. 558)
solum (p. 558)

1. Soils provide the foundation for animal and plant life and therefore are critical to Earth's ecosystems. Why is this true?
2. What are the differences among soil science, pedology, and edaphology?
3. Define pedon and polypedon, the basic spatial units of soil distribution.
4. Characterize the principal aspects of each soil horizon. Where does the main accumulation of organic material occur? Where does humus form? Explain the difference between the eluviated layer and the illuviated layer. Which horizons constitute the solum?

■ **Describe** soil properties, including colour, texture, structure, consistence, porosity, and soil moisture.

We use several physical properties to classify soils. Colour suggests composition and chemical makeup. Soil texture refers to the size of individual mineral particles and the proportion of different sizes. For example, **loam** is a balanced mixture of sand, silt, and clay. Soil structure refers to the arrangement of soil peds, which are the smallest natural cluster of particles in a soil. The cohesion of soil particles to each other is called soil consistence. Soil porosity refers to the size, alignment, shape, and location of spaces in the soil. Soil moisture refers to water in the soil pores and its availability to plants.

> loam (p. 559)

5. Soil colour is identified and compared using what technique?
6. Define a *soil separate*. What are the various sizes of particles in soil? What is loam? Why is loam regarded so highly by agriculturists?
7. What is a quick, hands-on method for determining soil consistence?
8. Summarize the five soil-moisture regimes common in mature soils.

■ ***Explain*** basic soil chemistry, including cation-exchange capacity, and ***relate*** these concepts to soil fertility.

Particles of clay and organic material form negatively charged **soil colloids** that attract and retain positively charged mineral ions in the soil. The capacity to exchange ions between colloids and roots is an ability called the **cation-exchange capacity (CEC)**. CEC is a measure of **soil fertility**, the ability of soil to sustain plants. Fertile soil contains organic substances and clay minerals that absorb water and retain certain elements needed by plants.

> soil colloids (p. 561)
> cation-exchange capacity (CEC) (p. 561)
> soil fertility (p. 561)

9. What are soil colloids? How are colloids related to cations and anions in the soil? Explain cation-exchange capacity.
10. What is meant by the concept of soil fertility?

■ ***Evaluate*** the principal soil formation factors, including the human element.

Environmental factors that affect soil formation include parent materials, climate, vegetation, topography, and time. Human influence is having a great impact on Earth's prime soils. Essential soils for agriculture and soil fertility are threatened by mismanagement, destruction, and conversion to other uses. Much soil loss is preventable through the application of known technologies, improved agricultural practices, and government policies.

11. Briefly describe the contributions of the following factors and the effects on soil formation: parent material, climate, vegetation, landforms, time, and human activity.
12. Explain some of the details that support the concern over loss of our most fertile soils. What cost estimates have been placed on soil erosion?

■ ***Describe*** the principal pedogenic processes that lead to the formation of soils under different environmental conditions.

Specific soil-forming processes keyed to climatic regions (not a basis for classification) are called **pedogenic regimes**: **laterization** (leaching in warm and humid climates, not present in Canada; see Oxisols is Appendix B), **salinization** (collection of salt residues in surface horizons in hot, dry climates; discussed with Solonetzic soils), **calcification** (accumulation of carbonates in the B and C horizons in drier continental climates; discussed with Chernozemic soils), **podzolization** (soil acidification in forest soils in cool climates; discussed with Podzolic soils), and **gleysation** (humus and clay accumulation in cold, wet climates with poor drainage; discussed with Gleysolic soils).

> pedogenic regimes (p. 563)
> laterization (p. 563)
> salinization (p. 563)
> calcification (p. 564)
> podzolization (p. 564)
> gleysation (p. 564)

■ ***Describe*** the 10 soil orders of the Canadian System of Soil Classification and ***explain*** the general occurrence of these orders.

The **Canadian System of Soil Classification (CSSC)** is built around an identification and analysis of physical properties of the soil that can be observed in the field. The system divides soils into five hierarchical categories: order, great group, subgroup, family, and series.

The 10 soil orders are **Brunisolic** (weakly developed, humid region soils), **Chernozemic** (grassland soils), **Cryosolic** (cold soils underlain by permafrost), **Gleysolic** (saturated, reducing soils), **Luvisolic** (woodland soils), **Organic** (peat, muck, bog, and fen soils), **Podzolic** (northern conifer forest soils), **Regosolic** (soils without B horizons), **Solonetzic** (soils with saline parent materials), and **Vertisolic** (expandable clay soils).

> Canadian System of Soil Classification (CSSC) (p. 564)
> Brunisolic (p. 565)
> Chernozemic (p. 566)
> Cryosolic (p. 569)
> Gleysolic (p. 569)
> Luvisolic (p. 569)
> Organic (p. 569)
> Podzolic (p. 569)
> Regosolic (p. 571)
> Solonetzic (p. 572)
> Vertisolic (p. 573)

13. Why did Canada adopt its own system of soil classification? Describe a brief history of events that led up to the modern CSSC system.

14. Which soil order is associated with the development of a bog? Account for the use of bog "soil" (peat) as a low-grade fuel.

15. Describe the podzolization process occurring in northern coniferous forests. What are the surface horizons like? What management strategies might enhance productivity in these soils? Name the soil order for these areas.

16. Compare and contrast Interior Plains soils with those of the southeastern Canadian Shield.

17. What processes inhibit soil development in the extreme north? Explain.

18. Briefly describe what you found on the *Soil Landscapes of Canada* (SLC) Web site. Try the SLC Internet Mapping feature for your specific area or region (http://sis.agr.gc.ca/cansis/nsdb/slc/intro.html).

19. Which of the 10 soil orders is characteristic of the area where you live?

Soil horizon in a sphagnum peat soil profile and drying blocks of peat on Mainland Island, in the Orkneys, north of Scotland. The bricks are used as fuel. These are Organic soils (Histosols in the FAO and *Soil Taxonomy* systems). [Bobbé Christopherson.]

MyGeosciencePlace

Visit **www.mygeoscienceplace.ca** for several figure animations, satellite loops, self-study quizzes, flashcards, interactive glossary, career links, RSS feeds, Pearson eText of *Geosystems*, and much more.

CHAPTER 19

Ecosystem Essentials

The transition from Boreal Forest to Arctic Tundra is marked by the lichen woodlands in which stunted black spruce trees speckle the landscape in a spacing of about 3 metres. The spruce trees are rooted in a mat of lichens, mosses, and shrubs. Lichens in these transition zones provide an important source of winter food for caribou. [Stephen Krasemann/All Canada Photos, Inc..]

KEY LEARNING CONCEPTS

After reading the chapter, you should be able to:

- ■ **Define** ecology, biogeography, and the ecosystem concept.
- ■ **Describe** communities, habitats, and niches.
- ■ **Explain** photosynthesis and respiration, and **derive** net photosynthesis and the world pattern of net primary productivity.
- ■ **Relate** abiotic ecosystem components to ecosystem operations, and **explain** trophic relationships.
- ■ **Relate** how biological evolution led to the biodiversity of life on Earth.
- ■ **Define** succession, and **outline** the stages of general ecological succession in both terrestrial and aquatic ecosystems.

Species' Distributions Shift with Climate Change

An ecosystem involves plants and animals and their interactions with the physical environment. Changing climate affects ecosystems because temperature and moisture are among the physical limiting factors on species distributions and ecosystem function. Either through a lack or through an excess, such factors limit biotic operations. Species are able to tolerate varying conditions for each limiting factor, but if conditions become too difficult, species must adapt or evolve, seek out new habitat elsewhere, or become extinct.

As temperatures increase, many animals are expanding their ranges into higher latitude areas with more favorable thermal conditions. Also, species are expanding their ranges to higher elevations—but existing high-elevation species are losing available range as temperatures increase. Shifting climatic conditions may exceed the rate at which some species can migrate, causing a contraction in suitable ranges at lower latitudes or elevations.

Changing climate in northern Canada is impacting the ranges of many species. Narwhals and beluga whales that inhabit cold Arctic waters face changed oceanographic conditions. Reduced sea ice will limit the opportunities for polar bears to access a principal food source—seals. Under a 4 C° increase in the collared lemming's territory—a keystone species in the food chain—a study predicted its range would decline by about 305 000 km^2, or 60%. Facing competition for habitat and resources from southern migrants, a number of species might be able to accommodate shifting their ranges further north, only to find that expansion limited by the Arctic Ocean.

A relatively long-term study in Yosemite National Park, California, found that over the course of a century, small mammal communities moved to higher elevations in response to warming temperatures. Scientists found that half the species monitored showed substantial movement toward cooler temperatures at higher elevations which is consistent with a 3 C° increase in minimum temperature during the last century (Figure GN 19.1).

Formerly low-elevation species expanded their ranges, and high-elevation species contracted their ranges. These animals are highly threatened by climate change. Because the latitudinal temperature gradient in the tropics is slight, tropical species are similarly at risk of mountaintop extinction as warming pushes climatically suitable conditions beyond the reaches of mountain peaks.

Global climate change is expected to affect forest distributions as well, although plant communities are slower to respond to environmental change. A recent study on 130 species of North American trees suggests that ranges will shift northward between 330 and 700 km, depending on the success of dispersal into new habitats. Thus, deciduous forests that are now common in the United States would be found in Canada by century's end, and the present range would be replaced by grasslands in some areas and by a different mix of tree species in other regions. Figure GN 19.2 shows a projected northward shift in the climatic envelope for one species, sugar maple, in eastern North America.

Working Group II in the 2007 Intergovernmental Panel on Climate Change's *Fourth Assessment Report* estimated that with a warming of 1.9 to 3.0 C°, more than 30% of species will be outside the range of their preferred environmental conditions, placing them at risk of extinction. For species to survive, they must adapt or evolve, or continue to shift to stay within their ranges. Thus, a physical geography text written 20 to 70 years from now may have to redo the biome maps to reflect these changes in species distributions. In this chapter, we discuss ecosystems and limiting factors; biomes are the focus of Chapter 20.

FIGURE GN 19.1 Montane species relocate in response to climate change. Species are moving to higher elevations in the Southern and Central Sierra Nevada as their preferred ranges shift to the higher mountains in the background. [Robert Christopherson.]

FIGURE GN 19.2 Projected climatic shift in range of sugar maple. Current and projected future range of sugar maple (*Acer saccharum*) based on the conditions for 2071–2100 modelled by the Canadian Centre for Climate Modelling and Analysis. [Reprinted by permission of University of California Press. *BioScience* 57:929-937, D.W. McKenney, J.H. Pedlar, K. Lawrence, K. Campbell and M.F. Hutchinson, Beyond Traditional Hardiness Zones: Using Climate Envelopes to Map Plant Range Limits. © 2007.]

Diversity is an impressive feature of the living Earth. The diversity of organisms is a response to the interaction of the atmosphere, hydrosphere, and lithosphere, which produce a variety of conditions within which the biosphere exists. The diversity of life also results from the intricate interplay of living organisms themselves. Strategies each species uses seem to work to maintain biodiversity and species coexistence. We, as part of this vast natural complex, seek to find our place and understand the feelings nature stimulates within us.

> The physical beauty of nature is certainly among its most powerful appeals to the human animal. The complexity of the aesthetic response is suggested by its wide-ranging expression from the contours of a mountain landscape to the ambient colors of a setting Sun to the fleeting vitality of a breaching whale. Each exerts a powerful aesthetic impact on most people, often accompanied by feelings of awe at the extraordinary physical appeal and beauty of the natural world.[1]

The biosphere, the sphere of life and organic activity, extends from the ocean floor to about 8 km altitude into the atmosphere. An **ecosystem** is a self-sustaining association of living plants and animals and their nonliving physical environment. The biosphere includes myriad ecosystems from simple to complex, each operating within general spatial boundaries. Earth's biosphere itself is a collection of ecosystems within the natural boundary of the atmosphere and Earth's crust.

Natural ecosystems are open systems for both solar energy and matter, with almost all ecosystem boundaries functioning as transition zones rather than as sharp demarcations. Distinct ecosystems—for example, forests, seas, mountaintops, deserts, beaches, islands, lakes, and ponds—make up the larger whole.

Ecology is the study of the relationships between organisms and their environment and among the various ecosystems in the biosphere. The word *ecology*, developed by German naturalist Ernst Haeckel in 1869, is derived from the Greek *oikos* ("household" or "place to live") and *logos* ("study of"). **Biogeography** is the study of the distribution of plants and animals, the diverse spatial patterns they create, and the physical and biological processes, past and present, that produce Earth's species richness.

The degree to which modern society understands Earth's biogeography and conserves Earth's living legacy will determine the extent of our success as a species and the long-term survival of a habitable Earth, as stated by geographer Gilbert White more than 30 years ago:

> The time is ripe to step up and expand current efforts to understand the great interlocking systems of air, water, and minerals nourishing the Earth. . . . Moreover, without vigorous action toward that goal,

nations will be seriously handicapped in trying to cope with proven and suspected threats to ecosystems and to human health and welfare resulting from alterations in the cycles of carbon, nitrogen, phosphorus, sulfur, and related materials. . . . Society depends upon this life-support system of planet Earth.[2]

Earth's most influential biotic (living) agents are humans. This is not arrogance; it is fact—because we powerfully influence every ecosystem on Earth. From the time humans first developed agriculture, the raising of animals, and the use of fire, we began a process that has led to our dominance over Earth's physical systems.

In this chapter: We explore ecosystems and the community, habitat, and niche concepts. Plants are the essential living component in the biosphere, translating solar energy into usable forms to energize life. The role of nonliving systems, including biogeochemical cycles, is examined. We cover the organization of living ecosystems along complex food chains and webs. The biodiversity of living organisms is seen as a product of biological evolution over the past 3.6+ billion years, approximately. Ecosystem stability and resilience, and how living landscapes change over space and time through the process of succession, are important. Included is coverage of the effects of global change on ecosystems and rates of succession. The chapter ends with a look at the Great Lakes environment and status.

Ecosystem Components and Cycles

An ecosystem is a complex of many variables, all functioning independently yet in concert, with complicated flows of energy and matter (Figure 19.1). The key is to understand the linkages and interconnections within and between systems. As the quote in the caption says, ". . . The effects of what you do in the world will always spread out like ripples in a pond." The aggregate demand for burning fossil fuels far away from the Gulf Coast, Gulf of Mexico, pushed the need for risky drilling schemes— and thus accidents occur. The Barataria wetlands and the Little Blue Heron habitat on the coast bear the brunt of the 2010 BP oil spill (Figure 19.1b and c).

An ecosystem includes both biotic (living) and abiotic (nonliving) components. Nearly all ecosystems depend on a direct input of solar energy; the few limited ones that exist in dark caves, in wells, or on the ocean floor depend on chemical reactions (chemosynthesis). Ecosystems are divided into subsystems, with the biotic portion composed of producers (plants), consumers (animals), and detritus feeders and decomposers (worms, mites, bacteria, fungi). The abiotic flows in an ecosystem include gaseous, hydrologic, and mineral cycles. Figure 19.2 illustrates these essential elements of an ecosystem.

[1]S. R. Kellert, "The biological basis for human values of nature," in S. R. Kellert and E. O. Wilson, eds., *The Biophilia Hypothesis* (Washington, DC: Island Press, 1993), p. 49.

[2]G. F. White and M. K. Tolba, *Global Life Support Systems*, United Nations Environment Programme Information, No. 47 (Nairobi, Kenya: United Nations, 1979), p. 1.

FIGURE 19.1 The web of life.

(a) Study the spider web as you read the following quotation:

> Life devours itself: everything that eats is itself eaten; everything that can be eaten is eaten; every chemical that is made by life can be broken down by life; all the sunlight that can be used is used. . . . The web of life has so many threads that a few can be broken without making it all unravel, and if this were not so, life could not have survived the normal accidents of weather and time, but still the snapping of each thread makes the whole web shudder, and weakens it. . . . You can never do just one thing: the effects of what you do in the world will always spread out like ripples in a pond.

(b) In the Barataria Preserve wetland in the Mississippi delta with bald cyprus trees, note the cypress knees; this is a swamp in the bayou. (c) A Little Blue Heron, near Sanibel Island, Florida, on the Gulf Coast. [(a) Robert Christopherson; quotation from Friends of the Earth and Amory Lovins, The U.N. Stockholm Conference, *Only One Earth* (London, England: Earth Island Limited, 1972), p. 20. (b) and (c) Bobbé Christopherson.]

 GEO REPORT 19.1 *Six Major Extinctions Affect Earth's Species*

Since life arose on the planet, six major extinctions have occurred. The fifth one was 65 million years ago, whereas the sixth is happening across the present decades (see Figure 11.1). Of all these extinction episodes, this is the only one of biotic origin, caused for the most part by human activity. We have enormous impact on most of Earth's natural systems and their associated species.

Communities

A convenient biotic subdivision within an ecosystem is a community. A **community** is formed by interactions among populations of living animals and plants at a particular time. An ecosystem is the interaction of many communities with the abiotic physical components of its environment.

For example, in a forest ecosystem, a specific community may exist on the forest floor, whereas another community functions in the canopy of leaves high above. Similarly, within a lake ecosystem, the plants and animals that flourish in the bottom sediments form one community, whereas those near the surface form another. A community is identified in several ways—by its physical appearance, the species present and the abundance of each, the complex patterns of their interdependence, and the trophic (feeding) structure of the community.

Within a community, two concepts are important: habitat and niche. **Habitat** is the type of environment where an organism resides or is biologically adapted to live. In terms of physical and natural factors, most species have specific habitat requirements with definite limits and a specific regimen of sustaining nutrients.

Niche (French *nicher*, "to nest") refers to the function, or occupation, of a life form within a given community. It is the way an organism obtains and sustains the physical, chemical, and biological factors it needs to survive. A niche has several facets. Among these are a habitat niche, a trophic (food) niche, and a reproductive niche.

FIGURE 19.2 Biotic and abiotic components of ecosystems.
(a) Solar energy is the input that drives the biotic and abiotic components. Heat energy and biomass are the outputs from the biosphere. (b) Biotic and abiotic ingredients operate together to form this rainforest floor ecosystem in Puerto Rico. (c) Five or six species of lichen function under extremely hostile climate conditions on Bear Island in the Barents Sea. Each little indentation in the rock provides some advantage to the lichen. (d) Brain coral in the Caribbean Sea, at a 3-m depth, lives in a symbiotic relationship with algae. [Bobbé Christopherson.]

FIGURE 19.3 Kittiwakes have a specific habitat and niche, here on a sheer steep cliff on the northern coast of Iceland. [Bobbé Christopherson.]

For example, the Red-winged Blackbird (*Agelaius phoeniceus*) inhabits most of Canada and the United States in meadow, pastureland, and marsh habitats. This species nests in blackberry tangles and thick vegetation in freshwater marshes, sloughs, and fields. Its trophic niche is weed seeds and cultivated seed crops throughout the year, adding insects to its diet during nesting season.

Habitat and niche may seem quite specific at times, such as with the Black-legged Kittiwake. These Kittiwakes nest on little available space, in Figure 19.3 on a cliff face in northern Iceland. The guano from thousands of birds and their nests fertilize moss growth on the rock. These seabirds eat fish, making the cliffs above the sea ideal nesting sites. The young fledges learn to fly from these cliffs and to fish.

In a stable community, no niche is left unfilled. The *competitive exclusion principle* states that no two species can occupy the same niche (food or space) successfully in a stable community. Thus, closely related species are spatially separated either by distance or by individual strategies. In other words, each species operates to reduce competition and to maximize its own reproduction rate—literally, species survival depends on successful reproduction. This strategy in turn leads to greater diversity as species shift and adapt to fill each niche.

Among the characteristics of the acacia tree (Family, *Mimosaceae*), found off the coast of Africa in the arid environment on Fogo Island, Cape Verde, are large thorns, which adapted from branchlike forms (Figure 19.4). The tree must operate to preserve fluids, such as by having small leaves that can be oriented to maximize insolation and minimize evapotranspiration. The upside-down umbrella shape maximizes light received. Virtually all parts of the tree are edible in some way, forming interrelationships with insects and animals, from ants to giraffes. Many species of acacia are found in Africa, Australia, Europe, and North America.

Some species are *symbiotic*—that is, in an arrangement where two or more species exist together in an overlapping relationship. One type of symbiosis, *mutualism*, occurs when each organism benefits and is sustained over an extended period by the relationship. For example, lichen (pronounced "liken") is made up of algae and fungi living together (Figure 19.2c). The alga is the producer and food source for the fungus, and the fungus provides structure and physical support. Their mutualism allows the two to occupy a niche in which neither could survive alone. Lichen developed from an earlier parasitic relationship in which the fungi broke into the algal cells. Today, the two organisms have evolved into a supportive harmony and symbiotic relationship. The partnership of corals and algae discussed in Chapter 16 is another example of mutualism in a symbiotic relationship (Figure 19.2d).

By contrast, another form of symbiosis is a *parasitic* relationship, which may eventually kill the host, thus

FIGURE 19.4 Thorned acacia trees in an arid climate.
(a) A woman hauls water, balanced on her head, several kilometres past acacia trees in western Africa. (b) Small leaves and stiff thorns are the acacia's defense in a dry climate. [Bobbé Christopherson.]

destroying the parasite's own niche and habitat. An example is parasitic mistletoe (*Phoradendron*), which lives on and may kill various kinds of trees. Some scientists are questioning whether our human society and the physical systems of Earth constitute a global-scale symbiotic relationship of mutualism, which is sustainable, or a parasitic one, which is unsustainable.

▌▌ **CRITICAL THINKING 19.1**

Mutualism? Parasitism? Where Do We Fit In?

This chapter states, "Some scientists are questioning whether our human society and the physical systems of Earth constitute a global-scale symbiotic relationship of mutualism, which is sustainable, or of parasitism, which is unsustainable." Referring to the definition of these terms, what is your response to that statement? How do you equate our planetary economic system with the need to sustain life-supporting natural systems? Mutualism? Parasitism? What is your characterization?

Plants: The Essential Biotic Component

Plants are the critical biotic link between solar energy and the biosphere. Ultimately, the fate of all members of the biosphere, including humans, rests on the success of plants and their ability to turn sunlight into food.

Land plants (and animals) became common about 430 million years ago, according to fossilized remains. **Vascular plants** developed conductive tissues and true roots for internal transport of fluid and nutrients. (*Vascular* is from a Latin word for "vessel-bearing," referring to the conducting cells.) Presently, about 270 000 species of plants are known to exist, and most are vascular. Many more species have yet to be identified. They represent a great untapped resource base. Only about 20 species of plants provide 90% of the world's food; just three—wheat, maize (corn), and rice—comprise half of the food supply. Plants are a major source of new medicines and chemical compounds that benefit humanity. Plants also are the core of healthy, functioning ecosystems that sustain all life.

Leaves are solar-powered chemical factories, wherein photochemical reactions take place. Veins in the leaf bring in water and nutrient supplies and carry off the sugars (food) produced by photosynthesis. The veins in each leaf connect to the stems and branches of the plant and to the main circulation system.

Flows of carbon dioxide, water, light, and oxygen enter and exit the surface of each leaf (see Figure 1.5 in Chapter 1). Gases flow into and out of a leaf through small pores, the **stomata** (singular: *stoma*), which usually are most numerous on the lower side of the leaf. Each stoma is surrounded by guard cells that open and close the pore, depending on the plant's changing needs. Water that moves through a plant exits the leaves through the stomata and evaporates from leaf surfaces, thereby assisting the plant's temperature regulation. As water evaporates from the leaves, a pressure deficit is created that allows atmospheric pressure to push water up through the plant all the way from the roots, in the same manner that a drinking straw

works. We can only imagine the complex operation of a 100-m tree!

Photosynthesis and Respiration

Powered by energy from certain wavelengths of visible light, **photosynthesis** unites carbon dioxide and hydrogen (hydrogen is derived from water in the plant). The term is descriptive: *photo-* refers to sunlight, and *-synthesis* describes the "manufacturing" of starches and sugars through reactions within plant leaves. The process releases oxygen and produces energy-rich food for the plant.

The largest concentration of light-responsive, photosynthetic structures (known as *organelles*) in a leaf rests below the leaf's upper layers. These organelle units within cells are the *chloroplasts*, and within each resides a green, light-sensitive pigment called **chlorophyll**. Within this pigment, light stimulates photochemistry. Consequently, competition for light is a dominant factor in the formation of plant communities. This competition is expressed in the height, orientation, distribution, and structure of plants.

Only about one-quarter of the light energy arriving at the surface of a leaf is useful to the light-sensitive chlorophyll. Chlorophyll absorbs only the orange-red and violet-blue wavelengths for photochemical operations, and it reflects predominantly green hues (and some yellow). That is why trees and other vegetation look green.

Photosynthesis essentially follows this equation:

$$6CO_2 + 6H_2O + \text{Light} \rightarrow C_6H_{12}O_6 + 6O_2$$

(carbon dioxide) (water) (solar energy) (glucose carbohydrate) (oxygen)

From the equation, you can see that photosynthesis removes carbon (in the form of CO_2) from Earth's atmosphere. The quantity is enormous: approximately 91 billion metric tons of carbon dioxide per year. Carbohydrates, the organic result of the photosynthetic process, are combinations of carbon, hydrogen, and oxygen. They can form simple sugars, such as *glucose* ($C_6H_{12}O_6$). Plants use glucose to build starches, which are more complex carbohydrates and the principal food stored in plants.

Plants store energy for later use. They consume this energy as needed through respiration by converting the carbohydrates to energy for their other operations. Thus, **respiration** is essentially a reverse of the photosynthetic process:

$$C_6H_{12}O_6 + 6O_2 \rightarrow 6CO_2 + 6H_2O + \text{energy}$$

(glucose carbohydrate) (oxygen) (carbon dioxide) (water) (heat energy)

In respiration, plants oxidize carbohydrates (stored energy), releasing carbon dioxide, water, and energy as heat. The overall growth of a plant depends on a surplus of carbohydrates beyond those lost through plant respiration. Figure 19.5 presents a simple schematic of this process, which produces plant growth.

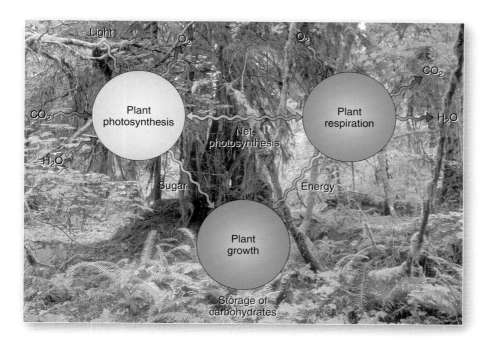

FIGURE 19.5 **How plants live and grow.**
The balance between photosynthesis and respiration determines net photosynthesis and plant growth. [Bobbé Christopherson.]

The *compensation point* is the break-even point between the production and consumption of organic material. Each leaf must operate on the production side of the compensation point, or else the plant eliminates it—something each of us has no doubt experienced with a houseplant that received inadequate water or light. The difference between photosynthetic production and respiration loss is *net photosynthesis*. The amount varies, depending on controlling environmental factors such as light, water, temperature, soil fertility, and the plant's site, elevation, and competition from other plants and animals.

The rapidly increasing carbon dioxide concentration in the atmosphere stimulates the photosynthetic processes. However, higher temperatures due to global warming result in higher respiration rates. Plants respire all the time but at night respiration processes are the plant's main operation, corresponding with the time that research shows present warming is greatest.

Plant productivity increases as light availability increases—up to a point. When the light level is too high,

light saturation occurs and most plants actually reduce their output in response. Some plants are adapted to shade, whereas others flourish in full sunlight. Crops such as rice, wheat, and sugarcane do well with high light intensity. Figure 19.6 portrays the general energy budget for green plants, showing energy receipt, energy utilization, and disposition of net primary production—how the energy is spent.

Net Primary Productivity The net photosynthesis for an entire plant community is its **net primary productivity**. This is the amount of stored chemical energy that the community generates for the ecosystem. **Biomass** is the net dry weight of all this organic material and its stored chemical energy.

Net primary productivity is measured as fixed carbon per square metre per year. ("Fixed" means chemically bound into plant tissues.) Study the map in Figure 19.7 and you can see that on land, net primary production tends to be highest between the Tropics of Cancer and Capricorn at

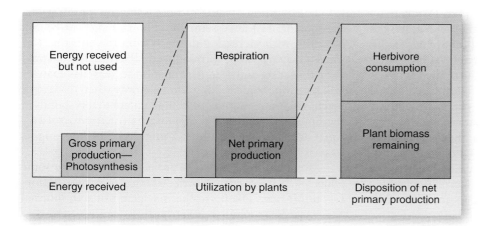

FIGURE 19.6 **Energy budget of the biosphere.**
Energy receipt, energy utilization, and energy disposition of net primary production by green plants.

FIGURE 19.7 **Net primary productivity.**
Worldwide net primary productivity in grams of carbon per square metre per year (approximate values).
[Based on D. E. Reichle, *Analysis of Temperate Forest Ecosystems* (Heidelberg, Germany: Springer, 1970.]

sea level and decreases toward higher latitudes and elevation. Precipitation also affects productivity, as evidenced by the correlations of abundant precipitation with high productivity adjacent to the equator and reduced precipitation with low productivity in the subtropical deserts. Even though deserts receive high amounts of solar radiation, other controlling factors limit productivity—namely, water availability and soil conditions.

In the oceans, differing nutrient levels control and limit productivity. Regions with nutrient-rich upwelling currents off western coastlines generally are the most productive. The map in Figure 19.7 shows that the tropical oceans and areas of subtropical high pressure are quite low in productivity.

In temperate and high latitudes, the rate at which carbon is fixed by vegetation varies seasonally. It increases in spring and summer as plants flourish with increasing solar input and, in some areas, with more available (nonfrozen) water, and it decreases in late fall and winter. Productivity rates in the tropics are high throughout the year, and turnover in the photosynthesis–respiration cycle is faster, exceeding by many times the rates experienced in a desert environment or in the far northern limits of the tundra. A lush hectare of sugarcane in the tropics might fix 45 metric tons of carbon in a year, whereas desert plants in an equivalent area might achieve only 1% of that amount.

Table 19.1 lists various ecosystems, their net primary productivity, and an estimate of net total biomass worldwide—154 billion metric tons of dry organic matter per year. Compare the various ecosystems, especially cultivated land (in *italics*), with most of the natural communities. Net

productivity is generally regarded as the most important aspect of any type of community, and the distribution of productivity over Earth's surface is an important subject of biogeography.

Abiotic Ecosystem Components

Critical in each ecosystem are the flow of energy and the cycling of nutrients and water in life-supporting systems. These abiotic (nonliving) components set the stage for ecosystem operations.

Light, Temperature, Water, and Climate Solar energy powers ecosystems, so the pattern of solar energy receipt is crucial. Solar energy enters an ecosystem by way of photosynthesis, and heat energy is dissipated from the system at many points. Of the total energy intercepted at Earth's surface and available for work, only about 1.0% is actually fixed by photosynthesis as carbohydrates in plants.

The duration of Sun exposure is the *photoperiod*. Along the equator, days are essentially 12 hours long year-round; however, with increasing distance from the equator, seasonal effects become pronounced. Plants have adapted their flowering and seed germination to seasonal changes in insolation. Some seeds germinate only when daylength reaches a certain number of hours. A plant that responds in the opposite manner is the poinsettia (*Euphorbia pulcherrima*), which requires at least 2 months of 14-hour nights to start flowering.

Monarch butterflies (*Danaus plexippus*) migrate some 3600 km from eastern North America to wintering forests in Mexico. The butterflies navigate using an internal

TABLE 19.1 Net Primary Productivity and Plant Biomass on Earth

Ecosystem	Area (10^6 km^2)	Net Primary Productivity per Unit Area (g · m^2 · yr) Normal Range	Mean	World Net Biomass (10^9 metric tonnes · yr)
Tropical rain forest	17.0	1000–3500	2200	33.9
Tropical seasonal forest	7.5	1000–2500	1600	10.9
Temperate evergreen forest	5.0	600–2500	1300	5.9
Temperate deciduous forest	7.0	600–2500	1200	7.6
Boreal forest	12.0	400–2000	800	8.7
Woodland and shrubland	8.5	250–1200	700	5.4
Savanna	15.0	200–2000	900	12.2
Temperate grassland	9.0	200–1500	600	4.9
Tundra and alpine region	8.0	10–400	140	1.0
Desert and semidesert scrub	18.0	10–250	90	1.5
Extreme desert, rock, sand, ice	24.0	0–10	3	0.06
Cultivated land	*14.0*	*100–3500*	*650*	*8.3*
Swamp and marsh	2.0	800–3500	2000	3.6
Lake and stream	2.0	100–1500	250	0.5
Total continental	**149.0**	—	773	104.5
Open ocean	332.0	2–400	125	37.6
Upwelling zones	0.4	400–1000	500	0.2
Continental shelf	26.6	200–600	360	8.7
Algal beds and reefs	0.6	500–4000	2500	1.5
Estuaries	1.4	200–3500	1500	1.9
Total marine	**361.0**	—	152	49.9
Grand total	**510.0**	—	333	154.37

Source: R. H. Whittaker, *Communities and Ecosystems* (Heidelberg, Germany: Springer, 1975), p. 224. Reprinted by permission.

time-compensated Sun compass to maintain their southwestward track while they compensate for time-of-day Sun changes. Researchers found receptors in their eyes sensitive to ultraviolet light that play the key role in accurate navigation. For Monarchs, ultraviolet light is an important abiotic component.

Other components are important to ecosystem processes. Air and soil temperatures determine the rates at which chemical reactions proceed. Significant temperature factors are seasonal variation and duration and the pattern of minimum and maximum temperatures.

Operations of the hydrologic cycle and water availability depend on precipitation and evaporation rates and their seasonal distribution. Water quality—its mineral content, salinity, and levels of pollution and toxicity—is important. Also, regional climates affect the pattern of vegetation and ultimately influence soil development. All of these factors work together to form the limits for ecosystems in a given location.

Figure 19.8 illustrates the general relationship among temperature, precipitation, and vegetation. Can you identify the characteristic vegetation type and related temperature and moisture regime that fit areas you know well? Such as a place you have lived, or an area around the school you attend.

Beyond these general conditions, each ecosystem further produces its own *microclimate*, which is specific to individual sites. For example, in a forest the insolation reaching the ground is reduced, and shade from its own trees blankets the forest floor. A pine forest cuts light by 20%–40%, whereas a birch–beech forest reduces it by as much as 50%–75%. Forests also are about 5% more humid than nonforested landscapes, have moderated temperatures (warmer winters and cooler summers), and experience reduced winds.

Life Zones Alexander von Humboldt (1769–1859), an explorer, geographer, and scientist, observed that plants and animals recur in related groupings wherever similar conditions occur in the abiotic environment. He synthesized in a systems approach the influence of atmospheric, oceanic, geologic, and ecologic parameters on vegetation distributions. Humboldt was far ahead of his time as an Earth systems scientist. And, as a true geographer, he thought of nature and Earth systems as spatial arrays of phenomena.

After several years of study in the Andes Mountains of Peru, he described a distinct relation between elevation and plant communities as his *life zone concept*. As he climbed the mountains, he noticed that the experience was

(e) Dry tundra, East Greenland

(f) Moist tundra, Spitsbergen, Arctic Ocean

(g) Needleleaf forest, Independence Pass, Colorado

(h) Deciduous forest near Chicago

(d) Cold desert, Arizona

(c) Sonoran Desert, Southwest U.S.

(b) Subtropical desert, Arizona

(i) Tropical rain forest, El Yunque, Puerto Rico

Cold

Temperature

Hot

(a)

Precipitation

Wet

Dry

FIGURE 19.8 How temperature and precipitation affect ecosystems.
(a) Climate controls (wetness, dryness, warmth, cold) and ecosystem types; (b) through (i) are representative photos of each area. [(c) Robert Christopherson. All others Bobbé Christopherson.]

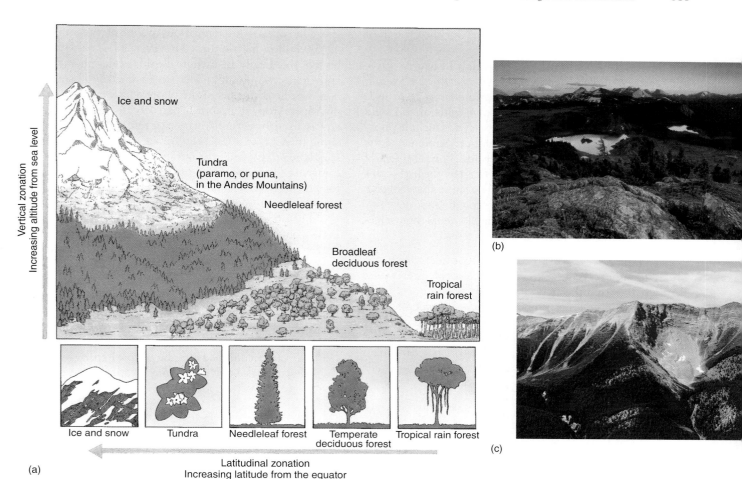

FIGURE 19.9 Vertical and latitudinal zonation of plant communities.
(a) Progression of plant community life zones with changing elevation or latitude. (b) Alpine tundra
ecosystem in the Canadian Rockies. (c) The timberline for a needleleaf forest in the Canadian Rockies. The
line of trees marks the limit of highest continuous forest, whereas the area above it marks the zone in which
no trees grow. [(b) Design Pics/Thinkstock; (c) Robert Christopherson.]

similar to that of travelling away from the equator toward higher latitudes (Figure 19.9a).

This zonation of plants is noticeable on any trip from lower valleys to higher elevations. Each **life zone** possesses its own temperature, precipitation, and insolation relations and therefore its own biotic communities. Scientific research now shows that climate change is causing plants and animals to move their range to higher elevations with more desirable temperatures, as established life zones shift. Evidence exists that some species have run out of mountain as environmental conditions simply have taken them "out-of-bounds," either elsewhere or into extinction.

Elemental Cycles

The most abundant natural elements in living matter are hydrogen (H), oxygen (O), and carbon (C). Together, these elements make up more than 99% of Earth's biomass; in fact, all life (organic molecules) contains hydrogen and carbon. In addition, nitrogen (N), calcium (Ca), potassium (K), magnesium (Mg), sulphur (S), and phosphorus (P) are

 GEO REPORT 19.2 *Earth's Magnetic Field Acts as an Abiotic Component*

The fact that birds and bees can detect Earth's magnetic field and use it for finding direction is well established. Small amounts of magnetically sensitive particles in the skull of the bird and the abdomen of the bee provide compass directions.

A team of biologists found that sea turtles detect magnetic fields of different strengths and inclinations (angles). This means that the turtles have a built-in navigation system that helps them know where they are on Earth (like our Global Positioning System, which requires multimillion-dollar satellites). Loggerhead sea turtles hatch in Florida, crawl into the water, and spend the next 70 years travelling thousands of miles between North America and Africa around the subtropical high-pressure gyre in the Atlantic Ocean. The females return to where they were hatched to lay their eggs. The researchers think that the hatchlings are imprinted with magnetic data unique to the beach where they hatched and then develop a more global sense of position as they live a life swimming across the ocean.

significant nutrients, elements necessary for the growth of a living organism.

Several key chemical cycles function in nature. Oxygen, carbon, and nitrogen each have *gaseous cycles*, which are partly in the atmosphere. Other elements have *sedimentary cycles*, which principally involve mineral and solid phases; major elements that have these cycles include phosphorus, calcium, potassium, and sulphur. Some elements combine gaseous and sedimentary cycles. The recycling of gases and sedimentary (nutrient) materials forms Earth's **biogeochemical cycles**, so called because they involve chemical reactions necessary for growth and development of living systems. The chemical elements themselves recycle over and over again in life processes.

Oxygen and Carbon Cycles We consider these two cycles together because they are so closely intertwined through photosynthesis and respiration (Figure 19.10). The atmosphere is the principal reserve of available oxygen. Larger reserves of oxygen exist in Earth's crust, but they are unavailable, being chemically bound with other elements, especially the silicate (SiO_2) and carbonate (CO_3) mineral families. Unoxidized reserves of fossil fuels and sediments also contain oxygen.

The oceans are enormous pools of carbon—about 42 900 billion metric tons. However, all of this carbon is bound chemically in carbon dioxide, calcium carbonate, and other compounds. The ocean initially absorbs carbon dioxide by means of the photosynthesis carried on by phytoplankton; it becomes part of the living organisms and is fixed in certain carbonate minerals, such as limestone ($CaCO_3$). In Chapter 16, we saw that excessive absorption of CO_2 from the atmosphere by the ocean is lowering pH. This condition of acidification makes it harder for plankton, corals, and other organisms to maintain calcium carbonate skeletons.

The atmosphere, which is the integrating link in the cycle, contains only about 700 billion metric tons of carbon (as carbon dioxide) at any moment. This is far less carbon than is stored in fossil fuels and oil shales (13 200 billion metric tons, as hydrocarbon molecules) or in living and dead organic matter (2500 billion metric tonnes, as carbohydrate molecules). Carbon dioxide is released into the atmosphere by the respiration of plants and animals, volcanic activity, and fossil fuel combustion by industry and transportation.

The carbon dumped into the atmosphere by human activity constitutes a vast geochemical experiment, using the

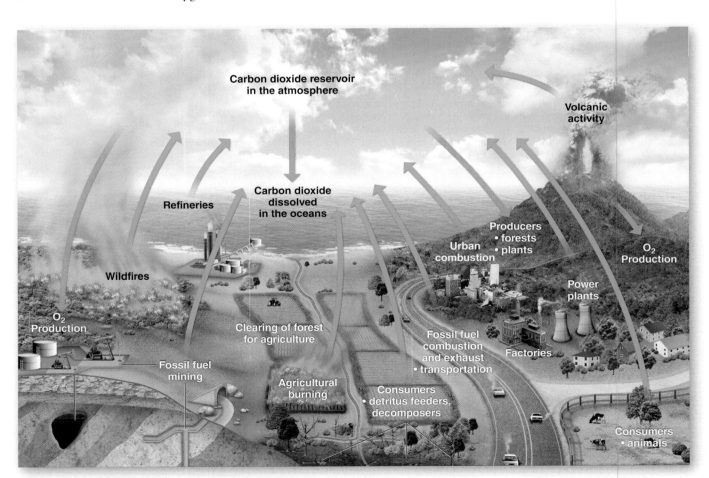

FIGURE 19.10 **The carbon and oxygen cycles.**
Carbon is fixed through photosynthesis and begins its passage through ecosystem operations. Respiration by living organisms, the burning of forests and grasslands, and the combustion of fossil fuels release carbon to the atmosphere. These cycles are greatly influenced by human activities.

real-time atmosphere as a laboratory. Annually, we are adding carbon to the atmospheric pool in an amount 400% greater than 1950 levels. Global emissions of carbon from fossil fuels continue to increase, with some 8.2 billion metric tons of carbon added to the atmosphere in 2007—compare this to the 1.47 billion metric tons in 1950, or 4.74 billion metric tons in 1980. About 50% of the carbon emitted since the beginning of the Industrial Revolution and not absorbed by oceans and organisms remains in the atmosphere, enhancing Earth's natural greenhouse effect—and thus global warming and climate change.

Nitrogen Cycle Nitrogen, which accounts for 78.084% of each breath we take, is the major constituent of the atmosphere. Nitrogen also is important in the makeup of organic molecules, especially proteins, and therefore is essential to living processes. A simplified view of the nitrogen cycle is portrayed in Figure 19.11.

Nitrogen-fixing bacteria, which live principally in the soil and are associated with the roots of certain plants, are the key link to life. The roots of legumes such as clover, alfalfa, soybeans, peas, beans, and peanuts have such bacteria. Bacteria colonies reside in nodules on the legume roots and chemically combine the nitrogen from the air in the form of nitrates (NO_3) and ammonia (NH_3). Plants use these chemically bound forms of nitrogen to produce their own organic matter. Anyone or anything feeding on the plants thus ingests the nitrogen. Finally, the nitrogen in the organic wastes of these consuming organisms is freed by denitrifying bacteria, which recycle nitrogen back to the atmosphere.

To improve agricultural yields, many farmers use synthetic inorganic fertilizers, as opposed to soil-building

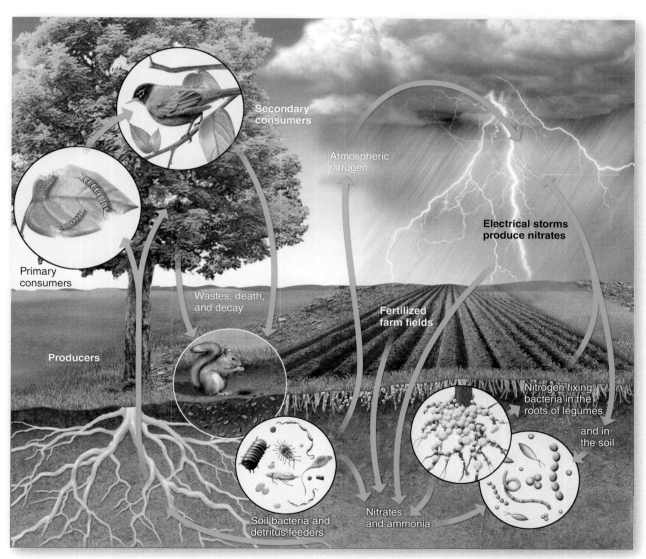

FIGURE 19.11 The nitrogen cycle.
The atmosphere is the essential reservoir of gaseous nitrogen. Atmospheric nitrogen gas is chemically fixed by bacteria to produce ammonia. Lightning and forest fires produce nitrates, and fossil-fuel combustion forms nitrogen compounds that are washed from the atmosphere by precipitation. Plants absorb nitrogen compounds and produce organic material.

organic fertilizers (manure and compost). Inorganic fertilizers are chemically produced through artificial nitrogen fixation at factories. Humans presently fix more nitrogen as synthetic fertilizer per year than all terrestrial sources combined—and the present production of synthetic fertilizers now is doubling every 8 years; some 1.82 million metric tons are produced every week, worldwide. The crossover point when anthropogenic sources of fixed nitrogen exceeded the normal range of naturally fixed nitrogen was 1970.

This surplus of usable nitrogen accumulates in Earth's ecosystems. Some is present as excess nutrients, washed from soil into waterways and eventually to the ocean. This excess nitrogen load begins a water pollution process that feeds an excessive growth of algae and phytoplankton, increases biochemical oxygen demand, diminishes dissolved oxygen reserves, and eventually disrupts the aquatic ecosystem. In addition, excess nitrogen compounds in air pollution are a component in acid deposition, further altering the nitrogen cycle in soils and waterways.

Figure 19.12 includes maps and images of the core region of the Gulf Coast dead zone, a region of oxygen-depleted water off the coast of Louisiana in the Gulf of Mexico. In 2008, researchers at Texas A&M University reported dead zone conditions stretching along the entire Texas Gulf Coast and extending in a discontinuous spread some 32 km from shore.

The Mississippi River carries agricultural fertilizers, farm sewage, and other wastes to the Gulf, causing huge spring blooms of phytoplankton: a greening of primary productivity. The Mississippi drainage system handles the runoff for 41% of the continental United States. By summer, the biological oxygen demand of bacteria feeding on the decay exceeds the dissolved oxygen; hypoxia (oxygen depletion) develops, killing any fish that venture into the area. These low-oxygen conditions act as a limiting factor on marine life. From 2002 on, the Gulf Coast dead zone has expanded to an area of more than 22 000 km² each year. The agricultural, feedlot, and fertilizer industries dispute the connection between their nutrient input and this extensive dead zone.

In other parts of the world, the connection is established. Similar coastal dead zones occur as the result of nutrient outflows from more than 400 river systems worldwide, affecting almost 250 000 km² of offshore oceans and seas. In Sweden and Denmark, a concerted effort to reduce nutrient flows into rivers reversed hypoxic conditions in the Kattegat Strait (between the Baltic and North Seas). And with the fall of the Soviet Union and state agriculture in 1990, fertilizer use is down more than 50% in the former Soviet republics. The Black Sea now gets several months' break from year-round hypoxia at river deltas.

As with most environmental situations, the cost of mitigation is cheaper than the cost of continued damage to

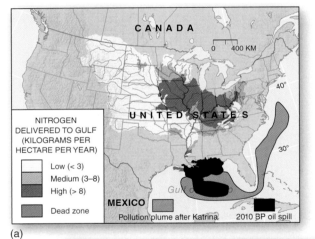

NITROGEN DELIVERED TO GULF (KILOGRAMS PER HECTARE PER YEAR)

Low (< 3)
Medium (3–8)
High (> 8)
Dead zone

Pollution plume after Katrina   2010 BP oil spill

(a)

FIGURE 19.12 The Gulf Coast dead zone.
(a) Mapped total nitrogen originating in the upstream watershed that feeds the Mississippi River system. (b) The flush of nutrients from the Mississippi River drainage basin enriches the offshore waters in the Gulf of Mexico, causing huge phytoplankton blooms in early spring (red areas). (c) By late summer, oxygen-depleted waters dominate what is known as the *dead zone.* Note the Katrina plume and an estimate of the 2010 Gulf oil disaster. [(a) Based on R. B. Alexander, R. A. Smith, and G. E. Schwarz, "Effect of stream channel size on the delivery of nitrogen to the Gulf of Mexico," *Nature* 403 (February 17, 2000): 761. (b) *SeaWiFS* image, NASA/GSFC.]

(b)

(c)

marine ecosystems. A 20% to 30% cut in nitrogen inflow upstream is estimated to increase dissolved oxygen levels by more than 50% in the dead zone region of the Gulf. One government estimate placed the application of excess nitrogen fertilizer at 20% more than needed in Iowa, Illinois, and Indiana. The initial step to resolving this issue might be to mandate applying only the levels of fertilizer needed—a savings in overhead costs for agricultural interests—and, secondly, to begin dealing with animal wastes from feedlots in the basin. Such nutrient management is already legislated for most of Canada.

Following Hurricane Katrina in 2005, the region was overwhelmed by discharge carrying sewage, chemical toxins, oil spills, household pesticides, animal wastes and carcasses, and nutrients. The plume, now mostly dissipated, from this event tracked around the Florida peninsula and northward up the Eastern seaboard (see the suggested plot in Figure 19.12a). Add to all this the 2010 *Deepwater Horizon* oil spill, where British, Swiss, and Cayman Island corporations, under the flag and regulations of the Marshall Islands, were operating in U.S. waters and caused the worst oil spill disaster in U.S. history. You will find more on this in Chapter 21.

Limiting Factors

The term **limiting factor** identifies the one physical or chemical abiotic component that most inhibits biotic operations, through either its lack or its excess. In most ecosystems, precipitation is the limiting factor. However, temperature, light levels, and soil nutrients certainly affect vegetation patterns. Here are a few examples of possible limiting factors:

- Low temperatures limit plant growth at high elevations;
- Lack of water limits growth in a desert;
- Excess water limits growth in a bog;
- Changes in salinity levels affect aquatic ecosystems;
- Lack of iron in ocean surface environments limits photosynthetic production;
- Low phosphorus content of soils limits plant growth; and
- General lack of active chlorophyll above 6100 m limits primary productivity.

Each organism possesses a range of tolerance for each limiting factor in its environment. This fact is illustrated in Figure 19.13, which shows the geographic range for two tree species and two bird species. The coast redwood (*Sequoia sempervirens*) is limited to a narrow section of the Coast Ranges in California, covering barely 9500 km², concentrated in areas that receive necessary summer advection fog. On the other hand, the red maple (*Acer rubrum*) thrives over a large area under varying conditions of moisture and temperature, thus demonstrating a broader tolerance to environmental variations.

The Mallard Duck (*Anas platyrhynchos*) and the Snail Kite (*Rostrhamus sociabilis*) also demonstrate a variation in tolerance and range (Figure 19.13b). The Mallard, a generalist, feeds from widely diverse sources, is easily domesticated, and is found throughout most of North America in at least one season of the year. By contrast, the Snail Kite is a specialist that feeds only on one specific type of snail.

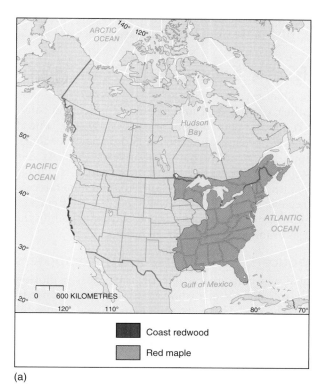

(a)

Coast redwood

Red maple

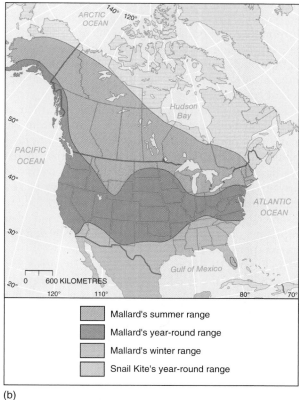

(b)

Mallard's summer range

Mallard's year-round range

Mallard's winter range

Snail Kite's year-round range

FIGURE 19.13 Limiting factors affect the distribution of every plant and animal species.
(a) Distributions of coast redwood and red maple demonstrate the effect of limiting factors, (b) as do the distributions of the Mallard Duck and the Snail Kite across North America. The Mallard is a generalist and feeds widely. In contrast, the range of its food, a single type of snail, limits the Snail Kite.

This single food source, then, is its limiting factor. Note its small habitat area near Lake Okeechobee in Florida.

Biotic Ecosystem Operations

The abiotic components of energy, atmosphere, water, weather, climate, and minerals make up the life support for the biotic components of each ecosystem. The flow of energy, cycling of nutrients, and trophic (feeding) relations determine the nature of an ecosystem. As energy cascades through this process-flow system, it is constantly replenished by the Sun. But nutrients and minerals cannot be replenished from an external source, so they constantly cycle within each ecosystem and through the biosphere. Let us examine these biotic operations.

Producers, Consumers, and Decomposers

Organisms that are capable of using carbon dioxide as their sole source of carbon are *autotrophs* (self-feeders), or **producers**. These are the plants. They chemically fix carbon through photosynthesis. Organisms that depend on producers as their carbon source are *heterotrophs* (feed on others), or **consumers**. Generally, these are animals (Figure 19.14).

Autotrophs are the essential producers in an ecosystem— capturing light energy and converting it to chemical energy, incorporating carbon, forming new plant tissue and biomass, and freeing oxygen. Solar energy enters each food chain through the producer plant or producer phytoplankton, subsequently flowing through higher and higher levels of consumers.

From the producers, which manufacture their own food, energy flows through the system along a **food chain** circuit, reaching consumers and eventually *detritivores*, dealing with refuse in the chain. Organisms that share the same basic foods are said to be at the same *trophic level*. Ecosystems generally are structured in a **food web**, a complex network of interconnected food chains. In a food web, consumers participate in several different food chains, comprising both *strong interactions* and *weak interactions* between species in the food web.

In Figure 19.14b a bearded seal (*Erignathus barbatus*), with body fat exceeding 30%, rests on a bergy bit, or small iceberg, in Arctic waters where they feed on fish and clams. Figure 19.14c shows a male polar bear (*Ursus maritimus*) hauling its bearded seal kill onto the ice. The polar bear, a marine mammal, is the dominant Arctic predator. In 19.14d, on the pack ice many kilometres from land we see a mother and her 6-month-old cubs-of-the-year feeding on a seal catch. Even though the cubs still nurse, they share the kill with mother. The polar bear consumes most of the seal except for the bones and intestines, which are quickly eaten by birds scavenging the leftovers—note the Glaucous Gulls and Ivory Gulls in the photo.

Primary consumers feed on producers. Because producers are always plants, the primary consumer is a **herbivore**, or plant eater, like the krill in Figure 19.15. A **carnivore** is a secondary consumer and primarily eats meat. A tertiary consumer eats primary and secondary consumers and is referred to as the "top carnivore" in the food chain, as with the leopard seal and orca in Antarctica and the polar bear in the Arctic. Orca, an oceanic dolphin, feeds mainly on fish in the Arctic region as well as other whales. A consumer that feeds on both producers (plants) and consumers (meat) is an **omnivore**—a category occupied by humans, among others.

Detritivores (detritus feeders and decomposers) are the final link in the endless chain. Detritivores renew the entire system by releasing simple inorganic compounds and nutrients with the breaking down of organic materials. Detritus refers to all the dead organic debris—remains, fallen leaves, and wastes—that living processes leave. Detritus feeders—worms, mites, termites, centipedes, snails, crabs, and even vultures, among others—work like an army to consume detritus and excrete nutrients that fuel an ecosystem. **Decomposers** are primarily bacteria and fungi that digest organic debris outside their bodies and absorb and release nutrients in the process. This metabolic work of microbial decomposers produces the rotting that breaks down detritus. Detritus feeders and decomposers, although different in operation, have a similar function in an ecosystem.

Examples of Complex Food Webs

An example of a complex community is the oceanic food web that includes krill, a primary consumer (Figure 19.15a). Krill (*Euphausia sp.*, at least a dozen species) is a shrimplike crustacean that is a major food for an interrelated group of organisms, including whales, fish, seabirds, seals, and squid in the Antarctic region. All of these organisms participate in numerous other food chains as well, some consuming and some being consumed.

Phytoplankton began this chain by harvesting solar energy in photosynthesis. *Herbivorous zooplankton* such as krill and other organisms eat phytoplankton. Consumers eat krill at the next trophic level. Because krill are a protein-rich, plentiful food, increasingly factory ships, such as those from Japan and Russia, seek them out. The annual krill harvest currently surpasses a million tons, principally as feed for chickens and livestock and as protein for human consumption. Many of the Antarctic dwelling birds depend on krill and on fish that eat krill.

Another example of a complex food web comes from eastern North America, and a temperate deciduous forest. As with the krill food web, the diagram in Figure 19.16 (page 605) is simplified from the actual complexity of nature. From our discussion find the primary producers and then locate the primary, secondary, and tertiary consumers in this community. Do you find the detritivores (worms are shown) playing a role as well? Bacteria act as decomposers in the system; do you find any other decomposers in the illustration?

Efficiency in a Food Web

Any assessment of world food resources depends on the level of consumer being targeted. Let us use humans as an example.

(b)

(c)

(d)

(a)

FIGURE 19.14 **Energy, nutrient, and food pathways in the environment.**
(a) The flow of energy, cycling of nutrients, and trophic (feeding) relationships portrayed for a generalized ecosystem. The operation is fueled by radiant energy supplied by sunlight and first captured by the plants. (b) A bearded seal on a bergy bit in the Arctic Ocean. (c) A solitary male polar bear drags its seal feast across pack ice. (d) A mother polar bear and cubs eat a meal on an iceberg after mom caught a seal; birds work on the leftovers. [Bobbé Christopherson.]

Many people can be fed if wheat is eaten directly. However, if the grain is first fed to cattle (herbivores) and then we eat the beef, the yield of available food energy is cut by 90% (810 kg of grain is reduced to 82 kg of meat); far fewer people can be fed from the same land area (Figure 19.17, page 605).

In terms of energy, only about 10% of the kilocalories (food Calories, not heat calories) in plant matter survive from the primary to the secondary trophic level. When humans consume meat instead of grain, there is a further loss of biomass and added inefficiency. More energy is lost to the environment at each progressive step in the food chain. You can see that an omnivorous diet such as with an average North American and European is quite expensive in terms of biomass and energy.

Food web concepts are becoming politicized as world food issues grow more critical. Today, approximately half of the cultivated acreage in Canada and the United States is planted for animal consumption—beef and dairy cattle, hogs, chickens, and turkeys. Livestock feed includes approximately 80% of the annual corn and non-exported soybean harvest (Figure 19.17b). In addition, some lands cleared of rain forest in Central and South America were converted to pasture to produce beef for export to restaurants, stores, and fast-food outlets in

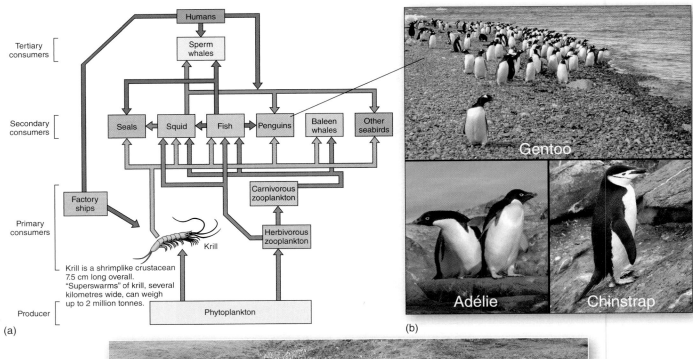

(a)

Tertiary consumers

Secondary consumers

Primary consumers

Producer

Krill is a shrimplike crustacean 7.5 cm long overall. "Superswarms" of krill, several kilometres wide, can weigh up to 2 million tonnes.

(b)

(c) King Penguins, Salisbury Plain, South Georgia Island, Antarctica

FIGURE 19.15 **A complex food web.**
(a) A simplified food web in Antarctic waters, from phytoplankton producers (bottom) through various consumers. Phytoplankton began this chain using photosynthesis to store solar energy. Krill and other herbivorous zooplankton eat the phytoplankton. Krill, in turn, are consumed by the next trophic level. (b) Gentoo penguins (*Pygoscelis papua*) on a rocky shore in Antarctica watch the water for leopard seal predators. Adélie penguins (*Pygoscelis adeliae*) depend on the ice as a base for feeding and are most threatened in Antarctica. Chinstrap penguins (*Pygoscelis antarctica*) show us that we mainly identify penguins by differences in black and white patterns on their heads. (c) Some 100 000 pairs of King Penguins (*Aptenodytes patagonicus*) and their young gather on Salisbury Plain, South Georgia Island. The parents take turns going to the Southern Ocean for fish in this food web, making a constant parade of clean, stomach-full Penguins returning to the juvenile or egg and dirty, empty Penguins head back to the sea. The juveniles are small and dark brown. [Bobbé Christopherson.]

developed countries. Thus, lifestyle decisions and dietary patterns in North America and Europe are perpetuating inefficient food webs, not to mention the destruction of valuable resources, both here and overseas. Developing countries continue to shift dietary patterns to less efficient meat-based food systems, increasing the demand for livestock products.

Ecosystems, Evolution, and Succession

Far from being static, Earth's ecosystems have been dynamic (vigorous and energetic) and ever changing from the beginning of life on the planet. Over time, communities of plants and animals have adapted, evolved, and in turn shaped their

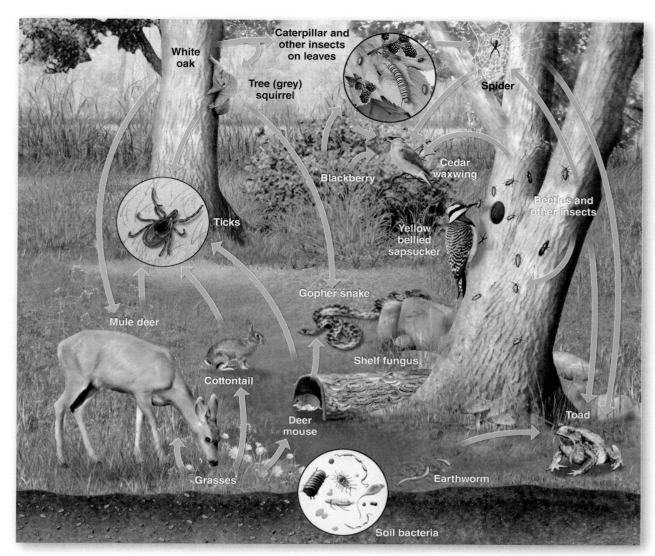

FIGURE 19.16 Temperate forest food webs.
A simplified illustration of food webs in a temperate forest. Examine the art and identify primary producers and primary, secondary, and tertiary consumers. Featured are strong interactions, but many weak interactions not illustrated hold such natural communities together, affirming the hypothesis that complexity is stabilizing and not weakening the community.

FIGURE 19.17 Efficiency and inefficiency in biomass consumption.
(a) Biomass pyramids illustrate a great difference in efficiency between direct and indirect consumption of grain. (b) A feedlot outside Dodge City, Kansas, processes 6500 head of livestock a day, 6 days a week.
[Bobbé Christopherson.]

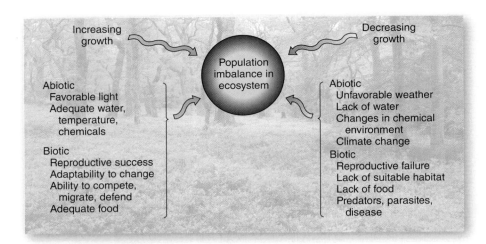

FIGURE 19.18 **Factors controlling the population balance of an ecosystem.** Potential growth factors and resistance factors ultimately determine the population of an ecosystem. [Scottish forest photo by Bobbé Christopherson.]

environments to produce great diversity. A constant interplay exists between a community's increasing growth and its decreasing growth, caused by resistance factors that create limits and disruptions (Figure 19.18). Each ecosystem is constantly adjusting to changing conditions and disturbances in the struggle to survive. The concept of change is key to understanding ecosystem stability.

The nature of change in natural ecosystems can range from gradual transitions from one equilibrium to another, balancing the factors in Figure 19.18, to extreme catastrophes such as an asteroid impact or severe volcanism. In the evolution of life, or the physical and chemical evolution of Earth's systems, such sudden changes created a punctuated equilibrium. Following each of the five major extinctions of life over the past 450 million years, there were great bursts of diversity and proliferation of new and different species, a process known as *speciation*. Although the extinctions temporarily limited biodiversity, each created evolutionary opportunities for speciation to occur.

For most of the last century, scientists thought that an undisturbed ecosystem—whether forest, grassland, aquatic, or other—would progress to a stage of equilibrium, a stable point, with maximum chemical storage and biomass. Modern research has determined, however, that ecosystems do not progress to some static conclusion. In other words, there is no "balance of nature"; instead think of a constant interplay of physical, chemical, and living factors in a dynamic equilibrium.

Biological Evolution Delivers Biodiversity

A critical aspect of ecosystem stability and vitality is **biodiversity**, or species richness of life (a combination of *biological* and *diversity*). Biodiversity includes species diversity, or the number and variety of different species; genetic diversity, or the number of genetic characteristics found within a species; and ecosystem diversity, which includes the number and variety of ecosystems, habitats, and communities on a landscape scale. A working estimate places the number of species presently populating Earth at 13.6 million; however, scientists have classified less than 2 million of these.

The origin of this diversity is embodied in the *theory of evolution*. (The definition of a *scientific theory* is given in Focus Study 1.1). **Evolution** states that single-cell organisms adapted, modified, and passed along inherited changes to multi-cellular organisms. The genetic makeup of successive generations was shaped by environmental factors, physiological functions, and behaviours that led to a greater rate of survival and reproduction. Thus, in this continuing process, traits that help a species survive and reproduce are passed along more frequently than are those that do not. A species refers to a population that can reproduce sexually and produce viable offspring. By definition, this means reproductive isolation from other species.

Each inherited trait is guided by a *gene* that is a segment of the primary genetic material, *DNA* (deoxyribonucleic acid), that resides in the nest of chromosomes in

---

🌐 **GEO REPORT 19.3**   *Poisoning a Food Web; Who Is at the Top?*

A study of food webs is a study of who eats what and where they do the eating. When chemical pesticides are applied to an ecosystem of producers and consumers, the food web concentrates some of these chemicals. Many chemicals are degraded or diluted in air and water and thus are rendered relatively harmless. Other chemicals, however, are long-lived, stable, and soluble in the fatty tissues of consumers. They become increasingly concentrated at each higher trophic level. The polar bears of the Barents Sea have some of the highest levels of persistent organic pollutants (POPs) in any animal in the world, despite their remoteness from civilization. The pollution arrived in ocean currents and the atmosphere.

Thus, pollution in a food web can efficiently poison the organism at the top. Many species are threatened in this manner, and, of course, humans are at the top of many food chains and can ingest concentrated chemicals in this way. This is called *biological amplification*, or *magnification*.

every cell nucleus. These traits—and especially the ones that are most successful at maximizing niches different from those of other species or that help the species adapt to environmental changes—are passed to successive generations. Such differential reproduction and adaptation passes along successful genes or groups of genes in a process of genetic favouritism called *natural selection*. The process of evolution follows generation after generation and tracks the passage of inherited characteristics that were successful—the failures passed into extinction. Thus, today's humans are the result of billions of years of positive change and affirmative natural selection.

New mixes in the *gene pool*, or all genes possessed by individuals in a given population, involve *mutations*. Mutation is a process that occurs when a random action, or perhaps an error as the DNA reproduces, forms new genetic material and inserts new traits into the inherited stream. Geography comes into play; physical environments affect natural selection and differ over space. For example, a species may disperse through migration to a different environment where new traits are favored. Imagine the evolutionary effects of migrations across ice bridges or land connections at times of low sea level. A species may also be separated from other species by a natural *vicariance* (fragmentation of the environment) event. Continental drift established natural barriers to species movement and resulted in the evolution of new species. The physical and chemical evolution of Earth's systems is therefore closely linked to the biological evolution of life.

The deciphering of complete species *genomes*, or the total genetic identity of an organism, is a scientific triumph and is disclosing a complex history and geography of each species—where species originated, how species are dispersed, what diseases and traumas were of consequence. Analysis of the human genome has indicated our origins and provided a road map of how we got to where we are.

Biodiversity Fosters Ecosystem Stability

Stable ecosystems are constantly changing. An ecosystem with *inertial stability* has the ability to resist some low-level disturbance. *Resilience* is an ecosystem's ability to recover from disturbance and return to its original state. In an ecosystem, a population of organisms can be stable yet not resilient. Further, some disturbances are too extreme for even a highly resilient ecosystem. Several of the dramatic asteroid impact episodes that triggered partial extinctions over the past 440 million years overcame the resilience of plant and animal communities. Think of resilience as an ecosystem's ability to recover from disturbance, its ability to absorb disturbance up to some threshold point before it snaps to a different set of relations, thus altering some logical ecological progression.

A tropical rain forest is a diverse, stable community that can withstand most natural disturbance. Yet this ecosystem has low resilience in terms of severe events; a cleared tract of rain forest will recover slowly because most of the nutrients are stored in the vegetation rather than in the soil. Changes in microclimates may also make regrowth of the same species difficult. In contrast, a midlatitude grassland is less diverse and low in stability, yet high in resilience. When burned, the community recovers rapidly due to extensive root systems that allow rapid regrowth.

In the context of ecosystem stability and resilience, consider the elimination of a full section of forest ecosystem on private land in southern Oregon, south-southeast of Crater Lake, shown in Figure 19.19. Note the high

FIGURE 19.19 Poor practices disrupt stable forest communities.
(a) An example of clear-cut timber harvesting that has devastated a stable forest community and produced drastic changes in microclimatic conditions. (b) A logged pine forest and logging road. About 10% of the Northwest's old-growth forests remain, as identified through satellite images and GIS analysis. [(a) Bobbé Christopherson. (b) Robert Christopherson.]

road density, the inadequate buffers along watercourses to prevent sedimentation of streams, the drag lines and skid trails to each pickup spot that pockmark the landscape. On nearby U.S. Forest Service land, the rules are clear: A full 95-m tree buffer is left on either side of a stream, road densities are minimized, and harvesting regimes that include partial removals, commercial thinning, and group selection harvests, among others, are all in contrast to the devastation on private lands in the photo. Scientists have determined that for sustainable forests the sole objective should never be the complete removal of the timber.

In the 1990s, field experiments in prairie ecosystems of Minnesota began to confirm an important scientific assumption: that greater biological diversity in an ecosystem leads to greater long-term stability and productivity. For instance, during a drought, some species of plants will be damaged. In a diverse ecosystem, however, other species with deeper roots and better water-obtaining ability will thrive. Ongoing experiments also suggest that a more diverse plant community is able to retain and use soil nutrients more efficiently than is one with less diversity. For more about this ongoing research effort at the Cedar Creek Ecosystem Science Reserve, see http://www.cedarcreek.umn.edu/about/.

The present loss of biodiversity is irreversible. Extinction is final no matter how complex the organism or how long it lived since it evolved. E. O. Wilson, the famed biologist, has written that all species, and all genes within species, must be considered together and that across the globe biodiversity is in trouble.

Recent efforts at ecosystem restoration have had some success in preserving biodiversity, although questions remain about the effects of such efforts on increasing or restoring ecosystem services. The goal of returning ecosystems to original conditions before human intervention is now being expanded to include consideration of "novel ecosystems," those combinations of species and habitats that have never occurred together. To sustain biodiversity and the way ecosystems function in our changing world may demand consideration of these human-altered ecosystems.

Agricultural Ecosystems and Change Humans simplify communities and ecosystems by eliminating biodiversity, thus making them more vulnerable to disturbance. An artificially produced monoculture community, such as a field of wheat, is singularly vulnerable to severe weather or attack from insects or plant disease. In some regions, simply planting multiple crops brings more stability to the ecosystem. This is an important principle of sustainable agriculture, a movement to make farming more ecologically compatible.

A modern agricultural ecosystem creates an enormous demand for energy, chemical pesticides and herbicides, artificial fertilizer, and irrigation water. The practice of harvesting and removing biomass from the land interrupts the cycling of materials into the soil (Figure 19.20). This

net loss of nutrients must be artificially replenished. The type of plantation agriculture in Figure 19.20b is depleting of soil nutrients over time; this farming practice requires subsidies of chemical fertilizers and herbicides to eliminate competing vegetation.

Increasing temperatures with climate change reduce yields and increase overhead costs. Imagine being a farmer in the latter part of this century when average summer conditions exceed the hottest extreme summer temperatures of today. The stress on agricultural ecosystems, crops, and livestock will be something experienced across the globe in tropical, subtropical, midlatitude, and subarctic regions.

Species distributions are also affected by climate change, as presented in this chapter's Geosystems Now. Current global change is occurring rapidly, at the rate of decades instead of millions of years. Thus, we see die-out and succession of different species along disadvantageous habitat margins. The displaced species may colonize new regions made more hospitable by climate change. Also shifting will be agricultural lands that produced wheat, corn, soybeans, and other commodities. Society will have to adapt to these changes.

Ecological Succession

Ecological succession occurs when newer communities of plants and animals (usually more complex) replace older ones (usually simpler)—a change of species composition. Each successive community of species modifies the physical environment in a manner suitable for a later community of species. Changes apparently move toward a more mature condition, although disturbances are common and constantly disrupt the sequence.

Succession often requires an initiating disturbance. Examples include a windstorm, severe flooding, a volcanic eruption, a devastating wildfire, an insect infestation, and an agricultural practice such as prolonged overgrazing (Figure 19.21). When existing organisms are disturbed or removed, new communities can emerge. At such times of nonequilibrium transition, the interrelationships among species produce elements of chance, and species having an adaptive edge will succeed in the competitive struggle for light, water, nutrients, space, time, reproduction, and survival.

Rather than thinking of ecosystems as uniform across the landscape, think of them as a patchwork mosaic of communities and habitats. This is the study of *patch dynamics*, or the interactions between and within disturbed portions of habitats. Individual patches may be undergoing different stages of succession, thus adding to complexity in the landscape. Most ecosystems are in actuality made up of patches of former landscapes. Biodiversity in some respects is the result of such patch dynamics.

Land and water experience different forms of succession. We first look at terrestrial succession, characterized by competition for sunlight, and then at aquatic succession, characterized by progressive changes in nutrient levels.

(a) Alfalfa feedstocks, central Minnesota

(b) Pinetree plantation in Ontario

(c) Harvesting oats near Dokka, Norway

(d) Broccoli, near San Luis Obispo, California

(e) Fish farming, Bay of Fundy, Nova Scotia

FIGURE 19.20 Examples of agricultural ecosystems.
[(a), (c), (d), and (e) by Bobbé Christopherson; (b) J. David Andrews/Masterfile.]

CRITICAL THINKING 19.2

Observe Ecosystem Disturbances

Over the next several days as you travel between home and campus, a job, or other areas, observe the landscape. What types of ecosystem disturbances do you see? Imagine that several hectares in the same area you are viewing had escaped any disruptions for a century or more. Describe what some of these ecosystems and communities might be like.

Terrestrial Succession

An area of bare rock or a disturbed site with no vestige of a former community can be a place for **primary succession**, the beginning of an ecosystem. Examples include new surfaces created by mass movement of land, areas exposed by a retreating glacier, cooled lava flows and volcanic eruption landscapes, or surface mining and clear-cut logging scars, or areas of sand dunes. Plants taking hold on new lava flows from the Kīlauea volcano, Hawai'i, illustrate primary

(a)

(b)

(c)

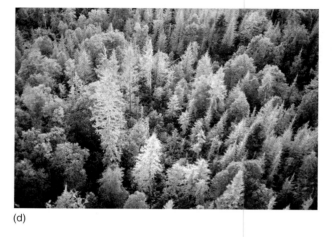
(d)

FIGURE 19.21 Disturbances in ecosystems alter succession patterns.
(a) After flooding along Rivière des Ha! Ha!, Québec, extensive aggradation renews the sediment supply to the valley. (b) Community development proceeds in a burned forest, progressing perhaps by chance, as species with an adaptive edge, such as fireweed (*Epilobium* sp.), succeed. (c) Unwise practices cause extensive soil erosion on a hog farm in Iowa; a disrupted prairie landscape. (d) Insect infestation (spruce budworm) weakens trees that turn grey and die off. [(a) Courtesy of the Geological Survey of Canada. Photo 1997-42KK by G. R. Brooks. Reproduced with the permission of Natural Resources Canada. © 2012; (b) Bobbé Christopherson; (c) USDA Natural Resources Conservation Service; (d) Natural Resources Canada, Reproduced with the permission of the Minister of Public Works and Government Services, 2012. Courtesy of the Canadian Forest Service.]

succession (Figure 19.22). In terrestrial ecosystems, succession begins with early species that form a **pioneer community**. Primary succession often begins with lichens, mosses, and ferns growing on bare rock. These early inhabitants prepare the way for further succession to grasses, shrubs, and trees.

More common in nature is **secondary succession**, which begins if some aspects of a previously functioning community are present. An area where the natural community has been destroyed or disturbed, but where the underlying soil remains intact, may experience secondary succession.

As succession progresses, soil develops, and a different set of plants and animals with different niche requirements may adapt. Further niche expansion follows as the community matures. Succession, which is really the developmental process forming new communities, is a dynamic set of interactions with sometimes unpredictable outcomes, steered by sometimes random, unpredictable events that trigger a threshold leap to a new set of relations—the basis of *dynamic ecology*.

Examples of secondary succession are most of the areas affected by the Mount St. Helens eruption and blast in 1980, which burned or blew down about 38 450 hectares of trees (Figure 19.23). Some soils, young trees, and plants were protected under ash and snow, so community development began almost immediately after the event. The areas

completely destroyed near the Mount St. Helens volcano or those buried beneath the massive landslide north of the mountain became candidates for primary succession.

As succession progresses, soil develops and a different set of plants and animals with different niche requirements may adapt. Further niche expansion follows as the community matures. Succession, which is really the developmental process forming new communities, is a dynamic set

FIGURE 19.22 Primary succession.
Ferns take hold as primary succession on new lava flows that came from the Kīlauea volcano in Hawai'i. [Bobbé Christopherson.]

(a)   1979

(b)   1980

2008—view from the ISS

(c)   1983

1999

(d)   1983

1999

(e)   1983

1999

(f)   1983

1999

FIGURE 19.23 **The pace of change in the region of Mount St. Helens.**
A 2008 astronaut photo of the volcano shows the devastation (north is to the right). The area north of the volcano—(a) before the eruption (1979) and (b) after the eruption (1980)—experienced profound change in all ecosystems. A series of four photo comparisons made in 1983 and 1999 of matching scenes illustrates the slow recovery of secondary succession: (c) and (d) at Meta Lake; (e) Spirit Lake panorama view (note the mat of floating logs after 19 years); (f) detail of the destroyed forest community. [*ISS* astronaut photo, NASA/GSFC. (a) 1979, 1980, and 1983 photos by Robert Christopherson; (b) all 1999 photos by Bobbé Christopherson.]

of interactions with sometimes unpredictable outcomes, steered by sometimes random, unpredictable events that trigger a threshold leap to a new set of relations—the basis of *dynamic ecology*.

Succession through the Ice Age Glaciation is a large-scale disturbance that well illustrates how succession operates. As Earth cycled through glacial and interglacial ages (Chapter 17), the ecological succession in all ecosystems was affected repeatedly. Imagine the milder midlatitude climate at the beginning of an interglacial warming, with lush herb and shrub vegetation slowly giving way to pioneer trees of birch, aspen, and pine. Winds and animals dispersed seeds, and changing communities readily spread in response to changing conditions. During the warm interglacial, trees increased shade and the organic content of soil increased. Deciduous trees such as oak, elm, and ash spread freely on well-drained soils; willow, cottonwood, and alder grew on poorly drained land.

As climates cooled with the approach of the next glacial, soils became more acidic, so podzolization (cool, moist, forested) processes dominated (see Chapter 18), helped by the acidity of spruce and fir trees. Ecosystems slowly returned to the vegetation community that existed at the beginning of the interglacial. The increased cold produced open regions of disturbed ecosystems. Freezing and the advance of ice disrupted highly acidic soils.

The Holocene (the past 10 000 years) is apparently atypical because of the development of human societies and agriculture. Civilization is creating an artificial and accelerated succession, similar in some ways to the closing centuries of an interglacial. The challenge for biogeographers is to understand such long-term developmental change principles, given the accelerated pace at which change is occurring in the industrial and postindustrial era.

Wildfire and Fire Ecology Fire and its effects are one of Earth's significant ecosystem and economic processes. In Canada and the United States since 2000, more than double the annual average area burned in wildfires. Each year's loss seemingly beat the record set the year before—in 2009, 72 000 fires burned nearly 2.3 million hectares in the United States. For more information, see the National Interagency Fire Center at http://www.nifc.gov/fire_info/nfn.htm.

Over the past 50 years, the role of fire in ecosystems has been the subject of much scientific research and experimentation. Today, fire is recognized as a natural component of most ecosystems and not the enemy of nature that it was once thought to be. In fact, in many forests, undergrowth and surface litter is purposely burned in controlled "cool fires" to remove fuel and prevent catastrophic and destructive "hot fires." Forestry experts have learned that, when fire-prevention strategies are rigidly followed, they can lead to the abundant undergrowth accumulation that fuels major fires.

Modern society's demand for fire prevention to protect property goes back to European forestry of the 1800s.

Fire prevention became an article of faith for forest managers in North America. But, in studies of the longleaf pine forest that stretches in a wide band from the Atlantic coastal plain to Texas, fire was discovered to be an integral part of regrowth following lumbering. In fact, seed dispersal of some pine species, such as the knobcone and Jack pine, do not occur unless assisted by a forest fire. Heat from the fire opens the cones, releasing seeds so they can fall to the ground for germination. Also, these fire-disturbed areas quickly recover with protein-rich woody growth, young plants, and a stimulated seed production that provides abundant food for animals.

The science of **fire ecology** imitates nature by recognizing fire as a dynamic ingredient in community succession. Controlled ground fires, deliberately set to prevent accumulation of forest undergrowth, now are widely regarded as a wise forest management practice and are used across North America. The Canadian Forest Service (CFS, a branch of Natural Resources Canada, http://www.nofc.cfs.nrcan.gc.ca), the agency that oversees the management of Canada's forests, recognizes that fire is an important natural disturbance in many of Canada's forest ecosystems. It is especially important in the boreal forest.

In the early 1900s, organized forest fire suppression began with the goal of reducing wildfire threat to public safety and to timber resources. The CFS researched the relationship between forest management and fire management since the 1920s, focusing on the development of an assessment system for evaluating wildfire threats both spatially and temporally; the creation of landscape-level fuel treatments; and the synthesis and distribution of information to mitigate wildfire threat in wildland-urban interface areas. In the United States, the U.S. Department of Agriculture's Forest Service first recognized the principle of fire ecology in the early 1940s and formally implemented the practice in 1972. Controlled ground fires, deliberately set to prevent accumulation of forest undergrowth, now are widely regarded as a wise forest management practice and are used across the country.

Wildland-urban interface areas are the places where urban or agricultural structures are located near trees and other vegetation. These areas in Canada and elsewhere present an increasingly serious problem because wildfires have the potential to burn both buildings and wildland vegetation simultaneously, in what fire managers call *interface fires*. For example, the Canadian Forest Service reports that in Canada during 1998, interface fires forced the evacuation of 18 000 residents, and another 46 000 were placed on evacuation alert. In 2003, interface fires caused massive destruction in Kelowna, British Columbia and the second costliest insured disaster in Canadian history resulted from the wildfire destruction of Slave Lake, Alberta in 2011. Information for living in the interface and suggestions for creating communities that are aware of fire dangers can be found on the CFS website (http://www.nofc.cfs.nrcan.gc.ca/pages/159). The connection between the record wildfires in the West since 2000 and climate change was reported in *Science* in 2006. These changes are occurring in Canada as well.

Higher spring and summer temperatures and earlier snowmelt are extending the wildfire season and increasing the intensity of wildfires in the western U.S. . . . Here, we show that large wildfire activity increased suddenly and markedly in the mid-1980s, with higher large-wildfire frequency. Longer wildfire durations, and longer wildfire seasons. . . strongly associated with increased spring and summer temperatures and an earlier spring snowmelt.[3]

[3]A. L. Westerling, H. G. Hidalgo, D. R. Cayan, and T. W. Swetnam, "Warming and earlier spring increase western U.S. forest wildfire activity," *Science* 313, no. 5789 (August 18, 2006): 940–943.

Aquatic Succession

Ecosystems occur in water as well as on land. Lakes, estuaries, ponds, and shorelines are complex ecosystems. The concepts that you just read about—stability and resilience, biodiversity, community succession—apply to open water, shoreline, and watershed systems as well.

Focus Study 19.1 examines ecosystems of the Great Lakes of North America. This is the largest lake system on Earth and is jointly managed by Canada and the United States.

When viewed across geologic time, a lake or pond is really a temporary feature on the landscape. Lakes and ponds exhibit successional stages as they fill with nutrients and sediment and as aquatic plants take root and grow. This growth captures more sediment and adds organic debris to the system (Figure 19.24). This gradual enrichment in

[text continued page 618]

FIGURE 19.24 Idealized lake–bog–meadow succession in temperate conditions.
(a) What begins as a lake gradually fills with organic and inorganic sediments, which successively shrink the area of the pond. A bog forms, then a marshy area, and finally a meadow completes the successional stages.
(b) Spring Mill Lake, Indiana. (c) Organic content increases as succession progresses in a mountain lake.
(d) The Richmond Nature Park and its Lulu Island Bog were ocean just 8000 years ago. Frasier River sediment created the mudflats and set the stage for the evolution of this sphagnum bog with acidic soils that "quakes" when you walk on it. Plants in the bog include moss, shore pine, hemlock, blueberry, salal shrubs, and Labrador tea, among others. [Bobbé Christopherson.]

FOCUS STUDY 19.1

Ecosystems of the Great Lakes

The Great Lakes—Superior, Michigan, Huron, Erie, and Ontario—contain 18% of the total volume of all freshwater lakes in the world and have dominated the history and development of North America. The basins of the Great Lakes are gifts of the last ice age, when glaciers advanced and retreated over this region (see Figure 17.29). Their combined surface area covers 244 000 km², a little less than the Atlantic Provinces excluding Labrador. The entire drainage basin embraces 528 000 km², or an area about the size of Manitoba.

This international waterway of lakes and connecting rivers spans more than 2771 km from west to east, with 18 000 km of coastline—many consider this Canada's fourth coastline (Figure 19.1.1). The lakes contain over 30 000 islands and diverse coastal environments, featuring

(a)

(b)

FIGURE 19.1.1 **The Great Lakes Basin.** (a) Elevations above sea level, depths below lake level, and principal urban areas are shown. The map outline is the limit of the drainage basin for the Great Lakes system. (b) The Great Lakes region on a rare cloudless day August 10, 2010. [(a) Map courtesy of Environment Canada, U.S. EPA, and Brock University cartography; (b) *Aqua* MODIS image, NASA/GSFC.]

FIGURE 19.1.2 Great Lakes elevation profile and lake levels.
Average depth and lake surface levels, 2010. The International Great Lakes Datum of 1985 is the standard baseline. [Data courtesy of the Canadian Hydrographic Service, Central Region, and the International Coordinating Committee on the Great Lakes Basin Hydraulic and Hydrographic Data.]

major dunes and sandy beaches, bedrock shorelines, gravel beaches, and adjoining coastal wetlands. Major agricultural regions surround the lakes, as do many centres of industrial activity, maritime commerce, and tourism.

Lake Superior is the highest in elevation, deepest, and largest in the system (Figure 19.1.2). It drains through St. Mary's River into Lake Huron, which is connected to and at the same surface elevation as Lake Michigan; the two lakes are joined through the Straits of Mackinac. Water then flows through the St. Clair River, Lake St. Clair and the Detroit River into Lake Erie, the shallowest of the Great Lakes. Compared to an average water retention time of 191 years in Lake Superior, Lake Erie has the shortest retention time of 2.6 years. The Niagara River transports water into Lake Ontario, which is drained by the St. Lawrence River into the St. Lawrence Estuary and Gulf of St. Lawrence and eventually into the North Atlantic Ocean.

Because of the large size of the overall Great Lakes system, its associated climate, soils, and topography vary widely. Dominating the north are colder microthermal climates, exposed portions of the Canadian Shield bedrock, and vast stands of conifers and acidic soils. To the south, warmer mesothermal climates and fertile, glacially deposited soils provide a vast agricultural base. Farms and urbanization replaced previous stands of mixed forest. The original landcover is almost completely disturbed.

Changing Lake Levels

Measurements of Great Lakes water levels extend back to 1860. Recently, water levels were slightly lower, with dry conditions across the region into 2010, as all lakes were below average by up to 0.3 m. Only Lake Ontario was about 2.5 cm above average in late 2010. Lake levels are higher in the summer after snowmelt and with increased summer maximum precipitation. Lake levels fluctuate annually, depending on precipitation and evaporation in the basin; near-drought conditions bring lower lake levels.

Climate change is forecasted to lower lake levels as evaporation increases from lake surfaces. Eleven major climate models forecast reductions from 0.3 m to as much as 1.5 m in a worst-case projection, reducing outflow into the St. Lawrence by 20% to 40%. When added to increased human consumption and water demand across the region, this is a double blow to lake levels. This will make wetlands even more vulnerable as the coastal shoreline retreats. Losses of wetlands translate to habitat loss for many species.

Wetlands and Coastal Ecosystems

Wetlands in the Great Lakes are tied to lake levels, which determine wetland distribution, vegetation composition, and ecological operations. Wetland ecosystems exist throughout the Great Lakes, along 18 000 km of shoreline and extensive connecting river channels, occurring as swamps, marshes, bogs, and fens.

Coastal wetlands occupy that key interface between the land and the water, storing and cycling organic material and nutrients into aquatic ecosystems. Among many important wetlands are the far western end of Lake Superior in the St. Louis River estuary, the area along Sturgeon Bay in the Door Peninsula of Wisconsin, and the far eastern end of Lake Ontario and its coastal lagoon. Over two-thirds of Great Lakes wetlands have been lost during this century, and those remaining are threatened by development, drainage, or pollution. These ecosystems are critically important for migratory waterfowl as seasonal habitat, for a number of amphibians, and for fisheries, as many Great Lakes species depend on

FIGURE 19.1.3 Land use in the Great Lakes Basin.
Generalized distribution map of land use, nonagricultural and agricultural, in the Great Lakes Basin.
[Environment Canada, U.S. EPA, and Brock University cartography.]

coastal wetlands as a reproduction niche. Wetlands also filter pollutants and anchor soils and sediment against wave erosion.

Society asks much of the Great Lakes and coastal ecosystems: to dilute wastes from cities and industry, to dissipate thermal pollution from power plants, to provide municipal drinking water and irrigation water, and to sustain unique and varied ecosystems—open lake, coastal shore, coastal wetland, lakeplain (former lake bed), inland wetland, and inland terrestrial (upland areas of forest, prairie, and barrens).

Land Use, Human Activities, and Impacts

Figure 19.1.3 portrays land use in the Great Lakes Basin. About 25% of Canada's population and 10% of the U.S. population live in the Great Lakes drainage basin. Major agricultural regions

and many centres of industrial activity surround the lakes. The eight Great Lakes states generate $18 billion per year in revenue from agriculture, pulp and paper, fisheries, transportation, and tourism, among other activities. Twenty-five percent of Canada's farm revenues are in the Great Lakes Basin along with an Ontario forestry industry that tops $19 billion and a commercial fishery with revenues exceeding $250 million.

Each activity has its own impact on lake systems. Runoff from agricultural areas contains chemicals, nutrients, and eroded soil. The pulp and paper industry was a major polluter, but has improved as more was learned about the dangers of pollution; for example, mercury contamination was halted in the 1970s, and better disposal methods for wastes were implemented. The forests were not always treated in a sustainable way in

terms of reforestation, and today forests may be regarded as a diminished resource in the basin. Recovery efforts are slow to make up for bad past practices, but progress is under way.

Lake Erie was the first of the Great Lakes to show severe effects of *cultural eutrophication*, for it is the shallowest and warmest of the five lakes. About a third of the overall population in the Great Lakes Basin lives in the drainage of Lake Erie, making it the major recipient of sewage effluent from treatment plants. Over the years, dissolved oxygen levels dropped as biochemical oxygen demand increased, caused by sewage-treatment discharges and algal decay, forming low-oxygen dead zones. Algae flourished in these eutrophic conditions and coated the beaches, turning the lake a greenish brown. In the 1950s and 1960s, the oily contaminated surface of the Cuyahoga River, flowing into Lake Erie through Cleveland, Ohio, caught fire several times. The 1969 fire finally spurred public opinion to demand action.

In the 1970s, environmental restrictions were implemented and inputs of phosphorus into Lake Erie were eventually reduced by 90%. The dead zone steadily declined. However, in the 1990s, a significant dead zone was again identified in Lake Erie, with scientists still trying to understand its return. Two hypotheses have emerged: First is the possibility that introduced species—such as exotic zebra and quagga mussels—are compounding the anoxic (lacking oxygen) or hypoxic (low oxygen) conditions along lake bottoms. Second is the effect of climate change on lake stratification. As discussed in the Chapter 7 *Geosystems Now*, warming temperatures extend the period of time when the lakes are stratified, isolating the cooler bottom waters for more weeks each year.

Lake stratification plays a role in the formation of these oxygen-depleted dead zones. In the summer, as in most lakes, the Great Lakes stratify as the surface waters warm and become less dense and the cooler waters collect to form the lower layer in the lake. Little mixing occurs between these two layers, so productivity is accelerated in the top layers—increased nutrients and light penetration cause this increase.

Normally, as the fall season matures, surface water cools and sinks, displacing deeper water and creating a turnover of the lake mass. By midwinter, the temperature from the surface to the bottom is uniformly around 4°C, the point at which water is densest; temperatures at the surface are near freezing—but this is changing.

Overall the lakes are warming with climate change. Lake Superior surface water reached 23.9°C in July of 2007. During August 2010, Lake Superior was 8 C° above normal water temperature and Lake Michigan 4 C° above normal—both new records. Scientists are analyzing the impact of these temperature increases on lake ecosystems and the prolonging of the period of lake stratification, which interrupts normal lake turnover.

Aquatic Ecosystems and Restoration

The Great Lakes support a food chain of producers and consumers, as does any aquatic ecosystem. Native fish populations have suffered from human activities: overfishing, introduction of exotic species, pollution from excess nutrients, toxic contamination, and disruption of spawning habitats. Commercial fishing peaked in the 1880s, but it wasn't until water pollution peaked in the 1960s and early 1970s that fisheries declined to their lowest levels.

Toxic chemicals such as polychlorinated biphenols (PCBs) and DDT—both banned in North America in the 1970s—accumulate and persist in lake sediments and organisms and are subject to biological amplification as they move up the food chain. In the Great Lakes, scientists have reported PCBs found in phytoplankton, rainbow smelt, lake trout, and, higher in the food chain, a herring gull eggshell.

In 1972, Canada and the United States signed the Great Lakes Water Quality Agreement, and the cleanup was under way. The governments implemented strong pollution-control programs, working in concert with citizens, industries, and private organizations. These efforts resulted in declining levels of PCBs and DDT in the lakes up until 1990, when rates of decline levelled off. Today, lake trout (in Lake Superior), sturgeon, herring, smelt, alewife, splake, yellow perch, pickerel (walleye), and white bass are fished. However, health advisories are occasionally issued warning of danger in consuming fish of certain species, sizes, and locales.

An ecosystem approach to management of the Great Lakes Basin is the key to recovery. This approach considers the physical, chemical, and biological components that constitute the total system. In 2010, the U.S. government approved $475 million in funding for the Great Lakes Restoration Initiative, the largest U.S. investment of federal dollars in the Great Lakes in 20 years. This initiative targets some of the greatest threats to the lakes—namely, invasive species and pollution of water and sediment. Priority areas also include restoring wetlands and other critical habitats (see http://greatlakesrestoration.us/).

For more information on Great Lakes ecosystems, go to Environment Canada's Great Lakes home page at http://www.ec.gc.ca/grandslacs-greatlakes/default.asp?lang=En and NOAA's Great Lakes Research Lab site at http://www.glerl.noaa.gov/. (For additional Great Lakes information, see http://www.seagrant.wisc.edu/outreach/.)

GEO REPORT 19.4 *Another Take on Lake–Bog Succession*

Research has uncovered an apparent opposite pattern to the lake–bog succession described, in areas that have been recently deglaciated. The new study points to the reality that succession is poorly understood in aquatic ecosystems. Scientists examined lakes in the Glacier Bay, Alaska, area and found that they had become more dilute, acidic, and unproductive—in other words, less eutrophic—during the past 10 000 years. Successional changes in the surrounding vegetation and soils seem to be linked to the aquatic ecosystem. These studies suggest that in various cool, moist, temperate rainforest climates with landscapes created by glacial retreat, different processes are at work in lakes.

water bodies is known as eutrophication (from the Greek *eutrophos*, meaning "well nourished").

In moist climates, a floating mat of vegetation grows outward from the shore to form a bog. Cattails and other marsh plants become established, and partially decomposed organic material accumulates in the basin, with additional vegetation bordering the remaining lake surface. Vegetation and soil and a meadow may fill in as water is displaced; willow trees follow, and perhaps cottonwood trees; and eventually the lake may evolve into a forest community.

The stages in lake succession are named for their nutrient levels: *oligotrophic* (low nutrients), *mesotrophic* (medium nutrients), and *eutrophic* (high nutrients). Greater primary productivity and resultant decreases in water transparency mark each stage, so that photosynthesis becomes concentrated near the surface. Energy flow shifts from production to respiration in the eutrophic stage, with oxygen demand exceeding oxygen availability.

Nutrient levels also vary spatially: Oligotrophic conditions occur in deep water, whereas eutrophic conditions occur along the shore, in shallow bays, or where sewage, fertilizer, or other nutrient inputs occur. Even large bodies of water may have eutrophic areas along the shore. As society dumps sewage, agricultural runoff, and pollution in waterways, the nutrient load is enhanced beyond the cleansing ability of natural biological processes. The result is *cultural eutrophication*, which hastens succession in aquatic systems.

GEOSYSTEMS CONNECTION

Earth's biosphere is a remarkable functioning entity of abiotic and biotic components, all interacting and interrelated through some 13.6 million species. Plants harvest sunlight through photosynthesis and thus begin vast food webs of energy and nutrition. Life evolved on Earth into a biologically diverse structure of organisms, communities, and ecosystems, seemingly gaining strength and resilience through their biodiversity. We next move to biomes and a synthesis of all the subjects from Chapters 2 through 19, as we bring it all together to form a portrait of our planet.

 APPLIED PHYSICAL GEOGRAPHY *Species Diversity and Species Richness*

The distribution of species in space is an important property examined by both biogeographers and ecologists. By examining patterns of diversity we gain insight into factors that cause the variation.

Diversity refers to the abundance of taxa that are present in a prescribed area. At its simplest, diversity is measured as species richness: the greater the number of different species in an area, the greater the species richness of that area.

More complex mathematical techniques also are available to measure diversity. These techniques combine information on species richness and the relative abundance of species. Using the expanded definition, an area that has many species (high species richness) and is not dominated by any one species has high diversity. Under this definition, a forest composed of 20% paper birch, 20% hemlock, 20% white pine, 20% white spruce, and 20% Manitoba maple would have a higher diversity (but the same species richness) than a forest of 95% paper birch, 2% hemlock, 1% white pine, 1% white spruce, and 1% Manitoba maple.

Three areas of eastern Canada were sampled in a study of tree diversity. The data are presented in Table 1.

Using the information in Table 1, we calculate the species richness of each area. This is simply a count of the number of species present. For Site A: Richness = 6, Site B: Richness = 5, and Site C: Richness = 5. By this measure, the sites appear to be relatively similar.

Species diversity can be calculated for each area using Simpson's Index of Diversity:

$$D = 1 - \Sigma(P_i)$$

where *D* is the diversity and *Pi* is the proportion of species *i* in the study area.

For Site A: D = 1 − 0.24
= 0.76

For Site B: D = 1 − 0.26
= 0.74

For Site C: D = 1 − 0.32
= 0.68

This measure shows that all sites differ in diversity. The diversity of the sites can be related to latitude, amongst other controls: The most diverse site is the most southerly, the middle in diversity is from the middle region, and the least diverse is from the most northerly region.

Biogeographical Similarity

The biogeographical similarity (also called ecological similarity) of two areas is measured by the similarity of the species found in one area when compared to the other area. Biogeographical similarity is measured mathematically. If two areas (even if far apart in space) have the same species present, they are considered to be similar.

To calculate the biogeographical similarity of the three sites, we use the Greig-Smith Index of Similarity:

$$I = 2c/a + b$$

where *I* is the difference between the two areas (I = 1, no difference; I = 0, completely different), *a* is the species richness of one site, *b* is the species richness of the other site, and *c* is the number of species common to both sites.

Compare Site A with Site B
$$I_{AB} = (2 \times 3/6) + 5$$
$$= 0.55$$

Compare Site B with Site C
$$I_{BC} = (2 \times 3/5) + 5$$
$$= 0.60$$

Compare Site C with Site A
$$I_{CA} = (2 \times 2/5) + 6$$
$$= 0.36$$

This comparison shows that sites A and B have a moderate similarity—A is in the Carolinian zone known as the Midlatitude broadleaf and mixed forest and B is in the transition zone to the needleleaf forest and montane forest. The two sites are relatively close to each other (A is closer to B than to C). Sites B and C have the greatest similarity—both are in the transition to Boreal forest (needleleaf forest and montane forest). Sites A and C are the greatest distance apart and are the least similar.

TABLE 1 Tree Diversity in Three Sites of Eastern Canada

Site A: Leamington, Ontario (42°03′ N)

Species	Number of Trees	Proportion
White Pine (*Pinus strobus*)	2	0.2
Beech (*Fagus grandifolia*)	4	0.4
Sugar Maple (*Acer saccharum*)	1	0.1
White Oak (*Quercus alba*)	1	0.1
Kentucky Coffee Tree (*Gymnocladus dioicus*)	1	0.1
Eastern Flowering Dogwood (*Cornus florida*)	1	0.1
Total	10	

Site B: Hamilton, Ontario (43°15′ N)

Species	Number of Trees	Proportion
White Pine (*Pinus strobus*)	2	0.2
Sugar Maple (*Acer saccharum*)	4	0.4
Paper Birch (*Betula papyrifera*)	2	0.2
Beech (*Fagus grandifolia*)	1	0.1
Black Cherry (*Prunus serotina*)	1	0.1
Total	10	

Site C: Hull, Québec (45°25′ N)

Species	Number of Trees	Proportion
White Pine (*Pinus strobus*)	10	0.5
White Spruce (*Picea glauca*)	2	0.1
Hemlock (*Tsuga Canadensis*)	2	0.1
Paper Birch (*Betula papyrifera*)	4	0.2
Sugar Maple (*Acer saccharum*)	2	0.1
Total	20	

KEY LEARNING CONCEPTS REVIEW

■ **Define** ecology, biogeography, and the ecosystem concept.

Earth's biosphere is unique in the Solar System; its ecosystems are the essence of life. **Ecosystems** are self-sustaining associations of living plants and animals and their nonliving physical environment. **Ecology** is the study of the relationships between organisms and their environment and among the various ecosystems in the biosphere.

Biogeography is the study of the distribution of plants and animals and the diverse spatial patterns they create. Biogeographers trace communities across the ages, considering plate tectonics and ancient dispersal of plants and animals.

ecosystem (p. 588)
ecology (p. 588)
biogeography (p. 588)

1. What is the relationship between the biosphere and an ecosystem? Define ecosystem, and give some examples.
2. What does biogeography include? Describe its relationship to ecology.
3. Briefly summarize what ecosystem operations imply about the complexity of life.

■ **Describe** communities, habitats, and niches.

A **community** is formed by the interactions among populations of living animals and plants at a particular time. Within a community, a **habitat** is the specific physical location of an organism—its address. A **niche** is the function or operation of a life form within a given community—its profession.

4. Define a community within an ecosystem.
5. What do the concepts of habitat and niche involve? Relate them to some specific plant and animal communities.
6. Describe symbiotic and parasitic relationships in nature. Draw an analogy between these relationships and human societies on our planet. Explain.

■ **Explain** photosynthesis and respiration, and **derive** net photosynthesis and the world pattern of net primary productivity.

As plants evolved, the **vascular plants** developed conductive tissues. **Stomata** on the underside of leaves are the portals through which the plant participates with the atmosphere and hydrosphere. Plants (primary producers) perform **photosynthesis** as sunlight stimulates a light-sensitive pigment called **chlorophyll**. This process produces food sugars and oxygen to drive biological processes. **Respiration** is essentially the reverse of photosynthesis and is the way the plant derives energy by oxidizing carbohydrates. **Net primary productivity** is the net photosynthesis (photosynthesis minus respiration) of an entire community. This stored chemical energy is the **biomass** that the community generates, or the net dry weight of organic material.

7. Define a vascular plant. How many plant species are there on Earth?
8. How do plants function to link the Sun's energy to living organisms? What is formed within the light-responsive cells of plants?
9. Compare photosynthesis and respiration and the derivation of net photosynthesis. What is the importance of knowing the net primary productivity of an ecosystem and how much biomass an ecosystem has accumulated?
10. Briefly describe the global pattern of net primary productivity.

■ **Relate** abiotic ecosystem components to ecosystem operations, and **explain** trophic relationships.

Light, temperature, water, and the cycling of gases and nutrients constitute the life-supporting abiotic components of ecosystems. Elevation and latitudinal position on Earth create a variety of physical environments. The zonation of plants with altitude is the **life zone concept** and is visible as you travel between different elevations.

Life is sustained by **biogeochemical cycles**, through which circulate the gases and sedimentary materials (nutrients) necessary for growth and development of living organisms. The environment may inhibit biotic operations, either through lack or excess. These **limiting factors** may be physical or chemical in nature.

Trophic refers to the feeding and nutrition relations in an ecosystem. It represents the flow of energy and cycling of nutrients. **Producers**, which fix the carbon they need from carbon dioxide, are the plants, including phytoplankton in aquatic eco-

systems. **Consumers**, generally animals including zooplankton in aquatic ecosystems, depend on the producers as their carbon source. Energy flows from the producers through the system along a **food chain** circuit. Within ecosystems, the feeding interrelationships are complex and arranged in a complex network of interconnected food chains in a **food web**.

The primary consumer is a **herbivore**, or plant eater. A **carnivore** (meat eater) is a secondary consumer. A consumer that eats both producers and consumers is an **omnivore**—a role occupied by humans. **Detritivores** are detritus feeders and decomposers that release simple inorganic compounds and nutrients as they break down organic materials. Detritus feeders, including worms, mites, termites, and centipedes, process debris. **Decomposers** are the bacteria and fungi that process organic debris outside their bodies and absorb nutrients in the process—the rotting that breaks down detritus. Biomass and population pyramids characterize the flow of energy and the numbers of producers, consumers, and decomposers operating in an ecosystem.

11. What are the principal abiotic components in terrestrial ecosystems?
12. Describe what Alexander von Humboldt found that led him to propose the life zone concept. What are life zones? Explain the interaction among elevation, latitude, and the types of communities that develop.
13. What are biogeochemical cycles? Describe several of the essential cycles.
14. What is a limiting factor? How does it function to control the spatial distribution of plant and animal species?
15. What role is played in an ecosystem by producers and consumers?
16. Describe the relationship among producers, consumers, and detritivores in an ecosystem. What is the trophic nature of an ecosystem? What is the place of humans in a trophic system?
17. What is biomass pyramid? Describe how this relates to the nature of food chains.

■ **Relate** how biological evolution led to the biodiversity of life on Earth.

Biodiversity (a combination of *bio*logical and *diversity*) includes the number of different species and quantity of each species, the genetic diversity in species (number of genetic characteristics), and ecosystem and habitat diversity. The greater the biodiversity within an ecosystem, the more stable and resilient it is, and the more productive it will be. Modern agriculture often creates a nondiverse monoculture that is particularly vulnerable to failure.

Evolution states that single-cell organisms adapted, modified, and passed along inherited changes to multicellular organisms.

The genetic makeup of successive generations was shaped by environmental factors, physiological functions, and behaviours that created a greater rate of survival and reproduction that were passed along through natural selection.

> biodiversity (p. 606)
> evolution (p. 606)

18. Give some of the reasons why biodiversity infers more stable, efficient, and sustainable ecosystems.
19. Referring back to Focus Study 1.1, define the scientific method.
20. What is meant by ecosystem stability?
21. What do prairie ecosystems teach us about communities and biodiversity?

■ **Define** succession, and **outline** the stages of general ecological succession in both terrestrial and aquatic ecosystems.

Ecological succession describes the process whereby older communities of plants and animals are replaced by newer communities that are usually more complex. Past glacial and interglacial climatic episodes have created a long-term succession. An area of bare rock and soil with no trace of a former community can be a site for **primary succession**. The initial community that occupies an area of early succession is a **pioneer community**. **Secondary succession** begins in an area that has a vestige of a previously functioning community in place. Rather than progressing smoothly to a definable stable point, ecosystems tend to operate in a dynamic condition, with succeeding communities overlapping in time and space.

Wildfire is one external factor that disrupts a successional community. The science of **fire ecology** has emerged in an effort to understand the natural role of fire in ecosystem maintenance and succession. Aquatic ecosystems also experience community succession, as exemplified by the eutrophication of a lake ecosystem.

> ecological succession (p. 608)
> primary succession (p. 609)
> pioneer community (p. 610)
> secondary succession (p. 610)
> fire ecology (p. 612)

22. How does ecological succession proceed? What are the relationships between existing communities and new, pioneer communities?
23. Assess the impact of climate change on natural communities and ecosystems. Consider changes in species' distributions (Geosystems Now) or western wildfire conditions, for example.
24. Discuss the concept of fire ecology in the context of current scientific understanding of fire.
25. How is the spread of urbanization into wilderness areas related to increasing wildfire risk?
26. Summarize the process of succession in a body of water. What is meant by cultural eutrophication?

MyGeosciencePlace

Visit **www.mygeoscienceplace.ca** for several figure animations, satellite loops, self-study quizzes, flashcards, interactive glossary, career links, RSS feeds, Pearson eText of *Geosystems*, and much more.

CHAPTER 20

Terrestrial Biomes

Winter on a farmstead near Bradford, Ontario. Deciduous trees are bare in this transition from broadleaf and mixed forest to boreal forest. Imagine this same scene in July with all the trees leafed out and the fields reaching harvest times. [Andrew McLachlan/All Canada Photos, Inc.]

KEY LEARNING CONCEPTS

After reading the chapter, you should be able to:

- **Describe** the concept of biogeographic realms of plants and animals, and **define** ecotone and terrestrial ecosystem.

- **Define** biome, and **illustrate** formation classes as a basis for describing plant communities within biomes.

- **Differentiate** between native and exotic species, and **detail** the threat they represent to communities, using several examples.

- **Describe** 10 major terrestrial biomes, and **locate** them on a world map.

- **Relate** human impacts, real and potential, to several of the biomes.

Invasive Species Arrive at Tristan da Cunha

Geosystems Now in Chapter 6 describes an accident that left an oil-drilling platform adrift in the ocean currents of the South Atlantic. Eventually, the drifting *Petrobras XXI* rig ran aground in Trypot Bay, Tristan da Cunha, a remote island archipelago in the South Atlantic. See photos of Tristan and the rig in Chapter 6.

Inspection of the rig's vacant kitchen, cafeteria, and living quarters found various foods left behind, but no rodents or terrestrial species. However, because the owners of the Brazilian rig had not cleaned it prior to towing, it carried 62 nonnative species of marine life on the underwater portion of the rig. These areas showed an intact subtropical reef community of nonnative species, providing a rare opportunity for scientists to assess a potential biological invasion.

Invasive species can devastate biodiversity, especially in isolated island ecosystems (Figure GN 20.1). If a nonnative species becomes invasive, it outcompetes native species for resources and may introduce new predators, pathogens, or parasites into an ecosystem.

Scientists made numerous dives to survey the newly arrived organisms to Tristan da Cunha. They developed a system of four assessed risk levels for the potential invasion: no threat from species that perished in transit; low threat from species that persist on the rig alone; medium threat from species that could

FIGURE GN 20.2 Nonnative species on the submerged portion of the oil-drilling rig.
(a) Coral skeletons and dead barnacle shells provide microhabitats for other nonnative marine species. (b) A native rock lobster inspects a drilling rig strut and its cargo of organisms.
[Sue Scott. All rights reserved.]

spread from the rig; and highest threat (level four) from breeding species with high invasive potential. Corals that died in transit provided skeleton microhabitats for small crabs, worms, amphipods, and other crustaceans. Where barnacle shells remained, small sponges, brown mussels, and urchins persisted (Figure GN 20.2).

For the first time ever reported, fin-fish species had swum along with the rig as it drifted. Two of these, the silver porgy and the variable blenny, pose the greatest threat to native communities. The blenny has a reproductive doubling time of 15 months; the porgy arrived in large number, as more than 60 were counted around the rig. Also found were porceline crabs and a balanidae (a type of barnacle), both assessed with a level-four invasion risk.

The scientific team stated, "Our findings show that towing biofouled structures across biogeographic boundaries presents unexcelled opportunities for invasion to a wide diversity of marine species."[1] Tristan's aquatic ecosystems and what the effects might be. For the 298 people of Tristan who depend on their small fishery for a community subsistence catch and on their commercial rock lobster (a crawfish) for export, the economic effects could be devastating.

The contaminated rig was towed to distant deep water and sunk in 2007. Another threat to Tristan emerged in March 2011. A Maltese cargo vessel filled with soy beans and 1500 tons of fuel oil ran aground on nearby Nightingale Island, an important part of their fishery. The ship was hundreds of kilometers off course, despite its modern navigation capabilities. The crew was rescued. The oil spill surrounded the island, home to 200 000 Northern Rockhopper Penguins (*Eudyptes moseleyi*). Tristanians came by boat to rescue as many birds as they could and to set traps for any fleeing rats from the wrecked ship.

Literally, the oil rig and ship groundings demonstrate how globalization can attack even the most distant archipelago. The economic future of the 298 Tristanians is uncertain. For more see the Tritan web site at http://www.tristandc.com/.

FIGURE GN 20.1 Native marine environment offshore from Tristan da Cunha.
(a) Natural healthy kelp forest and marine ecosystem. (b) Tristan rock lobster, a native species that is carefully managed to provide the community with a valuable export commodity. [Sue Scott. All rights reserved.]

[1]R. M. Wanless, S. Scott, et al., "Semi-submersible rigs: A vector transporting entire marine communities around the world," *Biological Invasions* 10.1007/s (November 29, 2009): 9666.

In 1874, Earth was viewed as offering few limits to human enterprise. But visionary American diplomat and conservationist George Perkins Marsh perceived the need to manage and to conserve the environment:

> We have now felled forest enough everywhere, in many districts far too much. Let us now restore this one element of material life to its normal proportions, and devise means of maintaining the permanence of its relations to the fields, the meadows, and the pastures, to the rain and the dews of heaven, to the springs and rivulets with which it waters the Earth.[2]

Unfortunately, his warning was ignored. The clearing of the forests is perhaps the most fundamental change wrought by humans in our transformation of Earth. The development and expansion of civilization was fuelled and built on the consumption of forests and other natural resources. The natural "work" supplied by Earth's physical, chemical, and biological systems have an estimated annual worth of some $35 trillion to the global economy.

Today we see that Earth's natural systems do pose limits to human activity. Scientists are measuring ecosystems carefully, and they are building elaborate computer models to simulate our evolving real-time human-environment experiment—in particular, shifting patterns of environmental factors (temperatures and changing frost periods; precipitation timing and amounts; air, water, and soil chemistry; and a redistribution of nutrients).

What will the quotations about Earth's environment be like 140 years from now, about the same time interval since Marsh made his assessment? Humans now have become the most powerful biotic agent on Earth, influencing all ecosystems on a planetary scale.

In this chapter: We explore Earth's major terrestrial ecosystems, grouped into 10 biomes. Each biome is an idealized assemblage because much alteration of the

[2]G. P. Marsh, *Physical Geography as Modified by Human Action* (New York: Scribner's, 1874), pp. 385–386.

natural environment has occurred. The discussion covers biome appearance, structure, and location; the present conditions of related plants, animals, and environment; and the state of biodiversity. Table 20.1 summarizes most of the information about Earth's physical systems that is presented through the pages of this text. Through biomes, we synthesize the physical geography of place and region.

Biogeographic Realms

Earth's biosphere can be classified based on assemblages of similar plant and animal communities. Figure 20.1 shows Earth's biogeographic realms. The map illustrates the botanical (plant) realms worldwide, and generally overlaps with the traditional zoological (animal) realms. Each realm contains many distinct ecosystems that distinguish it from other realms, and, in turn, each ecosystem contains many communities.

A **biogeographic realm** is a geographic region where a group of plant and animal species evolved. As you can see, these realms correspond generally to continents. Species distributions are constrained by climatic and topographic barriers; the main barriers separating these realms are the oceans. Recognition that such distinct regions of broadly similar flora (plants) and fauna (animals) exist was an early beginning for *biogeography* as a discipline.

The Australian realm is unique, giving rise to 450 species of *Eucalyptus* among its plants and 125 species of marsupials, animals such as kangaroos that carry their young in pouches, where gestation is completed (Figure 20.2). The presence of monotremes, egg-laying mammals such as the platypus, adds further distinctiveness to this realm. Australia's unique flora and fauna are the result of its early isolation from the other continents. During critical evolutionary times, Australia drifted away from Pangaea (see Chapter 11) and never again was reconnected by a land bridge, even when sea level lowered during repeated glacial ages. New Zealand, although relatively close in location, is isolated from Australia, and it has no native marsupials.

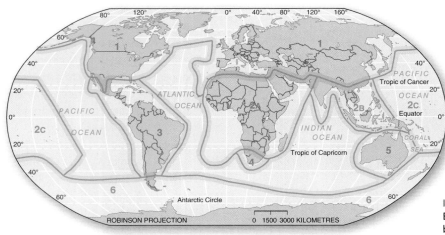

FIGURE 20.1 Biogeographic realms. Earth's biogeographic realms are roughly based on botanical realms.

FIGURE 20.2 **The unique Australian realm.**
The flora and fauna of Australia form a special assemblage of communities; here a western grey kangaroo near a dry river with eucalyptus trees and grasses. [A. Held/age fotostock.]

Transition Zones

Alfred Wallace (1823–1913), the first scholar of *zoogeography*, used the stark contrast in animal species among islands in present-day Indonesia to delimit a boundary between the Paleotropical and Australian realms (Figure 20.1). He thought that deep water in the straits had completely prevented species crossover. However, he later recognized that a boundary line actually is a wide transition zone, where one region grades into the other. Boundaries between natural systems are "zones of shared traits." Thus, despite distinctions among individual realms and our discussion of biomes, it is best to think of biome borders as transition zones of mixed identity and composition, rather than as rigidly defined boundaries.

A boundary transition zone between adjoining ecosystem regions is an **ecotone**. Because ecotones are defined by different physical factors, the width varies—again, think of a transition zone instead of a line. Ecosystems separated by different climatic conditions usually have gradual ecotones, whereas those separated by differences in soil or topography may form abrupt boundaries. For example, an ecotone formed by a landslide is abrupt, while an ecotone between prairies and northern forests may be many kilometres wide.

The range of environmental conditions found in ecotones makes these areas of high biodiversity and often larger population densities than communities on either side. Scientists have defined certain plant and animal species as having a range of tolerance for varying habitats; these "edge" species are often able to occupy habitat on either side of the ecotone. As human impacts cause ecosystem fragmentation, ecotones are becoming more numerous across the landscape. Although ecological response to climate change will occur at all levels in an ecosystem, the sensitivity of ecotones may make them more vulnerable.

Terrestrial Ecosystems

A **terrestrial ecosystem** is a self-sustaining association of land-based plants and animals and their abiotic environment, characterized by specific plant formation classes. Plants are the most visible part of the biotic landscape, and are key members of Earth's terrestrial ecosystems. In growth, form, and distribution, plants reflect Earth's physical systems: its energy patterns; atmospheric composition; temperature and winds; air masses; water quantity, quality, and seasonal timing; soils; regional climates; geomorphic processes; and ecosystem dynamics.

Specific characteristics are used for the structural classification of plants themselves. *Life-form designations* are based on the outward physical properties of individual plants or the general form and structure of a vegetation cover. These physical life forms include:

- *Trees* (large woody main trunk, perennial; heights usually exceed 3 m)
- *Lianas* (woody climbers and vines)
- *Shrubs* (smaller woody plants; stems branching at the ground)

 GEO REPORT 20.1   *Aquatic Ecosystems and Marine Protected Areas in Canada*

Oceans, estuaries, and freshwater bodies (streams and lakes) are home to aquatic ecosystems. Poor understanding of aquatic ecosystems has led to the demise of species such as herring in the Georges Bank of the Atlantic Ocean and an overall decline in fisheries worldwide. The conservation and protection of marine life and their habitats is the goal of marine protected areas (MPA). A marine protected area is an area of the sea within Canada's territory that is designated for conservation and protection.

As of 2011, 84 federal MPAs have been designated. The first MPA, designated in March 2003, is the Endeavour Hydrothermal Vents, which lies in 2250 m of water, 250 km southwest of Vancouver Island. The vents are part of the active spreading zone where new ocean floor is created. This MPA was designated to protect the vents that enrich seawater in the vicinity (see Figure 11.13b) and the unique associated ecosystems.

The second MPA, designated in May 2004, is the Gully, a part of the Eastern Scotian Shelf in the Atlantic Ocean located about 200 km east of Cape Breton Island, near Sable Island. The Gully is a canyon on the edge of the continental shelf where the ocean floor depth abruptly drops by over 2.5 km. The 65-km long and 15-km wide canyon was designated a marine protected area to safeguard and conserve the biological diversity of the region. Since 2004, 82 more MPAs have been designated, including locations in the Atlantic, Pacific and Arctic Oceans and the Great Lakes. In addition, there are over 700 provincial and territorial coastal protected areas that are considered to be MPAs. For more information see the MPA website http://www .dfo-mpo.gc.ca/oceans/management-gestion/marineprotection-protectionmarine/boo-fram2011/faq-eng.htm.

- *Herbs* (small plants without woody stems; includes grasses and other nonwoody vascular plants)
- *Bryophytes* (nonflowering, spore-producing plants; includes mosses and liverworts)
- *Epiphytes* (plants growing above the ground on other plants, using them for support)
- *Thallophytes* (lack true leaves, stems, or roots; includes bacteria, fungi, algae, lichens)

A **biome** is a large, stable, terrestrial ecosystem characterized by its dominant plant type and vegetation structure. Each biome usually is named for its dominant vegetation, or **formation class**, because that is the single most easily identified feature. We can generalize Earth's wide-ranging plant species into six broad groups: *forest, savanna, grassland, shrubland, desert,* and *tundra*. Within these, we can become more specific by formation class. For example, forests can be subdivided into rain forests, needleleaf forests, broadleaf forests, and seasonal forests. This leads to the designation of 10 global terrestrial biomes discussed in this chapter: tropical rain forest, tropical seasonal forest and scrub, tropical savanna, midlatitude broadleaf forest, needleleaf and montane forest, temperate rain forest, Mediterranean shrubland, midlatitude grassland, desert, and arctic and alpine tundra.

Because plant distributions respond to environmental conditions and reflect variations in climate and soil, the world climate map in Figure 10.6 is a helpful reference for this chapter. Although it was developed for terrestrial ecosystems, the biome concept can be applied to aquatic ecosystems: polar seas, temperate seas, tropical seas, seafloor, shoreline, and coral reef.

Invasive Species Our discussion of biomes involves species that are native to a region, meaning that their occurrence is a result of natural processes. These species have come to inhabit an area based on the evolutionary and physical factors previously discussed. Communities, ecosystems, and biomes can also be affected by species that are brought, or introduced, from elsewhere by humans, either accidentally as documented in the chapter opening *Geosystems Now*, or intentionally. These nonnative species are also known as *exotic species*, or *aliens*. After arriving in the new ecosystem, some species may then be disruptive and become **invasive species**.

Invasive plant and animal species are able to take over niches already occupied by native species. Typically around 90% of nonnative species fail when they try to move into established niches in a community. The 10% that succeed can alter community dynamics and lead to declines in native species. Prominent examples are Africanized "killer bees" in North and South America; brown tree snakes in Guam; kudzu vine across the U.S. southern region, zebra and quagga mussels in the Great Lakes; and common gorse (*Ulex europaeus*), a prickly, evergreen shrub, in temperate regions worldwide and mountainous areas of the tropics (Figure 20.3).

 (a)
 (b)
 (c)
 (d)
 (e)

FIGURE 20.3 Exotic species.
(a) A sign in Wallowa County, Washington, makes a plea for awareness in this agricultural country, listing noxious (nonnative, often problematic) weeds at the county line. (b) Invasive purple loosestrife near Lake Michigan and the Indiana Dunes National Lakeshore, Indiana (foreground and left center). (c) Kudzu, originally imported for cattle feed, spread from Texas to Pennsylvania; here it overruns pasture and forest in western Georgia. (d) Common gorse (yellow-flowering shrub), intended for barriers between pastures, runs wild across the landscape of West Point, Falkland Islands. (e) Zebra mussels literally cover most hard surfaces in the Great Lakes; they rapidly colonize on any surface, even sand, in freshwater environments. [(a), (b), (c), and (d) Bobbé Christopherson. (e) Wolfgang Poelzer/WaterFrame/Getty Images.]

For information on invasive species prevention and management, see http://invasions.bio.utk.edu/bio_invasions /index.html or http://www.invasivespecies.gov/.

As an example, Purple loosestrife (*Lythrum salicaria*) was introduced from Europe in the 1800s as a desired ornamental plant with some medicinal applications. The plant's seeds also arrived in ships that used soil for ballast. A hardy perennial, it escaped cultivation and invaded wetlands across the eastern portions of Canada and the United States, through the upper U.S. Midwest, and as far west as Vancouver Island, British Columbia, replacing native plants on which wildlife depend. The plant's invasive characteristics are its ability to produce vast quantities of seed during an extended flowering season and to spread vegetatively through underground stems and its tendency to form dense, homogeneous stands once established (Figure 20.3b).

In Canada and the United States, we humans are perpetuating a new type of terrestrial plant community. This type of *transition community* is somewhere between a grassland and a forest—an artificial successional stage produced by large-scale interruption and disturbance. We plant nonnative trees and lawns and then must invest energy, water, and capital to sustain such artificial modifications. Or we graze nonnative animals and plant crops that perpetuate this disturbed transitional state. It remains to be seen whether the land can return fully to its natural vegetation biomes if human influences are removed.

Now let us begin a tour of Earth's biomes, keeping in mind that these regions synthesize all we have learned about the atmosphere, hydrosphere, lithosphere, and biosphere in the pages of this text. Here we bring it all together.

Earth's Major Terrestrial Biomes

Few natural communities of plants and animals remain; most biomes have been greatly altered by human intervention. Thus, the "natural vegetation" identified on many biome maps reflects *ideal potential* mature vegetation, given the environmental characteristics in a region. For example, in Norway, the former needleleaf and montane forest today is a mix of second- and third-growth forests, farmlands, and altered landscapes (Figure 20.4). However,

II CRITICAL THINKING 20.1

Reality Check

Now is a good time to refer to the composite satellite images that appear inside the front cover of this text, one a cloudless view of Earth in natural colour typical of a local summer day, the other with clouds and atmospheric weather patterns. Compare the map in Figure 20.5 with these remarkable images and see what correlations you can make. Then compare the biomes in Figure 20.5 with population distribution as indicated by the nighttime lighting display also on the inside front cover. What generalizations do you make?

FIGURE 20.4 Needleleaf forest landscape modified by human activity.
Forests and farms in rural Norway, formerly covered in needleleaf forests. [Bobbé Christopherson.]

these ideal conditions form a basis for discussing natural ecological processes and the extent of human impacts.

Let us look at the global distribution of Earth's major terrestrial biomes as portrayed in Figure 20.5. Table 20.1 describes each biome on the map and summarizes other pertinent information gathered from throughout *Geosystems*.

Tropical Rain Forest

Earth is girdled with a lush biome—the **tropical rain forest**. In a climate of consistent year-round daylength (12 hours), high insolation, average annual temperatures around 25°C, and plentiful moisture, plant and animal populations have responded with the most diverse expressions of life on the planet.

The Amazon region is the largest tract of tropical rain forest, or *selva*. In addition, rain forests cover equatorial regions of Africa, Indonesia, the margins of Madagascar and Southeast Asia, the Pacific coast of Ecuador and Colombia, and the east coast of Central America, with small discontinuous patches elsewhere. The cloud forests of western Venezuela are such tracts of rain forest at high elevation, perpetuated by high humidity and cloud cover. Undisturbed tracts of rain forest are rare.

Rain forests represent approximately one-half of Earth's remaining forests, occupying about 7% of the total land area worldwide. This biome is stable in its natural state, resulting from the long-term residence of these continental plates near equatorial latitudes and lack of glacial activity.

The rainforest canopy forms three levels—see Figure 20.6a. The upper level is not continuous, but features emergent tall trees whose high crowns rise above the middle canopy. This upper level appears as a broken *overstory* of tall trees breaking through a middle canopy that is nearly continuous. The broad leaves block much of the light and create a darkened *understory* area and forest floor. The lower level is composed of seedlings, ferns, bamboo, and the like, leaving the litter-strewn ground level in deep shade and fairly open.

FIGURE 20.5 Major terrestrial biomes.
(a) The 10 major global terrestrial biomes. (b) Inset contains more detail for Canada. [(b) Adapted with the permission of Natural Resources Canada, 2012. Courtesy of The Atlas of Canada.]

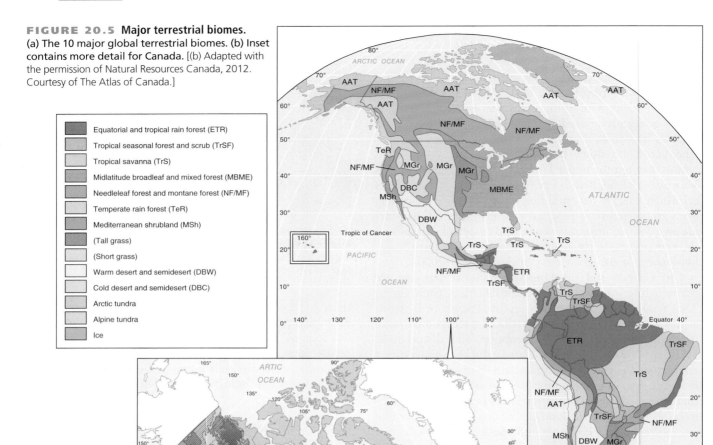

Equatorial and tropical rain forest (ETR)

Tropical seasonal forest and scrub (TrSF)

Tropical savanna (TrS)

Midlatitude broadleaf and mixed forest (MBME)

Needleleaf forest and montane forest (NF/MF)

Temperate rain forest (TeR)

Mediterranean shrubland (MSh)

(Tall grass)

(Short grass)

Warm desert and semidesert (DBW)

Cold desert and semidesert (DBC)

Arctic tundra

Alpine tundra

Ice

REGIONS:
Taiga plains
Boreal plains
Boreal shield
Boreal cordillera
Pacific maritime
Montane cordillera
Prairies
Atlantic maritime
Mixedwood plains

FOREST TYPES:
Coniferous forest
Broadleaf forest
Mixed forest
Transitional forest
Tundra and permafrost

Rain forests feature ecological niches that are distributed vertically rather than horizontally because of the competition for light. Biomass in a rain forest is concentrated high up in the canopy, that dense mass of overhead leaves. The canopy is filled with a rich variety of plants and animals. *Lianas* (vines) stretch from tree to tree, entwining them with cords that can reach 20 cm in diameter (Figure 20.7a). *Epiphytes* flourish there, too; these plants, such as orchids, bromeliads, and ferns, live entirely aboveground, supported physically, but not nutritionally, by the structures of other plants. Calm conditions on the forest floor make wind pollination difficult, so pollination is by insects, other animals, and self-pollination.

Aerial photographs of a rain forest, or views along riverbanks covered by dense vegetation, or the typical movie imagery of the "jungle" make it difficult to imagine the shadowy environment of the actual rainforest floor, which receives only about 1% of the sunlight arriving at the canopy (Figure 20.6b, page 631). The constant moisture, rotting fruit and moldy odours, strings of thin roots and vines dropping down from above, windless air, and echoing sounds of life in the trees together create a unique environment.

The smooth, slender trunks of rainforest trees are covered with thin bark and buttressed by large wall-like flanks that grow out from the trees to brace the trunks (Figure 20.7b). These buttresses form angular, open enclosures, a ready habitat for various animals. There are usually no branches for at least the lower two-thirds of the tree trunks.

The wood of many rainforest trees is extremely hard, heavy, and dense—in fact, some species will not even float in water. Exceptions are balsa and a few others, which are light.

MODIFIED GOODE'S HOMOLOSINE EQUAL-AREA PROJECTION

Varieties of trees include mahogany, ebony, and rosewood. Logging is difficult because individual species are widely scattered; a species may occur only once or twice per square kilometre. Selective cutting is required for species-specific logging, whereas pulpwood production takes everything.

Rainforest soils, principally Oxisols, are essentially infertile, yet these soils support rich vegetation. The trees have adapted to these soil conditions with root systems able to capture nutrients from litter decay at the soil surface. High precipitation levels and temperatures work to produce deeply weathered and leached soils, characteristic of the laterization process, with a claylike texture sometimes breaking up into a granular structure. Oxisols lack nutrients and colloidal material. With much investment in fertilizers, pesticides, and machinery, these soils can be productive.

The animal and insect life of the rain forest is diverse, ranging from small decomposers (bacteria) working the surface to many animals living exclusively in the upper stories of the trees. These tree dwellers are referred to as *arboreal*, from the Latin for "tree," and include sloths, monkeys, lemurs, parrots, and snakes. Beautiful birds of many colours, tree frogs, lizards, bats, and a rich insect community that includes more than 500 species of butterflies are found in rain forests. Surface animals include pigs (the bushpig and giant forest hog in Africa, wild boar and bearded pig in Asia,

and peccary in South America), species of small antelopes (bovids), and mammalian predators (the tiger in Asia, jaguar in South America, and leopard in Africa and Asia).

The present human assault on Earth's rain forests has put this diverse fauna and the varied flora at risk. It also jeopardizes an important recycling system for atmospheric carbon dioxide and a potential source of valuable pharmaceuticals and many types of new foods—and so much is still unknown and undiscovered.

Deforestation of the Tropics   More than half of Earth's original rain forest is gone, cleared for pasture, timber, fuel wood, and farming. Worldwide, an area larger than the maritime provinces is lost each year (169 000 km^2) and about a third more is disrupted by selective cutting of canopy trees, a damage that occurs along the *edges* of deforested areas.

When orbiting astronauts look down on the rain forests at night, they see thousands of human-set fires. During the day, the lower atmosphere in these regions is choked with the smoke. These fires are used to clear land for agriculture, which is intended to feed the domestic population as well as to produce accelerating cash exports of beef, rubber, coffee, soybeans, and other commodities. Edible fruits are not abundant in an undisturbed rain forest, but

TABLE 20.1 Major Terrestrial Biomes and Characteristics

Biome and Ecosystems (map symbol)	Vegetation Characteristics	Soil Orders of Soil Taxonomy[1]	Climate Type	Annual Precipitation Range	Temperature Patterns	Water Balance
Tropical Rain Forest (ETF) Evergreen broadleaf forest Selva	Leaf canopy thick and continuous; broadleaf evergreen trees, vines (lianas), epiphytes, tree ferns, palms	Oxisols Ultisols (on well-drained uplands)	*Tropical*	180–400 cm (>6cm/mo)	Always warm (21°–30°C; avg. 25°C)	Surpluses all year
Tropical Seasonal Forest and Scrub (TrSF) Tropical monsoon forest Tropical deciduous forest Scrub woodland and thorn forest	Transitional between rain forest and grasslands; broadleaf, some deciduous trees; open parkland to dense undergrowth; acacias and other thorn trees in open growth	Oxisols Ultisols Vertisols (in India) Some Alfisols	*Tropical monsoon, tropical savanna*	130–200 cm (>40 rainy days during 4 driest months)	Variable, always warm (>18°C)	Seasonal surpluses and deficits
Tropical Savanna (TrS) Tropical grassland Thorn tree scrub Thorn woodland	Transitional between seasonal forests, rain forests, and semiarid tropical steppes and desert; trees with flattened crowns, clumped grasses, and bush thickets; fire association	Alfisols (dry: Ultalfs) Ultisols Oxisols	*Tropical savanna*	9–150 cm, seasonal	No cold-weather limitations	Tends toward deficits, therefore fire- and drought-susceptible
Midlatitude Broadleaf and Mixed Forest (MBME) Temperate broadleaf Midlatitude deciduous Temperate needleleaf	Mixed broadleaf and needleleaf trees; deciduous broadleaf, losing leaves in winter; southern and eastern evergreen pines demonstrate fire association	Ultisols Some Alfisols	*Humid subtropical (warm summer) Humid continental (warm summer)*	75–150 cm	Temperate with cold season	Seasonal pattern with summer Maximum P and PE; no irrigation needed
Needleleaf Forest and Montane Forest (NF/MF) Taiga Boreal forest Other montane forests and highlands	Needleleaf conifers, mostly evergreen pine, spruce, fir; Russian larch, a deciduous needleleaf	Spodosols Histosols Inceptisols Alfisols (Boralfs: cold)	*Subarctic Humid continental (cool summer)*	30–100 cm	Short summer, cold winter	Low PE, moderate P; moist soils, some waterlogged and frozen in winter; no deficits
Temperate Rain Forest (TeR) West coast forest Coast redwoods (U.S.)	Narrow margin of lush evergreen and deciduous trees on windward slopes; redwoods, tallest trees on Earth	Spodosols Inceptisols (mountainous environs)	*Marine west coast*	150–500 cm	Mild summer and mild winter for latitude	Large surpluses and runoff
Mediterranean Shrubland (MSh) Sclerophyllous shrubs Australian eucalyptus forest	Short shrubs, drought adapted, tending to grassy woodlands and chaparral	Alfisols (Xeralfs) Mollisols (Xerolls)	*Mediterranean (dry summer)*	25–65 cm	Hot, dry summers, cool winters	Summer deficits, winter surpluses
Midlatitude Grasslands (MGr) Temperate grassland Sclerophyllous shrub	Tallgrass prairies and shortgrass steppes, highly modified by human activity; major areas of commercial grain farming; plains, pampas, and veld	Mollisols Aridisols	*Humid subtropical Humid continental (hot summer)*	25–75 cm	Temperate continental regimes	Soil moisture utilization and recharge balanced; irrigation and dry farming in drier areas
Warm Desert and Semidesert (DBW) Subtropical desert and scrubland	Bare ground graduating into xerophytic plants including succulents, cacti, and dry shrubs	Aridisols Entisols (sand dunes)	*Arid desert*	< 2 cm	Average annual temperature, around 18°C, highest temperatures on Earth	Chronic deficits, irregular precipitation events, P < ½ PE
Cold Desert and Semidesert (DBC) Midlatitude desert, scrubland, and steppe	Cold desert vegetation includes short grass and dry shrubs	Aridisols Entisols	*Semiarid steppe*	2–25 cm	Average annual temperature around 18°C	P > ½ PE
Arctic and Alpine Tundra (AAT)	Treeless; dwarf shrubs, stunted sedges, mosses, lichens, and short grasses; alpine, grass meadows	Gelisols Histosols Entisols (permafrost)	*Tundra Subarctic (very cold)*	15–180 cm	Warmest months > 10°C, only 2 or 3 months above freezing	Not applicable most of the year, poor drainage in summer
Ice			*Ice sheet, ice cap*			

[1]For Canadian Soil Order equivalents, see Table 18.4 in Chapter 18.

FIGURE 20.6 The three levels of a rainforest canopy.
(a) Lower, middle, and high levels of the rain forest. (b) Tropical rainforest canopy is thick, allowing little light to reach the forest floor, here in eastern Puerto Rico. [(b) Bobbé Christopherson.]

FIGURE 20.7 The rain forest.
(a) Lianas drape from the dense rainforest canopy to the forest floor. (b) The rainforest floor, with a typical buttressed tree, leaf litter, and lianas in the background. [Bobbé Christopherson.]

cultivated clearings produce bananas (plantains), mangos, jack fruit, guava, and starch-rich roots such as manioc and yams. Brazil has been the world's largest exporter of beef since 2004 and is the second leading country for soybean exports.

Because of the poor soil fertility, the cleared lands are quickly exhausted under intensive farming and are then generally abandoned in favour of newly burned and cleared lands, unless fertility is maintained artificially. The

dominant trees require from 100 to 250 years to reestablish themselves after major disturbances. Once cleared, the former forest becomes a mass of low bushes intertwined with vines and ferns, slowing the return of the forests.

Figure 20.8a and b shows satellite true-colour images of a portion of western Brazil called Rondônia, recorded in 2000 and 2009. These images give a sense of the level of rainforest destruction in progress. You can clearly see encroachment along new roads branching from highway

(a) 2000

(b) 2009

(c)

(d)

FIGURE 20.8 Amazon rainforest losses over three decades.
Satellite images of a portion of western Brazil called Rondônia, recorded in true colour in (a) 2000 and
(b) 2009, show large rainforest losses growing outward from highway BR364, the main artery in the region.
The branching pattern of feeder roads encroaches on the rain forest where you can see patch and edge
dynamics at work along new roadways. (c) Surface view of burning rain forest in the Amazon. (d) Brazilian
deforested areas clear cut in 2006–2011 in equivalent area in Canada. [(a) and (b) *Terra* MODIS, NASA/GSFC.
(c) Colin Jones/Photolibrary/Getty Images.]

BR364. The *edges* of every road and cleared area represent
a significant portion of the species habitat disturbance,
population dynamic changes, and carbon losses to the
atmosphere—more impact occurs along these edges than
in the tracts of clear-cut logging. The hotter, drier, and
windier edge conditions penetrate the forest up to 100 m.
Figure 20.8c shows a tract of former rain forest that has
just been burned to begin the clearing and road-building
process.

To give you a sense of the area of forest losses, Figure 20.8d shades in the equivalent area for given years.
Deforestation has decreased somewhat in the last couple
of years as Brazil's government has stepped up enforcement to preserve the forest; 2009–2010 combined losses
were down to approximately 18 000 km². The United

Nations Food and Agricultural Organization estimated
that, if this destruction to rain forests continues unabated,
these forests will be completely removed by 2050. By continent, rainforest losses are estimated at more than 50%
in Africa, more than 40% in Asia, and 40% in Central
and South America.

This is a highly charged issue, as can be seen by the
growth of Brazil's cattle industry, which uses these new
pasturelands. Cattle herds reached over 60 million head
by 2010, generating $3 billion in revenue. Among many
sites for further information, see the Tropical Rainforest Coalition at http://www.rainforest.org/, World
Resources Institute Global Forest Watch at http://www
.globalforestwatch.org/english/index.htm, or Rainforest
Action Network at http://www.ran.org/.

Focus Study 20.1 looks more closely at efforts to curb increasing rates of species extinction and loss of Earth's biodiversity, much of which is directly attributable to the loss of rain forests.

Tropical Seasonal Forest and Scrub

A varied biome on the margins of the rain forest is the **tropical seasonal forest and scrub**, which occupies regions of low and erratic rainfall. The shifting intertropical convergence zone (ITCZ) brings precipitation with the seasonally shifting high Sun of summer and then a season of dryness with the lower Sun of winter, producing a seasonal pattern of moisture deficits, some leaf loss, and dry-season flowering. The term *semideciduous* applies to some of the broadleaf trees that lose their leaves during the dry season.

Areas of this biome have fewer than 40 rainy days during the four consecutive driest months, yet heavy monsoon downpours characterize their summers (see Chapter 6, especially Figure 6.19). The climates *tropical monsoon* and *tropical savanna* apply to these transitional communities between rain forests and tropical grasslands.

Portraying such a varied biome is difficult. In many areas humans disturb the natural biome, so that the savanna grassland adjoins the rain forest directly. The biome does include a gradation from wetter to drier areas: monsoonal forests, to open woodlands and scrub woodland, to thorn forests, to drought-resistant scrub species (Figure 20.9). In South America, an area of transitional tropical deciduous forest surrounds an area of savanna in southeastern Brazil and portions of Paraguay.

The monsoonal forests average 15 m high with no continuous canopy of leaves, graduating into orchardlike parkland with grassy openings or into areas choked by dense undergrowth. In more open tracts, a common tree is the acacia, with its flat top and usually thorny stems. These trees have branches that look like an upside-down umbrella (spreading and open skyward), as do trees in the tropical savanna.

Local names are given to these communities: the *caatinga* of the Bahia State of northeastern Brazil, the *chaco* area of Paraguay and northern Argentina, the *brigalow* scrub of Australia, and the *dornveld* of southern Africa. Figure 20.5 shows areas of this biome in Africa, extending from eastern

(b)

FIGURE 20.9 Kenyan landscapes.
Two views of the open thorn forest and savanna near and in (a) the Samburu Reserve, Kenya, representing a broad ecotone between the two biomes, and (b) Maasai giraffes move across open country in Amboseli National Park, Kenya. [(a) Gael Summer. (b) Nigel Pavitt/John Warburton-Lee Photography/PhotoLibrary/Getty Images.]

Angola through Zambia to Tanzania and Kenya; in southeast Asia and portions of India, from interior Myanmar through northeastern Thailand; and in parts of Indonesia.

[text continued on page 636]

 GEO REPORT 20.2 *The Question of Food and Medicine*

Wheat, maize (corn), and rice—just three grains—fulfill about 50% of human planetary food demands. About 7000 plant species have been gathered for food throughout human history, but more than 30 000 plant species have edible parts. Undiscovered potential food resources are in nature waiting to be found and developed. Biodiversity, if preserved in each of the biomes, provides us a potential cushion for all future food needs, but only if species are identified, inventoried, and protected. The same is true for pharmaceuticals.

Nature's biodiversity is like a full medicine cabinet. Since 1959, 25% of all prescription drugs were originally derived from higher plants. Scientists have identified 3000 plants as having anticancer properties. The rosy periwinkle (*Catharanthus roseus*) of Madagascar contains two alkaloids that combat two forms of cancer. Yet less than 3% of flowering plants have been examined for alkaloid content. It defies common sense to throw away the medicine cabinet before we even open the door to see what is inside.

FOCUS STUDY 20.1

Species Diversity, Risks, and Biosphere Reserves

When the first European settlers landed on the Hawaiian Islands in the late 1700s, they counted 43 species of birds. Today, 15 of those species are extinct, and 19 more are threatened or endangered, with only one-fifth of the original species populations relatively healthy. In most of Hawai'i, no native species exist below 1220 m elevation because of an introduced avian virus. Humans have great impact on animals, plants, and global biodiversity. We are facing a loss of genetic diversity that may be unparalleled in Earth's history, even compared with the major extinctions over the geologic record.

As we learn more about Earth's ecosystems and their related communities, we understand their value to civilization and our interdependence with them. Natural ecosystems are a major source of new foods, chemicals, and medicines and are indicators of a healthy, functioning biosphere.

International efforts are under way to study and preserve specific segments of the biosphere: among others, the United Nations Environment Programme, World Resources Institute, World Conservation Union, Natural World Heritage Sites, Wetlands of International Importance, and Nature Conservancy. An important part of the effort is the setting aside of biosphere reserves and the focus provided by the World Conservation Monitoring Centre and its International Union for Conservation of Nature (IUCN) Red List of global endangered species at http://www.iucnredlist.org/. See also the home page of the Committee on the Status of Endangered Wildlife in Canada http://www.cosewic.gc.ca/eng/sct5/index_e.cfm, the endangered species home page of the U.S. Fish and Wildlife Service at http://www.fws.gov/endangered/ and the World Wildlife Fund at http://www.panda.org/.

FIGURE 20.1.1 The polar bear.
A male polar bear with snow on his face in northern Manitoba. One study predicts that the present polar bear population of 23 000 will be reduced by 67% by 2050 because of climate change and loss of sea ice—that will leave about 7 500 bears across the Arctic region. [Bobbé Christopherson.]

Species Threatened—Examples

The extinction of 67% of the known species of harlequin frogs in the tropics was discussed in Chapter 1 and Figure 1.7. In the Arctic region, the IUCN in 2006 listed the polar bear (*Ursus maritimus*) as "vulnerable" to extinction, a "threatened" category on its Red List of Threatened Species (Figure 20.1.1). Research released by the U.S. Geological Survey in September 2007 predicted that with the loss of Canadian, Alaskan, and Russian sea ice habitat, the number of polar bears will decrease by

FIGURE 20.1.2 Rhinoceros in Africa.
White rinoceros with young (*Ceratotherium simum*), Lake Nakuru National Park, Kenya, of the southern population. [Oleg Znamenskiy/Shutterstock.]

two-thirds by 2050 or earlier. The remaining 7500 bears will be struggling. Any action society takes now will hopefully result in a slowing of such sea-ice loss and the buying of a little adaptation time.

Black rhinos (*Diceros bicornis*) and white rhinos (*Ceratotherium simum*) in Africa exemplify species in jeopardy. Rhinos once grazed over much of the savannas and woodlands. Today they survive only in protected districts in heavily guarded sanctuaries and are threatened even there (Figure 20.1.2). In 1998, 2599 black rhinos remained, 96% fewer than the 70 000 in 1960. Populations have remained statistically stable through the last decade, and this count is supported by South Africa's guarding of about 50% of the herd. A slow recovery is under way, as numbers of black rhinos rose to 4240 in 2008, according to the IUCN/SSC's African Rhino Specialist Group. This is not the case with the western black rhino, a subspecies, which is down to its last few individuals.

Only 11 northern white rhinos existed in 1984, increasing to an estimated 29 by 1998 (Congo 25, Côte d'Ivoire 4), although the IUNC suggests this number might actually be lower. Political unrest in the Congo and the area of the Garamba National Park has led to the deaths of an unknown number of these few. The southern white rhino population reached 14 500 by 2008, an increase.

Rhinoceros horn sells for $29 000 per kilogram because it is thought to be an aphrodisiac (a false use of no medicinal effect). These large land mammals are nearing extinction and will survive only as a dwindling zoo population. The limited genetic pool that remains means that increasing the population size becomes more problematic.

Table 20.1.1 summarizes the numbers of known and estimated species on Earth. Scientists have classified only 1.75 million species of plants and animals of an estimated 13.6 million overall; this figure represents an increase in what scientists once thought to be the diversity of life on Earth. And those yet-to-be-discovered species represent a potential future resource for society. The wide range of estimates places the expected species count between a low of 3.6 million and a high of 112 million. Estimates of annual species loss range between 1000 and 30 000, although this range might be conservative. The possibility exists that over half of Earth's present species could be extinct within the next 100 years.

Biosphere Reserves

Formal natural reserves are a possible strategy for slowing the loss of biodiversity and protecting this resource base. Setting up a *biosphere reserve* involves principles of **island biogeography**. Island communities are special places for study because of their spatial isolation and the relatively small number of species present. Islands resemble natural experiments because the impact of individual factors, such as civilization, can be more easily assessed on islands than over larger continental areas.

Studies of islands also can assist in the study of mainland ecosystems, for in many ways a park or biosphere reserve, surrounded by modified areas and artificial boundaries, is like an island. Indeed, a biosphere reserve is conceived as an ecological island in the midst of change. The intent is to establish a core in which genetic material is protected from outside disturbances, surrounded by a buffer zone that is, in turn, surrounded by a transition zone and experimental research areas. An important variable to consider in setting aside a biosphere reserve is any change that might occur in temperature and precipitation patterns as a result of global change. A reserve selected to correspond with present climatic patterns could end up being outside the range of its species as climates change.

Not all protected areas are ideal bioregional entities by definition. Some are simply imposed on existing park space, and some remain in the planning stage, although the areas are officially designated. In Canada there are 16 biosphere reserve sites. The Ecological Monitoring and Assessment Network (http://www.ec.gc.ca/faunescience-wildlifescience/default.asp?lang=En&n=B0D89DF1-1/) is a network of organizations and individuals in Canada that monitors ecology and ecosystem changes. There are also 42 national parks (see http://www.pc.gc.ca/progs/np-pn/recherche-search_e.asp?p=1 for an alphabetical list) that exist to protect representative natural areas of Canadian significance. The stated goal of the National Parks Program is to promote public understanding, appreciation, and enjoyment of natural areas while maintaining the areas in an unimpaired state for future generations. The United States has 90 biosphere reserves under various jurisdictions.

Some of the best biosphere reserve examples have been in operation since the late 1970s and range from Everglades National Park in Florida, to the Changbai Reserve in China, to the Tai Forest on the Côte d'Ivoire (Ivory Coast), to the Charlevoix Biosphere Reserve in Québec, Canada. Added to these efforts is the work of the Nature Conservancy, which acquires land for preservation as a valuable part of the reserve.

The ultimate goal, about half achieved, is to establish at least one reserve in each of the 194 distinctive biogeographic communities presently identified. So far 6390 areas are designated, covering 657 million hectares. Scientists predict that designating new, undisturbed reserves may not be possible in a decade because pristine areas will be gone. The biosphere reserve program is coordinated by the Man and the Biosphere Programme of UNESCO (http://www.unesco.org/mab/). For other MAB links check http://www.unesco.org/new/en/natural-sciences/environment/ecological-sciences/man-and-biosphere-programme/networks/. More than 480 biosphere reserves are now operated voluntarily in 100 countries.

TABLE 20.1.1   Known and Estimated Species on Earth

Categories of Living Organisms	Number of Known Species	Estimated Number of Species			Accuracy
		High (000)	Low (000)	Working Estimate (000)	
Viruses	4 000	1 000	50	400	Very poor
Bacteria	4 000	3 000	50	1000	Very poor
Fungi	72 000	27 000	200	1500	Moderate
Protozoa	40 000	200	60	200	Very poor
Algae	40 000	1 000	150	400	Very poor
Plants	270 000	500	300	320	Good
Nematodes	25 000	1 000	100	400	Poor
Arthropods					
Crustaceans	40 000	200	75	150	Moderate
Arachnids	75 000	1 000	300	750	Moderate
Insects	950 000	100 000	2 000	8 000	Moderate
Mollusks	70 000	200	100	200	Moderate
Chordates	45 000	55	50	50	Good
Others	115 000	800	200	250	Moderate
Total	1 750 000	111 655	3 635	13 620	Very poor

Source: United Nations Environment Programme, *Global Biodiversity Assessment* (Cambridge, England: Cambridge University Press, 1995), Table 3.1–2, p. 118, used by permission.

▌▌ CRITICAL THINKING 20.2

Tropical Forests: A Global or Local Resource?

Given the information presented in this chapter about deforestation in the tropics and species extinction, assess the present situation. What are the main issues? What natural assets are at stake? How do we balance concerns for planetary natural resources against sovereign state rights? How are global biodiversity and greenhouse warming related to these issues? What is the perspective of the less-developed countries that possess most of the rain forest? What is the perspective of the more-developed countries and their transnational corporations? What kind of action plan would you develop to accommodate all parties?

The trees throughout most of this biome generally make poor lumber, but some, especially teak, may be valuable for fine cabinetry. In addition, some of the plants with dry-season adaptations produce usable waxes and gums, such as carnauba and palm-hard waxes. Animal life includes the koalas and cockatoos of Australia and the elephants, large cats, rodents, and ground-dwelling birds in other occurrences of this biome.

Tropical Savanna

The **tropical savanna** is large expanses of grassland, interrupted by trees and shrubs. This is a transitional biome between the tropical forests and semiarid tropical steppes and deserts. The savanna biome also includes treeless tracts of grasslands, and in dry savannas, grasses grow discontinuously in clumps, with bare ground between them. The trees of the savanna woodlands are characteristically flat-topped, in response to light and moisture regimes.

Savannas covered more than 40% of Earth's land surface before human intervention but were especially modified by human-caused fire. Fires occur annually throughout the biome. The timing of these fires is important. Early in the dry season they are beneficial and increase tree cover; late in the season they are very hot and kill trees and seeds. Savanna trees are adapted to resist the "cooler" fires.

Forests and elephant grasses averaging 5 m high once penetrated much farther into the dry regions, for they are known to survive there when protected; unprotected, coverage declines. Savanna grasslands are much richer in humus than the wetter tropics and are better drained, thereby providing a better base for agriculture and grazing. Sorghums, wheat, and groundnuts (peanuts) are common commodities.

Tropical savannas receive their precipitation during less than 6 months of the year, when these areas are influenced by the shifting ITCZ. The rest of the year is under the drier influence of shifting subtropical high-pressure cells. Savanna shrubs and trees are frequently *xerophytic*, or drought-resistant, with various adaptations to protect them from the dryness: small, thick leaves; rough bark; or leaf surfaces that are waxy or hairy.

Africa has the largest area of this biome, including the famous Serengeti Plains of Tanzania and Kenya and the Sahel region, south of the Sahara. Sections of Australia, India, and South America also are part of the savanna biome. Some of the local names for these lands include the *Llanos* in Venezuela, stretching along the coast and inland east of Lake Maricaibo and the Andes; the *Campo Cerrado* of Brazil and Guiana; and the *Pantanal* of southwestern Brazil.

Particularly in Africa, savannas are the home of large land mammals—zebra, giraffe, buffalo, gazelle, wildebeest, antelope, rhinoceros and elephant. These animals graze on savanna grasses (Figure 20.10), while others (lion, cheetah) feed upon the grazers themselves. Birds include the ostrich, martial eagle (largest of all eagles), and secretary bird. Many species of venomous snakes as well as the crocodile are present in this biome.

Midlatitude Broadleaf and Mixed Forest

Moist continental climates support a mixed forest in areas of warm to hot summers and cool to cold winters. This **midlatitude broadleaf and mixed forest** biome includes several distinct communities in North America, Europe, and Asia. Along the Gulf of Mexico, relatively lush evergreen broadleaf forests occur. Northward are mixed

(a)

(b)

FIGURE 20.10 Animals and plants of the Serengeti Plains.
(a) Savanna landscape of the Serengeti Plains, with wildebeest, zebras, and thorn forest. (b) Lions use sparse shade of an acacia tree. [(a) Stephen F. Cunha. (b) Michael & Christine Denis-Huot/Photolibrary/Getty Images.]

deciduous and evergreen needleleaf stands associated with sandy soils and burning. When areas are given fire protection, broadleaf trees quickly take over. Pines (longleaf, shortleaf, pitch, loblolly) predominate in the southeastern and Atlantic coastal plains. Into New England and westward in a narrow belt to the Great Lakes, white and red pines and eastern hemlock are the principal evergreens, mixed with deciduous oak, beech, hickory, maple, elm, chestnut, and many others (Figure 20.11). In Canada, part of this forest biome is known as Carolinian forest and occurs in a small area of extreme southwestern Ontario. The region is heavily populated, industrialized, and disturbed by agricultural activity. A nonprofit group called Carolinian Canada (http://www.carolinian.org/index.htm) works to protect and conserve this threatened forest ecosystem.

These mixed stands contain valuable timber and human activity has altered distribution patterns. Native stands of white pine in Michigan and Minnesota were removed before 1910; only later reforestation sustains a presence today. In northern China these forests have almost disappeared

as a result of centuries of harvest. The forest species that once flourished in China are similar to species in eastern North America: oak, ash, walnut, elm, maple, and birch.

This biome is quite consistent in appearance from continent to continent and at one time represented the principal vegetation of the *humid subtropical hot summer* and *marine west coast* (cool summer, winter drought) climatic regions of North America, Europe, and Asia.

A wide assortment of mammals, birds, reptiles, and amphibians is distributed throughout this biome. Representative animals (some migratory) include red fox, white-tail deer, southern flying squirrel, opossum, bear, and a great variety of birds, including tanager and cardinal. To the west of this biome in North America are the grasslands, and to the north are the poorer soils and colder climates that favour stands of coniferous trees and a gradual transition to the northern needleleaf forests.

Needleleaf Forest and Montane Forest

Stretching from the east coast of Canada and the Atlantic provinces westward to Alaska and continuing from Siberia across the entire extent of Russia to the European Plain is the northern **needleleaf forest** biome, or **boreal forest** (Figure 20.12). A more open form of boreal forest,

FIGURE 20.11 The mixed broadleaf forest.
(a) Pioneer Mothers' Memorial Forest near Paoli, Indiana, is 36 hectares of old-growth forest, virtually undisturbed since around 1816, featuring black walnut, white oak, yellow poplar, white ash, and beech trees, among others. (b) A young white-tailed deer grazes in the undergrowth of a mixed forest. [(a) and (b) Bobbé Christopherson.]

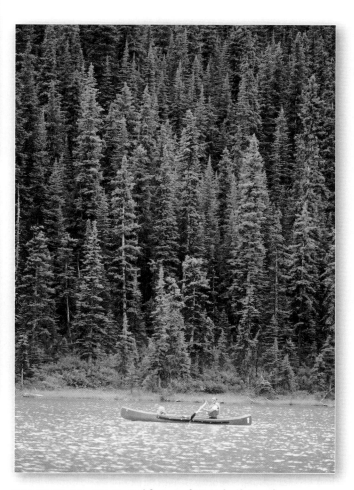

FIGURE 20.12 Boreal forest of Canada (*boreal* means "northern"). [Robert Christopherson.]

transitional to arctic and subarctic regions, is the **taiga**. The Southern Hemisphere, lacking *humid microthermal* climates, has no such biome except in a few mountainous locales. But **montane forests** of needleleaf trees exist worldwide at high elevations.

Boreal forests of pine, spruce, fir, and larch occupy most of the subarctic climates on Earth that are dominated by trees. Although these forests are similar in formation, individual species vary between North America and Eurasia. The larch (*Larix*) is interesting because it is the rare needleleaf tree that loses its needles in winter months, perhaps as a defence against the extreme cold of its native Siberia (see the Verkhoyansk climograph and photograph in Figure 10.21). Larches also occur in North America.

Boreal forest is Canada's largest biome and, to balance the demands placed on this forest, the Canadian Forest Service created the Model Forest Network (http://www.modelforest.net/) in 1992. Of the 14 Model Forests, 8 are boreal, 1 is subalpine/montane/boreal, and 1 is a transition between the boreal and prairie ecozones. Figure 20.13 portrays the locations of the Canadian Model Forests.

The Sierra Nevada, Rocky Mountains, Alps, and Himalayas have similar forest communities occurring at lower latitudes. Douglas fir and white fir grow in the western mountains in Canada and the United States. Economically,

these forests are important for lumbering, with trees for lumber occurring in the southern margins of the biome and for pulpwood throughout the middle and northern portions. Present logging practices and the sustainability of these yields are issues of increasing controversy.

In the Sierra Nevada montane forests of California, the giant sequoias naturally occur in 70 isolated groves. These trees are Earth's largest living things (in terms of biomass), although each began as a small seed (Figure 20.14a). Some of these *Sequoia gigantea* exceed 8 m in diameter and 83 m in height. The largest of these is the General Sherman tree in Sequoia National Park (Figure 20.14c); it is estimated to be 3500 years old. The bark is fibrous, 0.5 m thick, and lacks resins, so it effectively resists fire. Imagine the lightning strikes and fires that must have moved past the Sherman tree in 35 centuries! Standing among these giant trees is an overwhelming experience and creates a sense of the majesty of the biosphere.

Certain regions of the northern needleleaf biome experience permafrost conditions, discussed in Chapter 17. When coupled with rocky and poorly developed soils, these conditions generally limit the existence of trees to those with shallow rooting systems. The summer thaw of surface-active layers results in muskeg (moss-covered) bogs and organic soils of poor drainage and stability. Soils

FIGURE 20.13 Canadian Model Forest Network.
The Canadian Forestry Service and the Government of Canada cooperated to develop a program to manage the forests of Canada. Model Forests are a multi-stakeholder approach to addressing challenges within the forest and providing support for those who are reliant and dependent on the resource. By creating a neutral place of engagement for a wide range of forest-based interest groups, social, economic and environmental approaches to activities are the focus of the Model Forest. [Adapted with permission from Canadian Model Forest Network.]

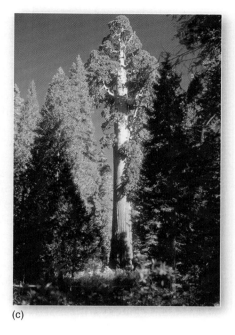

(a)   (b)

(c)

FIGURE 20.14 Sequoia: The seed, the seedling, the giant.
(a) A *Sequoia gigantea* seed. About 300 seeds are in each sequoia cone. (b) Seedling at approximately 50 years of age. (c) The General Sherman tree in Sequoia National Park, California. This tree is probably wider at the base—11.1 m—than a standard classroom. The first branch is 45 m off the ground and is 2 m in diameter! [Robert Christopherson.]

of the taiga are typically Podzolic (subject to podzolization), characteristically acidic and leached of humus and clays. Global warming is altering conditions in the high latitudes, causing increased melting and depth in the permafrost active layer. Some affected forests are dying in response to waterlogging in soils.

Representative fauna in this biome include wolf, elk, moose (the largest in the deer family), bear, lynx, beaver, wolverine, marten, small rodents, and migratory birds during the brief summer season. Birds include hawks and eagles, several species of grouse, pine grosbeak, Clark's nutcracker, and several owls. About 50 species of insects particularly adapted to the presence of coniferous trees inhabit the biome.

Temperate Rain Forest

Lush forests at middle and high latitudes are in the **temperate rain forest** biome. In North America, it occurs only along narrow margins of the Pacific Northwest (Figure 20.15a). Some similar types of forest exist in southern China, small portions of southern Japan, New Zealand, and a few areas of southern Chile.

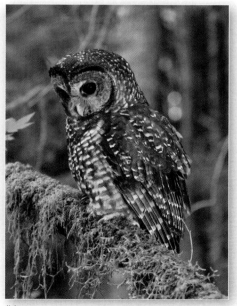

(a)

(b)

FIGURE 20.15 Temperate rain forest.
(a) An old temperate rain forest in the Pacific Northwest in the Gifford Pinchot National Forest features huge old-growth Douglas fir, redwoods, cedars, and a mix of deciduous trees, ferns, and mosses. Only a small percentage of these old-growth forests remains. (b) The northern spotted owl and fledgling is an indicator species of the temperate rain forest.
[(a) Bobbé Christopherson. (b) Danita Delimont/Gallo Images/Getty Images.]

This biome contrasts with the diversity of the equatorial and tropical rain forest in that only a few species make up the bulk of the trees. The rain forest of the Olympic Peninsula in Washington State is a mixture of broadleaf and needleleaf trees, huge ferns, and thick undergrowth. Precipitation approaching 400 cm per year on the western slopes, moderate air temperatures, summer fog, and an overall maritime influence produce this moist, lush vegetation community. Animals include bear, badger, deer, wild pig, wolf, bobcat, and fox. The trees are home to numerous bird species, including the famous spotted owl (Figure 20.15b).

The tallest trees in the world occur in this biome—the coastal redwoods (*Sequoia sempervirens*). The distribution is shown on the map in Figure 19.13a in Chapter 19. These trees can exceed 1500 years of age and typically range in height from 60 to 90 m, with some exceeding 100 m. Virgin stands of other representative trees, such as Douglas fir, spruce, cedar, and hemlock, have been reduced by timber harvests to a few remaining valleys in Oregon and Washington, less than 10% of the original forest. Replanting and secondary-growth forests are predominant. In similar forests in Chile, large-scale timber harvests and new mills began operations in 2000. Currently, U.S. corporations are shifting logging operations to these forests in the Chilean Lake District and northern Patagonia.

Many studies by the U.S. Forest Service and others noted the failing ecology of these forest ecosystems and suggested that timber management plans should include ecosystem preservation as a priority. The ultimate solution must be one of economic and ecological synthesis rather than continuing conflict and forest losses—the forests cannot be all cut down, nor can they be all preserved. The opposing sides in this conflict between logging and society interests should combine their efforts in a sustainable forestry model as was done for the boreal forest (http://cpaws.org/news/cpaws-proud-partner-in-new-boreal-forest-leadership-agreement, and specific to Canada, see http://canadianborealforestagreement.ca/).

Mediterranean Shrubland

The **Mediterranean shrubland** biome, also referred to as a temperate shrubland, occupies those regions poleward of the shifting subtropical high-pressure cells. As those cells shift poleward with the high summer Sun, the passage of storm systems and inputs of moisture are blocked. The presence of stable high pressure produces the characteristic *Mediterranean* (dry summer) climate and establishes conditions conducive to fire.

This biome is well adapted to frequent wildfires, for many of its characteristically deep-rooted plants have the ability to resprout from roots after a fire. The dominant shrub formations that occupy these regions are stunted and able to withstand hot-summer drought. The vegetation is *sclerophyllous* (from *sclero*, for "hard," and *phyllos*, for "leaf"). It averages a metre or two in height and has deep, well-developed roots, leathery leaves, and uneven low branches.

Typically, the vegetation varies between woody shrubs covering more than 50% of the ground and grassy woodlands covering 25%–60% of the ground. In California, the Spanish word *chaparro* for "scrubby evergreen" gives us the word **chaparral** for this vegetation type (Figure 20.16). This scrubland includes species such as manzanita, toyon, red bud, ceanothus, mountain mahogany, blue and live oaks, and poison oak.

A counterpart to the California chaparral in the Mediterranean region is the *maquis*, which includes live and cork oak trees (source of cork) as well as pine and olive trees. The overall similar appearance of the California and Spanish oak savannas is demonstrated in Figure 10.16c and d. In Chile, such a region is the *mattoral*, and in southwestern Australia, it is *mallee scrub*. In Australia, the bulk of the eucalyptus species are sclerophyllous in form and structure in whichever climate these occur.

As described in Chapter 10, *Mediterranean* climates are important in commercial agriculture for subtropical fruits, vegetables, and nuts, with many food types (e.g.,

FIGURE 20.16 Mediterranean chaparral.
Chaparral vegetation associated with the *Mediterranean* (dry summer) climate in southern California. [Bobbé Christopherson.]

artichokes, olives, almonds) produced only in this biome. Larger animals, such as several types of deer, are grazers and browsers, with coyote, wolf, and bobcat as predators. Many rodents, other small animals, and a variety of birds also proliferate.

Midlatitude Grasslands

Of all the natural biomes, the **midlatitude grasslands** are the most modified by human activity. Here are the world's "breadbaskets"—regions that produce bountiful grain (wheat and corn), soybeans, and livestock (hogs and cattle). Figure 20.17 shows a typical midlatitude grassland under cultivation for feedstock and crops. In these regions, the only naturally occurring trees were deciduous broadleaf trees along streams and other limited sites. These regions are called grasslands because of the predominance of grasslike plants before human intervention:

> In this study of vegetation, attention has been devoted to grass because grass is the dominant feature of the Plains and is at the same time an index to their history. Grass is the visible feature which distinguishes the Plains from the desert. Grass grows, has its natural habitat, in the transition area between timber and desert. . . . The history of the Plains is the history of the grasslands.[3]

In North America, tallgrass prairies once rose to heights of 2 m and extended westward to about the 98th meridian, with shortgrass prairies in the drier lands farther west. The 98th meridian is roughly the location of the 50 cm isohyet, with wetter conditions to the east and drier conditions to the west.

[3]From Walter Prescott Webb, *The Great Plains* (Needham Heights, MA: Ginn and Company, 1931), p. 32.

The deep, tough sod of these grasslands posed problems for the first European settlers, as did the climate. The self-scouring steel plough, introduced in 1837 by John Deere, allowed the interlaced grass sod to be broken apart, freeing the soils for agriculture. Other inventions were critical to opening this region and solving its unique spatial problems: barbed wire (the fencing material for a treeless prairie); well-drilling techniques developed by Pennsylvania oil drillers but used for water wells; windmills for pumping; and railroads to conquer long distances.

Few patches of the original prairies (tall grasslands) or steppes (short grasslands) remain within this biome. For prairies alone, the reduction of natural vegetation went from 100 million hectares down to a few areas of several hundred hectares each. The Nature Conservancy of Canada is working in conjunction with the Nature Conservancy in the United States to develop a natural corridor that will extend from Canada to the American Midwest. The northern extent of this corridor, the Manitoba Tallgrass Prairie Preserve, strives to preserve the last significant remnants of tallgrass prairie in Canada. More than 5000 hectares have been preserved, but another 4000 hectares are needed to make this preserve ecologically viable. The map in Figure 20.5 shows the natural location of these former prairie and steppe grasslands.

Outside North America, the Pampas of Argentina and Uruguay and the grasslands of Ukraine are characteristic midlatitude grassland biomes. In each region of the world where these grasslands have occurred, human development of them was critical to territorial expansion.

This biome is the home of large grazing animals, including deer, pronghorn, and bison (the almost complete annihilation of the latter is part of North American history, Figure 20.18). Grasshoppers and other insects feed on the grasses and crops as well, and gophers, prairie dogs, ground squirrels, turkey vultures, grouse, and prairie chickens are on the land. Predators include coyote, the nearly extinct black-footed ferret, badger, and birds of prey—hawks, eagles, and owls.

FIGURE 20.17 Farming in the grasslands of North America.
Midlatitude grasslands of Alberta, Canada, under cultivation. [Comstock/Thinkstock.]

FIGURE 20.18 **Bison graze on grassland.**
The Big Basin Prairie Preserve Wildlife Area, western Kansas.
Inset shows male and female, shedding winter coats. [Bobbé Christopherson.]

Deserts

Earth's **desert biomes** cover more than one-third of its land area, as is obvious in Figure 20.5. In Chapter 15, we examined desert landscapes and in Chapter 10, desert climates. We divide the desert lands into **warm desert and semidesert**, caused by the presence of dry air and low precipitation from subtropical high-pressure cells; and **cold desert and semidesert**, which tend toward higher latitudes, where subtropical high pressure is of influence less than 6 months of the year.

On a planet with such a rich biosphere, the deserts stand out as unique regions of fascinating adaptations for survival. Much as a group of humans in the desert might behave with short supplies, plant communities also compete for water and site advantage. Some desert plants, called *ephemerals*, wait years for a rainfall event, at which time their seeds quickly germinate and the plants develop, flower, and produce new seeds, which then rest again until the next rainfall event. The seeds of some xerophytic species open only when fractured by the tumbling, churning action of flash floods cascading down a desert arroyo, and, of course, such an event produces the moisture that a germinating seed needs.

Perennial desert plants employ other adaptive features to cope with the desert. Unique xerophytic features include

- Long, deep taproots (for example, the mesquite);
- Succulence (thick, fleshy, water-holding tissue, such as that of cacti),
- Spreading root systems to maximize water availability, waxy coatings and fine hairs on leaves to retard water loss, leafless conditions during dry periods (for example, palo verde and ocotillo),
- Reflective surfaces to reduce leaf temperatures, and
- Tissue that tastes bad to discourage herbivores.

The creosote bush (*Lorrea tridentata*) sends out a wide pattern of roots and contaminates the surrounding soil with toxins that prevent the germination of other creosote seeds, possible competitors for water. When a creosote bush dies, surrounding plants or germinating seeds will occupy the abandoned site, but must wait for infrequent rains to remove the toxins, according to one hypothesis.

The fauna of both warm and cold deserts are limited by the extreme conditions and include few resident large animals. Exceptions are the camel, which can lose up to 30% of its body weight in water without suffering (for humans, a 10%–12% loss is dangerous), and the desert bighorn sheep, in scattered populations in inaccessible mountains and places such as the Grand Canyon along rocky outcrops and cliffs, but not at the rim. Some representative desert animals are the ring-tail cat, kangaroo rat, lizards, scorpions, and snakes. Most of these animals are quite secretive and become active only at night, when temperatures are lower. In addition, various birds have adapted to desert conditions and available food sources—for example, roadrunners, thrashers, ravens, wrens, hawks, grouse, and nighthawks.

We are witnessing an unwanted expansion of the desert biome, discussed in Chapter 15. This process, known as *desertification*, is now a worldwide phenomenon along the margins of semiarid and arid lands.

Earth's deserts are subdivided into desert and semidesert associations, to distinguish those with expanses of bare ground from those covered by xerophytic plants of various types. The two broad associations are further separated into warm deserts, principally tropical and subtropical, and cold deserts, principally midlatitude.

Warm desert vegetation ranges from almost none to numerous xerophytic shrubs, succulents, and thorn tree forms. The lower Sonoran Desert of southern Arizona is an example (Figure 20.19). This desert landscape features the unique saguaro cactus (*Carnegiea gigantea*), which grows to many metres in height and up to 200 years in age if undisturbed. First blooms do not appear until it is 50 to 75 years old.

A few of the subtropical deserts—such as those in Chile, Western Sahara, and Namibia—are right on the seacoast and are influenced by cool offshore ocean currents. As a result, these true deserts experience summer fog that mists the plant and animal populations with needed moisture.

Arctic and Alpine Tundra

The **arctic tundra** is found in the extreme northern area of North America, around the coast of Greenland, and in Russia, bordering on the Arctic Ocean and generally north of the 10°C isotherm for the warmest month. Daylength varies greatly throughout the year, seasonally changing from almost continuous day to continuous night. The region, except for a few portions of Alaska and Siberia, was covered by ice during all of the Pleistocene glaciations. In

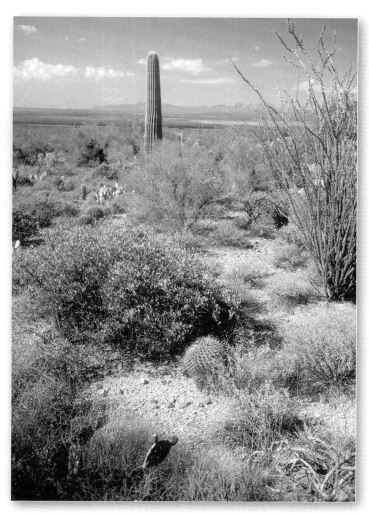

FIGURE 20.19 Sonoran Desert scene.
Characteristic vegetation in the Lower Sonoran Desert west of
Tucson, Arizona (32° N; elevation 900 m). [Robert Christopherson.]

terms of climate change, these regions have been warming at more than twice the rate of the rest of the planet over the past few decades; see the related discussions and photos in Figures 10.22 and 17.20–17.24. The impact of such heating on plants and animals, permafrost, First Nation peoples and their towns, glacial and sea ice, and decreasing ocean salinity are topics of active scientific inquiry and the International Polar Year for science and research that ended in March 2009.

Winters in this biome, which has a *tundra* climate, are long and cold; cool summers are brief. Intensely cold continental polar and arctic air masses and stable high-pressure anticyclones dominate winter. A growing season of sorts lasts only 60–80 days, and even then frosts can occur at any time. Vegetation is fragile in this flat, treeless world; soils are poorly developed periglacial surfaces that are underlain by permafrost. In the summer months, only the surface horizons thaw, thus producing a mucky surface of poor drainage. Roots can penetrate only to the depth of thawed ground, usually about a metre. In these periglacial regions, the surface is shaped by freeze–thaw cycles that create the frozen ground phenomena discussed in Chapter 17.

Tundra vegetation consists of low, ground-level herbaceous plant species, such as sedges, mosses, arctic meadow grass, snow lichen, and some woody dwarf willow (Figure 20.20). Owing to the short growing season, some perennials form flower buds one summer and open them for pollination the next. The tundra supports the musk ox, caribou, reindeer, rabbit, ptarmigan, lemming, and other small rodents, which are important food for the larger carnivores—the wolf, fox, weasel, snowy owl, polar bear. The tundra is an important breeding ground for geese, swans, and other waterfowl.

(a)

(b)

FIGURE 20.20 Arctic tundra.
(a) Tundra on the Kamchatka Peninsula, Russia. The Uzon Caldera is in the centre-background mountain range. (b) Lush by tundra standards, flowers, grasses, mosses, and dwarf willow flourish in the cold climate of the Arctic. [Bobbé Christopherson.]

FIGURE 20.21 Alpine tundra conditions.
An alpine setting at the edge of the forest and grazing
mountain goats in the Canadian Rockies. [Robert Christopherson.]

FIGURE 20.22 Arctic National Wildlife Refuge.
Caribou herd during summer migration in Alaska's Arctic
National Wildlife Refuge. Is this region destined for petroleum
exploration and development or for continued preservation as
wilderness? [Ted Kerasote/Photo Researchers/Getty Images.]

Alpine tundra is similar to arctic tundra, but it can occur at lower latitudes because it is associated with high elevations. This biome usually is described as above the timberline, that elevation above which trees cannot grow. Timberlines increase in elevation equatorward in both hemispheres. Alpine tundra communities occur in the Andes near the equator, the White Mountains and Sierra of California, the American and Canadian Rockies, the Alps, and Mount Kilimanjaro of equatorial Africa, as well as in mountains from the Middle East to Asia.

Alpine meadows feature grasses, herbaceous annuals (small plants), and stunted shrubs, such as willows and heaths. Because alpine locations are frequently windy sites, many plants appear to have been sculpted by the wind. Alpine tundra can experience permafrost conditions. Characteristic fauna include mountain goats, bighorn sheep, elk, and voles (Figure 20.21).

Because the tundra biome is of such low productivity, it is fragile. Disturbances such as tire tracks, hydroelectric projects, and mineral exploitation leave marks that persist for hundreds of years. As development continues, the region will face even greater challenges from oil spills, contamination, and disruption.

Planning continues for oil exploration and development of the Arctic National Wildlife Refuge (ANWR) on Alaska's North Slope. A U.S. Geological Survey assessment disclosed that the oil under the Arctic refuge coastal plain is likely held in many small reservoirs. Recovering this oil would require alteration of the ANWR landscape. Political and corporate pressure is continuous to exploit these expected reserves of fossil fuels.

This pristine wilderness is north of the Arctic Circle, bordering on Yukon Territory and the adjoining Beaufort Sea (Figure 20.22). The refuge area sustains almost 200 000 caribou, polar and grizzly bears, musk oxen, and wolves. Some have referred to it as "America's Serengeti," given the annual migration of hundreds of thousands of large animals. The 1002 Area is 6070 square kilometres in the ANWR with potential oil and gas resources, yet critical animal habitat for caribou and polar bears (http://energy.usgs.gov/alaska/anwr.html). The debate is ongoing; see http://justice.uaa.alaska.edu/rlinks/environment/ak_anwr.html.

 GEO REPORT 20.3 *The Porcupine Caribou Herd*

The Porcupine caribou herd is a population of tundra caribou that inhabit Yukon, Northwest Territories, and Alaska. Most of the herd migrates to the Alaska coastal plain to calve in early June. The calving area is small, and 80%–85% of the herd use it year after year. Oil exploration is not permitted in these areas because petroleum development can be devastating to Arctic wildlife. However, intense political pressure to relax any protection is ever present, and an aggressive campaign to overturn bans on exploration and drilling is active.

CRITICAL THINKING 20.3

Shifting Climate Hypothetical

Now that you have come to the end of this chapter, consider doing an exercise. Using Figure 20.5 (biomes), Figure 10.6 (climates), Figures 10.3 and 9.5 (precipitation), and Figure 8.2 (air masses), and the printed graphic scales on these maps, consider the following hypothetical scenario. Assume a northward climatic shift in Canada and the United States of 500 km; in other words, imagine moving North America 500 km south to simulate climatic categories shifting north. Describe your analysis of conditions through the Midwest from Texas to the prairies of Canada. Describe your analysis of conditions from New York through New England and into the Maritime Provinces. How will biomes change? What economic dislocations and relocations do you envision? For another region of the world, think about the climatic results if Australia shifted 500 km north—consider the new pattern of climate categories and ecosystems.

 GEOSYSTEMS CONNECTION

Earth's 10 biomes bring together all its natural systems into these specific regions. We see the patterns in the biosphere and the diversity of life. Real issues abound regarding preservation of this diversity and the influence of climate change on communities, ecosystems, and biomes. Physical geography and Earth systems science are in an important position to study these changes. The next chapter is a short, philosophical conclusion of our journey together through the pages of this book. Chapter 21 discusses the path ahead and asks key related questions.

APPLIED PHYSICAL GEOGRAPHY   *Landscape Pattern Analysis*

Landscapes are mosaics: patterns of homogeneous patches that vary in size, shape, and cover type. *Landscape pattern analysis* is an emerging field of study that applies quantitative methods to describe and understand the nature of landscape patterns. It can be used to analyze patterns in natural landscapes, anthropogenic landscapes, or natural landscapes affected by human activity. A key application of landscape pattern analysis is to assess how human activity causes fragmentation of natural landscapes and negatively impacts ecosystem functioning. Consider the patterns in Amazonian forests created by clearcutting shown in the satellite images in Figure 20.8: How would you describe—and then compare—those patterns quantitatively?

Quantitative descriptors of landscape patches are called *metrics*. Here we will compute three simple metrics for the two patches shown in Figure APG 20.1. The two patches have been outlined on a raster grid. The length of each side of the squares in the grid represents 50 m; therefore the area of one grid square is 50 m × 50 m = 2500 m². Because 100 m × 100 m = 10 000 m² = 1 hectare, we can also express the area

of a grid square as 2500 m² / 10 000 m² = 0.25 hectares.

The simplest metric that describes each patch is *area* (A). Both patches cover 12 grid squares, giving an area of 12 × 2500 = 30 000 m² (/10 000 = 3 hectares). However, the *perimeter* (P) length of Patch 1 is less than Patch B: 16 grid square sides × 50 m = 800 m vs. 24 sides × 50 m = 1200 m, respectively. Despite the similarity in area, the two patches clearly have different shapes which we can describe using the ratio of *perimeter:area* (m:m²). The units of this calculation are m⁻¹, but this metric is normally presented as a ratio without units. Patch 1 has a P:A ratio of 800/30 000 = 0.027 while the ratio of Patch 2 is 1200/30 000 = 0.040. Comparatively, the lower value for Patch 1 indicates a more compact shape; Patch 2 has a more elongated shape where a greater proportion of its area is closer to the edge of the patch.

Area and perimeter are primary metrics because the values can be measured directly. P:A ratio is a derived or secondary metric since it is calculated from other metrics. Note that P:A ratio is straightforward to calculate but it has a deficiency because if the shape of a patch is held constant, increasing patch area

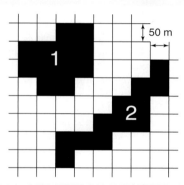

FIGURE APG 20.1 **Two homogeneous patches in a landscape.** Both patches have the same area, but Patch 2 has a longer perimeter and less compact shape than Patch 1.

causes the ratio to decrease. To overcome this problem, a more robust shape index metric can be computed.

Landscape pattern analysis is normally conducted on digital maps of real-world landscapes using a specialized software program or GIS. The number and complexity of metrics that can be calculated goes far beyond the simple metrics shown here. The leading software program for landscape pattern analysis is FRAGSTATS. To download the latest version of FRAGSTATS or to obtain documentation about it, visit http://www.umass.edu/landeco/research/fragstats/fragstats.html.

KEY LEARNING CONCEPTS REVIEW

■ **Describe** the concept of biogeographic realms of plants and animals, and **define** ecotone and terrestrial ecosystems.

The interplay among supporting physical factors within Earth's ecosystem determines the distribution of plant and animal communities and Earth's biodiversity. A **biogeographic realm** of plants and animals is a geographic region in which a group of species evolved. This recognition was a start at understanding distinct regions of flora and fauna and the broader pattern of terrestrial ecosystems. A boundary transition zone adjoining ecosystems is an **ecotone**. A **terrestrial ecosystem** is a self-sustaining association of plants and animals and their abiotic environment that is characterized by specific plant formation classes. Specific life-form designations include trees, lianas, shrubs, herbs, bryophytes, epiphytes (plants growing aboveground on other plants), and thallophytes (lacking true leaves, stems, or roots, including bacteria, fungi, algae, and lichens).

> biogeographic realm (p. 624)
> ecotone (p. 625)
> terrestrial ecosystem (p. 625)

1. Reread Marsh's quotations and analysis from 1874 at the beginning of this chapter. What seems to be our learning curve regarding the path ahead for Earth's forests and ecosystems? Is our future direction controllable? Is it sustainable? Explain.
2. What is a biogeographic realm? How is the world subdivided according to botanical (plant) types? What are some plant life-form designations?
3. Describe a transition zone between two ecosystems. How wide is an ecotone? Explain.

■ **Define** biome, and **illustrate** formation classes as a basis for describing plant communities within biomes.

A **biome** is a large, stable ecosystem characterized by specific plant and animal communities. Biomes carry the name of the dominant vegetation because it is the most easily identified feature: forest, savanna, grassland, shrubland, desert, tundra. Biomes are divided into more specific vegetation units called **formation classes**. The structure and appearance of the vegetation is described: rain forest, needleleaf forest, Mediterranean shrubland, arctic tundra, and so forth.

> biome (p. 626)
> formation classes (p. 626)

4. Define *biome*. What is the basis of the designation?
5. Distinguish between formation classes and life-form designations as a basis for spatial classification.

■ **Differentiate** between native and exotic species, and **detail** the threat they represent to communities, using several examples.

Communities, ecosystems, and biomes can be affected by species that are introduced from elsewhere by humans, either accidentally or intentionally. These nonnative species are known as *exotic species*, or *aliens*. After arriving in the new ecosystem, some species may then be disruptive and become **invasive species**.

> invasive species (p. 626)

6. Enumerate several examples of invasive species described in the text, and describe the impact of invasive species on natural systems.
7. What happened in the waters of Tristan da Cunha? Why was this subject first introduced in Chapter 6 of the text and then pursued in this chapter? What are the linkages between the chapters? What economic damage might evolve in Tristan's marine ecosystems?

■ **Describe** 10 major terrestrial biomes, and **locate** them on a world map.

Biomes are Earth's major terrestrial ecosystems, each named for its dominant plant community. The 10 major biomes are generalized from numerous formation classes that describe vegetation. Ideally, a biome represents a mature community of natural vegetation. In reality, few undisturbed biomes exist in the world, for most have been modified by human activity. Many of Earth's plant and animal communities are experiencing an accelerated rate of change that could produce dramatic alterations within our lifetime. **Island biogeography** is the study of island communities of plants and animals and their isolation and small numbers of species present.

For an overview of Earth's 10 major terrestrial biomes and their vegetation characteristics, soil orders, climate-type designations, annual precipitation range, temperature patterns, and water balance characteristics, review Table 20.1.

> tropical rain forest (p. 627)
> tropical seasonal forest and scrub (p. 633)
> island biogeography (p. 635)
> tropical savanna (p. 636)
> midlatitude broadleaf and mixed forest (p. 636)
> needleleaf forest (p. 637)
> boreal forest (p. 637)
> taiga (p. 638)
> montane forest (p. 638)
> temperate rain forest (p. 639)
> Mediterranean shrubland (p. 640)
> chaparral (p. 640)
> midlatitude grasslands (p. 641)
> desert biomes (p. 642)
> warm desert and semidesert (p. 642)
> cold desert and semidesert (p. 642)
> arctic tundra (p. 642)
> alpine tundra (p. 644)

8. Using the integrative chart in Table 20.1 and the world biome map in Figure 20.5, select any two biomes and study the correlation of vegetation characteristics, soil, moisture, and climate with their spatial distribution of the biomes. Then, contrast the two using each characteristic.
9. Describe the equatorial and tropical rain forests. Why is the rainforest floor somewhat clear of plant growth? Why are logging activities for specific species so difficult there?
10. What issues surround the deforestation of the rain forest? What is the impact of these losses on the rest of the biosphere? What new threat to the rain forest has emerged?
11. To what do the terms *caatinga*, *chaco*, *brigalow*, and *dornveld* refer to? Explain.

12. Describe the role of fire or fire ecology in the tropical savanna biome and the midlatitude broadleaf and mixed forest biome.
13. Why does the northern needleleaf forest biome not exist in the Southern Hemisphere, except in mountainous regions? Where is this biome located in the Northern Hemisphere, and what is its relationship to climate type?
14. In which biome do we find Earth's tallest trees? Which biome is dominated by small, stunted plants, lichens, and mosses?
15. What type of vegetation predominates in the Mediterranean (dry summer) climate? Describe the adaptations necessary for these plants to survive.
16. What is the significance of the 98th meridian in terms of North American grasslands? What types of inventions enabled humans to survive in the grasslands?
17. Describe some of the unique adaptations found in a desert biome.
18. What is desertification (see Chapter 15 and this chapter)? Explain its impact.
19. What physical weathering processes are specifically related to the tundra biome? What types of plants and animals are found there?

■ *Relate* human impacts, real and potential, to several of the biomes.

The tropical rainforest biome is undergoing rapid deforestation. Because the rain forest is Earth's most diverse biome and is important to the climate system, such losses are creating great concern among citizens, scientists, and nations. Efforts are under way worldwide to set aside and protect remaining representative sites within most of Earth's principal biomes. Knowing principles of **island biogeography** in studying isolated ecosystems are important in setting up biosphere reserves. Island communities are special places for study because of their spatial isolation and the relatively small number of species present.

island biogeography (p. 635)

20. What is the relationship between island biogeography and biosphere reserves? Describe a biosphere reserve. What are the goals of setting up reserves?
21. Compare the map in Figure 20.5 with the composite satellite image inside the front cover of this text. What correlations can you make between the local summertime portrait of Earth's biosphere and the biomes identified on the map?
22. Using credible Internet sources, what is the present status relative to ongoing, but halted, efforts to begin oil and gas exploration in ANWR?

MyGeosciencePlace

Visit **www.mygeoscienceplace.ca** for several figure animations, satellite loops, self-study quizzes, flashcards, interactive glossary, career links, RSS feeds, Pearson eText of *Geosystems*, and much more.

CHAPTER 21

Earth and the Human Denominator

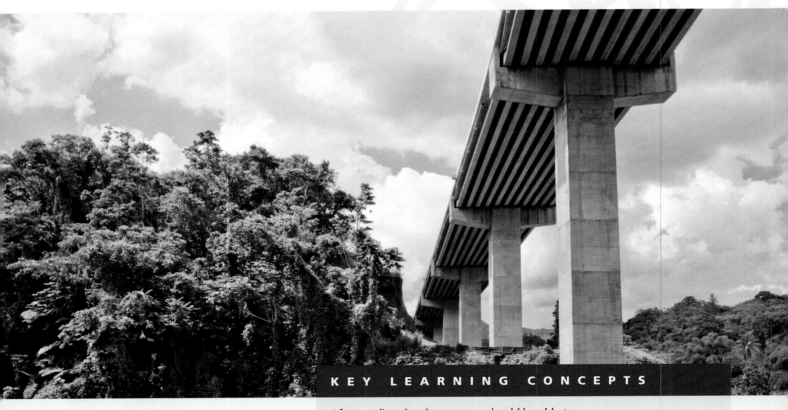

A new highway slices through a Puerto Rican rain forest. This is a remarkable reminder of humans as Earth's major geomorphic agent, and for considering the human denominator. [Bobbé Christopherson.]

KEY LEARNING CONCEPTS

After reading the chapter, you should be able to:

- **Determine** an answer for Carl Sagan's question, "Who speaks for Earth?"
- **Describe** the growth in human population, and **speculate** on possible future trends.
- **Analyze** "An Oily Bird," and **relate** your analysis to energy consumption patterns in Canada and the United States.
- **List** and **discuss** 12 key issues for Earth in the twenty-first century.
- **Appraise** your place in the biosphere, and **discover** your relation to Earth systems.

Seeing Earth and Ourselves from Space

Throughout history, the human perspective of Earth and our relation to Earth has evolved. There was a time when Earth systems were viewed much as the workings of a clock, which could be disassembled, controlled, and then put back together. Certainly, technology played its role to empower humans in modifying planetary systems.

Only in the last half century has an understanding emerged that Earth is a vast complex of interrelated systems, a synergistic whole that is greater than the sum of its component parts. There is serious thought that perhaps Earth behaves like an organism itself; self-maintaining, self-organizing, metabolizing—part of the Gaia Hypothesis.

In the 1950s and 1960s, during the young space age, humans began placing satellites and spacecraft in low orbit. With great strides in lift capability, a goal was set by the U.S. government for humans to go to the Moon before 1970. Scientists and philosophers alike began to speculate what the impact would be when humans first saw views of Earth from a distance, from space. How would society react to such a moment? People speculated about the cultural shock of seeing the planet isolated in the void of space. We had no mental framework, no imprinting to handle seeing Earth from far away, since the human experience is bound by gravity to the planet's surface.

In 1968, *Apollo VIII* launched on a journey to orbit the Moon. On their voyage, the astronauts made photos of Earth (Figure GN 21.1). Civilization now had photos of Earth from space and three witnesses to explain what they saw and how they felt.

A few months later *Apollo IX* was in Earth orbit testing all the systems needed to land on the lunar surface. During a spacewalk astronaut Rusty Schweickart had to stop work while NASA figured out a problem with some tools. In those few minutes of waiting, the drifting astronaut looked down as the entire Mediterranean

FIGURE GN 21.1 First distant views of our home planet.
From December 21 to 27, 1968, *Apollo VIII* was in flight between Earth and the Moon, successfully orbiting the Moon 10 times. The astronauts witnessed dramatic Earth-rises beyond the lunar surface. [NASA.]

swept by, then the Middle East. The impact of those moments in orbit was profound on him. In the world below, he could see "no frames and no boundaries."

The astronaut gave many talks when he returned to Earth about what he experienced both as an engineer and as a human being. In 1987, he wrote:

> During my space flight, I came to appreciate my profound connection to the home planet and the process of life evolving in our special corner of the Universe, and I grasped that I was part of a vast and mysterious dance whose outcome will be determined largely by human values and actions.[1]

In 1977, two *Voyager* spacecraft were launched to tour the outer planets, and we continue to this day to receive telemetry even though these craft are far beyond the Solar System in interstellar space. The cameras on board sent back images of this "Pale Blue Dot" we live on.

In 2006, the *Cassini–Huygens* spacecraft was studying Saturn and its many satellites. Scientists directed the craft so that Saturn was backlit by the Sun, a view of the rings that we never see from Earth (Figure GN 21.2). The small dot to the left of Saturn (see arrow), just inside

[1]R. Schweickart, *Discovery*, July 1987, p. 62.

FIGURE GN 21.2 View of Earth through Saturn's rings.
The *Cassini–Huygens* spacecraft made a surprise catch—a glimpse of Earth as a little pale dot, some 1.23 billion km distant. It was September 19, 2006, on Earth. [NASA/JPL.]

the bright ring, is Earth! All that we studied in the text and that we are trying to understand is on that small dot.

In May 2010, NASA's *Messenger* satellite, in orbit around the planet Mercury, was 183 million km from Earth. *Messenger*'s wide-angle camera caught a view of Earth and the Moon, bright with reflected sunlight (Figure GN 21.3).

We might ask, How have these views of Earth from space impacted society and culture? Have these views informed our relationship to Earth systems?

We have travelled together studying Earth this semester through the lens of physical geography and Earth systems science. Do you feel your perspective of the home planet changed during this journey through *Geosystems*? Perhaps find an Earth photo, print it, and display it in your room as a reminder.

FIGURE GN 21.3 The view of us from Mercury.
Messenger spacecraft in orbit about Mercury could see Earth and the Moon. [NASA/GSFC.]

We stand in the first decade of the twenty-first century. This century will be an adventure for the global society, historically unparalleled in experimenting with Earth's life-supporting systems. You will spend the majority of your life in this century. What preparations and "future thinking" can you do to understand all that is to occur?

Our vantage point in this book is that of physical geography. We examined Earth's many systems: its energy, atmosphere, winds, ocean currents, water, weather, climate, endogenic and exogenic systems, soils, ecosystems, and biomes. Earth can be observed and studied from profound vantage points, as described in *Geosystems Now*.

Since November 2000, the International Space Station (ISS) has operated at an orbital altitude between 350 and 400 km, in the upper reaches of Earth's thermosphere. A 16-nation coalition has completed a scientific workstation that is 44.5 m long, 78 m wide, and 27.5 m tall (Figure 21.1). The 455-metric-tonne complex has had more than 130 astronauts and scientists aboard in 392 m³ of pressurized work space (about the volume in a Boeing 747 jumbo jet). By 2011, the ISS completed nearly 70 000 orbits, some 2.7 billion km.

Several hundred scientific investigations and experiments have been completed or are under way to help us increase our understanding of Earth and life systems through research in the unique space environment. All life-support supplies must be brought from Earth. Water recycling and purification techniques provide the bulk of the water needed. Oxygen is electrolytically derived from water and supplemented by compressed oxygen. Enormous solar panel arrays generate electricity. Without plants, carbon dioxide must be scrubbed from the air the astronauts breathe. See http://www.nasa.gov/mission_pages/station/main/index.html for more information and updates.

This exploration has led us to an examination of the planet's most abundant large animal, *Homo sapiens*. In his 1980 book and public television series *Cosmos*, the late astronomer Carl Sagan asked:

What account would we give of our stewardship of the planet Earth? We have heard the rationales offered by the nuclear superpowers. We know who speaks for the nations. But who speaks for the human species? Who speaks for Earth?[2]

Indeed, who does speak for Earth? We might answer: Perhaps we physical geographers, and other scientists who have studied Earth and know the operations of the global ecosystem, should speak for Earth. However, some might say that questions of technology, environmental politics, and future thinking belong outside of science and that our job is merely to learn how Earth's processes work and to leave the spokesperson's role to others.

A fact of life is that Earth's more-developed countries (MDCs), through their economic dominance, speak for the billions who live in less-developed countries (LDCs). The scale of disparity on our home planet is difficult to comprehend. The fate of traditional modes of life may rest in some distant financial capital. But, economics aside, the reality is that the remote lands of Siberia are linked by Earth systems to the Pampas of Argentina, to the Great Plains in North America, and to the deserts of North Africa.

In this sense, Earth can be compared to a space station or spaceship. In the same way the members of a crew aboard the ISS are inextricably linked to each other's lives and survival, we too, are each connected through the operation of planetary systems. Growing international environmental awareness in the public sector is gradually prodding governments into action. People, when informed, generally favor environmental protection and public health progress over economic interests.

Understanding these linkages among Earth's myriad systems was our quest in *Geosystems*. We now see how there are global linkages among physical and living systems and how actions in one place can affect change elsewhere in the web of life. We presented 21 *Geosystems Now* case studies, which opened each chapter, stretching across the breadth of the discipline. Take a moment to review these essays of applied topics (Table 21.1).

[2]C. Sagan, *Cosmos* (New York: Random House, 1980), p. 329.

FIGURE 21.1 Our orbital perspective—Earth's Space Station.
The International Space Station (ISS) as it looked upon completion in spring 2010. The ISS began scientific operations in November 2000. The station orbits at a speed of 28 000 km · h⁻¹, orbiting Earth in 91.6 min, 15.7 times a day. [NASA.]

The Human Count

Because human influence is pervasive, we consider the totality of our impact the *human denominator*. Just as the denominator in a fraction tells how many parts a whole is divided into, so the growing human population and the increasing demand for resources and rising planetary impact suggest how much the whole Earth system must adjust. Yet Earth's resource base remains relatively fixed.

The human population of Earth passed 7 billion in October 2011; more people are alive today than at any previous point in the planet's long history, and we are unevenly arranged in 192 countries and numerous colonies. *Virtually all new population growth is in the LDCs*, which now possess 81%, or about 5.6 billion, of the total population. Over the span of human history, billion-mark milestones are occurring at closer intervals (Figure 21.2).

Living in just two countries is 36.6% of Earth's population (19.4% in China and 17.2% in India—2.56 billion people combined). Moreover, we are a young planetary population, with some 27% of those now alive under the age of 15 (2010 data from the Population Reference Bureau, at http://www.prb.org, and the U.S. Census Bureau's *POPClock Projection*, at http://www.census.gov/cgi-bin/popclock).

If you consider only the population count, the MDCs do not have a population growth problem. In fact, some European countries are actually declining in growth or are near replacement levels. However, people in the developed world produce a greater impact on the planet per person and therefore constitute a population impact crisis. An equation expresses this impact concept:

$$I = P \cdot A \cdot T$$

where I is planetary impact; P is *population;* A is *affluence*, or consumption per person; and T is *technology*, or the level of environmental impact per unit of production. Canada and the United States, with about 5% of the world's population between them, produce more than 25.8% ($1.6 trillion and $14.7 trillion in 2010) of the world's gross domestic product and use more than double the energy per capita of Europeans, more than 7 times that of Latin Americans, 10 times that of Asians, and 20 times that of Africans. Therefore, the impact on the state of Earth systems, natural resources, and sustainability of current practices in the MDCs is critical.

The concept of an individual's "footprint" has emerged—ecological footprint, carbon footprint, lifestyle footprint. These consider what your affluence and technology, the *A* and the *T* in the equation, cost planetary

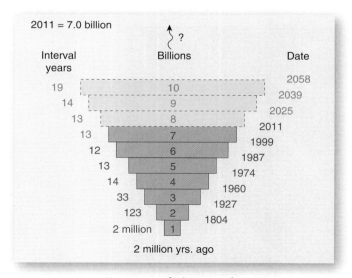

FIGURE 21.2 Human population growth.
The number of years required for the human population to add 1 billion to the count grows shorter and shorter. The twenty-first century should mark a slowing of this history of growth if policy actions are taken. Note the population forecasts for the next half-century—7 billion was reached in October 2011.

systems. Footprint assessment is grossly simplified, but it can give you an idea of your impact and even an estimate of how many planets it would take to sustain that lifestyle and economy if everyone lived like you. Your authors have taken action to neutralize the carbon footprint for the production and printing of these textbooks and the publisher used sustainable-forestry green paper for *Geosystems* to lessen ecological impacts. Many web links will help to calculate your footprint; here is a sample:

http://www.earthday.org/footprint-calculator

http://www.footprintnetwork.org

http://www.ecologicalfootprint.org/

http://www.carbonfootprint.com/calculator.html

https://www.econeutral.com/carboncalculator.html

http://www.ucsusa.org/publications/greentips/whats-your-carb.html

An Oily Bird

At first glance, the chain of events that exposes wildlife to oil contamination seems to stem from a technological problem. An oil tanker splits open at sea and releases its petroleum cargo, which is moved by ocean currents toward shore, where it coats coastal waters, beaches, and animals. In response, concerned citizens mobilize and try to save as much of the spoiled environment as possible (Figure 21.3). But the real problem goes far beyond the physical facts of the spill. What is the spatial and systems relation between an oily bird and ongoing global climate change?

In Prince William Sound off the southern coast of Alaska, in clear weather and calm seas, the *Exxon Valdez*, a single-hulled supertanker operated by Exxon Corporation,

FIGURE 21.3 An oily bird.
Oiled Brown Pelicans (*Pelecanus occidentalis*) struggle as they wait for cleaning and possible survival in the Gulf of Mexico wetlands. [Lee Celano/Reuters.]

struck a reef in 1989. The tanker spilled 42 million litres of oil. It took only 12 hours for the *Exxon Valdez* to spill its contents, yet a complete cleanup is impossible, and costs and private claims have exceeded $15 billion. Scientists are still finding damage and residual oil spill. Eventually, more than 2400 km of sensitive coastline were affected, including parts of three national parks and eight other protected areas (Figure 21.4).

The death toll of animals was massive: At least 5000 sea otters died, or about 30% of resident otters; about 300 000 birds and uncounted fish, shellfish, plants, and aquatic microorganisms also perished. Sublethal effects, namely mutations, now are appearing in fish. The Pacific herring is still in significant decline, as are the harbour seals; other species are in recovery, such as the bald eagle and common murre. More than two decades later, oil remains in mudflats and marsh soils beneath rocks.

The immediate problem of cleaning oil off a bird symbolizes a national and international concern with far-reaching spatial significance. And while we search for answers, oil slicks continue to contaminate. An average of 27 accidents a day occurs each day, 10 000 a year world-wide, ranging from a few disastrous spills to numerous small ones. There have been 50 spills equal to the *Exxon Valdez* or larger since 1970. In addition to oceanic oil spills, people improperly dispose of crankcase oil from their automobiles in a volume that annually exceeds all of these tanker spills.

The largest oil spill in U.S. history occurred in 2010. Somewhere between 50 000 and 95 000 barrels of oil a day for 86 days spewed from a wellhead on the seafloor; this is 7 to 15 million litres a day, or the equivalent of a 1989 *Exxon Valdez* oil spill every 4 days. The range in the estimated spill rate relates to the behaviour of the responsible oil company and a concerted effort to cover up the true nature of the spill because of potential financial liabilities. The well drilled by the *Deepwater Horizon*, at a depth of 1.6 km, was one of the deepest drilling attempts ever tried, and much of the technology remains untested or unknown. See the shaded area on the map in Figure 21.4 for a comparison of the 2010 *Deepwater Horizon* Gulf spill to the 1989 *Exxon Valdez* Alaskan spill. Scientists are analyzing many aspects of the tragedy to determine the extent of the biological effects on the gulf, wetlands, and beaches.

The immediate effect of global oil spills on wildlife is contamination and death. But the issues involved are much bigger than dead birds. Within the systems approach of this text, let us ask some fundamental questions about the *Exxon Valdez* and *Deepwater Horizon* accidents:

- Why was the *Exxon Valdez* oil tanker there in the first place?
- Why is it necessary for the *Deepwater Horizon* to drill in deep water with relatively limited technology?
- Why are only a few of the 28 tankers that traverse the Prince William Sound of the safer double-hulled design?

FIGURE 21.4 Worldwide oil spills, the 1989 *Exxon Valdez* accident, and the 2010 *Deepwater Horizon* disaster. (a) Location of visible oil slicks worldwide in the 1990s. (b) Track of spreading oil for the first 56 days of the Alaskan spill. The shaded area gives you a spatial equivalent of the 2010 oil spill in the Gulf of Mexico compared to the 1989 *Exxon Valdez* spill. (c) Louisiana coastal marsh coated with oil. [(a) Data from Organization for Economic Cooperation and Development. (b) and (c) NOAA.]

- Why is petroleum imported in such enormous quantities? Is the demand for petroleum products based on real need and the operation of efficient systems?
- The Canadian and U.S. demand for oil is higher per capita than the demand of any other country. Efficiencies and mileage ratings in the transportation sector have not improved for the cars, trucks, and SUVs (light trucks) leading in sales. And why is there not greater use of hybrid gas-electric or all-electric vehicles?

The spike in oil and gasoline prices in 2007–2011 coincided with a record decrease in distance driven, as drivers adjusted their driving habits with few difficulties—the economic principle is *price elasticity* of demand. This demonstrates the effectiveness of conservation and efficiency strategies used by individuals who have reduced demand.

Strangely, the word *conservation* was not used in media or political coverage during that time. One task of physical geography is to analyze all the spatial aspects of these environmental events and the ironies that are symbolized by an oily bird, and to make the connection with global climate change in such a planetary system.

The Century Before Us

Many of the thresholds discussed in *Geosystems* will occur during your lifetime. Many headline events are already signaling you of change. Assessing what is important at such a time is an important exercise in critical thinking. Many headline events are already signalling change, especially global climate change and all its impacts: changing habitats, niches, and biomes; rising sea level; increases in flood occurrences and weather intensities; the impact on human health as disease vectors spread to new regions; increases of extinctions of plants and animals; changes to freshwater resources; and changes to food, fiber, and forest production—among other issues.

As we conclude, a brief list of the dominant key issues of concern for humans in the twenty-first century seems appropriate. This list includes issues for which our present way of thinking is not working, issues that need to be addressed in new ways. A *paradigm* is the name given to a standard way of thinking about issues; this is thinking "in the box." A shift in a paradigm begins when we learn something new and begin to think "outside the box." These key issues are listed, in no particular order, as the basis for thinking and change to provide a useful framework for brainstorming and discussion of the central issues that affect us in the new century. Earth's physical geography and geographic science are important to the consideration of the paradigm shifts these 12 items infer—and perhaps require.

Twelve Key Issues for the Twenty-First Century

1. Population increases in the less-developed countries;
2. Planetary impact per person (on the biosphere and resources; $I = P \cdot A \cdot T$), an individual's ecological and carbon footprint;
3. Feeding the world's population;
4. Global and national disparities of wealth and resource allocation;
5. Status of women and children (health, welfare, rights);
6. Global climate change (temperatures, sea level, ocean chemistry, weather and climate patterns, disease, and biodiversity);
7. Energy supplies and energy demands; renewables and demand management;
8. Loss of biodiversity (habitats, genetic wealth, and species richness);
9. Pollution of air, surface water (quality and quantity), groundwater, oceans, and land;
10. The persistence of wilderness (biosphere reserves and biodiversity hot spots);
11. Globalization versus cultural diversity; and
12. Conflict resolution.

Who Speaks for Earth?

Geographic awareness and education is an increasingly positive force on Earth. Yet ideological and ethical differences still remain within society. This dichotomy was addressed by biologist Edward O. Wilson:

> The evidence of swift environmental change calls for an ethic uncoupled from other systems of belief. Those committed by religion to believe that life was put on Earth in one divine stroke will recognize that we are destroying the Creation; and those who perceive biodiversity to be the product of blind evolution will agree. . . . Defenders of both premises seem destined to gravitate toward the same position on conservation. . . . For what, in the final analysis, is morality but the command of conscience seasoned by a rational examination of consequences? . . . An enduring environmental ethic will aim to preserve not only the health and freedom of our species, but access to the world in which the human spirit was born.[3]

In an ideal sense, the human population holds all of Earth's systems in common. Now, what about Sagan's question mentioned at the beginning of the chapter? The late Carl Sagan asked, "Who speaks for Earth?" He gave us this answer:

> We have begun to contemplate our origins: starstuff pondering the stars; organized assemblages of ten billion billion billion atoms considering the evolution of atoms; tracing the long journey by which, here at least, consciousness arose. Our loyalties are to the species and the planet. We speak for Earth. Our obligation to survive is owed not just to ourselves but also to that Cosmos, ancient and vast, from which we spring.[4]

[3]E. O. Wilson, *The Diversity of Life* (Cambridge, MA: Harvard University Press, 1992), p. 351.

[4]C. Sagan, *Cosmos* (New York: Random House, 1980), p. 345.

CRITICAL THINKING 21.1

A Final Review

A. What part do you think technology, politics, and thinking about the future should play in science courses?

B. Assess population growth issues: the count, the impact per person, and future projection. What strategies do you see as important?

C. According to the discussion in the chapter, what worldwide factors led to the *Exxon Valdez* accident or the risky drilling in deep water in the Gulf of Mexico? Describe the complexity of that event from a global perspective. In your analysis, examine both supply-side (corporations and utilities) issues and demand-side (consumers) issues as well as environmental and strategic factors. And what about the concept of the oily bird?

D. After examining the list of 12 key issues for Earth in the twenty-first century, suggest items that need to be added to the list, omitted from the list, or expanded in coverage. Rearrange and organize the list as needed to match your concerns and sense of priorities as to importance of various shifts in view that are needed.

E. This chapter states that we already know many of the solutions to the problems we face. Why do you think these solutions are not being implemented at a faster pace?

F. Who speaks for Earth?

GEOSYSTEMS CONNECTION

As this icon of a bridge suggests, your journey leads to more courses and study—and the rest of the twenty-first century. Study hard and travel safely—with the wind at your back.

May we all perceive our spatial importance within Earth's ecosystems and do our part to maintain a life-supporting and sustaining Earth for ourselves and countless generations in the future.

MyGeosciencePlace

Visit **www.mygeoscienceplace.ca** for several figure animations, satellite loops, self-study quizzes, flashcards, interactive glossary, career links, RSS feeds, Pearson eText of *Geosystems*, and much more.

Maps in This Text and Topographic Maps

Maps Used in This Text

Geosystems uses several map projections: Goode's homolosine, Robinson, and Miller cylindrical, among others. Each was chosen to best present specific types of data. **Goode's homolosine projection** is an interrupted world map designed in 1923 by Dr. J. Paul Goode of the University of Chicago. Rand McNally published *Goode's Atlas*, which first used this projection in 1925. Goode's homolosine equal-area projection (Figure A.1) is a combination of two oval projections (*homolo*graphic and *sin*usoidal projections).

Two equal-area projections are cut and pasted together to improve the rendering of landmass shapes. A *sinusoidal projection* is used between 40° N and 40° S latitudes. Its central meridian is a straight line; all other meridians are drawn as sinusoidal curves (based on sine-wave curves) and parallels are evenly spaced. A *Mollweide projection*, also called a *homolographic projection*, is used from 40° N to the North Pole and from 40° S to the South Pole. Its central meridian is a straight line; all other meridians are drawn as elliptical arcs, and parallels are unequally spaced—farther apart at the equator, closer together poleward. This technique of combining two projections preserves areal size relationships, making the projection excellent for mapping spatial distributions when interruptions of oceans or continents do not pose a problem.

We use Goode's homolosine projection throughout this book. Examples include the world climate map and smaller climate type maps in Chapter 10, topographic regions and continental shields maps (Figures 12.3 and 12.4), world karst map (Figure 13.15), world sand regions and loess deposits (Figures 15.11 and 15.13), and the terrestrial biomes map in Chapter 20 (Figure 20.5).

Another projection we use is the **Robinson projection**, designed by the late Arthur Robinson in 1963 (Figure A.2). This projection is neither equal area nor true shape, but is a compromise between the two. The North and South poles appear as lines slightly more than half the length of the equator; thus higher latitudes are exaggerated less than on other oval and cylindrical projections. Some of the Robinson maps employed include the latitudinal geographic zones map in Chapter 1 (Figure 1.14), the daily net radiation map (Figure 2.11), the world temperature range map in Chapter 5 (Figure 5.18), the maps of lithospheric plates of crust and volcanoes and earthquakes in Chapter 11 (Figures 11.19 and 11.22), and the global oil spills map in Chapter 21 (Figure 21.4).

Another compromise map, the **Miller cylindrical projection**, is used in this text (Figure A.3). Examples of this projection include the world time zone map (Figure 1.21), global temperature maps in Chapter 5 (Figures 5.13 and 5.16), two global pressure maps in Chapter 6 (Figure 6.9), and the soil degradation map in Chapter 18 (Figure 18.8). This projection is neither true shape nor true area but is a compromise that avoids the severe scale distortion of the Mercator. The American Geographical Society presented Osborn Miller's map projection in 1942.

Mapping, Quadrangles, and Topographic Maps

The westward expansion across the vast North American continent demanded a land survey for the creation of accurate maps. Maps were needed to subdivide the land

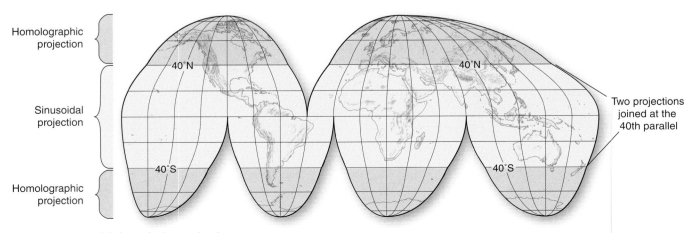

Homolographic projection

Sinusoidal projection

Homolographic projection

40°N

40°N

40°S

40°S

Two projections joined at the 40th parallel

FIGURE A.1 Goode's homolosine projection.
An equal-area map. [Copyright by the University of Chicago. Used by permission of the University of Chicago Press.]

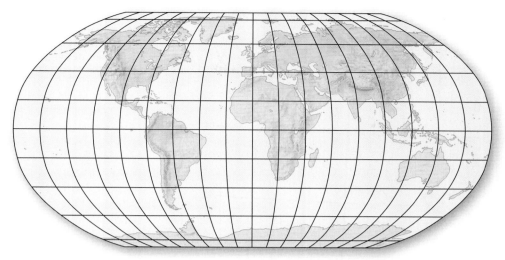

FIGURE A.2 **Robinson projection.**
A compromise between equal area and true shape. [Developed by Arthur H. Robinson, 1963.]

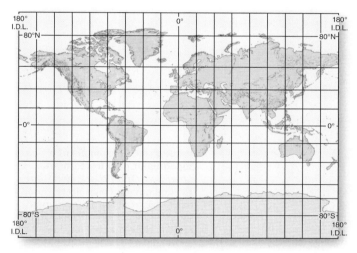

FIGURE A.3 **Miller cylindrical projection.**
A compromise map projection between equal area and true shape. [Developed by Osborn M. Miller, American Geographical Society, 1942.]

Topographic Maps

A **planimetric map** shows the horizontal position (latitude/longitude) of boundaries, land-use aspects, bodies of water, and economic and cultural features. A highway map is a common example of a planimetric map.

The most popular and widely used quadrangle maps are **topographic maps**. You will find topographic maps throughout *Geosystems* because they portray landscapes so effectively. As examples, see Figures 13.17 and 13.18, karst landscapes and sinkholes near Orleans, Indiana, and Winter Park, Florida; Figure 14.8, river drainage patterns; Figure 14.22, river meander scars; Figure 15.17, an alluvial fan in Montana; Figure 17.4, glaciers in Greenland; and Figure 17.19, drumlins in Peterborough, Ontario.

The National Topographic System (NTS) provides general-purpose topographic map coverage of Canada. The maps depict both the physical and human features of the landscape, including ground relief (landforms and terrain), drainage (lakes and rivers), forest cover, administrative areas, populated areas, transportation routes and facilities (including roads and railways), and other human-made features in detail. Natural Resources Canada produces maps that conform to the NTS and are available in two standard scales: 1:50 000 and 1:250 000. The area covered by a single 1:250 000 map is determined by its latitude and longitude and identified by a combination of grid zone number and a letter between A and P (Figure A.4). These map areas are then divided into 16 segments and numbered consecutively to form the blocks that make up the 1:50 000 map sheets.

The 1:50 000-scale topographic map is the most commonly used map series because it is an ideal scale for recreational activities (Figure A.5). At this scale, a sheet

and to guide travel, exploration, settlement, and transportation. In 1785, the U.S. Public Lands Survey System began surveying and mapping government land in the United States. In 1836, the clerk of surveys in the Land Office of the Department of the Interior directed public-land surveys. The Bureau of Land Management replaced this Land Office in 1946. The actual preparation and recording of survey information fell to the U.S. Geological Survey (USGS), also a branch of the Department of the Interior (see http://www.usgs.gov/pubprod/maps.html).

In Canada, Natural Resources Canada conducts the national mapping program. Canadian mapping includes base maps, thematic maps, aeronautical charts, federal topographic maps, and the *Atlas of Canada*, now in its sixth edition (see http://atlas.nrcan.gc.ca/).

Natural Resources Canada and the USGS depict survey information on quadrangle maps, so called because they are rectangular maps with four corner angles. The angles are junctures of parallels of latitude and meridians of longitude rather than political boundaries. These quadrangle maps utilize the Albers equal-area projection, from the conic class of map projections.

FIGURE A.4 **National Topographic System map index.**
The index displays the NTS system, in which the 1:250 000 map is 22F. Further subdivisions of the system are portrayed in this block (22F13 is a 1:50 000 map).

FIGURE A.5 **An example of a topographic map from Ontario.**
Creemore, Ontario, scanned from the Collingwood map sheet, number 41A8, from the 1:50 000 map series in the National Topographic System. Note the steeper slope (closely spaced contour lines) to the south and west of the Mad River and the flatter land (widely spaced contours) to the north and east.

(a) Perspective view of a
hypothetical landscape.
(b) Depiction of that landscape on a topographic
map. The contour interval
on the map is 6 m. [After the
U.S. Geological Survey.]

(a)

(b)

covers an area approximately 40 km by 28 km. Hills, valleys, lakes, rivers, streams, rapids, portages, trails and wooded areas; major, secondary, and side roads; and all human-made features such as buildings, power lines, dams, and cut lines are accurately represented on these maps. Maps at this scale are used by all levels of government and industry for flood control, forest-fire control, real-estate planning, development of natural resources, environmental issues, highway planning, and depiction of crop areas.

The 1:250 000-scale topographic map series is the next most common scale. Maps of this scale are commonly used for field reconnaissance. This scale is popular not only as an overview of a large area, but also as a road map for use when travelling. A standard 1:250 000-scale map shows an area approximately the size of Prince Edward Island.

The Centre for Topographic Information website (http://maps.nrcan.gc.ca/topo101/index_e.php) presents an online seminar called TOPO 101 that provides a list of commonly asked questions and explanations for topographic terms, and offers a legend of the many symbols used on Canadian topographic maps.

A topographic map adds a vertical component to a planimetric map to show topography (configuration of the land surface), including slope and relief (the vertical difference in local landscape elevation). These fine details are shown through the use of elevation contour lines (Figure A.6). A *contour line* connects all points at the same elevation. Elevations are shown above or below a vertical datum, or reference level, which is usually mean sea level.

The contour interval is the vertical distance in elevation between two adjacent contour lines (6 m in Figure A.6b).

The topographic map in Figure A.6b shows a hypothetical landscape, demonstrating how contour lines and intervals depict slope and relief, which are the three-dimensional aspects of terrain. The pattern of lines and the spacing between them indicates slope. The steeper a slope or cliff, the closer together the contour lines appear—in the figure, note the narrowly spaced contours that represent the cliffs to the left of the highway. A wider spacing of these contour lines portrays a more gradual slope, as you can see from the widely spaced lines on the beach and to the right of the river valley. In Figure A.7 are the standard symbols commonly used on these topographic maps.

The margins of a topographic map contain a wealth of information about its concept and content. In the margins of topographic maps, you find the name, position in the latitude–longitude and other coordinate systems, title, legend, magnetic declination (alignment of magnetic north) and compass information, datum plane, symbols used for roads and trails, the dates and history of the survey of that particular quad, and more.

In Canada, topographic maps may be purchased through various map dealers recommended by the Centre for Topographic Information, Natural Resources Canada (http://maps.nrcan.gc.ca/index_e.php). To find a list of authorized dealers, visit the Canada Map Office website (http://maps.nrcan.gc.ca/distribution_e.php). Topographic maps may be purchased in the U.S. directly from the USGS.

Control data and monuments
Vertical control

Third order or better, with tablet	BM ×16.3
Third order or better, recoverable mark	× 120.0
Bench mark at found section corner	BM! ×18.3
Spot elevation	× 5.3

Contours
Topographic

Intermediate	
Index	
Supplementary	
Depression	
Cut; fill	

Bathymetric

Intermediate	
Index	
Primary	
Index primary	
Supplementary	

Boundaries

National	
State or territorial	
County or equivalent	
Civil township or equivalent	
Incorporated city or equivalent	
Park, reservation, or monument	

Surface features

Levee	Levee
Sand or mud area, dunes, or shifting sand	(Sand)
Intricate surface area	(Strip mine)
Gravel beach or glacial moraine	(Gravel)
Tailings pond	(Tailings pond)

Mines and caves

Quarry or open pit mine	
Gravel, sand, clay, or borrow pit	
Mine dump	(Mine dump)
Tailings	(Tailings)

Vegetation

Woods	
Scrub	
Orchard	
Vineyard	
Mangrove	(Mangrove)

Glaciers and permanent snowfields

Contours and limits	
Form lines	

Marine shoreline
Topographic maps

Approximate mean high water	
Indefinite or unsurveyed	

Topographic-bathymetric maps

Mean high water	
Apparent (edge of vegetation)	

Coastal features

Foreshore flat	(Mud)
Rock or coral reef	(Reef)
Rock bare or awash	*
Group of rocks bare or awash	*** (***)
Exposed wreck	
Depth curve; sounding	3
Breakwater, pier, jetty, or wharf	
Seawall	

Rivers, lakes, and canals

Intermittent stream	
Intermittent river	
Disappearing stream	
Perennial stream	
Perennial river	
Small falls; small rapids	
Large falls; large rapids	
Masonry dam	
Dam with lock	
Dam carrying road	
Perennial lake; Intermittent lake or pond	
Dry lake	(Dry lake)
Narrow wash	
Wide wash	(Wide wash)
Canal, flume, or aquaduct with lock	
Well or spring; spring or seep	o ?

Submerged areas and bogs

Marsh or swamp	
Submerged marsh or swamp	
Wooded marsh or swamp	
Submerged wooded marsh or swamp	
Rice field	(Rice)
Land subject to inundation	Max pool 431

Buildings and related features

Building	
School; church	∎ ∎
Built-up area	
Racetrack	
Airport	
Landing strip	
Well (other than water); windmill	o
Tanks	●
Covered reservoir	●
Gaging station	o
Landmark object (feature as labeled)	⊙
Campground; picnic area	X
Cemetery: small; large	[Cem]

Roads and related features
Roads on Provisional edition maps are not classified as primary, secondary, or light duty. They are all symbolized as light duty roads.

Primary highway	
Secondary highway	
Light duty road	
Unimproved road	
Trail	
Dual highway	
Dual highway with median strip	

Railroads and related features

Standard gauge single track; station	
Standard gauge multiple track	
Abandoned	

Transmission lines and pipelines

Power transmission line; pole; tower	
Telephone line	Telephone
Aboveground oil or gas pipeline	
Underground oil or gas pipeline	Pipeline

FIGURE A.7 Standardized topographic map symbols used on USGS maps.
English units still prevail, although a few USGS maps are in metric. [From USGS, Topographic Maps, 1969.]

The 12 Soil Orders of the U.S. Soil Taxonomy

The U.S. soil classification system, *Soil Taxonomy—A Basic System of Soil Classification for Making and Interpreting Soil Surveys*, was published in 1975 and revised in a new second edition in 1999. Soil scientists refer to this publication simply as the **Soil Taxonomy**. Over the years, various revisions and clarifications in the system were published in *Keys to the Soil Taxonomy*, now in its 11th edition (2010, http://soils.usda.gov/technical/classification/tax_keys/), which includes all the revisions to the 1975 *Soil Taxonomy*. Major revisions include the addition of two new soil orders: Andisols (volcanic soils) in 1990 and Gelisols (cold and frozen soils) in 1998. Much of the information in this appendix is derived from these two keystone publications.

The classification system divides soils into six categories, creating a hierarchical sorting system (Table B.1). The smallest, most-detailed category is the soil series, which ideally includes only one polypedon but may include adjoining polypedons. In sequence from smallest category to the largest, the Soil Taxonomy recognizes *soil series, soil families, soil subgroups, soil great groups, soil suborders,* and *soil orders*.

Diagnostic Soil Horizons

To identify a specific soil series within the Soil Taxonomy, the U.S. Natural Resources Conservation Service describes diagnostic horizons in a pedon. A *diagnostic horizon* reflects a distinctive physical property (colour, texture, structure, consistence, porosity, moisture) or a dominant soil process (discussed with the soil types).

In the solum (A, E, and B horizons), two diagnostic horizons may be identified: the epipedon and the subsurface. The presence or absence of either of these diagnostic horizons usually distinguishes a soil for classification.

- The **epipedon** (literally, "over the soil") is the diagnostic horizon at the surface where most of the rock structure has been destroyed. It may extend downward through the A horizon, even including all or part of an illuviated B horizon. It is visibly darkened by organic matter and sometimes is leached of minerals. Excluded from the epipedon are alluvial deposits, eolian deposits, and cultivated areas, because soil-forming processes have lacked the time to erase these relatively short-lived characteristics.
- The **diagnostic subsurface horizon** originates below the surface at varying depths. It may include part of the A or B horizon or both. Many diagnostic subsurface horizons have been identified.

The 12 Soil Orders of the Soil Taxonomy

At the heart of the Soil Taxonomy are 12 general soil orders. Their worldwide distribution is shown in Figure B.1. Please consult this table and the map as you read the discussion of the Canadian System of Soil Classification (CSSC) in Chapter 18, where similar soil orders correlate. Because the Soil Taxonomy evaluates each soil order on its own characteristics, there is no priority to the classification. However, you will find a progression in the table and map legend, for the 12 orders are arranged loosely by latitude, beginning with Oxisols along the equator as in Chapter 10 (climates) and Chapter 20 (terrestrial biomes).

Table B.1 U.S. Soil Taxonomy

Soil Category	Number of Soils Included
Orders	12
Suborders	47
Great groups	230
Subgroups	1200
Families	6000
Series	15 000

FIGURE B .1 **Soil Taxonomy.**
Worldwide distribution of the
Soil Taxonomy's 12 soil orders.
[Adapted from maps prepared by
World Soil Resources Staff, Natural
Resources Conservation Service,
USDA, 1999, 2006.]

- Oxisols
- Aridisols
- Mollisols
- Alfisols
- Ultisols
- Spodosols
- Entisols
- Inceptisols
- Vertisols
- Histosols
- Andisols
- Gelisols
- Rock land
- Shifting sands
- Ice fields

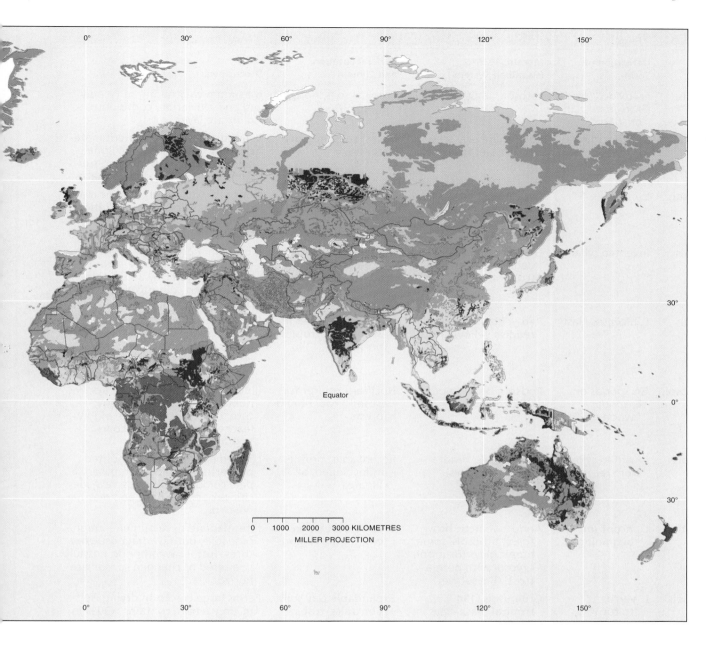

0   1000   2000   3000 KILOMETRES
MILLER PROJECTION

Equator

Table B.2 Soil Taxonomy Soil Orders

Order	Derivation of Term	Marbut, 1938* (Canadian System†)	General Location and Climate	Description
Oxisols	Fr. *oxide*, "oxide" Gr. *oxide*, "acid or sharp"	Latosols, lateritic soils	Tropical soils, hot, humid areas	Maximum weathering of Fe and Al and eluviation, continuous plinthite layer
Aridisols	L. *aridos*, "dry"	Reddish desert, grey desert, sierozems	Desert soils, hot, dry areas	Limited alteration of parent material, low climate activity, light colour, low humus content, subsurface illuviation of carbonates
Mollisols	L. *mollis*, "soft"	Chestnut, chernozem (Chernozemic)	Grassland soils; subhumid, semiarid lands	Noticeably dark with organic material, humus rich, base saturation high, friable surface with well-structured horizons
Alfisols	Invented syllable	Grey-brown podzolic, degraded chernozem (Luvisol)	Moderately weathered forest soils, humid temperate forests	B horizon high in clays, moderate to high degree of base saturation, illuviated clay accum., no pronounced colour change with depth
Ultisols	L. *ultimus*, "last"	Red-yellow podzolic, reddish yellow lateritic	Highly weathered forest soils, subtropical forests	Similar to Alfisols, B horizon high in clays, generally low amount of base saturation, strong weathering in subsurface horizons, redder than Alfisols
Spodosols	Gr. *spodos* or L. *spodus*, "wood ash"	Podzols, brown podzolic (Podzol)	Northern conifer forest soils, cool humid forests	Illuvial B horizon of Fe/Al clays, humus accum.; without structure, partially cemented; highly leached, strongly acid; coarse texture of low bases
Entisols	Invented syllable from *recent*	Azonal soils, tundra (some Regosols)	Recent soils, profile undeveloped, all climates	Limited development; inherited properties from parent material; pale colour, low humus, few specific properties; hard and massive when dry
Inceptisols	L. *inceptum*, "beginning"	Ando, subarctic brown forest lithosols, some humic gleys (Brunisol, Cryosol with permafrost, Gleysol wet)	Weakly developed soils, humid regions	Intermediate development; embryonic soils, but few diagnostic features; further weathering possible in altered or changed subsurface horizons
Vertisols	L. *verto*, "to turn"	Grumusols (1949) tropical black clays (Vertisolic)	Expandable clay soils; subtropics, tropics; sufficient dry period	Forms large cracks on drying, self-mixing action, contains >30% in swelling clays, light colour, low humus content
Histosols	Gr. *histos*, "tissue"	Peat, muck, bog (Organic)	Organic soils, wet places	Peat or bog, >20% organic matter, much with clay >40 cm thick, surface, organic layers, no diagnostic horizons
Andisols	L. *ando*, "volcanic ash"	—	Areas affected by frequent volcanic activity (formerly within Inceptisols and Entisols)	Volcanic parent materials, particularly ash and volcanic glass; weathering and mineral transformation important; high CEC and organic content, generally fertile
Gelisols	L. *gelatio*, "freezing"	Formerly Inceptisols and Entisols (Cryosols, some Brunisols)	High latitudes in Northern Hemisphere, southern limits near tree line	Permafrost within 100 cm of the soil surface; evidence of cryoturbation (frost churning) and/or an active layer; patterned-ground

*C. F. Marbut, USDA soil scientist, developed the first American system of soil classification in the 1930s, first published in the USDA *Yearbook of Agriculture* in 1938.

†For comparison, these are soil orders from the Canadian System of Soil Classification (CSSC), last revised in 1998.

The Köppen Climate Classification System

The Köppen climate classification system was designed by Wladimir Köppen (1846–1940), a German climatologist and botanist, and is widely used for its ease of comprehension. The basis of any empirical classification system is the choice of criteria used to draw lines on a map to designate different climates. Köppen-Geiger climate classification uses average monthly temperatures, average monthly precipitation, and total annual precipitation to devise its spatial categories and boundaries. But we must remember that boundaries really are transition zones of gradual change. The trends and overall patterns of boundary lines are more important than their precise placement, especially with the small scales generally used on world maps.

Take a few minutes to examine the Köppen system, the criteria, and the considerations for each of the principal climate categories. The modified Köppen-Geiger system has its drawbacks, however. It does not consider winds, temperature extremes, precipitation intensity, quantity of sunshine, cloud cover, or net radiation. Yet the system is important because its correlations with the actual world are reasonable and the input data are standardized and readily available.

Köppen's Climatic Designations

Figure 10.5 shows the distribution of each of Köppen's six climate classifications on the land. This generalized map shows the spatial pattern of climate. The Köppen system uses uppercase letters (A, B, C, D, E, H) to designate major climatic categories from the equator to the poles. The guidelines for each of the major categories are in the margins of Figure C.1.

Five of the climate categories are based on thermal criteria:

A   Tropical (equatorial regions)
C   Mesothermal (Mediterranean, humid subtropical, marine west coast regions)

D   Microthermal (humid continental, subarctic regions)
E   Polar (polar regions)
H   Highland (compared to lowlands at the same latitude, highlands have lower temperatures—recall the normal lapse rate—and more efficient precipitation due to lower evapotranspiration demand)

Only one climate classification is based on moisture as well as temperature:

B Dry (deserts and semiarid steppes)

Within each climate classification additional lowercase letters are used to signify temperature and moisture conditions. For example, in a tropical rain forest *Af* climate, the *A* tells us that the average coolest month is above 18°C (average temperature for the month), and the *f* indicates that the weather is constantly wet, with the driest month receiving at least 6 cm of precipitation. (The designation *f* is from the German *feucht*, for moist.) As you can see on the climate map, the tropical rain forest *Af* climate dominates along the equator and corresponds with the equatorial rain forest biome.

In a *Dfa* climate, the *D* means that the average warmest month is above 10°C, with at least one month falling below 0°C; the *f* says that at least 3 cm of precipitation falls during every month; and the *a* indicates a warmest summer month averaging above 22°C. Thus, a *Dfa* climate is a humid-continental, hot-summer climate in the *Geosystems* microthermal category.

Köppen Guidelines

The Köppen guidelines and map portrayal are in Figure C.1. First, check the guidelines for a climate type, then the colour legend for the subdivisions of the type, and then check out the distribution of that climate on the map. You may want to compare this with the *Geosystems* climate map in Figure 10.4 that presents causal elements that produce these climates.

FIGURE C.1 World climates and their guidelines according to the Köppen classification system.

Köppen Guidelines
Tropical Climates — A

Consistently warm with all months averaging above 18°C; annual water supply exceeds water demand.

Af — Tropical rain forest:
f = All months receive precipitation in excess of 6 cm.

Am — Tropical monsoon:
m = A marked short dry season with 1 or more months receiving less than 6 cm precipitation; an otherwise excessively wet rainy season. ITCZ 6–12 months dominant.

Aw — Tropical savanna:
w = Summer wet season, winter dry season; ITCZ dominant 6 months or less, winter water-balance deficits.

Mesothermal Climates — C

Warmest month above 10°C; coldest month above 0°C but below 18°C; seasonal climates.

Cfa, Cwa — Humid subtropical:
a = Hot summer; warmest month above 22°C.
f = Year-round precipitation.
w = Winter drought, summer wettest month 10 times more precipitation than driest winter month.

Cfb, Cfc — Marine west coast, mild-to-cool summer:
f = Receives year-round precipitation.
b = Warmest month below 22°C with 4 months above 10°C.
c = 1–3 months above 10°C.

Csa, Csb — Mediterranean summer dry:
s = Pronounced summer drought with 70% of precipitation in winter.
a = Hot summer with warmest month above 22°C.
b = Mild summer; warmest month below 22°C.

Microthermal Climates — D

Warmest month above 10°C; coldest month below 0°C; cool-temperature-to-cold conditions; snow climates. In Southern Hemisphere, occurs only in highland climates.

Dfa, Dwa — Humid continental:
a = Hot summer; warmest month above 22°C.
f = Year-round precipitation.
w = Winter drought.

Dfb, Dwb — Humid continental:
b = Mild summer; warmest month below 22°C.
f = Year-round precipitation.
w = Winter drought.

Dfc, Dwc, Dwd — Subarctic:
Cool summers, cold winters.
f = Year-round precipitation.
w = Winter drought.
c = 1–4 months above 10°C:
d = Coldest month below −38°C, in Siberia only.

Dry Arid and Semiarid Climates — B

Potential evapotranspiration* (natural moisture demand) exceeds precipitation (natural moisture supply) in all B climates. Subdivisions based on precipitation timing and amount and mean annual temperature.

Earth's arid climates.

BWh — Hot low-latitude desert

BWk — Cold midlatitude desert
BW = Precipitation less than half of natural moisture demand.
h = Mean annual temperature above 18°C.
k = Mean annual temperature below 18°C.

Earth's semiarid climates.

BSh — Hot low-latitude steppe

BSk — Cold midlatitude steppe
BS = Precipitation more than half of natural moisture demand but not equal to it.
h = Mean annual temperature above18°C.
k = Mean annual temperature below18°C.

Polar Climates — E

Warmest month below 10°C; always cold; ice climates.

ET — Tundra:
Warmest month 0–10°C; precipitation exceeds small potential evapotranspiration demand*; snow cover 8–10 months.

EF — Ice cap:
Warmest month below 0°C; precipitation exceeds a very small potential evapotranspiration demand; the polar regions.

EM — Polar marine:
All months above −7°C, warmest month above 0°C; annual temperature range ,17 C°.

*Potential evapotranspiration = the amount of water that would evaporate or transpire if it were available—the natural moisture demand in an environment; see Chapter 9.

MODIFIED GOODE'S HOMOLOSINE EQUAL-AREA PROJECTION

A TROPICAL CLIMATES

	Af	Tropical rain forest climate
	Am	Tropical monsoon climate
	Aw	Tropical savanna climate

C MESOTHERMAL CLIMATES

	Cfa	Humid subtropical, without dry season, hot summers
	Cwa **Cwb**	Humid subtropical, winter-dry
	Cfb **Cfc**	Marine west coast, without dry season, warm to cool summers
	Csa **Csb**	Mediterranean summer-dry

D MICROTHERMAL CLIMATES

	Dfa **Dwa**	Humid continental, hot summers
	Dfb **Dwb**	Humid continental, warm summers
	Dfc **Dwc**	Subarctic, cool summers
	Dfd **Dwd**	Subarctic, very cold winter

w Winter dry
f Without a dry season

B DRY ARID AND SEMIARID CLIMATES

	BW	Desert climate
	BS	Steppe climate

h Low-latitude hot **B** climates
k Midlatitude cold **B** climates

E POLAR CLIMATES
H HIGHLAND

	ET	Tundra climate
	EF **H**	Ice cap and sheets Denotes cold climate due to elevation

Common Conversions

Metric to Imperial

Metric Measure	Multiply by	Imperial Equivalent
Length		
Centimetres (cm)	0.3937	Inches (in.)
Metres (m)	3.2808	Feet (ft)
Metres (m)	1.0936	Yards (yd)
Kilometres (km)	0.6214	Miles (mi)
Nautical miles	1.15	Statute miles
Area		
Square centimetres (cm^2)	0.155	Square inches (in.^{2})
Square metres (m^2)	10.7639	Square feet (ft^2)
Square metres (m^2)	1.1960	Square yards (yd^2)
Square kilometres (km^2)	0.3831	Square miles (mi^2)
Hectares (ha) 10 000 (m^2)	2.4710	Acres (a)
Volume		
Cubic centimetres (cm^3)	0.06	Cubic inches (in.^{3})
Cubic metres (m^3)	35.30	Cubic feet (ft^3)
Cubic metres (m^3)	1.3079	Cubic yards (yd^3)
Cubic kilometres (km^3)	0.24	Cubic miles (mi^3)
Litres (l)	1.0567	Quarts (qt), U.S.
Litres (l)	0.88	Quarts (qt), Imperial
Litres (l)	0.26	Gallons (gal), U.S.
Litres (l)	0.22	Gallons (gal), Imperial
Mass		
Grams (g)	0.03527	Ounces (oz)
Kilograms (kg)	2.2046	Pounds (lb)
Metric tons (tonne) (t)	1.10	Short tons (tn), U.S.
Velocity		
Metres per second (m·s^{-1})	2.24	Miles per hour (mph)
Kilometres per hour (km·h^{-1})	0.62	Miles per hour (mph)
Knots (kn) (nautical mph)	1.15	Miles per hour (mph)
Temperature		
Degrees Celsius (°C)	1.80 (then add 32)	Degrees Fahrenheit (°F)
Celsius degrees (C°)	1.80	Fahrenheit degrees (F°)
Additional volume measurements		
Gallons (Imperial)	1.201	Gallons (U.S.)
Gallons (gal)	0.000003	Acre-feet

1 cubic foot per second per day = 86 400 cubic feet = 1.98 acre-feet

Additional energy and power measurements

1 watt (W) = 1 joule s^{-1}

1 joule = 0.239 calories

1 calorie = 4.186 joules

1 W · m^{-2} = 0.001433 cal/min

679.8 W · m^{-2} = 1 cal cm^{-2} min^{-1}

1 W · m^{-2} = 2.064 cal cm^{-3} day^{-1}

1 W · m^{-2} = 61.91 cal cm^{-2} month^{-1}

1 W · m^{-2} = 753.4 cal cm^{-2} year^{-1}

100 W · m^{-2} = 75 kcal cm^{-2} year^{-1}

Solar constant:

1372 W · m^{-2}

2 cal cm^{-2} min^{-1}

Imperial to Metric

Imperial Measure	Multiply by	Metric Equivalent
Length		
Inches (in.)	2.54	Centimetres (cm)
Feet (ft)	0.3048	Metres (m)
Yards (yd)	0.9144	Metres (m)
Miles (mi)	1.6094	Kilometres (km)
Statute miles	0.8684	Nautical miles
Area		
Square inches (in.^{2})	6.45	Square centimetres (cm^2)
Square feet (ft^2)	0.0929	Square metres (m^2)
Square yards (yd^2)	0.8361	Square metres (m^2)
Square miles (mi^2)	2.5900	Square kilometres (km^2)
Acres (a)	0.4047	Hectares (ha)
Volume		
Cubic inches (in.^{3})	16.39	Cubic centimetres (cm^3)
Cubic feet (ft^3)	0.028	Cubic metres (m^3)
Cubic yards (yd^3)	0.765	Cubic metres (m^3)
Cubic miles (mi^3)	4.17	Cubic kilometres (km^3)
Quarts (qt), U.S.	0.9463	Litres (l)
Quarts (qt), Imperial	1.14	Litres (l)
Gallons (gal), U.S.	3.8	Litres (l)
Gallons (gal), Imperial	4.55	Litres (l)
Mass		
Ounces (oz)	28.3495	Grams (g)
Pounds (lb)	0.4536	Kilograms (kg)
Short ton (tn), U.S.	0.91	Metric tons (tonne) (t)
Velocity		
Miles per hour (mph)	0.448	Metres per second (m·s^{-1})
Miles per hour (mph)	1.6094	Kilometres per hour (km·h^{-1})
Miles per hour (mph)	0.8684	Knots (kn) (nautical mph)
Temperature		
Degrees Fahrenheit (°F)	0.556 (after subtracting 32)	Degrees Celsius (°C)
Fahrenheit degrees (F°)	0.556	Celsius degrees (C°)
Additional water measurements		
Gallons (U.S.)	0.833	Gallons (Imperial)
Acre-feet	325 872	Gallons (gal)

Additional Notation

Multiples	Prefixes	
1 000 000 000 = 10^9	giga	G
1 000 000 = 10^6	mega	M
1000 = 10^3	kilo	k
100 = 10^2	hecto	h
10 = 10^1	deka	da
1 = 10^0		
0.1 = 10^{-1}	deci	d
0.01 = 10^{-2}	centi	c
0.001 = 10^{-3}	milli	m
0.000001 = 10^{-6}	micro	μ

The chapter in which each term appears is boldfaced in parentheses and is followed by a specific definition relevant to the term's usage in the chapter.

Aa (12) Rough, jagged, and clinkery basaltic lava with sharp edges. This texture is caused by the loss of trapped gases, a slow flow, and the development of a thick skin that cracks into the jagged surface.

Abiotic (1) Nonliving; Earth's nonliving systems of energy and materials.

Ablation (17) Loss of glacial ice through melting, sublimation, wind removal by deflation, or the calving of blocks of ice. (*See* deflation.)

Abrasion (14, 15, 17) Mechanical wearing and erosion of bedrock accomplished by the rolling and grinding of particles and rocks carried in a stream, removed by wind in a "sandblasting" action, or imbedded in glacial ice.

Absorption (4) Assimilation and conversion of radiation from one form to another in a medium. In the process, the temperature of the absorbing surface is raised, thereby affecting the rate and wavelength of radiation from that surface.

Active layer (17) A zone of seasonally frozen ground that exists between the subsurface permafrost layer and the ground surface. The active layer is subject to consistent daily and seasonal freeze–thaw cycles. (*See* permafrost, periglacial.)

Actual evapotranspiration (9) AE; the actual amount of evaporation and transpiration that occurs; derived in the water balance by subtracting the deficit (DEFIC) from potential evapotranspiration (PE).

Adiabatic (7) Pertaining to the cooling of an ascending parcel of air through expansion or the warming of a descending parcel of air through compression, without any exchange of heat between the parcel and the surrounding environment.

Advection (4) Horizontal movement of air or water from one place to another. (*Compare* convection.)

Advection fog (7) Active condensation formed when warm, moist air moves laterally over cooler water or land surfaces, causing the lower layers of the air to be chilled to the dew-point temperature.

Aerosols (3) Small particles of dust, soot, and pollution suspended in the air.

Aggradation (14) The general building of land surface because of deposition of material; opposite of degradation. When the sediment load of a stream exceeds the stream's capacity to carry it, the stream channel becomes filled through this process.

Air (3) A simple mixture of gases (N, O, Ar, CO_2, and trace gases) that is naturally odourless, colourless, tasteless, and formless, blended so thoroughly that it behaves as if it were a single gas.

Air mass (8) A distinctive, homogeneous body of air that has taken on the moisture and temperature characteristics of its source region.

Air pressure (3, 6) Pressure produced by the motion, size, and number of gas molecules in the air and exerted on surfaces in contact with the air; an average force at sea level of 1 kg · cm³. Normal sea-level pressure, as measured by the height of a column of mercury (Hg), is expressed as 1013.2 millibars, or 760 mm of Hg. Kilopascal equivalents are reported placing normal at 101.32 kPa; 10 mb = 1 kPa. Air pressure can be measured with mercury or aneroid barometers. (*See listings for both.*)

Albedo (4) The reflective quality of a surface, expressed as the percentage of reflected insolation to incoming insolation; a function of surface colour, angle of incidence, and surface texture.

Aleutian low (6) *See* subpolar low-pressure cell.

Alluvial fan (15) Fan-shaped fluvial landform at the mouth of a canyon; generally occurs in arid landscapes where streams are intermittent. (*See* bajada.)

Alluvial terraces (14) Level areas that appear as topographic steps above a stream, created by the stream as it scours with renewed downcutting into its floodplain; composed of unconsolidated alluvium. (*See* alluvium.)

Alluvium (14) General descriptive term for clay, silt, sand, gravel, or other unconsolidated rock and mineral fragments transported by running water and deposited as sorted or semisorted sediment on a floodplain, delta, or stream bed.

Alpine glacier (17) A glacier confined in a mountain valley or walled basin, consisting of three subtypes: valley glacier (within a valley), piedmont glacier (coalesced at the base of a mountain, spreading freely over nearby lowlands), and outlet glacier (flowing outward from a continental glacier).

Alpine tundra (20) Tundra conditions at high elevation. (*See* Arctic tundra.)

Altitude (2) The angular distance between the horizon (a horizontal plane) and the Sun (or any point in the sky).

Altocumulus (7) Middle-level, puffy clouds that occur in several forms: patchy rows, wave patterns, a "mackerel sky," or lens-shaped "lenticular" clouds.

Anemometer (6) A device that measures wind velocity.

Aneroid barometer (6) A device that measures air pressure using a partially evacuated, sealed cell. (*See* air pressure.)

Angle of repose (13) The steepness of a slope that results when loose particles come to rest; an angle of balance between driving and resisting forces, ranging between 33° and 37° from a horizontal plane.

Antarctic Circle (2) This latitude (66.5° S) denotes the northernmost parallel (in the Southern Hemisphere) that experiences a 24-hour period of darkness in winter or daylight in summer.

Antarctic high (6) A consistent high-pressure region centred over Antarctica; source region for an intense polar air mass that is dry and associated with the lowest temperatures on Earth.

Antarctic region (17) The Antarctic convergence defines the Antarctic region in a narrow zone that extends around the continent as a boundary between colder Antarctic water and warmer water at lower latitudes.

Anthropogenic atmosphere (3) Earth's future atmosphere, so named because humans appear to be the principal causative agent.

Anticline (12) Upfolded rock strata, in which layers slope downward from the axis of the fold, or central ridge. (*Compare* syncline.)

Anticyclone (6) A dynamically or thermally caused area of high atmospheric pressure with descending and diverging airflows that rotate clockwise in the Northern Hemisphere and counterclockwise in the Southern Hemisphere. (*Compare* cyclone.)

Aphelion (2) The point of Earth's greatest distance from the Sun in its elliptical orbit; reached on July 4 at a distance of 152 083 000 km; variable over a 100 000-year cycle. (*Compare* perihelion.)

Aquiclude (9) A body of rock that does not conduct groundwater in usable amounts; an impermeable rock layer, related to an aquitard that slows but does not block water flow. (*Compare* aquifer.)

Aquifer (9) A body of rock that conducts groundwater in usable amounts; a permeable layer of rock. (*Compare* aquiclude.)

Aquifer recharge area (9) The surface area where water enters an aquifer to recharge the water-bearing strata in a groundwater system.

Arctic Circle (2) This latitude (66.5° N) denotes the southernmost parallel (in the Northern Hemisphere) that experiences a 24-hour period of darkness in winter or daylight in summer.

Arctic region (17) The 10°C isotherm for July defines the Arctic region; coincides with the visible tree line—the boundary between the northern forests and tundra.

Arctic tundra (20) A biome in the northernmost portions of North America and northern Europe and Russia, featuring low, ground-level herbaceous plants as well as some woody plants.

Arête (17) A sharp ridge that divides two cirque basins. Derived from "knife edge" in French, these form sawtooth and serrated ridges in glaciated mountains.

Artesian water (9) Pressurized groundwater that rises in a well or a rock structure above the local water table; may flow out onto the ground without pumping. (*See* potentiometric surface.)

Asthenosphere (11) Region of the upper mantle just below the lithosphere; the least rigid portion of Earth's interior and known as the plastic layer, flowing very slowly under extreme heat and pressure.

Atmosphere (1) The thin veil of gases surrounding Earth, which forms a protective boundary between outer space and the biosphere; generally considered to extend out about 480 km from Earth's surface.

Aurora (2) A spectacular glowing light display in the ionosphere, stimulated by the interaction of the solar wind with oxygen and nitrogen gases and atoms at high latitudes, called aurora borealis in the Northern Hemisphere and aurora australis in the Southern Hemisphere.

Autumnal (September) equinox (2) The time around September 22–23 when the Sun's declination crosses the equatorial parallel (0° latitude) and all places on Earth experience days and nights of equal length. The Sun rises at the South Pole and sets at the North Pole. (*Compare* vernal equinox.)

Available water (9) The portion of capillary water that is accessible to plant roots; usable water held in soil moisture storage. (*See* capillary water.)

Axial parallelism (2) Earth's axis remains aligned the same throughout the year (it "remains parallel to itself"); thus, the axis extended from the North Pole points into space always near Polaris, the North Star.

Axial tilt (2) Earth's axis tilts 23.5° from a perpendicular to the plane of the ecliptic (plane of Earth's orbit around the Sun).

Axis (2) An imaginary line, extending through Earth from the geographic North Pole to the geographic South Pole, around which Earth rotates.

Azores high (6) A subtropical high-pressure cell that forms in the Northern Hemisphere in the eastern Atlantic (*see* Bermuda high); associated with warm, clear water and large quantities of sargassum, or gulf weed, characteristic of the Sargasso Sea.

Backswamp (14) A low-lying, swampy area of a floodplain; adjacent to a river, with the river's natural levee on one side and higher topography on the other. (*See* floodplain, yazoo tributary.)

Bajada (15) A continuous apron of coalesced alluvial fans, formed along the base of mountains in arid climates; presents a gently rolling surface from fan to fan. (See alluvial fan.)

Barrier beach (16) Narrow, long, depositional feature, generally composed of sand, that forms offshore roughly parallel to the coast; may appear as barrier islands and long chains of barrier beaches. (*See* barrier island.)

Barrier island (16) Generally, a broadened barrier beach. (*See* barrier beach.)

Barrier spit (16) A depositional landform that develops when transported sand or gravel in a barrier beach or island is deposited in long ridges that are attached at one end to the mainland and partially cross the mouth of a bay.

Basalt (11) A common extrusive igneous rock, fine-grained, comprising the bulk of the ocean-floor crust, lava flows, and volcanic forms; gabbro is its intrusive form.

Base level (14) A hypothetical level below which a stream cannot erode its valley, and thus the lowest operative level for denudation processes; in an absolute sense, it is represented by sea level, extending under the landscape.

Basin and Range Province (15) A region of dry climates, few permanent streams, and interior drainage patterns in the western United States; a faulted landscape composed of a sequence of horsts and grabens.

Batholith (11) The largest plutonic form exposed at the surface; an irregular intrusive mass; it invades crustal rocks, cooling slowly so that large crystals develop. (*See* pluton.)

Bay barrier (16) An extensive barrier spit of sand or gravel that encloses a bay, cutting it off completely from the ocean and forming a lagoon; produced by littoral drift and wave action; sometimes referred to as a baymouth bar. (*See* barrier spit, lagoon.)

Beach (16) The portion of the coastline where an accumulation of sediment is in motion.

Beach drift (16) Material, such as sand, gravel, and shells, that is moved by the longshore current in the effective direction of the waves.

Bed load (14) Coarse materials that are dragged along the bed of a stream by traction or by the rolling and bouncing motion of saltation; involves particles too large to remain in suspension. (*See* traction, saltation.)

Bedrock (13) The rock of Earth's crust that is below the soil and is basically unweathered; such solid crust sometimes is exposed as an outcrop.

Bergschrund (17) These form when a crevasse or wide crack opens along the headwall of a glacier; most visible in summer when covering snow is gone.

Bermuda high (6) A subtropical high-pressure cell that forms in the western North Atlantic. (*See* Azores high.)

Biodiversity (19) A principle of ecology and biogeography: the more diverse the species population in an ecosystem (in number of species, quantity of members in each species, and genetic content), the more risk is spread over the entire community, which results in greater overall stability, greater productivity, and increased use of nutrients, as compared to a monoculture of little or no diversity.

Biogeochemical cycle (19) One of several circuits of flowing elements and materials (carbon, oxygen, nitrogen, phosphorus, water) that combine Earth's biotic (living) and abiotic (nonliving) systems; the cycling of materials is continuous and renewed through the biosphere and the life processes.

Biogeographic realm (20) One of eight regions of the biosphere, each representative of evolutionary core areas of related flora (plants) and fauna (animals); a broad geographical classification scheme.

Biogeography (19) The study of the distribution of plants and animals and related ecosystems; the geographical relationships with their environments over time.

Biomass (19) The total mass of living organisms on Earth or per unit area of a landscape; also, the weight of the living organisms in an ecosystem.

Biome (20) A large terrestrial ecosystem characterized by specific plant communities and formations; usually named after the predominant vegetation in the region. (*See* terrestrial ecosystem.)

Biosphere (1) That area where the atmosphere, lithosphere, and hydrosphere function together to form the context within which life exists; an intricate web that connects all organisms with their physical environment.

Biotic (1) Living; referring to Earth's living system of organisms.

Blowout depression (15) Eolian (wind) erosion in which deflation forms a basin in areas of loose sediment. Diameter may range up to hundreds of metres. (*See* deflation.)

Bolson (15) The slope and basin area between the crests of two adjacent ridges in a dry region.

Boreal forest (20) (*See* needleleaf forest.)

Brackish (16) Descriptive of seawater with a salinity of less than 35‰; for example, the Baltic Sea. (*Contrast* to brine.)

Braided stream (14) A stream that becomes a maze of interconnected channels laced with excess sediment. Braiding often occurs with a reduction of discharge that reduces a stream's transporting ability or with an increase in sediment load.

Breaker (16) The point where a wave's height exceeds its vertical stability and the wave breaks as it approaches the shore.

Brine (16) Seawater with a salinity of more than 35‰; for example, the Persian Gulf. (*Contrast* to brackish.)

Brunisolic (18) A CSSC soil order with sufficiently developed horizons to distinguish it from the Regosolic order. Soils under forest cover with brownish horizons, although various colours are possible. Also, can be with mixed forest, shrubs, and grass.

Calcification (18) The illuviated (deposited) accumulation of calcium carbonate or magnesium carbonate in the B and C soil horizons.

Caldera (12) An interior sunken portion of a composite volcano's crater; usually steep-sided and circular, sometimes containing a lake; also can be found in conjunction with shield volcanoes.

Canadian System of Soil Classification (CSSC) (18) A soil classification system based on observable soil properties actually seen in the field; published in 1987 by the Canada Soil Survey Committee. Adapted to Canada's environment, the CSSC consists of 10 soil orders.

Capillary water (9) Soil moisture, most of which is accessible to plant roots; held in the soil by the water's surface tension and cohesive forces between water and soil. (*See also* available water, field capacity, hygroscopic water, and wilting point.)

Carbonation (13) A chemical weathering process in which weak carbonic acid (water and carbon dioxide) reacts with many minerals that contain calcium, magnesium, potassium, and sodium (especially limestone), transforming them into carbonates.

Carbon monoxide (3) An odourless, colourless, tasteless combination of carbon and oxygen produced by the incomplete combustion of fossil fuels or other carbon-containing substances; toxicity to humans is due to its affinity for haemoglobin, displacing oxygen in the bloodstream; CO.

Carnivore (19) A secondary consumer that principally eats meat for sustenance. The top carnivore in a food chain is considered a tertiary consumer. (*Compare* herbivore.)

Cartography (1) The making of maps and charts; a specialized science and art that blends aspects of geography, engineering, mathematics, graphics, computer science, and artistic specialties.

Cation-exchange capacity (CEC) (18) The ability of soil colloids to exchange cations between their surfaces and the soil solution; a measured potential that indicates soil fertility. (*See* soil colloid, soil fertility.)

Chaparral (20) Dominant shrub formations of Mediterranean dry-summer climates; characterized by sclerophyllous scrub and short, stunted, tough forests; derived from the Spanish *chaparro*; specific to California. (*See* Mediterranean shrubland.)

Chemical weathering (13) Decomposition and decay of the constituent minerals in rock through chemical alteration of those minerals. Water is essential, with rates keyed to temperature and precipitation values. Chemical reactions are active at microsites even in dry climates. Processes include hydrolysis, oxidation, carbonation, and solution.

Chernozemic (18) A CSSC soil order with well- to imperfectly-drained soils of the steppe–grassland–forest transition in Southern Alberta; Saskatchewan; Manitoba; Okanagan Valley, BC; and Palouse Prairie, BC. Accumulation of organic matter in surface horizon.

Chinook wind (8) North American term for a warm, dry, downslope airflow; characteristic of the rain-shadow region on the leeward side of mountains; known as fohn, or foehn, winds in Europe. (*See* rain shadow.)

Chlorofluorocarbons (CFC) (3) A manufactured molecule (polymer) made of chlorine, fluorine, and carbon; inert and possessing remarkable heat properties; also known as one of the halogens. After slow transport to the stratospheric ozone layer, CFCs react with ultraviolet radiation, freeing chlorine atoms that act as a catalyst to produce reactions that destroy ozone; manufacture banned by international treaties.

Chlorophyll (19) A light-sensitive pigment that resides within chloroplasts (organelles) in leaf cells of plants; the basis of photosynthesis.

Cinder cone (12) A volcanic landform of pyroclastics and scoria, usually small and cone-shaped and generally not more than 450 m in height, with a truncated top.

Circle of illumination (2) The division between light and dark on Earth; a day–night great circle.

Circum-Pacific belt (12) A tectonically and volcanically active region encircling the Pacific Ocean; also known as the "ring of fire."

Cirque (17) A scooped-out, amphitheatre-shaped basin at the head of an alpine glacier valley; an erosional landform.

Cirrus (7) Wispy, filamentous ice-crystal clouds that occur above 6000 m; appear in a variety of forms, from feathery hairlike fibres to veils of fused sheets.

Classification (10) The process of ordering or grouping data or phenomena in related classes; results in a regular distribution of information; a taxonomy.

Climate (10) The consistent, long-term behaviour of weather over time, including its variability; in contrast to weather, which is the condition of the atmosphere at any given place and time.

Climatic regions (10) An area of homogenous climate that features characteristic regional weather and air mass patterns.

Climatology (10) The scientific study of climate and climatic patterns and the consistent behaviour of weather, including its variability and extremes, over time in one place or region; includes the effects of climate change on human society and culture.

Climograph (10) A graph that plots daily, monthly, or annual temperature and precipitation values for a selected station; may also include additional weather information.

Closed system (1) A system that is shut off from the surrounding environment so that it is entirely self-contained in terms of energy and materials; Earth is a closed material system. (*Compare* open system.)

Cloud (7) An aggregate of tiny moisture droplets and ice crystals; classified by altitude of occurrence and shape.

Cloud-albedo forcing (4) An increase in albedo (the reflectivity of a surface) caused by clouds due to their reflection of incoming insolation.

Cloud-condensation nuclei (7) Microscopic particles necessary as matter on which water vapour condenses to form moisture droplets; can be sea salts, dust, soot, or ash.

Cloud-greenhouse forcing (4) An increase in greenhouse warming caused by clouds because they can act like insulation, trapping longwave (infrared) radiation.

Col (17) Formed by two headward-eroding cirques that reduce an arête (ridge crest) to form a high pass or saddlelike narrow depression.

Cold desert and semidesert (20) A type of desert biome found at higher latitudes than warm deserts. Interior location and rain-shadow locations produce these cold deserts in North America.

Cold front (8) The leading edge of an advancing cold air mass; identified on a weather map as a line marked with triangular spikes pointing in the direction of frontal movement. (*Compare* warm front.)

Community (19) A convenient biotic subdivision within an ecosystem; formed by interacting populations of animals and plants in an area.

Composite volcano (12) A volcano formed by a sequence of explosive volcanic eruptions; steep-sided, conical in shape; sometimes referred to as a stratovolcano, although composite is the preferred term. (*Compare* shield volcano.)

Conduction (4) The slow molecule-to-molecule transfer of heat through a medium, from warmer to cooler portions.

Cone of depression (9) The depressed shape of the water table around a well after active pumping. The water table adjacent to the well is drawn down by the water removal.

Confined aquifer (9) An aquifer that is bounded above and below by impermeable layers of rock or sediment. (*See* artesian water, unconfined aquifer.)

Constant isobaric surface (6) An elevated surface in the atmosphere on which all points have the same pressure, usually 500 mb. Along this constant-pressure surface, isobars mark the paths of upper-air winds.

Consumer (19) Organism in an ecosystem that depends on producers (organisms that use carbon dioxide as their sole source of carbon) for its source of nutrients; also called a heterotroph. (*Compare* producer.)

Consumptive use (9) A use that removes water from a water budget at one point and makes it unavailable further downstream (compare withdrawal).

Continental divide (14) A ridge or elevated area that separates drainage on a continental scale; specifically, that ridge in North America that separates drainage to the Pacific on the west side from drainage to the Atlantic and Gulf on the east side and to Hudson Bay and the Arctic Ocean in the north.

Continental drift (11) A proposal by Alfred Wegener in 1912 stating that Earth's landmasses have migrated over the past 225 million years from a supercontinent he called Pangaea to the present configuration; the widely accepted plate tectonics theory today. (*See* plate tectonics.)

Continental effect (5) A quality of regions that lack the temperature-moderating effects of the sea and that exhibit a greater range of minimum and maximum temperatures, both daily and annually. (*See* marine, land–water heating differences.)

Continental glacier (17) A continuous mass of unconfined ice, covering at least 50 000 km^2; most extensive at present as ice sheets covering Greenland and Antarctica. (*Compare* alpine glacier.)

Continental landmasses (12) The broadest category of landform, including those masses of crust that reside above or near sea level and the adjoining undersea continental shelves along the coastline; sometimes synonymous with continental platforms.

Continental shield (12) Generally, old, low-elevation heartland regions of continental crust; various cratons (granitic cores) and ancient mountains exposed at the surface.

Convection (4) Transfer of heat from one place to another through the physical movement of air; involves a strong vertical motion. (*Compare* to advection.)

Convectional lifting (8) Air passing over warm surfaces gains buoyancy and lifts, initiating adiabatic processes.

Convergent lifting (8) Airflows in conflict force lifting and displacement of air upward, initiating adiabatic processes.

Coordinated Universal Time (UTC) (1) The official reference time in all countries, formerly known as Greenwich Mean Time; now measured by primary standard atomic clocks, the time calculations are collected in Paris at the International Bureau of Weights and Measures (BIPM); the legal reference for time in all countries and broadcast worldwide.

Coral (16) A simple, cylindrical marine animal with a saclike body that secretes calcium carbonate to form a hard external skeleton and, cumulatively, landforms called reefs; lives symbiotically with nutrient-producing algae; presently in a worldwide state of decline due to bleaching (loss of algae).

Core (11) The deepest inner portion of Earth, representing one-third of its entire mass; differentiated into two zones—a solid-iron inner core surrounded by a dense, molten, fluid metallic-iron outer core.

Coriolis force (6) The apparent deflection of moving objects (wind, ocean currents, missiles) from travelling in a straight path, in proportion to the speed of Earth's rotation at different latitudes. Deflection is to the right in the Northern Hemisphere and to the left in the Southern Hemisphere; maximum at the poles and zero along the equator.

Crater (12) A circular surface depression formed by volcanism; built by accumulation, collapse, or explosion; usually located at a volcanic vent or pipe; can be at the summit or on the flank of a volcano.

Crevasse (17) A vertical crack that develops in a glacier as a result of friction between valley walls, or tension forces of extension on convex slopes, or compression forces on concave slopes.

Crust (11) Earth's outer shell of crystalline surface rock, ranging from 5 to 60 km in thickness from oceanic crust to mountain ranges. Average density of continental crust is 2.7 g · cm^2, whereas oceanic crust is 3.0 g · cm^3.

Cryosphere (1) The frozen portion of Earth's waters, including ice sheets, ice caps and fields, glaciers, ice shelves, sea ice, and subsurface ground ice and frozen ground (permafrost).

Crysolic (18) A CSSC soil order that dominates the northern third of Canada, with permafrost closer to the surface and composed of mineral and organic soil deposits. Generally found north of the treeline, or in fine-textured soils in subarctic forest, or in some organic soils in boreal forests.

Cumulonimbus (7) A towering, precipitation-producing cumulus cloud that is vertically developed across altitudes associated with other clouds; frequently associated with lightning and thunder and thus sometimes called a thunderhead.

Cumulus (7) Bright and puffy cumuliform clouds up to 2000 m in altitude.

Cyclogenesis (8) An atmospheric process that describes the birth of a midlatitude wave cyclone, usually along the polar front. Also refers to strengthening and development of a midlatitude cyclone along the eastern slope of the Rockies, other north–south mountain barriers, and along the North American and Asian east coasts. (*See* midlatitude cyclone, polar front.)

Cyclone (6) A dynamically or thermally caused area of low atmospheric pressure with converging and ascending airflows. Rotates counterclockwise in the Northern Hemisphere and clockwise in the Southern Hemisphere. (*Compare* anticyclone; *see* midlatitude cyclone, tropical cyclone.)

Daylength (2) Duration of exposure to insolation, varying during the year depending on latitude; an important aspect of seasonality.

Daylight saving time (1) Time is set ahead 1 hour in the spring and set back 1 hour in the fall in the Northern Hemisphere. In Canada and the United States, time is set ahead on the second Sunday in March and set back on the first Sunday in November—except in Hawai'i, Arizona, and Saskatchewan, which exempt themselves.

Debris avalanche (13) A mass of falling and tumbling rock, debris, and soil; can be dangerous because of the tremendous velocities achieved by the onrushing materials.

December solstice (2) *See* winter (December) solstice.

Declination (2) The latitude that receives direct overhead (perpendicular) insolation on a particular day; the subsolar point migrates annually through 47° of latitude between the Tropics of Cancer (23.5° N) and Capricorn (23.5° S).

Decomposer (19) Bacteria and fungi that digest organic debris outside their bodies and absorb and release nutrients in an ecosystem. (*See* detritivores.)

Deficit (9) D in a water balance, the amount of unmet (unsatisfied) potential evapotranspiration; a natural water shortage. (*See* potential evapotranspiration, PE.)

Deflation (15) A process of wind erosion that removes and lifts individual particles, literally blowing away unconsolidated, dry, or noncohesive sediments. (*See* blowout depression.)

Delta (14) A depositional plain formed where a river enters a lake or an ocean; named after the triangular shape of the Greek letter delta, Δ.

Denudation (13) A general term that refers to all processes that cause degradation of the landscape: weathering, mass movement, erosion, and transport.

Deposition (14) The process whereby weathered, wasted, and transported sediments are laid down by air, water, and ice.

Derechos (8) Strong linear winds in excess of 26 m·s^{-1}, associated with thunderstorms and bands of showers crossing a region. (*See* straight-line winds and plough winds.)

Desalination (9) In a water resources context, the removal of organics, debris, and salinity from seawater through distillation or reverse osmosis to produce potable water.

Desert biome (20) Arid landscapes of uniquely adapted dry-climate plants and animals.

Desertification (15) The expansion of deserts worldwide, related principally to poor agricultural practices (overgrazing and inappropriate agricultural practices), improper soil-moisture management, erosion and salinization, deforestation, and the ongoing climatic change; an unwanted semipermanent invasion into neighbouring biomes.

Desert pavement (15) On arid landscapes, a surface formed when wind deflation and sheetflow remove smaller particles, leaving residual pebbles and gravels to concentrate at the surface; resembles a cobblestone street. (*See* deflation, sheetflow.)

Detritivores (19) Detritus feeders and decomposers that consume, digest, and destroy organic wastes and debris. *Detritus feeders*—worms, mites, termites, centipedes, snails, crabs, and even vultures, among others—consume detritus and excrete nutrients and simple inorganic compounds that fuel an ecosystem. (*Compare* decomposers.)

Dew-point temperature (7) The temperature at which a given mass of air becomes saturated, holding all the water it can hold. Any further cooling or addition of water vapour results in active condensation.

Diagnostic subsurface horizon (Appendix B) A soil horizon that originates below the epipedon at varying depths; may be part of the A and B horizons; important in soil description as part of the Soil Taxonomy.

Differential weathering (13) The effect of different resistances in rock, coupled with variations in the intensity of physical and chemical weathering.

Diffuse radiation (4) The downward component of scattered incoming insolation from clouds and the atmosphere.

Discharge (14) The measured volume of flow in a river that passes by a given cross section of a stream in a given unit of time; expressed in cubic metres per second or cubic feet per second.

Dissolved load (14) Materials carried in chemical solution in a stream, derived from minerals such as limestone and dolomite, or from soluble salts.

Downburst (8) A powerful downdraft associated with thunderstorms and bands of showers.

Downwelling current (6) An area of the sea where a convergence or accumulation of water thrusts excess water downward; occurs, for example, at the western end of the equatorial current or along the margins of Antarctica. (*Compare* upwelling currents.)

Drainage basin (14) The basic spatial geomorphic unit of a river system; distinguished from a neighbouring basin by ridges and highlands that form divides, marking the limits of the catchment area of the drainage basin or its watershed.

Drainage density (14) A measure of the overall operational efficiency of a drainage basin, determined by the ratio of combined channel lengths to the unit area.

Drainage pattern (14) A distinctive geometric arrangement of streams in a region, determined by slope, differing rock resistance to weathering and erosion, climatic and hydrologic variability, and structural controls of the landscape.

Drawdown (9) *See* cone of depression.

Drought (9) Does not have a simple water-budget definition; rather, it can occur in at least four forms: *meteorological drought, agricultural drought, hydrologic drought,* and/or a *socioeconomic drought.*

Drumlin (17) A depositional landform related to glaciation that is composed of till (unstratified, unsorted) and is streamlined in the direction of continental ice movement—blunt end upstream and tapered end downstream with a rounded summit.

Dry adiabatic rate (DAR) (7) The rate at which an unsaturated parcel of air cools (if ascending) or heats (if descending); a rate of 10°C per 1000 m. (*See* adiabatic; *compare* moist adiabatic rate.)

Dune (15) A depositional feature of sand grains deposited in transient mounds, ridges, and hills; extensive areas of sand dunes are called sand seas.

Dust dome (4) A dome of airborne pollution associated with every major city; may be blown by winds into elongated plumes downwind from the city.

Dynamic equilibrium (1) Increasing or decreasing operations in a system demonstrate a trend over time, a change in average conditions.

Dynamic equilibrium model (13) The balancing act between tectonic uplift and erosion, between the resistance of crust materials and the work of denudation processes. Landscapes evidence ongoing adaptation to rock structure, climate, local relief, and elevation.

Earth systems science (1) An emerging science of Earth as a complete, systematic entity. An interacting set of physical, chemical, and biological systems that produce the processes of a whole Earth system. A study of planetary change resulting from system operations; includes a desire for a more quantitative understanding among components, rather than qualitative description.

Earthquake (12) A sharp release of energy that sends waves travelling through Earth's crust at the moment of rupture along a fault or in association with volcanic activity. The moment magnitude scale estimates earthquake magnitude; intensity is described by the Mercalli scale.

Ebb tide (16) Falling or lowering tide during the daily tidal cycle. (*Compare* flood tide.)

Ecological succession (19) The process whereby different and usually more complex assemblages of plants and animals replace older and usually simpler communities; communities are in a constant state of change as each species adapts to conditions. Ecosystems do not exhibit a stable point or successional climax condition as previously thought. (*Refer* to primary succession, secondary succession.)

Ecology (19) The science that studies the relations between organisms and their environment and among various ecosystems.

Ecosphere (1) Another name for the biosphere.

Ecosystem (19) A self-regulating association of living plants, animals, and their nonliving physical and chemical environments.

Ecotone (20) A boundary transition zone between adjoining ecosystems that may vary in width and represent areas of tension as similar species of plants and animals compete for the resources. (*See* ecosystem.)

Effusive eruption (12) A volcanic eruption characterized by low-viscosity basaltic magma and low-gas content, which readily escapes. Lava pours forth onto the surface with relatively small explosions and few pyroclastics; tends to form shield volcanoes. (*See* shield volcano, lava, pyroclastics; *compare* explosive eruption.)

Elastic-rebound theory (12) A concept describing the faulting process in Earth's crust, in which the two sides of a fault appear locked despite the motion of adjoining pieces of crust, but with accumulating strain they rupture suddenly, snapping to new positions relative to each other, generating an earthquake.

Electromagnetic spectrum (2) All the radiant energy produced by the Sun placed in an ordered range, divided according to wavelengths.

Eluviation (18) The removal of finer particles and minerals from the upper horizons of soil; an erosional process within a soil body. (*Compare* illuviation.)

Empirical classification (10) A climate classification based on weather statistics or other data; used to determine general climate categories. (*Compare* genetic classification.)

Endogenic system (11) The system internal to Earth, driven by radioactive heat derived from sources within the planet. In response, the surface fractures, mountain building occurs, and earthquakes and volcanoes are activated. (*Compare* exogenic system.)

Environmental lapse rate (3) The actual lapse rate in the lower atmosphere at any particular time under local weather conditions; may deviate above or below the normal lapse rate of 6.4°C per 1000 m. (*Compare* normal lapse rate.)

Eolian (15) Caused by wind; refers to the erosion, transportation, and deposition of materials; spelled "aeolian" in some countries.

Epipedon (Appendix B) The diagnostic soil horizon that forms at the surface; not to be confused with the A horizon; may include all or part of the illuviated B horizon.

Equal area (1) A trait of a map projection; indicates the equivalence of all areas on the surface of the map, although shape is distorted. (*See* map projections.)

Equatorial and tropical rain forest (20) A lush biome of tall broadleaf evergreen trees and diverse plants and animals, roughly between 23.5° N and 23.5° S. The dense canopy of leaves is usually arranged in three levels.

Equatorial low-pressure trough (6) A thermally caused low-pressure area that almost girdles Earth, with air converging and ascending all along its extent; also called the intertropical convergence zone (ITCZ).

Erg desert (15) A sandy desert, or area where sand is so extensive that it constitutes a sand sea.

Erosion (14) Denudation by wind, water, or ice, which dislodges, dissolves, or removes surface material.

Esker (17) A sinuously curving, narrow deposit of coarse gravel that forms along a meltwater stream channel, developing in a tunnel beneath a glacier.

Estuary (14) The point at which the mouth of a river enters the sea, where freshwater and seawater are mixed; a place where tides ebb and flow.

Eustasy (7) Refers to worldwide changes in sea level that are not related to movements of land but rather to a rise and fall in the volume of water in the oceans.

Evaporation (9) The movement of free water molecules away from a wet surface into air that is less than saturated; the phase change of water to water vapour.

Evaporation fog (7) A fog formed when cold air flows over the warm surface of a lake, ocean, or other body of water; forms as the water molecules evaporate from the water surface into the cold, overlying air; also known as steam fog or sea smoke.

Evaporation pan (9) A weather instrument consisting of a standardized pan from which evaporation occurs, with water automatically replaced and measured; an evaporimeter.

Evapotranspiration (9) The merging of evaporation and transpiration water loss into one term. (*See* potential and actual evapotranspiration.)

Evolution (19) A theory that single-cell organisms adapted, modified, and passed along inherited changes to multicellular organisms. The genetic makeup of successive generations is shaped by environmental factors, physiological functions, and behaviours that created a greater rate of survival and reproduction and were passed along through natural selection.

Exfoliation dome (13) A dome-shaped feature of weathering, produced by the response of granite to the overburden removal process, which relieves pressure from the rock. Layers of rock slough ("sluff") off in slabs or shells in a sheeting process.

Exogenic system (11) Earth's external surface system, powered by insolation, which energizes air, water, and ice and sets them in motion, under the influence of gravity. Includes all processes of landmass denudation. (*Compare* endogenic system.)

Exosphere (3) An extremely rarefied outer atmospheric halo beyond the thermopause at an altitude of 480 km; probably composed of hydrogen and helium atoms, with some oxygen atoms and nitrogen molecules present near the thermopause.

Exotic stream (14) A river that rises in a humid region and flows through an arid region, with discharge decreasing toward the mouth; for example, the Nile River and the Colorado River.

Explosive eruption (12) A violent and unpredictable volcanic eruption, the result of magma that is thicker (more viscous), stickier, and higher in gas and silica content than that of an effusive eruption; tends to form blockages within a volcano; produces composite volcanic landforms. (*See* composite volcano; *compare* effusive eruption.)

Faulting (12) The process whereby displacement and fracturing occur between two portions of Earth's crust; usually associated with earthquake activity.

Feedback loop (1) Created when a portion of system output is returned as an information input, causing changes that guide further system operation. (*See* negative feedback, positive feedback.)

Field capacity (9) Water held in the soil by hydrogen bonding against the pull of gravity, remaining after water drains from the larger pore spaces; the available water for plants. (*See* available water, capillary water.)

Fire ecology (19) The study of fire as a natural agent and dynamic factor in community succession.

Firn (17) Snow of a granular texture that is transitional in the slow transformation from snow to glacial ice; snow that has persisted through a summer season in the zone of accumulation.

Firn line (17) The snow line that is visible on the surface of a glacier, where winter snows survive the summer ablation season; analogous to a snow line on land. (*See* ablation.)

Fjord (17) A drowned glaciated valley, or glacial trough, along a seacoast.

Flash flood (15) A sudden and short-lived torrent of water that exceeds the capacity of a stream channel; associated with desert and semiarid washes.

Flood (14) A high water level that overflows the natural riverbank along any portion of a stream.

Floodplain (14) A flat, low-lying area along a stream channel, created by and subject to recurrent flooding; alluvial deposits generally mask underlying rock.

Flood tide (16) Rising tide during the daily tidal cycle. (*Compare* ebb tide.)

Fluvial (14) Stream-related processes; from the Latin *fluvius* for "river" or "running water."

Fog (7) A cloud, generally stratiform, in contact with the ground, with visibility usually reduced to less than 1 km.

Folding (12) The bending and deformation of beds of rock strata subjected to compressional forces.

Food chain, food chain circuit (19) The circuit along which energy flows from producers (plants), which manufacture their own food, to consumers (animals); a one-directional flow of chemical energy, ending with decomposers.

Food web (19) A complex network of interconnected food chains. (*See* food chain.)

Formation class (20) That portion of a biome that concerns the plant communities only, categorized by size, shape, and structure of the dominant vegetation.

Friction force (6) The effect of drag by the wind as it moves across a surface; may be operative through 500 m of altitude. Surface friction slows the wind and therefore reduces the effectiveness of the Coriolis force.

Frost action (13) A powerful mechanical force produced as water expands up to 9% of its volume as it freezes. Water freezing in a cavity in a rock can break the rock if it exceeds the rock's tensional strength.

Funnel cloud (8) The visible swirl extending from the bottom side of a cloud, which may or may not develop into a tornado. A tornado is a funnel cloud that has extended all the way to the ground. (*See* tornado.)

Fusion (2) The process of forcibly joining positively charged hydrogen and helium nuclei under extreme temperature and pressure; occurs naturally in thermonuclear reactions within stars, such as our Sun.

Gelifluction (13) Refers to soil flow in periglacial environments, a progressive, lateral movement; a type of solifluction formed under periglacial conditions of permafrost and frozen ground. (*See* solifluction.)

General circulation model (GCM) (10) Complex, computer-based climate model that produces generalizations of reality and forecasts of future weather and climate conditions. Complex GCMs (three-dimensional models) are in use in the United States and in other countries.

Genetic classification (10) A climate classification that uses causative factors to determine climatic regions; for example, an analysis of the effect of interacting air masses. (*Compare* empirical classification.)

Geodesy (1) The science that determines Earth's shape and size through surveys, mathematical means, and remote sensing. (*See* geoid.)

Geographic information system (GIS) (1) A computer-based data processing tool or methodology used for gathering, manipulating, and analyzing geographic information to produce a holistic, interactive analysis.

Geography (1) The science that studies the interdependence and interaction among geographic areas, natural systems, processes, society, and cultural activities over space—a spatial science. The five themes of geographic education are location, place, movement, regions, and human–Earth relationships.

Geoid (1) A word that describes Earth's shape; literally, "the shape of Earth is Earth-shaped." A theoretical surface at sea level that extends through the continents; deviates from a perfect sphere.

Geologic cycle (11) A general term characterizing the vast cycling that proceeds in the lithosphere. It encompasses the hydrologic cycle, tectonic cycle, and rock cycle.

Geologic time scale (11) A depiction of eras, periods, and epochs that span Earth's history; shows both the sequence of rock strata and their absolute dates, as determined by methods such as radioactive isotopic dating.

Geomagnetic reversal (11) A polarity change in Earth's magnetic field. With uneven regularity, the magnetic field fades to zero, then returns to full strength but with the magnetic poles reversed. Reversals have been recorded nine times during the past 4 million years.

Geomorphic threshold (13) The threshold up to which landforms change before lurching to a new set of relationships, with rapid realignments of landscape materials and slopes.

Geomorphology (13) The science that analyzes and describes the origin, evolution, form, classification, and spatial distribution of landforms.

Geostrophic wind (6) A wind moving between areas of different pressure along a path that is parallel to the isobars. It is a product of the pressure gradient force and the Coriolis force. (*See* isobar, pressure gradient force, Coriolis force.)

Geothermal energy (11) The energy in steam and hot water heated by subsurface magma near groundwater. Geothermal energy literally refers to heat from Earth's interior, whereas *geothermal power* relates to specific applied strategies of geothermal electric or geothermal direct applications. This energy is used in Iceland, New Zealand, Italy, and northern California, among other locations.

Glacial drift (17) The general term for all glacial deposits, both unsorted (till) and sorted (stratified drift).

Glacial ice (17) A hardened form of ice, very dense in comparison to normal snow or firn.

Glacier (17) A large mass of perennial ice resting on land or floating shelflike in the sea adjacent to the land; formed from the accumulation and recrystallization of snow in a process that forms glacial ice, which then flows slowly under the pressure of its own weight and the pull of gravity.

Glacier surge (17) The rapid, lurching, unexpected forward movement of a glacier.

Glacio-eustatic (7) Changes in sea level in response to changes in the amount of water stored on Earth as ice; the more water that is bound up in glaciers and ice sheets, the lower the sea level. (*Compare* eustasy.)

Gleysation (18) A process of humus and clay accumulation in cold, wet climates with poor drainage.

Gleysolic (18) A CSSC soil order defined on the basis of colour and mottling that results from chronic reducing conditions inherent in poorly drained mineral soils under wet conditions. High water table and long periods of water saturation.

Global dimming (4) The decline in sunlight reaching Earth's surface owing to pollution, aerosols, and clouds.

Global positioning system (GPS) (1) Latitude, longitude, and elevation are accurately calibrated using this handheld instrument that calibrates radio signals from satellites.

Goode's homolosine projection (Appendix A) An equal-area projection formed by splicing together a sinusoidal and a homolographic projection.

Graben (12) Pairs or groups of faults that produce downward-faulted blocks; characteristic of the basins of the interior western United States. (*Compare* horst; *see* Basin and Range Province.)

Graded stream (14) An idealized condition in which a stream's load and the landscape mutually adjust. This forms a dynamic equilibrium among erosion, transported load, deposition, and the stream's capacity.

Gradient (14) The drop in elevation from a stream's headwaters to its mouth, ideally forming a concave slope.

Granite (11) A coarse-grained (slow-cooling) intrusive igneous rock of 25% quartz and more than 50% potassium and sodium feldspars; characteristic of the continental crust.

Gravity (2) The mutual force exerted by the masses of objects that are attracted one to another and produced in an amount proportional to each object's mass.

Great circle (1) Any circle drawn on a globe with its centre coinciding with the centre of the globe. An infinite number of great circles can be drawn, but only one parallel is a great circle—the equator. (*Compare* small circle.)

Greenhouse effect (4) The process whereby radiatively active gases (carbon dioxide, water vapour, methane, and CFCs) absorb insolation and emit the energy at longer wavelengths, which are retained longer, delaying the loss of infrared to space. Thus, the lower troposphere is warmed through the radiation and reradiation of infrared wavelengths. The approximate similarity between this process and that of a greenhouse explains the name.

Greenwich Mean Time (GMT) (1) Former world standard time, now reported as Coordinated Universal Time (UTC). (*See* Coordinated Universal Time.)

Groundwater (9) Water beneath the surface that is beyond the soilroot zone; a major source of potable water.

Groundwater mining (9) Pumping an aquifer beyond its capacity to flow and recharge; an overuse of the groundwater resource.

Gulf Stream (5) A strong, northward-moving, warm current off the east coast of North America, which carries its water far into the North Atlantic.

Habitat (19) A physical location to which an organism is biologically suited. Most species have specific habitat parameters and limits. (*Compare* niche.)

Hail (8) A type of precipitation formed when a raindrop is repeatedly circulated above and below the freezing level in a cloud, with each cycle freezing more moisture onto the hailstone until it becomes too heavy to stay aloft.

Hair hygrometer (7) An instrument for measuring relative humidity; based on the principle that human hair will change as much as 4% in length between 0% and 100% relative humidity.

Heat (3) The flow of kinetic energy from one body to another because of a temperature difference between them.

Herbivore (19) The primary consumer in a food web, which eats plant material formed by a producer (plant) that has photosynthesized organic molecules. (*Compare* carnivore.)

Heterosphere (3) A zone of the atmosphere above the mesopause, 80 km in altitude; composed of rarefied layers of oxygen atoms and nitrogen molecules; includes the ionosphere.

Homosphere (3) A zone of the atmosphere from Earth's surface up to 80 km, composed of an even mixture of gases, including nitrogen, oxygen, argon, carbon dioxide, and trace gases.

Horn (17) A pyramidal, sharp-pointed peak that results when several cirque glaciers gouge an individual mountain summit from all sides.

Horst (12) Upward-faulted blocks produced by pairs or groups of faults; characteristic of the mountain ranges of the interior of the western United States. (*See* graben and Basin and Range Province.)

Hot spot (11) An individual point of upwelling material originating in the asthenosphere, or deeper in the mantle; tends to remain fixed relative to migrating plates; some 100 are identified worldwide, exemplified by Yellowstone National Park, Hawai'i, and Iceland.

Human–Earth relationships (1) One of the oldest themes of geography (the human-land tradition); includes the spatial analysis of settlement patterns, resource utilization and exploitation, hazard perception and planning, and the impact of environmental modification and artificial landscape creation.

Humidity (7) Water vapour content of the air. The capacity of the air to hold water vapour is mostly a function of the temperature of the air and the water vapour.

Humus (18) A mixture of organic debris in the soil worked by consumers and decomposers in the humification process; characteristically formed from plant and animal litter deposited at the surface.

Hurricane (8) A tropical cyclone that is fully organized and intensified in inward-spiraling rainbands; ranges from 160 to 960 km in diameter, with wind speeds in excess of 119 km·h^{-1}; a name used specifically in the Atlantic and eastern Pacific. (*Compare* typhoon.)

Hydration (13) A chemical weathering process involving water that is added to a mineral, which initiates swelling and stress within the rock, mechanically forcing grains apart as the constituents expand. (*Contrast* to hydrolysis.)

Hydraulic action (14) The erosive work accomplished by the turbulence of water; causes a squeezing and releasing action in joints in bedrock; capable of prying and lifting rocks.

Hydrograph (14) A graph of stream discharge (in cms or cfs) over a period of time (minutes, hours, days, years) at a specific place on a stream. The relationship between stream discharge and precipitation input is illustrated on the graph.

Hydrologic cycle (9) A simplified model of the flow of water, ice, and water vapour from place to place. Water flows through the atmosphere, across the land, where it is also stored as ice, and within groundwater. Solar energy empowers the cycle.

Hydrology (14) The science of water, its global circulation, distribution, and properties, specifically water at and below Earth's surface.

Hydrolysis (13) A chemical weathering process in which minerals chemically combine with water; a decomposition process that causes silicate minerals in rocks to break down and become altered. (*Contrast* to hydration.)

Hydrosphere (1) An abiotic open system that includes all of Earth's water.

Hygroscopic water (9) That portion of soil moisture that is so tightly bound to each soil particle that it is unavailable to plant roots; the water, along with some capillary water, that is left in the soil after the wilting point is reached. (*See* wilting point.)

Ice age (17) A cold episode, with accompanying alpine and continental ice accumulations, that has repeated roughly every 200 to 300 million years since the late Precambrian era (1.25 billion years ago); includes the most recent episode during the Pleistocene Ice Age, which began 1.65 million years ago.

Iceberg (17) Floating ice created by ice calving (a large piece breaking off) and floating adrift; a hazard to shipping because about nine-tenths of the ice is submerged and can be irregular in form.

Ice cap (17) A large, dome-shaped glacier, less extensive than an ice sheet (<50 000 km^2), although it buries mountain peaks and the local landscape.

Ice-crystal fog (7) A type of fog that develops at very low temperatures in a continental arctic air mass. Visibility is seriously limited when the air becomes full of ice crystals that have formed by sublimation.

Ice field (17) The least extensive form of a glacier, with mountain ridges and peaks visible above the ice; less than an ice cap or ice sheet.

Icelandic low (6) *See* subpolar low-pressure cell.

Ice sheet (17) An enormous continuous continental glacier. The bulk of glacial ice on Earth covers Antarctica and Greenland in two ice sheets.

Ice shelf (17) A very thick sheet of ice with a gently undulating to level surface that extends over the sea and floats on water. It is attached to the land along a coastal grounding line and also may be attached where ice flows around islands. On the seaward side, it is bounded by a steep cliff called the ice front that can be 2 to 50 m or more above sea level.

Ice storm (8) A major hazard in which supercooled precipitation freezes on contact with surfaces. The severity of the event is determined by the thickness of ice accumulation associated with a storm, the storm's duration, and the extent of area affected. Typically, an ice storm will last for 45 to 65 hours and will deposit, at most, 30 to 40 mm of ice.

Ice wedge (17) Formed when water enters a thermal contraction crack in permafrost and freezes. Repeated seasonal freezing and melting of the water progressively expands the wedge.

Igneous rock (11) One of the basic rock types; it has solidified and crystallized from a hot molten state (either magma or lava). (*Compare* metamorphic rock, sedimentary rock.)

Illuviation (18) The downward movement and deposition of finer particles and minerals from the upper horizon of the soil; a depositional process. Deposition usually is in the B horizon, where accumulations of clays, aluminum, carbonates, iron, and some humus occur. (*Compare* eluviation; *see* calcification.)

Industrial smog (3) Air pollution associated with coal-burning industries; it may contain sulphur oxides, particulates, carbon dioxide, and exotics.

Infiltration (9) Water access to subsurface regions of soil moisture storage through penetration of the soil surface.

Insolation (2) Solar radiation that is incoming to Earth systems.

Interception (9) Delays the fall of precipitation toward Earth's surface; caused by vegetation or other ground cover.

Internal drainage (14) In regions where rivers do not flow into the ocean, the outflow is through evaporation or subsurface gravitational flow. Portions of Africa, Asia, Australia, and the western United States have such drainage.

International Date Line (1) The meridian, an important corollary to the prime meridian on the opposite side of the planet; established by the treaty of 1884 to mark the place where each day officially begins.

Intertropical convergence zone (ITCZ) (6) *See* equatorial low-pressure trough.

Invasive species (20) Species that are brought, or introduced, from elsewhere by humans, either accidentally or intentionally. These nonnative species are also known as *exotic species* or *alien species*.

Ionosphere (3) A layer in the atmosphere above where gamma, X-ray, and some ultraviolet radiation is absorbed and converted into infrared and where the solar wind stimulates the auroras.

Island biogeography (20) A study of island communities that are special places because of their spatial isolation and the relatively small number of species present. Islands resemble natural experiments because the impact of individual factors, such as civilization, can be more easily assessed on islands than over larger continental areas.

Isobar (6) An isoline connecting all points of equal atmospheric pressure.

Isostasy (11) A state of equilibrium in Earth's crust formed by the interplay between portions of the lithosphere and the asthenosphere and the principle of buoyancy. The crust depresses under weight and recovers with its removal; for example, the melting of glacial ice. The uplift is known as isostatic rebound.

Isotherm (5) An isoline connecting all points of equal temperature.

Jet contrails (4) *Condensation trails* produced by aircraft exhaust, particulates, and water vapour can form high cirrus clouds, sometimes called *false cirrus clouds*.

Jet stream (6) The most prominent movement in upper-level westerly wind flows; irregular, concentrated, sinuous bands of geostrophic wind, travelling at 300 km·h^{-1}. (*See* polar jet stream, subtropical jet stream.)

Joint (13) A fracture or separation in rock that occurs without displacement of the sides; increases the surface area of rock exposed to weathering processes.

June solstice (2) *See* Summer (June) solstice.

Kame (17) A depositional feature of glaciation; a small hill of poorly sorted sand and gravel that accumulates in crevasses or in ice-caused indentations in the surface.

Karst topography (13) Distinctive topography formed in a region of chemically weathered limestone with poorly developed surface drainage and solution features that appear pitted and bumpy; originally named after the Krš Plateau in Slovenia.

Katabatic winds (6) Air drainage from elevated regions, flowing as gravity winds. Layers of air at the surface cool, become denser, and flow downslope; known worldwide by many local names.

Kettle (17) Forms when an isolated block of ice persists in a ground moraine, an outwash plain, or valley floor after a glacier retreats; as the block finally melts, it leaves behind a steep-sided hole that frequently fills with water.

Kinetic energy (3) The energy of motion in a body; derived from the vibration of the body's own movement and stated as temperature.

Köppen-Geiger climate classification (Appendix C) An empirical classification system that uses average monthly temperatures, average monthly precipitation, and total annual precipitation to establish regional climate designations.

Lagoon (16) An area of coastal seawater that is virtually cut off from the ocean by a bay barrier or barrier beach; also, the water surrounded and enclosed by an atoll.

Landfall (8) The location along a coast where a storm moves onshore.

Land–sea breeze (6) Wind along coastlines and adjoining interior areas created by different heating characteristics of land and water surfaces—onshore (landward) breeze in the afternoon and offshore (seaward) breeze at night.

Landslide (13) A sudden rapid downslope movement of a cohesive mass of regolith and/or bedrock in a variety of mass-movement forms under the influence of gravity; a form of mass movement.

Land–water heating difference (5) Differences in the degree and way that land and water heat, as a result of contrasts in transmission, evaporation, mixing, and specific heat capacities. Land surfaces heat and cool faster than water and have continentality, whereas water provides a marine influence.

Latent heat (7) Heat energy is stored in one of three states—ice, water, or water vapour. The energy is absorbed or released in each phase change from one state to another. Heat energy is absorbed as the latent heat of melting, vapourization, or evaporation. Heat energy is released as the latent heat of condensation and freezing (or fusion).

Latent heat of condensation (7) The heat energy released to the environment in a phase change from water vapour to liquid; under normal sea-level pressure, 540 calories are released from each gram of water vapour that changes phase to water at boiling, and 585 calories are released from each gram of water vapour that condenses at 20°C.

Latent heat of sublimation (7) The heat energy absorbed or released in the phase change from ice to water vapour or water vapour to ice—no liquid phase. The change from water vapour to ice is also called deposition.

Latent heat of vapourization (7) The heat energy absorbed from the environment in a phase change from liquid to water vapour at the boiling point; under normal sea-level pressure, 540 calories must be added to each gram of boiling water to achieve a phase change to water vapour.

Lateral moraine (17) Debris transported by a glacier that accumulates along the sides of the glacier and is deposited along these margins.

Laterization (18) A pedogenic process operating in well-drained soils that occur in warm and humid regions; typical of Oxisols. Plentiful precipitation leaches soluble minerals and soil constituents. Resulting soils usually are reddish or yellowish.

Latitude (1) The angular distance measured north or south of the equator from a point at the centre of Earth. A line connecting all points of the same latitudinal angle is called a parallel. (*Compare* longitude.)

Lava (11, 12) Magma that issues from volcanic activity onto the surface; the extrusive rock that results when magma solidifies. (*See* magma, aa, and pahoehoe.)

Life zone (19) A zonation by altitude of plants and animals that form distinctive communities. Each life zone possesses its own temperature and precipitation relations.

Lightning (8) Flashes of light caused by tens of millions of volts of electrical charge heating the air to temperatures of 15 000° to 30 000°C.

Limestone (11) The most common chemical sedimentary rock (nonclastic); it is lithified calcium carbonate; very susceptible to chemical weathering by acids in the environment, including carbonic acid in rainfall.

Limiting factor (19) The physical or chemical factor that most inhibits biotic processes, either through lack or excess.

Lithification (11) The compaction, cementation, and hardening of sediments into sedimentary rock.

Lithosphere (1) Earth's crust and that portion of the uppermost mantle directly below the crust, extending down to about 70 km. Some sources use this term to refer to the entire Earth.

Littoral drift (16) Transport of sand, gravel, sediment, and debris along the shore; a more comprehensive term, considers *beach drift* and *longshore drift* combined.

Littoral zone (16) A specific coastal environment; that region between the high-water line during a storm and a depth at which storm waves are unable to move sea-floor sediments.

Loam (18) A soil that is a mixture of sand, silt, and clay in almost equal proportions, with no one texture dominant; an ideal agricultural soil.

Location (1) A basic theme of geography dealing with the absolute and relative position of people, places, and things on Earth's surface.

Loess (15) Large quantities of fine-grained clays and silts left as glacial outwash deposits; subsequently blown by the wind great distances and redeposited as a generally unstratified, homogeneous blanket of material covering existing landscapes; in China, loess originated from desert lands.

Longitude (1) The angular distance measured east or west of a prime meridian from a point at the centre of Earth. A line connecting all points of the same longitude is called a meridian.

Longshore current (16) A current that forms parallel to a beach as waves arrive at an angle to the shore; generated in the surf zone by wave action, transporting large amounts of sand and sediment. (*See* littoral current, beach drift.)

Luvisolic (18) A CSSC soil order with eluviation-illuviation processes produce a light-coloured **Ae** horizon and a diagnostic **Bt** horizon. Soils of mixed deciduous–coniferous forests. Major occurrence is the St. Lawrence lowland. Luvisols do not have a solonetzic **B** horizon.

Lysimeter (9) A weather instrument for measuring potential and actual evapotranspiration; isolates a portion of a field so that the moisture moving through the plot is measured.

Magma (11) Molten rock from beneath Earth's surface; fluid, gaseous, under tremendous pressure, and either intruded into existing country rock or extruded onto the surface as lava. (*See* lava.)

Magnetosphere (2) Earth's magnetic force field, which is generated by dynamo-like motions within the planet's outer core; deflects the solar wind flow toward the upper atmosphere above each pole.

Mangrove swamp (16) A wetland ecosystem between 30° N or S and the equator; tends to form a distinctive community of mangrove plants. (*Compare* salt marsh.)

Mantle (11) An area within the planet representing about 80% of Earth's total volume, with densities increasing with depth and averaging 4.5 g · cm^3; occurs between the core and the crust; is rich in iron and magnesium oxides and silicates.

Map (1) A generalized view of an area, usually some portion of Earth's surface, as seen from above at a greatly reduced size. (*See* scale and map projection.)

Map projection (1) The reduction of a spherical globe onto a flat surface in some orderly and systematic realignment of the latitude and longitude grid.

Marine effect (5) A quality of regions that are dominated by the moderating effect of the ocean and that exhibit a smaller range of minimum and maximum temperature than continental stations. (*See* continentality, land–water heating differences.)

Mass movement (13) All unit movements of materials propelled by gravity; can range from dry to wet, slow to fast, small to large, and freefalling to gradual or intermittent.

Mass wasting (13) Gravitational movement of nonunified material downslope; a specific form of mass movement.

Meandering stream (14) The sinuous, curving pattern common to graded streams, with the energetic outer portion of each curve subjected to the greatest erosive action and the lower-energy inner portion receiving sediment deposits. (*See* graded stream.)

Mean sea level (MSL) (16) The average of tidal levels recorded hourly at a given site over a long period, which must be at least a full lunar tidal cycle.

Medial moraine (17) Debris transported by a glacier that accumulates down the middle of the glacier, resulting from two glaciers merging their lateral moraines; forms a depositional feature following glacial retreat.

Mediterranean shrubland (20) A major biome dominated by Mediterranean dry-summer climates and characterized by sclerophyllous scrub and short, stunted, tough forests. (*See* chapparal.)

Mercator projection (1) A true-shape projection, with meridians appearing as equally spaced straight lines and parallels appearing as straight lines that are spaced closer together near the equator. The poles are infinitely stretched, with the 84th north parallel and 84th south parallel fixed at the same length as that of the equator. It presents false notions of the size (area) of midlatitude and poleward landmasses but presents true compass direction. (*See* rhumb line.)

Mercury barometer (6) A device that measures air pressure using a column of mercury in a tube, one end of which is sealed, and the other end inserted in an open vessel of mercury. (*See* air pressure.)

Meridian (1) See longitude; a line designating an angle of longitude.

Mesocyclone (8) A large, rotating atmospheric circulation, initiated within a parent cumulonimbus cloud at midtroposphere elevation; generally produces heavy rain, large hail, blustery winds, and lightning; may lead to tornado activity.

Mesosphere (3) The upper region of the homosphere from 50 to 80 km above the ground; designated by temperature criteria; atmosphere extremely rarified.

Metamorphic rock (11) One of three basic rock types, it is existing igneous and sedimentary rock that has undergone profound physical and chemical changes under increased pressure and temperature. Constituent mineral structures may exhibit foliated or nonfoliated textures. (*Compare* igneous rock and sedimentary rock.)

Meteorology (8) The scientific study of the atmosphere, including its physical characteristics and motions; related chemical, physical, and geological processes; the complex linkages of atmospheric systems; and weather forecasting.

Microburst (8) Severe turbulence from a thunderstorm, smaller in size and speed than a downburst. (*See* downburst.)

Microclimatology (4) The study of local climates at or near Earth's surface, or that height above the Earth's surface where the effects of the surface are no longer of effect.

Midlatitude broadleaf and mixed forest (20) A biome in moist continental climates in areas of warm-to-hot summers and cool-to-cold winters; relatively lush stands of broadleaf forests trend northward into needleleaf evergreen stands.

Midlatitude cyclone (8) An organized area of low pressure, with converging and ascending airflow producing an interaction of air masses; migrates along storm tracks. Such lows or depressions form the dominant weather pattern in the middle and higher latitudes of both hemispheres.

Midlatitude grassland (20) The major biome most modified by human activity; so named because of the predominance of grasslike plants, although deciduous broadleafs appear along streams and other limited sites; location of the world's breadbaskets of grain and livestock production.

Mid-ocean ridge (11) A submarine mountain range that extends more than 65 000 km worldwide and averages more than 1000 km in width; centred along sea-floor spreading centres. (*See* sea-floor spreading.)

Milky Way Galaxy (2) A flattened, disk-shaped mass in space estimated to contain up to 300 billion stars; includes our Solar System.

Miller cylindrical projection (Appendix A) A compromise map projection that avoids the severe distortion of the Mercator projection. (*See* map projection.)

Mineral (11) An element or combination of elements that forms an inorganic natural compound; described by a specific formula and crystal structure.

Mirage (4) A refraction effect when an image appears near the horizon where light waves are refracted by layers of air at different temperatures (and consequently of different densities).

Model (1) A simplified version of a system, representing an idealized part of the real world.

Mohorovičić discontinuity, or Moho (11) The boundary between the crust and the rest of the lithospheric upper mantle; named for the Yugoslavian seismologist Mohorovičić; a zone of sharp material and density contrasts; also known as the Moho.

Moist adiabatic rate (MAR) (7) The rate at which a saturated parcel of air cools in ascent; a rate of 6 C° per 1000 m. This rate may vary, with moisture content and temperature, from 4 C° to 10 C° per 1000 m. (*See* adiabatic; *compare* dry adiabatic rate.)

Moisture droplet (7) A tiny water particle that constitutes the initial composition of clouds. Each droplet measures approximately 0.002 cm in diameter and is invisible to the unaided eye.

Moment magnitude scale (12) An earthquake magnitude scale. Considers the amount of fault slippage, the size of the area that ruptured, and the nature of the materials that faulted in estimating the magnitude of an earthquake—an assessment of the seismic moment. Replaces the Richter scale (amplitude magnitude); especially valuable in assessing larger magnitude events.

Monsoon (6) An annual cycle of dryness and wetness, with seasonally shifting winds produced by changing atmospheric pressure systems; affects India, Southeast Asia, Indonesia, northern Australia, and portions of Africa. From the Arabic word *mausim*, meaning "season."

Montane forest (20) Needleleaf forest associated with mountain elevations. (*See* needleleaf forest.)

Moraine (17) Marginal glacial deposits (lateral, medial, terminal, ground) of unsorted and unstratified material.

Mountain–valley breeze (6) A light wind produced as cooler mountain air flows downslope at night and as warmer valley air flows upslope during the day.

Movement (1) A major theme in geography involving migration, communication, and the interaction of people and processes across space.

Mudflow (13) Fluid downslope flows of material containing more water than earthflows.

Natural levee (14) A long, low ridge that forms on both sides of a stream in a developed floodplain; they are depositional products (coarse gravels and sand) of river flooding.

Neap tide (16) Unusually low tidal range produced during the first and third quarters of the Moon, with an offsetting pull from the Sun. (*Compare* spring tide.)

Needleleaf forest (20) Forests of pine, spruce, fir, and larch, stretching from the east coast of Canada westward to Alaska and continuing from Siberia westward across the entire extent of Russia to the European Plain; called the *taiga* (a Russian word) or the *boreal forest*; principally in the microthermal climates. Includes montane forests that may be at lower latitudes at higher elevation. (*See* taiga, boreal forest, montane forest.)

Negative feedback (1) Feedback that tends to slow or dampen response in a system; promotes self-regulation in a system; far more common than positive feedback in living systems. (*See* feedback loop, compare to positive feedback.)

Net primary productivity (19) The net photosynthesis (photosynthesis minus respiration) for a given community; considers all growth and all reduction factors that affect the amount of useful chemical energy (biomass) fixed in an ecosystem.

Net radiation (NET R) (4) The net all-wave radiation available at Earth's surface; the final outcome of the radiation balance process between incoming shortwave insolation and outgoing longwave energy.

Niche (19) The basic function, or occupation, of a life form within a given community; the way an organism obtains its food, air, and water.

Nickpoint (knickpoint) (14) The point at which the longitudinal profile of a stream is abruptly broken by a change in gradient; for example, a waterfall, rapids, or cascade.

Nimbostratus (7) Rain-producing, dark, grayish, stratiform clouds characterized by gentle drizzle.

Nitrogen dioxide (3) A noxious (harmful) reddish-brown gas produced in combustion engines; can be damaging to human respiratory tracts and to plants; participates in photochemical reactions and acid deposition.

Noctilucent cloud (3) A rare, shining band of ice crystals that may glow at high latitudes long after sunset; formed within the mesosphere, where cosmic and meteoric dust act as nuclei for the formation of ice crystals.

Normal fault (12) A type of geologic fault in rocks. Tension produces strain that breaks a rock, with one side moving vertically relative to the other side along an inclined fault plane. (*Compare* reverse fault.)

Normal lapse rate (3) The average rate of temperature decrease with increasing altitude in the lower atmosphere; an average value of 6.4 C° per km, or 1000 m. (*Compare* environmental lapse rate.)

Occluded front (8) In a cyclonic circulation, the overrunning of a surface warm front by a cold front and the subsequent lifting of the warm air wedge off the ground; initial precipitation is moderate to heavy.

Ocean basin (12) The physical container (a depression in the lithosphere) holding an ocean.

Omnivore (19) A consumer that feeds on both producers (plants) and consumers (meat)—a role occupied by humans, among other animals. (*Compare* consumer, producer.)

Open system (1) A system with inputs and outputs crossing back and forth between the system and the surrounding environment. Earth is an open system in terms of energy. (*Compare* closed system.)

Organic (18) A CSSC soil order with peat, bog, and muck soils, largely composed of organic material. Most are water-saturated for prolonged periods. Are widespread in association with poorly to very poorly drained depressions, although Folisols are found under upland forest environments. Exceed 17% organic carbon and 30% organic matter overall.

Orogenesis (12) The process of mountain building that occurs when large-scale compression leads to deformation and uplift of the crust; literally, the birth of mountains.

Orographic lifting (8) The uplift of a migrating air mass as it is forced to move upward over a mountain range—a topographic barrier. The lifted air cools adiabatically as it moves upslope; clouds may form and produce increased precipitation.

Outgassing (7) The release of trapped gases from rocks, forced out through cracks, fissures, and volcanoes from within Earth; the terrestrial source of Earth's water.

Outwash plain (17) Glacial stream deposits of stratified drift of meltwater-fed, braided, and overloaded streams; occurs beyond a glacier's morainal deposits.

Overland flow (9) Surplus water that flows across the land surface toward stream channels. Together with precipitation and subsurface flows, it constitutes the total runoff from an area.

Oxbow lake (14) A lake that was formerly part of the channel of a meandering stream; isolated when a stream eroded its outer bank forming a cut-off through the neck of the looping meander (see meandering stream). In Australia, known as a billabong (Aboriginal for "dead river").

Oxidation (13) A chemical weathering process in which oxygen dissolved in water oxidizes (combines with) certain metallic elements to form oxides; most familiar is the "rusting" of iron in a rock or soil (Ultisols, Oxisols), which produces a reddish-brown stain of iron oxide.

Ozone layer (3) *See* ozonosphere.

Ozonosphere (3) A layer of ozone occupying the full extent of the stratosphere (20 to 50 km) above the surface; the region of the atmosphere where ultraviolet wavelengths of insolation are extensively absorbed and converted into heat.

Pacific high (6) A high-pressure cell that dominates the Pacific in July, retreating southward in the Northern Hemisphere in January; also known as the *Hawaiian high.*

Pahoehoe (12) Basaltic lava that is more fluid than aa. Pahoehoe forms a thin crust that forms folds and appears "ropy," like coiled, twisted rope. (*Compare* to aa.)

Paleoclimatology (10) The science that studies the climates, and the causes of variations in climate, of past ages, throughout historic and geologic time.

Paleolake (17) An ancient lake, such as Lake Bonneville or Lake Lahonton, associated with former wet periods when the lake basins were filled to higher levels than today.

Pangaea (11) The supercontinent formed by the collision of all continental masses approximately 225 million years ago; named in the continental drift theory by Wegener in 1912. (*See* plate tectonics.)

Parallel (1) (*See* latitude.) A line, parallel to the equator, that designates an angle of latitude.

Parent material (13) The unconsolidated material, from both organic and mineral sources, that is the basis of soil development.

Particulate matter (PM) (3) Dust, dirt, soot, salt, sulphate aerosols, fugitive natural particles, or other material particles suspended in air.

Paternoster lake (17) One of a series of small, circular, stair-stepped lakes formed in individual rock basins aligned down the course of a glaciated valley; named because they look like a string of rosary (religious) beads.

Patterned ground (17) Areas in the periglacial environment where freezing and thawing of the ground create polygonal forms of arranged rocks at the surface; can be circles, polygons, stripes, nets, and steps.

Pedogenic regime (18) A specific soil-forming process keyed to a specific climatic regime: laterization, calcification, salinization, and podzolization, among others; not the basis for soil classification in the CSSC or the Soil Taxonomy.

Pedon (18) A soil profile extending from the surface to the lowest extent of plant roots or to the depth where regolith or bedrock is encountered; imagined as a hexagonal column; the basic soil sampling unit.

Percolation (9) The process by which water permeates the soil or porous rock into the subsurface environment.

Periglacial (17) Cold-climate processes, landforms, and topographic features along the margins of glaciers, past and present; periglacial characteristics exist on more than 20% of Earth's land surface; includes permafrost, frost action, and ground ice.

Perihelion (2) That point of Earth's closest approach to the Sun in its elliptical orbit; occurs on January 3 at 147 255 000 km; variable over a 100 000-year cycle. (*Compare* aphelion.)

Permafrost (17) Forms when soil or rock temperatures remain below 0°C for at least 2 years in areas considered periglacial; criterion is based on temperature and not on whether water is present. (*Compare* frozen ground; *see* periglacial.)

Permeability (9) The ability of water to flow through soil or rock; a function of the texture and structure of the medium.

Peroxyacetyl nitrate (PAN) (3) A pollutant formed from photochemical reactions involving nitric oxide (NO) and volatile organic compounds (VOCs). PAN produces no known human health effect, but it is particularly damaging to plants.

Phase change (7) The change in phase, or state, among ice, water, and water vapour; involves the absorption or release of latent heat. (*See* latent heat.)

Photochemical smog (3) Air pollution produced by the interaction of ultraviolet light, nitrogen dioxide, and hydrocarbons; produces ozone and PAN through a series of complex photochemical reactions. Automobiles are the major source of the contributive gases.

Photogrammetry (1) The science of obtaining accurate measurements from aerial photos and remote sensing; used to create and to improve surface maps.

Photosynthesis (19) The process by which plants produce their own food from carbon dioxide and water, powered by solar energy. The joining of carbon dioxide and hydrogen in plants, under the influence of certain wavelengths of visible light; releases oxygen and produces energy-rich organic material, sugars, and starches. (*Compare* respiration.)

Physical geography (1) The science concerned with the spatial aspects and interactions of the physical elements and processes that make up the environment: energy, air, water, weather, climate, landforms, soils, animals, plants, microorganisms, and Earth.

Physical weathering (13) The breaking and disintegrating of rock without any chemical alteration; sometimes referred to as mechanical or fragmentation weathering.

Pioneer community (19) The initial plant community in an area; usually found on new surfaces or those that have been stripped of life, as in beginning primary succession; including lichens, mosses, and ferns growing on bare rock. (*Compare* to primary succession.)

Place (1) A major theme in geography, focused on the tangible and intangible characteristics that make each location unique; no two places on Earth are alike.

Plane of the ecliptic (2) A plane (flat surface) intersecting all the points of Earth's orbit.

Planetesimal hypothesis (2) Proposes a process by which early protoplanets formed from the condensing masses of a nebular cloud of dust, gas, and icy comets; a formation process now being observed in other parts of the galaxy.

Planimetric map (Appendix A) A basic map showing the horizontal position of boundaries, land-use activities, and political, economic, and social outlines.

Plateau basalt (12) An accumulation of horizontal flows formed when lava spreads out from elongated fissures onto the surface in extensive sheets; associated with effusive eruptions; also known as flood basalts. (*See* basalt.)

Plate tectonics (11) The conceptual model and theory that encompasses continental drift, sea-floor spreading, and related aspects of crustal movement; accepted as the foundation of crustal tectonic processes. (*See* continental drift.)

Playa (15) An area of salt crust left behind by evaporation on a desert floor usually in the middle of a desert or semiarid bolson or valley; intermittently wet and dry.

Plough winds (8) Linear winds associated with thunderstorms and bands of showers that cause significant damage and crop losses. (*See* derechos.)

Pluton (11) A mass of intrusive igneous rock that has cooled slowly in the crust; forms in any size or shape. The largest partially exposed pluton is a batholith. (*See* batholith.)

Podzolic (18) A CSSC soil order of the coniferous forests and sometimes heath; leaching of overlying horizons occurs in moist, cool to cold climates.

Podzolization (18) A pedogenic process in cool, moist climates; forms a highly leached soil with strong surface acidity because of humus from acid-rich trees.

Point bar (14) In a stream the inner portion of a meander, where sediment fill is redeposited.

Polar easterlies (6) Variable weak, cold, and dry winds moving away from the polar region; an anticyclonic circulation.

Polar front (6) A significant zone of contrast between cold and warm air masses; roughly situated between 50° and 60° N and S latitude.

Polar high-pressure cells (6) A weak, anticyclonic, thermally produced pressure system positioned roughly over each pole; the region of the lowest temperatures on Earth. (*See* Antarctic high.)

Polypedon (18) The identifiable soil in an area, with distinctive characteristics differentiating it from surrounding polypedons that form the basic mapping unit; composed of many pedons. (*See* pedon.)

Porosity (9) The total volume of available pore space in soil; a result of the texture and structure of the soil.

Positive feedback (1) Feedback that amplifies or encourages responses in a system. (*Compare* to negative feedback, feedback loop.)

Potential evapotranspiration (PE) (9) The amount of moisture that would evaporate and transpire if adequate moisture were available; it is the amount lost under optimum moisture conditions, the moisture demand.

Potentiometric surface (9) A pressure level in a confined aquifer, defined by the level to which water rises in wells; caused by the fact that the water in a confined aquifer is under the pressure of its own weight; also known as a piezometric surface. This surface can extend above the surface of the land, causing water to rise above the water table in wells in confined aquifers. (*See* artesian water.)

Precipitation (9) Rain, snow, sleet, and hail—the moisture supply; called P, in the water balance.

Pressure gradient force (6) Causes air to move from an area of higher barometric pressure to an area of lower barometric pressure due to the pressure difference.

Primary succession (19) Succession that occurs among plant species in an area of new surfaces created by mass movement of land, areas exposed by a retreating glacier, cooled lava flows and volcanic eruption landscapes, surface mining and clear-cut logging scars, or an area of sand dunes, with no trace of a former community.

Prime meridian (1) An arbitrary meridian designated as longitude, the point from which longitudes are measured east or west, at Greenwich, England, selected by international agreement in an 1884 treaty.

Process (1) A set of actions and changes that occur in some special order; analysis of processes is central to modern geographic synthesis.

Producer (19) Organism (plant) in an ecosystem that uses carbon dioxide as its sole source of carbon, which it chemically fixes through photosynthesis to provide its own nourishment; also called an autotroph. (*Compare* consumer.)

Pyroclastic (12) An explosively ejected rock fragment launched by a volcanic eruption; sometimes described by the more general term tephra.

Radiation fog (7) Formed by radiative cooling of a land surface, especially on clear nights in areas of moist ground; occurs when the air layer directly above the surface is chilled to the dew-point temperature, thereby producing saturated conditions.

Rain gauge (9) A weather instrument; a standardized device that captures and measures rainfall.

Rain shadow (8) The area on the leeward slope of a mountain range, where precipitation receipt is greatly reduced compared to the windward slope on the other side. (*See* orographic lifting.)

Reflection (4) The portion of arriving insolation that is returned directly to space without being absorbed and converted into heat and without performing any work. (*See* albedo.)

Refraction (4) The bending effect on electromagnetic waves that occurs when insolation enters the atmosphere or another medium; the same process by which a crystal, or prism, disperses the component colours of the light passing through it.

Region (1) A geographic theme that focuses on areas that display unity and internal homogeneity of traits; includes the study of how a region forms, evolves, and interrelates with other regions.

Regolith (13) Partially weathered rock overlying bedrock, whether residual or transported.

Regosolic (18) A CSSC soil order with weakly developed limited soils, the result of any number of factors: young materials; fresh alluvial deposits; material instability; mass-wasted slopes; or dry, cold climatic conditions.

Relative humidity (7) The ratio of water vapour actually in the air (content) compared to the maximum water vapour possible (capacity) at that temperature; expressed as a percentage. (*Compare* vapour pressure, specific humidity.)

Relief (12) Elevation differences in a local landscape; an expression of local height difference of landforms.

Remote sensing (1) Information acquired from a distance, without physical contact with the subject; for example, photography, orbital imagery, or radar.

Respiration (19) The process by which plants use food to derive energy for their operations; essentially, the reverse of the photosynthetic process; releases carbon dioxide, water, and heat energy into the environment. (*Compare* photosynthesis.)

Reverse fault (12) Compressional forces produce strain that breaks a rock so that one side moves upward relative to the other side; also called a thrust fault. (*Compare* normal fault.)

Revolution (2) The annual orbital movement of Earth about the Sun; determines the length of the year and the seasons.

Rhumb line (1) A line of constant compass direction, or constant bearing, which crosses successive meridians at the same angle; appearing as a straight line only on a Mercator projection.

Richter scale (12) An open-ended, logarithmic scale that estimates earthquake magnitude; designed by Charles Richter in 1935; now replaced by the moment magnitude scale. (*See* moment magnitude scale.)

Rime fog (7) A fog that consists of supercooled water droplets that turn into rime frost on contact with freezing objects.

Ring of fire (12) *See* circum-Pacific belt.

Robinson projection (Appendix A) A compromise (neither equal area nor true shape) oval projection developed in 1963 by Arthur Robinson.

Roche moutonnée (17) A glacial erosion feature; an asymmetrical hill of exposed bedrock; displays a gently sloping upstream side that has been smoothed and polished by a glacier and an abrupt, steep downstream side.

Rock (11) An assemblage of minerals bound together, or sometimes a mass of a single mineral.

Rock cycle (11) A model representing the interrelationships among the three rock-forming processes: igneous, sedimentary, and metamorphic; shows how each can be transformed into another rock type.

Rockfall (13) Free-falling movement of debris from a cliff or steep slope, generally falling straight or bounding downslope.

Rossby wave (6) An undulating horizontal motion in the upper-air westerly circulation at middle and high latitudes.

Rotation (2) The turning of Earth on its axis, averaging about 24 hours in duration; determines day–night relation; counterclockwise when viewed from above the North Pole and from above the equator, west to east or eastward.

Salinity (16) The concentration of natural elements and compounds dissolved in solution, as solutes; measured by weight in parts per thousand (‰) in seawater.

Salinization (18) A pedogenic process that results from high potential evapotranspiration rates in deserts and semiarid regions. Soil water is drawn to surface horizons, and dissolved salts are deposited as the water evaporates.

Saltation (14) The transport of sand grains (usually larger than 0.2 mm) by stream or wind, bouncing the grains along the ground in asymmetrical paths.

Salt marsh (16) A wetland ecosystem characteristic of latitudes poleward of the 30th parallel. (*Compare* to mangrove swamp.)

Sand sea (15) An extensive area of sand and dunes; characteristic of Earth's erg deserts. (*Contrast* to reg deserts.)

Saturation (7) Air that is holding all the water vapour that it can hold at a given temperature, known as the dew-point temperature.

Scale (1) The ratio of the distance on a map to that in the real world; expressed as a representative fraction, graphic scale, or written scale.

Scarification (13) Human-induced mass movements of Earth materials, such as large-scale open-pit mining and strip mining.

Scattering (4) Deflection and redirection of insolation by atmospheric gases, dust, ice, and water vapour; the shorter the wavelength, the greater the scattering, and thus skies in the lower atmosphere are blue.

Scientific method (1) An approach that uses applied common sense in an organized and objective manner; based on observation, generalization, formulation, and testing of a hypothesis, and ultimately the development of a theory.

Sea-floor spreading (11) As proposed by Hess and Dietz, the mechanism driving the movement of the continents; associated with upwelling flows of magma along the worldwide system of mid-ocean ridges. (*See* mid-ocean ridge.)

Secondary succession (19) Succession that occurs among plant species in an area where vestiges of a previously functioning community are present; an area where the natural community has been destroyed or disturbed, but where the underlying soil remains intact.

Sediment (13) Fine-grained mineral matter that is transported and deposited by air, water, or ice.

Sedimentary rock (11) One of three basic rock types; formed from the compaction, cementation, and hardening of sediments derived from other rocks. (*Compare* igneous rock, metamorphic rock.)

Seismic wave (11) The shock wave sent through the planet by an earthquake or underground nuclear test. Transmission varies according to temperature and the density of various layers within the planet; provides indirect diagnostic evidence of Earth's internal structure.

Seismograph (12) A device that measures seismic waves of energy transmitted throughout Earth's interior or along the crust.

Sensible heat (3) Heat that can be measured with a thermometer; a measure of the concentration of kinetic energy from molecular motion.

Sheet flow (14) Surface water that moves downslope in a thin film as overland flow, not concentrated in channels larger than rills.

Sheeting (13) A form of weathering associated with fracturing or fragmentation of rock by pressure release; often related to exfoliation processes. (*See* exfoliation dome.)

Shield volcano (12) A symmetrical mountain landform built from effusive eruptions (low-viscosity magma); gently sloped, gradually rising from the surrounding landscape to a summit crater; typical of the Hawaiian Islands. (*Compare* effusive eruption; composite volcano.)

Sinkhole (13) Nearly circular depression created by the weathering of karst landscapes with subterranean drainage; also known as a doline in traditional studies; may collapse through the roof of an underground space. (*See* karst topography.)

Sleet (8) Freezing rain, ice glaze, or ice pellets.

Sling psychrometer (7) A weather instrument that measures relative humidity using two thermometers—a dry bulb and a wet bulb—mounted side-by-side.

Slipface (15) On a sand dune, formed as dune height increases above 30 cm on the leeward side at an angle at which loose material is stable—its angle of repose (30 to 34°).

Slope (13) A curved, inclined surface that bounds a landform.

Small circle (1) A circle on a globe's surface that does not share Earth's centre; for example, all parallels of latitude other than the equator. (*Compare* great circle.)

Snow line (17) A temporary line marking the elevation where winter snowfall persists throughout the summer; seasonally, the lowest elevation covered by snow during the summer.

Soil (18) A dynamic natural body made up of fine materials covering Earth's surface in which plants grow, composed of both mineral and organic matter.

Soil colloid (18) A tiny clay and organic particle in soil; provides chemically active sites for mineral ion adsorption. (*See* cation-exchange capacity.)

Soil creep (13) A persistent mass movement of surface soil where individual soil particles are lifted and disturbed by the expansion of soil moisture as it freezes or by grazing livestock or digging animals.

Soil fertility (18) The ability of soil to support plant productivity when it contains organic substances and clay minerals that absorb water and certain elemental ions needed by plants through adsorption. (*See* cation exchange capacity, CEC.)

Soil horizon (18) The various layers exposed in a pedon; roughly parallel to the surface and identified as O, A, Ae, B, C, and R (bedrock).

Soil-moisture recharge (9) Water entering available soil storage spaces.

Soil-moisture storage (9) ΔST, the retention of moisture within soil; it is a savings account that can accept deposits (soil-moisture recharge) or experiences withdrawals (soil-moisture utilization) as conditions change.

Soil-moisture utilization (9) The extraction of soil moisture by plants for their needs; efficiency of withdrawal decreases as the soil storage is reduced.

Soil science (18) Interdisciplinary science of soils. Pedology concerns the origin, classification, distribution, and description of soil. Edaphology focuses on soil as a medium for sustaining higher plants.

Soil Taxonomy (Appendix B) A soil classification system based on observable soil properties actually seen in the field; published in 1975 by the U.S. Soil Conservation Service and revised in 1990, 1998, and 2010 by the Natural Resources Conservation Service to include 12 soil orders.

Soil-water budget (9) An accounting system for soil moisture using inputs of precipitation and outputs of evapotranspiration and gravitational water.

Solar constant (2) The amount of insolation intercepted by Earth on a surface perpendicular to the Sun's rays when Earth is at its average distance from the Sun; a value of 1372 W · m², or 1.968 calories · cm², per minute; averaged over the entire globe at the thermopause.

Solar wind (2) Clouds of ionized (charged) gases emitted by the Sun and travelling in all directions from the Sun's surface. Effects on Earth include auroras, disturbance of radio signals, and possible influences on weather.

Solifluction (13) Gentle downslope movement of a saturated surface material (soil and regolith) in various climatic regimes where temperatures are above freezing. (*Compare* gelifluction.)

Solonetzic (18) A CSSC soil order where solonetz denotes saline or alkaline soils. Well- to imperfectly-drained mineral soils developed under grasses in semiarid to subhumid climates. Limited areas of central and north-central Alberta.

Solum (18) A true soil profile in the pedon; ideally, a combination of O, A, E, and B horizons. (*See* pedon.)

Spatial (1) The nature or character of physical space, as in an area; occupying or operating within a space. Geography is a spatial science; spatial analysis its essential approach.

Spatial analysis (1) The examination of spatial interactions, patterns, and variations over area and/or space; a key integrative approach of geography.

Specific heat (5) The increase of temperature in a material when energy is absorbed; water has a higher specific heat (can store more heat) than a comparable volume of soil or rock.

Specific humidity (7) The mass of water vapour (in grams) per unit mass of air (in kilograms) at any specified temperature. The maximum mass of water vapour possible in a kilogram of air at any specified temperature is termed its maximum specific humidity. (*Compare* vapour pressure, relative humidity.)

Speed of light (2) Specifically, 299 792 kilometres per second, or more than 9.4 trillion kilometres per year—a distance known as a light-year; at light speed Earth is 8 minutes and 20 seconds from the Sun.

Spheroidal weathering (13) A chemical weathering process in which the sharp edges and corners of boulders and rocks are weathered in thin plates that create a rounded, spheroidal form.

Spodosols (18) A soil order in the Soil Taxonomy classification that occurs in northern coniferous forests; best developed in cold, moist, forested climates; lacks humus and clay in the A horizons, with high acidity associated with podzolization processes.

Spring tide (16) The highest tidal range, which occurs when the Moon and the Sun are in conjunction (at new Moon) or in opposition (at full Moon) stages (compare neap tide).

Squall line (8) A zone slightly ahead of a fast-advancing cold front, where wind patterns are rapidly changing and blustery and precipitation is strong.

Stability (7) The condition of a parcel, whether it remains where it is or changes its initial position. The parcel is stable if it resists displacement upward, unstable if it continues to rise.

Stationary front (8) A frontal area of contact between contrasting air masses that shows little horizontal movement; winds in opposite direction on either side of the front flow parallel along the front.

Steady-state equilibrium (1) The condition that occurs in a system when rates of input and output are equal and the amounts of energy and stored matter are nearly constant around a stable average.

Stomata (19) A small opening on the undersides of leaves through which water and gasses pass.

Storm surge (8) A large quantity of seawater pushed inland by the strong winds associated with a tropical cyclone.

Storm tracks (8) Seasonally shifting paths followed by migrating low-pressure systems.

Straight-line winds (8) Linear winds associated with thunderstorms and bands of showers that cause significant damage and crop losses. (*See* derechos.)

Stratified drift (17) Sediments deposited by glacial meltwater that appear sorted; a specific form of glacial drift. (*Compare* till.)

Stratigraphy (11) A science that analyzes the sequence, spacing, geophysical and geochemical properties, and spatial distribution of rock strata.

Stratocumulus (7) A lumpy, grayish, low-level cloud, patchy with sky visible, sometimes present at the end of the day.

Stratosphere (3) That portion of the homosphere that ranges from 20 to 50 km above Earth's surface, with temperatures ranging from −57°C at the tropopause to 0°C at the stratopause. The functional ozonosphere is within the stratosphere.

Stratus (7) A stratiform (flat, horizontal) cloud generally below 2000 m.

Strike-slip fault (12) Horizontal movement along a faultline; that is, movement in the same direction as the fault; also known as a transcurrent fault. Such movement is described as right lateral or left lateral, depending on the relative motion observed across the fault. (*See* transform fault.)

Subduction zone (11) An area where two plates of crust collide and the denser oceanic crust dives beneath the less dense continental plate, forming deep oceanic trenches and seismically active regions.

Sublimation (7) A process in which ice evaporates directly to water vapour or water vapour freezes to ice (deposition).

Subpolar low-pressure cell (6) A region of low pressure centred approximately at 60° latitude in the North Atlantic near Iceland and in the North Pacific near the Aleutians, as well as in the Southern Hemisphere. Airflow is cyclonic; it weakens in summer and strengthens in winter. (*Refer* to cyclone.)

Subsolar point (2) The only point receiving perpendicular insolation at a given moment—the Sun directly overhead. (*See* declination.)

Subtropical high-pressure cell (6) One of several dynamic high-pressure areas covering roughly the region from 20° to 35° N and S latitudes; responsible for the hot, dry areas of Earth's arid and semiarid deserts. (*Refer* to anticyclone.)

Sulphate aerosols (3) Sulphur compounds in the atmosphere, principally sulphuric acid; principal sources relate to fossil fuel combustion; scatters and reflects insolation.

Sulphur dioxide (3) A colourless gas detected by its pungent odour; produced by the combustion of fossil fuels, especially coal, that contain sulphur as an impurity (SO_2); can react in the atmosphere to form sulphuric acid, a component of acid deposition.

Summer (June) solstice (2) The time when the Sun's declination is at the Tropic of Cancer, at 23.5° N latitude, June 20–21 each year. (*Compare* winter [December] solstice.)

Sunrise (2) That moment when the disk of the Sun first appears above the horizon.

Sunset (2) That moment when the disk of the Sun totally disappears.

Sunspot (2) Magnetic disturbances on the surface of the Sun, occurring in an average 11-year cycle; related flares, prominences, and outbreaks produce surges in solar wind.

Surface creep (15) A form of eolian transport that involves particles too large for saltation; a process whereby individual grains are impacted by moving grains and slide and roll.

Surplus (S) (9) The amount of moisture that exceeds potential evapotranspiration; moisture oversupply when soil moisture storage is at field capacity; extra or surplus water.

Suspended load (14) Fine particles held in suspension in a stream. The finest particles are not deposited until the stream velocity nears zero.

Swell (16) Regular patterns of smooth, rounded waves in open water; can range from small ripples to very large waves.

Syncline (12) A trough in folded strata, with beds that slope toward the axis of the downfold. (*Compare* anticline.)

System (1) Any ordered, interrelated set of materials or items existing separate from the environment or within a boundary; energy transformations and energy and matter storage and retrieval occur within a system.

Taiga (20) *See* needleleaf forest.

Talus slope (13) Formed by angular rock fragments that cascade down a slope along the base of a mountain; poorly sorted, cone-shaped deposits.

Tarn (17) A small mountain lake, especially one that collects in a cirque basin behind risers of rock material or in an ice-gouged depression.

Temperate rain forest (20) A major biome of lush forests at middle and high latitudes; occurs along narrow margins of the Pacific Northwest in North America, among other locations; includes the tallest trees in the world.

Temperature (5) A measure of sensible heat energy present in the atmosphere and other media; indicates the average kinetic energy of individual molecules within a substance.

Terminal moraine (17) Eroded debris that is dropped at a glacier's farthest extent.

Terrane (12) A migrating piece of Earth's crust, dragged about by processes of mantle convection and plate tectonics. Displaced terranes are distinct in their history, composition, and structure from the continents that accept them.

Terrestrial ecosystem (20) A self-regulating association characterized by specific plant formations; usually named for the predominant vegetation and known as a biome when large and stable. (*See* biome.)

Thermal equator (5) The isoline on an isothermal map that connects all points of highest mean temperature.

Thermohaline circulation (6) Deep ocean currents produced by differences in temperature and salinity with depth; Earth's deep currents.

Thermokarst (17) Topography of hummocky, irregular relief marked by cave-ins, bogs, small depressions, and pits formed as ground ice melts; an erosion process caused by ground ice melting; not related to solution processes and chemical weathering associated with limestone (karst).

Thermopause (2, 3) A zone approximately 480 km in altitude that serves conceptually as the top of the atmosphere; an altitude used for the determination of the solar constant.

Thermosphere (3) A region of the heterosphere extending from 80 to 480 km in altitude; contains the functional ionosphere layer.

Threshold (1) A moment in which a system can no longer maintain its character, so it lurches to a new operational level, which may not be compatible with previous conditions.

Thrust fault (12) A reverse fault where the fault plane forms a low angle relative to the horizontal; an overlying block moves over an underlying block.

Thunder (8) The violent expansion of suddenly heated air, created by lightning discharges, which send out shock waves as an audible sonic bang.

Tide (16) A pattern of daily oscillations in sea level produced by astronomical relations among the Sun, the Moon, and Earth; experienced in varying degrees around the world. (*See* neap and spring tides.)

Till (17) Direct ice deposits that appear unstratified and unsorted; a specific form of glacial drift. (*Compare* stratified drift.)

Till plain (17) A large, relatively flat plain composed of unsorted glacial deposits behind a terminal or end moraine. Low-rolling relief and unclear drainage patterns are characteristic.

Tombolo (16) A landform created when coastal sand deposits connect the shoreline with an offshore island outcrop or sea stack.

Topographic map (Appendix A) A map that portrays physical relief through the use of elevation contour lines that connect all points at the same elevation above or below a vertical datum, such as mean sea level.

Topography (12) The undulations and configurations, including its relief, that give Earth's surface its texture, portrayed on topographic maps.

Tornado (8) An intense, destructive cyclonic rotation, developed in response to extremely low pressure; generally associated with mesocyclone formation.

Total runoff (9) Surplus water that flows across a surface toward stream channels; formed by sheet flow, combined with precipitation and subsurface flows into those channels.

Traction (14) A type of sediment transport that drags coarser materials along the bed of a stream. (*See* bed load.)

Trade wind (6) Wind from the northeast and southeast that converges in the equatorial low-pressure trough, forming the intertropical convergence zone.

Transform fault (11) A type of geologic fault in rocks. An elongated zone along which faulting occurs between mid-ocean ridges; produces a relative horizontal motion with no new crust formed or consumed; strike-slip motion is either left or right lateral. (*See* strike-slip fault.)

Transmission (4) The passage of shortwave and longwave energy through space, the atmosphere, or water.

Transparency (5) The quality of a medium (air, water) that allows light to easily pass through it.

Transpiration (9) The movement of water vapour out through the pores in leaves; the water is drawn by the plant roots from soil-moisture storage.

Transport (14) The actual movement of weathered and eroded materials by air, water, and ice.

Tropical cyclone (8) A cyclonic circulation originating in the tropics, with winds between 39 and 73 mph; characterized by closed isobars, circular organization, and heavy rains. (*See* hurricane and typhoon.)

Tropical savanna (20) A major biome containing large expanses of grassland interrupted by trees and shrubs; a transitional area between the humid rain forests and tropical seasonal forests and the drier, semiarid tropical steppes and deserts.

Tropical seasonal forest and scrub (20) A variable biome on the margins of the rain forests, occupying regions of lesser and more erratic rainfall; the site of transitional communities between the rain forests and tropical grasslands.

Tropic of Cancer (2) The parallel that marks the farthest north the subsolar point migrates during the year; 23.5° north latitude. (*See* Tropic of Capricorn; summer or June solstice.)

Tropic of Capricorn (2) The parallel that marks the farthest south the subsolar point migrates during the year; 23.5° south latitude. (*See* Tropic of Cancer; winter or December solstice.)

Tropopause (3) The top zone of the troposphere defined by temperature; wherever −57°C occurs.

Troposphere (3) The home of the biosphere; the lowest layer of the homosphere, containing approximately 90% of the total mass of the atmosphere; extends up to the tropopause; occurring at an altitude of 18 km at the equator, 13 km in the middle latitudes, and at lower altitudes near the poles.

True shape (1) A map property showing the correct configuration of coastlines, a useful trait of conformality for navigational and aeronautical maps, although areal relationships are distorted. (*See* map projection; *compare* equal area.)

Tsunami (16) A seismic sea wave, travelling at high speeds across the ocean, formed by sudden motion in the sea floor, such as a sea-floor earthquake, submarine landslide, or eruption of an undersea volcano.

Typhoon (8) A tropical cyclone in excess of 74 m·h² that occurs in the western Pacific; same as a hurricane except for location.

Unconfined aquifer (9) An aquifer that is not bounded by impermeable strata. It is simply the zone of saturation in water-bearing rock strata with no impermeable overburden, and recharge is generally accomplished by water percolating down from above.

Undercut bank (14) In streams, a steep bank formed along the outer portion of a meandering stream; produced by lateral erosive action of a stream; sometimes called a cutbank. (*Compare* point bar.)

Uniformitarianism (11) An assumption that physical processes active in the environment today are operating at the same pace and intensity that has characterized them throughout geologic time; proposed by Hutton and Lyell. (*Compare* catastrophism.)

Upslope fog (7) Forms when moist air is forced to higher elevations along a hill or mountain and is thus cooled. (*Compare* valley fog.)

Upwelling current (6) An area of the sea where cool, deep waters, which are generally nutrient rich, rise to replace the vacating water, as occurs along the west coasts of North and South America. (*Compare* downwelling current.)

Urban heat island (4) An urban microclimate that is warmer on average than areas in the surrounding countryside because of the interaction of solar radiation and various surface characteristics.

Valley fog (7) The settling of cooler, more dense air in low-lying areas; produces saturated conditions and fog.

Vapour pressure (7) That portion of total air pressure that results from water vapour molecules, expressed in millibars (mb). At a given dew-point temperature, the maximum capacity of the air is termed its saturation vapour pressure.

Vascular plant (19) A plant having internal fluid and material flows through its tissues; almost 250 000 species exist on Earth.

Ventifact (15) A piece of rock etched and smoothed by eolian erosion— abrasion by windblown particles.

Vernal (March) equinox (2) The time around March 20–21 each year when the Sun's declination crosses the equatorial parallel and all places on Earth experience days and nights of equal length. The Sun rises at the North Pole and sets at the South Pole. (*Compare* autumnal equinox.)

Vertisolic (18) A CSSC soil order that occurs in heavy-textured material that is high in clay content (≥ 60% clay), especially smectite, a shrinking and swelling clay. These soils have little development of horizons, and are marked by slickensides and severe disruption.

Volatile organic compounds (VOCs) (3) Compounds, including hydrocarbons, produced by the combustion of gasoline, from surface coatings and from electric utility combustion; participates in the production of PAN through reactions with nitric oxides.

Volcano (12) A mountainous landform at the end of a magma conduit, which rises from below the crust and vents to the surface. Magma rises and collects in a magma chamber deep below, erupting effusively or explosively and forming composite, shield, or cinder-cone volcanoes.

Warm desert and semidesert (20) A desert biome caused by the presence of subtropical high-pressure cells; dry air and low precipitation.

Warm front (8) The leading edge of an advancing warm air mass, which is unable to push cooler, passive air out of the way; tends to push the cooler, underlying air into a wedge shape; identified on a weather map as a line with semicircles pointing in the direction of frontal movement. (*Compare* cold front.)

Wash (15) An intermittently dry streambed that fills with torrents of water after rare precipitation events in arid lands.

Water table (9) The upper surface of groundwater; that contact point between the zone of saturation and aeration in an unconfined aquifer. (*See* zone of aeration, zone of saturation.)

Wave (16) An undulation of ocean water produced by the conversion of solar energy to wind energy and then to wave energy; energy produced in a generating region or a stormy area of the sea.

Wave-cut platform (16) A flat or gently sloping tablelike bedrock surface that develops in the tidal zone, where wave action cuts a bench that extends from the cliff base out into the sea; sometimes termed *shore platform*.

Wave cyclone (8) *See* midlatitude cyclone.

Wavelength (2) A measurement of a wave; the distance between the crests of successive waves. The number of waves passing a fixed point in 1 second is called the frequency of the wavelength.

Wave refraction (16) A bending process that concentrates wave energy on headlands and disperses it in coves and bays; the long-term result is coastal straightening.

Weather (8) The short-term condition of the atmosphere, as compared to climate, which reflects long-term atmospheric conditions and extremes. Temperature, air pressure, relative humidity, wind speed and direction, daylength, and Sun angle are important measurable elements that contribute to the weather.

Weathering (13) The processes by which surface and subsurface rocks disintegrate, or dissolve, or are broken down. Rocks at or near Earth's surface are exposed to physical and chemical weathering processes.

Westerlies (6) The predominant surface and aloft windflow pattern from the subtropics to high latitudes in both hemispheres.

Western intensification (6) The piling up of ocean water along the western margin of each ocean basin, to a height of about 15 m; produced by the trade winds that drive the oceans westward in a concentrated channel.

Wetland (16) A narrow, vegetated strip occupying many coastal areas and estuaries worldwide; highly productive ecosystems with an ability to trap organic matter, nutrients, and sediment.

Wilting point (9) That point in the soil–moisture balance when only hygroscopic water and some bound capillary water remains. Plants wilt and eventually die after prolonged stress from a lack of available water.

Wind (6) The horizontal movement of air relative to Earth's surface; produced essentially by air pressure differences from place to place; its direction is influenced by the Coriolis force and surface friction.

Wind vane (6) A weather instrument used to determine wind direction; winds are named for the direction from which they originate.

Winter (December) solstice (2) That time when the Sun's declination is at the Tropic of Capricorn, at 23.5° S latitude, December 21–22 each year. The day is 24 hours long south of the Antarctic Circle. The night is 24 hours long north of the Arctic Circle. (*Compare* Summer [June] solstice.)

Withdrawal (9) Sometimes called *offstream use*, the removal of water from the natural supply, after which it is used for various purposes and then is returned to the water supply.

Yardang (15) A streamlined rock structure formed by deflation and abrasion; appears elongated and aligned with the most effective wind direction.

Yazoo tributary (14) A small tributary stream draining alongside a floodplain; blocked from joining the main river by its natural levees and elevated stream channel. (*See* backswamp.)

Zone of aeration (9) A zone above the water table that has air in its pore spaces and may or may not have water.

Zone of saturation (9) A groundwater zone below the water table in which all pore spaces are filled with water.